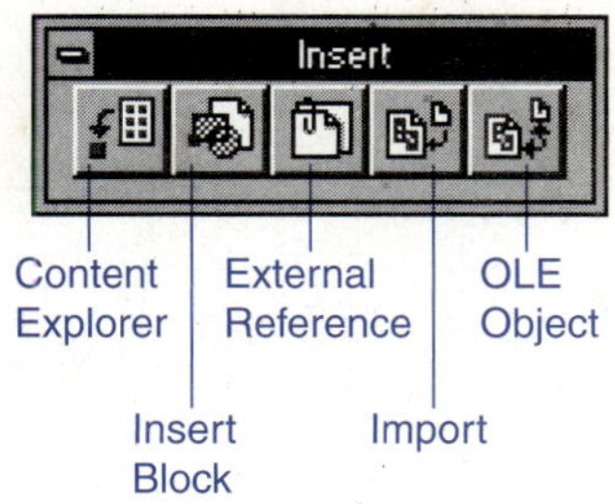
Insert
Content Explorer
Insert Block
External Reference
Import
OLE Object

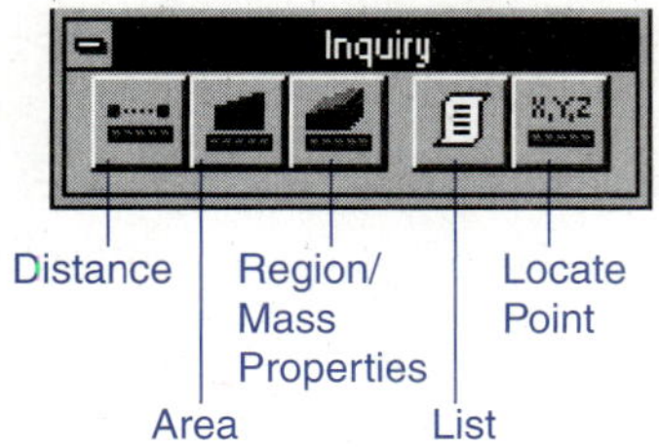
Inquiry
Distance
Area
Region/ Mass Properties
List
Locate Point

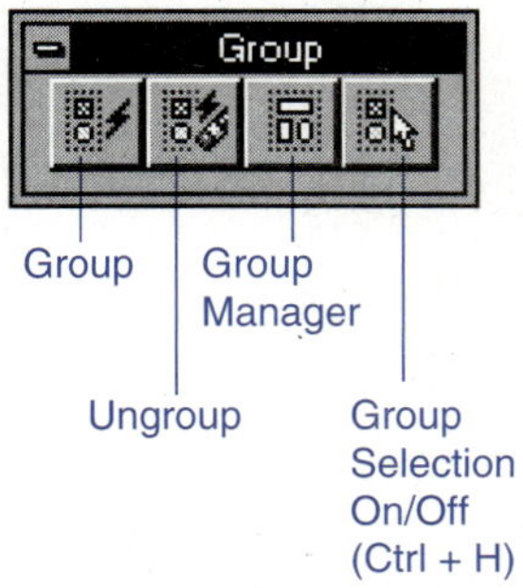
Group
Group
Ungroup
Group Manager
Group Selection On/Off (Ctrl + H)

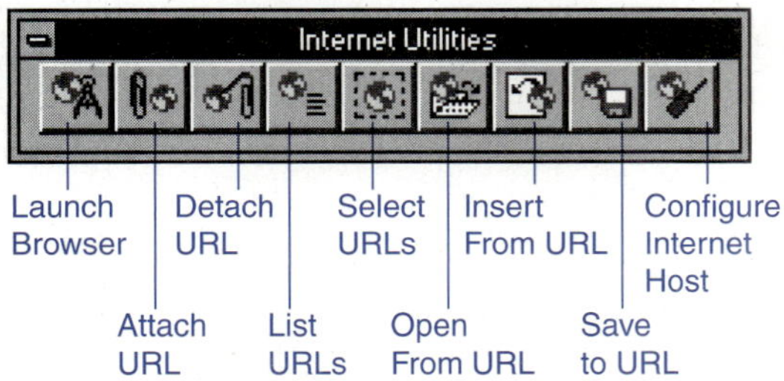
Internet Utilities
Launch Browser
Attach URL
Detach URL
List URLs
Select URLs
Open From URL
Insert From URL
Save to URL
Configure Internet Host

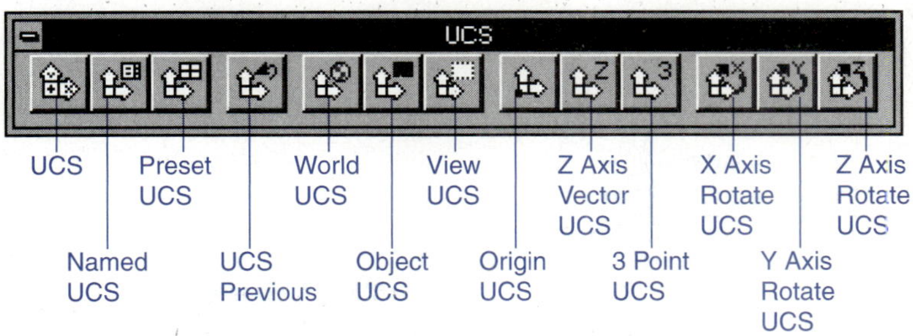
UCS
UCS
Named UCS
Preset UCS
UCS Previous
World UCS
Object UCS
View UCS
Origin UCS
Z Axis Vector UCS
3 Point UCS
X Axis Rotate UCS
Y Axis Rotate UCS
Z Axis Rotate UCS

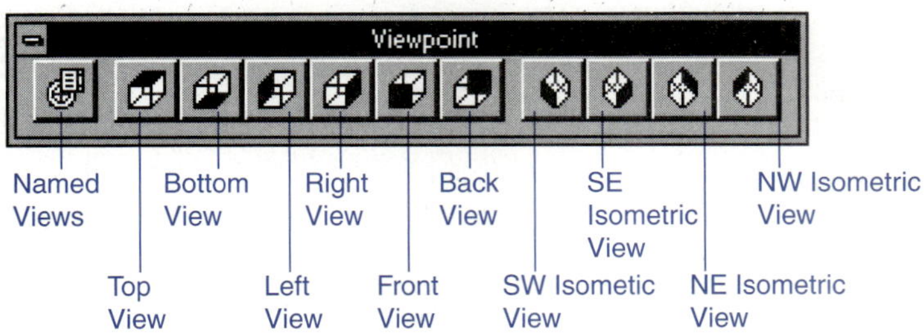
Viewpoint
Named Views
Top View
Bottom View
Left View
Right View
Front View
Back View
SW Isometric View
SE Isometric View
NE Isometric View
NW Isometric View

AutoCAD LT® 2000

Basics Through Advanced

AutoCAD LT® 2000

Basics Through Advanced

David A. Madsen

Chairman
Drafting Technology
Autodesk Premier Training Center

Clackamas Community College
Oregon City, OR

Former Board of Directors
American Design Drafting Association

Rod Rawls

Autodesk Certified Instructor
Autodesk Training Center Manager
Drafting Technology
Autodesk Premier Training Center

Clackamas Community College
Oregon City, OR

Prentice Hall

Upper Saddle River, New Jersey
Columbus, Ohio

Library of Congress Cataloging-in-Publication Data

Madsen, David A.
AutoCAD LT 2000 / basics through advanced / David A. Madsen, Rod Rawls.
p. cm.
ISBN 0-13-018174-9
1. Computer graphics. 2. AutoCAD. I. Rawls, Rod R. II. Title.

T385.M3235 2001
620′.0042′02855369—dc21 00-033983

Vice President and Publisher: Dave Garza
Editor in Chief: Stephen Helba
Acquisitions Editor: Debbie Yarnell
Associate Editor: Michelle Churma
Production Editor: Louise N. Sette
Production Supervision: Karen Fortgang, bookworks
Design Coordinator: Robin G. Chukes
Cover Designer: Jason Moore
Cover art: FLIR Systems, Inc., Alan Mascord, Design Associates, and Bruce Wilcox
Production Manager: Brian Fox

This book was set in Times Roman by STELLARViSIONs and was printed and bound by Courier Kendallville, Inc. The cover was printed by Phoenix Color Corp.

Prentice Hall

10 9 8 7 6 5 4 3 2 1
ISBN: 0-13-018174-9

Preface

AutoCAD LT® 2000: Basics Through Advanced is a text and workbook that provides complete coverage of AutoCAD LT. This text provides the beginning student and the drafting or engineering professional with a complete understanding of every AutoCAD LT command using professional drafting methods and techniques. All software commands are presented in a manner that shows each prompt with examples of the exact input you should use. This text also contains a variety of valuable features that help make learning AutoCAD LT easy for you:

- It is easy to read, use, and understand.
- Learning Goals are provided at the beginning of each chapter to identify what you will learn as a result of completing the chapter.
- The text includes Microsoft Windows® 95, Windows98, Windows NT, and Windows 2000 applications.
- Commands are presented in a manner that shows every prompt with the exact input you should use.
- Field Notes explain special applications, tricks, and professional tips for using AutoCAD LT.
- Through the Window ... is a unique feature that shares Windows95, Windows98, Windows NT, and Windows 2000 applications.
- Exercises are provided throughout for you to practice as you learn AutoCAD LT.
- Learning Checkpoints are questions that are placed throughout the text following each major topic discussion. Answering these questions provides you with an excellent way to review the previous information and check your knowledge and understanding.
- Multiple choice tests, matching exercises, and word scrambles are provided with each chapter to help you learn and have fun with AutoCAD LT.
- Multidisciplinary projects allow you to learn how to use AutoCAD LT in your drafting, engineering, or architectural field.
- The Instructor's Resource Manual contains project solutions and multiple choice, matching, and word scramble solutions. The Instructor's Resource Manual also has additional multiple choice tests, crosswords, word finds, and fill-in-the-blank activities related to each chapter in the text. Answers and solutions are also provided for these tests and activities.
- A Companion Website with additional review questions and drawing activities is available at www.prenhall.com/madsen.

Format of Text

The format of this text helps you learn how to use AutoCAD LT both by example and complete explanations of each feature.

Command Access Mapping

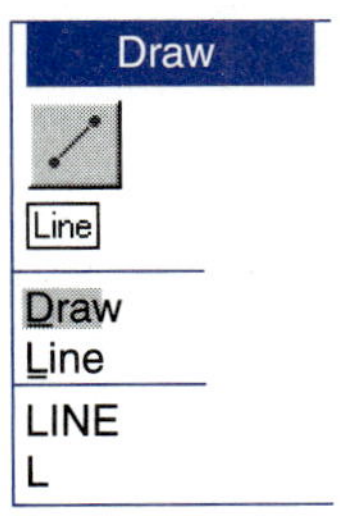

Every AutoCAD LT command discussion begins with a display of the available options for accessing that command. For example, the toolbar button that starts the LINE command is displayed at the top of the graphic image in the margin next to this paragraph. Also included is the name of the toolbar and the tooltip — for easier recognition. The second area shows the name and option used to access the command from the pull-down menu system. The command name and any default command shortcuts (aliases) or accelerator keystrokes are shown last.

Accessing AutoCAD LT Commands

In addition to the quick reference mapping of available command selection methods, all options are further described within the text. For example, the LINE command can be accessed by picking Line from the Draw pull-down menu, by picking Line in the Draw toolbar, or by typing **L** or **LINE** at the Command: prompt. The keyboard letter used to access the menu and the command is shown underlined just as it is in the AutoCAD LT menu system.

When a command sequence is discussed, examples of the command are presented as if you are typing at the keyboard, or as it appears when you pick the command from the toolbar or pull-down menu. When the command is presented as if it is typed at the keyboard, any available keyboard shortcut is always given before the full command name. One goal of this book is for you to see all of the methods of using AutoCAD LT commands and to decide which methods work best for you.

Understanding the Command Format Presented in This Text

When a command is issued at the keyboard, the command shortcut and full name are displayed in bold full caps and the return arrow symbol (↵) shows you when to press the Enter key. This is an example of how a command is displayed when entered at the keyboard:

Command: **L** or **LINE**↵

When the command prompts are answered by typing a value, the typed information is also presented in bold. For example, the following LINE command prompts are answered with coordinate values followed by pressing the Enter key:

Command: **L** or **LINE**↵
Specify first point: **4.5, 2.5**↵
Specify next point or [Undo]: **7.5, 8.5**↵
Specify next point or [Undo]: ↵
Command:

When you pick a point or use a technique other than typing, the prompt is followed by the suggested method presented in italics and angle brackets:

Command: **L** or **LINE**↵
Specify first point: ⟨*pick first point*⟩
Specify next point or [Undo]: ⟨*pick next point*⟩
Specify next point or [Undo]: ↵
Command:

After you have learned the different ways to respond to AutoCAD LT prompts, you can use the method that works best for you. For example, if the prompt reads

Specify first point: ⟨*pick first point*⟩

you can pick a point, as suggested, enter coordinate values, or use any other input method you prefer.

Presenting Command Options

When a prompt asks you to select a command option, the capitalized letter or letters within the option name must be entered at the keyboard. If a letter in more than one word is capitalized, you can enter either letter. The polyline command options are used in the following example:

Command: **PL** or **PLINE**↵
Specify start point: ⟨*pick a start point*⟩
Current line-width is 0.0000
Specify next point or [Arc/Close/Halfwidth/Length/Undo/Width]: **W**↵

If you are given a prompt with a value in brackets <>, you can specify a new value or press Enter to accept the value in the brackets like this:

Command: **PL** or **PLINE**↵
Specify start point: *⟨pick a start point⟩*
Current line-width is 0.0000
Specify next point or [Arc/Close/Halfwidth/Length/Undo/Width]: **W**↵
Specify starting width <0.0000>: **.25**↵
Specify ending width <0.2500>: ↵
Specify next point or [Arc/Close/Halfwidth/Length/Undo/Width]:

Identifying Key Words

Key words are ***bold italic*** for your ease in identification. These words relate to AutoCAD LT terminology and professional applications. These words are defined in the content of the text and in the glossary. Key words are an important part of your AutoCAD LT learning process, because they are part of the world of computer-aided drafting, drafting standards, and AutoCAD LT communication.

Special Features

AutoCAD LT 2000: Basics Through Advanced contains several special features that help you learn and use AutoCAD LT, Windows95, Windows98, and Windows NT as explained in the following paragraphs. Most features are shown here as they appear in the book.

LEARNING GOALS

- ☐ Use AutoCAD LT to prepare drawings in your field of interest or in a variety of disciplines.
- ☐ Answer questions related to AutoCAD LT.
- ☐ Use AutoCAD LT and drafting related terminology.
- ☐ Do exercises as you learn AutoCAD LT.
- ☐ Use matching, multiple choice, word scramble, and projects activities to learn AutoCAD LT and for fun.

Exercise P.1

1. An exercise is provided after each AutoCAD LT topic or command lesson.
2. The exercises allow you to practice what you have just learned. Practicing AutoCAD LT applications is one of the most important keys to learning the program effectively.
3. Exercises should be completed at a computer while using AutoCAD LT to reinforce what you have just studied.
4. Exercises are saved to disk and can be used only as practice or as classroom assignments.

LEARNING CHECKPOINT

- ☐ A Learning Checkpoint is provided after every major AutoCAD LT learning section in each chapter.
- ☐ Learning Checkpoints are questions that relate to the previous content of the chapter.
- ☐ These questions are key to what you should learn about AutoCAD LT.
- ☐ Learning Checkpoint questions can be used as review or as mini-tests for checking your progress.

AutoCAD LT Learning Assistance™ Integration

The Autodesk Learning Assistance CD provided with AutoCAD LT 2000 software offers a variety of multimedia-based tutorials and concept illustrations that can serve as a valuable supplement to the discussion material in this text. When material related to a text topic is available, the Learning Assistance icon is displayed after the Learning Checkpoint along with a listing of the relevant Learning Assistance topics. The format shows the folder title in italics and the topic title in bold text. For example:

Introducing the AutoCAD LT Interface

- Mastering the AutoCAD LT Graphical User Interface

Through the Window...

Through the Window . . . is a special feature that provides you with instructions and applications, plus insightful tips and tricks for using Windows95, Windows98, Windows NT, and Windows 2000 effectively with AutoCAD LT.

Windows95/Windows98/Windows NT 4.0/Windows 2000

The screen images used in *AutoCAD LT®2000: Basics Through Advanced* show the Windows 98 operating system being used, but all AutoCAD commands and functions work exactly the same whether you are using Windows95, Windows98, Windows NT, or Windows 2000.

Field Notes

Field Notes are another special feature of *AutoCAD LT®2000*: *Basics Through Advanced*. Field Notes are placed throughout the text to provide you with any one or more of the following advantages:

- Professional tips and applications
- Special features of AutoCAD LT
- Advanced applications
- Additional instruction about how certain features work

Multiple Choice Test

There is a multiple choice test at the end of each chapter. The multiple choice tests can be used to check your understanding of the chapter content or they can be used as review. The multiple choice tests allow you to quickly determine your knowledge and they are easy for you or your instructor to evaluate. Expanded comprehensive multiple choice tests are provided in the Instructor's Resource Manual and correlated with every chapter of the text.

Matching Exercises

At the end of every chapter there is a matching exercise that provides a word list and chapter-related statements. You match the word to the statement. This is a convenient way to review the key terminology related to the current chapter.

Word Scramble

Each chapter has a word scramble. These puzzles provide you with a fun way to review key words and commands that are important in the current chapter.

Projects

Drafting projects are one of the most important ways to complete and solidify your learning and understanding of AutoCAD LT. It has been said many times, in terms of learning AutoCAD, that if you do not practice you will forget. The projects allow you to put to practice what you have just learned. The projects are different from the exercises, because they combine a variety of commands that are used in the current chapter and in past chapters. Exercises focus only on using the currently discussed command. The projects at the end of every chapter are designed to provide AutoCAD LT practice for a variety of drafting fields. You or your instructor can select the projects that relate directly to the type of drafting you are doing. Projects are identified with the following icons that correlate to the related drafting field. This makes it easier for you to target the desired projects.

This icon identifies projects that are designed to develop AutoCAD LT skills in the area of mechanical drawing for the machine manufacturing industry.

This icon represents projects that are based on the architectural drafting and building construction industry.

This icon is used to identify projects that are designed to relate to the electrical and electronics drafting industry.

This icon is used to describe projects that relate to the industrial pipe drafting, plumbing, or the fluid power industry.

This icon is used to identify drawings that are done in the graphics industry. These projects include signs, logos, charts, graphs, and art-related topics.

Appendices

The appendices for this text are designed to help you use AutoCAD LT in the architectural, engineering, and drafting environments. The appendices contain the following valuable information:

- Installing AutoCAD LT 2000
- Drafting Standards
- Standard Support Libraries

Instructor's Resource Manual

The Instructor's Resource Manual for this text provides the following items:

- Introduction: How to Use this Text
- Chapter Learning Checkpoint Answers
- Chapter Multiple Choice Test Answers
- Chapter Matching Answers
- Chapter Word Scramble Answers
- Chapter Exercise Solutions
- Chapter Project Solutions
- Suggested Course Syllabi
- Handouts
- Companion Website Information

The Instructor's Resource Manual also contains for additional fun and training with AutoCAD LT:

- Comprehensive multiple choice tests and solutions
- Crossword puzzles and solutions for each chapter
- Word finds and solutions for each chapter
- Fill-in-the-blank questions and solutions for each chapter

Companion Website
http://www.prenhall.com/madsen

The Companion Website is a valuable instructional aid that benefits students and instructors alike. On the website you will find materials such as objective listings for each chapter, additional tests that can be taken on-line and e-mailed directly to the instructor, and current course syllabi (provided by your instructor). More than a simple evaluation method, these tests provide hints and, upon completion, immediate feedback to the student — transforming the Companion Website into a powerful learning tool.

Acknowledgments

We would like to express our appreciation to the reviewers of this text: Gerald Bacza, Fairmont State College; Thomas Hester, California Polytechnic University, Pomona; Scott MacKenzie; and Graham Walker, Manhattan College.

Warning and Disclaimer

This book is designed to provide tutorial information about the AutoCAD LT® 2000 computer program. Every effort has been made to make this book complete and as accurate as possible, but no warranty or fitness is implied. The information is provided on an "as-is" basis. The authors and Prentice-Hall, Inc. shall have neither liability nor responsibility to any person or entity with respect to any loss or damage in connection with or arising from information contained in this book.

Contents

Chapter 5
Using Layers and Managing Object Properties 159

Chapter 6
Precision Drafting Tools 197

Chapter 7

Editing Your Drawing 251

Chapter 14

3D Drafting with AutoCAD LT 663

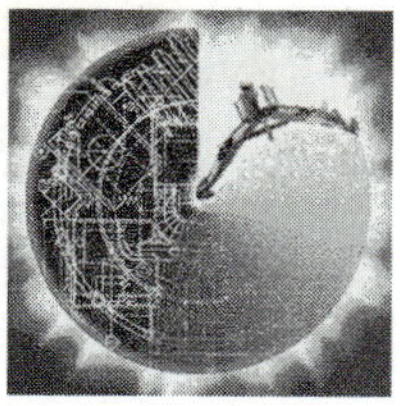

CHAPTER 1

An Introduction to AutoCAD LT

LEARNING GOALS

- Describe two principal computer-aided drafting concepts.
- Identify computer equipment and terminology.
- Start AutoCAD LT.
- Use the AutoCAD LT interface.

About Computer-Aided Drafting

The personal computer, or PC, is rapidly changing the way most things are done both in industry and at home. Today's PCs have the capability of storing, processing, and retrieving huge amounts of information very quickly. Its versatility and affordability have helped the PC to become the primary tool used by most industries for creating drawings and calculating engineering data. ***Computer-aided design and drafting*** (CADD) is the term that describes this growing technology. CADD technology provides many powerful engineering tools for the creation and analysis of precision technical drawings. Many of these drawings can be used as a source of information for creating computer-generated models. Analyzing such models helps the designer to find design flaws or potential failure points long before the first part is ever built. Industries using CADD can increase efficiency and speed up the process of bringing a product to market.

The area of CADD that is associated with the creation and editing of technical drawings is known as CAD, or ***computer-aided drafting.*** The use of a computer for drafting, rather than pencils, scales, and templates, has many benefits. One of the main benefits is accuracy. Modern CAD software programs provide a virtually unlimited drawing area, in which most objects can be drawn actual size regardless of how large or small they are. Your display can be changed quickly to show any area of the drawing. This means that, like a camera lens, you can zoom out or zoom in, allowing you to get very close to work with small features of your drawing, or to back off so you can see the whole picture. Computer-aided drafting programs can provide up to 16 decimal places of accuracy, with tools that allow you to use this precision easily in your drawings.

The greatest benefit to productivity within a drafting department comes from the fact that, with CAD, objects need only be drawn once, after which they can be used over and over again. For example, electronic schematic diagrams use symbols for resistors, transistors, capacitors, and other electronic components. Using CAD software, you can draw such a symbol once and then copy it to every location in your drawing where you need that symbol. It can even be saved permanently to a symbol library and used in other drawings. Companies using CAD benefit from these symbol libraries in their day-to-day drafting tasks.

Revisions to existing drawings can be done quickly and efficiently using CAD. After the required changes have been made, a new drawing can be produced within minutes using modern printers.

After a CAD drawing has been created, it can be transferred almost anywhere in the world within minutes using telephone communication lines. This feature plus PC affordability has made it possible for designers and drafters to operate their own businesses out of the home.

These and many other benefits have made PC CAD applications the primary tools for modern drafters.

LEARNING CHECKPOINT

- ☐ What are the advantages of using computer-aided drafting?
- ☐ What is the greatest benefit to productivity from using CAD?

Computer Equipment and Terminology

As you learn to use AutoCAD LT, you need to become familiar with the equipment used to run the program. Physical computer equipment is referred to as ***hardware,*** and the programs that the computer runs are called ***software.*** The central component of a personal computer system is the microcomputer, and the input and output devices are known as ***peripherals.*** A personal computer that is set up for work applications is commonly referred to as a ***workstation.*** Many possible combinations of equipment can be used in a PC system. The most common components are discussed here. The typical components of a PC-based CAD system are shown in Figure 1.1.

FIGURE 1.1 Typical components of a PC-based AutoCAD LT workstation.

Computer

The personal computer belongs to a class of computers known as *microcomputers.* The most commonly used microcomputer systems for CAD applications are IBM systems and systems made by other manufacturers that are referred to as IBM ***compatibles*** or ***clones.*** The particular brand name of the computer you are using does not matter, but the available resources such as memory and disk storage space are very important.

The primary component of your computer system is the ***central processing unit,*** or ***CPU.*** This is housed in a rectangular metal box along with your disk drives and other equipment necessary for your computer to function properly. The CPU does all of the actual data processing and numeric calculations required to run your software applications. AutoCAD LT 2000 is designed to run on a PC using an Intel Pentium® processor. The recommended minimum processor speed is 133 megahertz. Although you can run AutoCAD LT on a system with a slower processor, the software speeds may be less than acceptable.

Another very important feature of your computer is the amount of installed ***memory.*** Your system's memory is actually composed of several computer chips that can be used to store data temporarily while programs are running. Generally speaking, the more memory your computer has, the better off you are. Memory size is measured in ***bytes.*** One byte is the approximate space required by the computer to store one text character. Computer terminology uses the metric-style prefixes, so that one *kilo*byte is about one thousand bytes and a *mega*byte (MB) is about one million bytes.

Modern computers are typically sold with 32 to 64 MB of installed memory. The operating system you are using determines the minimum amount of memory required by your computer (operating systems are discussed later). The AutoCAD LT documentation recommends a minimum of 32 MB of memory be installed to run this software. Note that running the software with less than the recommended amount of memory may slow down performance. AutoCAD LT runs best with 64 MB or more of memory.

Additional components include printed circuit boards, often called *cards,* that plug into the larger main system board. Some of these cards merely provide a way for your computer to communicate with various peripheral devices such as your display monitor, pointing device, or printer. Other cards may control disk drives, provide the basis for a sound system, or give you network or telephone line access.

A detailed list of the minimum system requirements for running AutoCAD LT 2000 is provided in Appendix A.

Monitor

The display device for your computer is called a ***monitor.*** Desktop-style workstations usually use CRT (cathode-ray tube) monitors, similar to televisions. Laptop and portable computers often use LCD (liquid crystal diode) display systems.

The screen display is actually composed of many tiny rectangles called ***pixels.*** The term *pixel* is an acronym for *picture elements.* Display quality is measured by the total number of pixels that can be displayed on screen and the number of colors that can be used. The term used to indicate display quality is ***resolution.*** A typical resolution might be 800 × 600. This mean that the display is divided into 800 pixels horizontally and 600 vertically. Higher resolutions, such as 1280 × 1024, use smaller pixels and make the text and images appear smoother. The most common resolutions used on CAD systems provide 1024 × 768 × 256 or better. The last number (256) in this specification indicates how many colors can be displayed.

The resolutions available on your system are related not only to the monitor, but also to your ***video adapter card*** (also referred to as a *graphics card*). This is one of the printed circuit boards mentioned earlier that plugs into your computer to allow it to communicate with peripheral devices. The monitor is a peripheral device and requires an adapter card.

AutoCAD LT requires that you have a VGA (video graphics array) card or better in your system. It is recommended that your display be set to 800 × 600 × 256 or better for AutoCAD LT 2000. Your display looks much better if you have an SVGA (super VGA) or a graphics accelerator card.

Keyboard

The ***keyboard*** is one of the primary tools for communicating with your computer. If you have learned to touch-type then you have a strong advantage when learning to use AutoCAD LT. Although many of your CAD tools can be found through using the menu system, all of the tools are available by typing the proper command name or option using your keyboard. Experienced professionals often tell you that the keyboard is the fastest way to use your CAD application. Although it is not necessary in order to learn AutoCAD LT, regular practice or a course in typing may be helpful.

Many styles of keyboards are available in today's marketplace. Which keyboard you use is an important consideration. The old standard is the 101-key flat keyboard, as shown in Figure 1.2A. If you use one of these keyboards, you should follow certain guidelines to protect yourself from injury. Frequent typing with your wrists bent can cause unnecessary strain and may result in carpal tunnel syndrome or tendinitis. Most computer stores sell wrist pads that are placed in front of the keyboard to keep your wrists elevated and straight to reduce the risk of injury.

A B

FIGURE 1.2 Keyboards used at a CAD workstation. (A) A 101-key flat keyboard. (Courtesy of IBM) (B) A 104-key ergonomic keyboard. (Courtesy of Microsoft Corporation)

Modern keyboards are designed with the normal positions of your hands taken into consideration. These are often referred to as ergonomic keyboards, as shown in Figure 1.2B. These keyboards have features such as built-in wrist pads and contoured key positioning and are angled at the center to allow you to position the keyboard at the proper angle to match the normal position of your hands and to keep your wrists straight.

Pointing Devices

A pointing device is a very important part of your CAD system. Many of the features of your computer software are accessed by an onscreen symbol of an arrow, called a ***cursor.*** Within some applications, a vertical and horizontal line combination called ***crosshairs*** is used. The pointing device is used to move the screen cursor or crosshairs to the desired location. Many styles of pointing devices are available depending on your particular needs or preferences.

The most common device used for this purpose is the ***mouse*** (see Figure 1.3A). This is because the mouse is inexpensive and yet versatile enough to meet the needs of many different software applications. The most commonly used mouse is the mechanical mouse. This device contains a small ball on the underside that rolls when the mouse is moved across a flat surface. Sensors inside the mouse report the motion to your soft-

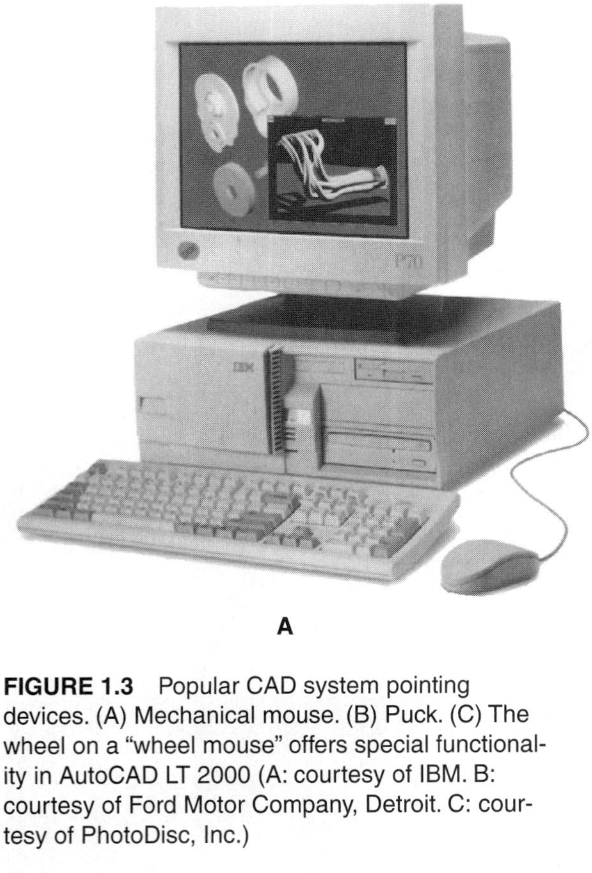

A

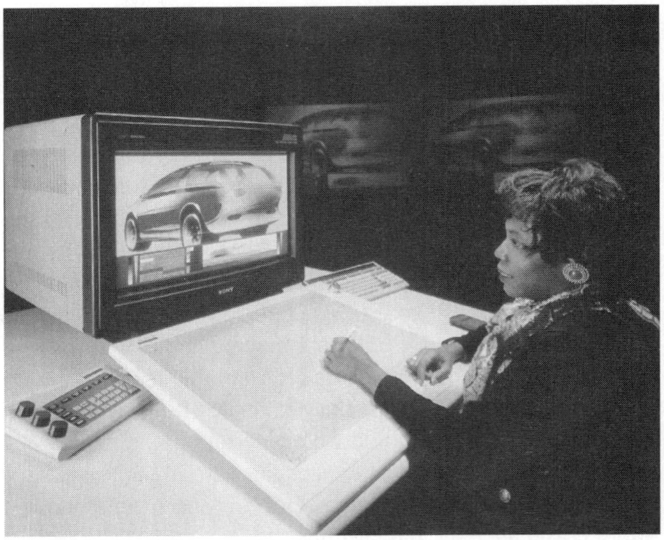

B

FIGURE 1.3 Popular CAD system pointing devices. (A) Mechanical mouse. (B) Puck. (C) The wheel on a "wheel mouse" offers special functionality in AutoCAD LT 2000 (A: courtesy of IBM. B: courtesy of Ford Motor Company, Detroit. C: courtesy of PhotoDisc, Inc.)

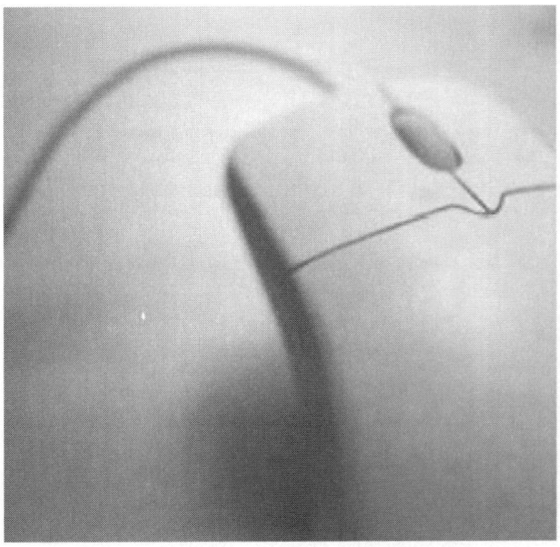

C

ware application and the screen cursor is moved appropriately. Once the cursor is in the desired position, the ***pick button*** can be pressed to cause an action. This action might be selection of a menu item or specification of an object location. A mouse typically has two or three buttons. The purpose of the additional buttons is often determined by your operating system.

Autodesk recommends the use of the Microsoft™ IntelliMouse® with the AutoCAD LT 2000 software. This mouse provides special functionality in the form of a small device between the two primary buttons that acts as both a wheel and a button. The wheel can be rolled, or pressing on it allows it to act as a button. The IntelliMouse is discussed in each area where it applies within this text.

Another style of mouse is the optical mouse. This mouse utilizes a reflective pad with nonreflective grid lines and a light and light sensor. In essence, the light "blinks" each time a grid line is crossed, and each "blink" represents a certain distance moved. Some newer optical mouse products can be used without the special reflective pad.

The trackball is also a popular pointing device. It works much like a mechanical mouse turned upside down. Rather than moving the device itself, the ball is rolled in place. Rolling the ball causes your screen cursor to change position. If you have difficulty using a mouse, the trackball is an excellent alternative.

More specialized types of pointing devices are also available. Two that are often used in CAD applications are the ***puck*** and the ***stylus.*** These two devices must be attached to a ***digitizer tablet.*** The digitizer tablet tracks the position of the pointing device on its surface. This makes it an excellent tool for digitizing existing drawings, or tracing them into the computer. Some tablets are very large to aid in tracing maps and other large drawings.

The puck, which looks somewhat like a mouse but only works on the surface of the digitizer tablet, is shown in Figure 1.3B and 1.4A. These devices usually have between 4 and 16 buttons. Each of the buttons on the puck can be assigned to a specific function.

The stylus is shaped like a pen (see Figure 1.4A). It is often used for more precise digitizing tasks, because it can be controlled much more accurately than a puck. A stylus is typically equipped with one or two buttons, one of which is the pick button.

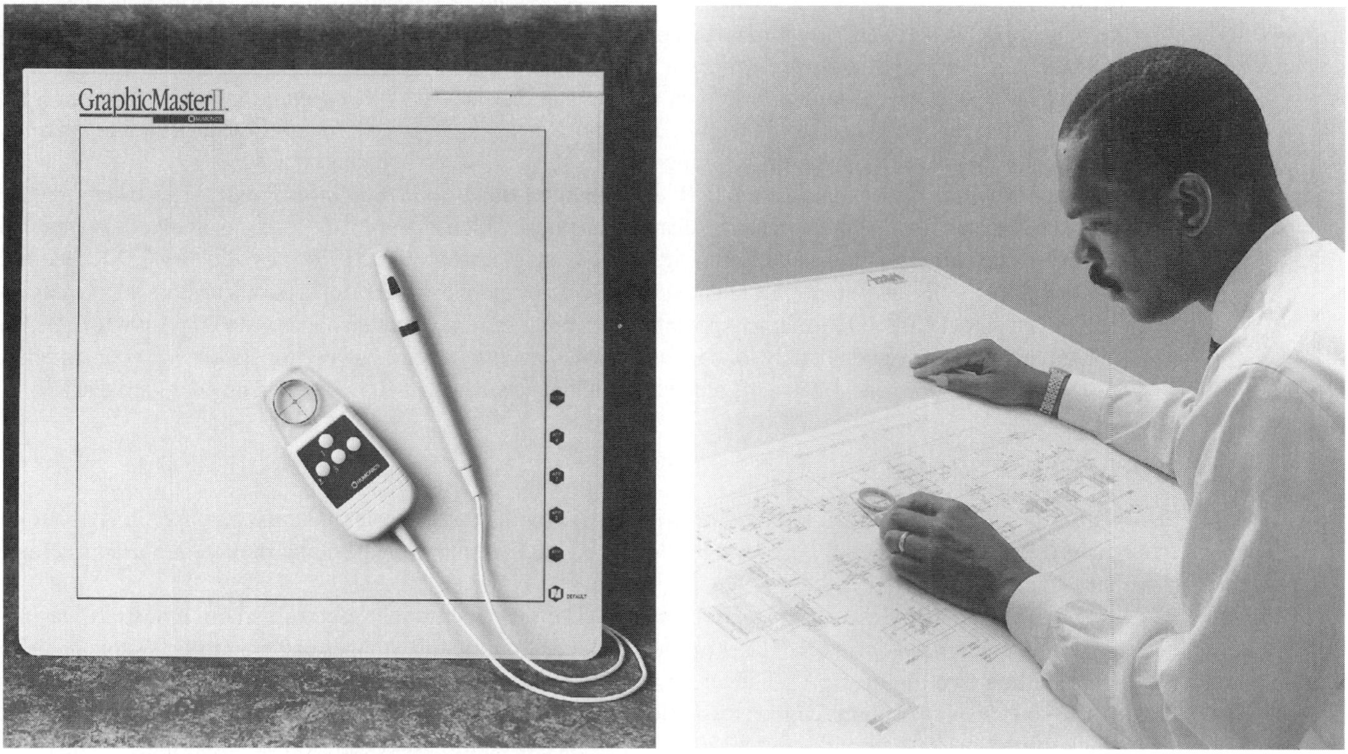

A B

FIGURE 1.4 Common CAD digitizing devices. (Courtesy of Numonics) (A) Digitizer puck; stylus. (B) Desktop digitizer tablet; large table digitizer.

A menu template can be placed on the digitizer tablet to give you access to commonly used menu picks for your AutoCAD LT software. A menu template placed on a digitizer is shown in Figure 1.4B. Many companies create custom templates designed to fit their specific needs.

Field Notes

Although a Microsoft™ Intellimouse® is officially recommended by AutoDesk, many other mouse manufacturers now offer a model with a wheel button. If you decide to purchase an alternative brand, be certain that the mouse has 100% Microsoft wheel functionality. This information should be indicated on the product packaging. Some wheel mouse products come with special software and drivers that provide customizable functionality. However, some of this software may interfere with the native AutoCAD LT wheel mouse functions. If so, uninstall the add-on mouse software to restore AutoCAD LT wheel mouse functionality.

Data Storage Devices

A typical CAD system has one or two disk drives that use floppy diskettes. These removable disks are most commonly used for transferring data to or from your computer. The current industry standard is the high-density 3½-in. diskette, which stores up to 1.44 MB of data files. For compatibility with older systems, your computer may also have a high-density 5¼-in. drive. These diskettes are less durable and less reliable than the 3½-inch style, and they cannot store as much data. Additionally, the 3½-in. diskette is enclosed in a hard protective case, which makes it very convenient to transport.

To be able to permanently store the program files required to run your software applications, personal computers typically use what are called ***hard disks*** or ***nonremovable drives.*** These drives come in many sizes, but as a rule you cannot have too much hard disk space. With the price of magnetic disks continuing to decrease, today's computers are often sold with 1 *giga*byte (one billion bytes) or more of storage space available. This may seem like a lot of space, but you need 73 MB of disk space just for the AutoCAD LT software. Depending on what software packages you are using, you may use up to a gigabyte just to store your operating system and original software program files. Then when you consider the space needed to store your drawings and documents, you may need several gigabytes of storage space.

Optical disk drives (commonly known as compact disk or CD) are a popular storage device as well. These drives use disks that can store up to 4 GB or more on a single disk. Some of these disks are ***rewritable,*** meaning that just like a magnetic drive, you can store, erase, and replace files as needed.

Another type of optical disk is the CD-ROM. The ***ROM*** stands for ***Read-Only Memory.*** This means that the disk can be read, but none of the files can be changed and no additional data can be stored on them. CDs are often used by software companies to deliver their programs. For example, AutoCAD LT is provided on a CD-ROM disk. The entire program fits on a single CD, but it would take 25 or more of the 3½-in. diskettes to store all the files required by AutoCAD LT 2000. (Refer to Appendix A for additional information about installing AutoCAD LT.) A CD-ROM drive is very useful not only for easy and convenient installations, but also for conserving your hard disk space. Many applications can run just off of the CD without needing to be fully installed on your hard disk.

Printers and Plotters

A ***printer*** or ***plotter*** allows you to take a drawing that is on the computer and place it on paper, referred to as ***hardcopy.*** Printers are typically used for producing smaller format drawings, and plotters are used to create larger format drawings.

Many different styles of printers are available. The most commonly used printers in industry today are ***laser printers*** and ***ink-jet printers.*** Laser printers produce high-quality images using up to 1200 dots per inch (dpi) resolution (see Figure 1.5A). The term ***resolution*** is used for printers and plotters in the same way it is used for your display system. Higher resolution values result in cleaner and more accurate printed images. Today's ink-jet printers provide up to 720-dpi or higher resolution and can print photographic-quality images. Ink-jet printers, shown in Figure 1.5B and 1.5C, generally print much slower than laser printers.

Printers are less expensive than plotters and, as a rule, they produce an image much faster than a plotter. For this reason, they are often used to produce check prints. But printers are typically limited to small sizes, such as A size (8.5 × 11 in.) or B size (11 × 17 in.), with some printers producing up to C size (17 × 22 in.) prints. Larger sizes are often produced using plotters.

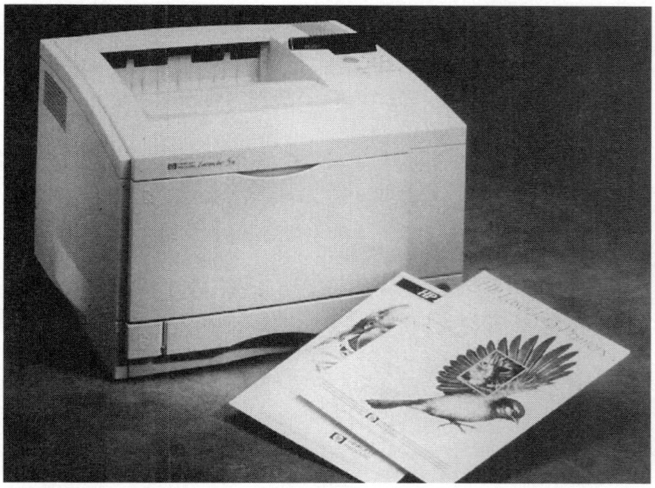

A

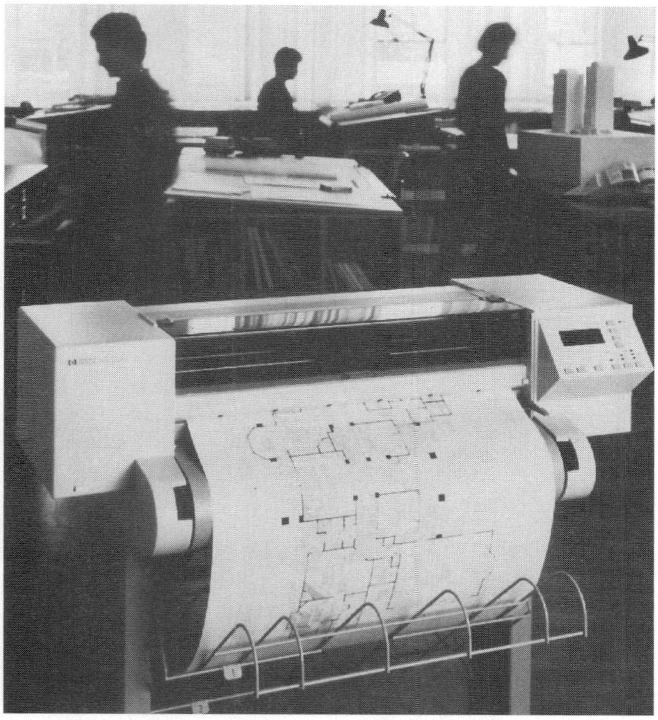

B

FIGURE 1.5 Printers are often used to produce check prints. (Photos courtesy of Hewlett-Packard Company)

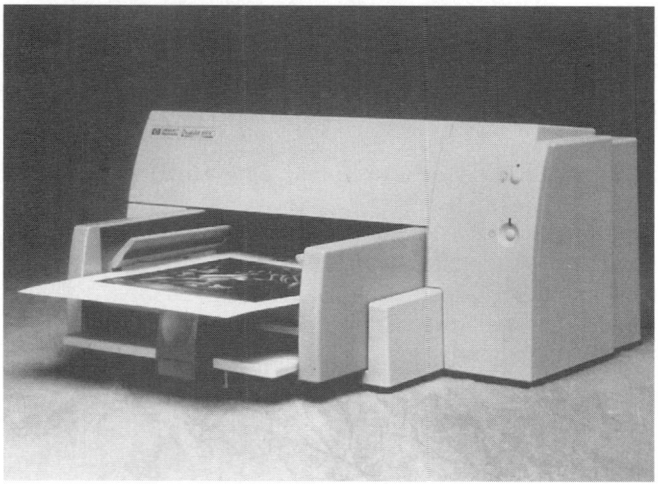

C

Plotters are often used in industry to produce high-quality final prints. A large-format plotter can produce any size drawing from A size to E size (34 × 44 in.) or larger. Some plotters are small enough to go on a desktop and produce only A size or B size drawings.

Pen plotters and ***pencil plotters*** produce the highest quality drawings, but a complex drawing can sometimes take up to an hour or more to complete. Ink-jet plotters can complete a high-quality large-format drawing in a few minutes. This, combined with low cost, has made ink-jet plotters very popular in industry. ***Electrophotographic plotters*** and ***thermal plotters*** are extremely fast and use 300- to 600-dpi resolution to produce a drawing. Many modern plotters can be loaded with an entire roll of paper for unattended plotting. Two styles of plotters are shown in Figure 1.6.

Computer Networks

In an engineering or drafting department where there is more than one workstation, it can be difficult to maintain drawing file control. This refers to ensuring that as a drawing is *edited,* or changed, only the latest revision of the drawing is used by the various people who need to access it. Problems can occur if two or more

A

B

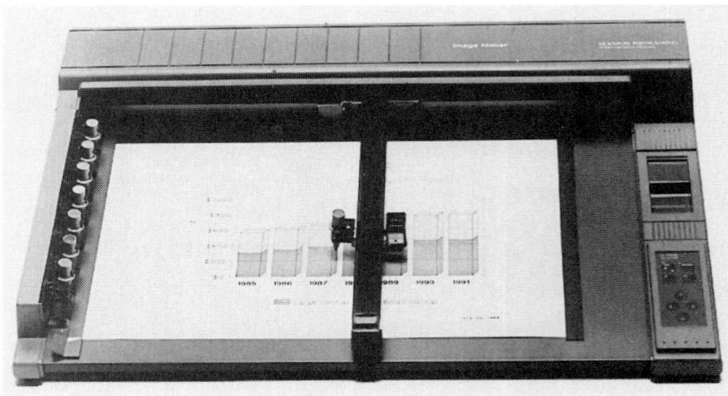

C

FIGURE 1.6 Plotters can produce high-quality final prints in large or small format. (A and B: courtesy of Hewlett-Packard Company; C: courtesy of CalComp Technology, Inc.)

workstations have a copy of the same drawing file, because separate editing can occur in each location, which can result in inconsistent versions of the same drawing being available.

Connecting all of your computer systems in a local-area network (LAN) can help to avoid this and many other possible problems. A typical CAD network uses one computer with a large amount of storage space as a ***file server***. This file server provides a central location for all of the company's or school's drawing files so only one working copy of each file exists. All of the other computers can be connected with a cable to this file server to provide access to the stored files. Networks provide various degrees of security for files, and can be set up so that they do not allow more than one person to work on the file at one time.

In addition to drawing file control, networks provide communication capabilities through the use of ***e-mail*** (electronic mail), security for sensitive data files, and accurate logs of time spent on projects.

Operating Systems

The software that controls your computer system, such as MS DOS or Windows (95/98/NT), is known as an ***operating system.*** AutoCAD LT 2000 can be run under Windows95, Windows98, or Windows NT operating systems. These operating systems provide the same style of interface, and AutoCAD LT works exactly the same in each operating system. Figure 1.7 shows an example of the Windows operating system desktop. The term ***desktop*** refers to the layout of icons and features on the operating system screen.

FIGURE 1.7 The Windows desktop.

Ergonomics in the Workplace

On-the-job injuries related to computer usage are very common today. Such injuries are referred to as musculoskeletal disorders, or MSDs. Most of these injuries are due to what is called *repetitive stress.* This has to do with making the same movements over and over again, such as typing at the keyboard or using a mouse. One of the most well-known repetitive stress injuries is known as *carpal tunnel syndrome. Tendinitis* is another common problem that can occur while working with computers. Both of these disorders can cause pain in your arms, wrists, and hands and can make movement difficult. Other common computer-related problems include neck, back, or leg pain and eye strain. The number of repetitive stress related injuries each year is high enough that, on November 22, 1999, the Occupational Safety & Health Administration (OSHA) proposed a complete set of ergonomic standards to help protect workers in high-risk jobs. If implemented, these proposed standards will require employers to provide ergonomically correct workspaces and equipment to match the physical makeup of each working individual. The OSHA Web site provides additional information on these proposed ergonomic standards (www.osha.gov).

Many of these problems can be prevented by designing your workstation ergonomically (see Figure 1.8). The term ***ergonomic*** in this sense refers to the science of adapting your workstation to fit your body

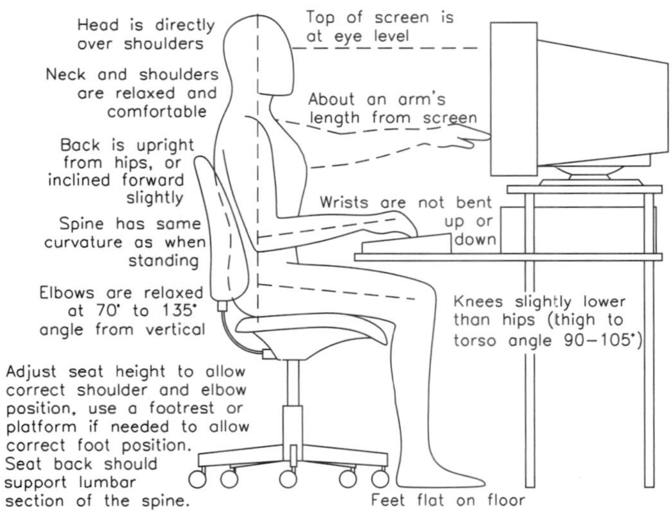

FIGURE 1.8 An ergonomic workstation.

comfortably. Many types of ergonomic equipment can be purchased for your workstation, but there are also many things you can do to your workstation and for yourself to help prevent this type of injury. The following is a listing of considerations and practices to help avoid various types of injuries and disorders:

Wrists and Arms

- Use an ergonomically designed keyboard and pointing device. These devices should fit your hands comfortably and keep your wrists straight while you are using them.
- If you rest your wrists while typing, be sure to use a wrist support pad to keep them straight. The best practice is to not rest your wrists while typing.
- Practice periodic stretching and exercising of shoulders, arms, and wrists.

Neck

- Place your monitor so the top of the screen is at eye level. This keeps you from having to tilt your head either up or down to view your screen.

Back

- Use a comfortable chair with good back support. Your chair should be adjustable for height and tilt and should have armrests.
- Maintain a good sitting posture.
- Take frequent breaks. Stand up and do stretches frequently throughout the day.

Legs

- Adjust the height of the chair so that your feet can rest flat on the floor.
- Use a tilted footrest under the desk to relieve the pressure on your legs while working.
- When possible, take a walk during breaks to stretch and exercise your legs.

Eyes

- The ideal distance from the monitor to your eyes is 18 to 30 inches.
- Keep your screen angled for minimum glare from lighting. If necessary, use a glare screen.
- At least once every 15 min, look away from the screen for a minute or two and focus your eyes on an object at least 20 ft away.

Working every day at the computer is a sedentary job. The only things that really receive regular exercise are your brain and your fingers, so it is important that you participate in sports or other physical activities as appropriate to maintain a healthy heart and lungs. Remember to check with your doctor before beginning a new exercise program.

Accessibility Options

Working at a computer workstation can provide special challenges for people with disabilities. Most of today's computer software applications provide options to adjust the size and colors of features on the screen to improve visibility, as well as alternative methods of entering commands or options. Many computer hardware options are available also, such as specialized pointing devices for users with varied levels of mobility and dexterity. Appendix D provides additional information on accessibility options.

Exercise 1.1 — Estimated time required: 30 min.

1. Write down a list of the equipment currently at your CAD workstation (home, school, or work) with a short description of each piece of equipment. Include settings such as display resolution, memory and hard disk sizes, etc.
2. Adjust your workstation to be as ergonomic as possible. Create a list of additional adjustments that could be made to reduce your risk of injury and increase your comfort while working.

LEARNING CHECKPOINT

- ☐ What are the primary components of a typical CAD workstation?
- ☐ How much memory is recommended for running AutoCAD LT?
- ☐ What is *resolution*? What is a good resolution for a CAD system?
- ☐ What two types of devices are used for creating hardcopy drawings?
- ☐ What is the most commonly used pointing device? Why?
- ☐ How can a network help you maintain drawing control?
- ☐ Why should your workstation be designed ergonomically?
- ☐ Why are breaks, stretching, and exercises an important part of each day?

About AutoCAD LT

AutoCAD LT 2000 software is a full-featured CAD package. This means that it provides many powerful drawing tools and is suitable for use by engineers, architects, drafters, and other design professionals. With more than 250,000 users worldwide, AutoCAD LT is the leading two-dimensional computer-aided drafting program.

The popularity of this software is due to several factors. It provides a full-featured CAD tool set and yet is relatively inexpensive when compared to other packages. Additionally, AutoCAD LT 2000 can directly share drawings with AutoCAD 2000. For companies that are not yet using solid modeling or other advanced features in their design process, AutoCAD LT represents an inexpensive alternative to AutoCAD. In fact, the two packages look and work much the same except for some of the advanced features in AutoCAD that are not present in AutoCAD LT. These missing items include solid modeling and photorealistic rendering, programming interfaces such as Visual LISP™ Visual Basic, Active X, and a few other items that are not required for most conventional two-dimensional drafting tasks.

AutoCAD LT is easy to learn, provides on-line help, and can be an ideal starting package for companies and individuals converting from manual to CAD drafting. Many design professionals who use AutoCAD at work have installed AutoCAD LT at home to enable them to work at home as well. Many drafting and engineering students also use AutoCAD LT because it so closely resembles AutoCAD, yet it costs much less.

In addition to its powerful tool set, AutoCAD LT provides an optional extensive library of predrawn drafting symbols and clip art. These tools can help you get started producing professional-quality drawings right away.

Starting AutoCAD LT

To start AutoCAD LT, the program must first be installed on the hard disk of your computer. The installation process makes copies of the program files on your hard disk. If you have not yet installed the software, refer to Appendix A for installation information.

During installation a new folder is placed in the Programs section of your Start menu. One way to start AutoCAD LT is to pick the Start button, pick Programs, pick the AutoCAD LT 2000 program folder, and then pick the AutoCAD LT 2000 program selection. This menu pick is shown in Figure 1.9. Another way to start AutoCAD LT is to double-click on the AutoCAD LT 2000 shortcut icon on the desktop. The term ***double-click*** means to press the mouse pick button twice very quickly. If it does not work the first time, try it again a little faster. The AutoCAD LT shortcut icon is placed on your desktop during the installation process. This icon is shown in Figure 1.10.

When you start to load the program, your cursor changes into an hourglass shape. This means that the Windows system is busy and that you must wait while the program loads into memory. After a moment or two, an AutoCAD LT logo screen appears in the center of your screen.

The logo screen then disappears and is replaced by the AutoCAD LT program window. You are now ready to begin to explore the AutoCAD LT interface. The term ***interface*** is used to describe the methods by which you communicate with a computer program.

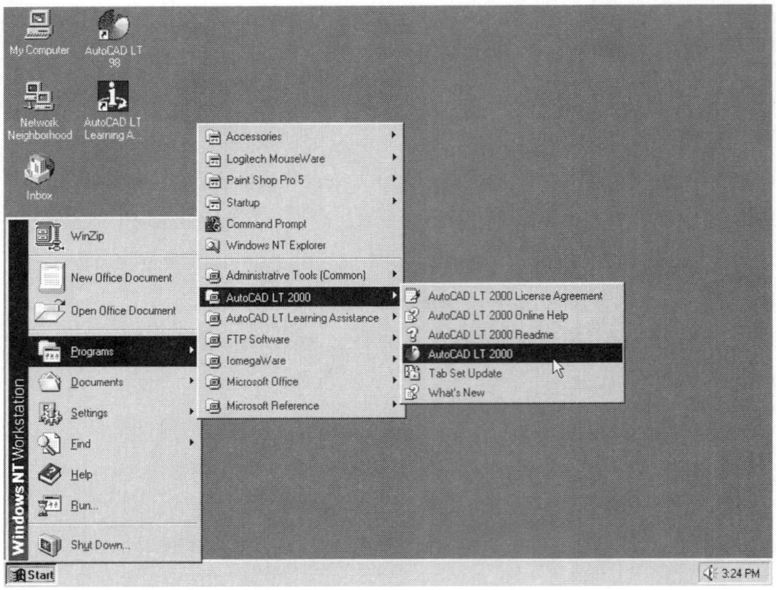

FIGURE 1.9 Starting AutoCAD LT.

FIGURE 1.10 The AutoCAD LT 2000 shortcut icon.

Through the Window...

If you are a new Windows user and have not yet mastered the double-click, you can change the Windows settings to accept a slower double-click. Here's how: Pick the Start button, then select Settings followed by Control Panel. Point at the Mouse icon and right-click (press the *right* mouse button), then pick Open. The Mouse Properties dialog box allows you to adjust and test the double-click speed. If you are using a Microsoft IntelliMouse, picking the Mouse icon launches the configuration software for the IntelliMouse, which can be used to specify your desired mouse settings.

Exercise 1.2 — Estimated time required: 15 min.

1. If AutoCAD LT is not yet installed on your system, refer to Appendix A and follow the described installation procedures. If you are using a school or work computer, ask your instructor or system administrator for guidance.
2. Use the appropriate method to start AutoCAD LT. When the AutoCAD LT program window appears, do not do anything else yet. Continue to read this text for a tour of the AutoCAD LT interface.

Using Dialog Boxes

The first thing AutoCAD LT does once it is running is display the Start Up ***dialog box.*** A dialog box looks somewhat like a program window with a title bar but no border. The purpose of a dialog box is to provide a means for you to enter instructions or settings for a software program with what is referred to as an ***intuitive interface.*** This means that the options are presented in a way to make them clear and easily recognizable. Additionally, dialog boxes require a minimum of typing. Many choices are made simply by moving your cursor to the desired selection and pressing the pick button. Most dialog boxes also provide what is known as ***on-line help.*** The term *on-line* used in this sense means "while you are working." Help is usually available without the need to exit the dialog box you are using, so it does not require an interruption of your work to get guidance or additional information.

Two different types of help are available for most dialog boxes. If you need more information about the features of a dialog box, pick the small question mark button on the title bar next to the Close button. This attaches a question mark to your cursor. Next, point at any dialog box feature and press the pick button. The help information is displayed in a box next to the cursor location. This feature is illustrated in Figure 1.11. The large help button displaying the text “Help” activates the full on-line help system. Using on-line help is discussed later in this chapter.

FIGURE 1.11 (A) The Help button. (B) A question mark is attached to the cursor. (C) Picking a dialog box feature displays additional information.

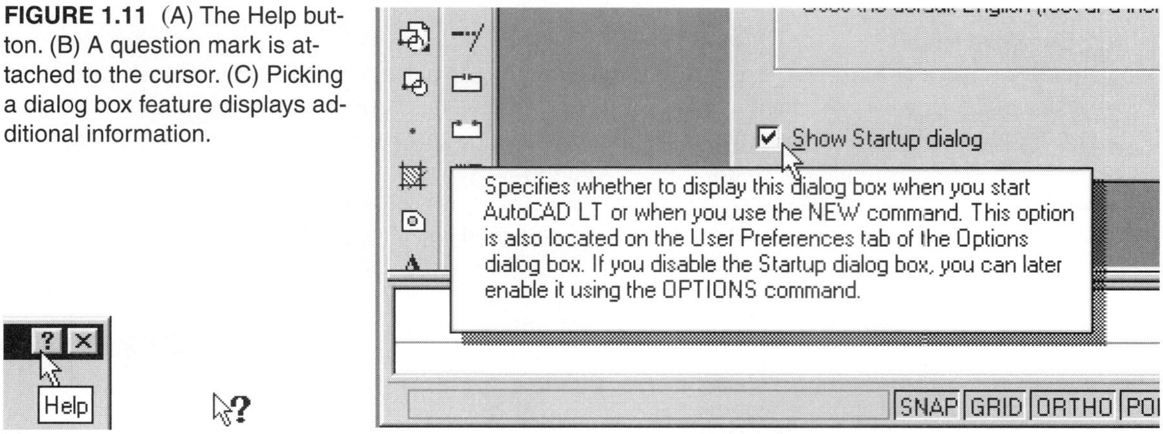

A B C

Dialog boxes in AutoCAD LT have standard features that accept information in a specific way. It is important to understand how to enter or change information using these various features and how to get help when you need it. The following descriptions give you an introduction to dialog box components and familiarize you with how they work.

Buttons

Dialog box buttons appear as slightly raised rectangular buttons. Buttons are most often used to start an action of some type. Every dialog box has at least one button that exits the dialog box. The OK and Cancel buttons are the two most common exit buttons. If you pick the OK button, all of the settings or changes you made in the dialog box are accepted; if you press Cancel, then any changes you made are discarded. Many dialog boxes also have a Help button that displays a help screen regarding the dialog box you are using. Figure 1.12 shows an OK, Cancel, and Help button arrangement as encountered in many dialog boxes. Note the bold outline around the OK button; this indicates that it is the default option, which is the option that will be selected if you press the Enter key on your keyboard.

FIGURE 1.12 The OK, Cancel, and Help buttons are found at the bottom of many of the AutoCAD LT dialog boxes.

Buttons that cause specific actions have a unique style of text label. For example, the *ellipsis* (three periods: ...) on a button indicates that a ***subdialog box*** will be displayed after you pick this button. A subdialog box is displayed and made active without hiding or ending the previous dialog box. When you finish working in the subdialog box, the previous dialog box is again made active.

When a button label is followed by the less than symbol (<), which resembles a left-facing arrow, then picking that button temporarily hides the current dialog box and allows you to provide input by picking an object or a location in the drawing.

List Boxes

When several options are available to you, they are often presented in the form of a list in a ***list box.*** A selection can be made by pointing to it and pressing the pick button on your mouse. If more options are available than can be displayed at once, a scroll bar and arrows are placed on the side of the list. You can use the scroll bar and arrows to move up or down in the list and display additional choices. In some lists, more than one selection can be made at one time. An example of a list box is shown in Figure 1.13.

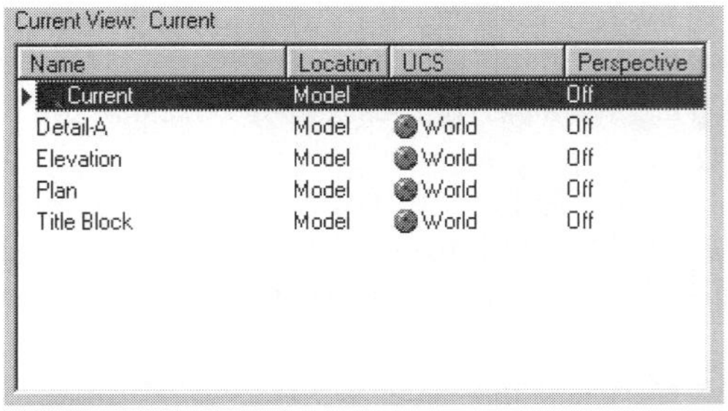

FIGURE 1.13 A list box can present several options.

Popup List Boxes

A popup list is similar to a list box, except that it must first be expanded to see the available selections. On the right side of a popup list is a button with a down arrow. Picking this button displays the options contained in the list. Another difference between popup lists and list boxes is that you can make only one selection at a time in a popup list. As with the list boxes, if more options are available than can be displayed at once in the list, a scroll bar and arrows are placed on the side of the list. The current selection is displayed when the list is collapsed. Figure 1.14 shows the same popup list in a collapsed and an expanded state.

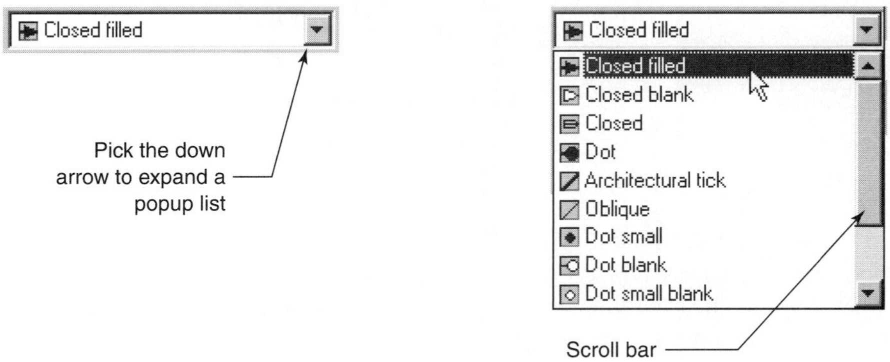

FIGURE 1.14 Picking a popup list expands it to display available options.

Radio Buttons

Radio buttons typically present a number of options, allowing only one item to be selected. Radio buttons are named after the buttons on a car radio. By pressing one of the buttons, you switch to a new setting and turn off the button that was previously selected. The same is true of radio buttons in a dialog box. A set of radio buttons is shown in Figure 1.15.

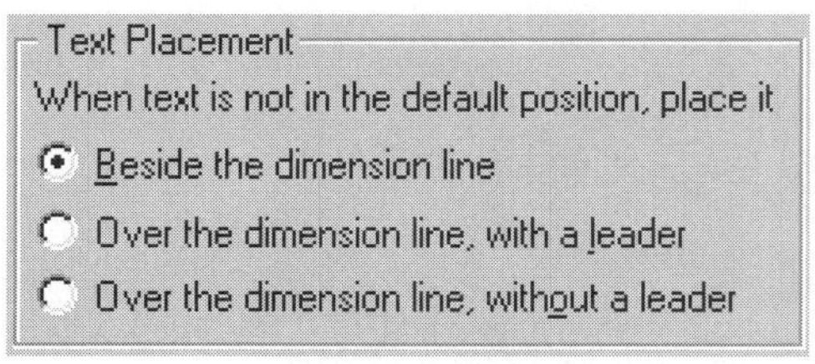

FIGURE 1.15 A set of radio buttons allows only one selection.

Edit Boxes

An ***edit box*** provides a means of entering text or number values into the dialog box. Edit boxes are sometimes referred to as *text boxes*. Some edit boxes allow only a limited number of characters to be entered, while others scroll from side to side to provide additional room for text. Edit boxes typically provide a text label that describes what type of information should be entered. Figure 1.16 shows an example of an edit box.

Images and Image Buttons

Dialog boxes often provide images within the dialog box that show the current settings. Some of these images are buttons, allowing you to pick an image directly and toggle through the available settings until you

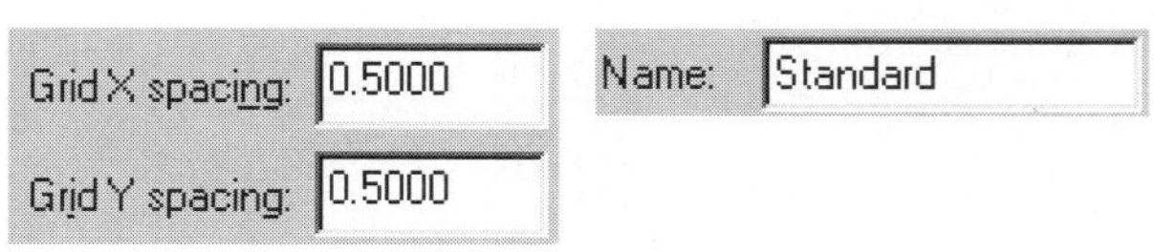

FIGURE 1.16 Edit boxes are used for entering text or number values.

Field Notes

When using edit boxes, you can edit the text using some of the tools available in most Windows text editing programs. These techniques can save you time and make your editing much easier:

- Use your arrow keys on the keyboard to move the cursor location.
- The Home key moves the cursor to the beginning of a line of text. The End key moves it to the end of the text.
- The Ctrl and Shift keys can be used in combination with the arrow keys for faster movement and highlighting text.
- Typing while all or part of the text is highlighted automatically replaces the highlighted text.
- Double-clicking in an edit box highlights the entire contents.
- The Delete key and Backspace key can be used to remove text as needed.
- Ctrl+C copies the highlighted text, Ctrl+V can be used to paste, and Ctrl+X cuts the text.

get the desired image. Other types of images include simple square color swatches that show color settings. Images help to make items in dialog boxes instantly recognizable. An example of an image button that controls the appearance of point objects is shown in Figure 1.17.

FIGURE 1.17 Some images are also buttons that can be selected directly.

Toggles

A *toggle,* like an electric light switch, turns a feature on or off. Each toggle, or *checkbox,* consists of a small square box and a label describing a feature. If the feature is on or active, a check mark or an X appears in the box. If the box is empty, the feature is turned off. Picking the label or the box switches the setting. Figure 1.18 shows an example of toggles.

FIGURE 1.18 Picking a toggle turns it either on or off, depending on the current value.

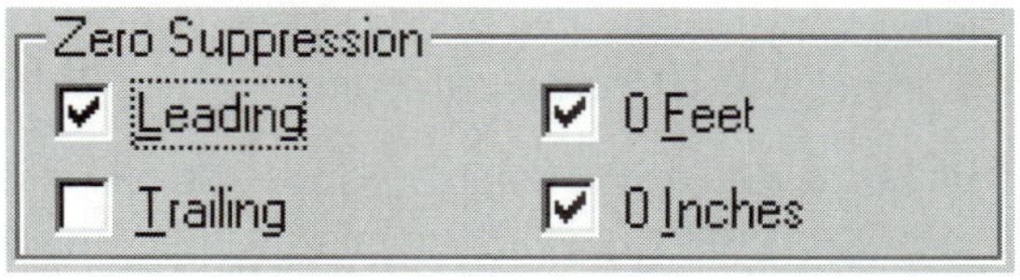

Sliders

Sliders are used to change values interactively. A slider can be adjusted by picking the arrows at either end, which moves the slider in small steps. Larger steps can be taken by picking the background area of the slider bar itself. You can also point to the elevator button, press, and hold your pick button and move the slider interactively. Releasing the pick button places the elevator button in its current location. The slider shown in Figure 1.19 changes the size of the square in the image to the right.

FIGURE 1.19 Sliders provide an interactive way to adjust values.

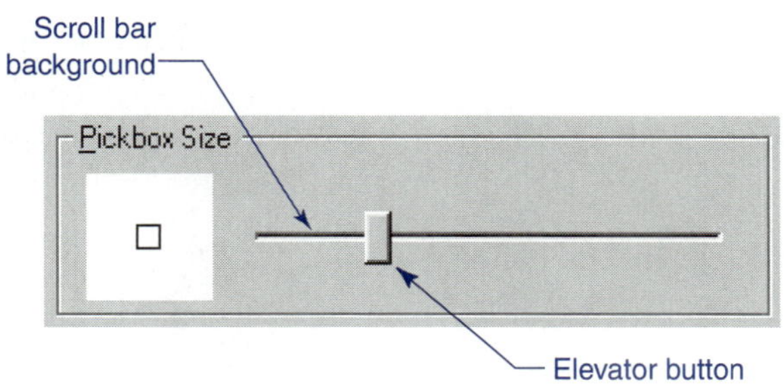

Dialog Box Error Messages

If a required value is omitted, or a value is entered incorrectly, most dialog boxes display an error message. Messages regarding warnings or errors are displayed in an ***alert box*** (see Figure 1.20). An alert box requires that you pick a button, usually an OK button, before you can proceed. It is important to read these messages, because sometimes the warnings are to prepare you for what might otherwise be unexpected results in your drawing efforts.

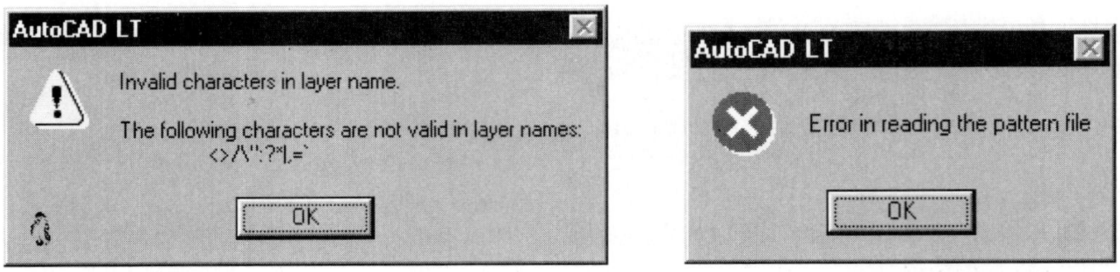

A Warning message **B** Error message

FIGURE 1.20 (A) Warning messages display an exclamation point. (B) Error messages display an X in a red circle.

Keyboard Shortcuts

Many of the labels on a dialog box show one character underlined. This provides you with the ability to access dialog box features using your keyboard. To access an item displaying an underscored character, press the Alt key in combination with the underscored character. For example, to access the Help button displayed in Figure 1.12, you press Alt+H.

When an item has keyboard focus (when it is highlighted), the value can be changed by typing a new value. Toggle values can be changed by pressing the spacebar; radio buttons can be cycled through using the arrow keys. In most cases, however, using your cursor is the easiest way to use a dialog box.

☑ LEARNING CHECKPOINT

- ☐ How is AutoCAD LT 2000 started?
- ☐ What are the advantages of a dialog-style interface?
- ☐ Describe the usage of buttons, lists, radio buttons, toggles, and sliders.
- ☐ Where are the two primary locations for error messages in a dialog session?
- ☐ How can dialog box features be accessed with the keyboard?

Accessing AutoCAD LT Commands and Features

AutoCAD LT provides several ways to access its commands and features. This adds versatility to the program and allows you to use the method that works best for you. Becoming familiar with the layout of the AutoCAD LT screen and how to access commands quickly is an important part of mastering the use of AutoCAD LT 2000.

The primary means of accessing AutoCAD LT commands and features is through the ***menu*** system. Like a menu at a restaurant, a menu in AutoCAD LT offers you a list of available options and commands from which to choose. This section introduces you to the techniques for using AutoCAD LT's menu system.

When you first start AutoCAD LT the Startup dialog box is displayed (see Figure 1.21). This dialog box is discussed in detail in Chapter 2. For now, dismiss this dialog box without making any changes by picking the Cancel button.

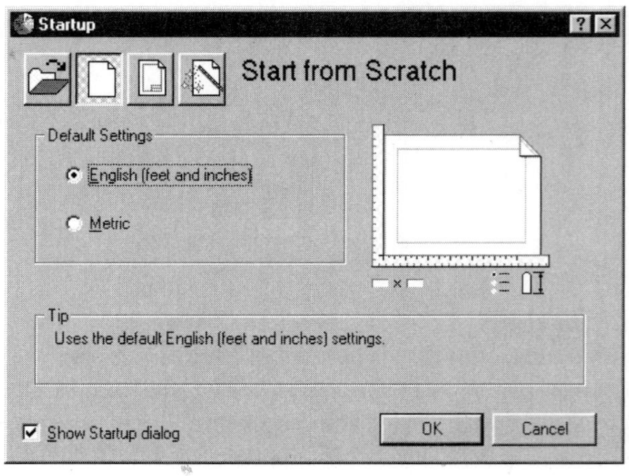

FIGURE 1.21 The Startup dialog box is displayed when you start AutoCAD LT.

After the Startup dialog box is dismissed, the AutoCAD LT graphics screen is completely visible. AutoCAD LT has two screens. The graphics screen is used for drawing and editing objects, and the text screen is used for obtaining text-based information about the drawing. The text screen is not visible at this time. The graphics screen layout is detailed in Figure 1.22. Study this figure along with the descriptions that follow. Note that in the Windows operating system, your task bar may be displayed at the bottom, depending on how you have your desktop configured.

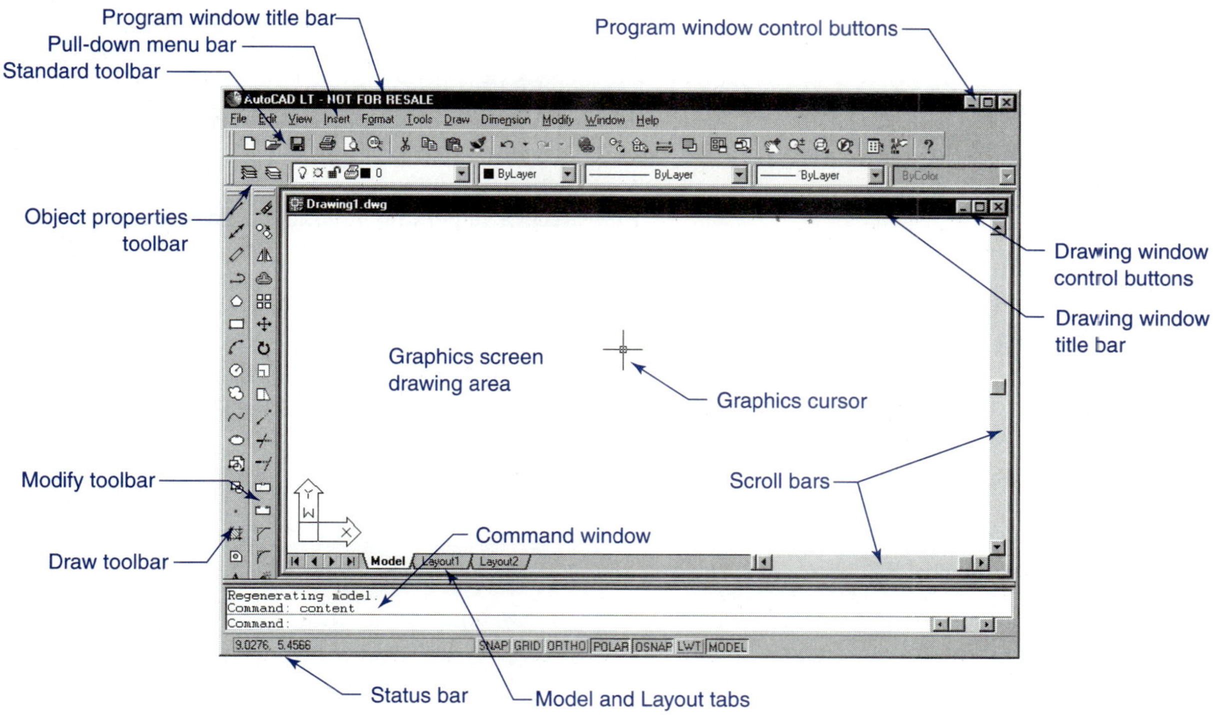

FIGURE 1.22 The AutoCAD LT graphics screen layout.

Brief descriptions of each of the AutoCAD LT graphics screen components are given here. Their usage is detailed in the sections that follow.

- **Title bar:** The title bar of the AutoCAD LT program window is a standard feature of all program windows. In AutoCAD, the title bar reports the name of the application and, when the drawing window is maximized, displays the name of the current drawing in square brackets. When the drawing window is not maximized, the drawing file name is displayed on the drawing window title bar. If you have not yet given the current drawing a name, the name *Drawing1.dwg* appears in the brackets.
- **Window control buttons:** These buttons appear at the top of all program windows. They provide a simple means to adjust the size of the AutoCAD LT window. The control buttons on the drawing window title bar are used to adjust the appearance of individual drawing windows.
- **Pull-down menu bar:** Each of the names on this menu bar is associated with a pull-down menu. Picking the menu name displays the associated menu.
- **Standard toolbar:** Each of the buttons on this toolbar starts a command or performs a function in AutoCAD LT. The toolbar buttons grouped in this toolbar include those for standard Windows tools, along with a selection of commonly used AutoCAD LT commands.

- **Object Properties toolbar:** This toolbar presents a set of tools that control the appearance and various properties of the objects in your drawing.
- **Draw toolbar:** The most commonly used drawing options are presented in this toolbar.
- **Modify toolbar:** This toolbar provides access to the most frequently used object modification options in AutoCAD LT.
- **Graphics screen drawing area:** This is where the current view of your drawing is displayed. As you work in your drawing, this is where you will most commonly interact with your drawing.
- **Horizontal and vertical scroll bars:** These scroll bars provide a convenient means to change the drawing display area to show another area of your drawing.
- **Command window:** This is where commands typed in will appear, along with prompts from AutoCAD LT requesting information from you.
- **Command window scroll bars:** These allow you to scroll up, down, right, or left as needed to view information not currently visible in the command window.
- **Status bar:** The status bar displays information about your drawing and the current settings for various features of AutoCAD LT. When you point at a toolbar button or menu item, a help string is displayed on the status bar.
- **Graphics cursor:** The cursor changes to this shape when the drawing and viewport where the cursor points are active.

Canceling an AutoCAD LT Command

Any instruction you give to AutoCAD LT is referred to as a ***command.*** AutoCAD LT has many commands available, some for creating drawing objects and others for modifying drawing objects. Frequently, after starting a command, you may decide that you want to stop the command without completing it. Most commands, even if they are currently in progress, can be canceled by pressing the Esc (Escape) key on your keyboard. The Esc key is found at the upper left corner of most keyboards. Pressing the Esc key once or twice returns AutoCAD LT to a ready state so another command can be entered, or even the same command using different options.

Using Pull-Down Menus in AutoCAD LT

The primary text-based menu structure in AutoCAD LT is the ***pull-down menu*** system. The pull-down menu bar shown in Figure 1.22 displays several options that can be picked to display a pull-down menu. To see how these menus work, point to the File option and press the pick button. The menu displayed appears to be pulled down from the menu bar (see Figure 1.23). As you move your cursor up and down the menu, the item you are currently pointing at appears highlighted. Another area to watch as you scroll through the menu choices is the lower left area of the screen. The status line is temporarily hidden and a ***help string*** is displayed in its place. A help string is a brief description that expresses the effect of the command associated with the menu selection at which you are pointing. The description ends with a colon (:), followed by the name of the command associated with that menu selection. Pressing the pick button selects the currently highlighted item and starts the associated command. As you point at the New … command in the File menu, note the help string message: *Creates a new drawing file: NEW.*

The underlined character in the menu bar titles and each of the menu options is referred to as a ***menu access key.*** These provide keyboard access to the pull-down menus. For example, to access the New … option from the File menu, first press an Alt+F keystroke to display the File menu. Then, press the N key to access the New … option.

If you have selected a menu that does not contain the option that you are looking for, simply pick another menu name. The previous menu is hidden and the new menu is then displayed. If you want to dismiss the currently displayed menu without making another selection, you can press the Esc key.

Many pull-down menu choices display a ***cascading submenu,*** also known as a *walking* or *hierarchical* menu, that presents a group of related commands. This allows a single pull-down menu to provide access to many more options without increasing the size of the menu. Menu selections that have a cascading submenu display an arrow on the right edge of the menu. When you select one of these options, the cascade is automatically displayed. Then you can pick the desired menu selection. Figure 1.24 shows the cascading submenu for the Drawing Utilities option on the File pull-down menu.

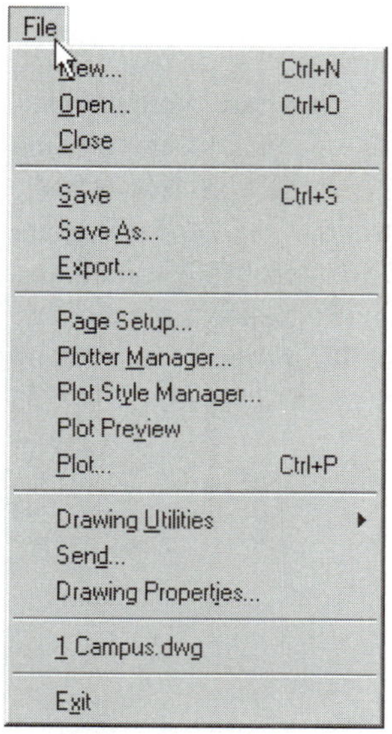

FIGURE 1.23 The File pull-down menu.

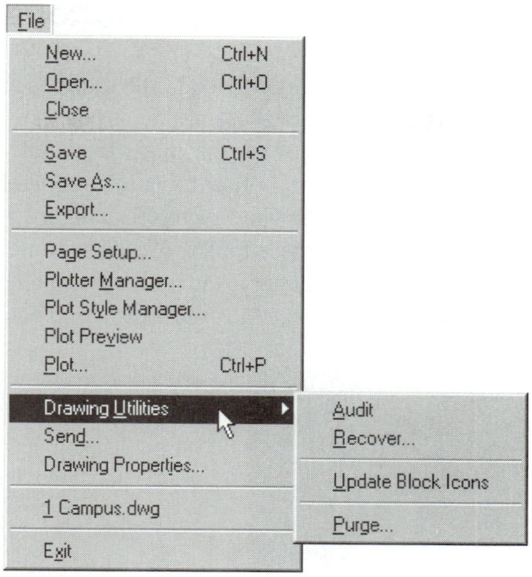

FIGURE 1.24 Cascading submenus display additional choices.

Accelerator Keys

On the File and Edit pull-down menus, some of the selections show a description of a keystroke combination that is referred to as an ***accelerator key.*** An accelerator key is an option provided for easy access to commonly used functions and commands. As an example, rather than picking the New ... command in the File menu, you could instead use the Ctrl+N keystroke to start the NEW command. To perform a Ctrl+N keystroke, press and hold the Ctrl button on your keyboard. Next, press the N key and then release both keys.

AutoCAD LT is said to be *Microsoft Windows logo-compliant,* meaning that the toolbars, menus, and accelerator keys are similar to those available in other Microsoft Windows applications, such as Word, Access, and Excel. If you currently use any of these applications, you may already be familiar with many of the accelerator keys available in AutoCAD LT 2000.

Field Notes

There are actually two completely different methods for using pull-down menus with your mouse. The first method requires making two or more individual picks. For example, to select the New ... command from the File menu:

1. Point to the menu bar and pick File by pressing and immediately releasing the pick button.
2. Point to the New ... command and press and release the pick button.

The second method is done by picking only once:

1. Point to the menu bar and pick File by pressing and continuing to hold the pick button.
2. Move the cursor to the New ... command and release the pick button.

Either method produces the same results. Use the method that you are most comfortable with.

AutoCAD LT Toolbars and Toolbar Buttons

The key features of the AutoCAD LT interface are the toolbars and toolbar buttons. These are typically preferred to the use of pull-down menus, because a toolbar button usually requires only one pick to start a command. Each toolbar displays a variety of buttons that start AutoCAD LT commands or functions. By default, the first time you start AutoCAD LT, only four toolbars are visible: the Standard toolbar, the Object Properties toolbar, the Draw toolbar, and the Modify toolbar. Figure 1.25 shows the Draw and Modify toolbars. There are many different buttons on these toolbars, each with its own unique image. In a short time most of these will be familiar to you and you will recognize them immediately. One of the primary features of AutoCAD LT that will help you in this area is the tooltip and help string displayed by each button.

FIGURE 1.25 The Draw and Modify toolbars.

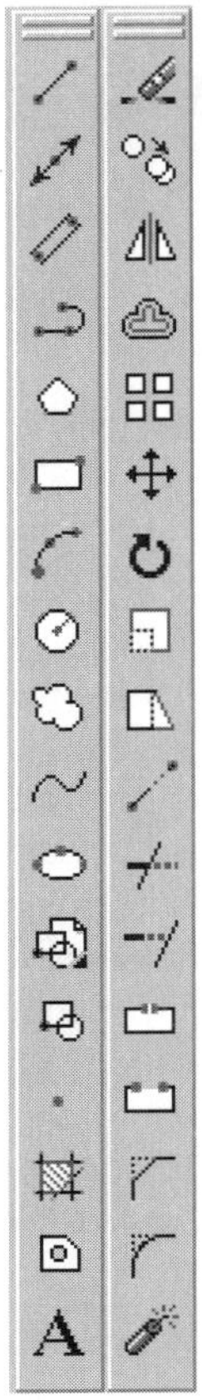

When you point at a toolbar button with your cursor and leave it there for about a half of a second or so, a small text box is displayed next to the cursor that gives the name of the button—this is called a ***tooltip***. When a tooltip is displayed, a help string also appears on the status line in the lower left area of the AutoCAD LT window. The tooltip most often serves as a reminder of what the graphic image on the button means. Using this feature you can quickly familiarize yourself with the appearance of the buttons you use frequently. The help strings for toolbar buttons are the same as described earlier regarding pull-down menu selections. For example, in Figure 1.26, note the tooltip for the New button and the help string displayed on the status line. The tooltip reminds you that the graphic image represents the NEW command. If you need to know more about the NEW command, read the description on the status line. This button displays the message: *Creates a new drawing file: NEW.* The help string for a command typically remains constant regardless of the method used to pick the command. If you need more information than is displayed in the help string, you can use AutoCAD LT's Help facility, which is discussed later in this chapter. Pointing to a toolbar button and picking it activates its command.

FIGURE 1.26 Tooltips and help strings help you to recognize toolbar buttons quickly.

Tooltip

Help string

Some of the toolbar buttons display an arrow in the lower right corner of the image. This type of button is known as a ***flyout.*** A flyout is a special type of button that is like a toolbar within a toolbar. To access the currently displayed button on the flyout, point to it and pick just as you would with any other button. The tooltip and help string for a flyout are displayed in the same manner as other toolbar buttons. To see how a flyout is different, point to it, press, and hold down the pick button.

A flyout will typically display a group of related commands. After displaying the flyout, move the cursor to the additional buttons. Continue to hold the pick button in until you are ready to make your choice. Note that you can display tooltips and help strings for each of the buttons on the flyout as well. Once you have made your decision, point to the desired button and release the pick button on the mouse. The command you are pointing to when you release the pick button is activated.

For example, in Figure 1.27, the flyout for the Zoom button on the Standard toolbar is shown. Note that the tooltip for the Zoom In button is visible. Releasing the pick button while pointing to the Zoom In button activates the appropriate command for changing the display. This command is covered in Chapter 4.

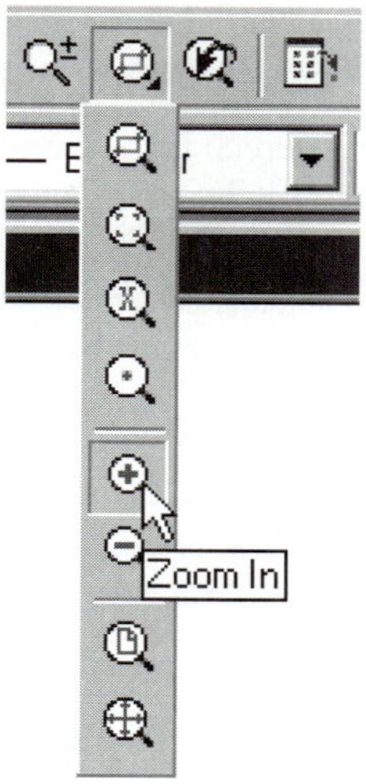

FIGURE 1.27 The Zoom flyout. Flyouts display additional related commands.

When you select an option from a flyout, the image for the most recent button selected from the flyout is displayed on the top-level button. The button displayed when the rest of the flyout is not visible is considered the top-level button.

After a selection is made, as shown in Figure 1.27, the Zoom In button becomes the top-level button. See the change in the Standard toolbar shown in Figure 1.28. If you need to access a different zooming option, you must display the flyout as you did to select the Zoom In button and use the same method to select the new option.

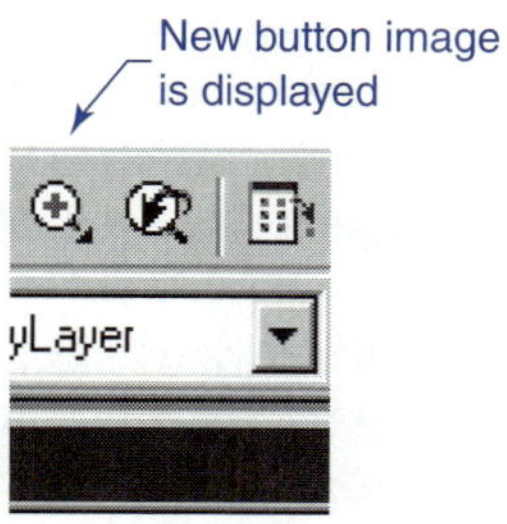

FIGURE 1.28 The most recently selected button becomes the top-level button on a flyout.

Field Notes

One common problem for new AutoCAD LT users comes from accidentally hiding a floating toolbar. Hiding a toolbar makes it unusable until it is again made visible. In Windows, a floating toolbar is hidden by picking the button in the upper right corner. By default, your toolbars are docked in the initial view. Floating and docking toolbars are covered later in this chapter.

If you do accidentally hide a toolbar, it is easy to make it visible again. Here's how:

1. Pick the View pull-down menu.
2. Select the Toolbars ... option to display the Toolbars dialog box.
3. Place a checkmark in the box next to the toolbar name (for example: Draw) by picking it.
4. Pick the OK button to return to your drawing.

The AutoCAD LT Command Window and the Text Screen

One of the primary areas to watch on the AutoCAD LT screen is the Command window (see Figure 1.29). If the command you are using does not use a dialog box, this is where AutoCAD LT communicates with you. Options for commands are listed in this area, and AutoCAD LT's requests for information, warnings, and error messages are found here as well. For example, if you start a LINE command, the prompt *From point:* appears in the command window. The term ***prompt*** refers to a request by AutoCAD LT for input.

FIGURE 1.29 Watch the Command window carefully to see what type of input is required.

You can also enter commands directly into the Command window using the keyboard. When you type a command or option at the command line, you must follow the command with an Enter keystroke. If you watch the Command window while picking a command using a toolbar button or a menu selection, you see the command entered in the Command window automatically. If you do type commands, you can type the full command name or for some commands you can type what is known as a ***command alias.*** A command alias is a shortened version of a command name made to boost your speed for Command window entries. As commands are discussed in this text, if a command alias exists it will be listed as well.

By default, the current line and the two previous lines of information are displayed in the Command window. To the right of the Command window are a vertical and a horizontal scroll bar. These can be used to view lines of text that have scrolled up and are no longer visible. In some cases, on lower resolution screens, some command option lines or messages may be too wide to be displayed in the Command window. Use the horizontal scroll bar to scroll right if you need to see the rest of the text.

It is very important to pay close attention to the Command window. If AutoCAD LT is currently prompting you with a Command: prompt, then it is awaiting entry of a command. The term *Command: prompt* is used to indicate a prompt on the bottom line of the command window that reads simply *Command:*. If a Command: prompt is not visible, then a command is already active. When a command is active, an ***option line*** is often displayed. An option line presents the available options for the currently active command.

Even so, some messages may scroll off of the Command window before you can completely read them. Or you may wish to check to see if you entered something incorrectly. You can view as many as 200 lines of text that have scrolled off of the Command window by opening AutoCAD LT's Text window.

Press the F2 function key on your keyboard to toggle back and forth between the graphics and text window. Figure 1.30 shows the appearance of the AutoCAD LT Text window. The scroll bars can be used if you need to review more information than is displayed currently in the Text window.

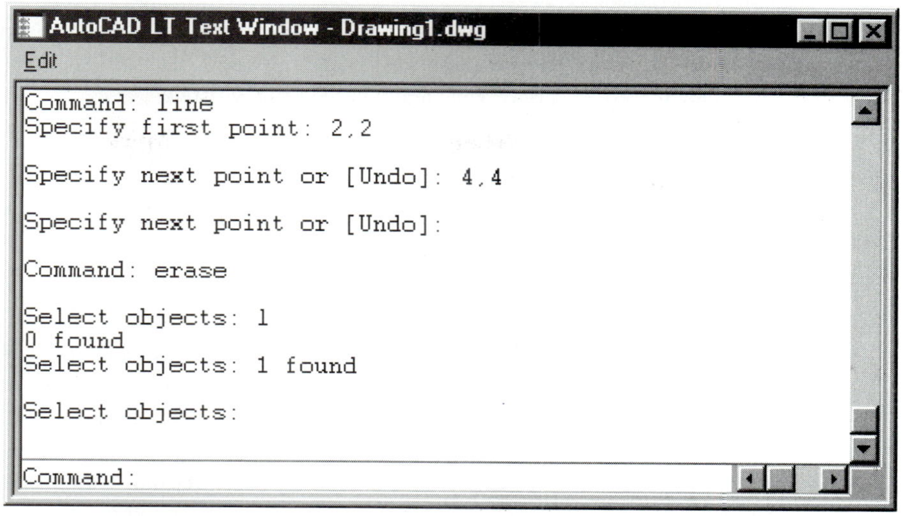

FIGURE 1.30 The Text window can be used to view text that has scrolled off of the Command window.

Field Notes

- Except when you are creating text in your drawing, pressing the spacebar is the same as pressing the Enter key.
- By pressing the up and down arrow keys on the keyboard, you can cycle through the command entries and options that you have entered previously. To reuse one of these options, press Enter when it is displayed.

Exercise 1.3

Estimated time required: 5 min.

1. Open the AutoCAD LT program.
2. In the Startup dialog box, press each of the buttons at the top. Note the changes in the dialog box content. Pick the Cancel button to dismiss the dialog box.
3. Use your mouse to explore the pull-down menus and toolbar buttons, reading the tooltips and help strings as you do so. If you accidentally start a command, press the Esc key to cancel it.
4. Use your mouse to pick the New ... option from the File pull-down menu. When the Create New Drawing dialog box appears, press the Esc key to cancel.
5. Use your keyboard to access the New ... option from the File pull-down menu. When the Create New Drawing dialog box appears, pick the Cancel button to cancel it.
6. Pick the New toolbar button from the Standard toolbar. When the Create New Drawing dialog box appears, pick the Close button at the upper right corner of the dialog box to cancel it.
7. Type **NEW** in at the Command: prompt and press Enter. Again, cancel the Create New Drawing dialog box.
8. Use the accelerator keystroke Ctrl+N to enter the NEW command and cancel the Create New Drawing dialog box.
9. Think about the many ways available to enter or to cancel an AutoCAD LT command. Consider the advantages and disadvantages of each method.

LEARNING CHECKPOINT

- ☐ What is the primary means of accessing AutoCAD LT commands?
- ☐ Name the primary text-based menu system in AutoCAD LT.
- ☐ What is a menu access key and how is it used?
- ☐ What are cascading submenus?
- ☐ List the four toolbars visible the first time you start AutoCAD LT.

- ☐ What are tooltips and help strings and how can they help you?
- ☐ How is a flyout used?
- ☐ What are accelerator keys and where are they listed?
- ☐ What is the Command: prompt?
- ☐ Why is it important to watch the Command window very carefully?
- ☐ What is the AutoCAD LT text screen and how can it be displayed?

Sizing and Positioning the AutoCAD LT Window

In Windows, programs that you run are displayed within a rectangular border known as a ***window.*** The program windows provide a great deal of flexibility, allowing you to move and size the windows as needed. Program windows in both operating systems provide the same capabilities, but provide different ways of doing things.

The reason for needing to size and move your program windows has to do with the capability in Windows operating systems of opening more than one document or one program at a time. This even applies to AutoCAD LT 2000, because you can open more than one drawing file at a time. This gives you the capability of sharing drawing data by copying objects from one drawing into another. Professional drafters are often able to reuse symbols or geometry from drawings created previously. Being able to open more than one drawing at a time makes it easy to copy things from one drawing to the other and can save a lot of time.

Whether you are editing multiple drawings in AutoCAD LT, running other applications, or just working in a single application, it is important to understand how to work with program windows.

In both operating systems, the ***title bar*** is the location of the controls for most of the window functions. The title bar is the area across the top of a program window that lists the program and the name of the currently opened file. The Windows operating system uses icons, or pictures, rather than text wherever possible. Figure 1.31A shows the AutoCAD LT 2000 title bar displayed in Windows and lists the features. In Figure 1.31B, note that the icon image associated with AutoCAD LT is displayed in the upper left corner. Picking this icon displays a menu. A menu is a listing of tasks or options that can be started simply by pointing to the desired item and pressing the pick button.

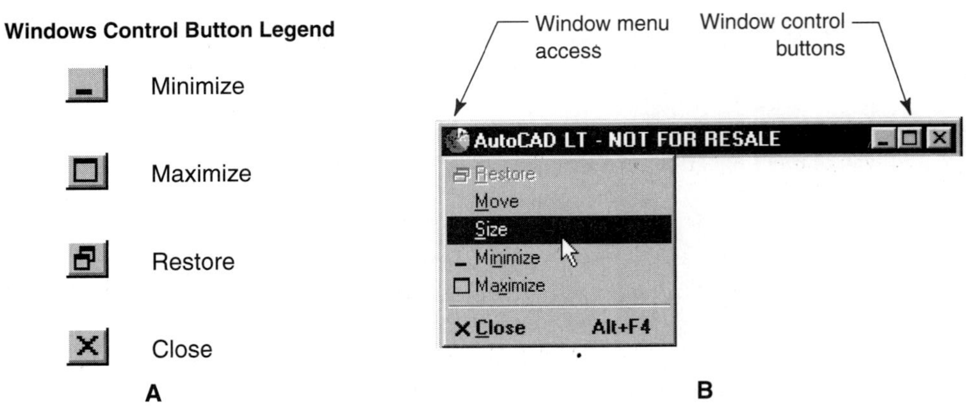

FIGURE 1.31 AutoCAD LT program window title bars.

The standard program window menus for both operating systems are shown in Figure 1.31B. Individual drawing windows also display a Next option for switching the active drawing. Items that are available to you are printed distinctly, and items that are not currently available appear to be somewhat transparent, or "grayed out." The options are described here:

- **Restore:** Available only when the program window is either maximized or minimized, this option restores the window to the last floating position.
- **Move:** Available only on floating windows, this option changes the cursor to a four-way arrow and allows you to move the window. Point to the title bar, press and hold the pick button, and move your mouse. Release the pick button to drop the window and leave it in its new position. Note that you can do the same task without picking Move first. Just point to the title bar with your standard cursor, press and hold pick, and move the window in the same way.
- **Size:** Available only on floating windows, this option changes the cursor to a four-way arrow

and allows you to change the size of the window. Point to the border on the edge of the window and the cursor changes shape to show you whether your resizing operation is horizontal, vertical, or diagonal. Note that you can do the same task without picking Size first. Just point to the border with your standard cursor, press and hold pick, and size the window in the same way.

- **Minimize:** This option reduces the program window to a task bar button. To return to the program window after minimizing, pick the task bar button or double-click the program icon.
- **Maximize:** Picking Maximize increases the size of the program window to fill the entire screen. This can also be done by double-clicking on the title bar of a floating window.
- **Close:** This option closes the application contained in the window. Basically, this is an off switch for the program running within the window.

To make the AutoCAD LT window as large as it can be on your screen, *maximize* it. This fills the screen with the AutoCAD LT program window. Any other program windows that are also open are hidden behind the AutoCAD LT window.

When you are using more than one program at a time and need to be able to see two or more applications at once, your windows should be floating. The term *floating* applies to a window that is neither maximized nor minimized. A floating window can be temporarily sized and positioned as needed. Floating windows can also be arranged so that multiple windows are visible at the same time. An example of a situation where you would want to use more than one program at a time might be if you are producing technical documentation in a word processor that uses drawings in the document.

If you need to work in another application for a period of time, but plan to return to AutoCAD LT and continue the work you are doing there, *minimize* the AutoCAD LT window. When you minimize the AutoCAD LT window it is not usable until it is restored to a floating or maximized position. In Windows, a minimized application is displayed as a button on the task bar.

Working with floating windows affords you the greatest flexibility in terms of window sizing and positioning capabilities. As mentioned previously, you do not need to select the Move or Size options in the window control menu in order to move or resize a window.

Through the Window...

If you need to work in more than one program at a time, but need your applications to be maximized, you can have each of the windows maximized and still easily switch from one application to another. Here's how: For each program you need to run, pick the Start button, start the application, and maximize each window by picking the maximize button or using the window control menu. Now, when you need to switch from one application to another, press and hold the Alt key on your keyboard. Press and release the Tab key while still holding the Alt key. A small window appears in the center of the screen with icons representing each of the applications that are currently running. Press and release the Tab key until the application you need is outlined. To select an application, release the Alt key.

To move the AutoCAD LT window when it is floating, move the cursor to the title bar area then press and hold the pick button. Move the cursor while continuing to hold the pick button down. Depending on your operating system and display configuration, you may see an outline representation of the window as it is moved (see Figure 1.32). When it is in the desired location, drop the window into position by releasing the pick button.

A program window can be sized in three different ways as described previously. The window can be resized horizontally, vertically, or diagonally. When sizing the window diagonally, you are actually sizing it both horizontally and vertically at the same time. To size a window horizontally, move the cursor to either the left or right vertical edge of the window until it changes its shape into a left and right arrow. Press and hold the pick button, and move your pointing device. Your movement is reflected by the program window. Figure 1.33 shows the AutoCAD LT program window being sized horizontally. When the window is the desired size, release the pick button.

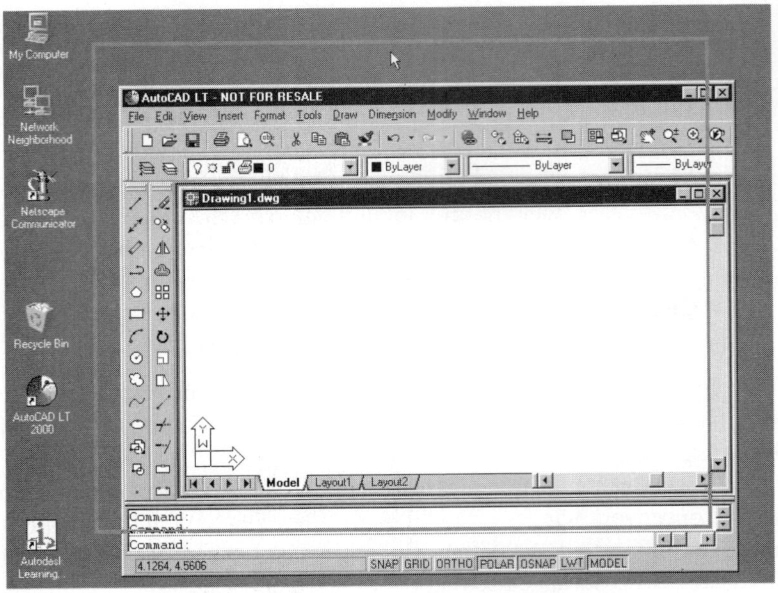

FIGURE 1.32 Moving a floating AutoCAD LT program window.

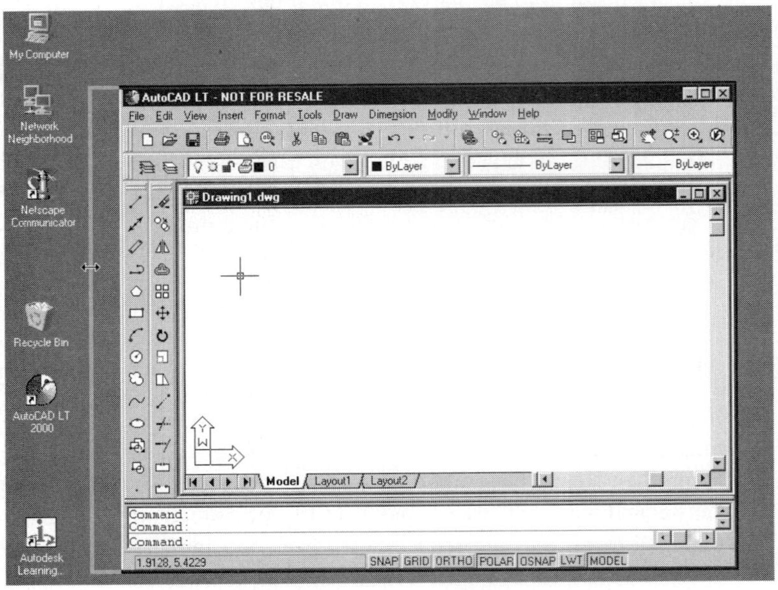

FIGURE 1.33 Sizing the AutoCAD LT window horizontally.

Figure 1.34 shows a vertical sizing operation. This is done in the same way as the horizontal sizing, except that you must initially point to either the top or the bottom edge of the window, and the movement cursor is an up and down arrow.

Resizing the window diagonally allows you to change both the height and the width of the window at the same time. This requires that you point to one of the four corners of the window then press and hold the pick button. This is shown in Figure 1.35; note the shape of the diagonal sizing cursor. As before, move the cursor until the window is the desired size; then release the pick button.

One of the most powerful features of the Windows operating systems is the capability to run more than one application at a time. In addition to running different programs at once, you can even run more than one session of AutoCAD LT. Using the positioning and sizing capabilities discussed previously, you can arrange your desktop as needed. In Figure 1.36, AutoCAD LT and a word processing application are both visible on the desktop. This gives you great flexibility in working with your applications. Such an arrangement may not be possible on systems with lower display resolution capabilities. For more information on adjusting your display resolution, see Appendix A.

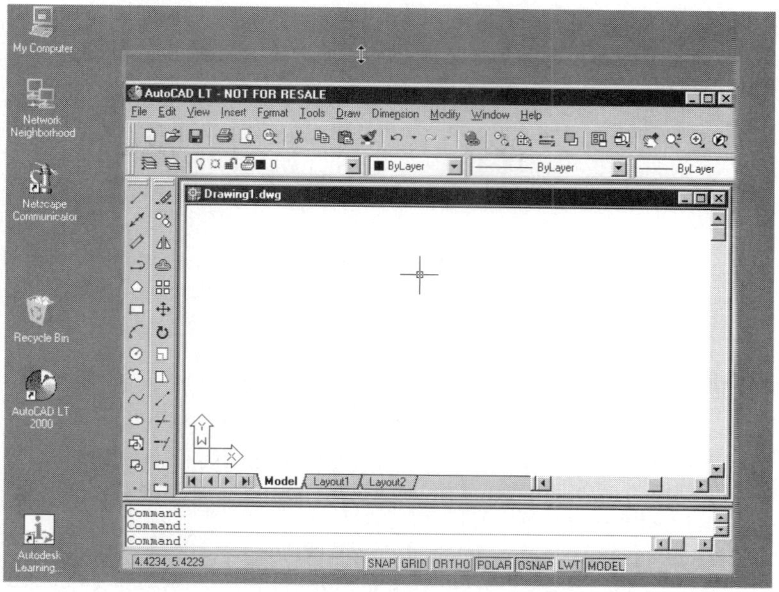

FIGURE 1.34 Sizing the program window vertically.

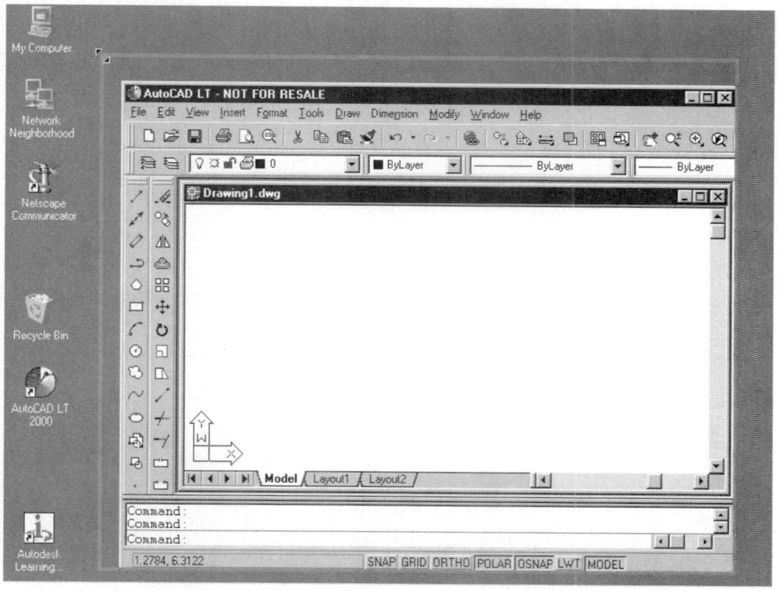

FIGURE 1.35 Sizing the window diagonally changes both horizontal and vertical size.

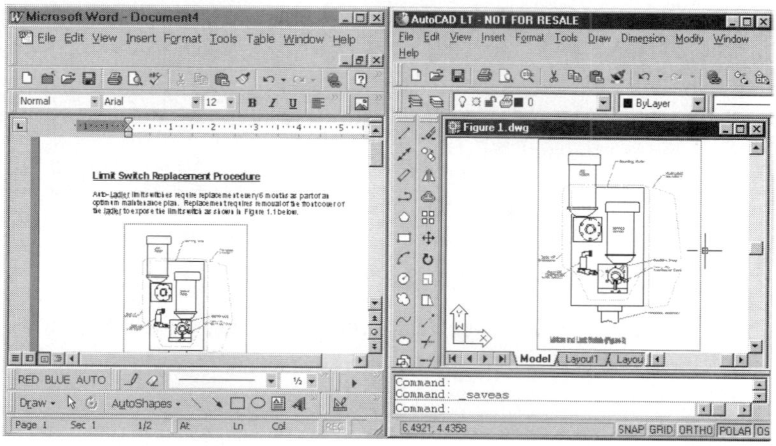

FIGURE 1.36 Two different program windows can be displayed simultaneously.

Through the Window...

When you need to display two or more program windows at once on your desktop, there is an easier way than manually sizing and positioning each window. Here's how: Point to the task bar (avoid any buttons) and press the right mouse button. The menu that is displayed provides options for arranging windows currently floating on your desktop. Cascade displays the windows overlapped. Pick the one you want and it comes to the top. Tile Horizontally or Tile Vertically displays your windows without overlapping them, sizing each window equally. This menu provides an option to Undo the last option, in case you do not like the results of the selected arrangement.

Sizing and Moving Toolbars

AutoCAD LT's toolbars can be moved and resized in much the same way as program windows. Pointing to the top, bottom, left, and right edges produces the resizing cursor. With toolbars, you cannot resize diagonally. To move a toolbar, point to the title bar, press and hold the cursor button and move the mouse—just as you would with program windows.

Toolbars can also be attached, or ***docked,*** at the edges of the AutoCAD LT window. Docking a toolbar removes the title bar and embeds it in the program window. The Standard toolbar and Object Properties toolbar are docked by default at the top of the screen (refer to Figure 1.22). To return a docked toolbar to a floating state, point to the grab bars, then press and hold the pick button and move the toolbar to the new location.

If you are trying to move the toolbar close to the edge, but do not want it docked, press the Ctrl key while you are moving the toolbar. This prevents docking. Refer to the topic "Customizing Toolbars and Toolbar Buttons" in Chapter 17 for complete information on working with toolbars.

Field Notes

If you right-click when you are pointing at the toolbar, a cursor menu is displayed. This menu allows you to control the visibility settings of the toolbars and offers an option to customize the toolbar buttons. Use this menu if you accidentally hide a toolbar and want it to be made visible again, but you should not select the Customize option until after you have reviewed the information in Chapter 17.

Exercise 1.4 — Estimated time required: 5 min.

1. Open the AutoCAD LT program.
2. Pick the Cancel button to dismiss the Startup dialog box.
3. Use the window control buttons found in the upper right corner of the program window to minimize the AutoCAD LT application.
4. Double-click on the Task Bar button to maximize the window.
5. Pick the Restore button to change to a floating window.
6. Use your cursor to resize the floating window horizontally, vertically, and diagonally.
7. Reposition the AutoCAD LT window into a new location on the screen.
8. Select the maximize button again.
9. Try steps 3 through 8 using selections from the window control menu in the upper left corner instead of the buttons.

LEARNING CHECKPOINT

- ☐ What is the primary reason for needing to size and move program windows?
- ☐ Where are most of the program window controls found?
- ☐ Name each of the available window control options.

- ☐ What reason might you have for needing two windows visible at once?
- ☐ Describe each of the alternate cursors used to move and size windows.
- ☐ What is the easiest way to close a program window?

Shortcut Menus

AutoCAD LT 2000 provides a system of context-sensitive *shortcut menus* that are accessed by pressing the second mouse button, commonly referred to as *right-clicking*. The shortcut menu appears at the current cursor location for fast and easy access and is sometimes referred to as a *cursor menu*. The options that appear on the shortcut menu are determined by the location of the cursor and what command or procedure is currently in process.

Figure 1.37 shows examples of different shortcut menus that are available in AutoCAD LT 2000. When no command is active and no object is currently selected, the first item on the shortcut menu is an option to repeat the previous command or menu selection (see Figure 1.37A). If an object is selected, the shortcut menu also displays a list of some of the more commonly used editing commands (see Figure 1.37B). When a command is active, any available options for the active command are displayed on the shortcut menu, as shown in Figure 1.37C. Right-clicking on a toolbar provides a menu for controlling toolbar visibility (Figure 1.37D). If the active command has no available options, then a right-click is the same as pressing the [Enter] key. The cascading menu that is available when you right-click in the floating command window provides immediate access to up to six of the most recently used commands (see Figure 1.37E). Additionally, many dialog boxes provide shortcut menus within list boxes or other areas that offer easy access to available options.

Use these shortcut menus to your best advantage. The shortcut menu system is a very powerful productivity tool that provides an immediately accessible list of options that apply to your current situation. Shortcut menus are discussed throughout the text wherever they apply.

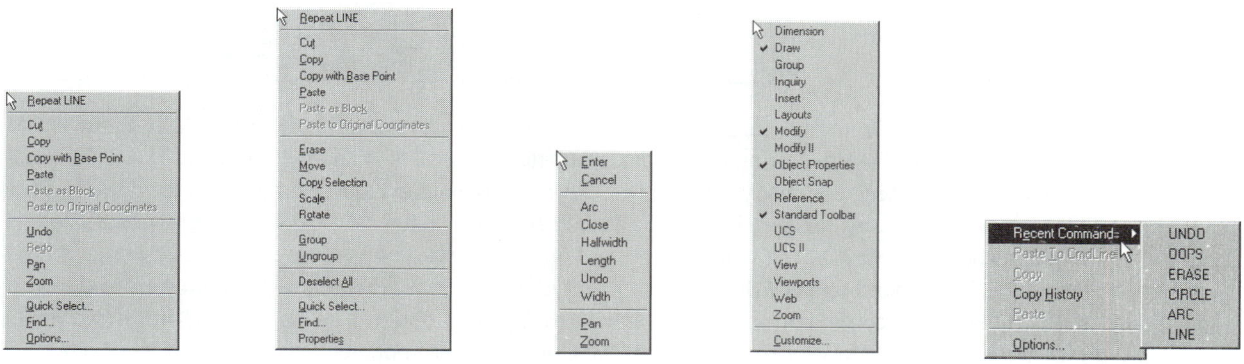

A B C D E

FIGURE 1.37 Shortcut menus provide context-sensitive choices, listing currently available options.

Field Notes

Shortcut menus can be customized to match personal preferences, or even fully disabled. If your shortcut menus have been disabled, you can enable them again in the Right-Click Customization dialog box, which is accessed from the Options dialog box. You can type OPTIONS at the Command: prompt, or select Options… from the Tools pull-down menu. On the User Preferences tab of the Options dialog box, pick the Right-click Customization button. You can then set your preferences for the right-click action.

Starting a Drawing Session

When you start a drawing session with AutoCAD LT, you either begin a new drawing or open an existing drawing to continue your work from a previous session. The Startup dialog box is displayed when you first start AutoCAD LT, and this gives you the option of opening an existing drawing or starting a new drawing using a variety of formats. The Startup dialog box is discussed in detail in Chapter 2.

Standard

New (Ctrl+N)

File
New

NEW
N
[Ctrl] + [N]

If you have already been working in AutoCAD LT and you wish to either start a new drawing or open an existing one, you need to enter the appropriate command to do so. The command to start a new drawing is NEW.

To enter the NEW command, press the New button on the Standard toolbar. You may also enter this command by picking the New … option from the File pull-down menu, by pressing Ctrl+N, or by typing **NEW** at the Command: prompt. The NEW command displays the Create New Drawing dialog box. This is the same as the Startup dialog box, except it does not provide an option for opening an existing drawing. The optional formats for starting your new drawing are discussed in detail in Chapter 2. To start your first new drawing, enter the NEW command by any of the methods described. When you get to the Create New Drawing dialog box, pick the Start from Scratch button as shown in Figure 1.38. This starts a drawing with the default options. In this example, the term *default* indicates that no custom settings have been made.

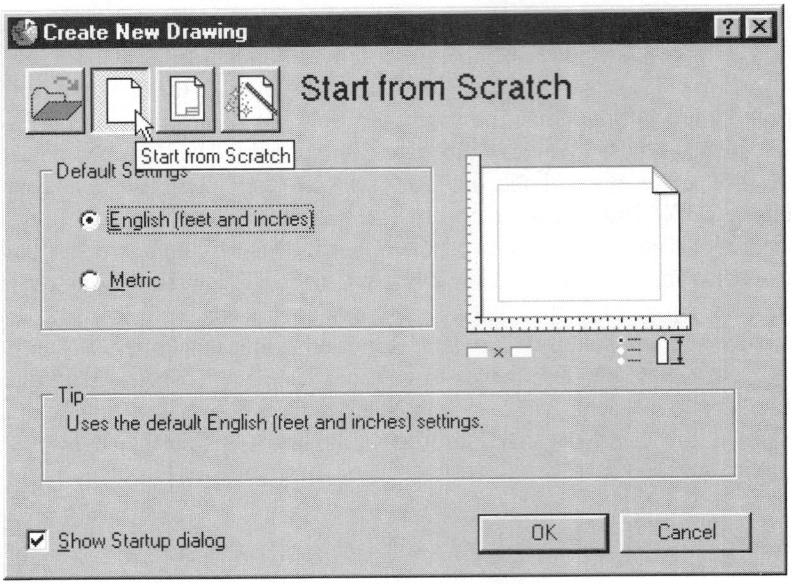

FIGURE 1.38 The NEW command displays the Create New Drawing dialog box.

Standard

Open (Ctrl+O)

File
Open

OPEN
[Ctrl] + [O]

After selecting Start from Scratch, pick the OK button and you are returned to the AutoCAD LT drawing editor. After a new drawing is started using this method, the title bar displays the name *[Drawing2.dwg]*. This indicates that the current drawing does not yet have a name. A name is assigned to a drawing when the drawing file is written to your disk drive using the Save Drawing As dialog box. This feature is also discussed further in Chapter 2.

If you want to open a drawing you have worked on previously, you can use the OPEN command.

The OPEN command opens a drawing file from your disk drive. Pick the Open button from the Standard toolbar to start this command. You can also pick the Open … option from the File … pull-down menu, use the Ctrl+O accelerator key, or type **OPEN** at the Command: prompt.

When you start the OPEN command, the Select File dialog box is displayed (Figure 1.39). In the upper left corner of the window is the File name: edit box. This shows the currently highlighted drawing name. When you first open this dialog box, the default file-type is Drawing (*.dwg). This is because AutoCAD LT drawing files are saved with a file extension of ".dwg." The list box directly below the Look in: dropdown list is the file list. This list shows the names of the drawings that are found in the current directory folder. In Figure 1.39, the current directory folder is C:\Program Files\AutoCAD LT 2000, as shown in the Look in: window.

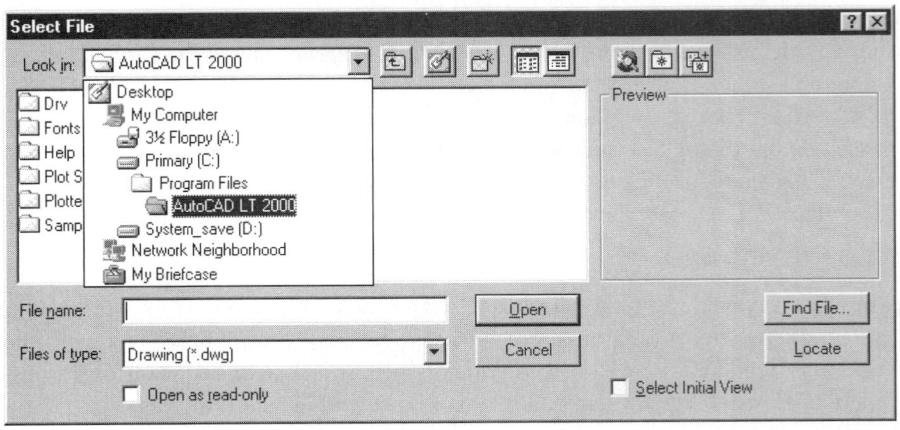

FIGURE 1.39 The Select File dialog box is displayed when you enter the OPEN command.

To look in another directory folder, double-click on the new folder. For example, to look in the sample folder, point to the folder and double-click. Now the contents of this folder are displayed in the file list. To move back to the AutoCAD LT 2000 directory, double-click on that folder again. If you need to look on another disk drive or folder, pick the Look in: dropdown list and select the new destination. If you are connected to a network, the available network drives are also displayed in this list.

The Files of type: popup list contains the specification Drawing (*.dwg), DXF (*.dxf), and Drawing Template File (*.dwt), because AutoCAD LT opens only these types of files directly. Some other types of files can be imported; this option is covered in Chapter 15.

The Preview box displays an image of the currently selected file. This can be very helpful when you are looking for a file but cannot remember its name. To use this feature, point to one of the drawings in the file list and press the pick button once. The name of the highlighted file is then displayed in the File name edit box and an image of the file is shown in the Preview image tile. Figure 1.40 shows a drawing selected, and its image is displayed in the Preview image tile. Picking the OK button will open the drawing currently highlighted, or you can double-click on the file name. To find out more about any feature of this dialog box, pick the question mark button on the title bar and then pick the feature.

FIGURE 1.40 The Preview image tile displays an image of the currently selected drawing file.

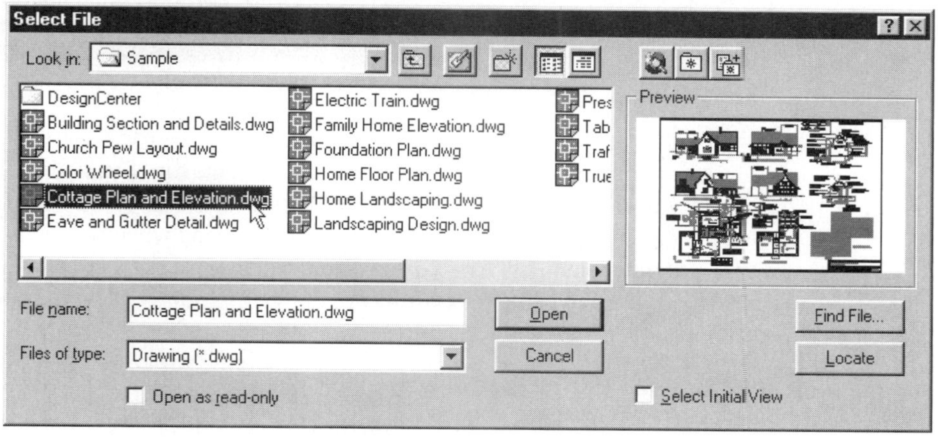

Through the Window...

When AutoCAD LT is installed on your computer, it registers the AutoCAD drawing file extension with Windows. This means that Windows associates files with the extension .dwg with the AutoCAD LT program and can automatically start the AutoCAD LT program with the requested file preloaded. Here's how:

In Windows Explorer, or My Computer, navigate to the appropriate disk drive and directory folder and find the desired drawing name. Point to the file icon with the cursor and double-click.

In the Windows environment, almost any file dialog box can be used to perform basic file-maintenance tasks, such as copying, renaming, moving, or even deleting files. To display a menu of your options, point at a file name in the file list area and right-click your mouse. Right click in a blank area, where no filename is highlighted, to display a menu of options for the list itself. These features are discussed in Chapter 15.

The Multiple Document Interface

A powerful feature of the AutoCAD LT 2000 software is the capability to open multiple drawings simultaneously. This is referred to as a *Multiple Document Interface (MDI)*. In AutoCAD LT it is sometimes called the *Multiple Design Interface*. When you are working on a drawing that is a part of a project consisting of many different drawings, you can open several or all of the drawings related to the project. With multiple drawings open, you can quickly refer to the appropriate drawings to get additional design information or even to reuse drawing content. AutoCAD LT allows you to simply drag and drop geometry and other drawing content from one drawing to another.

To ensure that you experience results consistent with this discussion of the MDI features, first close AutoCAD LT 2000. If asked whether or not to save changes, pick No. Next, start the AutoCAD LT software again and pick Cancel when the Startup dialog box is displayed.

The initial default condition of the drawing window is in a floating position and filling the drawing area. Each subsequent time that you run AutoCAD LT, the drawing window begins in the same state it was in when you last closed the software. You can restore the default state by picking Tile Horizontally from the Window pull-down menu.

You can begin a new drawing at any time. Starting a second concurrent drawing session displays the second drawing window floating above the first, as shown in Figure 1.41A.

FIGURE 1.41 (A) When floating, subsequent drawing windows are initially displayed on top of the previous windows. (B) Multiple windows are displayed in a cascade.

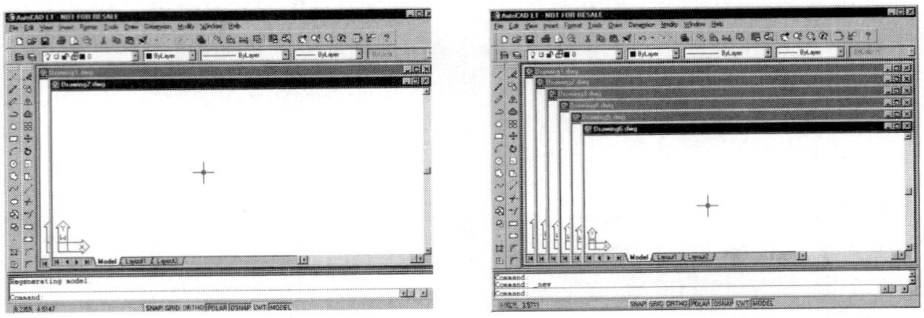

A B

Any number of drawings can be open at the same time, limited only by your available system memory. The behavior of drawing windows within the AutoCAD LT program window is very much like that of the program windows on the Windows desktop. The drawing windows are moved and resized in exactly the same way as program windows. They can be displayed in a cascade as shown in Figure 1.41B, or drawing windows can be tiled. You can control the display of drawing windows using the options provided on the Window pull-down menu (see Figure 1.42A).

FIGURE 1.42 (A) The Window pull-down menu provides options for arranging drawing windows. (B) The Select Window list.

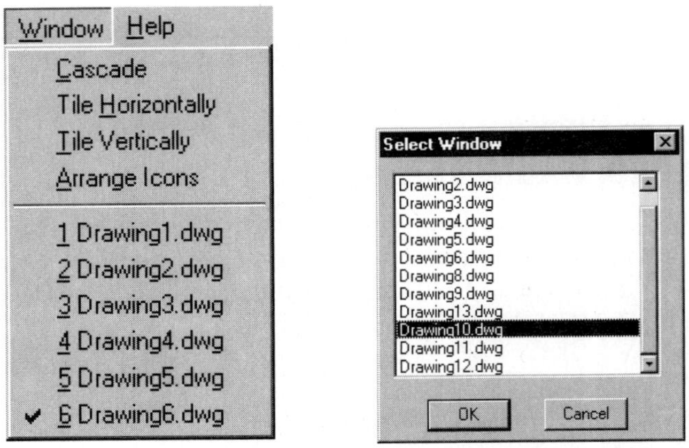

A B

Notice that the names of the currently open drawings are displayed on the Window menu. Picking a drawing name displays the appropriate drawing window. A checkmark is displayed next to the currently active drawing. If more than nine drawings are open, a More Windows... option appears at the bottom of the menu. Picking More Windows... displays the Select Window list, where you can select the desired drawing name (see Figure 1.42B). When multiple drawing windows are visible, you can pick inside the desired window to activate it.

Pick the drawing icon image on the drawing window title bar to display the window control menu. In addition to the standard window control options, this menu provides an option for switching to the Next drawing window. Alternatively, you can use the Ctrl + Tab or Ctrl + F6 keystroke combinations to move to the next drawing window. If you add the Shift key (pressing Ctrl + Shift + Tab), the order in which the windows are switched is reversed.

A tiled window arrangement using two windows is shown in Figure 1.43A. When too many windows are tiled, each drawing may be too small to work in effectively (see Figure 1.43B).

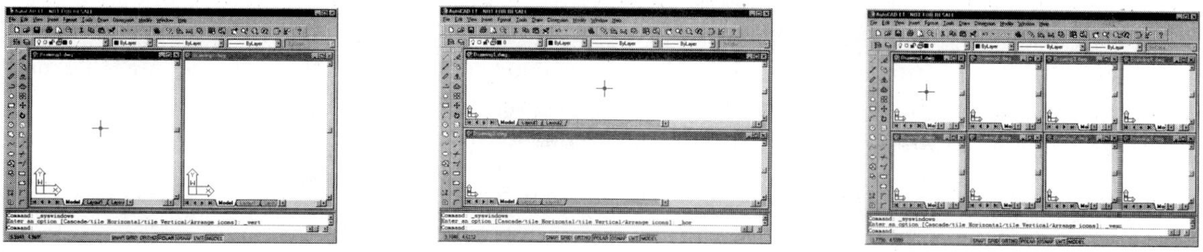

A B C

FIGURE 1.43 (A) Two drawing windows tiled vertically. (B) Two drawing windows tiled horizontally. (C) If too many windows are tiled, the drawing windows can be too small to use effectively.

Drawing windows can also be minimized within the AutoCAD LT program window. Minimized drawings are displayed as miniature versions of the drawing window title bars and are referred to as icons. You can minimize windows that are being used but are not needed at the moment. Figure 1.44 shows an arrangement of windows and minimized drawings.

FIGURE 1.44 Minimized drawing windows appear as icons in the AutoCAD LT program window.

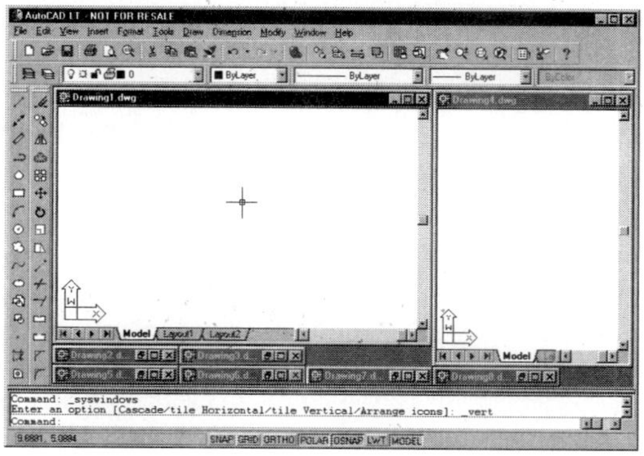

It is typically best to have only a single drawing visible unless you are doing something that requires more than one drawing to be visible. Having multiple drawings visible at the same time reduces your available workspace in each window. When you are working in a single drawing, maximizing the drawing window provides the largest available drawing area. Maximizing a drawing allows only a single drawing to be displayed, but if you switch to another drawing, it is also displayed in a maximized state.

Each drawing that you have open requires a certain amount of system resources. Having too many drawings open simultaneously can slow your system down. You should always close drawings that are no longer needed.

Another feature of the MDI is the capability to open multiple drawings at the same time. The OPEN command displays the Select File dialog box. You can pick any number of drawings using the standard Windows style file selection techniques. To select a sequence of files, pick the first file in the list, then hold the Shift key and select the last file. This method selects the files you pick and all the files listed between them. If you want to select multiple files that are not listed sequentially, hold the Ctrl key while picking the files. Figure 1.45 shows several files selected in the Select File dialog box. Each selected file is listed in the File name: edit box. When multiple files are selected, no drawing preview is displayed.

FIGURE 1.45 Multiple drawing files can be selected and opened simultaneously.

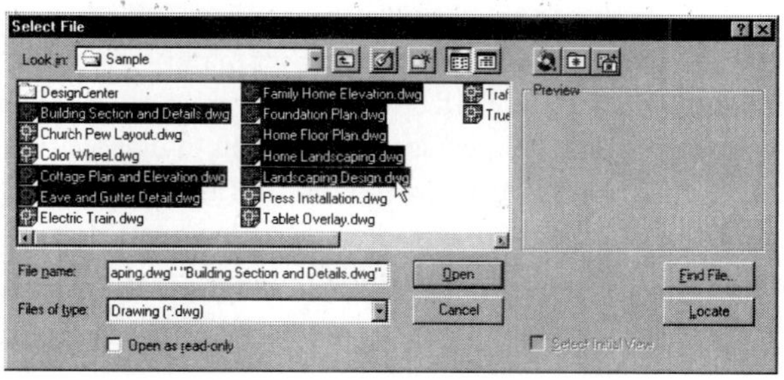

Ending a Drawing Session

File
Exit

QUIT
EXIT

After you complete your work in AutoCAD LT, you can exit the program most easily by pointing to the program window Close button. As discussed earlier, this is the button with the X found in the upper right corner of every program window (see Figure 1.31). Picking this button enters the QUIT command at the Command: prompt. The QUIT command can be typed at the Command: prompt as either QUIT or EXIT, or you can pick Exit from the File pull-down menu.

If you have made no changes to the drawings that are currently open, AutoCAD LT is closed with no further prompts. When a drawing has unsaved changes, you will see a dialog box asking you if you want to save these changes. Figure 1.46 shows this warning dialog box as it appears when the current drawing has not been named. If the drawing has been named, its name appears in place of *Drawing1.dwg.*

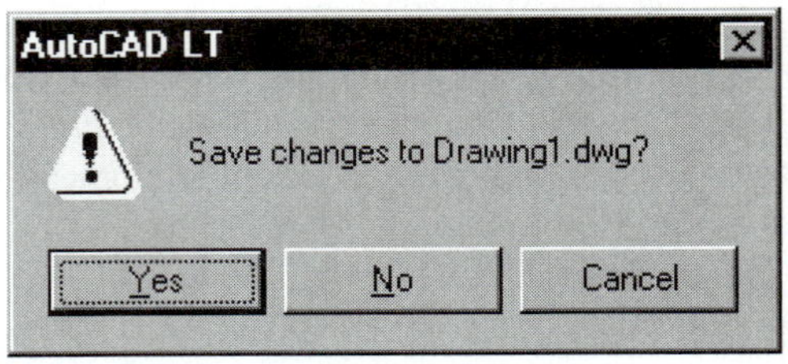

FIGURE 1.46 Select Yes to save changes, No to discard changes, or Cancel to remain in the drawing.

If you are finished working in the current drawing, but need to either open or begin another drawing, do not use the QUIT command. It is not necessary to close AutoCAD LT in order to exit the current drawing.

File
Close

CLOSE

The CLOSE command can be used to close the current drawing window and keep AutoCAD LT running. You can enter CLOSE at the Command: prompt, or pick Close from the File pull-down menu. If you close all drawing windows, the AutoCAD LT program window is left in what is called the *zero document state*. This means that no drawing files are currently open, and therefore, most AutoCAD LT commands and options are not available. This is why only a few tools and menu selections are available. Figure 1.47 shows the AutoCAD LT program window in the zero document state.

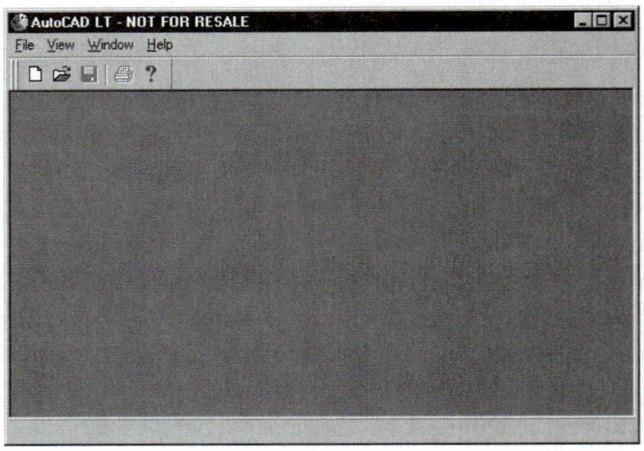

FIGURE 1.47 When no drawings are open, the AutoCAD LT window is displayed in the zero document state.

Field Notes

Settings in AutoCAD LT 2000 are stored by *system variables*. Many system variables are set within dialog boxes or by menu selections. In addition, you can change the value of many system variables by typing the variable name at the Command: prompt.

In order to maintain backward compatibility with older releases of AutoCAD LT, a variable called SDI (Single Document Interface) allows you to disable the MDI so that only one drawing file can be opened at a time. You can type SDI at the Command: prompt or use the OPTIONS command—on the System tab, under General Options, place a checkmark next to Single-drawing compatibility mode. The Single Document Interface is very restrictive and should not be used unless absolutely necessary.

Exercise 1.5 **Estimated time required: 5 min.**

1. Start the AutoCAD LT program.
2. Pick the Cancel button to dismiss the Startup dialog box.
3. Select Tile Horizontally from the Window menu.
4. Use your cursor to move and resize the drawing window.
5. Minimize the drawing window, then maximize it. Then, use the Restore button to return it to a floating state.
6. Start a second drawing session. Accept the default option in the Create New Drawing dialog box.
7. Cascade, then tile the drawing windows.
8. Use the OPEN command to open two drawings of your choice from the AutoCAD LT 2000\Sample folder.
9. Cascade and then tile the drawing windows.
10. Switch from one drawing to the next using each available option.
11. Use the CLOSE command to close each open drawing and leave AutoCAD LT in a zero document state. Pick No if asked whether to save changes.
12. Exit AutoCAD LT 2000.

LEARNING CHECKPOINT

- ☐ What command is used to start a new drawing session?
- ☐ How is an existing drawing opened for further editing?
- ☐ How can the drawing preview feature be used to your advantage?
- ☐ How can double-clicks be used in a Select File dialog box?
- ☐ What is the MDI?
- ☐ Describe the available options for arranging drawing windows.
- ☐ What keystrokes allow you to switch to a different drawing window?
- ☐ What are three different ways to exit AutoCAD LT?

Using On-Line Help in AutoCAD LT

Standard

Help

Help
AutoCAD LT Help

HELP
?
[F1]

AutoCAD LT provides a comprehensive help system for getting fast answers or guidance while you are working. You can access the help system at any time—even while another command is active. The on-line help in AutoCAD LT 2000 is started using the HELP command. If no command is currently active, you can type **HELP** or enter a question mark (**?**) at the Command: prompt. Optionally, you can press the F1 function key on your keyboard, pick the Help button on the Standard toolbar, or select AutoCAD LT Help from the Help pull-down menu. Figure 1.48 shows the AutoCAD LT 2000 Help System window, with the Contents tab active.

The AutoCAD LT 2000 Help System window displays navigation buttons, similar to those used in a web browser, along the top. The help system information is divided into a left and a right frame. The left frame, also called the *Contents Window*, is for navigation and searching. It has three tabs that display the table of **Contents**, the **Index**, and the **Search** tools. The frame on the right displays the actual help information. For many topics, this frame also displays three tabs used to control the type of information displayed. The **Concepts** tab provides conceptual information relevant to the selected topic. The **Procedures** tab shows step-by-step procedural information, and the **Reference** tab provides links to related information.

Browsing the Help Contents

When you enter the HELP command at the Command: prompt, the AutoCAD LT 2000 Help System window appears as shown in Figure 1.48. You can browse through the help system information using the Contents tab. The icons displayed in the Contents tab are illustrated and described here:

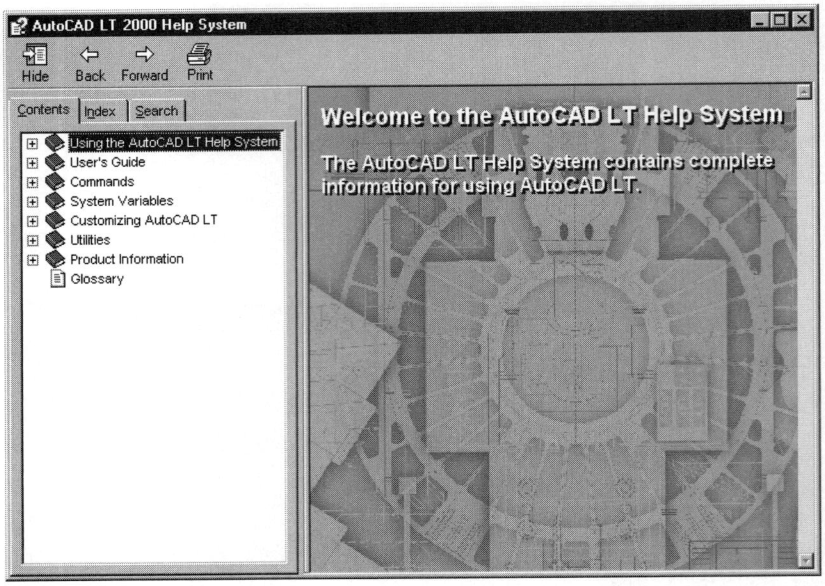

FIGURE 1.48 The Contents tab is active by default in the AutoCAD LT 2000 Help System window.

 Represents an unopened grouping of informational topics, such as Book, Chapter, or Section. Picking a book icon displays information in the frame to the right. Double-click on this icon (or pick the Plus Sign icon) to open it and display its contents.

 Represents an opened grouping of informational topics. Double-click on this icon (or pick the Minus Sign icon) to close it and hide its contents.

 **or**  Both of these icons represent a page of information. Picking one displays the topical information in the frame to the right. To hide page icons, close the book in which they are contained. Pages that show a red asterisk indicate a new feature in AutoCAD LT.

 A closed book displays a Plus Sign icon. Picking the plus sign, similar to double-clicking an unopened book, displays additional contents. Using the Plus Sign icons allows faster navigation because the book you open is not selected, so its information is not displayed.

 An open book displays a Minus Sign icon. Picking the minus sign closes the book and hides its contents.

The categories found under the Contents tab are divided into several categories, and where appropriate, these categories are further subdivided. The primary categories are as follows:

- **Using the AutoCAD Help System** — Contains information about using the help system.
- **User's Guide** — Provides conceptual and procedural information, with links to associated commands.
- **Commands** — Lists detailed information on all commands available in AutoCAD LT 2000, plus any available command options.
- **System Variables** — Provides detailed information on available settings within AutoCAD LT 2000 and their effects.
- **Customizing AutoCAD LT** — Details the options for customizing the AutoCAD LT 2000 software
- **Utilities** — Details the use of special tools available in AutoCAD LT 2000, along with available external utility programs.
- **Product Information** — Contains copyright and compatibility information.
- **Glossary** — Lists definitions for terms associated with AutoCAD LT 2000.

In the Contents tab, the shortcut menu displays three general options. Right-click anywhere in the Contents tab to display this menu. See Figure 1.49. The Open all selection expands all branches of the help file so that all books are opened and all available topics are visible in the Contents tab. Be careful—using this option may make it more difficult to find what you are looking for. The Close all option provides a convenient method for immediately closing all branches.

FIGURE 1.49 Right-clicking in the Contents tab area displays this shortcut menu.

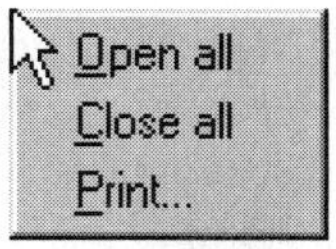

You can also print out help file information by picking the Print… option. This option displays a subsequent dialog box, as shown in Figure 1.50. Use only the first option: *Print the selected topic. The Print the selected heading and all subtopics* option cannot be used.

FIGURE 1.50 It is best to use the *Print the selected topic* option to avoid huge print jobs.

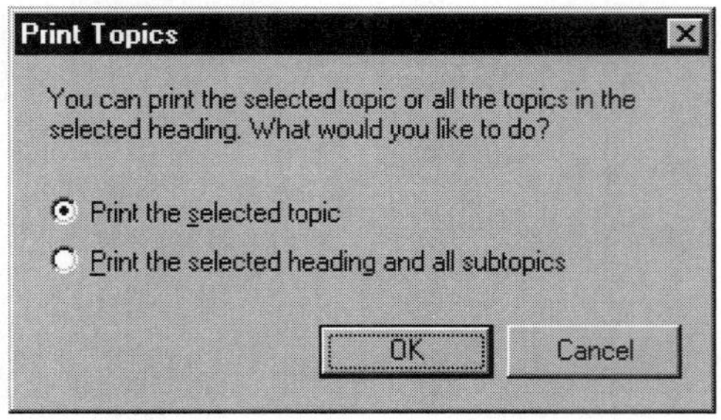

Once you have found the category of information you are looking for, you can hide the Contents window to reduce the amount of screen space required by the AutoCAD LT 2000 Help System window. Use the Show and Hide buttons found on the navigation bar to control the visibility of the Contents window. Figure 1.51 shows these two buttons. You can now arrange the Help System window to allow you to see the AutoCAD LT program window again. You can make the AutoCAD LT program window current by pointing to it and pressing the pick button on your mouse. The Help System window will stay "on top," meaning you will be able to see both windows at the same time. This feature allows you to view relevant help information while you work in AutoCAD LT.

To exit the help system completely, pick the X button in the upper right corner of the Help System window.

FIGURE 1.51 Use the Show and Hide buttons to control the visibility of the Contents window.

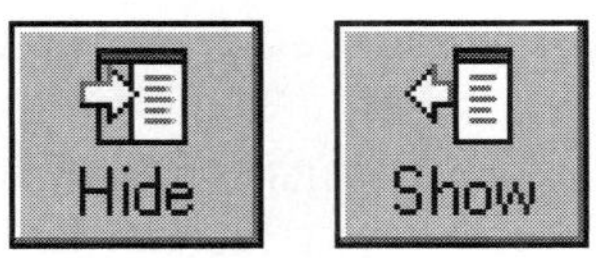

Help Information Display Controls

Many of the help information pages display three tabs at the top, as indicated earlier in this discussion. Use these tabs to specify the type of information you are looking for. The Concepts tab gives conceptual information, providing a foundation and appropriate context for learning about the current topic. The Procedures tab provides the "how to" information and links to associated pages of information. A *link*, often called a *hyperlink*, is blue underlined text that is linked to another document in the help system. To use a link, simply point your cursor to the text and pick it. The linked document is then displayed. If you have used another Windows-based help system, or if you have used a Web browser such as Netscape or Internet Explorer, you may already be familiar with the use of links. The third tab, the Reference tab, contains brief listings and links to related command and system variable help pages.

If you want to return to previously viewed information, one option is to select the Back button found on the navigation bar at the top of the Help System window. Optionally, you can right-click in the frame on the right and select Back from the shortcut menu.

Using the Index

Like any other reference manual, the AutoCAD LT 2000 Help System provides a comprehensive index to allow you to search an alphabetical list for a desired topic. To use the index, select the Index tab. In the edit box at the top of the Index area, type the entry you are looking for. As you type, the help system automatically displays the first index entry that matches the text you are entering, as shown in Figure 1.52. To display the information for any index entry, double-click on it. Some entries may have more than one relevant help page.

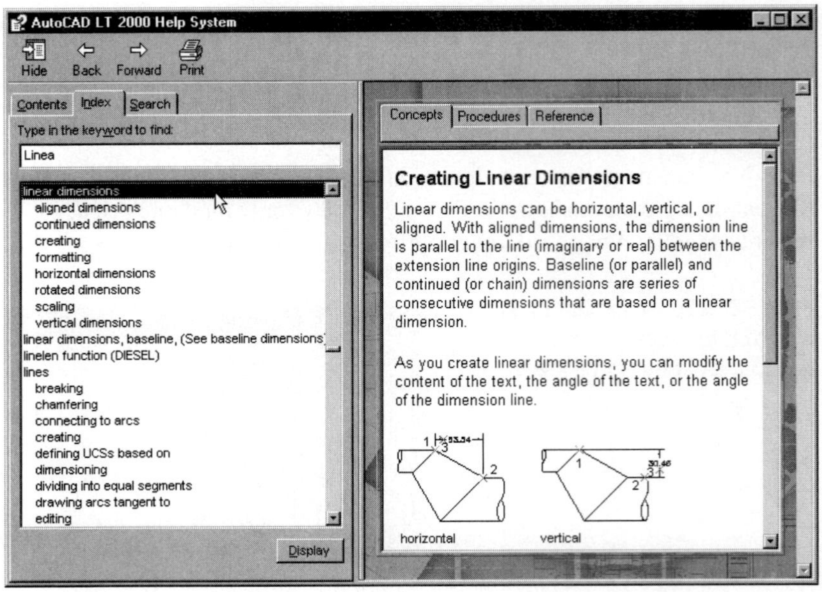

FIGURE 1.52 The Index tab displays topics that match your text entry. Double-click on an entry to see the help information.

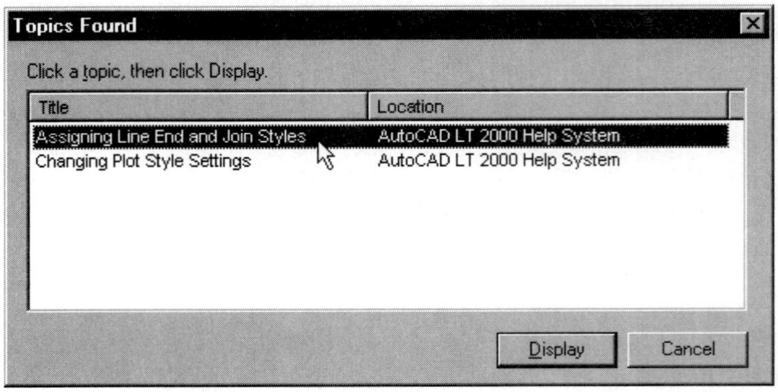

FIGURE 1.53 The Topics Found dialog box is displayed when more than one associated topic is available for an entry.

Double-clicking on an entry that has more than one associated help topic displays the Topics Found dialog box, where you can specify which topic is of interest to you. Figure 1.53 shows the Topics Found dialog box.

To print a topic found in the Index, select the Print button from the navigation bar at the top of the Help System window. Note that once you display the contents of a topic found in the Index, selecting the Contents tab then displays the page location in the table of contents, along with adjacent topics from which you can select.

Searching the Help System

In many cases, the fastest and most convenient method for finding information you need is by searching the help system. The Search tab allows you to specify a keyword and find all topics containing that word. First, enter a keyword pertaining to the topic you are interested in, then select the List Topics button. Now, double-click on the topic to see the associated help information. An example search is shown in Figure 1.54.

Using a keyword like *line* may produce undesirable results because 500 topics are found. You can use multiple words to narrow your search. If you type more than one keyword, only the topics that contain all the keywords are displayed. For example, if you enter the words *creating lines*, all the topics displayed contain both of these words, but, again, too many topics are displayed and many that have absolutely nothing to do with creating lines. To specify an exact phrase that you want to find, enclose it in quotation marks. Specifying a keyword as *"creating lines"* displays only nine topics, and because they contain the exact phrase "creating lines," most of the topics contain useful information. Avoid phrases that are too specific, such as *"creating a single line segment,"* because the wording in the help file may not contain this exact phrase, and your search produces no results.

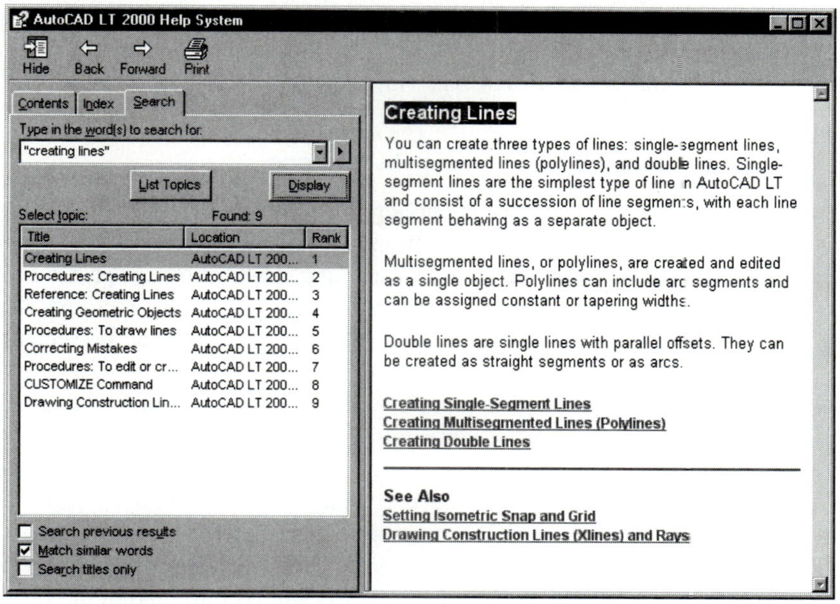

FIGURE 1.54 The Search tab provides a convenient way to search the help files for specific information.

Context-Sensitive Help

The single most useful feature of the AutoCAD LT 2000 Help System is *context-sensitive help*, which provides help on the currently active command. For example, if you are trying to use a command such as LINE, and you need assistance, just start the LINE command and then press F1. Alternatively you can pick the Help button, which appears on the Standard Toolbar as a question mark. When you do this, the help system is started and information on how to use the currently active command is automatically displayed.

Exercise 1.6 — Estimated time required: 5 min.

1. Start the AutoCAD LT 2000 Help System by typing HELP. Use the Content tab to find information on the LINE command. Exit the help system.
2. Start the AutoCAD LT 2000 Help System by picking the Help button from the Standard Toolbar. Use the Index tab to find information on the LINE command. Exit the help system.
3. Start the AutoCAD LT 2000 Help System by picking the AutoCAD LT Help selection from the Help pull-down menu. Use the Search tab to find information on the LINE command. Exit the help system.
4. Type **LINE** at the Command: prompt and press Enter. At the From point: prompt, press the F1 key.
5. Right-click in the Contents tab area and select Close all.
6. Open the *User's Guide* category, then open *Creating Geometric Objects* and *Creating Lines*.
7. Display the topic labeled *Creating Single-Segment Lines*.
8. Review the Concepts page, and then pick the Procedures tab. From the Procedures page, pick the LINE link at the bottom of this page.
9. Return to the previous topic by selecting the Back button. Pick the Reference tab.
10. In the Reference tab, pick the XLINE link.
11. Exit the help system.

AutoCAD LT Learning Assistance™

The AutoCAD LT Learning Assistance CD is an excellent on-demand supplement to instructor-led classroom training. This interactive multimedia tool supplements your learning with concept discussions and tutorials that use text, graphics, audio, and video presentations to illustrate a variety of AutoCAD LT topics. The Learning Assistance software comes with AutoCAD LT 2000 on a separate CD and must be installed before it can be used. See Appendix A for information on installing AutoCAD LT Learning Assistance.

The CD must be present in your CD ROM drive in order to play the multimedia presentations, but the text content can be viewed without the CD. Additionally, it is not necessary for AutoCAD LT to be running to review the Learning Assistance information.

Using AutoCAD LT Learning Assistance

When Learning Assistance material related to the text discussion is available, a listing of the relevant topics is provided at the end of the Learning Checkpoints section. The Learning Assistance presentations can be used as desired to supplement your learning. The video clips provide live-action demonstrations so you can watch each step of a process as it happens. You can use the Learning Assistance CD even if you do not have sound capability on your computer, because all the spoken presentation material is also provided as text content.

To start Learning Assistance, you can select Learning Assistance from the Help pull-down menu in AutoCAD LT. Optionally, you can simply put the CD in the drive and it will automatically start up. The Learning Assistance window looks similar to the layout of the standard AutoCAD LT Help System window discussed earlier in this chapter. If you have used a Web browser such as Netscape or Internet Explorer, the browser style interface will be familiar to you. Whether you have used a browser before or not, the first time you use the software you should pick the How to Use hyperlink on the opening page (see Figure 1.55). This displays several additional links to more detailed information on topics such as *Viewing Content, Playing Animation, Sound, and Other Media, Using Try It, Searching for Topics and Keywords,* and more.

FIGURE 1.55 The AutoCAD Learning Assistance layout is similar to the AutoCAD LT Help System. The cursor changes to a pointer finger when you are pointing at a hyperlink.

The Contents window on the left provides three tabs; **Contents, Index** and **Find**. These tabs have the same function as the tabs in the Help System. When a video clip is playing, a tab labeled **Media** is displayed. The icons displayed in the Contents tab of Learning Assistance are the same as those used in the Help System, except that a checkmark is placed on the icon of any topic that has been viewed. This feature is useful if you want to work through all the Learning Assistance topics; the topics you have not yet reviewed will not show a checkmark. In Figure 1.56, the checkmarks indicate that the first two topics in the Introducing the AutoCAD LT Workspace folder have been viewed.

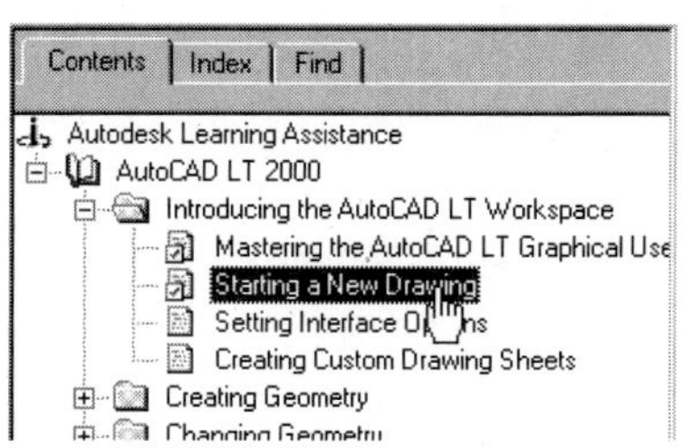

FIGURE 1.56 Previously viewed pages display a check-mark to help you track your progress.

Field Notes

- The Learning Assistance video clips were recorded at a screen resolution of 800 × 600, and when viewed smaller than the original size, the image quality is poor. For systems set to 800 × 600 resolution, the image quality is best when the video clip is displayed in full-screen mode. To use the full-screen mode option, point at the video and right-click. From the shortcut menu, select the Full Screen option.
- The *How to Use* topic in AutoCAD LT Learning Assistance describes a *Try It* feature, which does not exist.

AutoCAD LT Support Assistance™

AutoCAD LT 2000 provides a comprehensive on-line knowledge base of technical support information called Support Assistance. You can start Support Assistance by picking Support Assistance from the Help pull-down menu in AutoCAD LT. This knowledge base is designed to help you find solutions quickly. Troubleshooting and "how-to" topics are presented in a concise problem/solution format. Rather than simply being a source of information about AutoCAD LT features, like the Help System and Learning Assistance, the Support Assistance tool is designed to help you solve problems. When you want to know how to erase an object or learn about the different ways to draw a circle, you should check the Help System or Learning Assistance. When you get an error message you don't understand or you try to erase an object and it doesn't go away, use Support Assistance. Figure 1.57 shows the Support Assistance window.

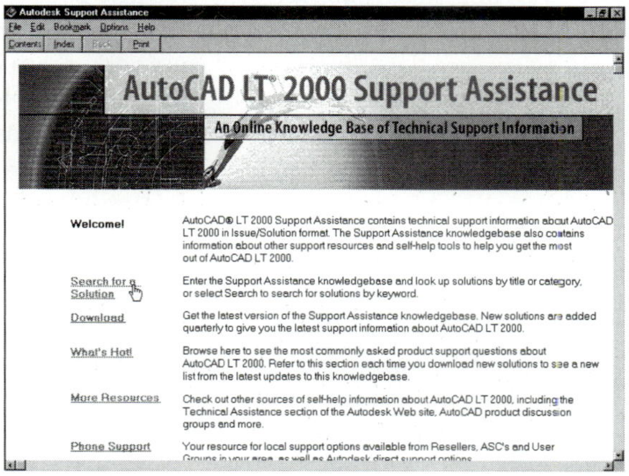

FIGURE 1.57 Support Assistance is an on-line knowledge base providing technical support for AutoCAD LT 2000.

The first time you use Support Assistance, you should scroll down to the bottom of the first screen and select the topic Getting the Most from Support Assistance. This topic offers guidance on how to use the search tools to find your solution fast.

The Support Assistance features include:

- **Search for a Solution** — Lets you browse through the knowledge base by category, or you can select the Search button to look for a specific solution.
- **What's Hot!** — Provides a list of the most commonly asked questions regarding AutoCAD LT 2000 and their solutions.
- **More Resources** — Links to World Wide Web–based resources such as the Autodesk Technical Assistance Web Site, AutoCAD LT Discussion Groups, and AutoCAD User Groups.
- **Phone Support** — A guide to Authorized Autodesk Resellers, Autodesk Systems Centers, phone support, and training options.

- **Getting the Most from Support Assistance** — A tutorial on using search tools, plus building and updating keyword lists to help you find what you are looking for quickly.

Selecting any of the links to Web-based resources automatically starts your Web browser and loads the selected resource page. Accessing these options requires Internet access.

Autodesk on the Web

Selecting Autodesk on the Web cascade on the Help pull-down menu in AutoCAD LT provides direct links to Web resources. As with all the previously discussed Web-based resources, an active Internet connection and a Web browser are required in order to access the Web sites. The links provided are as follows:

- **AutoCAD LT Home Page** — Provides product information, access to newsgroups, and other AutoCAD LT resources. One URL is http://www.autodesk.com/aclt2000user
- **Autodesk Home Page** — Provides product information and resources for all Autodesk products. The URL is http://www.autodesk.com/
- **Autodesk Product Support Services** — A technical assistance site for all Autodesk products. The URL is http://www.autodesk.com/support/
- **AutoCAD User's Group International** — An international organization that can connect you with local AutoCAD Users' Groups where you can network, share ideas, and field questions. This is actually a link to a file found in the AutoCAD LT 2000\Help folder, but the local page has links to the AUGI Web site.

Exercise 1.7 — Estimated time required: 10 min.

1. Review the Learning Checkpoint material following Exercise 1.3.
2. Start AutoCAD LT Learning Assistance.
3. Find and open the topic *Mastering the AutoCAD LT Graphical User Interface.*
4. Review the text information on this topic.
5. Pick the Play Video button and watch the video clip.
6. Pick the Related Topics icon.
7. In the Related Items dialog box, select Starting a New Drawing, and pick the Close button.
8. Pick the Home icon.
9. Close Learning Assistance.
10. Start Support Assistance and pick the Search for a Solution option.
11. Find the source of the error message: *Drawing file was created by an incompatible version.*
12. If you have Internet access, continue to work through this exercise.
13. Select the More Resources option.
14. Pick the link to The Autodesk Technical Assistance Web Site.
15. On the Technical Assistance Web page, pick the AutoCAD LT link in your browser, and on the subsequent page, select the AutoCAD LT 2000 link under the Hot Issues topic.
16. If you have access to a printer, print the Hot Issues page from your browser.

MULTIPLE CHOICE

Circle the choice or enter your response on an answer sheet by selecting the option that most accurately completes or answers the given statements.

1. AutoCAD LT documentation recommends __________ of memory be installed.
- **a.** 16 megabytes
- **b.** 256 megabytes
- **c.** 64 kilobytes
- **d.** 32 megabytes

2. Frequent typing with your wrists bent can result in:
- **a.** eye strain
- **b.** carpal tunnel syndrome
- **c.** backache
- **d.** foot odor

3. When the label of a dialog button is followed by this symbol, it means that picking the button opens a subdialog box:
- **a.** <
- **b.** ...
- **c.** >
- **d.** ?

4. To access a dialog box item with the keyboard, press the _____ key and the underscored character at the same time.
- **a.** Ctrl
- **b.** Enter
- **c.** Alt
- **d.** Esc

5. The key that cancels an operation in AutoCAD LT is:
- **a.** Ctrl
- **b.** Enter
- **c.** Alt
- **d.** Esc

6. The AutoCAD LT text screen can be viewed by pressing:
- **a.** F1
- **b.** F3
- **c.** F2
- **d.** F4

7. The NEW command *cannot* be started doing this:
- **a.** Ctrl+N
- **b.** Pick the New toolbar button.
- **c.** Pick New... from the File pull-down.
- **d.** Alt+N

8. A shortened version of a command name that you can type in at the Command: prompt is called a:
- **a.** command alias
- **b.** dialog box
- **c.** menu access key
- **d.** cancel

9. A toolbar that is attached to the edge of the AutoCAD LT program window is referred to as being:
- **a.** docked
- **b.** minimized
- **c.** floating
- **d.** maximized

10. The accelerator keystroke Ctrl+O starts the __________ command.
- **a.** NEW
- **b.** OPEN
- **c.** QUIT
- **d.** CLOSE

MATCHING

Match each term to the correct description by writing the appropriate number in each box at the left.

- ☐ Dialog box
- ☐ Tooltip
- ☐ Help string
- ☐ Radio button
- ☐ Edit box
- ☐ List box
- ☐ Toggle
- ☐ Image
- ☐ Exit button
- ☐ Close button
- ☐ Popup list
- ☐ Interface
- ☐ Menu access key
- ☐ Help
- ☐ Accelerator key

1. General term describing the way you communicate with the computer.
2. Turns something on or off.
3. Help located at the cursor.
4. Text is entered using this.
5. A combination keystroke to access a command quickly.
6. A button with an X located in the upper right corner.
7. A graphic element of a dialog box.
8. Pick this button to get assistance.
9. Used to present a listing of options in a dialog.
10. A button that allows only one selection.
11. Information on the status bar.
12. This list allows only one selection.
13. Provides an intuitive interface.
14. Usually OK or Cancel.
15. Provides keyboard access to pull-down menu items.

WORD SCRAMBLE

Unscramble the six scrambled words below, one letter to each square, to form six AutoCAD LT–related words:

NIDWOW

KETROWN

RORCUS

ROMINTO

CAPEES

NUME

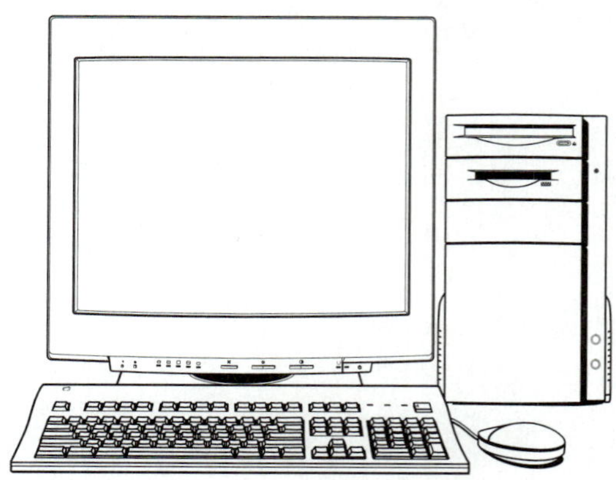

Unscramble the circled letters to form the special answer, as suggested by the illustration.

CHAPTER 2

Introduction to Drafting with AutoCAD LT

LEARNING GOALS

- Set up a quick AutoCAD LT drawing.
- Establish the drawing limits and set the units style.
- Use Grid and Snap to assist in making a drawing.
- Draw lines by picking points.
- Draw lines by entering distances, angles, and coordinates.
- Use the ORTHO command to assist in drawing lines.
- Use the REDRAW command to remove Blips from the screen.
- Erase objects by picking, windowing, and crossing.
- Use the ERASE command before or after selecting objects.
- Remove objects from a selection set.
- Use the OOPS, U, and REDO commands.
- Print or plot a drawing.

Drafting with AutoCAD LT

At the beginning of any drafting project, it is important to set up the AutoCAD LT 2000 interface options to suit your needs. *Interface options* are settings that control the way in which you interact with the AutoCAD LT software. There are many available options you can customize to fit the way that you work and your personal preferences. The use and effects of these options will be introduced throughout the text wherever they apply to the discussion material. The first step in any drawing project is to set up the drawing environment. The term *drawing environment* refers to the settings your drawing uses, such as the overall drawing size and the units of measurement. AutoCAD LT allows you to specify units in several different formats, such as feet and inches or decimal style units. The drawing area can be set up for creating very small mechanical parts or designing an entire office complex. This chapter discusses methods of setting up drawings and introduces the fundamentals of creating, editing, and printing drawings.

Setting AutoCAD LT Interface Options

One aspect of interface options is the capability to rearrange, resize, relocate, and reconfigure the AutoCAD LT program window features. At some screen resolutions, the command line text and toolbar buttons may appear too large or too small. You may wish to change the colors of the program window text and background to your preference. Additionally, you may find that relocating features within the window makes them easier to see or use.

When the Windows screen resolution is set to higher values, on-screen features are displayed at a smaller size. If the default size of the toolbar buttons in AutoCAD LT seems too small, you can increase the size at which they are displayed. To adjust the size at which the toolbar buttons are displayed, pick the Toolbars... option from the View menu found on the AutoCAD LT menu bar. In the Customize dialog box, select the Toolbars tab. As shown in Figure 2.1A, place a checkmark in the Large buttons checkbox by picking it.

Tools
Toolbars...
TOOLBAR
TO

The button size changes immediately. Remove the checkmark if you want to return the toolbar buttons to the default size. Pick Close to dismiss the dialog box. The comparative sizes of the large and small toolbar buttons are illustrated in Figure 2.1B.

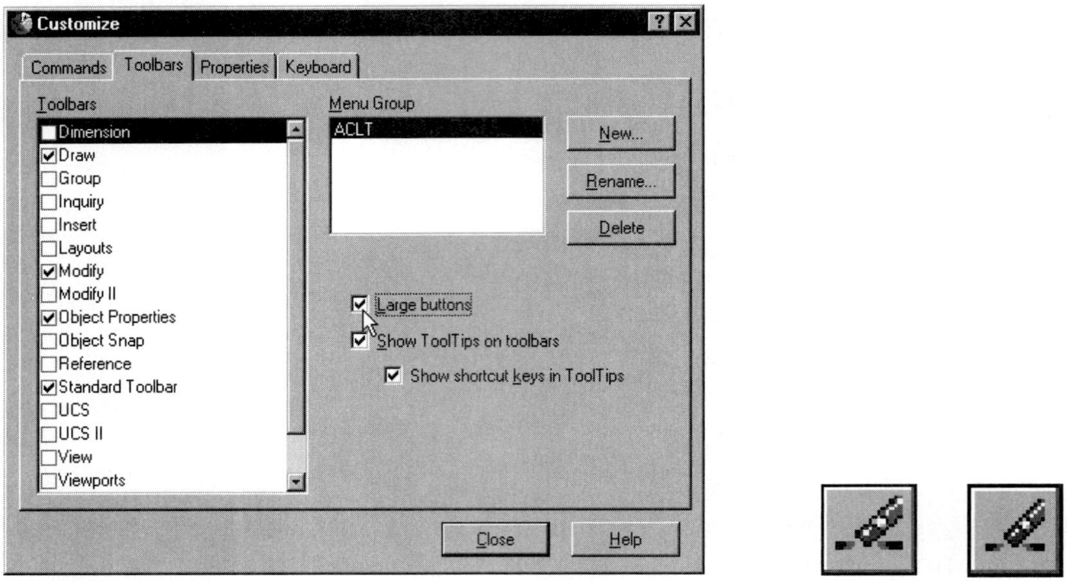

A B

FIGURE 2.1 Larger buttons can be easier to use on systems set to higher screen resolutions.

The floating command window displays three lines of text by default, but it can be adjusted to display more or fewer lines. It is recommended that the command window always show a *minimum* of three lines of text. When fewer than three lines of text are displayed, error messages and other important information may not be displayed. The easiest way to adjust the number of lines displayed is to use the resizing bar, as shown in Figure 2.2. When the resizing cursor is displayed, press and hold the pick button, then drag the bar to the desired size.

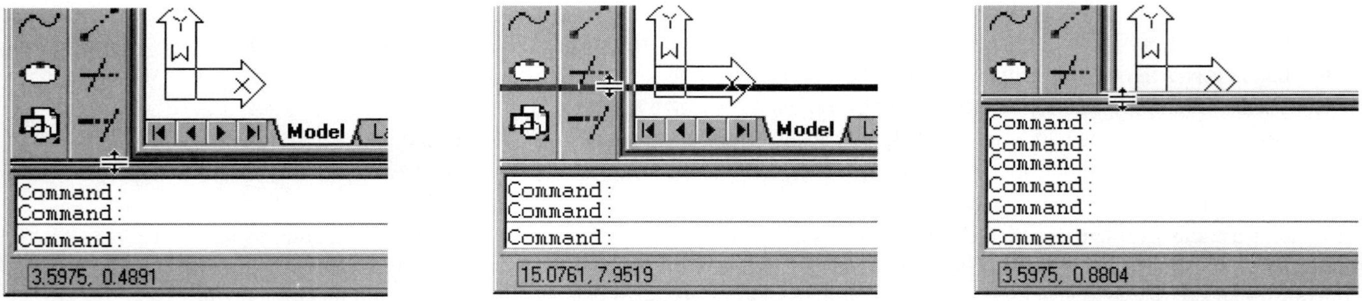

Press and hold the pick button | Drag the resizing bar into position | Release the pick button

FIGURE 2.2 Use the resizing bar to change the number of lines displayed in the Command: window.

Many new AutoCAD LT users prefer to relocate the command window to the top of the program window. You can drag the it to the top of the screen and dock it there, or you can place it in a floating position if desired. Docking the command window at the top places it at or near eye level, making it very easy to monitor.

Tools
Options...
OPTIONS
OP

You can adjust the height and font of the text displayed in the command window using the Options dialog box. To access the Options dialog box, pick Options... from the Tools pull-down menu, select Options… from a shortcut menu, or enter OPTIONS or OP at the Command: prompt. Select the Display tab in the Options dialog box, and pick the Fonts… button to access the Command Line Window Font dialog box. Figure 2.3A shows a 14-point bold Lucida Console font being selected.

To adjust the colors of AutoCAD LT program window features, select the Colors… button in the Options dialog box. Select a window element from the list, or point to the feature on the image tiles in the dialog box and press the pick button. Pick the new color from the drop-down list. The Default All button resets all features to their default colors.

FIGURE 2.3 You can adjust the properties of the AutoCAD LT program window features to match your preferences.

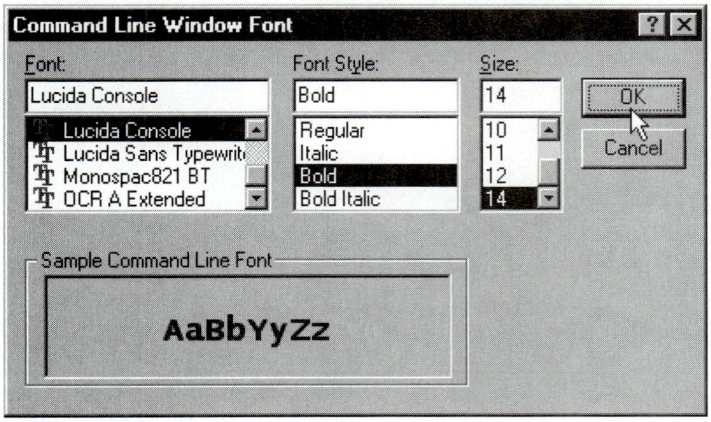

A

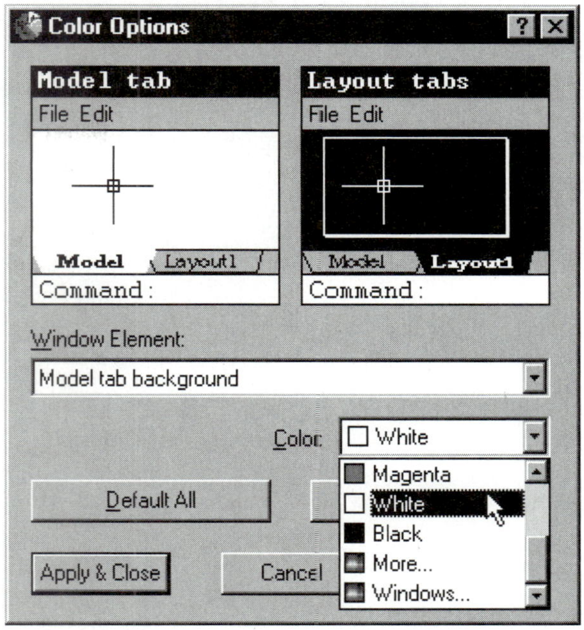

B

Field Notes

- AutoCAD LT provides an interface option that can be set to sound an audible alert when an incorrect entry is made. The appropriate error message is displayed, and the computer system beeps to warn you that your entry was not accepted.

  The *Beep on error in user input* control is in the General Options area of the System tab in the Options dialog box. Place a checkmark to enable the feature, or remove the check to disable the beep.
- The next section introduces the Startup dialog box. If the Startup dialog box has been disabled on your system, you can re-enable it by placing a check in the checkbox labeled Show Startup dialog in the General Options area on the System tab of the Options dialog box.

LEARNING CHECKPOINT

- □ Why is it important to set up the AutoCAD LT 2000 interface options?
- □ List your preferred settings for each of the available Interface Options discussed in this section.
- □ What is the fewest number of lines that should ever be displayed in the floating command window? Why?

The AutoCAD LT Drawing Setup Options

AutoCAD LT provides several methods for setting up your drawing, including *Wizards*, which you may have used in other Windows applications. A Wizard is an automated process that prompts you for information about how you want your document to be set up and then makes all the specific settings for you. The AutoCAD LT Wizards automatically adjust many drawing settings to match the size and type of your drawing. You can choose a Quick Setup, or for a more detailed setup process, you can use the Advanced Setup Wizard.

Using the Quick Setup

Standard

New (Ctrl+N)

File
New

NEW
N
[Ctrl] + [N]

When you open AutoCAD LT, you get the Startup dialog box shown in Figure 2.4. You can start a similar dialog box by picking New... in the File pull-down menu, but it is called the Create New Drawing dialog box and it does not offer the Open a Drawing option.

The Use a Wizard button lets you select Quick Setup or Advanced Setup. Advanced Setup is the default wizard option. You may also pick the Use a Template, Start from Scratch, or Open a Drawing buttons. Pick Use a Wizard to access the automated setup options. A description of the setup option that is highlighted is provided in the Wizard Description compartment (see Figure 2.4). To do a quick setup, double-click the Quick Setup Wizard or

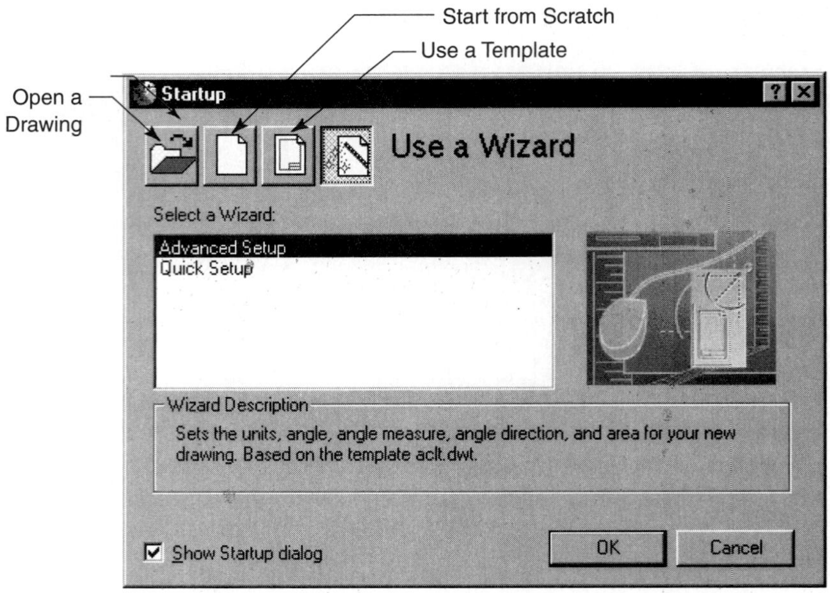

FIGURE 2.4 The Startup dialog box. Notice the Wizard Description of the Advanced Setup option.

pick Quick Setup and pick the OK button or press Enter. Now you get the Quick Setup dialog box shown in Figure 2.5. The Quick Setup dialog box allows you to set the drawing units and area to your specifications. AutoCAD LT then sets up the drawing area and changes settings such as text height to an appropriate scale based on the settings you make in this dialog box. Using Quick Setup is a fast way for you to get started using AutoCAD LT.

Setting Units of Measure

The Quick Setup dialog box gives you several options for setting your drawing units in the Units page. The initial setting is Decimal units, and there is an example of a typical decimal units display on the right (see Figure 2.5A). Select the units option that matches your drawing. When you pick a units option, the selected option becomes active and an example is displayed on the right. Figure 2.5B through E shows the selection and example displayed for each of the unit options. The following types of units are available:

- *Decimal:* This is the default setting and is the most versatile option. Decimal units are the best choice unless you prefer a specific format for specifying drawing information, such as feet and inches, or scientific units. In AutoCAD LT, decimal units can represent whatever your application requires. For example, if you are drawing a small mechanical part, drawing units may represent inches or millimeters. In larger drawing applications, such as maps, units may represent miles or kilometers. Figure 2.5A shows decimal units selected.
- *Engineering:* Drawing in engineering units is generally used in mapping and civil drafting projects such as dam and bridge construction, plot plans, and topography. This selection is shown in Figure 2.5B.
- *Architectural:* This units setting is used when you draw in feet, inches, and fractional inches for architectural drawings such as plans, sections, elevations, and details (see Figure 2.5C).
- *Fractional:* Fractional units are used when you are making a drawing that contains fractional parts of any common unit of measure. Look at Figure 2.5D.
- *Scientific:* These units of measure are used when very large or small values are required. The applications occur in businesses such as chemical engineering or astronomy. The example in Figure 2.5E displays 1.5500E+01. The E refers to an exponent value and the +01 is the exponent 10 to the first power.

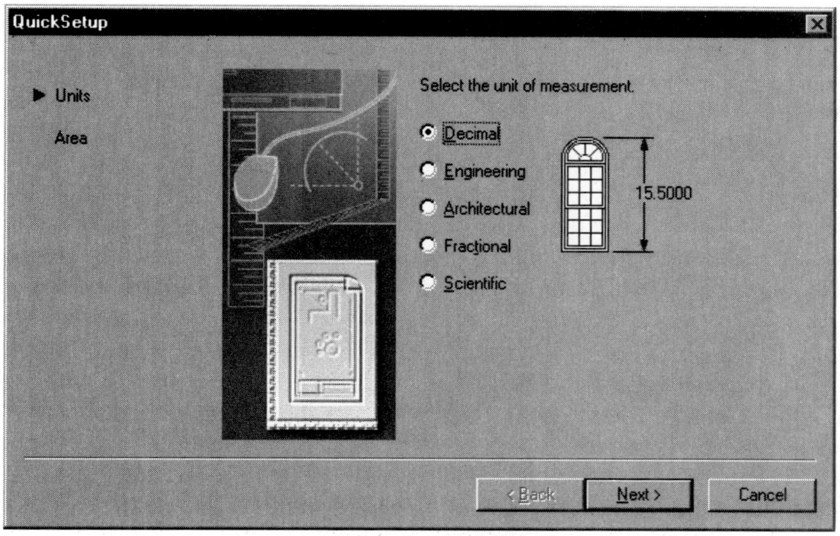

A Decimal units is the default setting.

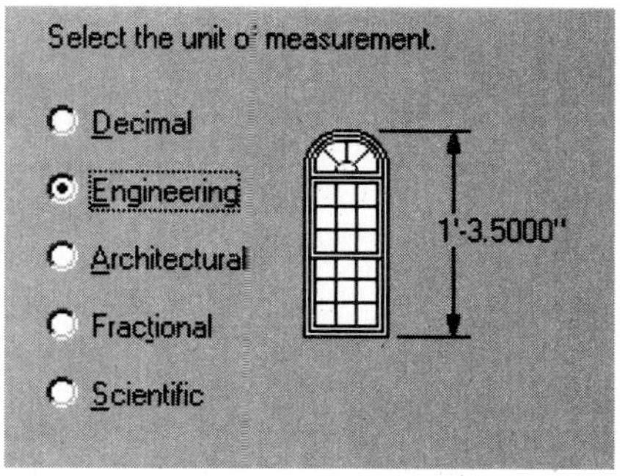

B Engineering units.

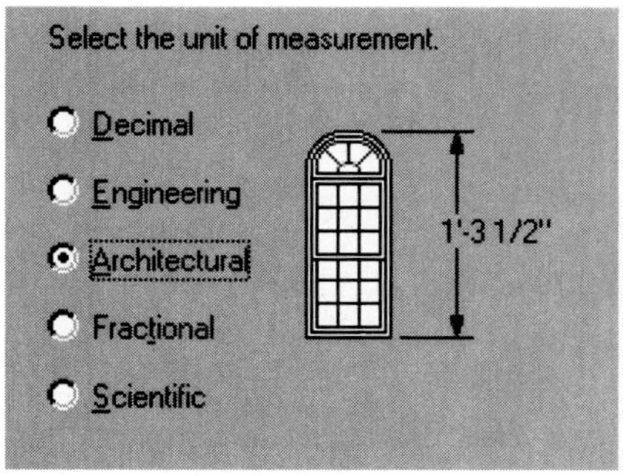

C Architectural units.

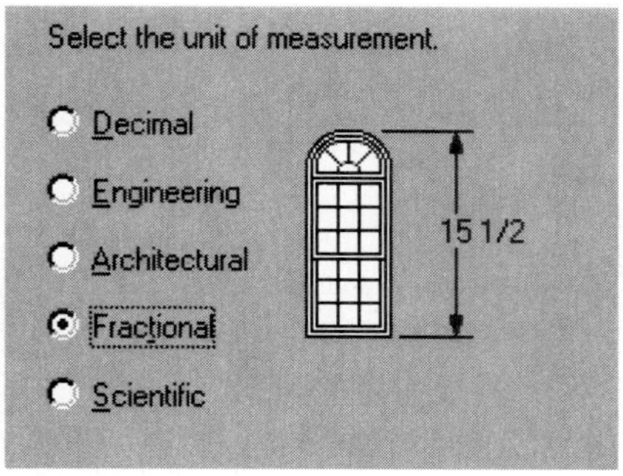

D Fractional units.

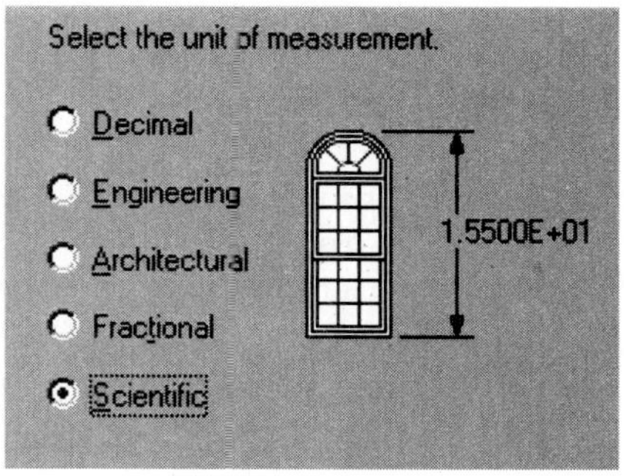

E Scientific units.

FIGURE 2.5 Units page of the Quick Setup dialog box.

Exercise 2.1 — Estimated time required: 5 min.

1. Access the Customize dialog box and change the button size to large.
2. Set the toolbar button size to your own preference and pick Close.
3. Use the cursor to resize the floating command window in AutoCAD LT so that seven lines of text are displayed. Change it back to three lines.
4. Move the floating toolbar to a docked position at the top of the AutoCAD LT program window. Return it to the bottom if that is your preference.
5. Access the Options dialog box.
6. Use the Command Line Text Window Font dialog box to try several different fonts. Set it to your own preference.
7. Using the Color Options dialog box, change the colors of the AutoCAD LT screen to match your preferences.
8. Open AutoCAD LT and look at the Startup dialog box. Pick New from the File pull-down menu to access the Create New Drawing dialog box if AutoCAD LT is already running.
9. Double-click on Quick Setup in the Select a Wizard box, or highlight Quick Setup and press Enter. Now you should see the Quick Setup dialog box.
10. Decimal units is the default unit of measure. Look at the example units.
11. Pick each of the unit options and notice how the example units display changes to represent each type of unit.
12. Pick the Next button, then pick Finish.

Setting the Drawing Size

AutoCAD LT provides a virtually unlimited amount of space in which you can create your drawing. When you use a Wizard, part of the setup procedure asks you to specify the dimensions of the area that your drawing will occupy. All objects created in AutoCAD LT are drawn at full scale, meaning that they are drawn at their actual size. When setting up your drawing space, make the area large enough to hold all necessary views of your drawing plus any required dimensions.

The drawing area can be very small if you are drawing small objects, or it can be large enough for a building, a residential development, a state map, or even larger if necessary. You can control how much of the drawing is displayed on your screen and specify the scale at which the drawing is to be printed. You can also change the size of the drawing area at any time later in a drawing session.

The drawing area that you specify is referred to as the model space **limits**. Model space is where you create a drawing in AutoCAD LT. You can set the model space drawing limits using the Area page in the Quick Setup dialog box. Keep in mind that this area indicates the amount of space required by the objects you are drawing and not the size of the sheet on which you will be printing.

Figure 2.6 shows the Area page of the Quick Setup dialog box with its default settings. Use your cursor to pick inside the text boxes labeled Width: and Length: to specify the size of your drawing area. Use the style of units you are working with to indicate the drawing size. If you are using architectural units, be sure to place the foot symbol (′) after a number indicating a value in feet or it is interpreted as inches. A drawing size of 17 × 11 is specified in Figure 2.7. Notice that the width value is the horizontal dimension, and the length value is the vertical dimension.

FIGURE 2.6 The Area page in the Quick Setup dialog box. Notice the example image.

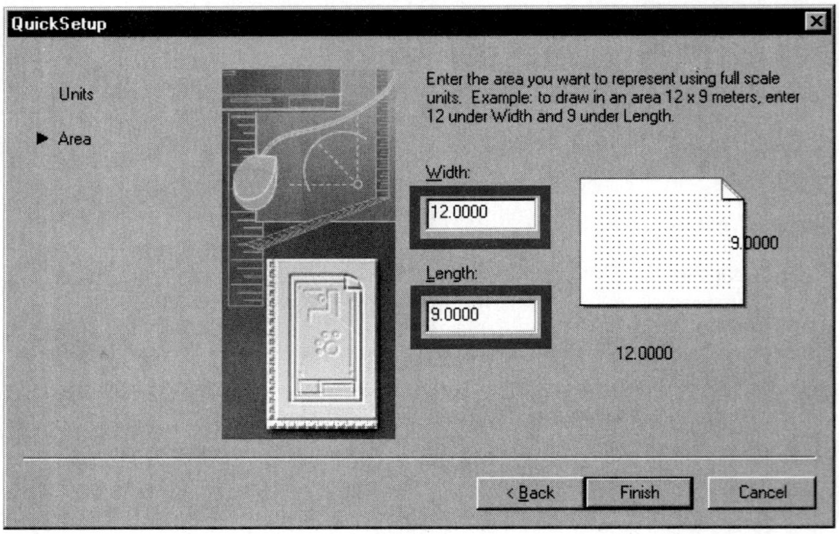

FIGURE 2.7 Changing the drawing area.

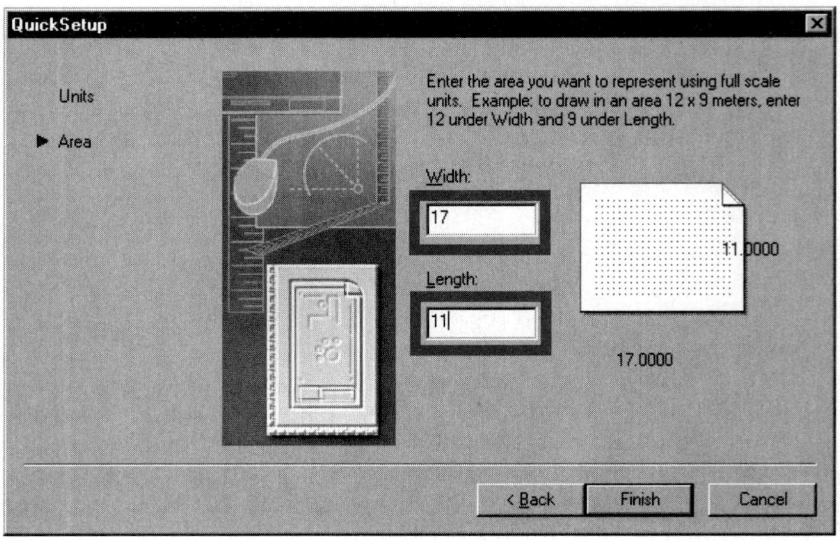

If you are new to drafting, then drawing in real units might seem like a good idea. However, if you have used manual drafting in the past, you may be wondering about the drawing scale. It is best to forget about drawing scale for now and think about drawing everything actual or full size. If drawing scales need to be set, this is done during the drawing layout process, which is discussed in the Multiview Drawing Layout section in Chapter 13.

Field Notes

Remember, when entering a new value in a text box, all you have to do is double-click on the current value to highlight it. Then just type the new value. It is not necessary to press the Backspace or Delete key first. The highlighted text is automatically replaced by the text you type.

More about Drawing Limits

The initial Model space drawing limits are set up in the Area page of the Quick Setup dialog box. Regardless of the settings you specify, the limits are turned off by default. When turned off, the limits have little effect on the drawing process. In addition, the limits setting can be changed at any time. Changing the limits settings is discussed in Chapter 3. The effects of the drawing limits are as follows:

- Specifies where the drawing grid is displayed (Chapter 3)
- Provides an easy display change option for displaying the entire drawing area. (Chapter 4)

The model space drawing limits are not related in any way to the final printed sheet size. The basic rule for determining the most appropriate initial limits setting is to specify an area that will contain your entire drawing. In a multiview drawing application, use your standard drawing layout guidelines based on school or company standards to calculate the required area. If you are drawing a floor plan, use the largest horizontal and vertical dimensions of the building and add enough area to contain dimensions or other required drawing data. You can always adjust the limits later if needed.

Introduction to Model Space and Paper Space

AutoCAD LT provides two drawing areas: **model space** and **paper space**. Model space is the primary area of the drawing. This is where your model (drawing) is created. All drawings are created in model space at actual size without consideration of the final layout or printed size and scale. When your drawing is complete, you then complete your drawing layout in paper space.

When using the Quick Setup wizard, you automatically begin your drawing session in model space. In later chapters, you will learn to use model space to create drawing layouts for industry-standard sheet sizes and print your drawings at industry-standard drawing scales. Unless otherwise indicated, all discussions, examples, and exercises are based on model space being active.

Model space is active when the Model tab at the bottom of the drawing area is selected. If you pick one of the layout tabs, the Page Setup dialog box is displayed. Creating a layout and using the Page Setup dialog box are discussed in later chapters. For now, if you accidentally pick a layout tab, just pick the Cancel button in the Page Setup dialog box, and then pick the Model tab to return to model space.

Exercise 2.2 — Estimated time required: 5 min.

1. Open AutoCAD LT if it is not already open. Use the Startup or Create Drawing dialog box and select Quick Setup.
2. Pick the Next > button.
3. Read the text description near the top.
4. The default limits are Width 12 and Length 9. Change the Width to 17 and the Length to 11.
5. Change the Width to 8.5 and notice the difference in the example.
6. Pick the Finish button.

LEARNING CHECKPOINT

- □ What information is given by the Wizard about Quick Setup?
- □ Name and give an example of each of the five types of units in AutoCAD LT.
- □ What is the purpose of the Limits setting?
- □ What are some of the advantages of an unlimited drawing area?

Introducing the AutoCAD LT Workspace

- Starting a New Drawing
- Setting Interface Options

Concept Animations

- Drawing Scale

Introduction to the AutoCAD LT Drawing Aids

AutoCAD LT provides you with drawing aids that help make drawing easy and accurate. Two of the drawing aids that you set up before beginning a drawing are called Grid and Snap. ***Grid*** is a pattern of dots displayed on the screen at any desired increment that you establish. ***Snap*** is an invisible grid that forces the screen cursor to move in exact increments. The idea behind these drawing aids is to give you a grid on the screen that matches units of measure on your drawing. This is similar to doing a pencil drawing on graph paper. The lines on the graph paper give you something to follow when making a sketch or drawing. The grid dots on the screen work the same way, and the snap spacing forces the screen cursor to follow the dots exactly as you move the pointing device. The Quick Setup automatically establishes equal grid and snap settings based on the units and drawing area you select.

Setting the Grid and Snap

Tools
Drafting Settings...
DSETTINGS
DS
SE

Status Bar
GRID
GRID
[Ctrl] + [G]
[F7]

Status Bar
SNAP
SNAP
[Ctrl] + [B]
[F9]

Grid and snap settings are controlled in the Drafting Settings dialog box. To access this dialog box, pick Drafting Settings… in the Tools pull-down menu, or type **DSETTINGS, DS,** or **SE** at the Command: prompt and press Enter. The Snap and Grid tab of the Drafting Settings dialog box is shown in Figure 2.8. The Snap On (F9) and Grid On (F7) checkboxes turn these features on or off. As indicated by the labels, the keyboard function keys F7 and F9 can also be used to toggle the state of the Snap and Grid. The function keys can be used whether or not the Drafting Settings dialog box is visible. The accelerator keys toggles are CTRL+G (grid) and CTRL+B (snap).

The default settings in the Snap type & style area should be set to Grid snap and Rectangular snap. If these settings are not currently active, pick the appropriate radio buttons to apply these settings. The other snap types and styles are discussed later in the text.

The X and Y spacing values control the distance between grid dots or snap points along the X and Y axes of the Cartesian coordinate system. The Cartesian coordinate system is detailed later in this chapter. The X spacing controls the horizontal spacing, and the Y spacing controls the vertical spacing. In Figure 2.8, the spacing is .5 on both axes for grid and snap. When you set an X spacing value, the Y spacing is automatically changed to match. The most common applications of grid and snap use equal X and Y spacing values. Some applications may work best with different X and Y spacing. In this case you need to set the X spacing first, then set the Y spacing.

The grid dots provide a visual aid but do not control cursor movement. The snap controls the cursor movement but does not display the increments on screen. When the grid and snap features are both on and set to the same values, the incremental cursor movement is restricted so that the cursor "snaps" directly to the grid dots on screen. If the grid is too dense, it can become distracting, and in some cases AutoCAD LT may report that the grid is too dense to display. For this reason it is common for grid and snap to be set to different values that complement each other. Various applications for grid and snap are discussed later. Figure 2.9 shows the appearance of the AutoCAD LT screen with grid and snap turned on and set to their default values.

The grid and snap settings can also be controlled at the command line by typing **GRID** or **SNAP** at the Command: prompt:

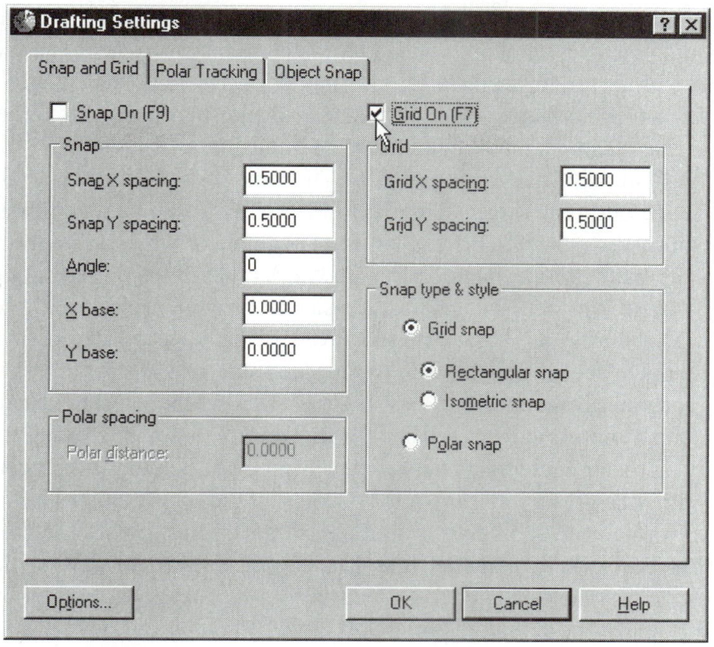

FIGURE 2.8 The Drafting Settings dialog box.

Command: **GRID↵**
Specify grid spacing(X) or [ON/OFF/Snap/Aspect] <0.5000>: **.25↵**
Command: **SNAP↵**
Specify snap spacing or [ON/OFF/Aspect/Rotate/Style/Type] <0.5000>: **.125↵**
Command:

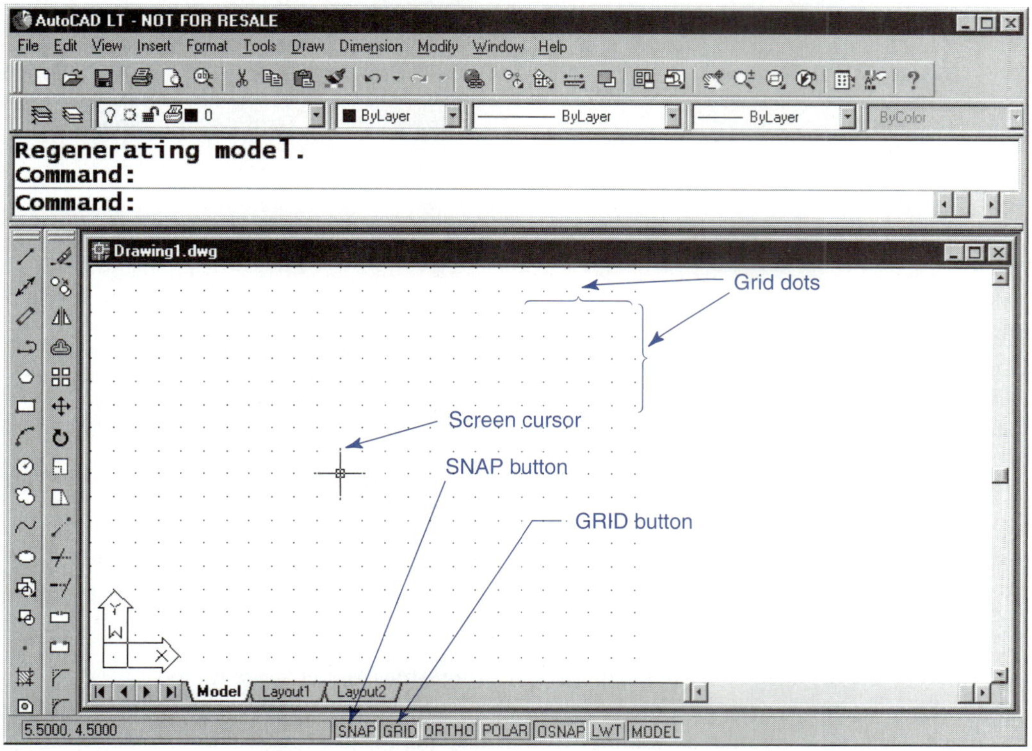

FIGURE 2.9 The AutoCAD LT screen with the grid displayed.

Things to Consider When Setting Drafting Settings

The Grid dots and Snap settings are usually spaced at some convenient unit of measure that matches units on your drawing. For example, you may be drawing an object in inches with a variety of measurements including .25, .50, .75, and 1.50 in. Then you might want to set the grid and snap spacing to the smallest measurement of .25. Now, when you move the screen cursor it automatically moves in .25-in. increments. Metric drawings might use 1-mm or 10-cm increments, depending on the drawing size. This makes it easy for you to draw the objects by picking points that match the measurements on the drawing. Another example might be for an architectural drawing with a variety of dimensions, including 6″, 1′0″, 1′6″, 4′0″, and 6′6″, for example. In this case, you may want to set the grid and snap spacing to 6″ because this makes it easy for you to draw the exact features that are found on the architectural drawing.

The Grid and Snap settings can be the same as with the AutoCAD LT Quick Setup default, or they can be set to different values. This is up to you. You will see the advantages of different settings as you begin to draw with AutoCAD LT. Here is an example of why you might choose different Grid and Snap settings: If the smallest increment on the drawing is .125 in., then setting the grid at this value places the grid dots very close together. The grid dots basically become useless, and, in some cases, may be too close for AutoCAD LT to display. If they are too close, the message "Grid too dense to display" is given in the Command window. The grid should be a general guide to assist your drawing, but the snap spacing should be very accurate. If the smallest dimension is .125 in., then a snap spacing of .125 and a grid spacing of .5 might be an option to consider. This allows the screen cursor to snap to the exact .125 measurement, and there are four snap increments between each set of grid dots. This forces the screen cursor to snap directly on the grid dots at every fourth snap. Whatever Grid and Snap settings you use, the snap and grid should be equal, or the snap should be a multiple of the grid setting. Some examples are given in Table 2.1. The exact snap and grid increments that you choose depend totally on the requirements for the particular drawing. Picking the GRID or SNAP buttons on the status bar at the bottom of the AutoCAD LT program windows toggles these features on or off. Right-clicking on the GRID or SNAP buttons displays shortcut menus that present related options. Pick Settings… from the shortcut menu to display the Drafting Settings dialog box, or pick the appropriate option to turn a feature on or off. Figure 2.10 shows these shortcut menus. The Polar Snap On option on the SNAP shortcut menu is discussed later. In this example, the Off options are disabled because the grid and snap are already off.

TABLE 2.1 Possible snap and grid settings for various applications

Mechanical Drawings				Architectural Drawings		Civil Drawings	
Snap	**Grid**	**Snap**	**Grid**	**Snap**	**Grid**	**Snap**	**Grid**
.0625	.125	1 mm	5 mm	4	12	1′	2′
.125	.25	2	10	6	12	1′	5′
.25	.5	5	20	6	24	2′	10′

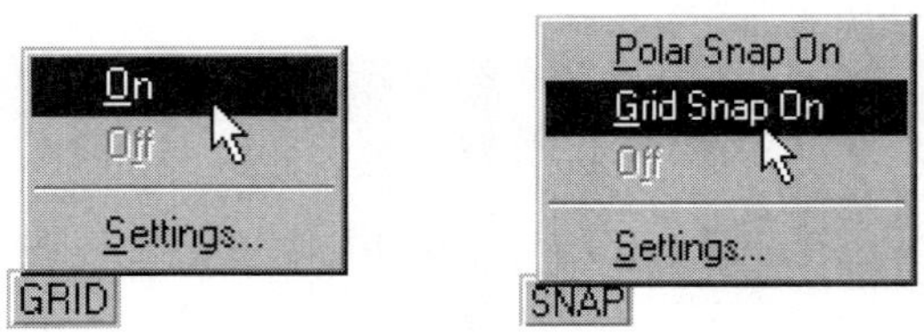

A B

FIGURE 2.10 Shortcut menus are displayed by right-clicking on the GRID or SNAP buttons on the status bar.

Field Notes

- Grid dots are displayed only in the defined drawing Area (Model space limits).
- The Snap feature is useful in some applications, but in some situations can be too restrictive. When you need to point to a location between snap points, just toggle the snap feature off.
- Remember that closing a dialog box by picking the X button on the title bar is the same as picking the Cancel button. If you use the X button to close the Drafting Settings dialog box instead of the OK button, any settings you made will be discarded.

Exercise 2.3

Estimated time required: 5 min.

1. Close the AutoCAD LT software if it is currently running. Restart AutoCAD LT and access the Quick Setup Wizard option from the Startup dialog box.
2. In the Quick Setup dialog box, accept the default Units setting of Decimal and pick the Next > button. Set the Area (Model space limits) Width to 11.5 and Length to 8 units. Pick Finish to close the dialog box.
3. Notice that Grid and Snap are both OFF by default.
4. Open the Drafting Settings dialog box by picking Drafting Settings... from the Tools pull-down menu. Pick the tab labeled Snap and Grid.
5. Place a checkmark in the Snap On and Grid On checkboxes to toggle these features on. Use the default snap and grid spacing values of .5.
6. Pick the OK button to close the Drafting Settings dialog box.
7. Move your cursor around in the drawing area and notice how the cursor "snaps" only to the grid dots.
8. Open the Drafting Settings dialog box by typing **DS** at the Command: prompt.
9. Set both the X and Y spacing for Snap to .25, and leave the Grid set to .5 spacing. Pick the OK button to close the dialog box.
10. Move your cursor around in the drawing area. Notice that the cursor now snaps not only to the grid dots but also to a point midway between each pair of grid dots.
11. Open the Drafting Settings dialog box by picking Settings... from the shortcut menu displayed by right-clicking on the SNAP button on the status bar.
12. Set the X and Y spacing for Snap to .0625, and set the Grid spacing to .25.
13. Close the dialog box and explore the results of the new settings.
14. Toggle the grid off using the GRID button on the status bar. Toggle it on again using the F7 function key. Toggle grid off using the Ctrl + G accelerator key. From the GRID button shortcut menu, select On to display the grid again.
15. Toggle the snap feature off and on using the SNAP button on the status bar, the F9 function key, the Ctrl + B accelerator key and finally by picking Grid Snap On from the SNAP button shortcut menu.
16. Open the Drafting Settings dialog box by typing **SE** at the Command: prompt.
17. Set the X and Y snap spacing to .25 and the X and Y grid spacing to .5. Both Grid and Snap should be toggled ON.
18. Pick the OK button to close the Drafting Settings dialog box.
19. Keep the drawing open to continue to the next exercise.

LEARNING CHECKPOINT

- □ Why does AutoCAD LT provide you with drafting settings?
- □ Describe *grid* and *snap.*
- □ Identify at least two things to consider when setting the Grid and Snap options.
- □ Name four ways to toggle the Grid settings and four ways to toggle the Snap setting.
- □ For both Grid and Snap, in what order must the X and Y spacing values be set when the X and Y spacing values are not the same?
- □ On the shortcut menu for the SNAP button on the status bar, which option has the same effect as placing a check in the checkbox labeled Snap On (F9) in the Drafting Settings dialog box?

Introducing the AutoCAD LT Workspace

- Starting a New Drawing

Drawing Lines with AutoCAD LT

Lines are used in drafting to communicate an idea. Some drafting fields such as mechanical drafting recommend strict standards for line presentation. Line standards for these drawings are provided in the ASME Y14.2M document. Other drafting fields, such as architectural, piping, and electrical, also have recommended line standards that are commonly used. Standard line examples that are commonly used in industry are displayed in Appendix B.

Draw

Line

Draw
Line

LINE
L

Drawing Lines by Picking Points

When drawing lines with AutoCAD LT, you use the LINE command. This command can be accessed in any of these ways:

- Pick Line from the Draw pull-down menu.
- Pick the Line button in the Draw toolbar.
- Type **L** or **LINE** at the Command: prompt.

When you enter the LINE command, you get this message at the prompt line:

Command: **L** or **LINE**↵
Specify first point:

Specify first point: means that AutoCAD LT is ready for you to enter the first point to begin drawing a line. If Grid and Snap are on, the screen cursor snaps to Snap points as you move the mouse. Also, as you move the screen cursor, the ***coordinate display*** indicates where the cursor is in relation to the drawing origin. The coordinate display may be turned on or off or changed from absolute coordinate to polar coordinate values using the F6 key, Ctrl + D, or by double-clicking on the coordinate display on the status bar. Absolute and polar coordinates are discussed later. The ***drawing origin,*** or *origin,* is in the lower left corner of the screen when you begin an AutoCAD LT drawing with the Quick Setup. Look at Figure 2.11. The drawing origin has a coordinate display of 0.0000,0.0000. As you move the mouse, the coordinate display changes to represent how far you have moved to the right and up from the origin. The coordinate display of 4.5000,4.5000 shown in Figure 2.11 means that the screen cursor is 4.5 units to the right and 4.5 units up from the origin.

Now, use the left mouse button to pick the point. The prompt reads:

FIGURE 2.11 Pick the point at coordinates 4.5000,4.5000. Notice the origin, command line, and coordinate display.

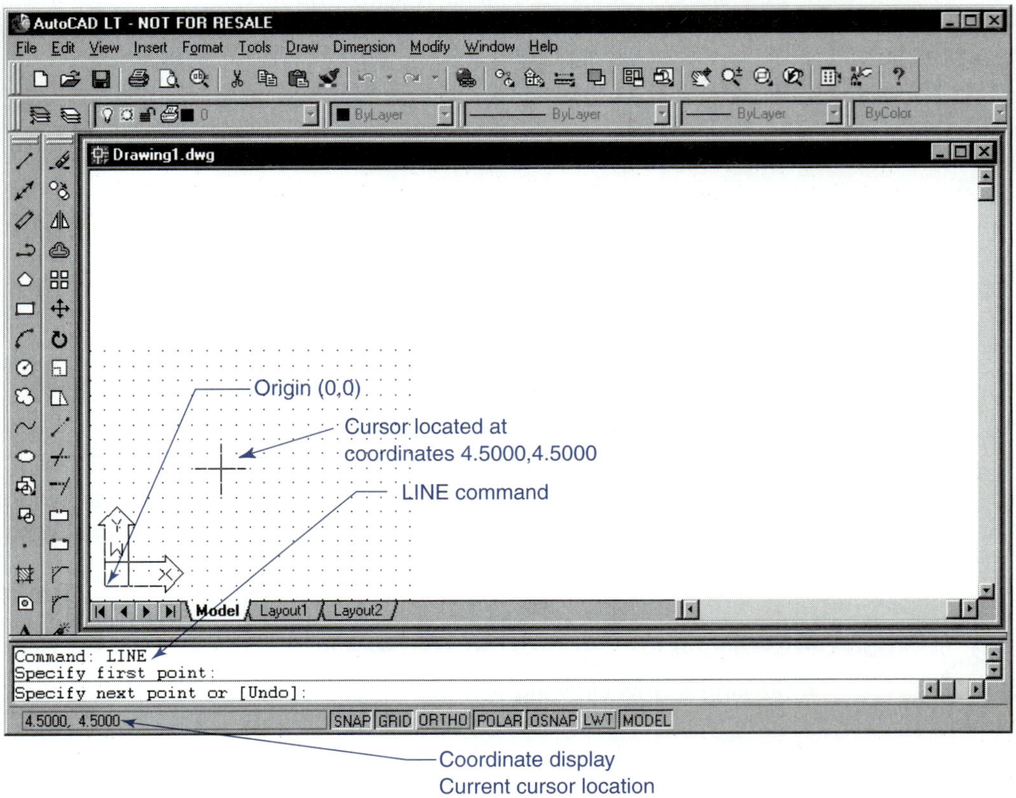

Command: **L** or **LINE**↵
Specify first point: ⟨*pick where the coordinates read 4.5000,4.5000*⟩
Specify next point or [Undo]:

AutoCAD LT prompts you to pick another point to define the line and presents a list of any available options. As you move the screen cursor, the coordinate display continues to tell you the distance to the right and up from the origin. At the same time, a temporary line is displayed between the first point you picked and the cursor location. This is called a ***rubber-band line.*** As you move the mouse, the rubber-band line also moves and shows you where the line would be if you picked the next point. Figure 2.12 shows coordinates 6.5000,6.5000 selected as the next point. You may continue drawing as many connected line segments as you wish, because AutoCAD LT continues to give you the To point: prompt until you cancel the LINE command. Exit the LINE command by pressing the Esc or Enter key or the space bar:

Command: **L** or **LINE**↵
Specify first point: ⟨*pick where the coordinates read 4.5000,4.5000*⟩
Specify next point or [Undo]: ⟨*pick where the coordinates read 6.5000,6.5000*⟩
Specify next point or [Undo]: **Cancel**
Command:

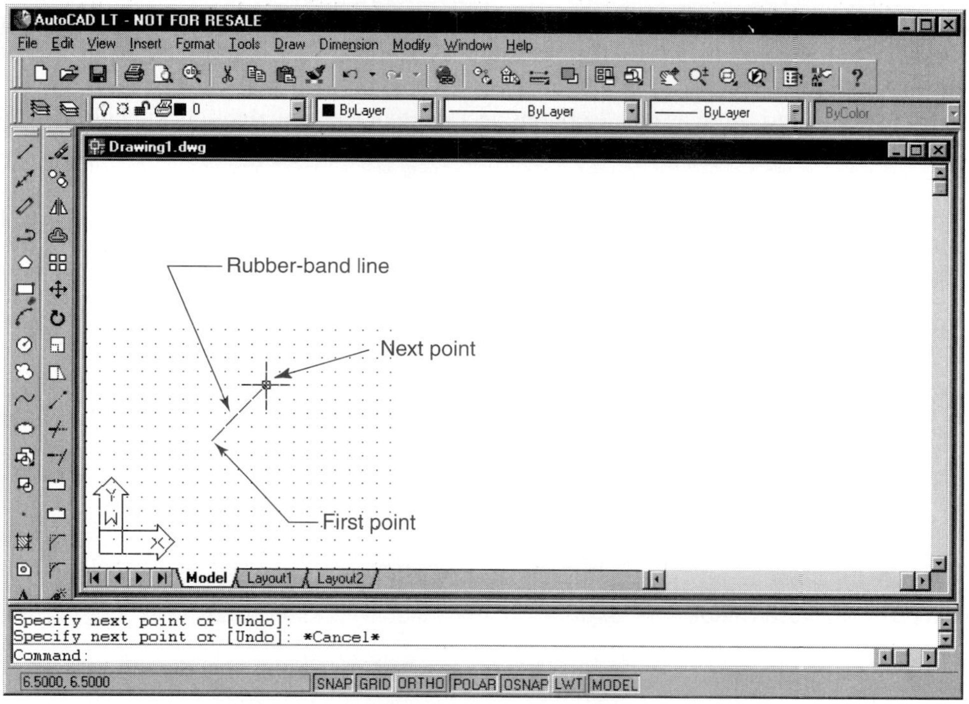

FIGURE 2.12 Pick the other end at coordinates 6.5000,6.5000.

Field Notes

- When you move your cursor during the LINE command, a polar tip may be displayed indicating the distance and direction of cursor travel. This is a feature of Polar Snap, which is discussed later.
- The size of the crosshair cursor in AutoCAD LT is an adjustable interface option. In the Display tab of the Options dialog box, the Crosshair size area provides an edit box and a slider bar that can be used to set the size between 1% and 100% of the screen size. The default crosshair size is 5%.
- This text shows typed commands in bold print to show you what must be entered at the command line. When you pick a command from a menu or a toolbar, it is entered by AutoCAD LT in a slightly different way at the Command: prompt. Commands accessed in this manner are preceded by an underscore character and the first prompt at the Command: line is automatically entered. For example,

    Command: _line Specify first point:

It can be typed this way as well, but the underscore is unnecessary, so it is not commonly used.

Using Command Options

Most commands provide a default course of action along with options that can be used when needed. When options are available, they are displayed within square brackets as part of the prompt. Although it is not listed at the prompts, an option to cancel the current operation by pressing the Esc key is typically available. If an option is displayed in angle brackets, it is activated by pressing the Enter key.

You can also display a list of available options on a shortcut menu by right-clicking in the drawing window. The shortcut menu shows any available command options for easy access. If no options are available, right-clicking is equivalent to pressing the Enter key.

No options are displayed when you first start the LINE command. The only available user responses at this time are to either specify the first point or cancel the command. Figure 2.13 shows each of the prompts issued by the LINE command, and the associated shortcut menu.

Command: **L** or **LINE**

Specify first point: *No shorcut menu available. Right-click = [Enter]*

Specify next point or [Undo]:

Specify next point or [Undo]:

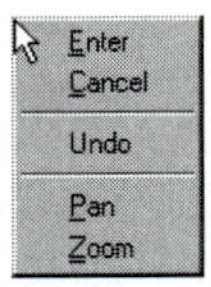

Specify next point or [Close/Undo]:

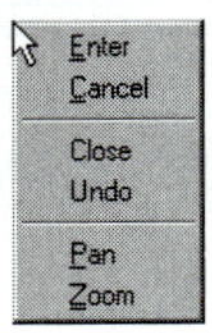

FIGURE 2.13 Command options are listed in square brackets as part of the prompt, or you can right-click in the drawing area to display the shortcut menu.

The LINE command options are as follows:

- **Enter** Produces the same effect as pressing the Enter key.
- **Cancel** Stops the current LINE command and returns to the Command: prompt.
- **Undo** The LINE command backs up one step, removing the effects of the last point specification.
- **Close** Available only after two line segments have been drawn, this draws a segment from the current location back to the first point specified in this use of the LINE command.
- **Pan & Zoom** These display change options are detailed in Chapter 4.

Save Your First Drawing

Standard

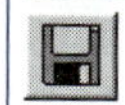

Save (Ctrl+S)

File
Save

SAVE
SA
[Ctrl] + [S]

You are asked to save the drawing in the next exercise. A drawing is saved so the work that you have done is protected and you can access it later. Before saving the drawing you need to decide on a name. For example, the next exercise asks you to save the drawing as EX2.5, where *EX* stands for exercise and *2.5* is Chapter 2, exercise number 5. Other drawing names may be selected to describe the type of drawing or project, such as FLOOR PLAN, or PART A-100.

Drawings that have not yet been saved are assigned a temporary name. The first drawing created in a drawing session is assigned the temporary name *Drawing1.dwg*, and subsequently created drawings use an incremented name (*Drawing2.dwg, Drawing3.dwg,* etc.). When a drawing is saved, a user-specified name is assigned to the drawing file. If your drawing windows are floating, whether cascaded, tiled, or minimized, the drawing name is displayed in the title bar of the drawing window. When the drawing window is maximized, the name of the currently active drawing is shown in square brackets on the AutoCAD LT program window title bar.

The SAVE command is used to save a drawing to a file. The SAVE command is accessed by picking Save from the File pull-down menu, by picking the Save button from the Standard toolbar, by typing **SAVE** or **SA** at the Command: prompt, or by using the Ctrl + S accelerator keystroke. If the drawing has not yet been saved, the SAVEAS command is automatically started and the Save Drawing As dialog box is displayed. The current drawing name is listed in the File name: edit box, and the Save in: drop-down list shows the name of the current folder. It is strongly recommended that you do not save your drawing files in the AutoCAD LT 2000 folder.

Starting with good file management practices can help you avoid potential problems in the future. The Save Drawing As dialog box provides a complete set of disk and file management tools. An in-depth discussion of disk and file management procedures is covered in Chapter 15. For now, you should at least create a simple set of folders where you can store your work. The following discussion shows how to create a folder for your drawing exercise files, but you should always ask your instructor or system administrator for guidance in setting up an appropriate file system.

In a drawing that has not been saved previously, use the SAVE command to display the Save Drawing As dialog box. Pick the Create New Folder button as shown in Figure 2.14A. The temporary folder name of New Folder is highlighted for you (Figure 2.14B). To rename the new folder, just begin typing the desired name and then press Enter. After renaming the folder, point at it with your cursor and double-click to open it (see Figure 2.14C). Once you have opened the new folder (Figure 2.14D), you can enter the name in the File name: edit box and pick the Save button to create the file. Figure 2.14E depicts the new folder location.

FIGURE 2.14 The Save Drawing As dialog box provides several important disk and file management tools. (A–D) A new folder is being created for storing drawing files created in your textbook exercises. (E) The new folder structure.

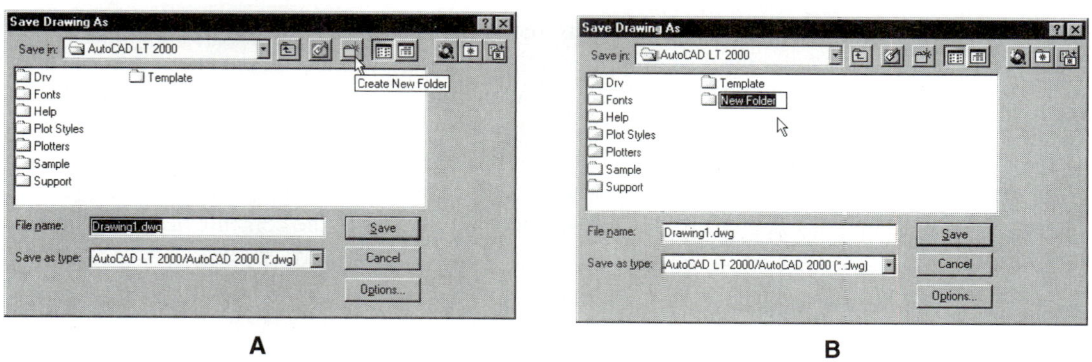

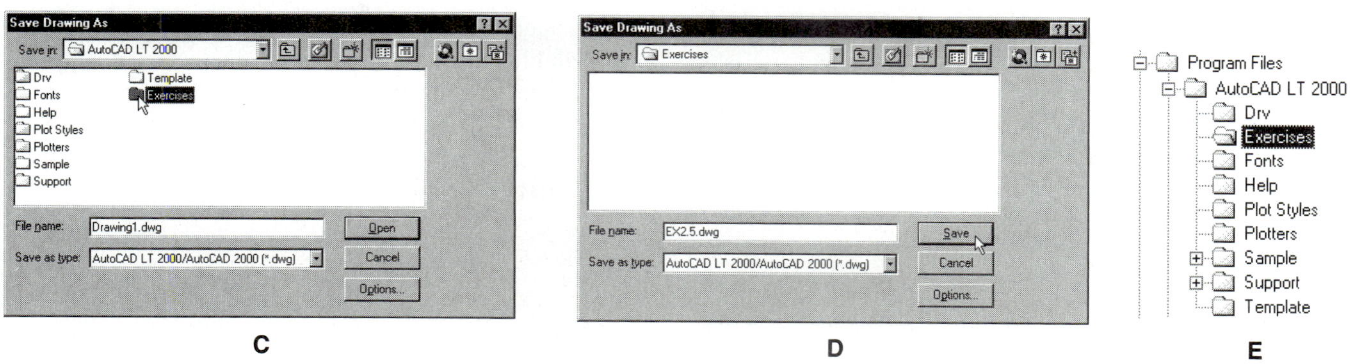

If a drawing file has been saved previously, the SAVE command does not ask for the file name. With no further prompting, the associated file is updated to reflect any changes to the drawing since the last time it was saved. Using the pull-down menu or the toolbar button to save a previously saved drawing issues the QSAVE command. QSAVE is functionally equivalent to the SAVE command.

It is important to develop proper habits for saving your work. Additions and modifications to drawings are stored temporarily in computer memory as you work. When you save a drawing, a more permanent record is written on your disk drive. If you experience a power failure or a system "crash," the information contained in computer memory is immediately lost; however, files saved on a disk are not typically affected. A system failure can mean a loss of all work completed since the last time you saved your drawing. As you begin working in AutoCAD LT you should get into the habit of saving your drawing every *10 to 15 minutes*. Losing 10 minutes' worth of work costs you much less than losing several hours of work. Most new CAD drafters learn this the hard way.

Another aspect of proper drawing file management is learning to reuse previous work. In many industries, a product line may include several products that are very similar. Some drafting projects may be similar enough that a few modifications to an existing drawing may be all that is needed to complete a new project. AutoCAD LT allows you to open any existing drawing project and save it under a new name without affecting the original drawing file. To save a drawing under a new name, use the SAVEAS command. You can start the SAVEAS command by picking Save As... from the File pull-down menu or by typing **SAVEAS** at the Command: prompt. This command always displays the Save Drawing As dialog box, where you can specify a new folder location and even a new file name as needed.

Field Notes

As with most Windows applications, right-clicking in an AutoCAD LT file dialog box displays context-sensitive shortcut menus. Right-clicking while your cursor is pointing to a folder or a file displays a shortcut menu with options such as *copy, rename,* and *delete*. The shortcut menu displayed by right-clicking in the empty space between files provides options for adjusting the file display style and creating new folders, as well as an Undo option.

Naming Your Drawings

A file name has two components, the actual name of the file and the file extension. A *file extension* is a suffix that identifies the type of file and tells the computer what software application is used to open the file. The file extension for AutoCAD LT 2000 drawing files is *.dwg*. You do not need to type the *.dwg* when saving a drawing because the *.dwg* file extension is automatically applied by AutoCAD LT.

Similar to any other file in the Windows operating system, a drawing file can be named using up to 256 characters and can include printable characters such as spaces, dashes, periods, commas, and underscores. Using this flexibility can help you accurately identify the contents of a drawing based on its name. Here are a few examples of descriptive file names that can be used:

Remodeling plan.dwg

Guest House. @60% complete, needs electrical and plumbing details.dwg

Allen Project, Phase 1.dwg

Some characters cannot be used in file names, including forward slashes (/), backslashes (\), equals signs (=), question marks (?), and asterisks (*). Although file names can be up to 256 characters, it is recommended that file names be kept as short as is practical for each application.

The folder path and file extension also count toward the 256-character limit. For example, the folder path *\Program Files\AutoCAD LT 2000\Exercises* is 41 characters long, and the file extension *.dwg* requires another 4 characters, limiting a file name in this folder to 211 characters.

Exercise 2.4

Estimated time required: 5 min.

1. Continue from Exercise 2.3.
2. Enter the LINE command using the pull-down menu. Cancel the command and enter the LINE command by picking the toolbar button. Cancel the command and type **LINE** (or the alias **L**) followed by pressing the Enter key or the space bar. Think about which method you like the best. You should now have a Specify first point: prompt.
3. Move the screen cursor and watch the coordinate display values change.
4. Move the screen cursor until you get coordinate values of 4.5000,4.5000, just like Figure 2.11.
5. Pick this point. You should now have a Specify next point [Undo]: prompt.
6. Move the screen cursor and watch the rubber-band cursor adjust to different line lengths as you move.
7. Move the screen cursor until you get coordinate values of 6.5000,6.5000, just like Figure 2.12.
8. Pick this point.
9. Watch the rubber-band cursor again as you move the mouse.
10. Pick some more points and cancel the LINE command when you are done.
11. Save as EX2.4 and close the drawing by picking Close from the File pull-down menu. Check with your instructor or system administrator for guidance on setting up your own folders.

Open a Saved Drawing

Standard
Open (Ctrl+O)
File Open
OPEN [Ctrl] + [O]

When starting AutoCAD LT, you can pick the Open a Drawing button in the Startup dialog box. The last four files that were opened in AutoCAD LT are shown in the Select a File: list. Selecting one of these provides a Preview image of the drawing. Double-click on the desired file or highlight it and pick OK to open. Pick the Browse … button to access the dialog box shown in Figure 2.10. Use the OPEN command if you need to work on an existing drawing without using the Startup dialog box. To do this, pick Open … in the File pull-down menu, use Ctrl+O, pick the Open toolbar button, or type **OPEN.** This displays the Select File dialog box, shown in Figure 2.15. If you want to open EX2.4 to work on it some more, find EX2.4 and pick it. EX2.4.dwg becomes highlighted and is displayed in the File name: edit box. An image of the drawing is shown in the Preview box to help you confirm the selection (see Figure 2.15). Pick Open to open the drawing when you are ready.

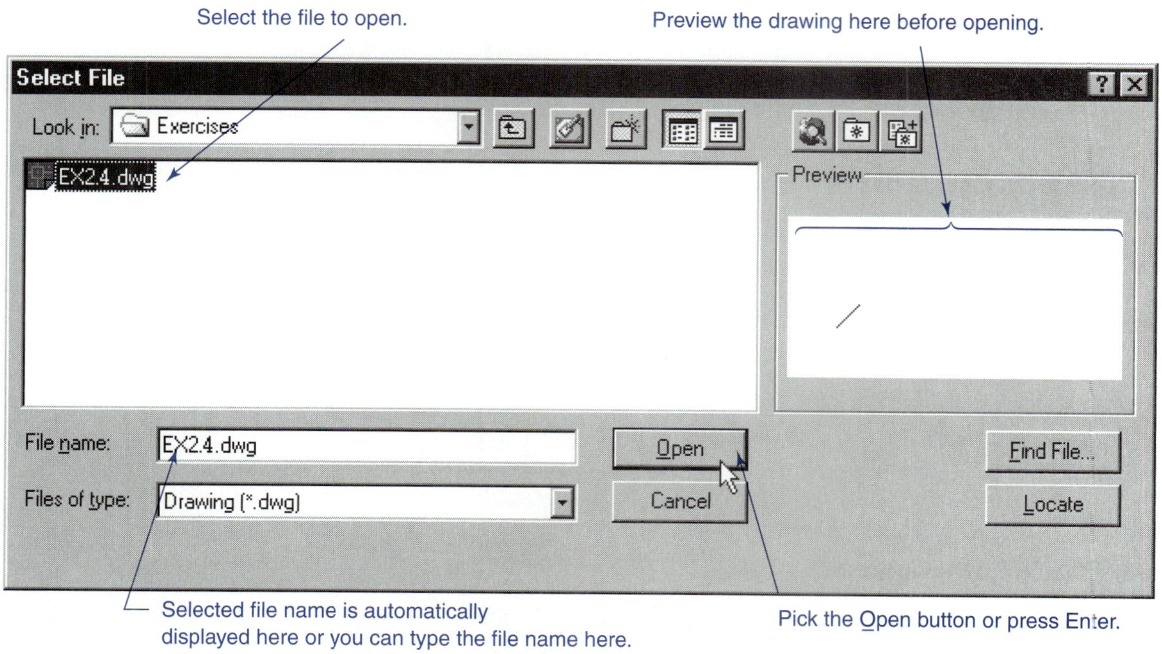

FIGURE 2.15 Open a drawing using the Select File dialog box. Notice the Preview image on the right.

Drawing Lines by Entering Distances, Angles, and Coordinates

In many situations, you can draw lines by picking points as you have just seen. This works if the Grid and Snap settings match the measurements on the object you plan to draw. There are also situations when picking points does not give you the accuracy or flexibility that you need. AutoCAD LT uses what is known as the Cartesian coordinate system. The ***Cartesian coordinate system*** relates to numbers that are used to locate points relative to two intersecting axes lines. There is a two-dimensional (2-D) system that relates to an X and Y axis and a three-dimensional (3-D) system that uses an additional Z axis. The 3-D system is discussed in Chapter 14. Points are located from the intersection of the X and Y axes, which is called the *origin.* This origin is the same as the drawing origin that was discussed earlier. When using this system, measurements along the X axis are either right (positive) or left (negative) from the origin, and distances along the Y axis are up (positive) or down (negative) from the origin. Points are always assigned two numbers, such as 5,4. These numbers are called ***coordinates.*** The first coordinate (5) is the X value and the second (4) is the Y value. Look at Figure 2.16.

Generally when you are drawing, the origin is in the lower left corner of the screen. This makes all the X and Y coordinates positive, which is usually easier to use while drawing. Figure 2.17 shows how some sample coordinates read if the origin is the lower left corner of the screen.

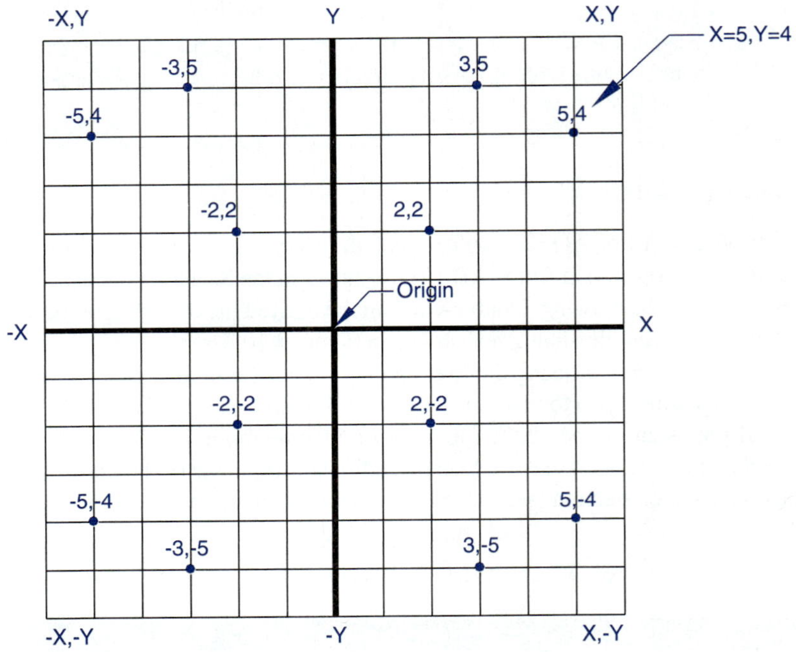

FIGURE 2.16 The Cartesian coordinate system.

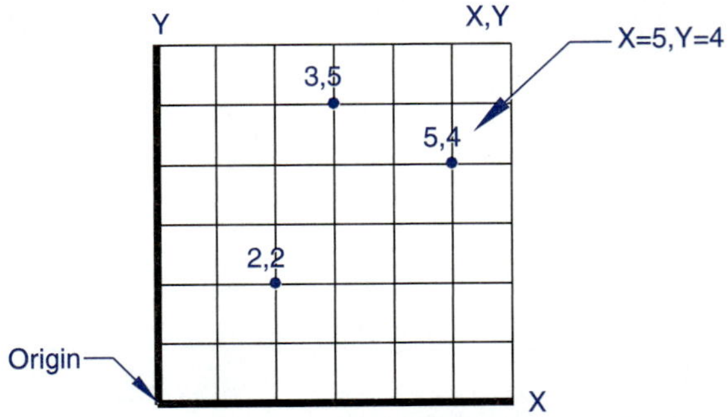

FIGURE 2.17 Coordinates with the origin in the lower left corner.

Coordinate Entry Options

The previous discussion introduced you to the Cartesian coordinate system. When you are working with AutoCAD LT, you have the option of entering coordinates to locate points using one of four coordinate entry options. These options are picking points (as you have already learned), absolute, relative, and polar coordinates.

Using Absolute Coordinates

Absolute coordinates are X and Y points that are always established based on their distance from the origin. The origin is coordinate 0,0. This works well in a situation where you know the location of points from the origin. If you want to draw a line from the point coordinate 2,2 to the point coordinate 7.5,6.25, you would use the following command sequence, as shown in Figure 2.18:

Command: **L** or **LINE**↵
Specify first point: **2,2**↵
Specify next point or [Undo]: **7.5,6.25**↵
Specify next point or [Undo]: ↵
Command:

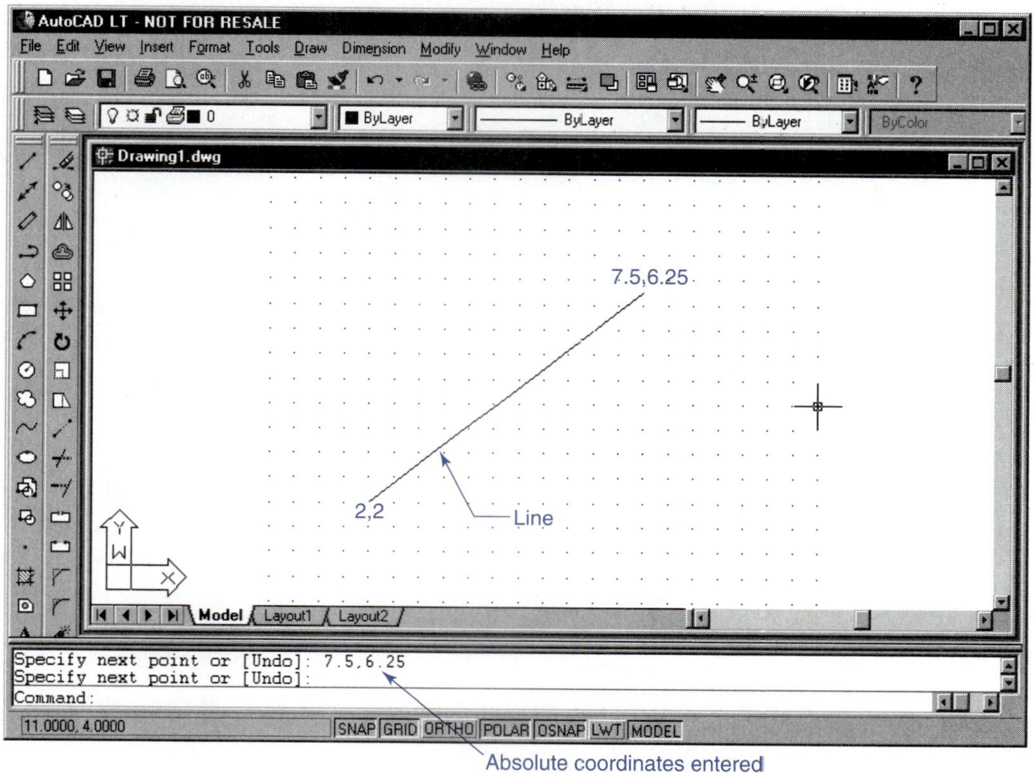

FIGURE 2.18 Drawing a line using absolute coordinates.

Exercise 2.5 — Estimated time required: 5 min.

1. Start a new drawing using the Quick Setup Wizard. Specify decimal units and a drawing area of 11 × 8.5 units. Toggle the Grid on using the default spacing.
2. Use the LINE command to draw the following shape, specifying absolute coordinates as shown:

Command: **LINE↵**
Specify first point: **2,2↵**
Specify next point or [Undo]: **4,2↵**
Specify next point or [Undo]: **4,3.5↵**
Specify next point or [Close/Undo]: **3,3.5↵**
Specify next point or [Close/Undo]: **3,4↵**
Specify next point or [Close/Undo]: **2,4↵**
Specify next point or [Close/Undo]: **2,2↵**
Specify next point or [Close/Undo]: ↵

Command: **LINE↵**
Specify first point: **2,2.75↵**
Specify next point or [Undo]: **4,2.75↵**
Specify next point or [Undo]: ↵

Command: **LINE↵**
Specify first point: **3,2↵**
Specify next point or [Undo]: **3,2.75↵**
Specify next point or [Undo]: ↵

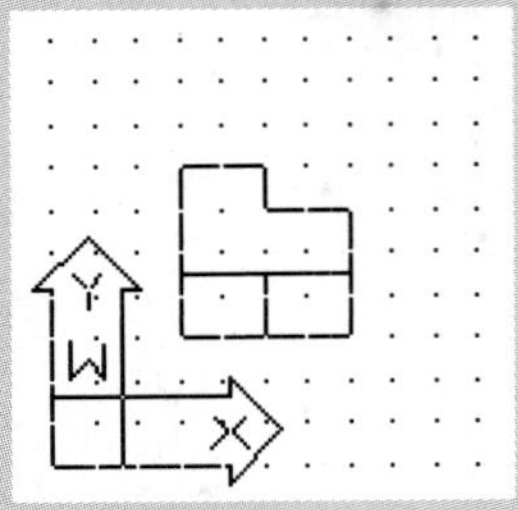

3. Save as EX2.5, and close the drawing.

Using Relative Coordinates

Relative coordinates are used when you want to establish a point based on an X axis and a Y axis distance from a previous point. Think of it as locating a point "relative" to another point. The first point of a line may be selected by picking or with absolute coordinates, and the next point is drawn relative to the first specifying the change in X and Y values, as shown in Figure 2.19. The X,Y entry for a relative coordinate must be preceded by the "@" symbol like this:

Command: **LINE↵**
Specify first point: **2,2↵**
Specify next point or [Undo]: **@5,4↵**
Specify next point or [Undo]: ↵
Command:

Figure 2.20 shows the results of this command sequence.

FIGURE 2.19 Using relative coordinates.

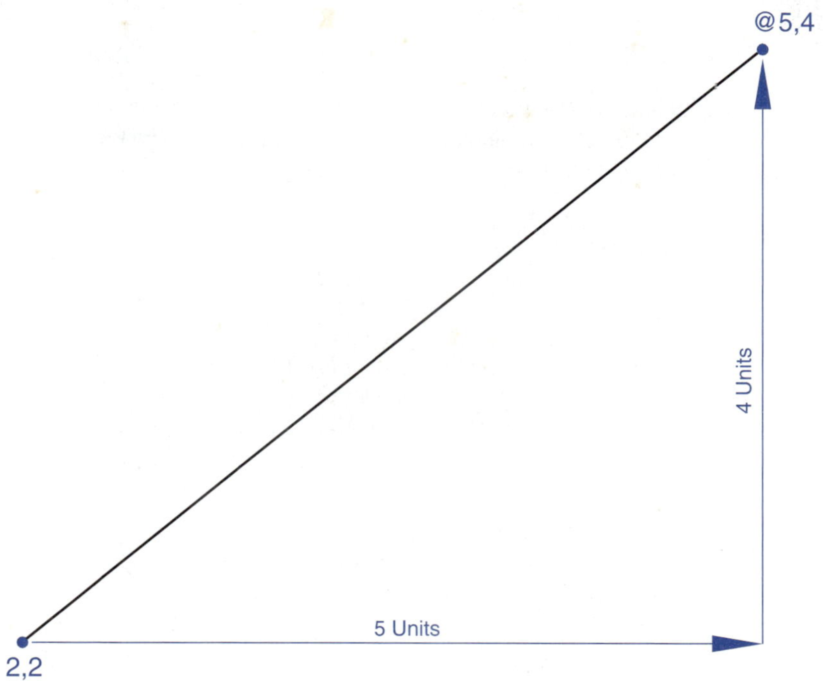

FIGURE 2.20 Drawing a line using relative coordinates.

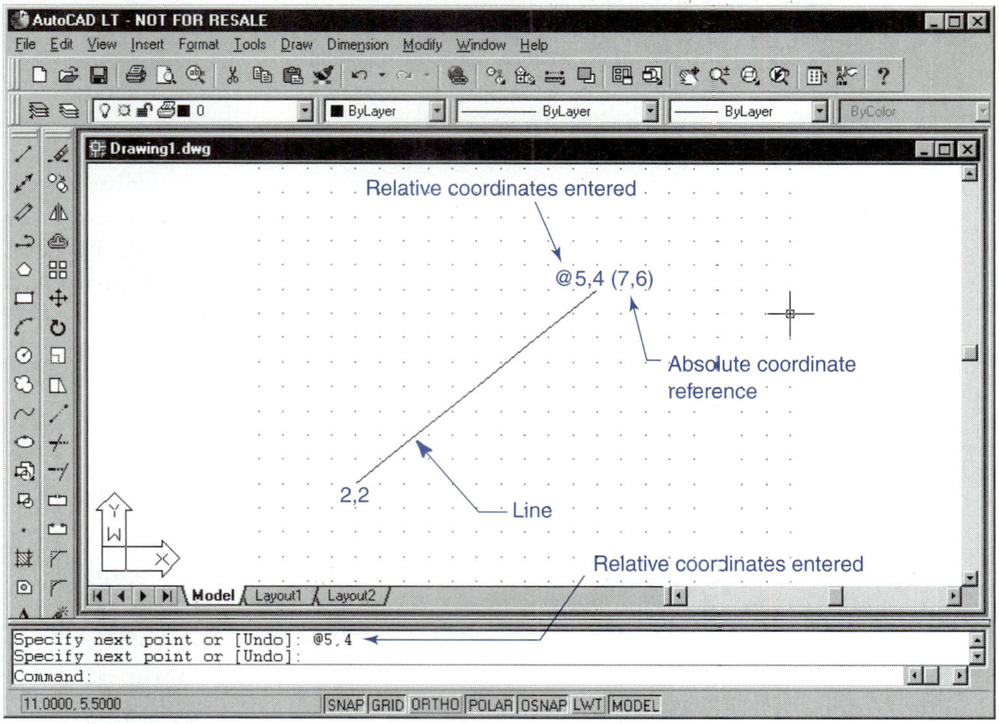

Exercise 2.6 **Estimated time required: 5 min.**

1. Open EX2.5 for editing.
2. Use the LINE command to draw the second view of the following object, specifying relative coordinates as shown.

Command: **LINE↵**
Specify first point: **6,2↵**
Specify next point or [Undo]: **@2,0↵**
Specify next point or [Undo]: **@0,2↵**
Specify next point or [Close/Undo]: **@-.75,0↵**
Specify next point or [Close/Undo]: **@0,-1.25↵**
Specify next point or [Close/Undo]: **@-1.25,0↵**
Specify next point or [Close/Undo]: **@0,-.75↵**
Specify next point or [Close/Undo]: ↵

Command: **LINE↵**
Specify first point: **@.5,0↵**
Specify next point or [Undo]: **@0,.75↵**
Specify next point or [Undo]:↵

Command: **LINE↵**
Specify first point: **@.75,.75↵**
Specify next point or [Undo]: **@.75,0↵**
Specify next point or [Undo]: ↵

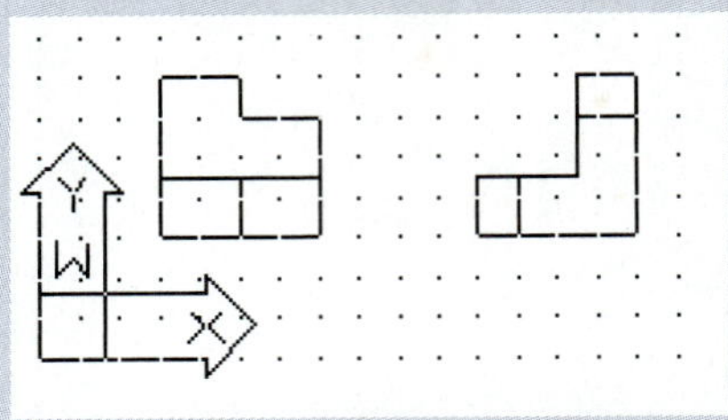

3. Save as EX2.6, and close the drawing.

Using Polar Coordinates

Polar coordinates are used when you want to establish a point based on a distance and an angle from a previous point. The angle from the previous point may be positive if measured in a counterclockwise direction or negative if measured in a clockwise direction. The angles are based on the degrees in a circle. There are 360° in a circle with each quarter of the circle being called a ***quadrant.*** Each quadrant is 90°, as shown in Figure 2.21.

FIGURE 2.21 The quadrants of a circle and a polar coordinate measurement.

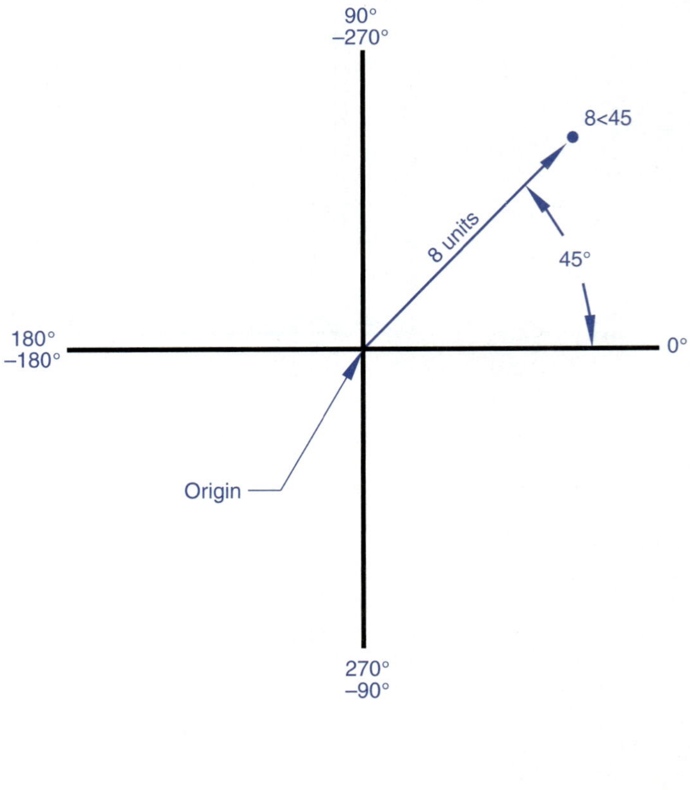

When you enter a polar coordinate, you enter the distance followed by the angle using an angle bracket (<). For example, if you want a point that is 8 units at a 45° angle from the origin (0,0), enter 8<45. The results are shown in Figure 2.21. The first point of a line may be selected by picking or with absolute coordinates and the next point drawn from the first using a unit distance and an angle. A polar coordinate must be preceded by the "@" symbol when referencing the previous point. The following command sequence draws the object shown in Figure 2.20:

Command: **LINE**↵
Specify first point: **3,4**↵
Specify next point or [Undo]: **@2<45**↵
Specify next point or [Undo]: **@2<315** or **@2<−45**↵
Specify next point or [Close/Undo]: **@1.5<270**↵ (or **@1.5<−90**)
Specify next point or [Close/Undo]: **@2.8284<180**↵
Specify next point or [Close/Undo]: **@1.5<90**↵
Specify next point or [Close/Undo]: ↵
Command:

FIGURE 2.22 Using polar coordinates.

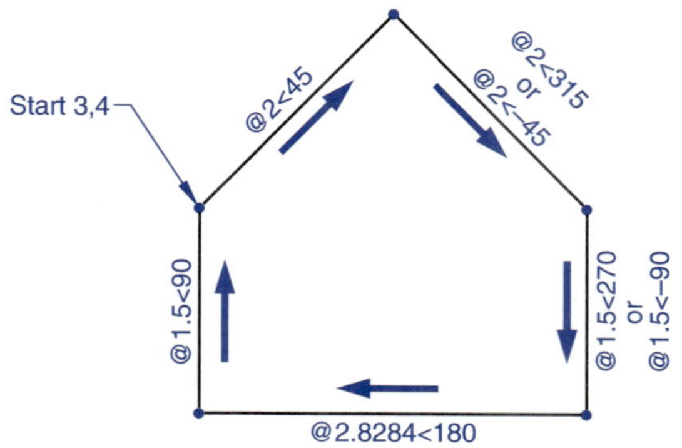

Field Notes

Press the F6 key to turn the coordinate display on or off or to change the display from absolute coordinate to polar coordinate values. The coordinate display may also be toggled using CTRL+D or by double-clicking on the display itself. When the coordinate display is turned off, it updates only when you pick a point. This means that it displays the location of the last point picked.

An absolute coordinate display looks like this:

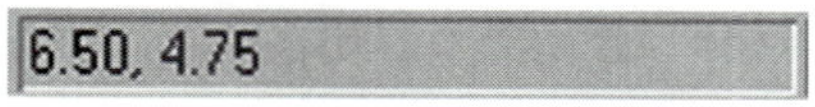

A polar coordinate display looks like this:

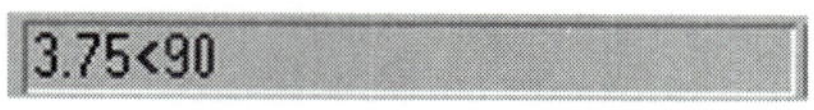

When the display is turned off, the coordinates are gray and update only when a point is picked.

Closing a Polygon

A ***polygon*** is a closed plane figure with straight sides. The object in Figure 2.22 is an example of a polygon. When drawing a polygon, the last line ends where the first line began. This can be done by entering the same coordinates for the end of the last line that were used for the start of the first line, as was done in the previous command sequence. An easier way to do this is to type **C** for Close at the To point: prompt for the last line, like this:

Command: **LINE**↵
Specify first point: **3,4**↵
Specify next point or [Undo]: **@2<45**↵
Specify next point or [Undo]: **@2<315**↵ (or **@2<−45)**
Specify next point or [Close/Undo]: **@1.5<270**↵ (or **@1.5<−90)**
Specify next point or [Close/Undo]: **@2.8284<180**↵
Specify next point or [Close/Undo]: **C**↵
Command:

Doing this automatically closes the polygon and returns the Command: prompt (see Figure 2.23). The Close option can also be picked from the LINE command shortcut menu after two or more segments have been drawn in the current line sequence.

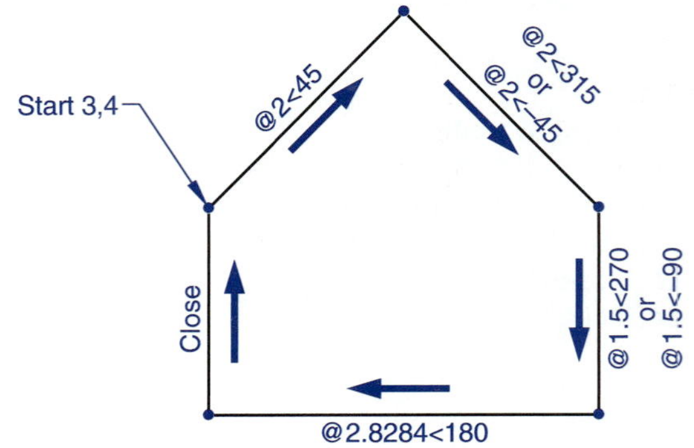

FIGURE 2.23 Using the Close option to close a polygon.

Repeating the Previous Command Quickly

You can easily repeat the previously used command by pressing the Enter key or the space bar. When you are not working with text, pressing the space bar has the same effect as pressing Enter. This practice saves time when compared to accessing the command in another manner. The following command sequence shows how this works:

Command: **LINE↵**
Specify first point: ⟨*pick a point*⟩
Specify next point or [Undo]: ⟨*pick another point*⟩
Specify next point or [Undo]: ⟨*pick another point*⟩
Specify next point or [Close/Undo]: **C↵**

Command: ⟨*press the Enter key or space bar*⟩
LINE Specify first point: ⟨*pick a point*⟩
Specify next point or [Undo]: ⟨*pick another point*⟩
Specify next point or [Undo]: **Cancel**

Field Notes

The previously used command can also be accessed by pressing the right mouse button to open the cursor menu. The first item in the menu repeats the previous command. For example, if the previous command was LINE, then the cursor menu item is Repeat LINE. Select this to repeat the LINE command.

Exercise 2.7 — Estimated time required: 5 min.

1. Open EX2.6 for editing.
2. Use the LINE command to draw the third view of the following object, specifying polar coordinates as shown:

Command: **LINE**↵
Specify first point: **2,6**↵
Specify next point or [Undo]: **@1<0**↵
Specify next point or [Undo]: **@.5<90**↵
Specify next point or [Close/Undo]: **@1<0**↵
Specify next point or [Close/Undo]: **@1.5<90**↵
Specify next point or [Close/Undo]: **@2<180**↵
Specify next point or [Close/Undo]: **@2<270**↵
Specify next point or [Close/Undo]:

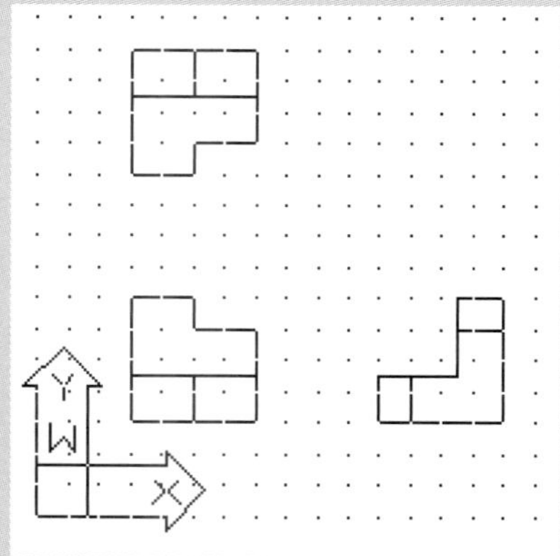

Command: **LINE**↵
Specify first point: **@1.25<90**↵
Specify next point or [Undo]: **@2<0**↵
Specify next point or [Undo]: ↵

Command: **LINE**↵
Specify first point: **@1<180**↵
Specify next point or [Undo]: **@.75<90**↵
Specify next point or [Undo]:

3. Save as EX2.7, and close the drawing.

Combining Coordinate Methods

All the available coordinate entry methods may cause some confusion for the beginning AutoCAD LT user. The best thing to do is practice using all the point entry methods until you become familiar with the way they work. You will then be able to select the entry method that works best for your specific situation. You can use any entry method at any point prompt as desired. For example, it may be easier to pick one point or use the absolute coordinate and then enter relative or polar coordinates for the next point.

When you are planning a drawing, it is usually best to sketch the object and establish the line endpoint coordinates on graph paper. This early planning saves a lot of time when you get ready to draw with AutoCAD LT. An example is shown with the electronic circuit speaker symbol laid out in Figure 2.24A. This layout shows the length of each line and the angle of lines where needed. The drafter made the sketch in Figure 2.24B showing the planned point entries for each corner of the object. With this preliminary work done, all you have to do is enter the coordinates:

Command: **L** or **LINE**↵
Specify first point: **3,4**↵
Specify next point or [Undo]: **@.75,0**↵
Specify next point or [Undo]: **@.75<−45**↵
Specify next point or [Close/Undo]: **@0,1.75**↵
Specify next point or [Close/Undo]: **@.75<225**↵
Specify next point or [Close/Undo]: **@.75<180**↵
Specify next point or [Close/Undo]: **C**↵
Command:

Other solutions to the problem may have worked just as well. Your goal is to select AutoCAD LT tools that help you create each drawing as quickly and accurately as possible.

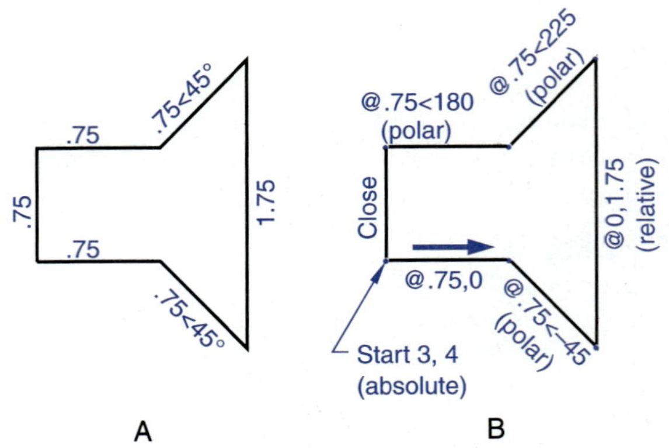

FIGURE 2.24 Using a combination of coordinate entry methods. (A) The engineering layout. (B) The coordinates entries used to draw the speaker symbol.

Exercise 2.8

Estimated time required: 5 min.

1. Open AutoCAD LT or pick New in the File pull-down menu if it is already open and use the Quick Setup with Decimal measurements and limits of 8.5 and 11.
2. Use the LINE command to make a drawing with the combination of coordinate entry methods displayed in Figure 2.24.
3. Save as EX2.8 and close the drawing.

Entering Units in AutoCAD LT

All the examples and exercises that you have studied so far have used generic decimal units for distance specifications. Many of your drawing applications may require a more specialized format for specifying distances. The rules of entry for each available linear unit format are as follows:

Decimal and Fractional Units

- Whole numbers do not require a decimal point.
  Example: 1 14 -22
- Numbers less than 1 do not require a leading zero.
  Example: .5 .0625 -.8477
- Large numbers do not require commas.
  Example: 1024 2844366.0122 -43771
- Trailing zeros do not increase accuracy. The numbers 1.5 and 1.500 give the exact same results.
- Unit specifications are not given for decimal units. For example, if your units represent inches or millimeters, do not include an inch symbol (″) or metric unit callout (mm) with your numeric entry.
- Either fractions or decimals may be used for linear units, but fractions must be separated from the whole number by a hyphen.
  Example: 1/2 2-1/16

Architectural and Engineering Units

- Numbers entered without a unit specification are interpreted as inches. A numeric entry of 3 is interpreted as 3″.
- Numbers intended to represent distances measured in feet must have the foot symbol (′).
  Example: 32′ 142′ -15′
- Foot and inch combinations can be entered with or without a hyphen.
  Example: 1′3 1′-3 1′-3″ -2′4″ -2′4″ -2′-4″
- Decimal or fractional foot and inch values are accepted.
  Example: 1.5′ -2.25′ 4.5 -3.875 1′3.5″ 1/2′
- Fractions of inches must be separated from the whole-inch value with a hyphen.
  Example: 1′3-1/2 1′3-1/2″ 1′-3-1/2″

Scientific Units

- Numbers can be entered as simple decimal values, without scientific notation.
  Example: 1.5 -3.61 377
- Scientific notation expresses a change in the decimal point location. A positive value indicates the decimal moves to the right, negative values mean the decimal point moves to the left.
  Example: 1.5E+3 is equivalent to 1500 1.5E-3 is equivalent to .0015
- Fractions cannot be used.

Field Notes

Coordinate entry is very versatile and accepts many variations of polarity (+ or –) and units style. For example, when drawing a line from an existing base point that extends vertically two units, you can use any of the following *polar* coordinate entries:

@2<90   @2<−270   @−2<270   @−2<−90

Some of these are unlikely applications, but this versatility gives you several added options when specifying coordinate point locations. Remember that when you are using polar coordinates, making either the distance or the angle negative reverses the direction.

LEARNING CHECKPOINT

- ☐ Identify three ways to access the LINE command in AutoCAD LT.
- ☐ What are the four coordinate entry options?
- ☐ What is the symbol @ used for?
- ☐ Why is it helpful to combine coordinate entry methods?
- ☐ How are feet, inches, and fractional inches specified in AutoCAD LT?
- ☐ How can you conveniently close the last segment of a polygon?
- ☐ What is the fastest way to repeat the previous command?

Concept Animations

- Coordinate Entry Method

More AutoCAD LT Drawing Aids

Earlier in this chapter you were introduced to the Grid and Snap drawing aids. Two other drawing aids are Ortho and Blips. When the Ortho option is on, your pointing device allows only horizontal or vertical movement during drawing and editing operations. ***Blips*** are temporary screen marks that are displayed when you pick points.

Using Ortho

Ortho is referred to as a mode. A ***mode*** is a setting or operating condition that you control. Ortho is a toggle setting, meaning that it can be either on or off. When Ortho is on, the pointing device is allowed only horizontal or vertical movement while drawing. If Ortho is off, then the pointing device may be moved at any angle. Ortho is off by default. An advantage of having Ortho on is seen when you need to draw an object made up of horizontal and vertical lines. Having Ortho on ensures that the lines you draw are exactly horizontal or vertical as needed. Ortho may be quickly turned on or off by picking the ORTHO button on the status bar or pressing the F8 key. If Ortho is off and you toggle it on, you get this status display at the Command: prompt:

> Status Bar
> ORTHO
>
> ORTHO
> OR
> [Ctrl] + [L]
> [F8]

Command: <Ortho on>

You can also turn Ortho on or off using the ORTHO button shortcut menu. Set Ortho at the Command: prompt by typing:

Command: **ORTHO↵**
Entermode [ON/OFF]<OFF>**: ON↵**

Now, practice drawing lines with Ortho on and off to notice the big difference in the way the cursor controls the lines you are drawing. Figure 2.25 shows the difference between drawing a line with Ortho on and off.

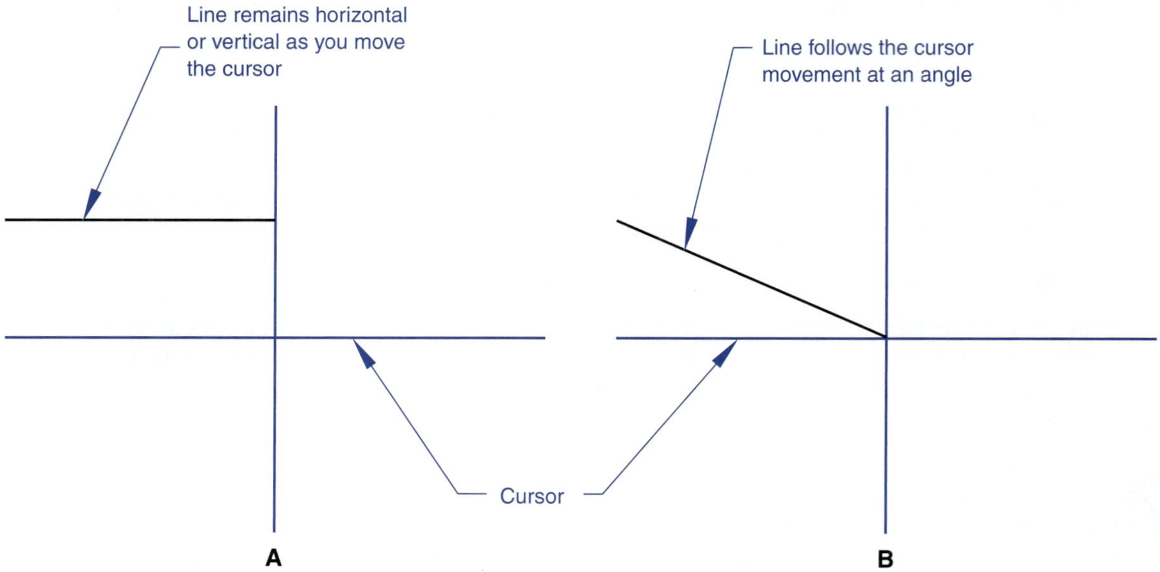

FIGURE 2.25 The difference between drawing a line with (A) Ortho on and (B) Ortho off.

Field Notes

The Ortho setting affects only points entered by picking with the pointing device. A typed coordinate entry, whether absolute, relative, or polar, is not affected by Ortho settings. The Snap settings, however, cannot override the Ortho control.

Another thing to remember about Ortho (and other toggles) is that the status is displayed on the command line when the toggle is activated. This means that if you begin to type a command, it appears after the status display. In the following example, Ortho is toggled on and Snap is toggled off prior to entering a line command:

Command: <Ortho on> <Snap off> **LINE↵**

A toggle status display appears in angle brackets (<>) and does not interfere with command entry.

An Introduction to Transparent Commands

A ***transparent command*** is a command that can be started while another command is in progress. Commands that are not transparent must be entered when you have a Command: prompt. A transparent command can be accessed by selection from a pull-down menu, status line button, or toolbar button or by typing the command name preceded by an apostrophe ('). DSETTINGS, GRID, SNAP, and ORTHO are transparent commands that you have learned so far. Double-click the ORTHO status line button or type **'ORTHO** (note the apostrophe) if you want to enter the ORTHO command transparently while inside the LINE command:

Command**: LINE↵**
Specify first point: ⟨*pick a point or enter coordinates*⟩
Specify next point or [Undo]: **'ORTHO**
>>Enter mode [ON/OFF] <OFF>: **ON**
Resuming LINE command.
Specify next point or [Undo]: ⟨*pick a point or enter coordinates*⟩
Specify next point or [Undo]: ⟨*enter another point or Cancel*⟩
Command**:**

AutoCAD LT lets you know that a transparent command prompt is being issued by showing double angle brackets (>>) in front of the prompt as shown in the previous command sequence. After you use the transparent command, AutoCAD LT tells you that you are resuming the command in progress.

Exercise 2.9 **Estimated time required: 5 min.**

1. Open AutoCAD LT or pick New in the File pull-down menu if it is already open and use the Quick Setup with Decimal measurements, limits of 8.5 and 11, and turn on the Grid and Snap.
2. With the Ortho default setting off, use the LINE command to make a rectangle at a size of your own choosing.
3. Turn Ortho on and draw another rectangle. Notice the difference in the control of the vertical and horizontal lines.
4. Turn Ortho on and off using the status bar button, F8 key, and at the command prompt to determine the method that works best for you.
5. Save as EX2.9 and close the drawing.

Marks on the Screen

The locations where you pick points to draw lines and other things can be displayed by temporary marks called blips. The blips are helpful in allowing you to visualize selected points more clearly. Blips are turned off, or not displayed, in AutoCAD LT by default. They can be turned on or off at the command prompt:

Command: **BM** or **BLIPMODE**↵
Enter mode [ON/OFF] <OFF>: **ON**↵
Command:

Exercise 2.10 **Estimated time required: 5 min.**

1. Open AutoCAD LT or pick New in the File pull-down menu if it is already open and use the Quick Setup with Decimal measurements, limits of 8.5 and 11, and turn on the Grid and Snap.
2. Turn the blips on using the BLIPMODE command.
3. Draw several lines of your own design and notice the Blips.
4. Turn the blips off.
5. Draw several more lines and notice the difference.
6. Save as EX2.10, and close the drawing.

Cleaning up the Screen

After you have done some drafting with blipmode turned on, the blips may become distracting. This is especially true after you have done some erasing, because blips remain even after lines are erased. Blips are easily removed from the screen with the REDRAW command. Access the REDRAW command by picking Redraw in the View pull-down menu, or type **R** or **REDRAW:**

Redraw View

View
Redraw

REDRAW
R

Command: **R** or **REDRAW**↵
Command:

REDRAW can be entered as a transparent command. Use it at any time to clean up the screen by typing **'R** or **'REDRAW** while inside a command, or pick Redraw from the View pull-down menu.

Exercise 2.11 **Estimated time required: 5 min.**

1. Open AutoCAD LT or pick New in the File pull-down menu if it is already open and use the Quick Setup with Decimal measurements, limits of 8.5 and 11, and turn on the Grid and Snap.
2. With Blipmode on, draw several lines of your own design.
3. Pick Redraw in the View pull-down menu and notice what happens to the blips.
4. Draw several more lines and then enter R at the command prompt followed by pressing the Enter key or the space bar.
5. Save as EX2.11, and close the drawing.

LEARNING CHECKPOINT

- ☐ What is the purpose of Ortho?
- ☐ When should you use Ortho, and when should it not be used?
- ☐ What is the purpose of blips?
- ☐ How do you remove blips from the screen?

Erasing Objects

Modify
Erase

Modify
Erase

ERASE
E
[Delete]

Any time you are changing a drawing by erasing, moving, copying, or altering objects in any way, it is referred to as ***editing.*** Erasing objects is a very common editing practice. Just as when you are drawing with pencil, you often need to erase. Throughout this book, you will learn that objects may be selected and then an editing task performed, or you may enter an editing command and then select objects to be edited. When you select objects for editing, the objects you choose are called a ***selection set.*** Although there are many ways to select objects, the following discussion introduces you to the basics.

Selecting Objects to Erase

Objects may be selected to erase by picking, by requesting the last object drawn, by placing a window around the object, or by placing a window partly across an object. Other selection methods are available, but these basic techniques are explained in the following discussion.

Entering the ERASE Command Before Selecting the Objects

You may enter an editing command and then select the objects to be edited, or you can select the objects and then enter the command. The first part of this explanation shows you how to enter the command before selecting objects.

Picking Objects

The ERASE command is accessed by picking Clear from the Edit pull-down menu, by picking the Erase toolbar button, or by typing **E** or **ERASE** at the Command: prompt like this:

Command: **E** or **ERASE** ↵
Select objects:

Now you get the *Select objects:* prompt, and the screen cursor changes to a small box called a ***pick box.*** Move the pick box to an object, such as a line, and pick it, as shown in Figure 2.26A, by pressing the pick button on the mouse. The object becomes highlighted when you pick it (see Figure 2.26B). You then get another Select objects: prompt. AutoCAD LT allows you to continue picking objects or to press Enter to end the selection process and have the object erased. The complete command sequence works like this and is displayed in Figure 2.26C:

Command: **E** or **ERASE**↵
Select objects: ⟨*pick an object or objects*⟩
Select objects: ⟨*pick more objects or press Enter*⟩
Select objects: ↵
Command:

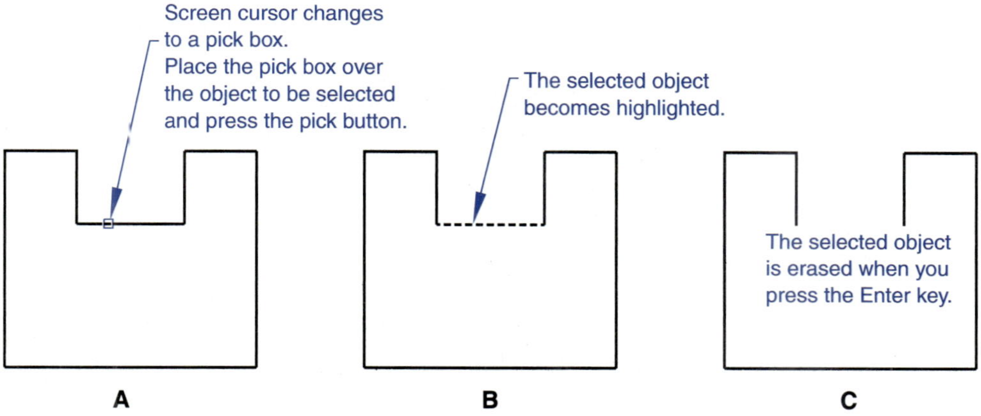

FIGURE 2.26 Picking an object to erase.

Erasing the Last Object Drawn

A handy way to erase the last object you drew is to enter **L** for *last* at the Select objects: prompt. This method erases only the last object that you created and it works like this:

Command: **E** or **ERASE**↵
Select objects: **L**↵
Select objects: ⟨*pick more objects or press Enter*⟩
Select objects: ↵
Command:

Exercise 2.12 — **Estimated time required: 5 min.**

1. Open AutoCAD LT or pick New in the File pull-down menu if it is already open and use the Quick Setup with Decimal measurements, limits of 8.5 and 11, and turn on the Grid and Snap.
2. Draw an object similar to Figure 2.26A.
3. Enter the ERASE command and pick a line to erase similar to Figure 2.26.
4. Draw a line anywhere and at any desired length.
5. Type **ERASE** and enter **L** at the Select objects: prompt followed by pressing the Enter key to erase the line you just drew.
6. Save as EX2.12, and close the drawing.

Selecting Objects with a Window

AutoCAD LT lets you automatically place a window around one or more objects to select by the way you pick and move the mouse. This is referred to as ***implied windowing*** and is accomplished by first picking a point on the screen where no object is found. Next, move the cursor and a dynamic rectangle is formed. If you move the cursor to the *right* of the pick point, the lines of the rectangle are solid and it is called a *window.* By surrounding objects with this window, they can be selected for editing operations. Note that a window must totally surround the object or objects to be selected. To erase objects with a window selection, use the following approach:

- First enter the ERASE command:

  Command: **E** or **ERASE** ↵
  Select objects: ⟨*continue with the following steps*⟩

- Move the cursor to a place at the lower (or upper) left of the object and pick. Refer to the window shown in Figure 2.27A. The cursor becomes a solid outline window as you move the mouse to the right.
- Move the mouse to the right until the window totally surrounds all of the objects to be erased and pick the other corner as shown in Figure 2.27A.
- The selected objects become highlighted as shown in Figure 2.27B.
- Press the Enter key or space bar at the Select objects: prompt and the selected objects are erased, as in Figure 2.27C.

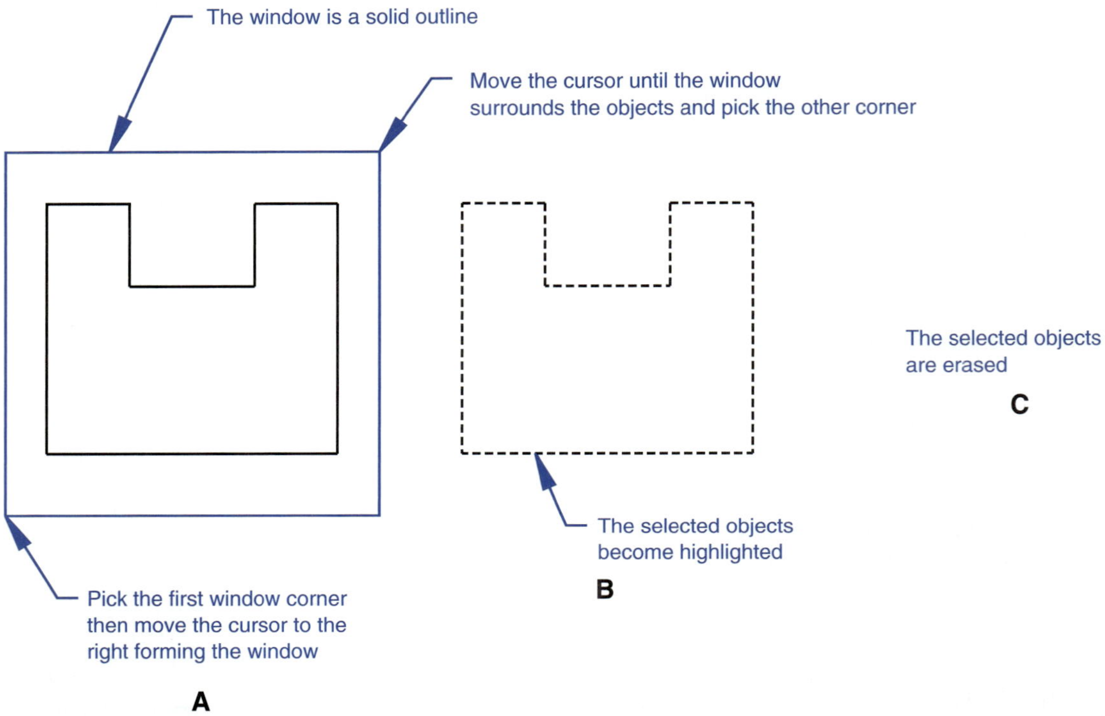

FIGURE 2.27 Selecting objects using a window.

Exercise 2.13 — **Estimated time required: 5 min.**

1. Open AutoCAD LT or pick New in the File pull-down menu if it is already open and use the Quick Setup with Decimal measurements, limits of 8.5 and 11, and turn on the Grid and Snap.
2. Using the LINE command, create a drawing similar to Figure 2.27A.
3. Enter the ERASE command and use the window to erase the objects as shown in Figures 2.27B and C.
4. Save as EX2.13, and close the drawing.

Erasing Objects with a Crossing Box

A crossing box is formed at an object selection prompt in the same way as a window is formed, except that the rectangle is dragged to the *left* rather than the right. Where the window must totally surround the entire object to be erased, the crossing box selects not only objects it surrounds, but also any objects that it touches, or *crosses*. Windows and crossing boxes each have their own advantages for specific selection needs. As you work in AutoCAD LT, you will find many situations where one or the other better suits your needs. To see a clear example of the difference between a window and a crossing box, do the following, and compare the results with those shown in Figure 2.27:

- First enter the ERASE command:

  Command: **E** or **ERASE**↵
  Select objects: ⟨*continue with the following steps*⟩

- Move the cursor to a place at the lower (or upper) *right* of the object and pick. Look at Figure 2.28A. The cursor becomes a dashed outline crossing box as you move the mouse to the left.
- Move the mouse to the left until the crossing box totally surrounds or crosses through the objects to be erased and pick the other corner as shown in Figure 2.28A.
- The selected objects become highlighted as shown in Figure 2.28B.
- Press the Enter key at the Select objects: prompt, and the selected objects are erased as in Figure 2.28C.

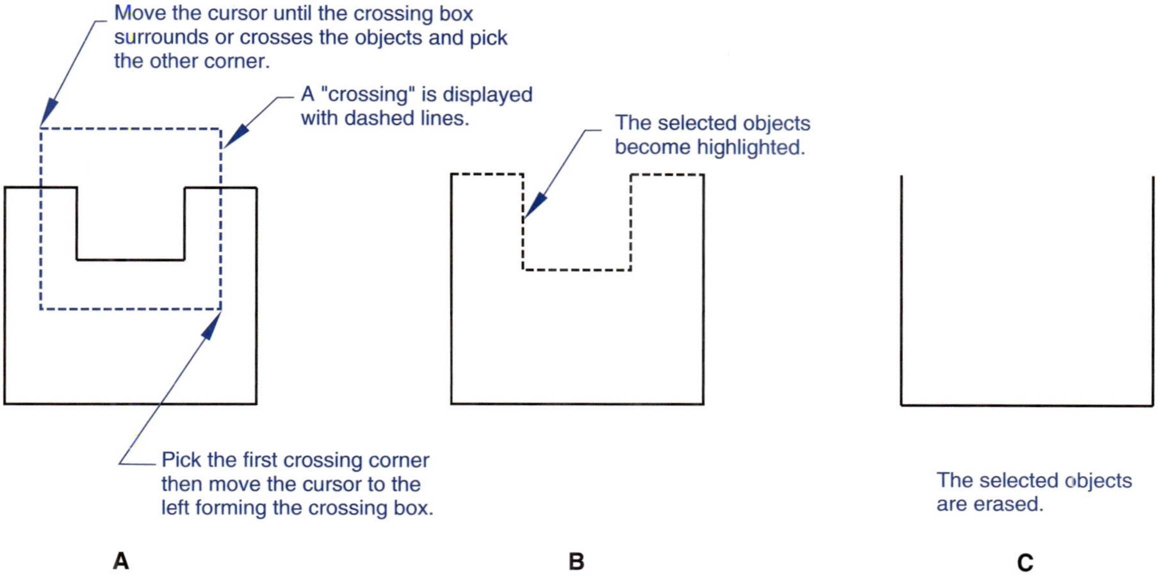

FIGURE 2.28 Selecting objects with a crossing box.

The window is formed by moving the cursor to the *right* of the pick point and a crossing box by moving to the *left*. You can immediately tell the difference between the window and crossing selections because the window is a solid rectangle and the crossing is a dashed rectangle.

Field Notes

- In some cases, the geometry of your drawing may be too dense or crowded to be able to pick in the desired location without picking an object. This can make implied windowing difficult or impossible to use. To use a window or a crossing box in such a situation, type W for window or C for crossing at an object selection prompt. The pick box will turn into crosshairs, allowing very accurate pointing, and will not pick any objects until your window or crossing box is completed.

  Also, if you use this method, it does not matter from which direction you form the rectangle. For example, if you enter a W for a window, you can form the window by moving to either the left or the right of the pick point.

Removing Selected Objects from the Selection Set

It is common to select a group of objects for editing and then decide that you want one or more of the objects removed from the selection set. This is easy to do by using the Remove option. The Remove option is used by typing **R** at the Select objects: prompt and pressing the Enter key. When you get the Remove objects:

prompt, use pick, window, or the crossing box to select objects to be removed from the selection set:

Command: **E** or **ERASE**↵
Select objects: ⟨*pick an object, use a window or crossing*⟩
Select objects: ⟨*pick more objects or press Enter*⟩
Select objects: **R**↵
Remove objects: ⟨*select the objects*⟩
Remove objects: ⟨*select more objects to remove or press Enter*⟩
Command:

When objects are removed from the selection set, they are no longer highlighted, and AutoCAD LT tells you how many objects were removed. Objects removed from a selection set are not affected by the editing command being used. AutoCAD LT also lets you change your mind again if you select objects to be removed and then want them added back to the selection set. To add objects back, use the Add option by typing **A** at the Remove objects: prompt. This returns the Select objects: prompt so you can select more objects:

Command: **E** or **ERASE**↵
Select objects: ⟨*pick an object, use a window or crossing*⟩
Select objects: **R**↵
Remove objects: ⟨*select the objects to be removed*⟩
Remove objects: **A**↵
Select objects: ⟨*pick an object, use a window or crossing*⟩
Select objects: ↵
Command:

Field Notes

You can also remove objects from a selection quickly and conveniently by pressing the Shift key while you pick a previously selected object. This way, you do not have to type **R** and then **A** to begin selecting again. To add new objects to the selection set, simply release the Shift key and continue to pick.

Pressing Shift to remove also works when you are using a window or a crossing box generated with implied windowing. Press the Shift key while you make the first pick to remove the selected objects from the selection set. Note that using Shift to remove does not work when you type **W** or **C** to begin a window or crossing box.

Exercise 2.14 — Estimated time required: 5 min.

1. Open AutoCAD LT or pick New in the File pull-down menu if it is already open and use the Quick Setup with Decimal measurements, limits of 8.5 and 11, and turn on the Grid and Snap.
2. Draw an object similar to Figure 2.28A.
3. Enter the ERASE command and use the crossing box to erase the objects similar to Figure 2.28.
4. Enter the ERASE command and pick the left vertical line to erase and then remove it from the selection. Use the Add option to reselect the same line and then remove it again.
5. Your drawing should still look like Figure 2.28C.
6. Select and deselect objects using the Shift key while picking. Try this with the window and crossing options as well.
7. Save as EX2.14, and close the drawing.

Noun/Verb Selection and an Introduction to Grips

In the previous discussion, you learned how to enter the ERASE command and then select the objects to erase. You can also select the objects before you enter the command. This is called ***noun/verb selection,*** because the object is specified first, then the action. You can use several of the selection methods that were explained earlier, such as picking, windowing, or crossing. The pick box is displayed at the crosshair intersection when no command is active. The available selection methods work just as they did in the previous discussion. This pick box is here just for the purpose of picking objects and it works the same as the standard pick box. The big difference is in what happens to the objects you select. For example, move the screen cursor to a line and pick it as shown in Figure 2.29. Notice the squares that are automatically displayed on the line. There is one square on each end and one in the middle. These squares are called ***grips.*** Many editing tasks can be performed with grips, as discussed in detail later in this book. What is important for now is that you can select objects and then enter an editing command, such as ERASE. These are the steps:

- Select the objects by picking, window, or crossing.
- Enter the ERASE command:

Command: **E** or **ERASE**↵
ERASE 4 found
Command:

AutoCAD LT automatically erases the objects, tells you how many objects were found to erase, and returns the Command: prompt. Note that only picking and implied windowing can be used for this type of object selection. An object or objects can be erased quickly after being selected by pressing the Delete key.

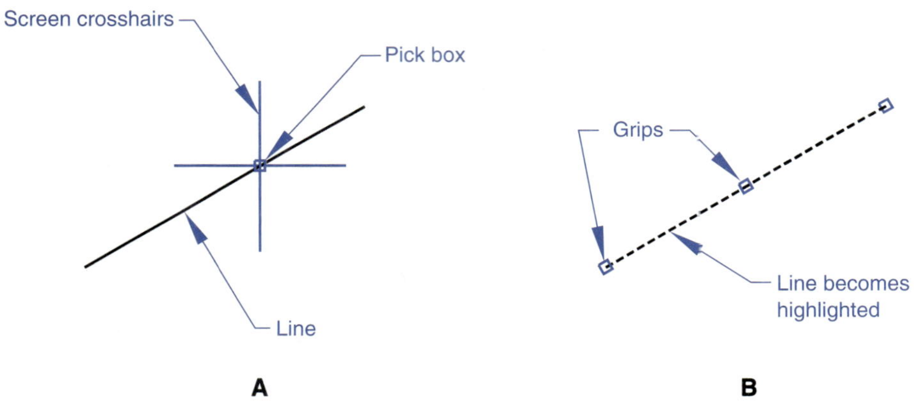

FIGURE 2.29 Selecting an object before entering the ERASE command. Notice the grips.

Field Notes

New users of AutoCAD LT may experience some initial difficulty in trying to get used to working with grips. These pointers will help you to get through some of the more common problems with grips:

- Not all editing commands allow objects to be preselected.
- If you accidentally pick objects, and you want to *un*select them, press the Esc key twice or pick Deselect All from the shortcut menu.
- When you accidentally start a selection window or crossing, press Esc once to abort the selection process.
- If the objects you select are automatically *un*selected when you enter an editing command and a Select objects: prompt is issued, change the value of the PICKFIRST system variable to 1 as follows:

Command: **PICKFIRST**↵
Enter new value for PICKFIRST <0>: **1**↵

Another method to set this variable is by setting the check box labeled Noun/Verb Selection in the Selection tab of the Options dialog box.

Using the OOPS Command

If you erase something and then decide that you want it back, you can use the OOPS command. This is an easy command name to remember, because "Oops!" is a common word to say when you accidentally erase objects that you still need. The OOPS command may be used to bring back the most recent objects that you erased like this:

Command: **OOPS↵**
Command:

Note that OOPS brings back only those objects removed by the last ERASE command.

Changing the Pick Box Size

The pick box size is preset by AutoCAD LT, but you can change it if you wish. The default pick box size is 3 pixels. (Pixels are the tiny dots that make up what is displayed on the computer screen, as discussed in Chapter 1.) Look at the pick box that is provided by AutoCAD LT at the intersection of the crosshairs. It is displayed anytime the Command: prompt is present without an active command. This pick box is the same size as the pick box displayed at a Select objects: prompt. You may want to make the pick box size bigger for ease in selecting objects. Or you might need to make the pick box smaller if you are trying to pick objects in a very complex drawing where objects are close together.

Change the pick box size on the Selection tab in the Options dialog box, in Figure 2.30. Use the slider to increase or decrease the pick box size. The image at the left shows the pick box size as you make adjustments. Pick the OK button when ready.

You can also change the pick box size using the PICKBOX system variable at the Command: prompt by typing the number of desired pixels:

Command: **PICKBOX↵**
Enter new value for PICKBOX <3>: **6↵**
Command:

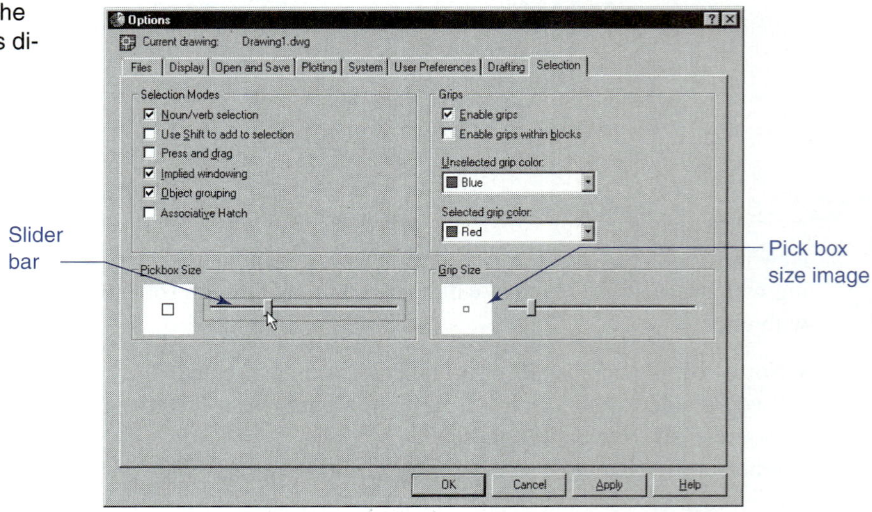

FIGURE 2.30 Changing the pick box size in the Options dialog box.

Exercise 2.15

Estimated time required: 6 min.

1. Open AutoCAD LT or pick New in the File pull-down menu if it is already open and use the Quick Setup with Decimal measurements, limits of 8.5 and 11, and turn on the Grid and Snap.
2. Draw a line similar to Figure 2.29A.
3. Pick the line.
4. Notice the grips displayed on the line and that the line is highlighted.
5. Type the **ERASE** command and press the Enter key.
6. The line is automatically erased.
7. Draw an object similar to the one shown in Figure 2.27A.
8. Select the entire object with a window and notice the grips.
9. Press the Delete key to erase the object.
10. Type the **OOPS** command and press Enter.
11. The previously erased object returns.
12. Experiment by increasing the pick box size larger than the default.
13. Pick a line on the drawing and erase it.
14. Use OOPS to bring the line back.
15. Decrease the pick box size smaller than the default.
16. Pick a line on the drawing and erase it.
17. Use OOPS to bring the line back.
18. Change the pick box size back to the default value.
19. Think about how changing the pick box size affected your ability to pick objects.
20. Save as EX2.15, and close the drawing.

☑ LEARNING CHECKPOINT

- □ What does the term *editing* refer to in an AutoCAD LT drawing?
- □ What is a selection set?
- □ Can you name three ways to access the ERASE command?
- □ What is the square selection cursor called?
- □ What are the differences between a selection window and a crossing box?
- □ How can you remove or add objects to a selection set?
- □ What are grips?
- □ How is noun/verb selection different from standard selection?
- □ In what way can altering the pick box size help your selection process?

Viewing, Selecting, and Using Precision Drawing Tools

- Using Selection Sets to Edit Multiple Objects

Concept Animations

- Selecting Objects

Undoing and Redoing

There are many times when a command or series of commands does not give you the desired results. You can remove the effects of the last command entered by using the **U** command:

Standard
Undo
Edit Undo
U [Ctrl] + [Z]

```
Command: E or ERASE↵
Select objects: L↵
1 found
Select objects: ↵
Command: U↵
ERASE
```

The name of the command that was undone is displayed at the command line. You can undo any number of commands one at a time using this method. Alternatively, you can press CTRL+Z, or select the Undo command from the Edit menu. The name of the command to be undone is displayed on this menu.

An undo button and list is available on the Standard tool bar. Picking the Undo button has the same effect as using the U command. By picking the Undo list, as shown in Figure 2.31A, you can undo a number of commands at the same time.

Standard

Redo

Edit
Redo

MREDO
[Ctrl] + [Y]

If you undo a previous command and then decide you did not want to undo it after all, you can redo the command. To redo a command, select Redo from the Edit pull-down menu, press CTRL+Y or select the Redo button or list from the Standard toolbar; or type MREDO at the Command: prompt.

Command: **MREDO**↵
All/Last/<Number>:

You can specify the number of commands to redo, redo just the last undone command, or redo all undone commands. When you need to redo multiple commands, it is usually easier to do so using the Redo list button on the Standard toolbar, as shown in Figure 2.31B.

FIGURE 2.31 The Undo and Redo lists can be used to undo or redo several commands at the same time.

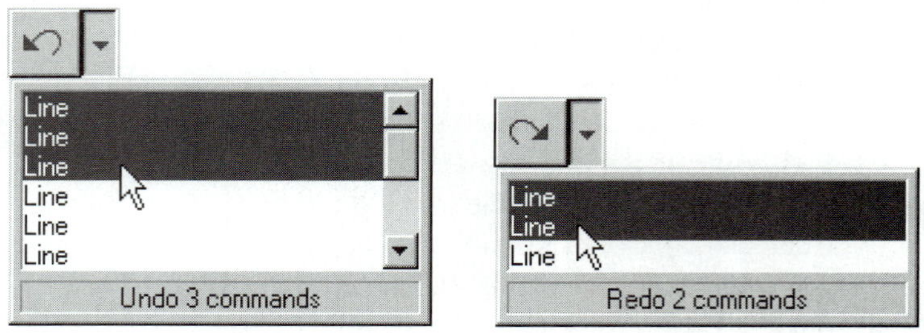

A B

Field Notes

Earlier versions of AutoCAD LT had only the REDO command. This limited predecessor to the MREDO command is still present in AutoCAD LT 2000. The REDO command reverses the effects of the last U or UNDO command (UNDO is discussed in Chapter 7). The REDO command, however, can be used only *immediately* after the U (or UNDO) command. If you undo a command and then use another command, such as LINE, you can no longer redo what was undone using the REDO command. This also means that REDO cannot be used several times in a row to redo more than one command.

Exercise 2.16

Estimated time required: 5 min.

1. Open EX2.15.
2. Use the ERASE command to erase all of the objects.
3. Pick the Undo toolbar icon. The previously erased objects return.
4. Repeat the first two steps, but this time enter the U command by typing **U** or picking Undo from the Edit pull-down menu. Decide which method works best for you.
5. Use the ERASE command to erase all of the objects.
6. Use the LINE command to draw a new line anywhere in the drawing.
7. Enter the U command, the line disappears.
8. Use the U command again. The erased objects return.
9. Enter the REDO command. The objects are erased again.
10. Use the REDO command again. Nothing happens.
11. Use the U command again. The erased objects return.
12. Erase the objects once again and draw a new line anywhere in the drawing.
13. Enter the OOPS command. Erased objects return and the new line remains as well.
14. Think about how this worked. OOPS is often a better option for returning erased objects, but U will undo the effects of almost any command.
15. Save as EX2.16, and close the drawing.

LEARNING CHECKPOINT

- □ What are three ways to undo the results of a command?
- □ How can you restore a command that has been undone?
- □ What is the limitation of the REDO command?
- □ Why is OOPS often a better option for restoring erased objects?

Printing Your First Drawing

When you create a CAD drawing, the drawing exists only as an electronic file and can be viewed only at a computer workstation unless you produce a hardcopy of the drawing using a printer or plotter. Producing a hardcopy is called *printing* or *plotting*. Plotting (or printing) a drawing serves several purposes in the design process. Most obviously, when a drawing project is completed, plotted drawings allow you to communicate design details to others. Plots (or prints) are required at remote locations, on the shop floors, or at any location where a computer workstation is not available. Other applications for printing include creating *check prints* for checking your drawing. Because the display monitor has a limited area and resolution, it is very common to find mistakes on larger printed copies that were not noticed on the computer screen.

This introduction to printing covers the fundamentals of printing drawings from model space. Printing from paper space and producing industry-standard drawing layouts are discussed in later chapters.

Standard
Plot (Ctrl+P)
File
Plot
PLOT
PRINT
[Ctrl] + [P]

Introduction to the Plot Dialog Box

Drawings are printed, or plotted, using the PLOT command. The PLOT command is accessed by picking Plot… from the File pull-down menu, picking the Plot button on the Standard toolbar, by typing **PLOT, PP,** or **PRINT** at the Command: prompt, or by using the Ctrl+P accelerator keystroke.

The Plot dialog box displays two tabs, Plot Device and Plot Settings. The first step is to set up your plotting device on the Plot Device tab. A drop-down list in the Plotter configuration area shows the names of the currently available plotting devices (see Figure 2.32). Your instructor or system administrator should have this set properly for you at this time. Adding a new plotter or printer to the list is discussed in Chapter 13.

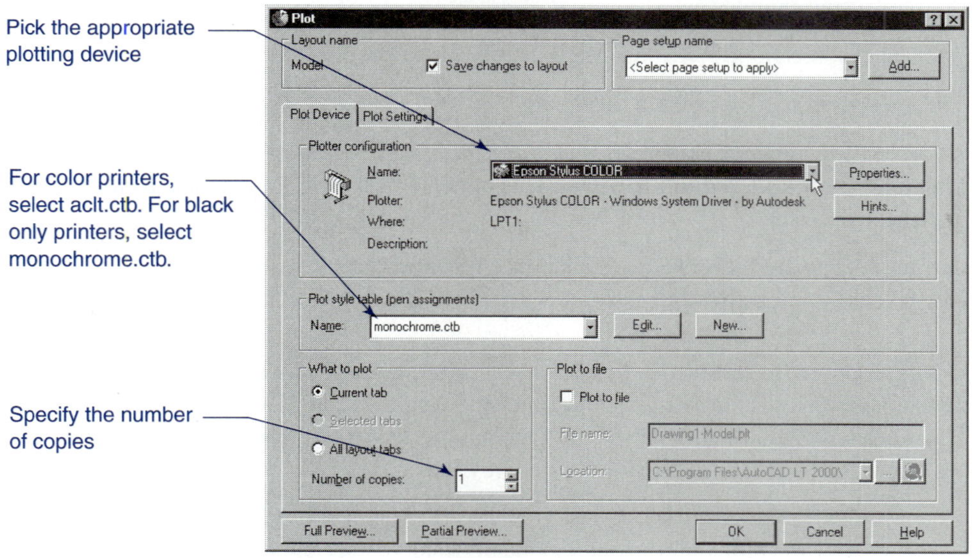

FIGURE 2.32 The Plot Device tab on the Plot dialog box.

Working with plot style tables is detailed in Chapter 13. For now, if you want to print in color, use the *aclt.ctb* option. For a black-only print, use the *monochrome.ctb* setting. If you try to print using colors on a black-only plotting device, the colors are displayed as various shades of grays. In the What to plot area, make sure that the Current tab is being plotted, and indicate how many copies should be printed.

Pick the Plot Settings tab to set up plotting options such as what area to plot, what scale to use, and to configure additional plotting parameters. The Plot Settings tab is shown in Figure 2.33.

FIGURE 2.33 The Plot Settings tab on the Plot dialog box.

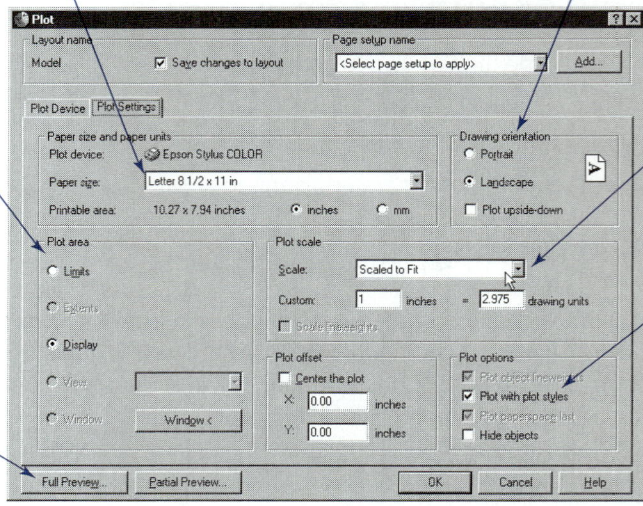

Paper Size and Paper Units

All available media sizes for the currently configured Plot device: are listed in the Paper size: drop-down list. When you select a sheet size, the printable area is displayed in the selected units format. The term *printable area* describes the area of the paper on which the plotting device is physically capable of printing.

Drawing Orientation

Set your drawing to print either in a Portrait or a Landscape orientation by picking the appropriate radio button. You can also print your drawing upsidedown by placing a check in the Plot upside-down checkbox. The text letter on the paper image provides a graphic representation of the current settings.

Plot Area

The Plot Area defines what area within the drawing is plotted. You can plot the entire drawing, or you can plot any desired portion. The options are defined as follows:

- **Limits** The defined limits of the current space. When plotting from the Model tab, this represents the Model space limits.
- **Extents** The smallest rectangle that contains all the objects in the drawing.
- **Display** The area currently displayed in the drawing window.
- **View** The area defined by the named drawing view specified in the drop-down list. Named drawing views are introduced in Chapter 4. This option is disabled if no named drawing views have been defined.
- **Window** Any user-defined rectangular area. Picking the Window < button temporarily hides the Plot dialog box and prompts you to specify corner points to define the rectangular area to be plotted.

Plot Scale

Specify a scale that is appropriate for the intended uses for your print. You can plot check prints at full scale or at a reduced scale to conserve paper. You can select an industry standard scale from the list, or you can select Scaled to Fit. The Scaled to Fit option scales the plot area as needed to fit the specified paper size. You can specify a custom size if the list does not provide the option you need.

Plot Offset

Placing a check in the Center of the plot checkbox automatically centers your plotted drawing on the sheet. The X: and Y: options allow you to specify the distance that the plot origin is placed from the paper origin.

Plot Options

These options will be detailed in Chapter 13. For now, just make sure that the Plot with plot styles option is checked when you plot.

Full Preview and Partial Preview

The preview features allow you to check the results of the current plot settings before you actually print. The Partial Preview… option provides a quick way to check that your orientation and plot area is correct (see Figure 2.34). The paper size, printable area, and effective area are displayed along with any applicable warnings.

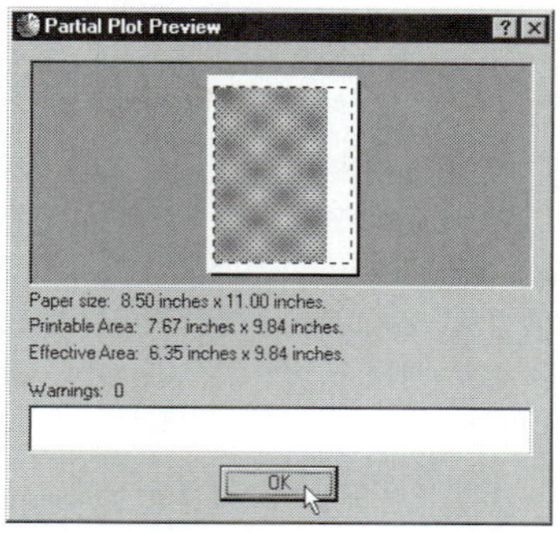

FIGURE 2.34 The Partial Plot Preview dialog box provides a fast and convenient way to check your plot settings.

The printable area of the paper is surrounded by a dashed line. The shaded area indicates the area of the plot, and the red triangle indicates the plot origin.

The Full Preview... option presents a WYSIWYG style preview (What You See Is What You Get) (see Figure 2.35). The paper is displayed and the drawing is shown as it will actually appear when it is plotted. The cursor changes into a magnifying glass with a plus/minus symbol (the real time zoom feature is detailed in Chapter 4). The shortcut menu provides additional options, including Exit and Plot. If you pick Exit, you are returned to the Plot dialog box. Picking Plot sends the plot directly to the plotter and returns you to the Command: prompt.

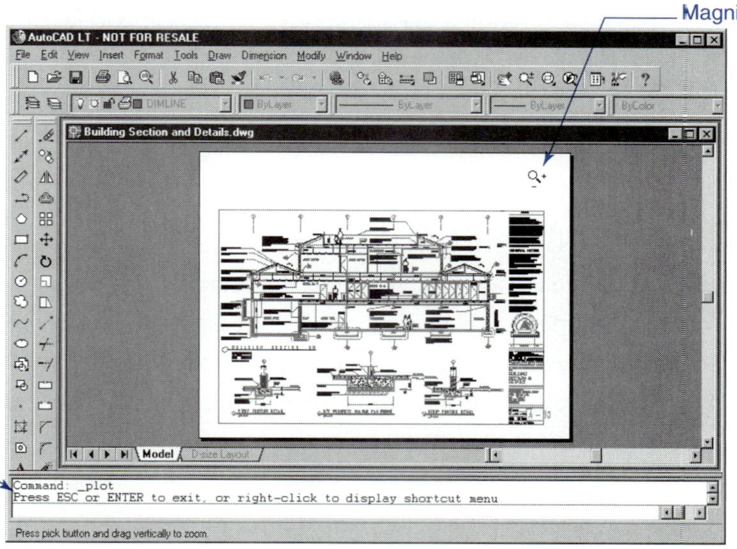

FIGURE 2.35 The full plot preview shows the drawing as it will actually appear when it is plotted.

Field Notes

When you are getting ready to do a plot, be sure the printer or plotter is turned on and paper is loaded. If you experience difficulty getting the desired results from your printer or plotter, review the pertinent material in this chapter. If you are still having difficulty, do not spend a lot of time working at it. It makes much more sense to go directly to your instructor or system administrator for assistance.

This is true for all of the subject matter in this text. When you cannot locate an answer to a question in the text in a reasonable amount of time, get immediate assistance whenever possible. Your instructor, system administrator, or an experienced coworker can often help you find a fast solution so that you can continue. This will keep you productive in your learning process and help to avoid unnecessary frustration.

Exercise 2.17 — Estimated time required: 10 min.

1. Open EX2.8 and prepare to make a print or plot, if approved by your instructor or supervisor.
2. With the Model tab active, start the PLOT command.
3. Specify an appropriate plotting device on the Plot Device tab. If your printer or plotter uses black ink only, specify the *monochrome.ctb* plot style table. If you are using a color printer, select the *acad.ctb* plot style table.
4. In the Plot Settings tab, specify the desired paper size.
5. Specify Limits as the plot area, and set the plot scale to 1:1.
6. Display a partial preview, then a full preview. Press Esc to return to the Plot dialog box.
7. Set the Plot Area to Display.
8. Display a partial preview, then a full preview. Press Esc to return to the Plot dialog box.
9. Set the Plot Area to Extents.
10. Display a full preview. Press Esc to return to the Plot dialog box.
11. Pick the Window < button to define a rectangle to plot. Draw a rectangle that surrounds all the drawing objects with a small margin.
12. Display a full preview. Press Esc to return to the Plot dialog box.
13. Preview the plot using both landscape and portrait orientation.
14. Use the options that you feel fit your needs best, and make a print or plot that includes all the objects in the drawing.
15. Save as EX2.17, and close the drawing.

☑ LEARNING CHECKPOINT

- □ What are the four ways to start the PLOT command?
- □ What is the difference between the Display, Extents, Limits, and Window Plot area options?
- □ How does the rotation angle affect the way the plot looks?
- □ What are the results and advantages of using partial or full plot previews?

MULTIPLE CHOICE

Circle the choice or enter your response on an answer sheet by selecting the option that most closely completes or answers the given statements.

1. The first page of the Quick Setup dialog box allows you to set:
- **a.** drawing aids
- **b.** limits
- **c.** units
- **d.** grid

2. The drawing area you specify is referred to as:
- **a.** sheet
- **b.** layout
- **c.** model space limits
- **d.** drafting space

3. A pattern of dots that is displayed on the screen at any desired interval:
- **a.** blips
- **b.** snap
- **c.** grid
- **d.** dots

4. An imaginary pattern that forces the screen cursor to move in exact increments:
- **a.** blips
- **b.** snap
- **c.** grid
- **d.** dots

5. Allows the pointing device only horizontal and vertical movement:
- **a.** snap
- **b.** grid
- **c.** ortho
- **d.** blip

6. Clean the screen of unwanted marks with this command:
- **a.** CLEAN
- **b.** REDRAW
- **c.** BLIPMODE
- **d.** VIEW

7. Changing a drawing by erasing, moving, copying, or altering objects in any way is referred to as:
- **a.** editing
- **b.** changing
- **c.** correcting
- **d.** modifying

8. When you enter the ERASE command and get the Select objects: prompt, the screen cursor changes to:
- **a.** crosshairs
- **b.** box
- **c.** dashed line
- **d.** pick box

9. Use this command as many times as you want to remove one or more previous commands:
- **a.** REMOVE
- **b.** OOPS
- **c.** U
- **d.** R

10. Use this command to save a new drawing for the first time:
- **a.** SAVE
- **b.** SAVEAS
- **c.** NEW
- **d.** OPEN

MATCHING

Match each term to the correct description by writing the appropriate number in each box at the left.

☐ Absolute	☐ Limits	☐ Polygon
☐ Architectural	☐ Mode	☐ Quadrant
☐ Blips	☐ Model	☐ Relative
☐ Cartesian	☐ Open	☐ REMOVE
☐ Coordinate	☐ OOPS	☐ SAVE
☐ Crossing	☐ Ortho	☐ SAVEAS
☐ Decimal	☐ Paper	☐ Selection
☐ Editing	☐ Pick	☐ Transparent
☐ Engineering	☐ Pixels	☐ Window
☐ Grid	☐ PLOT	

1. These units are used to specify distances in inches or millimeters.
2. Drawing in these units is generally used in mapping and civil drafting projects such as dams and bridges, plot plans, and topography.
3. These units are used when drawing in feet and inches and fractional inches.
4. This sets your drawing area.
5. The space in which you create your drawing.
6. AutoCAD LT provides you with this space where the drawing is organized and scaled as needed for the end product.
7. This is a pattern of dots that is displayed on the screen at any desired increment you establish.
8. As you move the screen cursor, this display indicates where the cursor is in relation to the drawing origin.
9. Use this command to save your drawing with a new name.
10. Use this command to save your work in progress.
11. Use this command if you want to work on a previous drawing.
12. This coordinate system relates to numbers that are used to locate points relative to two intersecting axes.
13. These coordinates are always established based on their X and Y distance from the origin.
14. These coordinates are used when you want to establish a point based on a distance from a previous point.
15. A quarter of a circle.
16. This is a closed plane figure with straight sides.
17. This is a setting or operating condition that you control.
18. These are temporary screen marks that are displayed when you pick a point.
19. With this on, the pointing device allows only horizontal and vertical movement.
20. This is a command that can be started while another command is in progress.
21. AutoCAD LT refers to changing a drawing as this process.
22. When you select objects with AutoCAD LT, the objects are referred to as this kind of a set.
23. When you get a Select objects: prompt, the screen cursor changes to this kind of a box.
24. A box that must totally surround an object to be erased.
25. A box that may either surround or cross through an object to erase it.
26. AutoCAD LT allows you to remove objects from a selection set by using this option.
27. If you erase something and then decide you want it back, you can use this command.
28. These are tiny dots that make up what is seen on the computer screen.
29. Prints are made using this command.

WORD SCRAMBLE

Unscramble the seven scrambled words below, one letter to each square, to form seven AutoCAD LT–related words:

LOARP

SIMTIL

NIROCADTOE

LOBASETU

LETAVIRE

PLIB

NOWDWI

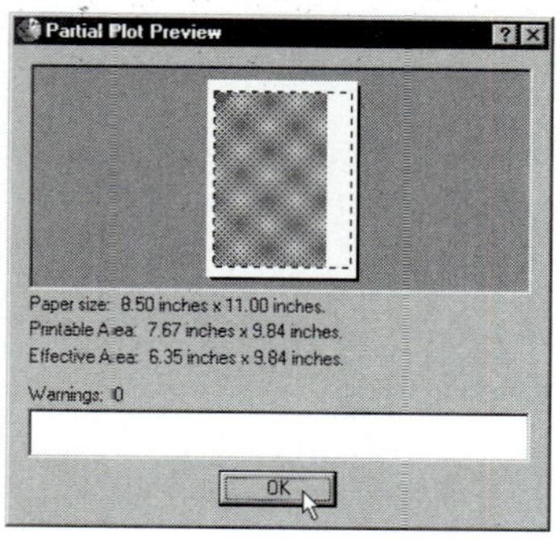

Unscramble the circled letters above to form the special answer, as suggested by the illustration.

PROJECTS

Draw Projects 2.1–2.5 using the Quick Setup and these settings:

- Decimal units
- 8.5 × 11 limits

2.1 Use the LINE command to draw a graphic design using the following absolute coordinates:

- 1.5,5.75
- 3.25,5.75
- 3.25,4.5
- 5,6.375
- 3.25,8.25
- 3.25,7
- 1.5,7
- 2.125,6.375
- 1.5,5.75
    - Cancel the line command.
    - Save as P2.1.
    - Print the drawing.

2.2 Use the LINE command to draw the sheet metal part using the following relative coordinates after the initial absolute coordinate:

- 2,2 (absolute)
- @3.25,0
- @0,1.875
- @−.875,0
- @0,.75
- @1.75,0
- @0,3.125
- @−.5,.5
- @−1.5,0
- @−.75,−.75
- @−.75,.75
- @−.25,0
- @0,−2
- @.25,0
- @0,−3.5
- @−.25,−.25
- @−.375,0
- Close
  - Save as P2.2.
  - Print the drawing.

2.3 Use the LINE command to draw the latch plate using the following polar coordinates after the initial absolute coordinate:

- 3,4 (absolute)
- @.5<0
- @.625<90
- @2.5<0
- @2.375<90
- @.75<180
- @1.5<270
- @2.25<180
- @.75<225
- @.375<270
- Close
  - Save as P2.3.
  - Print the drawing.

2.4 Use the LINE command to draw the trophy base using the following combination of coordinates:

- 1.5,3 (absolute)
- @5,0 (relative)
- @1<90 (polar)
- @5<180 (polar)
- Close.
- Press Enter or the space bar.
- 2.25,4 (absolute)
- @4.5<90 (polar)
- @1.75,1.75 (relative)
- @1.75,−1.75 (relative)
- @4.5<270 (polar)
- Cancel.
- Press Enter or the space bar.
- 2.75,4.75 (absolute)
- @2.5,0 (relative)

- @3.5<90 (polar)
- @2.5<180 (polar)
- Close.
  - Save as P2.4.
  - Print the drawing.

2.5 Use the LINE command to draw the picture frame using the following combination of coordinates:

- Point 1. 1,1 (absolute)
- Point 2. @6.5,0 (relative)
- Point 3. @9<90 (polar)
- Point 4. @−6.5,0 (relative)
- Close.
- Press Enter or the space bar.
- Point 5. 1.5,1.5 (absolute)
- Point 6. @5.5,0 (relative)
- Point 7. @8<90 (polar)
- Point 8. @5.5<180 (polar)
- Close.
- Set Grid to .5.
- Set Snap to .25 and turn Snap on.
- Enter the LINE command and do the following:
  - Pick point 1. *(Note: The point numbers refer to the points established by the previously numbered coordinate entries.)*
  - Pick point 5.
- Cancel.
- Press Enter or the space bar.
  - Pick point 2.
  - Pick point 6.
- Cancel.
- Press Enter or the space bar.
  - Pick point 3.
  - Pick point 7.
- Cancel.
- Press Enter or the space bar.
  - Pick point 4.
  - Pick point 8.
- Cancel.
  - Save as P2.5.
  - Print the drawing.

Draw Projects 2.6–2.14 using the Quick Setup and these settings:

- Units should correlate with the problem
- 8.5 × 11 limits
- .25 Grid
- .125 Snap

Use the LINE command by using the point entry methods that best fit each situation in each problem. It is suggested that you use sketches to determine a planned procedure and coordinates.

Make your drawings proportional to the given product. Dimensions (if any) are given to establish the size of the main feature. Sizes and locations of features that are not dimensioned may be determined to your own specifications. Do not include dimensions or notes on your drawing. Save each drawing as related to the project number, such as P2.6. Make a print or plot as specified by your instructor or supervisor.

2.6 Electrical Drawing: Shock Resistor

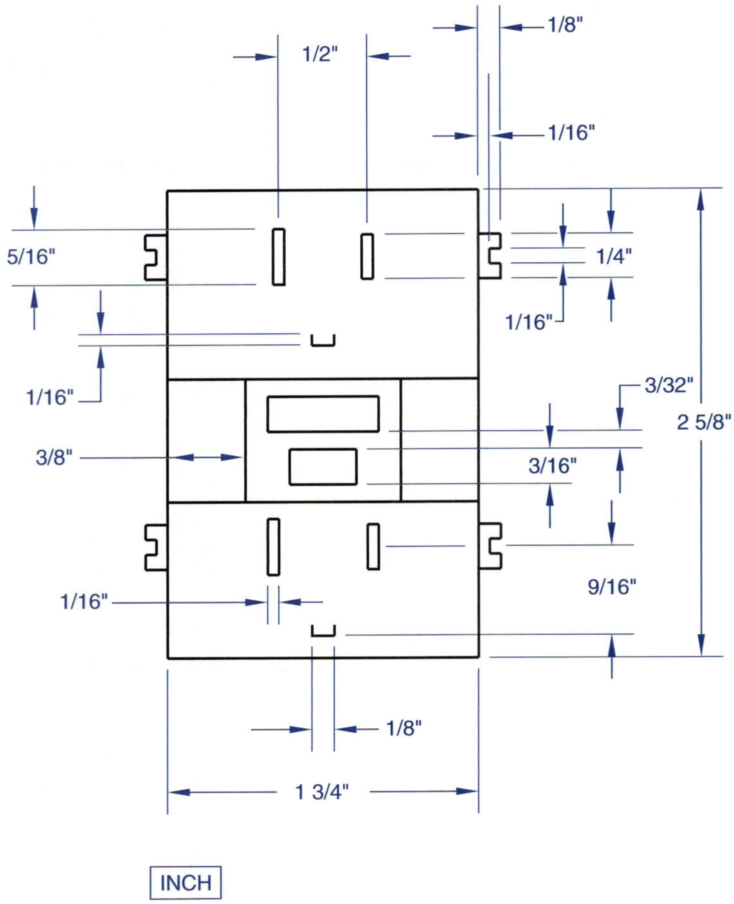

2.7 Mechanical Drawing: Clock Base

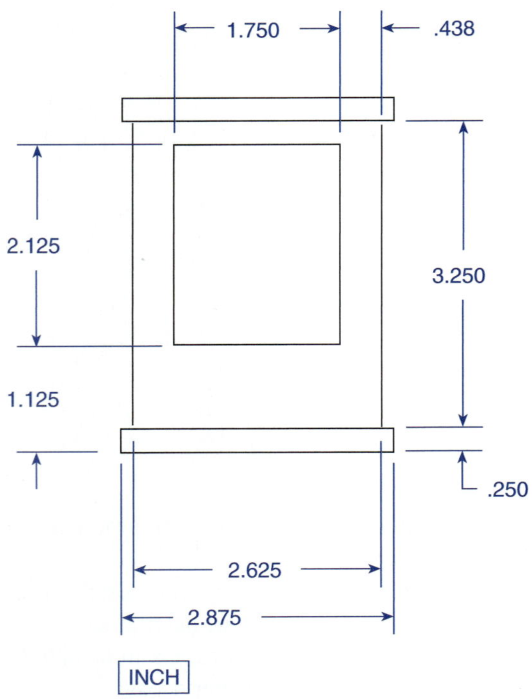

2.8 Architectural Drawing: Footing Detail

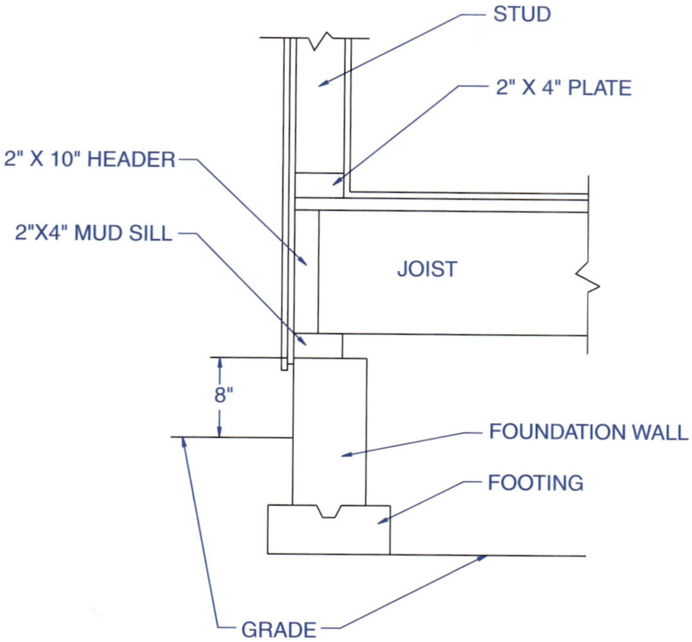

2.9 Electrical Drawing: Baseboard Heater Circuit

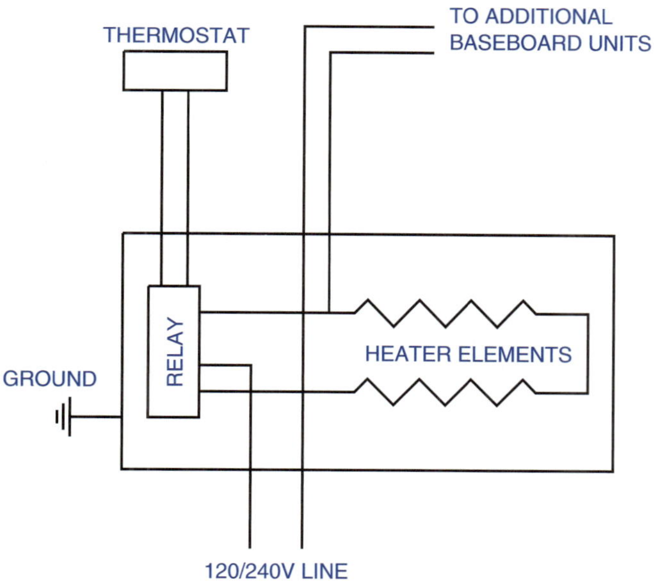

2.10 Pipe Drawing: Pipe Assembly

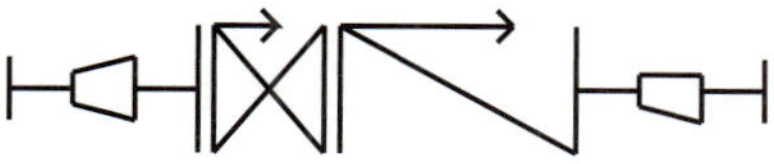

CHAPTER 3

Drawing Basic Objects

LEARNING GOALS

- Use the AutoCAD LT Advanced Setup option.
- Use an AutoCAD LT template.
- Create a template drawing.
- Customize existing template drawings.
- Draw circles, arcs, ellipses, and elliptical arcs.
- Draw regular polygons and rectangles.
- Use the DONUT command to draw filled rings and circles.
- Draw filled objects with the SOLID command.
- Turn the fill on and off to create different designs.

In Chapter 2 you learned how to quickly set up an AutoCAD LT drawing and practiced fundamental applications of drawing and erasing lines. This chapter provides you with additional setup options, including setting up your own custom drawing formats. Additionally, you will learn to draw basic shapes such as circles, arcs, polygons, and filled shapes.

Additional AutoCAD LT Setup Options

When you open AutoCAD LT, you get the Start Up dialog box and when using the NEW command, the Create New Drawing dialog box is displayed. These dialog boxes were introduced in Chapter 2 with the Quick Setup option. You also have a choice of these options: Advanced Setup, Use a Template, or Start from Scratch.

Using the Advanced Setup Option

The Advanced Setup option is one of the Wizards found in the Startup and Create New Drawing dialog boxes. The Quick Setup Wizard was introduced in Chapter 2. The Advanced Setup Wizard provides additional flexibility. In the Setup or Create New Drawing dialog boxes, double-click on Advanced Setup or highlight Advanced Setup and pick the OK button. This displays the Advanced Setup dialog box found in Figure 3.1. This dialog box allows you to make settings in five different areas, listed on the left side. A filled blue triangle is displayed next to the currently active area. Use the Next> and <Back buttons to move between areas.

Units

This area is the same as the Units area discussed with the Quick Setup Wizard in Chapter 2. This option allows you to select one of five different units of measure for your drawing. Refer to Setting Units of Measure in Chapter 2. The Precision: drop-down list shown in Figure 3.1 is a feature of the Advanced Setup tabs. Access this list to select the number of digits beyond the decimal point for the numeric display. The Sample Units image changes to match your choice.

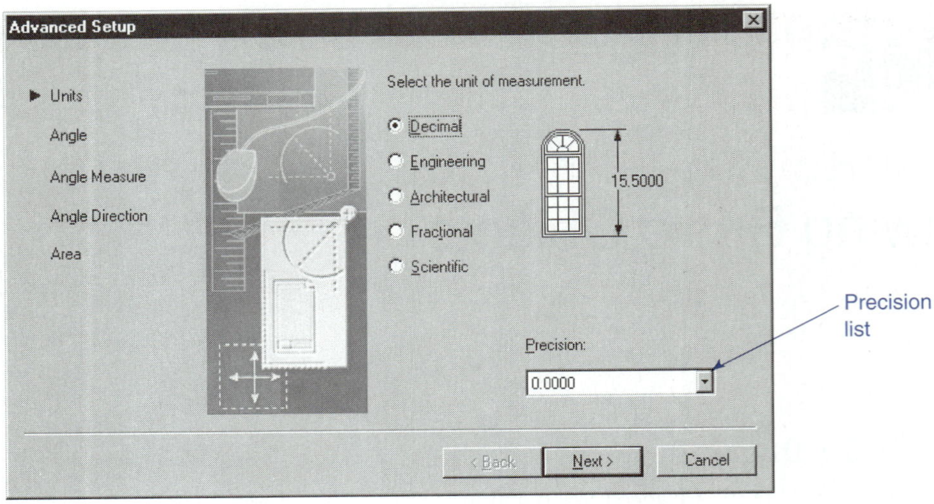

FIGURE 3.1 The Advanced Setup dialog box.

Field Notes

The precision setting does not affect the accuracy of a drawing. This setting controls only the precision at which AutoCAD LT displays drawing information such as coordinate locations, distances, and angles. Precise entries can be made regardless of the display precision.

Angle

Pick this tab to choose angular units and the display accuracy of angles you draw (see Figure 3.2). The angle measurement options are explained in the following list:

- **Decimal Degrees** — Decimal degrees is the default normally used in mechanical drafting where degrees and decimal parts of a degree are commonly used. Look at the example area in Figure 3.2. Pick the Precision down arrow to access the drop-down list. Pick the desired angle precision. Notice how the Sample Angle image changes to reflect the display precision you select.
- **Deg/Min/Sec** — The Degrees/Minutes/Seconds option is used in mechanical, architectural, structural, and civil drafting when it is necessary for angular measurements to contain accuracy related to minutes and seconds. Notice the example area in Figure 3.3. There are 60 minutes in one degree and 60 seconds in one minute. Access the Precision drop-down list to establish the display accuracy of seconds.

FIGURE 3.2 The Advanced Setup dialog box, Angle area. Decimal Degrees is the default. Notice the example image shown at the right.

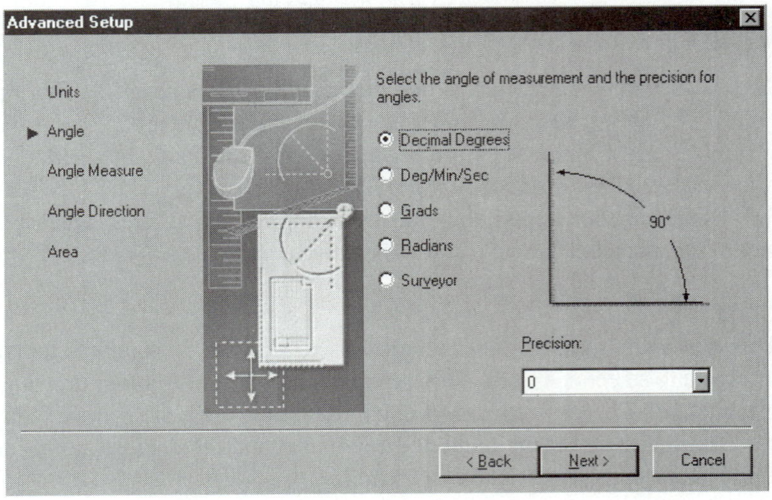

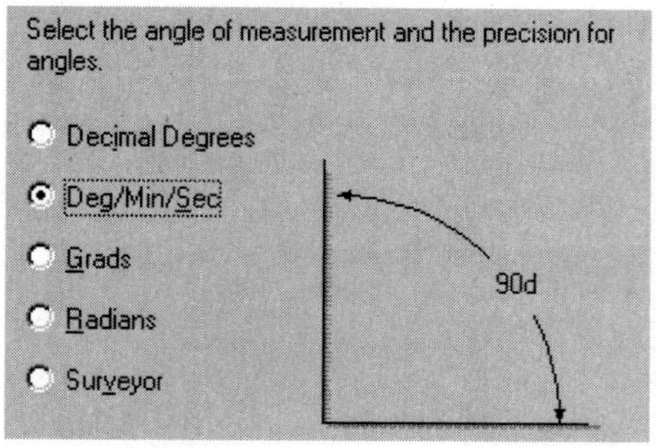

FIGURE 3.3 The Deg/Min/Sec (Degree/Minute/Second) angle option.

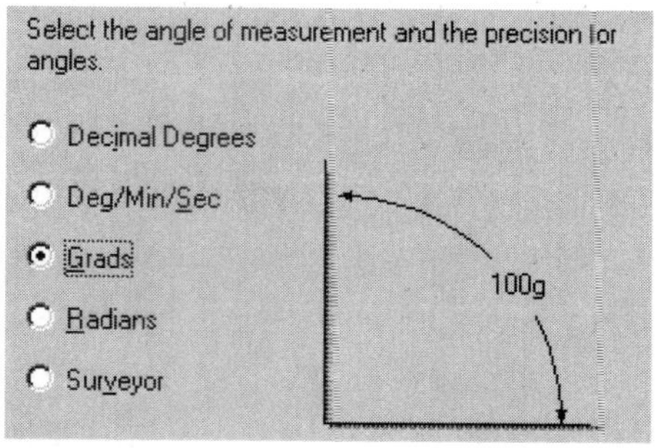

FIGURE 3.4 The Grads angle option.

- **Grads** — This refers to the abbreviation of ***gradient,*** which is a unit of angular measure. The angular value is followed by a "g," as shown in the example area in Figure 3.4. This is based on one-quarter of a circle having 100 grads. A full circle has 400 grads. A 45° angle, for example, has 50 grads. Use the Precision drop-down list to change the display number of decimal grads used.
- **Radians** — The ***radian*** is an angular unit, arc, or rotational measure where π radians = 180°. A 90° angle, for example, has $\pi/2$ radians and an arc length of $\pi/2$. Notice the example shown in Figure 3.5, which is displayed when Radians is active, and observe the results when you adjust the display precision.
- **Surveyor** — Surveyor angles are measured using bearings. The ***bearing*** of a line is its direction with respect to one of the quadrants of a compass. Bearings are measured clockwise or counterclockwise depending on the quadrant and beginning from either North or South. Bearings are measured in degrees, minutes, and seconds. An angle measured 45°30′15″ from north toward east is expressed as N45°30′15″E. Figure 3.6 shows the Advanced Setup Surveyor selection and the example image with sample bearings represented in relation to the quadrants of a compass. The Precision settings determine decimal display accuracy of the minutes settings.

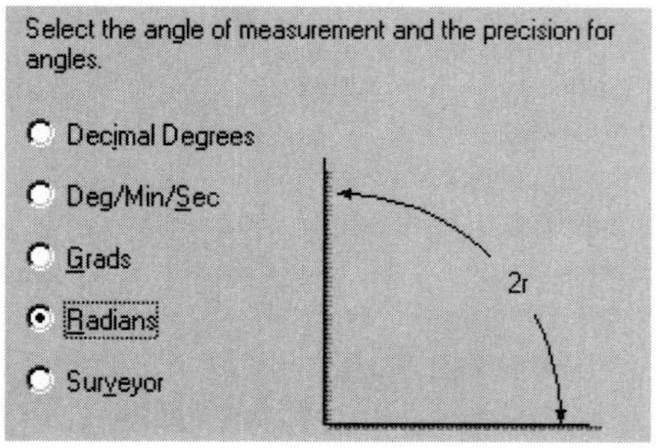

FIGURE 3.5 The Radians angle option.

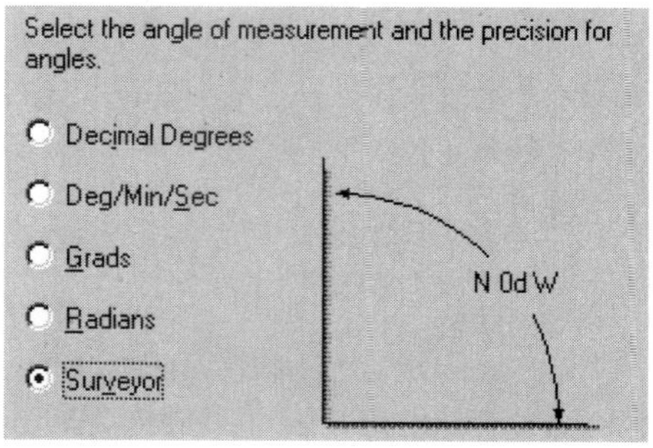

FIGURE 3.6 The Surveyor angle option and sample bearing example.

Angle Measure

This area lets you choose the compass position from which angles are measured. The AutoCAD LT default has angles measured in a counterclockwise direction beginning at 0° East on the right side of your screen. Notice the Angle Zero Direction image in Figure 3.7 that displays the 0° East (E) compass orientation. The orientation of the compass directions is the same as when you look at a map, with North at the top of your screen. This setting determines which direction is used as angle 0° (or 0r, 0g, etc.). The other options are North, West, South, and Other. The Other option requires that you type a desired starting angle. Use your cursor to pick each of the options and notice the change in the Angle Zero Direction image with each selection.

Angle Direction

The Angle Direction tab allows you to select Counter-Clockwise or Clockwise angle direction. The angle direction originates from the compass position that you used in the Angle Measure area. Figure 3.8 shows the Step

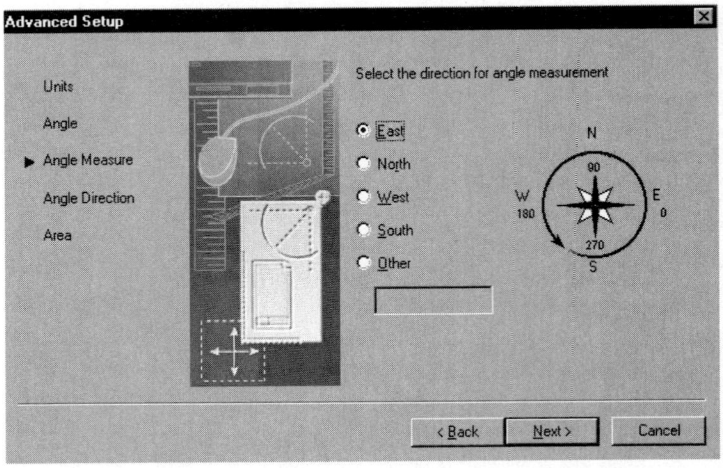

FIGURE 3.7 The Advanced Setup dialog box, Angle Measure area.

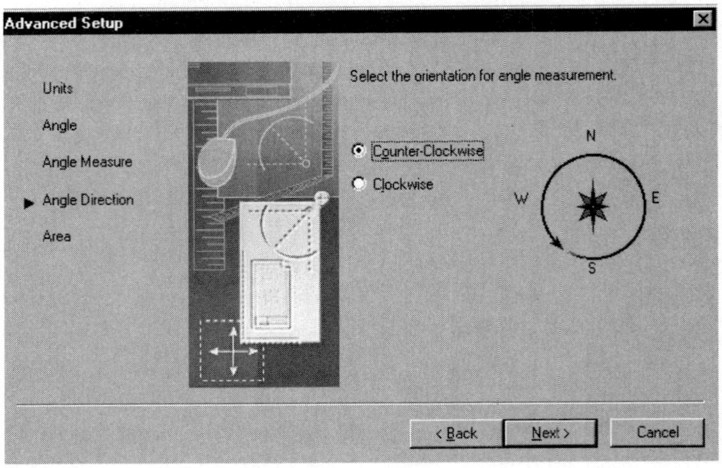

FIGURE 3.8 The Advanced Setup dialog box, Angle Direction area. Notice the counterclockwise example in the Angle Direction image.

4: Angle Direction area and the default Counter-Clockwise angle direction selection and related Angle Direction image. The default Counter-Clockwise setting is recommended in most applications.

Area

This works the same way as the Quick Setup discussion in Chapter 2. Refer to Setting the Drawing Size in Chapter 2 for a review if needed.

Exercise 3.1 — **Estimated time required: 5 min.**

1. Open AutoCAD LT if it is not already open. Use the Startup dialog box or if AutoCAD LT is open, use the NEW command to access the Create New Drawing dialog box and select Advanced Setup.
2. Notice the Sample Units image displayed for the decimal units default. As a review from Chapter 2, pick each of the other four unit options and observe the example image for each. Pick the Decimal option and set the precision to 0.000 before going on.
3. Open the Angle area. Change the Precision to a couple of different settings and look at the example image as you pick each of the angle unit options. Select Decimal Degrees and set the precision to 0.00 before you go on.
4. Access the Angle Measure area and pick each of the four compass orientation options. Notice how the Angle Zero Direction image changes with each selection. Pick the East option before going on.
5. Access the Angle Direction area and notice the Angle Direction image for the Counter-Clockwise default. Pick the Clockwise option and see the difference in the image representation. Pick Counter-Clockwise before going on.
6. Access the Area area and change the Width to 17 and the Length to 11.
7. Set Grid at .5 and Snap at .25. Draw a simple line object of your own design.
8. Save as EX3.1 and close the drawing.

Starting from Scratch

The AutoCAD LT Start Up and Create New Drawing dialog boxes have a Start from Scratch button. Select this option if you want to set up a drawing with your own options. When you pick Start from Scratch, AutoCAD LT lets you choose either English or Metric default settings (see Figure 3.9). Starting from scratch may not be the best choice for new AutoCAD LT users, because it requires you to set up all your layout conditions on your own.

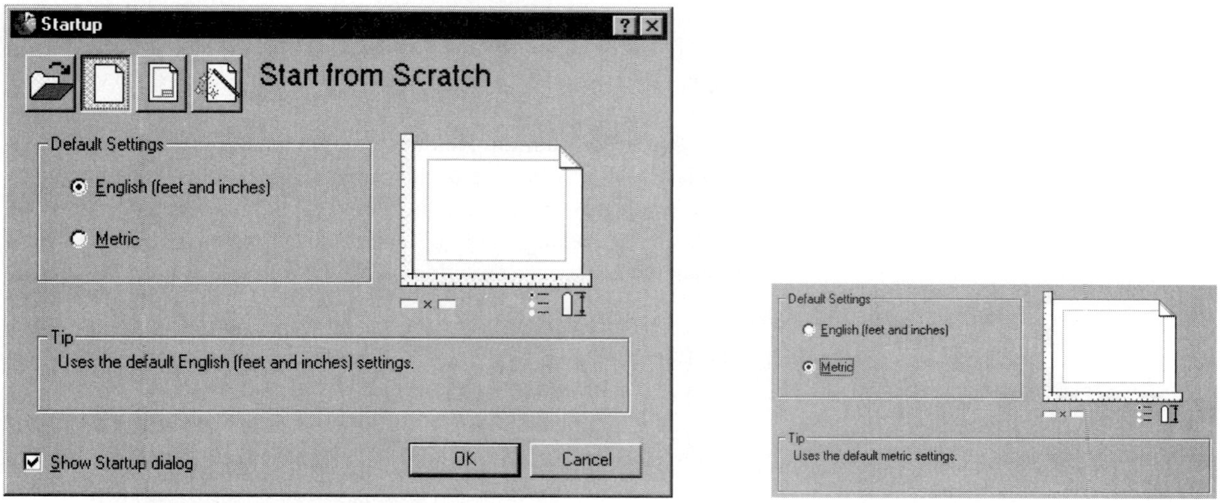

A B

FIGURE 3.9 The AutoCAD LT Start from Scratch option allows you to select either (A) English (feet and inch) or (B) Metric default settings.

Using an AutoCAD LT Template

A template is a drawing file with preestablished settings. A discussion about creating and using prototypes is given later in this chapter. To use one of these templates, pick the Use a Template option in the Start Up or Create New Drawing dialog box. Choose the desired template from the Select a Template list as shown in Figure 3.10. The template that you select is displayed in the image box and a Template Description is provided. In the Select a Template list, the aclt.dwt option allows you to start a drawing using feet and inch settings, whereas the acltiso.dwt choice is for metric settings. These options do not have title blocks. The .dwt file extension is for drawing templates.

FIGURE 3.10 In the AutoCAD LT Use a Template option, pick the desired template from the Select a Template list. Notice the selected template is displayed in the image box and a description is provided under the Template Description.

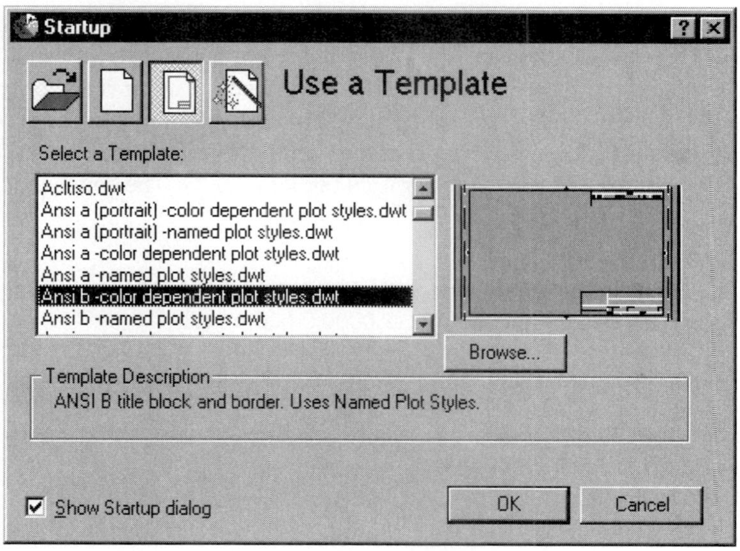

Setting Units and Limits Outside of the AutoCAD LT Setup

You have now seen how to set up an AutoCAD LT drawing using the Quick Setup and Advanced Setup options. Although this is a convenient way to set the drawing units and limits, you may need to change these settings during your drawing session, or you may just want additional flexibility.

Format
Units

DDUNITS
UNITS
UN

Use the UNITS command at any time during a drawing to set the units and angles to match your needs. The DrawingUnits dialog box is displayed for easy control of the settings. This command may be accessed by typing UN, UNITS, or DDUNITS, or by picking Units ... in the Format pull-down menu (see Figure 3.11A). Use the Drawing Units dialog box to pick the desired Length and Drawing Angle format. Access the Precision: drop-down list to set the number of digits to the right of the decimal point. The check box in the Angle area lets you specify Clockwise angle direction. The sample Output area at the bottom displays the results of the current settings.

Look at Figure 3.11A and notice the Direction ... button. Pick this button to access the Direction Control dialog box shown in Figure 3.11B. This dialog box has the standard East, North, West, and South options. You can also pick Other to activate the Angle text box and the Pick an angle button. The Angle text box allows you to specify the angle that you want to be the angle zero direction. Select the Pick an angle button to pick two points on the screen that establish the angle zero direction.

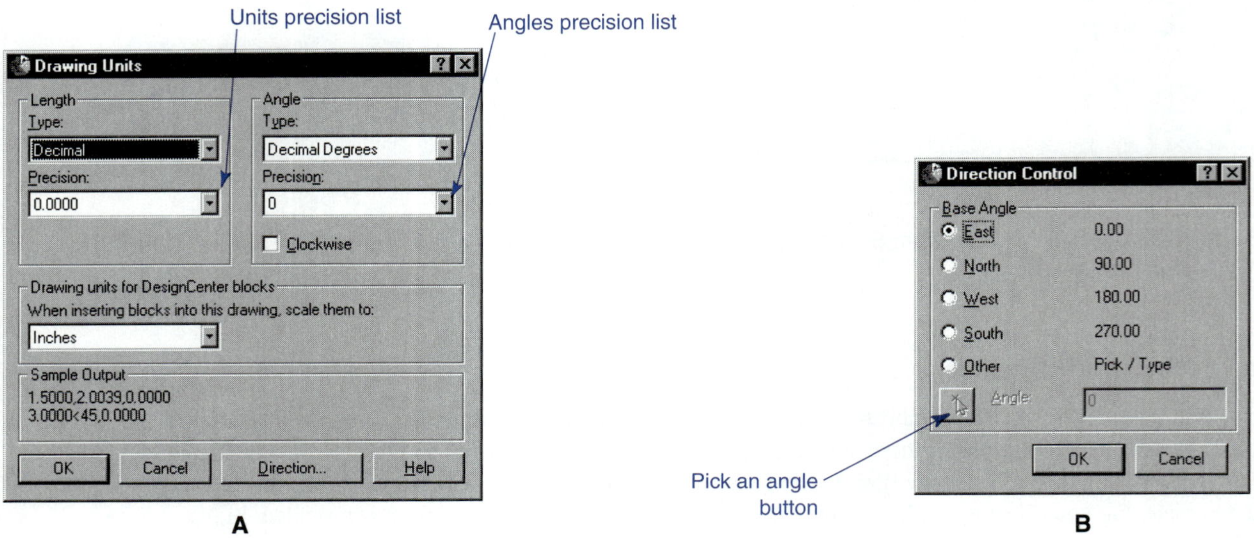

FIGURE 3.11 (A) Use the DDUNITS command to access the Drawing Units dialog box. (B) Pick the Direction... button in the Drawing Units dialog box to get the Direction Control dialog box.

Setting the size of the drawing area may also be done using the LIMITS command by typing **LM** or **LIMITS** or by picking Drawing Limits in the Format pull-down menu. The LIMITS command asks you to specify the coordinates of the lower left corner and the upper right corner of the drawing area. The lower left corner is usually 0,0 but you can specify something else <0,0> is the drawing default so press Enter to accept this coordinate. The upper right corner identifies the upper right corner of the drawing area. If you want a 17 × 11 drawing area, then the upper right corner is 17,11. The command works like this:

Command: **LM** or **LIMITS**↵
Reset Model space limits:
Specify lower left corner or [ON/OFF] <0.0000,0.0000>: ↵
Specify upper right corner <12.0000,9.0000>: **17,11**↵
Command:

The LIMITS command also provides an ON and an OFF option. Turning limits on has the effect of restricting the coordinates you can enter when drawing objects to the rectangular area defined by the limits settings. In the following example the limits are set to 0,0 and 17,11, and limits are turned on:

Command: **LIMITS↵**
Reset Model space limits:
Specify lower left corner or [ON/OFF] <0.0000,0.0000>: **OFF↵**
Command: **LINE↵**
Specify first point: **10,7.25↵**
Specify next point or [Undo]: **18,7.25↵**

**Outside limits
Specify next point or [Undo]: **@8<90↵**

**Outside limits
Specify next point or [Undo]: *Cancel*

Command: **LIMITS↵**
Reset Model space limits:
Specify lower left corner or [ON/OFF] <0.0000,0.0000>: **OFF↵**
Command:

Notice that the coordinate entry method does not matter. If the result is drawing an object that goes outside the limits, an error message is displayed and no object is drawn. Relatively few applications require limits to be turned on, so limits are off by default.

Field Notes

When you set the limits manually using the LIMITS command, the currently displayed area of your drawing does not change from the previous limits setting. To display your current limits, select the View pull-down menu, then pick the All option from the Zoom cascade. Additional display change commands and options are covered in Chapter 4.

Exercise 3.2

Estimated time required: 5 min.

1. Open AutoCAD LT if it is not already open. Use the Startup or Create New Drawing dialog box.
2. Pick Start from Scratch. Notice the Select Default Setting: that is highlighted. Look at the related Preview image and Description box.
3. If English is highlighted, pick Metric, or if Metric is highlighted, pick English. Now, look at the related Preview image and Description box to see the difference.
4. Pick the Use a Template button. Notice the list of Select a Template: options. Select each template in the list. Look at the Preview image and read the description as you make each selection.
5. Go to the Select a Template option that looked most interesting to you during Step 4 and double-click on that option. The AutoCAD LT screen displays the border and title block if the template that you selected contains one. As always, the screen cursor is available for you to make a drawing.
6. Turn the limits on and try to draw a line that extends beyond the limits area. While still at the To point: prompt, enter the limits command transparently by typing **'LM** and turn limits off. Try again to draw the same line.
7. Draw a shape of your own design. Print it from the Model tab if a printer is available.
8. Save as EX3.2, and close the drawing.

Using Template Drawings

As you learned earlier, templates are drawing files that contain established standards and settings. When you begin a new drawing with the Use a Template option, you are starting with a group of settings that are already set up and saved in the template file. When you begin a new drawing with the Quick Setup, Advanced Setup, or Start from Scratch options, you are working with a series of settings that you establish combined with standard AutoCAD LT settings. Every type of drawing you make should have a set of standards that you use. For example, there are different standards for mechanical, architectural, and electrical drawings. Templates typically contain correctly preset values for common drawing features, including:

- Standard limits with a border and title block
- Grid and snap settings
- Units and angle values
- Text standards and typical notes (Chapter 9)
- Dimensioning standards (Chapter 11)
- Plot Style Table settings

Most of the template names reference a plot style setting that is established in the drawing. The plot style table reference is either for a color-dependent plot style or a name plot style. The use of plot styles is discussed in Chapter 13. For now, select only templates that use color-dependent plot styles.

Customizing Existing Template Drawings

As previously discussed, AutoCAD LT has many templates available for you to use for the prototypes of your drawings. The Use a Template option lets you move directly into a border and title block format in a drawing where some or all the available settings are already configured for the type and size of drawing you are creating. However, the templates provided with AutoCAD LT 2000 have very generic settings and may need to be adjusted. After entering the desired format, you can establish additional drawing settings that are considered common for the type of drawing you are making. The following list shows basic settings that might be used for a drawing in the mechanical and architectural drafting fields:

	Mechanical	*Architectural*
Select a Template:	Ansi C	Architectural, English units
Grid	.5	12
Snap	.125	2

A template of this type is very fundamental. Additional settings such as text and dimension styles are discussed later in this text. You need to save your drawing as a template for later use after entering each of the specific desired settings. Follow these steps to save the template for future use:

1. Enter the SAVEAS command. This opens the Save Drawing As dialog box shown in Figure 3.12A.
2. Access the Drawing Template File (*.dwt) type in the Save as type: list, as shown in Figure 3.12B. The .dwt extension is a drawing template file.
3. Type a name for your drawing template in the File name: text box and then pick Save, as shown in Figure 3.12C. Give your template a name that correlates with the type of drawing you are creating. For example, choose something such as MECHANICAL_IN_B for a drawing to be done using ANSI standards, inch dimensions, and a B size (11 × 17-in.) sheet. Enter a name such as MECHANICAL_MM_A3 for a drawing to be done using ANSI or ISO standards, metric dimensions, and an A3 size (420 × 297-mm) sheet. Use a name such as ARCHIT_C for an architectural drawing done on a C size (18 × 24-in.) sheet.
4. The Template Description dialog box is automatically displayed. Type a description of your template in the Description text box, as shown in Figure 3.12D. A good description helps you identify the template later when you pick it from the Start Up or Create New Drawing dialog box. Use a description such as "Mechanical drawings using ANSI/IN. with B size layout and title block" or "Architectural drawing with C size layout and title block."
5. While still in the Template Description dialog box, pick the desired unit style, English (inch) or Metric, in the Measurement drop-down list. Pick OK when you are finished.

The new template file is saved in the Template folder with the .dwt extension. Now you can access the template any time you want it in the Select a Template: list of the Use a Template option in the Start Up or Create New Drawing dialog box.

Once you have a template established, you can use it as the beginning basis for each drawing of its type such as mechanical, architectural, or electrical, for example. Use the template to prepare the desired drawing

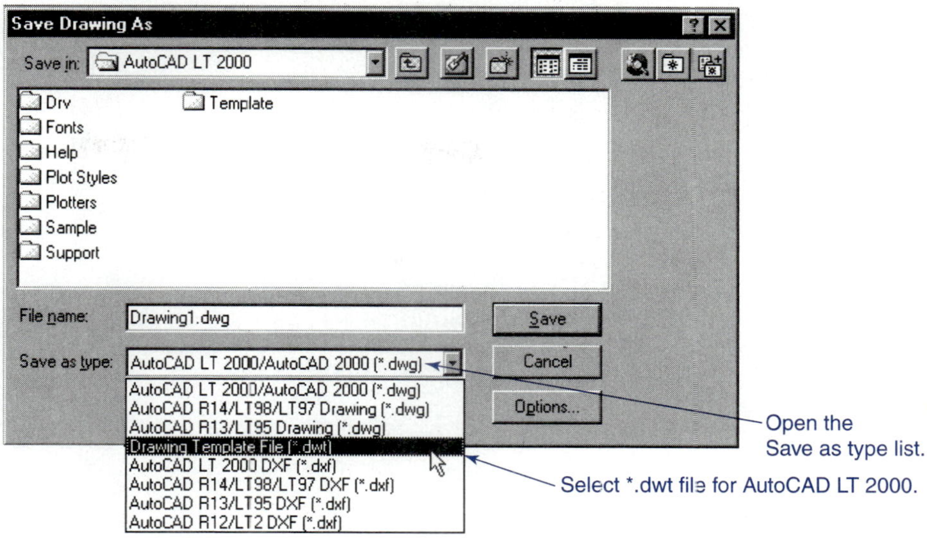

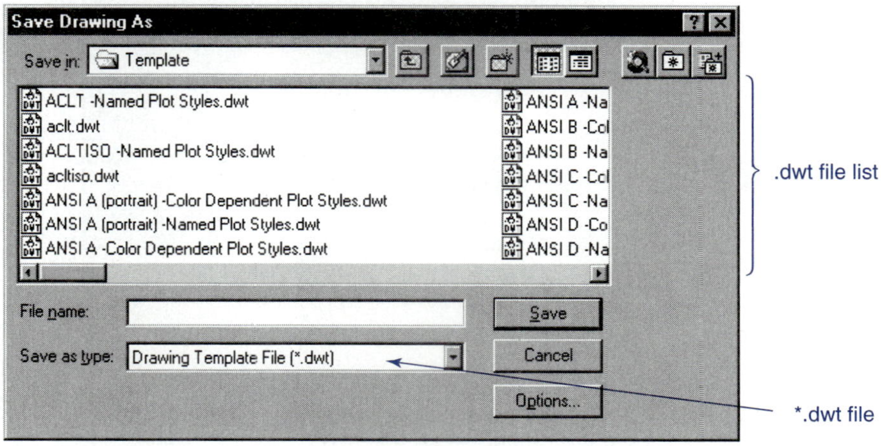

FIGURE 3.12 Naming, describing, and saving your template-drawing. (A) The Save Drawing As dialog box. (B) Access the Drawing Template File [*.dwt] in the Save as type: list. (C) Type the template name in the File name: text box and pick the Save button. (D) Type the description of your template in the Description text box and enter the desired units, inch or metric, in the Measurement text box. Pick OK when ready.

and then use the SAVEAS command to save the drawing with a file name that describes the specific drawing. This leaves the template unchanged for use each time you want it. Drawing names, for example, might relate to a part number or product in mechanical drawing, to a project name and drawing type such as a floor plan in architectural drawing, or to a product schematic in electronic drafting.

Field Notes

- When you save a new template file, you are automatically moved to the AutoCAD LT 2000\Template folder. By default, this is where AutoCAD LT looks to determine what templates are available, so only those files saved in this folder are displayed in the list of available templates. To look in other folders, pick More files ... from the list.
- You can tell AutoCAD LT to look in a different folder using the OPTIONS command. In the Options dialog box, pick the Files tab and change the folder name found under the *Template Drawing File Location* setting.
- You can also use an existing drawing as a template file. Use the OPEN command to open any existing drawing that already has settings and/or content that applies to your current project. After the file is open, use the SAVEAS command to save the drawing to a new location and file name.

FIGURE 3.12 *continued*

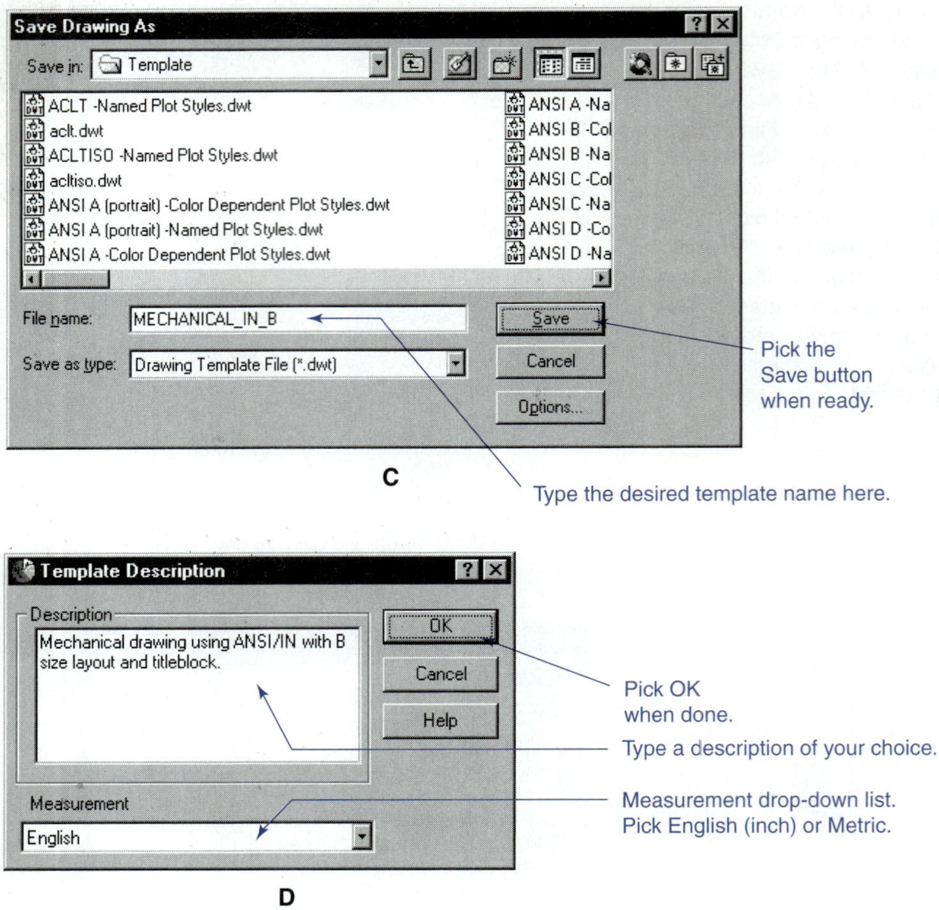

Through the Window...

Your file selection dialog boxes may display only file names and not the file extension. You can turn the display of file extensions on or off as desired. This is a function of the operating system, not AutoCAD LT. Here's how:

1. Pick the Start button from the task bar, select Programs and then Windows (95/98/NT) Explorer.
2. Select Options... from the View menu.
3. On the View tab of the Options dialog box, either place or remove the check mark next to Hide file extensions for known file types.
4. The change will take effect the next time you start AutoCAD LT 2000.

Exercise 3.3

Estimated time required: 8 min.

1. Open AutoCAD LT if it is not already open. Use the Startup or Create Drawing dialog box.
2. Pick Use a Template.
3. Access a template of your choice in the Select a Template: list. If you are interested in mechanical drafting, pick a template such as ansi_b.dwt for an inch drawing or iso_a2.dwt for a metric drawing. If you are working in architectural drafting, try the archeng.dwt template. Double-click or highlight the desired template and pick OK.
4. The template of your choice is now displayed on the screen. You can modify it in any way to suit your drafting needs. For a very fundamental custom template, enter the settings that may be used for a drawing in the mechanical or architectural drafting fields as you desire:

	Mechanical	*Architectural*
Grid	.5	12
Snap	.125	2

5. Enter the SAVEAS command and pick Drawing Template in the Save File as Type: file list.
6. Type a desired template name in the File Name: text box. Use a name of your choice or as described in the previous discussion.
7. Type a description of your template in the Template Description box. Select or type the desired units in the Measurement box. Pick the OK button.
8. Enter the NEW command and look through the Select a Template: list of the Create New Drawing dialog box until you find the name of the template you just created. Access the new template.
9. Make a simple drawing of your choice.
10. Save as EX3.3 and close the drawing.

LEARNING CHECKPOINT

- ☐ Where is the Advanced Setup option found?
- ☐ Write an example of decimal degrees and degrees/minutes/seconds.
- ☐ Make a sketch of the surveyor's angle N45°W.
- ☐ Name at least four standard border and title block formats provided by AutoCAD LT.
- ☐ What advantage is provided by using templates?

Introducing the AutoCAD LT Workspace

- Starting a New Drawing
- Setting Interface Options

Drawing Curved Objects

In Chapter 2 you learned how to draw lines and how to edit your drawing by erasing. The rest of the discussion in this chapter teaches you how to draw circles, arcs, ellipses, rectangles, polygons, and filled objects. As you go through this discussion, keep in mind that prompts answered with ⟨pick a point⟩ in the examples can also use absolute, polar, or relative coordinate entry.

Drawing Circles

Circles are drawn using the CIRCLE command, which is found by accessing the Circle cascade in the Draw pull-down menu, by picking the Circle button in the Draw toolbar, or by typing **C** or **CIRCLE** at the Command: prompt. Four options can be used to draw a circle. These options are based on features related to the circle and are discussed next.

Drawing a Circle with the Center and Radius

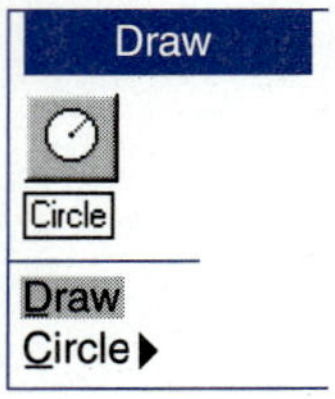

You can draw a circle by selecting a center point and then either picking or typing a radius value. The ***radius*** is the distance from the center to the circumference of the circle. To do this, go to the Draw pull-down menu and pick the Circle cascade followed by Center, Radius, or pick the Circle toolbar button, or type **C** or **Circle** at the Command: prompt. The Command: prompt asks you to pick a center point. After you select a center point, move the cursor to drag the circle to a desired radius and pick or type a specific radius value. If you pick a point, the distance between the center point and the next point you pick is used as the radius value (see Figure 3.13). The Command: looks like this as you draw a circle:

> Command: **C** or **CIRCLE**↵
> Specify center point for circle or [3P/2P/Ttr (tan tan radius)]: *<pick a center point>*
> Specify radius of circle or [Diameter]: *<type a radius value or pick the radius>*
> Command:

FIGURE 3.13 Drawing a circle using the Center, Radius option.

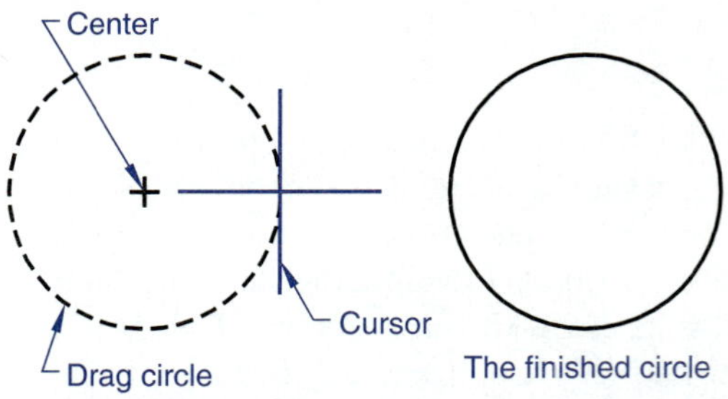

Field Notes

- When you are finished drawing a circle, you can press Enter or the space bar at the Command: prompt to immediately start the **CIRCLE** command again. The previously used radius value is displayed in angle brackets <>. The brackets are not visible for the first circle drawn in any drawing session. You can press Enter to accept this value or type a new value.
- AutoCAD LT stores the location of the last point picked in a system variable called LASTPOINT. You can access this point by using the @ symbol. This provides an easy way to create concentric circles:

> Command: **CIRCLE**↵
> Specify center point for circle or [3P/2P/Ttr (tan tan radius)]: *<pick center point>*
> Specify radius of circle or [Diameter] <1.6833>: **2**↵
> Command: ↵
> CIRCLE Specify center point for circle or [3P/2P/Ttr (tan tan radius)]: **@**↵
> Specify radius of circle or [Diameter] <2.5000>: **2.25**↵
> Command:

Drawing a Circle with the Center and Diameter

A circle can also be drawn by selecting a center point and then either picking or typing a diameter value. ***Diameter*** is the distance across the circle and passing through the center. To do this, go to the Draw pull-down menu and pick Circle followed by Center, Diameter. The Command: prompt asks you to pick a center point. After you select a center point, move the cursor to drag the circle to a desired diameter and pick or type a specific diameter value. When you use the Center, Diameter option, the screen cursor extends beyond the circle a distance equal to the radius. This process shows you the diameter as the distance between the center and the cursor (see Figure 3.14).

> Command: **C** or **CIRCLE**↵
> Specify center point for circle or [3P/2P/Ttr (tan tan radius)]: *<pick a center point>*
> Specify radius of circle or [Diameter]: _d Specify diameter of circle: *<type a diameter value or pick the diameter>*
> Command:

FIGURE 3.14 Drawing a circle using the Center, Diameter option.

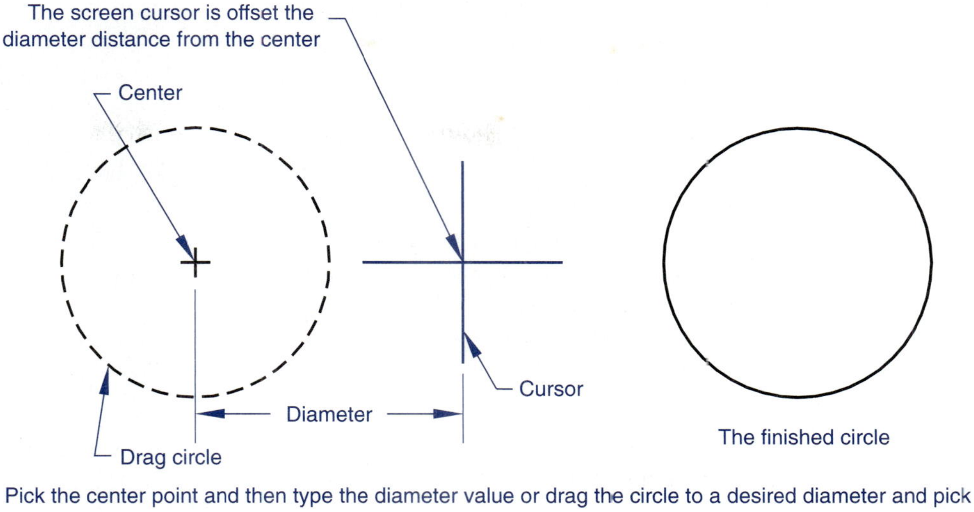

Additionally, you can type **C** or **CIRCLE** at the Command: prompt and use the Diameter option. When using the Diameter option at the keyboard, you need to type **D** at the Diameter/<Radius>: prompt like this:

Command: **C** or **CIRCLE**↵
Specify center point for circle or [3P/2P/Ttr (tan tan radius)]: *<pick a center point>*
Specify radius of circle or [Diameter]: **D**↵
Specify diameter of circle: *<type a diameter value or pick the diameter>*
Command:

If the Center, Diameter option is picked from the pull-down menu, the diameter option is automatically used. When you use the Diameter option, the screen cursor extends beyond the circle a distance equal to the radius.

Field Notes

When you enter a command by typing at the command line, the shortcut menu at the next Command: prompt provides an option to repeat the previous command—but this selection does not repeat the options you used. Many menu selections automatically enter some options, such as with the Center, Diameter option on the Circle cascade of the Draw menu. After you start a command using a menu pick, the shortcut menu at the next Command: prompt provides an option to repeat the menu option you used. For example, after you use the Center, Diameter option, the shortcut menu option reads: Repeat Center, Diameter.

Drawing a Circle with the 2 Points Option

A circle can be defined by specifying two points on the diameter of the circle. The points can be picked freehand or entered from the keyboard using any standard coordinate entry method. You can pick Circle from the Draw pull-down menu and select 2 Points, or use the 2P option at the command line (see Figure 3.15). The prompt sequence is as follows:

Command: **C** or **CIRCLE**↵
Specify center point for circle or [3P/2P/Ttr (tan tan radius)]: **2P**↵
Specify first end point of circle's diameter: *<pick the first point>*
Specify second end point of circle's diameter: *<pick the second point>*
Command:

FIGURE 3.15 Drawing a circle using the 2 Points option.

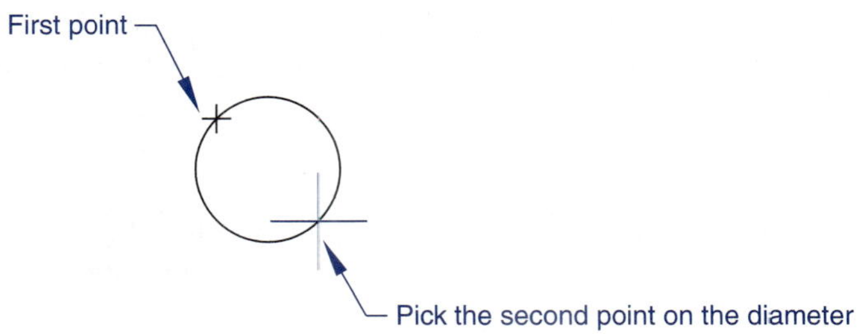

Drawing a Circle with the 3 Points Option

You can draw a circle by picking three points on the circumference. The ***circumference*** is the perimeter line of the circle. To do this, pick Circle and then 3 Points in the Draw pull-down menu or use the **3P** option at the command line. AutoCAD LT asks you to select the First point, Second point, and Third point. When using the pull-down menu, AutoCAD LT automatically asks for the points. After you pick the second point, AutoCAD LT drags the circle to the place where you pick the third point (see Figure 3.16). When using the keyboard, type **3P** like this:

Command: **C** or **CIRCLE**↵
Specify center point for circle or [3P/2P/Ttr (tan tan radius)]: **3P**↵
Specify first point on circle: *<pick first point>*
Specify second point on circle: *<pick second point>*
Specify third point on circle: *<pick third point>*
Command:

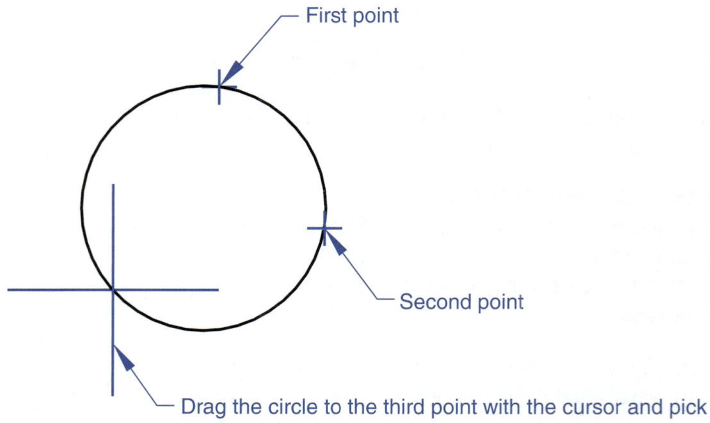

FIGURE 3.16 Drawing a circle with the 3 Points option.

Drawing a Circle Tangent to Two Objects

AutoCAD LT lets you easily draw a circle tangent to two other objects such as lines, arcs, and circles. ***Tangent*** means that the circle touches the objects at only one point without intersecting or crossing the objects. Draw a circle tangent to objects by picking Circle and then Tan, Tan, Radius in the Draw pull-down menu, or type the **TTR** option at the prompt line. When using this option, AutoCAD LT asks you to pick the object with which the circle is to be tangent, and then enter the radius of the circle. Figure 3.17 shows examples of drawing a circle tangent to two lines, to a line and a circle, and to two circles. When you select Tan, Tan, Radius from the pull-down menu, AutoCAD LT automatically issues the TTR option. After entering the TTR option, AutoCAD LT asks you to select the objects to which your circle will be tangent. Enter **TTR** at the keyboard like this:

Command: **C** or **CIRCLE**↵
Specify center point for circle or [3P/2P/Ttr (tan tan radius)]: **TTR**↵
Specify point on object for first tangent of circle: *<pick first object>*
Specify point on object for second tangent of circle: *<pick second object>*
Specify radius of circle <default>: *<specify radius>*
Command:

Field Notes

- When you point to an object to use for a tangency specification, a marker will appear at the cursor location. If you stop your cursor movement while the marker is visible, a tool tip–like feature called a *SnapTip* appears at the cursor location. These items are part of an important feature in AutoCAD LT called *AutoSnap.* In this application, the SnapTip reads Deferred Tangent… and it indicates that AutoCAD LT will attempt to find a location where tangency occurs, based on subsequent input. The AutoSnap feature is covered in detail in Chapter 6.
- If you are drawing a circle tangent to two angled line segments and the radius is too large, the circle is automatically placed beyond the lines. If the radius of the circle that you want tangent to two objects is too small, AutoCAD LT gives you the message "Circle does not exist."

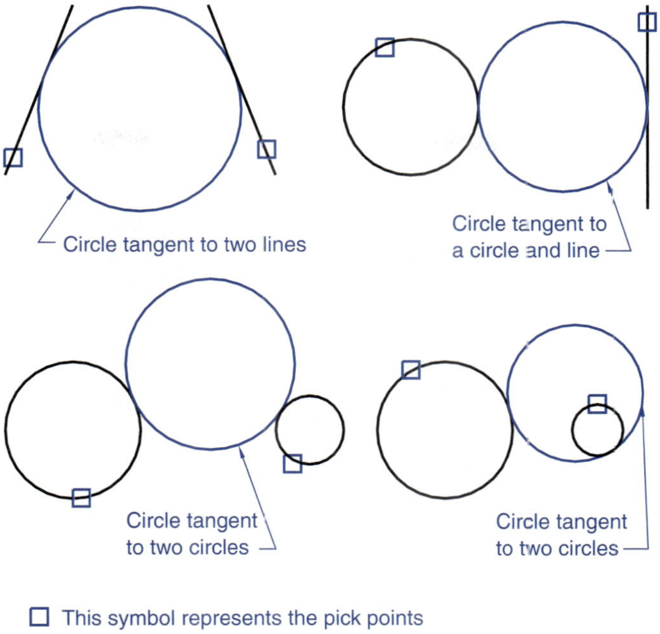

FIGURE 3.17 Drawing a circle using the Tangent, Tangent, Radius option.

Exercise 3.4

Estimated time required: 8 min.

1. Open AutoCAD LT if it is not already open. Use the setup option of your choice. A border and title block are not required.
2. Set limits at 8.5,11.
3. Draw the objects shown using the CIRCLE command options specified. The exact sizes are up to you, except for the objects where specific dimensions are given. Do not draw dimensions.
4. Save as EX3.4, and close the drawing.

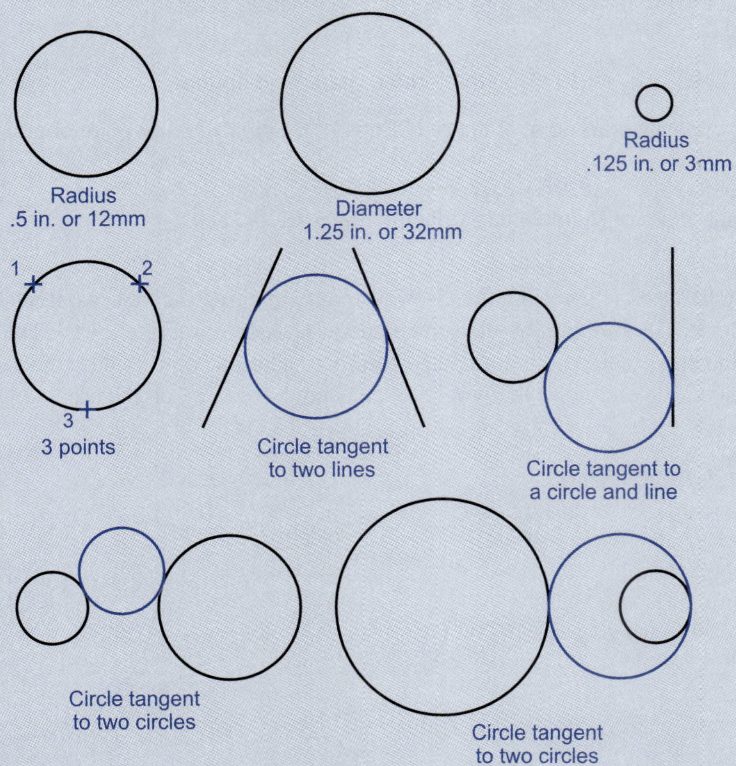

Drawing Arcs

AutoCAD LT provides several methods for drawing arcs. The variety of options gives you maximum flexibility when drawing arcs. The ARC command is found in the Draw pull-down menu and in the Draw toolbar, or you can type **A** or **ARC** at the Command: prompt.

Drawing Arcs by Specifying Three Points

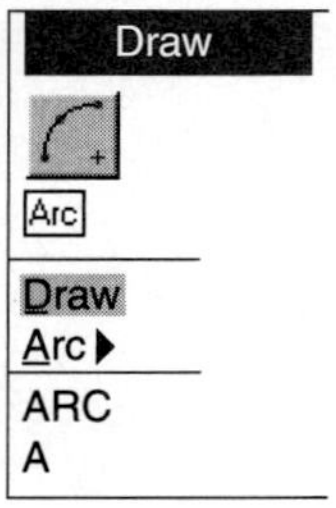

When the ARC command is entered at the keyboard, the default is an arc drawn by picking three points on the arc. The three-point method is also available by selecting Arc and then 3 Points in the Draw pull-down menu, or by picking the Arc toolbar button. AutoCAD LT asks for three points along the arc:

> Command: **A** or **ARC**↵
> Specify start point of arc or [CEnter]: *<pick first point on arc>*
> Specify second point of arc or [CEnter/ENd]: *<pick second point on arc>*
> Specify end point of arc: *<pick third point on arc>*
> Command:

After picking the second point, the arc is dragged into place as you decide where to place the third point. Figure 3.18 shows arcs drawn with the three-point option.

FIGURE 3.18 Drawing arcs using the 3 Points option.

Drawing Arcs Using the Start, Center, End Options

In some situations, you may know the location of the start point, the center of the arc, and the arc end point, or you may know the center location, the start, and the end. These options are found in the Draw pull-down menu by picking Arc followed by Start, Center, End or Center, Start, End in the cascading submenu. AutoCAD LT automatically answers the option prompts when you use the pull-down menu. This is the command sequence when using Start, Center, End:

> Command: _arc Specify start point of arc or [CEnter]: *<pick the start point>*
> Specify second point of arc or [CEnter/ENd]: _c Specify center point of arc: *<pick the center point>*
> Specify end point of arc or [Angle/chord Length]: *<pick the end point>*
> Command:

This is what AutoCAD LT asks when using the Center, Start, End option:

> Command: _arc Specify start point of arc or [CEnter]: _c Specify center point of arc: *<pick the center point>*
> Specify start point of arc: *<pick the start point>*
> Specify end point of arc or [Angle/chord Length]: *<pick the end point>*
> Command:

Something interesting happens when using these options. After picking the first two items, the arc is dragged in a default counterclockwise direction by the screen cursor as shown in Figure 3.19. This allows you to see the arc as you select the end point. At this time, the actual arc radius is controlled by the distance between the first point and the center. The end point that you pick does not have to be on the arc.

FIGURE 3.19 Drawing arcs using the Start, Center, and End options.

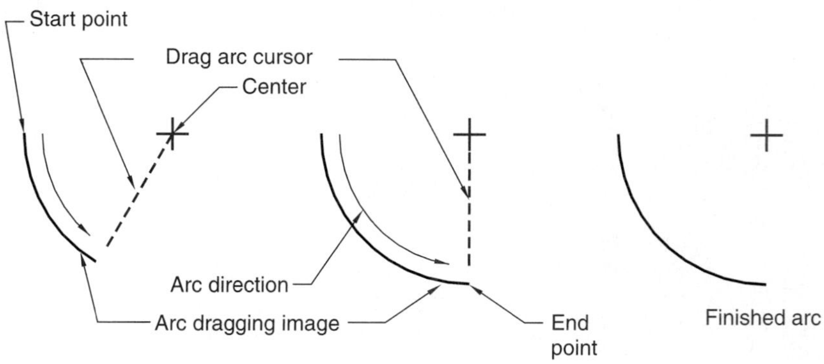

When entering these options at the keyboard, you need to type the capitalized letter of the desired option at the prompt line. The Start point option is the default at the first prompt, or you can begin with the Center option like this:

Command: **A** or **ARC**↵
Specify start point of arc or [CEnter]: **CE**↵
Specify center point of arc: *<pick the center point*
Specify start point of arc: *<pick the start point>*
Specify end point of arc or [Angle/chord Length]: *<pick the end point>*
Command:

Drawing Arcs Using the Angle Options

AutoCAD LT lets you draw arcs using a combination of the start point, end point, center, and included angle. The included angle specifies degrees in a counterclockwise direction. A negative angle can be used to draw the arc in a clockwise direction. An ***included angle*** is the angle formed between the start point, end point, and center of the arc as shown in Figure 3.20. These options are found in the Draw pull-down menu as Start, Center, Angle; Start, End, Angle; and Center, Start, Angle.

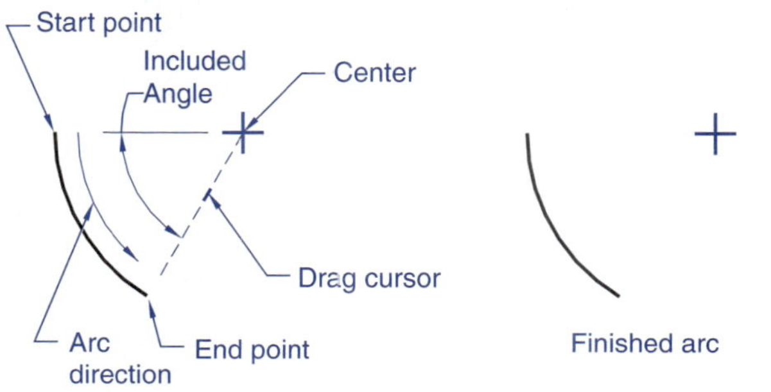

FIGURE 3.20 Drawing arcs using the Included Angle option.

When you select the desired option from the Draw pull-down menu, AutoCAD LT automatically issues the prompts based on the option chosen. This is an example of the prompts and responses when using the Start, Center, Angle option:

Command: _arc Specify start point of arc or [CEnter]: *<pick start point>*
Specify second point of arc or [CEnter/ENd]: _c Specify center point of arc: *<pick center point>*
Specify end point of arc or [Angle/chord Length]: _a Specify included angle: *<specify an angle>*
Command:

If you want to enter the ARC command using the Angle option at the keyboard, just enter **A** at the prompt. For example, use the Center, Start, Angle option like this:

Command: **A** or **ARC**↵
Specify start point of arc or [CEnter]: **CE**↵
Specify center point of arc: *<pick center point>*
Specify start point of arc: *<pick start point>*
Specify end point of arc or [Angle/chord Length]: **A**↵
Specify included angle: 60 *<or another desired angle value>*
Command:

Drawing Arcs Using the Length of Chord Option

A chord is defined as a line that connects two points on a curve. AutoCAD LT allows the definition of an arc based on the start point, center point, and the length of the chord. If the specified chord length is positive, the minor arc is drawn counterclockwise from the start point. If the length is negative the major arc is drawn counterclockwise. Figure 3.21 illustrates the creation of an arc using this method. The prompt sequence is shown here:

Command: **A** or **ARC**↵
Specify start point of arc or [CEnter]: *<pick start point>*
Specify second point of arc or [CEnter/ENd]: **CE**↵
Specify center point of arc: *<pick center point>*
Specify end point of arc or [Angle/chord Length]: **L**↵
Specify length of chord: **1.5**↵
Command:

FIGURE 3.21 Drawing arcs using the Length of Chord option.

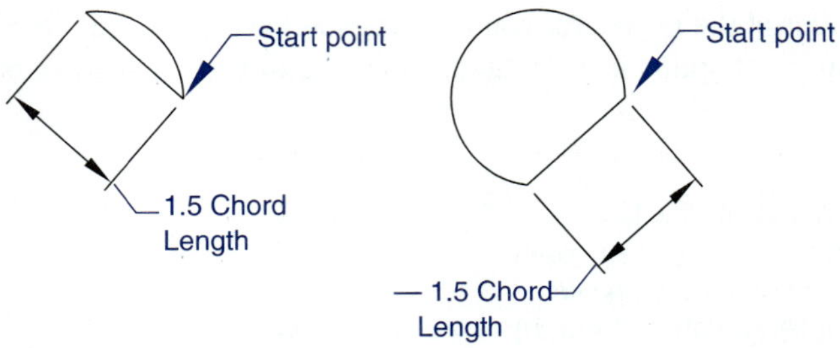

Drawing Arcs Using the Radius Option

The Radius option is used with the start and end points specified to define an arc. When a positive radius value is used, the minor arc is drawn. If the radius entry is negative, the major arc is drawn. Figure 3.22 illustrates the use of this option. The prompt sequence is as follows:

> Command: **A** or **ARC**↵
> Specify start point of arc or [CEnter]: *<pick start point>*
> Specify second point of arc or [CEnter/ENd]: **EN**↵
> Specify end point of arc: *<pick end point>*
> Specify center point of arc or [Angle/Direction/Radius]: **R**↵
> Specify radius of arc: **1**↵
> Command:

FIGURE 3.22 Drawing arcs using the Radius option.

Drawing Arcs Using the Direction Option

Using the Direction option, you can specify the direction of travel for an arc at its start point based on a specified start and end point. Because this option allows you to specify the direction of travel for the arc from its start point, it may not always be drawn counterclockwise. Figure 3.23 shows this option in use. The prompt sequence looks like this:

> Command: **A** or **ARC**↵
> Specify start point of arc or [CEnter]: *<pick start point>*
> Specify second point of arc or [CEnter/ENd]: **EN**↵
> Specify end point of arc: *<pick end point>*
> Specify center point of arc or [Angle/Direction/Radius]: **D**↵
> Specify tangent direction for the start point of arc: **45**↵
> Command:

FIGURE 3.23 Drawing arcs using the Direction option.

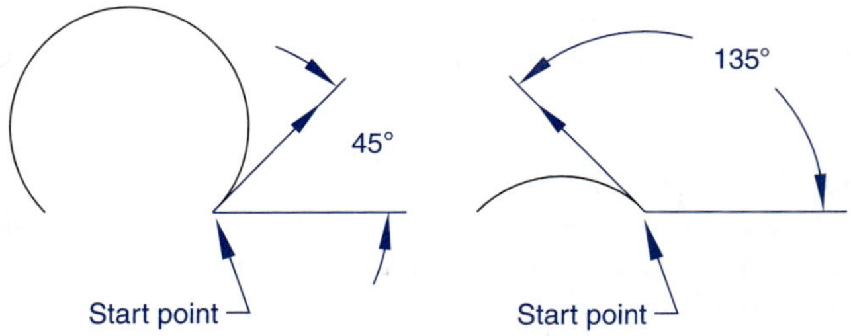

Drawing an Arc Tangent from a Previously Drawn Line or Arc

It is easy to draw an arc tangent to the end of a previously drawn line or arc. To do this, enter the ARC command immediately after drawing the line or arc that you plan to connect. After entering the ARC command, at the first prompt, press the Enter key or the space bar. Doing this automatically makes the end point of the previously drawn line or arc the start point of the new arc as shown in Figure 3.24. You can also use the Draw pull-down menu by selecting Arc followed by Continue. The command sequence looks like this:

> Command: **A** or **ARC**↵
> Specify start point of arc or [CEnter]: ↵
> Specify end point of arc: *<pick end point>*
> Command:

You can connect a series of tangent arcs by continuing this process until all of the desired arcs have been connected.

FIGURE 3.24 Drawing arcs continued from previous lines or arcs.

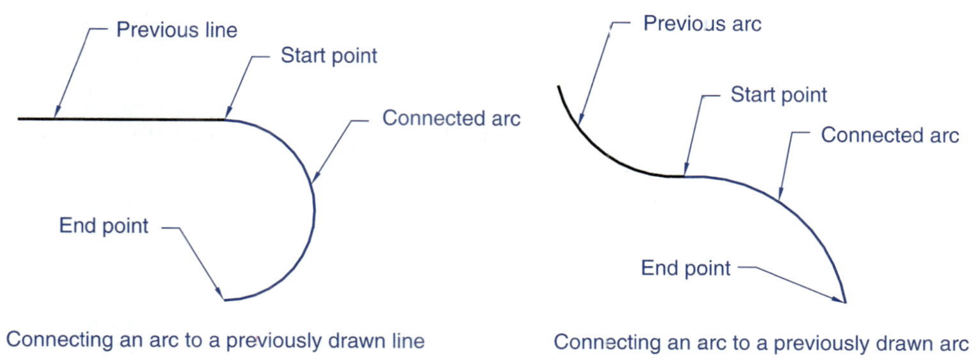

Field Notes

You can also draw a line tangent from a previously drawn arc (or connected to the previous line) by using the Continue option previously described. To do this, draw a desired arc and then enter the LINE command. Press the Enter key or space bar at the From point: prompt like this:

> Command: **L** or **LINE**↵
> Specify first point: ↵
> Length of line: *<enter desired length—angle is already established>*
> Specify next point or [Undo]: ↵
> Command:

Exercise 3.5 **Estimated time required: 5 min.**

1. Open AutoCAD LT if it is not already open. Use the setup option of your choice. A border and title block are not required.
2. Set limits at 8.5,11.
3. Draw the objects shown using the ARC command options specified. The exact sizes are up to you.

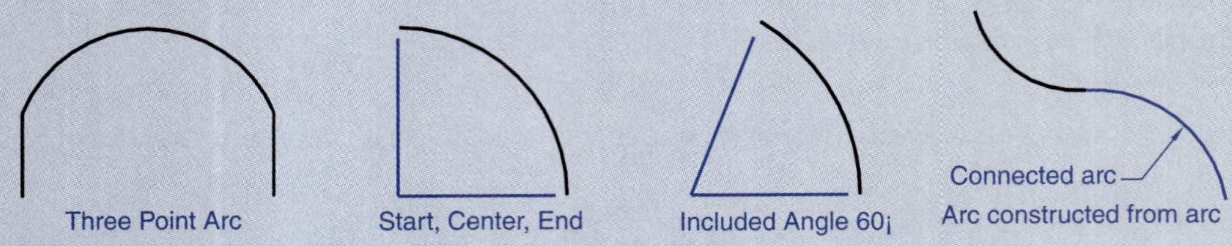

4. Use the following command entries to draw a slot that has a .5" radius and measures 2.5" from center to center:

Command: **ARC**↵
Specify start point of arc or [CEnter]: *<pick start point for first arc>*
Specify second point of arc or [CEnter/ENd]: **EN**↵
Specify end point of arc: **@1<90**↵
Specify center point of arc or [Angle/Direction/Radius]: **R**↵
Specify radius of arc: **.5**↵
Command: **LINE**↵
Specify first point: ↵
Length of line: **2.5**↵
Specify next point or [Undo]: ↵
Command: **ARC**↵
Specify start point of arc or [CEnter]:↵
Specify end point of arc: **@1<270**↵
Command: **LINE**↵
Specify first point: ↵
Length of line: **2.5**↵
Specify next point or [Undo]:↵
Command:

5. Now, draw a slot using this same method that has a .25" radius and measures 1.75" from center to center.
6. Save as EX3.5, and close the drawing.

Drawing Ellipses

Draw

Ellipse

Draw
Ellipse ▸

ELLIPSE
EL

An ***ellipse*** is commonly referred to as an oval, but the technical definition is an object that is drawn by a curve that has a constant value equal to the sum of its distance from two fixed points. One of the primary uses of an ellipse is for showing a circle on an inclined surface. The length of an ellipse is called the ***major axis*** and the width is the ***minor axis.*** The parts of an ellipse are shown in Figure 3.25. AutoCAD LT allows you to draw an ellipse by establishing the length of the major and minor axes, by selecting the center and the axial lengths, or by providing the length of an axis and a rotation angle. You can also draw an elliptical arc.

Drawing an Ellipse with the Axis End Points Option

You can draw an ellipse by establishing the axis end points. To do this select Ellipse and then Axis, End from the Draw pull-down menu, pick the Ellipse button on the Draw toolbar, or type **EL** or **ELLIPSE** at the Command:prompt. AutoCAD LT asks you for the first axis end points and then requests a distance from the center to the end of the other axis as shown in Figure 3.26. This is the command sequence:

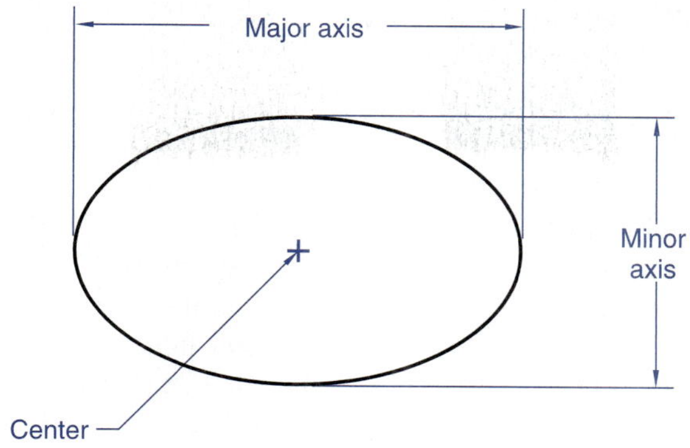

FIGURE 3.25 The parts of an ellipse.

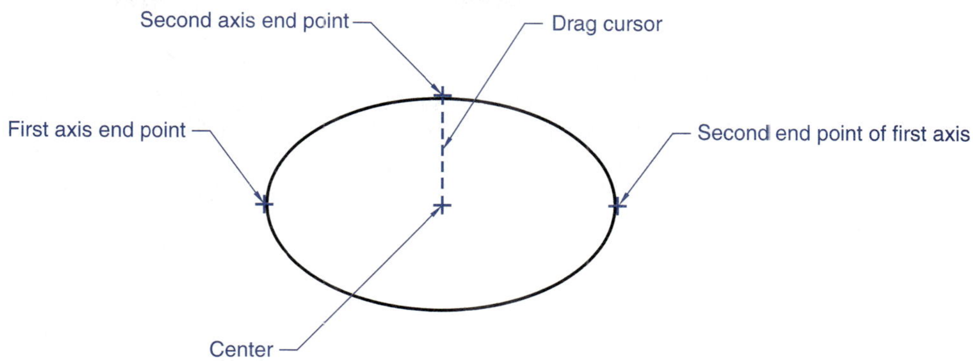

FIGURE 3.26 Drawing an ellipse using the Axis, End point option.

Command: **EL** or **ELLIPSE**↵
Specify axis endpoint of ellipse or [Arc/Center]: *<pick the first axis endpoint>*
Specify other endpoint of axis: *<pick the second axis endpoint>*
Specify distance to other axis or [Rotation]: *<pick the endpoint of the second axis or type a distance from the center to the axis endpoint>*
Command:

Drawing an Ellipse with the Center Option

You can automatically begin drawing an ellipse by picking the center if you choose Ellipse and then Center in the Draw pull-down menu. AutoCAD LT first asks you to select the center point followed by the distance to the first axis end point and then the distance to the end of the second axis. The command sequence looks like this, and the result is shown in Figure 3.27.

Command: _ellipse
Specify axis endpoint of ellipse or [Arc/Center]: _c
Specify center of ellipse: *<pick the center of the ellipse>*
Specify endpoint of axis: *<pick the first axis endpoint>*
Specify distance to other axis or [Rotation]: *<pick or type the distance to the second axis endpoint>*
Command:

If you use the keyboard to enter the ELLIPSE command, you need to enter **C** at the following prompt to use the Center option:

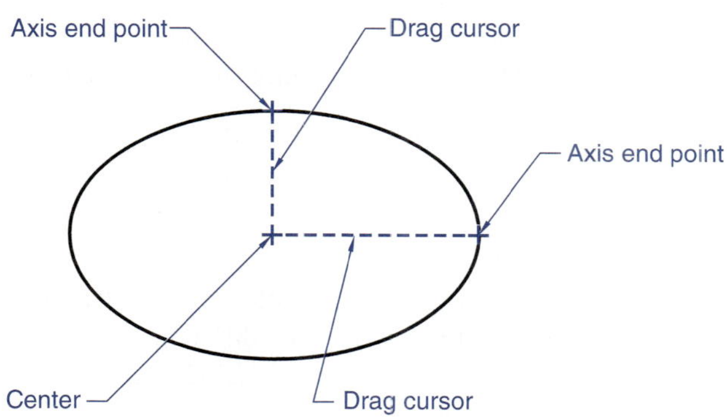

FIGURE 3.27 Drawing an ellipse using the Center option.

Command: **EL** or **ELLIPSE**↵
Specify axis endpoint of ellipse or [Arc/Center]: **C**↵

The command continues as previously shown.

Drawing an Ellipse by Using the Rotation Angle

You can draw an ellipse by typing or picking a desired rotation angle. You can visualize this by holding a coin. The coin looks like a circle when you look at the flat surface. Then, as you rotate the coin, it begins to look like an ellipse. The more you rotate the coin, the flatter it gets. The amount that you rotate the coin is the rotation angle. AutoCAD LT allows you to enter a rotation angle from 0 to 89.4°. A rotation angle of 0 creates a circle, whereas 89.4 is nearly a straight line. Figure 3.28 shows ellipses drawn using a variety of rotation angles. The ELLIPSE command may be accessed by any of the previously described means. The Rotation option is then accessed at the keyboard by typing **R** and then an exact rotation angle is usually typed for the best accuracy, like this:

Command: **EL** or **ELLIPSE**↵
Specify axis endpoint of ellipse or [Arc/Center]: *<pick the first axis endpoint>*
Specify other endpoint of axis: *<pick the second endpoint of the first axis>*
Specify distance to other axis or [Rotation]: **R**↵
Specify rotation around major axis: **60**↵ *<or any desired rotation angle>*
Command:

FIGURE 3.28 Various ellipse rotation angles.

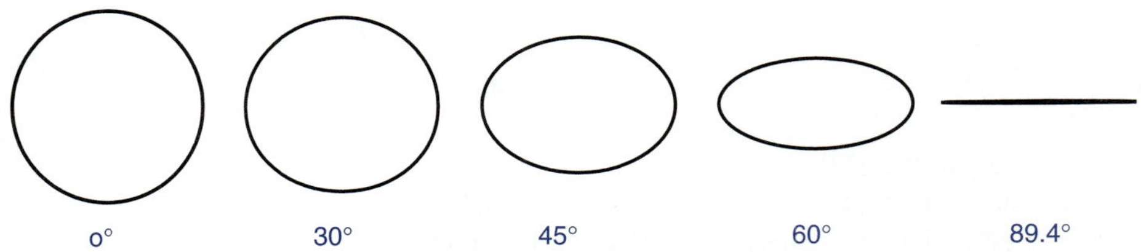

Drawing Elliptical Arcs

An elliptical arc is part of a full ellipse. An elliptical arc is drawn by accessing Ellipse and then Arc in the Draw pull-down menu or by entering the ELLIPSE command and then typing **A** to get the Arc option at the keyboard. Elliptical arcs are created by first defining an ellipse using one of the methods previously explained. Look at Figure 3.29A. You then have three options for creating the arc. You can select the start and end angles of the arc, the start angle and the included angle, or the arc parameters.

Drawing an Elliptical Arc with the Start and End Angles

The elliptical arc default asks you for a start and end angle. The start and end angles are measured from the first end point of the first axis. You can either pick desired angles or type a specific angle value at the keyboard. The angles are measured in a counterclockwise direction by default as shown in Figure 3.29B. The command looks like this when entered at the keyboard (see Figure 3.29):

Command: **EL** or **ELLIPSE**↵
Specify axis endpoint of ellipse or [Arc/Center]: **A**↵
Specify axis endpoint of elliptical arc or [Center]: *<pick first axis endpoint>*
Specify other endpoint of axis: *<pick the second endpoint of the first axis>*
Specify distance to other axis or [Rotation]: *<pick the second axis endpoint>*
Specify start angle or [Parameter]: **90**↵ *<this angle is measured from the first axis, with angle 0 being at the first axis endpoint specified>*
Specify end angle or [Parameter/Included angle]: **270**↵ *<this angle is also measured from the first axis>*
Command:

Field Notes

An elliptical arc is affected by the direction and base for angular measure. Elliptical arcs are still drawn counterclockwise, but the input angles are different.

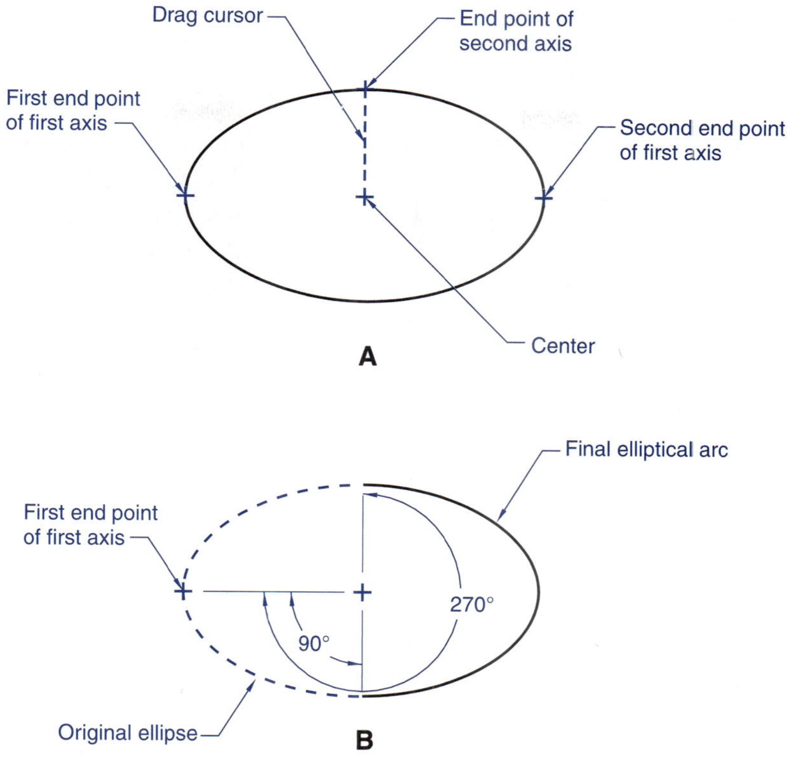

FIGURE 3.29 Drawing an elliptical arc using the Start and End Angle option.

Drawing an Elliptical Arc Using the Included Angles

An elliptical arc can also be drawn by entering a start angle followed by an included angle. The included angle is measured from the start angle as shown in Figure 3.30. After the initial ellipse is drawn, the prompts continue like this:

> Specify start angle or [Parameter]: **90↵**
> Specify end angle or [Parameter/Included angle]: **I↵**
> Specify included angle for arc <180>: **270↵**
> Command:

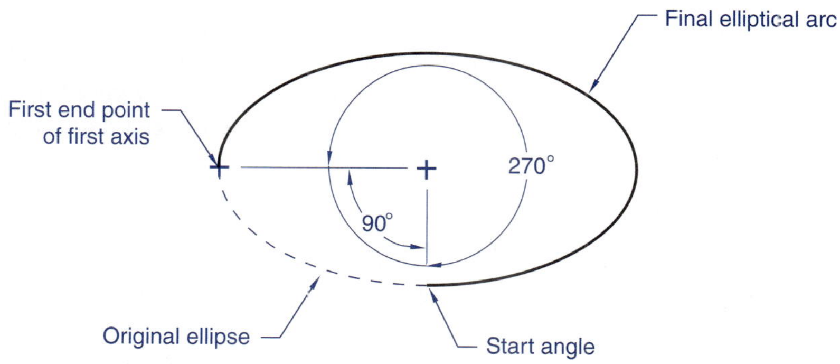

FIGURE 3.30 Drawing an elliptical angle using the Included Angle option.

Drawing an Elliptical Arc Using Parameters

The Parameter option uses the same basic input as the Start angle/End angle option but calculates the arc based on a parametric vector equation. The equation is $p(u) = c + a^* \cos(u) + b^* \sin(u)$, where c is the center of the ellipse, a is the major axis, and b is the minor axis. Some applications of this option may produce the same results as the angle specifications, whereas other applications may produce slightly different results.

Exercise 3.6 — **Estimated time required: 10 min.**

1. Open AutoCAD LT if it is not already open. Use the setup option of your choice. A border and title block are not required. Dimensions and notes are not needed.
2. Set limits at 8.5,11.
3. Draw an ellipse similar to the following:
   - Figure 3.28 with the Axis and End point option.
   - Figure 3.29 with the Center option.
   - Figure 3.30 with the Rotation option.
4. Draw elliptical arcs similar to the following:
   - Figure 3.31 with the Start and End Angle option.
   - Figure 3.32 with the Included Angle option.
5. Save as EX3.6, and close the drawing.

LEARNING CHECKPOINT

- ☐ Describe at least four ways to draw a circle.
- ☐ How do you make a circle tangent to two objects?
- ☐ What is the shortest way to enter the CIRCLE command at the keyboard?
- ☐ Identify at least three ways to draw an arc.
- ☐ How do you draw an arc from a previously drawn line or arc?
- ☐ Describe at least three ways to draw an ellipse.
- ☐ What is the difference between the Start and End Angle methods when compared with the Included Angle option for drawing elliptical arcs?
- ☐ How do you draw an elliptical arc with the Parameter option?

Creating Geometry

- Creating Arcs and Circles

Drawing Polygons

A ***polygon*** is a planar geometric object with three or more sides. ***Regular polygons*** have equal length sides. AutoCAD LT lets you easily draw any regular polygon with between 3 and 1024 equal-length sides. AutoCAD LT can also create rectangles. ***Rectangles*** are geometric figures with four sides and four right (90°) angles.

Drawing Polygons Based on a Circle

Draw

Draw
Polygon

POLYGON
POL

The POLYGON command is accessed by typing **POL** or **POLYGON** at the Command: prompt, by picking the Polygon toolbar button, or by picking Polygon from the Draw pull-down menu. You are asked for the number of sides and a center point for placement of the polygon, which is the center point for the imaginary circle AutoCAD LT uses in defining a polygon. The next prompt asks if the polygon is to be *inscribed in circle or circumscribed about circle.* Inscribed means *drawn inside,* and circumscribed means *drawn around.* Your choice depends on how you are defining the polygon.

If you know the distance across the flats of the polygon, enter a **C** for circumscribed about circle. This means that a regular polygon with the specified number of sides will be drawn around the circle you define. Note that a circle is not actually drawn; rather, its definition is used to create the polygon. The following sequence draws a six-sided figure (hexagon) that measures 2 units across the flats:

Command: **POL** or **POLYGON**↵
Enter number of sides <4>: **6**↵
Specify center of polygon or [Edge]: **4,4**↵
Enter an option [Inscribed in circle/Circumscribed about circle] <I>: **C**↵
Specify radius of circle: **1**↵
Command:

Notice that the radius is specified as 1 unit. This is because the radius is half the distance across the circle being used to define the polygon. The result of this command sequence is illustrated in Figure 3.31. Notice that the polygon is drawn around the defining circle.

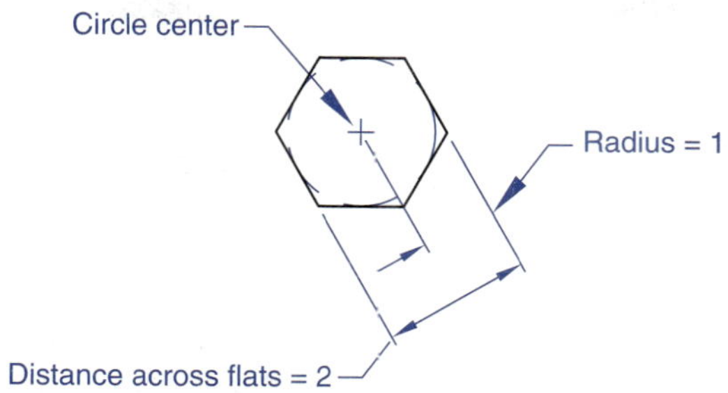

FIGURE 3.31 Using the *circumscribed* option defines a polygon by the distance across its flats.

If you are creating a polygon based on the distance across its points, you must use the Inscribed option. The following sequence creates the polygon shown in Figure 3.32, which is defined as being 2 units across its points.

Command: **POL** or **POLYGON**↵
Enter number of sides <6>: ↵
Specify center of polygon or [Edge]: **4,4**↵
Enter an option [Inscribed in circle/Circumscribed about circle] <C>: **I**↵
Specify radius of circle: **1**↵
Command:

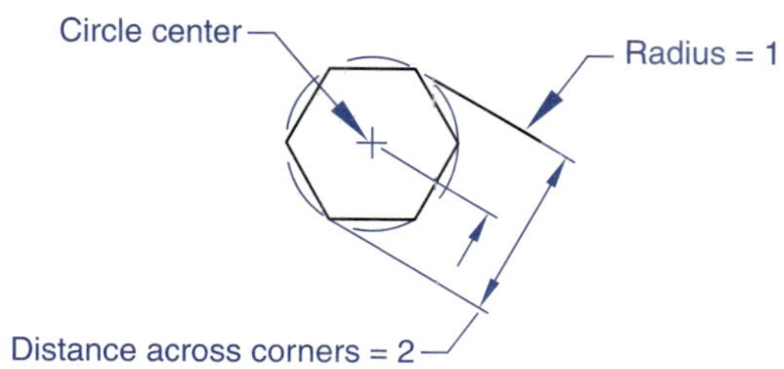

FIGURE 3.32 Using the *Inscribed* option defines a polygon by the distance across its points.

Drawing a Polygon Using the Edge Option

In some situations, you may know the length of the polygon edges. AutoCAD LT lets you use this information to easily draw the desired polygon. Figure 3.33 shows how to draw a hexagon with the Edge option. Use the Edge option by typing **E** at the prompt line to draw an octagon (a regular polygon with eight sides):

Command: **POL** or **POLYGON**↵
Enter number of sides <6>: **8**↵
Specify center of polygon or [Edge]: **E**↵
Specify first endpoint of edge: *<pick start point of edge>*
Specify second endpoint of edge: *<pick endpoint of edge>*
Command:

FIGURE 3.33 Drawing a regular polygon (octagon) using the Edge option.

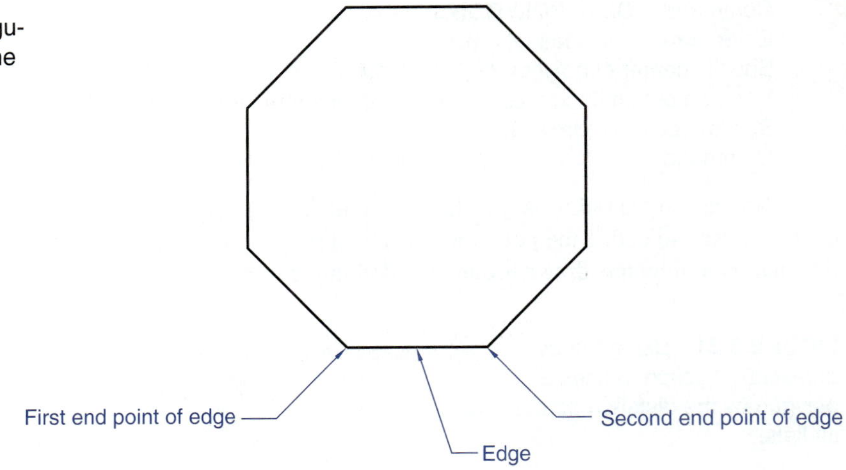

Drawing Rectangles

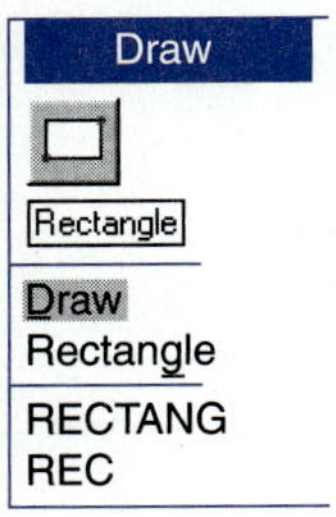

Rectangles can be drawn by picking Rectangle from the Draw pull-down menu, picking the Rectangle toolbar button, or typing **REC** or **RECTANG** at the Command: prompt. AutoCAD LT asks you to select the first corner of the rectangle. The cursor then turns into a rectangle as you drag to the right or left. Pick the opposite corner of the rectangle when the desired shape is established as shown in Figure 3.34. The command works like this:

Command: **REC** or **RECTANGLE**↵
Specify first corner point or [Chamfer/Elevation/Fillet/Thickness/Width]: *<pick first corner>*
Specify other corner point: *<pick opposite corner>*
Command:

FIGURE 3.34 Drawing a rectangle using the RECTANG command.

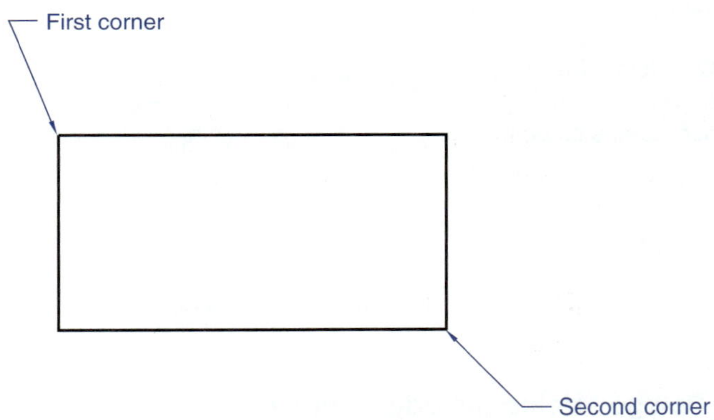

Field Notes

An easy way to draw an accurately sized rectangle is to specify the first corner as you would normally, then enter a relative coordinate at the Other corner: prompt. For example, if you wanted to create a rectangle that was 6 units wide and 4 units tall, the command sequence would look like this:

Command: _rectang
Chamfer/Elevation/Fillet/Thickness/Width/⟨First corner⟩**:** *⟨pick first corner⟩*
Other corner: **@6,4**↵

Notice in addition to the default <First corner> prompt, the RECTANG command has several other options:

Specify first corner point or [Chamfer/Elevation/Fillet/Thickness/Width]:

These other options are explained in the following:

- Chamfer: This option allows you to draw a rectangle with angled corners. The word ***chamfer*** comes from mechanical drafting and manufacturing as a reference to angled corners on an object, but chamfers on a rectangle can be used in any drafting field to make angled corners on a rectangular object. When you enter **C** to get the Chamfer option, AutoCAD LT asks you for the chamfer distances. The first chamfer distance you type is automatically set for the second chamfer distance. You can accept the second chamfer distance by pressing Enter or you can type another value. Equal chamfer distances make 45° corners on the rectangle, as shown in Figure 3.35A. This is the command sequence used to draw Figure 3.35A:

Command: **REC** or **RECTANGLE**↵
Specify first corner point or [Chamfer/Elevation/Fillet/Thickness/Width]: **C**↵
Specify first chamfer distance for rectangles <0.0000>: **.25**↵
Specify second chamfer distance for rectangles <0.2500>: ↵
Specify first corner point or [Chamfer/Elevation/Fillet/Thickness/Width]: *<pick first corner>*
Specify other corner point: *<pick opposite corner>*
Command:

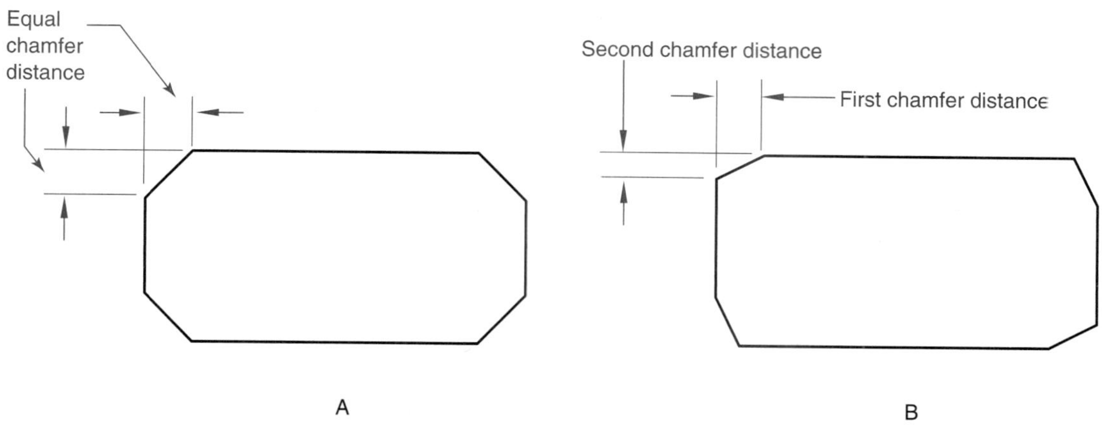

FIGURE 3.35 (A) A rectangle drawn with equal chamfer distances. (B) A rectangle drawn with different chamfer distances.

When you start AutoCAD LT, the initial default chamfer distance is 0.0000, which draws square corners. When you set a chamfer distance, such as .25, it remains in effect until changed. Figure 3.35B shows different chamfer distances drawn on a rectangle using these prompts:

Command: **REC** or **RECTANGLE**↵
Specify first corner point or [Chamfer/Elevation/Fillet/Thickness/Width]: **C**↵
Specify first chamfer distance for rectangles <0.0000>: **.25**↵
Specify second chamfer distance for rectangles <0.2500>: **.125**↵
Specify first corner point or [Chamfer/Elevation/Fillet/Thickness/Width]: *<pick first corner>*
Specify other corner point: *<pick opposite corner>*
Command:

Any settings that have been made to the rectangle modes are displayed above the prompt. For example, after the previous sequence, using the CHAMFER command displays the following:

Command: **REC** or **RECTANGLE**↵
Current rectangle modes: Chamfer=0.2500 x 0.1250
Specify first corner point or [Chamfer/Elevation/Fillet/Thickness/Width]:

- Elevation: This option allows you to enter a value for the Z coordinate location when drawing in 3-D. 3-D drafting with AutoCAD LT is covered in Chapter 14.
- Fillet: This option allows you to draw a rectangle with round corners. The word ***fillet*** comes from mechanical drafting and manufacturing as a reference to inside curved corners on an object, but fillets in AutoCAD LT can be inside or outside round corners. Fillets on a rectangle can be used in any drafting field to make arced corners on a rectangular object. When you enter **F** to get the Fillet option, AutoCAD LT asks you for the fillet radius. When you start AutoCAD LT, the initial default Fil-

let radius is 0.0000, which draws square corners. When you set a Fillet radius, such as .25, it remains in effect for chamfers and fillets until changed. A previously set Chamfer distance also becomes the default Fillet radius. Figure 3.36 shows fillets drawn on a rectangle using these prompts:

Command: **REC** or **RECTANGLE**↵
Specify first corner point or [Chamfer/Elevation/Fillet/Thickness/Width]: **F**↵
Specify fillet radius for rectangles <0.0000>: **.25**↵
Specify first corner point or [Chamfer/Elevation/Fillet/Thickness/Width]:
Specify other corner point:

FIGURE 3.36 Using the RECTANG command's fillet option to draw rounded corners on a rectangle.

- Thickness: This option is also use in AutoCAD LT 3-D applications. The thickness controls Z axis dimensions. See Chapter 14.
- Width: By default, the line used to create your rectangles has a width of zero. This option allows you to set a specific pen width for the line. Figure 3.37 shows a 6 × 4 rectangle with a .5 radius fillet and a line width of .125.

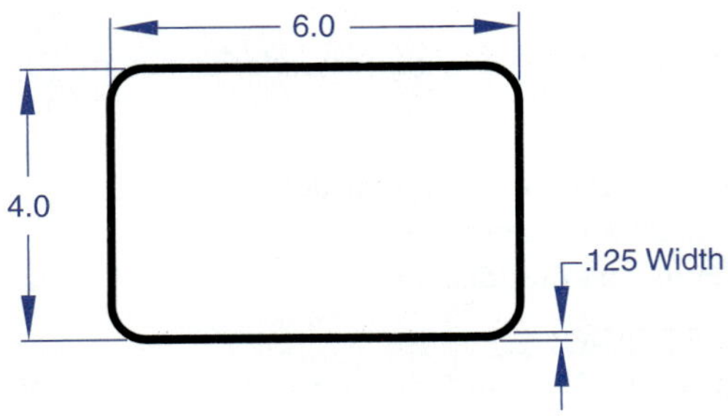

FIGURE 3.37 The Width option allows you to set a pen width for the lines of a rectangle.

Field Notes

- AutoCAD LT remembers the settings specified for the last rectangle you created and defaults to the same values. Even if you exit the current drawing and start a new drawing, the settings default to those used in the last rectangle you created.
- If you try to draw a rectangle and instead get a large, filled area on your screen, chances are that your width setting is too big for the size of rectangle you are drawing.

Exercise 3.7 — **Estimated time required: 8 min.**

1. Open AutoCAD LT if it is not already open. Use the setup option of your choice. A border and title block are not required. The placement of the objects is up to you.
2. Set limits at 8.5,11.
3. Draw the following regular polygons, each circumscribed around a .5-in. radius:
   - Square
   - Pentagon (five sides)
   - Hexagon
   - Octagon
4. Draw a hexagon with a horizontal edge measuring 1 in.
5. Draw a rectangle that is 4 in. (horizontal) × 2 in.
6. Save as EX3.7, and close the drawing.

Drawing Filled Objects

AutoCAD LT provides you with commands that can be used to create a variety of filled shapes. Filled circles, rings, and square or rectangular shapes are common, but other more creative shapes are possible. These shapes may be used for certain drafting practices such as the creation of symbols or used in a graphic design for custom artwork. The DONUT command is used for filled circular objects and SOLID for shapes that can be defined by a pattern of triangles. In Chapter 10, you will learn how to fill any closed shape or object with a solid pattern.

Drawing Donuts

Draw

Donut

Draw
Donut

DOUGHNUT
DONUT
DO

AutoCAD LT refers to filled circles and rings as *doughnuts,* or ***donuts*** for short, and they are drawn with the DONUT command. The DONUT command is found in the Draw pull-down menu by picking Donut, picking the Donut button in the Draw toolbar, or typing **DO** or **DONUT** or **DOUGHNUT** at the Command: prompt. The DONUT command asks you to create a solid ring or circle by giving the inside diameter and the outside diameter followed by the center point. Figure 3.38 shows the parts of a donut and donuts drawn with different specifications. The command continues to ask you to select the center of additional donuts. You can draw as many donuts as you wish and press Enter when finished:

Command: **DO** or **DONUT**
Specify inside diameter of donut <0.5000>: **.75**
Specify outside diameter of donut <1.0000>: **1.5**
Specify center of donut or <exit>: *<pick the center of the first donut>*
Specify center of donut or <exit>: *<pick the center of the next donut>*
Specify center of donut or <exit>:
Command:

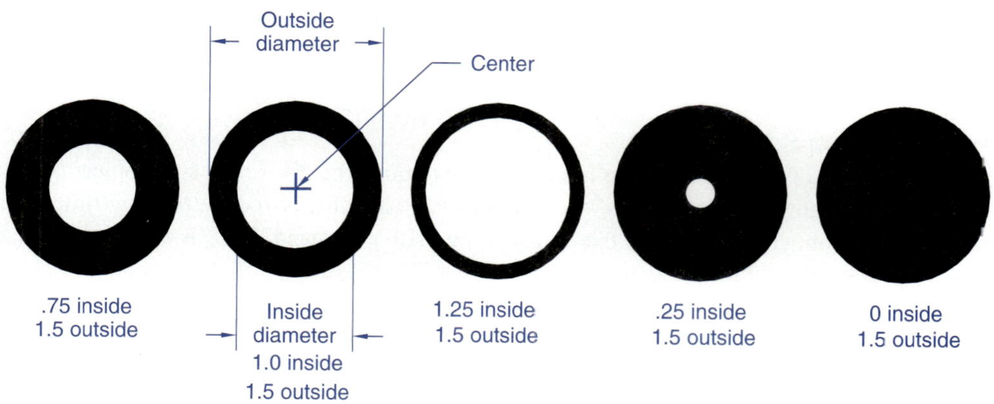

FIGURE 3.38 A variety of donuts with different specifications and the parts of a donut. Notice the solid circle at the right is a donut with 0 (zero) inside diameter.

Field Notes

A solid circle is a donut with a 0 (zero) inside diameter as shown in Figure 3.38. The original AutoCAD LT donut defaults are 0.50 inside diameter and 1.00 outside diameter. The previously set inside and outside diameters are given in brackets. These default values remain the same in the current drawing session until you change them.

Drawing Solids

SOLID
SO

A variety of filled objects can be drawn using the SOLID command. This command is accessed by typing **SO** or **SOLID** at the Command: prompt. When you enter the SOLID command, AutoCAD LT asks you to pick up to four points. If you pick three points and press Enter, you get a solid triangle as shown in Figure 3.39A. Press Enter again to exit the command. If you pick four points, you get a shape that varies depending on the order and position of the points. If you want a solid square or rectangle, you need to pick the corners in an order similar to the example in Figure 3.39B. Notice the object and order of points shown in Figure 3.39C. After picking four points, AutoCAD LT asks you to pick another third point and then another fourth point. You can press Enter at any time to end the point requests or keep picking points to create an infinite number of possibilities. Figure 3.39D shows an example of an object drawn by picking additional third and fourth points. This is the command sequence used to draw the object shown in Figure 3.39D:

Command: **SO** or **SOLID**↵
Specify first point: *<pick first point>*
Specify second point: *<pick second point>*
Specify third point: *<pick third point>*
Specify fourth point or <exit>: *<pick fourth point>*
Specify third point: *<pick fifth point>*
Specify fourth point or <exit>: *<pick sixth point>*
Specify third point: ↵
Command:

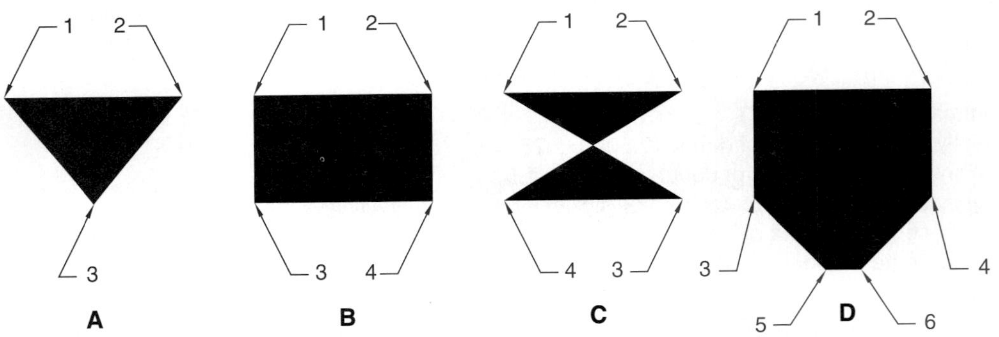

FIGURE 3.39 A variety of solid filled objects using the SOLID command. The numbers in the examples are the order in which points were picked.

Removing the Fill from Solid Objects

There may be a number of reasons why you might want to remove the fill from a solid object or donut. Removing the fill may create a desired design, speed up display changes, or reduce plotting time for a check plot. Whatever the reason, you can remove the fill using the FILL command. FILL is either on or off. FILL is on by default, but you can turn it off like this:

Command: **FILL**
Enter mode [ON/OFF] <ON>: **OFF**↵
Command:

If you have a solid filled object on the screen, turning FILL off does not automatically remove the fill from the object. Before you can see the difference, you need to update the drawing's screen display. AutoCAD LT refers to this as ***regenerating.*** You can regenerate the screen by using the REGEN command:

Command: **RE** or **REGEN**
Regenerating model.
Command:

AutoCAD LT gives you the message "Regenerating drawing" and automatically returns the Command: prompt. If you want to turn FILL back on, enter the FILL command, use the On option, and then use the REGEN command to update the screen display. Figure 3.40 shows the same objects that were in Figures 3.38 and 3.39 with the FILL turned off.

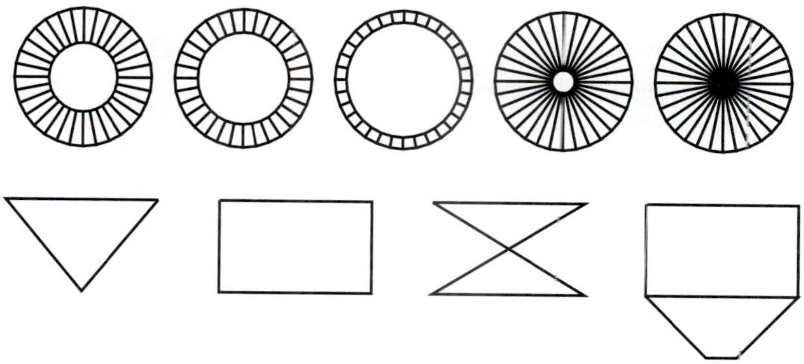

FIGURE 3.40 The same donuts and solids shown in Figures 3.38 and 3.39 with FILL turned off.

Exercise 3.8

Estimated time required: 10 min.

1. Open AutoCAD LT if it is not already open. Use the setup option of your choice. A border and title block are not required. The placement of the objects is up to you.
2. Set limits at 8.5,11.
3. Draw the donuts shown in Figure 3.38.
4. Draw solid shapes similar to those shown in Figure 3.39.
5. Turn the FILL off and then use the REGEN command. Notice the difference.
6. Turn the FILL back on and then use the REGEN command. Notice the difference again.
7. Save as EX3.8, and close the drawing.

LEARNING CHECKPOINT

- ☐ Identify two ways to draw regular polygons.
- ☐ Name the command used to draw rectangles.
- ☐ What command is used to draw filled rings?
- ☐ How do you draw a filled circle?
- ☐ Make a sketch of a filled rectangle with the corners numbered so as to identify the order in which points were picked.
- ☐ Explain what happens to solid filled objects when you turn FILL off.
- ☐ What is the purpose of the REGEN command with regard to turning FILL off and on?

MULTIPLE CHOICE

Circle the choice or enter your response on an answer sheet by selecting the option that most closely completes or answers the given statements.

1. The Advanced Setup Wizard does not set up this drawing feature:
- **a.** units style
- **b.** precision
- **c.** angle measurement
- **d.** drawing name

2. When using AutoCAD LT, you work on your drawing in what view?
- **a.** layout
- **b.** paper space
- **c.** model space
- **d.** title block

3. A drawing file with preestablished settings:
- **a.** prototype
- **b.** settings
- **c.** format
- **d.** layout

4. After drawing a circle, you can automatically enter the CIRCLE command again by:
- **a.** pressing the space bar
- **b.** pressing the Enter key
- **c.** either a or b
- **d.** neither a nor b

5. Do this to automatically make the endpoint of the previously drawn line or arc the start point of the new arc:
- **a.** press the space bar
- **b.** press the Enter key
- **c.** either a or b
- **d.** neither a nor b

6. AutoCAD LT does not ask for this information when creating a polygon:
- **a.** center of polygon
- **b.** radius of circle
- **c.** number of sides
- **d.** none of the above

7. Filled circles and rings are drawn with AutoCAD LT by using this command:
- **a.** DOUGHNUTS
- **b.** FILL
- **c.** SOLID
- **d.** DONUT

8. A variety of filled objects may be drawn using this command:
- **a.** SOLIDS
- **b.** FILL
- **c.** SOLID
- **d.** DONUT

9. This command allows you to set or change the size of the drawing area at any time during your drawing session:
- **a.** LIMIT
- **b.** LIMITS
- **c.** FORMAT
- **d.** UNITS

10. This command allows you to change the drawing units in the Units Control dialog box:
- **a.** UNITS
- **b.** UNIT
- **c.** DUNIT
- **d.** DDUNIT

MATCHING

Match each term to the correct description by writing the appropriate number in each box at the left.

- ☐ Bearing
- ☐ Counterclockwise
- ☐ Diameter
- ☐ Donut
- ☐ Enter
- ☐ Major
- ☐ Minor
- ☐ Polygon
- ☐ Template
- ☐ Radius
- ☐ Rectangle
- ☐ Solid
- ☐ Surveyor
- ☐ Tangent

1. These angles are measured using bearings.
2. This term refers to the angle of a line with its direction in respect to one of the quadrants of a compass.
3. The AutoCAD LT default has angles measured in this direction beginning at 0° East.
4. Using one of these to begin a drawing saves time.
5. This is the distance from the center to the circumference of the circle.
6. When you are finished drawing an object, you can press this or the space bar at the Command: prompt to get the same command again.
7. This is the distance across the circle passing through the center.
8. This means that the circle touches an object at only one point without intersecting or crossing the object.
9. The length of an ellipse is along this axis.
10. The width of an ellipse is along this axis.
11. A hexagon is drawn using this command.
12. This is drawn by picking the first corner and then moving the cursor to pick the other corner.
13. AutoCAD LT refers to filled circles and rings as this.
14. A filled rectangular shape may be drawn using this command.

WORD SCRAMBLE

Unscramble the seven scrambled words below, one letter to each square, to form seven AutoCAD LT–related words:

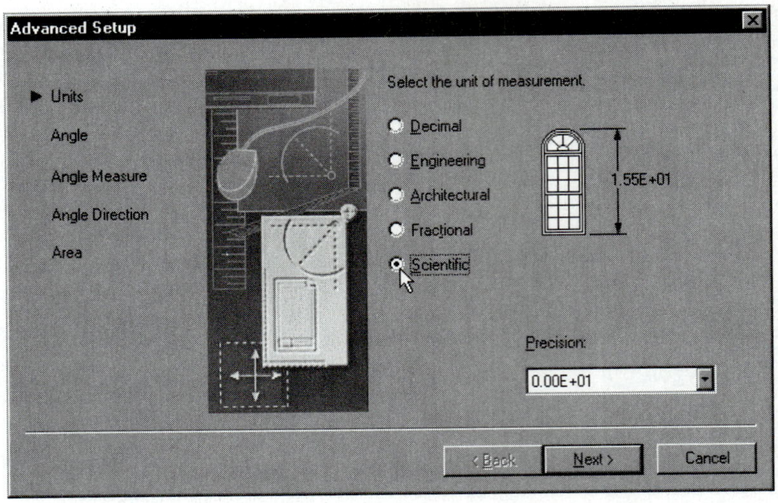

GRABINE

LICERC

PLESILE

CICELSOWK

TODNU

LOSDI

FINALTROAC

Unscramble the circled letters above to form the special answer, as suggested by the illustration.

PROJECTS

3.1 Porch Light

Design a porch light with features, sizes, and proportions similar to the one shown below. Save as P3.1.

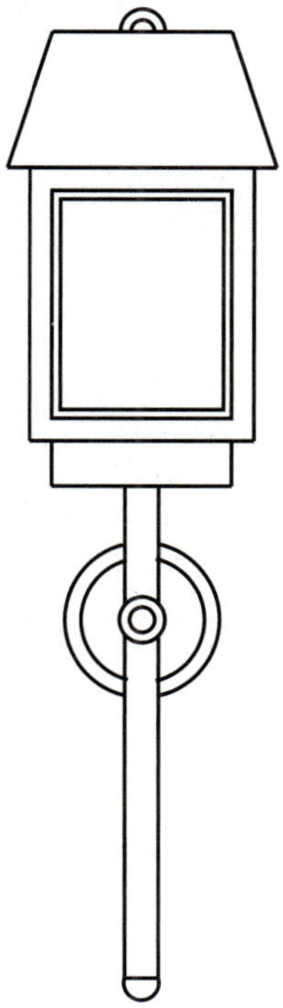

3.2 Duplex Convenience Outlet

Open P2.6 and make the changes shown below. Do not draw dimensions. Save as P3.2.

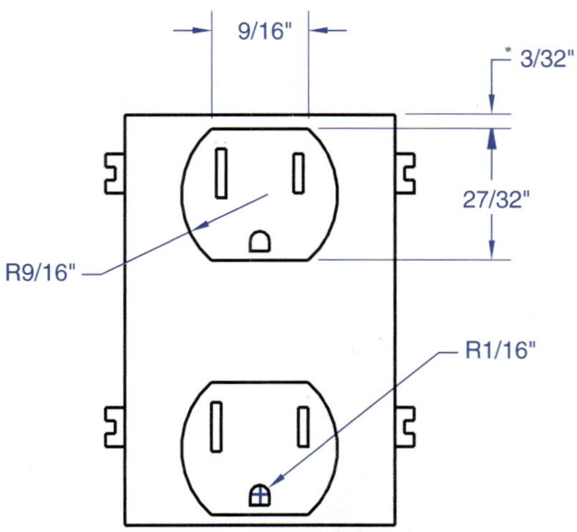

3.3 Clock
Open P2.7 and add the circles and ellipse shown below. Do not draw dimensions. Save as P3.3.

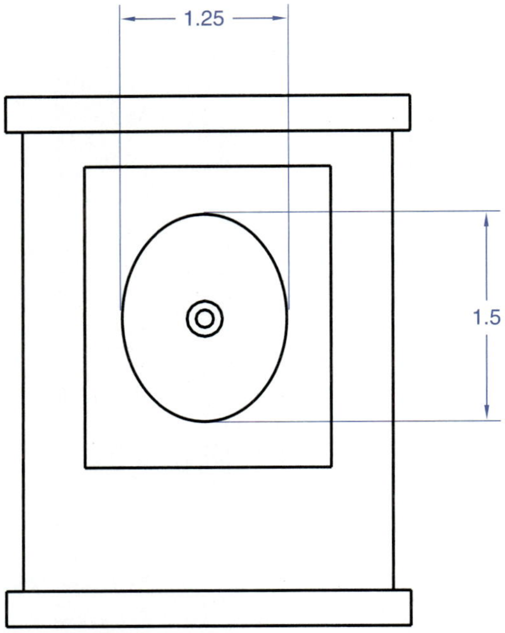

3.4 Cover Plate
Draw the object shown below without center lines or dimensions. Save as P3.4.

INCH

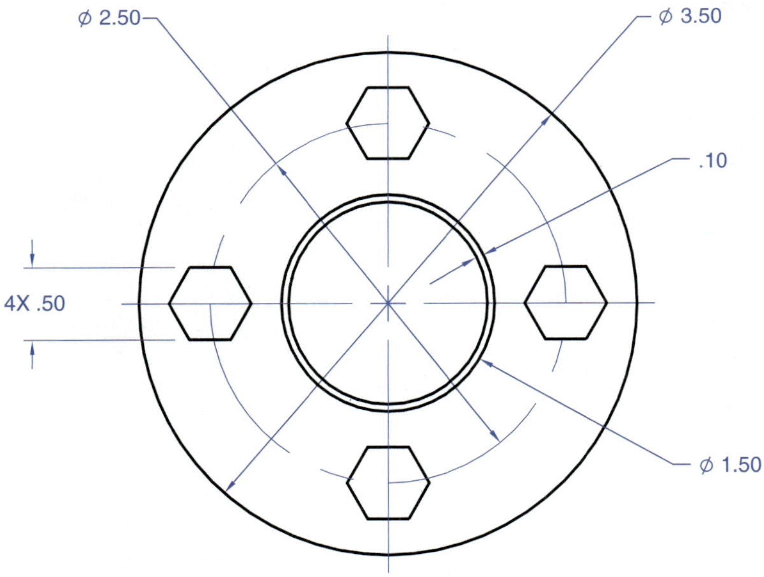

3.5 Cover Plate

Draw the object shown below without center lines or dimensions. Save as P3.5.

METRIC

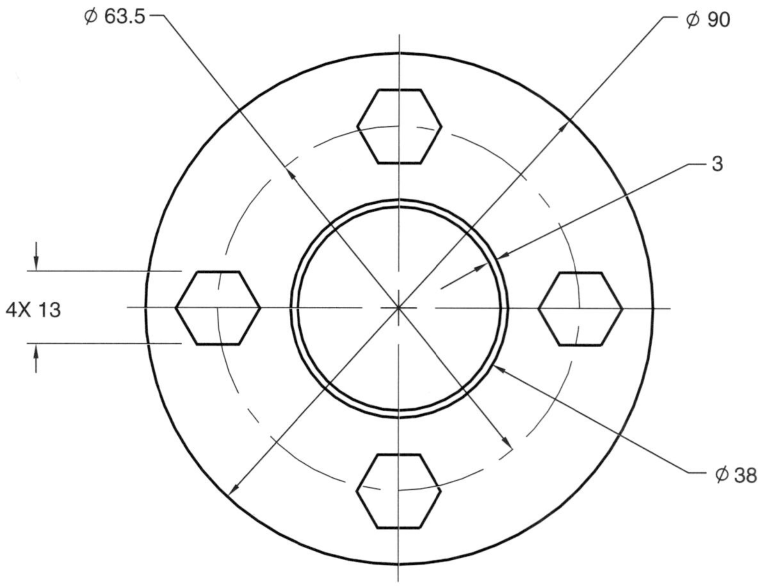

3.6 Gasket

Draw the object shown below without center lines or dimensions. Save as P3.6.

INCH

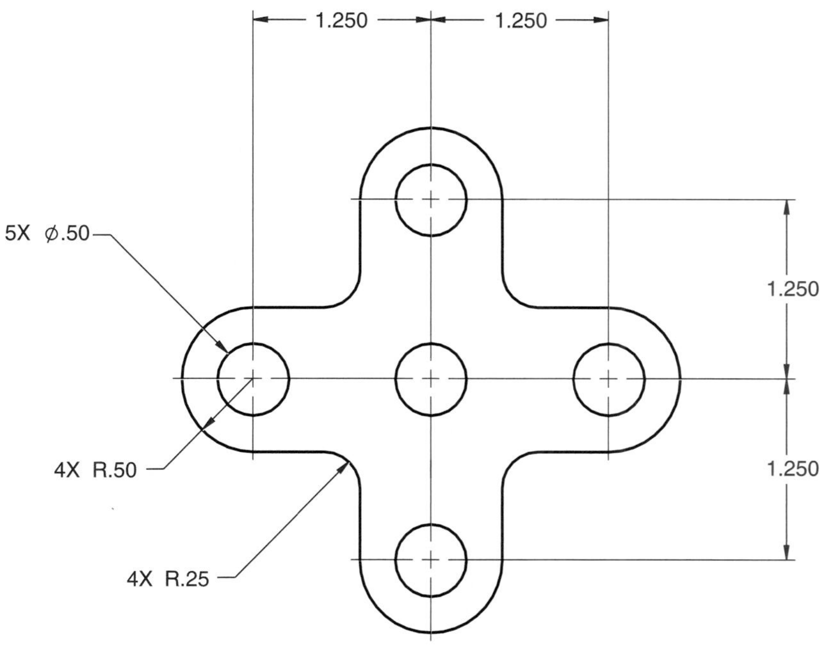

METRIC

3.7 Gasket

Draw the object shown below without center lines or dimensions. Save as P3.7.

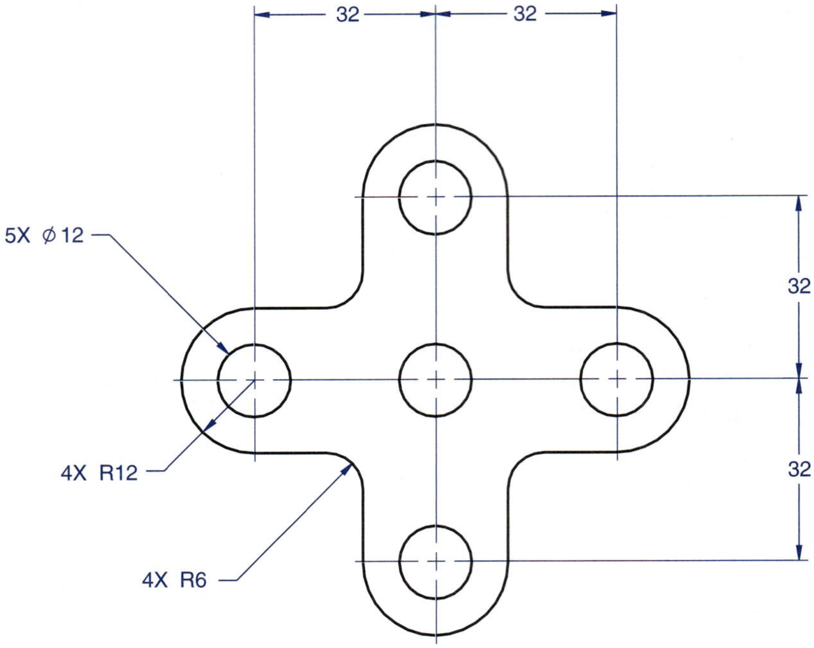

3.8 Gazebo

Draw a floor plan of the gazebo shown below. Draw the 8X Ø4″ POSTS as circles. Do not draw dimensions or notes. Save as P3.8. (Drawing courtesy of Mike W. Hehr.)

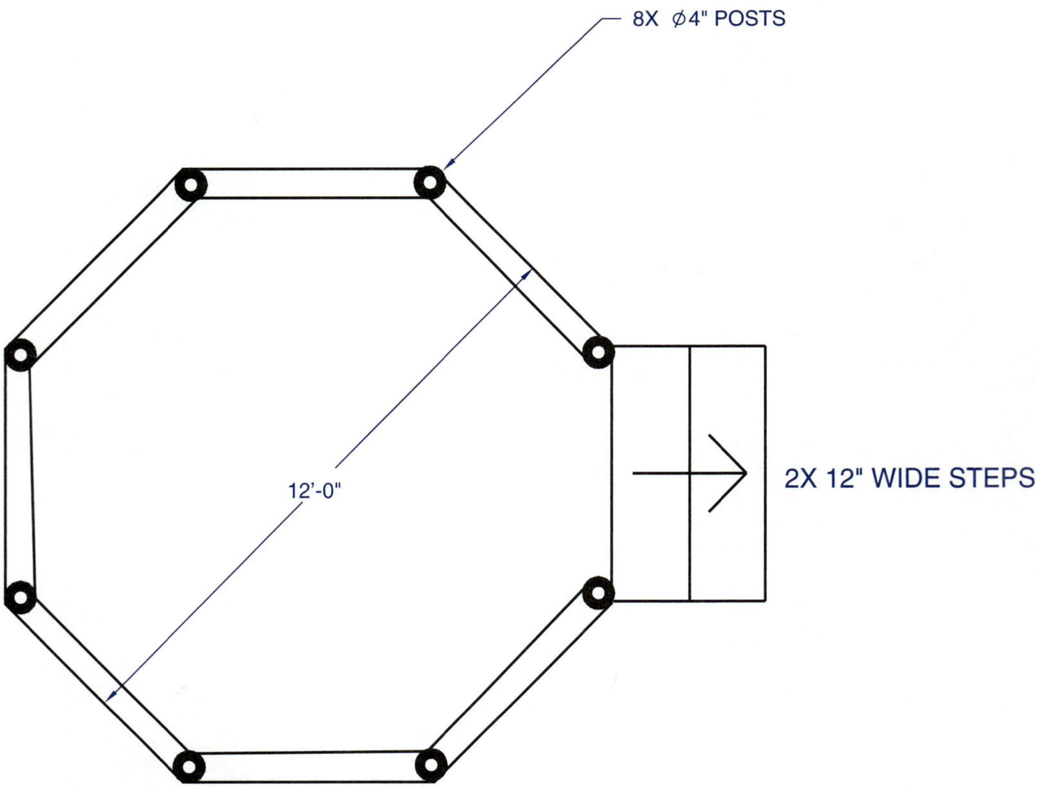

3.9 Clothes Dryer Circuit
Draw the schematic shown below. Do not draw dimensions or notes. Save as P3.9.

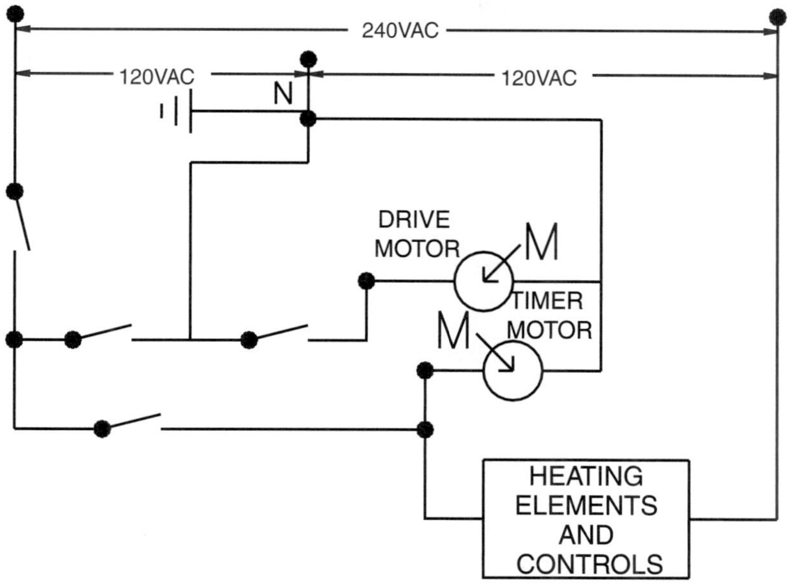

CLOTHES DRYER CIRCUIT

3.10 Piping Symbols
Draw the piping symbols shown below. Save as P3.10.

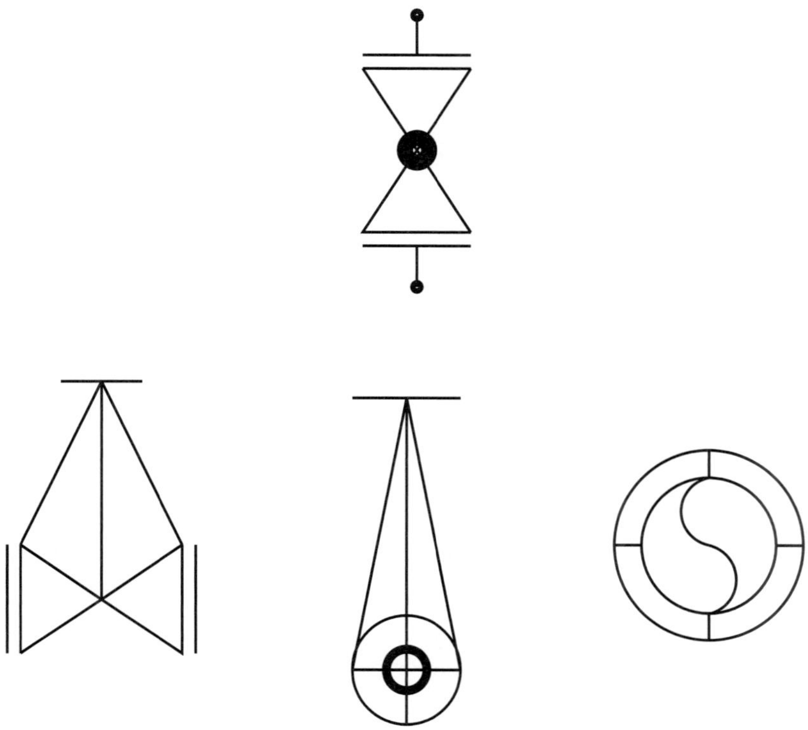

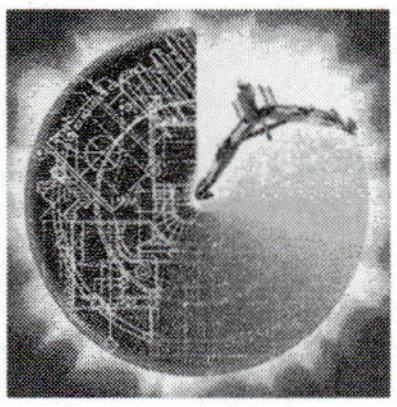

CHAPTER 4

Drawing Display Control

LEARNING GOALS

- Change the display area to magnify small details or reduce large areas.
- Display any area of the drawing on your screen.
- Use the Aerial View window to change the display area.
- Optimize display settings and options to speed your work.
- Create and manage named viewing areas in your drawing.

Changing Your View of the Drawing

Your computer monitor provides a small area in which you can display a drawing. An average 17-in. monitor actually provides a drawing area that is about 12 in. wide by 8 in. high, depending on your screen resolution and window arrangement. Unless your drawing layout is for an $8\frac{1}{2} \times 11$-in. sheet you cannot view the entire drawing at full size. Your CAD drawings may often have smaller details that are difficult or even impossible to see without changing the drawing display area.

AutoCAD LT provides a number of tools for changing the drawing display. Many of these display tools work in the same manner as a camera. With a camera, to ***zoom*** is to change the apparent size of the objects you are viewing. Changing the area that is displayed does not change the actual size of the objects, it merely changes the way in which you view them—this is the same for AutoCAD LT. To view something that appears small on your display, you *zoom in;* to increase the area displayed by shrinking the apparent size of the objects, you *zoom out.* Also similar to a camera, to view something outside of the current viewing area without changing the apparent size of the objects displayed, you can pan up, down, left, or right. The term ***pan*** indicates changing the location of the view without changing the magnification. If you think of your drawing display control as being like a camera, it makes the display change tools much easier to master. This first section covers the options for the ZOOM and PAN commands.

Using the ZOOM Command Options

ZOOM
Z

The ZOOM command has several different options to help you view any area of the drawing you need to see at virtually any magnification level. Entering the ZOOM command manually displays each of these options in the Command Window and allows you to specify the option you want to use:

> Command: **Z** or **ZOOM**↵
> Specify corner of window, enter a scale factor (nX or nXP), or
> [All/Center/Dynamic/Extents/Previous/Scale/Window] <real time>: *<enter an option>*

You can type the full command name if desired, but it is quicker and easier to use the shorter command alias (keyboard shortcut) by typing **Z**↵ instead. The option listing for any command presents the required entry in uppercase, meaning that most options can be accessed by typing only the first letter. Even so, the pull-down menu and toolbar button selections can be easier to use for some of the zooming options because of the automated command line input. The available zooming tools are explained in the following subsections.

Using the Zoom In Option

Zoom

Zoom In

View
Zoom ▶
In

A direct way to double the apparent size of the objects on the screen is to use the Zoom In option. You can pick the toolbar button from the Zoom flyout found on the Standard toolbar or pick the In option from the Zoom cascade on the View pull-down menu. If you look closely at the command line when using this option, you will notice that a 'ZOOM command is automatically entered by AutoCAD LT, followed by a 2X option. This is one way to use the Zoom Scale option. Entered at the keyboard, the command sequence looks like this:

> Command: **Z** or **ZOOM**↵
> Specify corner of window, enter a scale factor (nX or nXP), or
> [All/Center/Dynamic/Extents/Previous/Scale/Window] <real time>: **2X**↵

The scale option allows you to change the zoom factor relative to the current display. For example, the 2X (or 2 times) option zooms in closer to the drawing so that the objects appear twice (or two times) as large as they were (see Figure 4.1A). Notice that the center of the view remains the same. This is like adjusting your camera zoom lens to zoom in without moving the camera.

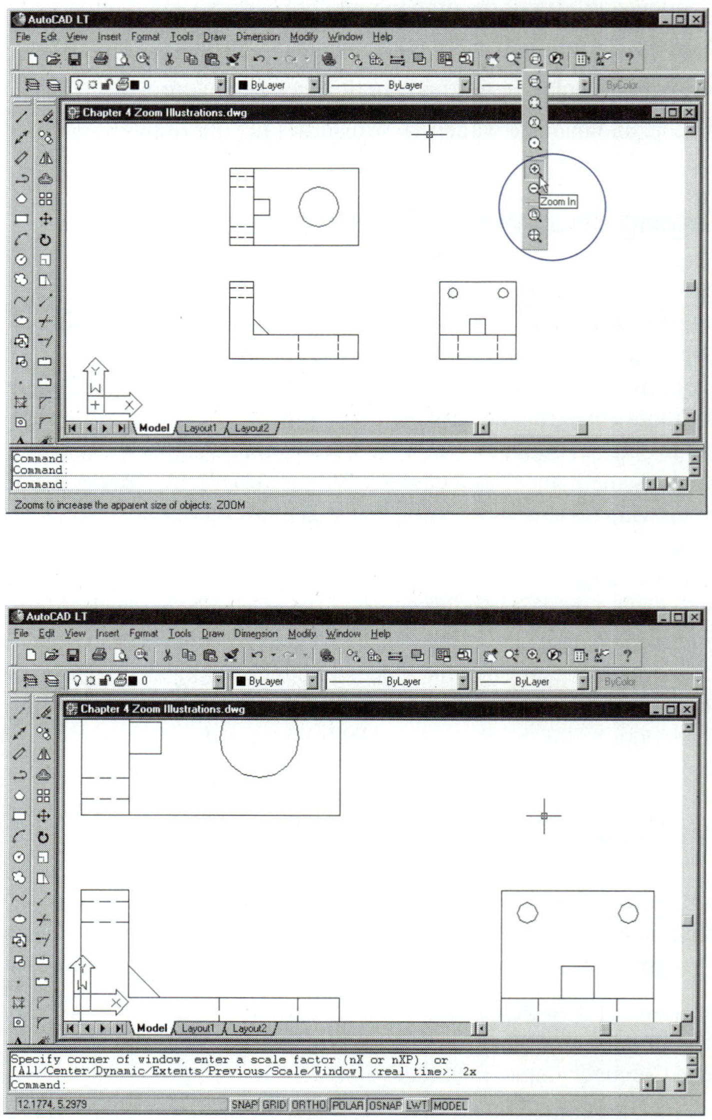

A

FIGURE 4.1 (A) Zoom 2X makes the objects on screen appear twice (2×) as large. (B) Zoom .5X makes the objects on screen appear half (0.5×) as large.

FIGURE 4.1 (continued)

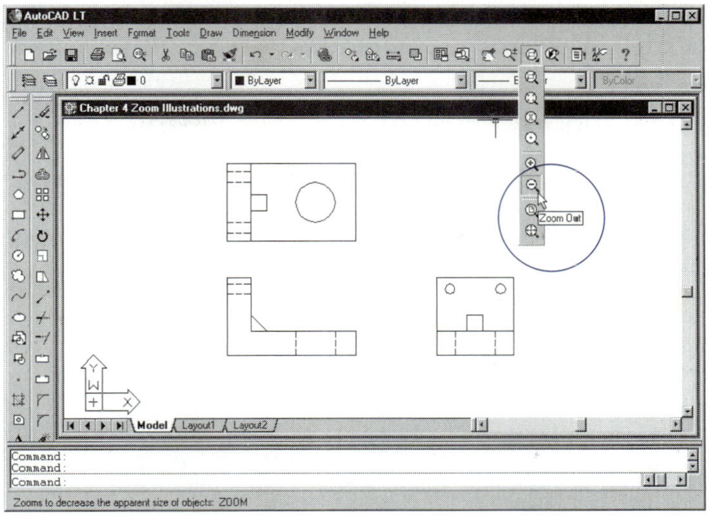

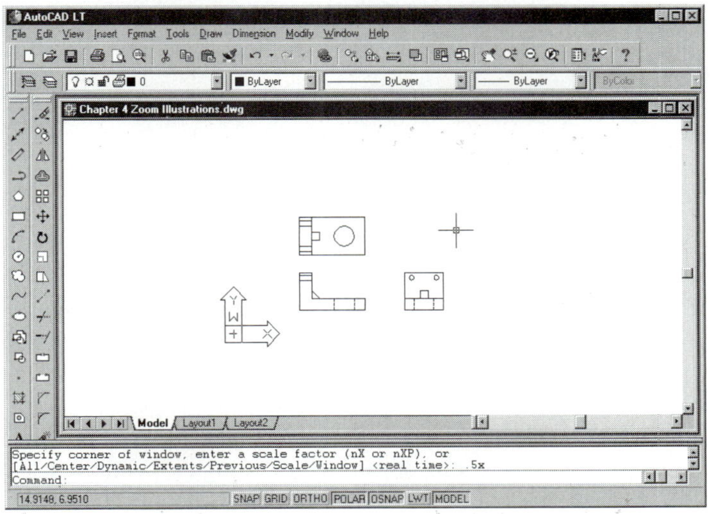

B

Using the Zoom Out Tool

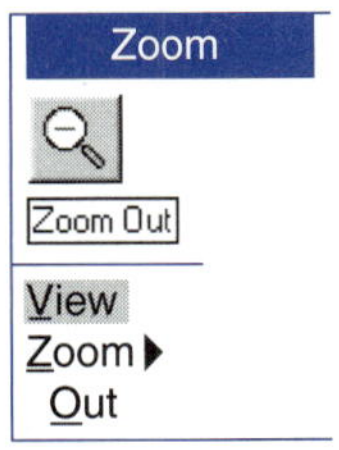

The Zoom Out tool is used to reduce the apparent size of the drawing to half its current size. Pick the Zoom Out button from the Zoom flyout on the Standard toolbar or select Out from the Zoom cascade on the View pull-down menu. This option changes the display so that the objects on screen appear to be one-half (0.5X) the size they appear in the current display (see Figure 4.1B). At the command line, the option is used like this:

> Command: **Z** or **ZOOM**↵
> Specify corner of window, enter a scale factor (nX or nXP), or
> [All/Center/Dynamic/Extents/Previous/Scale/Window] <real time>: **.5X**↵

Using the Zoom Scale Tool

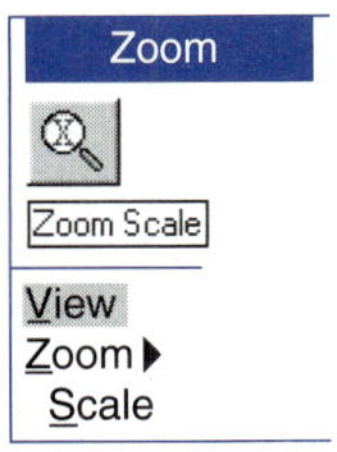

The Zoom Scale tool allows greater flexibility than the Zoom In and Zoom Out tools. You can pick the Zoom Scale tool from the Zoom flyout found on the Standard toolbar, or you can pick Scale from the Zoom cascade on the View menu.

The Zoom Scale tool activates the same Zoom command option used by Zoom In and Zoom Out, but prompts you to enter a zoom scale value. You can specify any number followed by an **X** (or **x**). This number serves as a multiplier for the apparent size of objects on the screen. The Zoom In tool, discussed earlier, automatically specifies a 2X value to double the apparent size of the objects. The Zoom Out tool automatically specifies .5X to decrease the apparent size of objects to one-half that of the current display. The Zoom Scale tool allows you to specify any desired magnification value using the keyboard.

To reduce the apparent size of the objects in the current view using this option, specify a decimal number greater than zero and less than one. For example, to reduce the zoom factor to one-fourth of the current view, enter **.25X** as the scale value:

> Command: **Z** or **ZOOM**↵
> Specify corner of window, enter a scale factor (nX or nXP), or
> [All/Center/Dynamic/Extents/Previous/Scale/Window] <real time>: **.25X**↵

If you want to get closer to your work, specify a number greater than one. For example, to increase the apparent size of the objects on screen by four times, use a 4X option:

> Command: **Z** or **ZOOM**↵
> Specify corner of window, enter a scale factor (nX or nXP), or
> [All/Center/Dynamic/Extents/Previous/Scale/Window] <real time>: **4X**↵

Exercise 4.1 — **Estimated time required: 5 min.**

1. Open a drawing from one of the exercises in Chapter 3.
2. Use the Zoom In and Zoom Out tools to enlarge and reduce the view size.
3. Use the Zoom Scale tool to try values that enlarge the display and then enter values to reduce the magnification.
4. Return the drawing to the original view and save it as EX4.1, then close the drawing.

Using the Zoom Window Tool

Zoom
Zoom Window
View
Zoom ▸
Window

The Zoom Window tool is probably one of the most commonly used zooming options in AutoCAD LT. While the Zoom Scale tool can be used to zoom in or out incrementally, the fact that it keeps the center of the screen the same can be limiting when the feature you want to see closer is not at the center of the current view.

You can select the Zoom Window tool from the Zoom flyout on the Standard toolbar, pick Window from the Zoom cascade on the View menu, or enter the ZOOM command from the keyboard and specify the Window option.

When Zoom Window is selected, you are then prompted to select the First corner and the Other corner. This is similar to when you are selecting objects to edit using the Window selection mode:

> Command: **Z** or **ZOOM**↵
> Specify corner of window, enter a scale factor (nX or nXP), or
> [All/Center/Dynamic/Extents/Previous/Scale/Window] <real time>: **W**↵
> Specify first corner: *<pick first corner>*
> Specify opposite corner: *<pick second corner>*
> Command:

The window you draw at the First corner: and Other corner: prompts can be of any ratio of height to width, but the resulting view change is displayed at the same proportion as the drawing area. This is because the shape of the drawing area in the AutoCAD LT window cannot change to match the shape of the window you draw. The new display shows *all the area contained in the window you define, centered on the screen.* Study the Zoom Window operations shown in Figures 4.2, 4.3, and 4.4 and compare the resulting display.

At the ZOOM command prompt line, it is not necessary to press **W**↵ to start the Window option. Instead, at the prompt, simply pick the first point with your cursor. It is understood that you are using the Window option, and AutoCAD LT then prompts you for the other corner of the window.

Using the Zoom All Tool

Zoom
Zoom All
View
Zoom ▸
All

The Zoom All tool lets you see the entire drawing. This tool zooms to display the limits of your drawing on the screen. If you have drawn objects outside of the limits, the view is expanded to include these objects as well. You can select Zoom All from the Zoom flyout on the Standard toolbar, pick All from the Zoom cascade of the View menu, or you can type it at the Command: prompt:

> Command: **Z** or **ZOOM**↵
> Specify corner of window, enter a scale factor (nX or nXP), or
> [All/Center/Dynamic/Extents/Previous/Scale/Window] <real time>: **A**↵
> Command:

FIGURE 4.2 (A) The top view of the part fills the window specified for the zoom operation.
(B) The resulting display shows everything that was in the window, centered in the display.

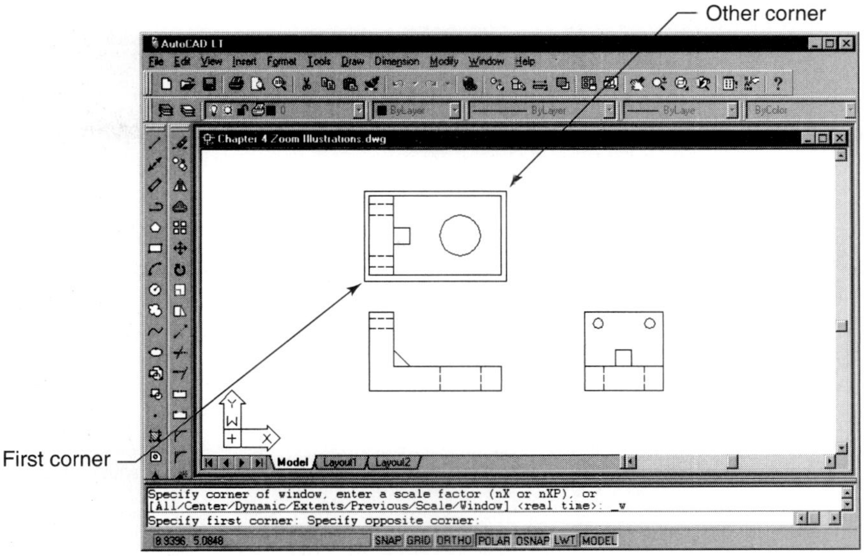

A

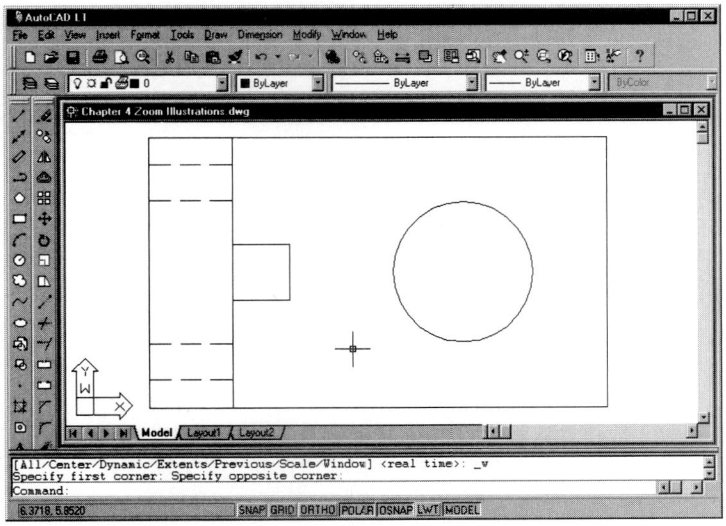

B

FIGURE 4.3 (A) The window picked is as wide as the part, but very short vertically. (B) The resulting display shows all that was windowed centered on the screen.

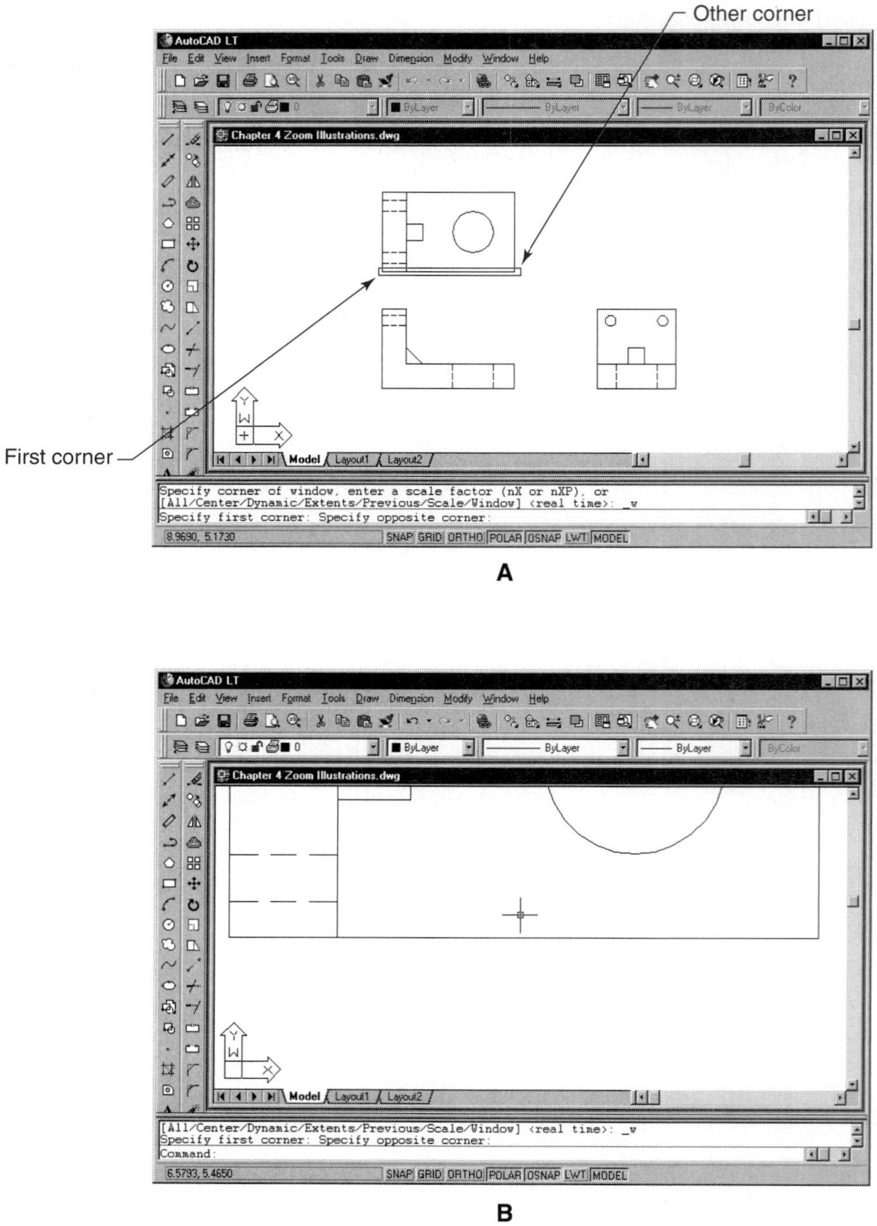

FIGURE 4.4 (A) The window picked is as tall as the part, but very short horizontally. (B) The resulting display shows the windowed area centered on the screen.

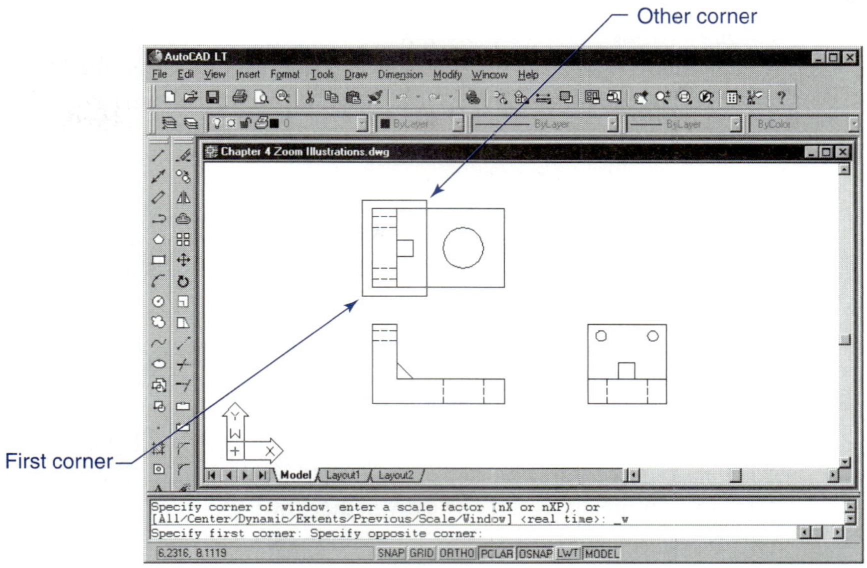

A

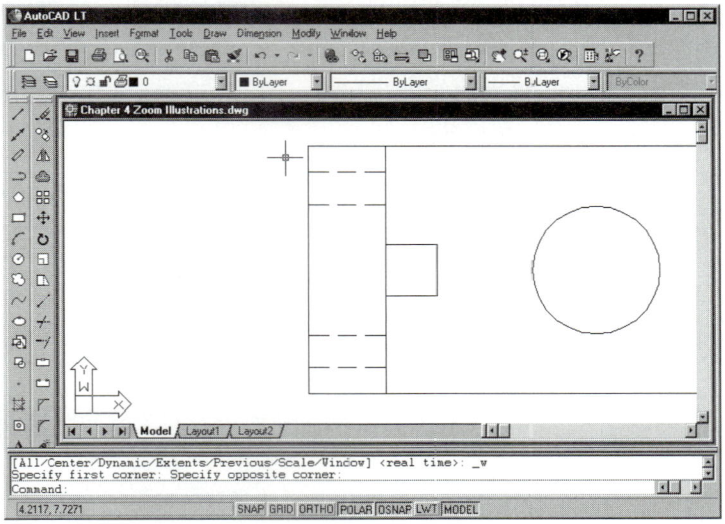

B

Using the Zoom Extents Tool

The Zoom Extents tool displays all of the objects in your drawing on screen at once, centered on the screen. The objects are shown as large as possible while still displaying all of the objects. Zoom Extents can be selected from the Zoom flyout on the Standard toolbar or you can pick Extents from the Zoom cascade of the View menu or type it:

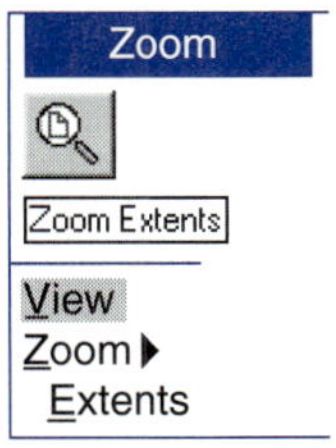

Command: **Z** or **ZOOM**↵
Specify corner of window, enter a scale factor (nX or nXP), or
[All/Center/Dynamic/Extents/Previous/Scale/Window] <real time>: **E**↵

Using the Zoom Center Tool

The Zoom Center tool allows you to change the display to be centered on a new point and specify the relative magnification or size of the area displayed. AutoCAD LT first prompts you to specify the point co-

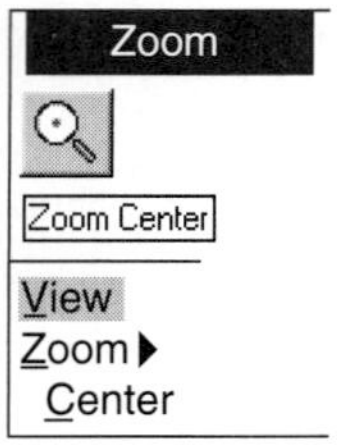

ordinate that is to be displayed at the center of the screen. You can type a coordinate or pick a point on the screen.

Zoom Center can be selected from the Zoom flyout on the Standard toolbar or you can pick Center from the Zoom cascade of the View menu or type it. This first example shows a point being picked and the magnification is doubled.

Command: **Z** or **ZOOM**↵
Specify corner of window, enter a scale factor (nX or nXP), or
[All/Center/Dynamic/Extents/Previous/Scale/Window] <real time>: **C**↵
Specify center point: <specify new display center point>
Enter magnification or height <9.0000>: **2X**↵

The magnification works the same as the Zoom Scale option: A number greater than one followed by an X zooms closer to your work and a number less than one zooms out. The magnification number is relative to the current display size shown in the default brackets. In the preceding example, the current display shows nine drawing units vertically, so 9.0000 is the default height. If you omit the X from the number you enter, AutoCAD LT considers the entry an absolute screen height. The absolute screen height indicates how many drawing units are displayed vertically in the drawing display area. In the example shown in Figure 4.5, the re-

FIGURE 4.5 (A) The Zoom Center tool allows you to locate the center of the display area. (B) The resulting display shows four drawing units vertically in the display area and is centered on the point 3.25,6.0.

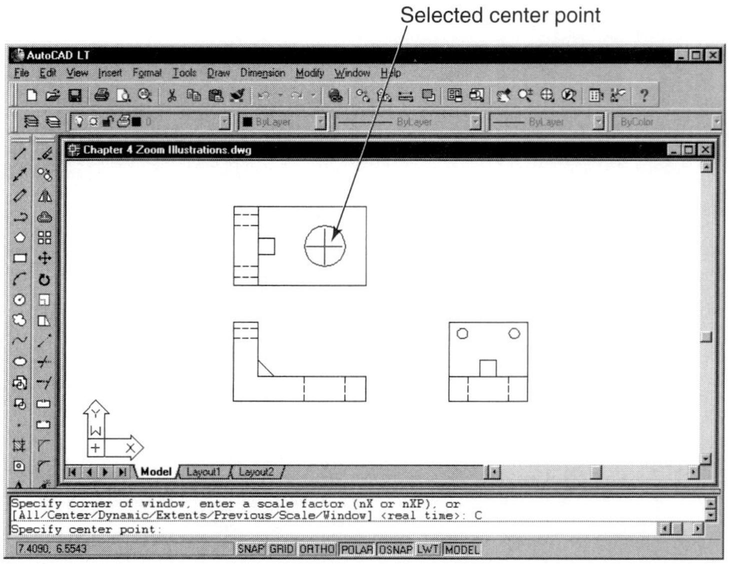

A

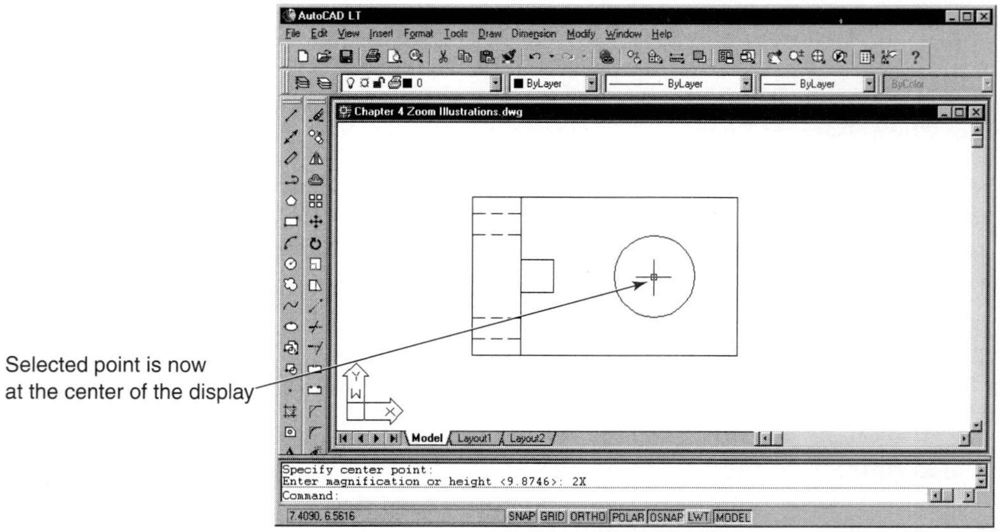

B

sulting display shows four drawing units vertically, and the point 3.25,6.0 (the center of the circle) is at the center of the screen:

Command: **Z** or **ZOOM**↵
Specify corner of window, enter a scale factor (nX or nXP), or
[All/Center/Dynamic/Extents/Previous/Scale/Window] <real time>: **C**↵
Specify center point: **325,6**
Enter magnification or height <9.0000>: **4**↵

Using the Zoom Previous Tool

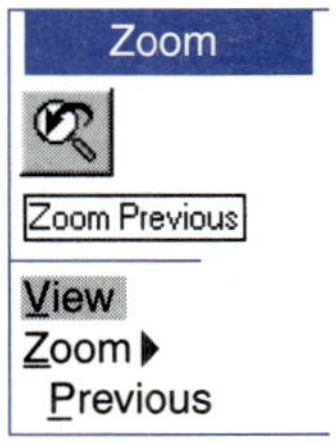

The Zoom Previous tool is likely to be the single most frequently used zooming option. The view that was displayed previously to the current view is displayed again when you select Zoom Previous. This makes it easy to get back to where you were before you zoomed to the current view. AutoCAD LT keeps the last 10 display areas available so that you can back up through a series of display changes to return to a desired view.

As with all display changes, returning to the previous view has no effect on the objects in the drawing. Although using the U command will undo a display change, using Zoom Previous does not undo any drawing or editing commands. You can pick the Zoom Previous toolbar button from the Standard Toolbar, pick Previous from the Zoom cascade of the View pull-down menu, or type the command at the Command: prompt:

Command: **Z** or **ZOOM**↵
Specify corner of window, enter a scale factor (nX or nXP), or
[All/Center/Dynamic/Extents/Previous/Scale/Window] <real time>: **P**↵

Exercise 4.2 **Estimated time required: 5 min.**

1. Open a drawing from one of the exercises in Chapter 3.
2. Use the Zoom Window and Zoom Previous tools to zoom in on various features of the drawing and then return to the previous display.
3. Try the Zoom All and Zoom Extents tools and note the differences. Draw an object outside of your limits and then try both of these tools again.
4. Use the Zoom Center tool to change the magnification of your display. Try setting an absolute screen height with this option.
5. Save as EX4.2 and close the drawing.

Using the Real-Time Zoom Tool

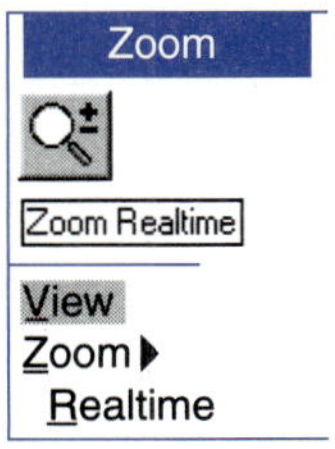

The Real-Time Zoom tool provides an interactive Zoom Scale process. This feature allows you to zoom in or out without having to enter a numeric value. Instead, moving your pointing device changes the display size as you watch, allowing you to decide when the display size fits your needs. The continuous feedback provided while you are adjusting the display makes this an ***interactive*** process. The Real-Time Zoom tool is available on the Standard toolbar, Real-Time can be picked from the Zoom cascade of the View pull-down menu, or it is the default option of the Zoom command prompt:

Command: **Z** or **ZOOM**↵
Specify corner of window, enter a scale factor (nX or nXP), or
[All/Center/Dynamic/Extents/Previous/Scale/Window] <real time>: ↵
Press Esc or Enter to exit, or right-click to display shortcut menu.

Notice that the cursor now changes shape to appear as a magnifying glass with a plus and a minus sign to the right, similar to the image on the toolbar button. To begin the interactive zooming process, press and hold the pick button. While holding the pick button down, move your cursor up to increase magnification or down to decrease magnification. You can continue this process, zooming in and out as needed, until your display appears the way you want it.

When you are zooming in or out, your cursor may reach the edge of the screen and not allow you to go any further. If this happens, release the pick button and reposition the cursor on screen. Then you can press and hold the pick button again and continue your zooming operation. Once the display appears the way you want it to, press either the Enter key or the Esc (Escape) key.

To display the real-time shortcut menu, press the right mouse button while in the real-time zoom command. The shortcut menu appears at the cursor location and presents the real-time display change options. See Figure 4.6.

FIGURE 4.6 The real-time shortcut menu appears at the cursor location when you right-click and presents the available real-time display change options.

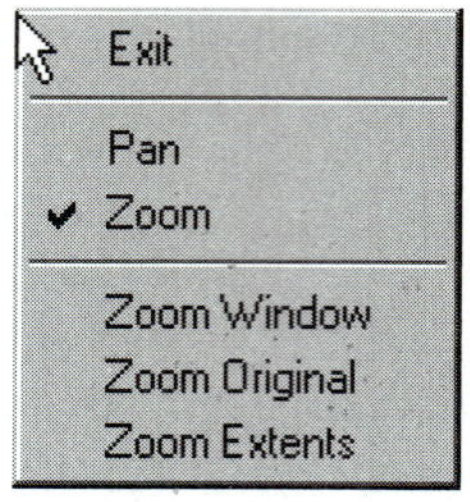

The options on this menu are as follows:

- **Exit** Exits the real-time zoom or pan command.
- **Pan** Toggles the display change tool to Pan (Pan is covered later in this chapter).
- **Zoom** Toggles the display change command to Zoom.
- **Zoom Window** Changes to a Window mode for zooming. This option requires that you *press and hold* the pick button, drag the mouse to form a window, and then release the pick button to accept the defined window.
- **Zoom Original** Returns the display to the state it was in when you started the real-time display change command.
- **Zoom Extents** Same as the regular Zoom extents option; shows the whole drawing.

Note that the real-time zooming option can be used only within the limits of what is called the logical extents. **Logical extents** refers to the area of the drawing that AutoCAD LT 2000 is currently keeping within video memory. This means that display changes outside this area require AutoCAD LT to regenerate the drawing. The topic of drawing regeneration is discussed later in this chapter. When you have zoomed in as far as possible without regenerating the drawing, the + sign disappears from your real-time zooming cursor. Likewise, when you have zoomed out as far as possible, the – sign disappears.

Field Notes

- If a display change does not occur as you expected and you want to try again, the quickest way to get back to where you were is to use the Zoom Previous tool.
- In a drawing where you have drawn several objects and Zoom All or Zoom Extents causes the objects to disappear, you may have accidentally created objects that are *very* far apart. If the objects are far enough apart, they may be too small to display properly and instead appear as small dots in opposing corners of the drawing. To check for this condition, after you zoom, check your coordinate display on the status bar as you move your cursor. If the coordinate numbers are much larger than your intended drawing area, this may be the case. If not, try a Zoom 0.9X to see if your objects are simply pushed up against the edges of the drawing area. Either way, a Zoom Previous takes you back to where you were.
- In earlier versions, entering RTZOOM activates the Real-Time Zoom command. AutoCAD LT 2000 still recognizes this command, but it is easier just to type **Z** and press Enter at the prompt.

LEARNING CHECKPOINT

- ☐ Which ZOOM command option is used by the Zoom In and Zoom Out tools?
- ☐ What is the primary limitation of the Zoom Scale option?
- ☐ Describe the use of the Zoom Window tool.

- ☐ What is the easiest way to return to the previously displayed view?
- ☐ What is the difference between Zoom All and Zoom Extents?
- ☐ Name the interactive zooming option and describe its use.

Zooming with the IntelliMouse

Autodesk recommends the use of the Microsoft IntelliMouse with AutoCAD LT 2000. There are many different brands of "wheel mouse" products on the market. Before you purchase an alternative product, be sure that it is 100% IntelliMouse compatible. If you have the IntelliMouse, you can zoom and pan transparently using the IntelliMouse wheel. The real-time zooming and panning features are subject to the same limitation as the actual commands, but the wheel provides an easier way to access these options.

To perform a real-time zoom, roll the wheel button without pressing it down. When you roll the wheel forward, the display is zoomed in, or made larger. When you roll the wheel backward, the display is zoomed out. Because it is a transparent function, it can be used within other commands. The zoom factor using the IntelliMouse is set using the ZOOMFACTOR system variable. Type ZOOMFACTOR at the Command: prompt to adjust this value. The default is 10%, meaning that each time you roll the wheel one "click," the display is zoomed up or down by 10%. You can set this value between 3 and 100%, but the default value works very well in most applications.

Pressing the wheel button down accesses the real-time panning feature. Then, just move your mouse to change the location of the display. The cursor changes to a hand, and your display moves in the direction you drag it. Note that the real-time panning feature works only if the MBUTTONPAN system variable is set to 1.

Using the PAN Command Options and Scrolling

The PAN command changes your view of the drawing without changing the magnification. This is very useful when you zoom into an area of the drawing and you need to see something that lies just outside of the currently visible area. Two Pan tools are available in AutoCAD LT: Real-Time Pan and Pan Point, or you can use the drawing area scroll bars.

Using Real-Time Pan Tool

The Real-Time Pan tool is the most convenient Pan option. It is an interactive display change tool similar to real-time zoom. Select the Real-Time Pan button from the Standard toolbar, pick Realtime from the Pan cascade of the View pull-down menu, or type **P** or **PAN** at the Command: prompt to use this tool.

Standard

Pan Realtime

View
Pan ▸
Realtime

Command: **P** or **PAN**↵
Press ESC or ENTER to exit, or right-click to display shortcut menu.

When this command is entered, your cursor changes to a small hand with a four-way arrow to the right similar to the image on the toolbar button. To use this option, press and hold the pick button, then move your cursor to slide the drawing around. You can release the pick button if you need to reposition the cursor and continue to pan the drawing in much the same way as the real-time zoom option.

Although this command appears to slide the drawing around, nothing in the drawing actually changes position—the only thing that changes is your view of the drawing. If a line was drawn from the point coordinate 2,2 to 4,4 and you slide the drawing six units to the right, the coordinates for the endpoints of the line are still 2,2 and 4,4.

Right-clicking while using the Real-Time Pan option displays the same popup menu as when using the Real-Time Zoom option. This menu was discussed in the previous section. Also, the Real-Time Pan option can be used only within the logical extents of the drawing. When you have reached the logical extent on the top, bottom, left, or right, the cursor displays a bar to show that you can go no further in that direction.

Using the Pan Point Tool

-PAN
-P

The Pan Point tool also allows you to slide the drawing display, but it is not interactive. Instead, with this option you can enter an X and Y displacement value or you can specify two points on the screen that describe how you want the drawing display to move.

To enter X and Y displacement values, type an **X,Y** value at the Displacement: prompt and press Enter at the Second point: prompt. For example, move the display so the drawing appears to be four units to the right and two units above its current location:

Command: **-P** or **-PAN**↵
Specify base point or displacement: **4,2**↵
Specify second point: ↵

The other way to use this option is to specify a point coordinate at each prompt. The points can be selected with your cursor or entered from the keyboard using absolute, relative, or polar coordinates. AutoCAD LT measures the distance between the two points on both the X and Y axes and pans the display accordingly. For example:

Command: **-P** or **-PAN**↵
Specify base point or displacement: **4,2**↵
Specify second point: **6,3**↵

This example moves the display so the drawing appears to be two units to the right and one unit above where it was previously. Figures 4.7 and 4.8 show the resulting display for these examples of the Pan Point tool. On

FIGURE 4.7 (A) The resulting display after entering a pan displacement value of 4 units on the X axis and 2 on the Y axis. (B) Pressing the Enter key at the Second point: prompt causes AutoCAD LT to use the value as an absolute displacement.

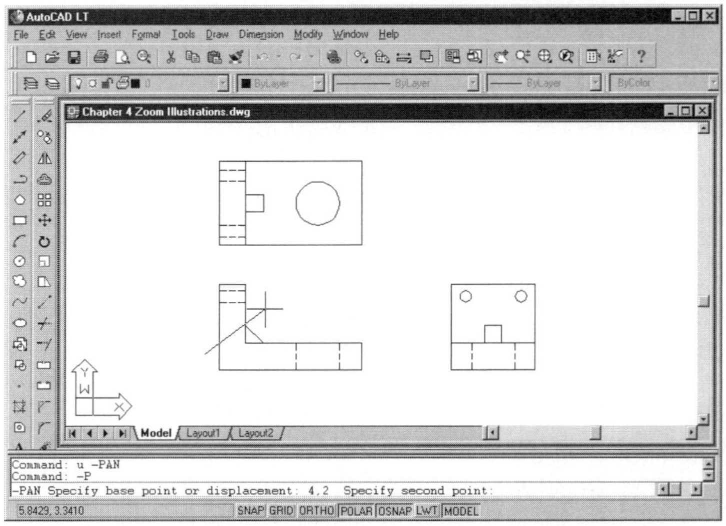

A

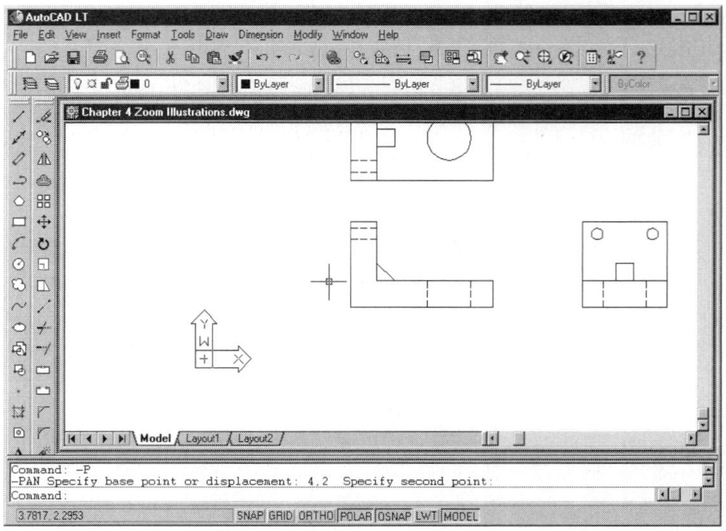

B

FIGURE 4.8 (A) The resulting display after entering a pan base point of 4,2 as the X,Y coordinate. (B) Enter a second point coordinate at the Second point: prompt and AutoCAD LT measures the distance and angle between the two points to use as the pan displacement value.

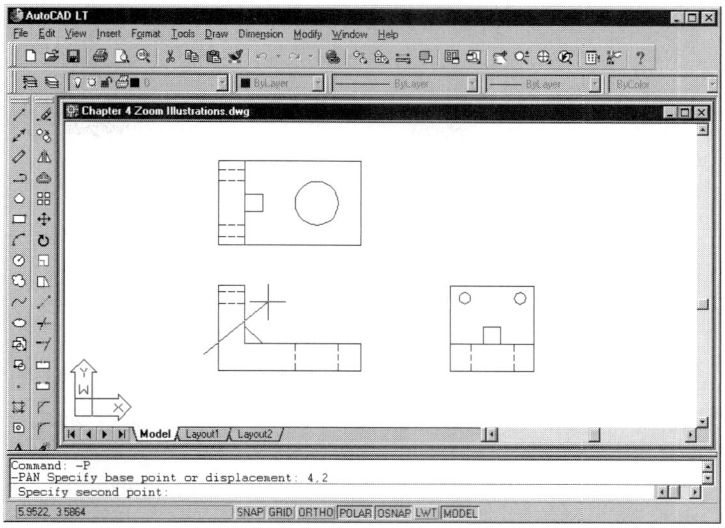

A

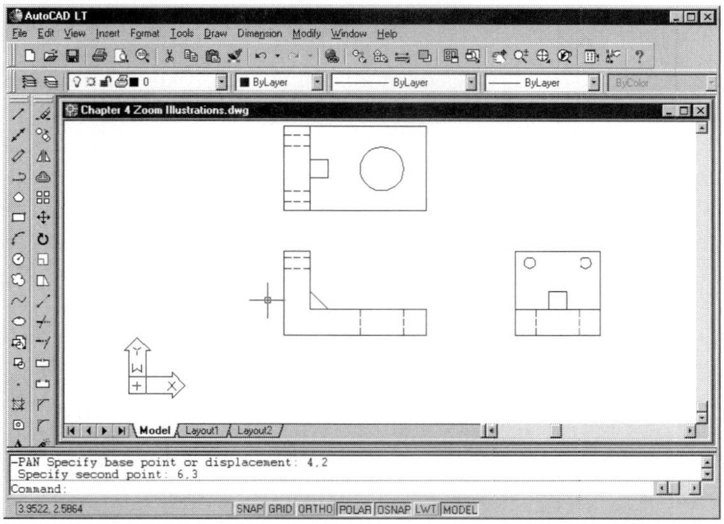

B

the Pan cascade of the View menu, AutoCAD LT presents four other options, Left, Right, Up, and Down. Selecting one of these options pans the display in the specified direction a distance equal to 20% of the current display height.

Using the Scroll Bars

The drawing area scroll bars are a quick and easy way to adjust the position of your drawing display. By default, AutoCAD LT displays scroll bars on the bottom and the right side of the drawing area. These are used like the scroll bars in any other Windows-based application.

At each end of a scroll bar is an arrow button. Picking this button moves the viewing area 10% in the direction indicated. You can move the display 80% by picking in the scroll bar background area; the side of the slider you point to when you pick is the direction the display is moved.

You can also point to the slider button, press and hold the pick button, and move the slider to a new position. The position of the slider relative to the scroll bar indicates where your current view is centered relative to the extents of the drawing. The ***drawing extents*** is the area of your drawing that contains objects, or the area that is displayed when you use the Zoom Extents tool. If you are not zoomed in too close, you can scroll freely through the extents of your drawing using the slider.

Field Notes

If scroll bars are not visible in your AutoCAD LT window, you can turn them on by using the OPTIONS command. On the Display page of the Options dialog box, place a check mark in the Display scrollbars in drawing window toggle. This toggle is located in the upper left area of the dialog box, labeled Window Elements. Pick the OK button to exit the dialog box and return to the drawing editor.

LEARNING CHECKPOINT

- ☐ Describe the use and advantages of the Real-Time Pan tool.
- ☐ What two methods can be used with the Pan Point tool?
- ☐ What are the three different ways the scroll bars can be used?

Viewing, Selecting, and Using Precision Drawing Tools

- Using Zooming and Panning to Control Drawing Display

How to Zoom Transparently

In Chapter 2 you were introduced to transparent commands. A ***transparent*** command can be used without interrupting a currently active command—as long as it does not require a drawing regeneration and it does not change the drawing database. The term ***drawing database*** refers to the information that AutoCAD LT stores to define the objects in a drawing file. Drawing and editing commands cannot be used transparently because they make direct changes to the drawing database.

AutoCAD LT maintains a certain area of the current drawing in memory, so you can quickly change the display area without the need to read the drawing file from your hard disk. This area is called the ***logical extents.*** If the requested display change shows an area that lies outside of the current logical extents, then AutoCAD LT must first regenerate your drawing. The term ***regenerate*** means that AutoCAD LT reads the current drawing database and redefines the virtual screen area. All of the objects in the new logical extents are loaded into memory from the current drawing database. Your drawing must also be regenerated if a display change shows an area that is extremely small in relationship to the current logical extents.

To increase your flexibility while drawing and editing, the zoom options can be used transparently as long as the results can be displayed using the current logical extents. The Pan tools and the scroll bars can also be used transparently under these same conditions.

When a display change option is selected from the menu, AutoCAD LT automatically checks to see if it can be done without a drawing regeneration. If so, the command is entered transparently. When entered at the Command: prompt, a transparent command behaves no differently than normal. However, entering a transparent command while another command is active temporarily stops the currently active command while the transparent command is processed. The following example shows the first point for a line object being picked. A zoom operation is done transparently to magnify part of the drawing and a second point is picked, then the previous display is returned to transparently:

Command: **LINE↵**
Specify first point:
Specify next point or [Undo]: **'Z↵**
>>Specify corner of window, enter a scale factor (nX or nXP), or
[All/Center/Dynamic/Extents/Previous/Scale/Window] <real time>: **W↵**
>>Specify first corner: *<pick first corner>*
>>Specify opposite corner: *<pick other corner>*
Resuming LINE command.
Specify next point or [Undo]:
Specify next point or [Undo]: **'Z↵**
>>Specify corner of window, enter a scale factor (nX or nXP), or
[All/Center/Dynamic/Extents/Previous/Scale/Window] <real time>: **P↵**
Resuming LINE command.
Specify next point or [Undo]:

As shown in the example, a transparent command has an apostrophe preceding the command name. The >> characters before the prompt indicate that you are working transparently while another command is active. Also in the previous example, notice that the W and the P are not preceded by an apostrophe. Command options entered for a transparent command do not require an apostrophe. When the transparent command is finished, a message is issued indicating that the active command is being resumed.

In the next example, the requested display change cannot be completed without a drawing regeneration. AutoCAD LT issues an appropriate message and resumes the active command:

Command: **LINE**↵
Specify first point:
Specify next point or [Undo]: **'Z**↵
>>Specify corner of window, enter a scale factor (nX or nXP), or
[All/Center/Dynamic/Extents/Previous/Scale/Window] <real time>: **W**↵
>>Specify first corner: *<pick first corner>*
>>Specify opposite corner: *<pick other corner>*
** Requires a regen, cannot be transparent.
Resuming LINE command.
Specify next point or [Undo]:

If the display change is required for you to continue, press the Esc key to cancel the currently active command and return to the Command: prompt. Now you can enter the display change option. You may notice that display changes requiring regenerations are somewhat slower than other display changes. This display speed difference is even more significant when working with larger drawings.

Field Notes

The VIEWRES command controls the accuracy level AutoCAD LT maintains for the display of curved objects. You may notice that when you make a significant change to the scale at which you are viewing your drawing that the circles and arcs may appear faceted—looking more like a polygon than a circle. The VIEWRES command prompt sequence is shown here:

Command: **VIEWRES**↵
Do you want fast zooms? [Yes/No] <Y>: ↵
Enter circle zoom percent (1–20000) <100>: **10000**↵
Regenerating model.

The prompt regarding fast zooms is not a functional feature, and fast zooms (transparent zooms) cannot be disabled. Set the circle zoom percent higher to avoid the faceting effect, or set it to a lower value to increase the speed of display changes in larger drawings.

Exercise 4.3 — Estimated time required: 10 min.

1. Open a drawing from one of the exercises in Chapter 3.
2. Zoom in and out with the Real-Time Zoom tool. See how far in and how far out you can zoom. Try Real-Time Pan, Pan Point, and panning using the scroll bars. Note the advantages and disadvantages of each method.
3. Start a drawing or editing command and use some of your display change tools transparently. Try entering a transparent display change using the keyboard.
4. On a piece of paper, write down the names of each of the display change tools. Indicate which ones can be used transparently and which cannot.
5. Save as EX4.3, and close the drawing.

LEARNING CHECKPOINT

- ☐ How can display change commands be used transparently?
- ☐ What types of commands cannot be used transparently?
- ☐ Which two Zoom options cannot be used transparently?
- ☐ What character precedes prompts to indicate the command is transparent?

Using the Aerial View Window

Standard
View
Aerial View
DSVIEWER
AV

The Aerial View window provides a powerful set of display management tools. This tool opens up a separate window where your entire drawing is displayed, and a number of display change options are available. The Aerial View window starts out as a small window initially displayed in the lower right area of the AutoCAD LT window, but can be moved and resized as needed. Figure 4.9 shows the Aerial View window.

The Aerial View window display is toggled by picking Aerial View from the View pull-down menu, or by typing **AV** or **DSVIEWER** at the Command: prompt. The DSVIEWER command is a toggle, meaning that if the Aerial View window is currently hidden, it will be displayed, and if it is currently visible, then this option hides it.

The Aerial View window toolbar and pull-down menus provide tooltips, and like any other window in a Windows environment, it can be resized or moved as desired.

Refer to Figure 4.10 for a map of the Aerial View window features.

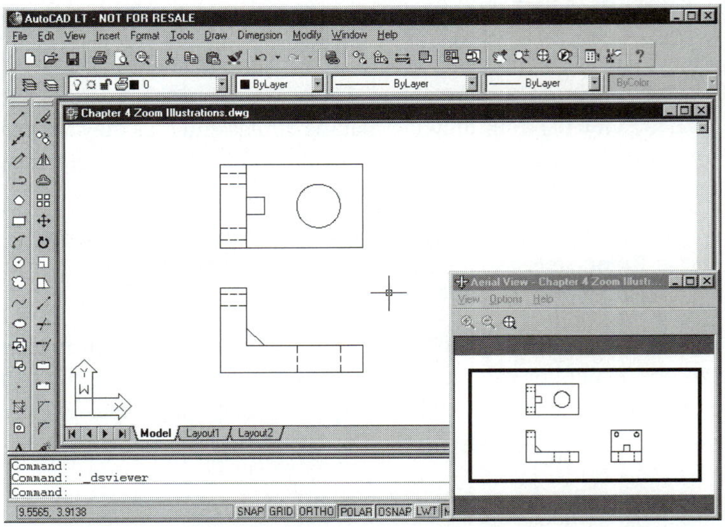

FIGURE 4.9 The Aerial View Window appears in the lower right area of the AutoCAD LT window by default but can be moved as desired.

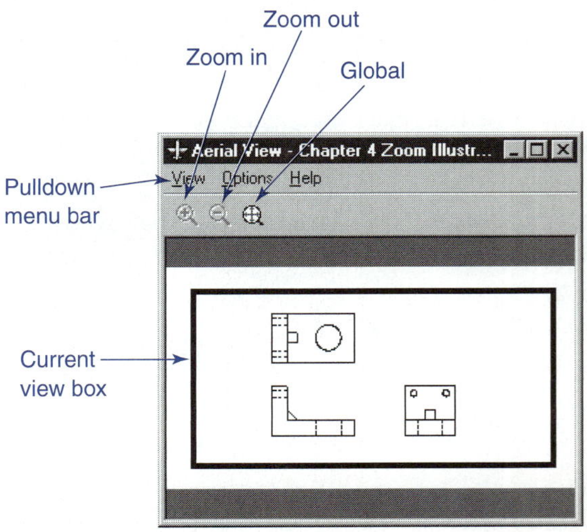

FIGURE 4.10 The features of the Aerial View window: Pull-down menu bar, Zoom In button, Zoom Out button, Global button, Current View box.

Using Aerial View

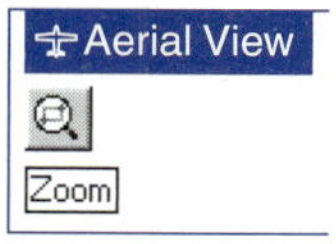

When you first start the Aerial View window, the entire drawing should be visible in the drawing display area. The currently displayed area of the drawing is shown outlined with the Current view box. As you move your cursor, you will move a rectangle the size of the Current view box with an X in the middle. This allows you to reposition the display area while maintaining the same zoom factor. If you press the pick button, an arrow appears on the right edge of the rectangle, and moving your cursor resizes the display area. Press the pick button at any time to toggle from resizing to repositioning mode. When you are happy with the display, right-click to accept it, and then move your cursor back to the main AutoCAD LT window and press the pick button to continue working in the new view.

One of the remarkable features of the Aerial View window is that even if the current view in the AutoCAD LT drawing display area is greatly magnified, the entire drawing still appears in the Aerial View window. This means that you can return to the Aerial View window to zoom to another area that is not even visible in the AutoCAD LT drawing display area.

Field Notes

- All Aerial View window display changes are entered transparently. If you attempt to make a display change that would require a regeneration, the request is ignored.
- You can return to a previous view using the Zoom Previous tool even when Aerial View was used to change the display.
- The U command has no effect on the DSVIEWER command, but will undo display changes made via the Aerial View window.

Exercise 4.4 — Estimated time required: 5 min.

1. Open a drawing from one of the exercises in Chapter 3.
2. Zoom in and out using the Aerial View window.
3. Pan using the Aerial View window.
4. Start a drawing or editing command and make a few transparent display changes using the Aerial View window.
5. Compare the use of the Aerial View window to other zooming options. Which display change tools are more convenient to use?
6. Save as EX4.4, and close the drawing .

Field Notes

The Aerial View window is meant to supplement the standard display change options available in AutoCAD LT, not replace them. Use all the available display change options to the best of your advantage.

Adjusting the Aerial View Window Display

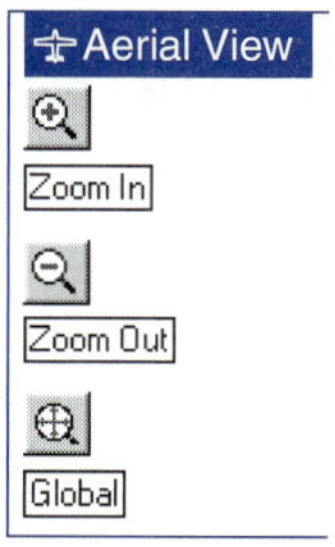

If you are working in a small area within a large drawing, you may wish to change the size of the image displayed in the Aerial View window to make the display changes easier. The Aerial View Zoom In tool increases the apparent size of the objects in the Aerial View window by 2X, and the Zoom Out tool reduces the apparent size by one-half. The Global tool is used to display the entire drawing. Each of these tools is available as toolbar buttons in the Aerial View window or on the View pull-down menu. Adjusting the size of the image displayed in the Aerial View window has no effect on the drawing display.

Controlling the Updating of the Aerial View Window

By default, the Aerial View window is updated dynamically. This means that when you make a change to your drawing, such as adding a new object or modifying an existing object, the changes are reflected in the

Aerial View window immediately. In small drawings, this is not likely to affect your system performance. In larger drawings this can affect your editing speed significantly if you have to wait on the Aerial View window to update each time you make a change.

You can turn off the dynamic update feature by picking Dynamic Update from the Options menu in the Aerial View window. When you pick this menu, a check mark is displayed by the menu selection if it is active. Picking the item toggles its current state.

If you turn off the dynamic update feature, the image is only updated when you move the cursor into the Aerial View window.

The AutoViewport selection on the Options menu controls whether the Aerial View window is automatically updated to display the contents of the current tiled viewport. This is discussed further in Chapter 13.

By default, any display changes made in the Aerial View window are reflected in real time in the main AutoCAD LT drawing area. You can disable this feature by picking the Realtime Zoom option from the Options menu.

Through the Window...

Using the Alt+Tab keystroke enables you to switch easily from one application window to another in Windows. However, this will not work for switching between the AutoCAD LT and Aerial View windows. This is because the Aerial View window is considered a *child* process of AutoCAD LT and not a separate application.

Since Aerial View is a child process of AutoCAD LT, if you minimize AutoCAD LT then Aerial View is minimized also, but it does not display its own icon or taskbar button.

Exercise 4.5 — Estimated time required: 5 min.

1. Open a drawing from one of the exercises in Chapter 3.
2. Start the Aerial View window.
3. Use the Aerial View window to change your drawing display.
4. Use the Zoom In and Zoom Out options to adjust the image displayed in the Aerial View window. Use the Global tool to reset the image to include the entire drawing.
5. Add some new objects to your drawing and edit existing objects. Watch the Aerial View window as you do so and note the automatic updates.
6. Turn the Dynamic Update feature off. Again, add some new objects to your drawing and edit existing objects. Force an update by moving your cursor into the Aerial View window.
7. Save as EX4.5, and close the drawing .

LEARNING CHECKPOINT

- ☐ What command starts the Aerial View window?
- ☐ What advantages are there to using the Aerial View options?
- ☐ Describe the options for updating the Aerial View window.

Standard

Named Views

View
Named Views...

DDVIEW
VIEW
V

Creating Named Views

When working in AutoCAD LT, you may find yourself frequently zooming to one or more specific views of the drawing. You can use the standard display change tools and the Aerial Viewer to zoom in and out as necessary. For greater speed and convenience you can assign names to the views and return directly to the named views from anywhere in the drawing. The Named Views tool allows you to create, manage, and restore named views in the drawing. Using named views can increase productivity by making display changes fast and accurate.

To display the View dialog box, select Named Views from the View flyout on the Standard toolbar, pick Named Views ... from the View pull-down menu, or type **VIEW** or **V** at the Command: prompt. The View Control dialog box is shown in Figure 4.11.

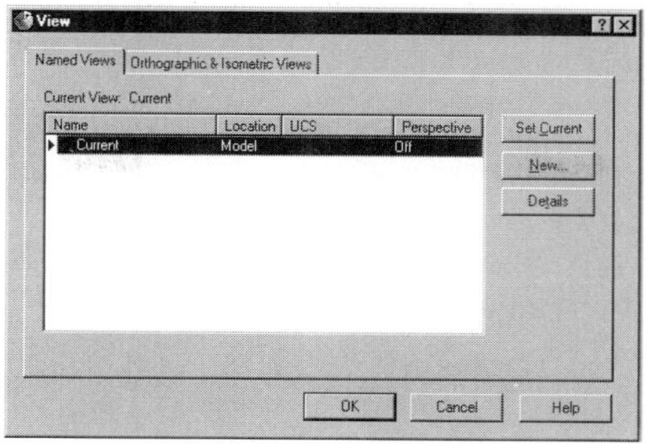

FIGURE 4.11 The View dialog box.

Defining Named Views

The Named Views tab of the View dialog box displays the names of each defined view in the current drawing and indicates whether they are in model space or paper space. The view named Current is always present in this dialog box. It is not actually a specific view, but a reference to whatever is the currently visible area of your drawing. To define your own named view, first pick the New ... button to display the New View dialog box (see Figure 4.12).

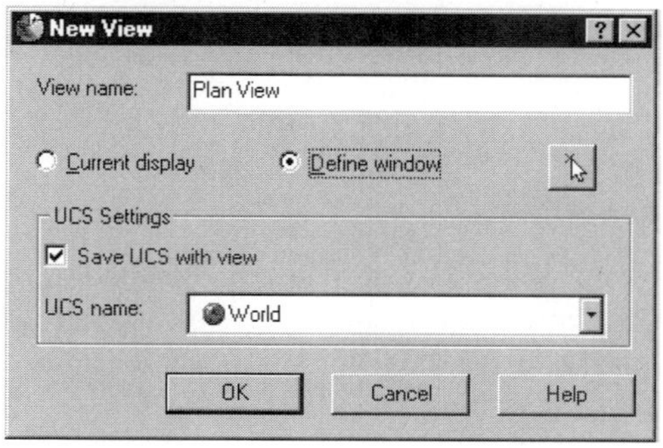

FIGURE 4.12 The New View dialog box.

It is usually a good idea to keep view names simple and descriptive so that it is easy to remember what area of the drawing each one displays. AutoCAD LT allows you to name a view using up to 255 characters. A view name can contain alphanumeric characters, spaces, and any character not used for other purposes, such as dollar signs ($), hyphens (-), and underscores (__). A view name cannot use asterisks, slashes, or question marks.

When defining a new view, you have a choice of assigning the view name to the Current Display or you can select Define Window. The Current Display option assigns the view name to the area that is currently displayed in the AutoCAD LT drawing display area.

The Define Window option assigns the view name to the display area described by picking two points. To define the window, pick the Define View Window button. You are then prompted, on the command line, to specify the two corners. You can pick the points or type the point coordinates using the keyboard. When defining the window, you can use transparent display change tools as needed to zoom in or out or pan the drawing.

Once you have defined the display area for the new view name, pick the OK button to save the view and return to the View dialog box.

Field Notes

- While using the View dialog box to define new views, if you select the Cancel button rather than the OK button, all of the views you have defined in this session of the View dialog will be discarded.
- Many of the features of the View dialog box, including the Orthographic & Isometric Views tab, are used only in 3-D applications and are discussed in later chapters.

If you define a named view and later want to change the definition, pick the New ... button in the View dialog box. Define the view with the desired changes and name it the same as the view you want to redefine. When you pick the OK button, an Alert box is displayed with a warning that the view name must be unique (see Figure 4.13). Pick the OK button, and when you return to the New View dialog box you can change the name. If you want to redefine the view represented by the selected view name, return to the View dialog box. Right-clicking on any existing view name displays a shortcut menu. Use the Delete option to remove the existing definition, then pick the New... button to define the view to meet your new requirements.

FIGURE 4.13 The alert box issues a warning if you try to recreate an existing view definition.

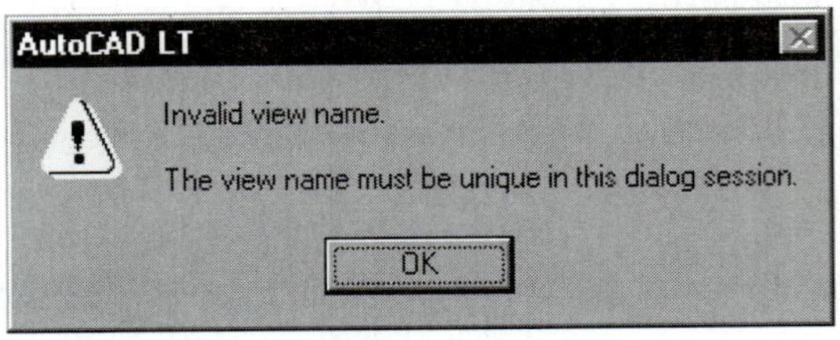

Getting Named View Descriptions

The Details... button in the View dialog box provides the defining information for the currently highlighted view displayed in the list. Much of the information displayed applies only to 3-D drawing, which is discussed in Chapter 13. The view Name and Area show you the name, location, and size of the view.

Restoring Named Views

To restore a named view, start the View dialog box by entering the VIEW command. Highlight the desired view, press the Set Current button, and pick OK. Optionally, you can double-click on the view name, or right-click and pick Set Current from the shortcut menu. The selected view is displayed when the dialog box disappears.

Deleting Named Views

When a named view is no longer needed, it can be removed from the list in the View dialog box. To delete a named view, highlight the view name in the list and pick Delete from the shortcut menu.

There is no further prompt when you pick the Delete button, the view is simply removed from the list. If you accidentally delete a view that you need, pick the Cancel button to discard all changes. If you do pick the OK button, you can use the U command to undo the changes made in the View Control dialog box.

Managing Views Transparently

-VIEW
-V

The VIEW command cannot be used transparently, but much of the real value of named views comes from transparent use. To manage named views transparently, use the '-VIEW command or type '-V. This example shows the '-VIEW command being used to restore a previously defined view during a LINE command sequence:

Command: LINE↵
Specify first point: *<pick a point>*
Specify next point or [Undo]: **'-V↵**

>>Enter an option [?/Orthographic/Delete/Restore/Save/Ucs/Window]: **R**↵
>>Enter view name to restore: **Plan View**↵
Resuming LINE command.
Specify next point or [Undo]:

The options of the -VIEW command are almost the same as the options of the VIEW command, but they are entered at the command line instead of in a dialog box. To save the current display as a named view, use the Save option. The Window option allows you to draw a window to describe a view and assign a name to it. The question mark, ?, gives you a listing of the currently defined views, and Delete removes named view definitions. Probably the most commonly used '-VIEW command option is Restore. Additional options are discussed in later chapters.

Field Notes

- If you use the VIEW command frequently, you will want to keep view names short. If you use very long view names, it may be faster to use the zooming and panning tools instead—especially if you are not a fast and accurate typist.
- Establishing a standard set of named views for all of your drawings can boost productivity. One way of doing this is to create an appropriate series of named views in each of your prototype drawings.

Exercise 4.6 Estimated time required: 10 min.

1. Open a drawing from one of the exercises in Chapter 3.
2. Start the View Control dialog box.
3. Create one named view that shows your entire drawing; name it ALL.
4. Create three or more views of different areas of your drawing and name them appropriately.
5. Use the Restore button in the View Control dialog box to restore each view.
6. Use the VIEW command to list the available views.
7. Draw a line that starts in one of your smaller views, then transparently restore another view and finish the line.
8. Save as EX4.6, and close the drawing .

LEARNING CHECKPOINT

- ☐ What are the four ways of starting the VIEW command?
- ☐ How can using named views increase your productivity?
- ☐ How can named views be restored transparently?

MULTIPLE CHOICE

Circle the choice or enter your response on an answer sheet by selecting the option that most accurately completes or answers the given statements.

1. To increase the apparent size of the objects on your screen, you should:

a. zoom out **c.** zoom in
b. wear glasses **d.** zoom extents

2. A Zoom Scale specification that would bring you closer to your work:

a. 1X **c.** .5X
b. 1/2X **d.** 2X

3. The Real-Time Zoom tool allows you to:
   a. zoom out
   b. zoom interactively
   c. zoom in
   d. all of the above
4. The zooming option that displays the drawing limits or extents, whichever is greater:
   a. Zoom All
   b. Zoom Out
   c. Zoom Extents
   d. Zoom Limits
5. A command that is issued while another command is active is a:
   a. hidden command
   b. transparent command
   c. error
   d. cancel
6. If you enter a coordinate at the first prompt of the PAN command and press Enter at the second prompt, the coordinate is considered to be:
   a. an exact value
   b. an incorrect value
   c. an error value
   d. a displacement value
7. To issue a command transparently, precede the command name with:
   a. Esc
   b. Alt
   c. an asterisk
   d. an apostrophe
8. Some commands can be used transparently if they do not require:
   a. user input
   b. a menu pick
   c. a regeneration
   d. a display change
9. The command that starts the Aerial View window is:
   a. DSVIEWER
   b. AVIEWER
   c. AV
   d. AERIAL
10. Named Views can be managed using the:
   a. Aerial View window
   b. REDRAW command
   c. View dialog box
   d. ZOOM command

MATCHING

Match each term to the correct description by writing the appropriate number in each box at the left.

- ☐ Zoom Window
- ☐ Zoom Extents
- ☐ Zoom All
- ☐ Zoom Previous
- ☐ Zoom Scale
- ☐ Real-Time Zoom
- ☐ Pan Point
- ☐ Real-Time Pan
- ☐ Scroll bars
- ☐ Arrow button
- ☐ Scroll bar background
- ☐ View Restore
- ☐ View Save
- ☐ View Window
- ☐ View Delete

1. Interactive panning tool.
2. Returns to the previously displayed view.
3. Interactive zooming tool.
4. A convenient means of sliding the drawing vertically or horizontally.
5. Displays the selected named view.
6. Pans the drawing display 80%.
7. Used to draw a window describing your display change.
8. Saves the current display area as a named view.
9. Magnifies or reduces the drawing display by a specified scale.
10. Saves a windowed area as a named view.
11. Shows all objects in your drawing.
12. Deletes a named view.
13. Pans the drawing display 10%.
14. Zooms to the limits or extents, whichever is greater.
15. Slides the drawing display by picking two points.

WORD SCRAMBLE

Unscramble the six scrambled words below, one letter to each square, to form six AutoCAD LT–related words:

NTXESET

CLORSL

SPRATANNERT

NCRESE

ETERRAGENION

MOZO

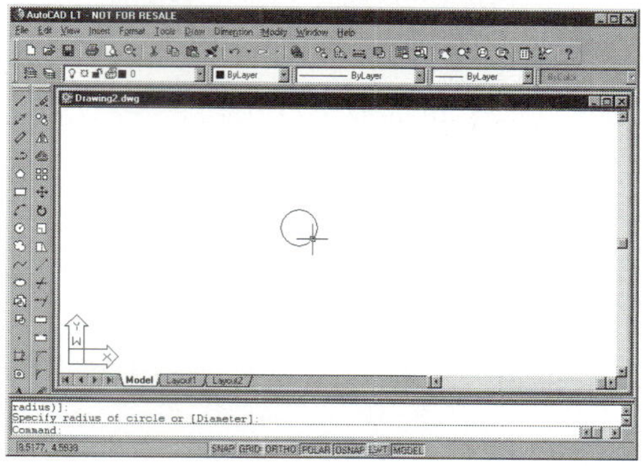

A

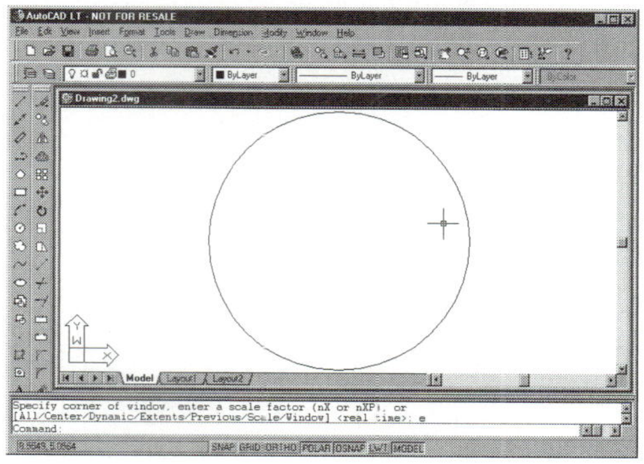

B

Unscramble the circled letters above to form the special answer, as suggested by the illustration.

PROJECTS

4.1 Open drawing P3.1 for editing. Create four named views as follows: HOOD, GLASS, MOUNT, ALL. The named views should show the appropriate area of the drawing. Save the drawing as P4.1.

4.2 Open drawing P3.2 for editing. Create three named views as follows: TOP-PLUG, BTM-PLUG, ALL. The named views should show the appropriate area of the drawing. Save the drawing as P4.2.

4.3 Open drawing P3.3 for editing. Create two named views as follows: ELLIPSE, ALL. The named views should show the appropriate area of the drawing. Save the drawing as P4.3.

4.4 Open drawing P3.4 for editing. Create five named views as follows: TOP-HEX, RGT-HEX, LFT-HEX, BTM-HEX, PLATE. The named views should show the appropriate area of the drawing. Save the drawing as P4.4.

4.5 Open drawing P3.5 for editing. Create five named views as follows: TOP-HEX, RGT-HEX, LFT-HEX, BTM-HEX, PLATE. The named views should show the appropriate area of the drawing. Save the drawing as P4.5.

4.6 Open drawing P3.6 for editing. Create six named views as follows: TOP, RGT, LFT, BTM, CTR, GASKET. The named views should show the appropriate area of the drawing. Save the drawing as P4.6.

4.7 Open drawing P3.7 for editing. Create six named views as follows: TOP, RGT, LFT, BTM, CTR, GASKET. The named views should show the appropriate area of the drawing. Save the drawing as P4.7.

4.8 Open drawing P3.8 for editing. Create two named views as follows: STAIRS, ALL. The named views should show the appropriate area of the drawing. Save the drawing as P4.8.

4.9 Open drawing P3.9 for editing. Create four named views as follows: DRIVE, TIMER, CONTROLS, CIRCUIT. The named views should show the appropriate area of the drawing. Save the drawing as P4.9.

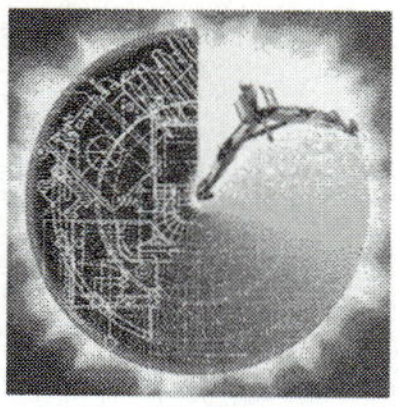

CHAPTER 5

Using Layers and Managing Object Properties

LEARNING GOALS

- ◎ Explain the importance of layers and good layer management.
- ◎ Create layers by name, color, and linetype.
- ◎ Draw objects on different layers.
- ◎ Adjust the linetype scale.
- ◎ Control layer visibility.
- ◎ Explain the difference between a frozen and a locked layer.
- ◎ Discuss why caution should be used when overriding layer settings.
- ◎ Manage object properties such as layer, linetype, and color.
- ◎ Filter layers.

An Introduction to AutoCAD LT Layers

A ***layer*** is defined by AutoCAD LT as a logical grouping of data, like transparent overlays on a manual drawing. Try to envision these overlays as clear sheets, each with its own specific type of drawing information. As you stack these clear sheets together, you can see through each sheet to the drawings on the sheets below. You can view overlays or layers individually or in combination. Layers might be considered as a series of drawing overlays. In architectural drafting, layers may be made up of several overlays including border and title block, floor plan, dimensions, notes, electrical, plumbing, and structural. Each layer can be displayed in its own color and plotted in color if a color plotter is available. Each layer can be displayed and plotted individually or together in any desired combination. Figure 5.1 provides a pictorial example of how layers work.

Layers for a mechanical drawing might be set up based on linetype. For example, you might create one layer each for object lines, hidden lines, center lines, and dimensions. The layers for each linetype may be set up using individual colors, which makes each linetype stand out clearly on the computer screen. During the plotting or printing process, each layer's color can be assigned a specific pen width. In this manner, line widths can be varied, with thick lines plotted 0.6 mm wide and thin lines plotted 0.3 mm wide to conform to ASME standards. These different widths provide line contrast even if the plot contains only black lines. Appendix B displays the recommended ASME linetypes and widths.

Managing Drawing Layers

A good layer management system and record keeping are very important. Layers may be managed by name or number, or by the project, or based on company or national standards. Layer names should be recorded in a procedures manual or drawing log with information about the content. The manual should provide the layer name, color, linetype, and specific information about the layer content and use. A good example of a layer management system is published in *CAD Layer Guidelines,* by the American Institute of Architects (AIA) Press, 1735 New York Avenue, N.W., Washington, D.C. 20006. In this format, layer names are based on abbreviations that are easy to recognize. Layer names are based on a logical grouping of objects in a drawing, such as A-DOOR for architectural doors or E-LITE for electrical lighting. AutoCAD LT lists layers alpha-

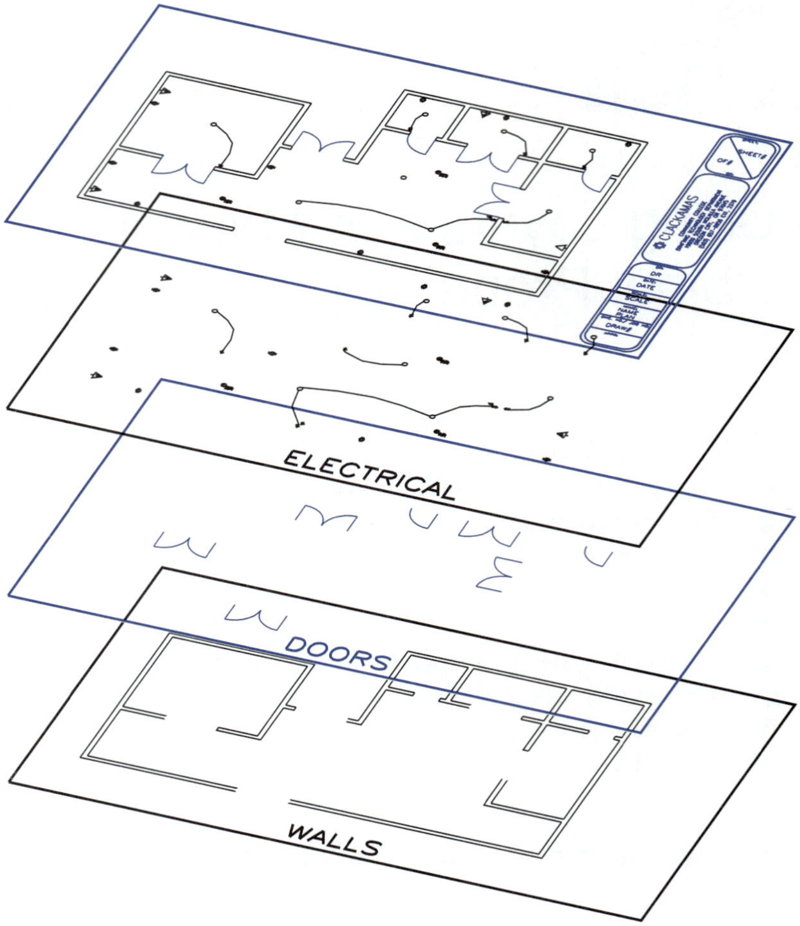

FIGURE 5.1 A pictorial representation of a CAD layering system showing how information is shared among drawings. (Drawing courtesy of Carl Backstrom.)

betically by name for ease of location. Use of a common prefix for all similar layers helps when you are trying to locate or sort layers. The AIA has established eight major groups of layer prefixes:

A	Architectural, interiors, and facility management
S	Structural
M	Mechanical
P	Plumbing
F	Fire protection
E	Electrical
C	Civil engineering and site work
L	Landscape architecture

You should determine if company, school, or national standards are available to follow when designing your layer names and content. If not, set up your layer naming system based on the information found in the drawing. Information regarding the CAD Layer Guidelines document can also be found at the AIA Online Network Web site. The URL is http://www.aia.org/

Creating Layers

Object Properties

Layer

Format
Layer...

LAYER
LA

Layers are created in the Layer Properties Manager dialog box. Access this dialog box by picking Layer ... in the Format pull-down menu, pick the Layer button in the Object Properties toolbar, or type **Layer** or **LA**. The Layer Properties Manager dialog box contains information about your layers. It also allows you to add or delete layers or to perform other layer management activities. When you start an AutoCAD LT drawing from scratch or with Quick Setup, the only layer listed is the default layer 0 (zero), as shown in Figure 5.2A. If you start an AutoCAD LT drawing from a template, additional layers may be listed. For example, look at Figure 5.2B and notice that the list includes the name, visibility setting, lock control, color, linetype, lineweight, plot style, and plot status for each layer. In Figure 5.2A, the Show details button has been selected to display the

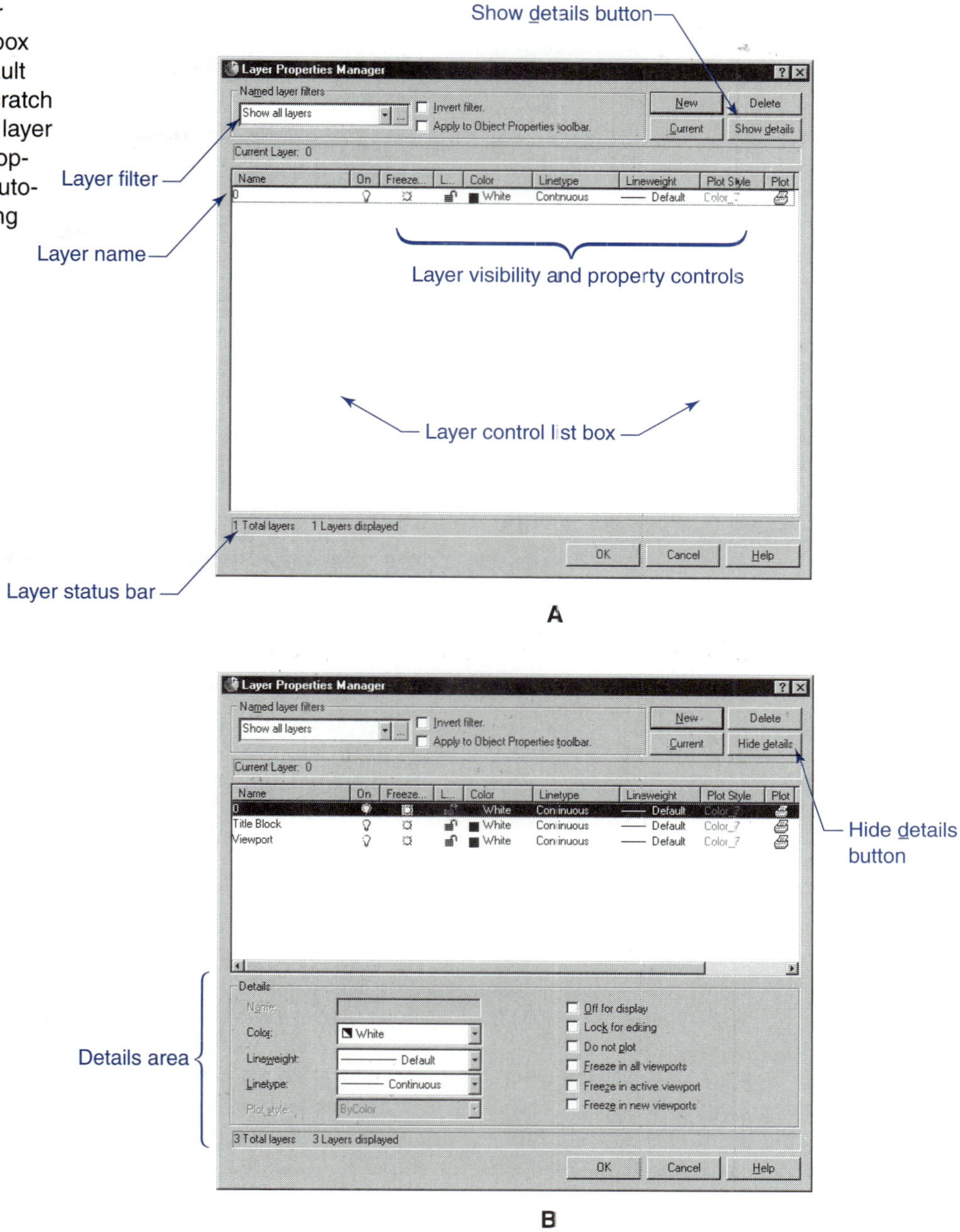

FIGURE 5.2 (A) The Layer Properties Manager dialog box shows the AutoCAD LT default layers when starting from scratch or using Quick Setup. The 0 layer is the default for all starting options. (B) Additional layers automatically added when starting with a template.

details area at the bottom of the dialog box. The details area provides access to the same controls available in the list using a different interface style. The 0 layer is listed with Title Block and Viewport. Pick the New button to add new layer names to the layer list. A new default layer named Layer1 is added to the list and highlighted when you pick the New button, as shown in Figure 5.3. New layers have the default state and properties. These features are discussed later. You can add default layers named Layer2, Layer3, etc., each time you pick the New button. The default layer names might work for some applications, but they usually are not descriptive enough for professional use.

When you pick the New button, the default Layer1 name is highlighted inside a text box. This allows you to immediately type a new layer name, such as Object, as shown in Figure 5.4. The Object layer might be used for drawing the object lines on a mechanical drawing. You can press Enter twice, after typing the desired layer name, to create another new layer. This is easier than pressing the New button. Then all you have to do is type another layer name in place of the default Layer name. An easy way to enter several layer names at the same time is to type each name, followed by a comma. Typing the comma drops the layer list to the next line, with the Layer1 name highlighted for you to type another new layer name. Figure 5.5 shows the layer names Center, Dimension, Hidden, and Section added to the list in this manner. These layers are used for displaying the type of line associated with the name. For example, the Center layer is used for centerlines and the Dimension layer is used for dimensions. AutoCAD LT displays layer names using the letter case you

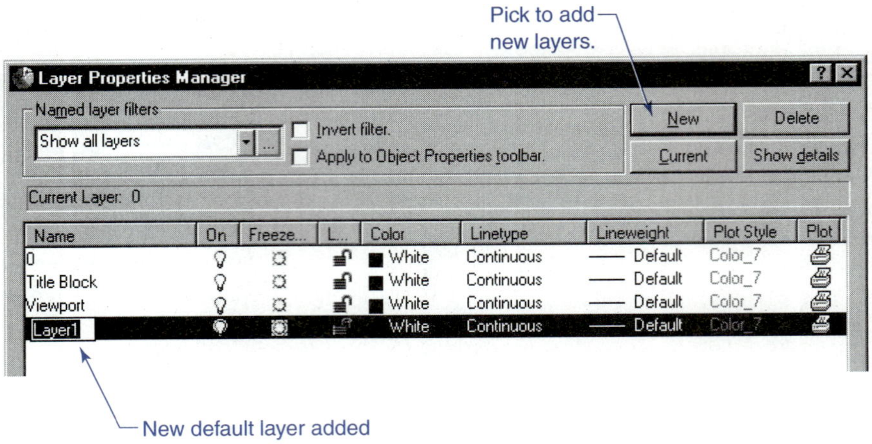

FIGURE 5.3 Pick the New button in the Layer Properties Manager dialog box to add a new layer. The default layer is named Layer1.

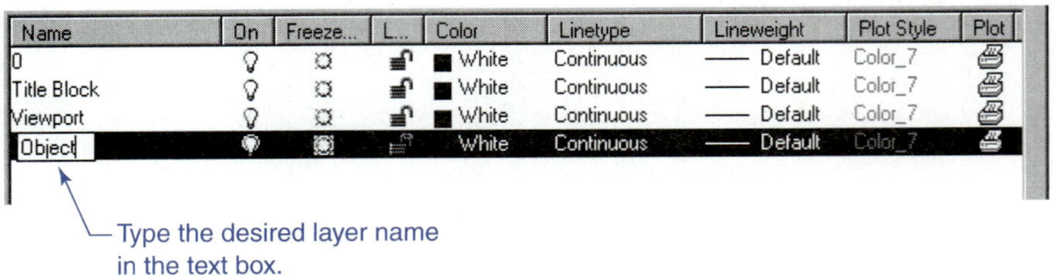

FIGURE 5.4 Type the desired layer name in the text box.

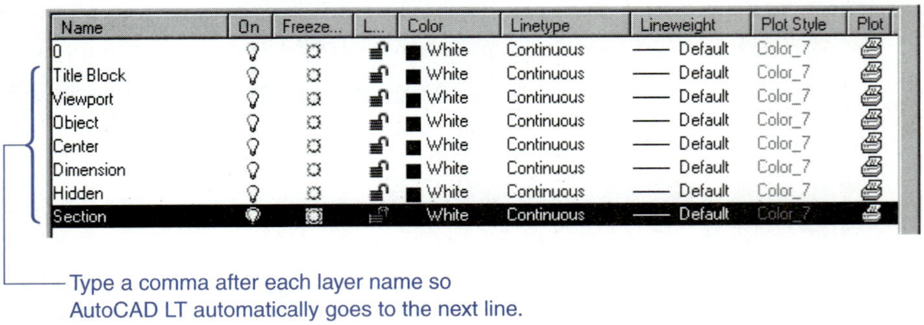

FIGURE 5.5 Type a comma after each layer name to have AutoCAD LT automatically go to the next line.

type when you create the layer, but layer names are not case sensitive. This means that you can type layer names using either caps or lowercase letters. Picking the Cancel button discards all changes and layers made during this dialog session. Pick the OK button to close the Layer Properties Manager dialog box when you are done working with layers.

Open the Layer Properties Manager dialog box again and you will see that AutoCAD LT has automatically arranged the layer names in alphabetical order, as shown in Figure 5.6. Every new layer has the default status and properties.

The following describes several ways to work with layers in the Name list:

- Pick a layer name to highlight it and then pick again to have a text box placed around the layer name. Now you can type a different layer name, if desired.

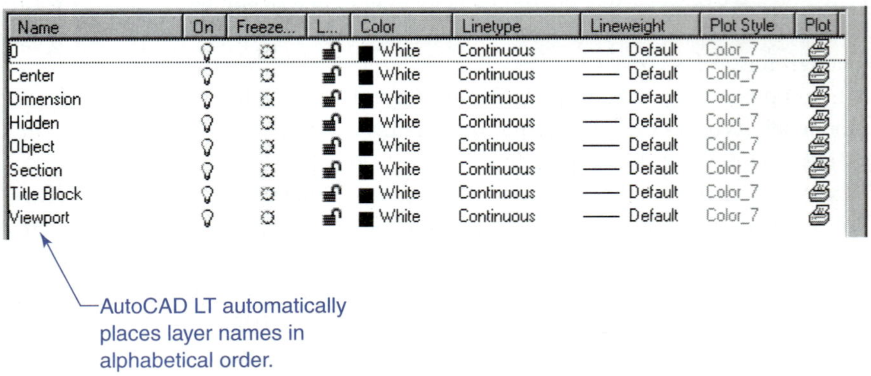

FIGURE 5.6 AutoCAD LT automatically lists layer names in alphabetical order.

- Pick a layer name and then hold the Shift key to have every layer name highlighted between the first pick and the second.
- Hold the Ctrl key while picking layer names to highlight multiple layer names when the names are not adjacent.
- Pick to highlight one or more layer names and then pick the Delete button to have the highlighted layers removed from the list. A layer cannot be removed if it is current or it contains objects.
- Move the cursor inside the layer list box and press the right mouse button. This displays the shortcut menu shown in Figure 5.7.

Layer names can have up to 255 characters and you can use letters, numbers, and special characters such as underscores (_), hyphens (-), dollar signs ($), and blank spaces.

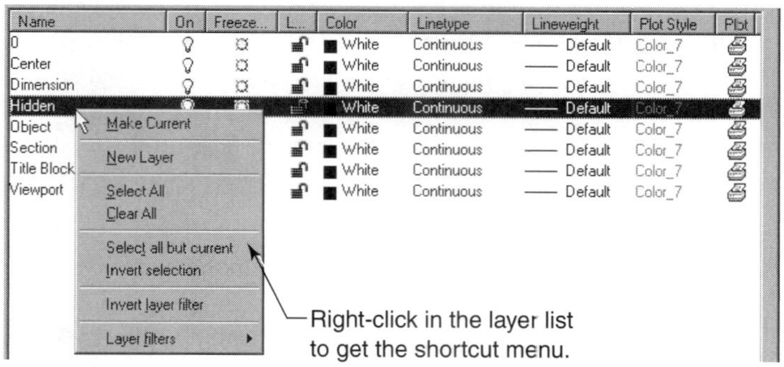

FIGURE 5.7 Move the cursor inside the layer list box and click on the right mouse button to get the cursor menu.

Using Layer Colors

As with many lists in Windows, the label at the top of each column in the layer list is actually a button. If you pick the button, the contents of the layer list are sorted alphabetically by the items in that column. Picking it again switches the sorting order from ascending (example: A, B, C, ...) to descending (example: Z, Y, X, ...). Move your cursor to the edge of any button to display the resizing cursor. Press and hold the pick button and move your mouse to adjust the width of a column. Also, the Layer Properties Manager can be resized in the same manner as a program window. Move your cursor to an edge or corner of the Layer Properties Manager, then press and hold the pick button and move the mouse. This can be useful in a drawing with very long layer names. Layer names that are wider than the Name column are displayed in an abbreviated format where the start and end of the layer name are visible, and the middle is represented by an ellipsis (see Figure 5.8A). If you have sized everything up as much as possible and still cannot view the full names of layers in your drawing, AutoCAD LT will display a tooltip showing the full name of the layer to which you are pointing. Figure 5.8B shows this feature.

Notice in Figure 5.6 that all of the listed layers are shown with the color white. The color white is white on a black display screen or it is black on a white display screen. Having all of the lines displayed with the color white is an option, but a better application is to assign each layer its own color. The standard AutoCAD LT colors are recognized by name and by color number. The following is a list of standard colors by name and number:

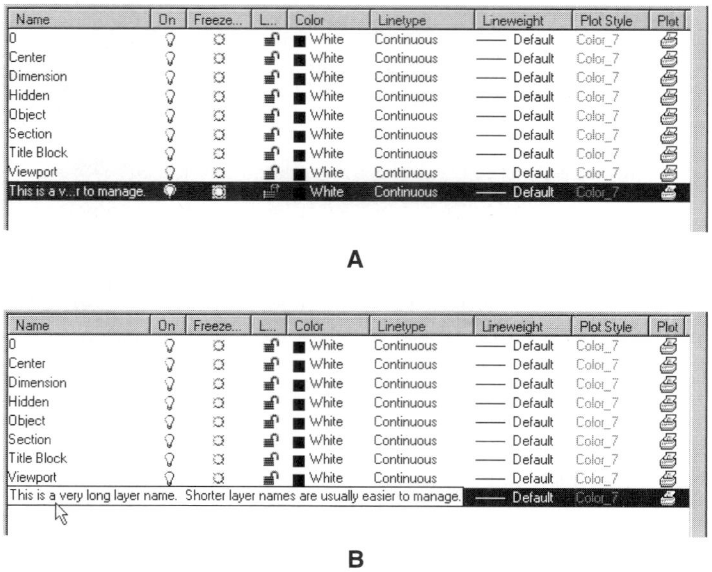

FIGURE 5.8 (A) Layer names that are too long to be completely displayed are abbreviated. (B) Pointing to an abbreviated layer name displays a tooltip with the full name.

Color	*Number*
RED	1
YELLOW	2
GREEN	3
CYAN	4
BLUE	5
MAGENTA	6
WHITE	7

Colors beyond the basic colors are identified only by numbers. The total color range runs from number 1 through 255.

To change a layer color, pick the color swatch or name associated with that layer. You can pick as many layers as you want to highlight and then pick any one of the highlighted colors. When you pick the color of a highlighted layer or layers, the Select Color dialog box is displayed. See Figure 5.9. The current color is displayed in the Color: text box. Move the cursor to a desired color, such as green, and pick. The color you pick is displayed in the Color: text box. Pick the OK button when you are ready. Colors can be picked in this manner or you can enter the color number in the text box. Change the layer color for all of the desired layers. Note that the selected color is assigned to all the currently highlighted layers. Figure 5.10 shows the selected layer colors for the previously named layers.

FIGURE 5.9 Pick the color swatch of the highlighted layer or layers to access the Select Color dialog box.

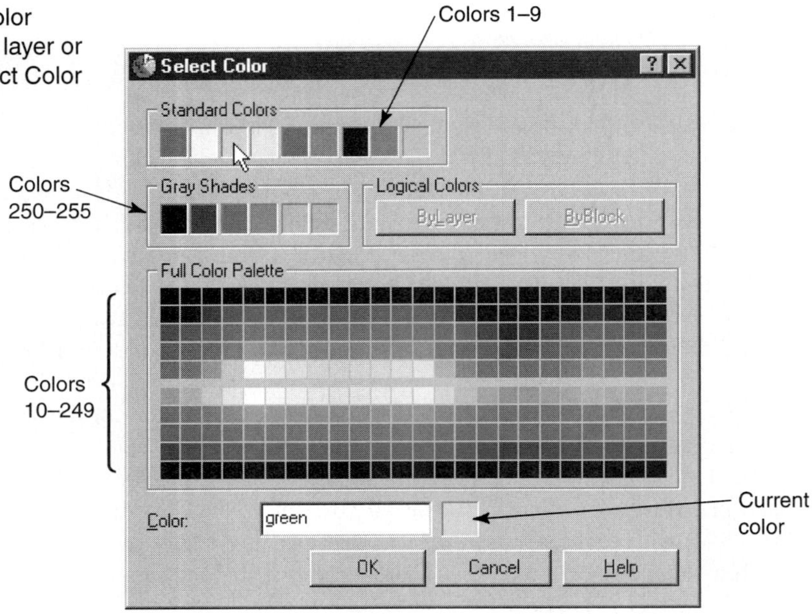

FIGURE 5.10 Pick the OK button in the Layer Properties Manager dialog box to accept the colors that were assigned to each layer.

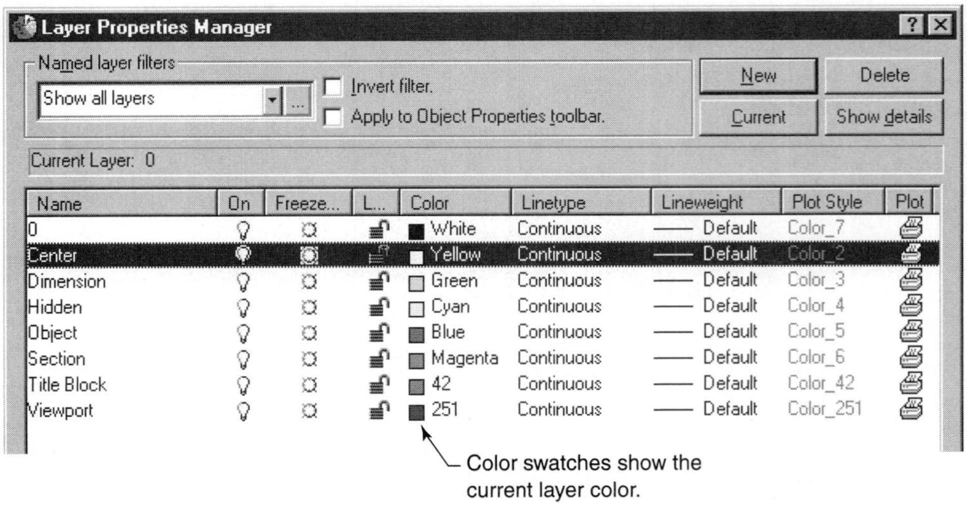

Field Notes

Defined layers can be used as templates for new layers. If an existing layers has some or all of the settings that you need on a new layer, highlight the existing layer name and pick the New button in the Layer Properties Manager. The new layer will be created with the same settings as the highlighted layer.

Using Layer Linetypes

The term ***linetype*** is AutoCAD LT's way of referring to types of drafting lines. Recommended linetypes are identified in the American National Standards Institute document *Line Conventions and Lettering* (ASME Y14.2M). These lines are shown in Appendix B. If needed, refer to the examples in that appendix for a review of drafting standards and practices.

When you initially name a new layer, the listed linetype is Continuous. Continuous linetypes are solid lines (without dashes). A Continuous linetype setting is used for object lines, section lines, and dimension lines, which should all be solid lines. However, for drawing lines to proper standards, you want to set lines in layers such as center, hidden, and phantom to their proper linetype representation. To do this, open the Layer Properties Manager dialog box, move the cursor to the linetype name of the desired layer, and pick. The Select Linetype dialog box shown in Figure 5.11 is displayed when you pick the desired linetype. The Select Linetype dialog box lists the available linetype names, shows what each line type looks like, and gives a short description. The only linetype listed in a drawing started from scratch is Continuous. You must load additional linetypes before they can be used with your layers. To load more linetypes, pick the Load ... button to get the Load or Reload Linetypes dialog box shown in Figure 5.12. The *aclt.lin* file contains ISO (International Organization for Standardization) inch linetypes with dots and dashes, standard ASME inch linetypes with dots and dashes, and complex linetypes with shapes and text. Use the down arrow or the scroll bar to access available linetypes, or you can resize this dialog box to expand the size of the list so you can view more linetypes at one time. Pick to highlight the desired linetypes and then pick the OK button to have them loaded into the Select Linetype dialog box. Figure 5.13 shows the Center, Hidden, and Phantom linetypes loaded along with the Continuous default linetype. Now, pick the desired linetype that matches the layer you chose and pick the OK button. Figure 5.14 shows the linetypes changed for the Center, Hidden, and a newly created Phantom layer. Pick the OK button in the Layer Properties Manager dialog box to have the layer linetype changes accepted by AutoCAD LT. Appendix C displays the *aclt.lin* linetypes.

Filters, the Current button, and the Show details button are explained later in this chapter.

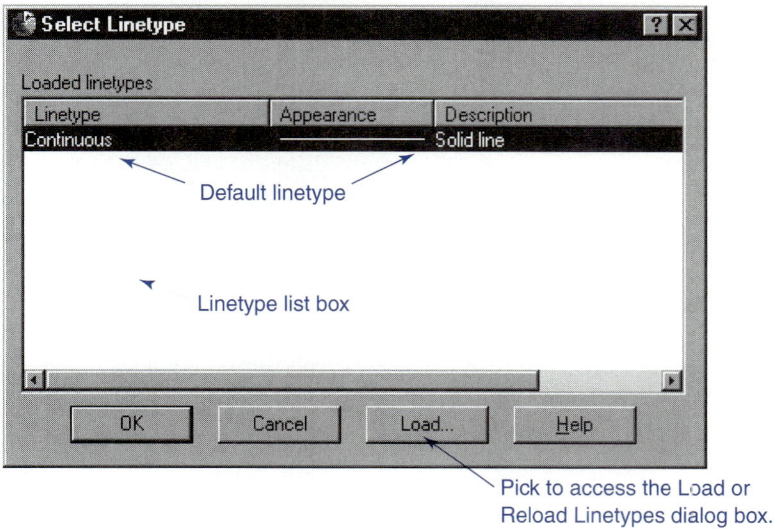

FIGURE 5.11 The Select Linetype displays the available linetypes. Continuous is the only linetype listed when you start AutoCAD LT. Pick the Load ... button to open the Load or Reload Linetypes dialog box where you can load additional linetypes.

Field Notes

The list of available linetypes is very long in the Load or Reload Linetypes dialog box. You can use the scroll bar or elevator button to locate the desired linetype, but this takes time. A quick way to find a linetype is to pick inside the Linetype window and then type the first letter of the linetype name. For example, if you type h, the list automatically advances and highlights the Hidden linetype. If you type p, the Phantom linetype is quickly highlighted.

FIGURE 5.12 Pick the Load ... button in the Select Linetype dialog box to open the Load or Reload Linetypes dialog box.

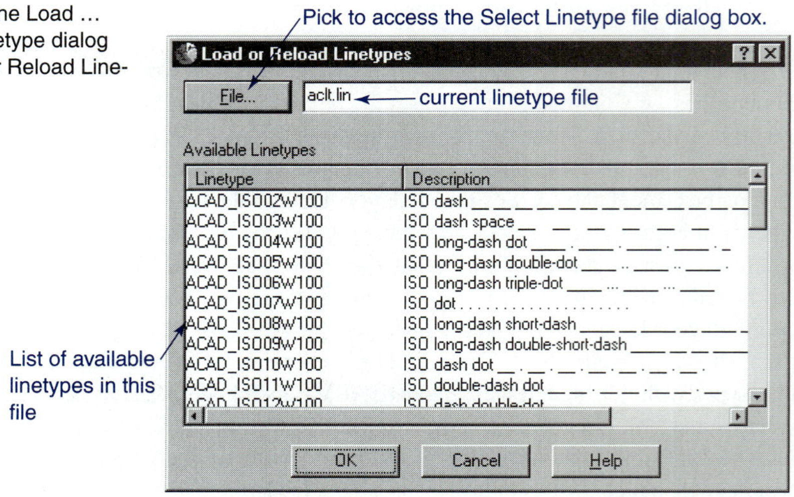

FIGURE 5.13 Linetypes loaded into the Select Linetype dialog box from the Load or Reload Linetypes dialog box.

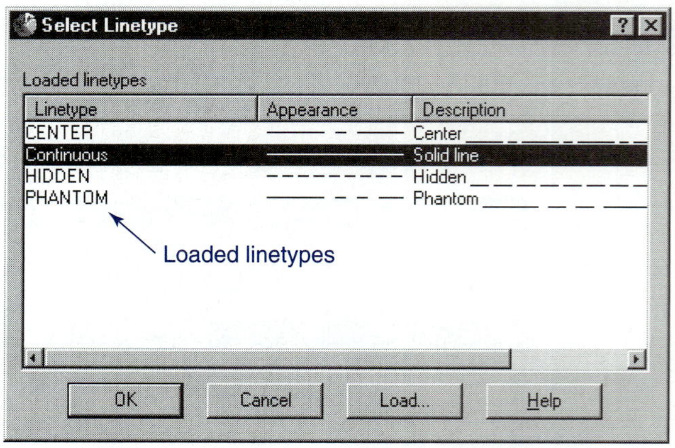

FIGURE 5.14 The desired linetypes are applied to their layers.

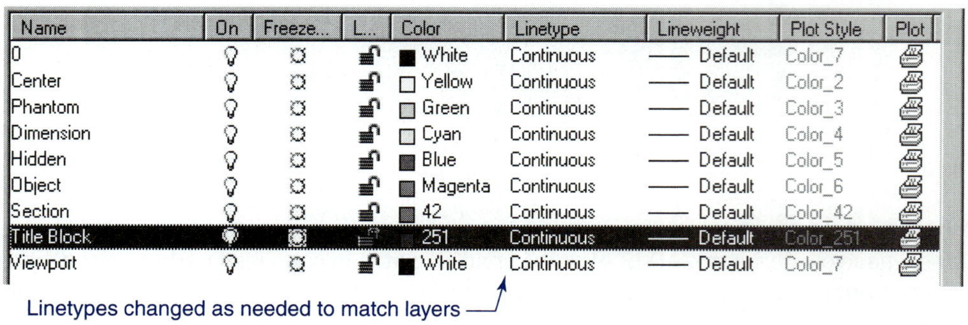

Field Notes

Notice the File ... button in Figure 5.12. Pick this button to access the Select Linetype File dialog box shown in Figure 5.15. There are two AutoCAD LT linetype files:

aclt.lin	These are the standard and complex linetypes for inch drawings.
acltiso.lin	These are the standard and complex linetypes for metric drawings.

Access the linetype file that contains the linetypes needed for your drawing and pick the OK button. These linetypes are now available in the Load or Reload Linetypes dialog box. Load the desired linetypes as previously explained.

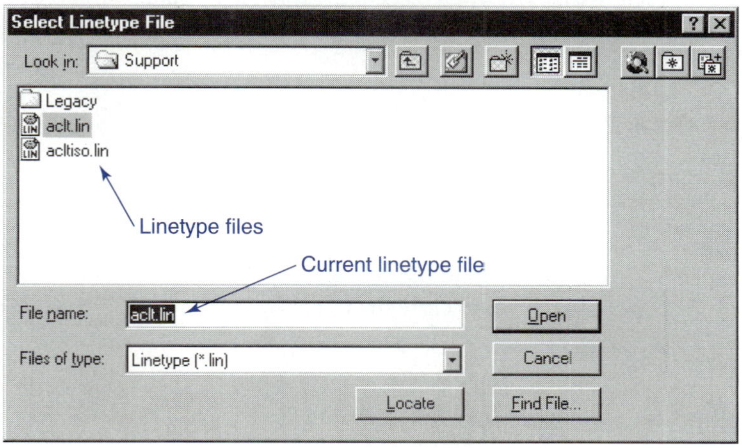

FIGURE 5.15 The Select Linetype File dialog box. Notice the two AutoCAD LT linetype LIN files: aclt and acltiso.

Format
Linetype...

LINETYPE
LT
DDLTYPE

You can also find and load linetypes by using the Linetype Manager dialog box. You can access the Linetype Manager dialog box by picking Other... in the Linetype drop-down list on the Object Properties toolbar, by picking Linetype ... in the Format pull-down menu, or by typing **LT**, **LINETYPE**, or **DDLTYPE**. The Linetype Manager is shown in Figure 5.16 with the previously loaded linetypes displayed. The Load ... button acts as previously discussed by opening the Load or Reload Linetypes dialog box. The Delete button is used to remove any highlighted linetypes from the list. Use of the linetype filters, the Current button, and the Show details button are explained later in this chapter.

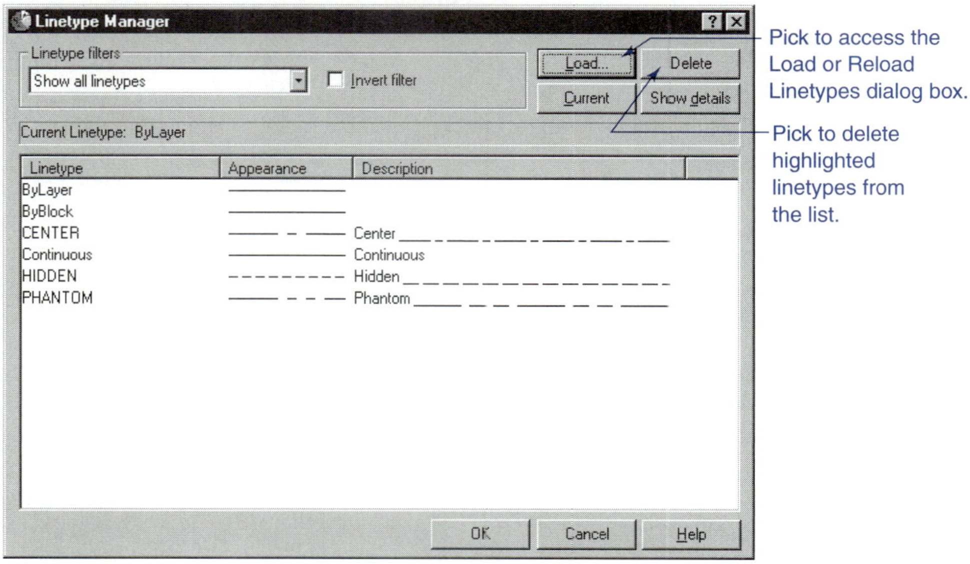

FIGURE 5.16 The Linetype Manager dialog box displays the previously loaded linetypes.

Exercise 5.1 **Estimated time required: 10 min.**

1. Open AutoCAD LT if it is not already open. Use the setup option of your choice, open an exercise from a previous chapter, or open a template.
2. A border and title block are optional.
3. Set limits at 8.5,11 unless your prototype contains other limits settings and is approved by your instructor or supervisor.
4. Establish the following layers by Name, Color, and Linetype:

Layer Name	*Color*	*Linetype*
CENTER	green	CENTER
CONSTRUCTION	red	CONTINUOUS
DIMENSION	blue	CONTINUOUS
HIDDEN	magenta	HIDDEN
OBJECT	white	CONTINUOUS
PHANTOM	yellow	PHANTOM
SECTION	cyan	CONTINUOUS

5. Open the Load or Reload Linetypes dialog box and pick the File ... button. This opens the Select Linetype File dialog box. The default aclt.lin file should be active. Pick the acltiso.lin file and then pick OK. Look at the available linetypes displayed in the Load or Reload Linetypes dialog box. Return to the aclt.lin file.
6. Save as EX5.1, and close the drawing.

Making a Layer Current

All objects drawn in AutoCAD LT are automatically placed on the currently active layer, typically referred to as the *current layer.* By default, the objects you draw automatically take on the properties assigned to that layer. For example, if the CENTER layer is current, its color is set to green and linetype to CENTER, then the objects you draw are displayed using green centerlines. A layer can be made current by using the Layer Properties Manager dialog box or by picking the Layer Control drop-down list.

In the Layer Properties Manager dialog box, either double-click a layer name or pick the desired layer to highlight it and then pick the Current: button. The selected layer name is displayed above the layer list. Pick the OK button, shown in Figure 5.17, when ready. The current layer with its color and linetype are displayed in the list boxes found in the Object Properties toolbar. (Figure 5.18). The term *ByLayer* in the layer color and linetype list boxes means that the objects drawn on a specific layer use the color and linetype assigned to that layer.

A layer can be made current faster by accessing the Layer Control list box in the Object Properties toolbar. When the list box is displayed, pick the desired layer to make it current automatically, as shown in Figure 5.19. The current layer with its color and linetype are then displayed as shown in Figure 5.18.

Object Properties

Make Object's Layer Current

AI_MOLC

You can also make the layer of an existing object on the drawing current. To do this, pick the Make Object's Layer Current button at the far left end of the Object Properties toolbar. AutoCAD LT then asks you to select an object. AutoCAD LT gives you a message indicating the layer of the object you selected is now current:

Command: ⟨*pick the Make Object's Layer Current button*⟩
Select object whose layer will become current: ⟨*pick the desired object*⟩
CENTER is now the current layer.
Command:

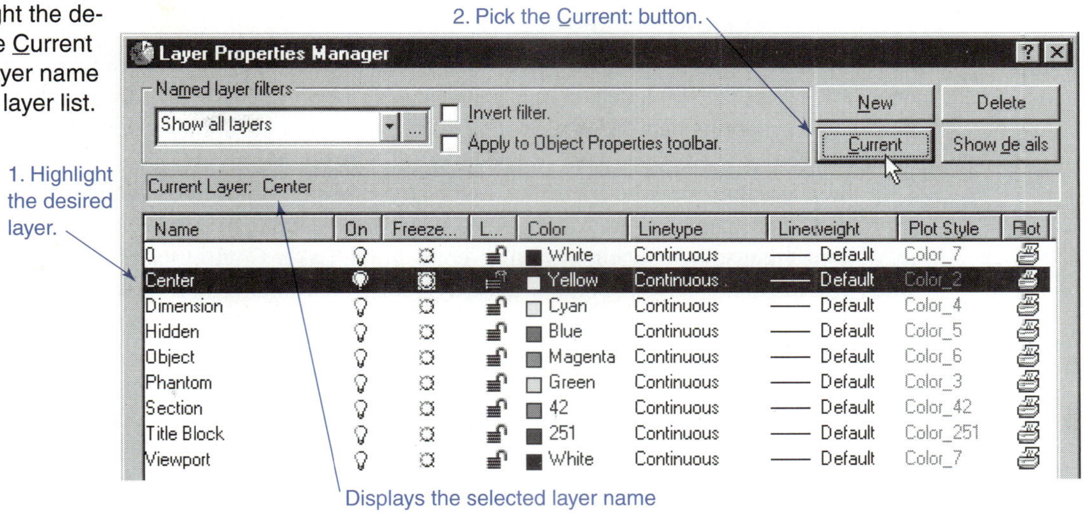

FIGURE 5.17 Highlight the desired layer and pick the Current button. The selected layer name is displayed above the layer list.

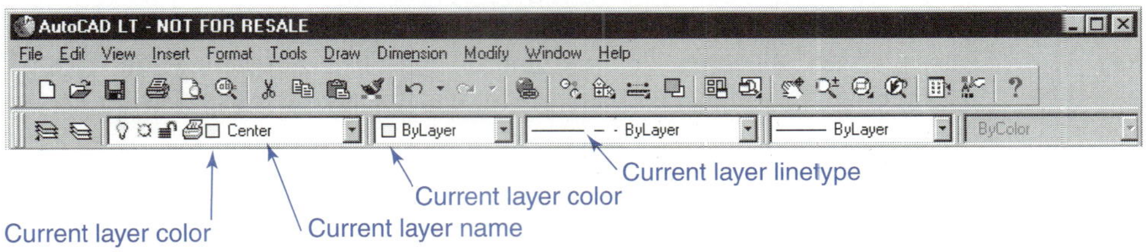

FIGURE 5.18 The current layer color and linetype are displayed in the list boxes found in the Object Properties toolbar.

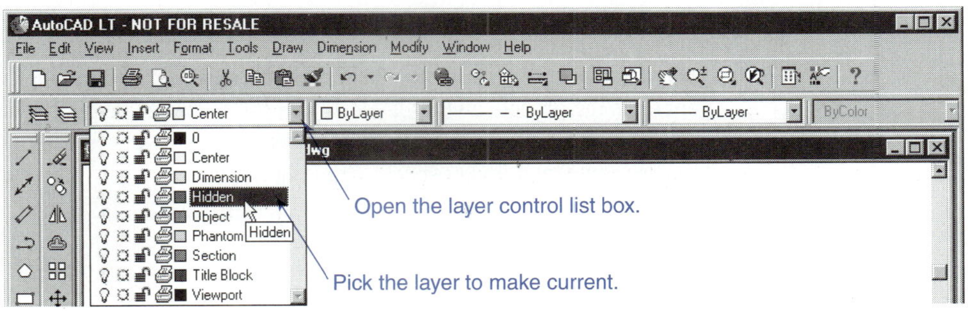

FIGURE 5.19 Open the Layer Control list box and select a layer to automatically make it current.

Field Notes

Use the scroll bar to access additional layers when more layers exist in the Layer Control list box than can be displayed in the list.

Controlling Layer Visibility

Layer visibility determines if the objects that have been drawn on a layer are visible or invisible. The objects on visible layers are displayed on the screen and can be plotted. The objects on nonvisible layers are not displayed and cannot be plotted. One reason for using layers is the ability to make the information on a specific layer visible if it needs to be seen or invisible if it is not in use.

Layer visibility can be controlled in the Layer Properties Manager dialog box and in the Layer Control list box. A layer name becomes highlighted when you pick one or more of the visibility options. The visibility options are displayed using symbolic icons. In the Layer Control list box a tooltip tells you the function when you move the cursor to one of these symbols. All you have to do to change the visibility of a specific layer is pick the desired symbol. The appearance of the symbol changes to represent the visibility status. The following displays the visibility symbols and what happens when they are used:

ON OFF

When a layer is on, it is visible and available for use. When a layer is off, objects on the layer are invisible and do not plot. You can turn off the current layer, but AutoCAD LT gives you a warning box that says, The current layer is turned off. If you turn off the current layer, you will not see the objects on the layer or any new objects you create.

THAWED FROZEN

When a layer is frozen, objects on the layer are invisible and cannot be plotted. A frozen layer does not regenerate when you change a view in the visible layers. Freezing layers can help speed up ZOOM, PAN, and decrease regeneration time for complex drawings. If you try to freeze the current layer, AutoCAD LT gives you this warning: Cannot freeze the current layer.

The following visibility controls are displayed only in the Layer Properties Manager and then only when working in a layout tab. These features are fully explained in later chapters.

Pick this symbol to freeze or thaw selected layers in the current viewport without affecting layer visibility in other viewports. A *viewport* is a window or windows in which the model space of a drawing is displayed in paper space. Viewports are fully explained in later chapters.

Pick this symbol to freeze or thaw selected layers in newly created viewports without affecting layer visibility in current viewports.

Field Notes

> Turning off a layer rather than freezing it can slow down drawing time, because AutoCAD LT regenerates the objects on that layer. If you often change layers between visible and invisible, turning unneeded layers off saves time. However, if layers are invisible for long periods of time, freezing unneeded layers speeds drawing time.

Locking and Unlocking Layers

LOCKED

UNLOCKED

A layer can be locked to keep you from accidentally editing it or to keep others from tampering with the contents of the layer. You cannot edit a locked layer, but you can look at it, you can add objects, and you can use inquiry commands. You can also freeze and thaw a locked layer and change its color and linetype setting Layers can be quickly locked or unlocked in the Layer Properties Manager dialog box and in the Layer Control list box at the top of the screen. Click on the lock symbol to either open or close the lock.

Using Layer Lineweights

Lineweights, or line widths, are used in drafting to provide additional contrast and clarity in a drawing. ASME standards require that some lines, such as object lines, be drawn using a lineweight of 0.6 mm. Other lines, such as hidden and center lines, use a thinner lineweight of 0.3 mm. Your specific company or school standards may have additional requirements.

In AutoCAD LT 2000, lineweights are controlled most effectively by assigning lineweights to layers. This way, when you draw on the Object layer, your lines are automatically created as continuous lines that are 0.6 mm wide. Or if you draw a line on the Hidden layer, it is automatically drawn using a hidden linetype and a 0.3 mm lineweight. In order for a new object to use the lineweight associated with the layer on which it was created, the Lineweight Control drop-down list must be set to ByLayer (see Figure 5.18).

Lineweights can be overridden using plot styles, which are discussed in Chapter 13. However, if you use the default *aclt.ctb* plot style, the lineweights you assign to your layers will also be used in plotting.

To assign a lineweight to a layer, access the Layer Properties Manager dialog box. Pick the current lineweight setting for the layer or layers you want to set to display the Lineweight dialog box (see Figure 5.20). Select the desired lineweight from the list. This presents a list of the most commonly used fixed drafting lineweights. If you need a lineweight that is not available on the list, you can set the new lineweight in a Plot Style Table (Chapter 13).

Pick the LWT button on the AutoCAD LT status bar to display lineweights on screen. Lineweights are relative, not absolute, in the Model tab. When you zoom in or out, the object lineweights do not change. This can adversely affect the display of closely grouped objects, as shown in Figure 5.21. If this happens, you can turn off the lineweight display by picking the LWT button again. Optionally, you can adjust the scale at which lineweights are displayed; this is discussed later in this chapter. Lineweights are absolute in plotting, so lineweights are dimensionally accurate on your hardcopy drawings.

Layer Plotting Control

The printer icon in the column labeled Plot in the Layer Properties Manager is used to turn plotting on or off for specific layers. By default, plotting is turned on for new layers unless you use an existing layer as a template. To toggle the plotting state, pick the printer icon. When the universal "NO" symbol (the red circle with a diagonal line) appears on the printer icon, plotting is turned off for that layer.

This feature allows you to control what part of a drawing is sent to the plotter without affecting the visibility for the specified layers. Figure 5.22 shows the Layer Properties Manager dialog box with plotting turned off for layer "0" and the "Viewport" layer. Common uses of this feature include turning off plotting for construction or reference layers, or for layers containing proprietary information.

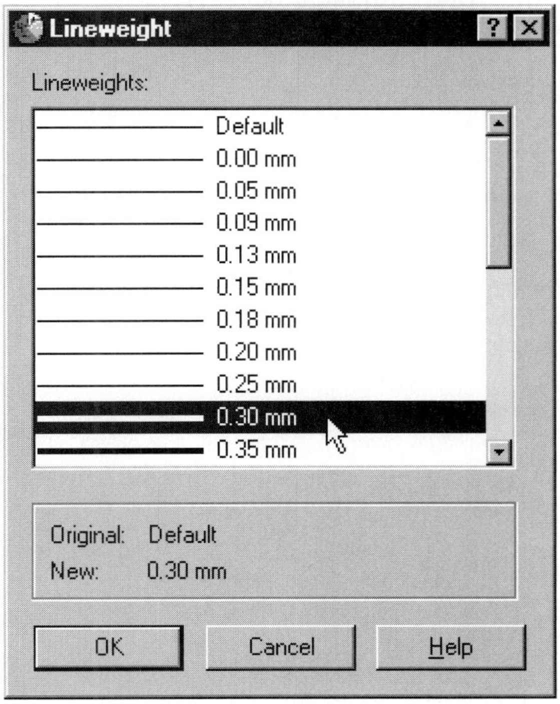

FIGURE 5.20 The Lineweight dialog box presents a list of the most commonly used drafting lineweights.

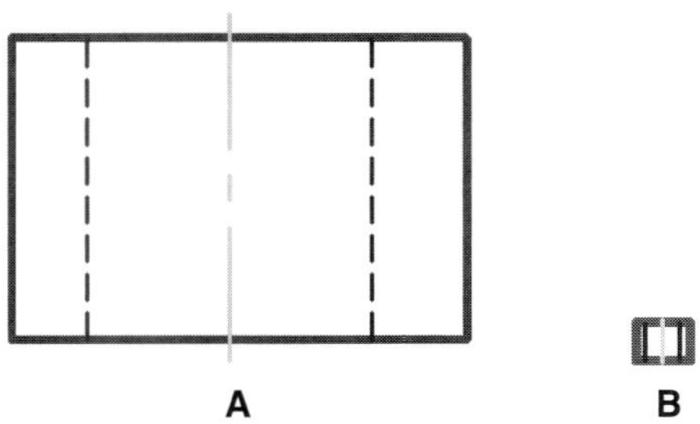

FIGURE 5.21 Lineweights are relative in the Model tab, not absolute. (A) When the objects are viewed closely, the lineweights display properly. (B) When zoomed out, the Model tab lineweights can get in the way.

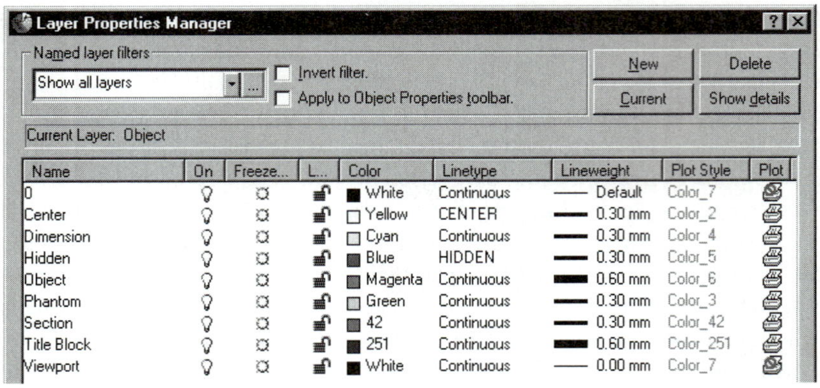

FIGURE 5.22 When layer plotting is turned off, the objects are not printed even if they are visible on-screen.

Exercise 5.2 — Estimated time required: 20 min.

1. Open AutoCAD LT if it is not already open and then open EX5.1.
2. Draw the schematic shown using the designated layers that were established in Exercise 5.1. The actual size is up to you. Do not include notes.

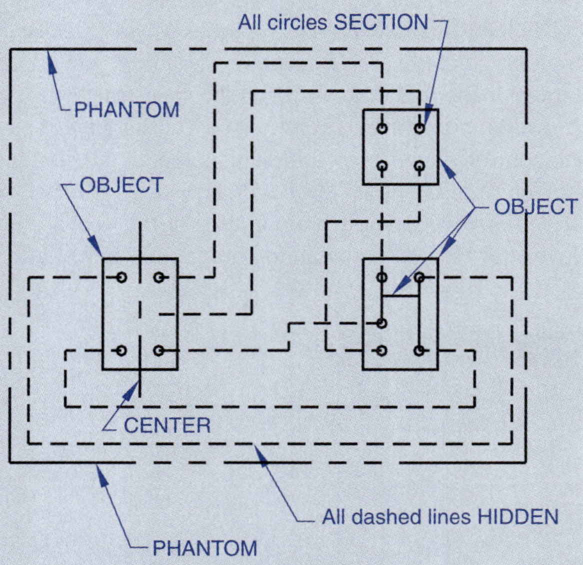

3. Adjust the linetype scale so each line clearly represents the proper linetype. Try a linetype scale of .5.
4. Turn off the PHANTOM layer and observe the results.
5. Freeze the HIDDEN layer and observe the results.
6. Change the lineweight of the Object layer to 0.6 mm and all other layers to 0.3 mm. Turn lineweight display on and view the results.
7. Right-click to open the cursor menu and then pick the Select All option in the Layer & Linetype Properties dialog box to turn on and thaw all layers.
8. Save as EX5.2, and close the drawing.

Layer and Linetype Control at the Command Line

-LAYER
-LA

Using the dialog box and the drop-down list is the easiest way to manage layers. You can also do these things, with the -LAYER command, at the keyboard if you like to type commands. To access the Layer command at the keyboard, type **-LA** or **-LAYER**. There is a hyphen (-) in front of the command name. The -LAYER command looks like this:

Command: **-LA** or **-LAYER**↵
Current layer: "Object"
Enter an option [?/Make/Set/New/ON/OFF/Color/Ltype/LWeight/Plot/Freeze/Thaw/LOck/Unlock]:

The options match the features you have already used in the previous discussions. Some of the options are self-explanatory, such as Freeze and Thaw. The following provides brief information about the other options:

- **?** Type a question mark (?) to get a list of available layers.
- **Make** Type **M** for the Make option to create a new layer and automatically make it current. If the layer you make already exists, it is simply made current.
- **Set** Type **S** for the Set option to set a new current layer.
- **New** Type **N** for the New option to create a new layer without changing the status of the current layer.
- **Ltype** Allows you to change the linetype setting for a layer. Linetypes are loaded as needed, if they are found in the currently referenced linetype file.

Field Notes

- If you are not creating a new layer or changing a layer's associated color, the Linetype Control drop-down list is the quickest and most convenient means of adjusting the most frequent layer settings. For creating new layers or changing colors, you will find that the Layer Properties Manager dialog box provides a more convenient and intuitive interface than is offered by the -LAYER command.
- The Layer Property Manager can be used transparently by picking the Layers toolbar button or by typing **'LA** at the current prompt. The Layer Control list box cannot be used transparently.

-LINETYPE
-LT

Linetypes can also be loaded and set at the command line, but it is not as convenient as using the dialog box. To do this, type **-LT** or **-LINETYPE** with a hyphen (-) typed before the command name. The -LINETYPE command gives you these options:

Command: **-LT** or **-LINETYPE**
Current line type: "ByLayer"
Enter an option [?/Create/Load/Set]:

The options are described as follows:

- **?** Type a question mark (?) to get a list of the currently loaded linetypes.
- **Create** This option is used to create custom linetypes and is explained in Chapter 16.
- **Load** Type **L** for the Load option if you want to load linetypes. The Load option asks you which linetypes you want to load. You can type one or more desired linetype names, separated by a comma; for example:

  Enter an option [?/Create/Load/Set]: **L↵**
  Enter linetype(s) to load: **HIDDEN,CENTER,PHANTOM↵**

  The Select Linetype File dialog box is now displayed. You select one of the linetype files as previously explained.
- **Set** Type **S** for the Set option if you want to set linetypes for use in the current drawing. This sets the current linetype. The default is BYLAYER, which means that linetypes are set based on layer controls.

Adjusting Linetype Scale

The ***linetype scale*** determines the relative length of dashes in linetypes such as hidden and centerlines. Setting a linetype scale ensures that the lines you draw are represented properly on the screen and when the drawing is plotted. Linetype scales also allow you to control the appearance of very short lines. When you draw a short center line, for example, AutoCAD LT does not display the dashes if there is not enough room. So, rather than getting a center line symbol, you may get a solid line. If this is not acceptable, you can reduce the linetype scale in an attempt to get the display you want. You can change the linetype scale for each line depending on the requirements or length of the line. Normally, however, it is not necessary to change the linetype scale except for special conditions.

The linetype scale can also be set to match the scale factor of the drawing or for individual objects. Setting the linetype scale for the entire drawing is referred to as a global scale factor. ***Global*** means that the setting affects everything on the entire drawing. If the linetype scale is set for drawing-specific objects, it is referred to as an individual object linetype scale factor. The term ***individual*** means that the setting affects only individually drawn objects without changing the entire drawing. The ***scale factor*** determines the final size of things such as text height, dimension characteristics, and linetype appearance when your drawing is plotted. For a full-scale (1:1) mechanical drawing, the scale factor is 1.0, which is the AutoCAD LT default. If the scale is half (1:2), the scale factor is 1/2, or 0.5. If you are making an architectural drawing that you plan to plot at 1/4″ = 1′0″, then the scale factor is 48. This is calculated as follows:

$$1/4 = 12$$
$$1 = 12 \times 4$$
$$1 = 48$$

You can change the linetype scale for the entire drawing or for new objects by using the Show details button in the Linetype Manager dialog box. Pick the Other... option in the Linetype Control List on the Object Properties toolbar, pick Linetype ... in the Format pull-down menu, or type **LT, LINETYPE,** or **DDLTYPE** at the Command: prompt to display this dialog box. Then highlight the desired linetype and pick the Show details button at the bottom of the dialog box. Picking this button expands the dialog box, as shown in Figure 5.23. The following identifies the features of the Details area:

- The Name: text box can be used to change the linetype name.
- The Description: text box can be used to change the linetype description.
- The Global scale factor: text box is where you change the linetype scale factor for the entire drawing. This feature is also controlled by LTSCALE, which is explained next.
- The Current object scale: text box is where you can set the linetype scale of new lines only. This change does not affect existing lines. The current object linetype scale is also controlled by the CELTSCALE system variable, where you can enter a scale factor at the prompt line.
- The Use paper space units for scaling check box is on by default. This scales linetypes the same for model space and paper space. This is also controlled at the prompt line using the PSLTSCALE system variable.
- The ISO pen width: list box is inactive unless you select an ISO linetype that allows for pen width adjustment.

FIGURE 5.23 Using the expanded details area of the linetype tab in the Linetype Manager dialog box.

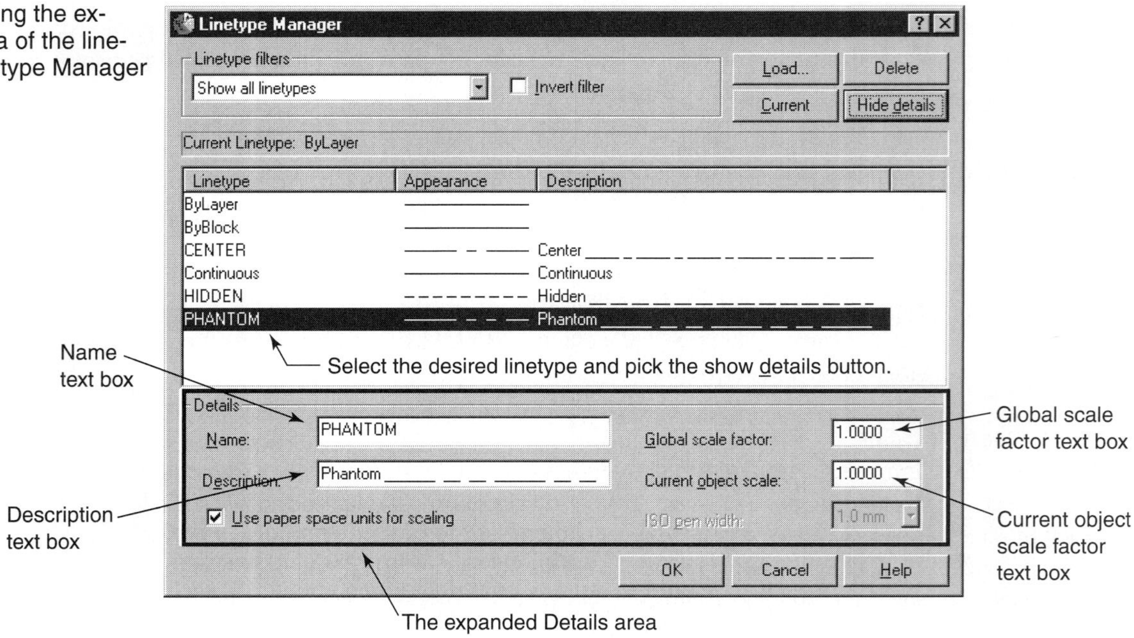

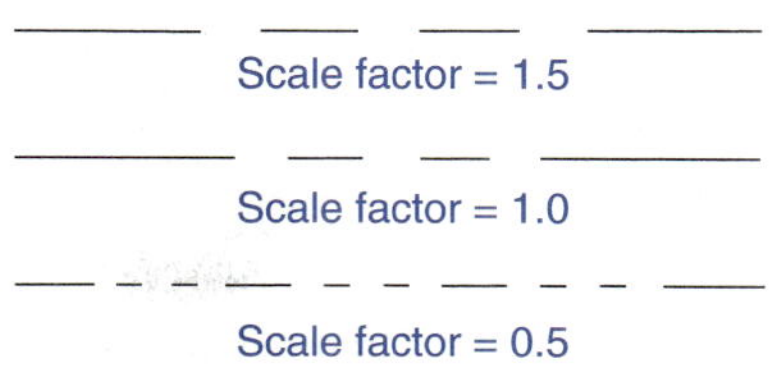

FIGURE 5.24 A comparison of different linetype scale settings.

Pick the Hide details button to return to the original Linetype Manager dialog box format. Pick the OK button when you are finished. Figure 5.24 gives you an example of using different linetype scales on a phantom line.

You can change the global linetype scale at the keyboard using the **LTS** or **LTSCALE** command. Making linetype scale changes in this manner alters the scale of every linetype on the drawing to match the specification you request. The command sequence looks like this:

Command: **LTS** or **LTSCALE**↵
Enter new linetype scale factor <1.000>: **.5**↵
Regenerating model.
Command:

Field Notes

Sometimes you need to adjust the scale factor for linetypes in small increments and look at the display after each adjustment until the desired appearance is achieved. The dash length you select should match American Society of Mechanical Engineers (ASME) or other standards you are using. Sample ASME standard lines are shown in Appendix B. If you choose a Linetype scale that is too big, some lines with dashes will appear solid.

LEARNING CHECKPOINT

- ☐ Briefly explain why layers are important.
- ☐ Why is a good layer naming system needed?
- ☐ How do you create a new layer in the Layer Properties Manager dialog box that is named HIDDEN, is assigned the color green, and is for the HIDDEN linetype?
- ☐ What is a CONTINUOUS linetype?
- ☐ Define linetype scale.
- ☐ Explain the difference between global and individual settings.
- ☐ What is the linetype scale of a drawing to be plotted at HALF (1:2) scale?
- ☐ What is the linetype scale of a drawing to be plotted at 1/4″ = 1′0″ scale?
- ☐ Describe two ways to make a layer current.
- ☐ With regard to layer visibility, what is the difference between Off and Freeze?
- ☐ How do you activate a frozen layer so it can be seen and used again?
- ☐ What is the purpose of locking a layer?

Setting and Changing Object Properties

- Organizing Objects Using Layers and Linetypes

Concept Animations

- Layering

Overriding Layer Settings

Layers are very important when designing and drafting with AutoCAD LT. When you see the term *ByLayer* in the control lists on the Object Properties toolbar, or in a dialog box, it means that the settings for that property reflect the settings of the layer on which the object is drawn. Objects are created using a ByLayer linetype and color by default in AutoCAD LT, and this indicates that the newly drawn objects take on the color, linetype, and lineweight properties as assigned to the layer that is current when they are created. In some cases you might want new objects to be on the same layer as others that they are associated with—yet use different colors or linetypes. This can be done with direct color and linetype settings.

Caution should be exercised when overriding layers. Overriding layers happens, for example, when you set an object color or linetype to a value other than By-Layer. An example of this situation is when you are drawing lines and decide to just change the color without regard to the color setting of the current layer. There may be some uses for this practice, but caution should be used because mixing colors and linetypes outside of layer control can result in a confusing drawing.

Overriding Layer Color

All objects are drawn in the current color. If the current color is ByLayer, the objects reference the current layer for their color value. If a color is specified, then the object is still created on the current layer, but the object is displayed in the current color rather than the color assigned to the current layer. The COLOR command allows you to set the default color of new objects you create.

The Select Color dialog box is accessed by typing **COL** or **COLOR** and is entered automatically when you pick Other ... in the Color Control drop-down list or Color ... from the Format pull-down menu. Refer to Figure 5.9 for a review of the Select Color dialog box. Notice that the Logical Colors area contains the BYLAYER and BYBLOCK buttons. Picking one of these buttons assigns the colors ByLayer or BYBLOCK as appropriate. BYBLOCK is explained in Chapter 12. Picking one of the colors sets a specific color for the objects to be drawn.

A quick way to change the current color is by using the Color Control list box located near the center of the Object Properties toolbar. The default color is set ByLayer, but you can change the color by opening the list and selecting the desired color, as shown in Figure 5.25. The last option in the Color Control list is Other ..., which opens the Select Color dialog box, where you can access additional colors.

Change the drawing color at the Command: prompt by typing **-COLOR** like this:

Command: **-COLOR**↵
Enter default object color <BYLAYER>**:** ⟨*type a color name or number such as* **RED**↵⟩
Command:

Notice that ByLayer is the default in the above command. Ignore the ByLayer default by typing a desired color name or number, or press Enter to accept the BYLAYER default. Type **BYLAYER** here later if you

FIGURE 5.25 The Color Control drop-down list.

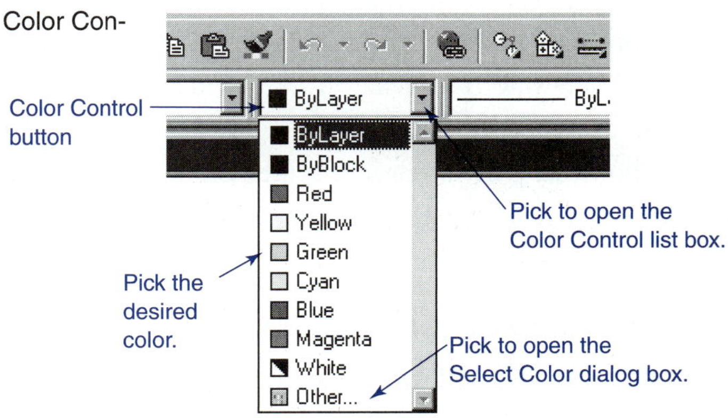

want to return to the layer control. The color for newly drawn objects can also be changed using the CECOLOR system variable.

Field Notes

The DDCOLOR command can be used transparently by picking Color ... from the Format menu or by typing **'COL,** or **'DDCOLOR** at the current prompt. The setting will take effect transparently during most commands. After finishing the command you will notice that the Color Control button is updated to show the new setting.

Overriding Layer Linetype

All objects are drawn with the current linetype. If the current linetype is ByLayer, then the current layer is referenced for the linetype value. If a specific linetype is used, then the object is still created on the current layer, but the object is displayed with the specific linetype rather than the linetype assigned to the current layer. You can set the linetype of any new objects you create by accessing the Linetype Manager dialog box box as previously discussed.

A quick way to change the current linetype is by using the Linetype Control list box located to the right of the Color Control list box in the Object Properties toolbar. The default linetype is set ByLayer, but you can change the linetype by opening the list and selecting the desired linetype, as shown in Figure 5.26. Linetypes must have been previously loaded before they are displayed in the Linetype Control drop-down list. Loading linetypes was explained earlier.

The -LINETYPE command can also be used to access a specific linetype. This command was previously discussed with regard to loading linetypes at the keyboard. The -LINETYPE command's Set option automatically loads a linetype if it is not already loaded, as long as the desired linetype is found in the currently referenced linetype file. Supportive information regarding the currently referenced linetype file was discussed previously with the loading linetypes explanation. Using the Set option in the -LINETYPE command to set a current linetype overrides the layer control. The set option sets a current linetype like this:

Command: **-LT** or **-LINETYPE**↵
Current line type: "ByLayer"
Enter an option [?/Create/Load/Set]: **S**↵
Specify linetype name or [?] <ByLayer>: **HIDDEN**↵
Enter an option [?/Create/Load/Set]: ↵
Command:

The options of the -LINETYPE command were explained previously.

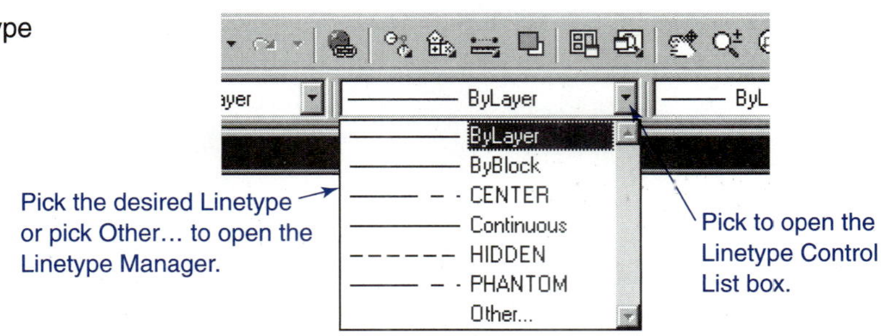

FIGURE 5.26 The Linetype Control list box.

Overriding Layer Lineweight

All objects are drawn using the current lineweight, which by default is ByLayer. As with color and linetype, this means that the lineweight used is the lineweight assigned to the layer that is current when the object is drawn. You can set a specific lineweight by selecting it from the Lineweight Control drop-down list on the Object Properties toolbar (Figure 5.27).

The Lineweight Settings dialog box provides complete control of lineweight settings and display options. To access the Lineweight Settings dialog box, pick Lineweight... from the Format menu, or type **LW**

FIGURE 5.27 The Lineweight Control list. Use the scrollbar to display additional lineweight options.

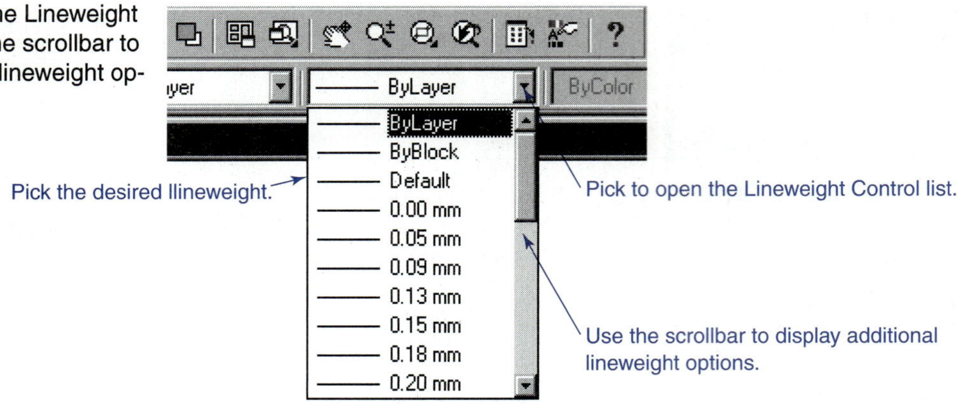

or **LINEWEIGHT** at the Command: prompt. The Lineweight Settings dialog box is shown in Figure 5.28. To set a new current lineweight, select the desired option from the Lineweights list. The Units for Listing controls whether lineweights are expressed in inches or in millimeters. For example, 0.3 mm is approximately equivalent to 0.012″. This lets you work with the system of measurement with which you are most comfortable. The Display Lineweight checkbox has the same effect as the LWT button on the status bar; a checkmark indicates that lineweights are displayed. Use the Default setting to control the default Lineweight that is assigned to layers. You can control the appearance of lineweights displayed on screen using the Adjust Display Scale slider bar.

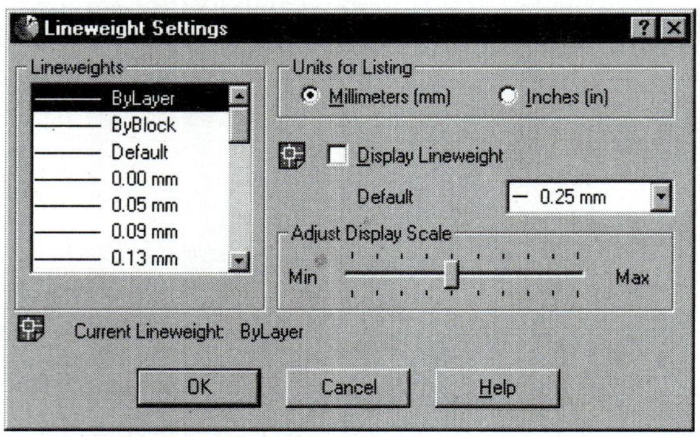

FIGURE 5.28 The Lineweight Settings dialog box.

Modifying Layers

Situations may occur that require you to change layer properties. You can change the linetype, color, and lineweight; you can also rename layers or control which layers are displayed in the layer name listing in the Layer Properties Manager dialog box.

Renaming Layers and Linetypes

Format
Rename...
DDRENAME
REN

It is easy to rename an existing layer using any one of three ways. One method uses the Layer Properties Manager dialog box. The second method opens the Rename dialog box with the RENAME command. The third method uses the -RENAME command at the keyboard.

To rename a layer in the Layer Properties Manager dialog box, pick the name of the layer you want to change, pause for a moment, then pick the layer name again. Do not double-click, as this simply sets the layer current. When you pick the name twice, the name appears in edit mode and you can type a new name and press Enter. If you are not comfortable with this style of interface, you can pick the Show details button and rename the layer in the Name: edit box. The details area is discussed later in this section.

The Rename dialog box is a powerful tool that can be used to rename layers, linetypes, and other named features in your drawing. The Rename dialog box, shown in Figure 5.29A, can be accessed by picking Rename... from the Format pull-down menu, or by typing **REN** or **RENAME** at the Command: prompt. A list of Named Objects is shown. Notice that Layers is the highlighted object. A list of the Items found in the named object is also displayed. Change a layer name by picking the desired layer name. OBJECT is selected in Figure 5.29A. The selected layer name is displayed in the Old Name: text box. Type a new name, such as **OBJECT-LINES,** in the Rename To: text box and pick the Rename To: button. The new layer name is now displayed in the Items list as shown in Figure 5.29B. Now, pick the OK button. Use the Rename dialog box to change a linetype name in the same manner.

A convenient way to rename layers or change color and linetype is to pick the Show details button of the Layer Properties Manager dialog box. Picking this button shows the Details area, as shown in Figure 5.30. The layer name can be changed in the Name: text box. The changed name is automatically displayed in the layer list. Change the layer properties as needed by picking a desired setting in the drop-down lists. Notice the right side of the Details area also has layer visibility check boxes. The displayed layer visibility options can be turned on and off as needed here.

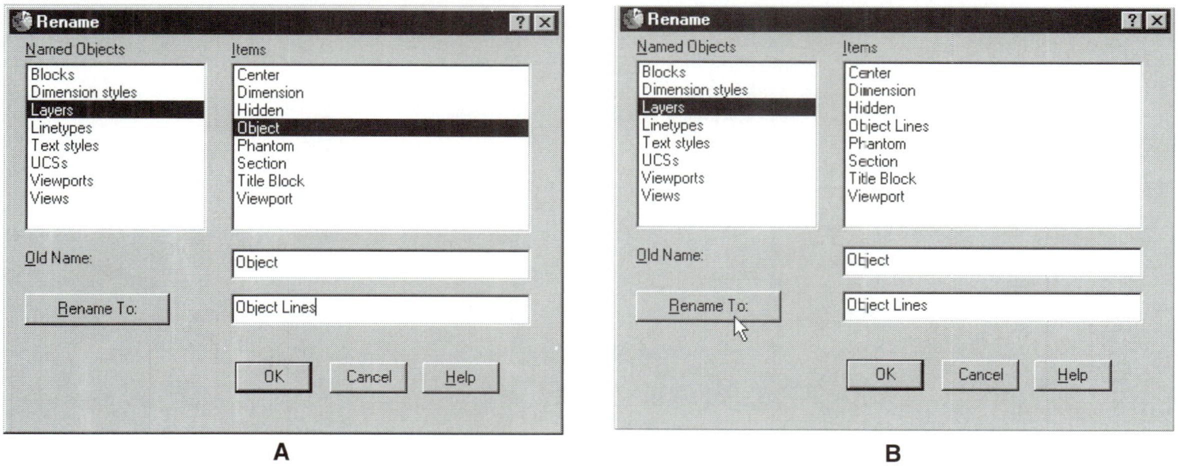

FIGURE 5.29 Using the Rename dialog box to rename a layer. (A) Pick Layer from the list of Named Objects. Pick the layer name to be changed from the Items list. Type a new name in the Rename To: text box, and then pick the Rename To: button. (B) The new layer name is now displayed in the Items list.

Changing an Object's Layer

Object Properties

Properties (Ctrl+1)

Modify
Properties

PROPERTIES
[Ctrl] + [1]

During creation of a drawing, you may discover that you forgot to change the layer before creating an object. If this happens, it is easy to change the objects to the correct layer. Changing an object's layer also changes the object to the color and linetype that is assigned to that layer if it was created using ByLayer settings. To do this, pick Properties ... from the Modify pull-down menu, pick the Properties toolbar button, or type **PROPERTIES** at the Command: line. The accelerator keystroke Ctrl+1 is a convenient way to access the PROPERTIES command. This command displays the Properties window, where you can edit many different properties of objects in your drawing. The Properties window is illustrated in Figure 5.31.

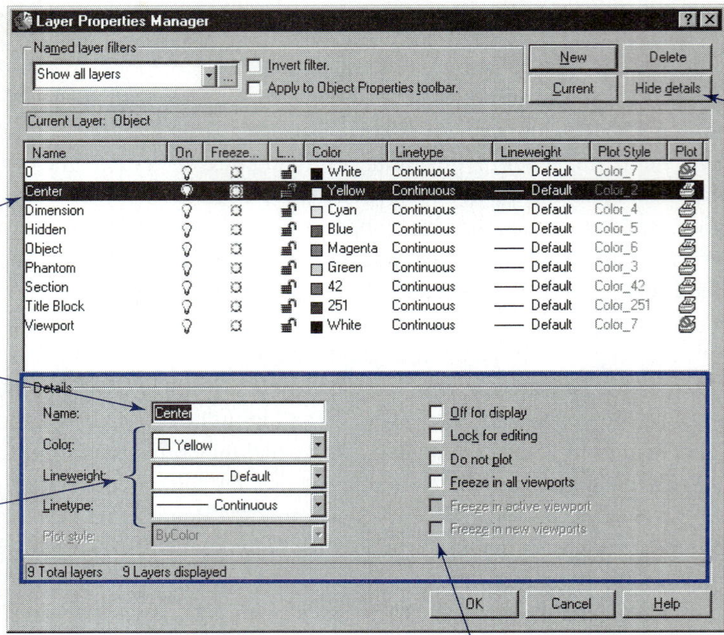

FIGURE 5.30 Pick the Show details button to access the Details area. Pick Hide details to close this area.

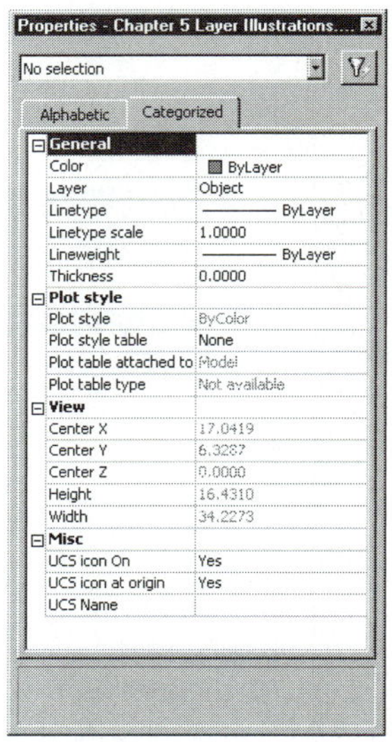

FIGURE 5.31 The Properties window.

The Properties window is what is referred to as a "modeless" dialog box, but it does not work like any of the dialog boxes introduced previously in this text. Notice that like a program or drawing window, it has a title bar and displays the current drawing name. Unlike a dialog box, the Properties window allows you to work in your drawing and use other commands, and stays visible until you dismiss it. Additionally, you can resize, relocate, or even dock the Properties window on the side of the AutoCAD LT program window. Figure 5.32 shows the Properties window in both a docked and a floating state. To resize the docked Properties window, move the cursor to the vertical bar between the Properties window and the docked toolbars. When the cursor changes to a resizing cursor, press and hold the pick button, then move your mouse to resize the window. Notice that increasing the size of the Properties window also reduces the size of the drawing display area.

When no objects are selected, the Properties window displays No selection in the drop-down list at the top, and any changes affect new objects created after the new setting is made. You will see the effect of changes to layer, linetype, color, and lineweight displayed in the list boxes in the Object Properties toolbar.

To edit an object, you must first select it. Because the Properties window does not display a selection prompt, you must grip-select the objects you want to modify. The Quick Select button provides advanced selection options. This feature is discussed in Chapter 7. The easiest method for most applications is to simply

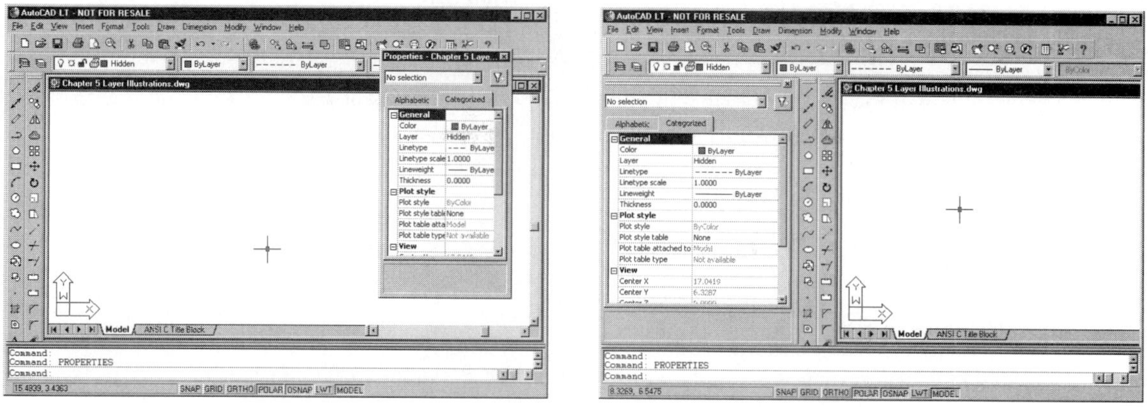

A B

FIGURE 5.32 The Properties window can be in a floating (A) or a docked (B) state.

use the grip-selection techniques discussed in Chapter 2. Grip-selected objects appear highlighted and display blue grip boxes. When you pick a single object, the type of object is shown in the drop-down list at the top, and all the properties of that object are displayed in the properties window. By default, the Categorized tab is displayed. This displays object properties in categories for easy access. If you are not sure under which category a property is found, you can use the Alphabetized tab. In the Categorized tab the layer, linetype, color, and lineweight settings are found in the first category, named General. Categories can be expanded or closed, similar to folders in Windows Explorer. Picking a plus sign (+) next to a category name expands that category, and picking a minus sign (−) closes that category.

To change the layer of a selected object, point to the value to the right of the Layer property and press the pick button. A drop-down list is displayed with the names of the available layers, from which you can pick a new layer. Also, by default, a description of the currently selected property is shown in the area at the bottom of the Properties window. In Figure 5.33, a single line object currently on the center layer is selected.

When multiple objects are selected, the Properties window displays only the properties that are common to all the currently selected objects. In Figure 5.34, the object selection includes lines, an arc, and a circle. The drop-down list shows that 5 objects are selected, and that any changes made in the Properties window will affect All (5) objects. You can also use the drop-down list to select a specific object type from the currently selected objects (see Figure 5.34B).

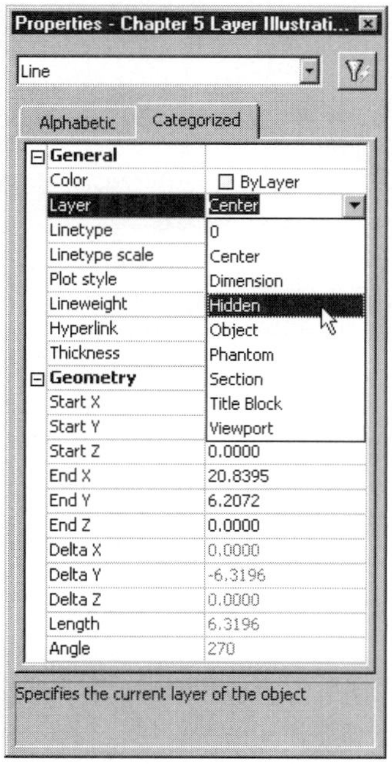

FIGURE 5.33 The Properties window provides easy control of object properties.

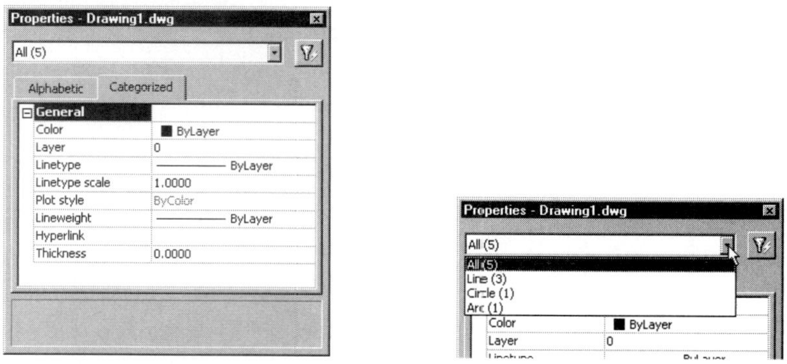

A B

FIGURE 5.34 (A) When multiple objects are selected, only the Properties common to all the selected objects are available. (B) All selected objects, or objects of a specific type, can be specified for editing.

Field Notes

The Properties window should be visible only while in use, because it takes up valuable screen space. To close the Properties window, pick the X button on the title bar, or enter the PROPERTIESCLOSE command. The easiest way to toggle the visibility of the Properties window is to use the Ctrl+1 accelerator keystroke.

Field Notes

- AutoCAD LT also provides a command line option for changing various properties of objects using the CHPROP command.
- If you have accessed an option of the CHPROP command such as Color or Linetype and the desired value is already present in the default brackets <>, pressing Enter accepts the default setting. The default always reflects the current setting. In the preceding example, the ByLayer setting was desired for linetype and color, so pressing Enter at the prompts preserved the default, which was <ByLayer>.

Using the Object Properties Toolbar

A quick way to change the layer, linetype, and color of an object or objects is to grip select the objects. Then you can use the Object Properties toolbar Layer list to change the layer of the selected objects. Use the Color list to select a different color for the selected objects, or access a different linetype from the Linetype list. After you have changed the object layer, color, or linetype as desired, press the Esc key twice to remove the grips.

Exercise 5.3 **Estimated time required: 10 min.**

1. Open AutoCAD LT if it is not already open and then open EX5.2.
2. Change the dashed lines to the CENTER layer.
3. Change the phantom lines to the HIDDEN layer.
4. Change the center line to the PHANTOM layer.
5. Change everything back to the condition found in the final drawing for Exercise 5.2.
6. Make the OBJECT layer current.
7. Load the TRACKS linetype from the aclt.lin linetype file.
8. Override the current layer color with red and the current layer linetype with TRACKS.
9. Use the LINE command to draw a line 0.5 in. away from and all around the current phantom line border. This line should be red and represented by the TRACKS linetype.
10. Override the current linetype scale with a setting of 2.
11. Use the LINE command to draw a line .5 in. away from and all around the current TRACKS line.
12. Change all settings back to the original ByLayer format and linetype scale.
13. Save as EX5.3, and close the drawing.

Adjusting Layer Listings

The Layer Properties Manager has several options for specifying which layers are displayed in the layer name list. These options are found in the Named layer filters drop-down list displayed in Figure 5.35. The following explains each of the options:

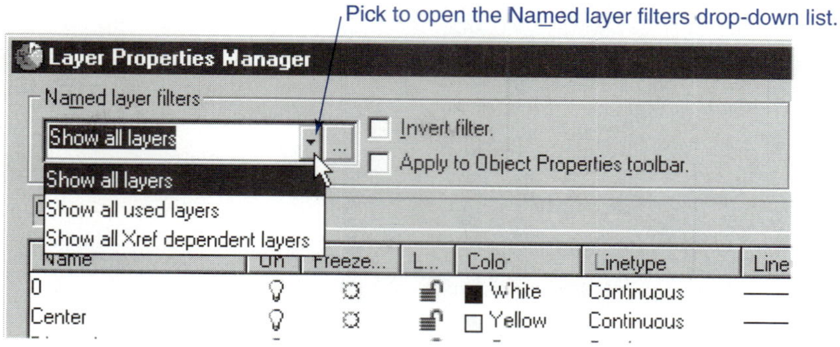

FIGURE 5.35 The Named layer filters list allows you to determine which layers are displayed in the layer name list.

- **Show all layers** — This is the default, which displays all layer names available in the drawing.
- **Show all used layers** — This option displays all of the layer names that are currently in use in the drawing. For example, you may have created 10 layers, but you have drawn objects on only 5 of the layers. The 5 layers that have been used in the drawing are displayed.
- **Show all xref dependent layers:** — Xref stands for external reference. *External references* are a source outside of the current drawing. Chapter 13 covers xrefs in detail. This option lists layer names that are xref-dependent.

You can reverse the function of any of these filters by placing a checkmark in the Invert filter button. If you have selected the Show all used layers filter and invert the filter, then only the layers that are not used are displayed. You can reduce the number of layer names displayed in the Layer Control drop-down list based on the active filter by picking the Apply to Object Properties toolbar toggle. The ellipsis button next to the drop-down list displays the Named Layer Filters dialog box, where you can define custom filters to meet your specific needs.

Using the Set Layer Filters Dialog Box

If you have many layers established, you can decide which to display in the list in the Layer Properties Manager. This works well if you are working on a large drawing with many layers, but you are using only a few key layers. Filtering the unneeded layers makes it easier for you to access the needed layers. You can filter layers based on names or status properties. When you filter layers, you are choosing the characteristics of layers that will be listed. Pick the ellipsis button next to the Named Layer filters drop-down list (see Figure 5.35). This opens the Named Layer Filters dialog box shown in Figure 5.36.

The Filter name: list displays the names of the currently defined filters. Pick the down-arrow button to view this list. Picking inside the text area of the Filter name: list activates a text cursor so you can enter a new name in the list. A filter name is subject to the same restrictions as a layer name. You can use very descriptive names, but you cannot use commas, periods, or other restricted characters. It does not matter whether you specify the filter name first or after defining the filter.

The Named Layer Filters dialog box provides several ways to filter the layer display.

The settings in the Named Layer Filters dialog box are cumulative. This means that you can look for layers that are both Off and Locked, or On, Frozen, and Red, for example. The filtering options for layers are as follows:

- **On/Off** — Pick the arrow to access the list shown in Figure 5.36B. The options include Both, which is the default. This filters layers by both on and off. In other words, all layers that are on and off are displayed. Pick On to filter layers that are turned on. This means that layers that are turned on are listed but layers that are turned off are not listed. Pick Off to filter layers that are turned off.

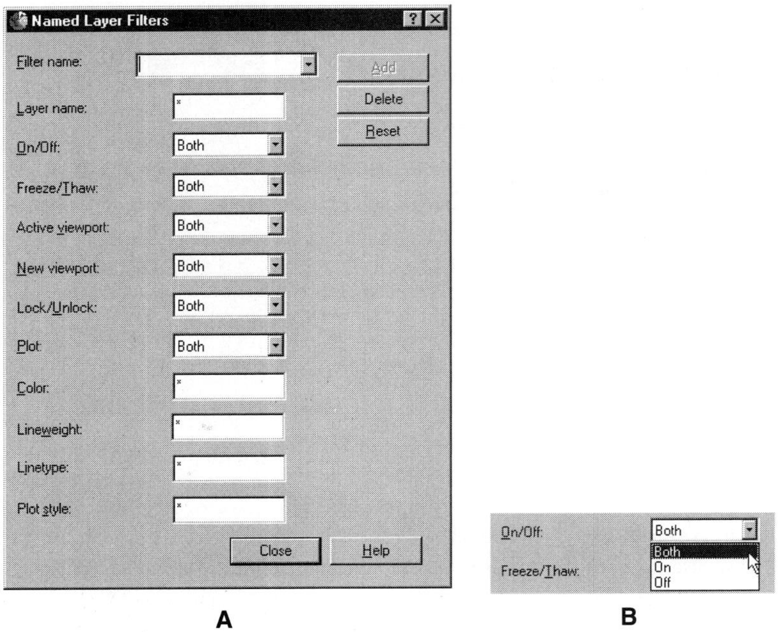

FIGURE 5.36 (A) Using the Named Layer Filters dialog box to filter layers. (B) Pick the down arrow to access the list.

- **Layer Name** There is a text box for this filtering application. The asterisk (*) shown is the default. The asterisk symbol is referred to as a wild card. A ***wild card*** allows you to match anything that is similar. For example, if you have several layers that begin with the name ELEC-, you can filter only those layers by entering ELEC-*. Now, only the ELEC- layers are listed. You can also remove the asterisk and type a desired layer name. You can also identify layers using question marks (?). For example, to find all layers that have E as the third letter, enter **??E*.** Another example might be one in which you want to find all layers that are related to the electrical plan on the fourth floor and the layer names look like ELEC-SW-4 and ELEC-WR-4. These could be found with the entry **ELEC-??-4.**
- **Freeze/Thaw** Filter layers that are frozen or thawed by picking Both, Frozen, or Thawed.
- **Active viewport and New viewport** Filter layers that are frozen or thawed in the active and new viewports by selecting Both, Frozen, or Thawed. Viewports are explained in Chapter 13.
- **Lock/Unlock** Filter layers that are locked or unlocked by picking Both, Locked or Unlocked.
- **Plot** Filter layers that are plotted or not plotted by picking Both, Plot, or Don't Plot.
- **Color** This allows you to filter layers by color names using the asterisk wild card or by individual color; or multiple criteria can be specified, separated by commas.
- **Lineweight** Specify a lineweight to filter. The text you enter must exactly match the listing shown in the layer list. For example, to specify a 0.3 mm line width you must type **0.3 mm**. A filter specification of **.3, 0.3,** or **.3** mm does not work. You can use wild cards. For example, **0.3*** would also find all layers with a 0.3 mm lineweight. Enter multiple lineweights separated by commas to filter more than one lineweight.
- **Linetype** This allows you to filter layers by linetype using the asterisk wild card or by individual linetype; or multiple criteria can be specified, separated by commas.
- **Plot style** Enter a plot style to filter using an exact name or wild cards.

You can pick the Reset button in the Named Layer Filters dialog box to reset all values back to the default settings. The Delete button removes the current Filter name: from the list. Use the Add button to add the new filter definition to the list. Also, if you select a filter and modify it, you must use the Add button again to actually make the changes.

Pick the Close button to accept the layer filters that you have set. The layer filter settings are now available for use. If no matching layer names are found, no layer names are displayed.

Adjusting Linetype Listings

The Linetype Manager dialog box has only preset options for specifying which linetypes are displayed in the linetype list. These options are found in the Linetype filters drop-down list displayed in Figure 5.37. The following explains each of the options:

- **Show all Linetypes** — This is the default option, which displays all the loaded linetypes in the Linetype list.
- **Show all used Linetypes** — This option displays all the loaded linetypes that are currently in use in the drawing. Linetypes that are not being used are not listed.
- **Show all Xref dependent Linetypes** — This option displays all xref-dependent linetypes that are loaded in the current drawing.

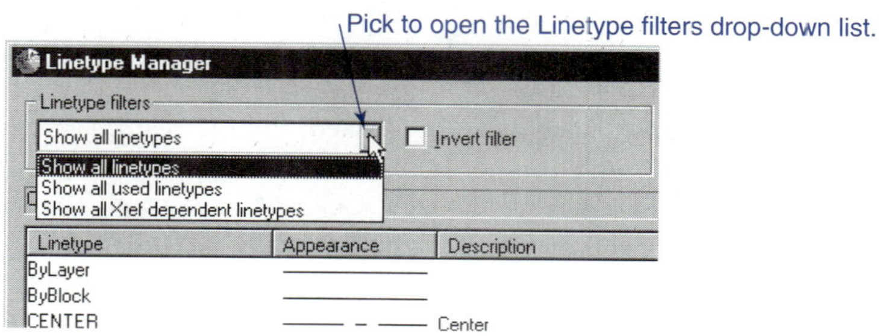

FIGURE 5.37 The Linetype filters list in the Linetype Manager allows you to determine which linetypes are displayed in the linetype list.

Pick the Invert filter checkbox to reverse the function of any of these filters. If you have selected the Show all used linetypes filter and invert the filter, then only the linetypes that are not used are displayed.

Exercise 5.4 **Estimated time required: 10 min.**

1. Open AutoCAD LT if it is not already open and then open EX5.2.
2. Use the Layer Properties Manager to change the Lineweight of the OBJECT layer lines to 0.60 mm width and all other layers lines to 0.30 mm.
3. Make a print or plot of the drawing displaying these line widths.
4. Experiment with layer filters by doing this:
   - Enter the Layer Properties Manager and pick the ellipsis button.
   - In the Named Layer Filters dialog box, set the On/Off: option to On, name the filter "All ON,"and pick Apply then Close.
   - Now, back in the Layer Control dialog box, turn Off at least two of your layers and see what happens—they should disappear from the layer list.
   - Pick the Invert filter checkbox to place a checkmark in it and see what happens—the layers that are off now appear in the layer list.
5. Experiment with filters. Design at least three named filters.
6. Save as EX5.4, and close the drawing.

LEARNING CHECKPOINT

- ☐ What does the term *ByLayer* mean?
- ☐ Why should caution be used when overriding layers?
- ☐ How do you rename a layer in the Layer Properties Manager?
- ☐ How do you access the Rename dialog box?
- ☐ Describe the process for changing the layer of a group of objects using the PROPERTIES command.
- ☐ Why would you want to filter layers?
- ☐ How do you set a specific layer to be plotted with wider lines than the other layers?

Introduction to AutoCAD DesignCenter

The fundamental benefit of using CAD is realized through reusing work you have already completed. The AutoCAD LT 2000 software provides simple ways to reuse drawing content from existing drawings. You can copy geometry from one drawing to another, or you can copy definitions for named objects, such as layers and linetypes. The primary tool for copying named object definitions is AutoCAD DesignCenter.

The command that starts AutoCAD DesignCenter is ADCENTER. You can access the ADCENTER command by picking the AutoCAD DesignCenter button from the Standard toolbar, by picking AutoCAD DesignCenter from the Tools menu, by typing **ADCENTER** or **ADC** at the Command: prompt, or with the accelerator keystroke Ctrl+2.

The DesignCenter window an be docked, floated, resized, or repositioned as needed, similar to the Properties window discussed earlier in this chapter. You can close the DesignCenter window by picking the X button on the title bar or by using the ADCCLOSE command. The Ctrl+2 keystroke functions as a toggle.

You can set DesignCenter to work only with the currently open drawings, or you can search your local hard disks, network drives, FTP sites, or Web pages for drawing content. The more advanced uses and features of DesignCenter are discussed in later chapters. This discussion covers how to copy layers and linetypes between drawings that are either open or available on local or network disk drives.

Controlling the DesignCenter Display

When you start DesignCenter, the window appears in the same state as the last time it was used. This includes the floating or docked state, the size and position, plus the content that was previously displayed. You can adjust the size and position as needed to meet your current needs. One important concern regarding DesignCenter is screen space. The DesignCenter window can be difficult to use if it is too small; however, making it larger reduces the display area available for the currently open drawings. For this reason, it is best to dismiss the DesignCenter window when it is no longer being used.

Some DesignCenter controls can be accessed by right-clicking to access context-sensitive shortcut menus. The title bar shortcut menu provides options to Move, Size, or Hide the DesignCenter window. The window border shortcut menu also allows you to Hide the window or indicate whether the DesignCenter window can be docked. Other shortcut menus are discussed later.

The DesignCenter window displays available drawing content sources. The term *drawing content* refers to the contents of a drawing. The specific content available using DesignCenter is named object definitions, such as layers, linetypes and additional named objects introduced later in this text. To access the content from all the currently open drawings, pick the Open Drawing button (see Figure 5.38). The folder at the top of the Tree View pane is labeled Open Drawings, and a listing of the currently open drawings appears below. In Figure 5.38 two drawings are currently open: the default drawing, which has not yet been named, and the drawing created in Exercise 5.1. Each drawing in the Tree View pane displays the plus sign (+), indicating that each contains additional branches. The contents of the currently selected item in the Tree View pane are displayed in the palette pane.

LEARNING CHECKPOINT

- ☐ What is the fundamental benefit of using CAD?
- ☐ List each option for starting AutoCAD DesignCenter.
- ☐ What are the names for the right and left panes of the DesignCenter window?
- ☐ Why does AutoCAD LT ignore duplicate names when copying named drawing content?

Sharing Data and Drawing Files

- Copying Objects and Layers Between Drawings

Concept Animations

- DesignCenter

Setting and Changing Object Properties

- Assigning Colors and Linetypes to Objects

Concept Animations

- Layering

MULTIPLE CHOICE

Circle the choice or enter your response on an answer sheet by selecting the option that most closely completes or answers the given statements.

1. A logical grouping of data, like transparent overlays on a drawing:
- **a.** transparencies
- **b.** overlays
- **c.** layers
- **d.** sheets

2. The LAYER command accesses this dialog box:
- **a.** Layer Properties Manager
- **b.** Select Color
- **c.** Select Linetype
- **d.** Change Properties

3. This is the AutoCAD LT default linetype:
- **a.** SOLID
- **b.** CONTINUOUS
- **c.** OBJECTS
- **d.** none of the above

4. This command or dialog box changes the linetype scale of every object on the drawing:
- **a.** LTSCALE
- **b.** Select Linetype dialog box
- **c.** SCALE
- **d.** DDLMODES

5. A layer is in this state when objects on the layer are invisible, and regenerations can occur when you restore the layer's visibility.
- **a.** On
- **b.** Off
- **c.** Locked
- **d.** Frozen

6. A layer is in this state if you want to keep people from accidentally editing or tampering with the layer contents:
- **a.** On
- **b.** Off
- **c.** Locked
- **d.** Frozen

7. Use this command to change the layer of several objects at one time:
- **a.** DDRENAME
- **b.** PROPERTIES
- **c.** DDMODIFY
- **d.** DDLAYER

8. This means that the setting affects everything on the entire drawing:
- **a.** individual
- **b.** specific
- **c.** all
- **d.** global

9. Adjust the linetype scale of individual objects using this command:
- **a.** LAYER
- **b.** LTSCALE
- **c.** DDLTYPE
- **d.** SELECTLT

10. The standard AutoCAD LT linetype file for metric drawings is
- **a.** aclt.lin
- **b.** Ltype.lin
- **c.** aclt.lty
- **d.** Ltype.lty

MATCHING

Match each term to the correct description by writing the appropriate number in each box at the left.

- ☐ Continuous
- ☐ Current
- ☐ PROPERTIES
- ☐ LAYER
- ☐ Ctrl+1
- ☐ Filtering
- ☐ Frozen
- ☐ Layer
- ☐ Locked
- ☐ Off
- ☐ Scale Factor

1. Defined by AutoCAD LT as a logical grouping of data, like transparent overlays on a drawing.
2. Access the Layer Properties Manager with this command.
3. What is the default linetype when you initially name a new layer?
4. This determines the final size of things such as text height, dimension characteristics, and linetype appearance.
5. A layer is in this state when it is active and ready for use.
6. A layer is in this state when objects on the layer are invisible and regenerations happen when visibility is restored.
7. A layer is in this state when objects on the layer are invisible and regenerations do not happen when visibility is restored.
8. Layers are in this state to keep people from tampering with the contents of the layer.
9. This command allows you to change the layer of several objects.
10. This keystroke accesses the command referred to in 9.
11. If you have a drawing with many layers but you are working with only a few layers, you can use this to have the unneeded layers removed from the layer list.

WORD SCRAMBLE

Unscramble the seven scrambled words below, one letter to each square, to form seven AutoCAD LT–related words:

ARLEY

NEYLTIEP

RUCETRN

IBITIVTIYSL

EZREFE

COKL

STOPPERIER

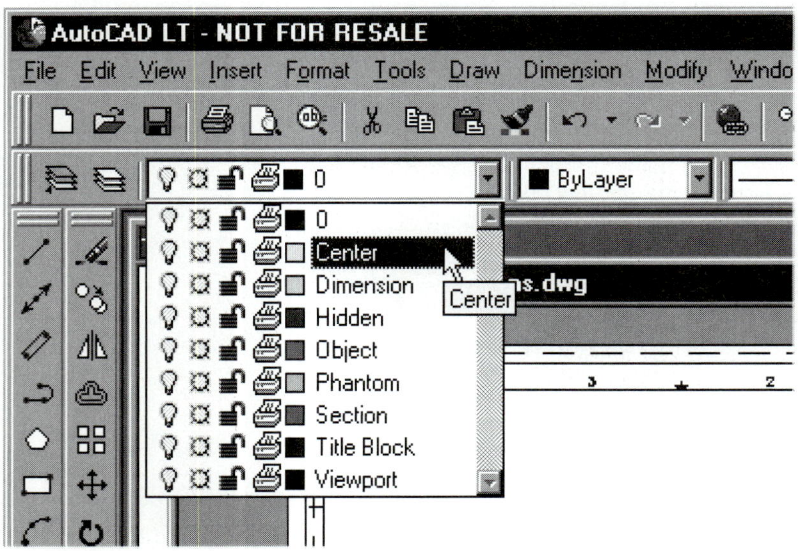

Unscramble the circled letters above to form the special answer, as suggested by the illustration.

PROJECTS

Set up the following drawing projects with layers that relate to the type of drawing as outlined and discussed in this chapter.

5.1 Amplifier Schematic

Draw the schematic shown below. Do not place text or connections that are shown as solid circles. Save as P5.1.

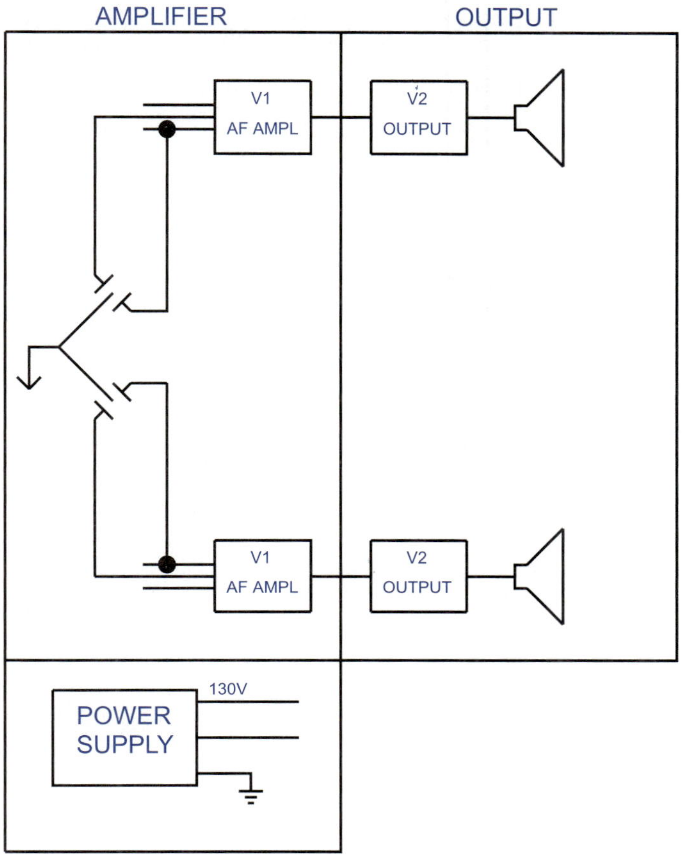

5.2 Hex Head Bolt

Draw the fastener shown below. Do not draw dimensions or notes. Save as P5.2.

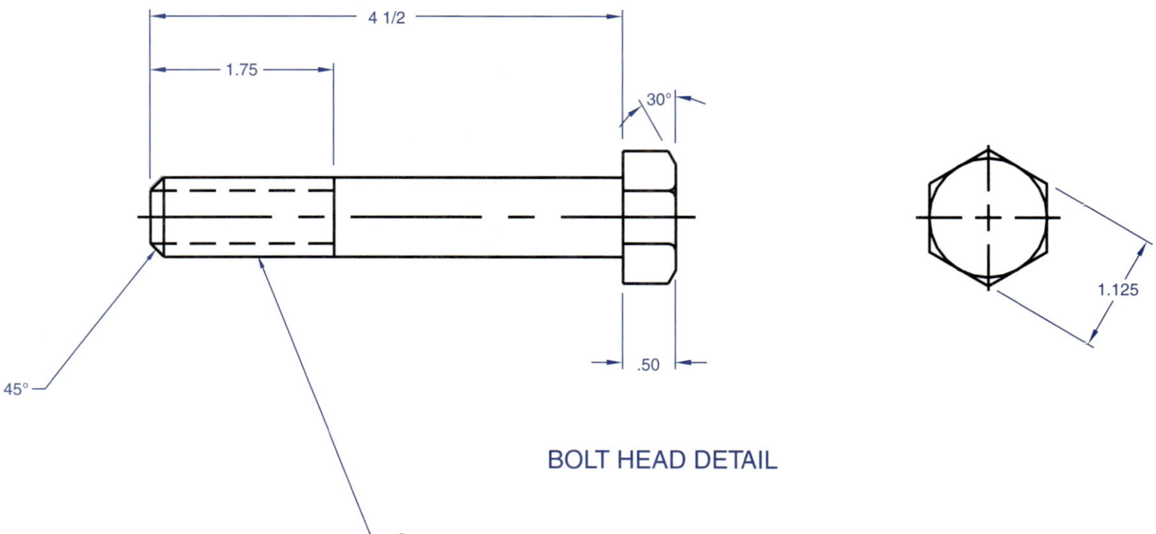

[*Note:* This note represents a 3/4 in. major (outside) diameter 10 threads per inch Unified National Course screw thread. Draw the hidden lines as a thread representation that is not to scale—placement is up to you.]

5.3 Kitchen Floor Plan

Draw the plan shown below without notes or dimensions. Save as P5.3.

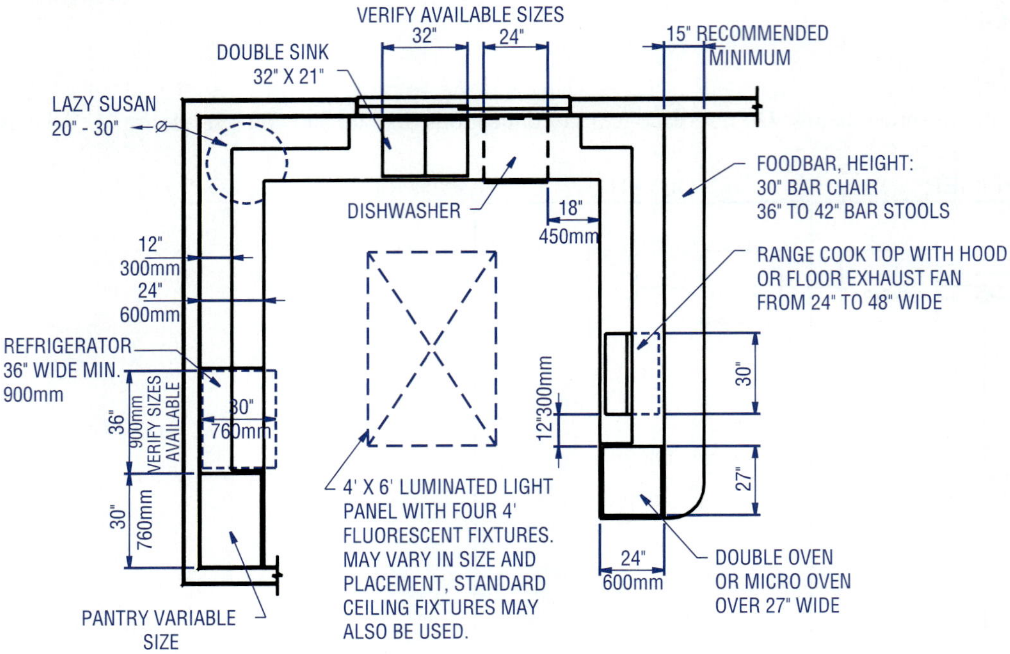

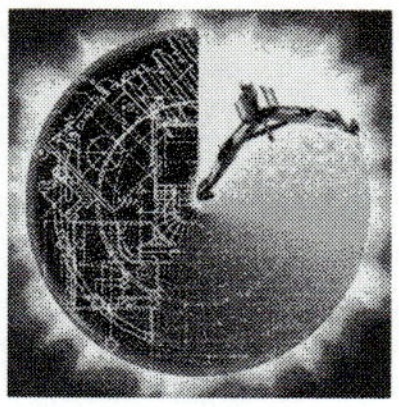

CHAPTER 6

Precision Drafting Tools

LEARNING GOALS

- Use Polar Tracking and Polar Snap features to simplify drawing tasks.
- Use AutoSnap features to place points quickly and accurately.
- Use the From option to establish a point from an existing point.
- Control the AutoSnap settings.
- Draw a variety of point styles and sizes.
- Divide objects into equal lengths.
- Establish equally spaced segments on an object.
- Use point filters to establish a point.
- Use the From option to draw objects using direct distance entry.
- Use tracking to determine a new point location from a series of directions and distances.
- Identify the coordinates of an existing point.
- Calculate distances, angles, and areas, and list object properties.
- Use the 2D Region Modeler to determine physical properties of shapes and areas.
- Use the built-in timer features.
- Draw construction lines using the XLINE command options and the RAY command.
- Adjust the Snap Angle and Origin options.

AutoCAD LT's Precision Drafting Tools

Learning to use the many precision drafting tools in AutoCAD LT 2000 allows you to create and use highly accurate drawings. Rather than trying to point accurately with the mouse, you can force AutoCAD LT to find exact points in your drawing with greater than eight decimal places of accuracy. Powerful inquiry tools allow you to extract manufacturing and engineering data from your drawing-including point locations, surface area calculations, centroids, moments of inertia, and more. AutoCAD LT even provides construction tools that let you use existing geometry to define new objects in your drawing.

The tools and commands discussed in this chapter will help you draw faster and more accurately and increase the usefulness of the drawings you create.

Polar Tracking and Polar Snap

In Chapter 2 you were introduced to the Polar Tracking feature, which displays the Polar tooltip indicating the distance and angle from the current cursor location to the previously selected point. By default, the Polar tooltip appears only when you drag the cursor along a horizontal or vertical alignment vector and does not restrict cursor movement along the vector. The term *vector* refers to a line describing a distance and angle. The AutoCAD LT help file refers to the dotted line displayed by Polar Tracking as either the *alignment vector* or the *alignment path*. The Polar Tracking and Polar Snap features provide additional options for more versatile control of dragging operations. These features can be used to reduce coordinate entry requirements while assuring complete accuracy.

The Polar feature is toggled on and off by picking the Polar button on the status bar, or using the F10 function key. The settings for the Polar feature are found in the Drafting Settings dialog box. There are two aspects to the Polar tools. Polar Tracking allows you to specify angles that define alignment paths, and Polar Snap allows you snap to specific increments along an alignment path.

Polar Tracking

To access the settings for Polar Tracking, right-click on the Polar button and pick Settings... from the shortcut menu. Optionally, you can start the Drafting Settings dialog box through any available method and just pick the Polar Tracking tab. The Polar Tracking tab is shown in Figure 6.1.

FIGURE 6.1 The Polar Tracking tab in the Drafting Settings dialog box.

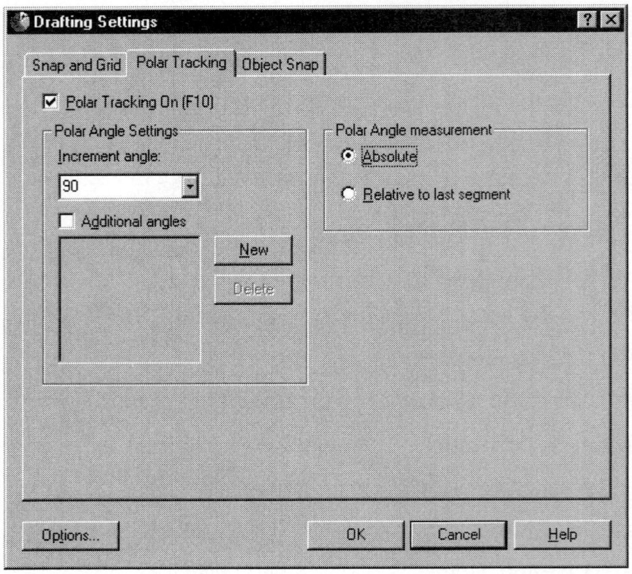

The Polar Tracking On (F10) checkbox turns the Polar Tracking feature on or off. The Polar Angle Settings area provides controls for specifying what angles are used for polar tracking. The default angle is 90°. This means that when you drag the cursor in a direction that is near 0, 90, 180, or 270, your cursor will track along the alignment vector. You can also select from other preset angles such as 45, 30, 15, or 5°. To select from preset angles, open the Increment angle: list and pick the desired angle. The preset angles are displayed in a format that matches the current angular measure system you are using. To specify an angle that is not found on the list, pick the Additional angles checkbox to activate the list and select from any of the listed angles. Pick the New button to add new angles to the list. To remove an unneeded angle, select the angle in the list and pick the Delete button.

The Polar Angle measurement allows you to specify whether the angle measurement is Absolute or Relative to last segment. Specifying Absolute means that the angles are measured according to the current angle 0 and angle direction settings. The Relative to last segment option pertains primarily to operations where you are drawing linear objects; this option means that each polar angle is measured using the angle of the last linear segment as angle 0.

Coordinate entry is simplified with Polar Tracking. Because the Polar Tracking feature defines the angle, you can use direct distance entry and simply enter the distance along the alignment vector. Figure 6.2 shows applications of the absolute polar tracking option. An application of relative polar tracking is illustrated in Figure 6.3. The command sequence for both figures is the same, and is shown here:

Command: **L** or **LINE**↵
Specify first point: **2,2**↵
Specify next point or [Undo]: **3**↵
Specify next point or [Undo]: **2**↵
Specify next point or [Close/Undo]: **3**↵
Specify next point or [Close/Undo]: **2**↵
Specify next point or [Close/Undo]: ↵
Command:

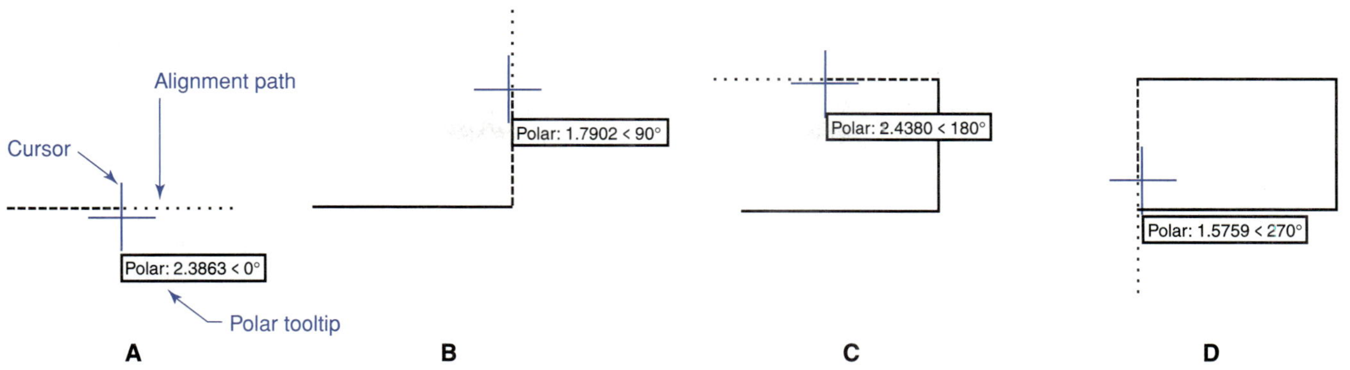

FIGURE 6.2 The Absolute option measures angles based on the default angle measurement in the current drawing.

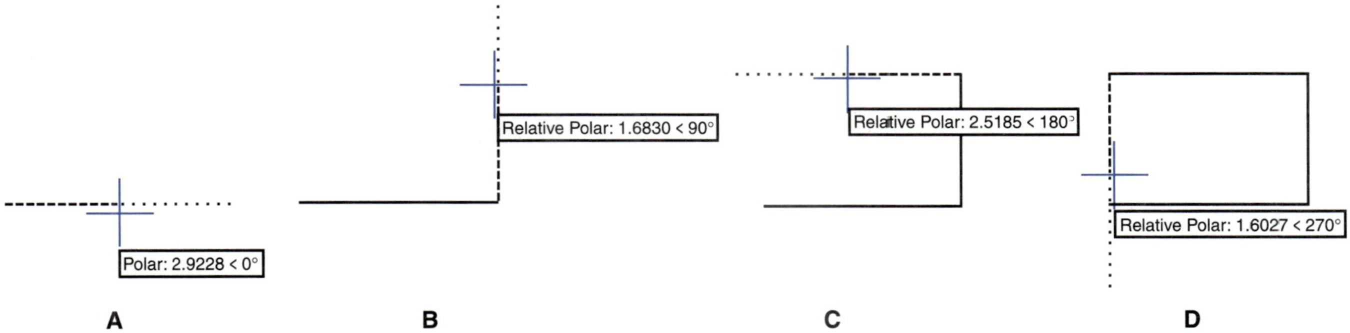

FIGURE 6.3 The Relative option measures angles based on the direction of the last segment.

Polar Snap

The Polar Snap feature can be used only in conjunction with the Polar Tracking feature. Polar Snap adds the additional capability of being able to automatically snap to specified increments along the alignment vector. The settings for Polar Snap are available on the Snap and Grid tab of the Drafting Settings dialog box (see Figure 6.4). Pick the Settings… option from the status bar SNAP button shortcut menu to display this tab.

FIGURE 6.4 The Snap and Grid tab in the Drafting Settings dialog box.

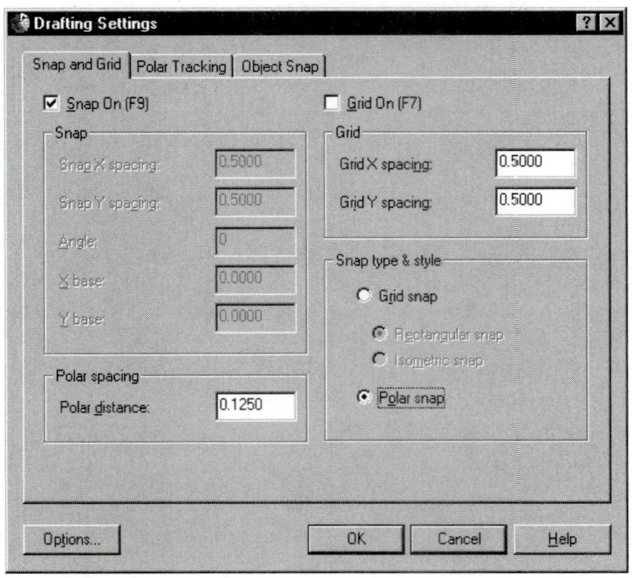

To use the Polar Snap feature, pick the Polar snap radio button in the Snap type & style area. This activates the Polar distance text box in the Polar spacing area and disables the settings for the grid snap feature. Enter the desired polar snap increment in the Polar distance text box. If the setting here is zero, the Snap X Spacing value of the grid snap is used. The Snap feature must be turned on. Figure 6.5 shows an application of the Polar Snap feature where each point specification is picked, and no typed coordinate entries are necessary. In this example, the polar angle measurement is absolute, set to 30°, and the Polar distance is 0.125.

Notice that in Figure 6.5D the Polar tooltip reads *Polar: Intersection*. When you move your cursor to a point where the alignment vector intersects an existing object, AutoCAD LT displays this tooltip. If you press the pick button when this tip is displayed, the point selected will be exactly where the alignment path intersects the object.

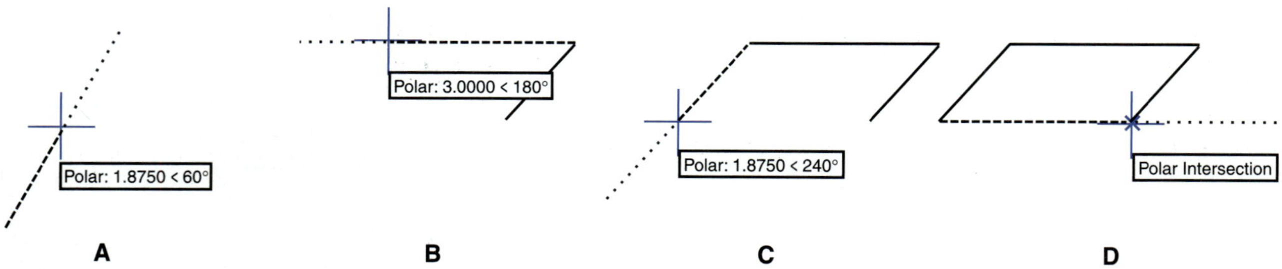

FIGURE 6.5 Using Polar Snap and Polar Tracking can greatly reduce coordinate entry requirements.

Polar Options

The Polar features have option settings available in the Options dialog box. You can start the OPTIONS command using any previously discussed method or by picking the Options... button in the Drafting Settings dialog box. On the Drafting tab you can specify whether the Polar Tracking vector and tooltip are displayed. For most applications, it is best to keep these features visible.

Field Notes

Typed coordinate entries will override any Polar Tracking or Polar Snap settings that are currently active. You can toggle the Polar features on or off as needed by picking the POLAR button on the status bar, by using the status bar POLAR and SNAP button shortcut menus or by using the F10 function key.

Exercise 6.1

Estimated time required: 10 min.

1. Open AutoCAD LT if it is not already open. Use the setup option of your choice.
2. Set limits at 8.5,11.
3. Set Polar Tracking and Polar Snap to your advantage for drawing the object shown below.
4. Do not draw dimensions.
5. Save as EX6.1, and close the drawing.

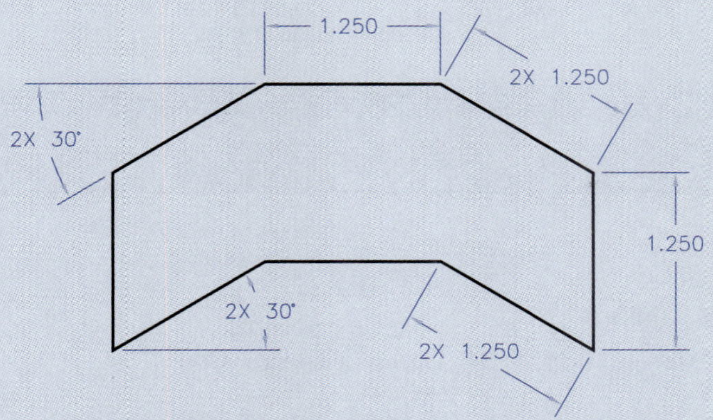

Object Snaps

Object snaps allow you to quickly pick exact locations on an object without having to be directly at the desired location. Object snaps are available for almost any need. Object snaps can be used any time AutoCAD LT asks you to select a point. When using object snaps, an AutoSnap marker is displayed at the snap location when you move the cursor to a related object or snap point. AutoSnap gives you a visual symbol, known as a marker, that lets you know which snap is being used. Also, if you pause just for a moment when you see the AutoSnap marker, a SnapTip is provided that tells you the name of the object snap being used. AutoSnap is on by default.

Object snaps can be accessed from the Object Snap toolbar, from the Object Snap cursor menu, or by typing the desired object snap abbreviation. Object snaps can be used at any point prompt or select objects prompt. Display the Object Snap toolbar by picking Toolbars ... in the View pull-down menu. This opens the Customize dialog box, with the Toolbars tab selected, as shown in Figure 6.6A. Pick the Object Snap option in the Toolbars list and then pick the Close button. Another method for toggling the toolbars display is to right-click on an existing toolbar button to get a popup cursor menu. See Figure 6.6B. A check by the toolbar

FIGURE 6.6 Selecting Object Snap in the Toolbars dialog box.

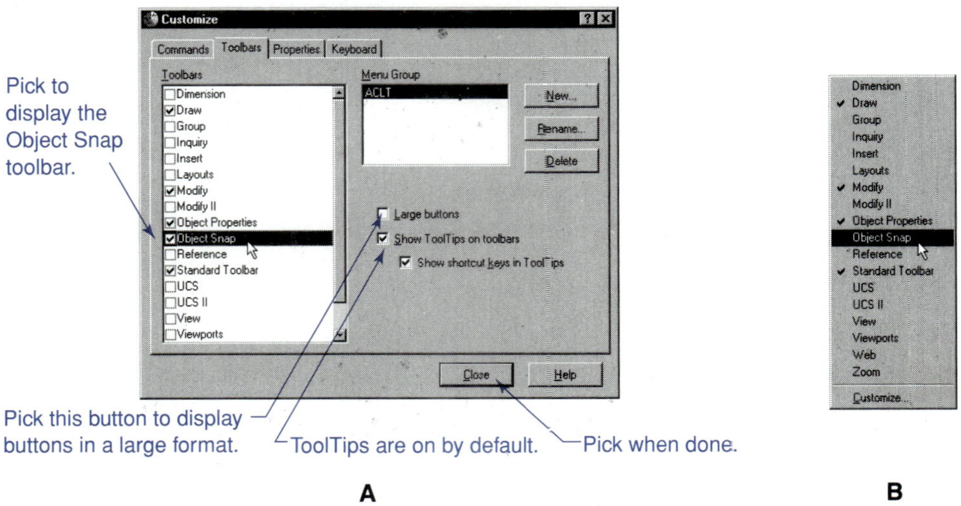

name indicates that it is currently displayed. Picking any toolbar name toggles its display either on or off. Picking the Customize... option at the bottom displays the Customize dialog box shown in Figure 6.6A. The Object Snap toolbar is shown in Figure 6.7 with each button name provided. The toolbar can be located where you want it on the screen or "docked" below the Object Properties toolbar or above the Command window. Refer to Chapter 1 for a review, if needed. When typed on the keyboard, each object snap uses the first three letters or more of the name, as shown in Figure 6.7.

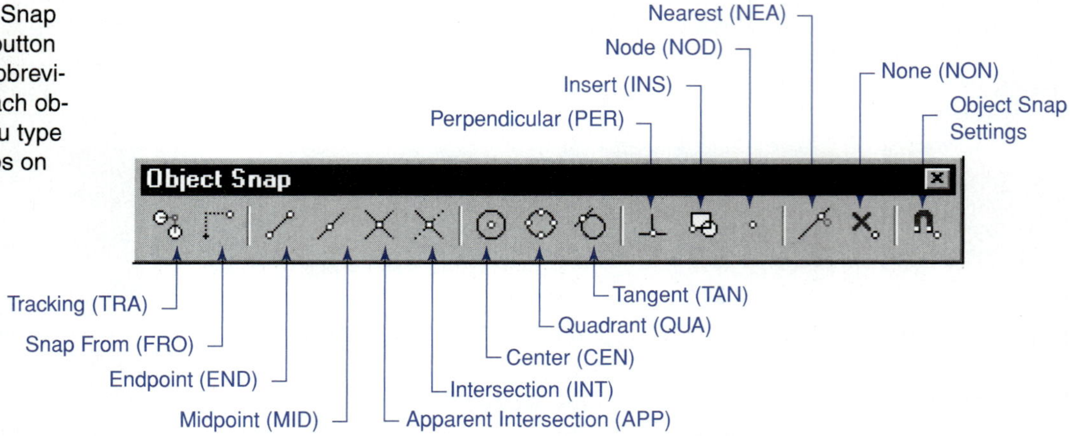

FIGURE 6.7 The Object Snap toolbar with each toolbar button labeled. The three-letter abbreviation in parentheses by each object snap name is what you type when entering object snaps on the keyboard.

There is also a cursor menu that contains the Object Snap options, as shown in Figure 6.8. The cursor menu is displayed where the cursor is located on the screen when you hold down the Shift key and press the right mouse button. The cursor menu disappears as soon as you pick the desired option. When the cursor menu is displayed, move the cursor arrow down the list of Object Snap options and pick the desired one.

The AutoSnap markers and the related SnapTips are displayed in Figure 6.9.

FIGURE 6.8 The Object Snap cursor menu is opened at the cursor location by pressing the Shift key and pressing the right mouse button.

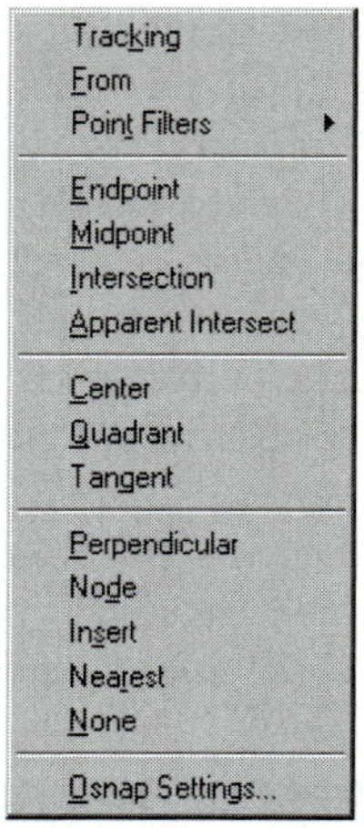

FIGURE 6.9 The AutoSnap markers and related SnapTips.

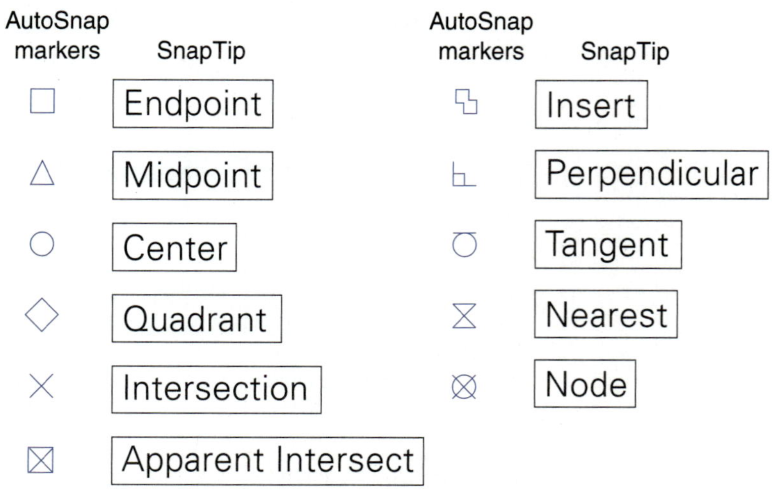

Snap to an Endpoint

Object Snap

ENDpoint

The Endpoint object snap is convenient for accurately picking the endpoint of an object such as a line or arc. For example, if you want to draw a line from the endpoint of an existing line, pick the Snap to Endpoint toolbar button, select Endpoint from the popup menu, or type **END** at the From point: prompt. Next, AutoCAD LT gives you the "of" prompt. This means that AutoCAD LT wants you to pick the object that you want to select the endpoint "of." If you want the endpoint of a line, move the crosshairs to anywhere "near" the end, and past the middle, of the desired line and pick on the object as shown in Figure 6.10. Notice the AutoSnap marker and SnapTip that provides you with visual identification that you have selected the correct point. The complete command sequence looks like this:

Command: **L** or **LINE**↵
Specify first point: **END**↵
of *<move the cursor near the endpoint and pick>*
Specify next point or [Undo]: *<pick the next point>*
Specify next point or [Undo]: ↵
Command:

The object snap is no longer active after the object is picked. Each object snap is active only for the next point selection, whether or not it is successful. An object snap is only successful if you pick a point where the cursor touches a visible object and the object has the requested feature. If, for example, you specify an Endpoint object snap and pick a point on a circle, no point is found. Also, the object snap you picked is deactivated and your point prompt is repeated. If you pick a point where the cursor does not touch any objects, again no point is found, the object snap is deactivated, and the point prompt is repeated. This is where the AutoSnap marker offers a great advantage, because you know the object is successfully picked when the marker is displayed at the desired location.

Field Notes

Notice that when you pick an Endpoint object snap from the menu that the entry at the prompt is _endp, and not _end. The reason for this is that END is also a command name in previous AutoCAD LT releases. If you were to accidentally enter END at a Command: prompt instead of a point selection prompt, your drawing would be automatically saved and AutoCAD LT would close. This could be very dangerous if you made changes that you did not want to save. Even if you were going to save the changes anyway, you would still experience the inconvenience of having to wait while exiting AutoCAD LT and then restarting it. It is strongly recommended that if you use the keyboard to enter your object snaps in previous AutoCAD LT releases, you should always type **ENDP** when you need Endpoint. However, the END command was discontinued in AutoCAD LT 97. This allows you to type END when using the Endpoint object snap on the keyboard.

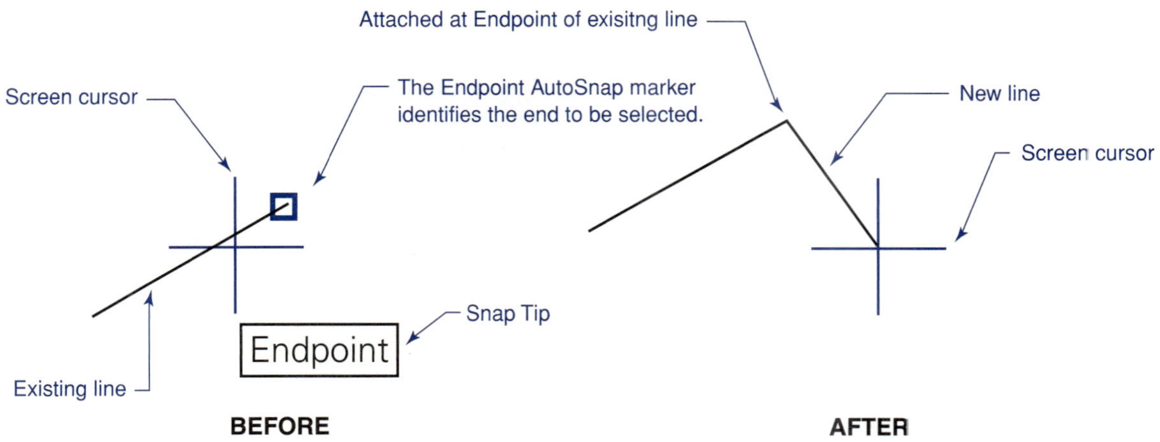

FIGURE 6.10 The object snap ENDpoint option finds the endpoint closest to the center of the screen cursor.

Snap to the Midpoint of an Object

Object Snap

MIDpoint

You can easily snap exactly to the middle of an object such as a line or arc. When you get a point prompt, select the Snap to Midpoint toolbar button, pick Midpoint in the cursor menu, or type **MID.** Move the cursor to any place on the line or arc and pick. Look at Figure 6.11 as you follow this command sequence:

> Command: **L** or **LINE**↵
> Specify first point: *<pick the first point>*
> Specify next point or [Undo]: **MID**↵
> of *<move the cursor near the midpoint and pick>*
> Specify next point or [Undo]: ↵
> Command:

FIGURE 6.11 Using the object snap MIDpoint option.

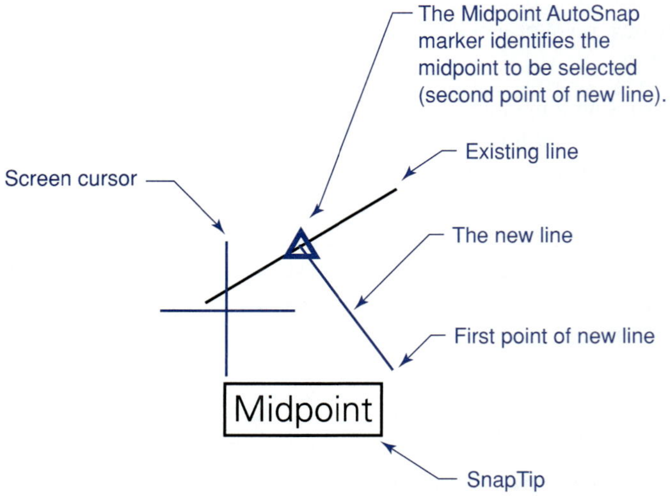

Snap to an Intersection

Object Snap

INTersection

It is a common drafting practice to connect a line to the intersection of other lines or objects. The Intersection object snap allows you to snap automatically to the intersection of objects such as lines, corners, arcs, and circles. Use this object snap by picking the Snap to Intersection toolbar button, selecting Intersection in the cursor menu, or typing **INT** when needed. Then move the cursor on or near the desired intersection or corner and pick. The following command sequence is shown in Figure 6.12A:

> Command: **L** or **E**↵
> Specify first point: *<pick the start point>*
> Specify next point or [Undo]: **INT**↵
> of *<move the cursor near the desired intersection and pick>*
> Specify next point or [Undo]:↵
> Command:

In some cases it may be inconvenient or even impossible to place the cursor on or very near the actual intersection. If this is the case, you can pick both objects individually and AutoCAD LT will find the point where they intersect. When you do this, you get the Extended Intersection AutoSnap marker and related SnapTip shown in Figure 6.12B when you pick the first object. You get the regular Intersection marker when you pick the second object.

FIGURE 6.12 (A) Using the object snap INTersect option to snap directly to an intersection. (B) Using the Extended Intersection to get an intersection of two objects.

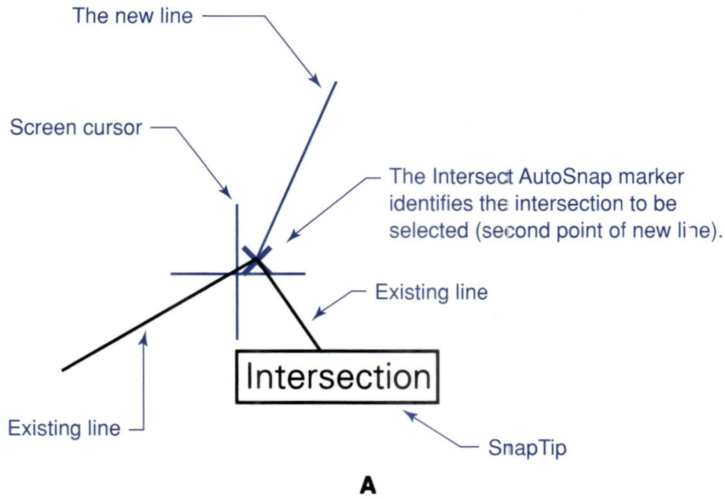

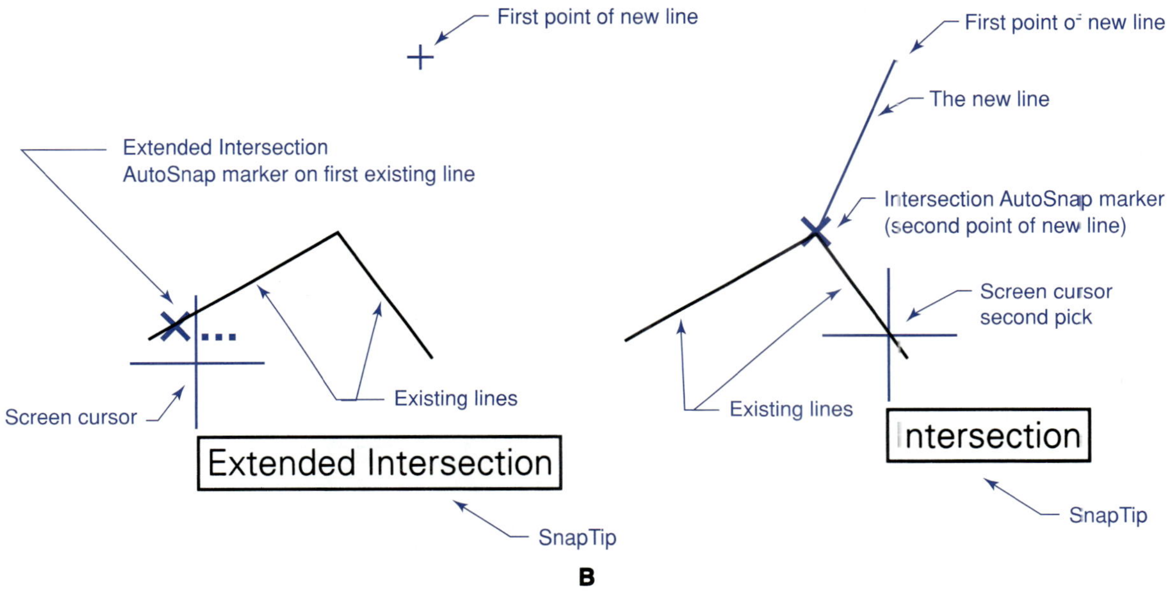

Field Notes

- As long as the objects you are picking are visible, the intersection can occur off screen and it will still be found.
- If the objects do not actually physically intersect, the point where they would intersect (if they were extended far enough) is found. This is true even for arcs, which are extended along their radius.

Snap Perpendicular to an Object

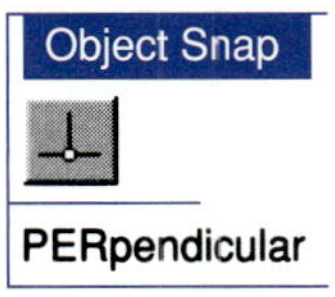

The Perpendicular object snap allows you to snap easily to an object perpendicular to another object. The term ***perpendicular*** means at right (90°) angles. To use the Perpendicular object snap, pick the Snap to Perpendicular toolbar button, select the Perpendicular option in the cursor menu, or type **PER.** Look at Figure 6.13 while you follow this command sequence:

Command: **L** or **LINE**↵
Specify first point: *<pick the first point>*
Specify next point or [Undo]: **PER**↵
of *<move the cursor near an existing object and pick>*
Specify next point or [Undo]: ↵
Command:

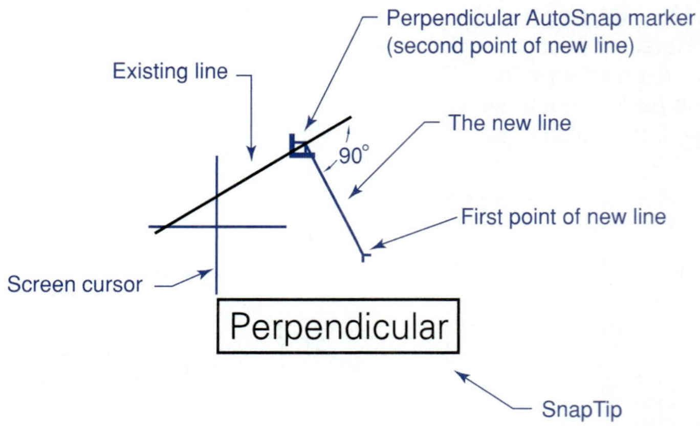

FIGURE 6.13 Using the object snap PERpendicular option.

In some situations, you may want to draw a line perpendicular to an existing object by selecting the existing object first, followed by selecting a point away from the object. When you do this, AutoCAD LT gives you the Deferred Perpendicular AutoSnap marker and related SnapTip. Deferred Perpendicular means that AutoCAD LT will establish the perpendicularity after waiting for you to pick the next point. Figure 6.14 shows how Deferred Perpendicular works.

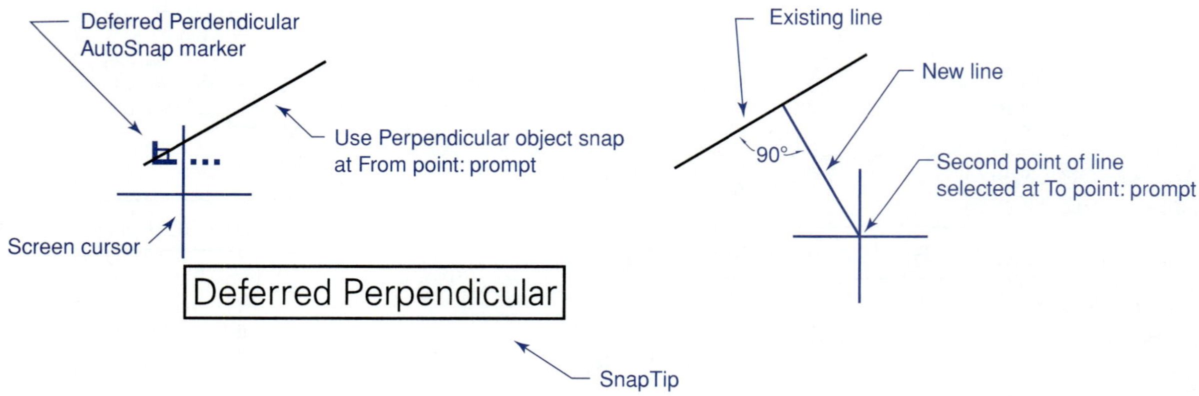

FIGURE 6.14 Using the Deferred Perpendicular object snap feature.

Field Notes

A common difficulty that you may encounter when using object snaps is accidentally picking the wrong menu item and activating an object snap other than the one you really need. If you do pick the wrong object snap and need to cancel it, here's how: Remember that simply picking any point deactivates the object snap whether or not the pick was successful, and if you pick a point where no object exists, then no point is found and the point prompt is reissued. You can use this feature to your advantage. When an incorrect object snap is selected, simply pick a point onscreen where no objects are found. The object snap is deactivated and the point prompt is reissued. Now you can select the correct object snap and continue working.

Exercise 6.2

Estimated time required: 10 min.

1. Open AutoCAD LT if it is not already open. Use the setup option of your choice. Dimensions and notes are not needed.
2. Set limits at 8.5,11.
3. Draw the object shown below using the steps given and suggested object snaps for accuracy.
4. Save as EX6.2, and close the drawing.

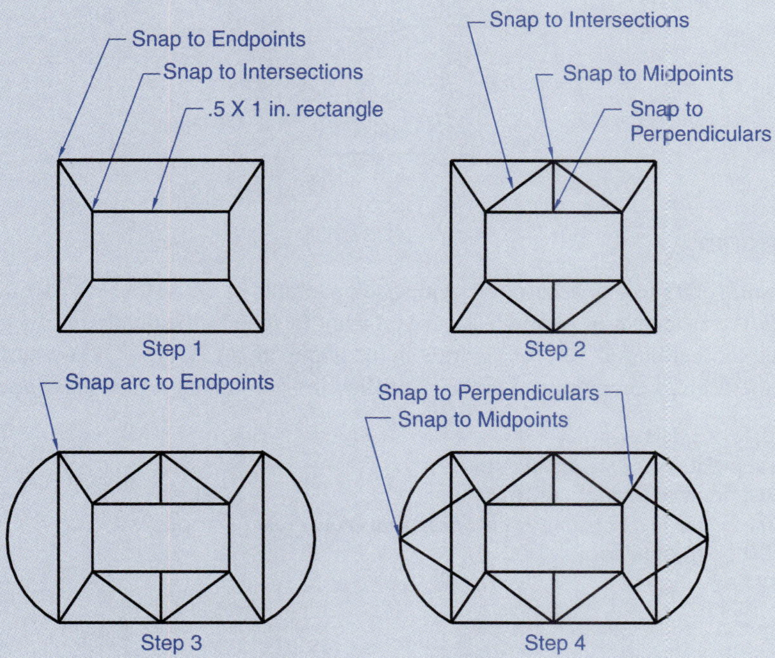

Snap to the Center

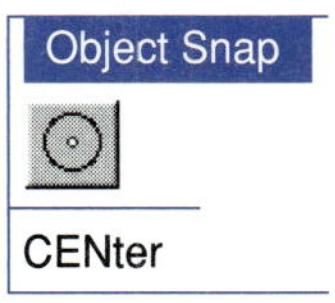

Snap an object to the center of a circle, arc, or ellipse by picking the Snap to Center toolbar button, selecting the Center option in the cursor menu, or typing **CEN** at the desired point prompt. Figure 6.15 shows a line drawn to the exact center of a circle by using the Center object snap. Move the cursor to anywhere on the circle and pick. Follow this command sequence:

Command: **L** or **LINE**↵
Specify first point: *<pick the first point>*
Specify next point or [Undo]: **CEN**↵
of *<move the cursor to an existing circle or arc and pick>*
Specify next point or [Undo]: ↵
Command:

Field Notes

One common mistake when learning to use the CENter object snap is trying to pick a point at the center of the circle. This does not work because in order for object snap to find a point associated with an object, the cursor must be touching the object itself. Remember, when snapping to the center of a circle, the cursor must be touching the circle when you pick. The exception to this rule is found when using running object snap, which is discussed later in this chapter.

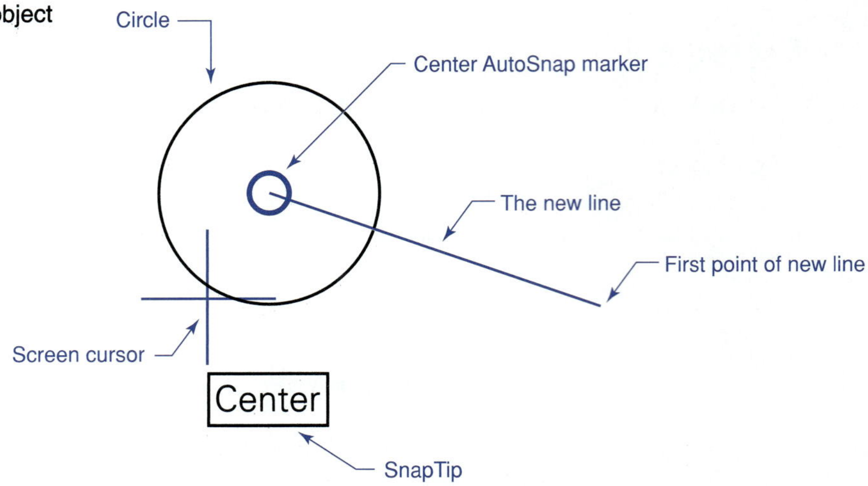

FIGURE 6.15 Using the object snap CENter option.

Snap to a Quadrant

Object Snap

QUAdrant

The term ***quadrant*** refers to a quarter of a circle. The quadrants of an AutoCAD LT circle are located at 0°, 90°, 180°, and 270°, as shown in Figure 6.16. If you want to snap to the quadrant of a circle or arc, pick the Snap to Quadrant toolbar button, select Quadrant in the popup menu, or type **QUA** when needed. Then, move the cursor near the desired quadrant and pick. The following command sequence is shown in Figure 6.17:

Command: **L** or **LINE**↵
Specify first point: *<pick the first point>*
Specify next point or [Undo]: **QUA**↵
of *<move the cursor to an existing circle or arc near a quadrant point and pick>*
Specify next point or [Undo]: ↵
Command:

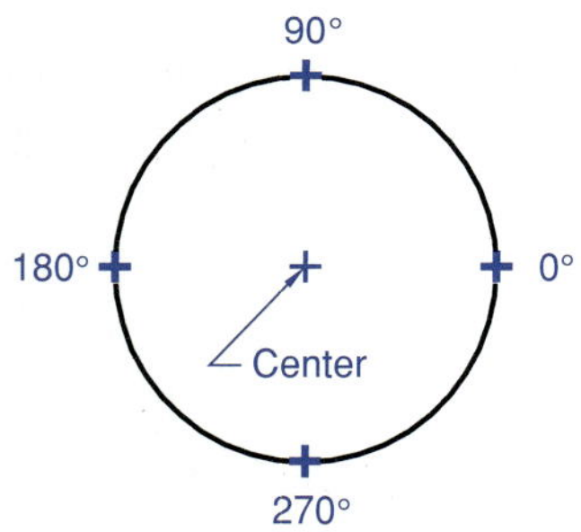

FIGURE 6.16 The quadrants of a circle.

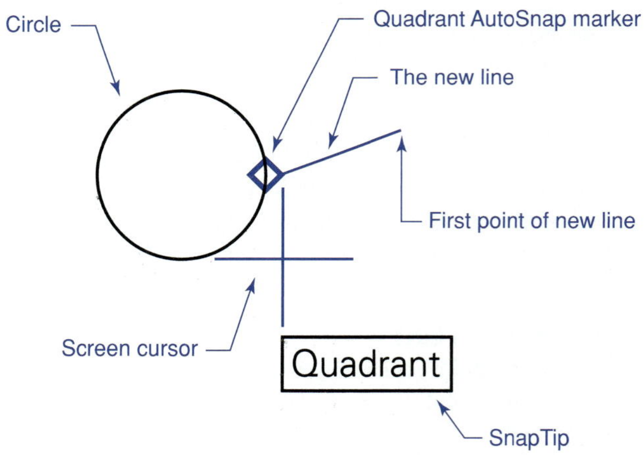

FIGURE 6.17 Using the object snap QUAdrant option.

Snap to a Tangent Point

Object Snap

TANgent

The Tangent object snap is used to snap accurately to the point of tangency of a curved object such as a circle, arc, or ellipse. Tangent means that a line, arc, circle, or ellipse touches another arc, circle, or ellipse at only one point, without crossing. To use this object snap option, pick the Snap to Tangent toolbar button, pick Tangent in the cursor menu, or type **TAN.** Move the cursor to a place on the circle near the intended point of tangency. Figure 6.18 shows a line drawn to the point of tangency of a circle. This is the command sequence:

Command: **L** or **LINE**↵
Specify first point: *<pick the first point>*
Specify next point or [Undo]: **TAN**↵
of *<move the cursor to an existing circle or arc near the desired tangent point and pick>*
Specify next point or [Undo]: ↵
Command:

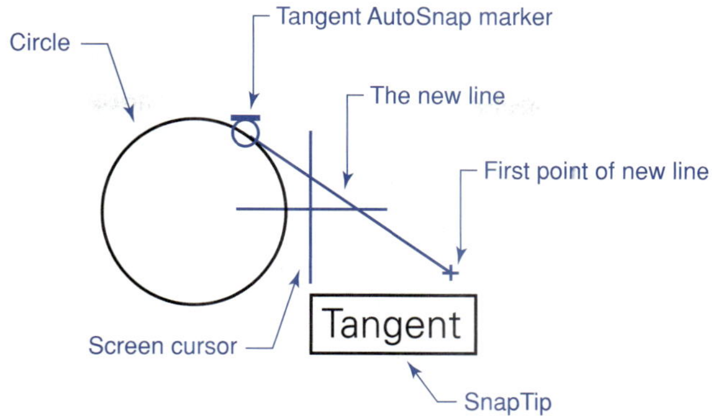

FIGURE 6.18 Using the object snap TANgent option.

In some situations, you may need to pick the tangent point first and then pick the second point. In this case, AutoCAD LT gives you the Deferred Tangent AutoSnap marker and related SnapTip. The Deferred Tangent AutoSnap marker looks like the Tangent marker with three dots following. Deferred Tangent means that AutoCAD LT will establish the actual point of tangency after waiting for you to pick the next point. The command sequence looks like this:

Command: **L** or **LINE**↵
Specify first point: **TAN**↵
of *<move the cursor to an existing circle or arc near the desired tangent point and pick>*
Specify next point or [Undo]: *<pick the next point>*
Specify next point or [Undo]: ↵
Command:

You can also draw circles and arcs tangent using the Three Point options. For example, you can draw a circle tangent to the three given circles in Figure 6.19 if you use the CIRCLE command's 3 Points option with each point tangent to a different circle. The command works like this:

Command: **C** or **CIRCLE**↵
Specify center point for circle or [3P/2P/Ttr (tan tan radius)]: **3P**↵
Specify first point on circle: **TAN**↵
to *<pick the first tangent point on circle 1>*
Specify second point on circle: **TAN**↵
to *<pick the second tangent point on circle 2>*
Specify third point on circle: **TAN**↵
to *<pick the third tangent point on circle 3>*
Command:

You can also draw a circle tangent to one other circle by using the CIRCLE command's Radius option if TANgent is used at the Radius prompt.

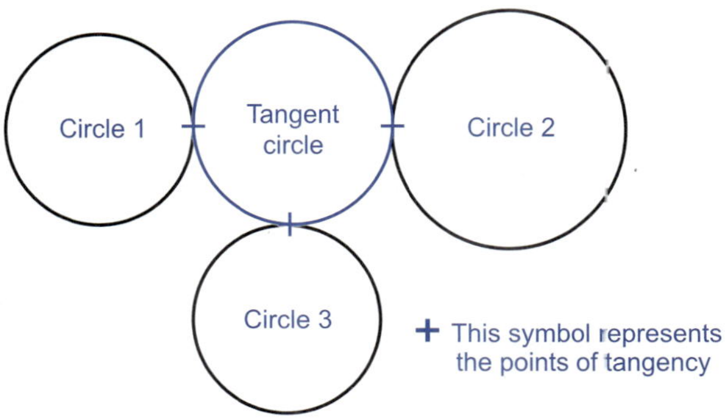

FIGURE 6.19 Using the CIRCLE command's Three Point option and the TANgent object snap to draw a circle tangent to three existing circles. *Note:* The AutoSnap markers and SnapTips are left off for clarity.

Field Notes

When picking Tan, Tan, Tan from the Circle cascade on the Draw pull-down menu, the TANgent entries are automatic, but if you pick where no object exists you will see an "invalid" 2D point message. To continue this command, you will need to restart the Tangent object snap mode. You can pick it from the menu, the tool bar, or enter it manually at the keyboard.

Exercise 6.3 — Estimated time required: 10 min.

1. Open AutoCAD LT if it is not already open. Use the setup option of your choice. Notes are not needed.
2. Set limits at 8.5,11.
3. Draw the object shown below using the steps given and suggested object snaps for accuracy. The exact size is up to you.
4. Save as EX6.3, and close the drawing.

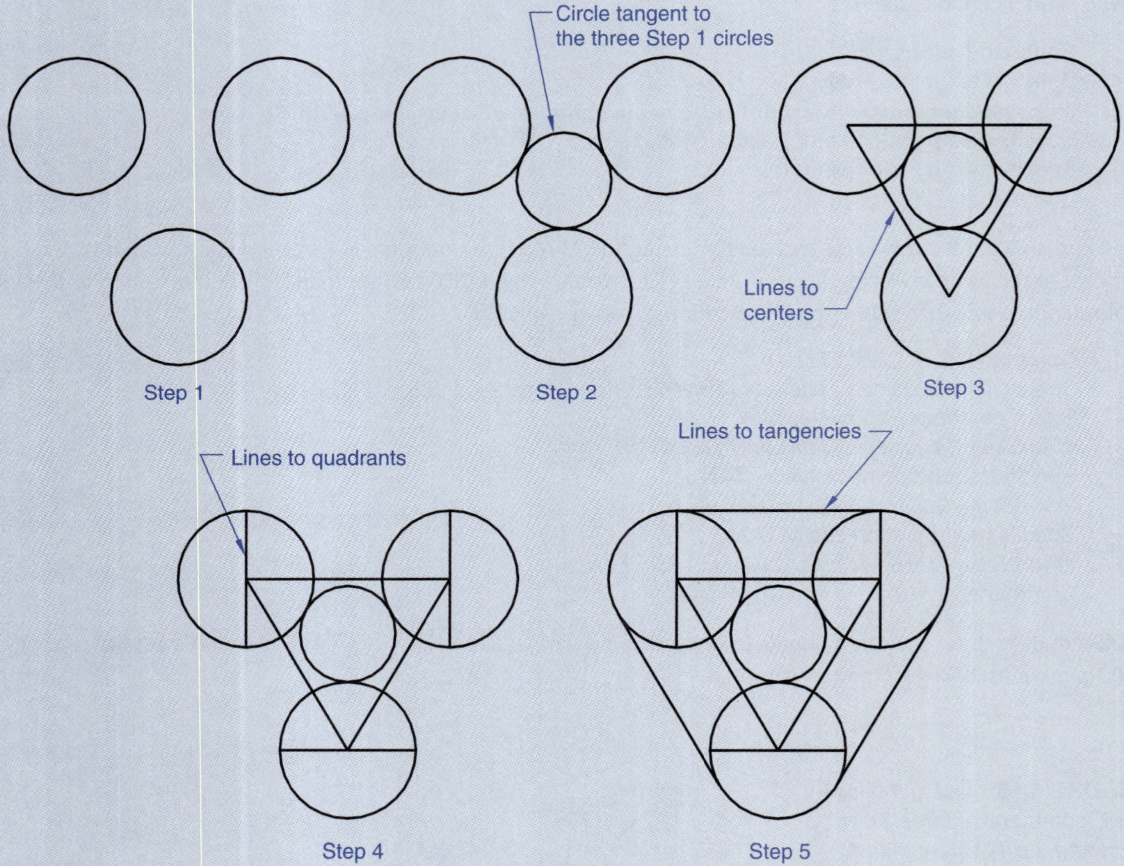

Snap to the Insertion Point

Object Snap

INSert

You will not use the Insert object snap until Chapters 9 and 12, but it is introduced here with the other object snap options. The Insert object snap is used to snap to the insertion point of text objects, blocks, attributes, and attribute definitions. ***Text*** is the AutoCAD LT term for letters and numbers. Text is explained in Chapter 9. The word ***block*** refers to an object, a group of objects, a drawing, or a symbol that is created as one object, generally for multiple use. An ***attribute*** contains information about a block. For example, an attribute might be a description or text within a block. An ***attribute definition*** describes the characteristics of the attribute. Blocks, attributes, and attribute definitions are explained in Chapter 12. Snap to an insertion point by picking the Snap to Insert toolbar

FIGURE 6.20 Using the object snap INSertion option.

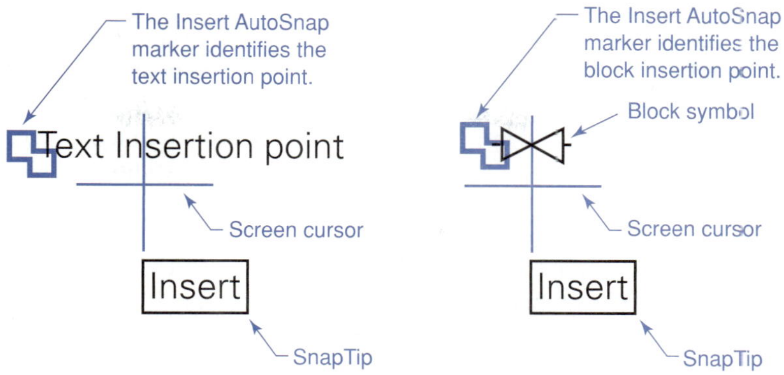

button, selecting Insert in the cursor menu, or typing **INS.** When you snap to an insertion point, you get the Insert AutoSnap marker and SnapTip. Figure 6.20 shows an example of a text and block insertion point.

Snap to a Node

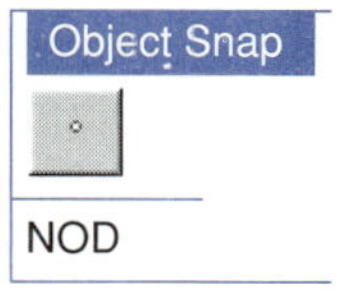

A ***node*** is a point object. Point objects are drawn using the POINT command, which is discussed later in this chapter. Snap to a node by picking the Snap to Node toolbar button, picking Node in the cursor menu, or typing **NOD** at the keyboard at a point prompt. When you snap to a point, you get the Node AutoSnap marker and SnapTip if AutoSnap is on.

Snap to the Nearest Point

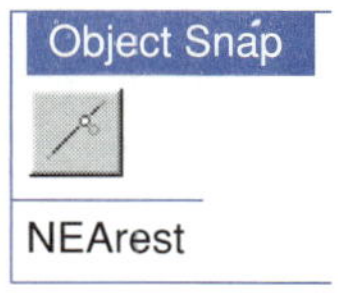

Oftentimes you may want to snap to an object, but the exact location of the point is not critical. The Nearest object snap allows you to snap to an object at a point that is closest to the cursor location. To access this object snap, pick the Snap to Nearest toolbar button, select Nearest in the cursor menu, or type **NEA.** Move the cursor as close as possible to the desired point and pick. When you use the Nearest object snap, you get the Nearest AutoSnap marker and SnapTip.

Snap to an Apparent Intersection

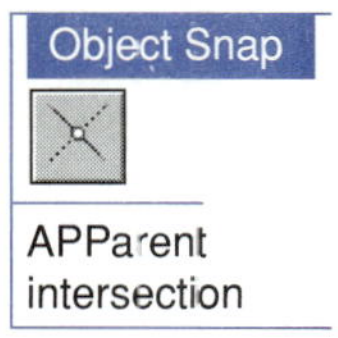

In 3-D drafting, objects that do not actually intersect physically may appear to intersect because of the angle you are viewing from. This is where the Apparent Intersection object snap is used. This option is discussed further in Chapter 14.

Disabling Object Snap

The None object snap option allows you to disable object snaps. This is most effective when you have a running object snap that you do not want to use for a specific application. (Running object snaps are explained later in this chapter.) When used during a command sequence, the None object snap allows only point entry without object snaps for the individual point when it is used. The None option needs to be used every time you want to temporarily disable a running object snap. To use this option, type **NON,** select None at the bottom of the cursor menu, or pick the Snap to None toolbar button.

Using Running Object Snaps

The term ***running object snap*** means that an object snap option or group of options can be set to run continuously. Running object snaps remain active until you change them or turn them off. Running object snaps are useful when you know that the drawing requires several of the same type of object snaps to be used. This saves a lot of time because the object snap that you set is automatically active when needed. You can set one or more object snaps to be active. If you set more than one running object snap, AutoCAD LT automatically uses the most appropriate object snap for the object you select. If two or more different possible object snap selections can be found, AutoCAD LT snaps to the selection that is closest to the cursor crossing. Running object snaps can be set in the Object Snap tab of the Drafting Settings dialog box or at the prompt line. Using the dialog box is most convenient.

Access the dialog box by selecting Drafting Settings ... from the Tools pull-down menu, pick the Object Snap Settings toolbar button, pick Settings... from the status bar OSNAP button, shortcut menu or type **OS** or **OSNAP**at the Command: prompt. The OSNAP display on the status line starts the OSNAP command only if no object snap modes are currently running. The Osnap Settings dialog box shown in Figure 6.21 displays all the object snap options. Turn on one or more desired running object snaps by picking the appropriate toggle. Figure 6.21 shows the Endpoint, Center, and Intersection running object snaps turned on. Pick the OK button when ready.

Entering running object snaps at the Command: line is more time consuming and is done by using the -OS or -OSNAP command. When you are asked to enter the desired object snap modes, type the abbreviated name of the object snap or group of object snaps. If you enter more than one object snap name, separate each name by a comma. Do this to set the Endpoint, Center, and Intersection running object snaps at the keyboard:

Command: **-O** or **-OSNAP↵**
Object snap modes: **END,CEN,INT↵**
Command:

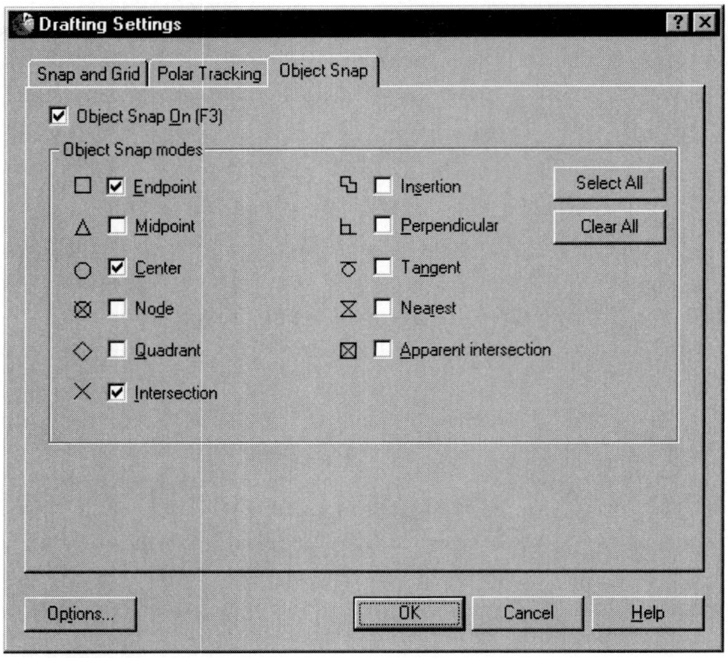

FIGURE 6.21 The Osnap Settings dialog box.

Turn off specific or all running object snaps if they are not needed. Pick the OSNAP button on the status line to toggle the running object snap feature. To turn running object snaps totally off, go back to the Osnap Settings dialog box and pick the Clear All button or toggle individual running object snaps as needed. You can also enter the -OSNAP command and either press Enter, or type **OFF NONE.**

This OSNAP toggle feature only works when there are object snap modes currently running. Setting running object snap modes automatically turns on the OSNAP button. Now the currently running object snap modes can be temporarily suspended by turning off the OSNAP button. Picking again resets the temporarily suspended running object snap modes. This is a very convenient tool because you do not have to use the OSNAP command to restore the previous settings.

Field Notes

- Picking the OSNAP button on the status line is very convenient to temporarily turn running object snaps on and off. Another option is to press Ctrl + F or use the F3 function key. There are times when you may want the running object snaps active and other times when they distract from your drawing performance.
- The one drawback to running object snaps comes when you forget to turn them off. If you are unaware of a running object snap mode, you may get very unexpected results while working in your drawing. There are two ways to recognize that a running object snap mode is active. First, at all point prompts, the aperture will appear, and AutoSnap markers and snap tips will appear on SnapTips. Second, the OSNAP button in the status line will be depressed. A quick pick on the OSNAP button immediately disables the running object snap modes.

Adjusting the Aperture Size

The AutoCAD LT default aperture size is fine for most uses. However, you may want to make the aperture smaller to work on a very crowded drawing or make it bigger for construction in large areas. The aperture size is measured in pixels. *Pixels* (short for *picture elements*) are the tiny dots that make up what is displayed on the computer screen. Review Chapter 1 for a full discussion of pixels. The AutoCAD LT default setting is 10 pixels. AutoCAD LT allows you to change the setting from 1 to 50 pixels. You can set pixel size using the APERTURE command or move the slider bar of the Aperture size area of the Drafting tab in the Options dialog box shown in Figure 6.21. When moving the slider, the image to the right shows the current aperture setting at actual size. When changing the aperture size at the command prompt, do this:

Command: **AP** or **APERTURE**↵
Object snap target height (1-50 pixels) <10>: **20**↵
Command:

Field Notes

- Changing the aperture size in the Options dialog is quick and easy. You can also see the size of the aperture, displayed in the image tile, as you move the slider bar.
- Aperture size can be adjusted as needed to fit any situation. Increasing the size of the aperture helps you to pick object snap points quickly and easily because you do not have to point so carefully. In a situation where there are many objects in your drawing and a large aperture is not accurate enough, reduce the size and you will be able to pick objects in a crowded area more accurately.

Changing Your AutoSnap Settings

You can make adjustments to your AutoSnap settings in the Drafting tab in the Options dialog box. Access this dialog box as previously discussed and then pick the Drafting tab, as shown in Figure 6.22. The AutoSnap settings are as follows:

- Marker: The marker is on by default. Pick this check box and remove the check to turn it off.
- Magnet: When the cursor is close enough, the magnet feature forces the cursor onto the snap point where the AutoSnap marker is located. This is on by default.
- Display AutoSnap tooltip: This is also on by default. This check box allows you to turn the SnapTip on or off.
- Display AutoSnap aperture box: The aperture box is located at the intersection of the screen cursor crosshairs when you snap to an object and when this check box is on. This option is off by default.

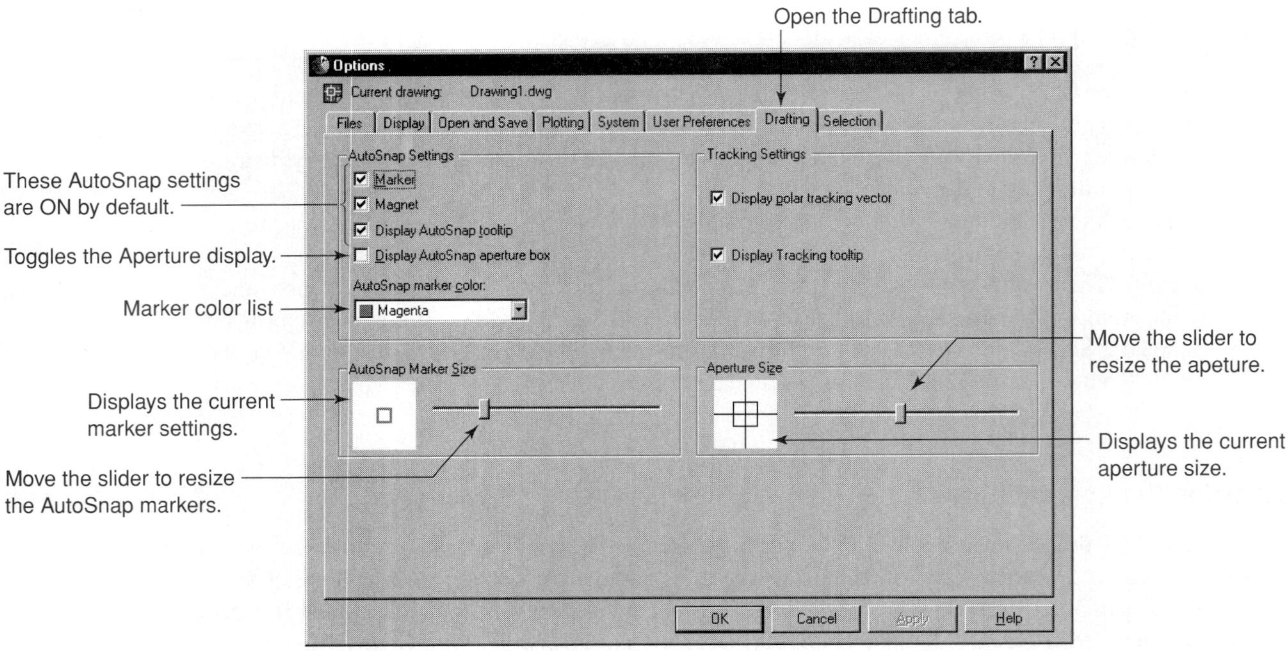

FIGURE 6.22 The Drafting tab is where you set AutoSnap options, change the marker size, or change the marker color.

The AutoSnap Marker Size: area has a slider bar that allows you to change the size of the AutoSnap markers. The image tile represents the marker size as you move the slider bar.

The Marker color: list box allows you to change the AutoSnap marker color to one of the seven standard colors, as desired.

Field Notes

When you use an object snap to select a point on an object, you can press the Tab key to cycle through all of the available locations that match the current object snap setting on the drawing. If you have more than one running object snap set, pressing the Tab key allows you to cycle through the available running object snaps that match related features on the drawing.

Exercise 6.4 **Estimated time required: 8 min.**

1. Open AutoCAD LT if it is not already open. Use the setup option of your choice. Notes and dimensions are not needed.
2. Set limits at 8.5,11.
3. Draw the object shown below using the steps given. Use Endpoint, Center, Intersect, and Tangent as running object snaps. The exact size is up to you.
4. Adjust the aperture size to help you make object snap selections.
5. Save as EX6.4, and close the drawing.

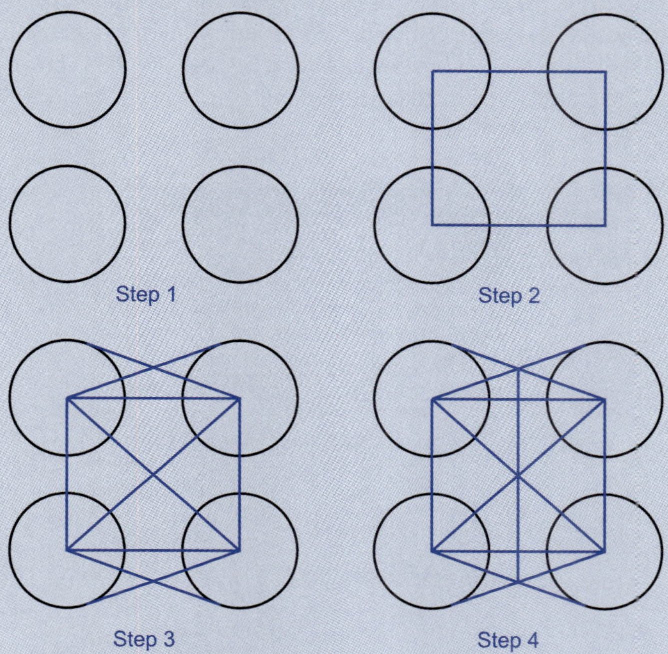

LEARNING CHECKPOINT

- ☐ What is the primary benefit of using Polar Tracking and Polar Snap?
- ☐ Describe the purpose of object snaps.
- ☐ How do you display the object snap cursor menu?
- ☐ Explain when and how object snaps are entered at the keyboard.
- ☐ List the names of at least 10 object snap options.
- ☐ Explain the function of the AutoSnap markers and SnapTips.
- ☐ Define a running object snap.
- ☐ Identify at least three ways to access the Osnap tab in the Drafting Settings dialog box.
- ☐ How are multiple running object snaps entered at the keyboard?
- ☐ How do you temporarily turn off or on running object snaps?
- ☐ Describe at least four ways to turn running object snaps off totally.
- ☐ How do you change the aperture size at the keyboard?
- ☐ Why is it desirable to change the aperture size using the Options dialog box?

Viewing, Selecting, and Using Precision Drawing Tools

- Drawing with Precision

Concept Animations

- Object Snaps

Reference Points and Other Point Objects

Draw
Point
Draw
Point ▸
POINT
PO

Points can be drawn using AutoCAD LT. The points you draw can look just like a grid dot, or a variety of point styles and sizes are available. Points can be placed on a drawing for reference, as markers, for design, or for snapping with the Node object snap option. The Point Style dialog box shown in Figure 6.23 contains the different point shapes and allows you to change the point size.

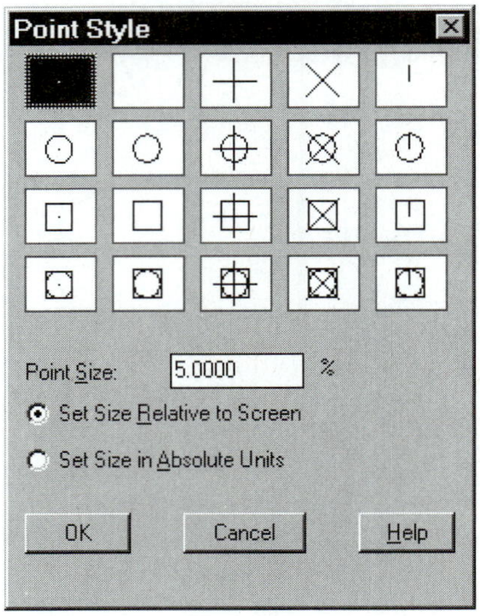

FIGURE 6.23 The Point Style dialog box.

Access the Point Style dialog box by picking Point Style ... in the Format pull-down menu or by typing **DDPTYPE.** The AutoCAD LT default point is a dot. To select a different point style, move the arrow cursor to the desired symbol image and pick; then pick the OK button. Among the many available options, you will notice that the second image tile from the left in the top row is blank. This style suppresses the display of points in your drawing and can be set current when you want to remove the points from your display, but not from your drawing. Two options are available for setting the point size format. The options are activated by picking one of the following radio buttons:

- Set Size Relative to Screen: This is the AutoCAD LT default. Pick this option if you want to set the point size as a percentage of the screen size. This kind of a point display changes when using the ZOOM command, but if you use the REGEN command, the point size returns to its correct size ratio to the screen. When this option is active, there is a percent (%) symbol next to the Point Size text box. Alter the size percentage by changing the value in the text box.
- Set Size in Absolute Units: Use this option if you want to set the point size in units that are specified in the Point Size text box. Points drawn using this format get larger or smaller when using the ZOOM command. When this option is active, Units is specified next to the Point Size text box. The units value you set is the same as your drawing units. For example, a setting of .25 is one-quarter of an inch on an inch drawing.

After using the Point Style dialog box to set the desired point style and size, you are ready to draw a point. To draw a single point, select Point and then Single Point from the Draw pull-down menu, pick the Point button in the Draw toolbar, or type **PO, PT,** or **POINT** at the Command: prompt. This command displays the current status and asks you to specify a point:

Command: **PO, PT** or **POINT**↵
Current point modes: PDMODE=0 PDSIZE=0.0000
Specify a point: *<pick a point or enter point coordinates>*
Command:

You can draw several points by picking Point and then Multiple Point in the Draw pull-down menu. The POINT command remains active for you to draw as many points as needed until you press Esc, Enter, or the space bar to exit the command.

Field Notes

You can draw several different point styles and sizes. However, when the drawing is regenerated, AutoCAD LT changes every point style and size to the same representation as the last point style and size drawn. So, in real practice, you can only have one currently active point style and size.

Exercise 6.5

Estimated time required: 5 min.

1. Open AutoCAD LT if it is not already open. Use the setup option of your choice.
2. Set limits at 8.5,11.
3. Open the Point Style dialog box, pick a point style of your own choosing, and draw it using the default size and format.
4. Do this again with a different point style.
5. Use the Point Style dialog box to select a different point style and set the size to 20%. Draw the point and notice the difference.
6. Use the Point Style dialog box to select a different point style and set the size to .25 units. Draw the point and notice the difference.
7. Use the Point Style dialog box to select a different point style and set the size to .50 units. Draw the point and notice the difference.
8. With all of the points that you just drew displayed on the screen, type REGEN at the Command: prompt and press Enter. Observe what happens.
9. Save as EX6.5, and close the drawing.

Measuring and Dividing Objects

Now that you know how to control the display of points, AutoCAD LT provides two commands that let you place points at specified distances along an object. These commands are DIVIDE and MEASURE. Before using the DIVIDE or MEASURE commands, you need to decide what you want the points to look like. To do this, use the Point Style dialog box to pick a point style and size. The default point style is a dot. The dot does not show when placed on an object, but it is there and can be snapped to using the Node object snap. If you want the point symbol to display clearly, then use one of the point styles that has a distinct shape. If the points are to be placed on the drawing for construction purposes, you might consider placing them on a construction layer so they can be frozen when not in use.

Using the Divide Command

The DIVIDE command is used to place evenly spaced points or blocks along the length, circumference, or perimeter of an object. Blocks are objects that are grouped together to make a single object or symbol. Blocks are explained in Chapter 12. To make evenly spaced divisions on an object, select Point and then Divide in the Draw pull-down menu or type **DIV** or **DIVIDE.** AutoCAD LT asks for a number of segments, for which you can enter between 2 and 32,767 divisions. Figure 6.24 shows how a line, a circle, and a rectangle are divided into eight segments using this command sequence:

Draw
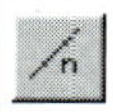
Divide

Draw
Point ▶

DIVIDE
DIV

Command: **DIV** or **DIVIDE**↵
Select object to divide: *<pick the object>*
Enter the number of segments or [Block]: **12**↵
Command:

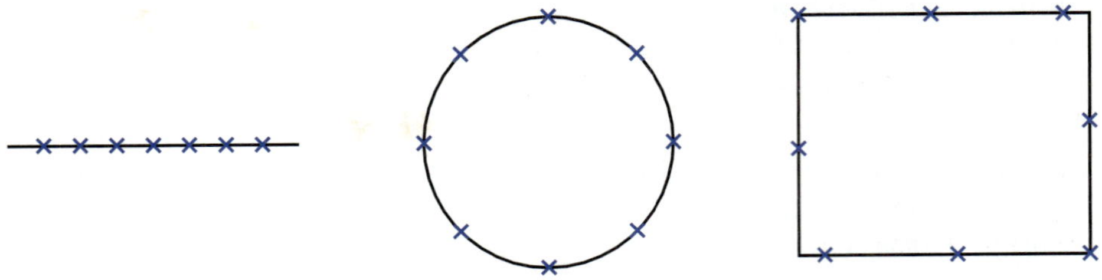

FIGURE 6.24 Using the DIVIDE command to make eight equally spaced divisions on three different objects.

Draw

Measure

Draw
Point ▸

MEASURE
ME

Using the Measure Command

The MEASURE command is used to place points or blocks a measured incremental distance along the length, circumference, or perimeter of an object. To place points a specified distance apart on an object, select Point and then Measure in the Draw pull-down menu or type **ME** or **MEASURE.** AutoCAD LT asks you for a segment length, which is the specified distance between points. The last segment length may be shorter than the specified length if the distance to the end of the object does not allow for a full length. Figure 6.25 shows the results of this command sequence:

Command: **ME** or **MEASURE**↵
Select object to measure: *<pick the object>*
Specify length of segment or [Block]: **.25**↵
Command:

FIGURE 6.25 Using the MEASURE command to mark three different objects with specific segment lengths.

Exercise 6.6 **Estimated time required: 5 min.**

1. Open AutoCAD LT if it is not already open. Use the setup option of your choice. A border and title block are not required.
2. Set limits at 8.5,11.
3. Open the Point Style dialog box. Pick the "X" point style and a size of 2%.
4. Draw a line, circle, and rectangle similar to those shown in Figure 6.24. Use the DIVIDE command to divide each object into eight equal parts.
5. Draw a line, circle, and rectangle similar to those shown in Figure 6.25. Use the MEASURE command to draw .25-in.-long segments on each object.
6. Save as EX6.6, and close the drawing.

Using the From Option to Establish a Point from an Existing Point

Object Snap

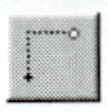

FROm

With object snaps, you snap to a specific point associated with an object. Yet, there are many situations when you may want to snap to a point that can be located using a specific point of reference. In this situation, you can use the From option. The From option allows you to specify a point, using relative or polar coordinates (or direct distance entry), that is at a specified location from a given point. The temporary reference point can be any point on an object such as an endpoint, midpoint, center, or any other known point in the drawing. One application might be when you want to draw a circle with its center a given X and Y distance from the corner of an object. It is easy to do this with the From option, which is accessed by picking the Snap From in the Object Snap toolbar button, selecting From in the Object Snap cursor menu, or typing **FRO.** Follow this command sequence, as you look at the steps in Figure 6.26, to draw a 0.25 circle with its center located .875,.625 from the corner of a plate:

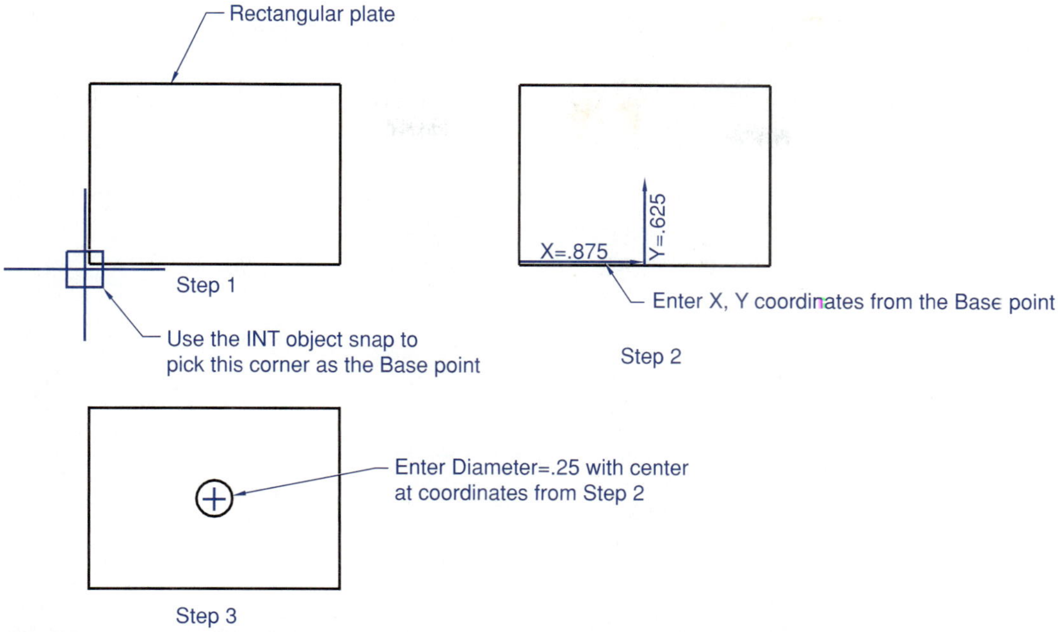

FIGURE 6.26 Using the From option to draw a line from a point perpendicular to a line.

Command: **C** or **CIRCLE**↵
Specify center point for circle or [3P/2P/Ttr (tan tan radius)]: **FRO**↵
Base point: **INT**↵
of <*pick the corner*> <Offset>: **@.875,.625**↵
Specify radius of circle or [Diameter] <0.5000>: **D**↵
Specify diameter of circle <1.0000>: **.25**↵
Command:

The following items are defined from the previous command sequence:

- **Base point** This is the point from which the From point is established. In this operation, the Base point is the corner of the rectangular plate in Figure 6.26.
- **Offset** This is the distance in relative or polar coordinates from the Base point. The Offset in the example is relative coordinates @.875,.625 from the Base point.

Any variety of operations may be performed using the From option. The possibilities depend on your specific application. Another example might have been to draw a circle a certain distance from the center of another circle or from the midpoint of a line.

Exercise 6.7 **Estimated time required: 5 min.**

1. Open AutoCAD LT if it is not already open. Use the setup option of your choice. Notes and dimensions are not needed.
2. Set limits at 8.5,11.
3. Draw the rectangular plate with four holes shown below using the From option to locate the holes from the corner of the rectangular plate. Do not draw dimensions and notes.
4. Save as EX6.7, and close the drawing.

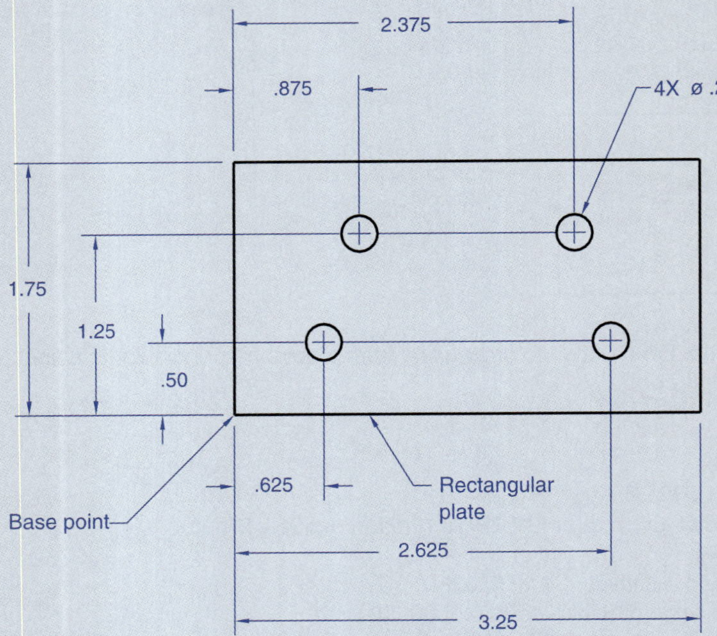

Using Point Filters

The term *filter* means to extract or remove certain information from something in order to create something else. ***Point filters*** are used to extract the X, Y, and Z coordinate values from individual points in order to create a new combined point. Point filters are also called ***coordinate filters.***

Using an X point filter works like drawing an imaginary horizontal line and a Y point filter establishes an imaginary vertical line. Z point filters are used for 3-D applications. Enter point filters by typing **.X** or **.Y** when AutoCAD LT asks you for point entry. Point filters work best when combined with object snaps to improve accuracy. An example of using point filters might be if you need to draw a circle with the center of its X and Y coordinates from the midpoint of the sides of the rectangular plate in Figure 6.27A. To do this, use the X and Y filters and the Midpoint object snaps as follows:

Command: **C** or **CIRCLE**↵
Specify center point for circle or [3P/2P/Ttr (tan tan radius)]: **.X**↵
of **MID**↵
of *<pick the bottom horizontal line>* (need YZ): **MID**↵
of *<pick left vertical line>*

The center of the circle automatically snaps to the intersection of the X and Y coordinates connected from the midpoints of the sides as shown in Figure 6.27B. Continue the CIRCLE command:

Specify radius of circle or [Diameter] <0.1250>: **.5**↵
Command:

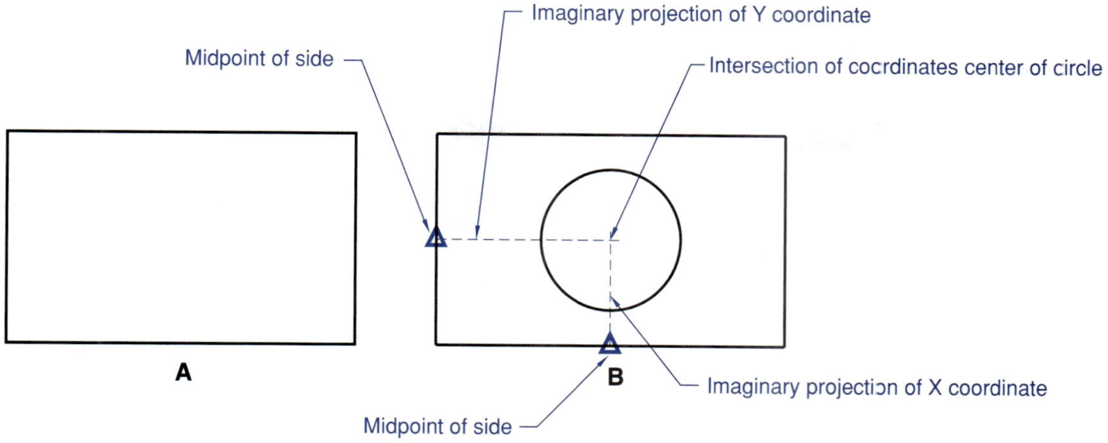

FIGURE 6.27 Using point filters to establish the intersection of X and Y coordinates from the midpoints of the sides of a rectangle. A circle is drawn with its center at the intersection.

Using Direct Distance Entry

A convenient way to enter point coordinate locations is by using ***direct distance entry.*** This feature allows you to point the cursor in the direction in which you want the next point to be placed and simply specify the distance. This feature works most accurately when ORTHO is on or you are using Polar Tracking. To try this first example, be sure that ORTHO is on. This sequence draws the rectangle shown in Figure 6.28, which is 4 units wide and 2 units high:

Command: **L** or **LINE**↵
Specify first point: **2,2**↵
Specify next point or [Undo]: <*drag cursor to the right, then type* **4**↵>
Specify next point or [Undo]: <*drag cursor up, then type* **2**↵ >
Specify next point or [Close/Undo]: <*drag cursor to the left, then type* **4**↵>
Specify next point or [Close/Undo]: **C**↵
Command:

FIGURE 6.28 Using direct distance entry to draw a rectangle.

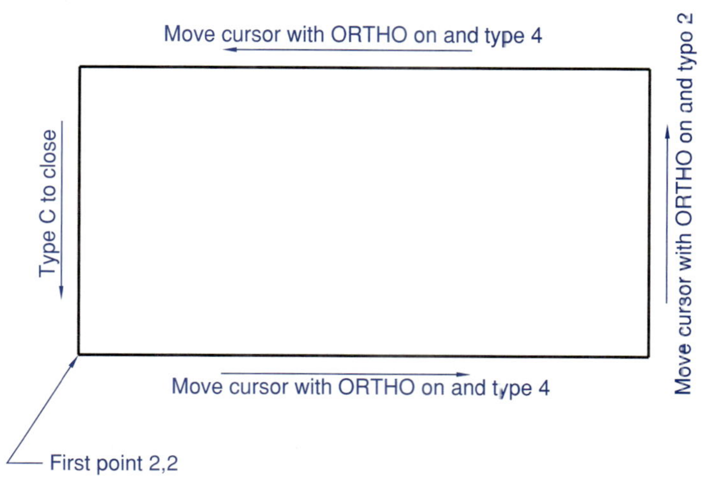

Field Notes

The idea of direct distance entry is to be able to find points quickly and easily with a minimum amount of input. Direct distance entry works very well for drawing perpendicular lines with the ORTHO or SNAP options on. Use polar coordinate entry if freehand pointing does not provide enough accuracy. Direct distance entry can be used anywhere that AutoCAD LT expects a point coordinate value, including both drawing and editing commands. It is also possible to use direct distance entry at the *first* point prompt, such as the From point: prompt of the LINE command. Typing in a single number finds a point that is at the same angle as the cursor in relationship to the LASTPOINT variable, at the specified distance.

Exercise 6.8 — Estimated time required: 5 min.

1. Open AutoCAD LT if it is not already open. Use the setup option of your choice.
2. Set limits at 8.5,11.
3. In the top portion of the drawing area, draw a rectangle similar to the one shown in Figure 6.27A.
4. Use point filters to draw a circle with the exact center at the X and Y intersection of a projection from the midpoints of the side and bottom of the rectangle. Use Figure 6.27B as an example.
5. Use Figure 6.28 as an example and follow the command sequence provided in the discussion about direct distance entry to draw a 4 × 2 rectangle. It is helpful to have ORTHO on when doing this part of the exercise.
6. Save as EX6.8, and close the drawing.

Tracking Points with AutoCAD LT

Object Snap

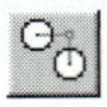

TRAcking
TK

Tracking is a way to locate a point relative to other points on the drawing. AutoCAD LT tracks a series of temporary points that you establish. Each point is found from the previous point. This allows you to determine a new point location from a series of directions and distances. The use of direct distance entry and object snaps assists in accurate tracking. Tracking can be used anytime AutoCAD LT asks for a point. The use of tracking is an easy way to find a point located at the imaginary intersection between two sides of an object. This example is similar to the illustration used in Figure 6.27 with the point filter discussion. Access tracking at any point prompt by picking the Tracking button in the Object Snap toolbar, picking Tracking in the Object Snap cursor menu, or typing **TK** or **TRA.** Press the Enter key to end tracking. Follow this command sequence while you look at Figure 6.29 to use tracking to draw a circle at the intersection of the X and Y projection between two points:

Command: **C** or **CIRCLE**↵
Specify center point for circle or [3P/2P/Ttr (tan tan radius)]: **TK**↵
First tracking point: **MID**↵
of *<pick the midpoint of the bottom horizontal line and move the cursor up>*
Next point (Press ENTER to end tracking): **MID**↵
of *<pick the midpoint of the left vertical line>*
Next point (Press ENTER to end tracking): ↵
Specify radius of circle or [Diameter] <0.5000>: **.5**↵
Command:

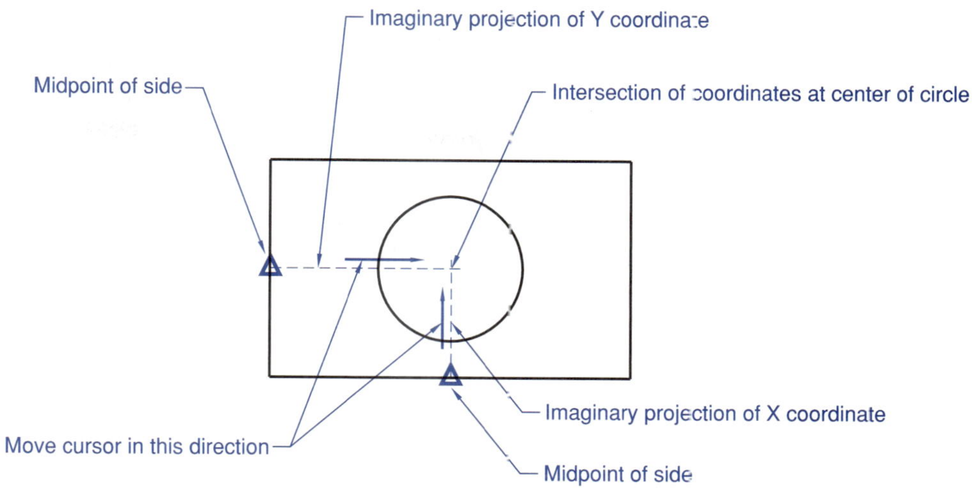

FIGURE 6.29 Using point tracking to establish an intersection from the midpoints of the sides of a rectangle. A circle is drawn with its center at the intersection.

Field Notes

When tracking from one point to the next, be sure that you move the cursor in the desired direction, otherwise unexpected results may occur. Press the Esc key and start again if something you dislike happens. AutoCAD LT continues to ask you for tracking points until you press Enter to turn tracking off.

Exercise 6.9

Estimated time required: 5 min.

1. Open AutoCAD LT if it is not already open. Use the setup option of your choice.
2. Set limits at 8.5,11.
3. Draw the rectangle object shown below.
4. Use point tracking to draw a circle with the exact center at the X and Y intersection of a projection from the midpoints of the side and bottom of the rectangle. Use Figure 6.29 as an example.
5. Use the FROM option to draw the other four circles from their adjacent corners.
6. Do not draw dimensions.
7. Save as EX6.9, and close the drawing.

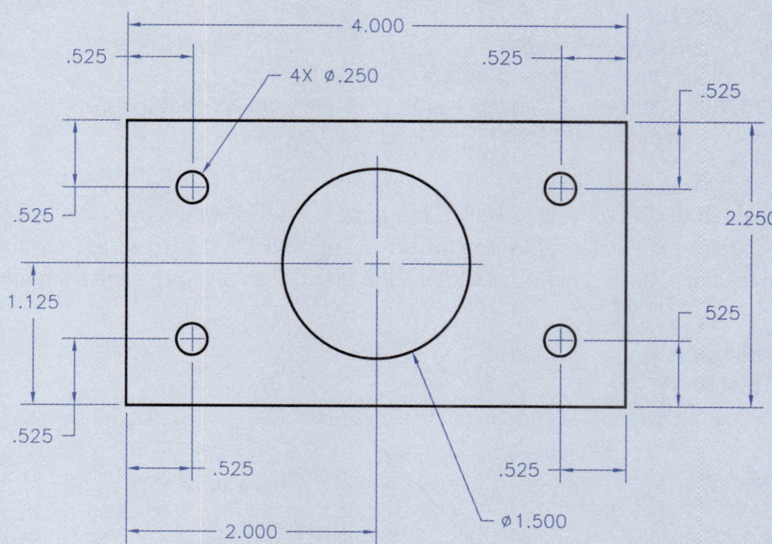

Drawing Inquiry Tools and Making Calculations

You can use AutoCAD LT to help you identify the location of points or to calculate distances, angles, and areas. You can also have AutoCAD LT list object properties and provide drawing information.

Identifying Points

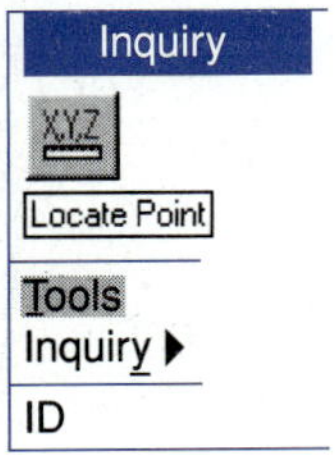

AutoCAD LT lets you determine the coordinates of a specific point and allows you to find a point by entering its coordinates. These tasks are done using a feature called ID Point. Access this feature by picking the Locate Point button from the inquiry flyout on the standard toolbar, pick ID Point from the Inquiry flyout of the Tools pull-down menu, or by typing **ID** at the Command: prompt. Use the command as follows when you want to identify a known point:

Command: **ID**↵
Specify point: ⟨*pick the point to identify*⟩

AutoCAD LT automatically gives you a listing of the X, Y, and Z coordinates of the point at the prompt line. For example, the point coordinates for the ID command might look like this:

X = 4.5000 Y = 7.0000 Z = 0.00000
Command:

Field Notes

- Obtaining the ID of a point without the aid of snap or object snap will give a reasonable estimate of the coordinate location, but for best results, use your available precision tools.
- The Inquiry flyout on the Standard toolbar is not labeled Inquiry when the toolbar is docked. This flyout contains the four buttons Distance, Area, List, and Locate Point. The Distance button is visible by default when you start AutoCAD LT. Like all flyouts, this one will display the most recently selected button.

Calculating Distances and Angles

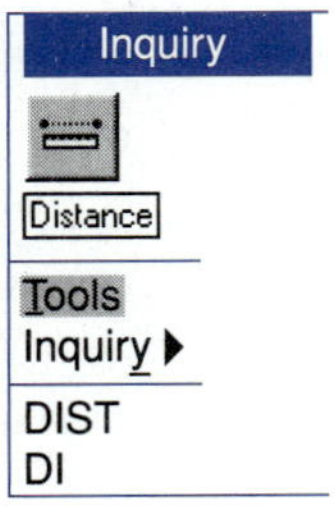

Two-dimensional and three-dimensional distances and angles are easily calculated with AutoCAD LT. This discussion explains how to find 2-D distances and angles. Finding 3-D distances and angles is covered in Chapter 13. To find the distance and angle between two points, pick the Distance button on the inquiry flyout of the standard toolbar, pick Inquiry and Distance in the Tools pull-down menu, or type **DI** or **DIST.** Next, pick the two points and AutoCAD LT automatically gives you information on the command line. An example looks like this:

Command: **DI** or **DIST**↵
Specify first point: ⟨*pick the first point*⟩
Specify second point: ⟨*pick the second point*⟩
Distance = 1.7678 Angle in XY Plane = 45 Angle from XY Plane = 0
Delta X = 1.2500, Delta Y = 1.2500, Delta Z = 0.0000
Command:

The Distance and Angle in the XY plane are shown in Figure 6.30. The Angle from the XY plane is a 3-D angle and is shown in Chapter 13. The term *Delta* in the preceding AutoCAD LT message is a mathematical word meaning a change in distance. In the previous example, the X and Y axis values were each increased by 1.25.

FIGURE 6.30 The distance and angle in the XY plane.

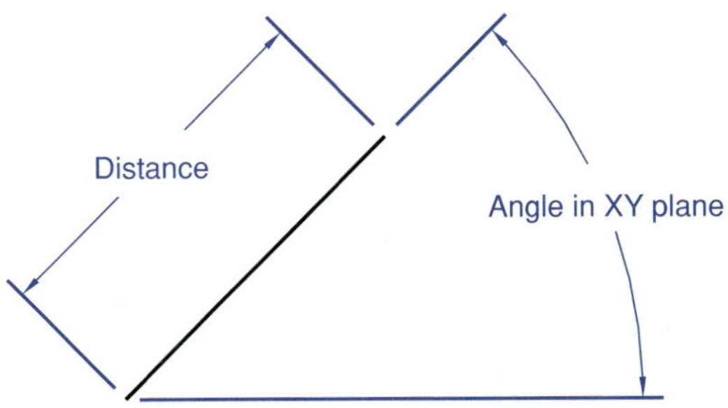

Calculating Areas

Inquiry
Area
Tools
Inquiry ▸
AREA
AA

AutoCAD LT allows you to calculate the area and perimeter of a feature by picking a series of points to define the object or by directly selecting certain objects. You can calculate a total area by adding and subtracting individual areas. To use this feature, pick the Area button from the standard toolbar, pick Inquiry and Area in the Tools pull-down menu, or type **AA** or **AREA.** The AREA command default option allows you to select a series of points enclosing the desired area. You start at one point and keep picking points around the object to the last point. To keep your area calculations accurate, always use object snap if possible. AutoCAD LT automatically closes the distance between the first point and the last point and displays the Area and Perimeter calculations. The following command calculates the area and perimeter of the object shown in Figure 6.31:

Command: **AA** or **AREA**↵
Specify first corner point or [Object/Add/Subtract]: *<pick point 1>*
Specify next corner point or press ENTER for total: *<pick point 2>*
Specify next corner point or press ENTER for total: *<pick point 3>*
Specify next corner point or press ENTER for total: *<pick point 4>*
Specify next corner point or press ENTER for total: *<pick point 5>*
Specify next corner point or press ENTER for total: *<pick point 6>*
Specify next corner point or press ENTER for total: *<pick point 7>*
Specify next corner point or press ENTER for total: ↵
Area = 2.1250, Perimeter = 6.2071
Command:

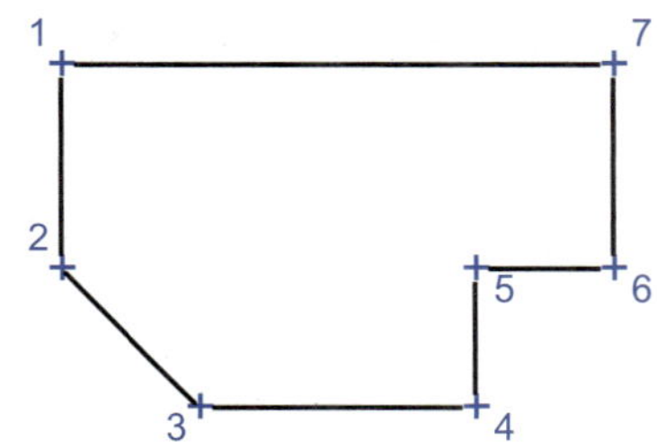

FIGURE 6.31 Defining a series of points to establish the area of an object.

If you have a closed area such as a circle, ellipse, or regular polygon, AutoCAD LT automatically calculates the area, and perimeter or circumference, using the Object option of the AREA command. You can also calculate the area and perimeter of open and closed polylines. A ***polyline*** is an AutoCAD LT object that is made up of one or more connecting segments that are treated as a single object. Chapter 8 is dedicated to explaining polylines. The circle shown in Figure 6.32 is calculated individually using the following Object option:

Command: **AA** or **AREA**↵
Specify first corner point or [Object/Add/Subtract]: **O**↵
Select objects: *<pick the circle>*
Area = 0.7854, Circumference = 3.1416
Command:

Many objects contain features that may need to be added or subtracted from the total area. The AREA command provides the Add and Subtract options to help you with this task. Look at the gasket object shown in Figure 6.33. The gasket contains five holes. We want to use the Add and Subtract options to calculate the area of the gasket without the holes. Begin with the Add option to calculate the area of the outside circle forming the entire gasket, and then Subtract the internal holes like this:

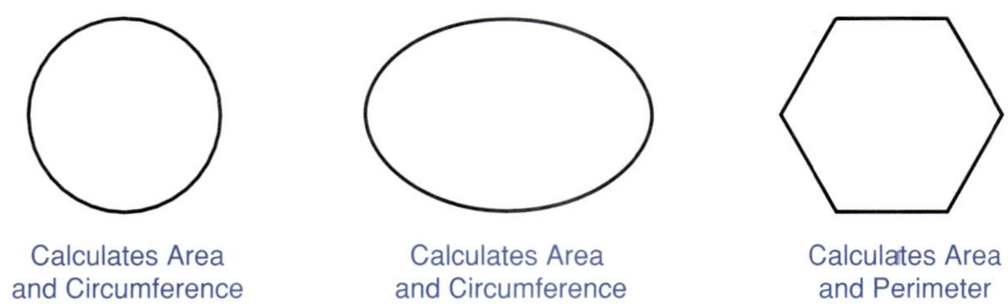

FIGURE 6.32 Calculating the area of a circle, ellipse, and hexagon.

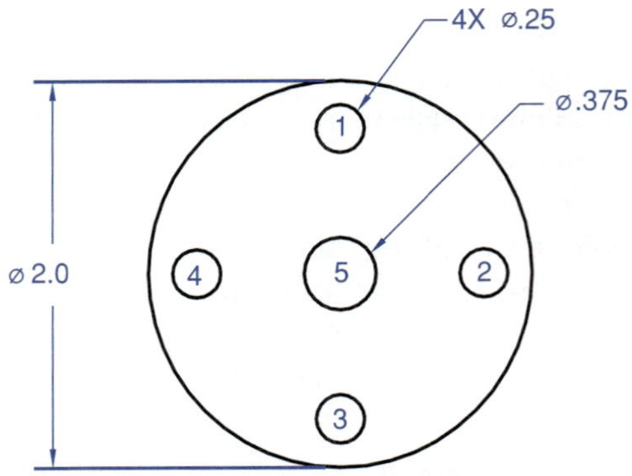

FIGURE 6.33 Using the Add and Subtract options of the AREA command to calculate the area of gasket material.

Command: **AA** or **AREA**↵
Specify first corner point or [Object/Add/Subtract]: **A**↵
Specify first corner point or [Object/Subtract]: **O**↵
(ADD mode) Select objects: *<pick the outside circle>*
Area = 3.1416, Circumference = 6.2832
Total area = 3.1416
(ADD mode) Select objects: ↵
Specify first corner point or [Object/Subtract]: **S**↵
Specify first corner point or [Object/Add]: **O**↵
(SUBTRACT mode) Select objects: *<pick circle 1>*
Area = 0.0491, Circumference = 0.7854
Total area = 3.0925
(SUBTRACT mode) Select objects: *<pick circle 2>*
Area = 0.0491, Circumference = 0.7854
Total area = 3.0434
(SUBTRACT mode) Select objects: *<pick circle 3>*
Area = 0.0491, Circumference = 0.7854
Total area = 2.9943
(SUBTRACT mode) Select objects: *<pick circle 4>*
Area = 0.0491, Circumference = 0.7854
Total area = 2.9452
(SUBTRACT mode) Select objects: *<pick circle 5>*
Area = 0.1104, Circumference = 1.1781
Total area = 2.8348
(SUBTRACT mode) Select objects: ↵
Specify first corner point or [Object/Add]: ↵
Command:

Listing Object Properties

Inquiry
List
Tools
Inquiry ▸
LIST
LI

AutoCAD LT provides information about your drawing or about objects in the drawing. The given information is displayed in the command area and in the AutoCAD LT text window. To list information about an object, pick the List button in the standard toolbar, pick Inquiry and List in the Tools pull-down menu, or type **LS** or **LIST.** The command works like this:

Command: **LS** or **LIST**↵
Select objects: *⟨pick the object or objects desired⟩*
Select objects: ↵
Command:

The information is displayed. Press the F2 key or pick the close button to remove the AutoCAD LT Text Window.

Field Notes

The AutoCAD LT Text Window displays object information one page at a time; it waits for the user before proceeding. If you have selected many objects to list, the information may require several pages to be displayed. You will see a message at the bottom of each page that says "Press ENTER to continue." Pressing the Enter key displays the next page of information. If you want to see information that has already scrolled off of the screen, you can use the scroll bars in the text window to scroll the text back down as needed.

Getting Information about Drawing Time

Tools
Inquiry ▶
TIME
TI

The TIME command provides information about key times and dates in the life of a drawing project. The TIME command is accessed by selecting Time from the Inquiry cascade on the Tools menu, or by typing TIME at the Command: prompt. The current time, the time that the current drawing was created and last updated, plus the total editing time are displayed.

```
Command: TIME↵
Current time: Saturday, July 24, 2000 at 8:20:08:890 PM
Times for this drawing:
Created: Friday, July 23, 2000 at 2:43:27:745 PM
Last updated: Saturday, January 02, 2000 at 4:21:53:665 PM
Enter option Total editing time: 1 days 05:36:41.145
Enter option Elapsed timer (on): 1 days 05:36:41.145
Enter option Next automatic save in: 0 days 00:45:48.790

Enter option [Display/ON/OFF/Reset]:
```

In addition, the TIME command provides a timer that can be used to time specific phases of a drawing for project tracking and control, or even for billing purposes. Before starting the timer, you will probably need to reset it to zero. Enter R for Reset at the prompt line. Next, use the ON option to start the timer running.

```
Enter option [Display/ON/OFF/Reset]: R↵
Timer reset to zero.
Enter option [Display/ON/OFF/Reset to zero]: ON↵
Timer on.
Enter option [Display/ON/OFF/Reset]:
```

When you have completed the task you are timing, view your results using the TIME command again. You can continue, turn the timer off, or reset it and enter the next phase of your project.

```
Current time: Saturday, July 24, 2000 at 8:35:22:884 PM
Times for this drawing:
Created: Friday, July 23, 2000 at 2:43:27:745 PM
Last updated: Saturday, January 02, 2000 at 4:21:53:665 PM
Total editing time: 1 days 05:51:55.139
Elapsed timer (on): 0 days 00:03:53.215
Next automatic save in: 0 days 00:30:34.796

Enter option [Display/ON/OFF/Reset]: OFF
Timer off.
```

Advanced Drawing Inquiries

The AREA command, discussed previously, provides the capability to determine the total area of a closed shape such as an ellipse, circle, or polygon. Even complex shapes composed of line segments can be checked for surface area. However, the AREA command does not provide an easy way to check a complex shape composed of irregular line and arc segments. For this purpose, AutoCAD LT provides a 2D region modeler. A region is a complex-shaped two-dimensional object created by any combination of lines, polylines, arcs, circles, ellipses, and splines that form a closed shape. Some of these object types are discussed in later chapters.

Region
Draw
Region
REGION
REG

To create a region, you must first draw an enclosed shape. Then, to model the region, you use the REGION command, which you can access by picking Region from the Draw pull-down menu or by typing REG or REGION at the Command: prompt. The following sequence was used to create a region from the objects shown in Figure 6.34. Notice that the two closed shapes are made into separate regions even when selected together.

Command: **REGION**↵
Select objects: *<pick first window corner>*
Specify opposite corner: *<pick second window corner>*
20 found
Select objects: ↵
2 loops extracted.
2 Regions created.
Command:

Using the AREA command on the large region in Figure 6.34 gives the following information:

Command: **AA** or **AREA**↵
Specify first corner point or [Object/Add/Subtract]: **A**↵
Specify first corner point or [Object/Subtract]: **O**↵
(ADD mode) Select objects: *<select large region>*
Area = 4.1912, Perimeter = 12.4000
Total area = 4.1912
(ADD mode) Select objects: ↵

You can use the Subtract option to get an overall surface area value:

Specify first corner point or [Object/Subtract]: **S**↵
Specify first corner point or [Object/Add]: **O**↵
(SUBTRACT mode) Select objects:
Area = 0.5900, Perimeter = 4.0712
Total area = 3.6012

Separate regions can be combined into single regions to provide even more flexibility. The methods of combining regions are referred to as *Boolean* operations. The three Boolean functions in AutoCAD LT 2000 are *union*, *subtract*, and *intersect*.

FIGURE 6.34 Complex shapes made of many different objects can be combined into a single object called a *region*.

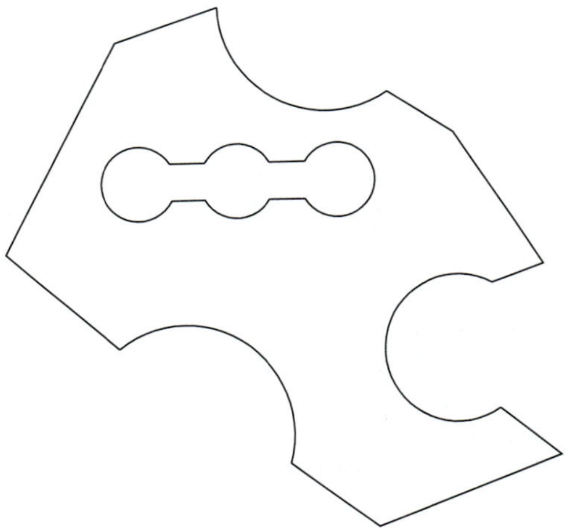

Using the UNION Command

Modify II
Union
Modify
Region ▸
UNION
UNI

The UNION command makes two or more separate regions into a single region by joining them together. You can access this command by picking Union from the Region cascade on the Modify pull-down menu, by picking the Union button on the Modify II toolbar, or by typing **UNI** or **UNION** at the Command: prompt. Figure 6.35 shows three regions being joined using UNION.

Command: **UNI** or **UNION**
Select objects: *<pick first window corner>*
Specify opposite corner: *<pick second window corner>*
3 found
Select objects: ↵
Command:

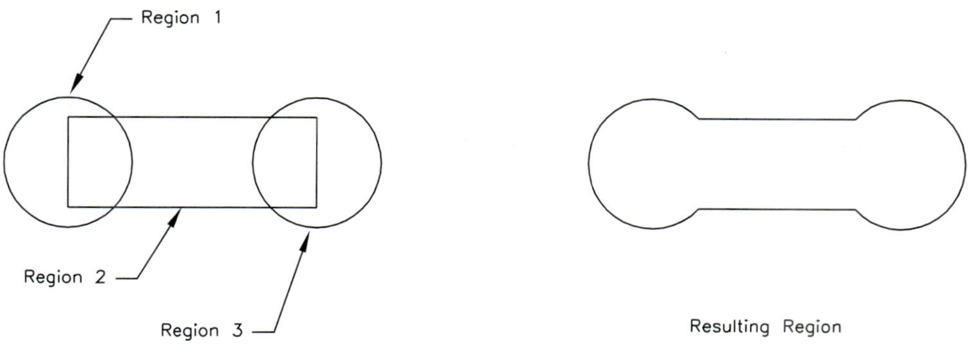

FIGURE 6.35 Separate regions can be joined using the UNION command.

Using the SUBTRACT Command

SUBTRACT creates a single region by subtracting a set of one or more regions from another set of one or more regions. You can access this command by picking Subtract from the Region cascade on the Modify pull-down menu, by picking the Subtract button on the Modify II toolbar, or by typing **SU** or **SUBTRACT** at the Command: prompt. The following sequence was used to perform the subtraction illustrated in Figure 6.36:

Modify II
Subtract
Modify
Region ▸
SUBTRACT
SU

Command: **SU** or **SUBTRACT**↵
Select regions to subtract from...
Select objects: *<select first region>*
1 found
Select objects: ↵
Select regions to subtract...
Select objects: 1 found
Select objects: 1 found
Select objects: ↵

FIGURE 6.36 The SUBTRACT command combines regions by subtraction.

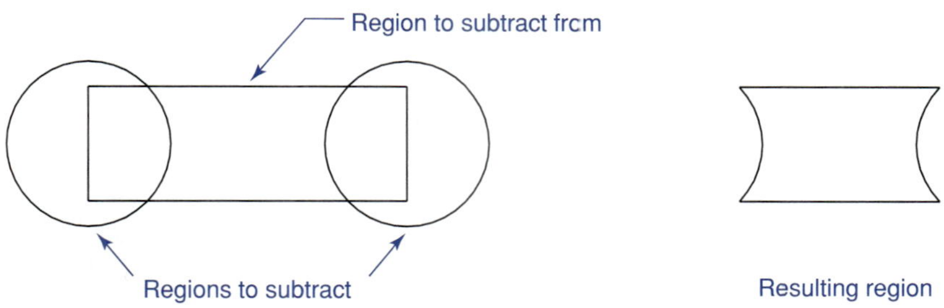

Using the INTERSECT Command

Intersect creates a single region from the shared area of two or more regions. The INTERSECT command is accessed by picking Intersect from the Region cascade on the Modify pull-down menu, picking the Intersect button from the Modify II toolbar, or by typing **IN** or **INTERSECT** at the Command: prompt. Figure 6.37 illustrates the use of the INTERSECT command.

Modify II
Intersect
Modify
Region ▸
INTERSECT
IN

Command: **INTERSECT**↵
Select objects: Other corner: 2 found
Select objects: ↵

FIGURE 6.37 The INTERSECT command creates a region from the shared area of two or more selected regions.

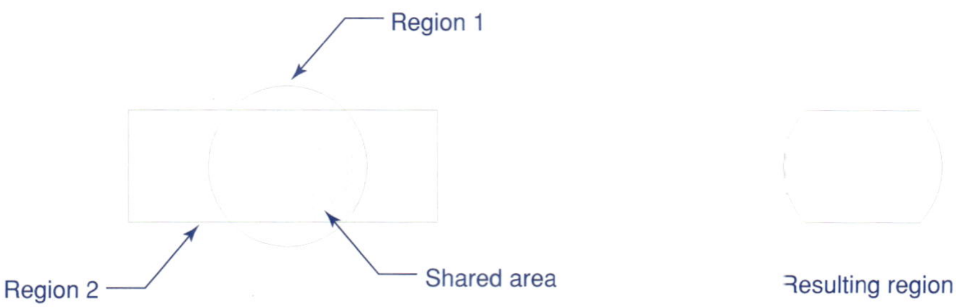

Listing Physical Properties of Regions

Modify II

Region/Mass Properties

Modify
Region ▸
MASSPROP

Regions also have physical properties that can be useful in engineering processes. A region can be used to find information such as the centroid (center of mass) and moments and products of inertia. The command used to determine these mass properties is **MASSPROP**. Here is the result of using the MASSPROP command on the large region in Figure 6.34:

```
Command: MASSPROP↵
Select objects: <select a region>
1 found
Select objects: ↵
--------------------   REGIONS   --------------------

Area:                    3.6012
Perimeter:               16.4712
Bounding box:            X: 3.8549   –   7.0300
                         Y: 2.0212   –   4.9189
Centroid:                X: 5.4199
                         Y: 3.4691
Moments of inertia:      X: 44.8351
                         Y: 108.0558
Product of inertia:      XY: 67.2972
Radii of gyration:       X: 3.5284
                         Y: 5.4777
Principal moments and X-Y directions about centroid:
                         I: 1.3132 along [0.9168 -0.3994]
                         J: 2.4477 along [0.3994 0.9168]

Write analysis to a file? [Yes/No] <N>:
```

You have the option of writing the output to a text file that you can reference later or print if needed. If you accept the default answer of no, you are returned to the Command: prompt.

Field Notes

- Regions that do not touch can be joined by the UNION command. The result is a single region object composed of any number of separate areas. Similarly, the SUBTRACT command can result in a single region composed of areas that do not touch one another.
- The INTERSECT command cannot be used on objects that do not touch, because there is no common area, or intersection, from which to make a resulting region.

Exercise 6.10 **Estimated time required: 15 min.**

1. Open AutoCAD LT if it is not already open. Use the setup option of your choice.
2. Set limits at 8.5,11.
3. Write the answer for each of the following requests on a separate sheet of paper.
4. Draw an object similar to the one shown in Figure 6.31. Do not draw the numbers. Calculate the area using the point method.
5. Draw a circle, ellipse, and a hexagon similar to the objects shown in Figure 6.30. Do not place the text. Calculate the area of each object.
6. Draw the gasket shown in Figure 6.33 using the dimensions given. Do not draw dimensions or numbers. The exact hole locations are not important, but the diameters are important. Make your drawing similar to the example in every other manner.
7. Use the ID command to get the coordinates at the center of each 0.25 hole.
8. Use the DIST command to determine the distance from the center of one 0.25 hole to the center of the opposite 0.25 hole.
9. Calculate the area of the gasket material.
10. Use the LIST command to get information about the outside circle.
11. Use the TIME command to see what is displayed.
12. Draw two shapes similar to those in Figure 6.34. Use the REGION command to make each into a region. Subtract the small region from the large one. Use the MASSPROP command to list the mass properties of the resulting region. Write the output to a file named EX6.10.TXT.
13. Save as EX6.10, and close the drawing.

☑ LEARNING CHECKPOINT

- ☐ Name at least three ways to access the Point Style dialog box.
- ☐ Describe two ways of setting point size.
- ☐ Explain the difference between the DIVIDE and the MEASURE commands.
- ☐ Discuss the purpose of the From option.
- ☐ Discuss the use of point filters.
- ☐ Explain how direct distance entry works.
- ☐ Define tracking.
- ☐ Name the command that is used to determine the coordinates of a point.
- ☐ How do you easily calculate the distance between two points?
- ☐ Identify two ways to calculate the area of objects.
- ☐ Name the command that keeps a running total of area calculations as you add and subtract individual areas of an object.
- ☐ What command allows you to get information about your drawing or about objects in the drawing?
- ☐ How do you use AutoCAD LT to get the current time?
- ☐ What is the best way to find the area of a complex closed shape made of different objects?
- ☐ Describe the four commands associated with regions.

Viewing, Selecting, and Using Precision Drawing Tools

- Drawing with Precision
- Measuring and Dividing Objects

An Introduction to Drawing Construction Lines

Construction lines have been used throughout the history of drafting. As the name implies, these lines are used as aids for the purpose of constructing parts of a drawing. Construction lines are generally removed when the drawing is finished. AutoCAD LT provides both construction lines (xlines) and rays. Xlines are infinite-length lines, and rays are semi-infinite in length. The difference is that construction lines extend in two directions from the origin and rays extend only in one direction from the origin. Some practical uses for construction lines might include the following:

- Making geometric constructions, such as bisecting angles or finding the center of a triangle.
- Projecting features from one view to the next in an orthographic projection for multiview drawings in mechanical drafting.
- Projecting between elevations in an architectural drawing.
- Establishing the projection of a bearing wall or partition in an architectural or structural layout.
- Creating temporary intersections for the use of object snaps.

Construction lines should be placed on a layer and in a color that clearly represents drawing development. A company or school practice might be to draw red construction lines on a CONSTRUCTION layer. When the drawing is completed, the CONSTRUCTION layer may be frozen or turned off, because the construction lines are no longer needed. Construction lines are usually not needed on the final plot. However, in some cases, they may be desirable on a check plot to help the checker determine how certain drawing features were established.

Drawing Construction Lines with the XLINE Command

XLINE
XL

AutoCAD LT gives you a lot of flexibility when drawing construction lines using the XLINE command. You can draw them between two points, from one point horizontally or vertically, at a designated angle, as the bisector of an angle, or offset from a given object. When construction lines are drawn, they extend into infinity, yet they do not alter the total drawing area or affect zooming operations. Construction lines are drawn by picking Construction Line from the Draw toolbar, by choosing Construction Line in the Draw pull-down menu, or by typing **XL** or **XLINE** at the Command: prompt.

Drawing Construction Lines between Two Points

The default construction line asks for two points. Look at the structural drawing example in Figure 6.38, which uses construction lines to establish the location of a gusset from the corners of an existing gusset using the following command sequence:

Command: **XL** or **XLINE**↵
Specify a point or [Hor/Ver/Ang/Bisect/Offset]: *<pick point 1>*
Specify through point: *<pick point 2>*
Specify through point: ↵
Command:

After drawing the first construction line, you keep getting the Specify through point: prompt, which allows you to draw additional construction lines from the first point. Press Enter to get back to the Command: prompt.

Drawing Horizontal and Vertical Construction Lines

Use the Horizontal option to draw a horizontal construction line from one point or the Vertical option to draw a vertical construction line from one point. Figures 6.39 and 6.40 show the horizontal and vertical projection to find the top and right side views from the front view of a mechanical drawing. This is the command sequence for drawing the horizontal construction lines:

Command: **XL** or **XLINE**↵
Specify a point or [Hor/Ver/Ang/Bisect/Offset]: **H**↵
Specify through point: *<pick point 1>*
Specify through point: *<pick point 2>*
Specify through point: *<pick point 3>*
Specify through point: ↵
Command:

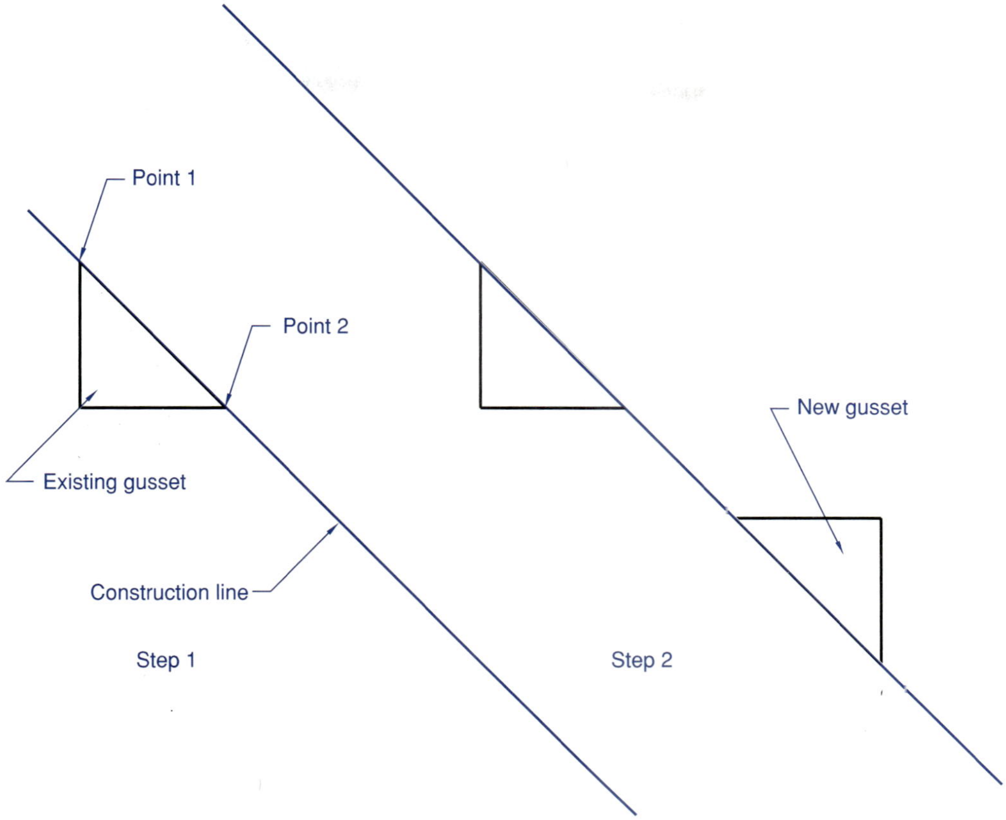

FIGURE 6.38 Using the XLINE command to draw a construction line between two points.

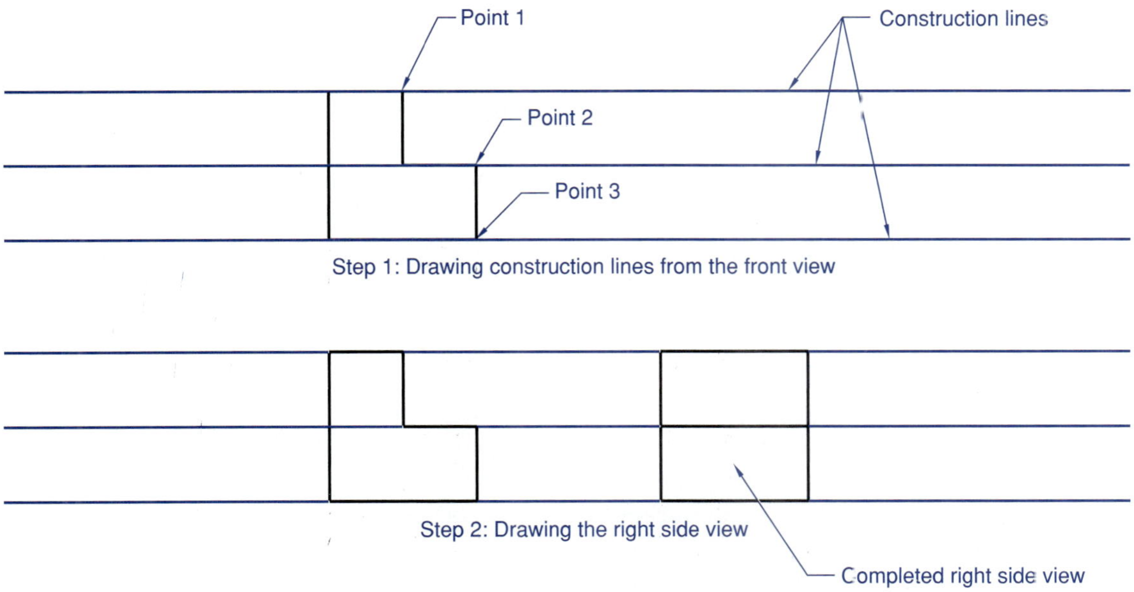

FIGURE 6.39 Using the XLINE command and the Horizontal option to draw construction lines.

FIGURE 6.40 Using the XLINE command and the Vertical option to draw construction lines.

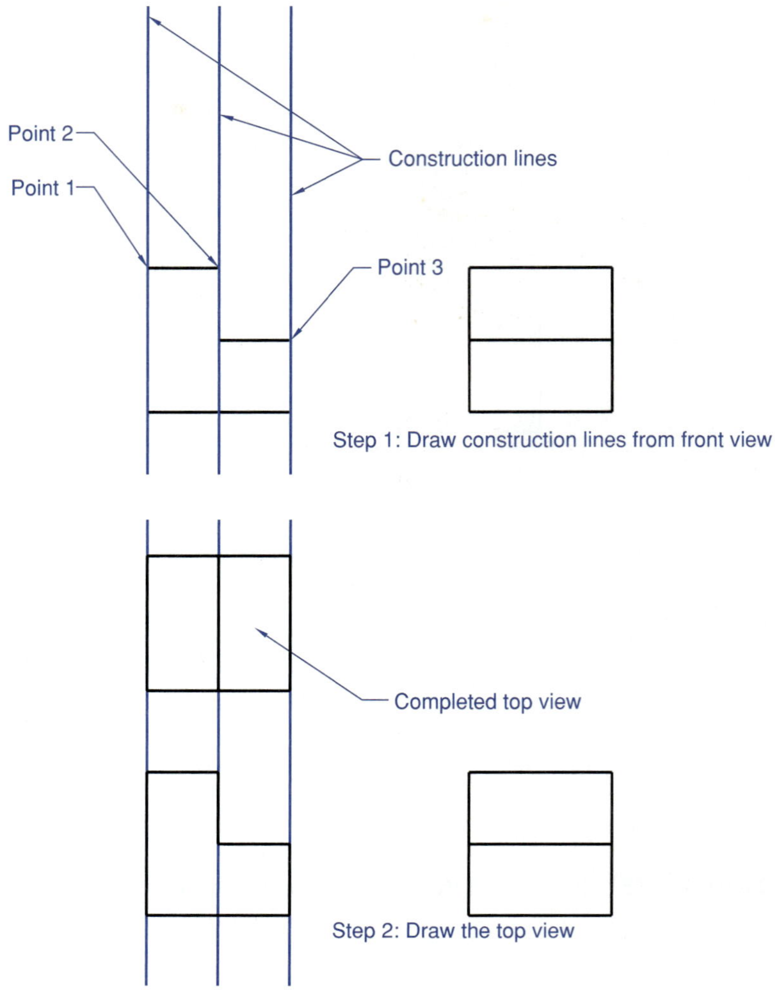

This is the command sequence for drawing the vertical construction lines:

Command: **XL** or **XLINE**↵
Specify a point or [Hor/Ver/Ang/Bisect/Offset]: **V**↵
Specify through point: *<pick point 1>*
Specify through point: *<pick point 2>*
Specify through point: *<pick point 3>*
Specify through point: ↵
Command:

Exercise 6.11

Estimated time required: 15 min.

1. Open AutoCAD LT if it is not already open. Use the setup option of your choice.
2. Set limits at 8.5,11.
3. Create a layer named CONSTRUCTION with a continuous linetype and red color for drawing the construction lines only.
4. Draw an existing gusset similar to the example in step 1 of Figure 6.38.
5. Draw the new gusset similar to the example in step 2 of Figure 6.38.
6. Draw a front view similar to the example in step 1 of Figure 6.39.
7. Use construction lines to draw a right side view (Figure 6.39) and a top view (Figure 6.40).
8. Freeze the CONSTRUCTION layer.
9. Save as EX6.11, and close the drawing.

Drawing Construction Lines at an Angle

Drawing construction lines at an angle is valuable for a number of practical applications, for example, constructing the slope of a roof or establishing an auxiliary view. The default of the Angle option asks you to specify an angle based on the current angle zero setting. This might be used to draw a roof slope at 22.5° as shown in this command sequence and demonstrated in Figure 6.41:

Command: **XL** or **XLINE**↵
Specify a point or [Hor/Ver/Ang/Bisect/Offset]: **A**↵
Enter angle of xline (0) or [Reference]: **22.5**↵
Specify through point: *<pick point 1>*
Specify through point: ↵
Command:

FIGURE 6.41 Using the XLINE command and the Angle option from horizontal to draw a construction line.

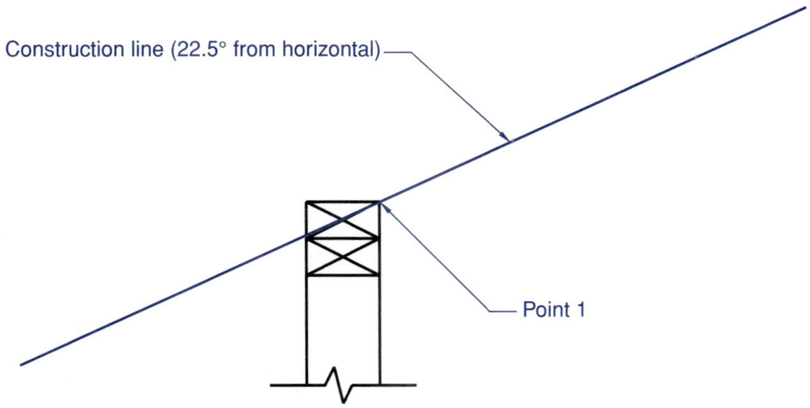

Field Notes

When you use the Angle option, the initial default angle is horizontal regardless of the angle zero setting. If the zero angle direction is not set to east, the default angle is adjusted appropriately.

The Angle option also has a Reference suboption, which may be handy when creating an auxiliary view for a mechanical drawing project. To use this option, select a reference line and designate an angle for the construction line to be drawn from the reference line. The following command sequence is shown in Figure 6.42:

Command: **XL** or **XLINE**↵
Specify a point or [Hor/Ver/Ang/Bisect/Offset]: **A**↵
Enter angle of xline (0) or [Reference]: **R**↵
Select a line object: *<pick the edge view of the slope surface in step 1>*
Enter angle of xline <0>: **90**↵
Specify through point: *<pick point 1>*
Specify through point: *<pick point 2>*
Specify through point: *<pick point 3>*
Specify through point: ↵
Command:

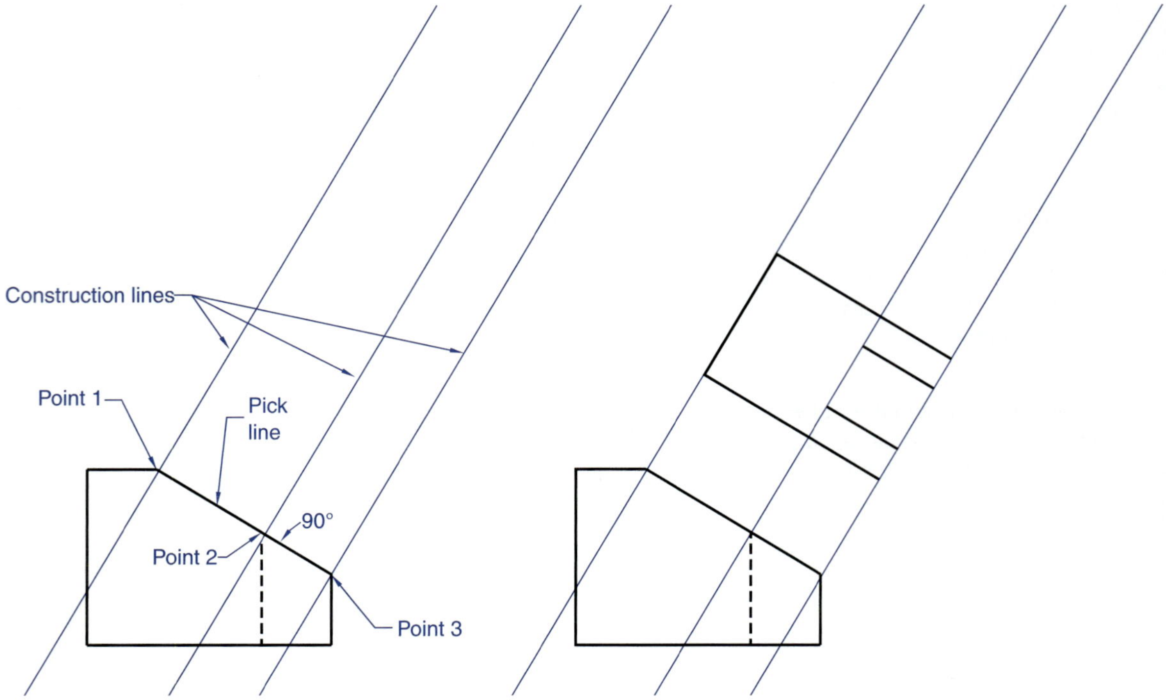

FIGURE 6.42 Using the XLINE command and the Angle option to draw construction lines from a reference line.

Exercise 6.12

Estimated time required: 5 min.

1. Open AutoCAD LT if it is not already open. Use the setup option of your choice. A border and title block are not required.
2. Set limits at 8.5,11.
3. Open EX6.11 and erase the objects to begin this drawing. If you did not do Exercise 6.11, create a layer named CONSTRUCTION with a continuous linetype and red color for drawing the construction lines only.
4. Use construction lines to help you when drawing a front view and auxiliary view that are approximately the same as those of Figure 6.42.
5. Freeze the CONSTRUCTION layer.
6. Save as EX6.12, and close the drawing.

Drawing the Bisector of an Angle

One of the XLINE command options allows you to draw the bisector of an existing angle. The bisector of an angle splits the angle in two equal parts. Look at Figure 6.43 as you follow this command sequence:

Command: **XL** or **XLINE**↵
Specify a point or [Hor/Ver/Ang/Bisect/Offset]: **O**↵
Specify angle vertex point: *<pick the vertex>*
Specify angle start point: *<pick a point on the first side>*
Specify angle end point: *<pick a point on the other side>*
Specify angle end point: ↵
Command:

Drawing a Construction Line Offset from Another Line

Many situations happen in which you need to draw a construction line to establish a feature parallel to an existing object. You can do this with the construction line Offset option. To do this, you determine the offset distance or pick a point, select the line, and specify the side of the line for the offset construction to be drawn. Figure 6.44 shows the construction of an outside rafter line parallel to the inside line that was drawn previously. This is the command sequence:

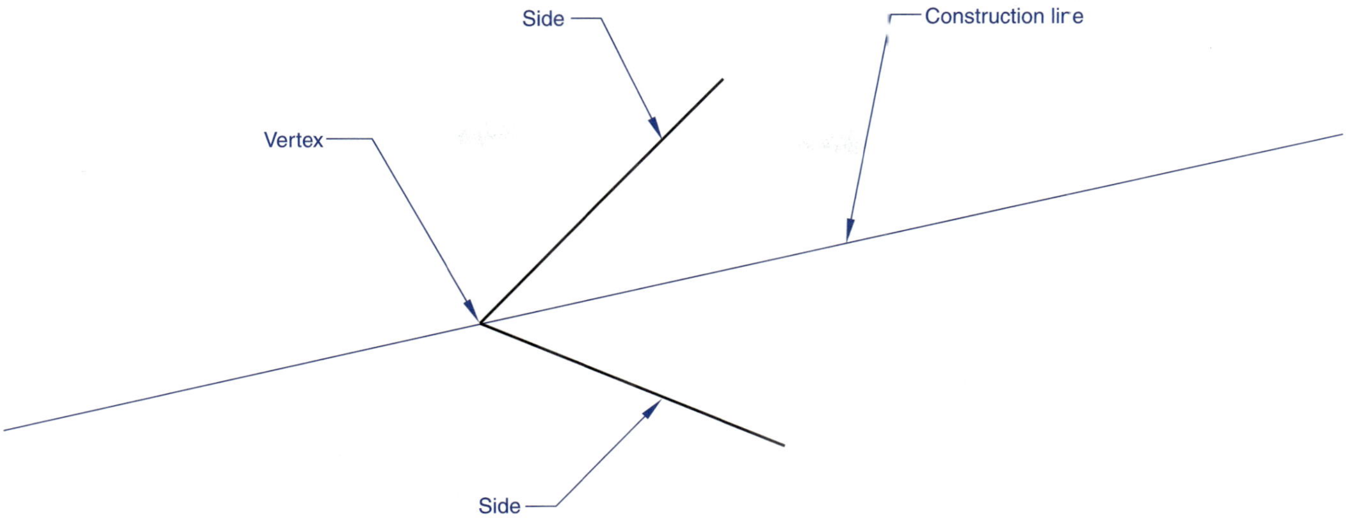

FIGURE 6.43 Using the XLINE command and the Bisect option to draw a construction line.

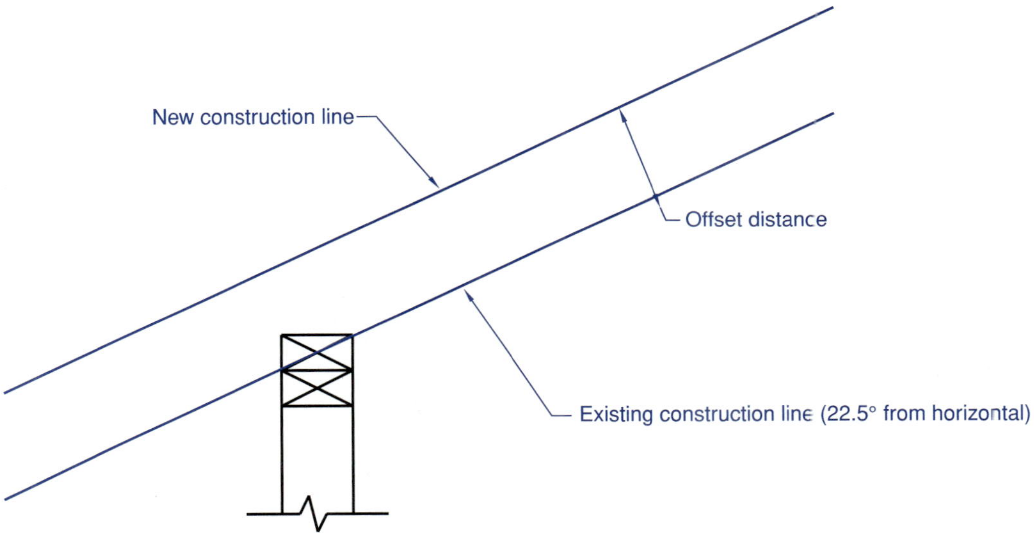

FIGURE 6.44 Using the XLINE command and the Offset option to draw a construction line parallel to an existing line.

Command: **XL** or **XLINE**↵
Specify a point or [Hor/Ver/Ang/Bisect/Offset]: **O**↵
Specify offset distance or [Through] <1.0000>: **.75**↵

"Through" refers to a point you pick through which the construction line goes. You can pick a point for the construction line to go through, or you can specify a distance from the selected object for the construction line to go through. The command continues:

Select a line object: *<pick a linear object>*
Specify side to offset: *<move the cursor to the side where you want the construction line and pick>*
Select a line object: ↵
Command:

Drawing Rays

Rays are also construction lines, but they are different from construction lines drawn with the XLINE command. XLINE construction lines extend in two directions from the point you pick, whereas rays extend in only one direction. The advantage of rays is that they go only in one direction and can provide less confusion on the drawing. Rays are drawn using the RAY command. The disadvantage of rays is that the RAY command only has one option, whereas the XLINE command has many options. Rays are drawn by typing **RAY**.

The command asks you for the first point and then the point through which you want the ray to pass. This is much like the two-point method of the XLINE command except the ray goes in only one direction from the first point. The RAY command works like this:

Command: **RAY**↵
Specify start point: ⟨*pick the first point to start the ray*⟩
Specify through point: ⟨*pick the second point for the ray to pass through*⟩
Specify through point: ⟨*more rays can be drawn from the first point or press Enter*⟩
Specify through point: ↵
Command:

Field Notes

Although xlines and rays can be used simply as guides and then frozen or deleted when you are finished, they can also be much more versatile. Editing commands discussed in Chapter 7 will show you how to break and trim existing drawing objects to suit your needs. When an xline is trimmed, it now has one endpoint—and is therefore transformed into a ray object. When you trim the infinite end of a ray, it has two endpoints—meaning it becomes a line object. Using these features allows your construction lines to be directly transformed into final geometry, reducing your drawing and editing time.

Exercise 6.13 — Estimated time required: 10 min.

1. Open AutoCAD LT if it is not already open. Use the setup option of your choice. A border and title block are not required.
2. Set limits at 8.5,11.
3. Open EX6.11 and erase the objects to begin this drawing. If you did not do Exercise 6.11, create a layer named CONSTRUCTION with a continuous linetype and red color for drawing the construction lines only.
4. Draw a double top plate and partial stud detail with a construction line 22.5° from horizontal similar to that shown in Figure 6.41. The scale and size are not important.
5. Draw the outside edge of the rafter using the Offset construction line option. Your drawing should look similar to Figure 6.44.
6. Draw an angle with a Bisector construction line similar to the example in Figure 6.43.
7. Save as EX6.13, and close the drawing.

Adjusting Snap Angle and Origin

You have been using Grid and Snap to make drawing easy and accurate. The Grid and Snap format you use places the grid dots in a horizontal and vertical pattern on the screen. The screen cursor also moves horizontally and vertically to match the grid. This works well for drawing horizontally and vertically oriented objects. When an object has features that are at an angle, it would be helpful if the Grid could be rotated to match the angle. AutoCAD LT has thought about this and allows you to adjust the Snap to any desired angle. When you do this, the Grid angle and the screen cursor also follow the same angle. The Snap angle is changed in the Snap and Grid tab of the Drafting Settings dialog box. Pick Drafting Settings... in the Tools pull-down menu to access the Drafting Settings dialog box. Picking the Settings... option on the status bar SNAP or GRID button shortcut menus takes you directly to the Snap and Grid tab of the Drafting Settings dialog box. The Snap area settings are enabled only when the Grid snap option in the Snap type & style area is active. To change the Snap Angle to 30°, for example, type **30** in the Angle: text box as shown in Figure 6.45 and pick OK. To return to the standard snap orientation, open the Drafting Settings dialog box again and change the angle back to zero.

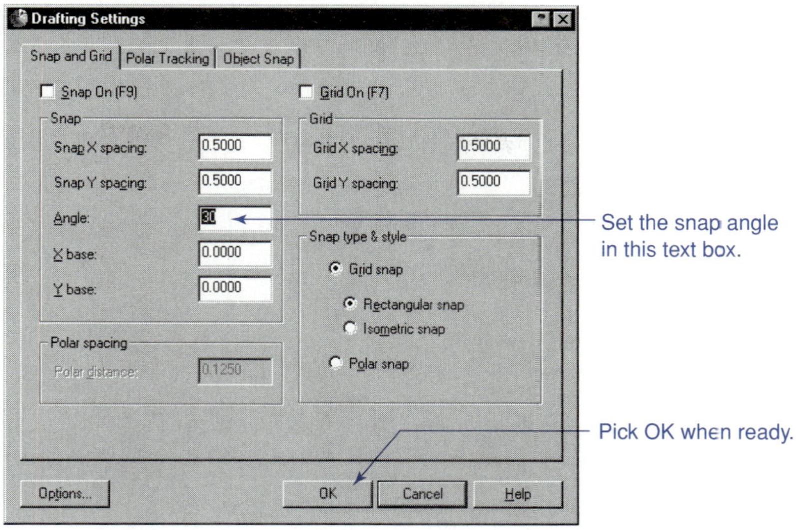

FIGURE 6.45 Changing the snap Angle to 30° in the Snap and Grid tab of the Drafting Settings dialog box.

The Snap origin, also known as the base point, is at the center point of the snap angle rotation by default. Look at Figure 6.45 and notice that the default X Base and Y Base settings are 0.0000. If you want to move the X and Y base points, enter the desired values in the text boxes.

In the discussion with Figure 6.42 you learned how to draw auxiliary views with constructions lines using the Angle option set at 90°. This method works well, although another technique is to rotate the snap and grid to match the angle of the slanted surface. This allows you to draw lines at right angles directly from the slanted surface. If you know the angle of the slanted surface, then enter that value in the Angle text box in the Drafting Settings dialog box shown in Figure 6.45. If you do not know the angle, use the LIST command and select the line of the slanted surface. For example, if the LIST command is used on the slanted surface in Figure 6.42, AutoCAD LT reports back Angle in XY Plane = 330. Use this value in the Angle text box and pick the OK button. Figure 6.46 shows the resulting Snap and Grid aligned with the slanted surface. Now, you can use a variety of the methods that you learned in this chapter to help you draw the auxiliary view.

1. Turn Ortho on.
2. Draw projection lines from the ends of the slanted surface. Place these lines on a Construction layer so they can be frozen later.
3. Use the DIST command to determine the exact length of the slanted line in the front view and the length from the lower end of the slanted line to the intersection of the hidden line.
4. Use the LINE command and direct distance entry to complete the perimeter of the auxiliary view, beginning at the end of one of the projection lines.
5. Use the Close option to complete the last line back to the start.

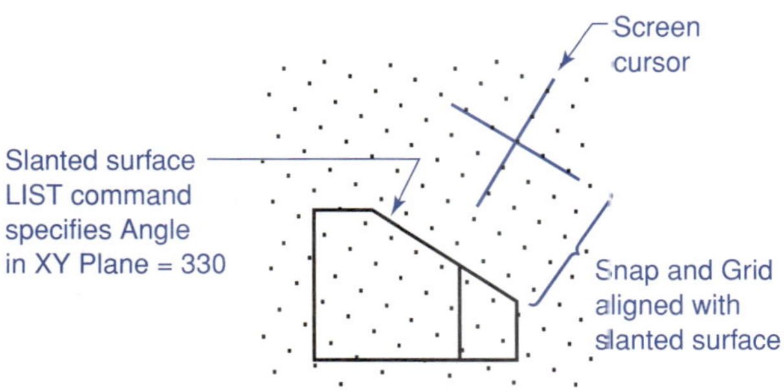

FIGURE 6.46 The Snap and Grid are aligned with the slanted surface to assist in drawing an auxiliary view.

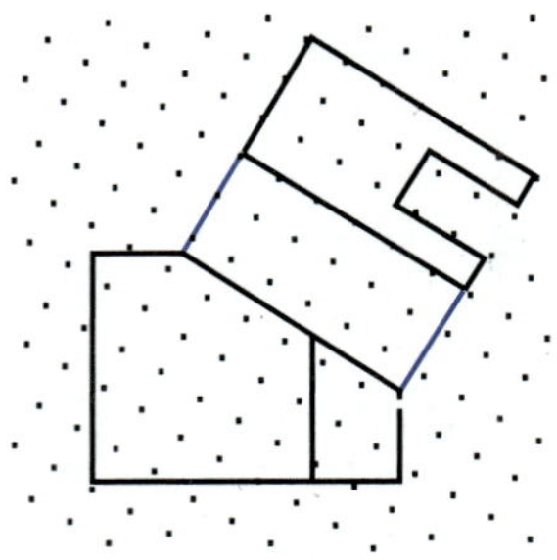

FIGURE 6.47 Projecting from the slanted surface to assist in creating an auxiliary view. Follow the steps outlined in the text.

Exercise 6.14 Estimated time required: 10 min.

1. Open EX6.12.
2. Erase the auxiliary view.
3. Set the snap and grid aligned with the slanted surface.
4. Use the steps described with Figure 6.47 to redraw the auxiliary view.
5. Save as EX6.14, and close the drawing.

LEARNING CHECKPOINT

- ☐ Why should construction lines be placed on a special layer?
- ☐ Describe the difference between making construction lines with the XLINE command compared with the RAY command.
- ☐ Use short statements to describe the function of the Horizontal, Vertical, Angle, Bisect, and Offset XLINE options.
- ☐ Discuss an advantage of changing the snap angle from the zero-degree default.

MULTIPLE CHOICE

Circle the choice or enter your response on an answer sheet by selecting the option that most closely completes or answers the given statements.

1. The object snap cursor menu is displayed when you perform this action:
   - a. Hold down the Ctrl key and press the left mouse button.
   - b. Hold down the Shift key and press the right mouse button.
   - c. Hold down the Shift key and press the left mouse button.
   - d. Hold down the Enter key and press the right mouse button.
2. The setting for this feature controls how close to an object the cursor must be when using AutoSnap.
   - a. cursor box
   - b. marker
   - c. pick box
   - d. aperture
3. This term refers to an object snap or group of object snap options that is set to run continuously:
   - a. continuous object snap
   - b. DDOSNAP
   - c. running object snap
   - d. OSNAP
4. This command is used to divide an object into a series of segmented lengths:
   - a. DIVIDE
   - b. MEASURE
5. This AutoCAD LT feature allows you to extract the X coordinate of one point and the Y coordinate of another point to come up with a new point coordinate.
   - a. extract
   - b. separate
   - c. remove
   - d. filter
6. This is a convenient way to enter point coordinate locations by pointing the cursor in the desired direction and specifying a distance:
   - a. point filters
   - b. From
   - c. tracking
   - d. direct distance entry
7. This command may be used to find the circumference of a circle:
   - a. DIST
   - b. LIST
   - c. AREA
   - d. OBJECT
8. This command allows you to get information about your drawing or about objects on the drawing:
   - a. DIST
   - b. LIST
   - c. AREA
   - d. OBJECT
9. Construction lines that extend an infinite distance in two directions from the pick point are drawn with this command:
   - a. XLINE
   - b. RAY
10. Picking this is a very convenient way to turn a running object snap on and off:
    - a. The OSNAP button on the status line
    - b. Running Object Snap toolbar button
    - c. Running Object Snap on the cursor menu
    - d. none of the above

MATCHING

Match each term to the correct description by writing the appropriate number in each box at the left.

- ☐ Area
- ☐ AutoSnap
- ☐ DDPTYPE
- ☐ Direct
- ☐ Dist
- ☐ Divide
- ☐ From
- ☐ Id
- ☐ List
- ☐ Marker
- ☐ Measure
- ☐ Midpoint
- ☐ Object
- ☐ Object snaps
- ☐ Node
- ☐ None
- ☐ Perpendicular
- ☐ Pixels
- ☐ PolarSnaps
- ☐ Ray
- ☐ Running
- ☐ Tangent
- ☐ Tracking
- ☐ Xline

1. These allow you to quickly pick exact locations on an object without having to be located directly at the desired location.
2. When you use an object snap, AutoCAD LT displays this at the object snap location when you move the cursor to the object.
3. You can easily snap to the middle of an object with this Object Snap option.
4. This term means at right angles.
5. Use this object snap for a line to touch a circle or arc at one point without intersecting.
6. Snap to a point with this object snap.
7. Disable object snap with this option.
8. This option allows you to specify a point that is at a specified location from a given point.
9. This object snap term means that an Object Snap option or group of options can be set to run continuously.
10. The aperture size is measured in these units.
11. Access the Point Style dialog box using this command.
12. This command is used to place evenly spaced points or blocks along the length, circumference, or perimeter of an object.
13. This command is used to place points or blocks a specified distance along the length, circumference, or perimeter of an object.
14. This distance entry feature allows you to point the cursor in the direction you want the next point and specify a distance from that point.
15. This allows you to determine a new point location from a series of directions and distances.
16. This command can be used to determine the coordinates of a point.
17. This command can be used to determine the distance and angle between two points.
18. This command can be used to calculate the perimeter of an object.
19. AutoCAD LT automatically calculates the circumference of a circle using this option.
20. Use this command to get information about an object.
21. This command draws construction lines that run in two directions from the pick point.
22. This command draws construction lines that run in one direction from the pick point.
23. Works with object snaps to display a marker when the cursor is near a snap point.
24. Allow you to drag angle and distance increments without entering values at the keyboard.

WORD SCRAMBLE

Unscramble the six scrambled words below, one letter to each square, to form six AutoCAD LT–related words:

RATEPUER

AGTENTN

ONSPA

EUSAMER

KGATNCIR

TNOCTUNORCIS

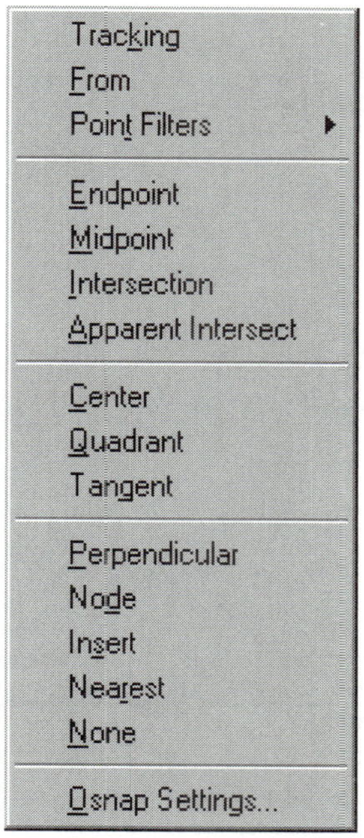

Unscramble the circled letters above to form the special answer, as suggested by the illustration.

PROJECTS

Set up the following drawing projects with layers that relate to the type of drawing as outlined and discussed in Chapter 5.

6.1 Piping Schematic
Draw the schemetic shown below. Save as P6.1.

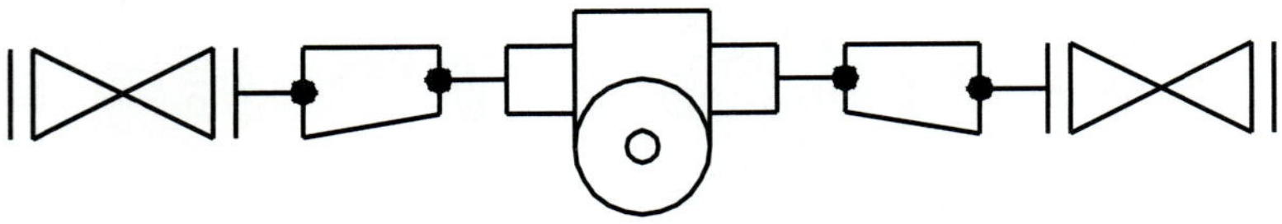

6.2 Doorbell Circuit
Draw the schematic shown below without text. Save as P6.2.

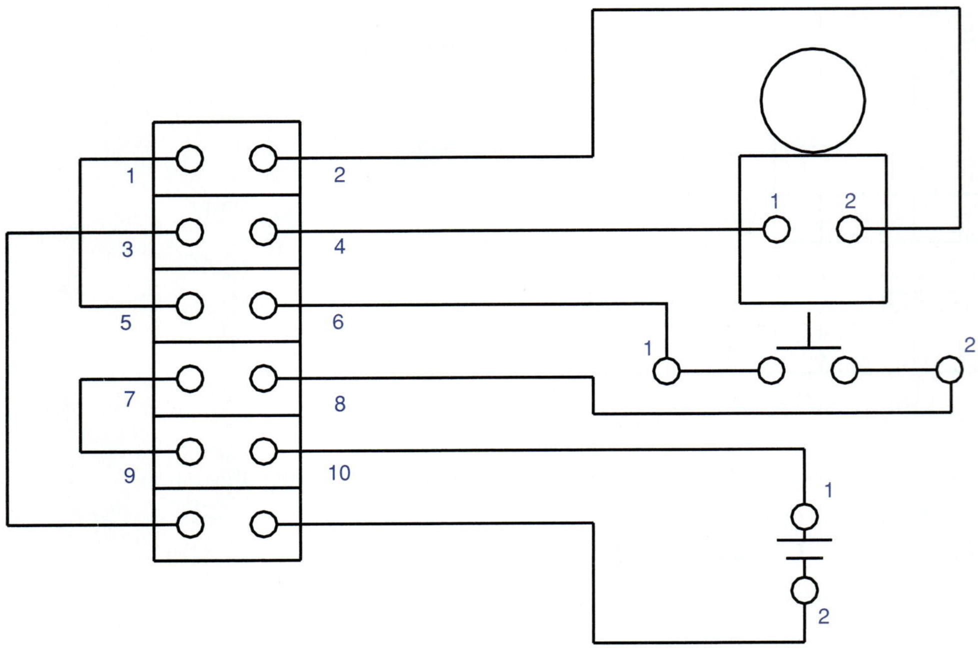

6.3 Eave Detail

Draw the detail shown below. Do not draw notes or dimensions. Save as P6.3.

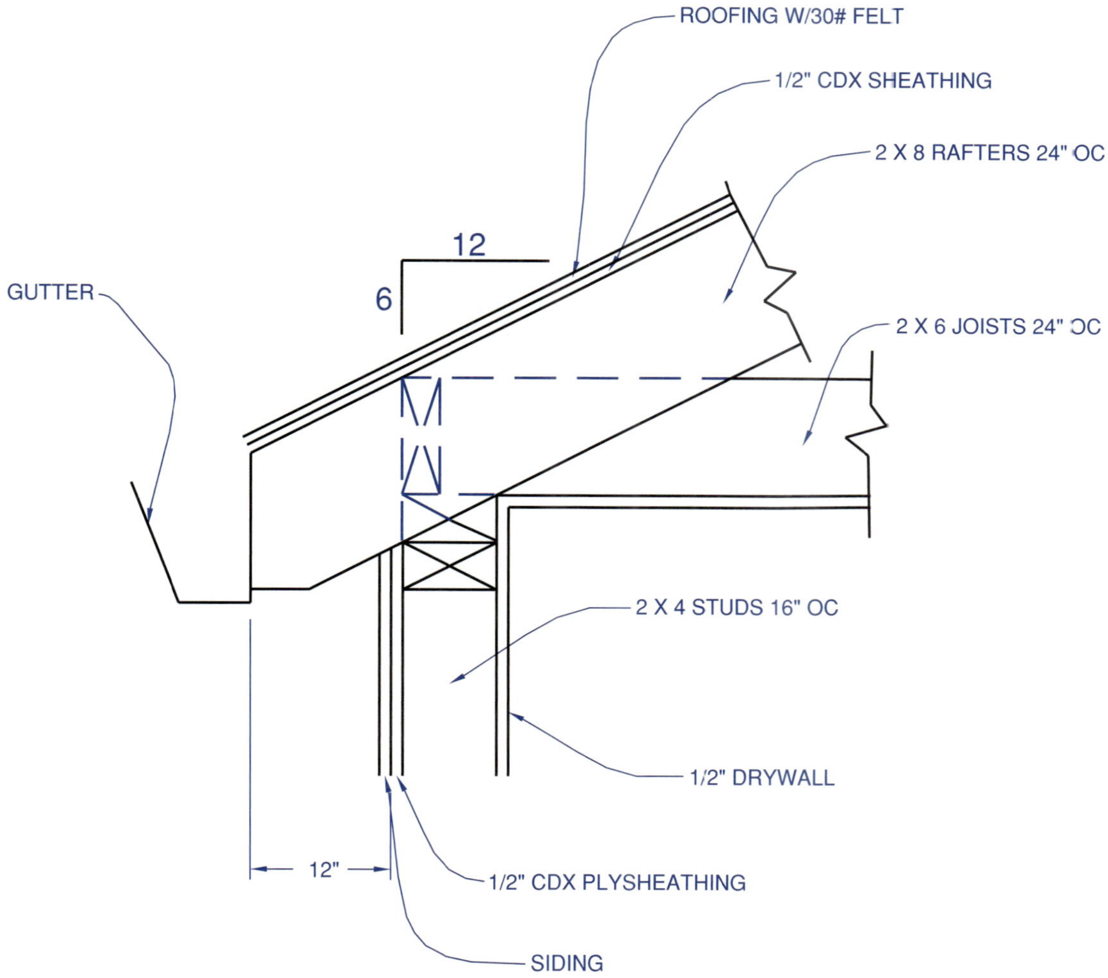

6.4 Rocker Arm

Draw the object shown below without notes or dimensions. Use construction lines to draw the initial layout and then draw arcs as needed. Save as P6.4.

INCH

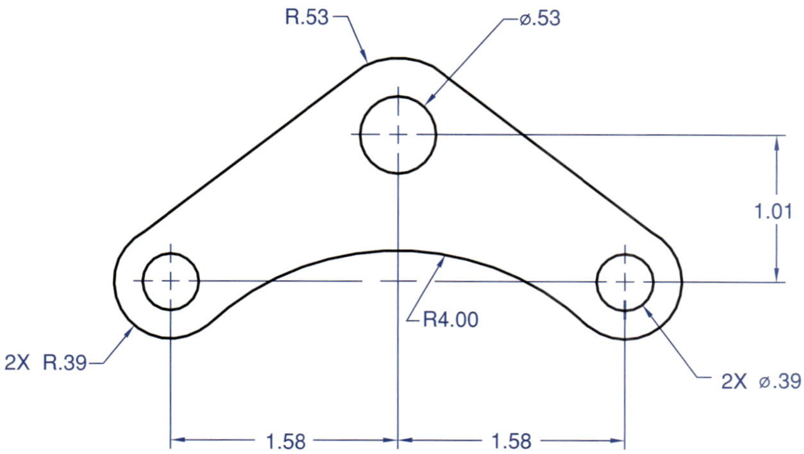

METRIC

6.5 Rocker Arm

Draw the object shown below without notes or dimensions. Use construction lines to draw the initial layout and then draw arcs as needed. Save as P6.5.

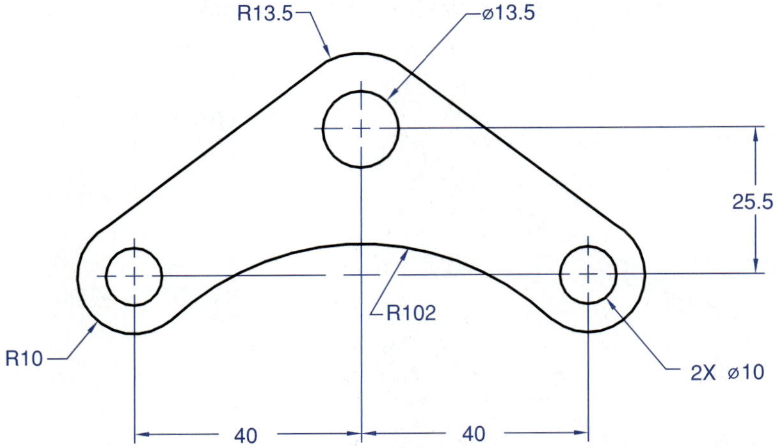

6.6 Boss Plate

Draw the object shown below without notes or dimensions. The phantom lines are shown for construction purposes and may be frozen on a construction layer after use. Save as P6.6.

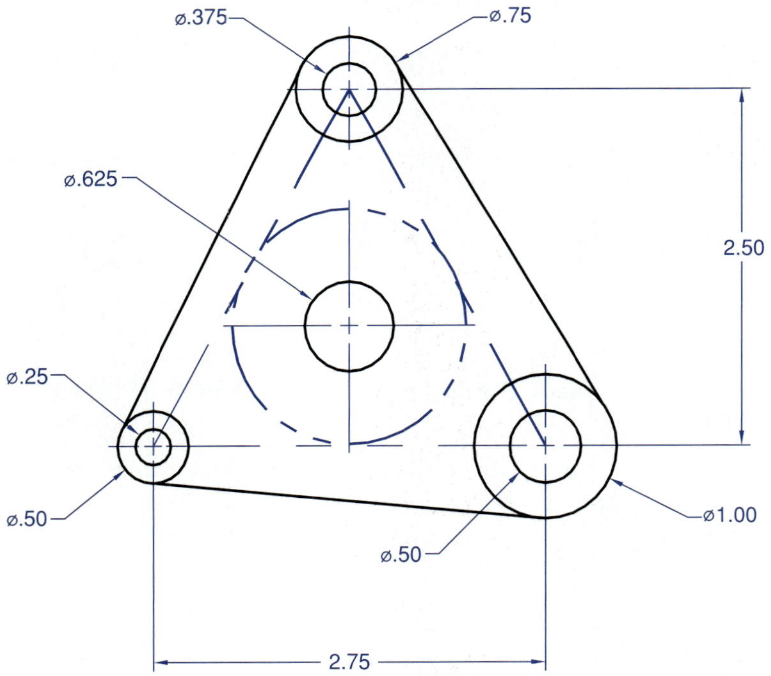

6.7 Ridge Gusset

Use PolarSnaps to assist you in drawing the following object. Do not draw dimensions. Save the drawing as P6.7.

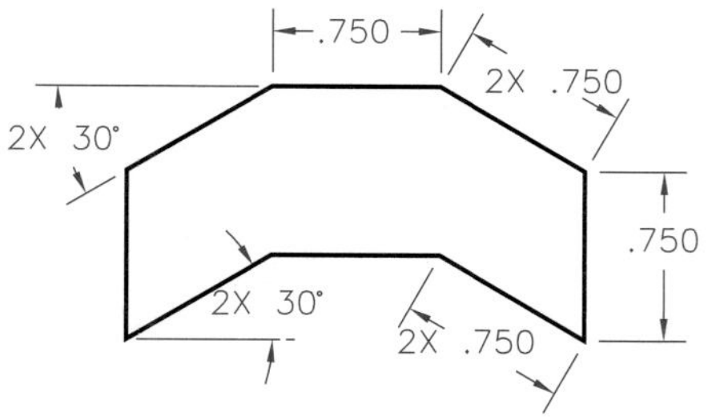

6.8 Angled Brace

Use PolarSnaps and direct distance entry to assist you in drawing the following object. Do not draw dimensions. Save the drawing as P6.8.

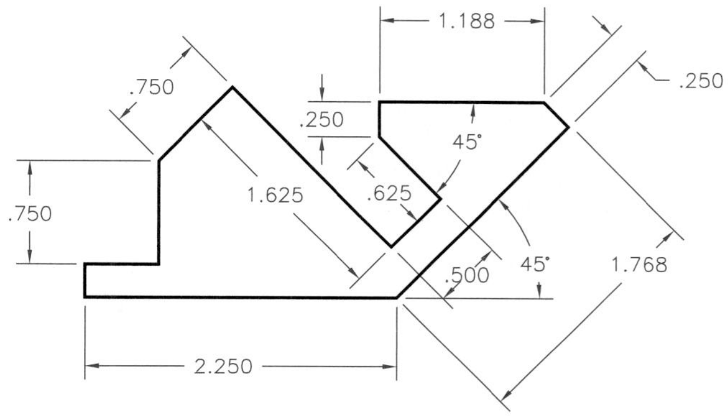

6.9 Step Block

Draw three views of the object shown below without notes or dimensions. Use construction lines as needed to establish the right side view. Save as P6.9.

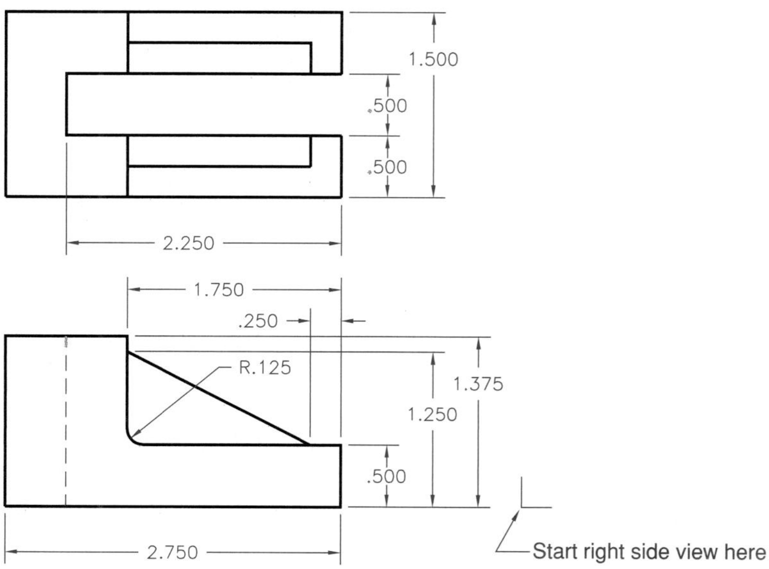

6.10 Slide Stop

Draw at least three views of the object shown below without notes or dimensions. Use construction lines as needed to align the views. Save as P6.10.

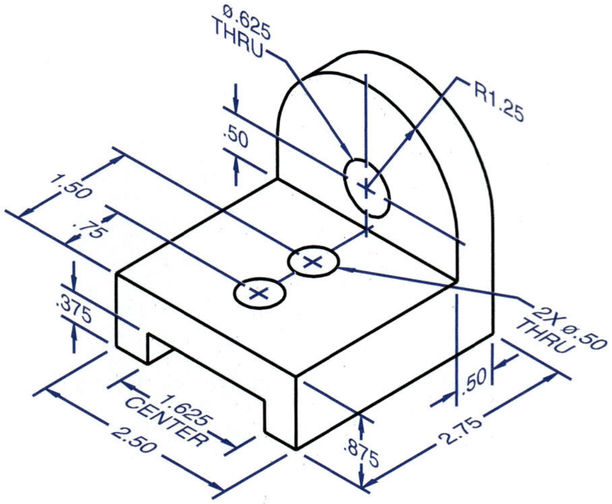

6.11 Angle Bracket

Draw at least three views (one view is an auxiliary view) of the object shown below without notes or dimensions. Use construction lines as needed to align the views. Save as P6.11.

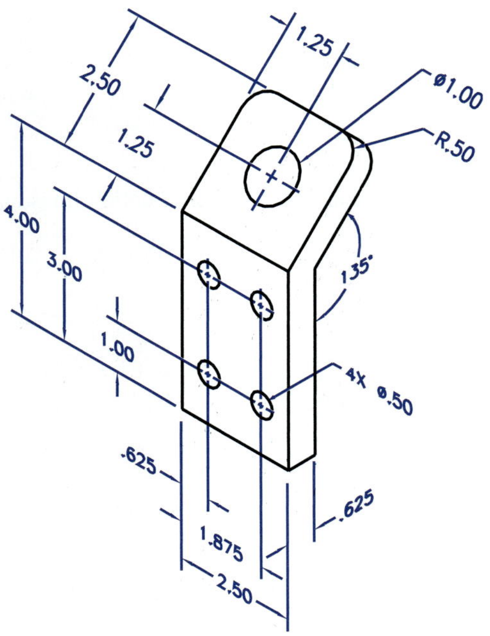

6.12 Spring

Draw at least three views (two views are needed as auxiliary views) of the object shown below without notes or dimensions. Use construction lines as needed to align the views. Save as P6.12.

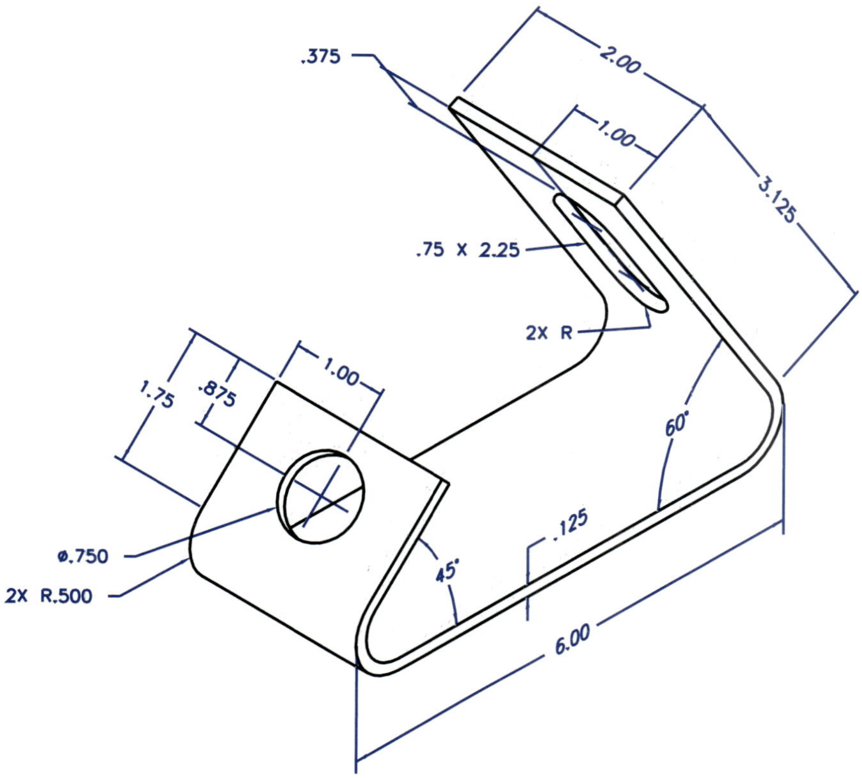

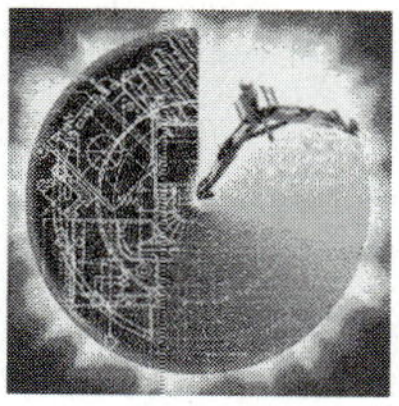

CHAPTER 7

Editing Your Drawing

LEARNING GOALS

- Use the Window Polygon, Crossing Polygon, and Fence selection options.
- Use selection cycling.
- Use the SELECT command and use the selected objects with the Previous option.
- Customize your selection options.
- Copy objects using the COPY, OFFSET, MIRROR, and ARRAY commands.
- Change objects using the MOVE, ROTATE, SCALE, LENGTHEN, and STRETCH commands.
- Select objects before entering commands.
- Use the grip STRETCH, MOVE, ROTATE, SCALE, and MIRROR commands.
- Break a portion out of objects.
- Trim and extend objects.
- Draw fillets and chamfers.
- Use the PROPERTIES command to quickly change individual objects.
- Use the Multiple Document Interface to copy data between drawings.

In Chapter 2 you learned to do some basic editing with the ERASE command. You also used OOPS, Undo, and REDO. You were introduced to selecting objects by picking and to use the Window and Crossing boxes. You discovered that commands can be entered before selecting the objects, or you can select the objects to activate grips before the command is entered. This chapter covers additional object selection options and the wide variety of AutoCAD LT editing commands.

Editing commands are far more powerful than drawing commands. Duplicating existing geometry and quickly editing it to meet your needs is far more productive than drawing each object from scratch. For example, consider how much faster it is to offset an existing line and then trim or extend it to meet your needs, rather than using a line command to create a completely new line. Also, the ability to copy and create arrays of objects represents an incredible time savings. Additionally, selecting objects before entering commands provides instant command line access to the more commonly used editing commands using GRIPS.

Object Selection Methods

When editing, you can select one object or a group of objects. The objects you select are called a selection set. AutoCAD LT defines a ***selection set*** as one or more objects that are specified for processing as a unit. The Window and Crossing selection options allow you to place a box around or through objects to be selected. This discussion explains the use of Window and Crossing Polygons and Fences to provide additional flexibility when selecting objects. You can select objects that are under other objects by cycling through the objects until you find the one you want. You can customize selection methods. You will also use grips for the ease of being able to issue several editing commands quickly after the objects have been selected.

In this section, the object selection methods that are discussed need to be entered at a *Select objects:* prompt. This prompt is issued whenever an editing command is entered. To work through the discussion topics in this section, use the ERASE command to activate the Select objects: prompt. To return the erased objects to the screen and proceed with each new topic, you can enter the OOPS command.

The Window and Crossing Polygon Selection Options

The Select Window and Crossing Polygon options work similar to the Window and Crossing boxes. Remember from Chapter 2 that a Window box must totally surround the objects to be selected, and a Crossing box may surround or cross through the objects to be selected. The Window and Crossing Polygon selection methods give you additional flexibility.

The Window Polygon selection option allows you to place a polygon of your own design around (totally enclosing) an object or group of objects that you want to select. The polygon may have three or more sides of any desired length and angle but may not touch or cross itself. The Window Polygon can be used by typing **WP** at the Select objects: prompt. Follow this Window Polygon sequence as you look at Figure 7.1:

Select objects: **WP**↵
First polygon point: 〈*pick the first point*〉
Specify endpoint of line or [Undo]: 〈*pick point 2*〉
Specify endpoint of line or [Undo]: 〈*pick point 3*〉
Specify endpoint of line or [Undo]: 〈*pick point 4*〉
Specify endpoint of line or [Undo]: 〈*pick point 5*〉
Specify endpoint of line or [Undo]: 〈*pick point 6*〉
Specify endpoint of line or [Undo]: ↵
8 found
Select objects: ↵

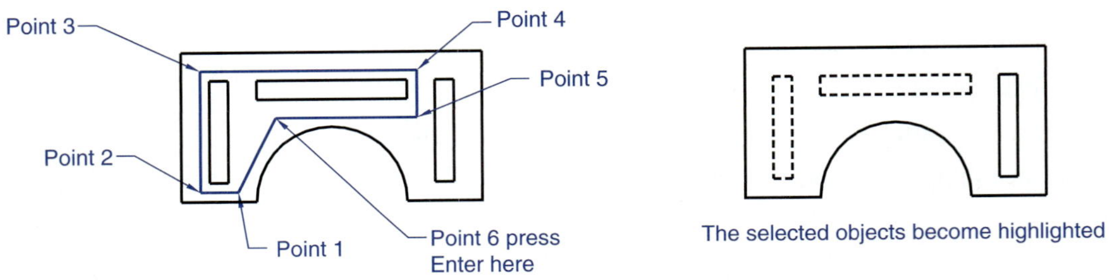

FIGURE 7.1 Use the Window Polygon to select objects that are enclosed within the polygon.

AutoCAD LT provides a solid cursor line to form the Window Polygon as you pick points. Press Enter after picking the last point. AutoCAD LT tells you how many objects were found and returns the Select objects: prompt. Press Enter again when you are satisfied with the polygon that you created. The selected objects become highlighted. When creating the sides of the Window Polygon, if you do not like where you placed one of the polygon sides, use the Undo option at any time:

Specify endpoint of line or [Undo]: 〈*pick point 3*〉
Specify endpoint of line or [Undo]: **U**↵
Specify endpoint of line or [Undo]: 〈*pick a new point 3*〉
Specify endpoint of line or [Undo]:

This removes the last polygon line and allows you to pick a new point.

The Crossing Polygon works just like the Window Polygon, except the cursor line is dashed and everything inside or crossing the polygon lines is selected. The Crossing Polygon can be used by typing **CP** at the Select objects: prompt. Follow this sequence as you look at Figure 7.2:

Select Objects: **CP**↵
First polygon point: 〈*pick the first point*〉
Specify endpoint of line or [Undo]: 〈*pick point 2*〉
Specify endpoint of line or [Undo]: 〈*pick point 3*〉
Specify endpoint of line or [Undo]: 〈*pick point 4*〉

Specify endpoint of line or [Undo]: ⟨*pick point 5*⟩
Specify endpoint of line or [Undo]: ⟨*pick point 6*⟩
Specify endpoint of line or [Undo]: ↵
10 found
Select objects: ↵

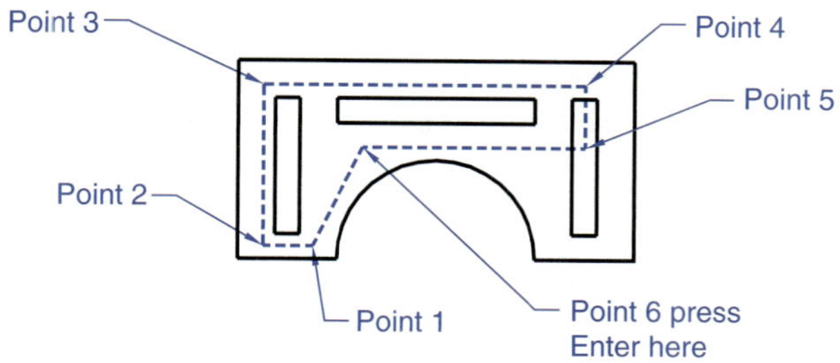

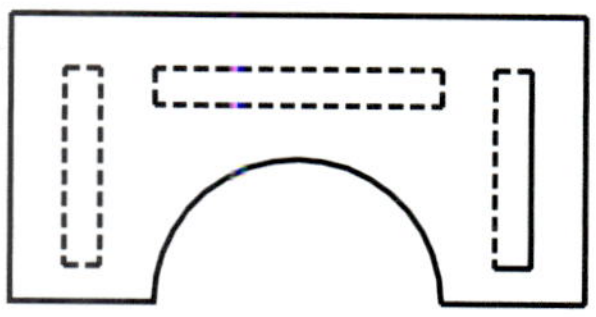

The selected objects become highlighted

FIGURE 7.2 Use the Crossing Polygon to select objects that are enclosed within and cross the polygon.

Exercise 7.1 **Estimated time required: 5 min.**

1. Begin a new drawing.
2. Draw an object similar to the original object shown in Figure 7.1.
3. Use the ERASE command and the Window Polygon option to select the same objects that are selected in Figure 7.1.
4. Enter OOPS to undo the previous command.
5. Use the ERASE command and the Crossing Polygon option to select the same objects that are selected in Figure 7.2.
6. Enter OOPS to undo the previous command.
7. Save as EX7.1, and close the drawing.

The Fence Selection Option

In some situations, it might be easier to place a selection line through objects to be selected rather than using a box or polygon. The Fence selection option draws a line that selects any object that it crosses. The Fence can be used by typing **F** at the Select objects: prompt. A Fence selection is shown in Figure 7.3 using this sequence:

Select Objects: **F**↵
First fence point: ⟨*pick the first point*⟩
Specify endpoint of line or [Undo]: ⟨*pick point 2*⟩
Specify endpoint of line or [Undo]: ⟨*pick point 3*⟩
Specify endpoint of line or [Undo]: ↵
3 found
Select objects: ↵

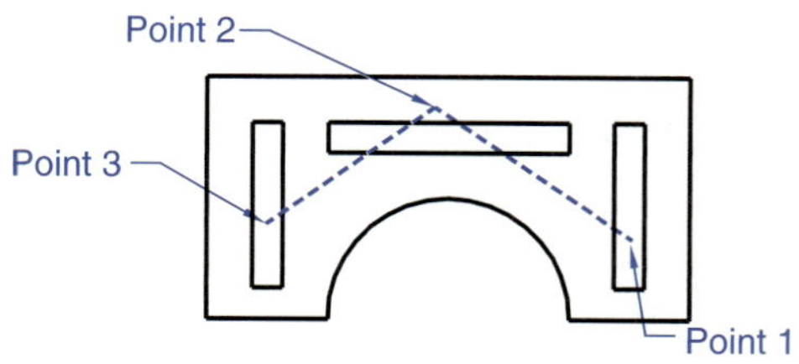

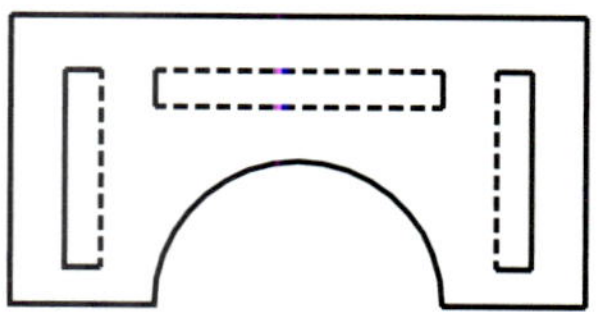

The selected objects become highlighted

FIGURE 7.3 Use the Fence option to select objects that cross the fence line.

Field Notes

- If you press the right mouse button at the Command: prompt, a shortcut menu with editing and display options is provided. The first option in this menu always repeats the previously used command or menu selection.
- The Add and Remove options were discussed in Chapter 2. Remember, if you select objects and then decide that you do not want one or more of them in the selection set, use the Remove option. Use the Add option to place more objects in the selection set after using Remove. A more convenient option is to press the Shift key while selecting objects to remove the specified objects from the selection set.

Exercise 7.2 — Estimated time required: 5 min.

1. Open EX7.1.
2. Use the ERASE command and the Fence option to select the same objects that are selected in Figure 7.3.
3. Use OOPS to undo the previous command.
4. Save as EX7.2, and close the drawing.

Selecting Objects that Are Very Close Together or Stacked

A drawing often contains objects that are very close together or on top of other objects. When objects are on top of other objects, they are referred to as being ***stacked.*** This may make it difficult to pick only the desired object. If the pick box touches multiple objects, AutoCAD LT selects the one that was created most recently, which may or may not be the one you want—which can be a frustrating experience. You can set the Pickbox variable to a very small value or use the ZOOM command when selecting objects that are very close together, but this does not solve the problem when objects are stacked. It is easy to overcome the problem of picking stacked objects by using what AutoCAD LT calls ***cycling.*** It is difficult to demonstrate cycling through stacked objects, because stacked objects appear to be one object, but Figure 7.4 makes the attempt. In this figure, the intersecting lines are stacked at the point of intersection. While it would be easy to simply move the pick box to the desired line and pick, this would not show how cycling works. If you pick at the intersection, as shown in Figure 7.4A, you may not select the line you want. To use cycling, press and hold the Ctrl key while you pick, and then release the Ctrl key. One of the objects becomes highlighted as shown in Figure 7.4B. Press the pick button again and the next eligible object becomes highlighted as shown in Figure 7.4C. Pick again to highlight another object as in Figure 7.4D. Press Enter to select the currently highlighted object. AutoCAD LT tells you when cycling is on and off like this:

Select objects: ⟨*press the Ctrl key and pick*⟩ <*Cycle on*>
⟨*the first object becomes highlighted*⟩
⟨*pick again; the second object becomes highlighted*⟩
⟨*pick again; the third object becomes highlighted*⟩
⟨*press Enter to select the highlighted object*⟩
<Cycle off> 1 found
Select objects: ↵

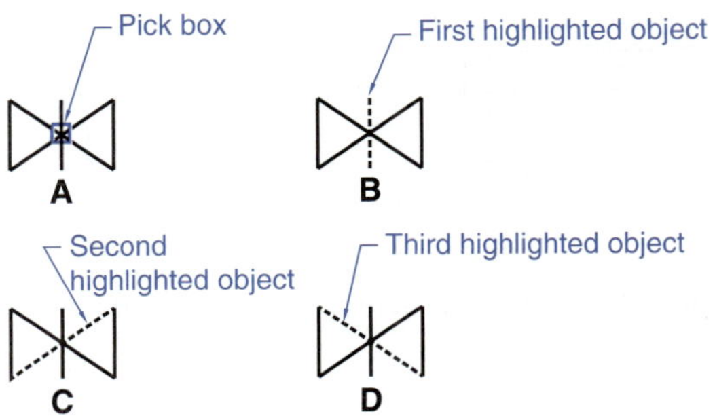

FIGURE 7.4 Cycling through objects for selection by picking while pressing the Ctrl key.

Using the SELECT Command

The SELECT command allows you to create a selection set with any of the typical selection options and then later use it in an editing application. The objects that are selected using the SELECT command are placed in an AutoCAD LT selection set called *previous.* You can access them when needed at a Select objects: prompt by typing **P** for previous. Type **SELECT** at the Command: prompt to use this command:

Command: **SELECT**↵
Select objects: ⟨*use any selection method*⟩
number found
Select objects: ↵
Command:

Select All can be picked from the Edit pull-down menu or by pressing Ctrl+A. This option selects all the objects in the drawing. The Select All option highlights all objects when you are at the Select objects: prompt or uses GRIP selection if you are at the Command: prompt. Optionally, you can type **ALL** at a Select objects: prompt.

Field Notes

Sometimes, the selection of a specific group of objects requires a complex and difficult selection process. Using the Previous option helps when you are performing two or more sequential editing operations on a selection set. If, however, you need to edit a different group of objects before continuing with the current selection set, you would not be able to continue to use the Previous selection option.

A simple feature of AutoCAD LT that can help to keep your Previous selection option available is found in the fact that any objects returned to the screen using the OOPS command immediately become the Previous selection set. So, this means that you can erase your complex selection set, edit the other group of objects, and then use the OOPS command to return the objects to the screen as your Previous selection set, as long as you *do not* use ERASE!

This can be unreliable if you erase another selection set, or if OOPS is used to return the objects and then the Undo option is used to undo the OOPS command. Either of these situations require you to undo all the way back to where the objects were erased.

Exercise 7.3

Estimated time required: 5 min.

1. Begin a new drawing.
2. Draw an object similar to the one shown in Figure 7.4A. Do not draw the pick box or the note.
3. Enter the ERASE command and use cycling to cycle through the objects as shown in Figure 7.4B, C, and D.
4. Press Enter when you have seen each object being cycled.
5. Press the Esc key at the Select objects: prompt.
6. Use the SELECT command to select the drawing and return to the Command: prompt.
7. Enter the ERASE command and type **P** at the Select objects: prompt. All of the objects that were selected with the previous SELECT command should be erased.
8. Use OOPS to undo the previous command.
9. Save as EX7.3, and close the drawing.

Customizing Selection Options

AutoCAD LT allows you to control how object selections are made. A group of system variables is available that can be used individually at the keyboard to control object selection methods. These are also accessed in the Selection tab of the Options dialog box by picking Options... in the Tools pull-down menu or by typing **OP** or **OPTIONS** at the Command: line prompt. The Selection tab with the default settings is shown in Fig-

FIGURE 7.5 The Object Selection Settings dialog box.

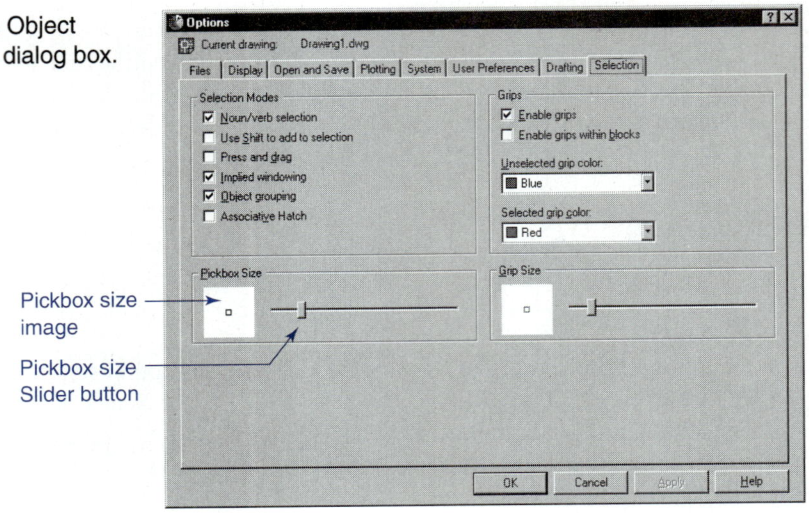

Tools
Options
OPTIONS
OP

ure 7.5. The discussions and examples in this text use the default settings. The Selection Modes are described as follows:

Noun/verb selection A check in this box allows you to select objects before entering a command. This option is turned on by default and allows you to pick objects first and then start an editing command using the preselected objects. If this option is off, then starting an editing command ignores any grip-selected objects and displays a Select objects: prompt.

Use Shift to add to selection Check this box if you want the convenience of pressing the Shift key to add objects to a selection set. Off by default this requires that the Shift key be held down in order to add items to the current selection. This means that if you pick an object at the Select objects: prompt, it is highlighted as normal. However, picking another object at the subsequent Select objects: prompt selects this object and removes any other currently selected items from the selection set. To add additional items to the selection set, you must hold the Shift key down while selecting.

Press and drag This option is off by default. When it is on, it changes the way that windows are drawn during object selections. Normally, you press and release the pick button at each desired corner. This option requires that you press and hold the pick button at the first corner, move the cursor to the other corner, and then release the pick button.

Implied windowing When set at its default setting of on, this option automatically places you in a Window/Crossing selection mode if a pick is made at a location where the pick box does not touch an object. If this option is off, the same pick simply reports no objects found.

Object grouping On by default, this means that all members of a group are selected when you select a single member. Object Groups are discussed in Chapter 12.

Associative Hatch This option is off by default. Turning it on means that selecting an associative hatch pattern also selects the boundary objects. Hatching is discussed in Chapter 10.

Field Notes

- Press and Drag or Implied Windowing must be on to automatically use a window or crossing box. If both are on, Implied Windowing does not work.
- Even with the Use Shift to Add option active, if you hold the Shift key and select objects that have already been selected, they are removed from the selection set as they would be normally.

With regard to Implied Windowing, if you are placed in the Window/Crossing selection mode, the setting of Press and Drag still affects the method by which the window must be drawn.

The Pickbox Size compartment allows you to move the slider button to get a desired pick box size. When moving the slider, the image to the right shows the current pick box setting at actual size. A smaller selection box can be used to pick within areas where objects are crowded close together, but if the pick box is too small, then general picking procedures are more difficult because more accuracy is required—this makes it easier to miss your target object. Larger pick boxes make general picking faster and easier, but cannot be used effectively in crowded areas. Finding a pick box size that is not too big or too small can help you be more productive. The pick box can also be sized by specifying the desired number of pixels using the PICKBOX command. Change from the default pixels of 3 like this:

Command: **PICKBOX** ↵
Enter new value for PICKBOX <3>: 6 ↵
Command:

Field Notes

- The DDSELECT command can be used transparently (**'SE** or **'DDSELECT**) to change your selection modes.
- Also, using **'PICKBOX** at any Select objects: prompt is a fast and convenient way to adjust the size of the pick box while working on your drawing.

Pick the User Preferences tab to access the Object Sort Methods settings; the default settings are shown in Figure 7.6. The object sort methods can be specified if the order in which the objects were created is important in your drawing or application. These options should not be set unless necessary, because object sorting requires additional processing time. In large or complex drawings, object sorting can result in decreased system performance. The following list explains the object sorting for each of the available options:

Object Selection When on, objects selected with a window style selection option are added to the selection set in the reverse order in which they were created. When off, the selection order is less predictable, but typically objects are added to the selection set in the order of proximity to the 0,0 coordinate point.

Object snap When on, if two qualifying objects are found in the aperture and the specified object snap point is the exact same distance from the picked point, the point referencing the most recently created object is used. When off, the results may not always be predictable.

Redraws When on, the REDRAW command draws objects in the reverse order in which they were created. When off, the objects are drawn according to their order in the display list managed by the display driver. With the speed of the display on most systems, you may not be able to see any difference between these settings.

Regens When on, the REGEN command regenerates objects in the drawing in the reverse order in which they were created. When off, the order is less predictable—typically starting in the lower left corner of the current view and working up and to the right.

Plotting When on, the PLOT command processes objects in the order in which they are found in the drawing database, from last to first. This has little value unless you are using a pen-style plotter and want to observe the plot as it is being generated.

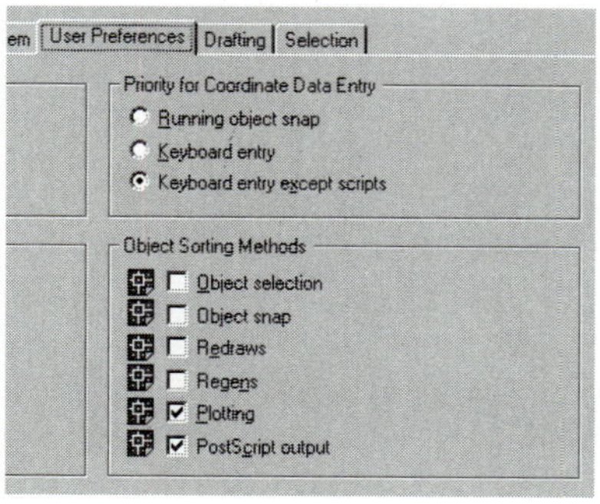

FIGURE 7.6 The Object Sort Methods settings are on the User Preferences tab of the Options dialog box.

PostScript Output When on, objects written to encapsulated PostScript files created using PSOUT are added to the file in the reverse order in which the objects were created. The PSOUT command is discussed in Chapter 15.

Selecting with Grips

Tools
Options
DDGRIPS
GR

AutoCAD LT places grips on an object when you select objects before entering a command. A brief introduction to grips was provided in Chapter 2. ***Grips*** are small squares that appear on objects you select while no command is active. The grips can be picked and dragged with the cursor to perform editing operations. Grips are displayed differently depending on the type of object. For example, grips are placed at the quadrants and center of a circle and at the ends and midpoint of a line. Figure 7.7 shows the location of grips on different objects. You can perform editing operations very quickly with grips. When you first select an object, the grips are blue boxes by default. These are called *unselected grips.* Press the Esc key twice to remove the grips from the object. The screen cursor snaps directly to a grip when it is moved over the grip. This allows you to easily use the grips for editing purposes. When you move the screen cursor to a grip and pick, the grip becomes solid red by default. These are called *selected grips.* The grip color may be changed if you wish. Press the Esc key once to return the solid red grip to the blue outline status. When you pick a grip and make it solid red, this grip is called the *base grip.* The base grip is the point from which the editing process occurs. Editing with grips is explained later in this chapter.

Grips are controlled by using the Selection tab of the Options dialog box shown in Figure 7.8. Access the Options dialog box by picking Options… in the Tools pull-down menu or by typing **GR** or **DDGRIPS** at the Command: line prompt. The Grips area has two primary options at the top. Grips are enabled by default. Turn grips off by picking to remove the check in the Enable grips check box. Grips are shown at the insertion point of a block as in Figure 7.7 by default. You can have grips displayed on every object within a block by picking the Enable grips within blocks check box. Blocks are explained in Chapter 12. You can change grip color using the two drop-down lists. Pick the Unselected grip color list to specify a new color for unselected grips. Pick the Selected grip color list to change the color of selected grips. Use the Grip Size area to change the grip size as needed. Move the slider button to get a desired grip size. When you move the slider, the image shows the current grip setting at actual size.

FIGURE 7.7 Grips displayed on a variety of objects.

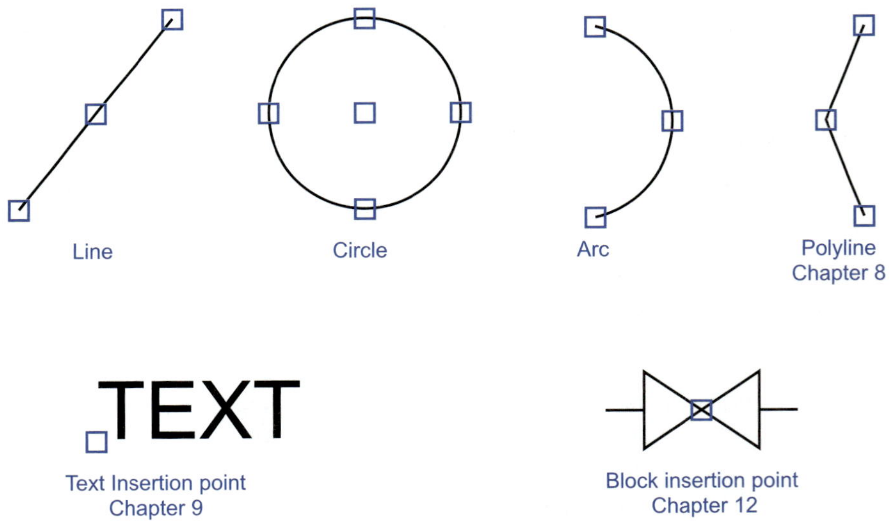

FIGURE 7.8 The Grips settings are found on the Selection tab of the Options dialog box.

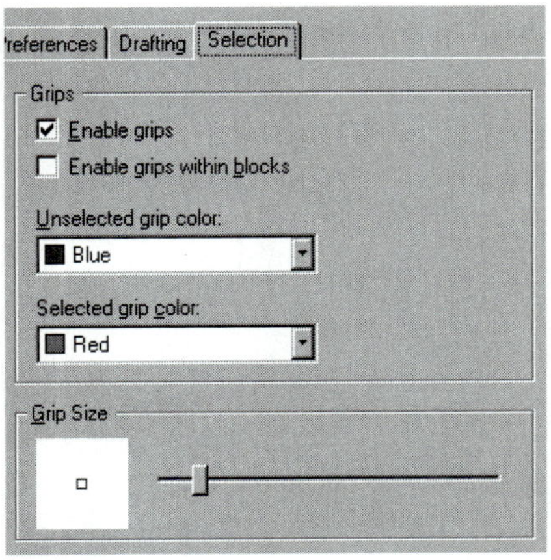

Field Notes

The Object Properties toolbar can be used to conveniently change the properties of grip selected objects. When a layer name is selected from the Layer Control list, grip selected objects are changed to the selected layer. Although the recommended setting for the rest of the tools is *By-layer*, if needed you can change the color, linetype, lineweight, or plot style using this same method. Once you have edited the desired properties, press the Esc key twice to clear the grips.

Exercise 7.4

Estimated time required: 5 min.

1. Begin a new drawing.
2. Draw a line, a circle, and an arc.
3. Select the line and observe the unselected grips. Pick one of the grips to make it a selected grip. Observe the results. Press the Esc key twice to remove the grips.
4. Do the same thing individually with the circle and arc.
5. Save as EX7.4, and close the drawing.

Using Quick Select

AutoCAD LT provides an advanced selection tool that allows you to select objects based on filter criteria that you specify. For example, you can select all objects on a specified layer or just objects of a given type. You can be very specific in your selection criteria, such as specifying all green hidden circles that have a 0.25 radius and a lineweight of 0.60 mm and are on layer 0. This selection criteria is specified using the Quick Select dialog box. You can access the Quick Select dialog box by picking Quick Select... from the Tools menu, or by typing **QSELECT** at the Command: prompt. The Quick Select dialog box is shown in Figure 7.9.

The Quick Select dialog box can be used only to grip select objects at the Command: prompt, and cannot be used at a Select objects: prompt. If no objects are currently grip-selected when you start the Quick Select dialog box, the Apply to: list box has a default value of Entire drawing. This means that all objects in the entire drawing will be checked to see if they match the filter criteria you specify. If one or more objects are already selected when you start the Quick Select dialog box, the default value in the Apply to: list is Current selection, allowing you to modify the current selection set. When Entire drawing is specified in the Apply to: list, the Object type: list shows

FIGURE 7.9 The Quick Select dialog box.

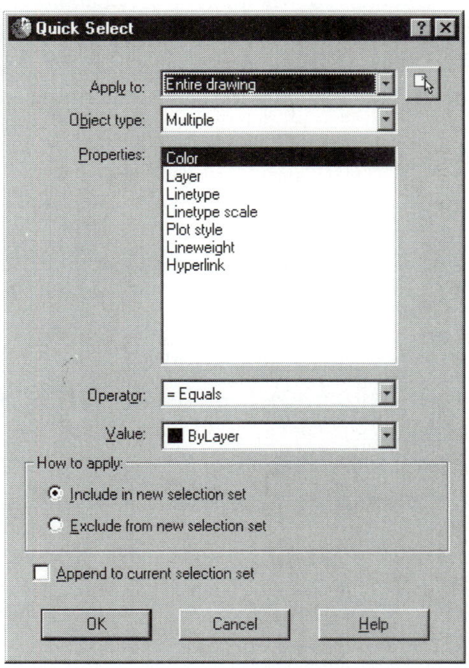

a listing of each of the object types found in the current drawing space; otherwise a list of the object types found in the current selection is displayed. The Select object button can be used to temporarily hide the dialog box while you create a new selection set. You can select a single object type from the Object type: list or use the Multiple option to select more than one type of object. The Properties: list shows a list of searchable properties applicable to the currently selected object type(s). For example, when Multiple is specified, only the general object properties common to all object types are listed (see Figure 7.9). Figure 7.10 shows the Quick Select dialog box when only lines are selected. Notice that additional properties that apply only to line objects are now added to the Properties: list.

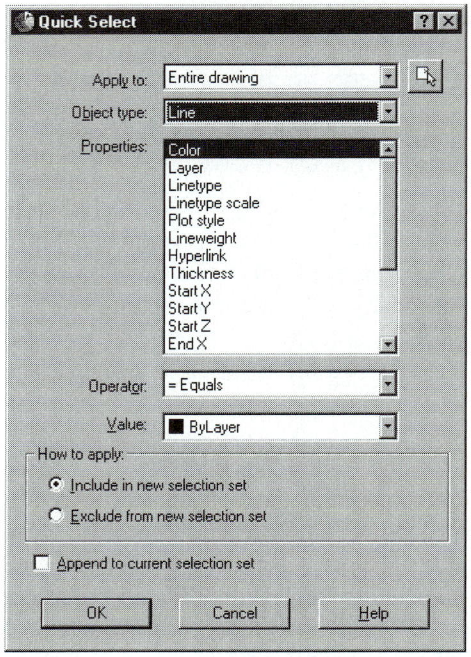

FIGURE 7.10 When specific object types are specified, the Properties list displays the searchable properties applicable to the specified object type.

The Operator: list allows you to define the way in which the property is applied. Operators include Equals, Not Equal To, Greater Than, Less Than, and Wildcard Match. The Greater Than and Less Than operators are available only for numeric values. A wildcard match can also be specified; refer to Chapter 5 if you need a review of wildcard options. Use the Value: field to specify the value of the filter. If the specified Property has preset values available, these values are displayed in the drop-down list. Otherwise, the Value: field is presented as a text box.

In the How to apply: area you indicate whether objects matching the specified criteria are to be used to create a new selection set or if the objects are to be removed from the current selection set. If you want to add the new objects to the current selection set place a checkmark next to Append to current selection set.

When you select OK, the objects matching the selection criteria are grip-selected and can be edited as needed.

Exercise 7.5

Estimated time required: 5 min.

1. Open EX5.2.dwg for editing.
2. Use the Quick Select dialog box to select all objects that are on the Object layer.
3. Erase the selected objects.
4. Use the Quick Select dialog box to select all LINE objects on the Hidden layer.
5. Erase the selected objects.
6. Save as EX7.5.dwg, and close the drawing.

LEARNING CHECKPOINT

- ☐ Define the term *selection set.*
- ☐ Explain the difference between WP and CP.

- ☐ How does the F selection option work?
- ☐ What is the purpose of cycling?
- ☐ Describe how the SELECT command works.
- ☐ What is Noun/Verb Selection?
- ☐ How does Press and Drag work?
- ☐ What is Implied Windowing?
- ☐ What is the main purpose of using sorting methods?
- ☐ How do you remove grips?
- ☐ Where are grips found on a circle?
- ☐ What happens to an unselected grip when you select it?
- ☐ What command starts the Quick Select dialog box?
- ☐ When can the Quick Select dialog box be used and what is its result?

Viewing, Selecting, and Using Precision Drawing Tools

- Using Selection Sets to Edit Multiple Objects

Concept Animations

- Selecting Objects

Copying Objects

AutoCAD LT supplies a group of commands that allow you to copy objects. These commands are useful for a variety of editing tasks that provide individual and multiple copies of objects in different arrangements. These commands include COPY, OFFSET, MIRROR, and ARRAY.

Using the COPY Command

Modify

Copy Object

Modify
Copy

COPY
CO
CP

Many projects contain features that are duplicated throughout the drawing. Once an object has been drawn, it can be copied as many times as needed. When copying objects, pick the Copy Object button from the Modify toolbar, pick Copy in the Modify pull-down menu, or type **CP** or **COPY** at the Command: prompt. The COPY command asks you to select the objects you want to copy and then asks for a base point. The ***base point*** is any specific reference point that has a meaningful relationship with the object. For example, circular features in a technical drawing are often located by dimensioning the center point of the circular profile. If you draw a hole in a part that is placed in several locations, the easiest way to locate the new copies accurately is to place them using the center of the circle as the reference point (i.e., the base point). Or, as shown in Figure 7.11, any specific point that can be used to locate the copy can be selected as a base point. The illustration shows a simplified piping symbol for a valve that is connected to the endpoint of a pipe. To copy this valve and place the copy at the endpoint of another pipe, a good base point selection is the MIDpoint of the line at the left side of the valve. The *Second point of displacement* label in Figure 7.11 specifies the new location of the base point in relation to the new copy of the valve. Specifying the ENDPoint of the second pipe accurately places the copy of the valve in the correct location. The COPY command works like this:

Command: **CP** or **COPY**↵
Select objects: *<select the objects to be copied>*
n found
Select objects: ↵
Specify base point or displacement, or [Multiple]: *<pick a base point>*
Specify second point of displacement or <use first point as displacement>: *<pick the location for the copy>*
Command:

The previous example allows you to make one copy of the desired objects. You can also make multiple copies by using the Multiple option. Follow this command sequence to make several copies of the same object:

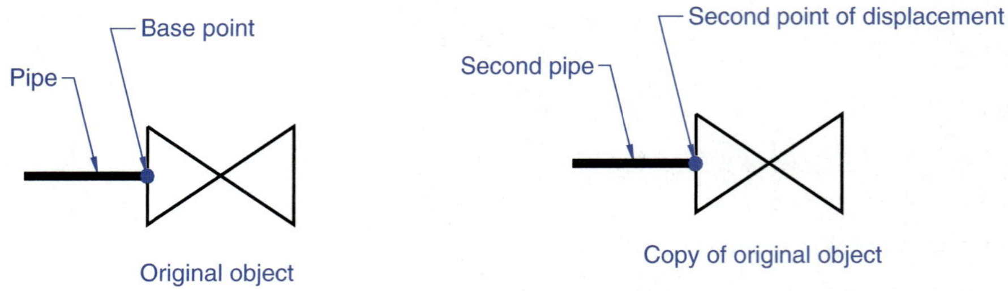

FIGURE 7.11 Selecting a base point and using the COPY command.

Command: **CP** or **COPY**↵
Select objects: *<select the objects to be copied>*
n found
Select objects: ↵
Specify base point or displacement, or [Multiple]: **M**↵
Specify base point: *<Pick a base point>*
Specify second point of displacement or <use first point as displacement>: *<pick the location for the first copy>*
Specify second point of displacement or <use first point as displacement>: *<pick the location for the second copy>*
Specify second point of displacement or <use first point as displacement>: *<pick the location for the third copy>*
Specify second point of displacement or <use first point as displacement>: ↵
Command:

The displacement option is used when you enter a coordinate at the "Specify base point or displacement, or [Multiple]:" prompt and press Enter at the "Specify second point of displacement or <use first point as displacement>:" prompt. The copies are then placed at a location that is the specified X and Y distances from the original. Also, this can be done by picking the first point and pressing Enter at the second prompt: the picked point is then used as the X and Y values for displacement.

Field Notes

- The displacement option can be a problem if you pick the first point and accidentally press Enter at the second point prompt—the copies are often made beyond the visible area of the drawing. For example, if you pick the point 11,8, then the copies are made 11 units over on the X axis and 8 units up on the Y axis. If the copies do not appear on screen, use Undo and try again, unless you want to copy off the screen.
- When objects are grip selected, Copy and Cut options are displayed on the shortcut menu. Do not use these options to copy objects within a drawing yet. These options start the COPYCLIP and CUTCLIP commands, which use the Windows clipboard to copy objects. The COPYCLIP, CUTCLIP, and PASTECLIP commands are discussed later in this chapter.

Exercise 7.6 — Estimated time required: 5 min.

1. Open EX7.4.
2. Use the COPY command's Multiple option to make three duplicates of the original object.
3. Save as EX7.6, and close the drawing.

Making Parallel Copies with the OFFSET Command

The OFFSET command can be used to create parallel copies of objects at a specified offset distance. Many objects can be offset, including lines, arcs, circles, polylines, construction lines, elliptical arcs, and ellipses. When offsetting a line, you create a duplicate line at a specified place parallel to the original line. Circles are offset by concentric placement either larger or smaller than the original circle. Create an offset copy by picking the Offset button from the Modify toolbar, by picking Offset in the Modify pull-down menu, or by typing **Of** or **OFFSET** at the Command: line prompt. The command asks you to specify an offset distance, select an object to offset, and choose which side of the original object you want to offset. Follow this command sequence as you refer to Figure 7.12:

Modify

Offset

Modify
Offset

OFFSET
O

Command: **O** or **OFFSET**↵
Specify offset distance or [Through] <1.0000>: *<offset distance,* **.25** *for example>*
Select object to offset or <exit>: *<pick the original object>*
Specify point on side to offset: *<pick a point on the side to offset>*

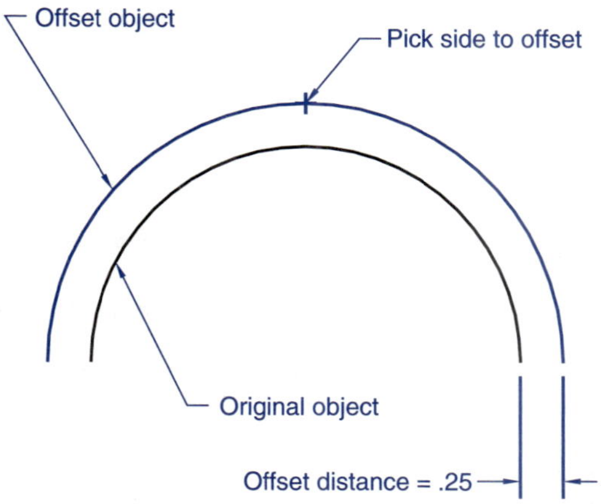

FIGURE 7.12 Using the OFFSET command.

AutoCAD LT continues to ask you to select an object to offset. This allows you to draw as many offsets, using the same distance, as desired:

Select object to offset or <exit>: *<pick an existing object>*
Specify point on side to offset: *<pick a point on the side to offset>*
Select object to offset or <exit>: *<continue by picking another object or press ↵>*
Command:

The OFFSET command allows you to pick a point through which the offset object is drawn. You can also pick two points in a drawing to specify a distance for the Through option. Consider using object snaps to your advantage when offsetting an object through a feature on an object. Use the Through option and follow this command sequence as you look at Figure 7.13:

Command: **O** or **OFFSET**↵
Specify offset distance or [Through] <0.2500>: **T**↵
Select object to offset or <exit>: *<pick the original object>*
Specify through point: *<pick a point for the copy to pass through>*
Select object to offset or <exit>: *<select another object or press ↵ >*
Command:

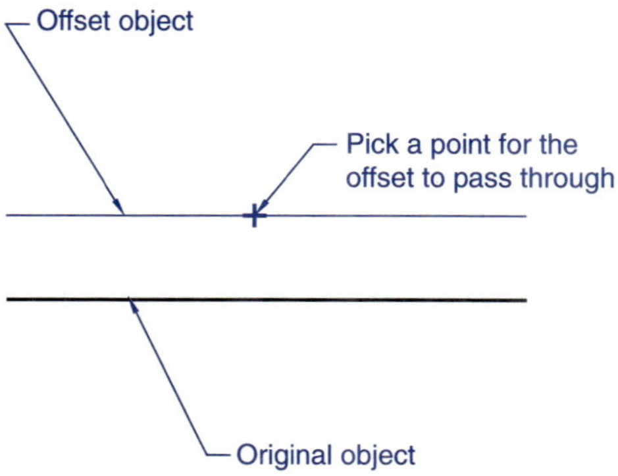

FIGURE 7.13 Using the OFFSET command's Through option.

Field Notes

- Some drafting productivity advantages result from the use of the OFFSET command. For example, when drawing a front view of an ortho drawing of a rectangularly shaped part, to get the right side view, use OFFSET Through to pick a location for one of the vertical lines in the right view and then use OFFSET with the distance being the width of the right side view. Horizontal lines can be handled in a similar manner. For example, draw a front view offset upward once using Through, and then the second time using the height of the top view as the distance.
- When using OFFSET to offset several features at varied offset values, a fast and easy way to change the offset distance for the next operation is to quickly press the space bar or Enter key twice. The first Enter ends the current OFFSET command and displays the Command: prompt. The second Enter restarts the OFFSET command and places you at the "Specify offset distance or [Through] <default>:" prompt. When you enter the new distance you can continue offsetting objects as before, using the new distance.

Exercise 7.7 — Estimated time required: 5 min.

1. Begin a new drawing.
2. Draw an arc similar to the original object shown in Figure 7.12.
3. Offset a distance of 0.25 outside of the original arc. The results should be similar to those shown in Figure 7.12.
4. Draw a line similar to the original object shown in Figure 7.13.
5. Use the OFFSET command's Through option to pick a point for the offset to pass through.
6. Save as EX7.7, and close the drawing.

Creating Mirror Images

Modify

Mirror

Modify
Mirror

MIRROR
MI

A mirror image of an object can be made and the original object can remain or it can be deleted. When you have a symmetrical object, you can draw half and then simply mirror the other half into position. Mirror images are drawn by picking the Mirror button on the Modify toolbar, by picking Mirror in the Modify pull-down menu, or by typing **MI** or **MIRROR** at the Command: prompt. The MIRROR command asks you to select the objects to mirror, establish a mirror line, and then decide if you want to keep or delete the old objects. The ***mirror line*** is an imaginary line across which the original object is mirrored. You are asked to pick the first and second point of the mirror line as shown in Figure 7.14. The mirror line may be located next to the original object or away from the original object. The distance between the mirror line and the original object is the same distance to the mirror image. The command sequence works like this:

Command: **MI** or **MIRROR**↵
Select objects: *<select the objects to mirror>*
n found
Select objects: ↵
Specify first point of mirror line: *<pick the first endpoint of the mirror line>*
Specify second point of mirror line: *<pick the other endpoint of the mirror line>*
Delete source objects? [Yes/No] <N>: ↵
Command:

Field Notes

It is easy to create a vertical or horizontal mirror line if you use ORTHO or Polar Tracking.

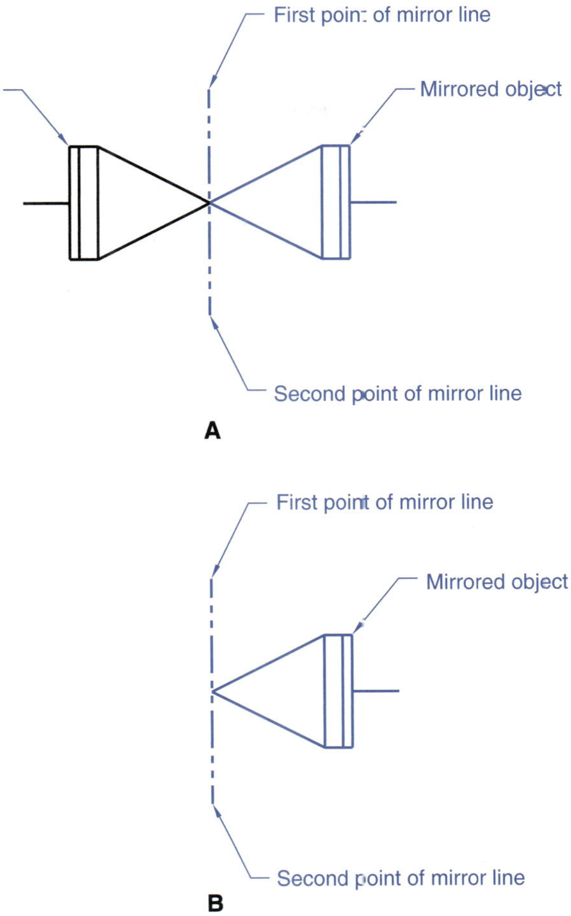

FIGURE 7.14 Using the MIRROR command. (A) The original object remaining after the command. (B) The second example deletes the original object while mirroring.

Exercise 7.8 **Estimated time required: 5 min.**

1. Begin a new drawing.
2. Draw an object similar to the original object shown in Figure 7.14.
3. Use the COPY command to duplicate the object directly below its current position.
4. Mirror the first object without deleting the original object, similar to Figure 7.14A.
5. Mirror the second object and delete its mate, similar to Figure 7.14B.
6. Save as EX7.8, and close the drawing.

Creating an Array of Objects

An **array** is a number of objects arranged in a pattern. The ARRAY command allows you to duplicate existing objects and place the new objects in a defined pattern. You can define rectangular patterns of rows and columns, or circular patterns. Before using the ARRAY command, you must create the original objects from which the pattern is to be made. The ARRAY command is accessed by picking Array … from the Modify pull-down menu, by picking the Array button from the Modify toolbar, or by typing **AR** or **ARRAY** at the Command: prompt. The ARRAY command displays the Array dialog box, where you define the pattern to create. Figure 7.15 shows the Array dialog box.

Modify
Array

Modify
Array

ARRAY
AR

Creating a Rectangular Array

To create a rectangular array, select the radio button at the top of the dialog box labeled Rectangular array. This displays the options for controlling the size and appearance of a rectangular array. At the top right corner is the Select objects button. Unlike most buttons that temporarily hide a dialog box, this and other buttons

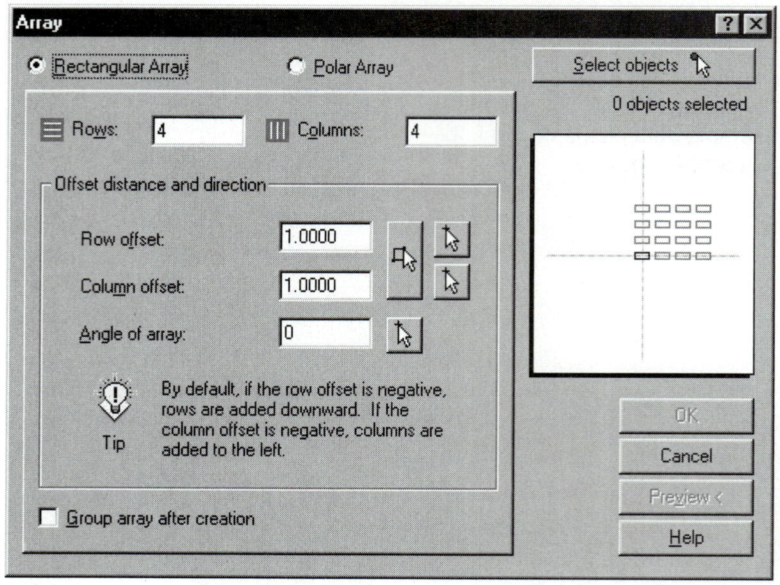

FIGURE 7.15 The Array dialog box is used to define a pattern of duplicated objects.

on this dialog box do not display the "<" symbol. Picking this button does hide the dialog box and allows you to select objects through any standard selection method. When you return to the Array dialog box, the number of objects you selected appears below this button. If you pick the Select objects button again, the previous selection set is discarded, and you must select all the objects to be used in the array.

The Rows: and Columns: settings allow you to control how many rows and columns will be created. A *row* is a horizontal arrangement of objects, and a *column* is a vertical arrangement. The offset values control the distance from one pattern element to the next. The offset values behave exactly like coordinates: positive values move upward (rows) and to the right (columns), and negative values move downward and to the left. Figure 7.16 illustrates these features. The default angle of the rows is 0°, or you can adjust this value in the Angle of array: box. With each adjustment, the preview image is updated to show the results of your current settings.

You can enter the row and column values, distances and angles by typing numbers in the text boxes, or you can pick the values directly on-screen. Figure 7.17 shows the function of each of the selection buttons. When picking a point on-screen, you can use any standard point specification method and apply any appropriate object snap modes.

To get a full preview of the results before accepting the settings, pick the Preview < button. This temporarily hides the dialog box and shows your drawing as it will appear after the currently defined array pattern is created. The dialog box that is displayed prompts you to accept, modify, or cancel the pattern. Picking Accept returns you immediately to the Command: prompt and implements the array settings as they are. Picking Modify returns you to the Array dialog box, and picking Cancel returns you to the Command: prompt after canceling the array command.

Field Notes

- An option at the bottom of the Array dialog box allows you to group the objects in the array pattern. Grouping objects allows them to be selected and edited as though they were a single object. The GROUP command and working with groups is detailed in Chapter 12. It would be best to review the discussion of groups prior to using this option.

Creating a Polar Array

The polar array creates a circular pattern of objects (see Figure 7.18). Select the Polar array radio button at the top of the Array dialog box to display the polar pattern options. As with the rectangular array, you must select the objects used to create the array pattern. The Center point: is established by typing X and Y values or by picking a point on-screen.

Scaling Objects

Modify

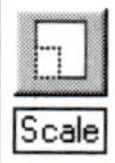

Modify
Scale

SCALE
SC

Existing objects in an AutoCAD LT drawing can be scaled up or scaled down using the SCALE command. When you ***scale*** an object, it means you are making the object larger or smaller as required. In some cases you may need to scale one or more features of a drawing due to a design change. Another common use for scaling is when similar features exist in a drawing that are different sizes. Rather than duplicate your efforts by drawing the objects again at the new size, it is easier to copy the existing objects and then scale the new copy to the correct size. To access the SCALE command, pick the Scale button from the Modify toolbar, pick Scale from the Modify pull-down menu, or type **SC** or **SCALE** at the Command: prompt.

Scaling can be used to either reduce or enlarge the size of objects. AutoCAD LT allows you to scale objects by specifying a scale factor or a reference dimension. The original size has a scale factor of 1. A scale factor of less than 1 is used to reduce the size of the object, and a scale factor of more than 1 enlarges the object. Scaling with a reference dimension is done by establishing an existing dimension and then a new desired specification.

Using a Scale Factor to Scale Objects

When scaling objects, AutoCAD LT asks you to select the objects, pick a base point, and type a scale factor. The specified scale factor is used as a multiplier for the size and relative positions of the objects being resized. Negative and zero scale factors are not allowed. Figure 7.22 shows how the SCALE command works and the results of using various scale factors. This is the command sequence:

Command: **SC** or **SCALE**↵
Select objects: <*select objects to scale*>
n found
Select objects: ↵
Specify base point: <*pick a base point*>
Specify scale factor or [Reference]: **2**↵
Command:

As with many numeric value prompts in AutoCAD LT, an alternative method of entry is to pick points in your drawing rather than entering them at the prompts. When asked for the scale factor, you can move the cursor to see the objects change in size and relative position. If you pick a point, the distance from the base point to the final cursor location is measured and used as the scale factor. For example, if the distance is 2.51 units, a scale factor of 2.51 is used.

FIGURE 7.22 Using the SCALE command with the Scale factor option.

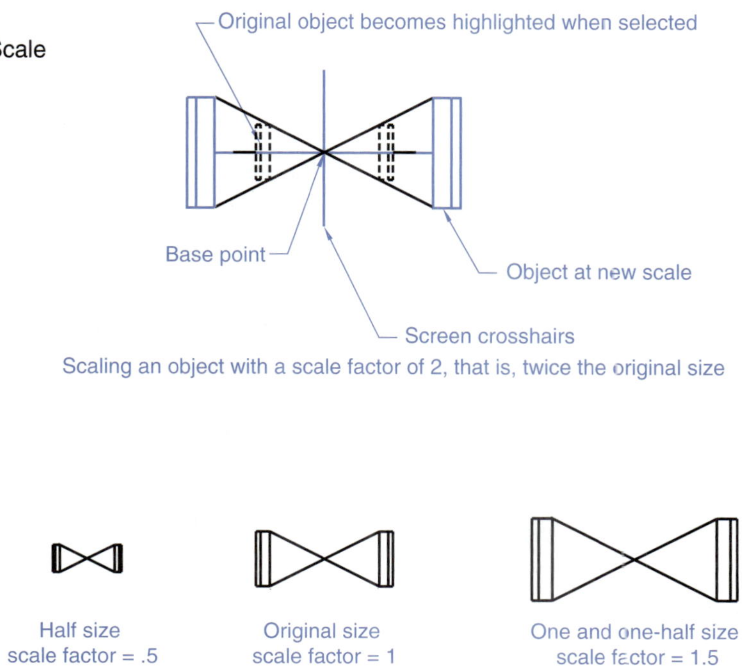

Using the Reference Option to Scale Objects

When using the Reference option to scale objects, you need to specify the reference length, which is the current length. The reference length can be 1, it can be the actual length of the object, or it can be established by picking two points on the object. You then specify a new length, which is either shorter or longer than the reference length. The new length can be the exact length that you want for the scaled object, or you can pick a point to where the object is to be scaled. The new length can also be established by dynamically dragging the object to the desired scale. The object is then scaled to match the new length. Refer to Figure 7.23 as you follow this command sequence:

Command: **SC** or **SCALE**↵
Select objects: *<select objects to scale>*
n found
Select objects: ↵
Specify base point: *<pick a base point>*
Specify scale factor or [Reference]: **R**↵
Specify reference length <1>: **.875**↵
Specify new length: **1.75**↵
Command:

FIGURE 7.23 Using the SCALE command with the Reference option.

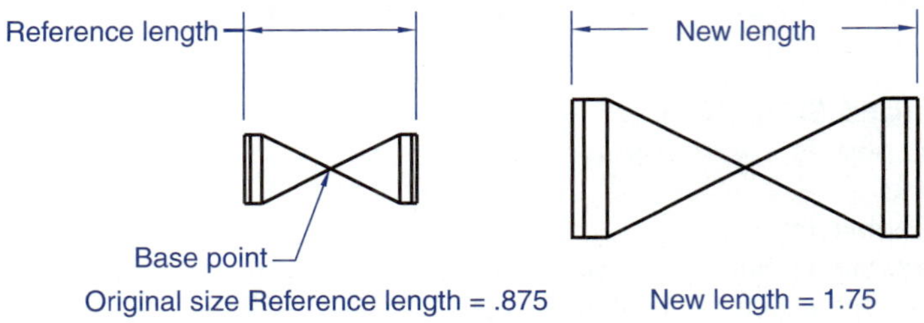

Field Notes

The following provides practical applications of the scaling Reference option:

- One example is when an object to be scaled is at a known size and the new size is also known, but determination of the actual required scale factor requires use of a calculator. To deal with this situation, enter the known reference size and the new size numerically using the keyboard.
- Another example is when a desired size is known but the current size is not. Now the reference length can be picked using any appropriate object snap mode and the new length typed.
- A third example is using either a picked or numerically entered reference length followed by picking a point that defines the new size as the distance from the specified base point to the picked point, with accuracy, using object snap or other precision drawing aids.

Exercise 7.12

Estimated time required: 5 min.

1. Open EX7.10.
2. Make six copies of the object with three above and three below.
3. Scale the top left object with a scale factor of .5.
4. Scale the top right object with a scale factor of 2.
5. Scale the bottom left object with a new length of .4375.
6. Scale the bottom right object with a scale factor of 1.75.
7. The middle objects in both rows remain at the original size for comparison.
8. Save as EX7.12, and close the drawing.

Lengthening Objects

The LENGTHEN command is provided in AutoCAD LT to change the length of objects and the included angle of arcs. An ***included angle*** is the angle formed between the start point, endpoint, and center of the arc as shown in Figure 3.20 (Chapter 3). The LENGTHEN command does not work on closed objects or objects that have no length definition. When asked to select an object to lengthen, the end of the object closest to the pick point is the end that gets changed. Access this command by picking the Lengthen button from the Modify toolbar, by picking Lengthen from the Modify pull-down menu, or by typing **LEN** or **LENGTHEN** at the Command: prompt. Several options become available when this command is entered:

Modify

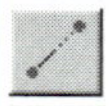

Lengthen

Modify
Lengthen

LENGTHEN
LEN

Command: **LEN** or **LENGTHEN**↵
Select an object or [DElta/Percent/Total/DYnamic]:

Using the Select Object Option

The Select an object option of the LENGTHEN command is the default and is simply used to give the length of an object and the included angle of an arc. Just pick any linear object or arc on the drawing and AutoCAD LT gives the length, and the included angle if the object is an arc. The object must have length definition. Objects that have length definition include lines, open or closed polylines, open or closed splines, arcs, circles, and ellipses. Several of these objects have limitations when using other lengthen options, but you can list the length of any of these object types.

Using the Delta Option

The Delta option of the LENGTHEN command is used to change the length of an object by a specified increment. Specify a positive increment to increase the length of a line or arc or a negative increment to decrease the length. Increase the length of an arc with a positive angle, or decrease an arc length with a negative angle. Note, however, that no object can be shortened to a zero length, and arcs cannot be lengthened to a full 360°. Several examples of the use of the Delta option are shown in Figure 7.24. The Delta option works like this:

Command: **LEN** or **LENGTHEN**↵
Select an object or [DElta/Percent/Total/DYnamic]: **DE**↵
Enter delta length or [Angle] <0.0000>: **.5**↵
Select an object to change or [Undo]: *<pick the object near the end to change>*

The command continues with the option to pick another object to change, type **U** to undo the last change, or press Enter to exit the command:

Select an object to change or [Undo]: ↵
Command:

The Angle suboption allows you to lengthen an arc by a positive included angle or shorten an arc with a negative included angle, as shown in Figure 7.22:

Command: **LEN** or **LENGTHEN**↵
Select an object or [DElta/Percent/Total/DYnamic]: **DE**↵

FIGURE 7.24 Using the LENGTHEN command's Delta option.

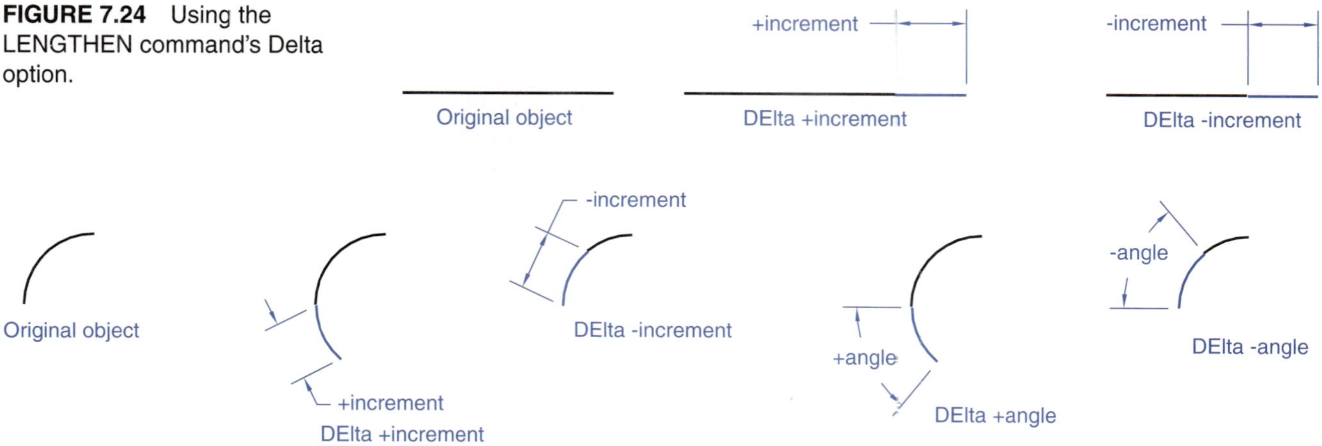

Enter delta length or [Angle] <0.0000>: **A↵**
Enter delta angle <0>: **30↵**
Select an object to change or [Undo]: *<pick the object near the end to change>*
Select an object to change or [Undo]: ↵
Command:

Using the Percent Option

The LENGTHEN command's Percent option is used to change the length of an object or the included angle of an arc by a specified percentage of the current length or included angle. The percentage is calculated according to the current length or included angle of the object selected at the time it is picked, and the percentage indicates total new length—not additional length. This means, for example, that if a percentage of 200% is specified, and a 1 unit long line is picked, it becomes 2 units long. Picking the same line again makes it 4 units long. A value of 100% has no effect, because 100% of anything is still the original value. Any changes made to the length of the line are made at the end nearest the pick point. Specify less than 100% to shorten an object or reduce the included angle, or indicate more than 100% to increase the length or included angle (see Figure 7.25). The following command sequence is used to increase the length of an object by 150%:

Command: **LEN** or **LENGTHEN↵**
Select an object or [DElta/Percent/Total/DYnamic]: **P↵**
Enter percentage length <100.0000>: **150↵**
Select an object to change or [Undo]: *<pick the object near the end to change>*
Select an object to change or [Undo]: ↵
Command:

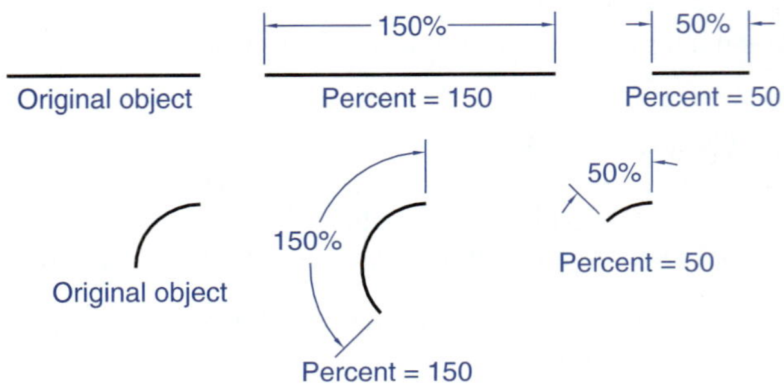

FIGURE 7.25 Using the LENGTHEN command's Percent option.

Field Notes

One common mistake users make when learning to use the percentage option is that they try to use decimal values instead of the intended percentage. For example, consider a user who is trying to reduce an object's length by one-half and specifies value of 0.5 as the percentage. Unfortunately, this is actually 0.5%, or one-half of 1%, and results in a *very* short object. The percentage specified to reduce an object length by one-half is 50%.

Using the Total Option

The LENGTHEN command's Total option is used to change the length of an object or the included angle of an arc to a specified total length or included angle. The shortening or lengthening required to change the total length of the object to the new specification is performed on the end nearest to the pick point. Therefore, the total length is actually measured from the opposite end, which remains fixed. This option makes it easy to specify an exact length or included angle. Figure 7.26 demonstrates this command sequence:

Command: **LEN** or **LENGTHEN↵**
Select an object or [DElta/Percent/Total/DYnamic]: **T↵**
Specify total length or [Angle] <1.0000)>: **1.25↵**
Select an object to change or [Undo]: *<pick the object near the end to change>*
Select an object to change or [Undo]: ↵
Command:

FIGURE 7.26 Using the LENGTHEN command's Total option.

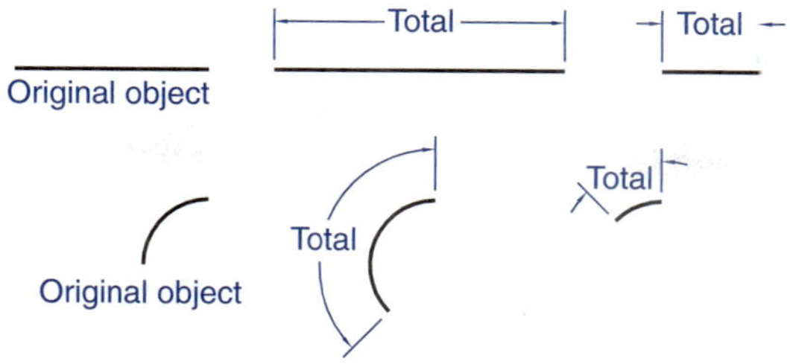

The Angle suboption asks you to enter the total included angle of an arc. Virtually any total value can be specified, but the smallest length value that AutoCAD LT uses is about 0.000001 units. When specifying angles for an arc, acceptable angles must be greater than 0.00005° and less than 360°.

Using the Dynamic Option

The LENGTHEN command's Dynamic option allows you to visually change the length of an object or the included angle of an arc by dragging one of the endpoints to the desired length. When dynamically lengthening an object such as a line, the new length is indicated by the distance between the fixed opposite end and the current cursor location. This can be used in combination with object snap, especially a PERpendicular mode, to accurately place the new location of the selected end. When using the Dynamic option on an arc, the true effects of your cursor movements may not be so obvious. A dragline connects the cursor to the original position of the selected arc endpoint, and moving your cursor either lengthens or shortens the arc. This is not a result of the current length of the dragline, as with a line object. What is actually happening is that the Dynamic option adjusts the included angle to match the absolute angle from the *arc center* to the *current cursor location.* This is used as a total value and is not relative to any current angle. Complex objects such as polylines and splines cannot be lengthened using the Dynamic option. This is the command sequence:

Command: **LEN** or **LENGTHEN**↵
Select an object or [DElta/Percent/Total/DYnamic]: **DY**↵
Select an object to change or [Undo]: ⟨*pick the object near the end to change*⟩
Specify new endpoint: ⟨*pick the new location for the endpoint being changed*⟩
Select an object to change or [Undo]: ↵
Command:

Field Notes

The Delta and Total options of the LENGTHEN command allow the value to be specified either by typing a numeric value or by picking two points on screen. However, one aspect of the Delta option can cause unexpected results when specifying the value by picking points. If the current delta value is positive, a picked distance is interpreted as a positive distance. When the current delta value is negative, any picked distance is automatically interpreted as a negative value. Therefore, if the current delta value is negative and you pick two points to describe a positive value of 4 units, for example, then the new delta value is −4.0 regardless of the direction of the pick or any other factors.

Exercise 7.13 **Estimated time required: 5 min.**

1. Begin a new drawing.
2. Draw a line 1.5 in. long and a quarter circle arc with a .5-in. radius similar to the original objects shown in Figure 7.22.
3. Make 7 copies (8 total) of the line and 9 copies (10 total) of the arc.
4. Do the following to each line:
   - + increment
   - − increment
   - 150%
   - 50%
   - 2.25 total
   - .5 total
   - + dynamic
   - − dynamic
5. Do the following to each arc:
   - + increment
   - − increment
   - Delta + angle
   - Delta − angle
   - 150%
   - 50%
   - 2.25 total
   - .5 total
   - + dynamic
   - − dynamic
6. Save as EX7.13, and close the drawing.

Stretching Objects

Modify

Stretch

Modify
Stretch

STRETCH
S

The STRETCH command is used to change the location of the defining points for one or more objects in a drawing. Depending on the object type, all or just some of the defining points can be relocated using STRETCH. For example, either one or both of the endpoints of a line can be relocated. If both points are moved the same relative distance, the effect is the same as a MOVE command. If only one of the endpoints is moved, the other remains fixed and the final effect is that the line is stretched to a new length, in a new direction, or both.

The points to be moved by a STRETCH command must be surrounded by a selection window option: Window, Crossing, Window Polygon, or Crossing Polygon. If you specify one window and then another, only the points surrounded by the last window are affected; any previous window specifications are discarded. Also, only the objects selected are affected, whether or not their defining points are surrounded. It is often easiest to use one of the crossing options because the desired points are surrounded and all of the needed objects are selected.

To access the STRETCH command, pick the Stretch button from the Modify toolbar, pick Stretch from the Modify pull-down menu, or type **S** or **STRETCH** at the Command: prompt. To learn the use of this command through an easy approach, start with selecting using a crossing box. Study the use and effects of the STRETCH command in Figure 7.27. The following command sequence is shown in Figure 7.27:

Command: **S** or **STRETCH**↵
Select objects to stretch by crossing-window or crossing-polygon...
Select objects: *<pick first corner of crossing-window>*
Specify opposite corner: *<pick other corner>*
6 found
Select objects: ↵
Specify base point or displacement: *<pick a base point>*
Specify second point of displacement: *<pick a second point of displacement>*
Command:

FIGURE 7.27 Using the STRETCH command.

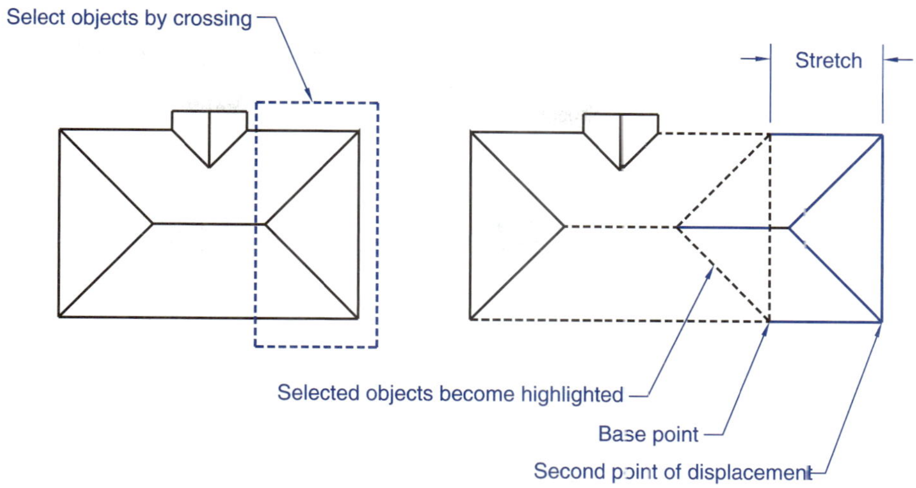

The example in Figure 7.27 can be selected easily by a crossing box. Notice that the three horizontal lines are stretched out, but the vertical line and angled lines are actually just moved. This is because the other ends of the horizontal lines were not surrounded by the selection window option, so they remain fixed. Both of the endpoints of the vertical line were surrounded and therefore both ends were moved the same distance.

This STRETCH command has a variety of uses and is very powerful when understood properly. The following examples help explain the effect of stretch on different object types and how different objects must be selected with the window specification to be affected:

- Circles are unaffected unless the center is surrounded.
- Arcs and lines must have one or both endpoints surrounded.
- Only surrounded vertices on polylines and splines are affected. Polylines are discussed in Chapter 8.
- A Crossing Polygon should be used for complex stretching needs.
- Use the Remove option to remove objects from the selection set with individual picks.
- The Window and Window Polygon options can be used, but their results may be undesirable.
- Objects to be stretched that are not selected by the Window options can be picked individually.
- You can use the pick box to pick a line or the Window option to surround a line, and you stretch the endpoint just as if you had selected using a Crossing box.
- The idea behind using the Crossing options is to select everything inside and crossing the box or polygon. These options are often a convenient selection method.

The STRETCH command can be used with a variety of selection options for different results, as shown in Figure 7.28.

Field Notes

- Consider using ORTHO or Polar Tracking in conjunction with STRETCH to conveniently stretch the object at a specific angle.
- If you specify one window, and then another, only the points surrounded by the last window are affected; any previous window specifications are discarded.

Exercise 7.14

Estimated time required: 5 min.

1. Begin a new drawing.
2. Draw a house roof plan similar to the original (left side) shown in Figure 7.27.
3. Stretch the roof similar to the operation shown in Figure 7.27.
4. Move the dormer to the center of the building by stretching and perform other stretching operations, as was done in Figure 7.28.
5. Save the drawing as EX7.14.

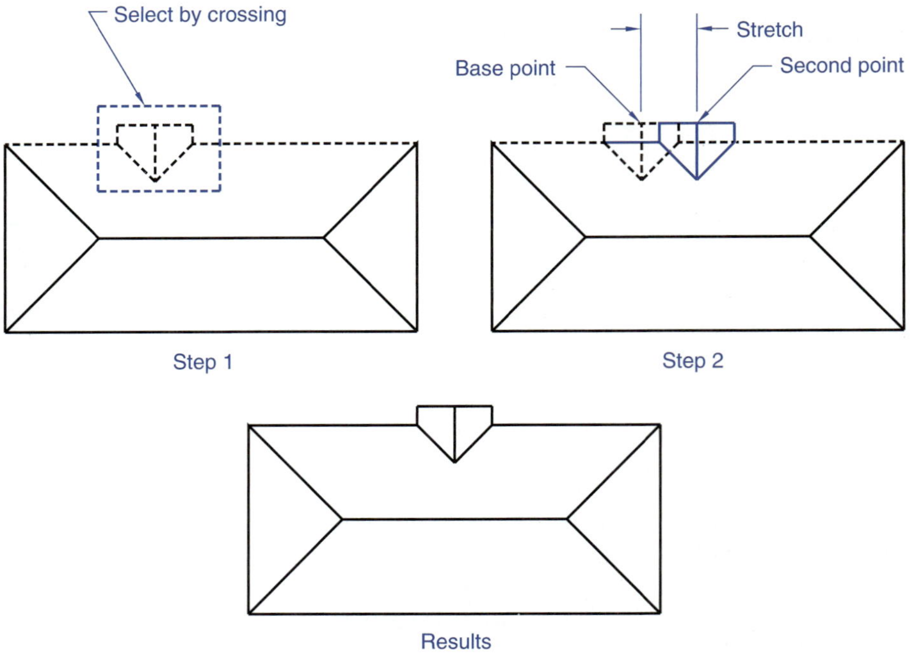

FIGURE 7.28 Moving objects with the STRETCH command.

LEARNING CHECKPOINT

- ☐ Identify at least five ways to enter the COPY command.
- ☐ What is the base point and what are commonly selected base points?
- ☐ What is the second point of displacement?
- ☐ Name the command that is used to make parallel copies.
- ☐ Describe the purpose of the mirror line.
- ☐ Define an array.
- ☐ What are two types of arrays?
- ☐ Explain the difference between the COPY and MOVE commands.
- ☐ Name the command that allows you to pivot objects at a base point to a desired angle.
- ☐ Describe the difference between the SCALE command's scale factor and reference options.
- ☐ What is the purpose of the LENGTHEN command?
- ☐ Discuss the primary difference between the LENGTHEN and STRETCH commands.

Changing Geometry

- Stretching, Trimming, and Extending Objects
- Copying Objects
- Rotating Objects

Concept Animations

- Introducing Base Points

Editing with Grips

As explained earlier, grips are displayed if you select objects before entering a command. In Chapter 2 you learned that you can select an object and then enter the ERASE command to have the object removed. This is the simplest form of selecting an object before entering the command. Grips allow you to perform several key editing operations quickly and conveniently, because you select objects and enter the command at the same time. To see how to use the grip commands, select a line object and then select the grip at the end of the line. The selected grip becomes solid red by default and the command line reads like this:

Command:
** STRETCH **
Specify stretch point or [Base point/Copy/Undo/eXit]:

STRETCH is the first command that is activated when you select a grip. Every time you press the space bar or Enter key, you get another command. The grip commands include STRETCH, MOVE, ROTATE, SCALE, and MIRROR. AutoCAD LT cycles through each of these commands as you press the space bar or Enter key. Keep cycling until you get the desired command like this:

Command:
** STRETCH **
Specify stretch point or [Base point/Copy/Undo/eXit]: ↵
** MOVE **
Specify move point or [Base point/Copy/Undo/eXit]: ↵
** ROTATE **
Specify rotation angle or [Base point/Copy/Undo/Reference/eXit]: ↵
** SCALE **
Specify scale factor or [Base point/Copy/Undo/Reference/eXit]: ↵
** MIRROR **
Specify second point or [Base point/Copy/Undo/eXit]: ↵
** STRETCH **
Specify stretch point or [Base point/Copy/Undo/eXit]:

The options associated with these commands should look familiar from the previous discussions. Exit the grip mode by typing **X** for exit or press the Esc key. Press Esc twice to remove the grips from the display. The first Esc keystroke deselects the highlighted object and the second hides the grips.

Field Notes

- You can press the space bar or Enter key to cycle through the grip editing commands or you can use the keyboard shortcut to go directly to the desired editing command. The keyboard shortcuts are ST for STRETCH, MO for MOVE, RO for ROTATE, SC for SCALE, MI for MIRROR.
- Another way to access the grip editing commands is to select a grip and then press the right mouse button. This displays the Grips shortcut menu. The menu has the editing options Move, Mirror, Rotate, Scale and Stretch. It also has the options Base Point, Copy, Reference, Undo, and Exit. The Properties option is explained later.
- The Base point option in each of the grip commands is used to pick a new base point. This does not change the selected grip, it just changes the base point. To use the Base point option, type **B** and press Enter. You then get the Base point: prompt. Now, pick a new base point.

Stretching with Grips

When you select a grip, the first command issued is STRETCH. This allows you to move the selected grip to a new location and stretch the object along with it. Figure 7.29 shows a line being stretched with grips following these steps:

Command:
** STRETCH **
Specify stretch point or [Base point/Copy/Undo/eXit]: *<move the selected grip to a desired location and pick—the line is now stretched as shown in Figure 7.29.>*

If you have more than one object to stretch at the same time, you can select two or more grips to edit by holding down the Shift key and picking the desired grips. Release the Shift key after the grips are selected and then pick one of the selected grips as the base point. Figure 7.30 shows how to stretch two lines by se-

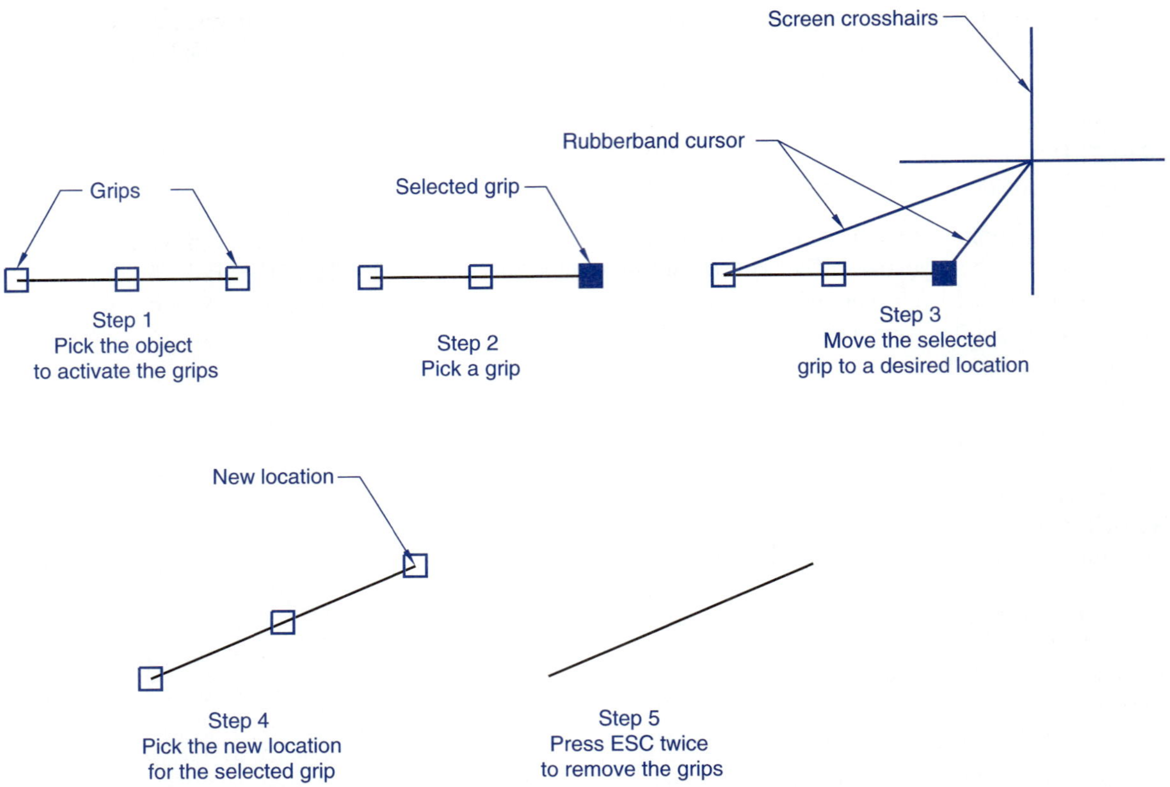

FIGURE 7.29 A line being stretched with grips.

lecting two grips, and how to stretch a roof by selecting three grips. One selected grip in each example is picked as the base point. Follow these steps to stretch each of the examples separately:

Select the objects. In the roof example, use a crossing box to select only the lines that will be stretched.
Hold down the Shift key and select the grips—two for the parallel line example and three for the roof example.
Release the Shift key and pick a selected grip to act as a base point.
Command:
** STRETCH **
Specify stretch point or [Base point/Copy/Undo/eXit]: <*move the selected grip to a desired location and pick—the objects are stretched separately as shown in Figure 7.30*>

Copying with the Grips STRETCH Command

The grips STRETCH command also has a Copy option that allows you to make multiple stretched copies of the object. Access this option using the shortcut menu or by typing **C** like this:

Select the objects.
Pick a grip to select and get this command:
Command:
** STRETCH **
Specify stretch point or [Base point/Copy/Undo/eXit]: **C↵**
** STRETCH (multiple) **
Specify stretch point or [Base point/Copy/Undo/eXit]: <*pick the desired location*>
** STRETCH (multiple) **
Specify stretch point or [Base point/Copy/Undo/eXit]: <*pick the desired location*>
** STRETCH (multiple) **
Specify stretch point or [Base point/Copy/Undo/eXit]: **X↵**
Command:

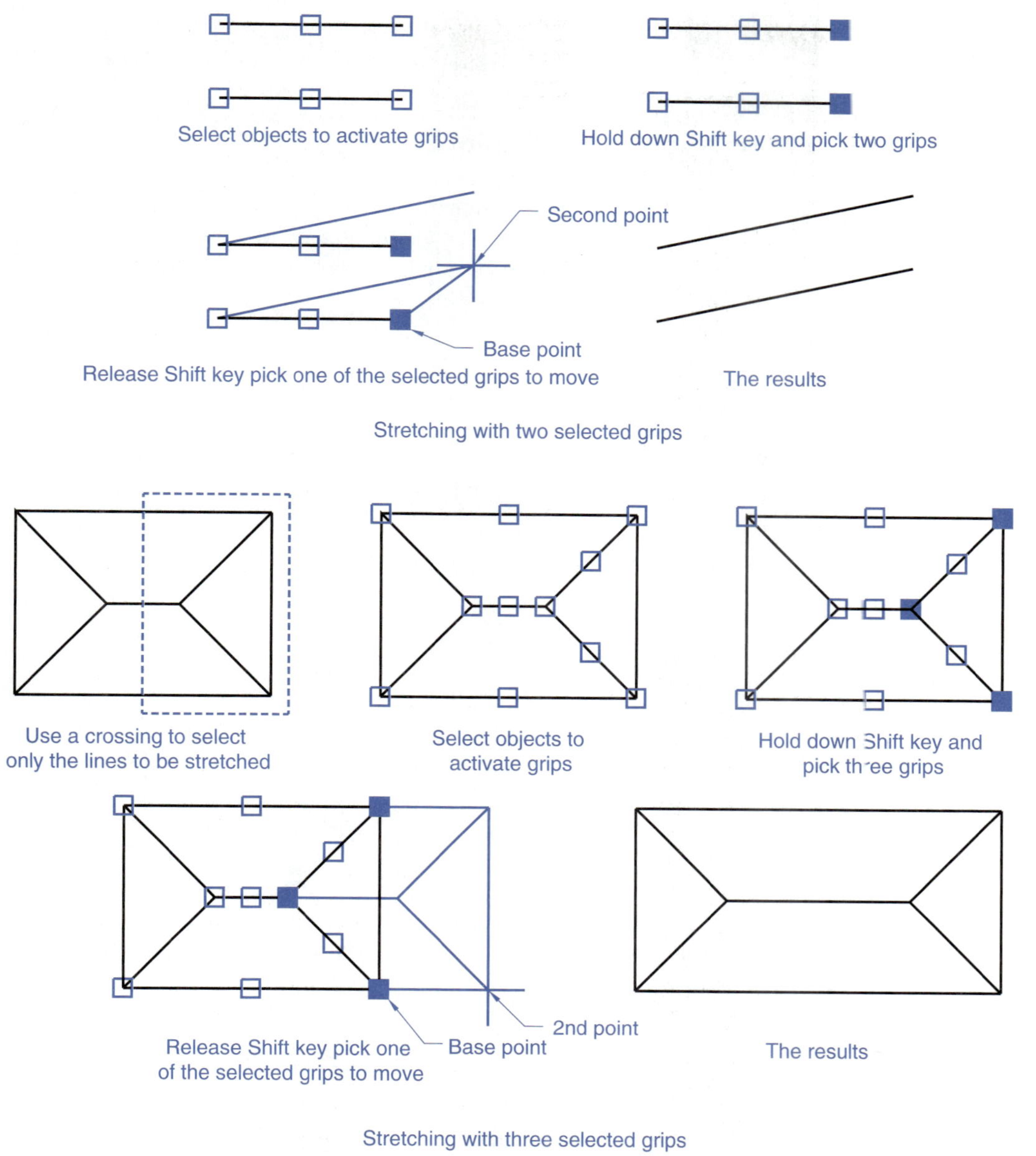

FIGURE 7.30 Stretching with more than one grip selected.

Field Notes

- If you hold down the Shift key while making the first pick and then release, each new pick creates a new copy at a freely picked point.
- If you hold down the Shift key while picking the new points, the copies are placed at an offset point based on the first two selected points.
- The selection process using grips is the same as normal selections. To remove objects from the selection set, press the Shift key while picking a single object, a window, or a crossing. Picking an object a second time in this manner hides its grips.
- When you are picking multiple grips to edit, you must press the Shift key while selecting each of the grips. If you accidentally miss the grip and pick a point on the selected object, it is then unselected. You can release the Shift key and pick it again to bring it back into the selection set.
- You can use the grips STRETCH command to move objects when you select a grip at the midpoint of a line, center of a circle, insertion point of text or a block, or on a point object.
- While inside a grip command, you can type **B** to establish a new base point together with the Copy option to make multiple copies at different base points.

Exercise 7.15 — Estimated time required: 5 min.

1. Begin a new drawing.
2. Draw a line similar to the one shown in Step 1 in Figure 7.29.
3. Use grips to stretch the line as shown in Figure 7.29.
4. Draw two parallel lines and use grips to stretch them as shown in the first example in Figure 7.30.
5. Draw a house roof plan similar to the second example shown in Figure 7.30.
6. Stretch the roof similar to the operation in the second example shown in Figure 7.30.
7. Save as EX7.15, and close the drawing.

Moving with Grips

To move objects using grips, all you have to do is select the objects, select a grip to be the base point, and then move to the desired location and pick. The MOVE command works like this:

Select the objects as shown in Figure 7.31.
Select a grip and then press the space bar or Enter key until you get this grip command, select Move from the shortcut menu, or type MO:
** MOVE **
Specify move point or [Base point/Copy/Undo/eXit]:
Move the cursor and pick a new location for the objects.

FIGURE 7.31 Moving an object with grips.

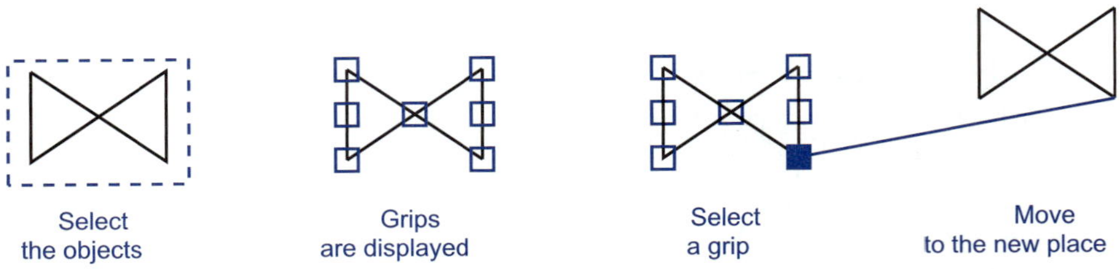

Field Notes

- All grip selected objects are moved, regardless of whether any other grips are selected.
- A new base point can be specified at *any time* for both single move operations or multiple copy operations.

Copying with the Grips MOVE Command

The grips MOVE command has a Copy option that allows you to copy objects. The Copy option can be used to pick the locations for copies, or you can use snap locations. The Copy option works like this to pick copy locations:

Select the objects as shown in Figure 7.32.
Select a grip and then select Copy from the popup menu, or press the space bar or Enter key until you get this grip command and type C:
** MOVE **
Specify move point or [Base point/Copy/Undo/eXit]: **C**↵
** MOVE (multiple) **
Specify move point or [Base point/Copy/Undo/eXit]:
The MOVE (multiple) command actually makes copies. Move the cursor and pick location for as many copies as desired. Press Enter when done.

You can also place multiple copies at regularly spaced intervals with offset snap locations. ***Offset snap locations*** are established by the distance between the selected object and the location of the first copy. All other copies are then placed at an offset distance equal to the first distance. Figure 7.32A displays this appli-

FIGURE 7.32 Copying an object with grips. (A) Making copies with the offset snap location method. (B) Picking the location of multiple copies.

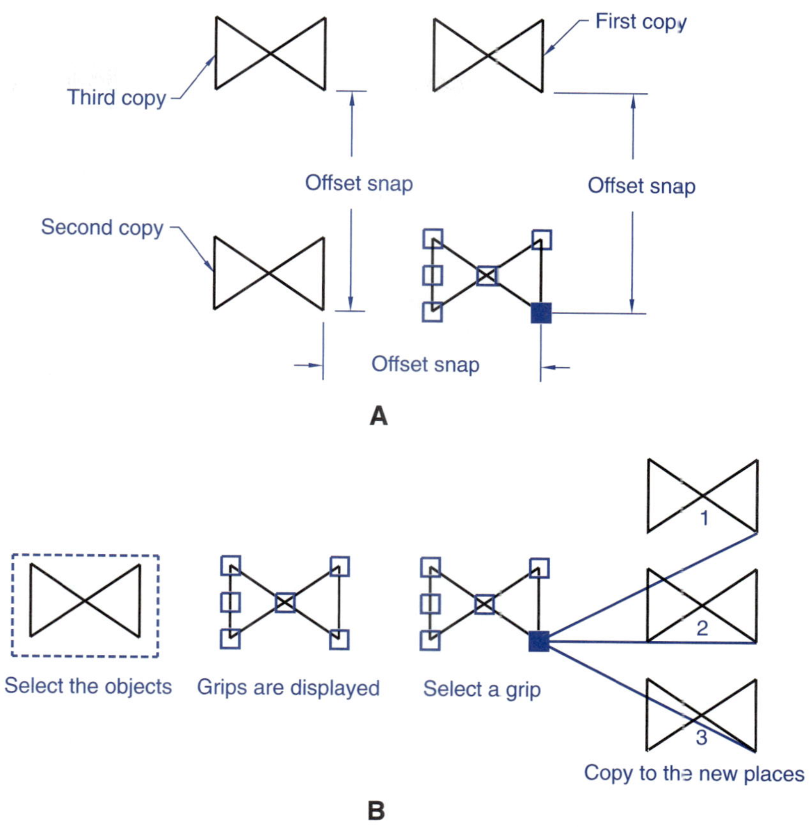

cation and allows you to see the difference between picking the copies in Figure 7.32B. The following sequence is used to demonstrate this process:

Select the objects as shown in Figure 7.32B.
Select a grip and then select Copy from the popup menu, or press the space bar or Enter key, or type MO to get this grip command and then type C:
** MOVE **
Specify move point or [Base point/Copy/Undo/eXit]: **C**↵
** MOVE (multiple) **
Specify move point or [Base point/Copy/Undo/eXit]:

- *Move the cursor and pick location for the first copy. The distance between the selected object and the first copy is the offset snap distance.*
- *Hold down the Shift key and place additional copies. The additional copies are automatically placed at the same offset snap distance.*
- *Press Enter when done.*

Exercise 7.16 **Estimated time required: 5 min.**

1. Begin a new drawing.
2. Draw an object similar to the original object shown in Figure 7.31.
3. Use grips to move the object as shown in Figure 7.31.
4. Use grips and the MOVE Copy option to make copies of the objects shown in Figures 7.32A and B.
5. Save as EX7.16, and close the drawing.

Rotating with Grips

You can use the ROTATE grip command to rotate objects by selecting a grip as a base point and then either rotating and picking the desired position or entering a rotation angle. The grip ROTATE command works like this:

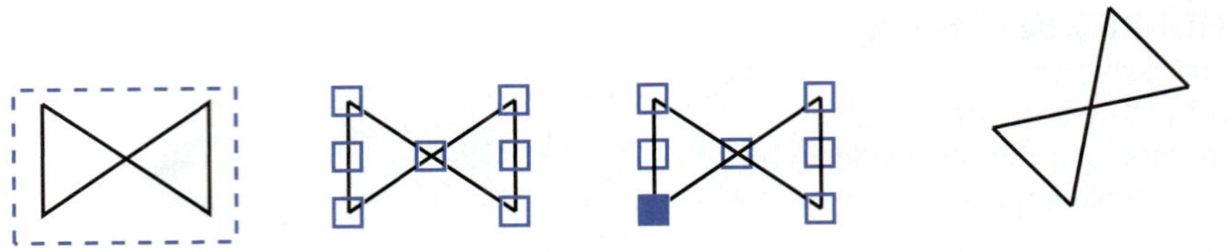

FIGURE 7.33 Rotating an object with grips.

Select the objects as shown in Figure 7.33.
Select a grip and then press the space bar or Enter key until you get this grip command, select Rotate from the shortcut menu, or type RO:
** ROTATE **
Specify rotation angle or [Base point/Copy/Undo/Reference/eXit]: ⟨*rotate by dragging and pick or type an angle such as* **45** *and press Enter*⟩

Field Notes

The ability to change the base point while determining a rotation specification, even between individual copies when using the multiple copy option, gives you maximum flexibility.

Making Multiple Rotations

The grip ROTATE command, as previously discussed, makes a single rotation unless you enter the Copy option. The Copy option lets you make multiple rotations. Enter the ROTATE Copy option like this:

Select the objects.
Select a grip and then press the space bar or Enter key until you get this grip command, select Rotate from the popup menu, or type RO:
** ROTATE **
Specify rotation angle or [Base point/Copy/Undo/Reference/eXit]: **C↵**
** ROTATE (multiple) **
Specify rotation angle or [Base point/Copy/Undo/Reference/eXit]: ⟨*drag the objects and pick the desired rotations or type angles and press Enter after each; press Enter when done.*⟩

Using the Grip Rotation Reference Option

The grip ROTATE command's Reference option works just like the ROTATE command Reference option discussed earlier in this chapter. Follow these steps:

Select the objects.
Select a grip and then press the space bar or Enter key until you get this grip command, select Rotate from the popup menu, or type RO:
** ROTATE **
Specify rotation angle or [Base point/Copy/Undo/Reference/eXit]: **R↵**
Specify reference angle <0>: ⟨*enter a reference angle or pick points*⟩
** ROTATE **
Specify new angle or [Base point/Copy/Undo/Reference/eXit]: ⟨*enter new angle or pick points*⟩

Exercise 7.17 — Estimated time required: 5 min.

1. Open EX7.16.
2. Select one of the objects.
3. Use grips to rotate the object as shown in Figure 7.33.
4. Select another one of the objects.
5. Use grips and the ROTATE command's Copy option to make three rotated copies of the object.
6. Save as EX7.17, and close the drawing.

Scaling with Grips

You can resize objects by using the grips SCALE command. This command allows you to select a grip and then scale the objects by moving the cursor to dynamically drag the objects to the desired scale, or you can type a scale factor and press Enter. You can also use the Reference option, which works the same way as previously described when using the Reference option to scale objects. Follow these steps when scaling objects with grips (see Figure 7.34):

Select the objects.
Select a grip and then press the space bar or Enter key until you get this grip command, select Scale from the popup menu, or type SC:
** SCALE **
Specify scale factor or [Base point/Copy/Undo/Reference/eXit]: ⟨*move the cursor to size the object or type a scale factor such as* **.5** *to scale down or* **1.5** *to scale up and press Enter* ↵⟩

FIGURE 7.34 Using the Scale factor option to scale objects with grips.

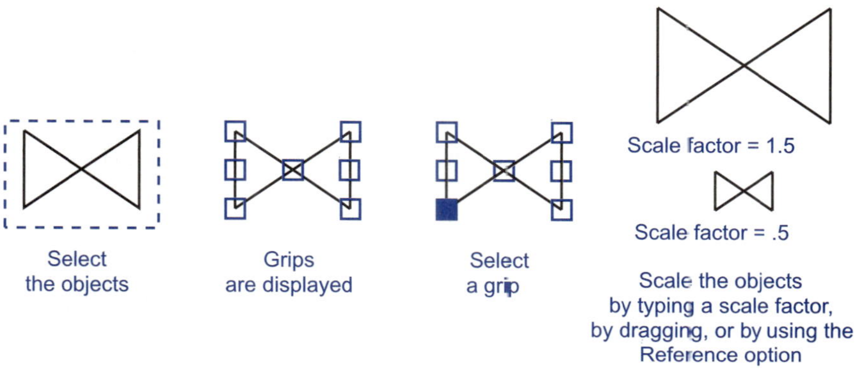

Field Notes

The ability to change the base point while determining a scale factor, even between individual copies when using the multiple copy option, gives you maximum flexibility.

Exercise 7.18 — Estimated time required: 5 min.

1. Open EX7.17.
2. Select one of the objects.
3. Use grips to scale the object with a 0.5 scale factor.
4. Select another one of the objects and use the grips to scale the object with a 1.5 scale factor.
5. Save as EX7.18, and close the drawing.

Mirroring with Grips

You can easily mirror objects with grips by selecting the objects, selecting a grip, and then accessing the grip MIRROR command. The grip you select automatically becomes the first point of the mirror line. Now, move the cursor and pick the second point of the mirror line. Having ORTHO on helps establish a vertical or horizontal mirror line. Use the Base point option if you want to select another point to be the first mirror line point. The MIRROR command automatically removes the original object, as shown in Figure 7.35.

Field Notes

The base point for the mirror line need not be a grip point. It can be picked anywhere, typed with coordinates, or picked using object snap or any other valid point entry method. This is true for all of the grip command options.

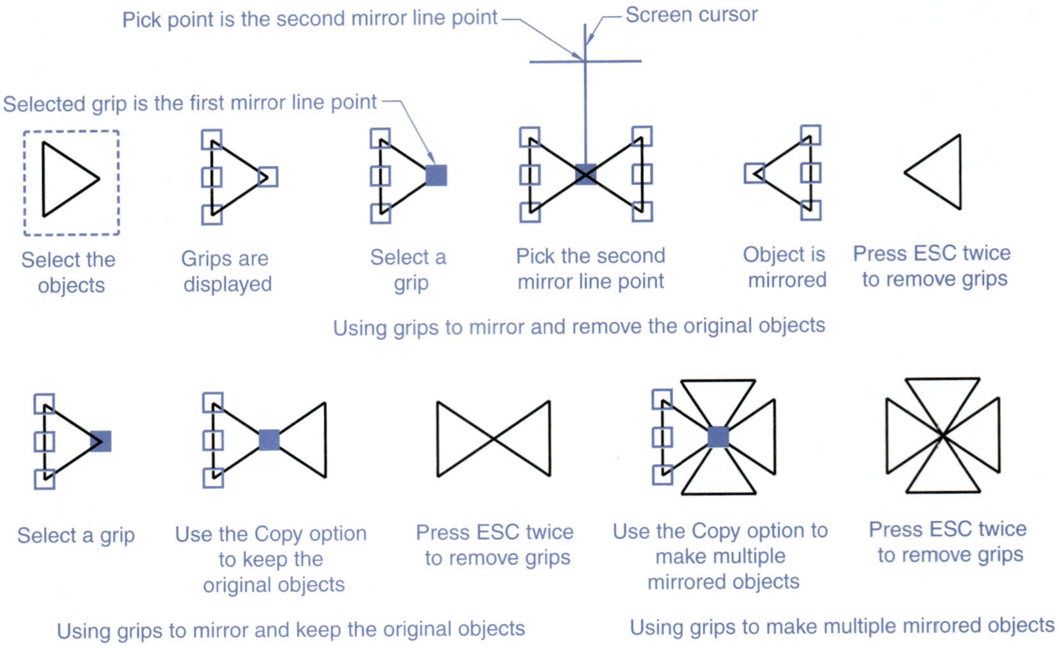

FIGURE 7.35 Mirroring objects with grips.

Use the Copy option or hold down the Shift key when picking the second point of the mirror line. This activates the multiple MIRROR command and keeps the original object while allowing you to mirror more than one of the objects if needed. Press Enter or type **X** for exit to get back to the Command: prompt. Use the Base point and Copy options together to change base points while making one or more mirrored objects (see Figure 7.35). The grips MIRROR command works like this:

Select the objects as shown in Figure 7.35.
Select a grip and then press the space bar or Enter key until you get this grip command, select Mirror from the shortcut menu, or type MI:
** MIRROR **
Specify second point or [Base point/Copy/Undo/eXit]: ⟨*pick the second point of the mirror line*⟩
Command:

Exercise 7.19

Estimated time required: 5 min.

1. Begin a new drawing.
2. Draw an object similar to the original object shown in the upper left corner of Figure 7.35.
3. Copy the object to two other locations.
4. Use grips to mirror one of the objects without keeping the original object. Use an object that is similar to the top example in Figure 7.35.
5. Use grips to mirror another one of the objects while keeping the object being mirrored. Use an object that is similar to the lower left example in Figure 7.35.
6. Select another one of the objects and make multiple mirrored objects. Use an object that is similar to the lower right example in Figure 7.35.
7. Save as EX7.19, and close the drawing.

Changing the Properties of an Object with Grips

If you pick an object to activate the grips and then select a grip to make it hot, you can press the right mouse button to get the Grips popup menu shown in Figure 7.36A. This popup menu is connected to the screen cursor drag line when you pick the right mouse button. Near the bottom of this menu is the Properties option. The other options are the grip editing commands and related functions that were explained earlier. Picking

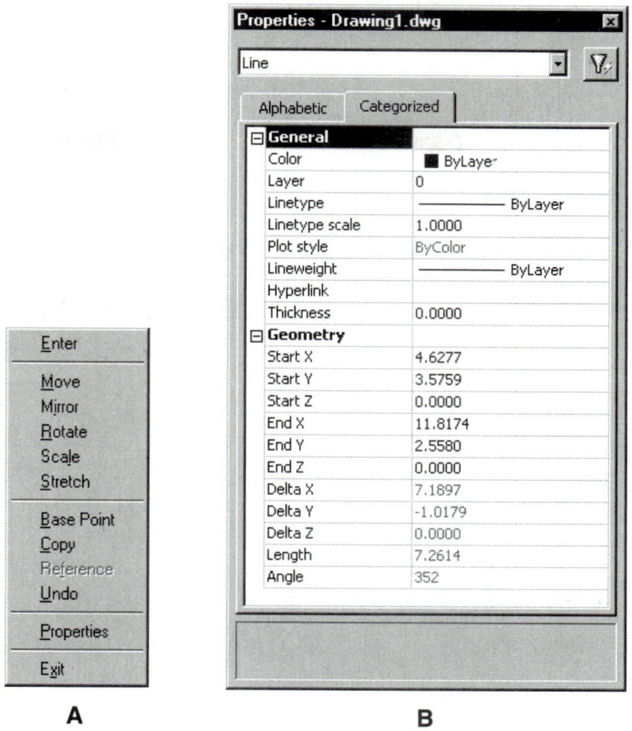

FIGURE 7.36 (A) The Grips shortcut menu is opened by pressing the right mouse button after selecting a grip. Then pick the Properties option to open the Properties window. (B) The Properties window with a single line selected.

the Properties option opens the Properties window using the currently selected objects. This allows you to edit any of the adjustable properties for the selected objects. Picking this options while a single object is selected provides the greatest flexibility. Figure 7.36B shows the Properties window contents when a single line is selected.

Exercise 7.20

Estimated time required: 5 min.

1. Begin a new drawing.
2. Draw a line, a circle, and an arc based on your own design and specifications.
3. Pick each of the objects individually to activate the grips. Select a grip to make it hot, then open the Properties window. Make changes to the properties of each object. Observe the speed and convenience available in changing objects in this manner.
4. Save as EX7.20, and close the drawing.

LEARNING CHECKPOINT

- ☐ Identify at least one advantage of editing with grips.
- ☐ What happens to a grip when you select it?
- ☐ List the grip edit commands.
- ☐ How do you cycle through the grip edit commands?
- ☐ What do you do if you want to access a specific grip command without cycling through the grip commands?
- ☐ How do you select multiple grips?
- ☐ How do you copy with grips?

Changing Geometry

- Using Grips to Edit Objects Quickly

Trimming and Extending Objects

AutoCAD LT provides you with commands that can be used to remove a portion of an object, trim objects to create clean intersections, or extend objects to meet other objects.

Removing a Portion from an Object

Modify
Break

Modify
Break

BREAK
BR

The BREAK command is used to remove a portion of an object or to provide a break at one point to create two separate objects. This command can be used in a number of different ways that are determined by how you enter the command. The BREAK command can be accessed by picking Break in the Modify pull-down menu, by picking the Break button in the Modify toolbar, or by typing **BR** or **BREAK** at the Command: prompt.

Breaking an Object at One Point

An object can be broken at one point when you want to split a single object into two objects. The object is broken at one point, yet it still looks like the original object, but it is now two objects connected at the break point. When you enter the BREAK command, you are asked to select an object. If you select an object by picking, the point you pick becomes the first break point. AutoCAD LT then asks you to Enter the second point. You can pick the second point exactly at the first point by entering the @ symbol and then pressing Enter. The object is now broken at one point. The command sequence looks like this:

Command: **BR** or **BREAK**↵
Select object: *<pick the object at the point where you want it broken>*
Specify second break point or [First point]: **@**↵
Command:

After selecting an object to break, you decide that you want to break the object at a single point that is different from the selected point; you can use the F option. The F option allows you to select a new first point like this:

Command: **BR** or **BREAK**↵
Select object: *<pick the object>*
Specify second break point or [First point]: **F**↵
Specify first break point: *<specify the location where you want it broken>*
Specify second break point: **@**↵
Command:

Field Notes

The reason AutoCAD LT provides the BREAK command's First point option is to allow a coordinate entry or an object snap point to be specified for a more accurate break point specification.

Breaking an Object at Two Points

An object can be broken at two points by picking an object to break. The point of selection becomes the first break point, and then you pick a second break point, as shown in Figure 7.37. The command looks like this:

Command: **BR** or **BREAK**↵
Select object: *<pick the object at the desired break point>*
Specify second break point or [First point]: *<specify the end of the break>*
Command:

If you select an object to break and then decide that you want to pick another first break point, you can use the F option. Doing this allows you to select another first break point like this:

Command: **BR** or **BREAK**↵
Select object: *<pick the object>*
Specify second break point or [First point]: **F**↵
Specify first break point: *<specify the first point of the break>*
Specify second break point: *<specify the end of the break>*
Command:

FIGURE 7.37 Breaking a line object between two points.

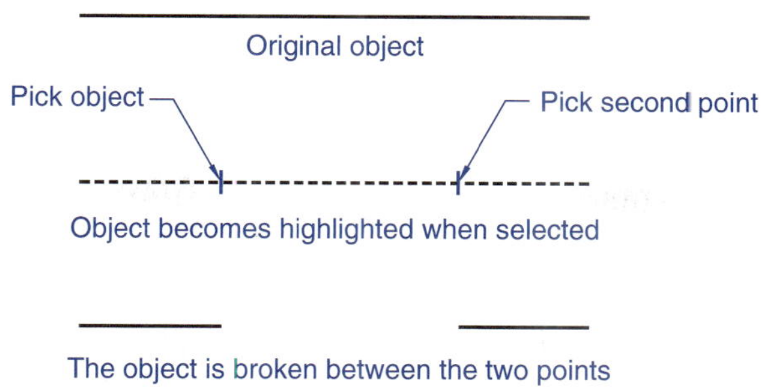

Field Notes

The break happens in a counterclockwise direction when breaking a portion out of a circle, arc, ellipse, or closed spline object. Splines are discussed in Chapter 8. Figure 7.38 demonstrates what happens when breaking a circle depending on how you pick the points.

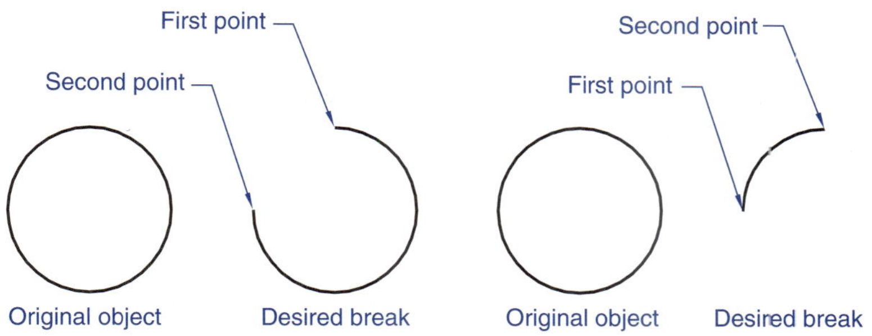

FIGURE 7.38 Breaking a circle between two points. Notice how the break points are selected.

Exercise 7.21 — Estimated time required: 5 min.

1. Begin a new drawing.
2. Draw a line and break it similar to Figure 7.37.
3. Draw a circle and make a copy of it.
4. Break the first circle by picking points in a counterclockwise direction similar to the example shown on the left in Figure 7.38.
5. Break the second circle by picking points in a clockwise direction similar to the example shown on the right in Figure 7.38.
6. Save as EX7.21, and close the drawing.

Trimming Objects

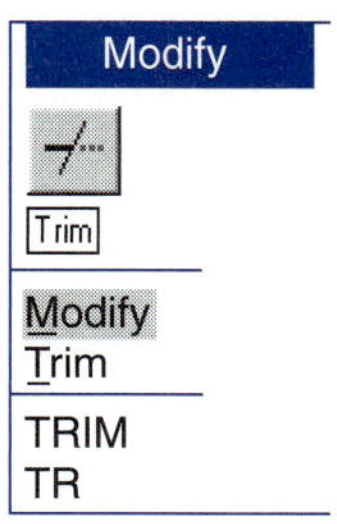

The TRIM command is a useful tool when you need to trim objects to meet other objects. The command is accessed by picking the Trim toolbar button, by picking Trim in the Modify pull-down menu, or by typing **TR** or **TRIM** at the Command: prompt. When you enter this command, AutoCAD LT asks you to select the cutting edges. ***Cutting edges*** are objects selected that specify the point where a trimmed object is to be trimmed back to. This point is located at the intersection of the cutting edge object and the object to be trimmed. You can think of the cutting edge objects as the blades used to cut the object being trimmed. Most normal drawing objects having an edge definition that can be used as cutting edges. These edges include lines, arcs, circles, polylines, splines, ellipses, text, xlines, and rays. Objects with no edge definitions cannot be used, such as solids, point objects, and blocks. After selecting the cutting edges, you are asked to select the objects to trim. Look at Figure 7.39 as you follow this command:

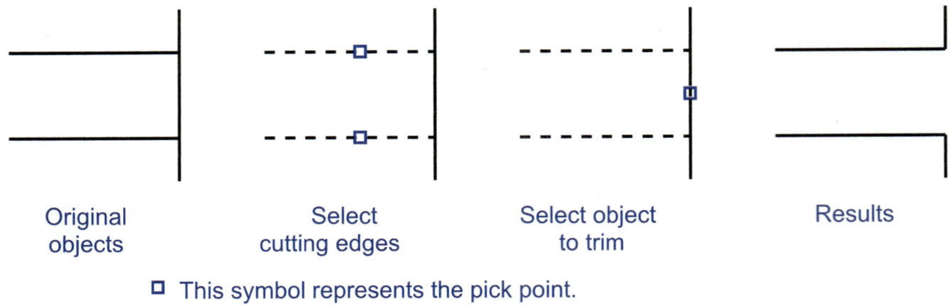

FIGURE 7.39 Using the TRIM command.

Command: **TR** or **TRIM**↵
Current settings: Projection=UCS Edge=None
Select cutting edges ...
Select objects: *<pick the cutting edges>*
n found
Select objects: ↵
Select object to trim or [Project/Edge/Undo]: *<pick objects near the end to trim>*
Select object to trim or [Project/Edge/Undo]: ↵
Command:

In some applications, the cutting edges and the objects to trim are the same. Objects that have been specified as cutting edges can be trimmed just like any other object if they intersect a cutting edge. An example is the keyway that needs to be drawn in the hub shown in Figure 7.40. Notice the selection of cutting edges and objects to trim.

The cutting edge determines where an object is trimmed; the point that you pick when specifying the object to trim determines which side is removed and which side stays. The side that is picked is trimmed, and the remaining portion of the object is left on the other side of the cutting edge. When using a wide polyline cutting edge, the actual trim location is at its center line. Polylines are explained in Chapter 8.

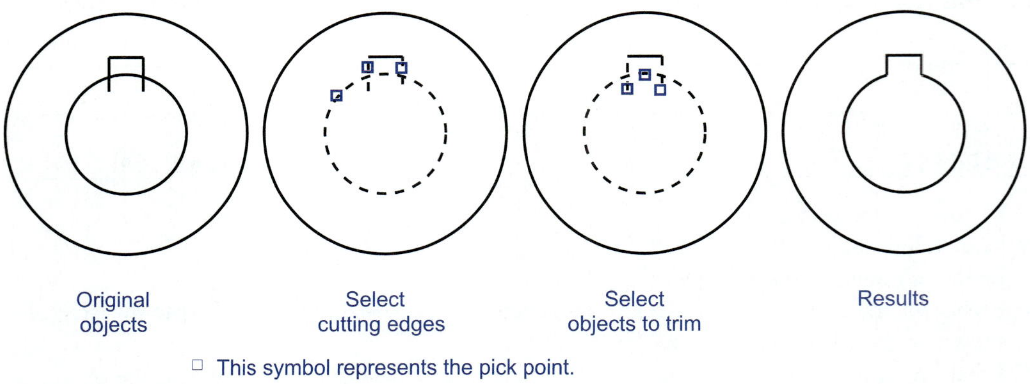

FIGURE 7.40 Using the TRIM command.

To be able to be trimmed, an object must have a portion remaining on the other side of the cutting edge after the trim is complete. To understand why, it helps to visualize the cutting edge again as a blade and the line segment as the material being cut. The material has been brought up to the edge of the blade but does not actually cross the blade's path. If it does not cross the cut path, then the blade cannot cut it. To remove such a line segment, use the ERASE command. Attempting to trim an object that does not cross the cutting edge produces the message:

Object does not intersect an edge.

Some closed objects, such as circles, ellipses, and closed splines must intersect a cutting edge in more than one location. If a line intersects only one cutting edge, the section from the cutting edge to the end is trimmed. A circle has no end to trim off. So, if the circle intersects only one cutting edge and only in one location, both ends of the trim section are at the same point and there is nothing to trim. Such an attempt produces the message:

Circle must intersect twice.

If you try to trim an object that cannot be trimmed, such as text or a block, the following message is displayed:

Cannot TRIM this object.

If the trim operation that you are trying to do comes up with unexpected results, use the Undo option within the TRIM command and try again.

Trimming Multiple Objects

Many situations happen that require you to trim several objects at the same time. This is common, as shown in the example of Figure 7.41A, where a series of lines must be trimmed back to another line. In this example, the Fence selection option is used to conveniently pick all the lines to be trimmed. The command sequence works like this, and the results are demonstrated in Figure 7.41:

Command: **TR** or **TRIM**↵
Current settings: Projection=UCS Edge=None
Select cutting edges ...
Select objects: <*pick the cutting edges*>
n found
Select objects: ↵
Select object to trim or [Project/Edge/Undo]: **F**↵
First fence point: <*pick first point of fence*>
Specify endpoint of line or [Undo]: <*pick additional fence points*>
Specify endpoint of line or [Undo]: ↵
Select object to trim or [Project/Edge/Undo]: ↵
Command:

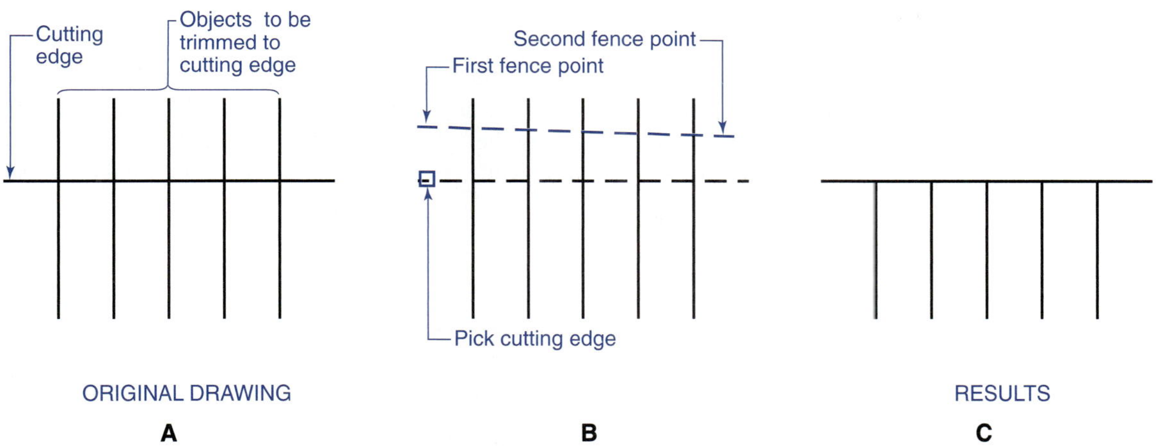

FIGURE 7.41 Trimming several objects back to a cutting edge with the Fence selection option.

Trimming to an Extended Intersection

The TRIM command can be used in a way that does not require a specified cutting edge to actually touch the object being trimmed. Instead, if an extended intersection exists, it can be used as the trim point. The term ***extended intersection*** describes the point at which one object would intersect another if both objects were extended far enough along their natural paths of extension. For example, an arc being checked for extended intersection is extended along its natural radius path.

To trim to an extended intersection, the Edge option of the TRIM command must first be set properly. If you look back to previous examples of TRIM, you will see in the initial status report that "Edge = None." This means that extended intersections are not checked for and only cutting edges that physically intersect the object being trimmed are used. The following command sequence sets the Edgemode to Extend and continues to trim the line as shown in Figure 7.42:

Command: **TR** or **TRIM**↵
Current settings: Projection=UCS Edge=None
Select cutting edges ...
Select objects: <*pick the cutting edge*>
n found

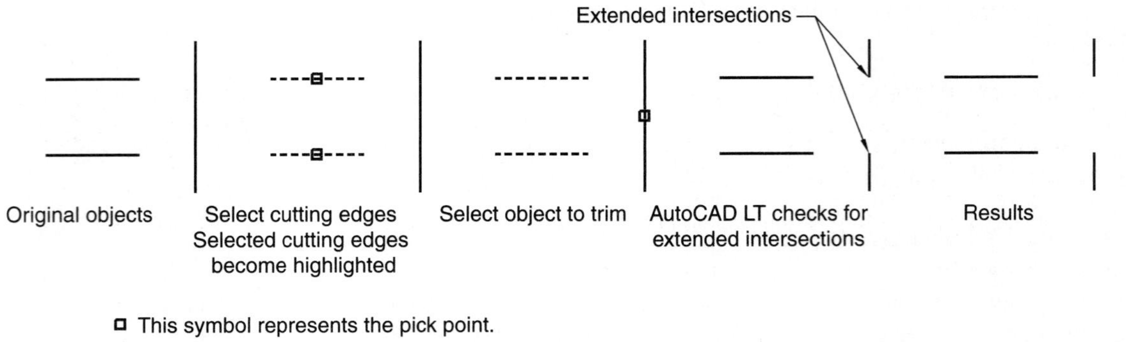

FIGURE 7.42 Using the TRIM command with an implied intersection.

```
Select objects: ↵
Select object to trim or [Project/Edge/Undo]: E↵
Enter an implied edge extension mode [Extend/No extend] <No extend>: E↵
Select object to trim or [Project/Edge/Undo]: <select the object to trim>
Select object to trim or [Project/Edge/Undo]: ↵
Command:
```

Notice that the TRIM command now reports the changed status of Edgemode:

```
Command: TR or TRIM↵
Current settings: Projection=UCS Edge=Extend
Select cutting edges ...
Select objects:
```

EDGEMODE is a system variable that can be set in either the TRIM or EXTEND commands. If EDGEMODE is set in TRIM then it also has the same setting for the use of EXTEND, which is discussed next in this chapter. Previously, you saw the Edge option set during the TRIM command. The Edge option can also be set with EDGEMODE. No extend is a 0 (zero) setting, while Extend is a 1 setting. EDGEMODE works like this:

```
Command: EDGEMODE↵
Enter new value for EDGEMODE <0>: 1↵
Command:
```

Using AutoCAD LT Smart Trimming

AutoCAD LT is smart enough to look for the closest intersecting object or extended intersecting object in the direction of your pick. This object is then used as the cutting edge. This feature is called the *smart* mode. To activate the smart mode, press Enter when you are asked to Select cutting edges. The selected object is automatically trimmed using the following sequence:

```
Command: TR or TRIM↵
Current settings: Projection=UCS Edge=Extend
Select cutting edges ...
Select objects: ↵
Select object to trim or [Project/Edge/Undo]: <pick objects to trim>
Select object to trim or [Project/Edge/Undo]: ↵
Command:
```

The smart mode has the following conditions:

- The EDGEMODE setting for an extended intersection affects the smart mode.
- AutoCAD LT uses an actual intersection if found before an extendied intersection.
- The object must be visible on the screen and cannot be a block or xref object. Blocks and xrefs are explained in Chapter 12.
- Trimming cannot be done between one actual and one extended intersection, but it can be done between two actual intersections, or two extended intersections.

Field Notes

A common architectural application of the TRIM command is the clean up of intersecting walls similar to the example shown in Figure 7.43A. All four wall lines are selected as cutting edges and then the short internal line segments are selected as the objects to trim. This is an excellent application of the smart mode. With the smart mode, there is no need to select cutting edges, just pick the locations to be trimmed as shown in Figure 7.43B.

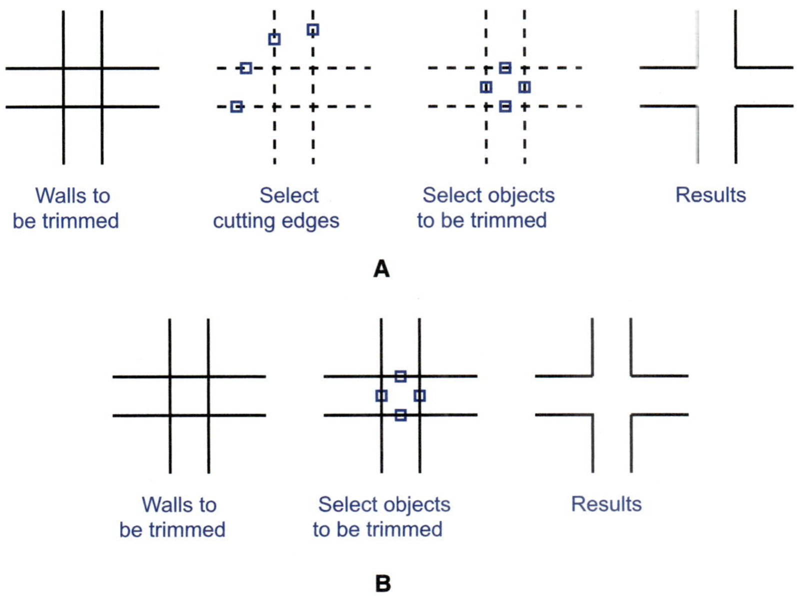

□ This symbol represents the pick point.

FIGURE 7.43 Using the TRIM command on intersecting lines. (A) Selecting objects to be trimmed and selecting the cutting edges. (B) Using the smart mode.

Exercise 7.22 — Estimated time required: 10 min.

1. Begin a new drawing.
2. Make a drawing similar to the original objects shown in Figure 7.39.
3. Trim the vertical line similar to the results shown in Figure 7.39.
4. Draw two concentric circles and the start of a keyway similar to the original objects shown in Figure 7.40.
5. Trim the keyway similar to the results shown in Figure 7.40.
6. Make a drawing similar to Figure 7.41A and use the Fence selection option to help trim the line extensions back to the cutting edge, as in Figure 7.41C.
7. Make a drawing similar to the original objects shown in Figure 7.42.
8. Trim the vertical line to the implied intersection with the horizontal lines similar to the results shown in Figure 7.42.
9. Draw two intersecting walls similar to the walls to be trimmed in Figure 7.43A.
10. Use the TRIM command to remove the lines inside the walls as was done in Figure 7.43A.
11. Draw two intersecting walls similar to the walls to be trimmed in Figure 7.43B.
12. Use the TRIM command in the smart mode to trim the lines inside the walls as was done in Figure 7.43B.
13. Save as EX7.22, and close the drawing.

Extending Objects

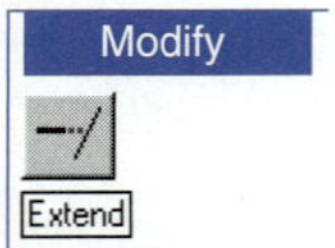

Modify
Extend

EXTEND
EX

The EXTEND command provides the opposite function of the TRIM command. EXTEND allows you to extend objects to meet other objects. The objects that you extend to are called the ***boundary edges.*** AutoCAD LT asks you to select the boundary edges and then select the objects to extend. For example, extending lines to circles is easy with the EXTEND command. The spokes of the wheel in Figure 7.44 are extended to the wheel and the hub with convenience and accuracy. This command is accessed by picking Extend from the Modify pull-down menu, by selecting the Extend button from the Modify toolbar, or by typing **EX** or **EXTEND** at the Command: prompt. Follow this command sequence to extend the spokes in Figure 7.44:

Command: **EX** or **EXTEND**↵
Current settings: Projection=UCS Edge=None
Select boundary edges ...
Select objects: *<select boundary edge objects (highlighted in Fig.7.44)>*
n found
Select objects: ↵
Select object to extend or [Project/Edge/Undo]: *<pick near the end of each spoke line>*
Select object to extend or [Project/Edge/Undo]: ↵
Command:

FIGURE 7.44 Using the EXTEND command.

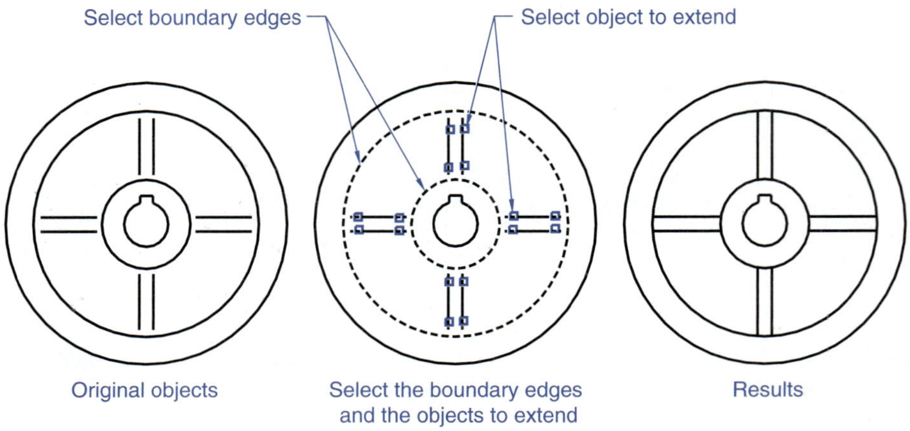

Field Notes

- The Edge option in the EXTEND command is used for extending objects to an implied intersection. The edge option works the same as in the TRIM command but rather than trimming at an implied intersection, the EXTEND command's Edge option extends the selected object. Remember from an earlier discussion that the EDGEMODE system variable also affects the EXTEND command's use with implied intersections.
- The Project option in the TRIM and EXTEND commands is used for trimming and extending objects in 3-D applications and is discussed in Chapter 14.
- The Undo option is available in these editing commands to let you undo the previous selection in case you make a mistake or change your mind.
- Attempting to extend an object that does not cross the boundary edge produces the message:

  No edge in that direction.

If you try to extend an object that cannot be extended, such as text or a block, the following message is displayed:

  Cannot EXTEND this object.

Using AutoCAD LT Smart Extending

The smart mode was explained earlier in the discussion of the TRIM command. Smart mode can also be used with the EXTEND command by automatically looking for the closest intersecting object or extended intersecting object in the direction of your pick. This object is then used as the boundary edge. To activate the smart mode, press Enter when you are asked to select boundary edges. The selected object is automatically extended using the following sequence:

Command: **EX** or **EXTEND**↵
Current settings: Projection=UCS Edge=None
Select boundary edges ...
Select objects: ↵
Select object to extend or [Project/Edge/Undo]: *<pick the object near the end to trim>*
Select object to extend or [Project/Edge/Undo]: ↵
Command:

Trim and Extend are two of the default options on the popup cursor menu when you right-click at the Command: prompt. When selected this way, these commands are automatically put into "smart" mode.

Exercise 7.23 **Estimated time required: 10 min.**

1. Begin a new drawing.
2. Make a drawing similar to the original objects shown in Figure 7.44.
3. Make a copy of this drawing.
4. Use one drawing to extend the spoke lines to meet the hub and wheel similar to the results shown in Figure 7.44.
5. Use the other drawing to extend the spoke lines to meet the hub and wheel using the smart mode. The task is easier, but the results are similar to the results shown in Figure 7.44.
6. Save as EX7.23, and close the drawing.

Drawing Fillets and Chamfers

AutoCAD LT allows you to easily draw rounded corners called ***fillets*** and angled corners called ***chamfers.*** In mechanical drafting for the manufacturing industry, fillets are rounded inside corners and rounds are rounded outside corners, but AutoCAD LT treats them all as fillets. Chamfers in mechanical drafting are slightly angled corners. AutoCAD LT lets you make rounded and angled corners to any desired specification and for any drafting field by using the FILLET and CHAMFER commands. Draw rounded corners by picking Fillet in the Modify pull-down menu, by picking the Fillet button in the Modify toolbar, or by typing **F** or **FILLET.** Draw angled corners by picking Chamfer in the Modify pull-down menu, by picking the Chamfer toolbar button, or by typing **CHA** or **CHAMFER** at the Command: prompt.

Drawing Fillets

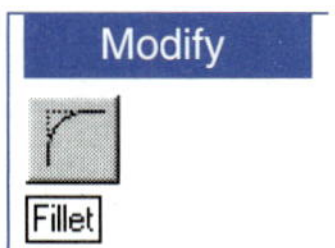

Modify
Fillet

FILLET
F

Fillets are drawn by specifying a radius and then selecting the objects to be filleted. The objects can be intersecting or nonintersecting. If objects do not intersect, the FILLET command extends the objects to where they would meet the radius or trims them, as needed, after applying a fillet. You can fillet lines, xlines, rays, circles, arcs, and true ellipses. You can also fillet all of the corners of a rectangle and polyline at one time. For the corners of a rectangle to all be filleted at one time, the rectangle must have been drawn with the RECTANG command. Polylines are explained in Chapter 8. Fillets are drawn on the current layer, in the current color, and with the current linetype. Be sure to properly set the current layer if you want the fillet to match the layer of the connecting objects.

If the objects being filleted are on the same layer, the fillet radius is created on that layer. If the objects are on different layers the radius is created on the current layer. This is also true of color and linetype—if the objects are the same color/linetype then that color/linetype is used, otherwise the current color/linetype is used.

Setting the Fillet Radius

Before drawing fillets, you need to consider the fillet radius. The initial default fillet radius is 0.5 and once it has been changed, the default is the same as the previous setting. The fillet radius is set by entering the Radius option and then typing a radius value like this:

Command: **F** or **FILLET**↵
Current settings: Mode = TRIM, Radius = 0.5000
Select first object or [Polyline/Radius/Trim]: **R**↵
Specify fillet radius <0.5000>: **.25**↵
Command:

The Command: prompt returns, but you can press the Enter key or space bar to immediately reenter the FILLET command and select objects to fillet. Figure 7.45 shows fillets drawn on several different objects and situations. This is the command sequence:

Command: ↵
Current settings: Mode = TRIM, Radius = 0.2500
Select first object or [Polyline/Radius/Trim]: *<pick the first object>*
Select second object: *<pick second object>*
Command:

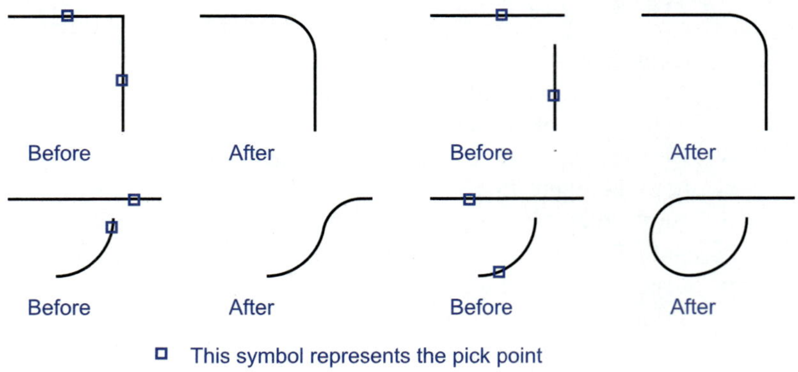

FIGURE 7.45 The results of applying the FILLET command to different objects.

The following points represent some very important applications and practices when drawing fillets:

- Look at Figure 7.45 and notice the pick point associated with drawing fillets to the line and arc objects. The original objects are the same, but the results are different depending on where you pick the original objects.
- A fillet radius of 0 (zero) can be used to connect two nonintersecting objects or to remove a fillet from a polyline as shown in Figure 7.46. This option is commonly used in drafting and is a convenient way for cleaning up corner intersections. If the rounded corner is where two line objects intersect with a fillet, the result of applying a 0 (zero) FILLET Radius is a corner, but the rounded fillet remains.
- The Polyline option is used to fillet the corners of a polyline. If the polyline is closed, the Close option must have been used to close the last segment for all of the corners to be filleted or chamfered. Use this option by typing **P** and then picking the polyline. Polylines are discussed in Chapter 8. If a line and adjacent polyline are filleted, the line becomes part of the polyline.

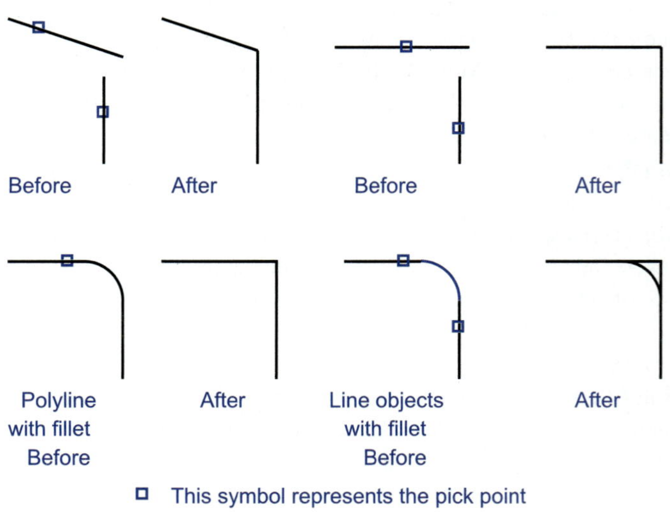

FIGURE 7.46 The results of applying a 0 (zero) FILLET Radius to different objects.

Using the FILLET Command's Trim Option

Fillets are usually set with a specified radius to use for rounding corners. The Trim option of the FILLET command allows you to decide if you want to keep or remove the original corner during the filleting process. The corner is trimmed by the initial default. The default then changes to the current setting. Figure 7.47 shows the difference between Trim and No trim. If you want to keep the corner, enter the Trim option like this and type **N** for No trim:

Command: **F** or **FILLET↵**
Current settings: Mode = TRIM, Radius = 0.2500
Select first object or [Polyline/Radius/Trim]: **T↵**
Enter Trim mode option [Trim/No trim] <Trim>: **N↵**
Select first object or [Polyline/Radius/Trim]: *<pick first object>*
Select second object: *<pick second object>*
Command:

FIGURE 7.47 A comparison between the FILLET command's Trim and No trim options.

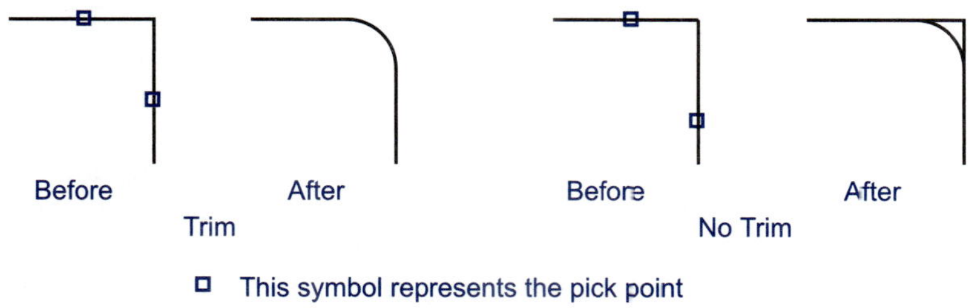

Field Notes

The current setting of the Trim option in the FILLET command is the same for the CHAMFER command, which is discussed next. Trim set in either the FILLET command or the CHAMFER command affects both commands. The Trim can be set within the command as previously shown or set using the TRIMMODE system variable. When TRIMMODE is 0 (zero), the Trim option is active. When TRIMMODE is 1, the No trim option is active. The TRIMMODE variable works like this:

Command: **TRIMMODE↵**
Enter new value for TRIMMODE <1>: **0↵**

Filleting Parallel Lines

The FILLET command can be used to make a rounded connection between two parallel objects such as lines, xlines, and rays. When you select two parallel lines for filleting, AutoCAD LT ignores the current fillet radius setting and automatically draws a round with a diameter that is equal to the distance between lines, as shown in Figure 7.48. If the parallel lines are unequal in length and you pick the longest line, the shortest line is extended to meet the radius. If you pick the shortest line, the longest line is automatically trimmed to meet the radius. This application is controlled by the current TRIMMODE setting.

FIGURE 7.48 Filleting parallel lines.

Exercise 7.24 **Estimated time required: 10 min.**

1. Open EX7.23.
2. Use a 0.125 fillet radius to fillet where the spokes intersect the wheel and hub.
3. Make drawings similar to the before objects shown in Figure 7.45.
4. Set a desired fillet radius and fillet the objects as shown in the results in Figure 7.45.
5. Make drawings similar to the before objects shown in Figure 7.46.
6. Set a 0 (zero) fillet radius and fillet the objects as shown in the results in Figure 7.46.
7. Make drawings similar to the before objects shown in Figure 7.47.
8. Set a desired fillet radius and fillet the objects as shown in the results in Figure 7.47. One object has Trim on and the other has No trim.
9. Make a drawing similar to the before object shown in Figure 7.48.
10. Pick the objects for filleting to get the results shown in Figure 7.48.
11. Save as EX7.24, and close the drawing.

Drawing Chamfers

Modify

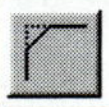

Chamfer

Modify
Chamfer

CHAMFER
CHA

AutoCAD LT provides you with a variety of options for drawing chamfers to intersecting or nonintersecting lines, polylines, xlines, and rays. The CHAMFER command lets you specify a distance for the chamfer lengths, which is referred to as the *Distance method.* You can also specify an angle and distance to establish the chamfer. This is called the *Angle method.* You can switch between methods when using the CHAMFER command by using the Method option and then typing either **D** for Distance or **A** for Angle like this:

Command: **CHA** or **CHAMFER**↵
(NOTRIM mode) Current chamfer Dist1 = 0.5000, Dist2 = 0.5000
Select first line or [Polyline/Distance/Angle/Trim/Method]: **M**↵
Enter trim method [Distance/Angle] <Distance>: *<enter* **D** *or* **A** *or press Enter for the default>*
Select first line or [Polyline/Distance/Angle/Trim/Method]:

Drawing Chamfers with Distances

You can specify equal or different horizontal and vertical chamfer distances with the Distance option. Equal chamfer distances result in a chamfer that is at a 45° angle. The value that you set for the first chamfer distance is automatically set as the default for the second chamfer distance. Accept this default by pressing Enter or type a new value and press Enter:

Command: **CHA** or **CHAMFER**↵
(NOTRIM mode) Current chamfer Dist1 = 0.5000, Dist2 = 0.5000
Select first line or [Polyline/Distance/Angle/Trim/Method]: **D**↵
Specify first chamfer distance <0.5000>: **.75**↵
Specify second chamfer distance <0.7500>: **.5**↵
Command:

Now, press the space bar or the Enter key to begin the CHAMFER command again to draw a chamfer with the distance setting that you just made. Look at Figure 7.49 as you follow this command sequence:

Command: ↵
(NOTRIM mode) Current chamfer Dist1 = 0.7500, Dist2 = 0.5000
Select first line or [Polyline/Distance/Angle/Trim/Method]: *<pick the first line>*
Select second line: *<pick the second line>*
Command:

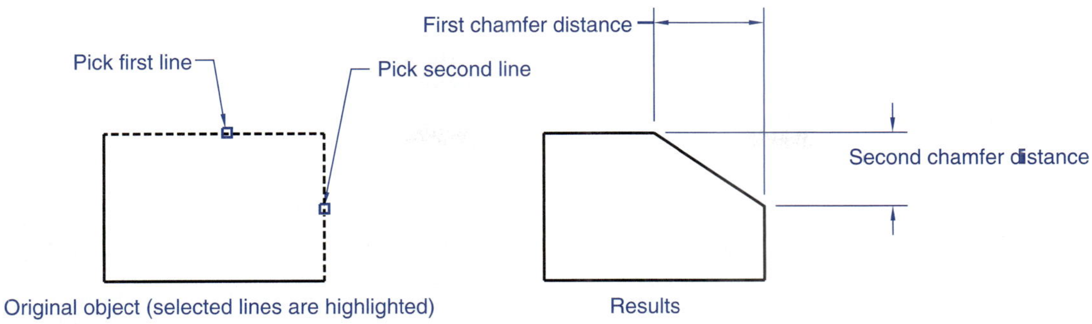

FIGURE 7.49 Using the CHAMFER command to draw a chamfer with distances.

Field Notes

- The chamfering process extends lines or trims lines as needed to create the chamfer in the same manner that this happens with the FILLET command as previously shown.
- If you set both chamfer distances to 0 (zero), the CHAMFER command extends or trims lines as needed to create a corner, but no chamfer is drawn.
- The Polyline option is used to chamfer the corners of polylines in the same manner as discussed with the FILLET command. Polylines are covered in Chapter 8.

Drawing Chamfers with the Distance and Angle Option

In some cases, you may know a chamfer distance and the angle. Use the Angle option to draw a chamfer in this manner. Enter the Angle option to set the chamfer distance and angle line like this:

Command: **CHA** or **CHAMFER**↵
(NOTRIM mode) Current chamfer Dist1 = 0.7500, Dist2 = 0.5000
Select first line or [Polyline/Distance/Angle/Trim/Method]: **A**↵
Specify chamfer length on the first line <1.0000>: **.75**↵
Specify chamfer angle from the first line <0>: **30**↵
Command:

Enter the CHAMFER command again and set the Method to the Angle option if it was previously set to the Distance option, and then draw the desired chamfer as shown in Figure 7.50:

Command: ↵
(NOTRIM mode) Current chamfer Dist1 = 0.7500, Dist2 = 0.5000
Select first line or [Polyline/Distance/Angle/Trim/Method]: **M**↵
Enter trim method [Distance/Angle] <Distance>: **A**↵
Select first line or [Polyline/Distance/Angle/Trim/Method]: *<pick the first line>*
Select second line: *<pick the second line>*
Command:

FIGURE 7.50 Using the CHAMFER command to draw a chamfer with distance and angle.

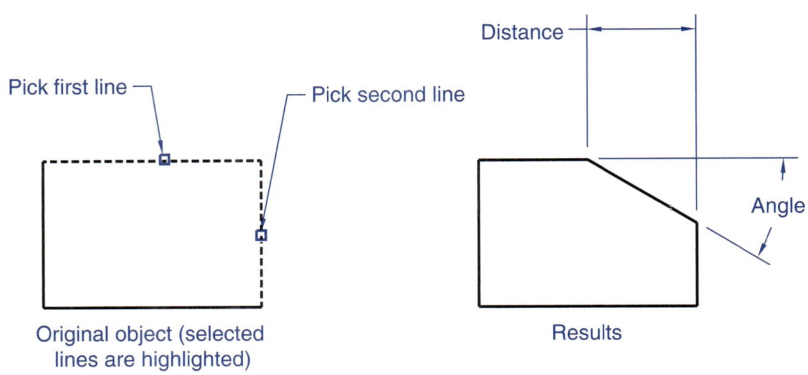

Using the Trim Option

The CHAMFER command's Trim option works just like the Trim option in the Fillet command. The options are Trim and No trim. With Trim on, the original corner is trimmed or extended as necessary. If No trim is active, the original corners are not extended or trimmed.

Exercise 7.25 **Estimated time required: 5 min.**

1. Begin a new drawing.
2. Make a drawing similar to the original object shown in Figure 7.49.
3. Set the chamfer distances to 0.75 and 0.5 and then use the Distance option to draw a chamfer similar to the results shown in Figure 7.49.
4. Make a drawing similar to the original object shown in Figure 7.50.
5. Set the chamfer distances to 0.75 and the angle to 30° and then use the Angle option to draw a chamfer similar to the results shown in Figure 7.50.
6. Save as EX7.25, and close the drawing.

Using the Properties Window to Edit Objects

Object Properties

Properties (Ctrl+1)

Modify
Properties

PROPERTIES
[Ctrl] + [1]

The PROPERTIES command was briefly introduced in Chapter 5 with regard to changing an object's color, layer, linetype, lineweight, and linetype scale. This command is also handy for making quick changes to geometric features. This was introduced to you earlier in this chapter when you picked Properties from the Grips popup menu to open the Properties window (see Figure 7.36). The easiest way to start this command is by picking the Properties button from the Object Properties toolbar, or you can type **PROPERTIES** or Ctrl+1 at the Command: prompt. After the Properties window is displayed, pick an object in your drawing. The Properties window displays the properties for the selected object (see Figure 7.51).

FIGURE 7.51 The Properties window can be used to change geometric features.

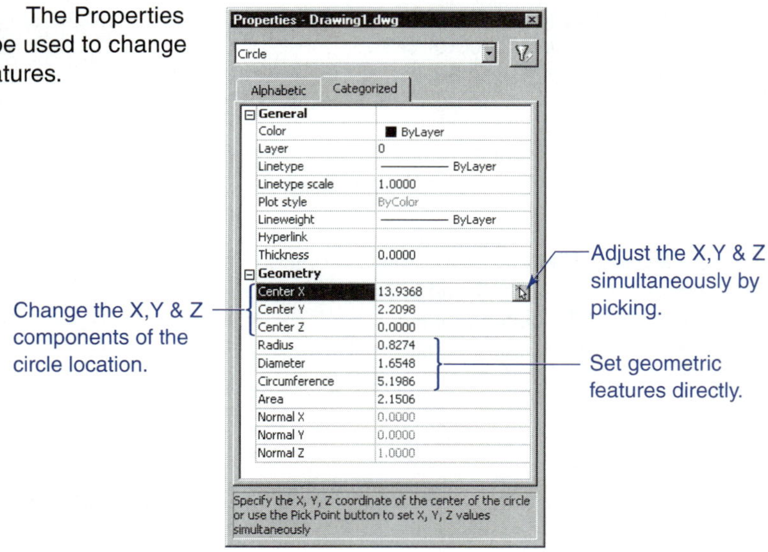

When you change the geometric features of an object, it may directly affect other features as well. For example, if you change the Area of a circle, the Radius and Circumference values must also be changed. AutoCAD LT automatically adjusts related properties as needed to match the values for the properties that you change.

Exercise 7.26 **Estimated time required: 5 min.**

1. Begin a new drawing.
2. Draw a .5-in.-diameter circle.
3. Use the Modify Circle dialog box to change the location of the circle and change the diameter to 1.5.
4. Draw a line 1 in. long.
5. Use the Modify Line dialog box to change the length of the line to 2.5 in.
6. Use the Arc Center option to draw an arc with a .75-in. radius with the start point at 0° and the endpoint at 90°.
7. Use the Modify Arc dialog box to change the start angle to 90° and the end angle to 130°. Change the radius to 1.5.
8. Save as EX7.26, and close the drawing.

Using the Multiple Document Interface

As discussed in previous chapters, AutoCAD LT provides a Multiple Document Interface (MDI)—meaning that you can open two or more drawings simultaneously. Most projects involve more than a single drawing, and it is often necessary to reference information or geometry in an existing drawing when you are creating a new drawing. In Chapter 5, you were introduced to copying named object definitions between drawings using DesignCenter and the standard Windows "drag-and-drop" interface. You can also use the convenient drag-and-drop interface to move or copy objects within a single drawing or between two different drawing files. Additionally, you can copy and store objects in the Windows Clipboard and then paste them into other drawings.

Drag-and-Drop Editing Options

When you need to move geometry precisely within a drawing, use the MOVE or PROPERTIES command as appropriate. However, if you simply need to relocate something to an approximate location, it can be faster and easier to use the drag-and-drop interface. This process is illustrated in Figure 7.52. First, grip-select the objects to be moved. Figure 7.52A shows a crossing box selection. Next, point at one of the selected objects and press and hold the pick button (Figure 7.52B). Figure 7.52C shows the drag-and-drop cursor displayed when you drag the objects. Release the pick button to drop the objects at the new location.

FIGURE 7.52 The drag-and-drop interface provides a fast and easy way to relocate objects in a drawing.

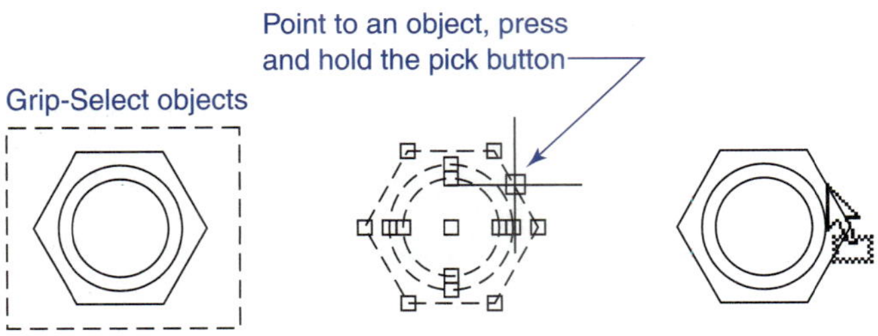

The drag-and-drop interface can also be used to copy objects. Similar to working with files in Windows Explorer, to copy instead of move, press the Ctrl key as you drag the objects. A small plus sign (+) appears next to the cursor to indicate that a copy is being made.

To access additional options when using the drag-and-drop interface, press and hold the right mouse button rather than the pick button. When you drop the objects by releasing the right mouse button, a shortcut menu is displayed (see Figure 7.53). The options on the shortcut menu are as follows:

- **Move Here** Moves the selection set to the new location.
- **Copy Here** Places a copy of the selected objects in the new location.
- **Paste as Block** Creates a block from the selected objects and inserts a block reference. Blocks are discussed in Chapter 12.
- **Cancel** Cancels the drag-and drop-operation.

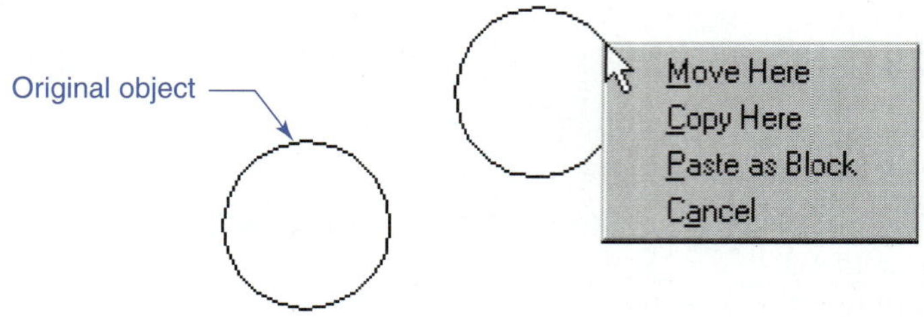

FIGURE 7.53 Use the right mouse button when dragging objects to display the shortcut menu.

Copying Objects between Drawings

When multiple drawings are open and visible, the drag-and-drop interface can be used to copy objects from one drawing to another. To drag objects from one drawing to another, both drawing windows must be visible at the same time. The process is the same as when dragging objects within a single drawing—grip-select the objects, then point at one of the selected objects and press and hold the pick button. While you are dragging objects, the cursor indicates where you can drag the objects to. When the cursor is pointing to a window feature or a toolbar, it appears as the universal "no" symbol (a circle with a diagonal line). Dropping the objects when the cursor displays this symbol cancels the drag-and-drop. As you move the cursor into the drawing area of another drawing window, it once again displays the objects you are dragging—indicating that the objects can now be dropped. Even though this process does not display the plus sign, dropping the object creates a copy and does not affect the original objects in the source drawing.

Using the right mouse button when dragging displays the shortcut menu. In Figure 7.54 the circle object has been dragged from Drawing1 to Drawing2 using the right mouse button. This menu does not provide a Move option, and it has one additional option:

- **Paste to Orig Coords** Pastes the objects into the new drawing at the same coordinate location as in the original drawing.

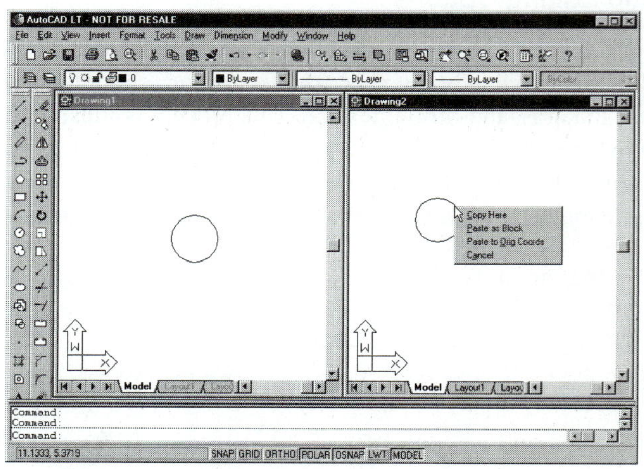

FIGURE 7.54 The shortcut menu provides different options when dragging objects between drawing files.

Using the Windows Clipboard

The drag-and-drop method of copying objects from one drawing to another is fast and convenient when the copied objects have a single destination. When you need to copy objects into multiple drawings or you need to reference a specific base point, the Windows Clipboard–based tools can provide additional flexibility. The basic Clipboard functions are described in this chapter. More advanced Clipboard functions are discussed in Chapter 15.

You can use all or part of an AutoCAD LT drawing in other AutoCAD LT drawings or in applications such as in a Windows document. To do this, you can either cut or copy the desired objects to the Windows Clipboard. The ***Clipboard*** is a place where objects are temporarily stored. AutoCAD LT objects are placed on the Clipboard by using the CUTCLIP or COPYCLIP commands. The CUTCLIP command removes the objects from the drawing and stores them on the Clipboard. The COPYCLIP command copies the objects from the drawing and stores them on the Clipboard. The objects that you place on the Clipboard stay there until you use the CUTCLIP or COPYCLIP commands again because each time you use one of these commands, the newly selected objects replace the objects that were there before. When the objects are on the Clipboard, they are available to be pasted into other Windows applications or into other AutoCAD LT drawings. The objects are transferred to other applications using the PASTECLIP command.

Cutting Objects

Objects can be cut from an AutoCAD LT drawing by picking Cut from the Edit pull-down menu, by picking the Cut to Clipboard button from the Standard toolbar, by pressing the Ctrl key and the X key (Ctrl+X), or by typing CUTCLIP. The command works like this:

Standard

Cut to Clipboard (Ctrl+X)

Edit
Cut

CUTCLIP
[Ctrl] + [X]

Command: **CUTCLIP**↵
Select objects: ⟨*use any selection method*⟩
Select objects: ↵
Command:

Caution is advised when using the CUTCLIP command, because the objects are removed from the drawing. The OOPS command can be used to bring the objects back, or you can undo the CUTCLIP command. Note that undoing this command in AutoCAD LT does not affect the contents of the Clipboard, so the cut items are still there.

Copying Objects

The COPYCLIP command works just like the CUTCLIP command except that the objects that are copied to the Clipboard remain in the drawing. This command is accessed by picking Copy from the Edit pull-down menu, by picking the Copy to Clipboard button from the Standard toolbar, by pressing the Ctrl key and the C key (Ctrl+C), or by typing COPYCLIP. The COPYCLIP command works like this:

Standard

Copy to Clipboard (Ctrl+C

Edit
Copy

COPYCLIP
[Ctrl] + [C]

Command: **COPYCLIP**↵
Select objects: ⟨*use any selection method*⟩
Select objects: ↵
Command:

The objects are copied in vector format. A ***vector*** is a mathematical object with exact direction and length but without specific location. The objects you copy to the Clipboard are stored there as WMF files (Windows metafiles). However, AutoCAD LT can transfer objects to other applications using a variety of formats.

Pasting AutoCAD LT Drawings

Pasting is the function of taking objects that are stored on the Clipboard and inserting them into a Windows application or into an AutoCAD LT drawing. Objects must be placed on the Clipboard before they can be pasted. The command used to paste objects to an AutoCAD LT drawing is PASTECLIP. This command is inactive until an object is placed on the Clipboard. To access this command, pick Paste from the Clipboard button in the Standard toolbar, type **PASTECLIP** at the Command: prompt, pick Paste from the Edit pull-down menu, or press the Ctrl+V accelerator key. This command asks for an insertion point. This is a point at the lower left corner of the object you selected. The objects are dynamically dragged with the screen cursor so you can see the image for placement. Pick the insertion point or enter desired coordinates. After objects are on the Clipboard, the PASTECLIP command works like this:

Standard

Paste from Clipboard

Edit
Paste

PASTECLIP
[Ctrl] + [V]

Command: **PASTECLIP**↵
Specify insertion point: ⟨*pick an insertion point*⟩
Command:

If you select the Paste as Block option, the pasted objects are inserted as a block object. This means that the individual objects you copied to the Clipboard are now combined and treated as though they are a single object. Any editing you do affects the entire object. You need to use the EXPLODE command if you want to convert the objects to the individual components. Access this command by picking Explode in the Modify pull-down menu, by picking the Explode button in the Modify toolbar, or by typing **X** or **EXPLODE** at the Command: prompt. The EXPLODE command asks you to select the objects. A single pick highlights the objects, and the objects are converted to their original condition when you press Enter.

Modify

Explode

Modify
Explode

EXPLODE
X

The following is a sequence to use when copying or moving information from one AutoCAD LT drawing to another:

1. Open the AutoCAD LT drawing that contains the desired information.
2. Use the COPYCLIP or CUTCLIP command to select the desired objects for placement on the Clipboard.
3. Open the AutoCAD LT drawing where you want the objects inserted.
4. Use the PASTECLIP command to insert the contents of the Clipboard into the desired drawing.

Exercise 7.27 **Estimated time required: 5 min.**

1. Open EX7.23.
2. Copy (COPYCLIP) the wheel with spokes and hub to the Clipboard.
3. Exit the drawing and save the changes upon exiting.
4. Start a new drawing.
5. Paste the contents of the Clipboard into this drawing.
6. Save as EX7.27, and close the drawing.

LEARNING CHECKPOINT

- ☐ Name the command that is used to remove a portion from an object or create two objects from one object.
- ☐ What command is used to remove a portion from an object back to another object?
- ☐ Define a cutting edge.
- ☐ What is an implied intersection?
- ☐ How do you activate the smart mode and what does it do?
- ☐ Name the command that lets you lengthen an object to meet another object.
- ☐ Define boundary edges.
- ☐ Name the command used to make rounded corners.
- ☐ What command is used to draw angled corners?
- ☐ Name the command that allows you to edit a single object using a dialog box.
- ☐ Define Clipboard.
- ☐ What command is used to place an object on the Clipboard without removing it from the drawing?
- ☐ Define pasting.
- ☐ Name the command that is used to place an object from the Clipboard into a drawing.

Changing Geometry

- Stretching, Trimming, and Extending Objects
- Creating Fillets and Chamfers

Copying an Object's Properties

Standard

Match Properties

MATCHPROP
MA

In the editing process, it is much faster to copy an existing object than to create a new object from scratch. When you are editing the properties of an object, it is often much faster to simply copy the properties of an existing object in your drawing by using the Match Properties tool. You can select the Match Properties button from the Standard toolbar, or you can type **MA** or **MATCHPROP** at the Command: prompt. You are prompted to select the *source object*. The source object is the object whose properties are to be copied. When you pick the source object, AutoCAD LT reports the "current active settings," indicating which properties will be copied. By default, all properties are active. In the following sequence, the source object is selected, and then the Settings option is used to change the currently active settings. This displays the Property Settings dialog box, shown in Figure 7.55. After the settings are adjusted, you are prompted to select the *destination objects* to which the copied properties are to be applied.

Command: **MA** or **MATCHPROP**↵
Select source object: *<pick the object whose properties you want to copy>*
Current active settings: Color Layer Ltype Ltscale Lineweight Thickness Text Dim Hatch
Select destination object(s) or [Settings]: **S**↵
Current active settings: Color Ltype Lineweight Text Dim Hatch
Select destination object(s) or [Settings]: *<pick objects to apply copied properties to>*
Select destination object(s) or [Settings]: *<pick objects to apply copied properties to>*
Select destination object(s) or [Settings]: ↵
Command:

The Settings option displays the currently active properties in the Property Settings dialog box shown in Figure 7.55. Here, you can select which properties will be applied to the destination objects. The effect of each of these settings is as follows:

- **Color** Applies the color setting of the source object to the destination objects.
- **Layer** Moves destination objects to the same layer as the source object.
- **Linetype** Applies the linetype setting of the source object to the destination objects.
- **Linetype Scale** Applies the object linetype scale of the source object to the destination objects.
- **Thickness** Applies the 3D thickness setting of the source object to the destination objects.
- **Lineweight** Applies the lineweight of the source object to the destination objects.
- **Dimension** Applies the dimension style of the source object to all selected dimension, leader, and tolerance objects.
- **Text** Changes the text style of the destination text objects to that of the source object.
- **Hatch** Applies the associative hatch pattern properties of the source object to selected associative hatch patterns.

FIGURE 7.55 The Property Settings dialog box controls which properties are applied to the destination objects.

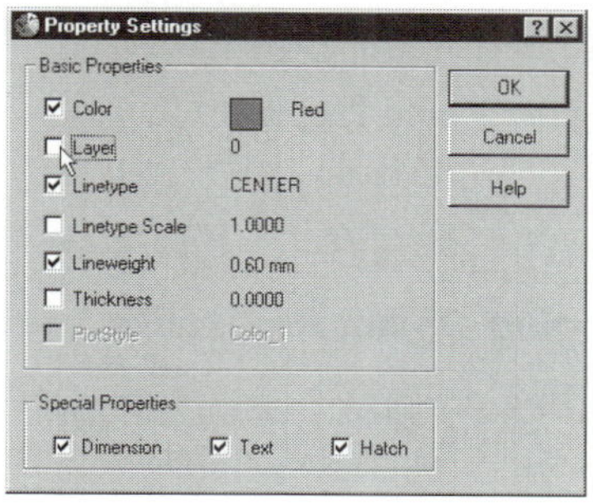

Figure 7.56 shows the color, lineweight, and linetype of the source object being applied to two other objects. One distinct advantage of using the Property Painter is that you can change multiple properties at the same time. Another advantage is that you do not need to know the values to which you want to set them—you can simply match an object that already has the correct settings.

FIGURE 7.56 The color and linetype properties of the source object are applied to the destination objects in the example.

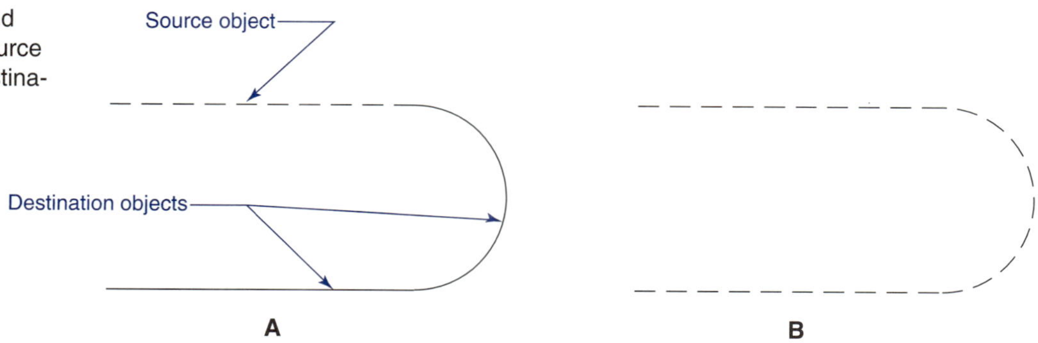

Field Notes

One extremely powerful capability of the Match Properties tool is found in conjunction with the Multiple Document Interface. When multiple drawings are open and visible, the source and destination objects can be in separate drawings. This means that you can select a source object in one drawing and apply the properties to destination objects in one or more different drawings.

Exercise 7.28 — Estimated time required: 5 min.

1. Start a new drawing session from scratch using Metric settings.
2. Define two new layers, and assign color and linetype settings of your own design.
3. Draw a 40-mm-diameter circle on each of the new layers, using BYLAYER color and linetypes.
4. Draw two more circles on these layers using specific colors and linetypes that override layer settings.
5. Draw four rectangles on layer 0 with BYLAYER settings.
6. Using Match Properties, assign all the properties of one circle to one of the rectangles. Repeat this procedure for the remaining circles and rectangles.
7. Use the Match Properties to assign BYLAYER colors to the objects in your drawing that currently override layer settings.
8. Save as EX7.28, and close the drawing.

LEARNING CHECKPOINT

- ☐ Name the command that starts the Match Properties tool.
- ☐ What are the advantages of using the Match Properties tool?

Setting and Changing Object Properties

- Using the Properties Window

MULTIPLE CHOICE

Circle the choice or enter your response on an answer sheet by selecting the option that most closely completes or answers the given statements.

1. One or more objects that are specified for processing as a unit is called a:
- **a.** selection
- **b.** selection set
- **c.** processing unit
- **d.** group

2. Make a selection by placing a polygon of your own design totally around an object or group of objects using a:
- **a.** window
- **b.** crossing
- **c.** window polygon
- **d.** window crossing

3. This option allows you to automatically create a window or crossing box by picking the first and second corners:
- **a.** Noun/Verb Selection
- **b.** Press and Drag
- **c.** Use Shift to Add
- **d.** Implied Windowing

4. Small squares that appear on objects you select are called:
- **a.** pick boxes
- **b.** pixels
- **c.** grips
- **d.** aperture

5. Create the other half of a symmetrical object with this command:
- **a.** COPY
- **b.** OFFSET
- **c.** MIRROR
- **d.** ARRAY

6. Make multiple copies of objects in a pattern with this command:
- **a.** COPY
- **b.** OFFSET
- **c.** MIRROR
- **d.** ARRAY

7. This command allows you to place objects in a new location:
- **a.** MOVE
- **b.** SCALE
- **c.** ROTATE
- **d.** STRETCH

8. The grip MIRROR command automatically does this to the original object:
- **a.** keeps
- **b.** asks to remove or keep
- **c.** removes
- **d.** none of the above

9. The size of the arc for the FILLET command is established with a:
- **a.** diameter
- **b.** radius
- **c.** center
- **d.** endpoints

10. The AutoCAD LT command that allows you to move objects that have been placed in temporary storage to an AutoCAD LT drawing or other Windows application is called:
- **a.** COPY
- **b.** COPYCLIP
- **c.** CUTCLIP
- **d.** PASTECLIP

MATCHING

Match each term to the correct description by writing the appropriate number in each box at the left.

- ☐ ARRAY
- ☐ BREAK
- ☐ CHAMFER
- ☐ Clipboard
- ☐ COPY
- ☐ DDMODIFY
- ☐ EXTEND
- ☐ Fence
- ☐ FILLET
- ☐ Grips
- ☐ LENGTHEN
- ☐ MIRROR
- ☐ MOVE
- ☐ OFFSET
- ☐ PASTECLIP
- ☐ ROTATE
- ☐ SCALE
- ☐ STRETCH
- ☐ TRIM
- ☐ WP

1. Edit objects so they are longer to meet other objects.
2. Place objects in a new location.
3. Edit objects so they are shorter to meet other objects.
4. Remove a portion from an object.
5. Lengthen or shorten objects.
6. Make duplicates of objects for placement anywhere on a drawing.
7. Copy objects into a specific pattern.
8. Use this command to place an object onto a drawing from the Clipboard.
9. Use this selection option to totally surround objects with a polygon of your design.
10. Use this command to lengthen or shorten closed objects.
11. Draw a corner.
12. Edit objects with these after selecting.
13. Use this to select objects and then access them later with the Previous option.
14. Use this selection option to place a line through objects to select.
15. Move objects to a desired angle.
16. Rounded corners.
17. Make an object bigger or smaller.
18. Make symmetrical copies.
19. Make parallel copies of objects.
20. Edit single objects in a dialog box.
21. Copy objects to here for temporary storage.

WORD SCRAMBLE

Unscramble the seven scrambled words below, one letter to each square, to form seven AutoCAD LT–related words:

RIROMR

ACSEL

NECFE

DXEETN

RKABE

ETOTRA

HNGELTNE

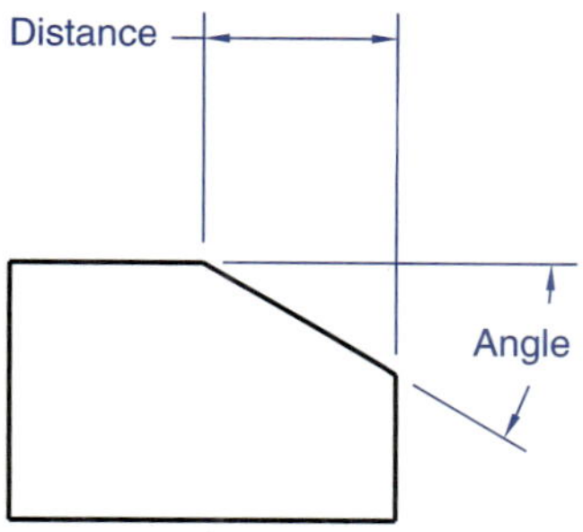

Unscramble the circled letters above to form the special answer, as suggested by the illustration.

PROJECTS

Set up the following drawing projects with layers that relate to the type of drawing as outlined and discussed in Chapter 5.

7.1 Clock
Open P3.3 and add the fillets to the clock, as shown below. Save as P7.1.

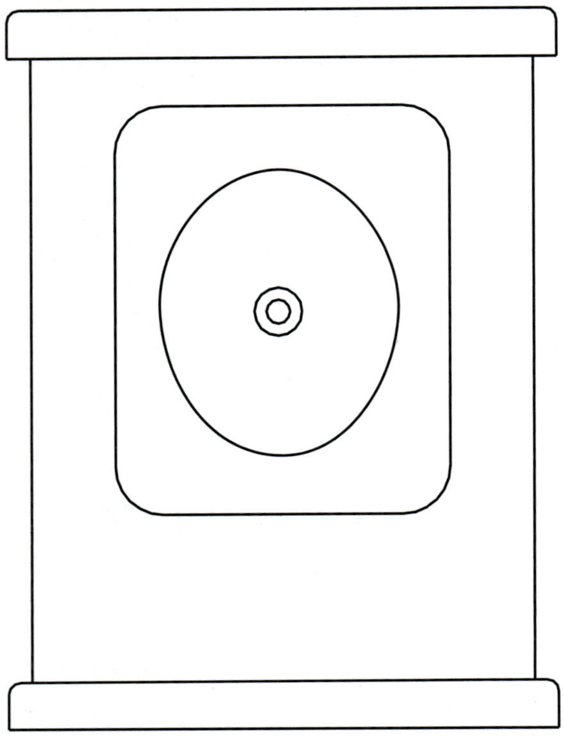

7.2 Piping Drawing
Open P3.10 and edit the symbols as needed to create the drawing shown below. Save as P7.2.

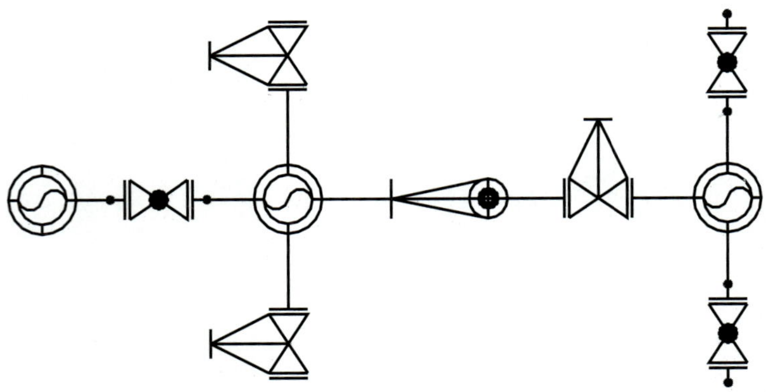

7.3 Chassis Divider
Draw the view shown below. Do not draw dimensions. Save as P7.3.

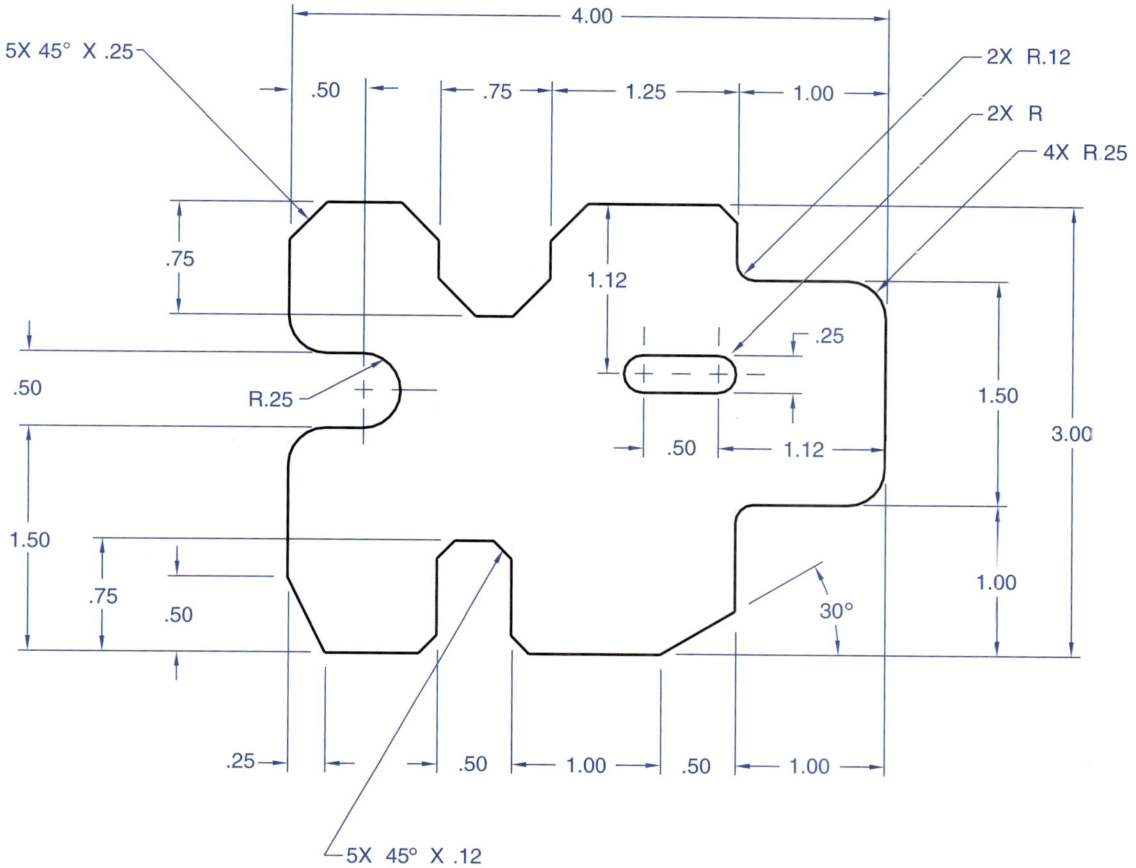

7.4 GFCI Schematic
Paste P2.6 and P3.2 into the drawing to create the schematic shown below without text. Save as P7.4.

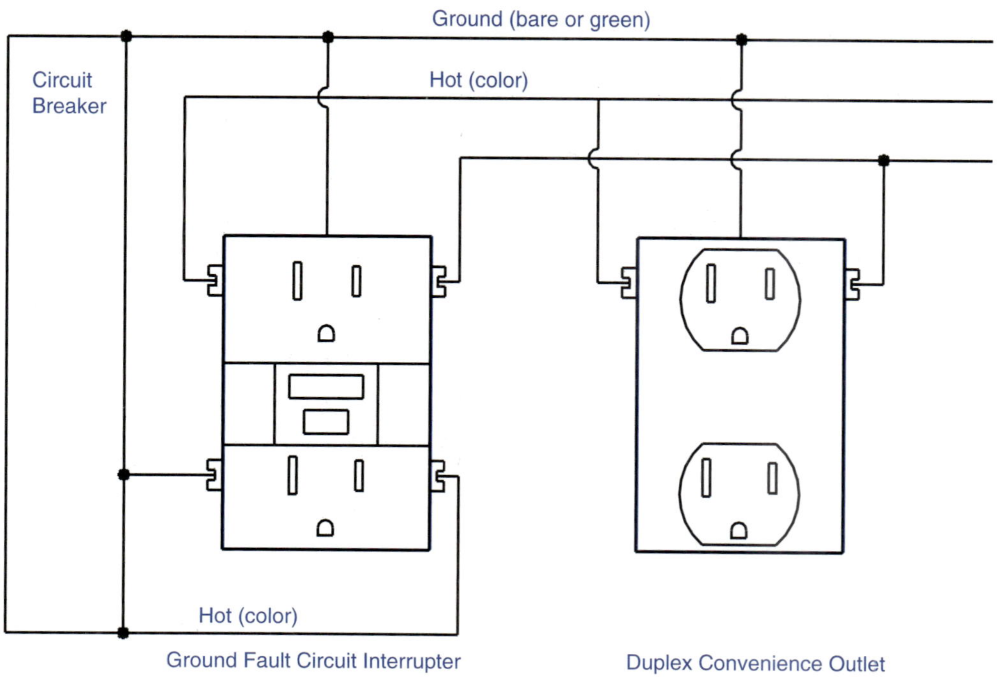

7.5 Integrated Circuit Schematic
Draw the schematic shown below without text . Save as P7.5.

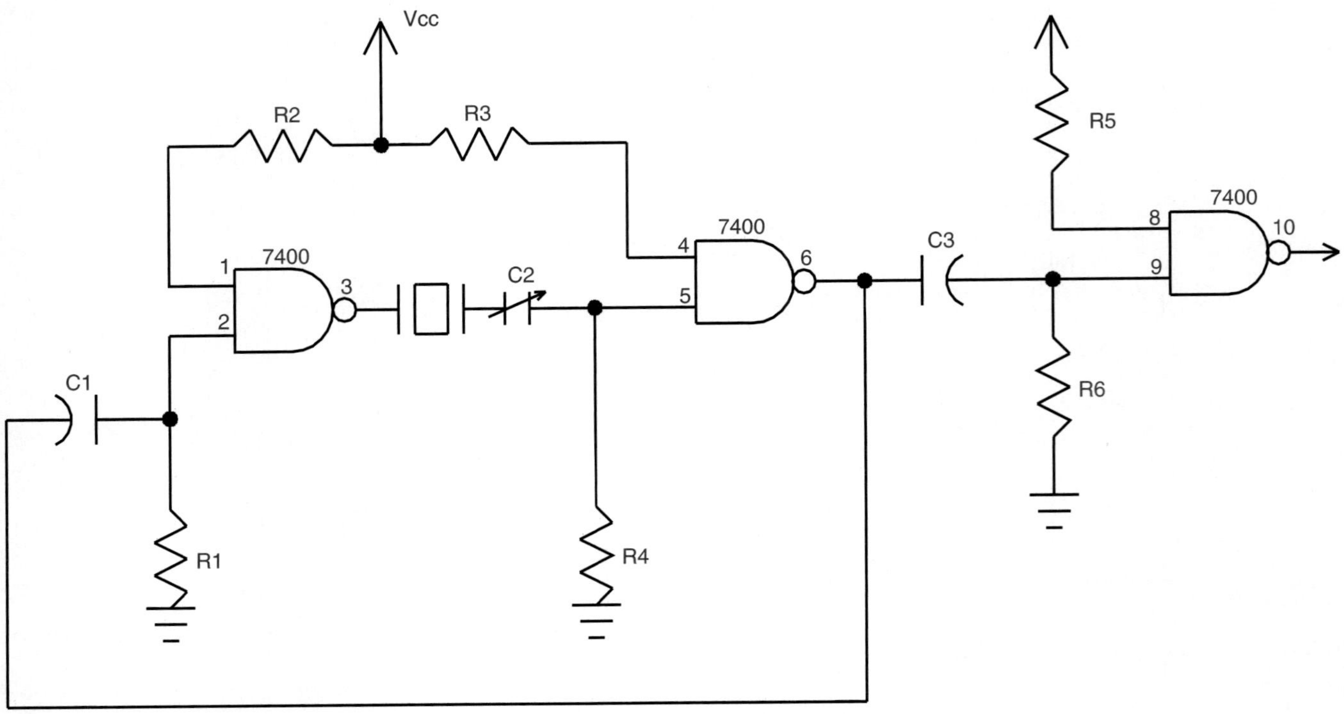

7.6 Electrical One-Line Diagram

Draw the diagram shown below without text or connectors. Draw the dimensioned examples first and then use the editing commands as needed to complete the diagram. Do not draw dimensions. Save as P7.6.

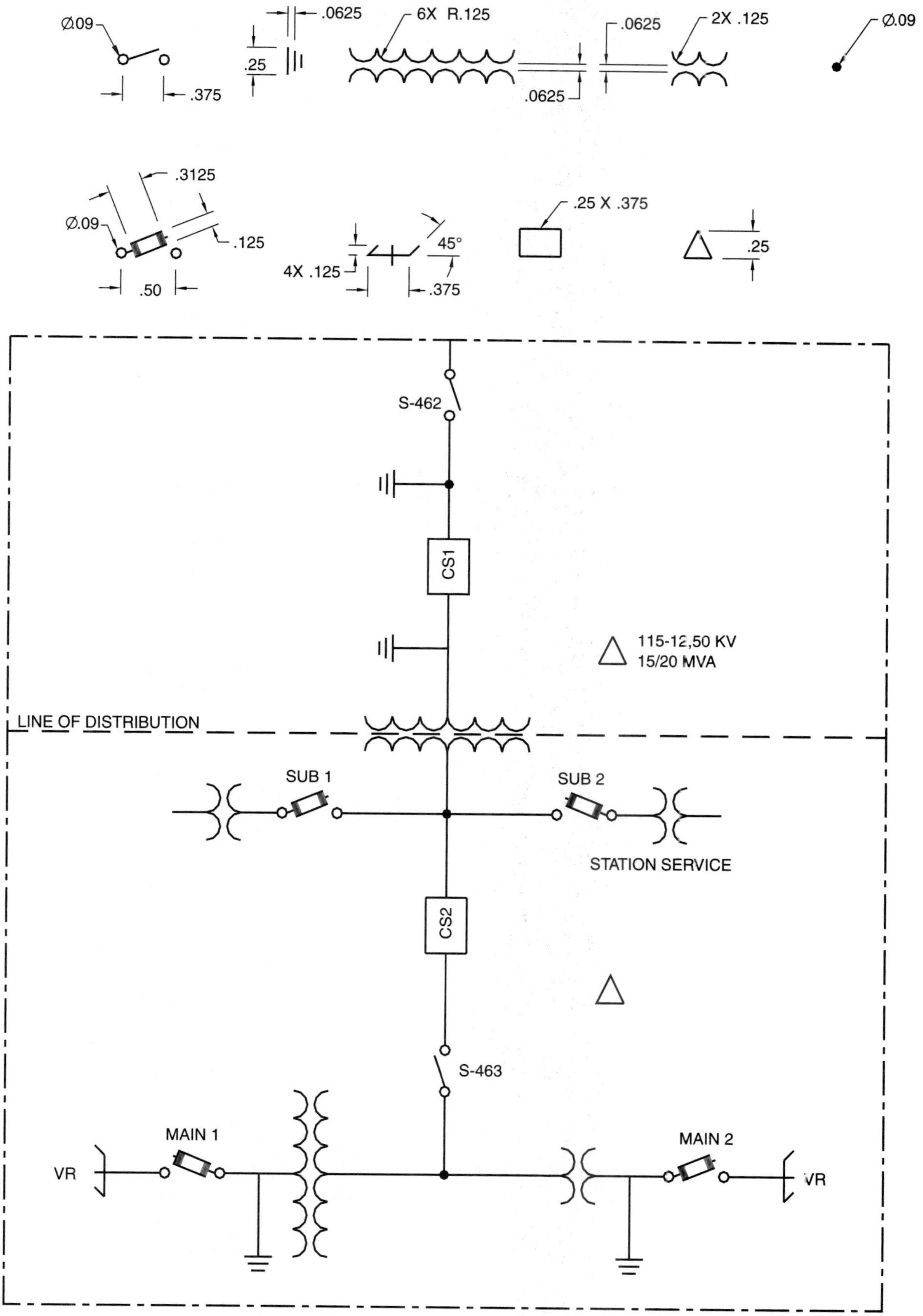

7.7 Gasket
Draw the half view shown below. Mirror along the symmetrical center line to create the other half. Do not draw notes or dimensions. Save as P7.7.

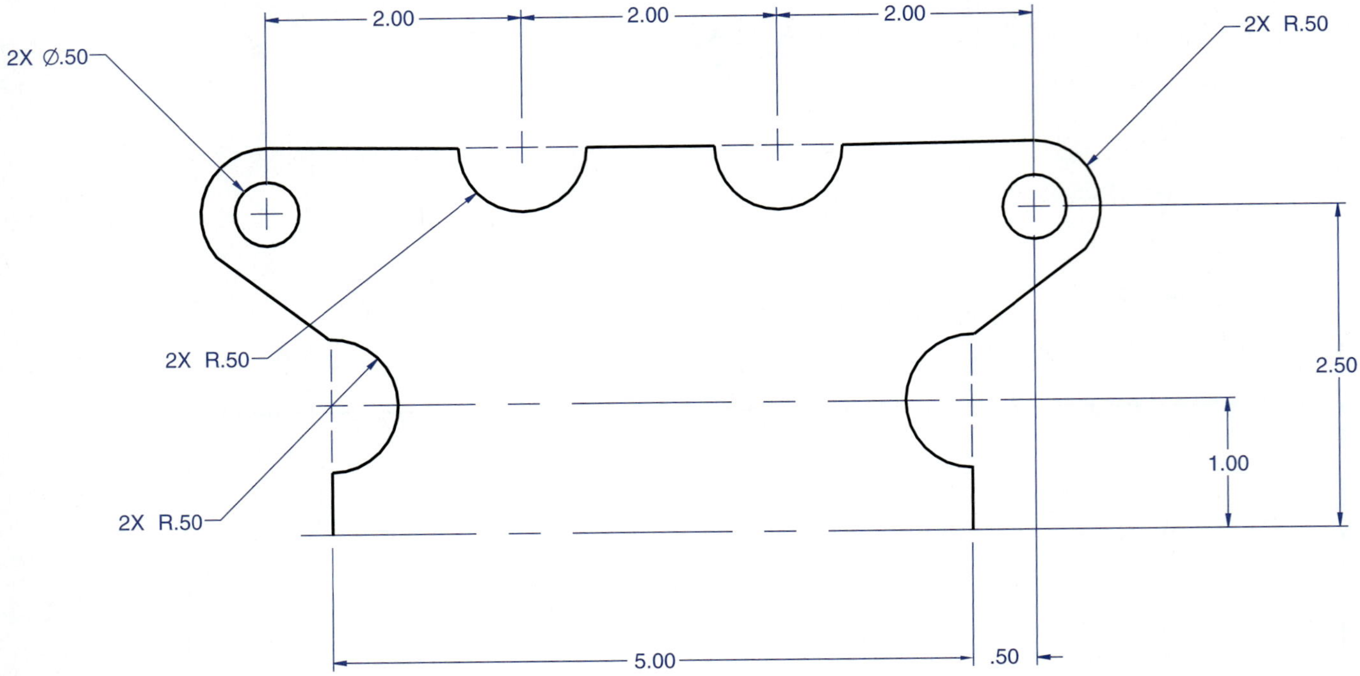

7.8 Wheel

Draw the object shown below without notes or dimensions. Save as P7.8.

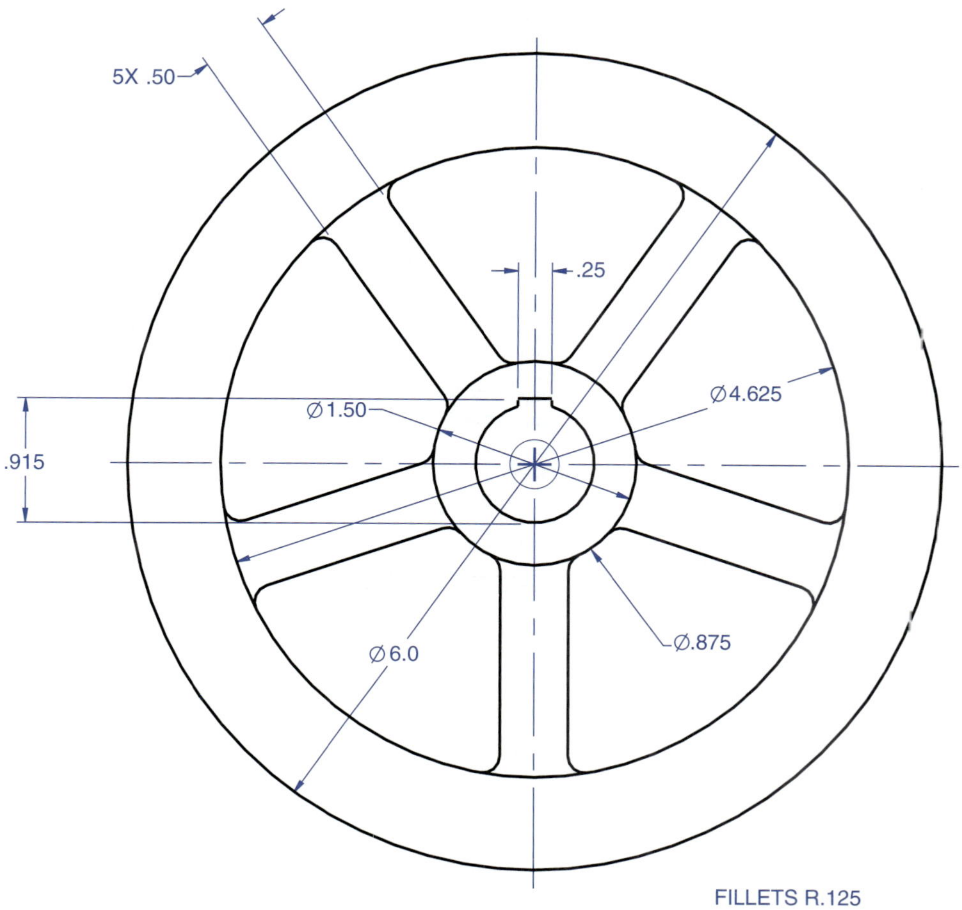

7.9 Drift Boat
Draw the views shown below to your own specifications. Save as P7.9.

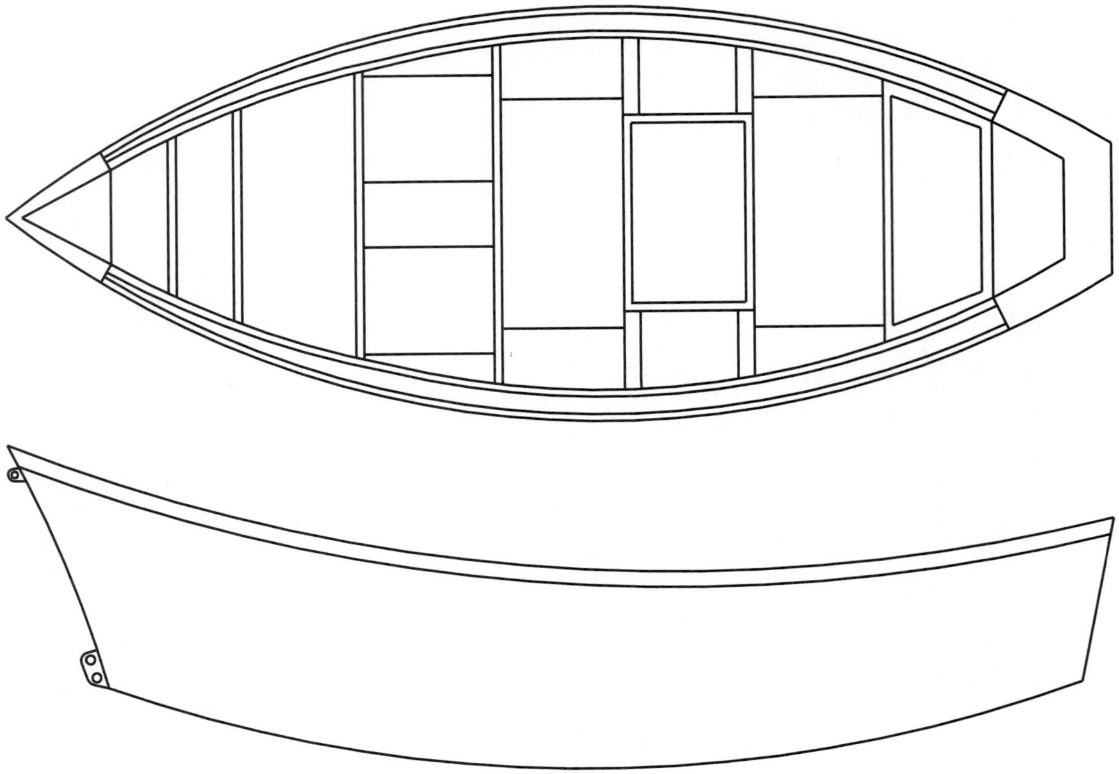

7.10 Plot Plan
Draw the plot plan shown below without dimensions. Save as P7.10.

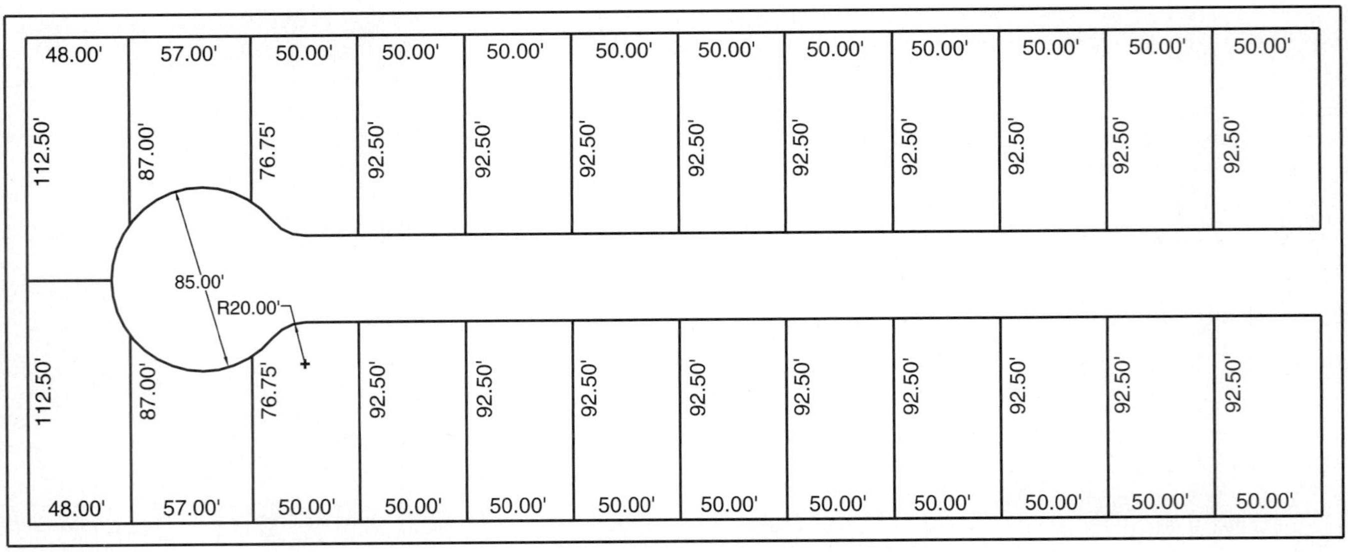

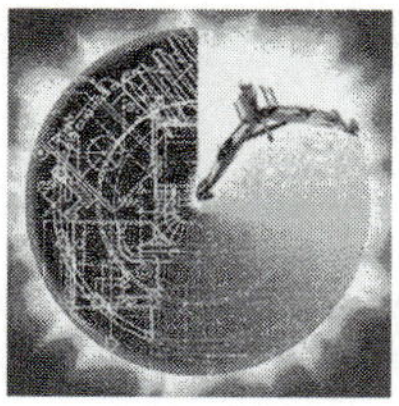

CHAPTER 8

Drawing and Editing Polylines and Double Lines

LEARNING GOALS

- ◎ Use the PLINE command options to draw a variety of polyline shapes and designs.
- ◎ Use the PEDIT command options to perform several polyline editing operations.
- ◎ Explain how to calculate the area of a closed polyline object.
- ◎ Make curves out of straight polyline segments.
- ◎ Draw fillets and chamfers on polylines.
- ◎ Explode a polyline.
- ◎ Draw and edit spline curves.
- ◎ Use the DLINE command to draw double lines with several design options.
- ◎ Set up and draw Revision Clouds.

Introduction to Polylines and Double Lines

AutoCAD LT provides you with the flexibility of creating interconnected line or line and arc segments in any width and of any desired design. These objects are called polylines. AutoCAD LT defines ***polylines*** as objects composed of one or more line segments or circular arcs that are treated as a single object. Polylines are also called ***plines*** (pronounced "p-lines") because they are drawn using the PLINE command. Polylines allow you to create objects that are limited only by your imagination, or you can simply use them to trace the boundary of a group of objects for the convenience of making area calculations. The REVCLOUD command uses polylines to construct revision clouds within your drawings. Revision clouds are cloudlike shapes in a drawing used to call attention to revised areas of a drawing. Rectangles created using the RECTANG command are also created using a single polyline object.

AutoCAD LT also provides a powerful tool for simultaneously drawing two parallel lines. The format of the lines can be of any width and design you select, including straight and arc double lines. For example, you can draw double lines spaced as needed for the walls of an architectural floor plan. AutoCAD LT calls these ***double lines,*** and they are drawn using the DLINE command.

Drawing Polylines

Draw

Polyline

Draw
Polyline

PLINE
PL

Each segment in a series of connected lines or connected lines and arcs is a single object when you draw using the LINE and ARC commands. The PLINE command, however, allows you to draw connected line and arc segments that together form a single object. These polylines offer you some editing flexibility that is not available with individual line and arc segments. For example, in Chapter 7 you learned how to draw fillets and chamfers by selecting two objects. The FILLET and CHAMFER commands have a Polyline option that allows you to pick a polyline and automatically have all of the corners filleted or chamfered as needed. Additionally, polylines offer you unlimited design opportunities by making thick or tapered line and arc objects.

Polylines are drawn by picking the Polyline button in the Draw toolbar, by picking Polyline in the Draw pull-down menu, or by typing **PL** or **PLINE** at the Command: prompt.

Using the PLINE Command Options

The initial prompt of the PLINE command is just like the LINE command. You are asked for the From point:, which is the first point of the polyline segment. You are then given several options, but the default asks for the endpoint of the line. The default width of a polyline is 0 (zero). The following command sequence draws the polyline shown in Figure 8.1:

Command: **PL** or **PLINE**↵
Specify start point: *<pick a point>*
Current line-width is 0.0000
Specify next point or [Arc/Close/Halfwidth/Length/Undo/Width]: *<pick a point>*
Specify next point or [Arc/Close/Halfwidth/Length/Undo/Width]: *<pick a point>*
Specify next point or [Arc/Close/Halfwidth/Length/Undo/Width]: ↵
Command:

FIGURE 8.1 Drawing a two-straight-segment polyline.

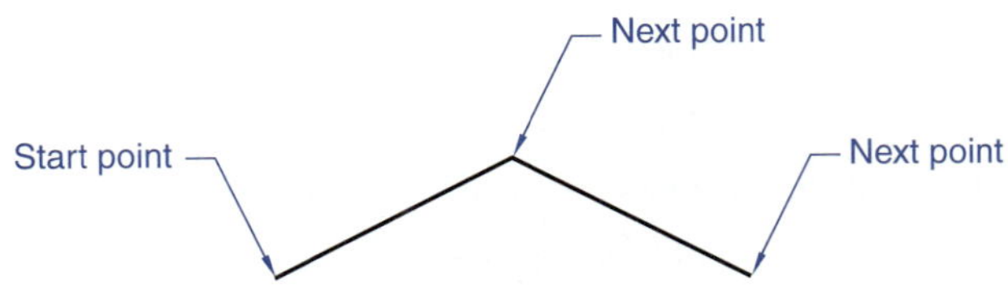

Although the object in Figure 8.1 looks like two line segments, it is really one object. All you have to do to erase the whole thing is to pick any place on the polyline at the Select objects: prompt of the ERASE command.

Closing and Undoing Polylines

The Close option in the PLINE command works just like the Close option for the LINE command. The Close option connects the last segment drawn with the start point of the first segment as shown in Figure 8.2. If you are drawing a polyline that you know is going to be closed, just use the Close option to automatically have the last segment closed to the beginning of the first segment like this:

Command: **PL** or **PLINE**↵
Specify start point: *<pick a point>*
Current line-width is 0.0000
Specify next point or [Arc/Close/Halfwidth/Length/Undo/Width]: *<pick a point>*
Specify next point or [Arc/Close/Halfwidth/Length/Undo/Width]: *<pick a point>*
Specify next point or [Arc/Close/Halfwidth/Length/Undo/Width]: **C**↵
Command:

FIGURE 8.2 Closing a polyline with the Close option.

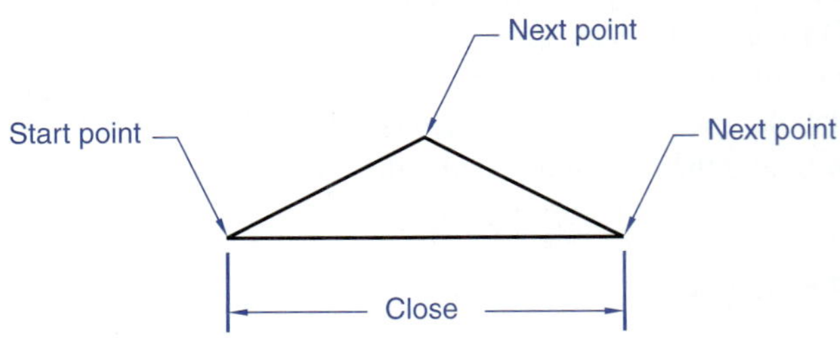

The Undo option is used within the PLINE command to undo the previously drawn polyline segment. This provides you with the convenience of undoing as many previously drawn polyline segments as needed without leaving the PLINE command. To do this, type **U** and press Enter at this PLINE prompt:

Specify next point or [Arc/Close/Halfwidth/Length/Undo/Width]: **U**↵

Once you have left the polyline command, you can undo all of the segments drawn in the previous PLINE command by typing **U** at the Command: prompt and pressing Enter.

Exercise 8.1 **Estimated time required: 5 min.**

1. Start a new drawing.
2. Draw two straight polyline segments like those shown in Figure 8.1.
3. Draw a closed polyline like that in Figure 8.2.
4. Save as EX8.1, and close the drawing.

Drawing Polyline Arcs

The PLINE command's Arc option can be used at any time while you are in the PLINE command to draw an arc segment connected to the previous straight or arc polyline segment. After you enter the PLINE command and pick the first point, you can enter the Arc option like this:

Command: **PL** or **PLINE**↵
Specify start point: *<pick a point>*
Current line-width is 0.0000
Specify next point or [Arc/Close/Halfwidth/Length/Undo/Width]: **A**↵
Specify endpoint of arc or [Angle/CEnter/CLose/Direction/Halfwidth/Line/Radius/Second pt/Undo/Width]: *<pick arc endpoint>*
Specify endpoint of arc or [Angle/CEnter/CLose/Direction/Halfwidth/Line/Radius/Second pt/Undo/Width]: ↵
Command:

As you can see, there are many suboptions. The default allows you to move the cursor and pick or type the coordinates of an endpoint of the arc. The coordinates can be entered as absolute, relative, or polar coordinates, or by using direct distance entry, if desired. Notice in Figure 8.3 that the direction in which the arc is drawn depends on which way you move the cursor after picking the first point. In a new drawing, if the cursor is dragged upward, the arc is drawn counterclockwise. If the cursor is dragged downward, the arc is drawn clockwise.

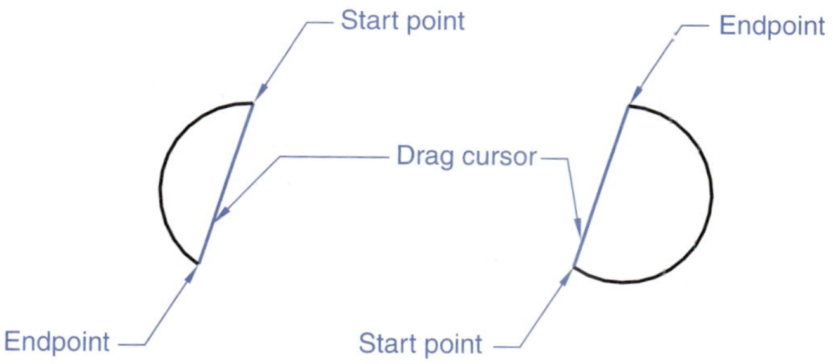

FIGURE 8.3 The direction in which the polyline arc is drawn depends on the direction you move the cursor after picking the first point.

A series of connecting arcs can be drawn if you continue to move the cursor and pick additional arc endpoints. You can also draw polyline arcs connected to straight segments by entering the Arc option and the Line option as needed. Polyline arc segments are drawn tangent to the previous polyline segment by default. Line segments can be drawn at a tangent using the Length option. When you enter the Length option, you are prompted only for the length of the line. The line is drawn the specified length in a direction that makes it tangent to the previous segment. If the previous segment is a line rather than an arc, the line is drawn in the same direction as the previous line segment. The results of the following command sequence are displayed in Figure 8.4. This sequence draws a straight segment followed by two arcs and then another straight segment:

Command: **PL** or **PLINE**↵
Specify start point: *<pick line start point>*
Current line-width is 0.0000
Specify next point or [Arc/Close/Halfwidth/Length/Undo/Width]: *<pick line endpoint>*
Specify next point or [Arc/Close/Halfwidth/Length/Undo/Width]: **A**↵
Specify endpoint of arc or [Angle/CEnter/CLose/Direction/Halfwidth/Line/Radius/Second pt/Undo/Width]: *<pick arc endpoint>*
Specify endpoint of arc or [Angle/CEnter/CLose/Direction/Halfwidth/Line/Radius/Second pt/Undo/Width]: *<pick arc endpoint>*
Specify endpoint of arc or [Angle/CEnter/CLose/Direction/Halfwidth/Line/Radius/Second pt/Undo/Width]: **L**↵

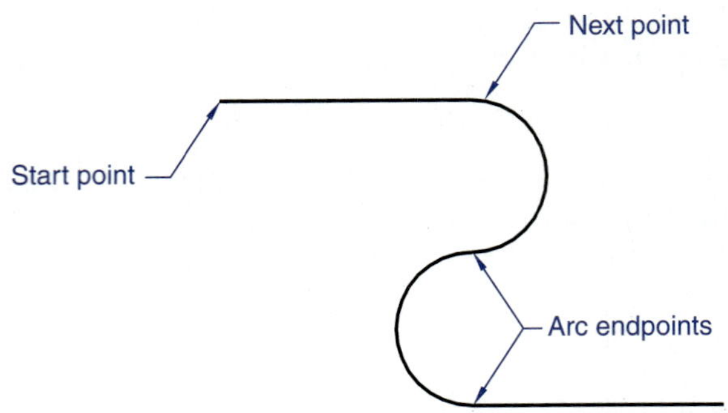

FIGURE 8.4 Drawing a polyline with a straight segment followed by two arc segments and then another straight segment, using the Length option.

Specify next point or [Arc/Close/Halfwidth/Length/Undo/Width]: **L**↵
Specify length of line: <*specify length of tangent line*>
Specify next point or [Arc/Close/Halfwidth/Length/Undo/Width]: ↵
Command:

Field Notes

Remember to use ORTHO to your advantage when drawing horizontal and vertical straight polyline segments. Use Polar Snap to assist with angled segments.

The other Arc suboptions that provide you with added flexibility when drawing polyline arcs are similar to the ARC command options that were discussed in Chapter 3. Figure 8.5 shows the results of each of the Arc suboptions. These suboptions are briefly described as follows:

Angle: Type **A** and press Enter to get a Specify included angle: prompt. Type or pick the desired included angle and then select the arc endpoint or use the Center or Radius option. The prompts work like this:

Specify endpoint of arc or [Angle/CEnter/CLose/Direction/Halfwidth/Line/Radius/Second pt/Undo/Width]: **A**↵
Specify included angle: <*pick or type an angle*>
Specify endpoint of arc or [CEnter/Radius]: <*pick an endpoint or type* **C** *or* **R**>

FIGURE 8.5 The results of using the PLINE Arc options.

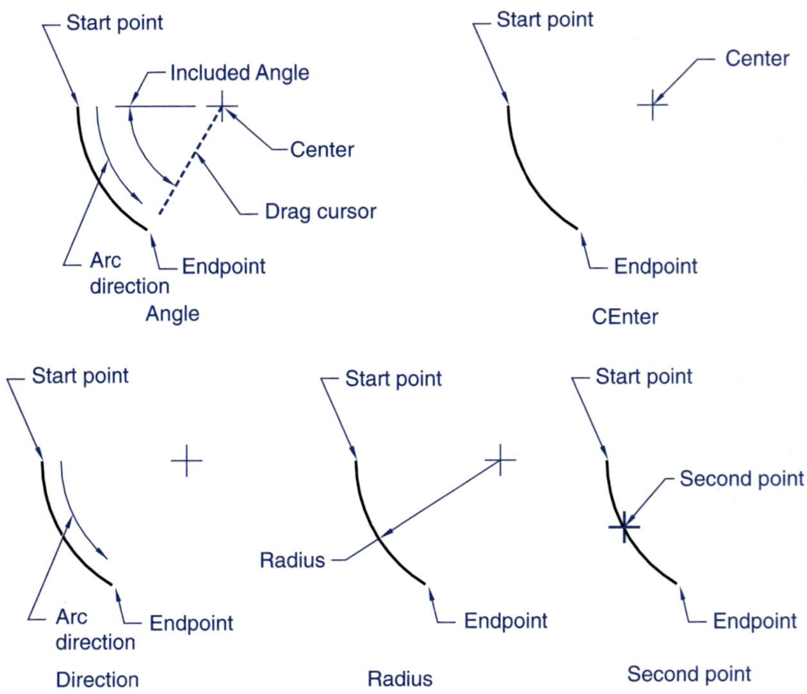

CEnter: Type **CE** to have the option to pick the arc's center point. You are then asked to pick an endpoint, or use either the Angle or Length option:

Specify endpoint of arc or [Angle/CEnter/CLose/Direction/Halfwidth/Line/Radius/Second pt/Undo/Width]: **CE**↵
Specify center point of arc: <*pick the center point*>
Specify endpoint of arc or [Angle/Length]: <*pick an endpoint or type* **A** *or* **L**>

The results of the CEnter option may not create an arc that is tangent to the previous arc.

Direction: Type **D** to be asked for the arc direction followed by the endpoint:

Specify endpoint of arc or [Angle/CEnter/CLose/Direction/Halfwidth/Line/Radius/Second pt/Undo/Width]: **D**↵
Specify the tangent direction for the start point of arc: <*pick or type an angle for the arc starting direction*>
Specify endpoint of the arc: <*pick the endpoint*>

Radius: Type **R** to be asked to enter the arc radius followed by picking the endpoint or using the angle option:

Specify endpoint of arc or [Angle/CEnter/CLose/Direction/Halfwidth/Line/Radius/Second pt/Undo/Width]: **R**↵
Specify radius of arc: <*pick or type a radius value*>
Specify endpoint of arc or [Angle]: <*pick the endpoint or type* **A**>

Second pt: Type **S** to get the Second point: prompt followed by the Endpoint: prompt:

Specify endpoint of arc or [Angle/CEnter/CLose/Direction/Halfwidth/Line/Radius/Second pt/Undo/Width]: **S**↵
Specify second point on arc: <*pick the second arc point*>
Specify end point of arc: <*pick the arc endpoint*>

The results of this option may not provide tangent arcs.

The Arc option also contains the CLose and Undo options that were explained earlier. However, this CLose option requires that you type **CL.** The previous Close option used only a **C.** The remaining Arc options are explained in the next few subsections.

Field Notes

- Keep in mind that you type the capitalized letter or letters of the option name.
- When accessing options of any command, keep in mind that you need to type only the letters that are capitalized in the option prompt.
- Remember that any prompt for a point, distance, or angle can be answered either by entering a value at the keyboard or by picking with the cursor.

Exercise 8.2

Estimated time required: 5 min.

1. Start a new drawing.
2. Draw connecting straight and arc polyline segments similar to those shown in Figure 8.4.
3. Save as EX8.2, and close the drawing.

Adjusting Polyline Width

The initial polyline width is 0 (zero), which makes a thin line or arc. When you change the polyline width, the new value becomes the default until it is changed again. The PLINE Width option allows you to draw polylines with any desired starting and ending widths. For example, follow this command sequence to draw the .25-in.-wide polyline shown in Figure 8.6:

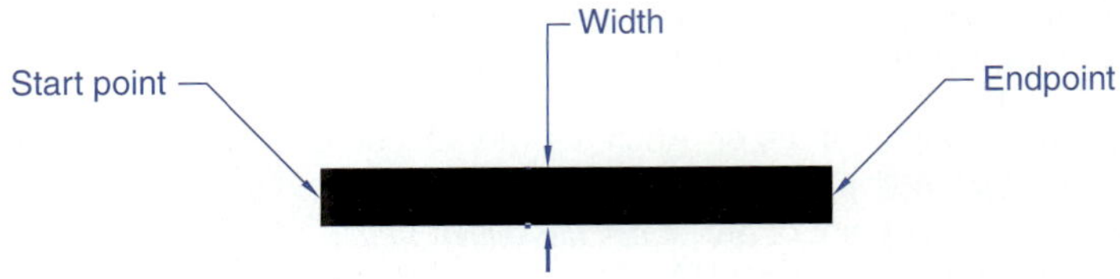

FIGURE 8.6 The elements of a wide polyline.

Command: **PL** or **PLINE**↵
Specify start point: *<pick a point>*
Current line-width is 0.0000
Specify next point or [Arc/Close/Halfwidth/Length/Undo/Width]: **W**↵
Specify starting width <0.0000>: **.25**↵
Specify ending width <0.2500>: ↵
Specify next point or [Arc/Close/Halfwidth/Length/Undo/Width]: *<pick the endpoint>*
Specify next point or [Arc/Close/Halfwidth/Length/Undo/Width]: ↵
Command:

Field Notes

Notice in the Width option command sequence that the default value for the ending width is automatically the same as the value you entered for the starting width. All you have to do is press Enter to accept the default. Also look at Figure 8.6 and notice that the points you pick to establish the length are at the center of the wide polyline.

The width you set applies to the polyline arcs just as it does for the straight segments. If you want to draw a tapered polyline, enter a different starting and ending width. If you want to draw a polyline with a sharp point, such as an arrow, use 0 (zero) for the starting width and some other value for the ending width. You can also change the polyline width at the beginning of each segment to create a variety of effects. Figure 8.7 shows the results of some different polyline width applications.

FIGURE 8.7 The results of some different polyline width applications.

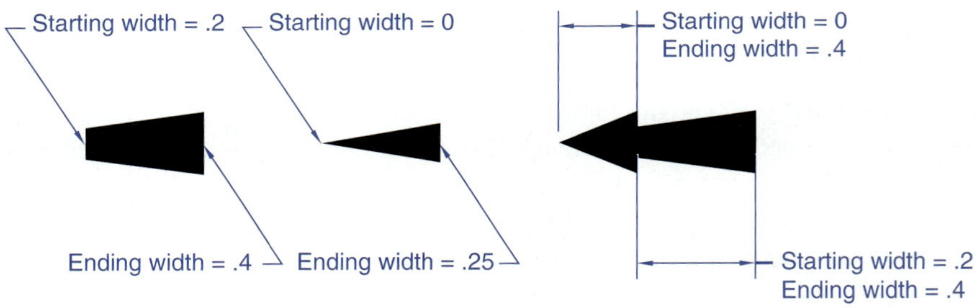

The PLINE command also has a Halfwidth option for drawing wide polylines that are measured from the center to the outside edge. A halfwidth polyline is shown in Figure 8.8 and drawn using this command sequence:

Command: **PL** or **PLINE**↵
Specify start point: *<pick a point>*
Current line-width is 0.0000
Specify next point or [Arc/Close/Halfwidth/Length/Undo/Width]: **H**↵
Specify starting half-width <0.0000>: **.25**↵
Specify ending half-width <0.2500>: **.5**↵
Specify next point or [Arc/Close/Halfwidth/Length/Undo/Width]: *<pick the endpoint>*
Specify next point or [Arc/Close/Halfwidth/Length/Undo/Width]: ↵
Command:

FIGURE 8.8 Using the PLINE Halfwidth option.

Field Notes

As you begin to work with wide polylines you will frequently need to select them for editing. A wide polyline is defined by its boundary and must be picked on an edge to be selected. Picking in the fill area of a polyline finds no object and begins an implied window selection, prompting you to select the other corner. You can either press Esc to cancel and pick the edge, or you can drag the implied crossing box out to where it touches the edge of the polyline and pick.

Exercise 8.3 — Estimated time required: 5 min.

1. Start a new drawing.
2. Draw a straight polyline segment with a 0.25 starting and ending width similar to that shown in Figure 8.6.
3. Draw three different polyline objects using a variety of width options, as was done in Figure 8.7.
4. Draw a halfwidth object similar to Figure 8.8.
5. Save as EX8.3, and close the drawing.

LEARNING CHECKPOINT

- ☐ What is the default polyline width?
- ☐ How do you draw a polyline arc connected to a straight pline segment?
- ☐ After drawing a polyline arc, how do you draw a connecting pline straight segment?
- ☐ How do you automatically set the same polyline starting and ending widths?
- ☐ Explain how to draw a polyline that looks like an arrowhead.
- ☐ Describe the results of the PLINE Halfwidth option.

Creating Geometry

- Drawing and Editing Complex Curves

Editing Polylines

AutoCAD LT provides several options for editing polylines. For example, you can change the width of polyline segments or of the entire polyline object. You can open or close polyline shapes. Straight polyline segments can be made into polyline curves. If polyline objects and nonpolyline objects meet at the endpoints, they can be joined as one polyline object. You can change the vertices of polylines. The ***vertices*** are the points at which polyline segments meet; a single instance is called a ***vertex.*** The editing you can do at vertices includes moving and deleting vertices and straightening between vertices. Polylines are edited with the PEDIT command. To start this command, type **PE** or **PEDIT** at the Command: prompt or pick Polyline in the Object cascade of the Modify pull-down menu.

Using the PEDIT Command Options

Modify II

Modify
Object ▸
Polyline

PEDIT
PE

When you enter the PEDIT command, you get the following prompt, which asks you to select a polyline:

Command: **PE** or **PEDIT**↵
Select polyline: *<pick a polyline object>*
Enter an option [Close/Join/Width/Edit vertex/Fit/Spline/Decurve/Ltype gen/Undo]:

When picking a wide polyline, remember to pick it on the edge. The Select polyline: prompt does not offer all the options of a standard Select objects: prompt. You cannot select the polyline using a window, crossing, or any other specialized selection option. The PEDIT command requires you to select a single polyline object using the pick box. The implied window feature is disabled, so if you pick inside of a wide polyline instead of picking the edge, the Select polyline: prompt is repeated.

After you have performed edits using the PEDIT command, you can use the Undo option to undo the edits one at a time. As with other command options, to undo the entire operation, return to the Command: prompt and use the **U** command. To return to the Command: prompt, you can press Enter at the Enter an option [...]: prompt or press the Esc key.

The PEDIT command offers many several editing options to fine-tune the appearance of the polylines in your drawing. Because all the segments of a polyline are part of a single object, the editing process can be more involved than working with individual line and arc segments. The PEDIT options are explained in the following discussion.

Closing and Opening Polylines

The Close option of the PEDIT command lets you close an open polyline by drawing a segment from the end of the last segment to the beginning of the first segment. After using the Close option, the prompt changes to Show the Open option. Type **O** and press Enter if you want to automatically open the polyline you just closed, as shown in Figure 8.9. The command sequence looks like this:

Command: **PE** or **PEDIT**↵
Select polyline: *<pick the polyline>*
Enter an option [Close/Join/Width/Edit vertex/Fit/Spline/Decurve/Ltype gen/Undo]: **C**↵
Enter an option [Open/Join/Width/Edit vertex/Fit/Spline/Decurve/Ltype gen/Undo]: **O**↵
Enter an option [Close/Join/Width/Edit vertex/Fit/Spline/Decurve/Ltype gen/Undo]: ↵
Command:

FIGURE 8.9 Closing an open polyline and then opening a closed polyline with the PEDIT command.

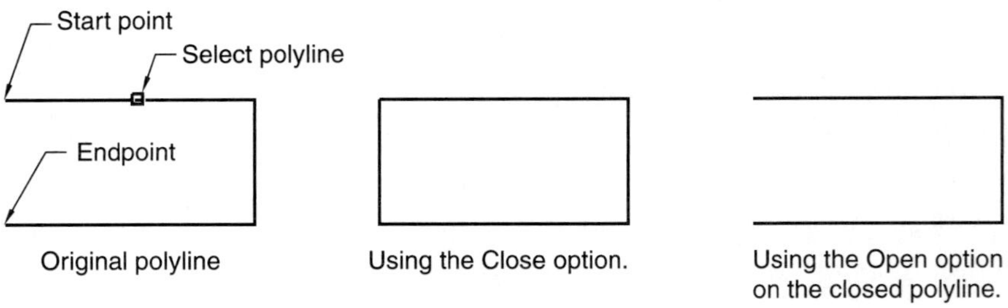

Joining Objects to a Polyline

The Join option of the PEDIT command allows you to join lines, arcs, or other polylines to a polyline if they meet at the endpoints. The Join option removes the curve fitting from a polyline. Curve fitting is discussed later in this chapter. When an object is joined with a polyline, the object and the polyline become one object and the object being joined takes on the same width characteristics as the polyline. Any joined objects are made part of the first selected polyline. Also, the color, layer, lineweight, and linetype of the first polyline are inherited by the joined objects. The prompts work as follows and the result of this sequence is shown in Figure 8.10:

Command: **PE** or **PEDIT**↵
Select polyline: *<pick the polyline line segment>*
Enter an option [Close/Join/Width/Edit vertex/Fit/Spline/Decurve/Ltype gen/Undo]: **J**↵
Select objects: *<pick arc object>*
1 found
Select objects: ↵
1 segments added to polyline
Enter an option [Close/Join/Width/Edit vertex/Fit/Spline/Decurve/Ltype gen/Undo]: ↵
Command:

FIGURE 8.10 Using the PEDIT Join option to connect an object to a polyline and have the object take on the characteristics of the polyline.

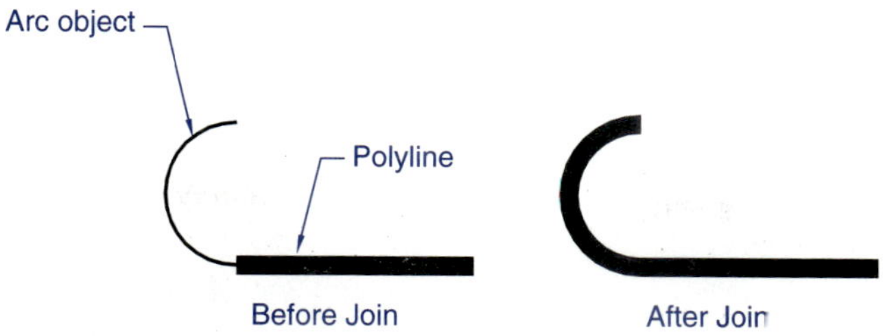

Field Notes

- After picking a polyline object at the Select polyline: prompt, it is not necessary to reselect the same polyline at the Select objects: prompt of the Join option. All you need to do is to select the objects that are to be joined to the first polyline object.
- An object can be joined to a polyline only if one of its endpoints is at the *exact* same location as an endpoint of the polyline. If there is any distance between the endpoints, however small, the objects cannot be joined.
- When the objects selected to join to a polyline are simple line and arc segments, the width setting of the original polyline is applied to the new segments. If the object you are joining is also a polyline, it maintains its original width setting regardless of the width of the original polyline.

Changing Connected Line and Arc Segments to a Polyline and Calculating the Area of a Closed Polyline

In Chapter 6 you learned about calculating the area of objects that were drawn using the LINE command and commands that created closed objects such as circles and polygons. However, you were unable to calculate the area of an object that was made up of connected lines and arcs. To calculate the area of objects like this, you can do one of three things. You can draw the original object using polyline lines and arcs, creating an outline of the object which is a continuous closed polyline. If the object is already drawn using line and arc segments, you can trace the outline of the object using the PLINE command and its options.

If the object is already drawn using line and arc segments, you can change these segments to a continuous polyline. Do this using the PEDIT command. When the PEDIT command asks you to Select polyline:, pick one of the line or arc objects. AutoCAD LT then tells you that "Object selected is not a polyline—Do you want to turn it into one? Y>" After answering yes to this question, AutoCAD LT turns the selected line or arc into a polyline and then gives you the typical PEDIT options. Now, use the Join option to connect the other arc and line segments to the new polyline segment followed by using the AREA command like this:

Command: **PE** or **PEDIT**↵
Select polyline: *<pick one of the line or arc objects>*
Object selected is not a polyline
Do you want to turn it into one? <Y> ↵
Enter an option [Close/Join/Width/Edit vertex/Fit/Spline/Decurve/Ltype gen/Undo]: **J**↵
Select objects: *<select the remaining line and arc objects>*
Select objects: ↵
3 segments added to polyline
Enter an option [Open/Join/Width/Edit vertex/Fit/Spline/Decurve/Ltype gen/Undo]: ↵

Command: **AA** or **AREA**↵
Specify first corner point or [Object/Add/Subtract]: **O**↵
Select objects: **L**↵ *<the polyline is now the last object added to the drawing>*
Area = 19.0686, Perimeter = 17.4248
Command:

Changing Polyline Width

The PEDIT Width option allows you to change the entire width of a polyline to a uniform value that you specify. Look at Figure 8.11 as you follow this command sequence:

Command: **PE** or **PEDIT**↵
Select polyline: *<pick the polyline>*
Enter an option [Close/Join/Width/Edit vertex/Fit/Spline/Decurve/Ltype gen/Undo]: **W**↵
Specify new width for all segments: **.1**↵
Enter an option [Close/Join/Width/Edit vertex/Fit/Spline/Decurve/Ltype gen/Undo]: ↵
Command:

FIGURE 8.11 Using the PEDIT Width option to uniformly change the width of an entire polyline.

Exercise 8.4 — Estimated time required: 5 min.

1. Start a new drawing.
2. Draw an open polyline similar to the original polyline in Figure 8.9; close the polyline; and then open it using the process shown in Figure 8.9.
3. Draw an arc connected to a polyline similar to that shown in Figure 8.10 and then join the arc to the polyline.
4. Draw a polyline similar to the before width change example shown in Figure 8.11 and then perform a width change similar to that in Figure 8.11.
5. Save as EX8.4, and close the drawing.

Editing Polyline Vertices

The Edit vertex option of the PEDIT command allows you to make several different changes to polyline vertices. When you enter the Edit vertex option, AutoCAD LT places an X at the first point of the polyline. You can move the X to another vertex by using the Next or Previous suboptions. This lets you edit the vertex where the X is located. The Next suboption is the initial default and then the default changes to the current application of Next or Previous. Figure 8.12 shows the X located at the vertices of a polyline. The vertex order is the same as when the polyline object was originally created. In this example, the polyline is closed, meaning that the first vertex and the last vertex are in the same location. In Figure 8.12A, the Next option moves the marker toward the last vertex, and in Figure 8.12B the Previous option moves the marker toward the first vertex. The following command sequence demonstrates the process of moving the vertex marker using the Next and Previous options:

Command: **PE** or **PEDIT**↵
Select polyline: *<pick the polyline>*
Enter an option [Open/Join/Width/Edit vertex/Fit/Spline/Decurve/Ltype gen/Undo]: **E**↵
Enter a vertex editing option
[Next/Previous/Break/Insert/Move/Regen/Straighten/Tangent/Width/eXit] <N>: ↵
Enter a vertex editing option
[Next/Previous/Break/Insert/Move/Regen/Straighten/Tangent/Width/eXit] <N>: ↵
Enter a vertex editing option
[Next/Previous/Break/Insert/Move/Regen/Straighten/Tangent/Width/eXit] <N>: **P**↵
Enter a vertex editing option
[Next/Previous/Break/Insert/Move/Regen/Straighten/Tangent/Width/eXit] <P>: ↵
Enter a vertex editing option
[Next/Previous/Break/Insert/Move/Regen/Straighten/Tangent/Width/eXit] <P>: **N**↵
Enter a vertex editing option
[Next/Previous/Break/Insert/Move/Regen/Straighten/Tangent/Width/eXit] <N>:

Locating the X at the desired vertex allows you to specify where the Edit vertex option is applied. The Edit vertex options are explained in the following list:

- **Break:** The Break option breaks the polyline between the two vertices you specify. First, use the Next or Previous option to move the marker to the vertex where you want the break to begin. Then enter the Break option. The Break option allows you to move the X marker to the Next or Previous vertex until you get to the vertex where you want the break to end. Use the Go option to make the break between where the X marker was when you entered the Break option and where you moved the X marker before entering Go. When the first vertex is specified as the start of the break, it is removed from the polyline and the marker snaps to the vertex at the end of the break. Otherwise, the marker snaps back to the start of the break. If you break an open polyline, two separate polylines are created. The sequence used in Figure 8.13 is as follows:

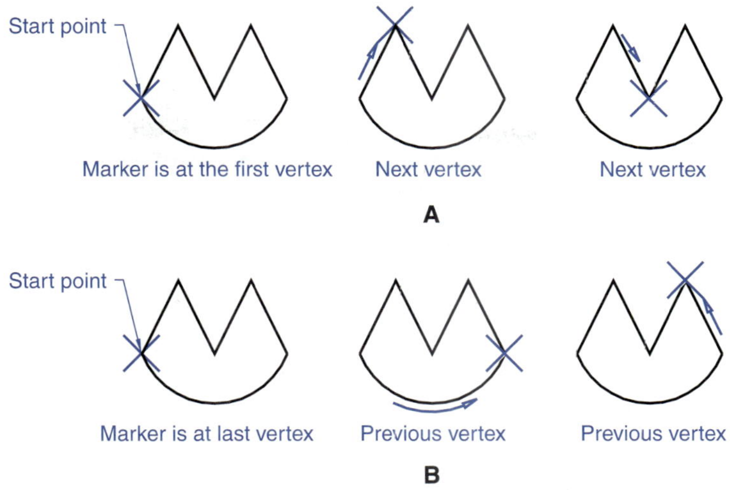

FIGURE 8.12 Using the Edit vertex (A) Next and (B) Previous options.

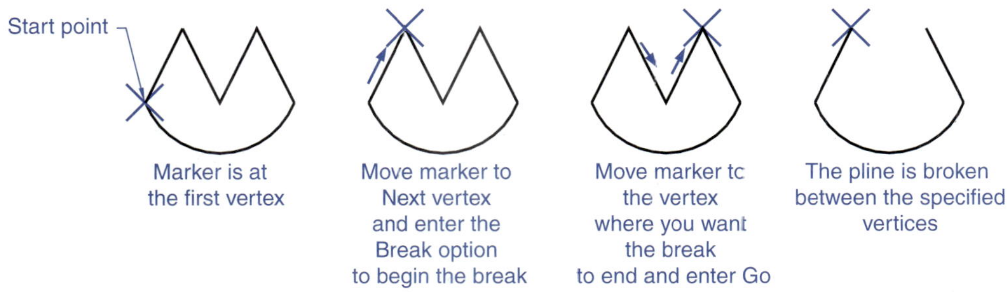

FIGURE 8.13 Using the PEDIT Break option.

Command: **PE** or **PEDIT**↵
Select polyline: <*pick a polyline*>
Enter an option [Open/Join/Width/Edit vertex/Fit/Spline/Decurve/Ltype gen/Undo]: **E**↵
Enter a vertex editing option
[Next/Previous/Break/Insert/Move/Regen/Straighten/Tangent/Width/eXit] <N>: **N**↵
Enter a vertex editing option
[Next/Previous/Break/Insert/Move/Regen/Straighten/Tangent/Width/eXit] <N>: **B**↵
Enter an option [Next/Previous/Go/eXit] <N>: ↵
Enter an option [Next/Previous/Go/eXit] <N>: ↵
Enter an option [Next/Previous/Go/eXit] <N>: **G**↵
Enter a vertex editing option
[Next/Previous/Break/Insert/Move/Regen/Straighten/Tangent/Width/eXit] <N>: **X**↵
Enter an option [Close/Join/Width/Edit vertex/Fit/Spline/Decurve/Ltype gen/Undo]: ↵
Command:

The Break option can also be used to break at a specific vertex without removing any segments if Break is used and Go is specified without moving the vertex marker. When Break is used, the polyline is made into two separate polylines—even closed polylines are affected this way.

- **Insert:** This Edit vertex option allows you to insert a new vertex. To do this, move the marker to the vertex previous to where you want the new vertex and then type **I** and press Enter for the Insert option. You are then asked to enter the location of the new vertex. A rubber-band cursor is connected to the screen crosshairs to assist you in placing the new vertex. A polar or relative coordinate or direct distance entry uses the current vertex as a base point. The new vertex is connected between the vertex at the marker location and the next vertex as shown in Figure 8.14:

Command: **PE** or **PEDIT**↵
Select polyline: <*pick the polyline*>
Enter an option [Open/Join/Width/Edit vertex/Fit/Spline/Decurve/Ltype gen/Undo]: **E**↵
Enter a vertex editing option
[Next/Previous/Break/Insert/Move/Regen/Straighten/Tangent/Width/eXit] <N>: ↵
Enter a vertex editing option

[Next/Previous/Break/Insert/Move/Regen/Straighten/Tangent/Width/eXit] <N>: ↵
Enter a vertex editing option
[Next/Previous/Break/Insert/Move/Regen/Straighten/Tangent/Width/eXit] <N>: **I**↵
Specify location for new vertex: *<pick or type new location>*
Enter a vertex editing option
[Next/Previous/Break/Insert/Move/Regen/Straighten/Tangent/Width/eXit] <N>: **X**↵
Enter an option [Open/Join/Width/Edit vertex/Fit/Spline/Decurve/Ltype gen/Undo]: ↵
Command:

FIGURE 8.14 Using the PEDIT Insert option to insert a new vertex.

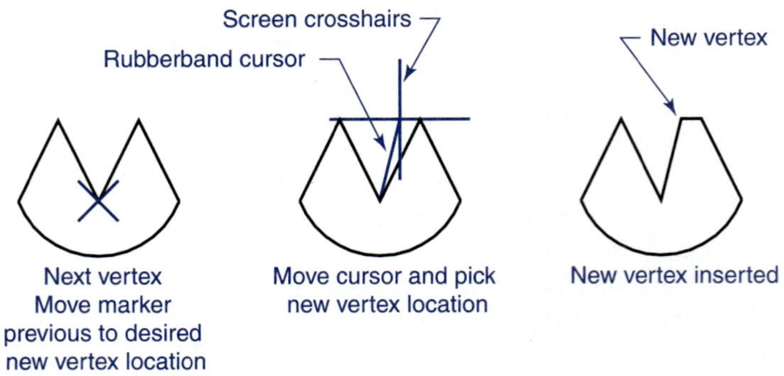

- **Move:** This Edit vertex option allows you to move a vertex to a new position as shown in Figure 8.15. A polar, relative, or absolute coordinate can be entered, or direct distance entry, a pick, or an object snap can be used to indicate the new location. This is the command sequence:

Command: **PE** or **PEDIT**↵
Select polyline: *<pick the polyline>*
Enter an option [Open/Join/Width/Edit vertex/Fit/Spline/Decurve/Ltype gen/Undo]: **E**↵
Enter a vertex editing option
[Next/Previous/Break/Insert/Move/Regen/Straighten/Tangent/Width/eXit] <N>: ↵
Enter a vertex editing option
[Next/Previous/Break/Insert/Move/Regen/Straighten/Tangent/Width/eXit] <N>: ↵
Enter a vertex editing option
[Next/Previous/Break/Insert/Move/Regen/Straighten/Tangent/Width/eXit] <N>: **M**↵
Specify new location for marked vertex: *<pick or type new location>*
Enter a vertex editing option
[Next/Previous/Break/Insert/Move/Regen/Straighten/Tangent/Width/eXit] <N>: **X**↵
Enter an option [Open/Join/Width/Edit vertex/Fit/Spline/Decurve/Ltype gen/Undo]: ↵
Command:

FIGURE 8.15 Using the PEDIT Move option to move a vertex.

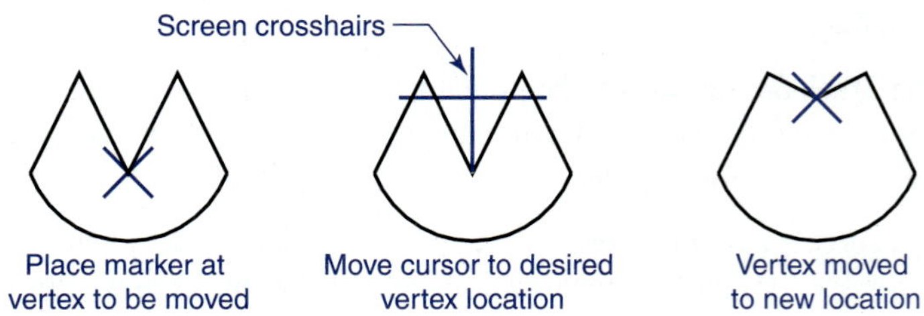

- **Regen:** This Edit vertex option regenerates the computer screen and recomputes the screen coordinates for the vertices that you have edited. This option is very useful for vertext editing options that are not immediately displayed, such as segment width changes.
- **Straighten:** The Straighten option removes the vertices of a polyline between the vertices you specify. First, use the Next or Previous option to move the marker to the vertex where you want the straightening to begin. Then enter the Straighten option. The Straighten option allows you to move the X marker to the Next or Previous vertex until you get to the

vertex where you want the straightening to end. Use the Go option to make the break between where you placed the X marker after entering the Straighten option and where you moved the X marker before entering Go. The marker then snaps back to the vertex where you started the straightening process as shown in Figure 8.16. The command sequence is shown here:

```
Command: PE or PEDIT↵
Select polyline: <pick the polyline>
Enter an option [Open/Join/Width/Edit vertex/Fit/Spline/Decurve/Ltype gen/Undo]: E↵
Enter a vertex editing option
[Next/Previous/Break/Insert/Move/Regen/Straighten/Tangent/Width/eXit] <N>: ↵
Enter a vertex editing option
[Next/Previous/Break/Insert/Move/Regen/Straighten/Tangent/Width/eXit] <N>: S↵
Enter an option [Next/Previous/Go/eXit] <N>: ↵
Enter an option [Next/Previous/Go/eXit] <N>: ↵
Enter an option [Next/Previous/Go/eXit] <N>: G↵
Enter a vertex editing option
[Next/Previous/Break/Insert/Move/Regen/Straighten/Tangent/Width/eXit] <N>: X↵
Enter an option [Open/Join/Width/Edit vertex/Fit/Spline/Decurve/Ltype gen/Undo]: ↵
Command:
```

FIGURE 8.16 Using the PEDIT Straighten option.

- **Tangent:** This Edit vertex option allows you to attach a specific tangency direction to individual vertices for later use in curve fitting. Changes to tangency are not evident until curve fitting is applied to a polyline, so applications of the Tangent option are discussed under the heading **Fitting Curves to Polyline Vertices,** which follows this discussion.
- **Width:** The Edit vertex Width option allows you to change the width of each polyline segment. To do this, move the marker to the start of the polyline segment where you want the width change to begin and then enter the Width option. AutoCAD LT prompts for a beginning and an ending width. To change the width of the segment to a uniform width, enter the same value for both the beginning and the ending width. Specifying different beginning and ending widths creates a tapered segment. The specified width values are applied to the segment that begins at the current vertex. The following command sequence shows how to change the width of the two polyline segments shown in Figure 8.17:

```
Command: PE or PEDIT
Select polyline: <pick a polyline>
Enter an option [Open/Join/Width/Edit vertex/Fit/Spline/Decurve/Ltype gen/Undo]: E↵
Enter a vertex editing option
[Next/Previous/Break/Insert/Move/Regen/Straighten/Tangent/Width/eXit] <N>: ↵
Enter a vertex editing option
[Next/Previous/Break/Insert/Move/Regen/Straighten/Tangent/Width/eXit] <N>: W↵
Specify starting width for next segment <0.0000>: ↵
Specify ending width for next segment <0.0000>: .2↵
Enter a vertex editing option
[Next/Previous/Break/Insert/Move/Regen/Straighten/Tangent/Width/eXit] <N>: ↵
Enter a vertex editing option
[Next/Previous/Break/Insert/Move/Regen/Straighten/Tangent/Width/eXit] <N>: W↵
```

Specify starting width for next segment <0.0000>: **.2**↵
Specify ending width for next segment <0.2000>: **0**↵
Enter a vertex editing option
[Next/Previous/Break/Insert/Move/Regen/Straighten/Tangent/Width/eXit] <N>: **X**↵
Enter an option [Open/Join/Width/Edit vertex/Fit/Spline/Decurve/Ltype gen/Undo]: ↵
Command:

FIGURE 8.17 Using the Edit vertex Width option to change the widths of polyline segments.

Exercise 8.5

Estimated time required: 10 min.

1. Start a new drawing.
2. Draw a polyline similar to the upper left object shown in Figure 8.12. Use the Direction option to make the last arc segment.
3. Make five copies of the object. You should have a total of six objects.
4. Enter the PEDIT command, select one of the objects, and move the marker around on the object as was done in Figure 8.12.
5. Break the polyline similar to the results in Figure 8.13.
6. Select another one of the objects and establish a new vertex similar to that shown in Figure 8.14.
7. Select another one of the objects and move a vertex to obtain results like those shown in Figure 8.15.
8. Select another one of the objects and straighten a section as was done in Figure 8.16.
9. Select another one of the objects and change the width of two segments as shown in Figure 8.17.
10. Save as EX8.5, and close the drawing.

Fitting Curves to Polyline Vertices

The Fit option of the PEDIT command allows curve fitting of existing polylines. The term *curve fitting* refers to the creation of a smooth curve from a series of tangent arcs that pass through each of the vertices in a polyline. A fit curve operation is performed on a polyline in Figure 8.18 using the tangency defaults. Study the following command sequence:

Command: **PE** or **PEDIT**↵
Select polyline: *<pick the polyline>*
Enter an option [Close/Join/Width/Edit vertex/Fit/Spline/Decurve/Ltype gen/Undo]: **F**↵
Enter an option [Close/Join/Width/Edit vertex/Fit/Spline/Decurve/Ltype gen/Undo]: ↵
Command:

FIGURE 8.18 Using the PEDIT Fit option to make curves out of polyline segments. The Fit curve passes through the polyline vertices.

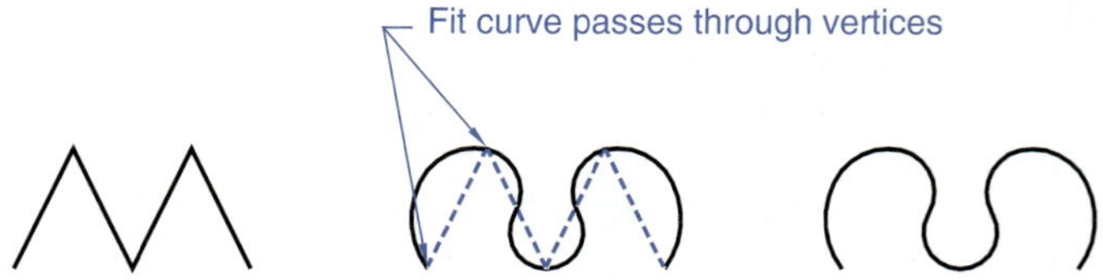

The appearance of a curve fit polyline is controlled by the tangency specification for each individual vertex. By default, the curves are calculated to maintain tangency between adjoining arc segments while using the smallest possible "bulge" on the arcs. Figure 8.19A shows a curve-fitting application that uses the default vertex tangency directions. The Edit vertex Tangent option of the PEDIT command allows you to attach a specific tangency direction to individual vertices. This makes it possible to fine-tune the appearance of curve-fitted polylines to suit a variety of applications.

First, enter the Edit vertex option of PEDIT and move the marker to the desired vertex. When you enter the Tangent option AutoCAD LT prompts you to specify the direction of vertex tangent and attaches a rubber-band line from the vertex to the cursor. The tangency direction can be specified numerically or by dragging the cursor in the desired direction and pressing the pick button. When the vertex marker is on a vertex that has been assigned a specific tangency, the standard "X" marker displays an arrow pointing in the direction of tangency (see Figure 8.19B). The results of specifying a tangent direction are not evident until curve fitting is applied. If you modify the tangency specifications for a polyline that has already had curve fitting applied, the changes are not displayed until the Fit option is used again.

The illustration in Figure 8.19 demonstrates the curve-fitting results using default tangency compared with a possible application of the Tangent option. The command sequence for the Tangent option is as follows:

```
Command: PE or PEDIT↵
Select polyline: <pick the polyline>
Enter an option [Close/Join/Width/Edit vertex/Fit/Spline/Decurve/Ltype gen/Undo]: E↵
Enter a vertex editing option
[Next/Previous/Break/Insert/Move/Regen/Straighten/Tangent/Width/eXit] <N>: ↵
Enter a vertex editing option
[Next/Previous/Break/Insert/Move/Regen/Straighten/Tangent/Width/eXit] <N>: T↵
Specify direction of vertex tangent: <pick or type an angle>
Enter a vertex editing option
[Next/Previous/Break/Insert/Move/Regen/Straighten/Tangent/Width/eXit] <N>: X↵
Enter an option [Close/Join/Width/Edit vertex/Fit/Spline/Decurve/Ltype gen/Undo]: ↵
Command:
```

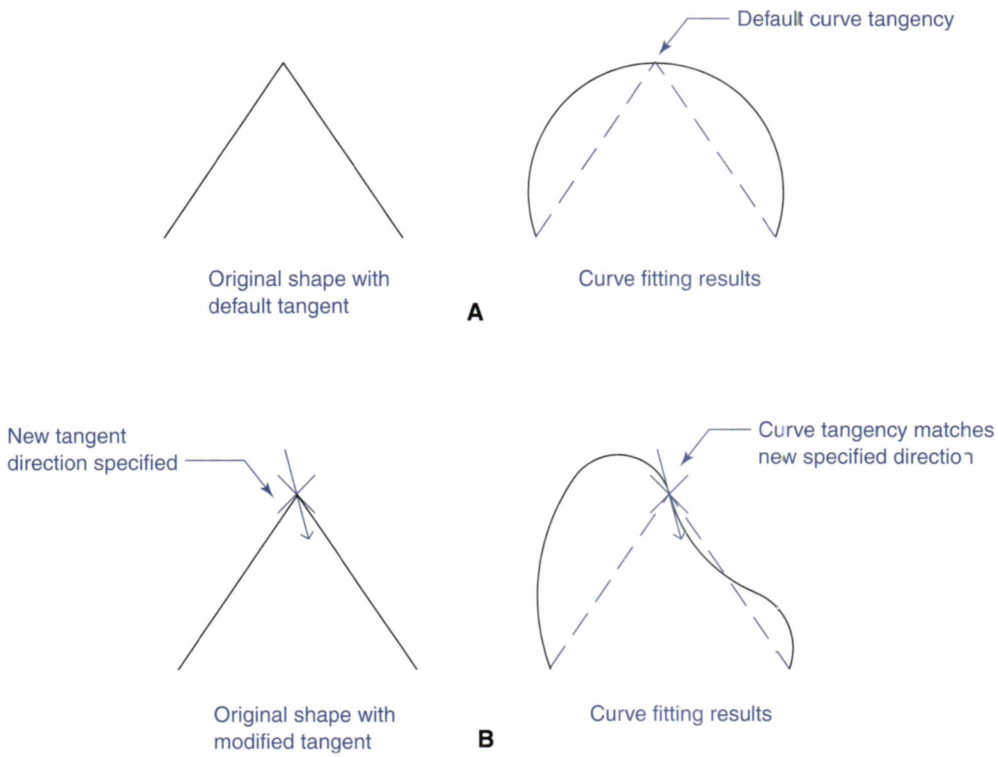

FIGURE 8.19 The Edit vertex Tangent option allows specific directions of tangency to be attached to individual vertices in order to control the results of curve fitting.

Field Notes

- The Fit option works well when you need to smooth the line between the points of a graph or sheet metal pattern layout that is originally created by connecting points with straight polyline segments, as shown in Figure 8.20.

FIGURE 8.20 The PEDIT Fit option works well to smooth the polyline segments that are used to connect the points of a graph.

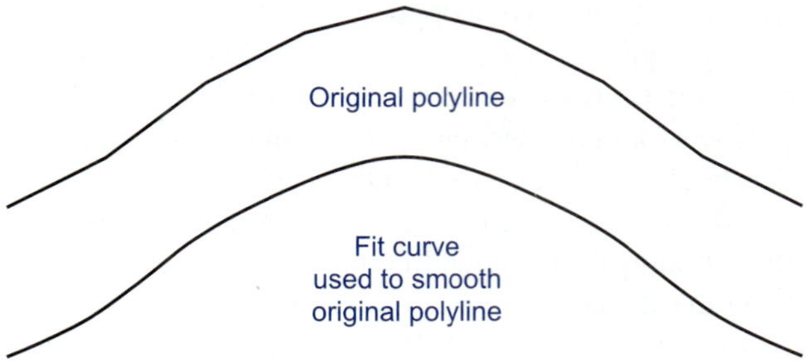

- If a tangency direction is set to be the same angle as an adjoining straight pline segment, that segment remains straight when a fit curve is applied.
- The polyline data are removed when you EXPLODE a curve-fit polyline, but the shape remains the same. You can use the PEDIT command to turn the object back into a polyline.
- The STRETCH, TRIM, and EXTEND commands affect a curve-fit polyline. For example, stretching a curve-fit pline does not cause a refit and may leave arcs no longer tangent to each other. Trimming or breaking a curve-fit pline makes the curve fitting permanent. This means that the curves are converted to actual pline arc segments, so the temporary vertices inserted by curve fitting are incorporated into the pline definition. You can still use the decurve option. However, a decurve reveals new vertex locations that were not used in the initial pline definition.

Creating Spline Curves

The Spline option of the PEDIT command also smoothes polyline segments. This option produces a spline approximation, called a B-spline. This type of spline curve is not as accurate as a true spline, which is created with the SPLINE command (discussed later). The difference between the Fit curve and the Spline curve is that the Fit curve passes through the vertices and the Spline curve uses the vertices as a frame for the curve development. The Spline curve only passes through the first and last vertices, and is pulled toward the others but does not necessarily pass through them. A comparison between the Fit and Spline curve options is shown in Figure 8.21. The Spline curve option works like this:

Command: **PE** or **PEDIT**↵
Select polyline: *<pick the polyline>*
Enter an option [Close/Join/Width/Edit vertex/Fit/Spline/Decurve/Ltype gen/Undo]: **S**↵
Enter an option [Close/Join/Width/Edit vertex/Fit/Spline/Decurve/Ltype gen/Undo]: ↵
Command:

FIGURE 8.21 Using the PEDIT Spline option to make curves out of polyline segments. The Spline curve does not pass through the polyline vertices.

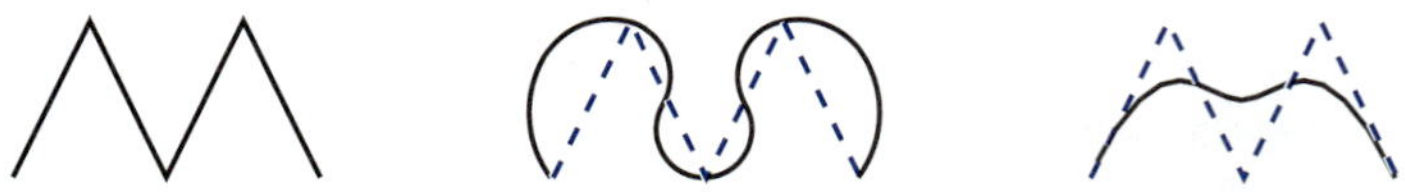

Additional Curve Options

There are two B-spline curve options that are accessed using the SPLINETYPE system variable. The default setting of 6 creates a ***cubic curve*** when using the PEDIT Spline option. If you change the SPLINETYPE setting to 5, you get a ***quadratic curve.*** The cubic curve default is smoother than the quadratic curve. Change the SPLINETYPE like this:

Command**: SPLINETYPE**↵
Enter new value for SPLINETYPE <6>**: 5**↵
Command**:**

You can also adjust the number of segments that are used to create a spline curve. The number of segments is established with the SPLINESEGS variable. The default number of segments is 8, which produces a smooth curve that requires little regeneration time and file size. If you increase the number of segments, you get a smoother curve, but you also increase file size and regeneration time. The SPLINESEGS variable is changed like this:

Command: **SPLINESEGS↵**
Enter new value for SPLINESEGS <8>: **12↵**
Command:

The SPLINESEGS can also be set in the Display tab of the Options dialog box. Enter the desired value in the text box labeled *Segments in a polyline curve* found in the Display resolution area.

Field Notes

Editing commands behave in the following different ways when used on spline-fit plines:

- The STRETCH command stretches the frame such that the spline is recalculated and a new curve is produced.
- OFFSET produces a spline-fit pline with no frame.
- DIVIDE, MEASURE, AREA Object, HATCH, FILLET, and CHAMFER see only the spline, not the frame.
- PEDIT's Join option automatically decurves spline fits for all plines being joined.
- PEDIT's Edit vertex option subcommands move the vertex marker (X) only to the vertices of the frame, whether visible or not. Edit vertex option effects include the following: Break will discard the spline; Insert, Move, Straighten, and Width cause an automatic refit (Width behaves as usual, displaying only if Regen is used when exiting the Edit vertex mode); Tangent specifications on vertices have no effect on a spline-fit curve. The spline frame is discussed later in this chapter.
- Object snap sees the spline, not the frame. To snap to control points, do a grip selection or decurve the spline.
- EXTEND adds a new vertex at the intersection of the frame with the boundary geometry.
- You can also edit with grips by selecting the spline-fit curve. The grips are displayed at the vertices. Use any of the desired grip edit commands to change the spline-fit curve accordingly.

Removing the Curve from a Fit or Spline Curve

The PEDIT command Decurve option allows you to remove the curve of a polyline that was edited with the Fit or Spline options. This process changes the curved object back to its original polyline segments. The command sequence is provided in the following and an example is displayed in Figure 8.22:

Command: **PE** or **PEDIT↵**
Select polyline: *<pick the polyline>*
Enter an option [Close/Join/Width/Edit vertex/Fit/Spline/Decurve/Ltype gen/Undo]: **D↵**
Enter an option [Close/Join/Width/Edit vertex/Fit/Spline/Decurve/Ltype gen/Undo]: ↵
Command:

FIGURE 8.22 Using the PEDIT Decurve option.

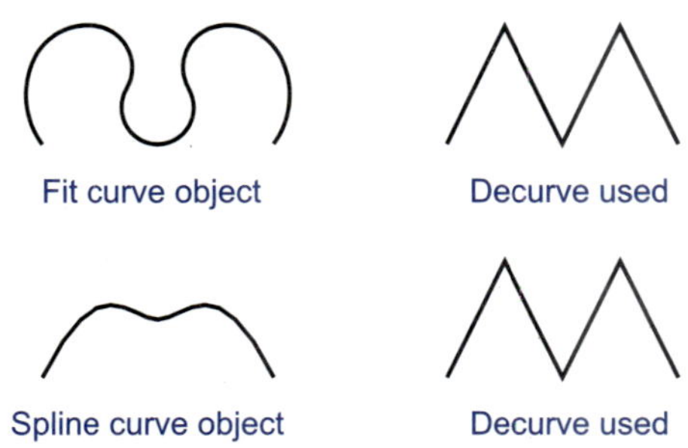

Field Notes

- The arc is straightened when the Decurve option is used on curved segments that were created using the Arc option of the PLINE command.
- User assigned tangencies are not lost by decurving. They remain intact and are used by any future curve-fitting operations.
- If a spline-fit polyline is edited using commands such as BREAK and TRIM, the spline frame is lost and any future attempt to decurve the spline back to its original frame has no effect. Also, since the spline no longer has an associated frame, the curve is now generated using standard polyline arc segments, resulting in many new vertices being inserted.

Exercise 8.6

Estimated time required: 10 min.

1. Start a new drawing.
2. Draw an open polyline similar to the original polyline shown in Figure 8.18.
3. Make three copies of the polyline.
4. Use the PEDIT Fit option on the first polyline. You should have results similar to Figure 8.18.
5. Use the Edit vertex Tangent option to adjust the tangency directions for the vertices on the two peaks of the second polyline. Next, use the PEDIT Fit option and compare the results with the curve fit created in step 4.
6. Use the PEDIT Spline option on the third other polylines. You should have results similar to Figure 8.20.
7. Use the Fit option on the fourth polyline and then use the Decurve option to remove the curve.
8. Save as EX8.6, and close the drawing.

Controlling the Appearance of Polyline Linetypes

The Ltype gen option in the PEDIT command lets you control the way patterned linetypes are drawn in relationship to the vertices of the polyline. The Ltype gen option has ON and OFF settings. OFF is the initial default, which draws linetypes starting and ending with a dash at each vertex. The dashes are placed uniformly with the vertices. When Ltype gen is ON, the linetype is drawn with the dashes uniformly spaced without regard to the vertices. An example of a polyline edited with Ltype gen OFF and ON is shown in Figure 8.23. This is the command sequence:

Command: **PE** or **PEDIT**↵
Select polyline: *<pick a polyline>*
Enter an option [Close/Join/Width/Edit vertex/Fit/Spline/Decurve/Ltype gen/Undo]: **L**↵
Enter polyline linetype generation option [ON/OFF] <Off>: **ON**↵
Enter an option [Close/Join/Width/Edit vertex/Fit/Spline/Decurve/Ltype gen/Undo]: ↵
Command:

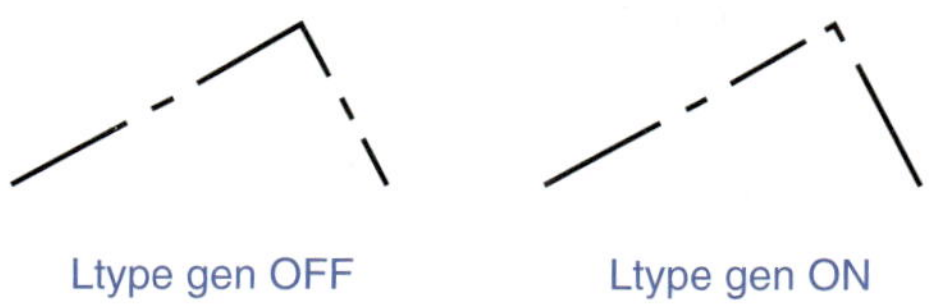

FIGURE 8.23 A comparison of the PEDIT Ltype gen options.

Field Notes

When Ltype gen is ON, short segments display a dashed line, but a corner may not be visible if the corner lines up with a gap.

Drawing Fillets and Chamfers on Polylines

Drawing fillets and chamfers were discussed in Chapter 7 with a brief mention of the Polyline option in the FILLET and CHAMFER commands. The Polyline option allows you to pick a polyline and automatically have all of the corners either filleted or chamfered with the current FILLET or CHAMFER settings. For all of the corners of a closed polyline to be filleted or chamfered, the last segment must have been closed using the Close option. Figure 8.24 shows the difference between drawing fillets and chamfers on closed polylines with and without using the Close option on the last segment. The Fillet command's Polyline option works like this:

Command: **F** or **FILLET**↵
Current settings: Mode = TRIM, Radius = 0.5000
Select first object or [Polyline/Radius/Trim]: **P**↵
Select 2D polyline: <*pick the polyline*>
4 lines were filleted
Command:

FIGURE 8.24 Using the FILLET command to round the corners of a polyline. The Close option must have been used to connect the last polyline line segment in order for all corners to be rounded.

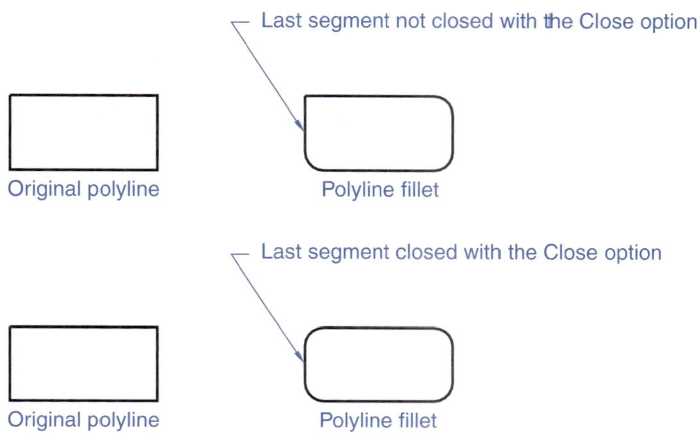

If you want to fillet or chamfer only one corner of a closed polyline, for example, use the Select first object: and Select second object: prompts just as you would when dealing with line objects.

Field Notes

When an object such as a line is filleted or chamfered with a polyline, the result is a desired fillet or chamfer and the line becomes part of the polyline.

Exploding Polylines

Polylines segments can be changed to individual lines and arcs by using the EXPLODE command. If you explode a wide polyline, as shown in Figure 8.25, the result is a series of individual thin lines and arcs that follow along the center of the original wide polyline. Access this command by picking the Explode button in the Modify toolbar, by picking Explode in the Modify pull-down menu, or by typing **EXPLODE** at the Command: prompt. This is how the EXPLODE command works:

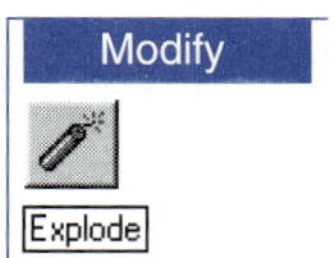

Modify
Explode
EXPLODE
X

Command: **EXPLODE**↵
Select objects: ⟨*pick the polyline*⟩
Select objects: ↵
Exploding this polyline has lost width information
The UNDO command will restore it.
Command:

If the polyline you are exploding has width or tangency specifications, AutoCAD LT warns you about the loss of width information when using the EXPLODE command. You are also reminded that using the UNDO command restores the polyline to its original condition.

FIGURE 8.25 Using the EXPLODE command to remove the polyline data.

Exercise 8.7 — Estimated time required: 5 min.

1. Open a new drawing.
2. Draw a polyline using a center linetype similar to the example at left in Figure 8.23 and then make a copy of the polyline.
3. Use the PEDIT command, select the second polyline, and turn the Ltype gen option ON. Observe the difference between the polylines. The first polyline has Ltype gen OFF by default.
4. Draw a rectangular polyline without using the Close option on the last segment and then fillet the polyline corners as was done to the top example in Figure 8.24.
5. Draw a rectangular polyline using the Close option on the last segment and then fillet the polyline corners as was done to the bottom example in Figure 8.24.
6. Draw an object similar to the original polyline in Figure 8.25 and then use the EXPLODE command to remove the polyline data.
7. Save as EX8.7, and close the drawing.

LEARNING CHECKPOINT

- ☐ How do you exit the PEDIT command?
- ☐ Describe the results of using the PEDIT Join option.
- ☐ Identify at least three ways to calculate the area of objects made up of line and arc segments.
- ☐ Name the PEDIT option that is used to change the entire width of a polyline to a uniform value.
- ☐ How do you select the desired polyline vertex when using the PEDIT command?
- ☐ Name the Edit vertex option that allows you to change the width of individual polyline segments.
- ☐ What is the difference between the Edit vertex Insert and Move options?
- ☐ Describe the difference between a Fit and a Spline curve.
- ☐ What is the effect of Ltype gen ON and OFF?
- ☐ How must a closed polyline be constructed to automatically have all corners rounded with the FILLET command?
- ☐ What is the result of exploding a polyline?

Creating Geometry

- Drawing and Editing Complex Curves

Drawing and Editing Spline Curves

Draw
Spline
Draw
Spline
SPLINE
SPL

Earlier, you learned how to create a spline curve from an existing polyline by using the Spline option of the PEDIT command. You can draw true spline curves of your own design using the SPLINE command. A true spline curve passes through the vertices. The spline curve created by AutoCAD LT is called a *nonuniform rational B-spline,* commonly referred to as NURBS. The smoothed polylines that you created with the Fit and Spline options of the PEDIT command are referred to as ***spline-fit curves.*** The differences between NURBS and spline-fit curves are as follows:

- NURBS are true spline curves that pass through the control points.
- Spline-fit polylines are a linear approximation of a true spline.
- NURBS create curved objects more accurately than spline-fit curves.
- True spline curves can be edited with several options using the SPLINEDIT command to be discussed later. Spline-fit curves are converted to splines when edited with the SPLINEDIT command.
- When a true spline and spline-fit curve have about the same shape, the true spline takes up less disk space.
- Both true splines and spline-fit curves can be edited with grips, but the true spline maintains its definition.

Access the SPLINE command by picking the Spline button in the Draw toolbar, by picking Spline in the Draw pull-down menu, or by typing **SPL** or **SPLINE** at the Command: prompt. When you enter the SPLINE command, you are asked to enter a series of two or more points. When you have picked the desired number of points and pressed Enter, the cursor moves back to the start point and you are asked to enter the start tangent. The start tangent determines how the beginning of the spline looks. You can pick a start tangent in any direction. After picking a start tangent, the cursor moves back to the end of the spline and you are asked to enter an end tangent. The end tangent controls the appearance of the spline end. You can press Enter at the tangent requests to have AutoCAD LT use the default tangency directions or you can enter specific tangent directions. Figure 8.26 shows the results of a spline drawn with different tangent endings. The SPLINE command works like this:

Command: **SPL** or **SPLINE**↵
Specify first point or [Object]: *<pick a point>*
Specify next point: *<pick another point>*
Specify next point or [Close/Fit tolerance] <start tangent>: *<pick another point>*
Specify next point or [Close/Fit tolerance] <start tangent>: *<pick another point>*
Specify next point or [Close/Fit tolerance] <start tangent>: *<pick another point>*
Specify next point or [Close/Fit tolerance] <start tangent>: *<pick another point>*
Specify next point or [Close/Fit tolerance] <start tangent>: ↵
Specify start tangent: *<pick a tangency direction or press Enter to accept the default>*
Specify end tangent: *<pick a tangency direction or press Enter to accept the default>*
Command:

FIGURE 8.26 Several different Spline curve starting and ending tangency options on open splines.

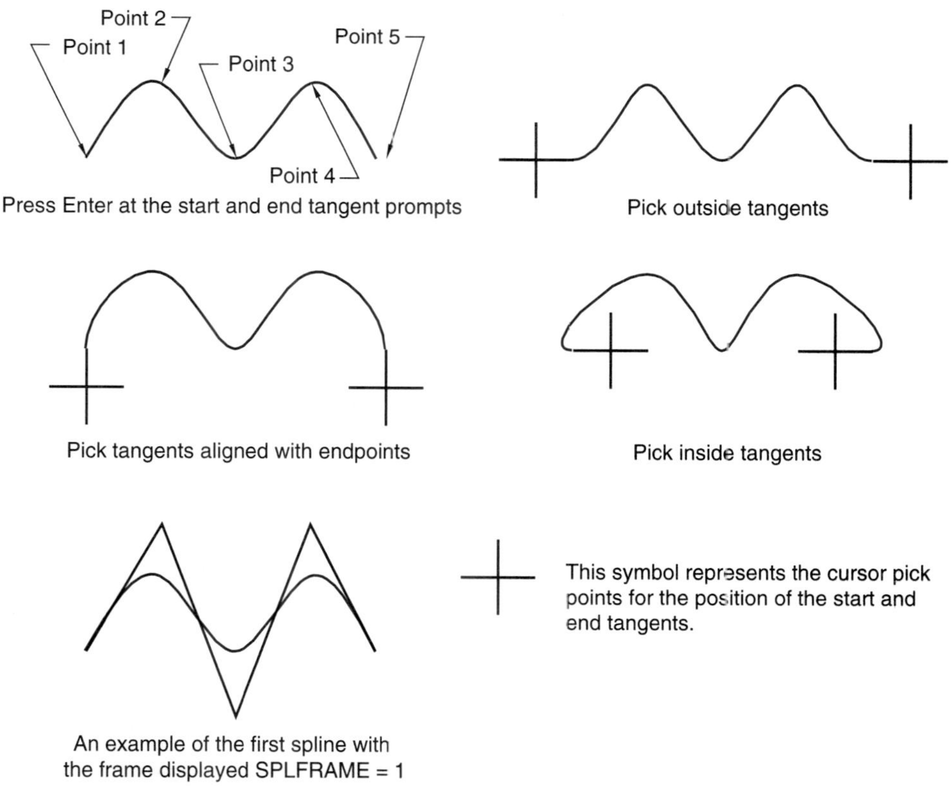

Displaying the Spline Frame

The spline frame is a display of the original polyline frame that is used to create either spline-fit or true spline curves. The spline frame is not displayed by default, but it can be displayed using the SPLFRAME system variable. The initial setting of SPLFRAME is 0 (zero), which means the spline frame is turned off. To show the spline frame, set the value to 1 (on) like this:

Command: **SPLFRAME**↵
Enter new value for SPLFRAME <0>: **1**↵
Command:

When SPLFRAME is on, the spline frame is automatically displayed when you create a true spline with the SPLINE command, or when you use PEDIT, on a polyline, to create a spline curve with the Spline option. If you turn SPLFRAME on after drawing spline curves, the spline frame is not immediately displayed. You need to type REGEN at the Command: prompt and press Enter to have the frame shown. Figures 8.26 and 8.27 show examples of the spline frame when displayed.

Field Notes

The SPLFRAME variable affects all spline objects, but the SPLINESEGS and SPLINETYPE variables affect only spline-fit polylines.

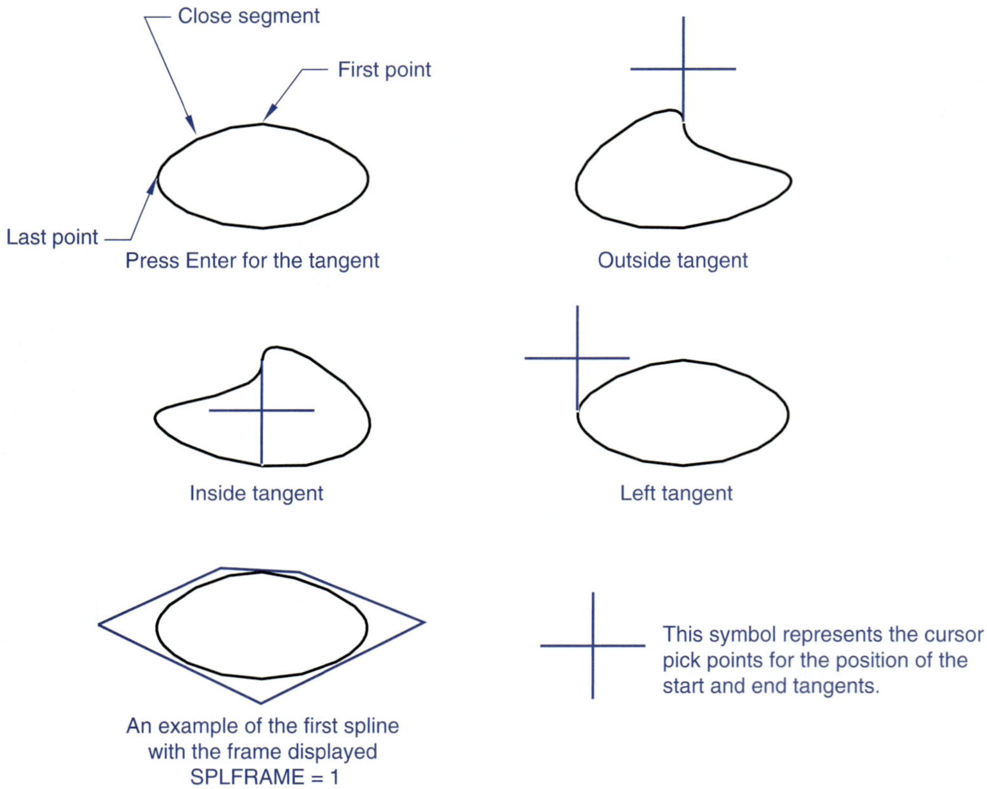

FIGURE 8.27 Several different Spline curve starting and ending tangency options on closed splines.

Exercise 8.8 Estimated time required: 5 min.

1. Open a new drawing.
2. Turn SPLFRAME on.
3. Draw four spline curves each with different ending tangents similar to the four examples shown in Figure 8.26.
4. Notice the spline frame display with the spline curves you create.
5. Turn SPLFRAME off.
6. Type REGEN at the Command: prompt and press Enter.
7. Notice that the spline frames are gone.
8. Save as EX8.8, and close the drawing.

Converting Spline Polylines to True Splines

You can convert a spline polyline into a true spline using the Object option of the SPLINE command. This works on curves that are created using the PEDIT Spline option but not on curves made using the PEDIT Fit option. AutoCAD LT asks you to select the objects:

Command: **SPL** or **SPLINE**↵
Specify first point or [Object]: **O**↵
Select objects to convert to splines
Select objects: *<pick one or more spline-fit polylines>*
n found
Select objects: ↵
Command:

Only a spline that still has an associated frame can be converted. If a spline-fit polyline has lost its frame, the PEDIT Spline option can be used again to restore the frame. Then the resulting polyline object can be successfully converted into a SPLINE object.

The DELOBJ system variable is used to show or delete objects that are used to create other objects, such as the spline frame. If DELOBJ is ON (1) the original spline-fit pline is deleted when the spline object is created. When OFF (0), the original object is retained. DELOBJ is ON by default.

Field Notes

Keep in mind that **U** can be typed at the SPLINE prompt, followed by pressing ENTER, to undo as many of the drawn segments as necessary—even though the option does not appear in the prompt.

Closing a Spline

The Spline command's Close option allows you to close the spline between the endpoint and the first point. After using the Close option, you are asked to enter a single tangent direction. This is because the start and end are a single point in a closed spline. The tangent you select affects the results of the closed spline in a variety of ways, as shown in Figure 8.27. This is the command sequence:

Command: **SPL** or **SPLINE**↵
Specify first point or [Object]: *<pick a point>*
Specify next point: *<pick another point>*
Specify next point or [Close/Fit tolerance] <start tangent>: *<pick another point>*
Specify next point or [Close/Fit tolerance] <start tangent>: *<pick another point>*
Specify next point or [Close/Fit tolerance] <start tangent>: C↵
Specify tangent: *<pick a tangency direction or press Enter to accept the default>*
Command:

Exercise 8.9 **Estimated time required: 5 min.**

1. Open a new drawing.
2. Draw four spline curves using the Close option. Each polyline should have different ending tangents similar to the four examples shown in Figure 8.27.
3. Save as EX8.9, and close the drawing.

Adjusting the Fit Tolerance of a Spline

The SPLINE command has a Fit Tolerance option that allows you to control how close the spline curve comes to the pick points. The default fit tolerance is 0 (zero). This forces the curve to be drawn so it passes directly through the pick points. Values greater than zero create different results and force the curve away from the pick points. The Fit Tolerance value is a proportional value, meaning that the value must be increased to affect larger splines in the same way. The results of different fit tolerances are shown in Figure 8.28 and the option works like this:

Command: **SPL** or **SPLINE**↵
Specify first point or [Object]: *<pick a point>*
Specify next point: *<pick another point>*
Specify next point or [Close/Fit tolerance] <start tangent>: **F**↵
Specify fit tolerance <0.0000>: **1**↵
Specify next point or [Close/Fit tolerance] <start tangent>: *<pick another point>*
Specify next point or [Close/Fit tolerance] <start tangent>: *<pick another point>*
Specify next point or [Close/Fit tolerance] <start tangent>: ↵
Specify start tangent: *<pick a tangency direction or press Enter to accept the default>*
Specify end tangent: *<pick a tangency direction or press Enter to accept the default>*
Command:

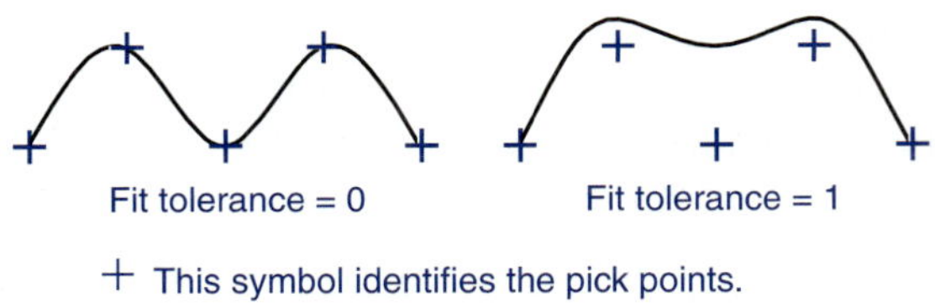

FIGURE 8.28 The results of different Fit Tolerance settings.

Field Notes

- The spline shown in Figure 8.28 is drawn using a 1 × 1 snap grid so each pick point is 1 unit away from the next on each axis. If this same fit tolerance of 1.0 were used on a spline whose pick points were 20 units or so from each other, the effect would be less visible.
- You can type either **F** or **T** to access the Fit Tolerance option.
- Although the Fit Tolerance is displayed at each prompt and can be changed at any time, the value is not local to the current vertex; instead, it affects the entire spline.

Exercise 8.10 **Estimated time required: 5 min.**

1. Open a new drawing.
2. Draw eight spline curves each with different Fit Tolerance settings, similar to the examples shown in Figure 8.28.
3. Save as EX8.10, and close the drawing.

Editing Splines

Modify II

Edit Spline

Modify
Object ▸
Spline

SPLINEDIT
SPE

AutoCAD LT provides you with several ways to edit spline curves. For example, you can reduce or increase the number of fit points of a spline. More fit points increase the accuracy. You can move fit points to change the shape of the spline. Spline curves are edited by picking Spline in the Object cascade of the Modify pull-down menu or by typing **SPLINEDIT** at the Command: prompt. Selecting a spline-fit pline with SPLINEDIT automatically converts the pline object into a SPLINE object and the command continues as it normally would. After entering the command and selecting a spline, grips are displayed at the control points. The spline edit options follow:

Command: **SPE** or **SPLINEDIT**↵
Select spline: *<pick the spline object>*
Enter an option [Fit data/Close/Move vertex/Refine/rEverse/Undo]:

The Undo and eXit options function as previously discussed.

Field Notes

There are two types of fit points. One type is called an ***interpolation point,*** which is a point through which a curve or surface passes to define the curve or surface. The other is an ***approximation point,*** which is a point that a curve or surface follows, but depending on the Fit tolerance, might not pass through.

Changing the Spline-Fit Data

Fit data include specific information about a spline such as the fit points, the fit tolerance, and all tangents associated with splines created using the SPLINE command. Spline-fit polylines converted into spline objects have no fit data. Also, some options of the SPLINEDIT command result in the loss of fit data, which somewhat reduces your flexibility for editing that spline. The Fit Data option of the SPLINEDIT command allows you to perform several editing tasks with the fit points. The Fit Data options are available when you type **F** and press Enter as follows:

Command: **SPE** or **SPLINEDIT**↵
Select spline: *<pick the spline object>*
Enter an option [Fit data/Close/Move vertex/Refine/rEverse/Undo]: **F**↵
Enter a fit data option
[Add/Close/Delete/Move/Purge/Tangents/toLerance/eXit] <eXit>:

The Fit Data options are explained next.

Add: This option allows you to add one or more fit points to the spline curve. To do this, select a grip as shown in Figure 8.29 and follow these prompts:

Enter an option [Fit data/Close/Move vertex/Refine/rEverse/Undo]: **F**↵
Enter a fit data option
[Add/Close/Delete/Move/Purge/Tangents/toLerance/eXit] <eXit>: **A**↵
Specify control point <exit>: *<select a control point grip>*
Specify new point <exit>: *<pick a location for the new control point>*
Specify new point <exit>: ↵
Specify control point <exit>: *<pick another control point grip or press Enter>*
Enter a fit data option
[Add/Close/Delete/Move/Purge/Tangents/toLerance/eXit] <eXit>: ↵
Enter an option [Fit data/Close/Move vertex/Refine/rEverse/Undo]: ↵
Command:

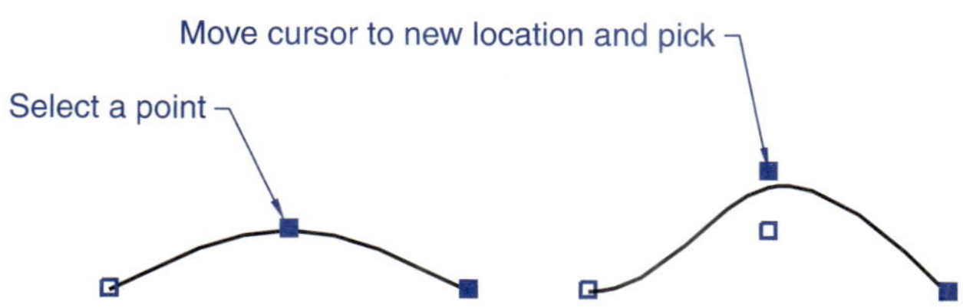

FIGURE 8.29 Adding a fit point with the SPLINEDIT Fit Data Add option.

Field Notes

- When the option contains two capitalized words, you can type either capitalized letter. For example, with the option Fit Data, you can enter either **F** or **D.**
- The examples used to demonstrate editing splines show the new points being picked. Remember that you can also use coordinate or direct distance entry.

Close: The Close option lets you close an open spline. If the spline you select for editing is already closed, then the Fit Data option is Open, which allows you to open a closed spline. Using the Close suboption of Fit Data preserves the fit data after closing the spline. This is different from the Close option presented at the initial prompt, which removes fit data when it closes the spline.

Delete: This Fit Data option lets you delete a fit point by selecting it. If there are only three fit points in the spline, and you delete one, the result is a straight segment between the two remaining points. You can select a control point by targeting it with the crosshairs and picking. When control points are deleted, the curve is recalculated using the remaining points and fit data.

Field Notes

The result of a straight line only occurs when the default tangency directions are used. If tangents other than the default are used, the resulting spline is still a curve, even when all fit points are removed. If you delete all of the control points except for the last two, the following message is issued:

```
Cannot delete beyond this.
```

Move: Use this option to move a fit point to a new location. When you select a spline and enter this option, you get Next and Previous prompts that allow you to progressively select different points along the spline until you get to the desired point. The cursor is connected to the selected point and the spline changes shape as you move the cursor. Look at Figure 8.30 as you follow these prompts:

```
Enter an option [Fit data/Close/Move vertex/Refine/rEverse/Undo]: F↵
Enter a fit data option
[Add/Close/Delete/Move/Purge/Tangents/toLerance/eXit] <eXit>: M↵
Specify new location or [Next/Previous/Select point/eXit] <N>: ↵
Specify new location or [Next/Previous/Select point/eXit] <N>: <pick a new location>
Specify new location or [Next/Previous/Select point/eXit] <N>: X↵
Enter a fit data option
[Add/Close/Delete/Move/Purge/Tangents/toLerance/eXit] <eXit>: ↵
Enter an option [Fit data/Close/Move vertex/Refine/rEverse/Undo]: ↵
Command:
```

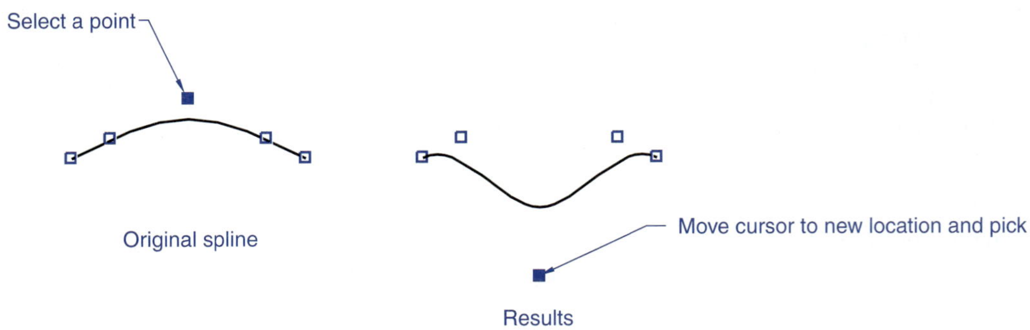

FIGURE 8.30 Moving a fit point with the SPLINEDIT Move Vertex option.

You can also use the Select Point option by typing **S** and pressing Enter. This lets you move the cursor to a desired point and pick it:

Specify new location or [Next/Previous/Select point/eXit] <N>: **S↵**
Specify control point <exit>: *<select a control point grip>*

Purge: This Fit Data option simplifies spline curves by removing fit data. Once Purge has been used, the spline can no longer be edited with the Fit Data option. The Purge option can be used to reduce the file size of very large drawings by simplifying the splines. The Undo option in the next prompt can be used to restore the Fit data.

Tangents: This option allows you to change the start and end tangents of an open spline or edit the tangency of points in a closed spline. The results can affect the spline in a manner that is similar to the tangency displayed in Figures 8.26 and 8.27. When you select a spline and use the Tangents option, the first tangent point is automatically selected for editing. After changing the first tangent point, the cursor switches to the second tangent point for editing. Use of the Tangents option gives the following command sequence:

Enter an option [Fit data/Close/Move vertex/Refine/rEverse/Undo]: **F↵**
Enter a fit data option
[Add/Close/Delete/Move/Purge/Tangents/toLerance/eXit] <eXit>: **T↵**
Specify start tangent or [System default]: *<edit the start tangent>*
Specify end tangent or [System default]: *<edit the end tangent>*
Enter a fit data option
[Add/Close/Delete/Move/Purge/Tangents/toLerance/eXit] <eXit>:

If you do not want to change the tangent points to your own specifications, you can accept the System Default option by typing **S** or **D** and pressing Enter:

Enter an option [Fit data/Close/Move vertex/Refine/rEverse/Undo]: **F↵**
Enter a fit data option
[Add/Close/Delete/Move/Purge/Tangents/toLerance/eXit] <eXit>: **T↵**
Specify start tangent or [System default]: **S↵**
Specify end tangent or [System default]: **S↵**
Enter a fit data option
[Add/Close/Delete/Move/Purge/Tangents/toLerance/eXit] <eXit>:

toLerance: Use this option to change the fit tolerance data. The prompt asks you to enter a new value for the fit tolerance. Adjusting the fit tolerance was discussed earlier and shown in Figure 8.28.

Exercise 8.11

Estimated time required: 5 min.

1. Open a new drawing.
2. Draw a spline curve similar to the original spline shown in Figure 8.29.
3. Make three copies of the spline.
4. Use the SPLINEDIT Fit Data Add option to add a fit point to one of the spline curves similar to those shown in Figure 8.29.
5. Use the Fit Data Move option to move a fit point on one of the spline curves similar to those shown in Figure 8.29.
6. Use the Fit Data Delete option to delete one of the fit points on one of the splines.
7. Use the Fit Data Close option to close one of the splines.
8. Save as EX8.11, and close the drawing.

Using the SPLINEDIT Close/Open Option

If you use the SPLINEDIT command and select an open spline, you get the Close option with the other options. If you select a closed spline, you automatically get the Open option listed. These options perform the operations implied by their names. After closing an open spline, the option changes from Close to Open. Using either of these options removes all fit data from the spline.

Moving a Spline Vertex

The SPLINEDIT's Move Vertex option allows you to move any spline control point to a new location. When you select a spline and enter this option, you get Next and Previous prompts that allow you to progressively select different points along the spline until you get to the desired point. The cursor is connected to the selected point and the spline changes shape as you move the cursor. Look at Figure 8.30 as you follow these prompts:

Enter an option [Fit data/Close/Move vertex/Refine/rEverse/Undo]: **M**↵
Specify new location or [Next/Previous/Select point/eXit] <N>: ↵
Specify new location or [Next/Previous/Select point/eXit] <N>: *<pick a new location>*
Specify new location or [Next/Previous/Select point/eXit] <N>: **X**↵
Enter an option [Close/Move vertex/Refine/rEverse/Undo/eXit] <eXit>:
Command:

You can also use the Select Point option by typing **S** and pressing Enter. This lets you move the cursor to a desired point and pick it.

Specify new location or [Next/Previous/Select point/eXit] <N>: **S**↵
Specify control point <exit>: *<select a control point grip>*

Refining Spline Curves

The SPLINEDIT command's Refine option is used to modify a spline shape by increasing the number of control points in a portion of the spline. You can change a spline's order. When you increase a spline's order, you increase the number of control points. You can also change the weight of a control point. Changing the weight of a control point forces the spline curve either further from or closer to the point where the change occurs. The options look like this:

Command: **SPE** or **SPLINEDIT**↵
Select spline: *<select a spline object>*
Enter an option [Close/Move vertex/Refine/rEverse/Undo/eXit] <eXit>: **R**↵
Enter a refine option [Add control point/Elevate order/Weight/eXit] <eXit>:

The SPLINEDIT Refine options are explained next.

Add control point: Use this option to add new control points to an existing spline. Each time you pick or enter a point coordinate, a new control point is added between the two points that control the portion of the spline closest to the specified location. The new control points are positioned as close to your pick point as possible without changing the current appearance of the spline curve. The reason for adding new points is to allow tighter control and greater flexibility for further editing procedures, such as moving vertices. You can add as many control points as you wish, but you should avoid doing so unnecessarily. This option also removes fit data. Figure 8.31 shows two control points added using this sequence:

Enter an option [Close/Move vertex/Refine/rEverse/Undo/eXit] <eXit>: **R**↵
Enter a refine option [Add control point/Elevate order/Weight/eXit] <eXit>: **A**↵
Specify a point on the spline <exit>: *<pick a point>*
Specify a point on the spline <exit>: *<pick a point>*
Specify a point on the spline <exit>: ↵
Enter a refine option [Add control point/Elevate order/Weight/eXit] <eXit>:

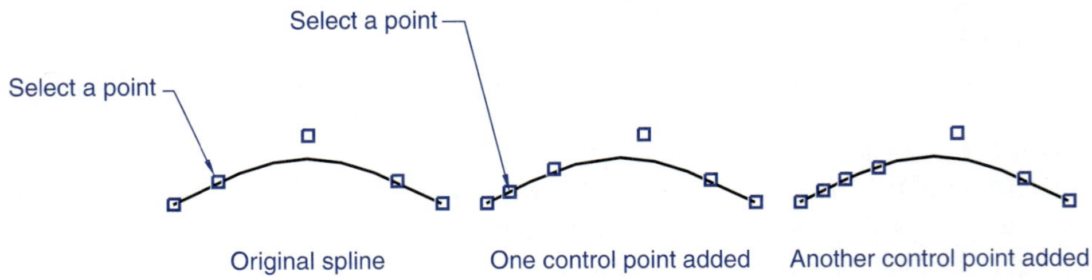

FIGURE 8.31 Adding control points with the SPLINEDIT Add control point option.

Elevate order: Elevating the order of a spline increases the number of control points for greater control uniformly across the spline. The default setting for the order is 4, which allows for four total control points on a one-segment spline, one at the start, one at the end, and two curve control points. AutoCAD LT supports settings of up to 26 for the order of the spline. A single-segment spline with an order of 26 has 24 curve control points, and 26 total control points. When the spline has multiple segments, each segment shares control points with the adjacent segments, which means that a spline initially defined using two segments and elevated in order to 26 will not have 52 total control points. Such a spline would have only 49 control points because 3 of the points belong to both segments. Since it would require AutoCAD LT to arbitrarily remove control points, the order of a spline cannot be reduced after it has been elevated. Because there is no easy way to lower the order of the spline, it is advised that you elevate the order only when necessary. Also, elevating the order of a spline removes all fit data. Figure 8.32 shows a spline with an order of 4 and then the elevated order of 10 as done with this SPLINEDIT command sequence:

Enter an option [Close/Move vertex/Refine/rEverse/Undo/eXit] <eXit>: **R↵**
Enter a refine option [Add control point/Elevate order/Weight/eXit] <eXit>: **E↵**
Enter new order <4>: **10↵**
Enter a refine option [Add control point/Elevate order/Weight/eXit] <eXit>:

FIGURE 8.32 Elevating the order of control points.

Notice that the resulting spline shows 17 total control points. The original spline definition used two segments, and the order is then elevated to 10. Each segment now has 10 total control points, with 3 being shared, making a total of 17.

Field Notes

- The order of a spline is defined as the degree of the spline polynomial plus 1. What this actually refers to is the equation used to calculate the curve of the spline. A cubic spline is calculated using a third-degree polynomial, so the order of a cubic spline is 4. The curve calculated using a third-degree polynomial has either two or no turning points. This can be easily demonstrated by first generating a spline with just two points, a start and an end (use the default tangencies). The result is a straight spline with no turning points. If you grip select the spline, you see that two control points appear on the spline. Use the GRIP Stretch option to move each of these grips. Now the spline has two turning points. Next, use the SPLINEDIT Refine–Elevate Order option to elevate the order to 5 and return to the Command: prompt. The resulting curve is now calculated using a fourth-degree polynomial, and so the degree of the polynomial plus 1 is equal to 5. When you grip select the spline this time you see an extra control point on the spline. Using your GRIP Stretch option you can now produce 3 turning points on the spline segment.
- When you elevate the order of a spline by 1, you are adding a single new control point on each segment of the spline. Elevating the order by 3 adds three new points on each segment and so on.

Weight: The weight of a fit point determines how much pull the point has on the spline curve. When all control points have the same weight, they all maintain the same amount of control over the spline. The default weight is 1. If you increase the weight of one or more fit points, you force the spline to pull closer to those points. The Weight prompts allow you to move to the next or previous fit points or use the Select Point option to pick the desired point. Adjusting the weight to higher values can cause the curve to pass through the control point regardless of the fit tolerance. Also, adjusting the weight removes fit data. The following sequence selects the desired point and increases the weight, as demonstrated in Figure 8.33:

Enter an option [Fit data/Close/Move vertex/Refine/rEverse/Undo]: **R**↵
Enter a refine option [Add control point/Elevate order/Weight/eXit] <eXit>: **W**↵
Spline is not rational. Will make it so.
Enter new weight (current = 1.0000) or [Next/Previous/Select point/eXit] <N>: **S**↵
Specify control point <exit>: *<pick the control point grip>*
Enter new weight (current = 1.0000) or [Next/Previous/Select point/eXit] <N>: **4**↵
Enter new weight (current = 4.0000) or [Next/Previous/Select point/eXit] <N>: **X**↵
Enter a refine option [Add control point/Elevate order/Weight/eXit] <eXit>:

FIGURE 8.33 Using the SPLINEDIT Weight option.

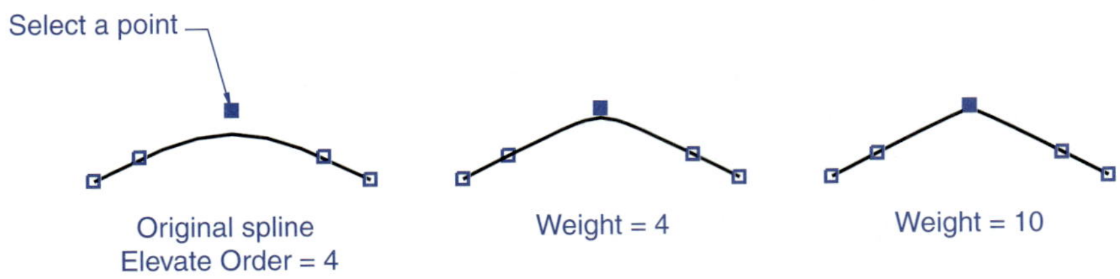

Exercise 8.12 — Estimated time required: 5 min.

1. Open a new drawing.
2. Draw a spline curve similar to the original spline shown in Figure 8.31.
3. Make two copies of the spline.
4. Use the SPLINEDIT Refine Add option to add two fit points to one of the splines as was done in Figure 8.31.
5. Use the Refine Elevate Order option to increase the order of one of the splines to 10 as was done in Figure 8.32.
6. Use the Fit Data Delete option to delete one of the fit points on one of the splines.
7. Use the Refine Weight option to increase the weight of one of the spline's control points to 10 as was done in Figure 8.33.
8. Save as EX8.12, and close the drawing.

Using the rEverse Option of the SPLINEDIT Command

This makes the existing endpoint into the start point and reverses the direction of movement when using options that offer a Next and Previous option for selecting control points. If you want to reverse the order of the spline curve control points, type **E** and press Enter to access the rEverse option.

Field Notes

To make fine adjustments to a spline, it is sometimes quicker and easier to use the GRIP Stretch option to move individual fit data points and adjust the curve as needed. If no previous operation has removed the fit data, when you grip select the spline, the fit data points are also available for adjustment. However, if you move one of the control points, the fit data are lost. To be sure which grips are fit points and which are control points, you need to observe the fit-point locations before selecting the splines.

LEARNING CHECKPOINT

- ☐ Name the command that allows you to draw spline curves of your own design.
- ☐ What is the function of the Fit Tolerance option?
- ☐ Explain the purpose of the SPLINEDIT Fit Data Purge option.
- ☐ Describe two ways to select a desired fit point when using the SPLINEDIT Move Vertex option.
- ☐ What is the purpose of the Elevate Order option?
- ☐ Describe the results of increasing the weight of a control point.

Drawing Double Lines

AutoCAD LT provides you with an excellent tool for drawing pairs of parallel lines and arcs that may be used for drawing the walls of architectural floor and foundation plans. Double lines can be drawn any desired width apart. They can be capped and they can be edited to break where they meet so they look like properly drawn wall intersections. Double lines are drawn using the DLINE command, which is accessed by picking Double Line in the Draw pull-down menu, by picking the Double Line button in the Draw toolbar, or by typing **DL** or **DLINE** at the Command: prompt.

Draw

Double Line

Draw
Double Line

DLINE
DL

Field Notes

There is no actual "double line" object type. The result of using the DLINE command is a sequence of LINE and ARC segments. Although the command creates *double lines,* after they are created they are just *lines.*

Using the DLINE Command

Double lines are drawn in a manner similar to that used to draw lines. In addition to a number of options, you are asked to pick a start point and the next point. The DLINE command is demonstrated in Figure 8.34 and works like this:

Command: **DL** or **DLINE**↵
Specify start point or [Break/Caps/Dragline/Offset/Snap/Undo/Width]: *<pick a start point>*
Specify next point or [Arc/Break/CAps/CLose/Dragline/Snap/Undo/Width]: *<pick another point>*
Specify next point or [Arc/Break/CAps/CLose/Dragline/Snap/Undo/Width]: *<pick another point>*
Specify next point or [Arc/Break/CAps/CLose/Dragline/Snap/Undo/Width]: ↵
Command:

FIGURE 8.34 The elements of a double line.

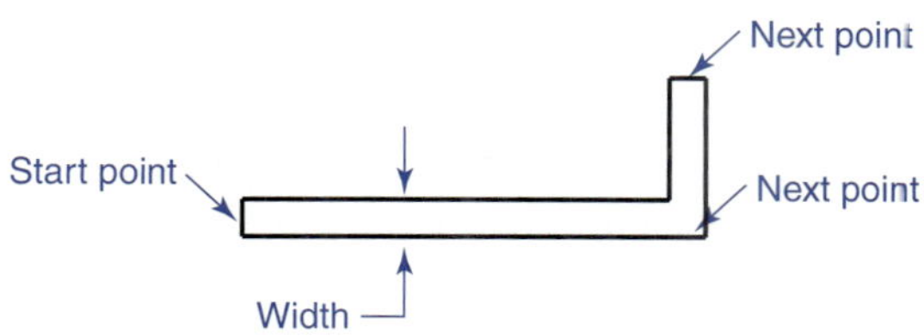

The DLINE command has the Undo and Close options that work just as they do with other applications. The Close option allows you to have AutoCAD LT automatically close the end of the last double line segment with the start of the first segment. The Undo option works while you are inside of the DLINE command to undo the previously drawn double line segments. Use Undo as many times as you need to undo consecutive previous segments.

Setting the Double Line Width

The double line width is one of the first options that you may want to set. This establishes the distance between the two parallel lines. If you are working on an architectural floor plan, you probably want to set the width to 6 in. for exterior walls and 5 in. for interior walls. The initial default width is 0.05. Figure 8.34 shows the double line width. This is how you set the width:

Command: **DL** or **DLINE**↵
Specify start point or [Break/Caps/Dragline/Offset/Snap/Undo/Width]: **W**↵
Specify width of dline <0.0500>: **6**↵
Specify start point or [Break/Caps/Dragline/Offset/Snap/Undo/Width]:

Field Notes

Be sure that the displayed drawing area is large enough prior to trying to draw 6-in.-wide walls. If not, drawing in a small area may produce unexpected results. The width of the double lines depends on the type and size of the drawing.

Setting the Dragline

After you set the width, you probably want to set how the double line is drawn. As you pick the points to draw the double line, a rubber-band cursor guides the placement of the double line to your pick points. AutoCAD LT refers to this as the *dragline*. The Dragline option has three settings. Set the Left option like this:

Command: **DL** or **DLINE**↵
Specify start point or [Break/Caps/Dragline/Offset/Snap/Undo/Width]: **D**↵
Enter offset from center or dragline position option [Left/Center/Right] <0.0000>: **L**↵
Specify start point or [Break/Caps/Dragline/Offset/Snap/Undo/Width]:

FIGURE 8.35 The DLINE Dragline options.

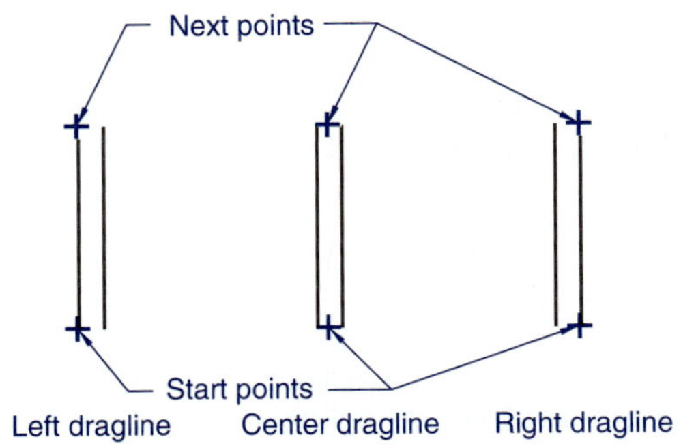

Figure 8.35 shows the difference between the Dragline options, which are explained in the following list:

- **Center:** The initial AutoCAD LT default setting draws double lines placed with your pick points in the center of the two lines. The Dragline setting remains the same until you change it. If you change to another setting, go back to the Center option by typing **C** and pressing Enter. When the Center option is used, the Offset from center = 0 prompt is issued. When the setting is Center, the resulting lines are drawn offset parallel to the dragline half of the width setting in each direction.
- **Left:** The Left option is accessed by typing **L** and pressing Enter. This places the dragline on the left side of the double line as you go from the start point to the next point. The Offset from center prompt gives a negative value when the left option is used. The value is half the distance from the center to the dragline. When the setting is left, the offset is the full width to the right.
- **Right:** The Right option is accessed by typing **R** and pressing Enter. This places the dragline on the right side of the double line as you go from the start point to the next point. When the setting is right, the offset is the full width to the left.

Field Notes

- The Left and Right options are based on a line drawn at 90° upward.
- When drawn counterclockwise, the Left option offsets outward and the right option offsets inward. When drawn clockwise, the Right option offsets outward and the Left option offsets inward.
- When using double lines for the walls in an architectural floor plan, the exterior walls are drawn using either the left or right option with the total wall width inside. This is because dimensions are normally made to the face of exterior studs. The interior walls and partitions are usually drawn using the center option because these walls are normally dimensioned to their centers.

Exercise 8.13 **Estimated time required: 5 min.**

1. Begin a new drawing.
2. Set double line width to .25.
3. Draw three double line segments with each of the dragline options, similar to the segments shown in Figure 8.35.
4. Save as EX8.13, and close the drawing.

Placing Caps on Double Lines

AutoCAD LT allows you to place caps on the ends of double lines. Caps are line segments that connect the ends of double lines. You have the choice of drawing double lines without caps, with caps on both ends, or with a cap on either the beginning or ending. You can change the way caps are placed at any time while drawing double lines. The initial option is Caps, which is accessed by typing **C** and pressing Enter. After picking the start point, the option changes to CAps, which requires you to type **CA** and press Enter to get the Caps option. The Caps option works like this:

Command: **DL** or **DLINE**↵
Specify start point or [Break/Caps/Dragline/Offset/Snap/Undo/Width]: **C**↵
Enter option for drawing endcaps [Both/End/None/Start/Auto] <Auto>: **B**↵
Specify start point or [Break/Caps/Dragline/Offset/Snap/Undo/Width]: *<pick a point>*
Specify next point or [Arc/Break/CAps/CLose/Dragline/Snap/Undo/Width]: **CA**↵
Enter option for drawing endcaps [Both/End/None/Start/Auto] <Auto>:

FIGURE 8.36 The DLINE Caps options.

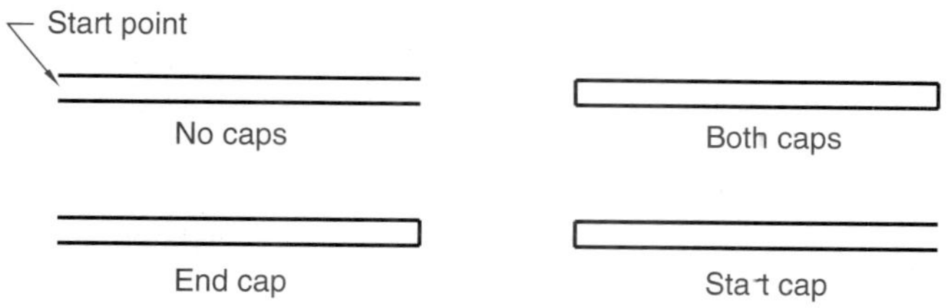

The caps options are shown in Figure 8.36 and explained in the following discussion:

- **Both:** This option places a cap at the start and end of open double lines.
- **End:** Use this option to place a cap only at the end of a double line.
- **None:** This option is used to place no end caps on a double line.
- **Start:** This option places a cap at the start of a double line.
- **Auto:** Use the Auto option if you want AutoCAD LT to automatically place a cap at the ends of double lines except when snapping to other objects. Snapping to other objects is explained later.

Exercise 8.14 **Estimated time required: 5 min.**

1. Begin a new drawing.
2. Set double line width to .25.
3. Draw four double line segments with each of the cap options, similar to the segments shown in Figure 8.36.
4. Save as EX8.14, and close the drawing.

Offsetting the Start of a Double Line

The DLINE's Offset option is used to begin a double line at a specified distance and angle from a known point. This is convenient for drawing a door opening in a floor plan, for example. When you enter the Offset option, AutoCAD LT issues the Offset from: prompt so that you can pick the point where you want the offset to begin.

You are then asked to pick the direction "toward" the beginning of the double line. Finally, enter the offset distance. The default value is the same as the distance between the "from" point and the "toward" point. Press Enter to accept this distance or type a new value such as 48 for a 48-in. doorway in an architectural floor plan. Draw the first double line with an end cap to establish the first part of the doorway. Use the Caps option to place a start cap at the other side of the doorway. Look at Figure 8.37 as you follow this command sequence:

Command: **DL** or **DLINE**↵
Specify start point or [Break/Caps/Dragline/Offset/Snap/Undo/Width]: **C**↵
Enter option for drawing endcaps [Both/End/None/Start/Auto] <Auto>: **S**↵
Specify start point or [Break/Caps/Dragline/Offset/Snap/Undo/Width]: **O**↵
Specify base point to offset from: *<pick the start of the offset>*
Specify point to indicate offset direction: *<move the cursor in the direction of the offset and pick>*
Specify distance of offset <4'>: *<accept the default you picked or enter a new distance>*
Specify next point or [Arc/Break/CAps/CLose/Dragline/Snap/Undo/Width]: *<pick the next point>*
Specify next point or [Arc/Break/CAps/CLose/Dragline/Snap/Undo/Width]: ↵
Command:

FIGURE 8.37 Using the DLINE Offset option.

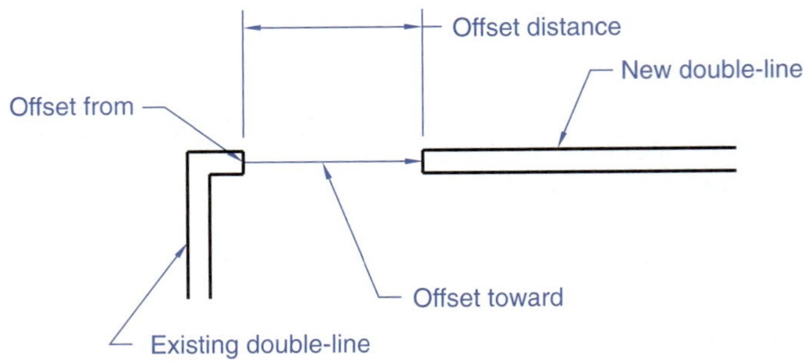

Exercise 8.15

Estimated time required: 5 min.

1. Begin a new drawing.
2. Set double line width to .25.
3. Draw a double line with an end cap similar to the existing double line shown in Figure 8.37.
4. Set the end cap to start and use the Offset option to offset the beginning of the next double line a distance of 1.25 from the endpoint of the previous double line, as was done in Figure 8.37.
5. Save as EX8.15, and close the drawing.

Drawing Double Line Arcs

The DLINE command allows you to draw double line separate arcs or arcs connected to straight double line segments. The Arc option is entered after picking the start point. The Arc option allows you to draw a double line arc by picking three points by default, or by typing **CE** to enter the CEnter option. The CEnter option is used to specify the center of the double line arc radius. You can also use the Endpoint option by picking an arc endpoint or by specifying the included angle. After entering the Arc option, the next prompt replaces the Arc option with the Line option. The Line option is used if you want to continue drawing a straight double line segment at the end of a double line arc segment. The following command sequence draws the closed double line with an arc segment that is displayed in Figure 8.38:

Command: **DL** or **DLINE**↵
Specify start point or [Break/Caps/Dragline/Offset/Snap/Undo/Width]: *<pick a point>*
Specify next point or [Arc/Break/CAps/CLose/Dragline/Snap/Undo/Width]: *<pick the next point>*
Specify next point or [Arc/Break/CAps/CLose/Dragline/Snap/Undo/Width]: **A**↵
Break/CAps/CEnter/CLose/Dragline/Endpoint/Line/Snap/Undo/Width/<second point>: *<pick a point or use the CEnter or Endpoint option>*
Endpoint: *<pick the endpoint>*
Break/CAps/CEnter/CLose/Dragline/Endpoint/Line/Snap/Undo/Width/<second point>: **L**↵
Specify next point or [Arc/Break/CAps/CLose/Dragline/Snap/Undo/Width]: *<pick a point>*
Specify next point or [Arc/Break/CAps/CLose/Dragline/Snap/Undo/Width]: **CL**↵
Command:

FIGURE 8.38 Drawing a closed double line with an arc segment.

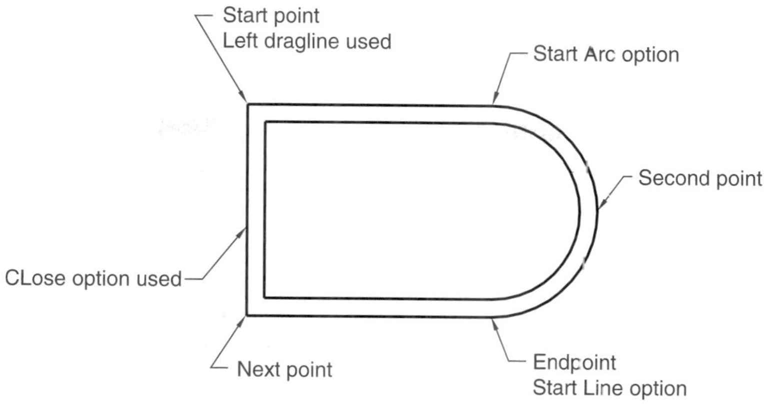

The CEnter suboption of the Arc option can be used if you want to draw the double line arc by first picking the start point followed by the center and then either picking the arc endpoint or using the Angle option to specify the included angle. The prompts work like this:

Command: **DL** or **DLINE**↵
Specify start point or [Break/Caps/Dragline/Offset/Snap/Undo/Width]: *<pick a point>*
Specify next point or [Arc/Break/CAps/CLose/Dragline/Snap/Undo/Width]: **A**↵
Break/CAps/CEnter/CLose/Dragline/Endpoint/Line/Snap/Undo/Width/<second point>: **CE**↵
Center point: *<pick the center point>*
Angle/<Endpoint>: *<press Enter for Endpoint or type* **A**↵ *for Angle>*
Endpoint: *<pick the endpoint>*
Break/CAps/CEnter/CLose/Dragline/Endpoint/Line/Snap/Undo/Width/<second point>: ↵
Command:

You can make sequential arcs using the CEnter option or by picking a second point and endpoint of the next continuous arc.

Exercise 8.16 **Estimated time required: 5 min.**

1. Begin a new drawing.
2. Set double line width to .25 and Dragline to Left.
3. Draw a double line similar to the one shown in Figure 8.38.
4. Save as EX8.16, and close the drawing.

Snapping a Double Line to Other Objects

A double line can be connected to another double line or to other objects by using the Snap option. You can use this option to either start or end a double line at another object. When using the Snap option, AutoCAD LT automatically trims or extends the ends of the double line to meet exactly with the desired object. The Snap option has a ***search area*** where AutoCAD LT looks for the object to which the double line will snap. No connection happens if the object is outside of the search area. The size of the search area is set in pixels. The available Snap options include turning Snap ON or OFF or setting the Size, which refers to the search area. The default size is 3 pixels. You can set the Size from 1 to 10 pixels. Set the search area to 5 pixels as follows:

Command: **DL** or **DLINE**↵
Specify start point or [Break/Caps/Dragline/Offset/Snap/Undo/Width]: *<pick a point>*
Specify next point or [Arc/Break/CAps/CLose/Dragline/Snap/Undo/Width]: **S**↵
Enter snap option [Size/OFF/ON] <ON>: **S**↵
Enter size of snap area (1-10) <10) <3>: **5**↵
Specify next point or [Arc/Break/CAps/CLose/Dragline/Snap/Undo/Width]: *<pick the next point>*
Specify next point or [Arc/Break/CAps/CLose/Dragline/Snap/Undo/Width]: ↵
Command:

Setting the Snap Size also turns Snap on for the next point. Turn snap on for each desired connection to an object. The result of the previous command is shown in Figure 8.39.

FIGURE 8.39 Using the DLINE Snap option to connect a double line with another object.

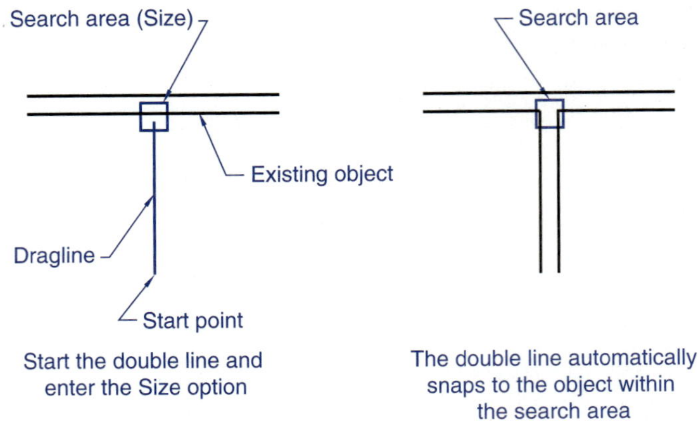

Field Notes

- To give you a clear picture of how big the search area is, set your pick box size using the PICKBOX command and specify the desired number. The search area is square like the pick box, meaning that the diagonal search distance is greater than either the horizontal or vertical distance.
- When you start the DLINE command, any running object snap modes are temporarily suspended, but you can still use object snap overrides as desired.

Breaking an Object Where the Double Line Meets

When you snap a double line to an object, you can have the object broken or unbroken where the endpoints of the double line meet the object. Having the object break at the double line is convenient for architectural applications where walls meet. Set the Break option like this:

Command: **DL** or **DLINE**↵
Specify start point or [Break/Caps/Dragline/Offset/Snap/Undo/Width]: **B**↵
Break dlines at start and endpoints [OFf/ON] <ON>: ↵
Specify start point or [Break/Caps/Dragline/Offset/Snap/Undo/Width]:

Break is on by default. Figure 8.40 shows the difference between Break ON and OFF.

FIGURE 8.40 A comparison between using the DLINE Snap option with the Break option ON and OFF.

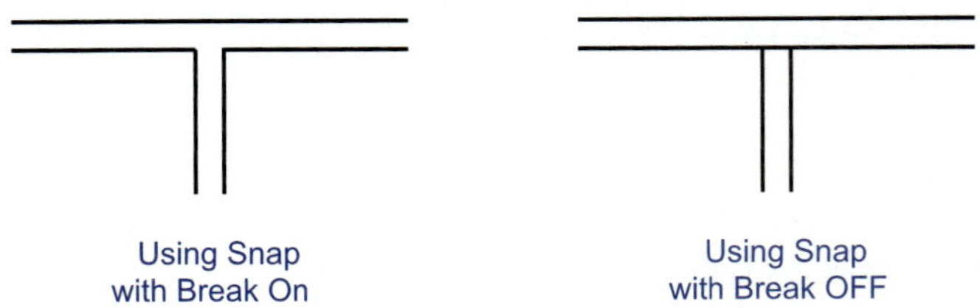

Exercise 8.17 — Estimated time required: 5 min.

1. Begin a new drawing.
2. Set the double line width to .25.
3. Draw a horizontal double line with the Dragline set to Left similar to the existing object shown in Figure 8.39.
4. Be sure Break is ON.
5. Draw a double line with a Center Dragline and with the Snap option ON to connect the Existing object, as was done in Figure 8.39.
6. Save as EX8.17, and close the drawing.

LEARNING CHECKPOINT

- ☐ Where is the double line width measured?
- ☐ Explain how the Dragline option works.
- ☐ Discuss the results obtained when using the DLINE Caps option.
- ☐ Explain how the DLINE Offset option works.
- ☐ How do you draw a double line arc connected to a straight double line segment and followed by a straight segment?
- ☐ What is the Snap option search area?
- ☐ When snapping a double line to an existing object, how can you be sure the object will break at the snap location?

Creating Geometry

- Drawing Lines and Specifying Points

Drawing Revision Clouds

Draw

Revcloud

Tools
Revision Cloud

REVCLOUD
RC

Revision clouds are often used in a drawing to draw attention to a revised area of a drawing. Revision clouds consist of connected arc segments created from a polyline object. The REVCLOUD command is accessed by picking the Revcloud button from the Draw toolbar, selecting Revision Cloud from the Tools menu, or typing **RC** or **REVCLOUD** on the keyboard. The REVCLOUD command issues the following prompt:

Command: **RC** or **REVCLOUD**↵
Current arc length: 0.5000
Specify start point or [Arc length]:

Enter an arc length that is appropriate for your drawing. Let us say, for example, you are drawing a floor plan that is to be printed at a scale of ¼″=1′, and you want the length of the arcs to be ½″ on the print. A scale of ¼″=1′ equals a scale factor of 1/48. To adjust drawing feature sizes to match this scale take the reciprocal of the fraction, that is, 48/1 or 48. Multiply the desired arc length by this number to find the correct length, which in this case is 24″ (48 x 0.5 = 24). If you have already set an appropriate Dimensioning Scale (DimScale) for your drawing, the specified arc length is automatically multiplied by the set scale. Setting the DIMSCALE is discussed in Chapter 11.

Command: **RC** or **REVCLOUD**↵
Current arc length: 0.5000
Specify start point or [Arc length]: **A**↵
Specify length of arc <0.5000>: **24**↵
Specify start point of cloud: *<pick a point on screen>*
Guide crosshairs along cloud path...
<Move the cursor along the desired path of the revision cloud, finally returning to the start point>
Revision cloud finished.
Command

After specifying the starting point, it is not necessary to use the pick button again. Using the pick button specifies the endpoints of new arc segments, but these will be shorter than the specified arc length and will result in a less uniform cloud. Any running object snap modes are temporarily disabled while you draw the revision cloud. Move the crosshairs along the desired path of the revision cloud. The arcs are drawn as you move your cursor. To finish the revision cloud, move the cursor back to the start point. When your cursor comes within the specified arc length of the start point, the revision cloud is closed and you are returned to the Command: prompt. Figure 8.41 shows the creation of a revision cloud.

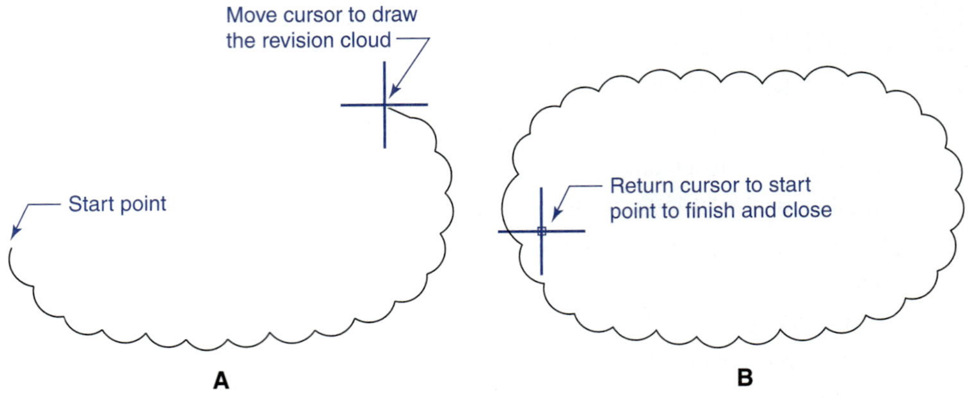

FIGURE 8.41 The REVCLOUD command automatically draws arc segments along the path that you move your cursor.

Field Notes

- You cannot undo individual arc segments within the REVCLOUD command. If you make a mistake while drawing a revision cloud, you can press the Esc key to stop the command, then the space bar to restart it.
- The REVCLOUD command can accurately track the cursor movements only when the cursor is visible in the drawing area of the AutoCAD LT window. If you are drawing a revision cloud near the edge of the screen and your cursor moves out of the drawing area, the next arc segment will be drawn to the point where your cursor reenters the drawing area.
- The REVCLOUD command creates a Polyline object that can be edited using the PEDIT command discussed earlier in this chapter. Minor adjustments can also be made using grips (see Chapter 7).

Creating Geometry

- Marking Revisions

MULTIPLE CHOICE

Circle the choice or enter your response on an answer sheet by selecting the option that most closely completes or answers the given statements.

1. Objects composed of one or more line or arc segments treated as a single object are called a:

a. line **b.** polyline **c.** double line **d.** arc

2. The initial polyline width default is:

a. 0 **b.** 0.05 **c.** none **d.** 1

3. If you want to draw a polyline that looks like an arrow with a point at one end and a width of .25 at the other end, use these settings:

a. start 0, end .25 **b.** start .25, end 0 **c.** either a or b **d.** neither a nor b

4. Use this PEDIT option to join an object with a polyline and have the joined object take on the same characteristics as the polyline:

a. Fit **b.** Edit vertex **c.** Join **d.** Undo

5. Use this PEDIT option to change the width of an entire polyline to a new uniform value:

a. Width **b.** Join **c.** Edit vertex **d.** Fit

6. This Edit vertex option allows you to change the width of different polyline segments as desired:
   - a. Fit
   - b. Spline
   - c. Width
   - d. Starting width
7. You must do this if you want a closed polyline to have all corners automatically chamfered using the CHAMFER command:
   - a. Close the last segment with the Close option.
   - b. Manually close the last segment.
8. Change a polyline to individual line and arc segments using this command:
   - a. X
   - b. Pick the Explode toolbar button.
   - c. EXPLODE
   - d. all of the above
9. When drawing a .25-in.-wide double line with the Left Dragline option, the Offset from center prompt reads:
   - a. .125
   - b. −.125
   - c. .25
   - d. −.25
10. A spline drawn between two points results in a:
    - a. curve between the points
    - b. straight segment between the two points
    - c. cannot draw a spline between two points
    - d. none of the above

MATCHING

Match each term to the correct description by writing the appropriate number in each box at the left.

- ☐ Caps
- ☐ Close
- ☐ Edit vertex
- ☐ EXPLODE
- ☐ Fit
- ☐ Join
- ☐ Offset
- ☐ PEDIT
- ☐ PLINE
- ☐ Polyline
- ☐ Snap
- ☐ Spline
- ☐ Weight

1. Allows you to connect a double line exactly to another object.
2. Used to make one or more changes to polyline vertices.
3. Changes polyline segments to individual lines and arcs.
4. Used to draw a double line from a known point.
5. An object composed of one or more segments that are treated as one.
6. Lines that connect the endpoints of double lines.
7. This uses the polyline vertices as a frame for curve development.
8. The command used to draw polylines.
9. Used to connect the last point with the first point.
10. Used to edit polylines.
11. Used to create smooth curves that pass through polyline vertices.
12. This option forces a spline to pull closer or farther from the control points.
13. Used to connect an object to a polyline and make it part of the polyline.

WORD SCRAMBLE

Unscramble the five scrambled words below, one letter to each square, to form five AutoCAD LT–related words:

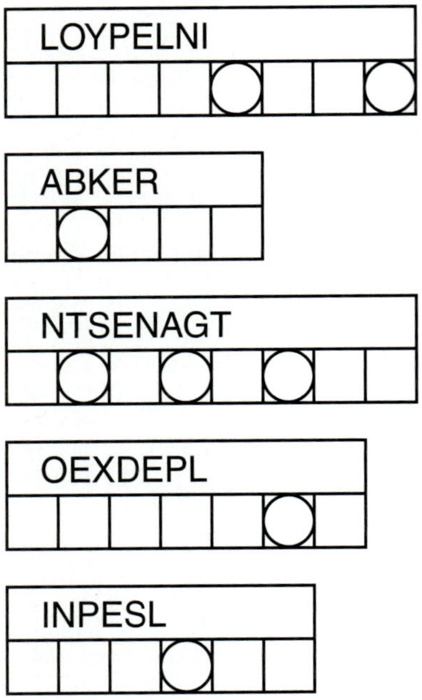

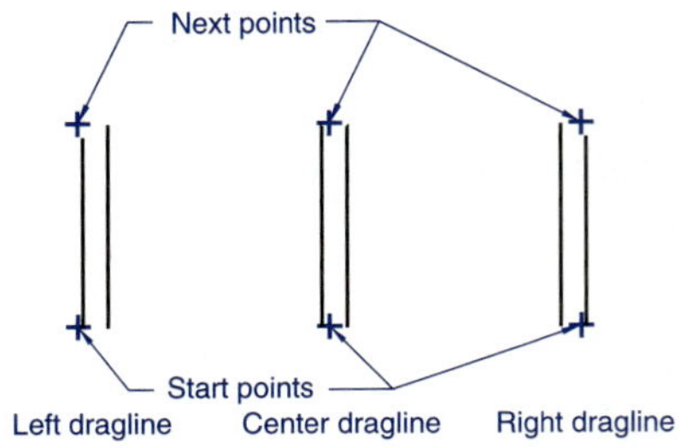

Unscramble the circled letters above to form the special answer, as suggested by the illustration.

PROJECTS

Set up the following drawing projects with layers that relate to the type of drawing as outlined and discussed in Chapter 5.

8.1 Arrow
Draw the arrow shown below without dimensions. Save as P8.1.

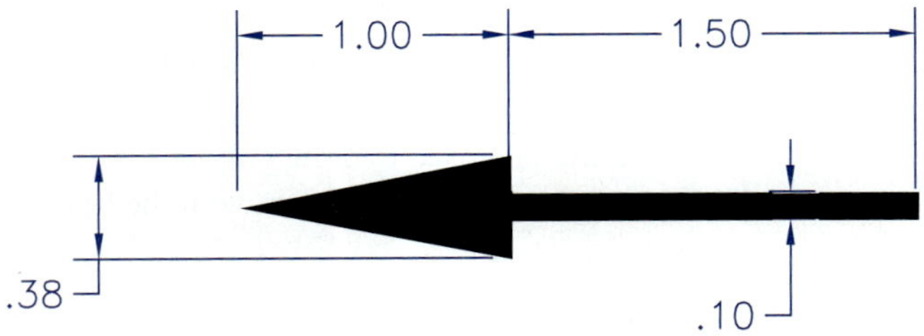

8.2 Graphic Symbol
Draw the symbol shown at the left below without dimensions. Use the ARC command to draw the ends and the PLINE command to draw .1 wide straight polyline segments connecting the arcs. Then use the PEDIT command's Join option to create the symbol shown at the right. Save as P8.2.

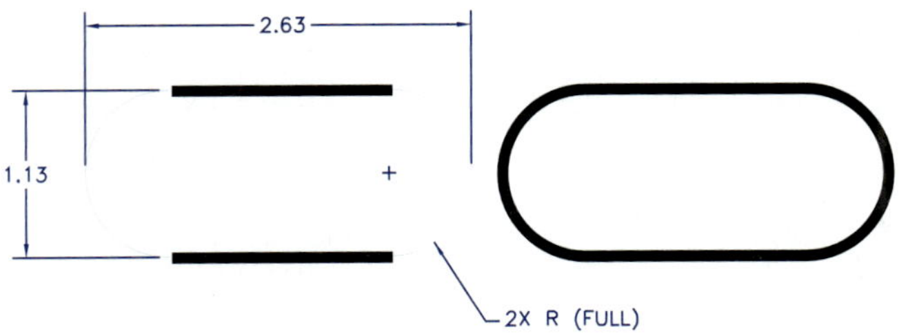

8.3 Graphic Symbol
Draw the symbol shown below without dimensions. Save as P8.3.

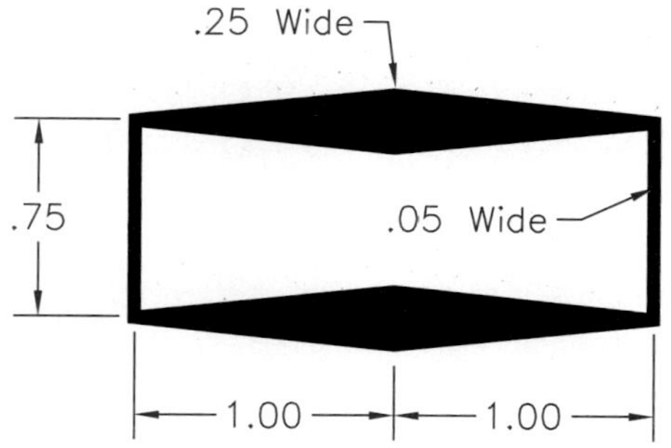

8.4 Graphic Symbol
Draw the symbol shown below without dimensions. Save as P8.4.

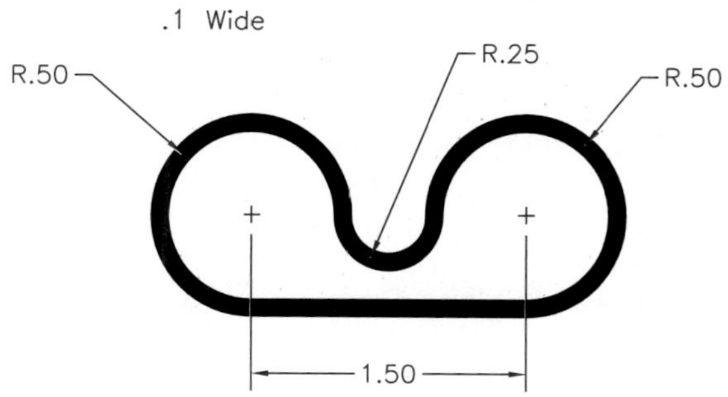

8.5 Arrow
Draw an arrow similar to the one shown below. Save as P8.5.

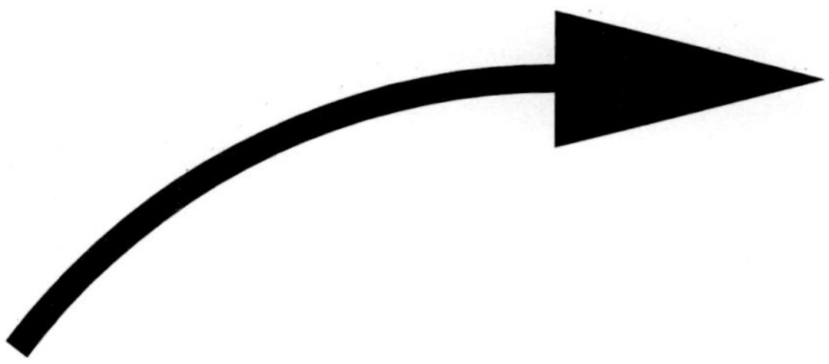

8.6 Graph
Draw two representations of the graph shown below without dimensions as follows:
Set up the graph grid on a blue layer and the graph line on a red layer. Draw one graph by connecting the grid intersection points with continuous straight polyline segments and then use the PEDIT Fit option to create the smooth curve. Draw the other graph using the SPLINE command. Save as P8.6.

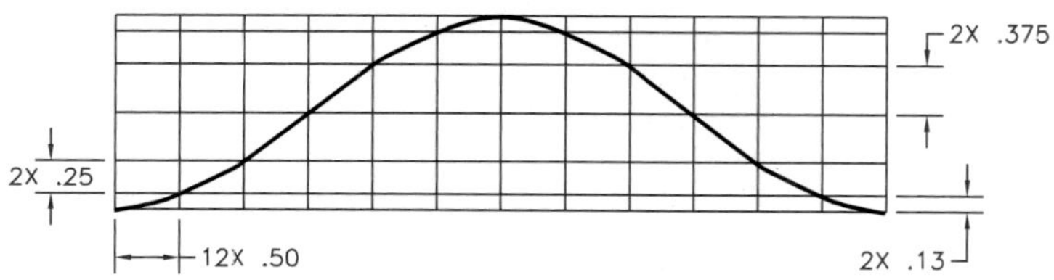

8.7 Clock
Open P7.1 and add the clock hands as shown below. Save as P8.7.

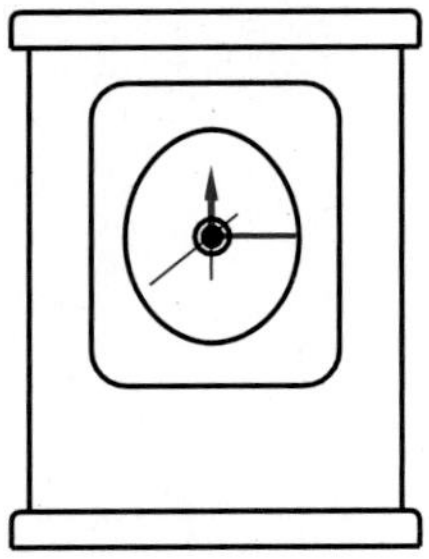

8.8 Star
Draw an object similar to the one shown below. Save as P8.8.

8.9 Floor Plan
Draw the partial floor plan below to your own specifications using double lines. Do not draw text. Save as P8.9.

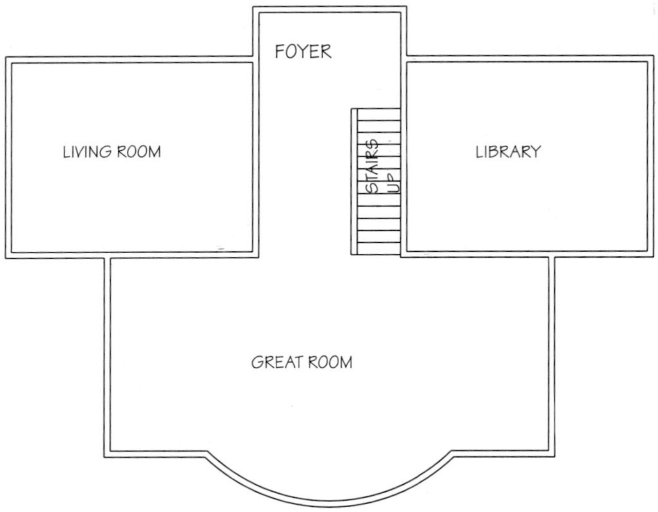

8.10 Floor Plan
Draw the floor plan below to your own specifications using double lines. Place doors, windows, and other objects using your own design. Do not draw text. Save as P8.10.

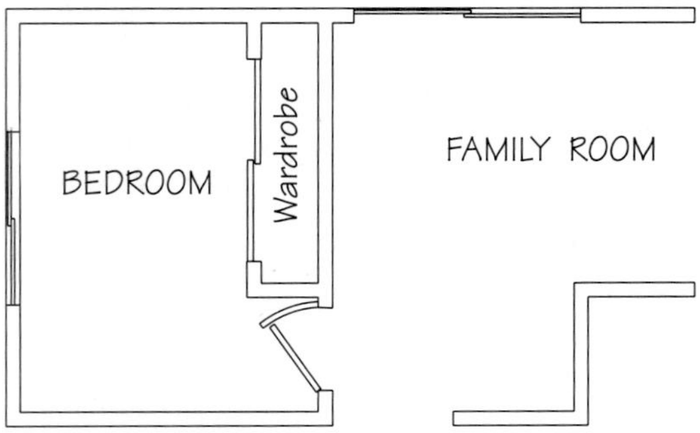

8.11 Revision Cloud
Open the drawing from problem P8.10 for editing. Use the REVCLOUD command to create a revision cloud that surrounds the Wardrobe in the existing drawing. Be sure that the arc length is appropriate to the scale of the drawing. Save as P8.11.

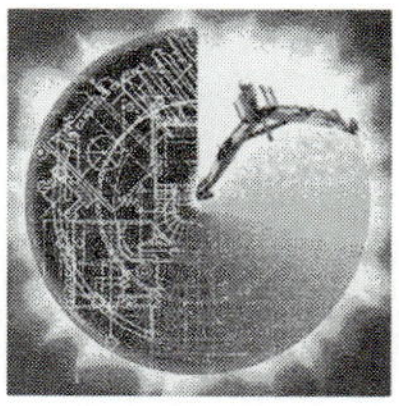

CHAPTER 9

Placing Text on a Drawing

LEARNING GOALS

- Use the DTEXT command to draw single-line text.
- Use the MTEXT command to draw paragraph text.
- Place text with different justification options.
- Create and use text styles.
- Draw special characters and symbols with text.
- Paste text from the Clipboard.
- Drag and drop text into AutoCAD LT.
- Edit text content and properties.
- Control the effects of mirroring on text objects.
- Use quick text.
- Check your spelling.
- Create a custom dictionary.

Introduction to Drawing Text

The letters and numbers you place in an AutoCAD LT drawing are referred to as ***text.*** When manual drafting is used, text is called lettering. Manual lettering on drawings has traditionally been a tedious and time-consuming process. Many professional drafters are able to create quality hand lettering that looks consistent between drawings, but it is often difficult for drafters to match the lettering of others. With AutoCAD LT, the practice of lettering becomes very easy. AutoCAD LT text not only looks the same on every drawing, it can be customized for application on different types of drawings. For example, the smooth uniform appearance of vertical Gothic lettering on mechanical drawings or the artistic look of lettering on architectural drawings can be easily accomplished.

AutoCAD LT provides a wide variety of text styles and options. Text can be prepared as single line or multiline. Every line of single-line text can be edited individually, whereas multiline text can be entered and edited in paragraph form. AutoCAD LT also allows you to check the spelling of words you place on the drawing.

Creating Single-Line Text

AutoCAD LT allows you to create ***single-line text*** that is referred to as ***line text.*** Line text is usually used for short text entries of one or more lines. Each line of line text is an individual object that can be edited separately from the other line text. Line text is drawn with the DTEXT command.

AutoCAD LT provides a variety of text fonts that can be used to create custom text styles. A ***text font*** is a complete set of characters, including letters, numbers, marks, and symbols, that is of unique proportion and design. A ***text style*** is defined as settings that determine the appearance of text characters. The AutoCAD LT text styles can be modified to suit your drafting practices. For example, you can slant, stretch, or compress the text styles for specific applications. Text styles can be defined to duplicate traditional smooth letters and numbers for mechanical drawing or present an artistic style that closely matches architectural hand lettering.

Using the DTEXT Command

Dtext

Draw
Text ▸
Single Line Text

DTEXT
DT

Line text is created using the DTEXT command. DTEXT stands for Dynamic TEXT; DTEXT allows you to see the text on the screen as you type. The DTEXT command can be accessed by picking Single Line Text from the Text cascade in the Draw pull-down menu or by typing **DT** or **DTEXT** at the Command: prompt. When entering the DTEXT commands, you are asked for a Start point. The Start point is the point where the text is entered on the screen. The Start point is also called the insertion point. Other options include Justify and Style. The Justify option determines how lines of text are aligned. The Justify options are explained later. The Style option is used to change text fonts. The Style option is also discussed later in this chapter.

After you enter the command and pick the Start point, you are asked for the text Height and Rotation angle. The text height should be set to match the desired height of letters and numbers on your drawing or for the specific application. Standard drawing text height is .125 in. or 3 mm. Other text heights such as 5/32 in. (4 mm) can be used depending on your company or school practices. Titles are often drawn .188 (5 mm) or .25 in. (6 mm) high. The initial AutoCAD LT text height depends on the setup or template used. The Start from Scratch option sets the text height at 0.200. The templates set the text height at varied values depending on the size of the sheet and the number system used.

The rotation angle determines the angle the text is placed at in relation to horizontal. The initial rotation angle default is 0, which makes all text horizontal. After you pick the Start point and enter the Height and Rotation angle, you get a Text: prompt and a text cursor is displayed on the screen. The text cursor is equal in size to the height specified for the text. This cursor moves as you type the desired text. After you type a line of text, press Enter to get the Text: prompt again. Press Enter every time you want to type a new line of text. This causes the cursor to drop down one line and be placed directly below the justification point. Pressing Enter on a blank line ends the DTEXT command. At the end of the last line of text, you can press Enter twice to return to the Command: prompt. Figure 9.1 shows the elements of AutoCAD LT text using the DTEXT command's Start point option:

Command: **DT** or **DTEXT**↵
Current text style: "Standard" Text height: 0.2000
Specify start point of text or [Justify/Style]: *<pick a start point for the first line of text>*
Specify height <0.2000>: **.25**↵
Specify rotation angle of text <0>: ↵
Enter text: **AutoCAD LT text is easy to draw and provides.**↵
Enter text: **you with a variety of fonts and styles.**↵
Enter text: ↵
Command:

While the DTEXT cursor is visible, you can pick any new location on the drawing and continue entering new lines of text as desired. You can also use the Backspace key to clear entered text and reenter as needed. Also, during the DTEXT command, any number of previously typed lines can be backspaced through. If you use the Backspace key to remove text from the current entry, you cannot retrieve it. The removed text must be retyped if you decide you need it after all.

FIGURE 9.1 (A) The steps in drawing AutoCAD LT text using the DTEXT command. (B) A variety of text rotation angle examples.

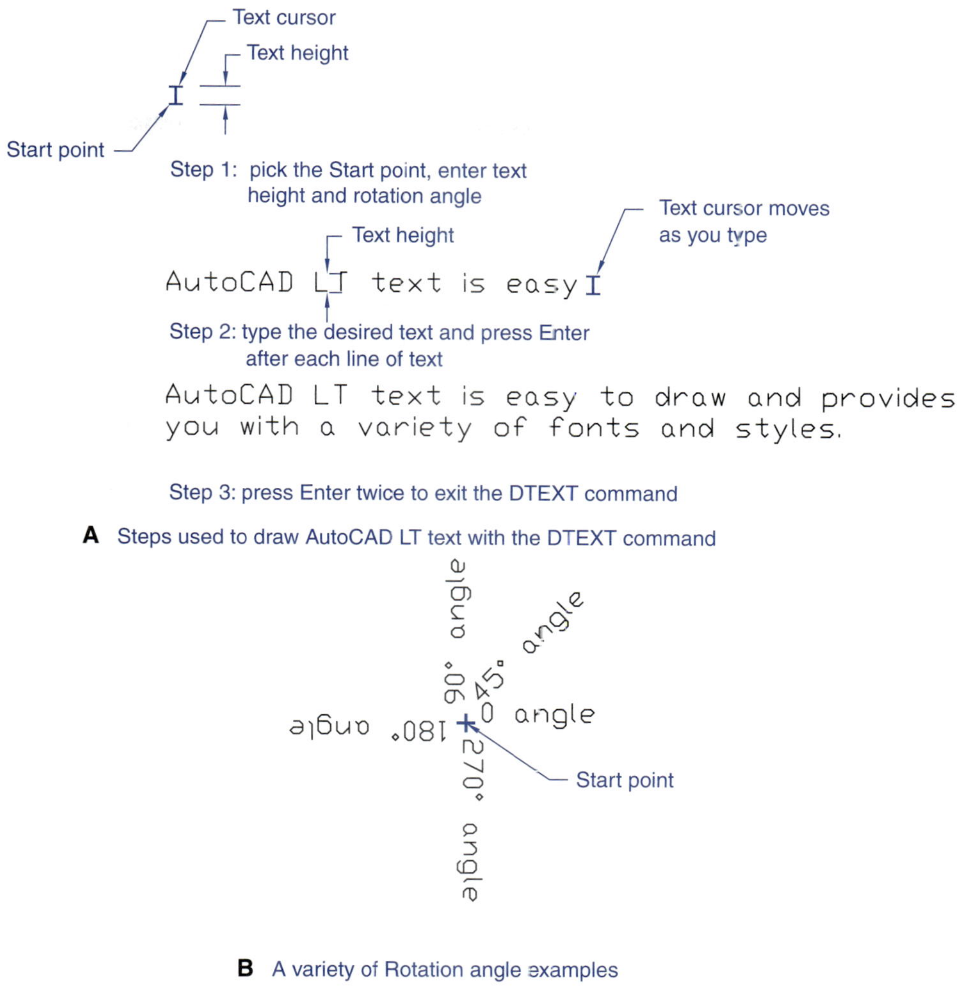

Field Notes

- The Start point option justifies lines of text along a left edge. This is referred to as left-justified text, as shown in Figure 9.1.
- If you enter the DTEXT command and press Enter at the Start point prompt, AutoCAD LT automatically places the text cursor one line below the last line of text. This is true even if the last line of text has been moved. The new line of text uses the same justification method as the previous line, just as if the text is created during the same DTEXT command.

Exercise 9.1 — Estimated time required: 5 min.

1. Begin a new drawing.
2. Make the text height .125 in. and the rotation angle 0 for all applications.
3. Use the DTEXT command's Start point option to type the text shown in Figure 9.1A.
4. Use the DTEXT command's Start point option and test the variety of rotation angles shown in Figure 9.1B. Use the same Start point for each line of text.
5. Save as EX9.1, and close the drawing.

Text Alignment Options

Text ***justification*** determines how text is aligned with the insertion point. AutoCAD LT provides you with several justification options that are available when you enter the DTEXT command's Justify option. The default option, Start point, creates text that is justified along the left side, and the bottom left corner of the first line is located at the specified insertion point. The other justification options are accessed like this:

Command: **DT** or **DTEXT**↵
Current text style: "Standard" Text height: 0.2000
Specify start point of text or [Justify/Style]: **J**↵
Enter an option [Align/Fit/Center/Middle/Right/TL/TC/TR/ML/MC/MR/BL/BC/BR]:

The following discussion explains how each Justify option works and the results:

Align: This option is used to specify two points that control the beginning and ending of the lines of text. The text you enter is placed within the points and the text height is adjusted between the points. Each line of text is automatically adjusted between the two initial points. When typing, the text appears to go beyond or fall short of the second point until you press Enter twice to complete the command. The text being typed is adjusted to the justification method after all text has been entered and you return to the Command: prompt. You need to keep track of the two points so you do not end up with more text between the points than you desire. The result of too much text between the points is very small text; too little text between the points results in big text. The points you pick also control the rotation angle of the text. Also, picking an endpoint that is to the left of the start point results in upside-down text. The following prompts are issued and demonstrated in Figure 9.2:

Command: **DT** or **DTEXT**↵
Current text style: "Standard" Text height: 0.2000
Specify start point of text or [Justify/Style]: **J**↵
Enter an option [Align/Fit/Center/Middle/Right/TL/TC/TR/ML/MC/MR/BL/BC/BR]: **A**↵
Specify first endpoint of text baseline: *<pick the beginning point for the text>*
Specify second endpoint of text baseline: *<pick the ending point>*
Enter text: **The Align option allows you to pick**↵
Enter text: **the beginning and end of the line of**↵
Enter text: text. **The text height is adjusted as needed to**↵
Enter text: **fit the text between the justification points.**↵
Enter text: ↵
Command:

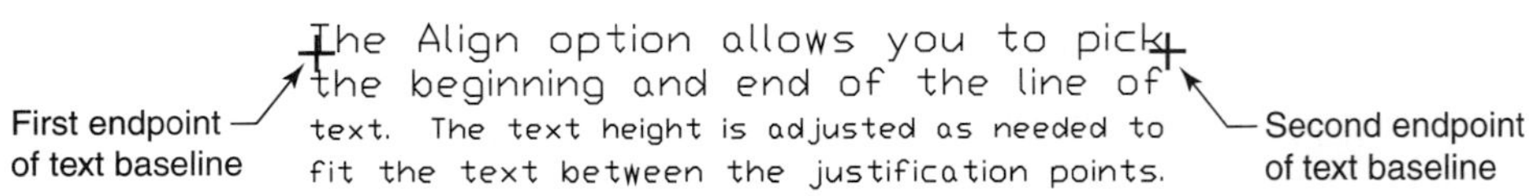

FIGURE 9.2 Using the Align option of the DTEXT Justify option. Notice how the height of the text varies depending on how much text is typed between the selected points.

Fit: The Fit option is similar to the Align option, because you pick two points to control the length of the lines of text. However, the Fit option also asks for the text height. The text height remains the same as the value you specify, but the text width varies depending on how much you type between the points. The points you pick control the rotation angle of the text. Look at Figure 9.3 as you follow these prompts:

Command: **DT** or **DTEXT**↵
Current text style: "Standard" Text height: 0.2000
Specify start point of text or [Justify/Style]: **J**↵
Enter an option [Align/Fit/Center/Middle/Right/TL/TC/TR/ML/MC/MR/BL/BC/BR]: **F**↵
Specify first endpoint of text baseline: *<pick the beginning point for the text>*
Specify second endpoint of text baseline: *<pick the ending point>*
Specify height <0.2000>: **.125**↵
Enter text: **The Fit option allows you to pick**↵
Enter text: **the beginning and end of the line of**↵
Enter text: **text and also control the text height.**↵
Enter text: **The text width is adjusted between the points.**↵
Enter text: ↵
Command:

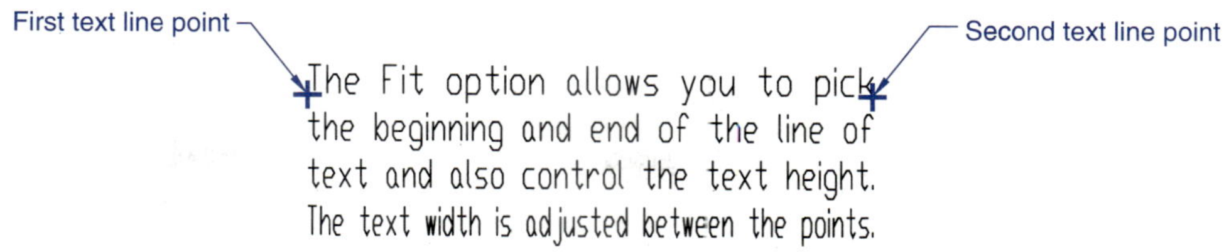

FIGURE 9.3 Using the Fit option of the DTEXT Justify option. Notice how the width of the text varies depending on how much text is typed between the selected points, while the text height remains the same as the value you specify.

Field Notes

The Fit text option comes in handy when a line of text is a little too long to fit in a desired area, such as in a title block, bill of materials, parts list, or schedule. Use the Fit option to squeeze the text into these limited areas rather than lowering the text height.

Center: This Justify option allows you to place text by specifying the center. The center is located along the baseline of the text and centered on each line of text you type. When you begin the Center option, the text cursor and the text you type move to the right of the pick point. Do not let this alarm you, because the text is automatically centered when you press Enter twice and leave the command. Figure 9.4 shows the result of the following Center option:

Command: **DT** or **DTEXT**↵
Current text style: "Standard" Text height: 0.2000
Specify start point of text or [Justify/Style]: **J**↵
Enter an option [Align/Fit/Center/Middle/Right/TL/TC/TR/ML/MC/MR/BL/BC/BR]: **M**↵
Specify center point of text: <*pick the center point*>
Specify height <0.1250>: ↵
Specify rotation angle of text <0>: ↵
Enter text: **The Center option allows you to pick.**↵
Enter text: **the center point of the line or lines of text.**↵
Enter text: ↵
Command:

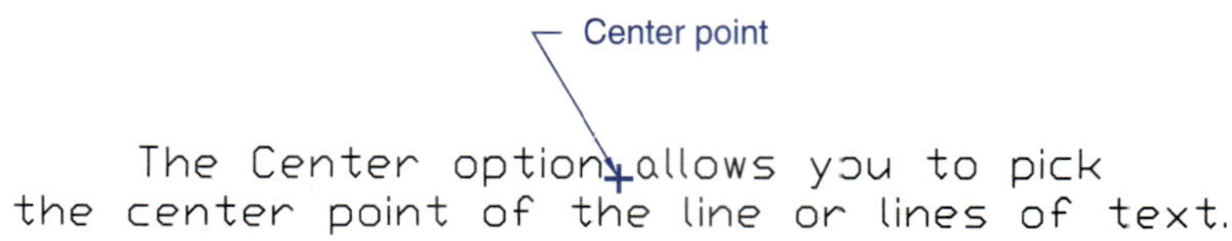

FIGURE 9.4 Using the Center Justify option of the DTEXT command.

Middle: This option allows you to specify the middle of a line of text. The middle is located in the middle of the text height and centered on each line of text you type. When you begin the Middle option, the text cursor and the text you type move to the right of the pick point, just like the Center option. Figure 9.5 shows the result of using the following Middle option:

Command: **DT** or **DTEXT**↵
Current text style: "Standard" Text height: 0.2000
Specify start point of text or [Justify/Style]: **J**↵
Enter an option [Align/Fit/Center/Middle/Right/TL/TC/TR/ML/MC/MR/BL/BC/BR]: **M**↵
Specify middle point of text: <*pick the middle point*>
Specify height <0.1250>: ↵
Specify rotation angle of text <0>: ↵
Enter text: **The Middle option allows you to pick.**↵
Enter text: **the midpoint of the line or lines of text.**↵
Enter text: **and centers the text at that point.**↵
Enter text: ↵
Command:

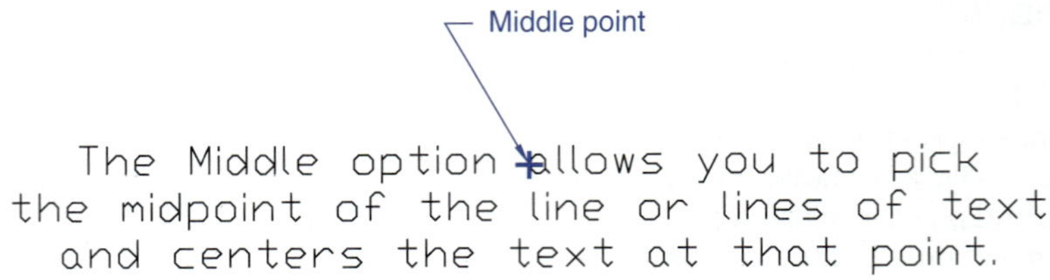

FIGURE 9.5 Using the Middle Justify option of the DTEXT command.

Right: The Right option justifies lines of text along a right edge as shown in Figure 9.6. The prompts work like this:

Command: **DT** or **DTEXT**↵
Current text style: "Standard" Text height: 0.2000
Specify start point of text or [Justify/Style]: **J**↵
Enter an option [Align/Fit/Center/Middle/Right/TL/TC/TR/ML/MC/MR/BL/BC/BR]: **R**↵
Specify right endpoint of text baseline: *<pick the endpoint of the text>*
Specify height <0.1250>: ↵
Specify rotation angle of text <0>: ↵
Enter text: **The Right option aligns text.**↵
Enter text: **along a right margin.**↵
Enter text: **This results in random length lines at the left.**↵
Enter text: ↵
Command:

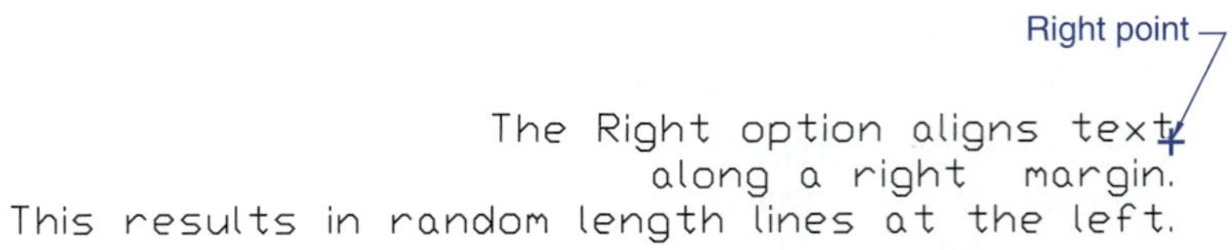

FIGURE 9.6 Using the Right Justify option of the DTEXT command.

In addition to the basic alignment options, AutoCAD LT offers nine more specialized alignment options. The justification points include Top Left, Top Center, Top Right, Middle Left, Middle Center, Middle Right, Bottom Left, Bottom Center, and Bottom Right. Figure 9.7 illustrates these justification points.

When specifying an alignment method, it is not necessary to first type the **J** for Justify at the first prompt. Use this option whenever you need a reminder of what the available options are. If you already know what option you need, simply type the option at the Start point: prompt, as shown here:

Command: **DT** or **DTEXT**↵
Current text style: "Standard" Text height: 0.2000
Specify start point of text or [Justify/Style]: **TR**↵
Specify top-right point of text:

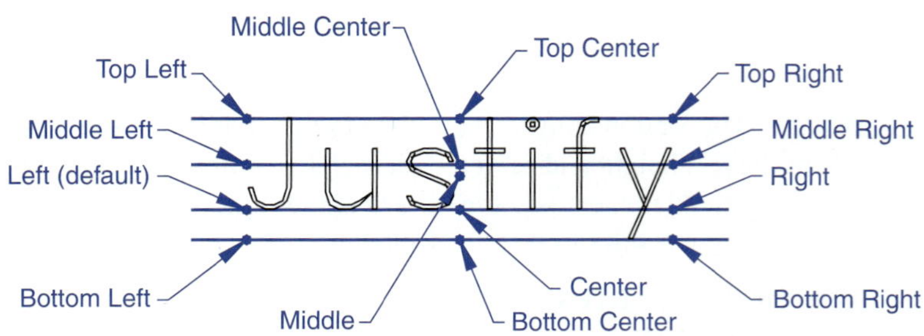

FIGURE 9.7 Justification options available for single-line text.

Field Notes

- The INSert object snap mode accesses the justification point specified when creating the text. The INSert point of Fit or Aligned text is the bottom-left point.
- Although single-line text does not provide the powerful tools found in a word processor or in multiline text, there are some tools available to make text entries easier. When typing text at the command line, you can use your arrow keys to go back and correct text on the current line without having to use the backspace button, which erases text as it goes. You can place your cursor anywhere in the text on the command line by pointing to the desired location and picking. You can also use the Home and End keys to go to the start or end of the line of text. The Ins key switches the command line from insert mode to overwrite mode.

Exercise 9.2 **Estimated time required: 15 min.**

1. Begin a new drawing.
2. Make the text height .125 in. and the rotation angle 0 for all applications.
3. Use the DTEXT command's Align option to type the text shown in Figure 9.2.
4. Use the DTEXT command's Fit option to type the text shown in Figure 9.3.
5. Use the DTEXT command's Center option to type the text shown in Figure 9.4.
6. Use the DTEXT command's Middle option to type the text shown in Figure 9.5.
7. Use the DTEXT command's Right option to type the text shown in Figure 9.6.
8. Create one line of text using each of the available specialized justification options. The text height should be .2 units. Type the justification description for the text content (Top/Left, Top/Center, etc.).
9. Draw a donut object, using an inside diameter of 0 and an outside of .1, at the INSert point of each text object in this drawing.
10. Save as EX9.2, and close the drawing.

Creating and Using Text Styles

There are two important AutoCAD LT terms that relate to the use of text. These terms are font file and text style. A general definition was provided earlier in this chapter. Further clarification will help you understand the following discussion. A ***font file*** is a font definition resource where a complete font is available for your use. A ***text style*** is a definition, within a drawing, of a particular application of text that includes the name of the font file along with any specific properties that you assign. A font file can be used by more than one text style. For example, your company may have text standards that are used on drawings. These standards are probably text styles that use font files in different manners. A text style is defined by you or your company to contain the desired text characteristics. In the process of defining a text style, you often load a font file to use as the basis for creating the text style.

The DTEXT and MTEXT commands both have a Style option. The MTEXT command is for drawing multiline text and is discussed later. The Style option is used to set the text style. In drawings based on any of the standard AutoCAD LT template files, the default style is called STANDARD, which uses the TXT.SHX font file. This is the font that has been used in the previous examples in this chapter. The STANDARD style is also referred to as a ***fast font*** because it is drawn and regenerated very quickly, but it does not look very good for most applications.

Field Notes

Other default text styles may be provided when you use a template, depending on which template you use.

AutoCAD LT provides you with a wide variety of standard text and symbol fonts defined in font files. The standard text and symbol font files have an .SHX extension. For example, the file ROMANS.SHX defines a Roman Simplex font. This font has smooth characters and is commonly used on drawings. Complex fonts such as COMPLEX.SHX provide you with characters that have serifs. ***Serifs*** are fine artistic lines projecting from, generally, the top and bottom of a letter. Gothic fonts such as GOTHICE.SHX are an old English style. The symbol fonts are used for applications such as mapping and math and can produce symbols not found on the keyboard. These fonts substitute symbols for standard keyboard characters. The mapping symbol font is called SYMAP.SHX.

Field Notes

> The names of .SHX files have specific meaning. For example, ROMANS = Roman Simplex, ROMANC = Roman Complex, ROMAND = Roman Duplex, and ROMANT = Roman Triplex. The characteristics of each font are established by the number of lines in the characters. The Simplex has one line, Duplex has two lines, and Triplex has three lines. This standard is maintained across many different .SHX font files.

AutoCAD LT provides True Type fonts that provide greater detail than the standard fonts. You may want to use the City Blueprint, Country Blueprint, or Stylus BT font for your architectural drawings because they closely resemble the artistic hand lettering used by architectural drafters.

Setting and Creating Text Styles

Format
Text Style...
STYLE
ST

The Style option found in the DTEXT and MTEXT commands is used to set a text style. You set a text style by typing the name after entering the Style option. However, before a text style can be used with one of these commands, the style must be defined. If you try to use the Style option and enter a text style, such as ROMANS, before it has been defined, AutoCAD LT gives you this message:

```
Command: DT or DTEXT↵
Current text style:  "Standard"  Text height:  0.1250
Specify start point of text or [Justify/Style]:  S↵
Enter style name or [?] <Standard>: ROMANS↵
Cannot find text style "ROMANS".
Enter style name or [?] <Standard>:
```

To solve this problem, you need to define the ROMANS text style. Text styles are defined using the DDSTYLE command. This command is accessed by picking Text Style ... in the Format pull-down menu or by typing **ST** or **STYLE** at the Command: prompt. The STYLE command opens the Text Style dialog box shown in Figure 9.8.

FIGURE 9.8 The Text Style dialog box.

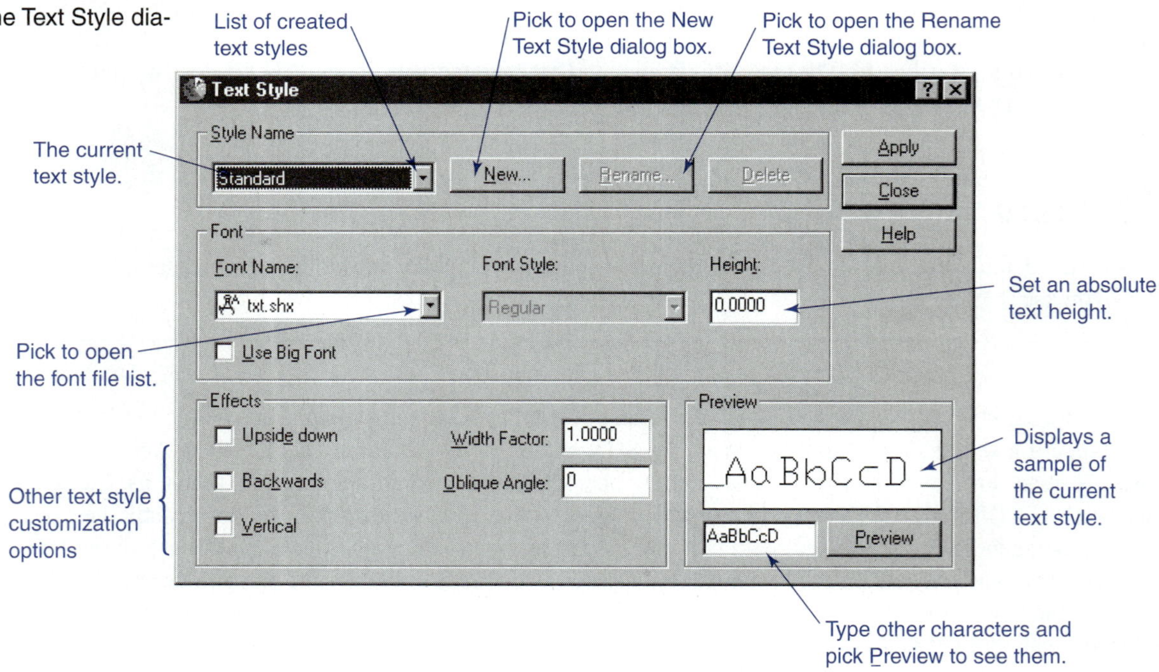

The following provides a brief description of the Text Style dialog box:

Style Name: This area is where the names of existing text styles are listed. You can modify, rename, or delete a listed text style.

The New ... button is used to create a new text style. Picking the New ... button opens the New Text Style dialog box shown in Figure 9.9. By default, STYLE1 is automatically displayed in the Style Name: text box. If you pick the OK button, a new style named STYLE1 is added to the list. Any future picks under the same conditions produce incrementally named styles, such as STYLE2 and STYLE3. It is very convenient to type a desired style name and then pick the OK button. You can type a style name that relates to your drawing, such as MECHANICAL for mechanical drawings or ARCHITECTURAL for architectural drawings. If a style named STYLE1 is created, you can use the Rename ... button to change the name if you wish. Text style names use the same standards as other named objects such as layers. The name can use up to 255 characters, but cannot use special characters like commas, question marks, or asterisks.

FIGURE 9.9 The New Text Style dialog box.

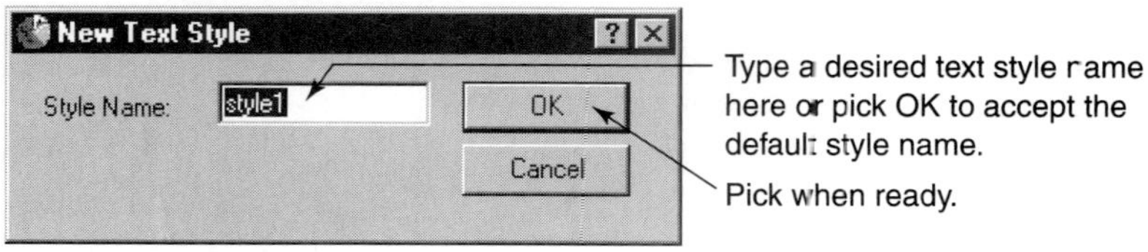

The Rename ... button is used to rename a current text style. To use this option, highlight a text style in the list to make it current and then pick the Rename ... button. This opens the Rename Text Style dialog box shown in Figure 9.10. Type a new text style name and pick OK. The current text style takes on the revised name.

FIGURE 9.10 The Rename Text Style dialog box.

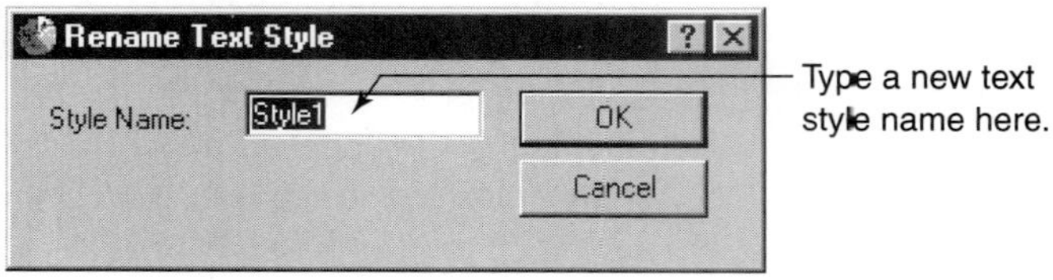

The Delete button is used to remove a current text style from the list. Notice in Figure 9.8 that the Rename ... and Delete buttons are not active. This is because the only text style listed is the AutoCAD LT STANDARD font, which you cannot rename or delete. When you pick the Delete button, Auto CAD LT issues an aclt Alert, which gives you a chance to change your mind.

Field Notes

- If you try to rename the STANDARD style name, the Text Style dialog box tells you that you cannot do this. However, the STANDARD text style can be renamed using the DDRENAME command. Even if the STANDARD style is renamed, it cannot be deleted from the Text Style dialog box.
- Text styles that are currently in use cannot be deleted. A style is *in use* when one or more text objects based on that style currently exist in the drawing.
- The ? option of the DTEXT command can be used to list the defined style names. Just type "?" at the Style name (or ?) <>: prompt and press Enter to get a list of the defined style names.

Font: The Font area of the Text Style dialog box is where you select the font you want to use in a text style. Open the Font Name: list to find the available fonts. The romans font is commonly used on mechanical drawings because it closely duplicates the traditional style recommended by ASME. So, if you named the text style MECHANICAL, find the romans.shx file and pick it, as shown in Figure 9.11.

FIGURE 9.11 The Font Name: list in the Text Style dialog box.

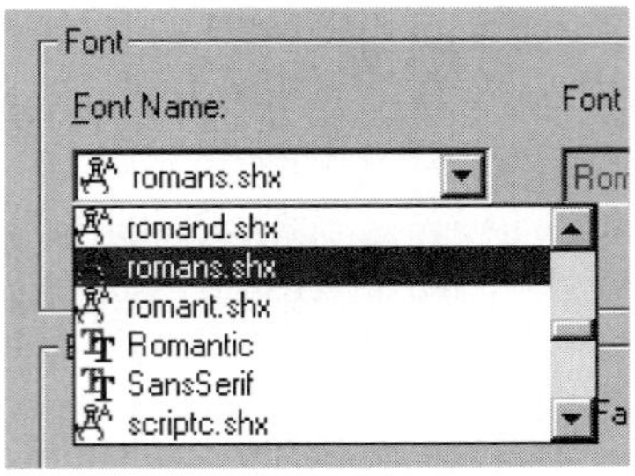

The Font Style: list is active only when you pick a font name that has its own style options. The romans.shx font has no additional style options. If you pick a font name such as SansSerif, the Font Style: list provides options that can be used to change the appearance of the font. See Figure 9.12.

FIGURE 9.12 The Font Style: list is available for some TrueType fonts. This provides different characteristics for the specified font.

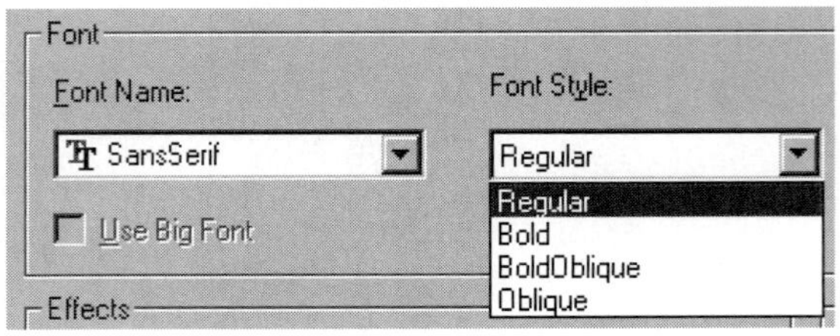

The Height: text box is where you specify the desired text height. The default text height value is 0 (zero). A zero text height entered here allows you to specify the text height every time you enter the DTEXT or MTEXT commands. This provides you with the flexibility to change the text height when you use these commands or simply press Enter to accept the current default. If you specify a value other than zero in the Height: text box, then this height becomes fixed for every time you use this text style. Specifying a fixed text height is an advantage when you know that the height for a particular text style is not going to change. However, this can cause unexpected results when a fixed height is specified for a style you need to use at different heights in a drawing. If you are creating text and no prompt is issued for height, it is because a fixed height has been applied to the style. If you find that a style has a fixed height, and you want it to be variable, you can redefine the style using a 0 height. This does not affect any previously drawn text, but any future uses of this style provide the text height prompt.

The Use Big Font check box is off by default and is active only with .shx fonts. Asian and other large-format fonts are called ***big fonts***. The big font is used as a supplement to define many symbols not available in normal font files. The Big Font: list replaces the Font Style: list when you pick the Use Big Font check box. An example of the effects of a big font can be seen by loading a normal font file and a big font file to be used as a text style.

Effects: The Effects area of the Text Style dialog box is where you can choose options for customizing a text font. You have several customization options, which include making text upside down, backwards, or vertical. You can also specify different heights, widths, and character slant. These options are designed into the text style by using the Effects area of the Text Style dialog box. First define a text style, as previously discussed. Next, change the effects as desired before picking the Apply button and closing the dialog box. You can change the effects individually and see the changes displayed immediately in the Character Preview image for any effect caused by a toggle, except the Vertical option. This allows you to view the effects of the design before making a decision to use it. The different elements of the Effects compartment in the Text Style dialog box are explained and demonstrated in the following list:

- **Upside down** Pick this toggle to have the text placed upside down as shown in Figure 9.13.

FIGURE 9.13 Setting the style as upside-down text.

- **Backwards** Check this toggle to have text drawn backwards, as shown in Figure 9.14. Backwards text is placed at a 180° angle relative to the specified rotation angle. Backwards text is very useful for plastic and metal cast part tools, where the text must be backwards on the tool for it to be forward on the part.

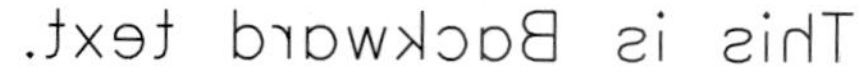

FIGURE 9.14 Setting the style as backwards text.

- **Vertical** This option places text vertically, as shown in Figure 9.15. A 0° rotation angle produced downward text.

FIGURE 9.15 Setting the text style as vertical text.

- **Width Factor** This text box allows you to change the width of text characters. The default width is 1. A width of less than 1 compresses the characters, and a width greater than 1 expands the characters. Figure 9.16 displays a variety of different text width specifications.

FIGURE 9.16 Examples of different text width settings.

- **Obliquing Angle** The obliquing angle establishes the slant of the characters. A positive obliquing angle slants the text to the right, and a negative angle slants text to the left. Text without any slant has an obliquing angle of 0 (zero). Some drafting fields such as structural, or rivers shown on maps, use text that is slanted to the right, usually at 15°. Few applications exist that go beyond ±30°. AutoCAD LT limits the obliquing angle to between ±85°. Figure 9.17 shows the results of changing the text obliquing angle.

FIGURE 9.17 Examples of different text obliquing angle settings.

Preview: This area displays several characters of the current text font. This is a good way to see what the text style looks like before you select it for use in a drawing. The preview image automatically shows the first few characters of a font. You can look at different characters by typing them in the text box to the left of the Preview button. For example, the image in Figure 9.8 displays an upper- and lowercase example of ABC. If you want to see what the numbers for this font look like, type them in the text box and pick the Preview button.

- **Apply** Pick this button to apply the selected style or style changes to all of the text in the current drawings.
- **Close** Pick this button to close the Text Style dialog box.

Steps in Creating a Text Style

The previous discussion explained how to create a text style using the Text Style dialog box. The following provides you with a quick step-by-step sequence to use when creating your first text style:

1. Think about the name for your text style. You can name the text style anything you want, but the name normally identifies its use. For example, you can have a text style named MECHANICAL for the general information found on your mechanical drawings. You can have a specific name for titles, such as MECHANICAL-TITLES. You can use similar style names for your architectural drawings, such as ARCH-TITLES. Use abbreviations, if you wish. You can also name a text style with the font name. For example, you can pick a text style name of ROMANS to be used with romans font on your mechanical drawings. Good fonts to use on architectural drawings are StylusBT, CityBlueprint, and CountryBlueprint.

Field Notes

It is best to keep a log of the text styles you create. You can refer to the log as a reminder of the text style characteristics used with the text style name.

2. Open the Text Style dialog box using one of the ways to access the STYLE command.
3. Pick the New... button to open the New Text Style dialog box. Type the desired text style name, such as MECHANICAL, in the Style Name: text box. Pick OK.
4. Open the Font Name: list and pick romans.shx.
5. Leave the Height: as 0 so you can specify the desired text height when you are drawing text.
6. Leave all other options at their default settings, because the romans font named MECHANICAL with flexible text height is what you want at this time.
7. Pick the Apply button.
8. Pick the Close button.

Exercise 9.3 **Estimated time required: 5 min.**

1. Open EX9.2.
2. Use the DDSTYLE command to define romans as a new text style using the romans font file.
3. Make the romans style the current text style in this drawing by picking Apply, and Close the dialog box.
4. Use the romans text style and type the upper- and lowercase alphabet and numbers 1 through 10 with .125-in.-high characters.
5. Notice the difference between the STANDARD style from the previous exercise and the romans style.
6. Save as EX9.3, and close the drawing.

Field Notes

If you use the Text Style dialog box to make a change to an existing text style and then select a different Style name before picking Apply, AutoCAD LT gives you this message:

> The current style has been modified.
> Do you want to save your changes?

If you answer Yes, the changes are saved to the current text style. Pick No to return to the Text Style dialog box with no changes made.

Exercise 9.4 — Estimated time required: 10 min.

1. Open EX9.3.
2. Erase the drawing.
3. Use the Text Style dialog box to set upside-down text and then use the DTEXT command to enter the text shown in Figure 9.12.
4. Use the Text Style dialog box to remove the previous effect and set backward text. Use the DTEXT command to enter the text shown in Figure 9.13.
5. Use the Text Style dialog box to remove the previous effect and set vertical text. Use the DTEXT command to enter the text shown in Figure 9.14.
6. Use the Text Style dialog box to remove the previous effect and set the width factor to a variety of values similar to those shown in Figure 9.15. Use the DTEXT command to enter the text after each setting.
7. Use the Text Style dialog box to remove the previous effect and set the obliquing angle to a variety of values similar to those shown in Figure 9.16. Use the DTEXT command to enter the text after each setting.
8. Save as EX9.4, and close the drawing.

Customizing Text Styles

Working with AutoCAD LT text becomes an easy task if you customize the text styles for the drawings you create and have them available in a template. Commonly customized text styles might include a variety such as those shown in Table 9.1.

TABLE 9.1 Common customized text styles

Mechanical Drawings					
Name	**Use**	**Font**	**Height**	**Width**	**Angle**
MECH	Drawing field	ROMANS	0.125	1.0	0
MECH-TITLES	View titles	ROMAND	0.25	1.5	0
MECH-PLANES	Cutting planes	ROMANS	0.25	1.0	0
MECH-DIM	Dimensions	GDT	0.125	1.0	0
Architectural Drawings					
Name	**Use**	**Font**	**Height**	**Width**	**Angle**
ARCH	Drawing field	StylusBT	0.125	1.0	0
ARCH-TITLES	Drawing titles	StylusBT	0.25	1.5	0

Exercise 9.5 — Estimated time required: 5 min.

1. Begin a new drawing, or open a previously developed mechanical or architectural template as appropriate.
2. Use the STYLE command to customize the following text styles for use in either your mechanical drawings or your architectural drawings, whichever you prefer:

Mechanical Drawings

Name	Font	Height	Width	Angle
MECH	ROMANS	0.125	1.0	0
MECH-TITLES	ROMAND	0.25	1.5	0
MECH-PLANES	ROMANS	0.25	1.0	0
MECH-DIM	GDT	0.125	1.0	0

Architectural Drawings

Name	Font	Height	Width	Angle
ARCH	StylusBT	0.125	1.0	0
ARCH-TITLES	StylusBT	0.25	1.5	0

3. Save as EX9.5, and close the drawing.

Loading Text Styles Using AutoCAD DesignCenter

It is always best to begin a drawing using a customized template that has been defined based on your company or school standards. Your templates should have drawing content such as text styles already defined and ready to use. However, creating new drawings is only part of the job for most drafters and designers. You will frequently be working on drawings created by other drafters. Many of these drawings will come from clients or vendors who may not use the same standards as your company. AutoCAD DesignCenter provides a fast and easy way to access text style definitions that are found in existing drawings or template files.

AutoCAD DesignCenter was introduced in Chapter 5 as a way to import layer and linetype definitions using a simple drag-and-drop interface. Like layers and linetypes, text styles are named object definitions that are accessible through DesignCenter.

Use the ADC command or the Ctrl+2 accelerator keystroke to activate the DesignCenter window. Arrange the window to match your preferences, and make sure that the drawing from which you are importing the style is visible. If the drawing that contains the style you need is currently closed, pick the Open Drawings button to display all the currently open drawings in the Tree View pane. Pick the plus sign next to the drawing icon to display the content categories. Select the Textstyles icon to display the available styles in the palette pane. Now, simply drag and drop the desired styles into your drawing (see Figure 9.18).

In Figure 9.18, all the highlighted text styles were imported into the new drawing. Opening the Style Name list in the Text Style dialog box verifies that all the text style definitions were successfully imported (see Figure 9.19).

If the drawing with the needed content is not currently open, you can access it using one of the other DesignCenter options as follows:

- *If you have recently accessed this file:* Pick the History button. All your recently opened files are displayed (Figure 9.20). Find the correct file and double-click on it to load the content in the palette pane.

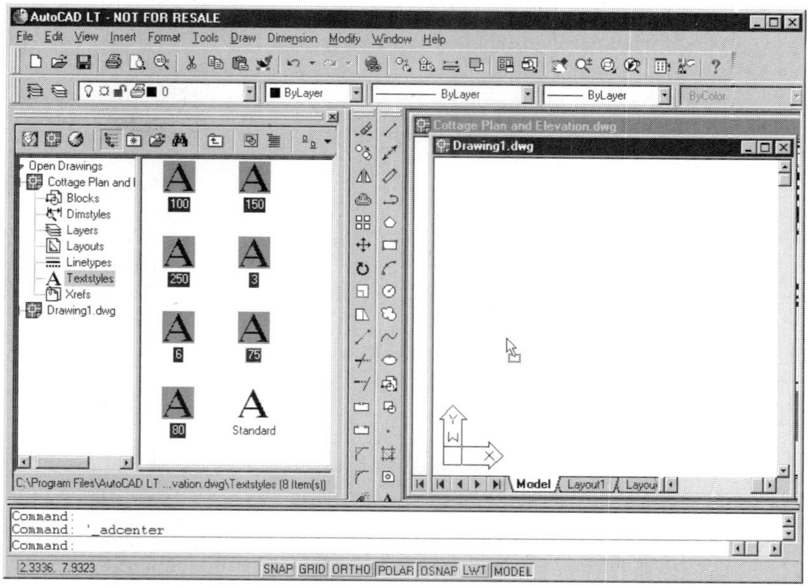

FIGURE 9.18 AutoCAD DesignCenter allows you to access and reuse previously defined drawing content such as text styles, increasing drafting productivity and helping implement accepted drawing standards.

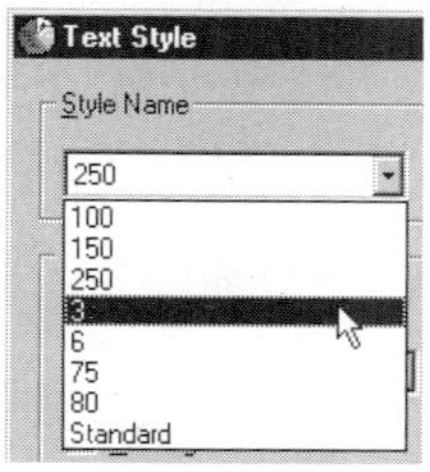

FIGURE 9.19 The imported styles are displayed in the Style Name list in the Text Style dialog box.

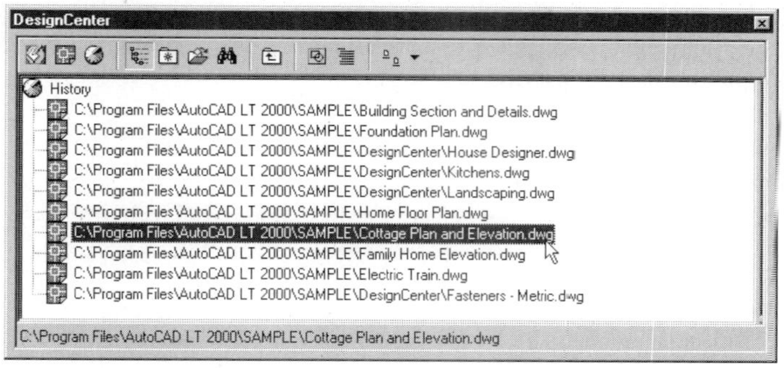

FIGURE 9.20 The History button displays the drawings that you have recently accessed with DesignCenter.

- *If you know the location of the file:* Pick the Desktop button and use the Tree View pane to access the correct drive and folder to locate the desired file. Double-click on it to load its content in the palette pane.
- *If you know the filename but can't locate it:* Pick the Find button. In the Find dialog box, pick the Drawings option from the Look for list, enter the filename in the Search for the word(s) box, select the File Name option from the In the field(s) list, then pick the Find Now button. Files matching the specified name are listed at the bottom of the Find dialog box (see Figure 9.21). Double-click on the file to load its content in the palette pane.

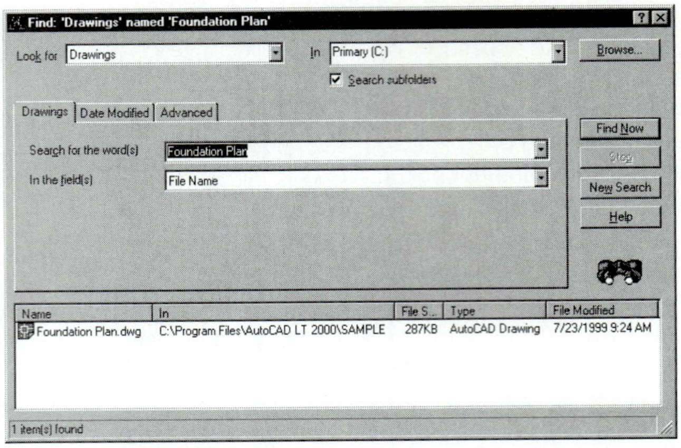

FIGURE 9.21 The Find tool in DesignCenter lets you quickly search all local and network drives and folders for the drawing file for which you are looking.

- *If you don't know the name or location of the file, but you know the name of the text style (or other drawing content) that you need:*

Pick the Find button. In the Find dialog box, pick the appropriate content type from the Look for list. Enter the name of the content item in the Search for the name box, and pick the Find Now button. The listing shows the content item and displays the name and location of the source drawing. With this method, it is not necessary to load the drawing content into the palette pane—you can simply drag and drop the content item from the Find dialog box directly into your drawing.

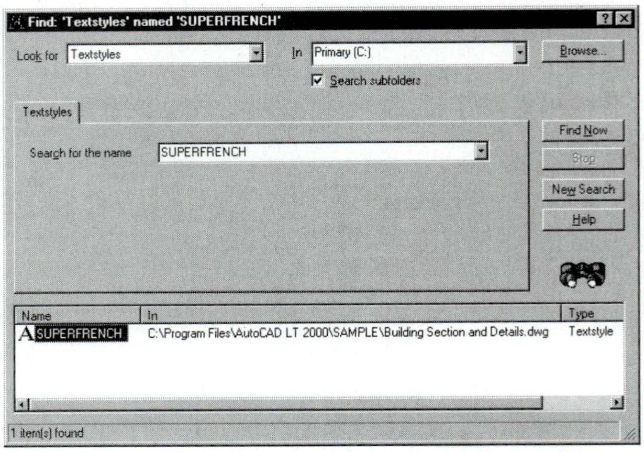

FIGURE 9.22 The Find dialog box can also be used to find specific content even if you don't know the name of the drawing in which the content is found. In this example, the text style "SuperFrench" was located by entering only the style name.

LEARNING CHECKPOINT

- ☐ What is single-line text?
- ☐ Define the term *text font.*
- ☐ What does the Justify option do?
- ☐ Describe the DTEXT Justify options: Start point, Align, Fit, Center, Middle, and Right. Be sure to explain the main difference between Align and Fit.
- ☐ How do you access the Text Style dialog box?
- ☐ Explain how to see different characters for the currently displayed font in the Preview image.
- ☐ How do you display a new font image in the Preview box?
- ☐ Discuss the effects of changing the text width factor and obliquing angle.
- ☐ Outline the six steps used to customize a text style called TITLES with ROMAND font, 0.25 height, and 1.5 width.

- ☐ How can DesignCenter be used to define new text styles in a drawing?
- ☐ Which tool displays a selectable list of files recently accessed using DesignCenter?
- ☐ Explain in detail how to use DesignCenter to search for drawing content when the drawing name and location are not known.

Working with Text and Symbols

- Controlling Text Appearance

Creating Multiline Text

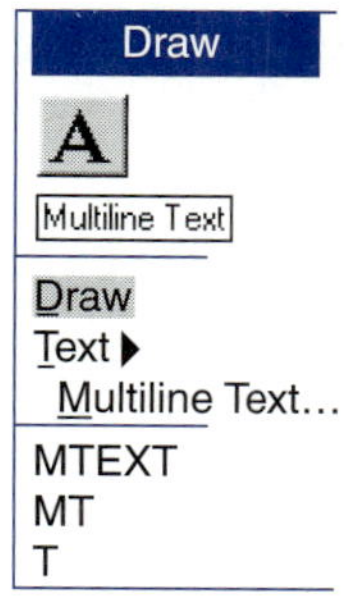

Multiline text is also referred to as paragraph text. AutoCAD LT defines ***paragraph text*** as consisting of a number of text lines or paragraphs that fit within a width you specify. Each set of lines or paragraphs is one object. This is very different from the previously discussed line text. With line text, every line of text is an individual object. All of the same parameters that affect line text, such as height, width, obliquing angle, and justification options, also work with paragraph text. Paragraph text is much more flexible than line text, allowing individual portions of the text to have varying properties. Multiline text is drawn by picking the Multiline Text button in the Draw toolbar, by picking Multiline Text... from the Text cascade on the Draw pull-down menu, or by typing **T**, **MT**, or **MTEXT**:

> Command: **T, MT,** or **MTEXT**↵
> Current text style: "ROMANS" Text height: 0.2000
> Specify first corner: *<pick the first corner of the text boundary>*
> Specify opposite corner or [Height/Justify/Line spacing/Rotation/Style/Width]: *<pick the opposite corner of the text boundary>*

The Specify first corner prompt is issued for you to pick the first corner of a box. The Specify opposite corner prompt asks you to move the cursor to form a box that is approximately equal in size to the area where you want the paragraph text to be placed. You can move the cursor in any direction from the first corner. Pick the opposite corner of the box when you have the desired size. In Figure 9.23, note that the box is the text boundary. The ***text boundary*** establishes the width of the paragraph of text. It is important that the text boundary width you establish accurately defines the width of the desired paragraph. The actual width of the paragraph may not be exactly the same as the width you specify, due to word length and wrapping. ***Word wrapping*** is the process by which the words that exceed the boundary width are automatically placed or "wrapped" to the next line. Some lines of text may be wider than others, but none is wider than the defined boundary. If a single word exceeds the defined paragraph width, the text is not wrapped, but is allowed to extend beyond the boundary. In this case, the paragraph width is not changed and all other text is wrapped as usual.

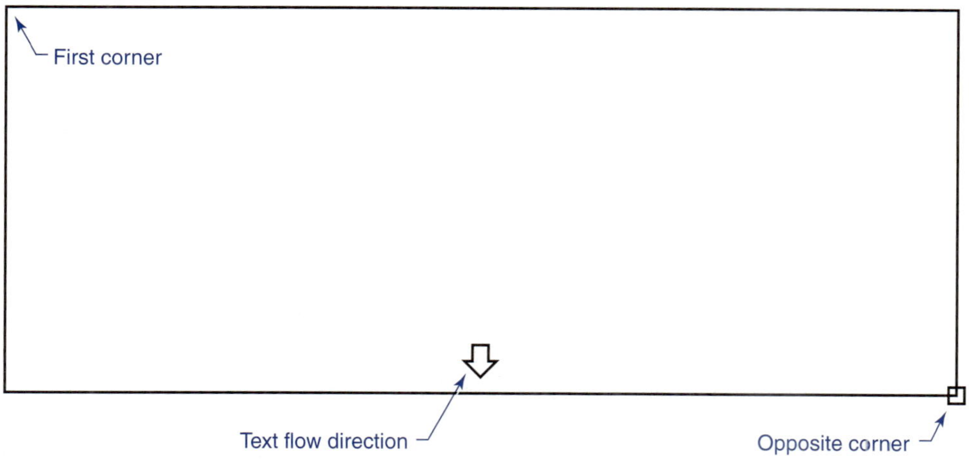

FIGURE 9.23 Establishing the text boundary for the MTEXT paragraph.

The height of the text boundary does not have to be exact, because AutoCAD LT automatically adjusts the text boundary to match the actual height of the paragraph you type. The flow arrow in Figure 9.23 gives you a reference for the direction the text will flow when it is entered in the boundary. This is related to the multiline text justification, which is discussed later. This flow arrow points down for any top-justified text, up for bottom-justification, or up and down for center-justified text.

The Height, Justify, Rotation, and Style options work as they do with the DTEXT command that was discussed earlier. These options are explained again later in this chapter with the information about the Multiline Text Editor.

The Width option is used by typing **W** and then pressing Enter. The Width option allows you to establish the width of the text boundary. A rubber-band cursor then connects the first point to the next point you pick to establish the width. The prompts are as follows:

Command: **T, MT,** or **MTEXT**↵
Current text style: "ROMANS" Text height: 0.2000
Specify first corner: *<pick the first corner of the text boundary>*
Specify opposite corner or [Height/Justify/Line spacing/Rotation/Style/Width]: **W**↵
Specify width: *<pick or type the width for the paragraph>*

You can also enter a numeric value at the keyboard. If you enter a 0 (zero), the multiline text continues on the same line until you press Enter. Used with a 0 width, no boundary is attached to the paragraph, and no automatic word wrapping occurs. Also, later grip editing of the width is not possible, although positioning can still be changed with grips.

Immediately after you specify the text boundary width, AutoCAD LT opens the Multiline Text Editor shown in Figure 9.24A. The text cursor is available for you to begin typing the paragraph. The lines of text you type automatically end at the text boundary and continue on the next line. You can move the text cursor to any desired place within the text boundary. Pick where you want the text cursor placed, and then backspace to move the cursor back or press the space bar to move it forward. Backspace to remove text or pick and hold while moving the cursor to highlight text. Press the backspace key or space bar to have highlighted text removed. Type more text as needed. You can press the Enter key at any time to go to the next line. The Multiline Text Editor works just like a word processor. The following list shows additional keystroke options that can be used when working in the Multiline Text Editor dialog box:

Keystroke	*Results*
Ctrl+→ Ctrl+←	Moves the cursor one word in the direction indicated. (Note: The "+" symbol means that you press the keys before and after the + at the same time.)
Arrow keys	Moves the cursor through the text one position in the direction of the arrow key used.
Home	Moves the cursor to the start of the current line.
End	Moves the cursor to the end of the current line.
Delete	Removes the character directly to the right of the cursor.
Ctrl+Delete	Removes the word directly to the right of the cursor.
← Backspace	The Backspace key removes one character to the left as it moves.
Ctrl+C	Copies the selected text to the Clipboard.
Ctrl+V	Pastes the Clipboard contents to the cursor position.
Ctrl+Shift+Space	Inserts nonbreaking space, keeping the words on either side on one line.
Ctrl + Backspace	Removes the word to the left of the cursor.
Ctrl+X	Cuts the highlighted selection to the Clipboard.
Ctrl+Z	Undoes the previous operation.
Ctrl+Space	Inserts a nonbreaking space. Used to keep text from wrapping to the next line.
Page Up	Moves the cursor to the beginning of the paragraph.
Page Down	Moves the cursor to the end of the paragraph.
Ctrl+Page Up	Moves the cursor to the beginning of the currently visible page.
Ctrl+Page Down	Moves the cursor to the end of the currently visible page.
Ctrl+Home	Moves the cursor to Line 1, Column 1.
Ctrl+End	Moves the cursor to the end of the text.
Ctrl+A	Selects and highlights all of the text.
Shift + → Shift + ←	Highlights text one character at a time in the arrow direction.

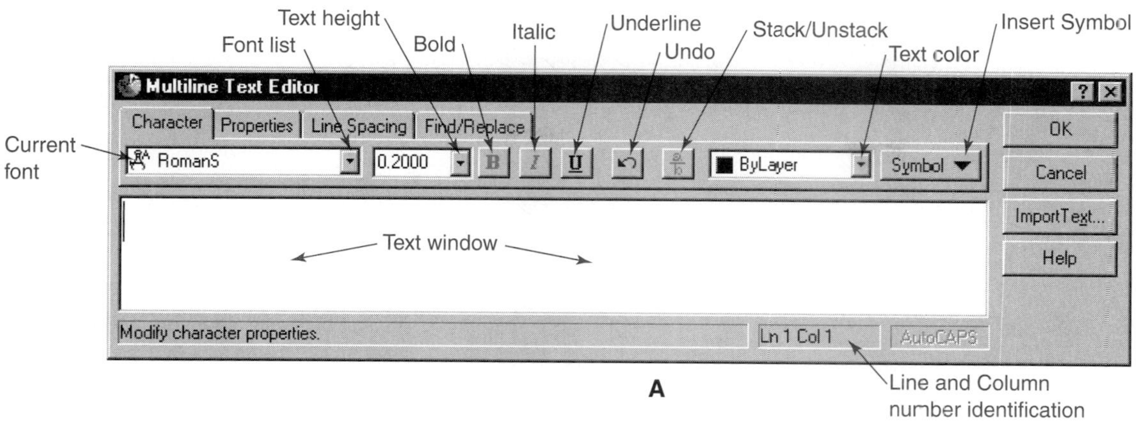

A

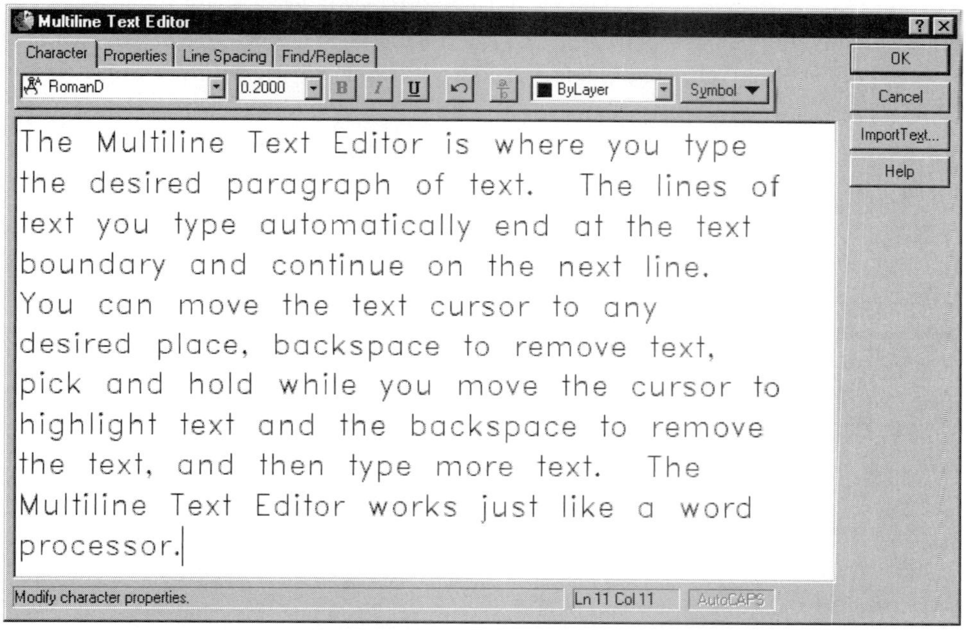

B

FIGURE 9.24 (A) The Multiline Text Editor. Text is typed—just as if you are using a word processor. (B) A paragraph of text is typed in the Multiline Text Editor.

Shift + ↑	Highlights the line of text in front of and above the cursor.
Shift + ↓	Highlights the line of text behind and below the cursor.
Esc	Closes the Multiline Text Editor (you loose any entries made).

In addition to the key strokes used to help you edit text, a shortcut menu is available. The menu shown in Figure 9.25 is opened by moving the screen cursor inside the text window and right-clicking. As with all context sensitive menus, the available options will vary based on current status, activity, and location. When an item of text is selected, the menu appears as shown in Figure 9.25. These options are described as follows:

- **Undo:** Pick this option to undo the last multiline text activity.
- **Cut:** This option cuts highlighted text from the paragraph and places it on the Clipboard.
- **Copy:** Pick this to copy highlighted text to the Clipboard.
- **Paste:** This option is used to paste items from the Clipboard into the text window at the text cursor location.
- **Select All:** Pick this option to select and highlight all the text in the current document.
- **Change Case:** This cascade offers options to change the selected text to either all UPPERCASE or all lowercase letters.

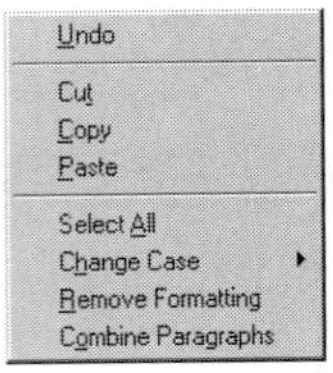

FIGURE 9.25 The Multiline Text Editor shortcut menu is displayed when you move the screen cursor inside the text window and right-click .

- **Remove Formatting:** Removes any formatting applied to the text in the Multiline Text Editor. This affects all text in the editor, not just selected text.
- **Combine Paragraphs:** Removes carriage returns from the selection to combine multiple paragraphs into a single paragraph.

Look at the paragraph that has been typed in Figure 9.24.B

When you have typed and edited the desired paragraph of text, pick the OK button to have the text placed on the screen in the location where you located the text boundary. Figure 9.26 shows the text that was typed in the Multiline Text Editor dialog box in Figure 9.24. You can use the MOVE command if you want to place the paragraph in a new location, or you can grip select the insertion point and use the GRIP Stretch or Move option.

The Multiline Text Editor is where you type the desired paragraph of text. The lines of text you type automatically end at the text boundary and continue on the next line. You can move the text cursor to any desired place, backspace to remove text, pick and hold while you move the cursor to highlight text and then backspace to remove the text, and then type more text. The Multiline Text Editor works just like a word processor.

FIGURE 9.26 The result of the text that was entered in the Multiline Text Editor dialog box in Figure 9.24B using the MTEXT command.

Field Notes

- The final appearance of the text can be different than the display in the Multiline Text Editor. Differences can happen depending on the type of font and the available space on each line. If the font width in the MTEXT editor is not proportionate to the width displayed in the editor, the resulting word wrap may be different with the onscreen text.
- Grip selection of paragraph text displays the four grips that represent the paragraph text boundary. These grips can be used to make adjustments to the width of the paragraph, but they do not affect the height.

As you look at Figure 9.24, notice that the Multiline Text Editor has four tabs, the Character, Properties, Line Spacing, and Find/Replace tabs. The Character tab is open when the editor initially appears. This is where you type in the text window, as previously shown. The other features of the Character tab are explained in the following:

- **Font:** The current style font is displayed when you enter the Multiline Text Editor. You can open the Font list to use a different font for text typed at the cursor location. You can also pick a font from the list to have it used in highlighted text within the paragraph.

- **Font height:** The value specified is the height of the current text style. You can change the value for text typed at the cursor location or for highlighted text within the paragraph.
- **Bold:** Pick this button to have highlighted text become bold or to change bold text back to regular text. This does not work on .shx text but is active for some TrueType fonts.
- **Italic:** Pick this button to have highlighted text become italicized or to change bold text back to regular text. This does not work on .shx text but is active for some TrueType fonts.
- **Underline:** Pick this button to underline highlighted text or to change underlined text back to regular text.
- **Undo:** Pick this button to undo the previous action.

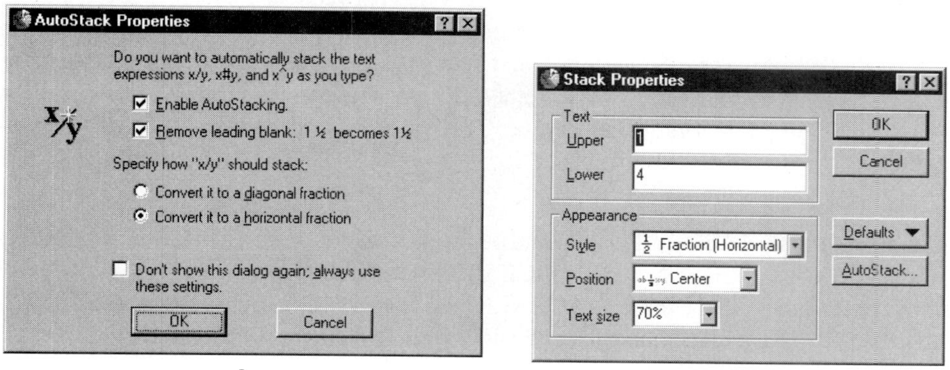

A B

FIGURE 9.27 (A) The AutoStack Properties dialog box controls how and when AutoStacking is implemented. (B) Stacked text is edited using the Stack Properties dialog box.

- **Stack/Unstack:** This button is used to manually stack text, such as fractions, or to unstack stacked text. Before using this button, a forward slash (/) needs to be typed between the text characters to be stacked. Then highlight the characters and pick the button. Use a caret symbol (^) between characters to stack without a dividing bar between.

Stacking text manually is not necessary, because the Multiline Text Editor can automatically stack fractions and tolerance text as you type. The first time you type a fraction (for example: 1/4" or 1 1/2") in the editor and press either the spacebar or Enter, the AutoStack Properties dialog box is displayed. The AutoStack Properties dialog box is shown in Figure 9.27A. This dialog box asks whether you want to have certain text expressions automatically stacked. If so, place a check in the box labeled Enable AutoStacking. The AutoStack Properties dialog box also allows you to specify how and when AutoStacking is implemented. The text expressions x/y or x#y, where x and y are integer values (whole numbers without a decimal), are recognized as fractions. By default, x/y is stacked vertically separated by a horizontal bar. The settings under the heading Specify how "x/y" should stack can be set so the fraction is stacked diagonally. The x#y entry is always stacked as a diagonal fraction and cannot be changed. The text x^y, where x and y are decimal numbers, is always stacked as a tolerance.

When mixed numbers are typed, it is common to separate the whole number from the fraction with a blank space. Otherwise, a fraction such as 1 1/4 (one and one-fourth) might be interpreted as 11/4 (eleven-fourths). After stacking, the fraction appears as 1 ¼ or 1 $\frac{1}{4}$, so there is little chance of misinterpretation. Checking the Remove leading blank option removes the leading space after the fraction is stacked, resulting in a number that appears as 1¼ or 1$\frac{1}{4}$.

By default, the AutoStack dialog box is displayed each time stackable text is detected by the Multiline Text Editor. If you are satisfied with the current settings you can place a check next to the *Don't show this dialog again; always use these settings* option. The dialog box can be turned back on at a later time if needed.

Stacked text cannot be edited like normal text. You can unstack it as described previously, edit it, and then restack it—but this is unnecessary for most editing needs. An easier way is to right-click on the text object and pick Properties from the shortcut menu. This displays the Stack Properties dialog box, where you can change the text content or appearance (see Figure 9.27B). The settings and options in this dialog box are as follows:

- **Text**
  - **Upper:** Edits the text content at the top of the stack.
  - **Lower:** Edits the text content at the bottom of the stack.
- **Appearance**
  - **Style:** Sets stacking style. The options are Fraction (Horizontal), Fraction (Diagonal), and Tolerance.
  - **Position:** Controls vertical justification within the text line for all stacked text items in the current text object. Options are Top, Center, and Bottom alignment. This value is saved in the TSTACKALIGN system variable.
  - **Text size:** Sizes the stacked text to a value between 50% to 100% percent of its original height. It is important to understand that this percentage is not relative to the text size of the sentence or paragraph containing the stacked text. Rather, this is relative to the original size of the text before it was stacked. This value is saved in the TSTACKSIZE system variable.
- **Defaults ▾**
  - **Restore From Defaults:** Sets the Position and Text size values to match the current TSTACKALIGN and TSTACKSIZE system variable settings.
  - **Save Current Settings:** Sets the TSTACKALIGN and TSTACKSIZE system variables to match the current Position and Text size values.
- **AutoStack:** Displays the AutoStack Properties dialog box. This is how to access the AutoStack Properties dialog box if the *Don't show this dialog again*; option has been picked.
- **Text Color:** The text color defaults to the current color setting in the drawing, but you can set the color for new text or change the color of selected text.
- **Symbol:** This drop-down menu, shown in Figure 9.28, provides commonly used symbols and a selection for Non-breaking Space, which keeps two words together when at the end of a line of text. Place a symbol at the cursor location by picking the desired item from the list. Pick Other... to open the Character Map shown in Figure 9.29. This provides you with many additional symbols to use in your text. Insert a symbol from the Character Map dialog box using the following features:
  - **Font:** This provides a list of available font character maps.
  - **Select:** When a character or symbol in the Character Map window is picked, it is framed within its compartment. If you press and hold the pick button, the characters you point at are enlarged for easier viewing.The following steps can be used to insert the symbol or characters into your document:

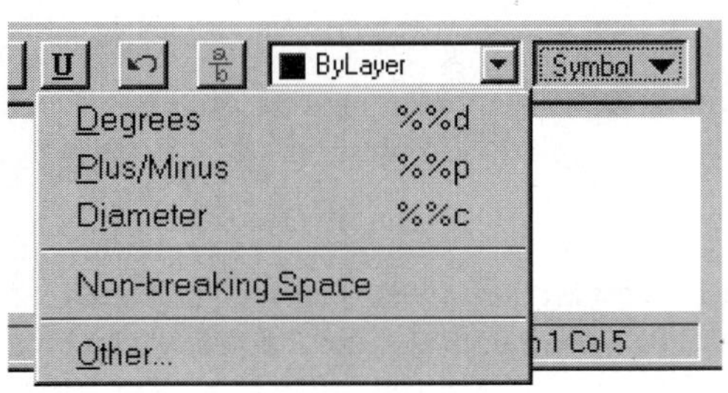

FIGURE 9.28 The Insert Symbol drop-down menu found in the Character tab of the Multiline Text Editor.

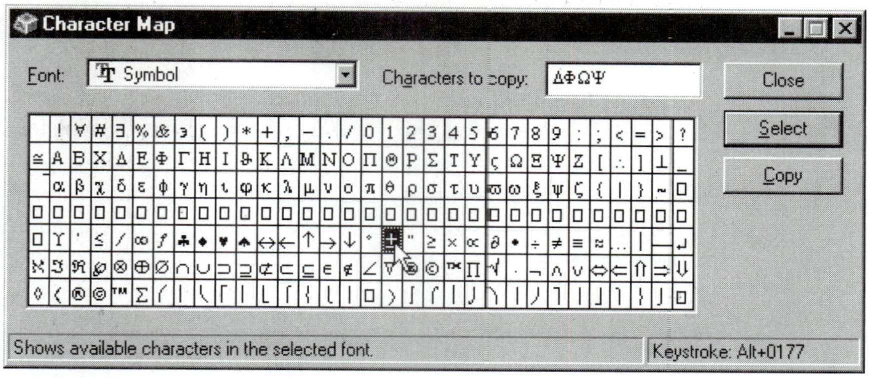

FIGURE 9.29 The Character Map dialog box is opened when you pick Other ... from the Symbol drop-down menu.

1. Pick the Select button. This displays the selected character or symbol in the Characters to Copy: box. You can continue in this manner to display as many items in the Characters to Copy: box as you wish. Optionally, you can double-click a character to place it in the Characters to Copy: box. Items can be removed from the Characters to Copy: box by picking and highlighting the desired characters and then pressing the Del key on your keyboard.
2. When you have the desired items in the Characters to Copy: box, pick the Copy button to have them copied to the Clipboard.
3. Pick the Close button to close the Character Map dialog box.
4. Now you are back in the Multiline Text Editor. Move the text cursor to where you want the symbol placed.
5. Move the screen cursor inside the text window and press the right mouse button to open the shortcut menu shown in Figure 9.25.
6. Pick the Paste option to have the symbol inserted in the document. The term *document* refers to the text you are entering in the Multiline Text Editor. A document, in general, is any text or drawing that you are working with on the screen or what you print.

Field Notes

- Using the Character Map dialog box requires a few steps, but it becomes easy after a little practice. The Unicode Character Map dialog box provides you with many optional symbols and a visual place to select the symbols. You can also enter the same symbols in your document by using the Unicode value that matches the desired symbol. Notice the lower right corner of the Character Map dialog box in Figure 9.29. When a symbol is picked, this displays the Unicode number. In many cases, this number can be used to enter the same symbol at the text cursor location by typing \u+number. For example, if the number is 00b1, you type \u+00b1. The actual symbol appears in your document when you pick OK to complete the multiline text. This method might work if you use a few symbols commonly and remember the Unicode values.
- If you need to insert the same symbol many times, you can speed up the process by using the Character Map dialog box to insert the first symbol, followed by copying and pasting the symbol in the document as needed.

Import Text...: Pick this button to import text into the Multiline Text Editor from an existing text file. This button accesses the Open dialog box, where you can find an existing text file. Select the desired file to have it imported into the current document. If you pick a text file that is too large, AutoCAD LT gives you this message: This file is too large to import as an MTEXT entity. Maximum size is 16k. To import text that is in a file greater than 16k, go directly to the program where the document is located and copy the desired material to the Clipboard. Then, return to the Multiline Text Editor in AutoCAD LT and paste the material into your document. Using this method, the maximum file size is just under 32k.

Line and Column location: Notice in the lower right corner of Figure 9.24B, there is a box that says Ln11Col11. This constantly updates the location of the text cursor location as it moves. Ln11 refers to the vertical-text cursor location, which is the eleventh line down from the beginning of the document.

Col11 refers to the horizontal-text cursor location, which is eleven characters to the right of the left margin.

AutoCAPS: Double-click on this feature to toggle it on or off. Gray text means that is it currently disabled. When enabled, this feature converts all newly typed text and imported text to all uppercase letters. In addition, this feature overrides the Caps Lock key—AutoCAPS cannot be turned off from the keyboard. Right-clicking on AutoCAPS displays a shortcut menu with two items. Picking AutoCAPS from this menu also toggles this feature on and off. The second selection is Toggle Caps. This selection toggles the Caps Lock key on the keyboard, but it works only when AutoCAPS is disabled.

Exercise 9.6 **Estimated time required: 10 min.**

1. Open EX9.5.
2. Use the Multiline Text Editor to type the paragraph shown in Figure 9.26.
3. Save as EX9.6, and close the drawing.

Adjusting Multiline Text Properties

The Properties tab of the Multiline Text Editor allows you to change features such as the text style, justification, boundary width, and text rotation angle. See Figure 9.30. The Properties tab options are explained in the following:

Style: This is a drop-down list that contains the created text styles.

Justification: The tooltip calls this Object Alignment, which is the justification of the current paragraph. There are several options shown in Figure 9.31. The options are identified in the Justification list, with an icon representing the appearance of the justification format, the name, and the abbreviation. The following explains each of the options:

- **Top Left** This is the default justification, which places the insertion point at the left of the top line and justifies the paragraph along the left edge.
- **Top Center** The insertion point is centered on the first line and the paragraph is justified along the center of each line of text.
- **Top Right** This option places the insertion point at the right of the top line and justifies the paragraph along the right edge.
- **Middle Left** The insertion point is located at the middle left edge of the text boundary and the text is justified along the left edge.
- **Middle Center** The insertion point is centered at the middle of the paragraph and the paragraph is justified along the center of each line of text.
- **Middle Right** The insertion point is located at the middle of the right edge of the text boundary and the text is justified along the right edge.

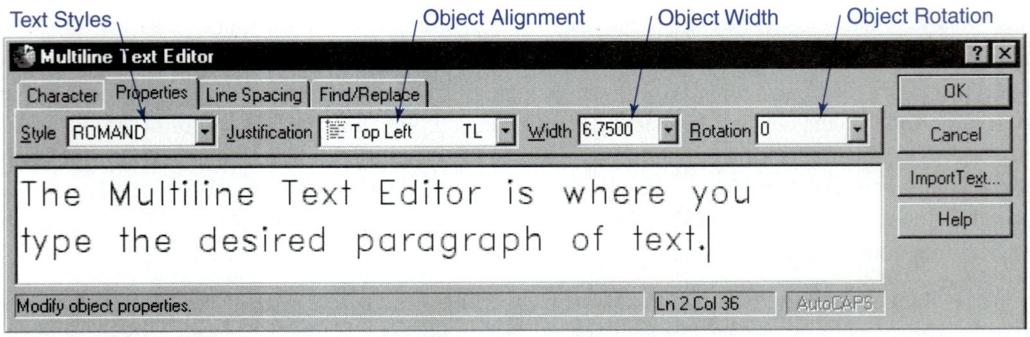

FIGURE 9.30 The Properties tab of the Multiline Text Editor.

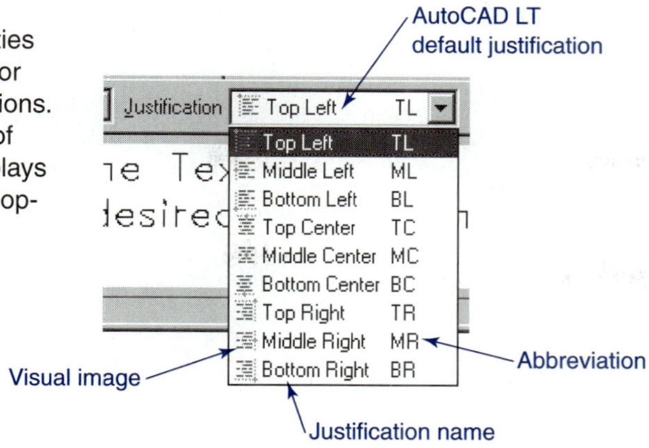

FIGURE 9.31 The Object Alignment list in the Properties tab of the Multiline Text Editor displays the justification options. Notice the icon at the right of each justification name displays an example of the resulting option.

- **Bottom Left** Places the insertion point at the left of the bottom line and justifies the paragraph along the left edge.
- **Bottom Center** The insertion point is centered on the bottom line and the paragraph is justified along the center of each line of text.
- **Bottom Right** This option places the insertion point at the right of the bottom line and justifies the paragraph along the right edge.

The MTEXT justification options can also be entered at the keyboard by using the Justify option:

Command: **T, MT,** or **MTEXT**↵
Current text style: "ROMANS" Text height: 0.2000
Specify first corner: *<pick first text boundary corner>*
Specify opposite corner or [Height/Justify/Line spacing/Rotation/Style/Width]: **J**↵
Enter justification [TL/TC/TR/ML/MC/MR/BL/BC/BR] <TL>:

These options are shown as the abbreviation of the MTEXT justification options that were previously discussed with the Multiline Text Editor. To set a justification option at the keyboard, type the letters representing the desired option and press Enter. The following list matches the abbreviation with the related option:

TL = Top Left ML = Middle Left BL = Bottom Left
TC = Top Center MC = Middle Center BC = Bottom Center
TR = Top Right MR = Middle Right BR = Bottom Right

Width: Use this text box to conveniently change the text boundary width. Double-click in the text box to highlight the current value and then type a new value. The previously used boundary widths are available in the list for your reference and use. There is also a no-wrap option, which allows you to type text beyond the text boundary.

Rotation: This text box allows you to enter any desired text rotation angle. The entire multiline text object is rotated at the specified angle. Zero rotation is the default, and the list gives you optional rotation angles in 15° increments. You can enter a numeric angle of your choice by selecting the text and entering a new value.

Exercise 9.7 **Estimated time required: 10 min.**

1. Open EX9.6.
2. Use the Multiline Text Editor to do each of the following: (the exact selections are up to you)

   Change the font of selected text.

   Change the text height of selected text.

   Type new text and make a selection bold and another selection italic.

   Underline a selection of text.

   Type a fraction and stack it.

   Change the color of selected text.

   Enter each of the following symbols directly from the Symbol list: degrees, plus/minus, and diameter.

   Insert the following symbols from the Character Map dialog box: ©, π, and ≥.
3. Save as EX9.7, and close the drawing.

Controlling Line Spacing

The Line Spacing tab in the Multiline Text Editor provides control options for line spacing in the text object. There are two aspects to line spacing control in AutoCAD LT, the type of spacing and the actual spacing setting. These settings are controlled using the two drop-down lists on this tab. Figure 9.32 shows the Line Spacing tab of the Multiline Text Editor.

The tooltip displayed next to the list on the left is Type. The line spacing type has two options, as follows:

- **At Least** This option allows for adjustment of line spacing on a per-line basis. The line value specified in the Spacing list sets the minimum spacing, and the spacing for each line is adjusted based on the size of the largest text character on that line. This flexible setting helps to prevent text from overlapping when multiple font sizes are used in the same text object.
- **Exactly** This option forces uniform line spacing throughout the multiline text object, using the exact value indicated in the Spacing list. No adjustment is made regardless of any text size variations.

The Spacing list sets the actual line spacing value. The line spacing value represents the distance between the bottom of one line of text and the top of the text on the next line below. The three options on the Spacing list are *Single (1.0x), 1.5 Lines (1.5x),* and *Double (2.0x)*. These values represent multiples of single-line spacing, but you are not limited to these options. The Spacing can be set to any value between 0.25x and 4x. Absolute values, such as 0.5, can also be specified as long as the value falls between the equivalent 0.25x and 4x multiples of single-line spacing based on the current text size.

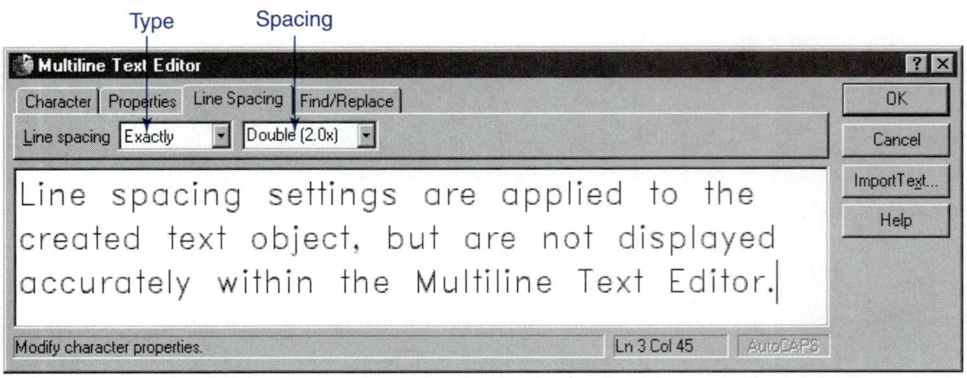

FIGURE 9.32 The Line Spacing tab of the Multiline Text Editor.

Finding and Replacing Multiline Text Items

The Multiline Text Editor has a Find/Replace tab, which allows you to conveniently find specific text within the document and replace it with other text. The Find/Replace tab is shown in Figure 9.33, and its features are explained in the following:

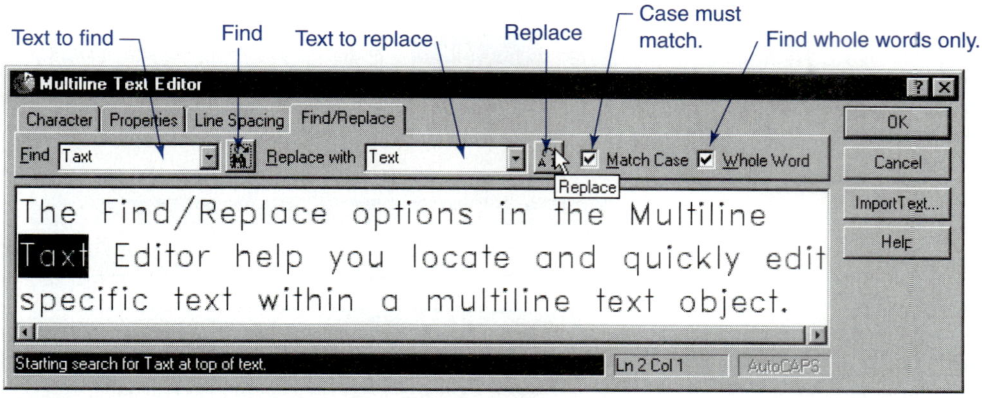

FIGURE 9.33 The Find/Replace tab of the Multiline Text Editor.

Find: This is a text box where you type the text that you want to find. For example, type *desired* in this text box if you want to find this word in the document. Pick the Find button to have the entered text located and highlighted, as shown in Figure 9.34A.

Replace with: This is a text box where you type the text you want to replace with the text you entered in the Find box. Figure 9.34B shows the word *preferred* typed in the Replace with box. Pick the Replace button to have the current word replaced with the new word, as shown in Figure 9.34C. Words that were used previously in the Find and Replace with boxes are stored in the list of each box for your convenience in selecting them later, if you wish.

Match Case: This check box is off by default, which forces AutoCAD LT to find a match for the specified word regardless of the text case. The term *character case* refers to the use of uppercase and lowercase text. For example, if Match Case is off and you want to find the word drill, AutoCAD LT will find it if it is entered as drill, Drill, or DRILL. If Match Case is on, the word is found only if it is entered exactly as you have it typed in the Find box.

Whole Word: This check box is off by default, which locates the word in the Find box even if it is part of another word. That is, if you type *bore* in the Find box, AutoCAD LT finds it even if it is part of the word *counterbore*, for instance. If this check box is on, AutoCAD LT finds only the single word that matches the word in the Find box.

Exercise 9.8 — Estimated time required: 5 min.

1. Open EX9.6.
2. Use the Multiline Text Editor to find the desired word and replace it with the preferred text as shown in Figure 9.34.
3. Type the new word DRILL. Type drill in the Find box. With the Match Case option on, pick the Find button. Turn Match Case off and pick the Find button again. Notice the difference.
4. Type the new word counterbore. Type bore in the Find box. With Whole Word on, pick the Find button. Turn Whole Word off and pick the find button again. Notice the difference.
5. Save as EX9.8, and close the drawing.

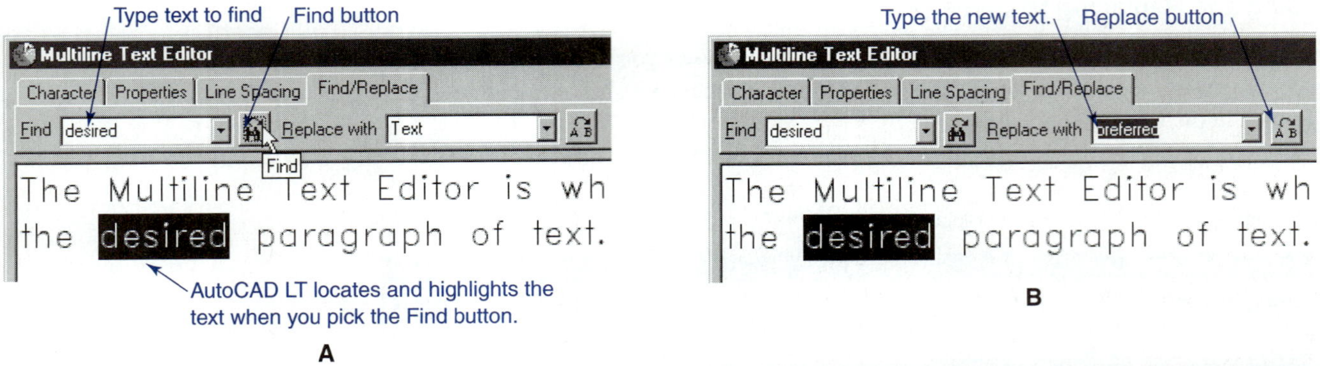

FIGURE 9.34 (A) Type the text that you want to find in the Find box and then pick the Find button. (B) Type the text that you want to replace in the Replace with box and then pick the Replace button. (C) The word that you typed in the Find box is replaced with the word that you typed in the Replace with box.

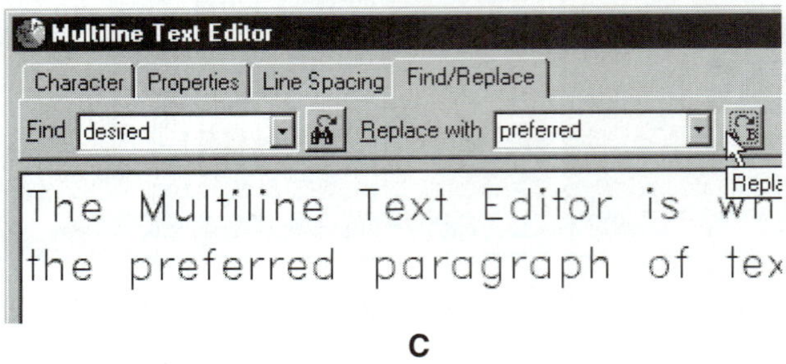

Placing Paragraph Text at the Prompt Line

The Multiline Text Editor provides a screen for entering paragraph text within the text boundary, but multiline text can also be typed at the prompt line. Use the -MT or -MTEXT command to enter paragraph text at the prompt. This is a hyphen (-) typed before MT or MTEXT. All prompts and options are the same as those for using MTEXT and accessing the Multiline Text Editor, except they are all used at the prompt line like this:

Command: **-MT** or **-MTEXT↵**
Current text style: "ROMANS" Text height: 0.2000
Specify first corner: *<pick the first text boundary corner>*
Specify opposite corner or [Height/Justify/Line spacing/Rotation/Style/Width]: *<pick the opposite corner>*
MText: **The desired paragraph text is typed at the prompt line rather than in the Multiline Text Editor. You can keep typing without concern for the end of the text line. AutoCAD LT automatically inserts the text within the text boundary when you are finished and have exited the command.↵**
MText: ↵
Command:

When using the -MTEXT command, type the desired paragraph text at the prompt line rather than in the Multiline Text Editor. Keep typing without concern for the end of the text line, or press the Enter key to go to the next line. AutoCAD LT automatically inserts the text within the text boundary when you are finished and have exited the command.

Exercise 9.9 **Estimated time required: 10 min.**

1. Open EX9.5.
2. Use the MECH text style with all of the design options set to default values.
3. Use the -MTEXT command to type the paragraph shown with this command in the previous discussion.
4. Save as EX9.9, and close the drawing.

LEARNING CHECKPOINT

- ☐ Define the term *paragraph text.*
- ☐ What is the difference between line and paragraph text?
- ☐ Describe the text boundary and its purpose.
- ☐ Explain three ways to establish a text boundary.
- ☐ Discuss how text is typed and edited within the Multiline Text Editor.
- ☐ What is the command for and how do you type paragraph text at the prompt line?

Additional Line and Paragraph Text Applications

You can create special symbols, paste text from the Clipboard, and drag a text file into AutoCAD LT. ***Control codes*** allow you to insert special drafting symbols such as diameter (∅), degree (°), and plus-or-minus (±). Codes are also used to format paragraph text with features such as underline or text height changes within the paragraph. Additional applications include pasting text from the Clipboard and dragging a text file into AutoCAD LT.

Using Special Characters and Symbols

Drafting symbols such as diameter (∅), degree (°), plus-or-minus (±), and underline require special codes when used with the DTEXT or MTEXT commands. The code used to draw symbols with the DTEXT command is a pair of percent signs (%%) and a key letter or symbol typed where the symbol is needed. Table 9.2 lists the codes as applied to drawing different features. Notice that the overline and underline examples require that you enter the code *before* and *after* where you want the overline or underline to happen. You can overline and underline at the same time by typing both codes before and after the desired text, like this: %%o%%uSAMPLE%%o%%u = $\overline{\underline{\text{SAMPLE}}}$.

TABLE 9.2 Control codes for symbols used with the DTEXT command

Code	Result	Type This:	Result
%%c	∅	%%c1.75	∅1.75
%%d	°	45%%d	45°
%%p	±	%%p.625	±.625
%%o	Overline	%%oSAMPLE%%o	$\overline{\text{SAMPLE}}$
%%u	Underline	%%uSAMPLE%%u	$\underline{\text{SAMPLE}}$
%%%	%	50%%%	50%

Exercise 9.10

Estimated time required: 5 min.

1. Open EX9.5.
2. Use the text style of your choice.
3. Use the DTEXT command to type the following:

   ∅1.75

   45°

   ±.625

   $\overline{\text{SAMPLE}}$

   $\underline{\text{SAMPLE}}$

   $\overline{\underline{\text{SAMPLE}}}$

4. Save as EX9.10, and close the drawing.

Special control codes can also be used when placing drafting symbols with the MTEXT command. These codes were introduced with the Multiline Text Editor earlier in the chapter. The %%c = ∅, %%d = °, and %%p = ± codes can be used with the MTEXT command, but %%o and %%u cannot be used. In addition to these codes, special Unicode characters can be used to draw the symbols listed in Table 9.3. The Unicode characters can also be used to draw the same symbols with DTEXT and -MTEXT commands.

TABLE 9.3 Control codes for symbols used with the MTEXT, TEXT, DTEXT, and -MTEXT commands

Unicode	Result	Type This:	Result
\U+2205	∅	\U+22051.75	∅1.75
\U+00B0	°	45\U+00B0	45°
\U+00B1	±	\U+00B1.625	±.625

The Unicodes and %% codes can be used to draw symbols as previously shown, but other codes are required to do special formatting of paragraph text when using the -MTEXT command. Table 9.4 shows the format codes and the results you can expect. When using the format codes, use opening braces ({) before and closing braces (}) after the intended feature to apply a format to the text items that are enclosed within other text items.

TABLE 9.4 Formatting codes

Format Code	Result	Type This:	Result
\O	Overline on		
\o	Overline off	\OSAMPLE\o	$\overline{\text{SAMPLE}}$
\L	Underline on		
\l	Underline off	\LSAMPLE\l	$\underline{\text{SAMPLE}}$
\~	Nonbreaking space at line end	Do\~not\~break\~these\~words	Do not break these words
\\	Backslash	INCH\\METRIC	INCH\METRIC
\{	Open brace		
\}	Close brace	\{SAMPLE\}	{SAMPLE}
\Hx;	Change height	SAMPLE \H.25;TEXT	SAMPLE TEXT
\Cx;	Change color	SAMPLE \C1;COLOR	SAMPLE COLOR
\Ffont;	Change font	SAMPLE \Fromans;TEXT	SAMPLE TEXT
\Sx^x;	Stacks text	SAMPLE \SOVER^UNDER;	SAMPLE $\genfrac{}{}{0pt}{}{\text{OVER}}{\text{UNDER}}$
\Sx/x;	Stacks text with dividing line	SAMPLE\SOVER\UNDER;	SAMPLE $\frac{\text{OVER;}}{\text{UNDER}}$
\Tx;	Adjusts width	\T2;SAMPLE	SAMPLE
\Ax;	Aligns fractions 0 = bottom (\A0;) 1 = center (\A1;) 2 = top (\A2;)		
\S	Stacks	\A1;SAMPLE \S5/8	SAMPLE $\frac{1}{2}$
\P	End paragraph	paragraph\Pparagraph	paragraph paragraph

Note: The x given in the format code refers to the variable value, such as text height factor, color, width, or font.

Exercise 9.11 **Estimated time required: 5 min.**

1. Open EX9.10.
2. Use the -MTEXT command and Unicodes or Format codes to type the following:

Ø1.75	SAMPLE TEXT
45°	SAMPLE TEXT
±.625	SAMPLE $\frac{5}{8}$
$\overline{\text{SAMPLE}}$	
$\underline{\text{SAMPLE}}$	

3. Save as EX9.11, and close the drawing.

Pasting Text from the Clipboard

Formatted text that is copied from a word processing program such as Microsoft Word or WordPerfect can be copied and pasted into an AutoCAD LT drawing. If the text is selected and pasted directly into the Multiline Text Editor, all the formatting is preserved in the new Mtext object. Pasting text from one of these applications into the drawing using the PASTECLIP command results in an OLE object that cannot be edited in AutoCAD LT. OLE applications are discussed in Chapter 15. Another option is to paste the text at the prompt line of a DTEXT or -MTEXT command. When the Enter text: prompt of DTEXT or the Mtext: prompt of the –MTEXT command is displayed, move your cursor into the floating command window and press the pick button to make the command window current. Next, right-click inside the command window and pick the Paste option. All formatting is lost, but the copied text now becomes usable single-line or multiline text.

If your word processor and your AutoCAD LT drawing window are both visible at the same time, you can simply select the desired text and conveniently drag and drop it into the Multiline Text Editor in an AutoCAD LT drawing. Similar to using the PASTECLIP command, dropping the text into the drawing area produces an OLE object that cannot be directly edited with AutoCAD LT.

The drag-and-drop method also works with standard text files. To work properly, the text file must contain only plain text and must have a file extension of .txt. Additionally, the text file must be under 32 kB in size. Using the Windows Explorer, just drag and drop the file into the drawing area. The text file is placed in the drawing and converted into a multiline text object.

Field Notes

- If you drag and drop a text file that is larger than 32 kB into AutoCAD LT, a message is displayed stating that the file was too large and was truncated. This indicates that AutoCAD LT read as much of the file as it could and ignored the rest. The result is that the incoming text is incomplete.
- If you accidentally place an OLE object in your drawing, point to the object and right-click to display the shortcut menu. Pick the Clear option to remove the OLE object.

LEARNING CHECKPOINT

- ☐ What are control codes?
- ☐ Give the %% control codes for these applications: diameter, degrees, plus-or-minus, overline, and underline.
- ☐ Give the Unicode for these applications: diameter, degrees, and plus-or-minus.
- ☐ How does the Unicode presentation differ between MTEXT, -MTEXT, and DTEXT command use?
- ☐ Describe how to place text from the Clipboard into the drawing.
- ☐ Briefly describe how drag and drop works for inserting a text file into an AutoCAD LT drawing.

Editing Existing Text

AutoCAD LT provides you with many options for editing text. Editing commands such as MOVE, COPY, SCALE, and ROTATE can be used on text objects. You can enter the command first and then select the text or select the text and use the grips for the desired editing operation. You can also mirror text. When mirroring text, you can decide to have the text mirrored in reverse image or readable. Other text editing commands allow you to change the content, font, and other features. You can also check your spelling.

Using the DDEDIT Command

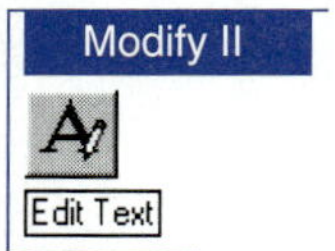

Modify
Object ▸
Text...

DDEDIT
ED

You can change the content of line text and you can change the content and justification of paragraph text with the DDEDIT command. This command is accessed by picking the Edit Text button in the Modify II toolbar, by picking Text ... in the Object cascade of the Modify pull-down menu, or by typing either **ED** or **DDEDIT** at the Command: prompt. When using this command, AutoCAD LT asks you to select an annotation. An ***annotation*** is anything that has to do with text, such as notes, dimensions, and text symbols. The command works like this:

Command: **ED** or **DDEDIT**↵
Select an annotation object or [Undo]:

The Undo option allows you to undo the previous edit while still inside of the DDEDIT command.

Editing Line Text with DDEDIT

You can select one line of line text at a time for editing with the DDEDIT command. This allows you to change the content as needed. When you select the line of text, you get the Edit Text dialog box shown in Figure 9.35. When the Edit Text dialog box is first displayed, the text inside is highlighted. You can work with this text in one of the following ways:

FIGURE 9.35 Using the DDEDIT command to edit a single line of text. (A) The existing text is displayed in the Edit Text dialog box. (B) The text is edited as needed.

- Begin typing. Everything that was highlighted is gone, allowing you to type a new line of text.
- Press the space bar, Delete key, or the Backspace key to have the text removed and then type the new text line.
- Move the cursor to a desired place within the text line and pick. This removes the highlighting but keeps the existing text. There is now a text cursor at the place you picked.
- Use the text cursor to backspace or go forward as needed.
- Type any desired text at the location of the text cursor. Notice the revised text that has been typed in Figure 9.35B.
- If the line of text is too long to see both ends in the Edit Text dialog box, press the Ctrl key and the right arrow key to move the cursor to the right or the left arrow key to move the cursor to the left. The line is fully exposed when you move the cursor all the way to the desired end. The arrow key can be used alone to move one character at a time or with the Ctrl key to move to the start of the next word in the direction the arrow key points. The Home key can be used to go directly to the start of the text and the End key to go to the end of the text line. Also, the Ctrl+C, Ctrl+X, and Ctrl+V combinations can be used in the Edit Text dialog box as previously discussed.
- You can pick and hold while dragging the cursor to highlight specific text. Then just press the space bar, Delete key, or the Backspace key to have the text removed; or begin typing new text to automatically remove the highlighted text while entering new text.
- When you are editing long text objects, it can be helpful to resize the Edit Text dialog box to accommodate more text. The Edit Text dialog box can be resized horizontally, but not vertically.

After you are done editing the line of text, pick the OK button or press Enter to return to the screen. The text is changed and the select annotation prompt remains for further editing of the same line or other lines of text. The complete command sequence works like this:

Command: **ED** or **DDEDIT**↵
Select an annotation object or [Undo]: *<pick the line of text to open the Edit Text dialog box. Pick the OK button when done.>*
Select an annotation object or [Undo]: ↵
Command:

Editing Paragraph Text with DDEDIT

The DDEDIT command can be used to change both content and justification of paragraph text. When you enter the DDEDIT command and select paragraph text, the familiar Multiline Text Editor appears. This works just like a word processor, as previously discussed. In addition to changing the text content you can easily change the other options, as previously explained. Refer back to Figure 9.24B. The command sequence works like this:

Command: **ED** or **DDEDIT**↵
Select an annotation object or [Undo]: *<pick the paragraph of text to open the Multiline Text Editor. Pick the OK button when done.>*
Select an annotation object or [Undo]: ↵
Command:

Exercise 9.12 **Estimated time required: 5 min.**

1. Open EX9.5.
2. Use the MECH text style.
3. Use the DTEXT command to type the following:

   Line text edited with the DDEDIT command.

4. Use the DDEDIT command to change the text to read:

   Line text is easily edited by using the DDEDIT command to access the Edit Text dialog box.

5. Use the MTEXT command to type the following inside of a 3-in.-wide text boundary:

   The DDEDIT command can be used to change the content of paragraph text.

6. Use the DDEDIT command to change the text to read:

   The DDEDIT command can be used to edit the content of paragraph text and change the justification.

7. Change the Justification to Top Center before picking OK.
8. Save as EX9.12, and close the drawing.

Using the PROPERTIES Command

The DDEDIT command provides a means of editing text content for both single- and multiline text but does not provide sufficient access to the many defining properties of the text object itself. The Multiline Text Editor provides a few options, but the Edit Text dialog box can change only text content, and nothing more. When you need complete access for modifying all aspects of a text object, it is best to use the PROPERTIES command.

Standard

Properties (Ctrl+1)

Modify
Properties...

PROPERTIES
[Ctrl] + [1]
MO

Editing Text with the Properties Window

Figure 9.36A shows the Properties window with a single-line text object selected for editing. The Properties window in Figure 9.36B has a multiline text object selected for editing. The Properties window allows you to modify virtually any characteristic of the selected object. The following list highlights each of the available options:

FIGURE 9.36 (A) The Properties window with a single-line text object selected for editing. (B) The Properties window with a Multiline text object selected for editing.

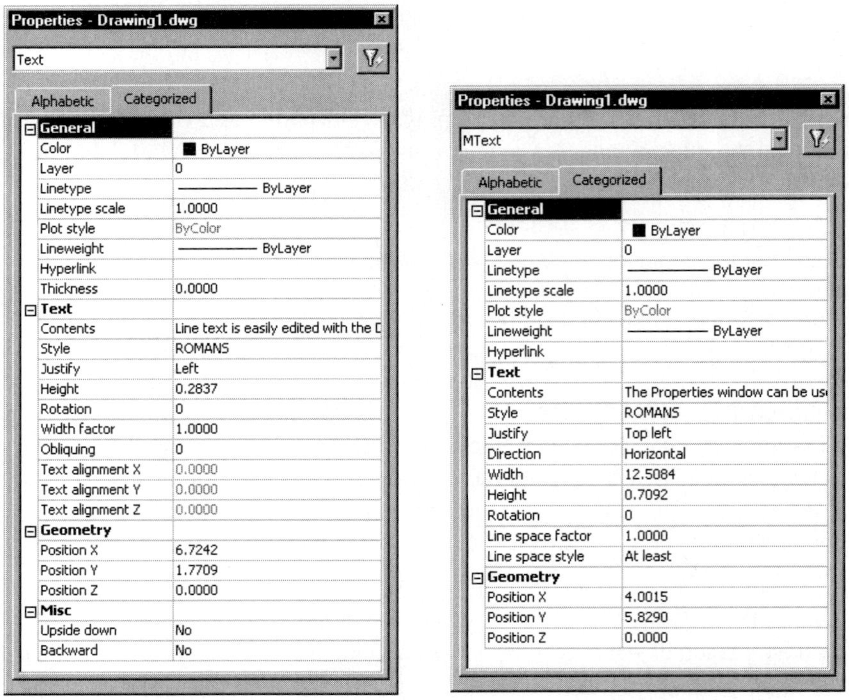

A B

- **General**
  - **Color** — Pick from the color control list or the Select Color dialog box to change the object color.
  - **Layer** — Pick from the layer list to move the object to a different layer.
  - **Linetype** — Linetype does not affect text display.
  - **Linetype Scale** — Linetype scale does not affect text display.
  - **Plot Style** — A ByColor plot style cannot be changed.
  - **Lineweight** — Specify an object lineweight by picking from the list.
  - **Hyperlink** — Display the Insert Hyperlink dialog box
  - **Thickness** — Change the extrusion value for text in 3-D drawings.
- **Text**
  - **Contents** — Directly edit text content for single-line text. The Multiline Text Editor is displayed when editing Mtext content.
  - **Style** — Assign a new text style by picking from the list of defined styles.
  - **Justify** — Select the new justification from the list of available options.
  - **Direction** — Reorient Mtext direction with a quick pick.
  - **Width** — Change the width of an Mtext object by typing a new value.
  - **Height** — Type a new value for the text height.
  - **Rotation** — Type a new rotation angle for the text.
  - **Width factor**
  - **Obliquing** — Adjust the width factor or obliquing angle of the individual text object without modifying the text style definition.
  - **Text alignment X**
  - **Text alignment Y**
  - **Text alignment Z** — } Adjust the alignment data for justified single-line text.
  - **Line space factor** — Pick or type a new line spacing for Mtext.
  - **Line space style** — Select the Mtext line spacing style from a list.
- **Geometry**
  - **Position X**
  - **Position Y**
  - **Position Z** — } Fine tune the text position by entering exact X, Y, and Z point coordinates, or use the select point option for an easy move.
- **Misc**
  - **Upside down**
  - **Backward** — Pick Yes or No to modify the appearance of the text object without modifying the text style definition.

Exercise 9.13 — Estimated time required: 10 min.

1. Open EX9.12.
2. Use the PROPERTIES command to change the line text to read:

   Line text is easy to edit by using the PROPERTIES command.

3. Experiment on the line text by making the following changes. Use the PROPERTIES command to select the line text between each change to observe the effects:
   - Change the insertion point with the Pick Point < button.
   - Change the height to .188.
   - Change the rotation to 45.
   - Change the width to 1.5.
   - Change the obliquing angle to 15.
   - Use a variety of justification options of your own choosing.
   - Change the style.
   - Try the Upside down and Backward options if you wish.
4. Use the PROPERTIES command to change the paragraph text to read:

   The PROPERTIES command is used to open the Properties window. You can then edit the content and change the justification.

5. Back in the Properties window, do experimentation on the line text by making the following changes. Use the PROPERTIES command to select the paragraph text between each change to observe the effects:
   - Change the insertion point.
   - Change the text height to 0.25.
   - Change the style.
6. Save as EX9.13, and close the drawing.

Editing Text Using the Find and Replace Tool

Standard

Find and Replace

Edit
Find

FIND

In very large drawings or in drawings containing many different text objects, the Find and Replace feature can help you quickly locate specific text items and can even automatically edit them for you. The Find and Replace dialog box is where you specify what the search criteria is and what should happen when the text is located. To display the Find and Replace dialog box, pick the Find and Replace button from the Standard toolbar, pick Find... from the Edit pull-down menu, or type **FIND** at the Command: prompt. The Find and Replace dialog box is shown in Figure 9.37.

Use the Find text string: box to specify what text to find. Opening the list displays the last six entries. Select from one of these or pick inside the text box and enter the words or text that you want to find. Use the Search in: list to control the general scope of the search. If objects were grip-selected when the Find and Replace tool was started, then Current select is the default option; otherwise, Entire drawing is the default, and Current selection is disabled. The Select objects button temporarily hides the Find and Replace dialog box, allowing you to create a selection set if desired. Enter a value in the Replace with: box if you want to replace the search item with new text. This list also displays the last six entries for your convenience. You do not have to replace the text items. This tool can also be used to find and review text without changing it. The Options button displays the Find and Replace Options dialog box, which is discussed later. Once you have specified you search criteria and any replacement value you want to apply, pick the Find Next button.

If the search text is found, it is displayed in the Context box along with the adjacent text. The search text is highlighted, as shown in Figure 9.37. To replace only the currently highlighted text, pick the Replace button, or select Replace All to replace all further occurrences found. A message is then displayed in the box near the bottom of the dialog box indicating how many occurrences were replaced.

In addition to the text replacement function, the Find and Replace dialog box provides other useful capabilities. When you need to work with text objects, but only text objects containing a specific text element, you can use the Select All button to refine a selection set by removing all text objects from the current selection that do not contain the specified text. This feature is enabled only when the Search in: specification is set

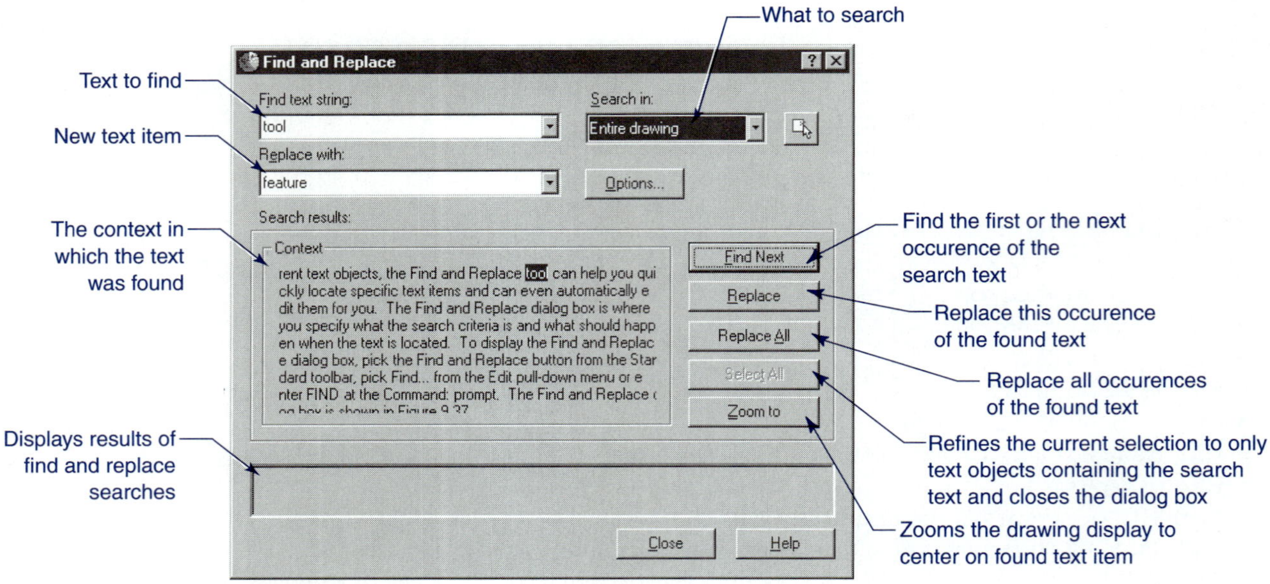

FIGURE 9.37 The Find and Replace dialog box.

to Current selection. You can specify the selection set before starting the FIND command, or you can use the Select objects button in the Find and Replace dialog box. Enter the text element that the text object should contain in the Find text string: box, and pick the Select All button. The Find and Replace dialog box is dismissed, and the selection set is refined to display only the text objects that contain the desired text.

Pick the Zoom to button to zoom the drawing display to the location of the currently found text item. The found text is then displayed near the center of the drawing area, and the Find and Replace dialog box is moved toward the edge of the screen so you can view the text item. This feature is very reliable when the found text is part of a single-line text object but gives mixed results when the text is part of a multiline text object.

The Find and Replace Options dialog box is displayed by picking the Options button in the Find and Replace dialog box. The Find and Replace Options dialog box is shown in Figure 9.38. The available options are as follows:

- **Include:** This area lets you check which types of annotation objects are to be searched for the specified text.
  - **Block Attribute Value** This refers to text values attached to complex symbols. Blocks and block attributes are discussed in Chapter 12.
  - **Dimension Annotation Text** Searches the text component of dimension objects.
  - **Text (Mtext, Dtext, Text)** Includes all types of text objects in the search.
  - **Hyperlink Description** Searches the Description field of hyperlinks attached to objects in the drawing.
  - **Hyperlink** Includes hyperlink URL values in the search.
- **Match case** When selected, this restricts the search to find only items that match the search text exactly, including the case of each character.
- **Find whole words only** When selected, this limits the search to find only occurrences of the search text that are whole words. For example, if this option is not active, a search for "*the*" could produce results such as "lea*the*r" or "*the*me."

FIGURE 9.38 The Find and Replace Options dialog box controls the search results.

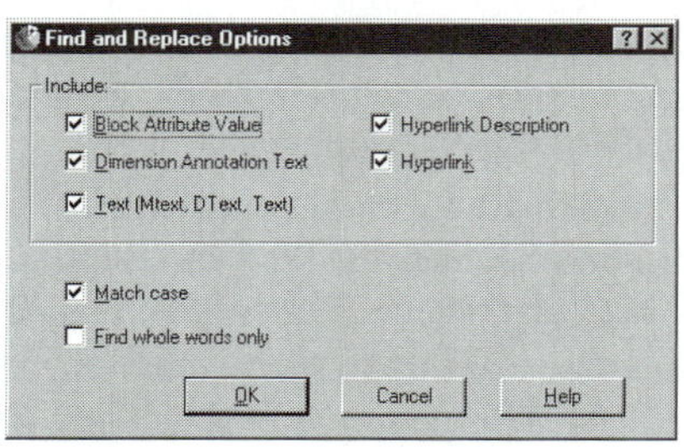

Field Notes

Special characters in text that has been imported from a word processing application and some characters found in the Character Map are represented in the Multiline Text Editor as a Unicode specification. For example, the ellipsis character (…) shows in the Multiline Text Editor as **\U+2026**. In some cases, the Find and Replace tool will not read a text object beyond this Unicode specification—meaning that it may not find every occurrence of the text you are looking for within a text object that uses these codes. Most characters, including the commonly used specifications for the degree, plus-or-minus, and diameter symbols, do not cause this problem. Most of the characters that cause this problem are not commonly used in technical drawings.

An easy solution for the ellipsis character is to use three periods instead of the single character. Unfortunately, not all the special characters offer such an easy solution.

Keep this limitation of the Find and Replace tool in mind if you use special characters in your text objects.

Exercise 9.14

Estimated time required: 5 min.

1. Open EX9.6.
2. Start the FIND command. Enter "text" (without the quotes) in the Find text string: box, and specify Entire drawing in the Search in: list; pick the Find button.
3. Pick the Find Next button until no more occurrences are found.
4. Pick the Options button to display the Find and Replace Options dialog box.
5. Place a checkmark next to the Match Case option.
6. Again search for the word "text." Notice the difference in results.
7. Specify a new search string using "just like," enter the text "similar to" in the Replace with: box (without the quotes), and pick the Find button.
8. When the string is found, pick the Zoom to button and view the results.
9. Pick the Replace button to change the text.
10. Select the previous entry "text" in the Find text string: box and enter "words" in the Replace with: box (without the quotes). Pick the Replace All button.
11. Save as EX9.14, and close the drawing.

Mirroring Objects with Text

Modify

Mirror

Modify
Mirror

MIRROR
MI

The MIRROR command was introduced in Chapter 7. This command is accessed by picking Mirror in the Modify pull-down menu, by picking the Mirror button in the Modify toolbar, or by typing **MI** or **MIRROR** at the Command: prompt. When mirroring text or objects with text, the text can be mirrored in reverse image or upside down depending on how the object is mirrored. You can also set the text to be readable when mirrored. The MIRRTEXT system variable controls how text is displayed when mirrored. The MIRRTEXT options are 1 (on), which reverses or places the mirrored text upside down, and 0 (off), which makes mirrored text readable. The system variable works like this:

Command: **MIRRTEXT**↵
Enter new value for MIRRTEXT <1>: **0**↵
Command:

Figure 9.39 shows the results of changing the MIRRTEXT variable.

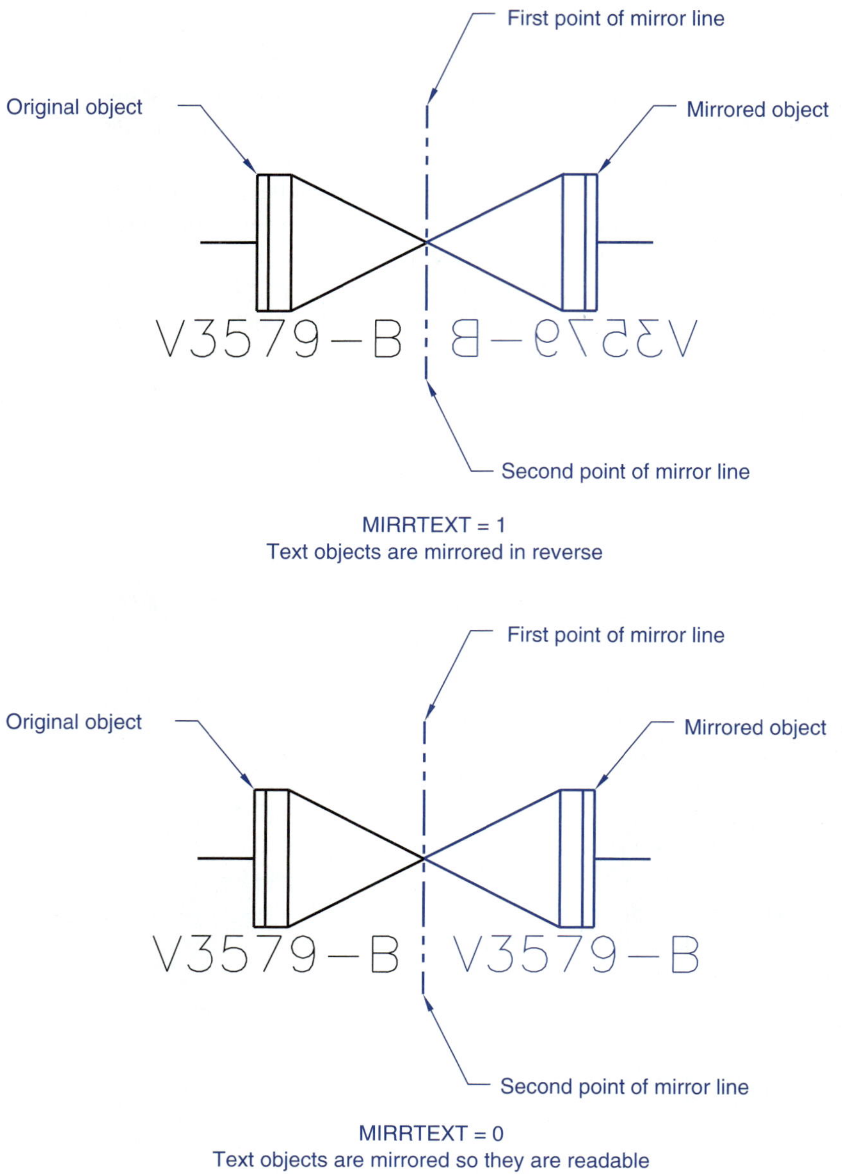

FIGURE 9.39 Using the MIRROR command with the MIRRTEXT system variable set to ON and OFF.

Making Quick Text

Quick text is used when you have a large drawing that contains a lot of text, and you want to increase display speed during a time when you do not plan to be drawing any text. Quick text changes the appearance of text to rectangles that represent only the frame of the text. To make this happen, use the QTEXT command by typing **QT** or **QTEXT** at the Command: prompt. The options are ON and OFF. OFF is the default that keeps the normal text display. Turn QTEXT on like this:

> Command: **QT** or **QTEXT**↵
> Enter mode [ON/OFF] <OFF>: **ON**↵
> Command:

To activate the quick text setting, type the REGEN command and press Enter. The difference between QTEXT ON and OFF is shown in Figure 9.40.

FIGURE 9.40 The difference between QTEXT OFF and ON.

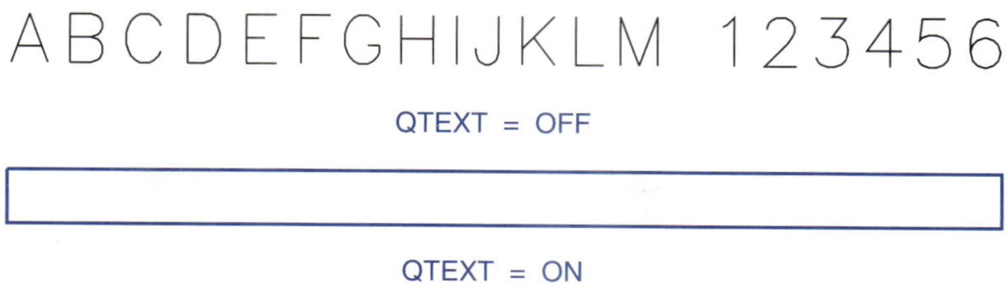

Field Notes

- In a drawing that has many objects that use True Type Fonts, selecting objects can be much slower. Turning QTEXT on helps avoid this problem.

Exercise 9.15 **Estimated time required: 5 min.**

1. Begin a new drawing, set a text style that has ROMANS font, and allow the text height to be adjustable each time you use the commands to draw text.
2. Make a drawing similar to the one shown in Figure 9.39, using MIRRTEXT ON and OFF.
3. Type something of your own choosing with technical content. For example, a general note from a textbook, drawing, or set of specifications.
4. Turn QTEXT on and type a new line of text. Notice that the new text is shown as a boundary only, but the existing text in unaffected.
5. Use the REGEN command to update the drawing. Observe the results.
6. Turn QTEXT off and type a new line of single line text. Use the REGEN command to update the drawing.
7. Save as EX9.15, and close the drawing.

Checking Your Spelling

Tools
Spelling

SPELL
SP

AutoCAD LT provides you with a spelling checker that has dictionaries available in several different languages. Each dictionary contains a standard word list. You can also create a custom dictionary by adding your own words, abbreviations, or commonly used text. The AutoCAD LT spell checker is accessed by picking Spelling in the Tools pull-down menu, or by typing **SP** or **SPELL** at the Command: prompt. You get the Select objects: prompt when you enter the SPELL command. You can select any number of lines or paragraphs of text, or you can type ALL to select all of the text on the drawing. If you select text that has no spelling errors, an AutoCAD LT Message tells you "Spelling check complete." Pick the OK button or press Enter to return to the Command: prompt. You also get this message when there are spelling problems and you have successfully completed checking. You get the Check Spelling dialog box shown in Figure 9.41 when you select text that has spelling problems. The command works like this:

Command: **SP** or **SPELL**↵
Select objects: ⟨*select the text or type ALL and press Enter for all text*⟩
Select objects: ↵

The AutoCAD LT spelling checker has many features. Look at the Check Spelling dialog box in Figure 9.41 as you review these features:

- **Context** First look at the bottom of the Check Spelling dialog box and notice the Context compartment. This displays all or part of the text that you selected. If part of the text is displayed, it is the text that surrounds the current word AutoCAD LT has identified as being misspelled.
- **Current dictionary:** This identifies the current dictionary that is being used. The current dictionary in Figure 9.41 is identified as American English at the top of the Check Spelling dialog box.

- **Current word** — In this compartment, AutoCAD LT displays the current word that is misspelled or is not in the dictionary.
- **Suggestions:** — This is a list of words that AutoCAD LT thinks might be the correct spelling of the current word. The first word is in a text box and is AutoCAD LT's best suggestion. These are the options allowed with the Suggestions:

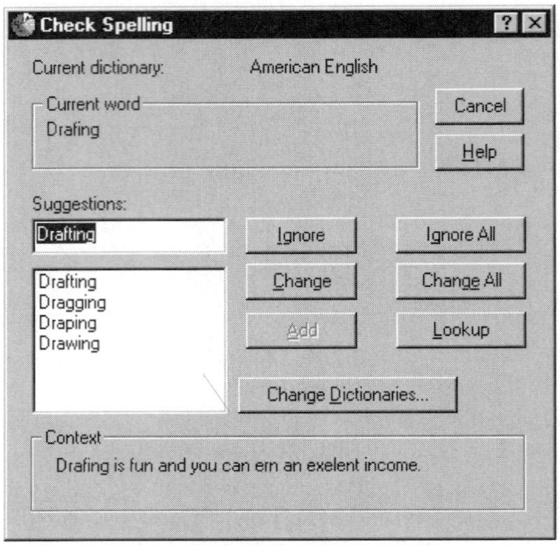

FIGURE 9.41 Using the SPELL command to select text and access the Check Spelling dialog box.

- Keep AutoCAD LT's best suggestion in the text box or pick one of the other words in the list to substitute. If you do not like the best suggestion or any of the other words in the list, you can change the word in the text box to a word that you like better.
- Continue this process until all words have been checked and AutoCAD LT issues the "Spelling check complete" message where you pick the OK button or press Enter to return to the drawing editor.

- **Ignore** — Pick this button if you want to accept this word as is and go on to the next word.
- **Ignore All** — Pick this button if you want AutoCAD LT to ignore this word each time it is found in the selected text.
- **Change** — Pick this button if you want AutoCAD LT to change the Current word to the word that is highlighted in the Suggestions: text box.
- **Change All** — Pick this button if you want AutoCAD LT to change the Current word, each time it is found in the selected text, for the word that is highlighted in the Suggestions: text box.
- **Add** — This button is active if there is a custom dictionary. Pick this button if you want to leave the suggested word unchanged and have it added to the custom dictionary. The maximum word length is 63 characters.
- **Lookup** — Pick this button if you want AutoCAD LT to list additional words that are similar to the word in the Suggestions: box.
- **Change Dictionaries ...** — Pick this button to open the Change Dictionaries dialog box, shown in Figure 9.42.

Changing, Using, and Creating Dictionaries

The Change Dictionaries ... button in the Check Spelling dialog box (Figure 9.41) is used to access the Change Dictionaries dialog box shown in Figure 9.42. The features of the Change Dictionaries dialog box are explained in the following:

- **Main dictionary** — This list box displays the available dictionary options. Pick the down arrow and select a new current dictionary for your spell checking.

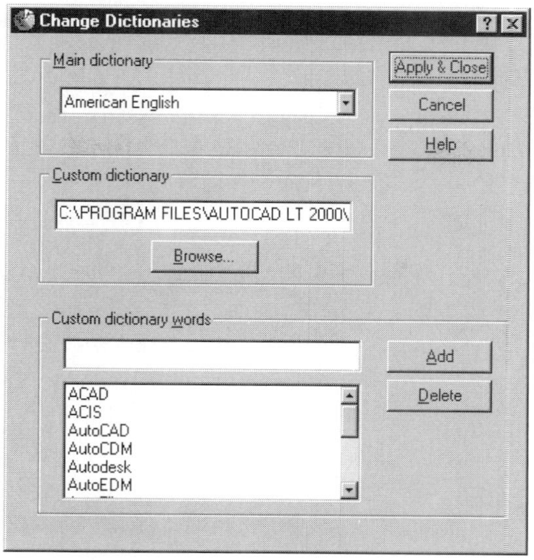

FIGURE 9.42 The Change Dictionaries dialog box.

- **Custom dictionary** Use the text box to type the drive, directory, and file name of a custom dictionary that you want to use for spell checking. Custom dictionaries have the file extension .CUS. If no custom dictionaries have been created, you can create one. Custom dictionaries are designed by you and your company to include words that are not in the main dictionary. The custom dictionary has words, abbreviations, and technical terms that are used in your drafting field or business.

Follow these steps to create a custom dictionary:

- Check the spelling of text entered in your drawing.
- For this example, you are doing a civil (mapping) drawing, and the Spell Checker picks up the word cadastral as a misspelled word. You know it is spelled correctly. Therefore, the word is not in the Main Dictionary. You want to add it to a custom dictionary.
- Pick the Change Dictionaries ... button.
- Enter a name in the Custom dictionary text box and then pick the OK button. The name CIVIL is entered in Figure 9.43 to create a custom dictionary for words used in map drawings and civil engineering projects. AutoCAD LT has a sample custom dictionary called C:\Program Files\AutoCAD LT 2000\support\sample.cus. You can have your custom dictionaries saved in the same directory by substituting your dictionary name, CIVIL, for the word sample, like this: C:\Program Files\AutoCAD LT 2000\support\CIVIL.cus. Pick the Apply & Close button.
- The Check Spelling dialog box returns and the Add button is active to accept words to be added to the custom dictionary. If AutoCAD LT displays a current word that is correctly spelled, then it is not in the main dictionary.
- If this is a word that you want in the custom dictionary, pick the Add button. The Current word, cadastral, is shown in Figure 9.44 and the Add button is being picked.

Follow these steps if a custom dictionary is already created and you want to add words to it:

- Pick the Change Dictionaries ... button. The Change Dictionaries dialog box shown in Figure 9.45 is displayed with the Custom dictionary specified as C:\Program Files\AutoCAD LT 2000\support\civil.cus. If the desired custom dictionary is not active, type a new dictionary drive, directory, and file name or pick the Browse ... button to get the Select Custom Dictionary dialog box.
- The Custom dictionary words compartment has a text box and list of words found in the civil dictionary.
- Continue placing words in the CIVIL custom dictionary by typing each word in the Custom dictionary words box and pick the Add button after each entry. The word quadrangle is being added in Figure 9.45. When the Custom dictionary words list gets long, a scroll bar is available to help you find words. The spell checker is not case sensitive, so you can enter words using upper- or lowercase.
- To remove a word from the custom dictionary, highlight the word in the custom dictionary words list and pick the Delete button.

FIGURE 9.43 Adding a custom dictionary.

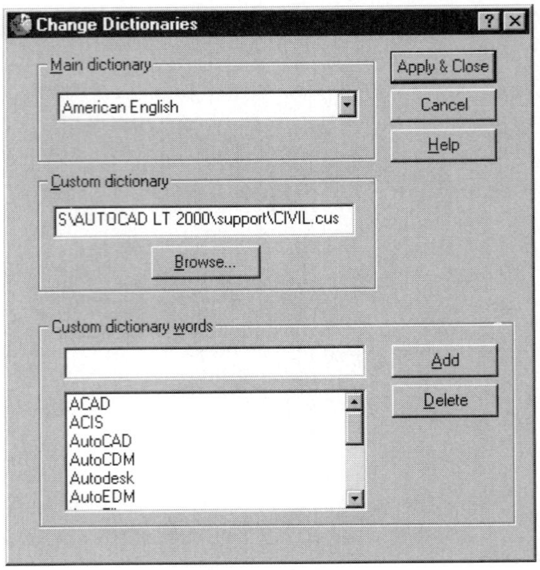

FIGURE 9.44 Adding words to the custom dictionary while in the Check Spelling dialog box.

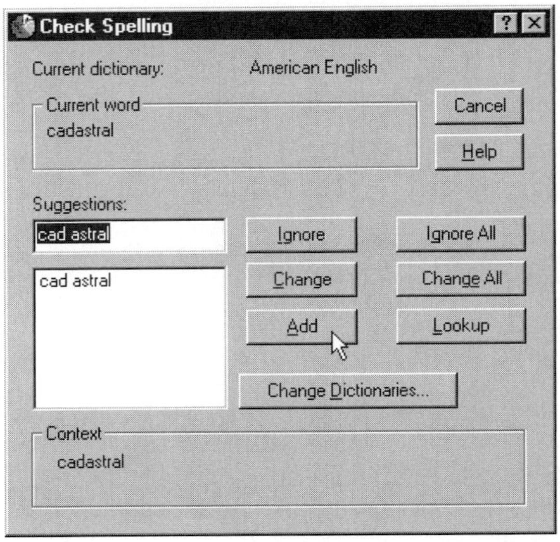

FIGURE 9.45 Adding words to the custom dictionary while in the Change Dictionaries dialog box.

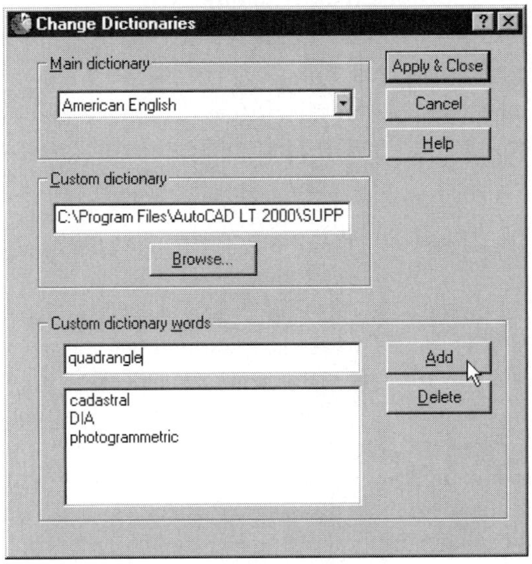

Exercise 9.16 **Estimated time required: 10 min.**

1. Open EX9.15.
2. Check the spelling of the text in this drawing.
3. If no spelling errors exist, use the DDEDIT or DDMODIFY command to add some spelling errors to the text.
4. Check the spelling again and correct the errors.
5. Create a custom dictionary with the name of your favorite drafting discipline or that of the type of drafting you currently perform.
6. Return to the drawing and type several words that you feel are unique to your field of drafting.
7. Use the spell checker on the words, and place any words not found in the main dictionary into your custom dictionary.
8. Save as EX9.16, and close the drawing.

LEARNING CHECKPOINT

- ☐ Explain the difference between using the DDEDIT command on line and on paragraph text.
- ☐ Explain the difference between using the PROPERTIES command on line and on paragraph text.
- ☐ What are the key differences between the DDEDIT and PROPERTIES commands?
- ☐ How do you mirror objects with text and get the text to be readable?
- ☐ What is the result and purpose of using quick text?
- ☐ Describe the primary features of the Check Spelling dialog box.
- ☐ Briefly explain how to create a custom dictionary.

Working with Text and Symbols

- Using the Multiline Text Editor

MULTIPLE CHOICE

Circle the choice or enter your response on an answer sheet by selecting the option that most closely completes or answers the given statements.

1. A complete set of characters made up of letters, numbers, marks, and symbols all of unique proportion and design:

a. characters **c.** style
b. font **d.** text

2. This command places text on the screen while you type:

a. DTEXT **c.** MTEXT
b. TEXT **d.** STYLE

3. Determines how lines of text are aligned:

a. alignment **c.** position
b. rotation **d.** justify

4. This option allows you to place text between two points with control over height:

a. Align **c.** Fit
b. Left **d.** Right

5. This command opens the Text Style dialog box:

a. STY **c.** DDEDIT
b. STYLE **d.** DDMODIFY

6. Multiline text is entered in the:
- **a.** Multiline Text Editor
- **b.** Mtext dialog box
- **c.** Edit MText dialog box
- **d.** Edit Text dialog box

7. Use this control code to draw a diameter symbol with your text:
- **a.** %%c
- **b.** %%d
- **c.** %%p
- **d.** %%u

8. Change the content of line text and the content and justification of paragraph text with:
- **a.** DDEDIT
- **b.** DDMODIFY
- **c.** CHANGE
- **d.** EDIT

9. Type this to edit an MText object:
- **a.** ED
- **b.** DDMODIFY
- **c.** TE
- **d.** all the above

10. Use this command to check your spelling:
- **a.** SPELLCHK
- **b.** SPELLING
- **c.** SP
- **d.** SPELL

MATCHING

Match each term to the correct description by writing the appropriate number in each box at the left.

- ☐ Annotation
- ☐ DDEDIT
- ☐ PROPERTIES
- ☐ DDSTYLE
- ☐ DTEXT
- ☐ Font
- ☐ Justify
- ☐ MTEXT
- ☐ -MTEXT
- ☐ %%c
- ☐ %%d
- ☐ Rotation
- ☐ SPELL
- ☐ Style
- ☐ Width

1. Complete set of characters, made up of letters, numbers, marks, and symbols of unique proportion and design.
2. Used to place paragraph text at the prompt line.
3. Used to change the content, justification, and other features of line and paragraph text.
4. Used to check the spelling.
5. Any text.
6. Determines how lines of text are aligned.
7. Stretches or compresses text characters.
8. Used to change the content of line text and the content and justification of paragraph text.
9. Control code for degree symbol.
10. Used to draw line text.
11. Used to draw paragraph text in a dialog box.
12. Settings that determine the appearance of text characters.
13. Load and customize text styles.
14. Control code for diameter symbol.
15. Text angle from horizontal.

WORD SCRAMBLE

Unscramble the seven scrambled words below, one letter to each square, to form seven AutoCAD LT–related words:

IRESTOPPER

XETMT

FJYTSIU

TNTANANOIO

TDDEID

DSATRDNA

NTOF

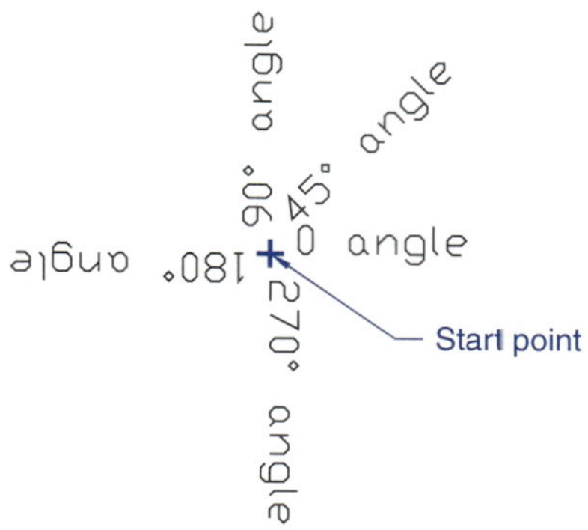

Unscramble the circled letters above to form the special answer, as suggested by the illustration.

PROJECTS

Set up the following drawing projects with layers that relate to the type of drawing as outlined and discussed in Chapter 5.

9.1 Open P2.9 and add text. Use ROMANS font. Save as P9.1.

9.2 Open P3.9 and add text. Use ROMANS font. Save as P9.2.

9.3 Open P5.1 and add text. Use ROMANS font. Save as P9.3.

9.4 Open P6.4 and add text. Use ROMANS font. Save as P9.4.

9.5 Open P7.7 and add text. Use ROMANS font. Save as P9.5.

9.6 Open P7.5 and add text. Use ROMANS font. Save as P9.6.

9.7 Open P7.6 and add text. Use ROMANS font. Save as P9.7.

9.8 Open P8.9 and add text. Use CIBT font. Save as P9.8.

9.9 Open P8.10 and add text. Use CIBT font. Save as P9.9.

9.10 Clock
Open P8.7 and add text as shown below. Use GOTHICE and ROMAND fonts. Save as P9.10.

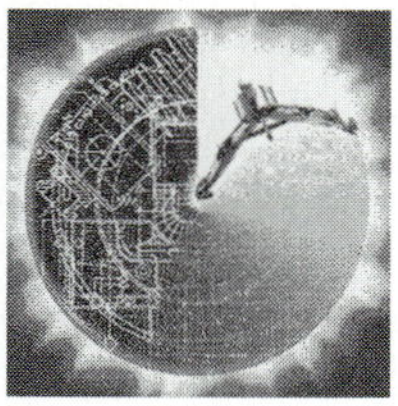

CHAPTER 10

Drawing Patterns and Section Lines

LEARNING GOALS

- Use the BHATCH and HATCH commands to draw hatch patterns.
- Select and draw several different pattern types.
- Change the pattern scale and angle.
- Create user-defined hatch patterns.
- Remove islands from a hatch pattern.
- Define the boundary set in a complex drawing.
- Use the style options.
- Have a new hatch pattern inherit the properties of an existing pattern.
- Perform and observe the difference between editing an associative and nonassociative hatch pattern.
- Use direct hatching.
- Hatch around text.
- Edit hatch patterns.

Introduction to Drawing Patterns and Section Lines

AutoCAD LT provides you with a library of 68 hatch patterns. The term ***hatch*** is used to describe the various patterns that can be used to fill in areas of your drawing. The AutoCAD LT standard hatch patterns are defined in the AutoCAD LT aclt.pat and acltiso.pat files and are displayed in Appendix C of this text. Hatch patterns are often used when drawing sectional views. AutoCAD LT provides the common material section line patterns for mechanical drafting. In mechanical drafting, standard hatch patterns are used to represent different materials, such as cast iron, brass, and aluminum. These standard hatch patterns are identified with ANSI numbers. For example, ANSI31 is the standard section symbol used to represent cast iron or general material in section. The American National Standard Institute document that recommends section line practice is ANSI Y14.3, *Multi and Sectional View Drawings.* AutoCAD LT also provides hatch patterns for materials such as concrete and earth for architectural sections. Drawing architectural elevations is made easier with material patterns for items such as brick and roofing. Hatch patterns can be used as an effective aid if you are designing charts and graphs. The uses are unlimited and can be applied to any drafting discipline, engineering field, or artistic design.

Hatch patterns are drawn in AutoCAD LT with the BHATCH and HATCH commands. The BHATCH command allows you to prepare hatch patterns using the Boundary Hatch dialog box and automatically hatches any enclosed area. BHATCH patterns can be ***associative hatch patterns,*** which means that the pattern is automatically revised if the boundary is changed. The ***hatch boundary*** is the shape that encloses the hatch pattern. The hatch boundary can be various objects that make up a shape or shapes. The HATCH command is used to draw hatch patterns using keyboard entry. Hatch patterns drawn with the HATCH command are ***nonassociative hatch patterns,*** which means that they are not revised when the hatch boundary is edited. The HATCH command can be used to hatch selected objects, or you can define a hatch boundary without selecting objects.

Hatch patterns can be edited using the HATCHEDIT command. This command allows you to change an existing associative hatch pattern.

Using the BHATCH Command

Draw
Hatch
Draw
Hatch...
BHATCH
H

The BHATCH command allows you to automatically hatch any enclosed area using the Boundary Hatch dialog box shown in Figure 10.1. The BHATCH command is accessed by picking Hatch . . . from the Draw pull-down menu, by picking the Hatch button in the Draw toolbar, or by typing **H** or **BHATCH** at the Command: prompt.

The Boundary Hatch dialog box provides a convenient way to set up hatch pattern properties and draw hatch patterns. As you look at Figure 10.1, notice that some of the Boundary Hatch dialog box features are inactive. These items become active during certain applications, which are discussed later in this chapter. The following explanations discuss the various features of the Boundary Hatch dialog box.

Hatch Pattern Types

Three types of hatch patterns are available in AutoCAD LT. You can select from *Predefined, User Defined,* or *Custom* using the Type: list on the Quick tab of the Boundary Hatch dialog box. The default option is Predefined, which refers to the hatch pattern definitions provided with the AutoCAD LT software. A total of 68 predefined hatch patterns are available. These patterns conform to accepted industry standards and are available in two formats. By default, a metric drawing uses ISO standard definitions, and inch drawings implement the ANSI standard. The ANSI standard pattern definitions are found in a text file named aclt.pat located in the Support folder. The acltiso.pat file provides the definitions for the ISO standard patterns. The ANSI and ISO pattern definitions are exactly the same, except the ISO patterns are scaled up by a factor of 25.4.

The User Defined pattern type allows an on-the-fly definition of a simple hatch pattern based on user input. The User Defined pattern options are limited, but where a fast and simple pattern is all that is needed, it can be a good solution.

Custom patterns are also user defined, but this method provides the same flexibility as the Predefined pattern style. Custom patterns must be defined in a .pat file before they can be used. Defining and using Custom hatch patterns is discussed in Chapter 17.

Field Notes

The hatch pattern standard used by AutoCAD LT depends on the current setting of the MEASUREMENT system variable. The MEASUREMENT system variable sets the units in AutoCAD LT as English or Metric. A value of 0 indicates inches (aclt.pat is used), and a value of 1 is metric (acltiso.pat is used).

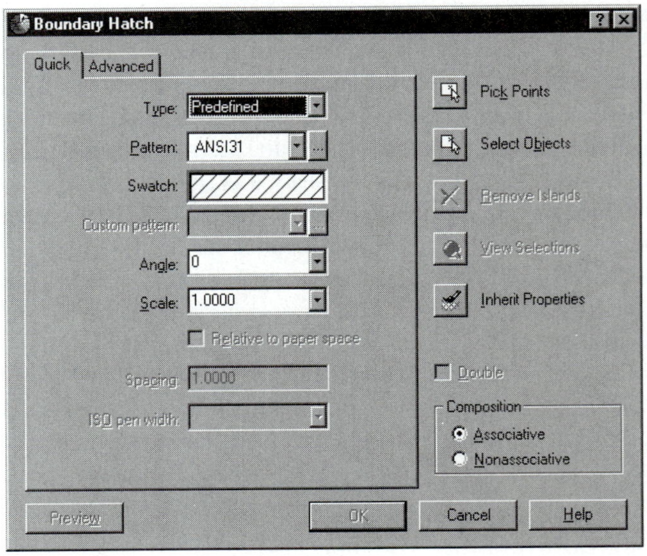

FIGURE 10.1 The Boundary Hatch dialog box is accessed with the BHATCH command.

Selecting a Predefined Hatch Pattern

Predefined patterns are the easiest to use and will meet the needs of most drafting projects. You can select a pattern from the Pattern: list, where all 68 patterns are presented in an alphabetized list. Up to six of the most recently used patterns (in the current drawing session) are displayed at the very top of the list. When you select a pattern name, a preview image showing the pattern appearance is displayed in the image tile labeled Swatch:. The swatch does not display the patterns to scale; each pattern is scaled as needed to fit the image tile.

If you prefer to browse through the patterns visually to select one, pick the ellipsis button just to the right of the Pattern: list to display the Hatch Pattern Palette dialog box. Picking the Swatch: image tile also displays the Hatch Pattern Palette dialog box. The patterns in this dialog box are grouped into four categories: ANSI, ISO, Other Predefined, and Custom. The Custom category is empty until a user-defined pattern file is made available. Creating user-defined pattern files is discussed in Chapter 17.

Figure 10.2A shows the Hatch Pattern Palette dialog box with the ANSI tab visible. This tab provides eight ANSI standard hatch patterns. To select a pattern, pick it and pick OK, or just double-click on it. You are returned to the Boundary Hatch dialog box with the selected pattern active, as shown in Figure 10.2B.

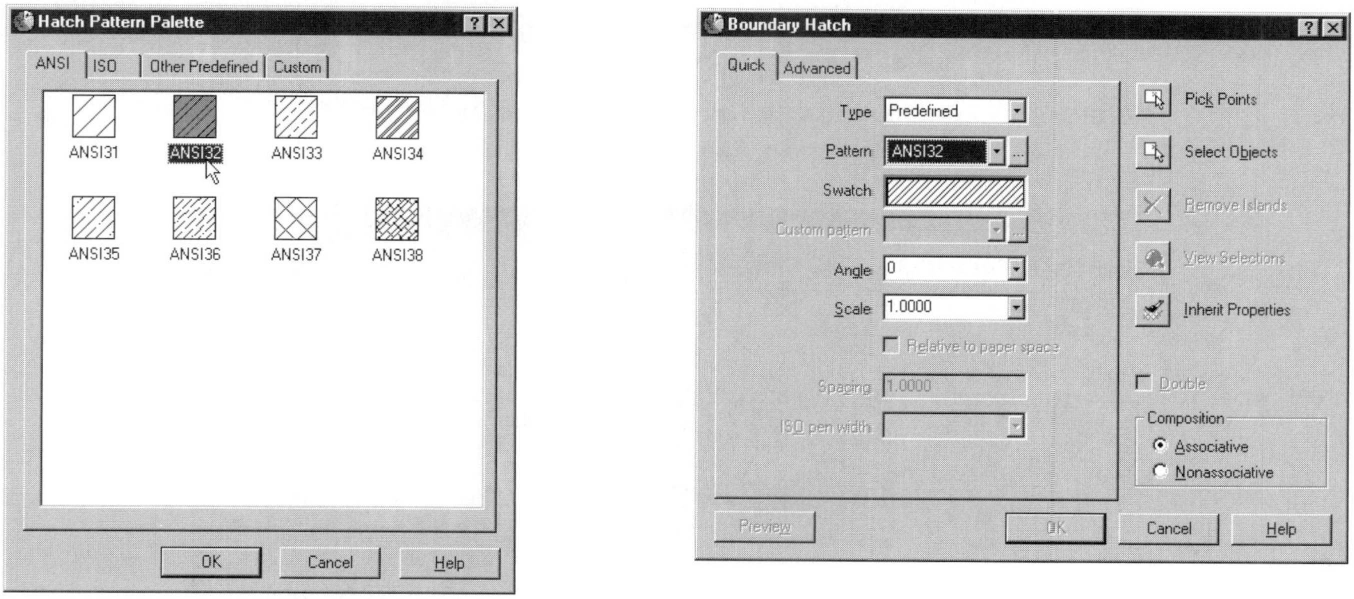

A B

FIGURE 10.2 (A) The ANSI tab of the Hatch Pattern Palette provides access to all the predefined ANSI standard hatch patterns. Select a pattern icon and pick the OK button or double-click on the pattern icon to select it. (B) The Boundary Hatch dialog box displays the new pattern information.

The ISO tab displays the ISO standard patterns; the architectural patterns and general graphic fill patterns are found on the Other Predefined tab. All hatch patterns are defined using lined patterns except for Solid. The Solid pattern provides a solid fill color and does not show a lined pattern. Figure 10.3 shows the contents of these two tabs. With the Hatch Pattern Palette at its default size, not all the Other Predefined patterns can be viewed at once. You can use the scroll bar, or as with many of the AutoCAD LT dialog boxes, you can point to an edge or corner to display the resizing cursor and then resize the dialog box as needed to increase the dialog box display size. Figure 10.4 shows the Hatch Pattern Palette dialog box expanded to show all the available patterns on the Other Predefined tab. The Custom tab remains empty until one or more custom hatch patterns have been created.

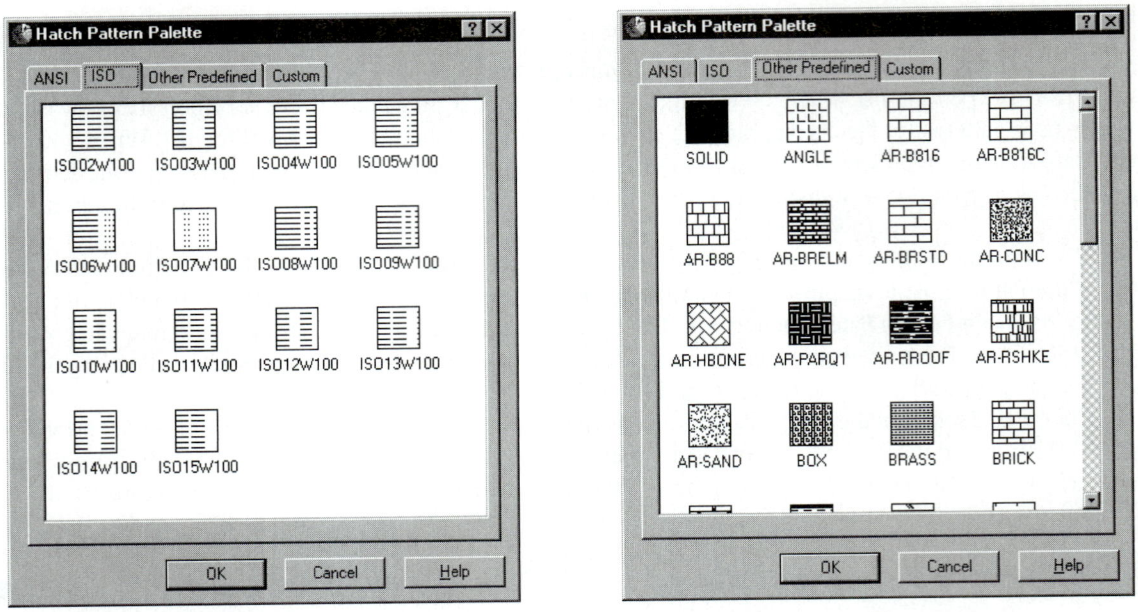

FIGURE 10.3 (A) The ISO tab of the Hatch Pattern Palette dialog box and (B) the Other Predefined tab.

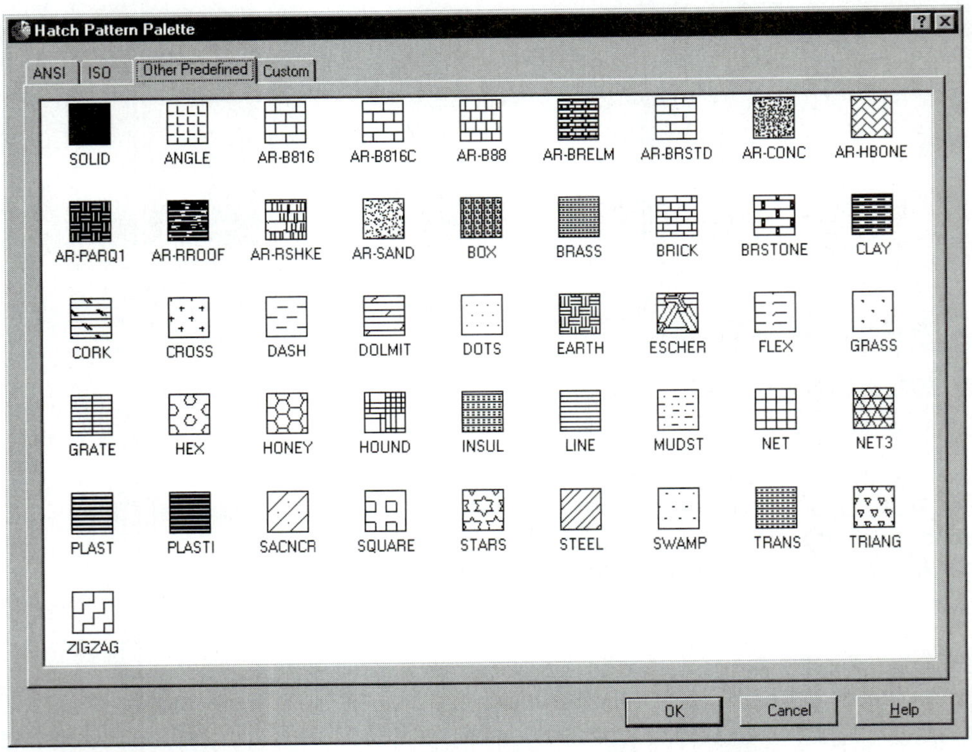

FIGURE 10.4 The Hatch Pattern Palette dialog box can be resized to show more of the available patterns.

Field Notes

The pattern type and values displayed in Figure 10.1 are the initial AutoCAD LT defaults. The values depend on the drawing area specified in the AutoCAD LT setup. When you make changes in the Boundary hatch dialog box, these changes remain active in the current drawing, until they are changed again.

Exercise 10.1 **Estimated time required: 5 min.**

1. Begin a new drawing, starting from scratch using English settings.
2. Open the Boundary Hatch dialog box.
3. Select a new pattern name from the Pattern: list and observe the new image in the Swatch: image tile.
4. Pick the ellipsis button to display the Hatch Pattern Palette dialog box. Browse through each of the tabs. Select a pattern and pick the OK button to return to the Boundary hatch dialog box.
5. Pick the Swatch: image tile. Pick the Cancel button to close the Hatch Pattern Palette dialog box.
6. Keep this drawing open for use in Exercise10.2.

Changing Pattern Properties

The pattern properties are controlled in the Boundary Hatch dialog box; you can modify the selected hatch pattern to fit your own specifications. Notice in Figure 10.1 that the available property settings include Scale: and Angle:.

Changing the Pattern Scale

The initial default pattern scale is 1.0000 unit as shown in the Scale: box in Figure 10.5. The 1 unit scale represents full scale. You can set the scale to any desired value depending on your drawing requirements. Selecting the drop-down list button displays a list of common scale factors. These preset options range from 0.25 to 2.0 at 0.25 increments. You can specify your own scale by double-clicking on the current value and typing a new scale. Figure 10.7 displays the same hatch pattern drawn using several different scale factors.

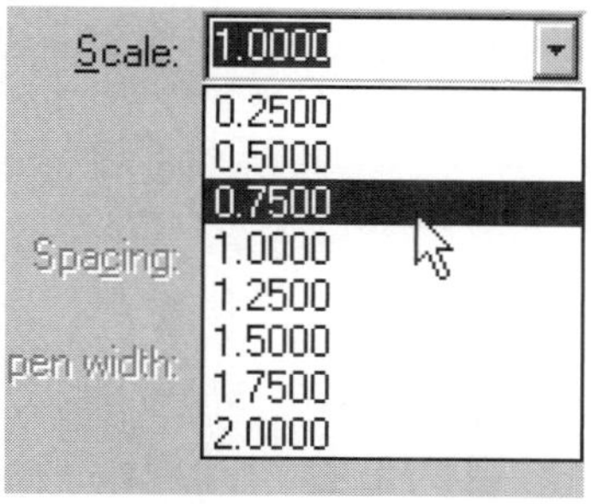

FIGURE 10.5 The Scale: drop-down list provides common scale factors, or a new scale factor can be typed.

Changing the Pattern Angle

The default pattern angle is 0 as shown in the Angle: box in Figure 10.6. This default angle displays the hatch pattern as represented in the image tile and in the symbol library shown in Appendix C. You can adjust the hatch pattern angle by entering a new value in the Angle: box. Preset angle options are listed at 15° increments, or you can type a different value. Various hatch pattern angles are illustrated in Figure 10.8, using the ANSI31 pattern as an example.

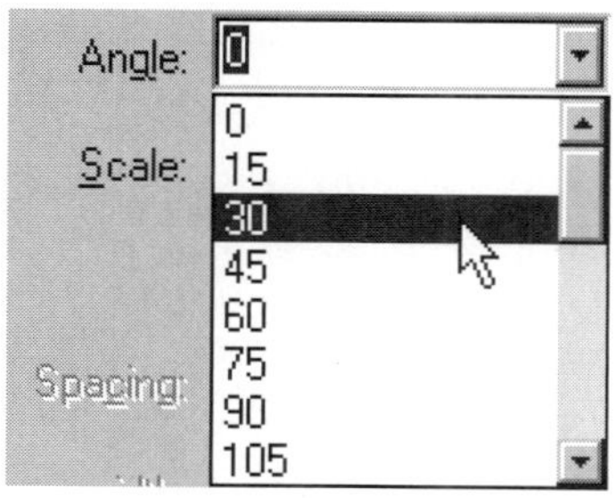

FIGURE 10.6 The Angle: drop-down list provides preset angle options at 15° increments, or you can enter a different angle.

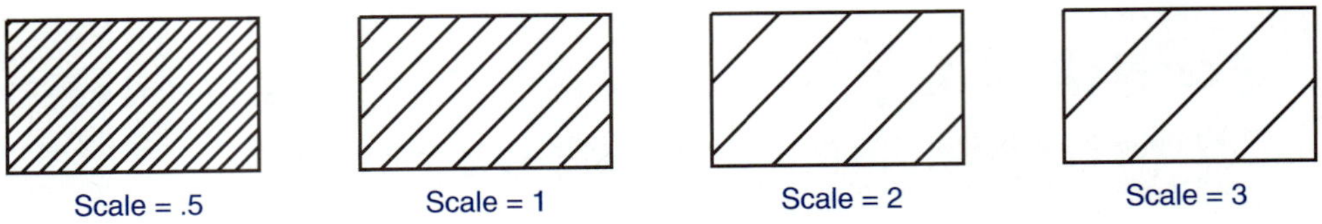

FIGURE 10.7 A hatch pattern drawn using different scale factors.

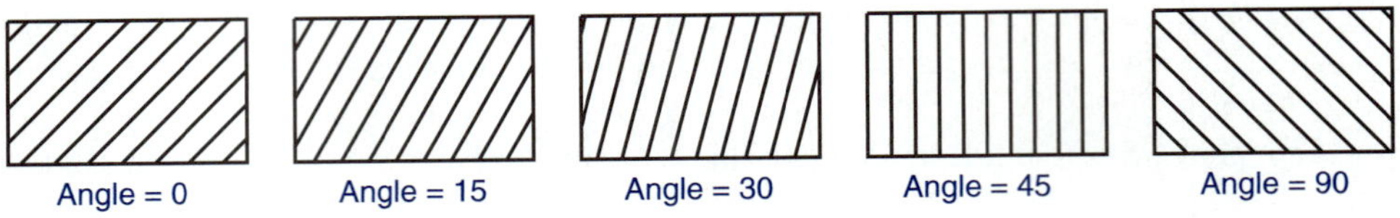

FIGURE 10.8 A hatch pattern drawn using different angle values.

Field Notes

The default pattern angle of 0 used on the ANSI31 pattern type actually draws lines at 45°. Be careful when using hatch patterns because the actual angle of the hatch lines and the rotation angle may be different as they are with the ANSI31 hatch pattern.

The recommended angle for section lines in mechanical drawings is 45°. In mechanical drafting, it is recommended that section lines not be drawn parallel or perpendicular to other adjacent lines on the drawing. To avoid this, you may need to set the hatch pattern so the actual angle of the hatch lines is between 15° and 75°. Vertical and horizontal section lines should be avoided in mechanical drawings.

Accessing the ISO Pattern Types

AutoCAD LT provides you with 14 standard ISO hatch pattern types. ISO stands for the International Organization for Standardization. When you select one of the ISO patterns, the ISO Pen Width: box is activated as shown in Figure 10.9A. Pick the down arrow to access the list of available ISO pen widths. Select the desired pen width as shown in Figure 10.9B. Selecting a pen width from this list establishes the scale for an ISO hatch pattern. Setting the number shown in the ISO Pen Width list updates the Scale value to match. Both the ISO Pen Width and Scale options set the value of the HPSCALE system variable and therefore affect the appearance of the pattern in the same manner.

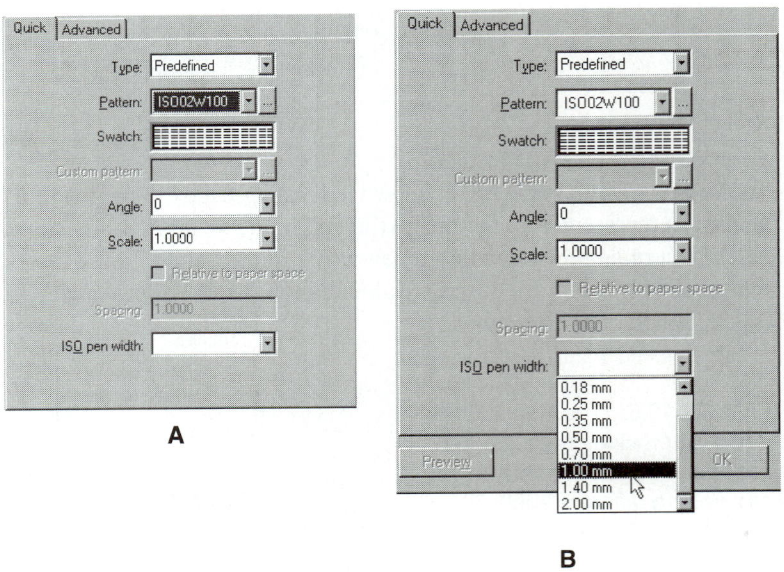

FIGURE 10.9 (A) Selecting an ISO pattern type. (B) The ISO Pen Width: list.

Field Notes

When the Measurement field on the User page of the Preferences dialog box is set to metric, the acltiso.pat file is used. This automatically scales hatch pattern definitions for metric equivalency.

The Other Pattern Type List Options

Earlier, you were introduced to the Predefined option in the Type: list. Two other options are also available in the list. Pick the down arrow to access the User-defined and Custom options. Pick the User-defined option as shown in Figure 10.10A if you want to create your own simple hatch pattern. When the User-defined option is selected, the Spacing: and Double options are now active for the first time, as you can see in Figure 10.10B. Notice also in Figure 10.10B that the image tile now displays the appearance of the user-defined pattern, based on the current settings.

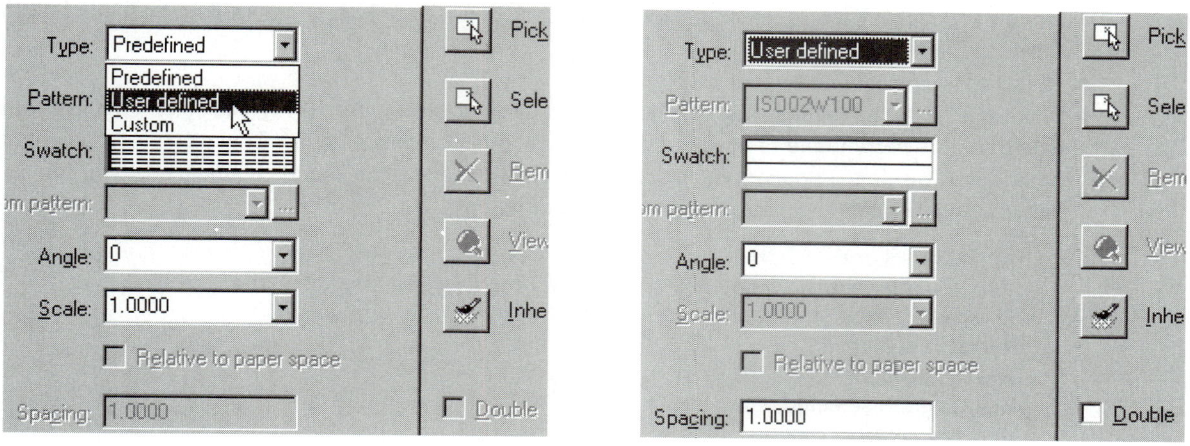

A B

FIGURE 10.10 (A) Pick the User-defined option in the Type list to create your own simple hatch pattern. (B) When the User-defined option is selected, the Spacing: box and Double toggle check box become active.

To define your own simple hatch pattern, set the angle, spacing between pattern lines, and the display of single or double lines. The Angle: box works just as previously described to set the desired angle for your pattern. In the User-defined application, pattern angles are measured from 0 (zero) as horizontal. The Spacing: box allows you to set the spacing between pattern lines. The 1.0000 default provides 1 unit of spacing between lines. The amount of spacing depends on your drawing size. A spacing of 0.125 might be good for an inch mechanical drawing, whereas 6 might be a valid setting for a metric mechanical drawing. An architectural drawing might use a setting of 2, depending on the application. The Double toggle should be off if you want a pattern with single lines. Check this toggle if you want double lines in your pattern. Double lines are created by placing two sets of lines that intersect at 90°. Figure 10.11 shows the results of a variety of user-defined hatch pattern designs.

The Custom option in the Type: list is used to access third-party hatch pattern files that can be used with AutoCAD LT. When you pick the Custom option, the Custom Pattern: box becomes active. If you have other hatch pattern files available, enter the pattern name here for access. The hatch pattern name and file name must be the same.

FIGURE 10.11 Examples of several different user-defined hatch patterns.

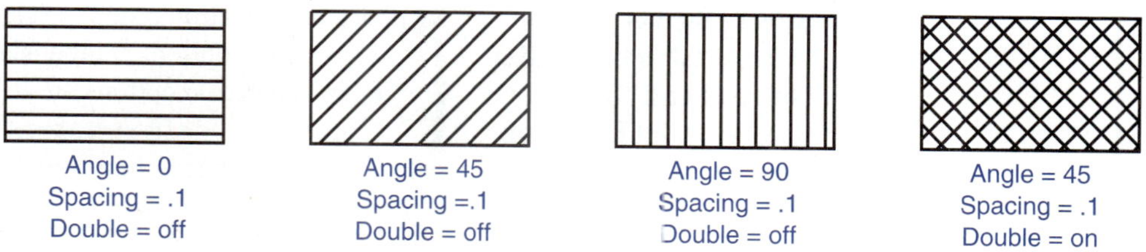

Field Notes

> Custom pattern definition files can contain only a single definition that defines a pattern having the same name as the file. Custom definitions can be added to the aclt.pat or acltiso.pat files as desired and are then available using the predefined option.

Drawing a Hatch Pattern

So far you have learned how to set up hatch pattern types. Now, you can either draw standard AutoCAD LT hatch patterns or create the simple user-defined hatch patterns. Follow these steps to draw one of the standard hatch patterns:

- Draw objects that you want to place hatch patterns within. For starters, consider drawing a closed rectangle with the LINE or PLINE command.
- Enter the BHATCH command to open the Boundary Hatch dialog box.
- Go to the Pattern: list and select the pattern by name, or use the Hatch Pattern Palette dialog box to select a pattern.
- Adjust the scale and angle as desired.
- Pick the Pick Points button. Look back at Figure 10.1 or see Figure 10.13. The screen returns with the crosshairs present and the prompt asks you to "Select internal point." This refers to selecting a point that is inside the boundary you want to hatch. You can select a single boundary, or you can select multiple boundaries to hatch in a single operation.

  Command: **H** or **BHATCH**↵
  ⟨*The Boundary Hatch dialog box opens. Pick the Pick Points button.*⟩
  Select internal point: ⟨*move the crosshairs within the boundary and pick*⟩
  Selecting everything . . .
  Selecting everything visible . . .
  Analyzing the selected data . . .
  Analyzing internal islands . . .
  Select internal point: ↵

- AutoCAD LT gives you several messages as it evaluates the hatch boundary. The first message is "Selecting everything…", which indicates that no boundary set was predefined. A boundary set is a smaller selection set identified for use in the current hatching operation. Creation and use of boundary sets is discussed later in this chapter. The next message is "Selecting everything visible…"; boundary hatching can be used only on objects that are currently visible on screen. The messages "Analyzing the selected data…" and "Analyzing internal islands…" indicate that AutoCAD LT is trying to determine how and where the hatch pattern should be applied based on the objects you have selected.
- When you have picked inside all the desired boundary areas, you can press Enter to return to the Boundary Hatch dialog box. Optionally, you can right-click to get the shortcut menu (see Figure 10.12). The options on the shortcut menu are as follows:
  - **Enter** — This is the same as pressing the Enter key. This returns you to the Boundary Hatch dialog box.
  - **Undo last Select/Pick** — This selection does not work in some releases of AutoCAD LT 2000. If not, you can also undo the last selection by typing **U**↵ at the Select internal point: prompt.
  - **Clear all** — Clears the current selection, allowing you to restart the selection process.
  - **Pick Internal Point** — Switches the selection mode to look for boundaries.
  - **Select Objects** — Switches the selection mode to select individual objects.
  - **Normal Island Detection**
  - **Outer Island Detection**
  - **Ignore Island Detection** — These three options set the island detection mode. Island detection options are discussed later in this chapter.
  - **Preview** — Allows you to preview the results of the current hatch pattern specifications.

- When back in the Boundary Hatch dialog box, you can pick the Preview button. This is a great AutoCAD LT feature that lets you preview the results of your hatch drawing before the hatch is applied. Picking the Preview button returns the screen with the hatch pattern temporarily placed and the message <Hit enter or right-click to return to the dialog>. The advantage of using preview is that if you do not like the way the preview looks, you can return to the Boundary Hatch dialog box and try again without starting over. You do not have to use the preview, and it may not be very important in a simple drawing like this. However, it might save you considerable time when hatching in a complex drawing.
- If you are satisfied with the results of the preview, pick the OK button at the bottom of the Boundary Hatch dialog box. This removes the dialog box and applies the hatch as you specified.

Through the Window...

There are some easy ways to use list boxes in Windows. For example, after popping the list down, you can use the keyboard cursor keys to move up or down through the list, and even use the Page Up, Page Down, Home, and End keys. The most convenient option is to press an alphabetic character key, which moves up or down the list to highlight the first item in the list beginning with the character you type.

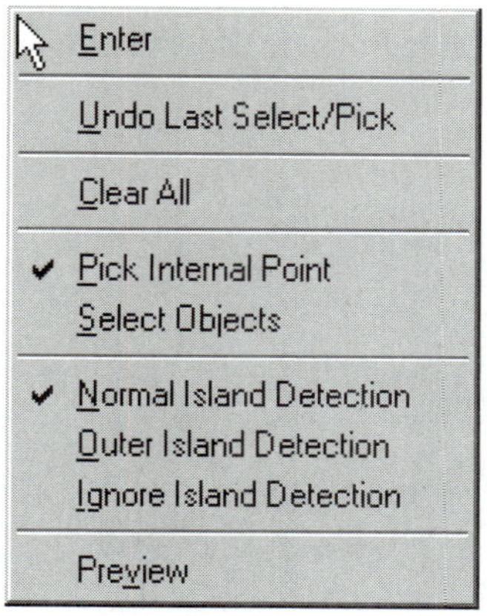

FIGURE 10.12 Right-clicking while selecting hatch boundaries displays the Boundary Hatch shortcut menu.

Field Notes

- If the hatch boundary is not properly closed, using the Pick Points option results in an error message. This happens if there are any gaps in the hatch boundary. If you get this error message, carefully check the hatch boundary to be sure the perimeter is closed.
- When you are inside the BHATCH command at the Select internal point: prompt, you can type U to undo the previous pick if you decide it was not what you wanted.
- If you complete the BHATCH command, and decide the results are not what you want, you can type U at the Command: prompt to undo the previous hatch.
- The Preview button is an excellent way to look at an object that you have hatched before you accept it. If you discover that the hatch properties are not what you expected, you can change them and try again. However, when you pick the same object again, you get a Boundary Definition Error alert box. The message in the box reads "Boundary duplicates an existing boundary." Pick the OK button and continue the process.

Exercise 10.2 **Estimated time required: 10 min.**

1. Use the drawing from Exercise 10.1, or begin a new drawing from scratch using English settings.
2. Use the LINE or PLINE command to draw a closed rectangle, similar to one of the rectangles shown in Figure 10.7. Copy the rectangle three times. You should have four rectangles similar to those shown in Figure 10.7.
3. Hatch inside the four rectangles using the ANSI31 pattern type and change the scale for each application, as was done in Figure 10.7. Be sure to use the Preview button to preview each hatch before applying.
4. Make five more rectangles and use the ANSI31 pattern to hatch each rectangle with a different angle, as was done in Figure 10.8.
5. Draw four more rectangles and create a different user-defined hatch pattern for each rectangle. The results should look like Figure 10.11.
6. Draw as many more rectangles as you desire and experiment by placing a different standard hatch pattern in each rectangle. This gives you a chance to see what some of the other patterns look like.
7. Save as EX10.2, and close the drawing.

Using the Additional Features of the Boundary Hatch Dialog Box

The Boundary Hatch dialog box has several buttons, as shown in Figure 10.13. The purpose of these buttons is explained in the following:

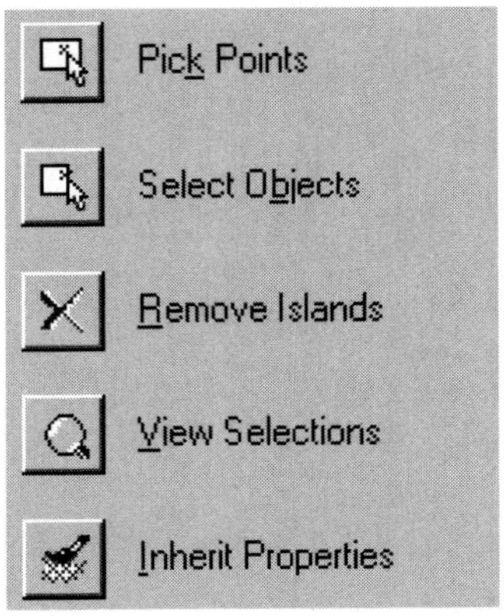

FIGURE 10.13 The Boundary Hatch dialog box feature buttons.

Using the Pick Points Button

The Pick Points button was explained in the previous discussion. This button is used to hatch a closed area by picking a point inside that area.

Using the Select Objects Button

The Select Objects button is used if you want to use one of the AutoCAD LT selection methods to select objects for hatching. Rather than the Select internal point: prompt that you get when using the Pick Points button, you get the Select objects: prompt. This is what the command sequence looks like when using the Select Objects button:

Command: **H** or **BHATCH**↵
⟨*The Boundary Hatch dialog box opens. Pick the Select Objects button.*⟩
Select objects: ⟨*pick the objects to hatch*⟩
Select objects: ↵

The Boundary Hatch dialog box returns for you to complete the hatching process. Now, use the Preview button to see if the defined hatch is okay. Right-click and pick the OK button if you are satisfied with the preview.

In addition to providing you with another way to draw hatches, the Select Objects button is useful when hatching multiple objects or an area that is separated by other objects. For example, the rectangle and circle in Figure 10.14 are divided by line objects and the plan is to hatch the entire circle and rectangle. The Select Objects option works well in this example, because it is easier to pick the rectangle and the circle to have the hatch drawn through the entire object. The rectangle must have been drawn with the PLINE or RECTANG command to use one pick. If the LINE command is used to draw the rectangle, each line object must be selected.

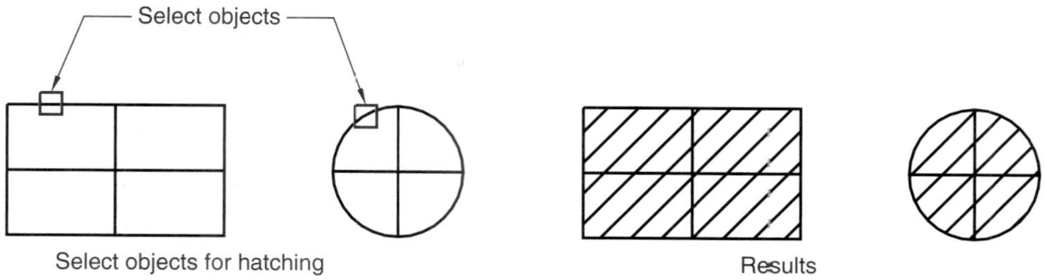

FIGURE 10.14 Using the Select Objects button to hatch objects.

Exercise 10.3

Estimated time required: 5 min.

1. Open a new drawing.
2. Draw a rectangle and circle with a horizontal and vertical line crossing each, similar to the original objects shown in Figure 10.14. Use the PLINE or RECTANG command to draw the rectangle.
3. Enter the Boundary Hatch dialog box and use the Pick Points button to pick a single point within the rectangle and circle. Return to the Boundary Hatch dialog box and Preview the results. Notice that only one quarter of each object is hatched.
4. Pick the Select Objects button, and this time pick the rectangle and the circle at the places shown in Figure 10.14. Return to the Boundary Hatch dialog box and Preview the results. The entire rectangle and circle should be hatched as in Figure 10.14. If you are satisfied with the preview, pick the Apply button.
5. Save as EX10.3, and close the drawing.

Using the Remove Islands Button

The Remove Islands button is used to select islands to hatch within a hatch area. AutoCAD LT defines an ***island*** as an enclosed area within the hatch boundary area as shown in Figure 10.15A. The Remove Islands button is inactive until you use the Pick Points button. If you use the Pick Points button, and pick between the hatch boundary and the island, the island is automatically left unhatched as shown in Figure 10.15B. If you want to hatch through the island, you can do the following:

- Enter the BHATCH command and use the Pick Points button to pick between the hatch boundary and the island as shown in Figure 10.15C. The following command sequence is used:

  Command: **H** or **BHATCH**↵

The Boundary Hatch dialog box opens. Pick the Pick Points button.

Select internal point: ⟨*pick between the boundary and the island*⟩
Selecting everything . . .
Selecting everything visible . . .
Analyzing the selected data . . .
Analyzing internal islands . . .
Select internal point: ↵

- The Boundary Hatch dialog box returns. Pick the Remove Islands button. The screen returns and you get this prompt:

  Select island to remove: ⟨*pick the island as shown in Figure 10.15D*⟩
  <Select island to remove>/Undo: ↵

- The Boundary Hatch dialog box returns again. Preview the hatch and if it is what you expect, right-click, then pick the OK button. The result is shown in Figure 10.15E.

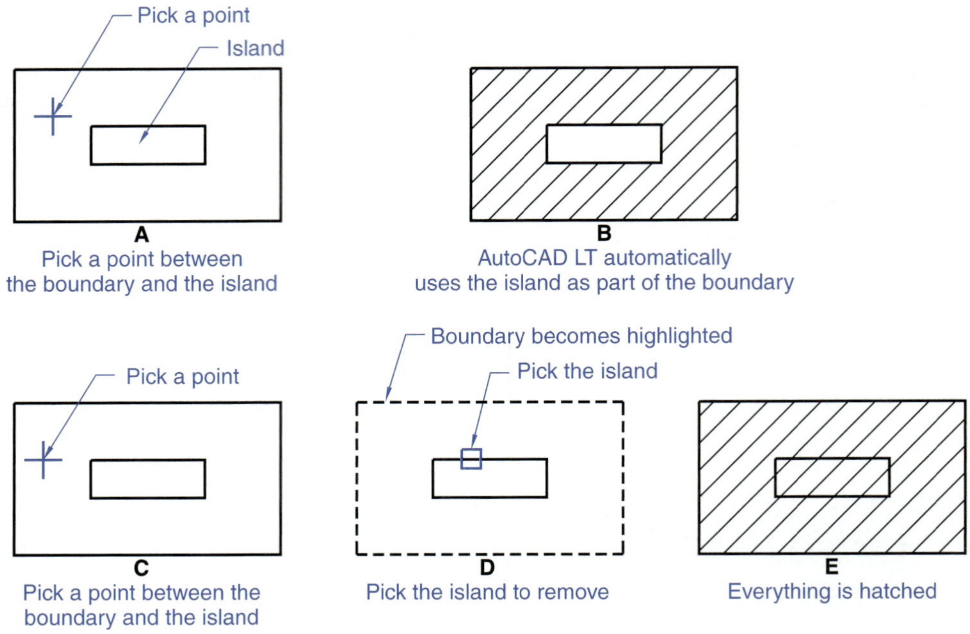

FIGURE 10.15 (A) An island is an enclosed area within a hatch boundary. (B) Using the Pick Points button to hatch between the hatch boundary and the island. (C)–(E) Hatching through an island by using the Remove Islands button.

4

Exercise 10.4 **Estimated time required: 5 min.**

1. Open a new drawing or one of your prototypes.
2. Draw an object similar to that shown in Figure 10.15A using the PLINE command.
3. Make two copies of the object.
4. Hatch the first object in a manner similar to Figure 10.15B.
5. Hatch the second object in a manner similar to Figure 10.15E.
6. Save as EX10.4, and close the drawing.

Using the View Selection Button

The View Selection button is active only after you have used the Pick Points or Select Objects button to establish a hatch boundary. When you pick the View Selection button, the screen returns and the hatch boundaries are highlighted for you to see. This just gives you a chance to see the selected hatch boundaries to confirm if they are what you intended. Right-click or press Enter when you are ready to return to the Boundary Hatch dialog box.

Using the Advanced Tab

Picking the Advanced tab displays the advanced options shown in Figure 10.16. These features are explained in the following discussion.

FIGURE 10.16 The Advanced tab displays the advanced options for hatching.

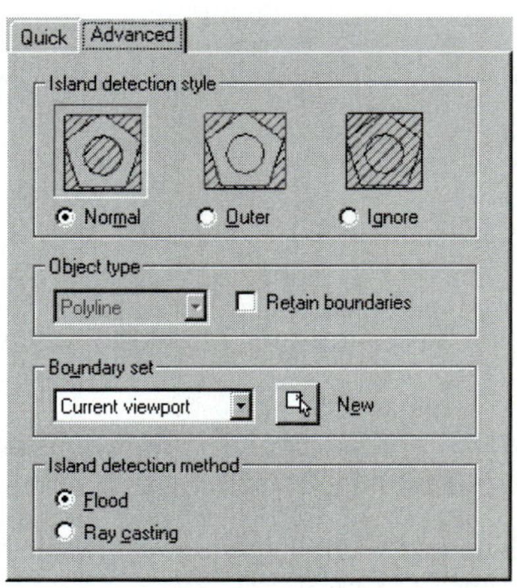

Specifying an Island Detection Style

The Island detection style controls how hatching is applied to objects that have internal islands. The Island detection style area displays image tiles depicting the effect of each style (see Figure 10.16). The Normal option, as the example image tile shows, hatches every other boundary level encountered. This is the initial default hatching method. The second method, Outer, hatches only the outermost boundary area and does not apply hatching to any internal boundaries. The Ignore option applies hatching as if the outermost boundary were selected using the Select Objects option; this option hatches through any internal objects. You can specify an Island detection style either by selecting the radio button or by picking the image tile for the desired option.

Defining a New Boundary Set

The term ***boundary set*** refers to the objects that are analyzed by AutoCAD LT to determine how the hatch pattern should be applied. The default option is Current viewport, which means that all objects in the current viewport are analyzed in the hatch boundary definition process. In very large drawings, this can be a slow process. You can define a smaller selection set to be used by picking the New button in the Boundary set area. When you pick the New button, the Boundary Hatch dialog box is hidden temporarily, and a Select objects: prompt is displayed on the command line. Select all objects that you want to be considered in the hatch boundary definition process and press Enter at a Select objects: prompt when you are finished. Any standard selection option can be used. The Boundary set list now shows the option Existing set, meaning that only the selected objects are analyzed for hatching. As an example, if you want to hatch a small area in the structural drawing shown in Figure 10.17 using a custom boundary set, follow this sequence:

Command: **H** or **BHATCH**↵

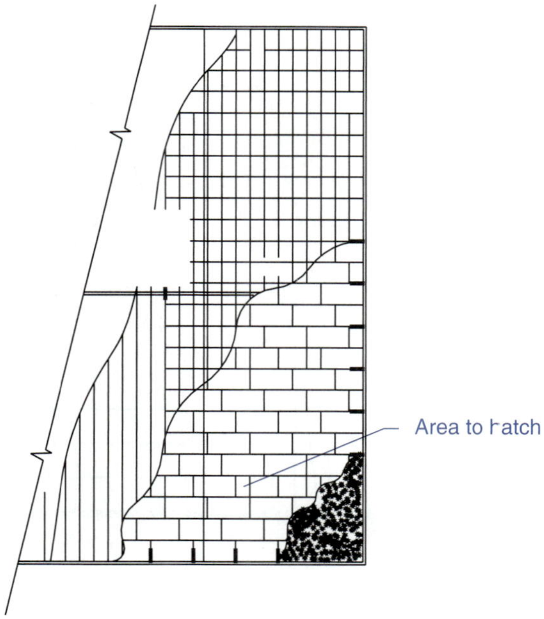

FIGURE 10.17 Defining a custom Boundary Set to quickly hatch a small area in a complex drawing.

The Boundary Hatch dialog box opens. Pick the Advanced tab. Pick the New button in the Boundary set area, and you get the Select objects: prompt. Use a Window or Crossing box to select the objects to be used for a boundary set. Any selection option works, but a Crossing box selects all the objects the box encloses or crosses:

Select objects: ⟨*use a Crossing box as shown in Figure 10.18*⟩
Select objects: ↵

The Boundary Hatch dialog box returns. Pick the Pick Points button and then pick a point inside the area to be hatched:

Analyzing the selected data . . .
Select internal point: ⟨*pick a point*⟩
Analyzing internal islands . . .
Select internal point: ↵

FIGURE 10.18 Using a Crossing selection box to select the area for a new boundary set.

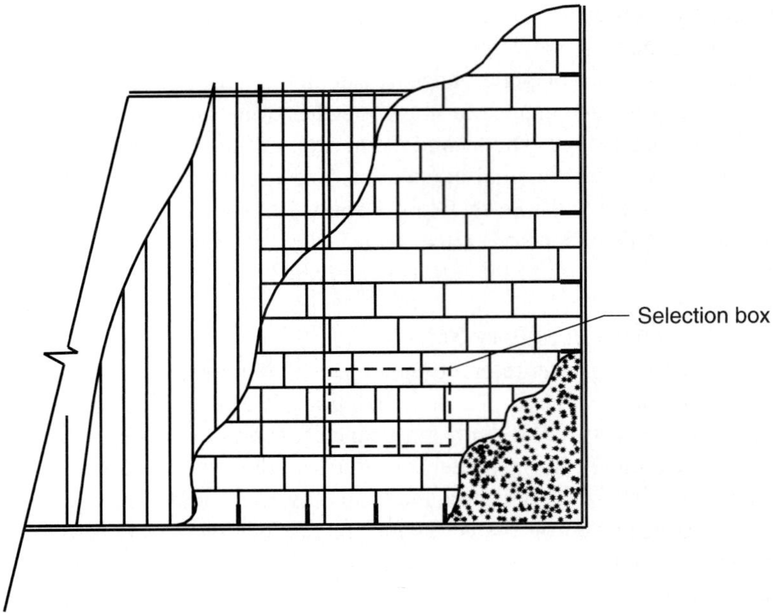

The Boundary Hatch dialog box returns. Preview the hatch and if it is acceptable, pick the OK button. The hatch is complete as shown in Figure 10.19.

FIGURE 10.19 Hatching within the small area of the complex drawing shown in Figures 10.17 and 10.18.

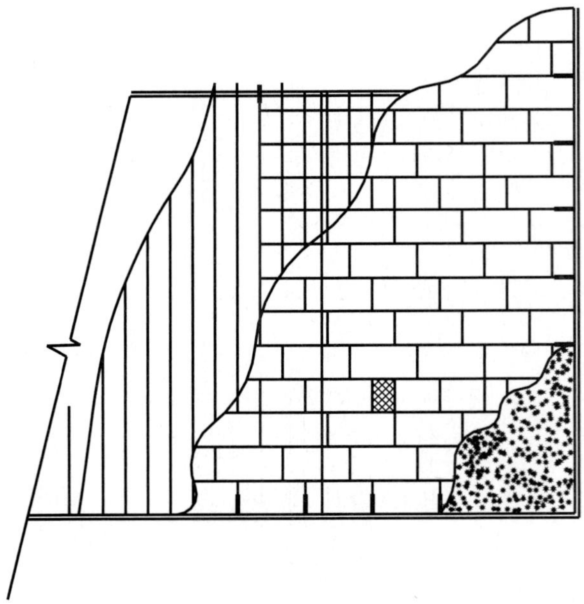

Island Detection Method

The Island detection method controls the recognition of internal islands. The Flood method is most commonly used, and is the initial default. The Flood and Ray casting options are described as follows:

- **Flood** This option includes islands as boundary objects.
- **Ray casting** This option runs an imaginary line from the point you pick to the nearest surrounding object and traces the boundary in a counterclockwise direction. This method excludes all islands from being boundary objects. The result is the same as using the Ignore Island detection style.

Exercise 10.5 **Estimated time required: 5 min.**

1. Open a new drawing.
2. Draw an object similar to the representation in the Island detection style image tile in Figure 10.16, without hatching.
3. Make two copies of the object.
4. Hatch the first object using the Normal style. The results should be similar to the image tile.
5. Hatch the second object using the Outer style. The results should be similar to the image tile.
6. Hatch the third object using the Ignore style. The results should be similar to the image tile.
7. Save as EX10.5, and close the drawing.

Using the Retain Boundaries Toggle

The Retain Boundaries toggle is off by default. The hatch boundaries that are created to establish a hatch pattern are temporary if this toggle is off. This means that the temporary hatch boundary does not remain as part of the drawing when the hatching process is over. As soon as the hatch pattern is drawn, the boundary is removed. Turning the Retain Boundaries toggle on keeps each hatch boundary as a polyline or a region. This stacks a new polyline or region on top of the existing boundary objects. This new object can be edited or erased if desired. You might want to do this if the original boundary is made up of line objects and you want a polyline or region boundary that you can use for purposes such as calculating the area.

Specifying the Boundary Object Type

The boundary objects created by the Retain Boundaries option are created as either regions or polylines, based on the setting in the Object Type list. Regions are discussed in Chapter 6, and polylines in Chapter 8. Using a region allows access to some data not available from a polyline object.

Using the Inherit Properties Button

The Inherit Properties button allows you to pick a hatch pattern that already exists on your drawing and use it as the pattern for hatching other areas. Doing this allows you to quickly and accurately duplicate an existing hatch pattern that is already in your drawing. This can save you time and maintain consistency in your drawing. To use this option, enter the BHATCH command and follow these steps:

Command: **H** or **BHATCH**↵

The Boundary Hatch dialog box opens. Pick the Inherit Properties button to get this prompt:

Select associative hatch object: ⟨*pick an existing associative hatch pattern on your drawing*⟩

When the Select associative hatch object: prompt is displayed, the cursor is shown as a pick box with a small paintbrush beside it (see Figure 10.20A). Use this pick box to select the hatch pattern whose properties you want to inherit. The name and properties of the pattern you select are displayed, and the following prompt is issued:

Inherited Properties: Name <ANSI36>, Scale <1.0000>, Angle <0>
Select internal point: <*specify the boundary area for the new pattern*>

At the Select internal point: prompt, the cursor changes to crosshairs with a large paintbrush (see Figure 10.20B). Either select an internal point or right-click and use the shortcut menu to switch to Select Objects mode. In the Select Objects mode the cursor changes to a pick box with the large paintbrush.

When you return to the Boundary Hatch dialog box, pick the OK button to accept the new hatching, or make any needed adjustments.

FIGURE 10.20 Using the Inherit Properties option allows you to hatch a new area using the same properties used by an existing hatch pattern. (A) When the existing pattern is selected, the cursor displays a small paintbrush. (B) The cursor displays a large paintbrush when boundary areas for the new hatch pattern are selected.

Exercise 10.6 — Estimated time required: 5 min.

1. Open a new drawing.
2. Draw a circle and hatch it with the AR-HBONE pattern using a scale of 0.75 and an angle of 0.
3. Draw another circle the same size as the first. Hatch this circle with AR-PARQ1, using a scale of 0.75 and an angle of 0.
4. Draw another circle the same size as the first two. Go to the Boundary Hatch dialog box and pick the Inherit Properties button. Select the hatch pattern in the first circle and apply it to the third circle.
5. Save as EX10.6, and close the drawing.

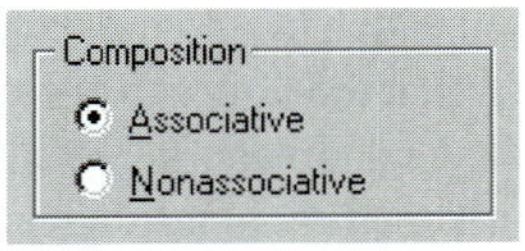

FIGURE 10.21 The Composition area of the Boundary Hatch dialog box controls whether the hatch pattern composition is Associative or Nonassociative.

Associative and Nonassociative Composition

Earlier, you learned that hatch patterns drawn with the BHATCH command are associative by default. This means that the pattern is automatically revised if the boundary is changed. An associative hatch pattern is treated as a single hatch object. The Associative radio button in the Composition area of the Boundary Hatch dialog box is on by initial default. See Figure 10.21. For most applications, the associative feature is left on, but you can turn it off in this area. While the Composition is set to Nonassociative, all hatch patterns drawn with the BHATCH command are nonassociative. This means that the pattern is not automatically updated. Figure 10.22A shows the results of stretching a hatched object with the associative feature on and off. You can use any of the available editing commands, such as ROTATE and SCALE, to modify objects with associative hatch patterns and have the pattern automatically change with the edit to the boundary. If you have an associative hatched object with an island, moving the island outside the boundary causes the boundary to be fully hatched and the moved island to also become hatched, as shown in Figure 10.22B. The area where the island in Figure 10.22B was moved became filled in with the hatch pattern. This also happens with an associative hatch pattern if you erase an island. This process is referred to as **healing**. As you can see with these examples, associative hatch patterns have the advantages of being able to edit the hatch boundary and having the hatch pattern automatically updated to match.

Field Notes

- When you are editing objects with hatch patterns, be sure that you select *only* the hatch boundary; do not select the hatch pattern.
- Be careful with edits that open a hatch boundary, such as the BREAK command. These types of edits can cause the associativity to be removed.
- Edits that add objects to the boundary, such as those occurring when using the FILLET or CHAMFER commands, may not properly update the pattern.

FIGURE 10.22 (A) The results of using the STRETCH command to edit a hatched object with associative and nonassociative hatching. (B) The results of using the MOVE command to move an island outside the boundary of an associatively hatched area.

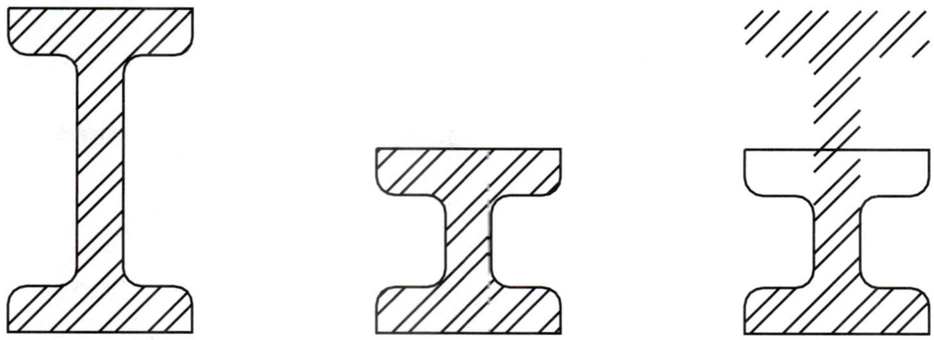

The original hatched object

The object edited using the STRETCH command with an associative hatch pattern

The object edited using the STRETCH comman with a nonassociative hatch pattern

A

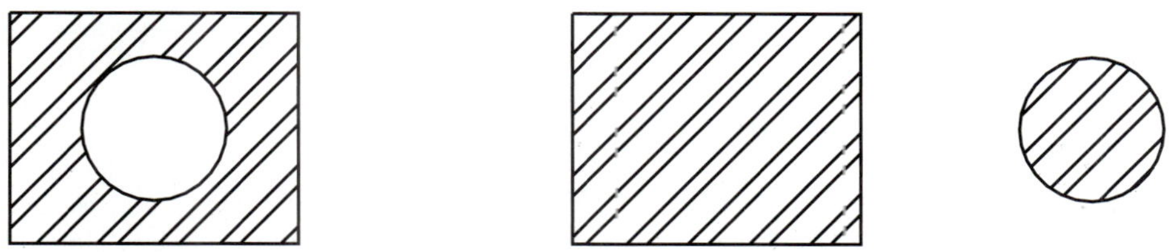

The original associative hatched object with an island

The results of using the MOVE command to move the island outside of the hatch boundary

B

Using the Relative to Paper Space Scaling Feature

This option is available only from within a layout tab. This makes it easy to create hatch patterns that display at a scale appropriate to your layout scale. The current scale of the viewport is used to calculate the correct scale factor to apply to the hatch pattern. Working with viewports and layouts is discussed in Chapter 13.

Field Notes

In some early versions of AutoCAD LT 2000, picking the Help button in the Boundary Hatch dialog box incorrectly displays help on the BOUNDARY command instead of the BHATCH command.

Exercise 10.7 **Estimated time required: 10 min.**

1. Open a new drawing or use one of your prototypes.
2. Draw an object similar to the original hatched object shown in Figure 10.22A without hatching.
3. Make a copy of the object.
4. Use the BHATCH command to hatch the first object with the ANSI32 pattern. Be sure the Associative feature is on.
5. Turn the Associative feature off and hatch the second object with the same pattern.
6. Use the STRETCH command on both objects and observe the results.
7. Turn the Associative feature on.
8. Draw and hatch the object shown at the left in Figure 10.22B.
9. Make two copies of the object to the right.
10. Use the MOVE command on one new object to move the island outside of the hatch boundary as shown on the right side of Figure 10.22B. Use transparent ZOOM to help as needed.
11. Erase the island from the other new object. Notice how the hatch pattern is "healed" where the island is erased.
12. Save as EX10.7, and close the drawing.

LEARNING CHECKPOINT

- ☐ List three ways to access the BHATCH command.
- ☐ Discuss two ways to change the Pattern: in the Boundary Hatch dialog box.
- ☐ Briefly discuss the user-defined pattern type.
- ☐ Explain the purpose and importance of the hatch preview.
- ☐ Describe the difference between using the Pick Points and the Select Objects buttons.
- ☐ What is an island?
- ☐ How does the Remove Islands button work?
- ☐ Discuss the purpose of the New Boundary set button.
- ☐ List and describe the Island detection style options.
- ☐ How does the Inherit Properties button work?
- ☐ Define associative hatch pattern.
- ☐ Identify at least one major advantage of using associative hatching.

Creating Geometry

- Filling Areas

Drag-and-Drop Hatch Patterns

The AutoCAD DesignCenter feature was discussed in earlier chapters, showing how it can be used to drag and drop drawing content into a drawing. AutoCAD DesignCenter can also be used to drag and drop hatch patterns into a drawing. This provides a convenient interface that allows quick and easy application of hatch patterns.

Accessing Hatch Patterns Using DesignCenter

To access hatch patterns for drag-and-drop application using AutoCAD DesignCenter, first activate the DesignCenter window using the ADC command or by pressing Ctrl+2. Pick the Desktop button to display the contents of your desktop in the Tree View pane. Next, use the Tree View pane to open the \Program Files\AutoCAD LT 2000\Support folder and pick the desired pattern file. By default, the *aclt.pat* and *acltiso.pat* files will be available.

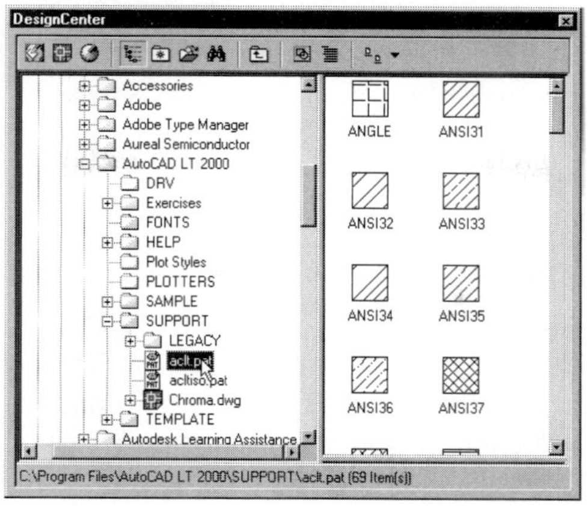

FIGURE 10.23 The AutoCAD DesignCenter window can be used to access hatch pattern content found in a .pat file.

When you select a .pat file in the Tree View pane, the Palette pane shows the available content items. Figure 10.23 shows the AutoCAD DesignCenter window with the contents of the *aclt.pat* file displayed in the Palette pane.

To apply a pattern using the current default hatch settings, just point to a pattern, and press and hold the pick button. Drag the cursor into the boundary area to hatch and release the pick button. When you are dragging the pattern, a box appears at the cursor location to show the appearance of the hatch pattern you are dragging. If this box is not visible, it is because the current default settings result in a pattern that is too dense to display. Figure 10.24A shows the cursor appearance when dragging a pattern into a drawing. Figure 10.24B illustrates the cursor appearance when the pattern defaults are too dense.

A B

FIGURE 10.24 (A) The hatch pattern appearance is shown at the cursor location as you drag the pattern into your drawing. (B) If the current settings would produce a hatch pattern that is too dense to display, the cursor does not display the pattern.

Figure 10.25 shows the application of a hatch pattern by dragging and dropping from AutoCAD DesignCenter. This method allows only one boundary to be defined and uses the current default hatch pattern properties for scale and angle.

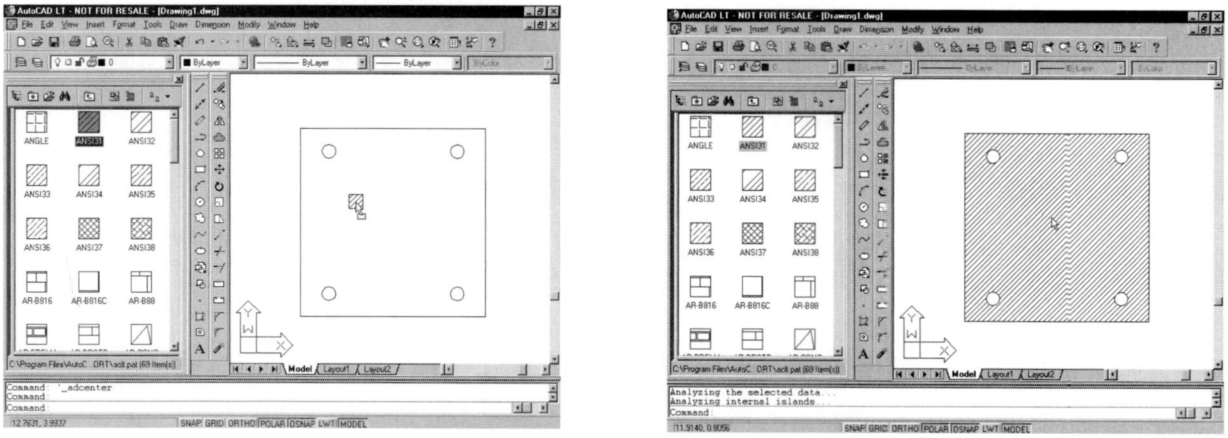

A B

FIGURE 10.25 (A) Dragging a hatch pattern from AutoCAD DesignCenter. (B) Dropping the pattern into a boundary.

Another method that can be used is to right-click on the pattern icon in DesignCenter and select Copy from the shortcut menu. This copies the hatch pattern definition to the Windows clipboard. Press Ctrl+V or pick Paste from either the Edit pull-down menu or from the shortcut menu in the drawing area to paste the pattern into the drawing. The hatch pattern will be displayed in a small box at the cursor location. Point anywhere inside the desired hatch boundary, and press the pick button to apply the hatch pattern.

Controlling Drag-and-Drop Hatch Pattern Properties

Patterns dragged into the drawing use the current default hatch pattern properties, which may not always work. If you know what the scale and angle of the new pattern should be, you can preset them using the HPSCALE and HPANG system variables. Like any other variable, these can be set at the command line by typing the variable name at the Command: prompt as follows:

Command: **HPSCALE↵**
Enter new value for HPSCALE <1.0000>: **24↵**
Command: **HPANG↵**
Enter new value for HPANG <0.00>: **45↵**

Another way to control the properties of patterns brought in from DesignCenter is by right-clicking on the pattern icon in DesignCenter and selecting BHATCH..., which starts the BHATCH command in AutoCAD LT using the selected pattern.

If you drag a pattern into the drawing using the right mouse button, a shortcut menu is displayed when you release the mouse button. The shortcut menu is illustrated in Figure 10.26, and the options on this menu are as follows:

■ Apply Hatch	Applies the hatch pattern just as if you used the pick button to drag the pattern.
■ Apply and Edit Hatch...	Applies the hatch pattern and starts the HATCHEDIT command. HATCHEDIT is discussed later in this chapter.
■ Apply Hatch to Multiple Objects	Applies the hatch pattern to the current boundary and lets you pick inside any number of additional boundaries.
■ BHATCH...	Starts the BHATCH command with the selected pattern.
■ Cancel	Cancels the operation.

FIGURE 10.26 The shortcut menu provides additional options when dragging hatch patterns from DesignCenter.

Exercise 10.8 **Estimated time required: 5 min.**

1. Open EX10.7 for editing.
2. Erase the existing hatch patterns, leaving the boundaries in place.
3. Re-Hatch the objects using the drag-and-drop method from DesignCenter. Be sure to edit settings where necessary.
4. Save as EX10.8, and close the drawing.

LEARNING CHECKPOINT

- ☐ Name the options for accessing DesignCenter.
- ☐ How can hatch patterns be inserted from DesignCenter?
- ☐ How can you access the BHATCH command from DesignCenter?
- ☐ How can the Windows Clipboard be used to inset patterns from DesignCenter?
- ☐ How can multiple pick points be specified when hatching from DesignCenter?

Concept Animations

- DesignCenter

Using the HATCH Command

HATCH
-H

The HATCH command does not use a dialog box. Instead, its prompts are issued in the floating command window and the responses are entered at the keyboard. Hatch patterns drawn using the HATCH command are nonassociative. The HATCH command is less intuitive than BHATCH because its prompts are issued one at a time. You also cannot preview with the HATCH command and then go back and change values as you can with the BHATCH command. As you follow through the HATCH command prompts, you will see many of the same features identified earlier when using the BHATCH command. However, the HATCH command offers certain features that are not available when using BHATCH. The HATCH command can be accessed by typing **HATCH** or **-H**. This is a hyphen (-) typed before H. The HATCH command provides the following sequence of prompts:

Command: **-H** or **HATCH↵**
Enter a pattern name or [?/Solid/User defined] <ANSI31>:

Notice that ANSI31 is the initial default hatch pattern type. You can accept this pattern type by pressing Enter or you can type one of the other pattern names. Appendix C shows the available standard hatch patterns and their names. You can also type **?** to specify particular pattern names, or press Enter again to accept the <*> wild card and get a list of the available patterns in a text window:

Enter a pattern name or [?/Solid/User defined] <ANSI31>: **?↵**
Enter pattern(s) to list <*>: ↵

The AutoCAD LT Text Window is displayed with a listing of the names and short descriptions of all available standard hatch patterns. Close the text window when finished looking at the list. The Command: prompt returns after you look through the list of available pattern options. Reenter the HATCH command by pressing Enter and accept the default pattern, or type another pattern name and press Enter:

Command: ↵
Enter a pattern name or [?/Solid/User defined] <ANSI31>:

The next prompt asks you for the pattern scale. Look back at Figure 10.7 and its related discussion on scale. Accept the default scale or enter a new value:

Specify a scale for the pattern <1.0000>: ↵

The next prompt requests a pattern angle. Review Figure 10.8 and the explanation about pattern angle:

Specify an angle for the pattern <0>: ↵

Next, you get the familiar Select objects: prompt. Use any of the AutoCAD LT selection options to select objects for hatching as shown in Figure 10.27:

Select objects to define hatch boundary or <direct hatch>,
Select objects: ⟨*pick or select the objects for hatching*⟩
Select objects: ↵
Command:

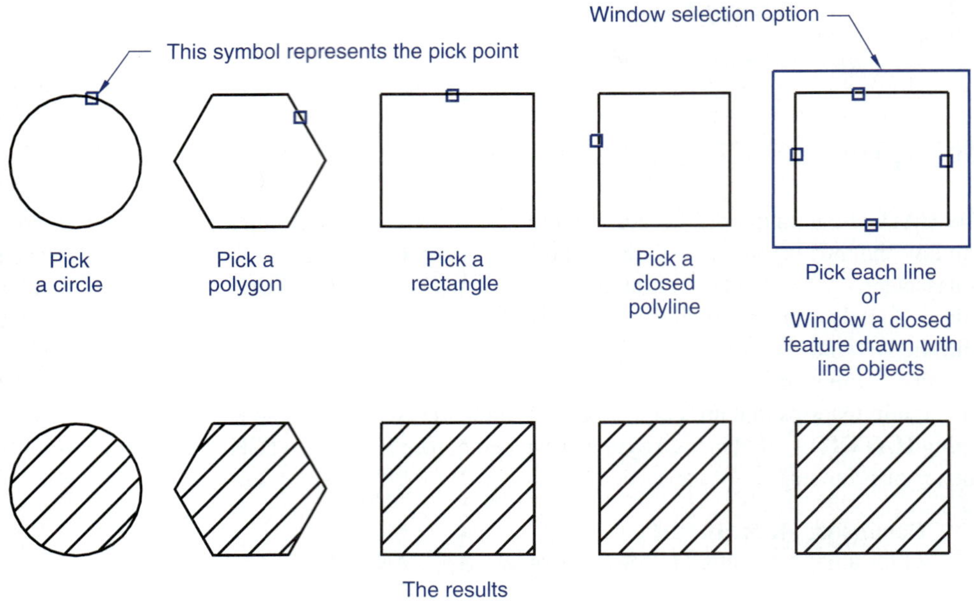

FIGURE 10.27 Selecting objects to hatch using the HATCH command.

Hatching Objects Solid

The Solid option of the HATCH command allows you to fill objects in solid. The results are the same as applying the SOLID hatch pattern using the Hatch Boundary dialog box except for associativity. You can solid-hatch any closed object, such as those shown in Figure 10.27. You can also solid-hatch irregular-shaped objects such as the slot or polyline curves shown in Figure 10.28. The Solid option works like this:

Command: **-H** or **HATCH**↵
Enter a pattern name or [?/Solid/User defined] <ANSI31>: **S**↵
Select objects to define hatch boundary or <direct hatch>,
Select objects: *<select objects to hatch>*
Select objects: ↵
Command:

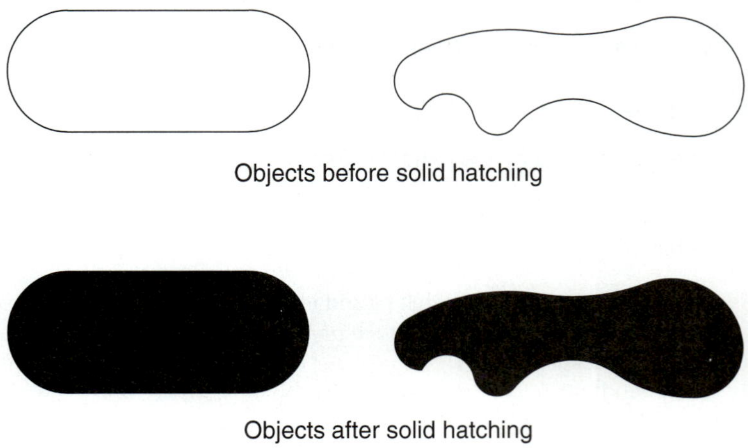

FIGURE 10.28 Using the Solid hatching pattern.

Field Notes

- When using the HATCH command, you should select individual objects such as circles, polygons drawn with the POLYGON command, rectangles drawn with the RECTANG command, or closed polylines. Any of these objects can be picked for hatching. Closed objects drawn with the LINE command require that you use one of the selection options such as Window or Crossing. Unexpected results can happen when selecting connected objects that are drawn with the LINE command. For example, if you try to hatch one side of two or more connected objects, the hatch lines can extend partly into the adjacent area. Do not worry if this happens. Undo the command and use the BHATCH command's Pick Points button to hatch the desired area.
- If you draw a hatch pattern and then immediately access the HATCH command by pressing Enter at the Command: prompt, AutoCAD LT takes you directly to the Select objects: prompt using the same hatch pattern from the previous command sequence.
- If you hatch more than one separate object while inside the HATCH command, the hatch pattern for all the objects are modified together when using editing commands. To avoid this, hatch each object separately with its own HATCH command.

Exercise 10.9 — Estimated time required: 10 min.

1. Open a new drawing.
2. Draw a circle, a hexagon, a rectangle using the RECTANG command, a closed polyline, and a closed rectangle using the LINE command. These should be similar to the objects shown at the top of Figure 10.27.
3. Hatch each object using the HATCH command. The results should be similar to those shown in the bottom part of Figure 10.27
4. Draw objects similar to the objects before hatching in Figure 10.28. Use arcs and lines to draw the slot, and use polyline arcs to draw the shape on the right. Be sure the objects are closed. Copy the objects below the original objects.
5. Use the Solid option of the HATCH command to solid-hatch the original two objects.
6. Use the BHATCH command SOLID pattern to hatch the other two objects.
7. Save as EX10.9, and close the drawing.

Drawing User-Defined Hatch Patterns with the HATCH Command

The User-defined option in the Type list of the Boundary Hatch dialog box allows you to draw simple hatch pattern designs like those shown in Figure 10.11. You can also do this in the HATCH command with the User-defined option. The User-defined option allows you to establish a simple hatch pattern with hatch lines at a specified angle and spacing, and either single or double. These are the prompts:

Command: **-H** or **HATCH↵**
Enter a pattern name or [?/Solid/User defined] <ANSI31>: **U↵**
Specify angle for crosshatch lines <0>: **45↵**
Specify spacing between the lines <1.0000>: **.125↵**
Double hatch area? [Yes/No] <N>: **Y↵**
Select objects to define hatch boundary or <direct hatch>,
Select objects: <*select objects to hatch*>
Select objects: ↵
Command:

The results of the previous sequence are shown in Figure 10.29.

FIGURE 10.29 Creating a simple user-defined hatch pattern with the HATCH command.

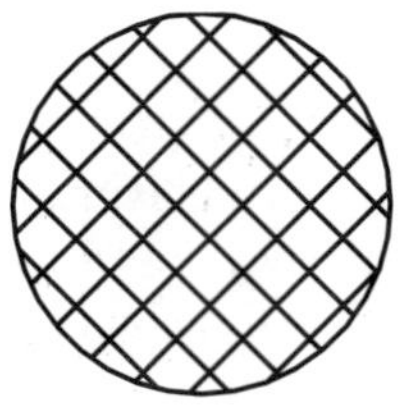

Using Direct Hatching with the HATCH Command

The HATCH command allows you to skip the Select objects: prompt and perform what is referred to as direct hatching. ***Direct hatching*** is used when you want to define a hatch boundary where the hatch pattern is to be placed, and then either keep the boundary or have it removed during the hatching process. You can use direct hatching to hatch individual areas within interconnected areas or for hatching where no boundary exists. AutoCAD LT reminds you that direct hatching is available by providing this message: "Select hatch boundaries or press Enter for direct hatch options." Press Enter at the Select objects: prompt to use the direct hatching feature. Any valid point entry method is acceptable, including osnap points, polar and relative coordinates, or direct distance entry:

Command: **-H** or **HATCH**↵
Enter a pattern name or [?/Solid/User defined] <ANSI31>: **EARTH**↵
Specify a scale for the pattern <1.0000>: ↵
Specify an angle for the pattern <0>: ↵
Select objects to define hatch boundary or <direct hatch>,
Select objects: ↵

Next, AutoCAD LT asks if you want to keep the polyline boundary. Answer Y or N:

Retain polyline boundary? [Yes/No] <N>: **Y**↵

Now you get prompts that allow you to draw a polyline boundary:

Specify start point: *<pick the first point>*
Specify next point or [Arc/Close/Length/Undo]: *<pick the next point>*
Specify next point or [Arc/Close/Length/Undo]: *<pick the next point>*
Specify next point or [Arc/Close/Length/Undo]: *<pick the next point>*
Specify next point or [Arc/Close/Length/Undo]: **C**↵

The Close option is used in the previous sequence to close the polyline boundary. Next, AutoCAD LT gives you a prompt that allows you to continue drawing additional polyline boundaries or to press Enter to apply the hatch:

Specify start point for new boundary or <apply hatch>: ↵
Command:

The hatch is applied and the polyline boundary is kept as shown in Figure 10.30A. Figure 10.30B shows a footing detail with the earth hatch pattern drawn using direct hatch and without keeping the polyline boundary.

The other options found in direct hatching are described as follows:

- **Arc:** This option allows you to draw a polyline arc using one of the PLINE arc options. Continue drawing arcs by picking the arc endpoints or by using one of the other options, or change to drawing straight polyline segments by entering the Line option. The prompts read like this when using the Arc option:

Specify start point: *<pick the first point>*
Specify next point or [Arc/Close/Length/Undo]: **A**↵
Enter an arc boundary option
[Angle/CEnter/CLose/Direction/Line/Radius/Second pt/Undo/Endpoint of arc] <Endpoint>: *<pick an arc endpoint or use another option>*
Enter an arc boundary option
[Angle/CEnter/CLose/Direction/Line/Radius/Second pt/Undo/Endpoint of arc] <Endpoint>: **L**↵
Specify next point or [Arc/Close/Length/Undo]: *<pick a point>*
Specify next point or [Arc/Close/Length/Undo]: *<pick a point>*
Specify next point or [Arc/Close/Length/Undo]: **C**↵
Specify start point for new boundary or <apply hatch>: ↵
Command:

FIGURE 10.30 (A) Using direct hatching with the polyline boundary. (B) Using direct hatching without the polyline boundary.

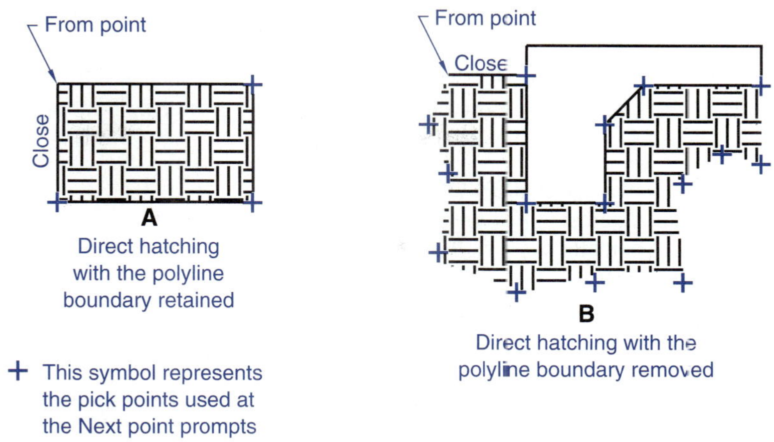

Refer to Chapter 8 for a complete review of the PLINE Arc options.

- **Close:** The Close option is used by typing C and pressing Enter to close a polyline boundary.
- **Length:** The Length option is used if you want to specify the length of a line in the last angle selected. If the previous segment was a line segment, the segment created using Length continues in the same direction. If the previous segment was an arc, the line segment drawn using Length continues at an angle tangent to the end of the arc segment. If the Length option is used on the first segment, the value stored in the LASTANGLE system variable is used.
- **Undo:** The Undo option is available to let you undo the previous polyline element.

Exercise 10.10

Estimated time required: 5 min.

1. Open a new drawing.
2. Use direct hatching to draw the earth pattern inside of a polyline boundary similar to the one shown in Figure 10.30A.
3. Draw a footing detail without hatching similar to that shown in Figure 10.30B. Use direct hatching to hatch the earth symbol around the footing without the boundary displayed. The results should look like Figure 10.30B.
4. Save as EX10.10, and close the drawing.

Field Notes

- If you draw more than one separate direct hatched area using the same HATCH command, all areas are treated as one when editing.
- You can draw a hatch pattern without a boundary using the direct hatching option of the HATCH command. You can also draw a hatch pattern within a boundary using either the HATCH or BHATCH command, and then erase the boundary if you want a pattern without a boundary displayed.

Drawing a Hatch Pattern with Individual Elements

When you use the HATCH command, the entire hatch pattern is a single block. You can also draw a hatch pattern where every element within the pattern is an individual object. This might be useful if you want to edit parts of the hatch pattern without affecting the entire pattern. To do this, enter the pattern name after an asterisk (*) like this:

Command: **-H** or **HATCH**↵
Enter a pattern name or [?/Solid/User defined] <ANSI31>: ***ANSI31**↵

Modify

Explode

Modify
Explode

EXPLODE
X

Now, continue drawing the hatch pattern as usual.

Existing hatch patterns can also be made into individual objects using the EXPLODE command. The EXPLODE command, which was introduced earlier, is accessed by typing **X** or **EXPLODE**, by picking Explode in the Modify pull-down menu, or by picking the Explode toolbar button. The command works like this:

Command: **X** or **EXPLODE**↵
Select objects: ⟨*pick the hatch pattern*⟩
Select objects: ↵
Command:

Use Undo if you want to undo a previously used EXPLODE command.

Exercise 10.11 **Estimated time required: 5 min.**

1. Open EX10.9.
2. Use the EXPLODE command on one of your hatch patterns.
3. Use the ERASE command by picking the exploded hatch pattern. Notice that each line of the hatch pattern is now an individual object.
4. Exit the drawing without saving, or save as EX10.11, and close the drawing, if preferred by your instructor or supervisor.

Hatching around Text

Text may be placed in an area that requires hatching. In these situations, you probably do not want the hatch pattern to run through the text. Text is hatched around when using the BHATCH command if the Style: is set to Normal or Outer and you use the Pick Points button to pick between the boundary and the text. You can also use the Select Objects button and select both the hatch boundary and the text. See Figure 10.31.

When using the HATCH command, you can hatch around text if you pick the object to be hatched then pick the text like this:

Command: **-H** or **HATCH**↵
Enter a pattern name or [?/Solid/User defined] <ANSI31>: ↵
Specify a scale for the pattern <1.0000>: ↵
Specify an angle for the pattern <0>: ↵
Select objects to define hatch boundary or <direct hatch>,
Select objects: <*select the objects to hatch*>
Select objects: <*select the text objects*>
Select objects: ↵
Command:

Figure 10.31 illustrates the use of the BHATCH and HATCH commands to hatch around text.

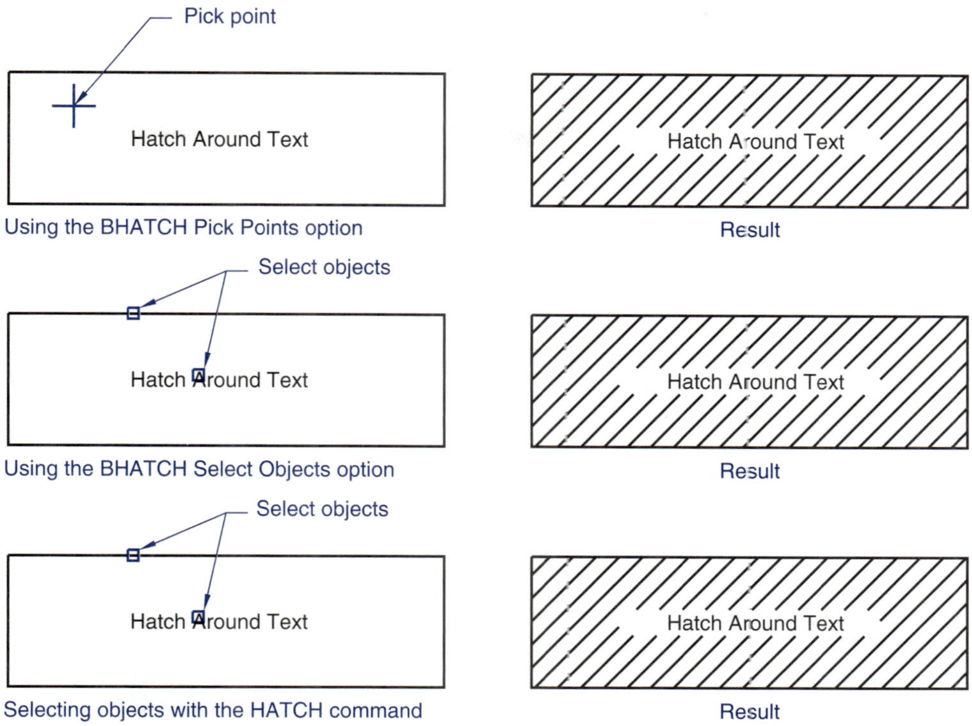

FIGURE 10.31 Hatching around text.

Field Notes

Now that you have learned how to use the BHATCH and HATCH commands, you might want to become familiar with the MaxHatch setting. This can be of value to help avoid exhausting your system resources by creating extremely large hatch patterns, or by specifying an extremely small scale for a complex hatch pattern in a very large area. This variable limits the number of objects that can be created by a single HATCH or BHATCH command. The value of this variable is used as the maximum number of objects that can be created to form a hatch pattern. If the hatch pattern parameters specified require more objects than indicated in MaxHatch, an error message is displayed and the pattern is not created. This variable can be set between 100 and 10,000,000. The default is 10,000. To change the value of the MaxHatch registry variable, use the SETENV command. Note that when you type the name of the variable to change, the variable is *case sensitive* and must be typed as MaxHatch.

Exercise 10.12 — Estimated time required: 8 min.

1. Open a new drawing or use one of your prototypes.
2. Draw three rectangles with the text "Hatch Around Text" in the middle of each rectangle. The drawings should be similar to the objects shown on the left side of Figure 10.31.
3. Hatch the first object using the BHATCH Pick Points option.
4. Hatch the second object using the BHATCH Select Objects option.
5. Hatch the third object using the HATCH command.
6. The results should be similar to the objects shown at the right in Figure 10.31.
7. Save as EX10.12, and close the drawing.

LEARNING CHECKPOINT

- ☐ List at least two key differences between the BHATCH and HATCH commands.
- ☐ How do you set a style option in the HATCH command?
- ☐ What is direct hatching?
- ☐ How do you tell AutoCAD LT to perform direct hatching with or without leaving the polyline boundary?
- ☐ What is the method used to instruct the HATCH pattern command to draw a hatch with individual elements?
- ☐ Identify two ways to hatch around text with the BHATCH command and at least one way with the HATCH command.

Editing Hatch Patterns and Using the HATCHEDIT Command

Any associative hatch pattern drawn using the BHATCH command can be edited along with any changes you make to the hatch boundary. For this to be true, the hatch pattern must have been drawn with the Associative toggle on. You can edit associative hatched objects with any of the grip editing commands or enter the COPY, MOVE, ROTATE, SCALE, and STRETCH commands before selecting the objects. You saw the effects of the STRETCH command on an associative and nonassociative hatch pattern in Figure 10.22A and the results of moving an island in an associative hatch pattern in Figure 10.22B. You can erase any hatched object just as you can any other object. When you are editing objects with hatch patterns, be sure that you select *only* the hatch boundary; do not select the hatch pattern.

Modify II

Edit Hatch

Modify
Object ▸
HATCH...

HATCHEDIT
HE

Associative hatch pattern properties can be edited using the HATCHEDIT command. The HATCHEDIT command is accessed by typing **HE** or **HATCHEDIT** at the Command: prompt, by picking the Edit Hatch button in the Modify II toolbar, or by picking Hatch ... in the Object cascade of the Modify pull-down menu. This command asks you to select a hatch object:

Command: **HE** or **HATCHEDIT**↵
Select associative hatch object: *<pick an associative hatch object>*

Selecting a hatch object opens the Hatch Edit dialog box shown in Figure 10.32. The Hatch Edit dialog box should look familiar to you because it is the same as the Boundary Hatch dialog box. The only difference from the Boundary Hatch dialog box is that the Boundary area selection buttons are not available. Notice in Figure 10.32 that these buttons are inactive. After selecting a hatch pattern, you can use the Hatch Edit dialog box to do any of the following edits:

- Change pattern Type.
- Change the pattern properties in the Scale: and Angle: boxes. If a User-defined hatch pattern is selected, the Spacing: box and Double toggle become active.
- Use the Inherit Properties button to pick an existing hatch pattern for your selected hatch pattern to match.
- Turn off the Associative feature. The Composition area is inactive if you pick a pattern drawn with the HATCH command.
- Pick the Advanced tab. The only active features in the Advanced tab are the Island detection style options. You can change the style and then pick the OK button.

After making all the desired changes in the Hatch Edit dialog box, pick the Preview Hatch button to see if the results are what you expected. Pick the Apply button to apply the changes.The changes are now represented in the selected hatch pattern.

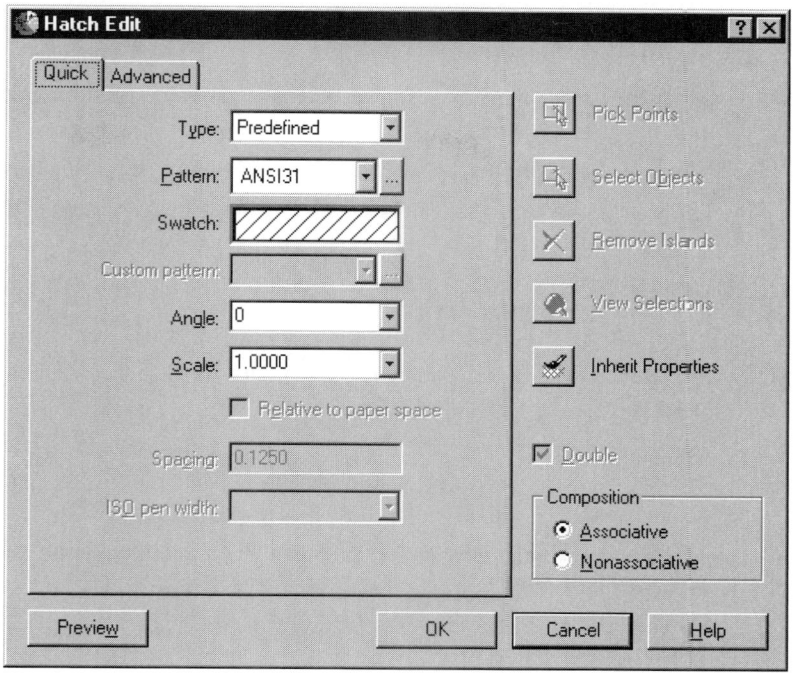

FIGURE 10.32 The Hatch Edit dialog box is accessed with the HATCHEDIT command.

If you enter -HATCHEDIT at the Command: prompt, you get this:

Command: **-HATCHEDIT**↵
Select associative hatch object: *<select an associative hatch object>*
Enter hatch option [Disassociate/Style/Properties] <Properties>:

The Disassociate option removes the associative quality from an associative hatch. The Style option allows you to change the hatch pattern style. Normal is the default, but you can use Ignore or Outer. Refer to Figure 10.21 for a review of these options. The Style prompt looks like this:

Enter hatch option [Disassociate/Style/Properties] <Properties>: **S**↵
Enter hatching style [Ignore/Outer/Normal] <Normal>:

The Properties option allows you to specify new hatch properties using the keyboard. These are the familiar prompts when using the Properties option:

Enter hatch option [Disassociate/Style/Properties] <Properties>: ↵
Enter a pattern name or [?/Solid/User defined] <ANSI31>: *<specify new pattern or press ↵>*
Specify a scale for the pattern <1.0000>: *<enter new scale or press ↵>*
Specify an angle for the pattern <0>: *<enter new angle or press ↵>*
Command:

Exercise 10.13

Estimated time required: 5 min.

1. Open EX10.5.
2. Use the HATCHEDIT command to change the pattern type to a different pattern for each object. Pick the Apply button.
3. Use the HATCHEDIT command to change the scale and angle of the pattern in each object to a different value. Pick the Apply button.
4. Use the HATCHEDIT command to change the object with the Ignore style to the Normal style. Pick the Apply button.
5. Save as EX10.13, and close the drawing.

LEARNING CHECKPOINT

- ☐ What conditions must exist for a hatch pattern to change automatically when the hatch boundary is edited?
- ☐ Describe the difference between the Hatch Edit and Boundary Hatch dialog boxes.
- ☐ List at least six edits that can be made to a hatch pattern when using the HATCHEDIT command.

MULTIPLE CHOICE

Circle the choice or enter your response on an answer sheet by selecting the option that most closely completes or answers the given statements.

1. This term is used to describe the variety of patterns that can be used to fill in areas of your drawing:
- **a.** patterns
- **b.** symbols
- **c.** hatch
- **d.** library

2. These patterns are automatically changed when the boundary is edited:
- **a.** associative
- **b.** change
- **c.** update
- **d.** modify

3. The shape that encloses the hatch pattern:
- **a.** polyline
- **b.** boundary
- **c.** border
- **d.** outline

4. This command allows you to draw associative hatch patterns:
- **a.** HATCH
- **b.** BHATCH
- **c.** BHAT
- **d.** STYLE

5. Use this button if you want to look at the hatch pattern before applying it to the drawing:
- **a.** Inherit Properties
- **b.** Preview Hatch
- **c.** View Selections
- **d.** Select Objects

6. This is an enclosed area within a hatch area:
- **a.** island
- **b.** object
- **c.** boundary
- **d.** space

7. When this command is used, the hatch pattern becomes individual objects.
- **a.** BHATCH
- **b.** EXPLODE
- **c.** HATCH
- **d.** DETACH

8. This terminology is used to describe the process of placing a hatch pattern by defining the boundary and either keeping or removing the boundary:
- **a.** direct hatch
- **b.** boundary definition
- **c.** boundary hatch
- **d.** polyline boundary

9. Use the HATCH command to draw a hatch pattern with its individual elements displayed by entering the hatch name like this:
- **a.** -ANSI31
- **b.** +ANSI31
- **c.** <ANSI31>
- **d.** *ANSI31

10. This command is used to edit existing hatch patterns:
- **a.** HEDIT
- **b.** HATCHEDIT
- **c.** EDITHATCH
- **d.** HATCHED

MATCHING

Match each term to the correct description by writing the appropriate number in each box at the left.

- ☐ Associative
- ☐ BHATCH
- ☐ Boundary
- ☐ Boundary set
- ☐ Direct
- ☐ HATCH
- ☐ HATCHEDIT
- ☐ Island
- ☐ Preview
- ☐ Solid
- ☐ Style
- ☐ User-defined

1. This hatch pattern allows you to fill objects.
2. This command is used to draw associative hatch patterns.
3. This command is used to change existing hatch patterns.
4. This option allows you to create simple hatch patterns.
5. These hatch patterns are automatically changed when the hatch boundary is edited.
6. This allows you to look at the hatch pattern before it is applied to the drawing.
7. This command is used to draw hatch patterns at the keyboard.
8. This is a closed feature within a hatch boundary.
9. This is the shape that encloses the hatch pattern.
10. This hatch option is used when you want to define a hatch boundary and either keep or remove the boundary when done.
11. This option is used to determine how internal features are hatched.
12. This is the object that AutoCAD LT analyzes when you pick a point.

WORD SCRAMBLE

Unscramble the five scrambled words below, one letter to each square, to form five AutoCAD LT–related words:

RBYODUAN

TAHHC

EIVPWER

AESLC

ADINLS

Unscramble the circled letters to the left to form the special answer, as suggested by the illustration.

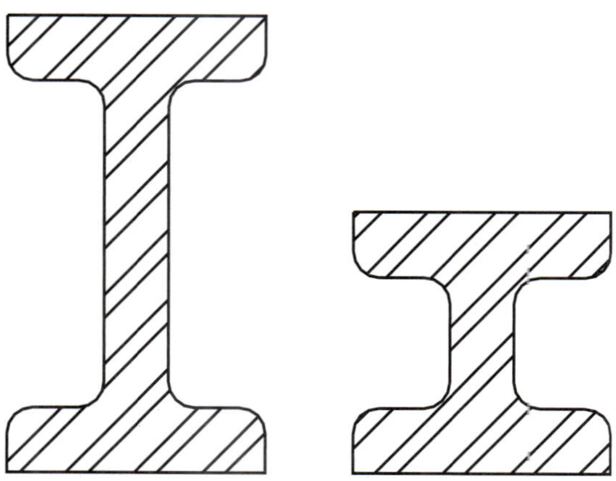

PROJECTS

Set up the following drawing projects with layers that relate to the type of drawing as outlined and discussed in Chapter 5.

INCH

10.1 Collar

Given the pictorial drawing of the object below, draw a front view and half sectional view. Do not draw dimensions. Save as P10.1.

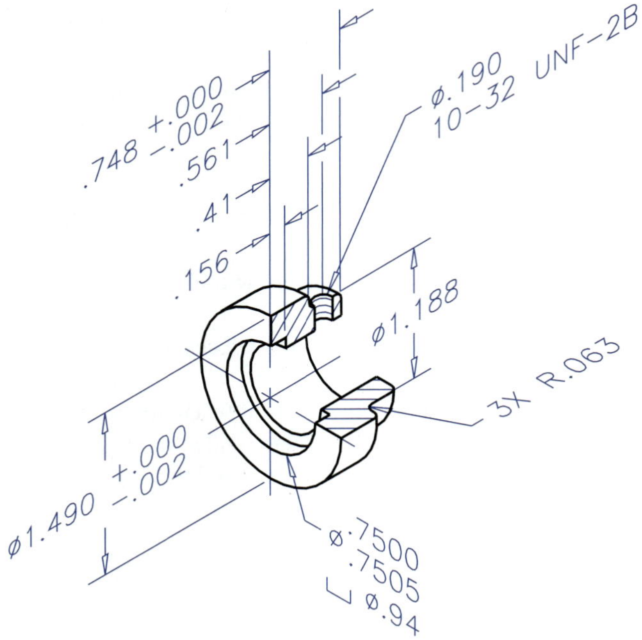

INCH

10.2 Pipe Connector

Given the pictorial drawing of the object below, draw a front and top view and a full sectional view. Do not draw dimensions. Save as P10.2. (Note: Only half of the object is shown in the pictorial.)

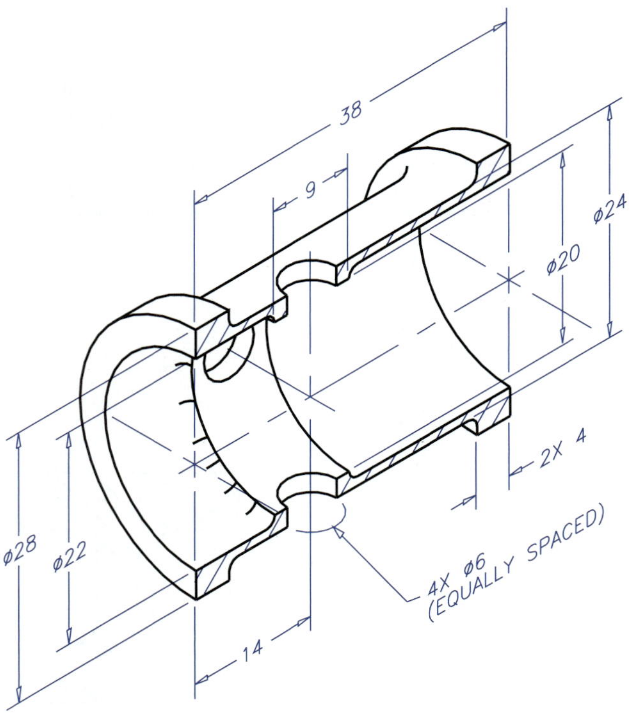

INCH

10.3 Arm

Given the pictorial drawing of the object below, draw a front and side view and a revolved section. Do not draw dimensions. Save as P10.3.

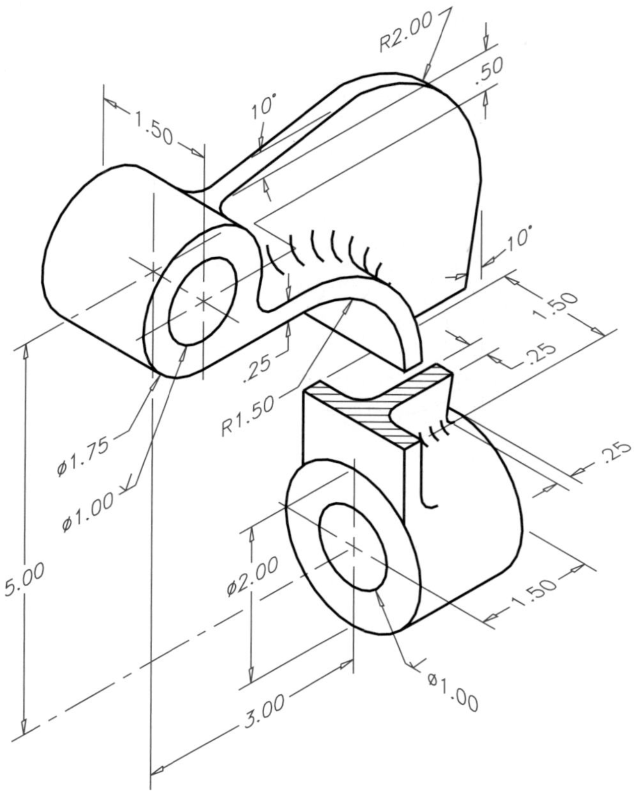

INCH

10.4 Spur Gear
Draw the views of the gear and provide the spur gear data chart. Do not draw dimensions. Save as P10.4. *Note:* Make undimensioned features approximate for students who have not studied gears and gear formulas.

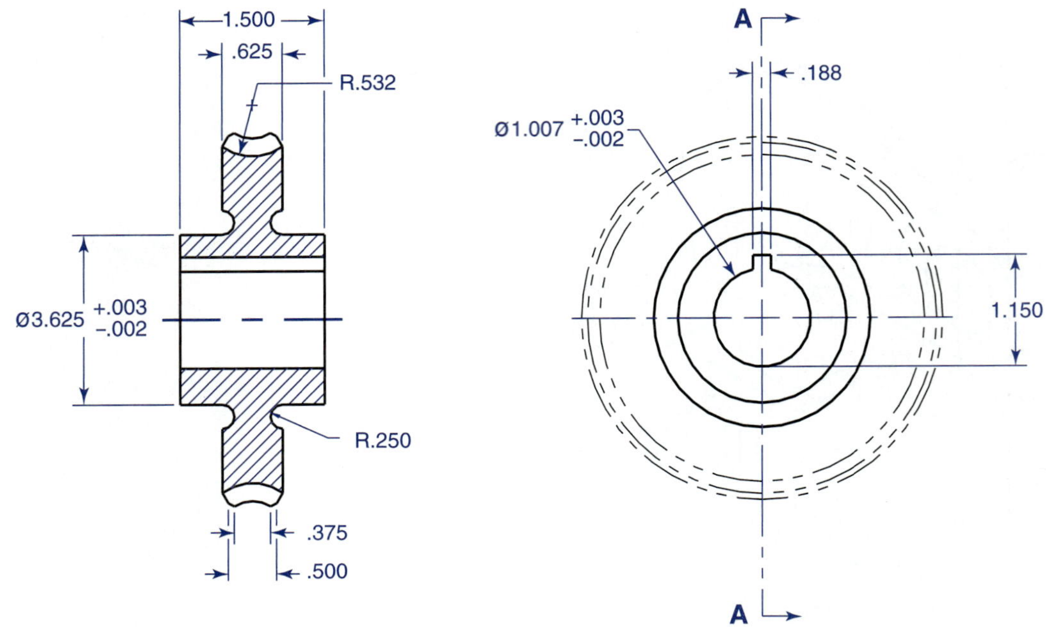

SECTION A–A

SPUR GEAR DATA	
DIAMETRAL PITCH	8
NUMBER OF TEETH	27
PRESSURE ANGLE	20°
PITCH DIAMETER	3.375
BASE CIRCLE DIAMETER	3.6187
CIRCULAR PITCH	.3927
CIRCULAR THICKNESS	.1964
ROOT DIAMETER	3.125

10.5 Draw the structural detail without dimensions and notes. Save as P10.5.

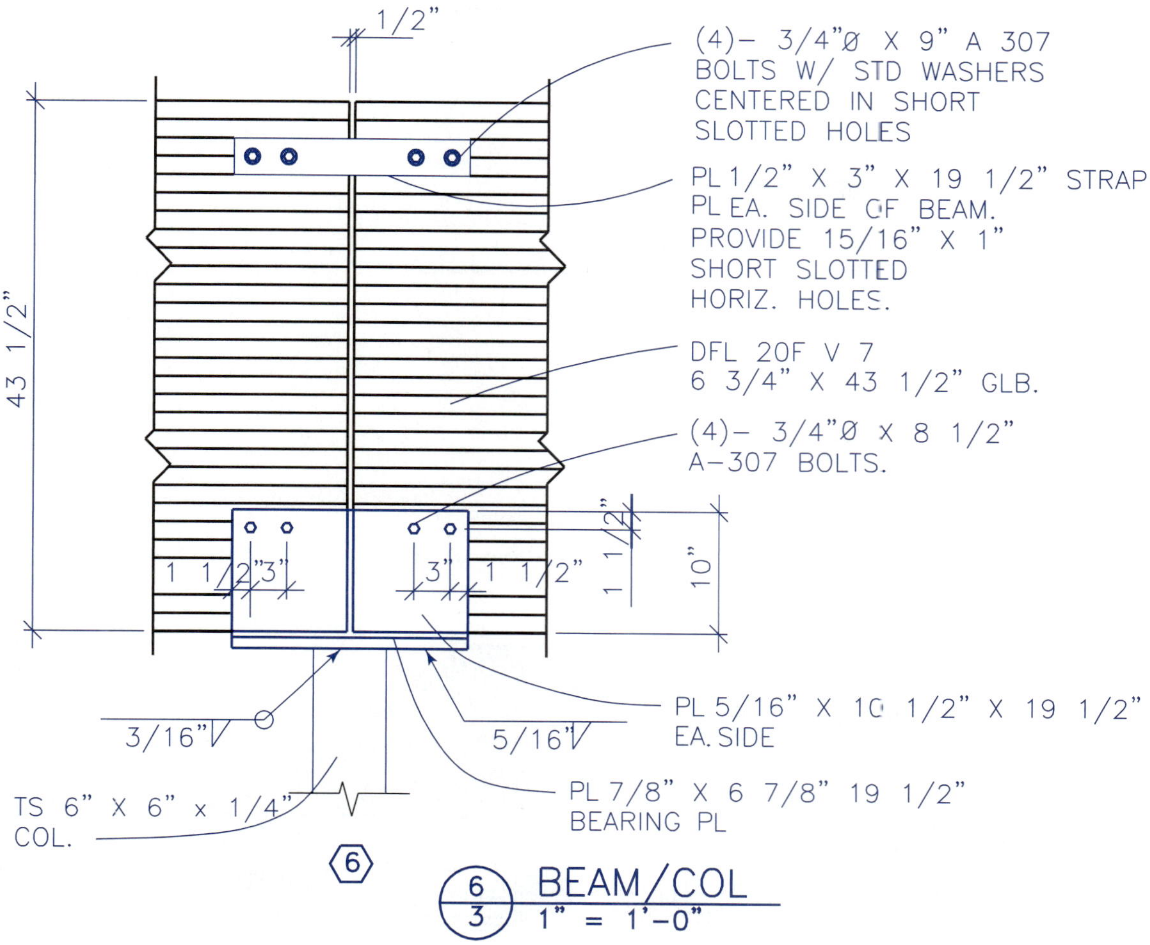

10.6 Draw the floor plan symbols without notes. Save as P10.6. (Note: Use similar symbols if the exact representation is not available.)

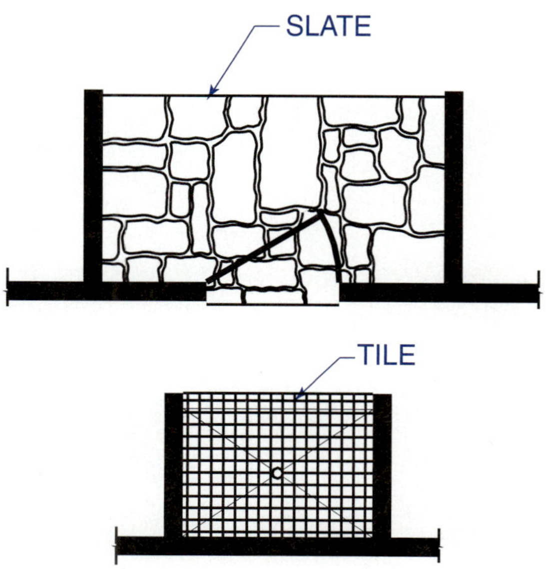

10.7 Draw the floor plan fireplace without notes or dimensions. Save as P10.7.

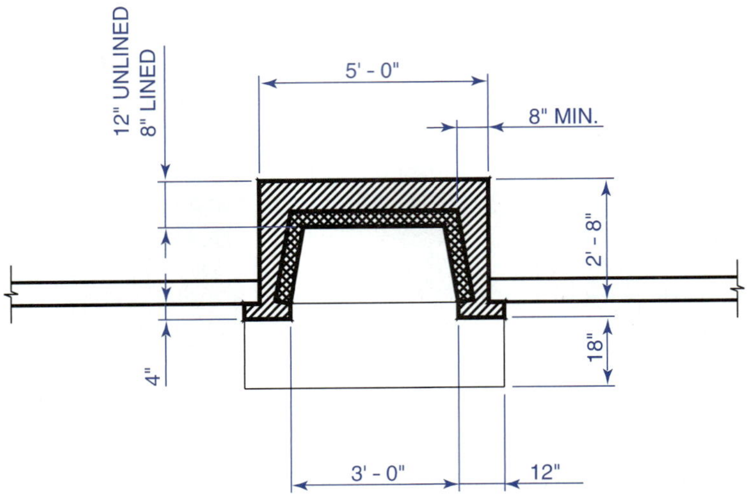

10.8 Draw the elevation shown below. The exact dimensions are up to you. Save as P10.8.

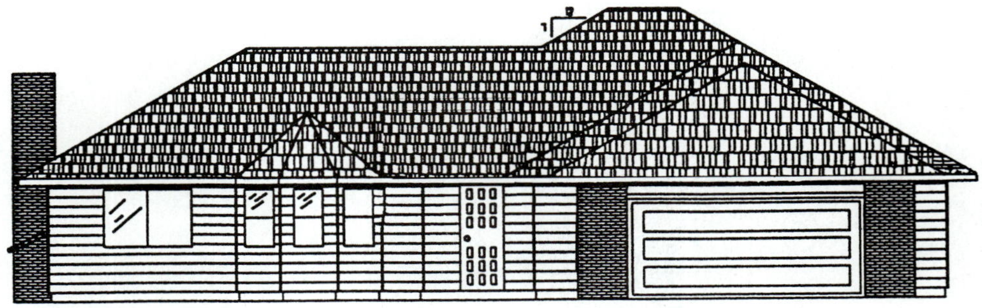

10.9 Design a company logo similar to the one shown below. Use the CityBlueprint or Stylus BT font. Save as P10.9.

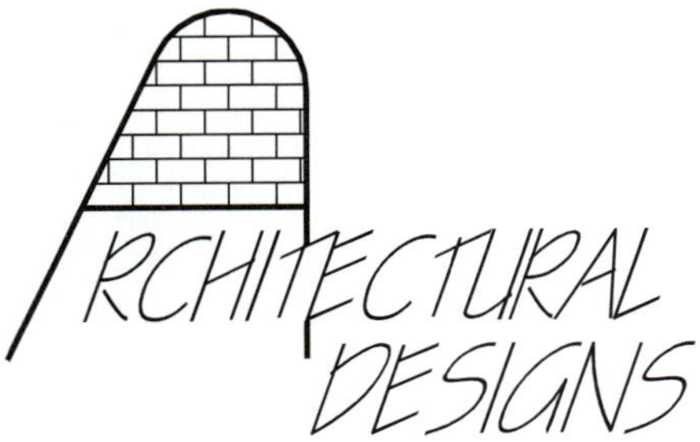

10.10 Draw the bar graph shown below. Use the ROMANS and ROMAND fonts. Save as P10.10.

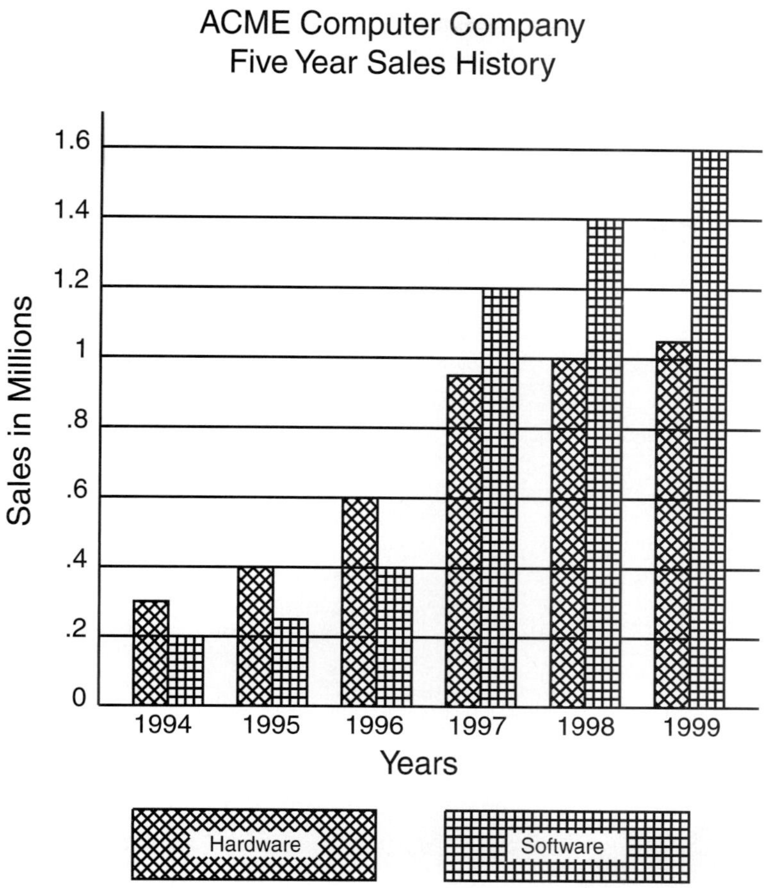

10.11 Design one of the holes for a golf course. Include the same features shown in the following proposal. Label each area with CityBlueprint or Stylus BT font. Be sure the hatch patterns do not cross the text. Save the drawing as P10.11.

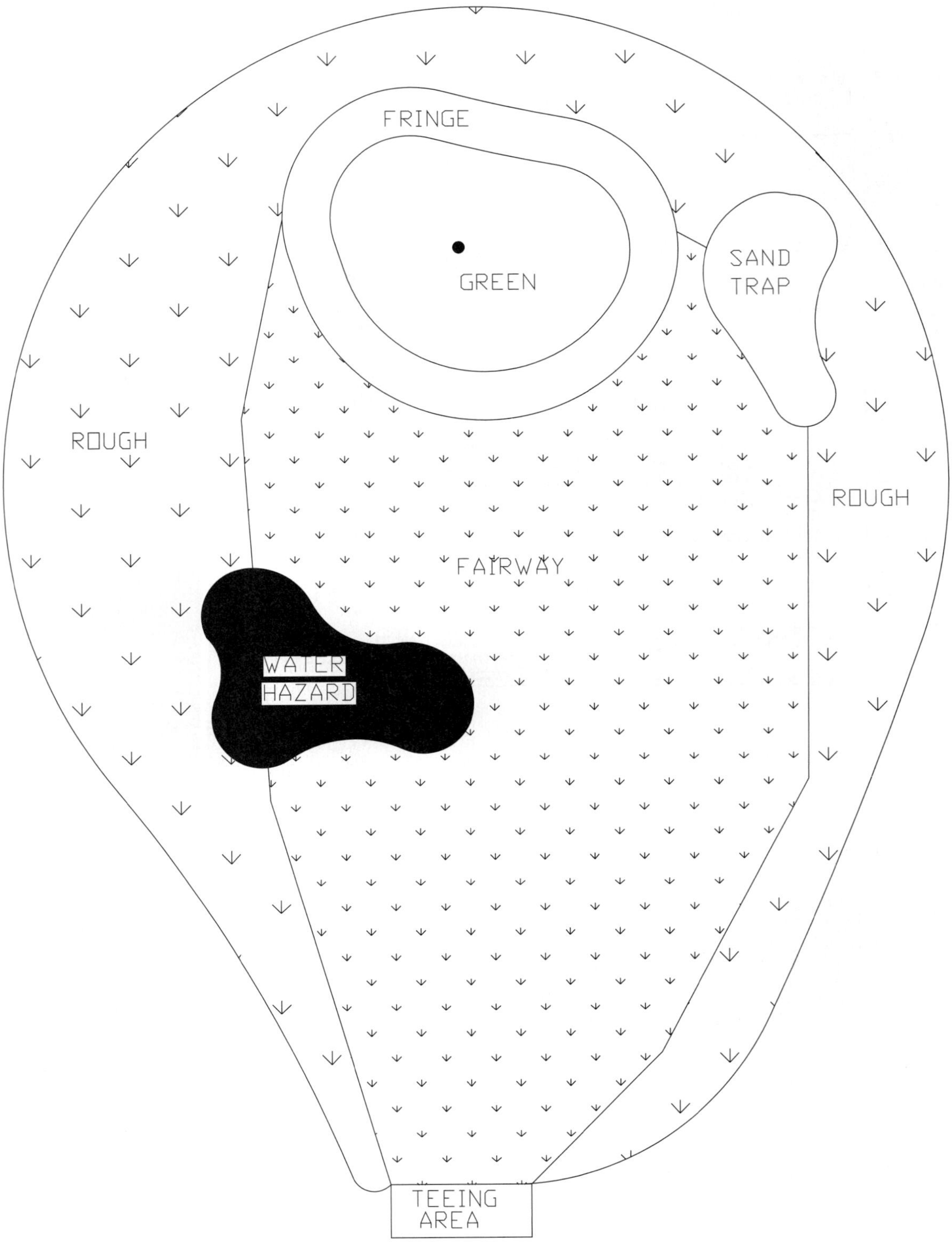

10.12 Design a landscaping plan similar to the following example. Include all the same characteristics, linetypes, hatch patterns, and shapes. Include the legend and display all text. Use CityBlueprint or Stylus BT font. Save the drawing as P10.12.

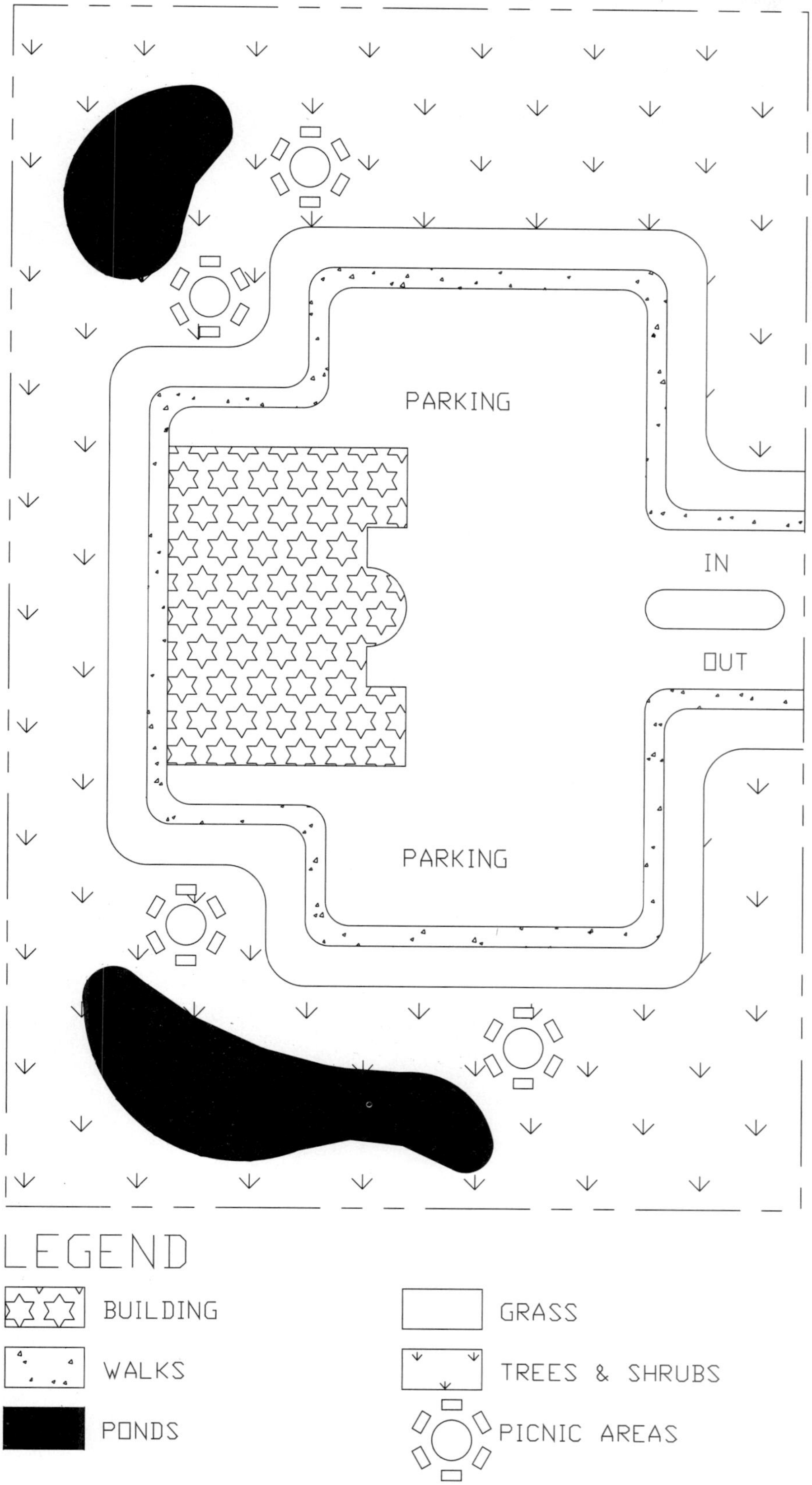

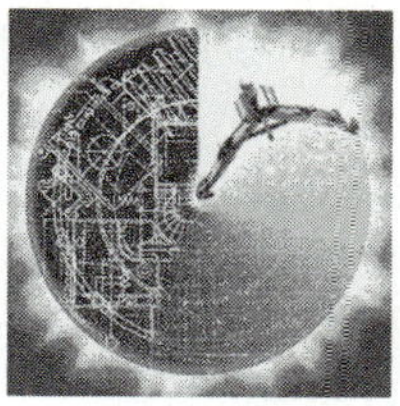

CHAPTER 11

Dimensioning a Drawing

LEARNING GOALS

- Draw linear dimensions.
- Select objects for direct dimensioning.
- Create chain and datum dimensions.
- Draw dimensions on slanted objects and angles.
- Dimension circles and arcs.
- Create arrowless (ordinate) dimensions.
- Manage dimension styles for your applications.
- Change dimension variables.
- Set tolerance values with dimension text.
- Draw a geometric tolerance symbol.
- Establish prefixes and suffixes with dimension text.
- Draw leader lines and notes.
- Edit existing dimensions.
- Change the variables of existing dimensions.
- Perform dimensioning at the command line.

So far, you have learned how to draw and edit objects, place text on a drawing, and prepare sections and other graphic designs. Drawings for manufacturing, architecture, construction, and other fields are usually incomplete without dimensions. ***Dimensions*** are defined as numerical values expressed in appropriate units of measure and indicated on a drawing and in other documents. Dimension numerals are placed along with lines, symbols, and notes to define the size and geometric or construction characteristics of a feature, part, or construction process or building component. Dimension numerals in mechanical manufacturing drafting are given in decimal inches or in metric units of millimeters. Mechanical drafting usually uses ***unidirectional dimensioning,*** in which all of the dimension numerals are placed horizontally and read from the bottom of the sheet. Dimensions in architectural drafting are given in feet and inches or in millimeters or meters. Civil drafting projects for mapping often use feet and decimal feet or metric units in millimeters, meters, and kilometers. Architectural, structural, and civil drafting usually use ***aligned dimensioning,*** in which text for horizontal dimensions is placed horizontally and reads from the bottom of the sheet, text for vertical dimensions is placed vertically and reads from the right side of the sheet, and dimensions placed at an angle have the text placed at the same angle. Electronic drafting projects use either decimal inches or millimeters and use either unidirectional or aligned dimensioning.

Dimensions fall into two types, size dimensions and location dimensions. ***Size dimensions*** are used to provide the measurements for the size of features and objects. ***Location dimensions*** are used to locate features and objects. Notes are also placed on drawings. ***Notes*** are not normally part of the dimensions but they may contain dimensional information. The two types of notes are general notes and specific notes. ***General notes*** supply information that applies to the entire drawing. ***Specific notes,*** also known as local notes, apply to specific features on the drawing and may be connected to the feature with a leader line.

Dimensioning standards for mechanical manufacturing drafting are recommended by the American Society of Mechanical Engineers in the document ASME Y14.5M-1994, *Dimensioning and Tolerancing.* Examples of many dimensioning standards and practices are displayed in Appendix B of this text. Dimensioning practices for architectural, structural, electronic, and precision sheet metal drafting applications are different from mechanical drafting and all practices are discussed throughout this chapter.

AutoCAD LT provides powerful dimensioning capabilities for two-dimensional drawings. AutoCAD LT allows you to dimension linear and angular features as well as circles and arcs with diameter and radius dimensions. AutoCAD LT also lets you draw ordinate dimensions that are sometimes referred to as *arrowless dimensions.* Ordinate dimensions are drawn without the traditional dimension lines and arrowheads. Figure 11.1A shows dimension elements using traditional dimensioning, and Figure 11.1B is an example of ordinate dimensioning.

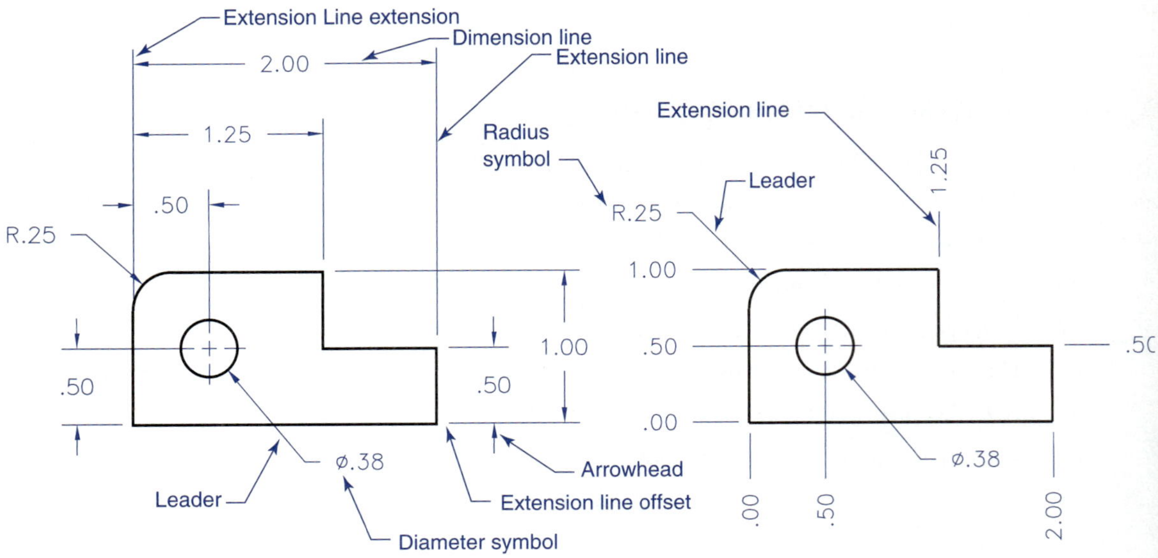

FIGURE 11.1 Basic dimensioning elements and practices. (A) Traditional dimension placement with extension and dimension lines having arrowheads. (B) Ordinate dimensioning, also known as arrowless dimensioning because there are no dimension lines and arrowheads.

The dimensioning variables can be set to control the way dimensions are presented. For example, you can control the size of the gap where the extension line meets the object, the arrowhead size and type, and the text style, height, and position.

This chapter shows you how to create dimension styles which contain the settings that are used on the types of drawings done at your school or company.

Field Notes

- When you dimension objects with AutoCAD LT, the objects are automatically measured exactly as you have drawn them. This makes it important for you to draw the original geometry accurately.
- Use the object snaps to your best advantage when dimensioning. AutoCAD LT dimensioning practices require that you locate features such as the extension line origin. This is accurately accomplished if you use an object snap such as INTersection. Setting the appropriate object snaps is a good idea when dimensioning.
- You should organize dimensions on a specific layer with an appropriate name and color suitable to your industry application.

Creating Dimensions

AutoCAD LT has a large variety of dimensioning capabilities that fall into five basic categories: linear, angular, diameter, radius, and ordinate.

Field Notes

Loading and docking toolbars was covered in Chapter 1. The easiest way to display the Dimension toolbar is to right-click on an existing toolbar button and pick Dimension from the shortcut menu. Optionally, you can pick Toolbars… from the View pull-down menu and place a check mark next to Dimension in the Toolbars list.

Drawing Linear Dimensions

Dimension

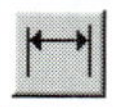

Linear Dimension

Dimension
Linear

DIMLINEAR
DLI

Linear dimensions are placed in a straight line that can be horizontal, vertical, or at an angle. Linear dimensions can be drawn by picking the Linear button in the Dimension toolbar, picking Linear from the Dimension pull-down menu, or by typing **DLI** or **DIMLINEAR** at the Command: prompt. When drawing linear dimensions, AutoCAD LT asks you to pick the first and second extension line origins followed by the dimension line location as shown in Figure 11.2. The command sequence works like this:

Command: **DLI** or **DIMLINEAR**↵
Specify first extension line origin or <select object>: ⟨*pick the first extension line origin*⟩
Specify second extension line origin: ⟨*pick the second extension line origin*⟩
Specify dimension line location or [Mtext/Text/Angle/Horizontal/Vertical/Rotated]: ⟨*pick the dimension line location*⟩
Dimension text = 2.2500
Command:

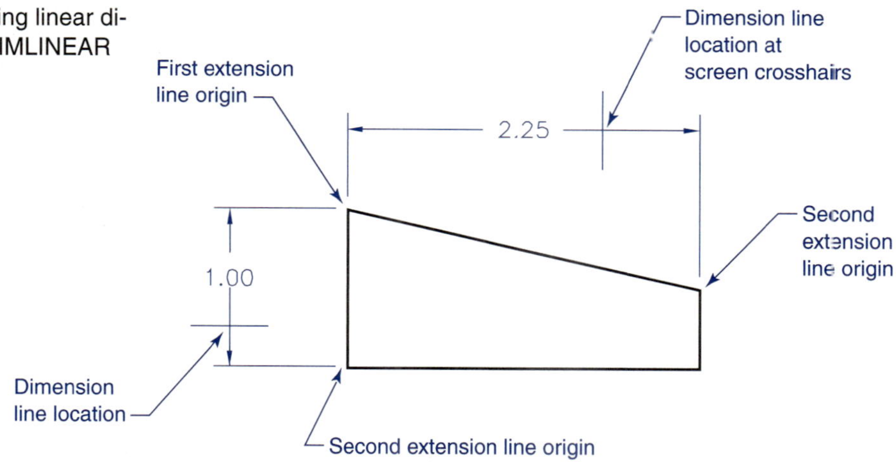

FIGURE 11.2 Placing linear dimensions with the DIMLINEAR command.

When you select the dimension line location, AutoCAD LT automatically centers the dimension text in a space provided in the dimension line. Later in this chapter you will learn how to place the text offset from center or above the dimension line for specific applications.

The first extension line origin can be on either end of a horizontal or vertical dimension. This is true unless the space between the extension lines is too small to accept the numeral with dimension line and arrowheads. When this happens, the first extension line origin establishes where the text is placed, as shown in Figure 11.3.

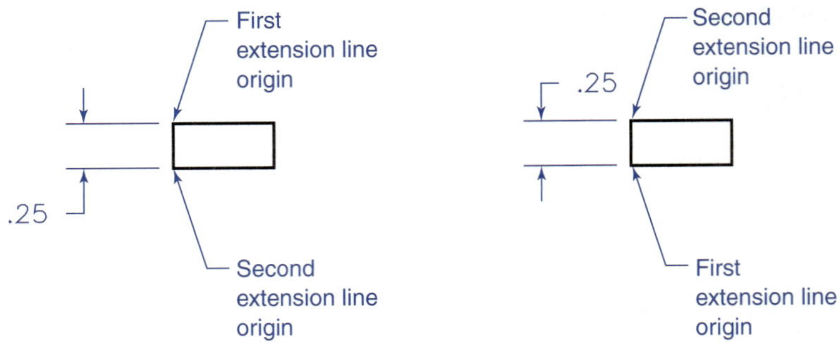

FIGURE 11.3 Placing linear dimensions in limited places. The first extension line origin determines the location of the dimension text.

Exercise 11.1 — Estimated time required: 5 min.

1. Begin a new drawing.
2. Draw an object and place a horizontal and vertical linear dimension similar to Figure 11.2.
3. Draw and dimension two objects similar to Figure 11.3.
4. Save as EX11.1, and close the drawing.

Selecting Objects to Dimension

The DIMLINEAR command can also be used to select objects for automatic dimensioning without picking the extension line origins. To do this, press the Enter key when you see the "Specify first extension line origin or <select object>:" prompt. You then get a Select objects prompt and a pick box for you to select the desired object on which to locate the dimension line and approve the dimension text or enter a new dimension numeral. Figure 11.4 shows this method being used to quickly dimension objects. The command sequence works like this:

Command: **DLI** or **DIMLINEAR**↵
Specify first extension line origin or <select object>: ↵
Select object to dimension: ⟨*pick the object*⟩
Specify dimension line location or [Mtext/Text/Angle/Horizontal/Vertical/Rotated]: ⟨*pick the dimension line location*⟩
Dimension text = 1.0000
Command:

FIGURE 11.4 Dimensioning objects directly by pressing Enter to select objects to dimension option of the DIMLINEAR command.

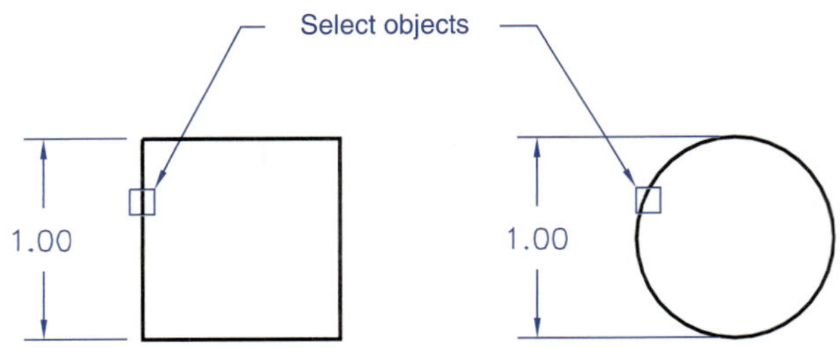

Exercise 11.2 — Estimated time required: 5 min.

1. Begin a new drawing.
2. Draw two objects and place a horizontal or vertical linear dimension similar to that shown in Figure 11.4 by pressing Enter to select object option of the DIMLINEAR command.
3. Save as EX11.2, and close the drawing.

Using the Other DIMLINEAR Options

The DIMLINEAR command has options that allow you to change the dimension text value, change the text angle, place the dimension either only horizontally or vertically, or place the dimension line at a desired angle other than horizontal or vertical. The options are found in the "Specify dimension line location or [Mtext/Text/ Angle/Horizontal/Vertical/Rotated]:" prompt. The following discussion explains each of the DIMLINEAR options:

Mtext—Type **M** and press Enter to use the Mtext option. Doing this opens the Multiline Text Editor shown in Figure 11.5. When this dialog box opens, the text cursor is in front of angle bracket (<>) symbols, which represent the default text. The default text is the actual distance between the extension lines. If you want to place a diameter symbol in front of the current text, open the Symbol list and pick Diameter or type the symbol code %%c. If you want to add the abbreviation MAX after the current text, move the text cursor following the angle brackets and type MAX. If you want to change the value, remove the angle brackets and type a new text value. You can also make any other changes available in the Multiline Text Editor. Pick the OK button when done. Figure 11.6 shows the objects from Figure 11.4 with text changes. Refer to Chapter 9 for additional information about using the Multiline Text Editor.

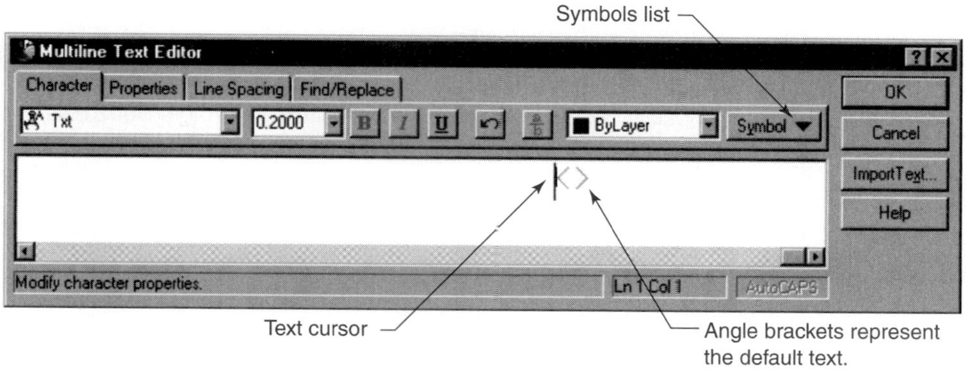

FIGURE 11.5 The Multiline Text Editor is accessed when using the Mtext option of the DIMLINEAR command. Use the cursor to enter additional text or change the current text. The angle brackets (<>) represent the actual dimension.

Text—Type **T** and press Enter to change dimension text at the prompt line. When you do this, AutoCAD LT identifies the current measurement in angle brackets. You can accept this value by pressing Enter, or you can type something else. For example, you can type angle brackets followed by MAX to have the current value placed in the drawing with the abbreviation MAX. Typing angle brackets keeps the current value, as shown in the following sequence:

Command: **DLI** or **DIMLINEAR**↵
Specify first extension line origin or <select object>: ↵
Select object to dimension: ⟨*pick object to dimension*⟩
Specify dimension line location or [Mtext/Text/Angle/Horizontal/Vertical/Rotated]: **T**↵
Enter dimension text <1.0000>: **<> MAX**↵
Specify dimension line location or [Mtext/Text/Angle/Horizontal/Vertical/Rotated]: ⟨*pick dimension line location*⟩
Dimension text = 1.0000
Command:

Type a different value if desired. To enter a symbol, such as diameter, type the control code. The control code for diameter is %%c. Refer to Chapter 9 for a refresher if needed.

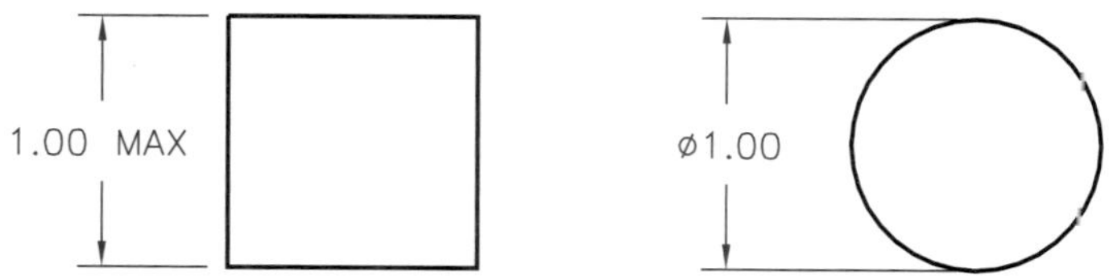

FIGURE 11.6 Using the Mtext option of the DIMLINEAR command to add text to the current value. The diameter symbol is added to the circle dimension.

Field Notes

It is recommended to leave the angle brackets as part of the dimension text when using the Mtext or Text options, because the angle brackets represent the default text. This is what maintains the associative nature of the dimension. If you want the flexibility of being able to edit dimensioned objects later, then they need to remain associative. Associative dimensions are automatically updated to match the change. Editing dimensions is discussed later in this chapter.

Angle—Type **A** and press Enter to use the Angle option. This option allows you to change the text angle as shown in Figure 11.7. For example, if you want to change the text angle from the horizontal default to 45°, type **45** when asked for the text angle and press Enter like this:

Specify dimension line location or [Mtext/Text/Angle/Horizontal/Vertical/Rotated]: **A↵**
Specify angle of dimension text: **45↵**
Specify dimension line location or [Mtext/Text/Angle/Horizontal/Vertical/Rotated]: ⟨*pick the dimension line location*⟩
Command:

A 45° text angle might not be commonly used, but rotating the text 90° is a typical application.

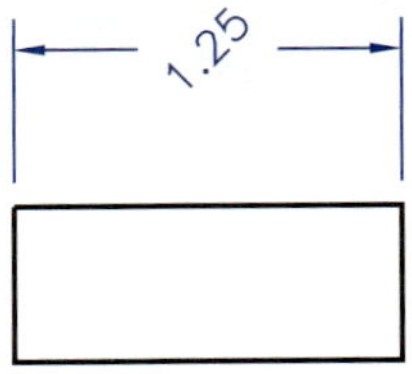

FIGURE 11.7 Using the Angle option of the DIMLINEAR command to place the text at an angle.

Horizontal or Vertical—AutoCAD LT interprets linear dimensions as being either vertical or horizontal by the distance from the origin to the dimension line. If the distance from the origin to the dimension line location is greatest on the Y axis, the dimension is interpreted to be horizontal. If the X axis distance is farther, the dimension is interpreted as vertical. You can see this work by moving the cursor to different locations as you drag the dimension line. If the default interpretation does not represent the type of dimension that you want to create, the Horizontal or Vertical option can be used to specify the type of dimension you want. To do this, type either **H** or **V,** as desired, and press Enter. AutoCAD LT then asks you to pick the dimension line location and also provides the Text and Angle options again in case you need them:

Specify dimension line location or [Mtext/Text/Angle/Horizontal/Vertical/Rotated]: **H↵**
Specify dimension line location or [Mtext/Text/Angle]: ⟨*pick the dimension line location or enter another option*⟩

Rotated—This option lets you rotate the dimension line to any desired angle. This is used for situations when the object is at an angle and you want the dimension line parallel to the object. The command sequence for the dimension placed in Figure 11.8 is as follows:

Command: **DLI** or **DIMLINEAR**
Specify first extension line origin or <select object>: ⟨*pick first extension line origin*⟩
Specify second extension line origin: ⟨*pick second extension line origin*⟩
Specify dimension line location or [Mtext/Text/Angle/Horizontal/Vertical/Rotated]: RO↵
Specify angle of dimension line <0>: 15↵
Specify dimension line location or [Mtext/Text/Angle/Horizontal/Vertical/Rotated]: ⟨*pick dimension line location*⟩
Dimension text = 2.00
Command:

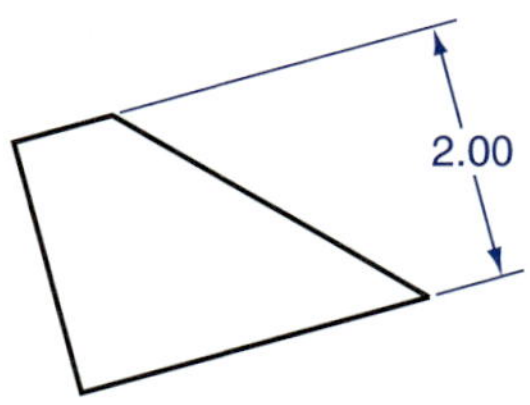

FIGURE 11.8 Using the Rotated option of the DIMLINEAR command to place the dimension line at a desired angle.

Exercise 11.3 — Estimated time required: 5 min.

1. Begin a new drawing or use one of your prototypes.
2. Draw two objects and place vertical linear dimensions using the Text option to change the dimension text similar to that shown in Figure 11.6.
3. Draw an object and dimension it with text at an angle similar to that of Figure 11.7.
4. Draw an object and dimension it similar to that of Figure 11.8. Use a rotation angle that matches the rotation of the part.
5. Save as EX11.3, and close the drawing.

Drawing Chain and Datum Dimensions

Dimension

Continue Dimension

Dimension
Continue

DIMCONTINUE
DCO

Chain dimensioning is where the next dimension continues from the previous dimension. This is also referred to as *point-to-point dimensioning* and is called *continuous dimensioning* by AutoCAD LT. Chain dimensioning is commonly used in architectural drafting but can be used in mechanical drafting depending on the design factors. The initial dimension must be placed before drawing the attached chain dimensions. After placing the first dimension, AutoCAD LT automatically connects the next dimensions as you pick the second extension line origin. You can perform chain dimensioning by picking the Continue Dimension button in the Dimension toolbar, by picking Continue in the Dimension pull-down menu, or by typing **DCO** or **DIMCONTINUE** at the Command: prompt. The command sequence works like this and is displayed in Figure 11.9:

Command: **DLI** or **DIMLINEAR**↵
Specify first extension line origin or <select object>: ⟨*pick the first extension line origin*⟩
Specify second extension line origin: ⟨*pick the second extension line origin*⟩
Specify dimension line location or [Mtext/Text/Angle/Horizontal/Vertical/Rotated]: ⟨*pick the dimension line location*⟩
Dimension text = 1.50
Command: DCO or DIMCONTINUE↵
Specify a second extension line origin or [Undo/Select] <Select>: ⟨*pick the next extension line origin*⟩
Dimension text = 1.25
Specify a second extension line origin or [Undo/Select] <Select>: ⟨*pick the next extension line origin*⟩
Dimension text = 1.25
Specify a second extension line origin or [Undo/Select] <Select>: ↵
Select continued dimension: ↵
Command:

The previous command sequence placed chain dimensions immediately after placing the first linear dimension. You can also come back and place chain dimensions any time by using the Select continued dimension: option of the DIMCONTINUE command. The Select continued dimension: option is automatically

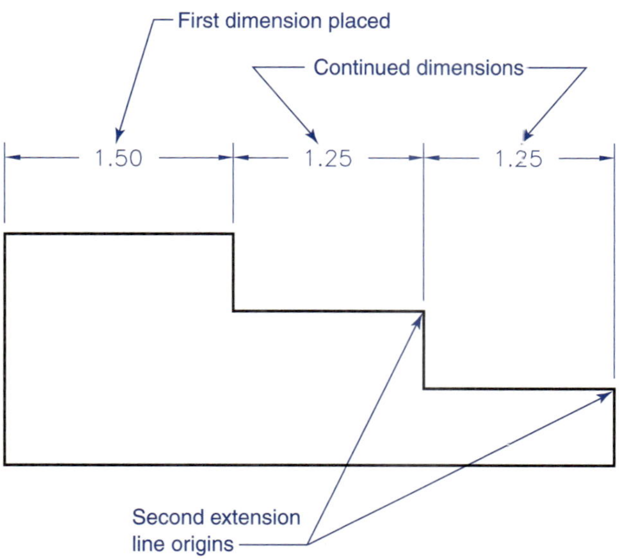

FIGURE 11.9 Creating chain dimensions with the DIMCONTINUE command.

issued at the end of the DIMCONTINUE command sequence, as you can see in the previous example. This prompt wants you to select an existing dimension to continue dimensions from. You can also use the Select option to get the Select continued dimension: prompt immediately:

Command: **DCO** or **DIMCONTINUE**↵
Specify a second extension line origin or [Undo/Select] <Select>: ↵
Select continued dimension: ⟨*pick the dimension to continue from*⟩
Specify a second extension line origin or [Undo/Select] <Select>: ⟨*pick the next extension line origin*⟩
Dimension text = 1.25
Specify a second extension line origin or [Undo/Select] <Select>: ↵
Select continued dimension: ↵
Command:

The Undo option allows you to undo the previously placed continue dimension. Just type **U** and press Enter:

Specify a second extension line origin or [Undo/Select] <Select>: **U**↵
Specify a second extension line origin or [Undo/Select] <Select>: **U**↵
Command has been completely undone.
Specify a second extension line origin or [Undo/Select] <Select>: ⟨*pick the next extension line origin or enter an option*⟩

Dimension
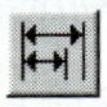
Baseline Dimension

Dimension
Baseline

DIMBASELINE
DBA

In ***datum dimensioning*** every dimension begins at the same starting place. AutoCAD LT calls this ***baseline dimensioning.*** Datum dimensioning is commonly used in mechanical drafting when the dimensions of a particular feature or features must be independent of other dimensions. Datum dimensioning is similar to chain dimensioning in the way it is created. The initial dimension must be placed before additional datum dimensions can be established. After placing the first dimension, AutoCAD LT automatically connects the next dimensions as you pick the second extension line origin. You can perform datum dimensioning by picking the Baseline Dimension button in the Dimension toolbar, by picking Baseline in the Dimension pull-down menu, or by typing **DBA** or **DIMBASELINE** at the Command: prompt. The command sequence works like this after placing the first dimension. Figure 11.10 illustrates the process:

Command: **DBA** or **DIMBASELINE**↵
Specify a second extension line origin or [Undo/Select] <Select>: ⟨*pick the next extension line origin*⟩
Dimension text = 2.75
Specify a second extension line origin or [Undo/Select] <Select>: ⟨*pick the next extension line origin*⟩
Dimension text = 4.00
Specify a second extension line origin or [Undo/Select] <Select>: ↵
Select base dimension: ↵
Command:

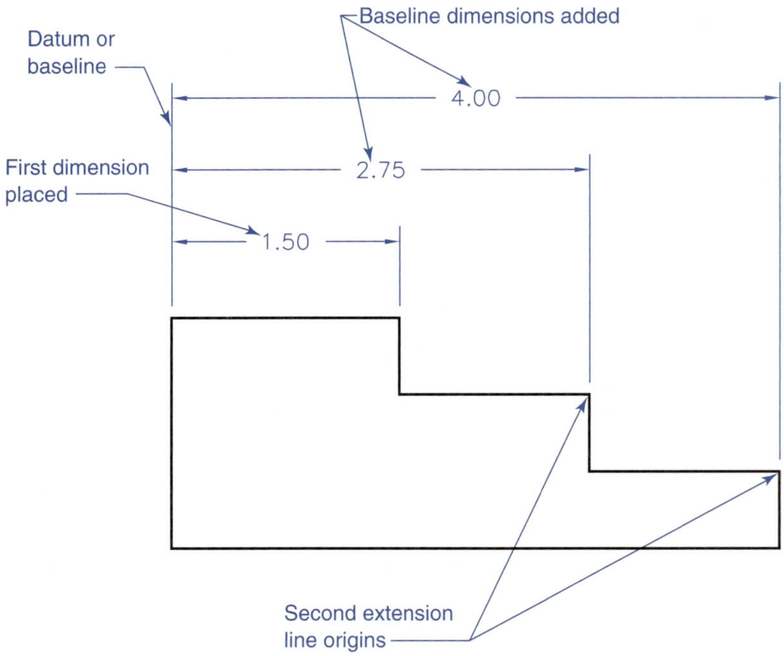

FIGURE 11.10 Creating datum dimensions with the DIMBASE command.

If you want to come back later and add datum dimensions to an existing dimension, you can use the Select base dimension: prompt or the Select option in the same manner as was demonstrated with chain dimensioning in the previous discussion. The Undo option also works, as previously described.

Field Notes

When continuing a baseline or continuous dimension that was created previously, it is important to select an appropriate point at the "Select base dimension:" or "Select continued dimension:" prompt. Pick a point on the dimension that is near the origin point of the extension line from which the new dimensions are to be constructed.

Exercise 11.4 — Estimated time required: 5 min.

1. Begin a new drawing.
2. Draw an object and place chain dimensions as shown in Figure 11.9.
3. Draw an object and place datum dimensions as shown in Figure 11.10.
4. Save as EX11.4, and close the drawing.

Drawing Dimensions Aligned with an Angled Object

Dimension

Aligned Dimension

Dimension
Aligned

DIMALIGNED
DAL

Dimensions can be drawn aligned to a slanted object by using the Rotated option of the DIMLINEAR command as previously explained, or by using the DIMALIGNED command. With the Rotated option, you must specify the angle, but with DIMALIGNED the dimension line is automatically aligned with the extension line origin points. These dimensions are placed by picking the Aligned Dimension button in the Dimension toolbar, by picking Aligned in the Dimension pull-down menu, or by typing **DAL** or **DIMALIGNED** at the Command: prompt. Look at Figure 11.11 as you follow this command sequence:

Command: **DAL** or **DIMALIGNED**↵
Specify first extension line origin or <select object>: ⟨*pick first extension line origin*⟩
Specify second extension line origin: ⟨*pick next extension line origin*⟩
Specify dimension line location or [Mtext/Text/Angle]: ⟨*pick the dimension line location*⟩
Dimension text = 1.41
Command:

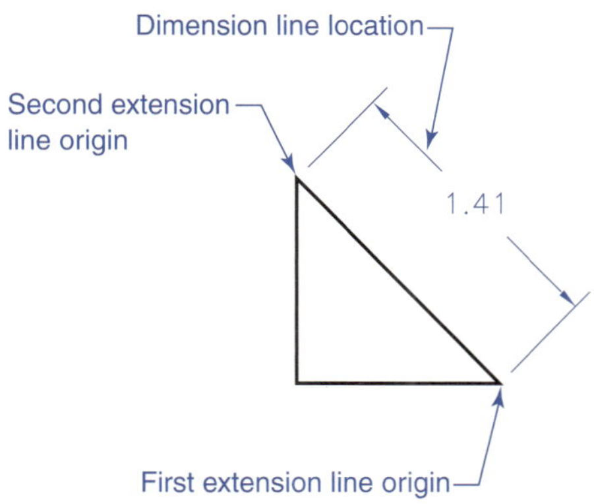

FIGURE 11.11 Placing dimensions at an angle with the DIMALIGNED command.

As with the other dimensioning commands, you can press Enter to pick objects directly for dimensioning when you see the press Enter to select prompt. You can also change the text value or the text angle by using the Mtext/Text/Angle options, as previously explained.

Exercise 11.5 — Estimated time required: 5 min.

1. Begin a new drawing.
2. Draw an object and place an aligned dimension as shown in Figure 11.11.
3. Save as EX11.5, and close the drawing.

Dimensioning Angles

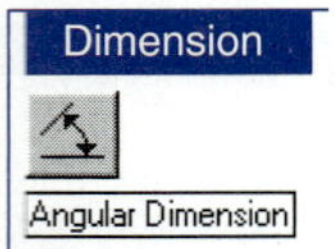

Dimension
Angular

DIMANGULAR
DAN

Angles are dimensioned in degrees with an arc-shaped dimension line. This is done by picking the Angular Dimension button in the Dimension toolbar, by picking Angular in the Dimension pull-down menu, or by typing **DAN** or **DIMANGULAR** at the Command: prompt. When entering this command, AutoCAD LT asks you to select an arc, circle, or line. After selecting the objects, you move the cursor to dynamically place the desired dimension line and text location. As you look at Figure 11.12, follow this command sequence for creating an angular dimension to line objects:

Command: **DAN** or **DIMANGULAR**↵
Select arc, circle, line, or <specify vertex>: ⟨*pick the first line*⟩
Select second line: ⟨*pick the second line*⟩
Specify dimension arc line location or [Mtext/Text/Angle]: ⟨*pick the dimension line location*⟩
Dimension text = 45.00
Command:

FIGURE 11.12 Drawing angular dimensions with the DIMANGULAR command. (A) Dimension numeral placed within the dimension line. (B) Dimension numeral placed outside the dimension line due to the limited space inside the dimension line.

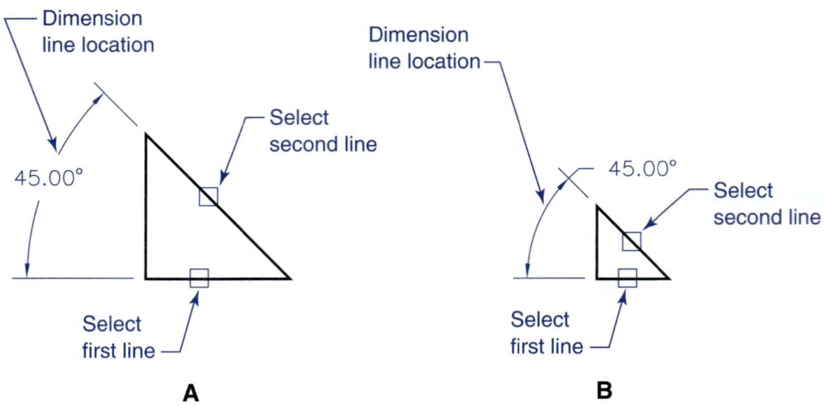

You can also apply an angular dimension to an arc or circle. When selecting an arc, the angle vertex is at the arc center and the angular measurement is to the arc endpoints. When selecting a circle, the angle vertex is at the center of the circle and the angle is established where you pick on the circle. Figure 11.13 shows an angle dimensioned to an arc and circle.

FIGURE 11.13 Using the DIMANGULAR command to dimension to an arc and circle.

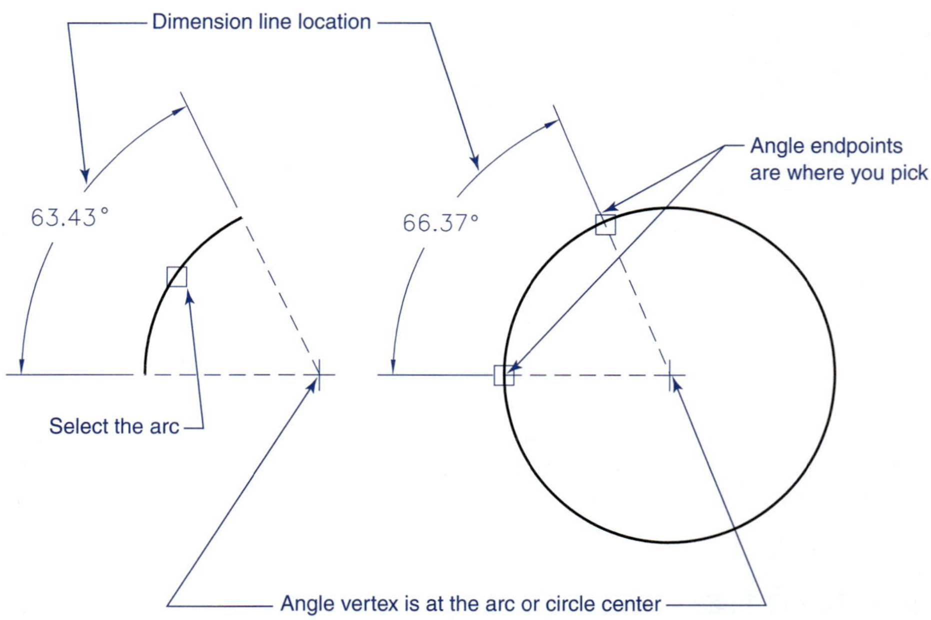

When you press Enter at the first DIMANGULAR prompt, you are asked to pick the angle vertex and the angle endpoints. This gives you the flexibility to pick these points on an object or to place an angle dimension without an object. The command sequence works like this and is displayed in Figure 11.14:

Command: **DAN** or **DIMANGULAR**↵
Select arc, circle, line, or <specify vertex>: ↵
Specify angle vertex: ⟨*pick angle vertex location*⟩
Specify first angle endpoint: ⟨*pick the first endpoint of the angle*⟩
Specify second angle endpoint: ⟨*pick the second endpoint of the angle*⟩
Specify dimension arc line location or [Mtext/Text/Angle]: ⟨*pick the dimension line location*⟩
Dimension text = 45
Command:

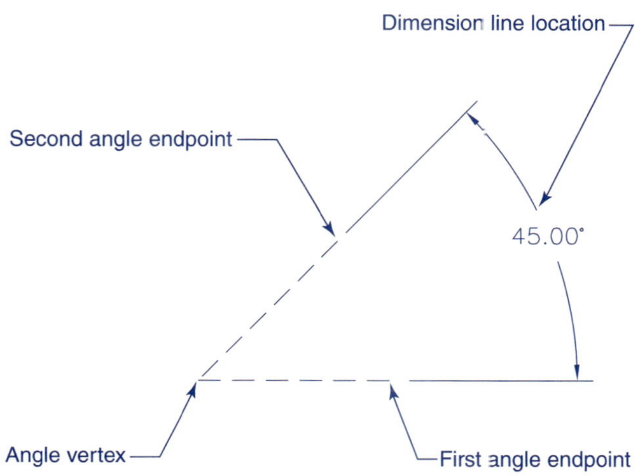

FIGURE 11.14 Using the DIMANGULAR command's RETURN option to dimension an angle based on selecting the vertex and angle endpoints.

Exercise 11.6 — Estimated time required: 5 min.

1. Begin a new drawing.
2. Draw objects and place angular dimensions as shown in Figure 11.12.
3. Draw objects and place angular dimensions as shown in Figure 11.13.
4. Draw an angular dimension similar to that shown in Figure 11.14.
5. Save as EX11.6, and close the drawing.

Dimensioning Circles and Arcs

Dimension

Diameter Dimension

Dimension
Diameter

DIMDIAMETER
DDI

The American National Standards Institute (ANSI) and the American Society of Mechanical Engineers (ASME) recommend that a circle be dimensioned with a diameter and an arc be dimensioned with a radius. AutoCAD LT makes this practice easy by automatically placing a diameter symbol (∅) in front of the numeral when dimensioning a circle and a radius symbol (R) in front of the numeral when dimensioning an arc. You can dimension an arc or circle with a diameter or radius dimension, but the ANSI/ASME recommendation is the normal practice.

Circles are dimensioned by picking Diameter in the Dimension pull-down menu, by picking the Diameter Dimension button on the Dimension toolbar, or by typing **DDI** or **DIMDIAMETER** at the Command: prompt. Look at Figure 11.15 as you follow this command sequence:

Command: **DDI** or **DIMDIAMETER**↵
Select arc or circle: ⟨*pick the circle*⟩
Dimension text = 1.50
Specify dimension line location or [Mtext/Text/Angle]: ⟨*pick the leader location*⟩
Command:

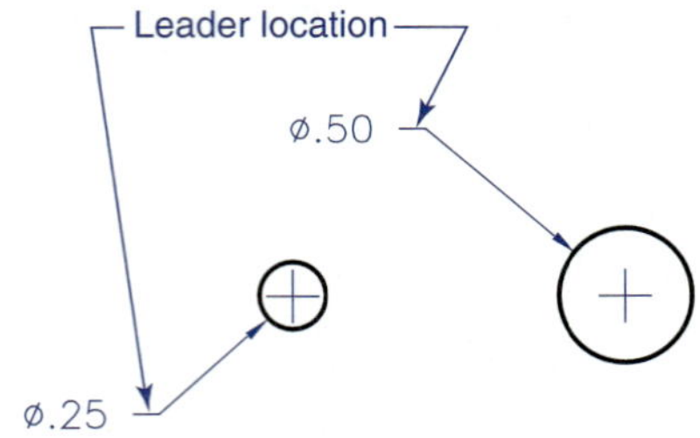

FIGURE 11.15 Dimensioning circles with the DIMDIAMETER command.

The previous command sequence allows you to change the dimension text. AutoCAD LT automatically places the diameter symbol with the default value. If you change the dimension text and remove the default text brackets (< >), to keep the diameter symbol, you need to type the code %%c before the new text. When asked for the dimension line location, you can drag the leader and pick the desired location. A leader and the diameter value are placed outside and a center mark is placed inside the circle. The leader automatically points to the center, as recommended by the ANSI/ASME standard. See Figure 11.15. Dimension variables that allow you more flexibility in the placement of the diameter dimension are used later in this chapter. The Mtext/Text/Angle options are available, as previously discussed.

Dimension

Radius Dimension

Dimension
Radius

DIMRADIUS
DRA

Arcs are dimensioned by picking Radius in the Dimension pull-down menu, by picking the Radius Dimension button in the Dimension toolbar, or by typing **DRA** or **DIMRADIUS.** Look at Figure 11.16 as you follow this command sequence:

Command: **DRA** or **DIMRADIUS**↵
Select arc or circle: ⟨*pick the arc*⟩
Dimension text = 0.75
Specify dimension line location or [Mtext/Text/Angle]: ⟨*pick the leader location*⟩
Command:

FIGURE 11.16 Dimensioning arcs with the DIMRADIUS command.

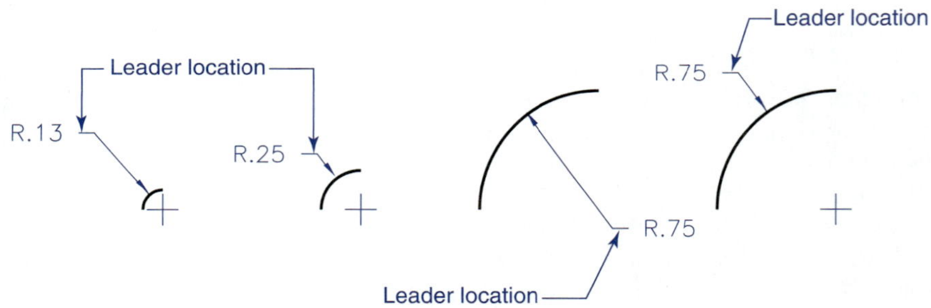

Dimensioning an arc is similar to dimensioning a circle. The size of the arc and the movement of your cursor determine the position of the dimension leader and text. AutoCAD LT automatically places the leader line pointing toward or through the arc or circle center as recommended by the ANSI/ASME standard. The Mtext/Text/Angle options are available, as previously discussed.

Field Notes

- If you want to add additional text to any dimension, you can add the desired text in front of or behind the default text angle brackets. This way, the default text is preserved—including diameter or radius symbols.
- The command aliases for dimensions are easier to master if you remember that they all follow the same simple rule. Look at the full command name, for example, DIMRADIUS or DIMDIAMETER. Use the first "D," skip the "IM" and use the next two letters. So the alias for **D**IM**RA**DIUS is **DRA**, and the alias for **D**IM**DI**AMETER is **DDI**.

Exercise 11.7 **Estimated time required: 5 min.**

1. Begin a new drawing.
2. Draw objects and place diameter dimensions as shown in Figure 11.15.
3. Draw objects and place radius dimensions as shown in Figure 11.16.
4. Save as EX11.7, and close the drawing.

Creating Ordinate Dimensions

Dimension

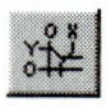

Ordinate Dimension

Dimension
Ordinate

DIMORDINATE
DOR

Ordinate dimensions are drawn without the traditional dimension lines and arrowheads. Ordinate dimensions are sometimes referred to as *arrowless dimensions* and are also called *arrowless tabular dimensions* when a table is used to give the size and specifications of features such as holes. (Figure 11.1 shows a comparison between traditional dimensioning and ordinate dimensioning.) Ordinate dimensions are drawn by picking the Ordinate Dimension button in the Dimension toolbar, by picking Ordinate in the Dimension pull-down menu, or by typing **DOR** or **DIMORDINATE** at the Command: prompt.

AutoCAD LT automatically places the ordinate dimension numeral at the end of an extension line from the feature you select. With ordinate dimensioning, the dimensions originate from datums. ***Datums*** are planes, points, surfaces, lines, or axes from which measurements are made. The datums on a part are usually zero, and dimensions to features on the part increase or decrease depending on their distance from the datums in the X and Y axes. By default, all coordinate locations are based on the WCS (World Coordinate System). The WCS is the base coordinate system that has been used throughout the text material to this point. You can define any number of new, customized coordinate systems. A custom coordinate system is called a User Coordinate System (UCS). Creating a new UCS can simplify many 3-D drafting procedures and also has many uses in 2-D drafting applications. Because the Ordinate dimensions in AutoCAD LT show the distance on the X or Y axis from the current origin point, the datum point must be at the 0,0 point coordinate location. By defining a new UCS, you can locate the 0,0 origin point anywhere in the drawing. You can create a new UCS for each view to dimension and return to the WCS when you are done dimensioning.

To create a new UCS for ordinate dimensioning applications, use the New option of the UCS command. This option prompts you to specify an origin point for the new UCS; you can enter a coordinate at the keyboard or pick a point on the screen. To prepare for dimensioning the part shown in Figure 11.17, the new origin is located at the lower left corner of the part.

Command: **UCS↵**
Current ucs name: *WORLD*
Enter an option [New/Move/orthoGraphic/Prev/Restore/Save/Del/?/World] <World>: **N↵**
Specify origin of new UCS or [ZAxis/3point/OBject/Face/View/X/Y/Z] <0,0,0>: 〈*enter the coordinates or pick the desired origin point*〉
Command

Unless the default drawing options have been changed, the UCS icon will appear at the new origin point. Because the WCS coordinate system is no longer active, the icon does not display the "W." After you finish dimensioning the view, you can restore the WCS by using the default "World" option of the UCS command:

Command: **UCS↵**
Current ucs name: *NO NAME*
Enter an option [New/Move/orthoGraphic/Prev/Restore/Save/Del/?/World] <World>: ↵
Command:

Dimension

Center Mark

Dimension
Center Mark

DIMCENTER
DCE

Now you are ready to dimension the features of the object unless the features are circles and arcs. For circles and arcs, you should dimension from a center mark, which needs to be drawn first. Center marks are drawn by picking the Center Mark button in the Dimension toolbar, by picking Center Mark in the Dimension pull-down menu, or by typing **DCE** or **DIMCENTER** at the Command: prompt. Figure 11.17B shows the center marks placed using this command:

Command: **DCE** or **DIMCENTER ↵**
Select arc or circle: 〈*pick the arc or circle*〉
Command:

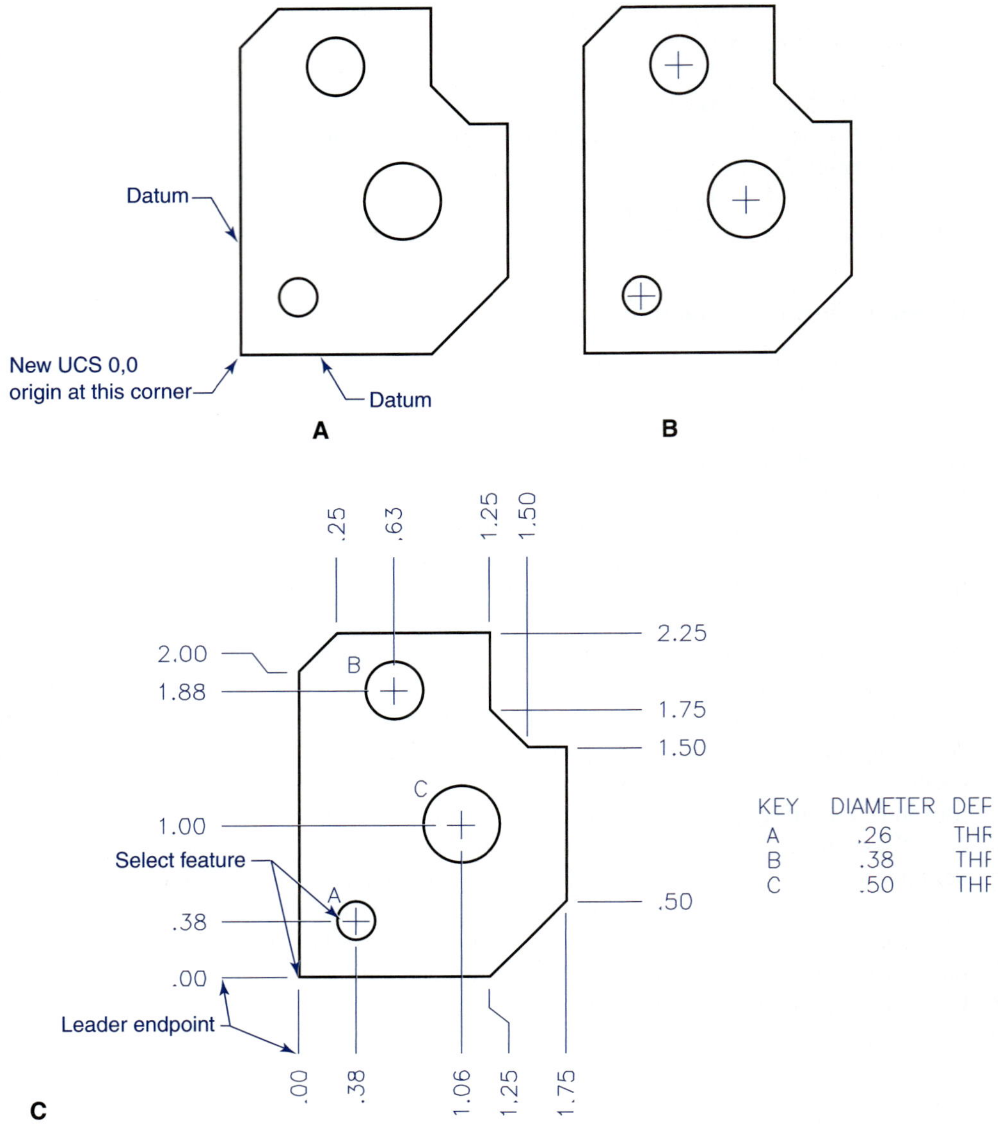

FIGURE 11.17 Datum dimensioning with the DIMORDINATE command. (A) The object to be dimensioned is shown with the datums identified and the UCS origin (0,0) placed to the intersection of the two datum surfaces. (B) The center marks are placed in the circle using the DIMCENTER command. (C) The object is completely dimensioned using the DIMORDINATE command. The hole key and table were added using the DTEXT command.

Now you are really ready to use the DIMORDINATE command. When using the DIMORDINATE command, you are asked to select the feature to dimension. You should use the object snaps for best advantage. For example, use the ENDpoint or INTersect object snap for corners and use the ENDpoint to snap to the center marks of circles and arcs. AutoCAD LT automatically offsets the extension line a short distance from the point you pick. This leaves the desired extension line gap between the object and the start of the extension line. During the ordinate dimensioning process, you select the feature to dimension and then move the screen cursor to pick the extension line endpoint. AutoCAD LT refers to the extension line endpoint as a *leader endpoint.* The extension line is dragged into place as you move the cursor. Look at Figure 11.17C as you follow this command sequence:

Command: **DOR** or **DIMORDINATE**↵
Specify feature location: ⟨*pick the feature to dimension*⟩
Specify leader endpoint or [Xdatum/Ydatum/Mtext/Text/Angle]: ⟨*pick the leader endpoint*⟩
Dimension text = .38
Command:

In Figure 11.17C the hole key and table are added using the MTEXT command.

Mechanical drafting practices often use ***unidirectional dimensioning,*** in which all of the dimensions and notes read from the bottom of the sheet. AutoCAD LT automatically places ordinate dimensions in the aligned dimensioning format. ***Aligned dimensioning*** is used when you want to read the dimensions from the bottom of the sheet for horizontal dimensions and from the right side of the sheet for vertical dimensions. Notice that aligned dimensioning is used in Figure 11.17C, whereas unidirectional dimensioning is used in all previous figures.

Sometimes a dimension might overlap another dimension if placed with a straight extension line from the object. This happens when the features are too close together. AutoCAD LT helps you with this problem by automatically offsetting the extension line between the feature and the extension line end that you pick. The result of this offset extension line is shown in Figure 11.17C and clarified in Figure 11.18. To create ordinate dimensions that use a straight line, turn ORTHO on while you are placing the dimension. ORTHO must be off to create an offset ordinate dimension.

FIGURE 11.18 AutoCAD LT automatically offsets the extension line when you pick an offset leader endpoint.

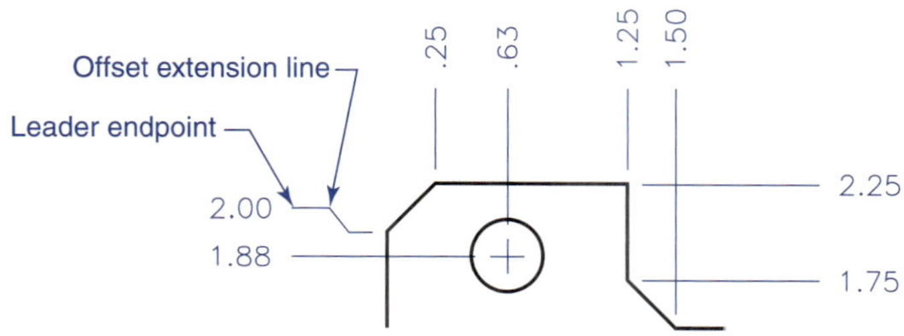

> **Exercise 11.8** — **Estimated time required: 10 min.**
>
> 1. Begin a new drawing.
> 2. Draw and dimension the object shown in Figure 11.17C.
> 3. Save as EX11.8, and close the drawing.

Creating Oblique Dimensions

An ***oblique dimension*** is one that has the extension lines placed at an angle from the feature being dimensioned. Oblique dimensions are sometimes used in situations where the dimension is crowded if the extension lines are projected horizontally or vertically from the object. This technique is sometimes used when dimensioning curves that are not defined by a radius. Oblique dimensions are placed by picking Oblique from the Dimension pull-down menu or by typing **DIMEDIT** at the Command: prompt and using the Oblique option. Before dimensions can be placed at an oblique angle, they need to be drawn as regular horizontal or vertical linear dimensions. The Oblique option is then used to rotate the dimension to the desired obliquing angle. Any positive angle from 1° to 179° can be entered. If an angle greater than 180° is entered, the 180° is subtracted and the resulting angle is used. Figure 11.19A shows dimensions place vertically and then changed to oblique as shown in Figure 11.19B. The DIMEDIT command sequence works like this:

Dimension

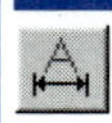

Dimension Edit

Dimension
Oblique

DIMEDIT
DED

Command: **DED** or **DIMEDIT**↵
Enter type of dimension editing [Home/New/Rotate/Oblique] <Home>: **O**↵
Select objects: ⟨*select dimensions to oblique*⟩
Select objects: ↵
Enter obliquing angle (press ENTER for none): **145**↵
Command:

FIGURE 11.19 Drawing oblique dimensions with the DIM or DIMEDIT command's Oblique option.

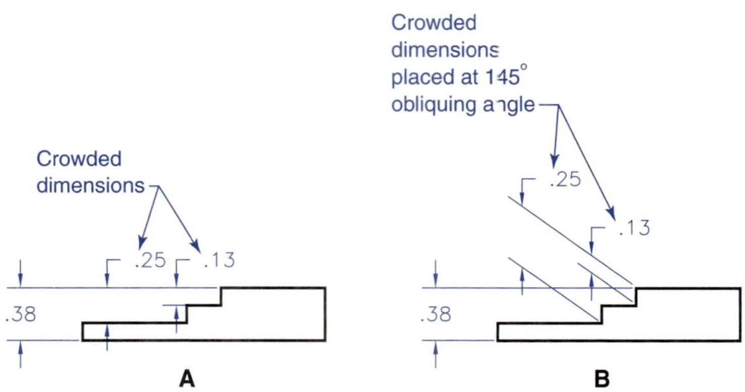

Oblique dimensions can also be created using the DIM command and the OBLIQUE option like this:

Command: **DIM**↵
Dim: **OBL** or **OBLIQUE**↵
Select objects: ⟨*pick the dimensions to oblique*⟩
Select objects: ↵
Enter obliquing angle (press Enter for none): **145**↵
Dim: ⟨*Press the Esc key*⟩
Command:

Additional discussion about the DIMEDIT and DIM commands is provided later in this chapter.

Field Notes

The Oblique option of the DIMEDIT command is used in the creation of isometric dimensions as well. Instruction on creation of isometric dimensions is provided in Chapter 14.

Exercise 11.9 — Estimated time required: 5 min.

1. Begin a new drawing.
2. Draw and dimension the object shown in Figure 11.19B.
3. Save as EX11.9, and close the drawing.

LEARNING CHECKPOINT

- ☐ Define the term *dimensions.*
- ☐ Explain the difference between size and location dimensions.
- ☐ List two types of notes.
- ☐ What are linear dimensions?
- ☐ How do you access the command used for drawing linear dimensions?
- ☐ Explain how to place linear dimensions by selecting the object directly.
- ☐ Describe how to change dimension text in the Multiline Text Editor dialog box.
- ☐ Explain two ways to rotate the dimension line to be aligned with a slanted object.
- ☐ How is chain dimensioning done?
- ☐ Describe the process for making datum dimensions.
- ☐ Name the command used to dimension angles.
- ☐ What command automatically places a diameter symbol when dimensioning circles and arcs?
- ☐ Name the command that automatically places a radius symbol when dimensioning arcs and circles.
- ☐ Name the command used to do arrowless dimensioning.
- ☐ Why is it important to define a UCS origin at the datum origin of the object when doing arrowless dimensioning?
- ☐ How do you offset the ordinate dimension extension line when needed to avoid crowding?
- ☐ Describe oblique dimensions.

Dimensioning Drawings

- Creating Linear, Angular, and Radial Dimensions
- Creating Ordinate Dimensions
- Creating Center Marks and Leaders

Concept Animations

- Dimensioning

Managing Dimension Styles

Dimension styles are saved sets of dimension variable settings that determine the appearance of the dimensions. Dimension styles are usually set up based on the type of drafting field for which they are used. ***Dimension variables*** are AutoCAD LT system variables that help you control the way dimensions look. A dimension style is established by changing the dimension variables as needed to accomplish the desired dimension appearance. For example, the dimension style for mechanical drafting probably has ROMANS or GDT text font placed in a break in the dimension line, and the dimension lines are capped with arrowheads. The dimension style for architectural drafting may use CityBlueprint text font placed above the dimension line, and dimension lines are terminated with slashes. See Figure 11.20. The dimension style can have dimensions based on national standards such as the ANSI/ASME or Architectural Graphic Standards, or set up to match company applications and standards. Dimension styles can also have a family of settings that allow you to assign different settings for each specific type of dimension if desired.

FIGURE 11.20 Dimensions drawn with two different dimension styles. (A) Mechanical drafting dimension. (B) Architectural drafting dimension.

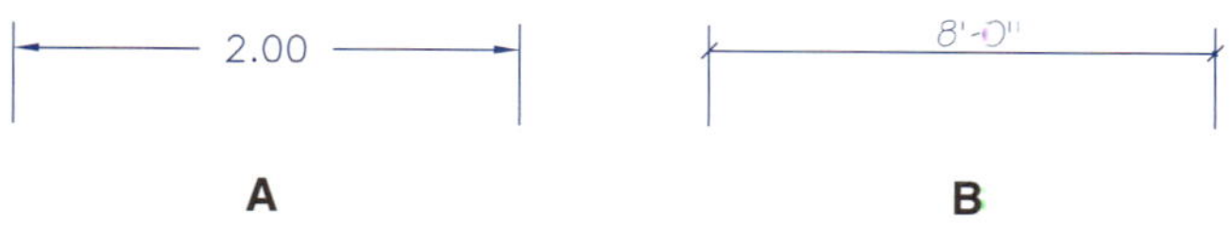

Creating New Dimension Styles

Dimension
Dimension Style
Dimension
Style...
DDIM
D

Dimension styles are created using the Dimension Style Manager dialog box shown in Figure 11.21. This dialog box is accessed by picking the Dimension Style button in the Dimension toolbar, by picking Style ... in the Dimension pull-down menu, or by typing **D** or **DDIM** at the Command: prompt.

Saving and Renaming Dimension Styles

The currently active dimension style is listed above the Styles: list in the Dimension Style Manager, as shown in Figure 11.21. All available styles defined in the current drawing are shown in the Styles: list. Picking *Styles in use* from the drop-down list below Styles: filters the display to show only the styles that are currently being used in the drawing. The image tile provides a preview of the style currently selected in the Styles: list.

The Dimension Style Manager provides a dialog interface for all the primary dimension style management options. You can set the current style, create a new dimension style, or modify an existing one. Other options include setting dimension style overrides and comparing different dimension styles. Pick a name from the list to make another dimension style current. The STANDARD dimension style is the AutoCAD LT default.

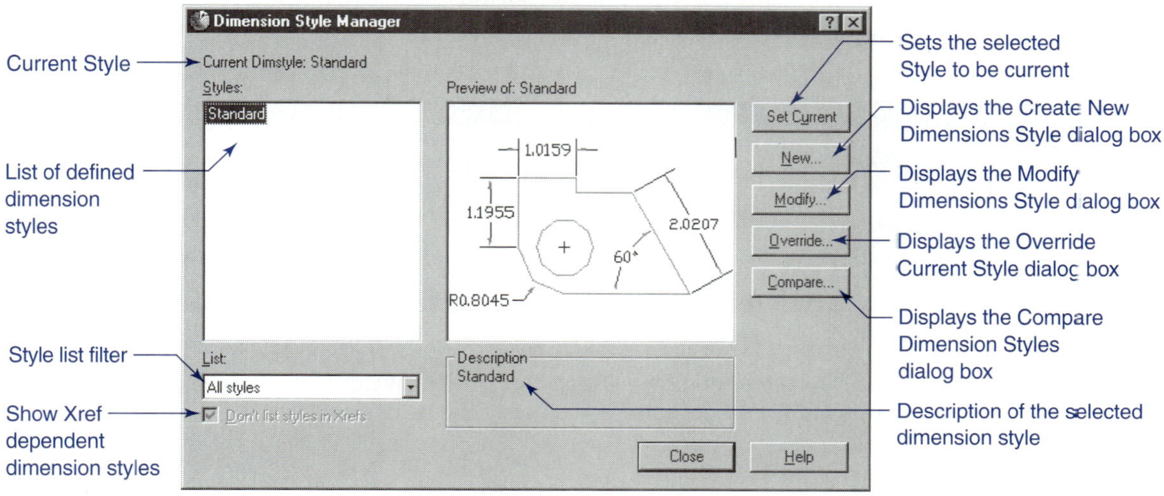

FIGURE 11.21 The Dimension Style Manager dialog box. The initial default style in use for drawings started using the aclt.dwt template is standard.

Changing Dimension Variables

The individual dimension style settings that control the appearance and application of dimensions are referred to as Dimension Variables, or ***dimvars***. The initial settings for the dimvars define a dimension style, but it is frequently necessary to change some of the settings to meet specialized dimensioning needs within a drawing. The Dimension Style Manager provides an intuitive interface for defining new dimension styles, making permanent modifications, or for setting up temporary dimension style overrides. After you learn the names and setting options of the dimvars, you may find it more convenient to change the values at the command line as needed.

As you are introduced to dimvars, keep in mind that dimvar settings can be changed at the Command: prompt by typing the name of the variable and entering a new value. All dimensioning variables begin with "DIM"; however, during a dimensioning command the variable name can be shortened by leaving off the "DIM" prefix.

The settings in the following discussion are presented in the New Dimension Style dialog box, which is accessed by picking the New… button in the Dimension Style Manager. The Modify Dimension Style and Override Dimension Style dialog boxes are exactly the same in appearance and access the same settings as the New Dimension Style dialog box. The use of dimension style overrides is discussed later in this chapter.

Changing Dimension Style Geometry

Pick the New… button in the Dimension Style Manager to open the Create New Dimension Style dialog box (see Figure 11.22). Although you can change any of the values to meet your needs, a new style must be based on an existing style to determine the default values for each setting. The Start With: list is used to select the existing style on which the new style will be based. The New Style Name: box starts with a default name based on the value in the Start With: list. In Figure 11.22A, the value is "Copy of Standard," because Standard is specified in the Start With: box. You can select any defined style to start with and modify the new style name as desired.

The Use for: list determines the scope of the new settings. Typically, the values you set will apply to all types of dimensions within the new style. In some cases, you may want different settings for different types of dimensions in your drawing. For example, you may want diameter dimensions to have center lines that extend beyond the diameter of the circle being dimensioned; however, you may want radius dimensions to use a center mark but not center lines. Specifying a specific dimension type in the Use for: box disables the New Style Name box because you are not creating a new style. Rather, you are creating what is called a *substyle* of the current dimension style. Working with dimension substyles is discussed later in this chapter. For now, the Use for: box should be set to All dimensions.

In Figure 11.22B, the new style name is specified as Mechanical-ASME. After a new style name is specified and the Continue button in the Create New Dimension Style dialog box is picked, the New Dimension Style: Mechanical-ASME dialog box is displayed. The name of the new style is displayed on the title bar (see Figure 11.23).

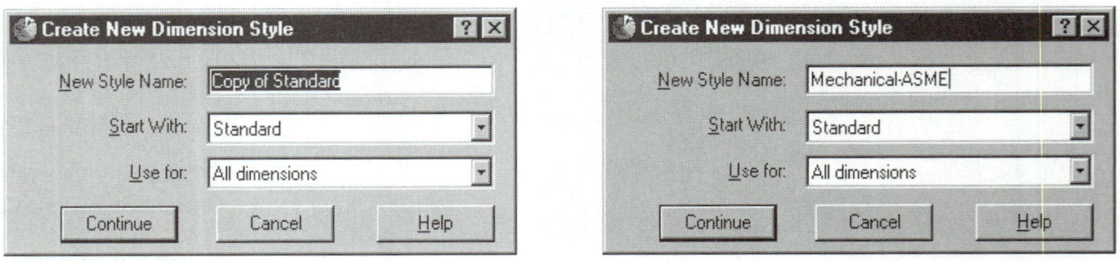

A B

FIGURE 11.22 The Create New Dimension Style dialog box. (A) The default style name is based on the style settings with which you start. (B) A new name can be specified as desired.

The New Dimension Style: dialog box has six tabs, each of which displays a specific category of settings. All settings specific to dimension lines, extension lines, and arrowheads are on the Lines and Arrows tab, as shown in Figure 11.23. The other tabs are introduced later in this discussion.

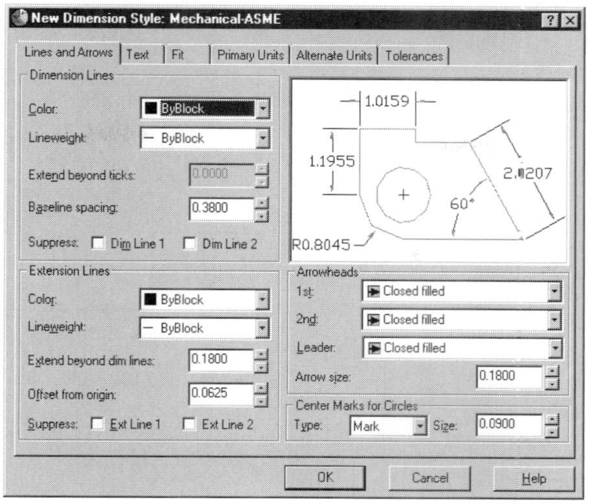

FIGURE 11.23 The New Dimension Style: dialog box is where new dimension styles are defined. The name of the new style appears on the title bar.

As you work through this section, check the image tile after each adjustment to get a preview of the dimension appearance based on the current settings. This preview shows sample linear, aligned, radius, and angular dimensions.

Changing the Dimension Line Presentation

The Dimension Lines area of the Lines and Arrows tab is used to change the format of the dimension line with the following dimension variables:

- **Color:** Pick a color from the drop-down list, or pick the Other... option at the bottom of the list to open the Select Color dialog box, where you can assign a color to the dimension lines. The color is normally assigned BYBLOCK, which is the default, and indicates that the dimension assumes the currently active color setting. Different color settings are normally used only for pen width considerations when plotting the drawing. The command line equivalent is DIMCLRD (**C**o**L**o**R** of **D**imension line).

- **Lineweight:** This setting controls the lineweight applied to the dimension lines, if it is to be different from the rest of the dimension object. The default is BYBLOCK. The command line equivalent is DIMLWD (**L**ine**W**eight for **D**imension lines).

- **Extend beyond ticks:** This box is inactive unless you are using tick marks instead of arrowheads. Tick marks, also called *oblique arrowheads,* are often used when dimensioning architectural drawings. The different settings for arrowhead styles are explained later. In this style of dimensioning, the dimension lines often cross over the extension lines. The ***extension*** represents how far the dimension line extends beyond the extension line. When this text box is active, you can change the value from the .00 default. The command line dimension variable is DIMDLE (**D**imension **L**ine **E**xtension).

- **Baseline spacing:** This text box allows you to change the spacing between dimension lines in baseline dimensions. Optionally, you can use the up and down arrows to adjust the value, but it is usually faster to just double-click inside the box and enter a new value using the keyboard. The default spacing is .38 units. AutoCAD LT automatically spaces the dimension lines this distance when you use the DIMBASELINE command. Figure 11.24 shows the dimension line spacing. This setting may need to be changed, depending on the specified dimension text size, and whether the dimension is horizontal or vertical. The command line equivalent is DIMDLI (**Di**mension **L**ine **I**ncrement), which asks you to enter a new value.

- **Suppress:** *Suppress* means to keep from being displayed. The Suppress: option consists of two toggles that allow you to keep either the first or second or

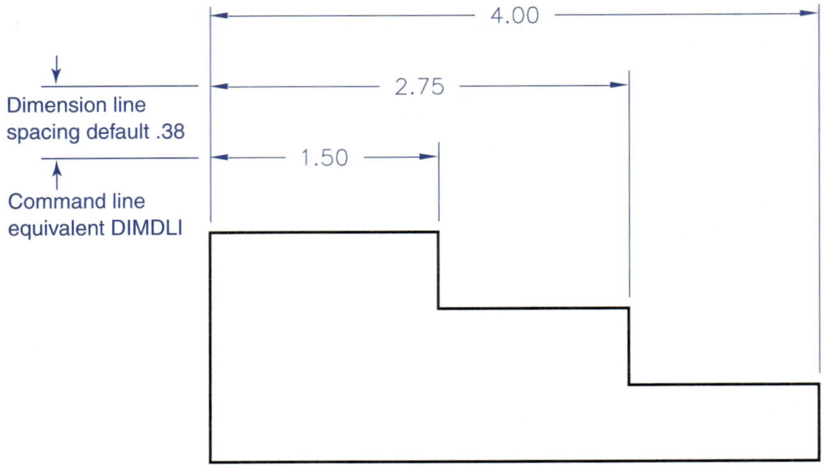

FIGURE 11.24 Using the Baseline spacing: setting. The command line equivalent is DIMDLI.

both dimension lines and their arrowheads from being displayed. The Dim Line 1 and Dim Line 2 toggles refer to the first and second points picked when the dimension was created. These are off by default, meaning that dimension lines and arrowheads *are* displayed. The command line equivalents for these dimension variables are DIMSD1 and DIMSD2 (**S**uppress **D**imension lines 1 and 2). When entering the value for variables that are either on or off, you can type **ON** or **OFF,** or you can use 0 and 1. A value of 0 means off, and 1 means on.

Changing the Extension Line Presentation

The Extension Line area of the Lines and Arrows tab is used to change the format of the extension lines with the following dimension variables:

- **Color:** The color list is used to change the extension line color. The default is BYBLOCK, and the command line equivalent is DIMCLRE (**C**o**L**o**R** of **E**xtension line).
- **Lineweight:** This setting controls the lineweight applied to the extension lines, if it is to be different from the rest of the dimension object. The default is BYBLOCK. The command line equivalent is DIMLWE (**L**ine**W**eight for **E**xtension lines).
- **Extend beyond dim lines:** This text box is used to set the extension line extension, which is the distance the extension line runs past the dimension line as shown in Figure 11.25. The default is .18, and the command line equivalent is DIMEXE (**EX**tension line **E**xtension). A common extension line extension is .125 in., but it depends on the type and size of drawing.

FIGURE 11.25 The extension line extension default is .18 and the command line dimension variable is DIMEXE.

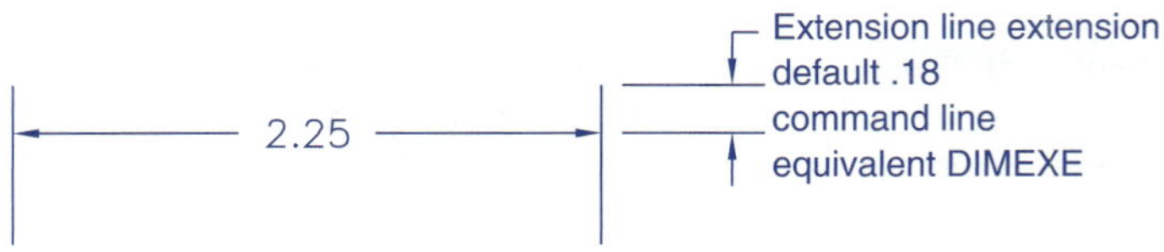

- **Offset from origin:** This text box is used to change the distance between the object and the beginning of the extension line as shown in Figure 11.26. Most applications require a small space, and the default is .06. It is recommended that no gap exist when an extension line meets a center line as shown in Figure 11.27. The command line equivalent is DIMEXO (**EX**tension line **O**ffset).

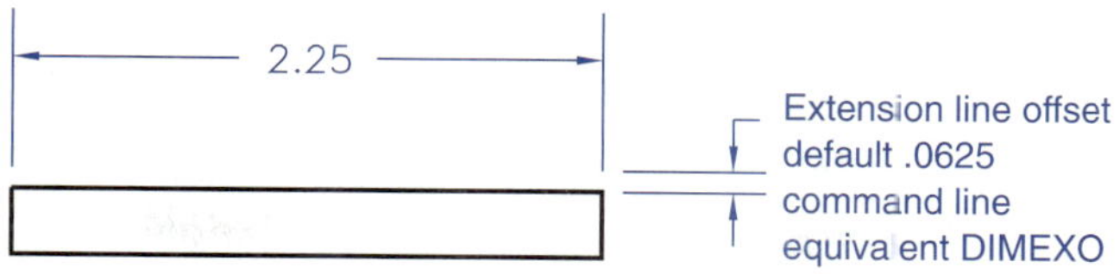

FIGURE 11.26 The extension line offset default is .0625 and the command line dimension variable is DIMEXO.

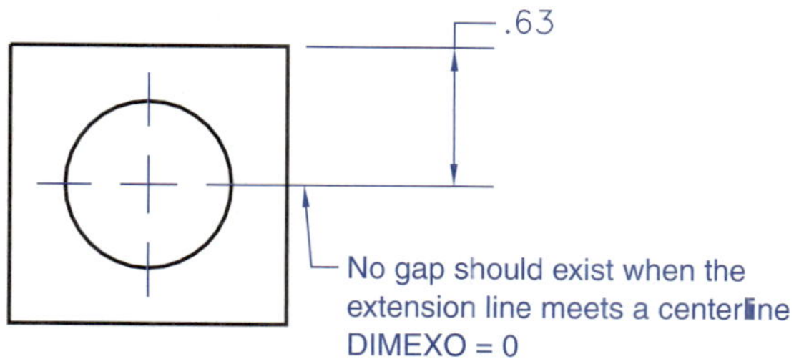

FIGURE 11.27 The extension line offset should be zero when an extension line meets a center line.

- **Suppress:** This option is used to suppress either the first extension line or the second or both as desired. These toggles are off by default and all extension lines are displayed. You might want to suppress an extension line if it coincides with an object line or if you do not want it displayed for any reason. The command line entries are DIMSE1 and DIMSE2 (**S**uppress **E**xtension lines 1 and 2).

Changing the Arrowhead Appearance

AutoCAD LT provides several different arrowhead options. These options are available in the Arrowheads area of the Lines and Arrows tab. The default arrowhead is Closed Filled as displayed in the 1st: and 2nd: list boxes and in the image tiles above the list boxes shown in Figure 11.28A. Open the list box to access the entire list of arrowhead options as shown in Figure 11.28B. If you pick a new arrowhead in the first list, AutoCAD LT automatically makes the same selection for the second list and the examples in the image tiles are changed to match. If you want a different arrowhead for each end of the dimension line, pick the desired first arrowhead and then open the second list and pick another. Figure 11.28C shows a different arrowhead selected for each end of the line.

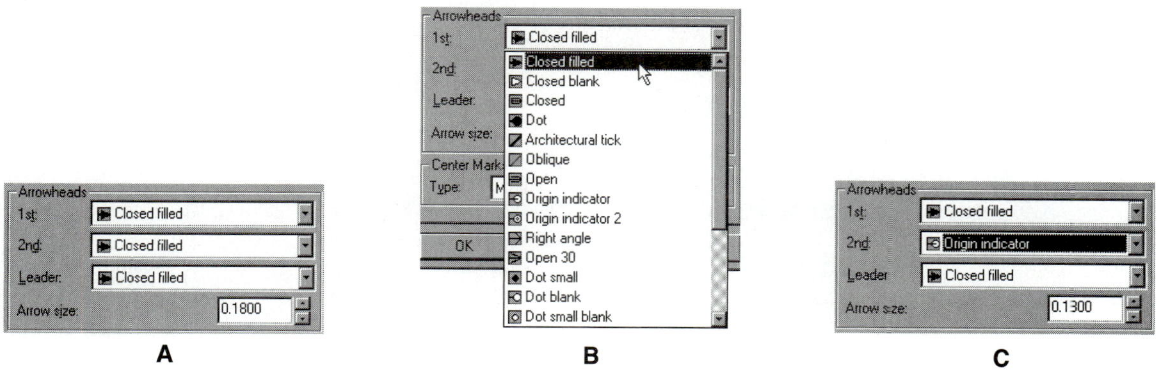

FIGURE 11.28 (A) The arrowhead area of the Lines and Arrows tab displays the first and second arrowhead name and image tile. (B) Access the list of optional arrowhead symbols. (C) Displaying different arrowhead symbols for each end of the dimension line.

Several different arrowhead options are provided by AutoCAD LT, or you can create your own arrowhead design with the User Arrow ... option.

When changing dimension arrowheads at the command line using dimvars, the variables used are DIMBLK, DIMBLK1, DIMBLK2, and DIMSAH. If both arrowheads are to be the same, the only variable that needs changed is the DIMBLK (**BL**oc**K**) variable. This accepts a text value that is the name of the arrowhead style you wish to use. Each of the names is listed in the arrowhead descriptions that follow. To set up separate arrowheads, first set DIMSAH (**S**eparate **A**rrow**H**eads) to on. The arrowheads that are used by the first and second dimension lines are set by using DIMBLK1 and DIMBLK2.

The various types of arrowheads are commonly used for the following applications, but you should check with your school, office, or appropriate national standards:

- **Architectural** Architectural Tick, Dot, Closed Filled, Oblique, Open, Right Angle, Open 30, or Dot Small. The Architectural Tick, Dot, and Closed Filled are the most commonly used.
- **Mechanical** Closed Filled, Closed, Closed Blank, or Open. The Closed Filled is the most commonly used and is represented in the ANSI/ASME standards. The Closed Filled is often used as the arrowhead for leaders in many drafting fields. The Small Dot symbol is used when a leader points to a surface.

Many of the AutoCAD LT arrowhead options are displayed and named in Figure 11.29. The arrowhead symbols are all displayed with the same size setting.

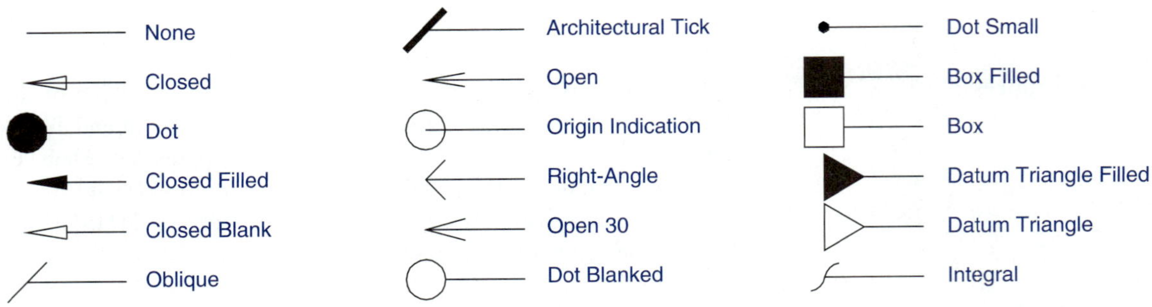

FIGURE 11.29 Standard AutoCAD LT arrowhead options.

The User Arrow ... option in the Arrowheads list requires that you create a block of the desired arrowhead design. A block is a commonly used symbol and the creation of blocks is discussed in Chapter 12. After a block is made and named, you can pick the User Arrow ... option to open the Select Custom Arrow dialog box shown in Figure 11.30A. In this dialog box you select a defined block name from the list that matches the name of the arrowhead block that you created. Doing this activates the block to be used as the arrowheads for the dimension on your drawing. Figure 11.30B shows a variety of custom arrows that can be commonly used or can have special applications. The user arrow is controlled at the command line by the DIMBLK variable by typing the name of the block.

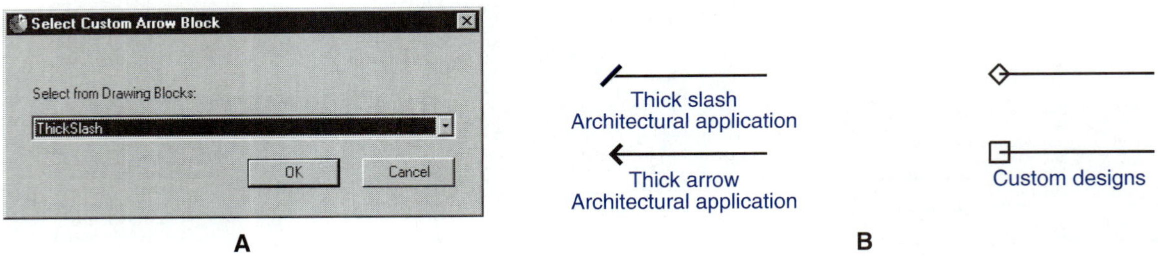

FIGURE 11.30 (A) The Select Custom Arrow dialog box. (B) Sample custom user arrows.

When you access the Oblique arrowhead option, the Extend beyond ticks: box in the Dimension Line area is activated. This allows you to enter a value for a dimension line projection beyond the extension line. The default value is zero, but some architectural companies like to project the dimension line past the extension line by setting this to a desired value as shown in Figure 11.31. This is controlled at the command line with the DIMDLE dimension variable.

The Leader: box is used to specify the type of arrowhead used by leaders. Leaders need to be set separate from the 1st and 2nd arrowheads, for example, when in an architectural drawing where the dimension arrowheads are specified as tick marks.

FIGURE 11.31 The dimension line extension option is active when you pick the Oblique arrowhead option. This is the DIMDLE dimension variable.

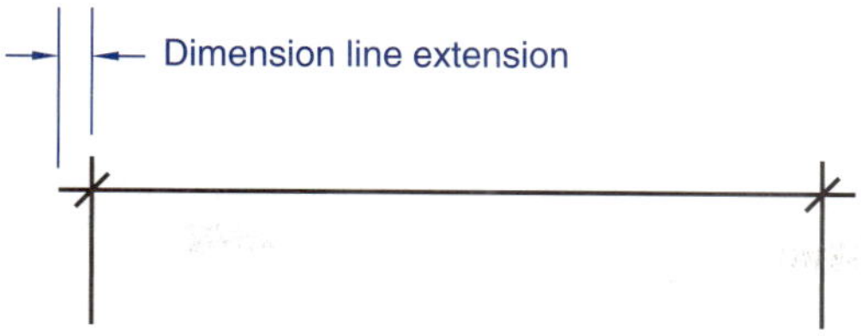

Changing Arrowhead Size

The Arrow si<u>z</u>e: box in the Arrowheads area of the Lines and Arrows tab allows you to change the size of any selected arrowhead. The default value is .18. Arrowheads are commonly .125 in. but vary depending on the drawing size. The arrowhead size can also be changed at the command line with the DIMASZ (**Ar**rowhead **SiZ**e) dimension variable.

Using Center Marks in Circles and Arcs

The Center Marks for Circles area of the Lines and Arrows tab allows you to select the way center marks are placed in circles and arcs. The three listed options are identified as Mark, Line, and None. None provides for no center marks to be placed in circles and arcs. The preview image displays the effect of the currently selected option. The Mark option is used to place center marks only, and the Line option places center marks and center lines as displayed in the Figure 11.32 image tiles. The None option is used when no center marks are desired. You can also change the center mark option by picking directly on the image tile. After selecting either the Mark or Line center mark option, you can place center marks on circles and arcs by using the DIMCENTER command. This command is accessed by picking the Center Mark button in the Dimension toolbar, by picking Center <u>M</u>ark in the Dime<u>n</u>sion pull-down menu, or by typing **DCE** or **DIMCENTER** at the Command: prompt. The command asks you to select the arc or circle:

Dimension

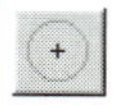

Center Mark

Dime<u>n</u>sion
Center <u>M</u>ark

DIMCENTER
DCE

Command: **DCE** or **DIMCENTER**↵
Select the arc or circle: ⟨*pick the arc or circle*⟩
Command:

FIGURE 11.32 (A) The Mark option and the related preview image. (B) The Line option and the related preview image.

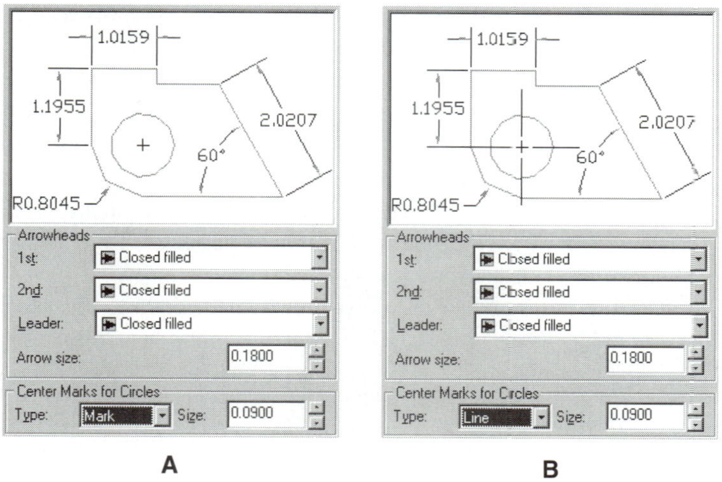

The current DIMCEN variable settings are also used when applying radius or diameter dimensions. The center marks applied using the DIMCENTER command are not associative dimensions and cannot be automatically updated. When the center mark is applied as part of a radius or diameter dimension, it is associative and can be updated to match new settings if desired.

Changing the Center Mark Size

The Si<u>z</u>e: box in the Center Marks for Circles area of the Lines and Arrows tab is used to change the size of the center mark presentation. The default size is .09. The size specification controls the Mark and Line options in different ways, as shown in Figure 11.33.

The center mark option can also be changed at the Command: prompt by using the DIMCEN (**CEN**ter) dimension variable. Entering a positive value provides for the mark option as shown in Figure 11.33A. Entering a negative value provides for the line option as shown in Figure 11.33B. Keep in mind that only positive values need to be entered in the Si<u>z</u>e: box of the Geometry dialog box. The following shows a negative value used to provide for the line option to be used:

Command: **DIMCEN↵**
Enter new value for DIMCEN <0.09>: **−.125↵**
Command:

Remember that the DIMCENTER command is used to actually place the center marks after setting the dimension variable. Also, unlike most dimvars, the "DIM" prefix for DIMCEN cannot be omitted at a dimensioning prompt. This is because typing **CEN** at a point prompt is interpreted as an Object Snap specification.

FIGURE 11.33 (A) The size related to using the Mark option. (B) The size related to using the Line option.

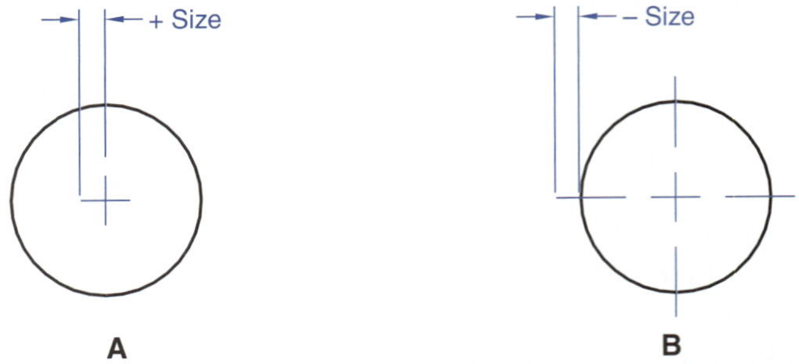

Exercise 11.10

Estimated time required: 8 min.

1. Begin a new drawing.
2. Open the Dimension Style Manager dialog box and notice STANDARD as the current dimension style.
3. Create a new dimension style named Mechanical or Architectural, based on your preferred drafting field.
4. Look at the Dimension Lines area as you refer to Figure 11.24 as a reference to dimension line spacing.
5. Look at the Extension Lines area as you refer to Figure 11.25 as a reference to the extension line extension and Figure 11.26 for the extension line offset.
6. Look at the Arrowheads area and pick each of the arrowhead options; watch the example in the preview image change to match your selection. Try making the first and second arrowheads the same and different. Notice when you pick the Oblique arrowhead that the Extension: box in the Dimension Line area becomes active. Look at Figure 11.31 to see the results of a value entered in this box.
7. Look at the Center Marks for Circles area as you pick each of the list options and see how the preview image changes to match the selection. Look at Figure 11.33 to see the results of changing the center mark size.
8. Use the Lines and Arrows tab to make the following settings based on your preferred drafting field:

Setting	*Mechanical*	*Architectural*
Baseline spacing	.50	.75
Extend beyond dim lines	.125	.18
Offset from origin	.0625	.08
Arrowheads	Closed, Blank, Closed Filled, or Open	Dot, Closed Filled, or Architectural Tick
Arrowhead size	.125	.18
Center	Line	Mark
Center size	.25	.25

9. Pick the OK button. You are now back in the Dimension Style Manager dialog box. Notice the new dimension style added to the list.
10. Look at the Description box to see the text description.
11. Pick the Set Current button. The dimension style you created should now be listed as the current style.
12. Pick Close.
13. Save as EX11.10, and keep the drawing open for the next exercise.

Changing the Dimension Text Format

The dimension text format establishes the way dimension text appears on the drawing and the relationship with the positioning of the dimension lines and arrowheads. These controls are adjusted in the Text tab in the New Dimension Style dialog box. The Text tab is shown in Figure 11.34.

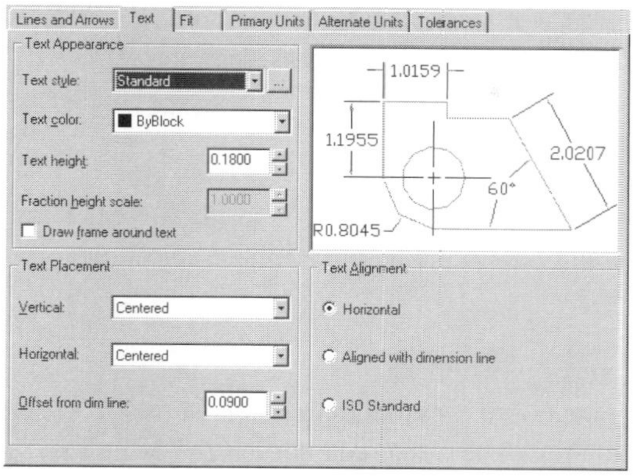

FIGURE 11.34 The Text tab in the New Dimension Style: dialog box.

Setting Dimension Text Appearance Options

The Text Appearance area of the Text tab is used to set the dimension text style, height, fraction appearance, and color. These options are explained as follows:

- **Text style:** The dimension text style uses the STANDARD text style by default. Text styles must be defined in the current drawing before they are available for use in dimension text. You can access the list of loaded text styles by clicking the down arrow of the Style: list as shown in Figure 11.35. The ellipsis button next to the Text style list displays the Text Style dialog box, where you can define or modify text styles as needed. Dimension text styles are changed at the Command: prompt by using the DIMTXSTY variable.

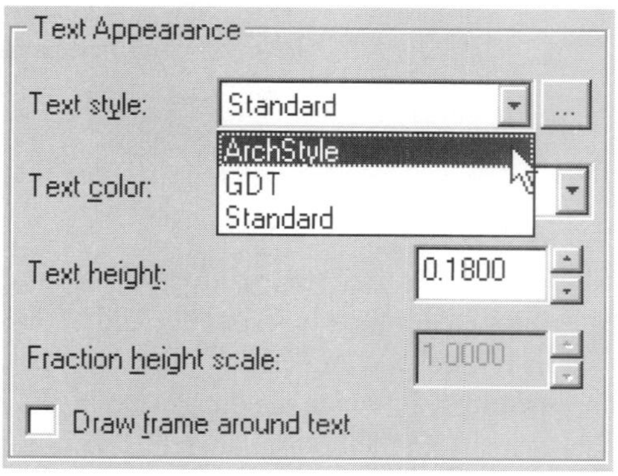

FIGURE 11.35 Open the Text Style: list to determine which dimension text styles have been loaded.

- **Text color:** Pick a color from the list or access the Select Color dialog box if you want to change the color of dimension text. The dimension color default is BYBLOCK. The dimension text color is changed at the Command: prompt with the DIMCLRT (**C**o**L**o**R** of **T**ext) variable.
- **Height:** The dimension text height is set by entering the desired value in the Height: box. Dimension text height is generally the same as the rest of the text height found on the drawing. The text height for other drawing text is set using the STYLE command. The default dimension text height is .18, which is an acceptable standard. Many companies use a text height of .125 in. The ASME standard recommends text heights between .125 and .188 in. Dimension text height can be set at the Command: prompt with the DIMTXT variable.

- **Fraction height scale:** Sets the scale factor used to calculate the height of text used to represent fraction values and dimensional tolerances. This number is a multiplier based on the dimension text height. This value can be changed at the command line using the DIMTFAC (**T**olerance scale **FAC**tor) variable.
- **Draw frame around text:** Creates a frame around text used to denote a basic dimension. This sets the DIMGAP variable to a negative value. An additional DIMGAP discussion is provided later.

Setting the Dimension Text Placement

Dimension text location and orientation is controlled in the Text Placement area on the Text tab. These settings control the vertical and horizontal justification and placement of the dimension text relative to the rest of the dimension features.

Setting the Vertical Text Alignment

The Vertical Justification area of the Format dialog box is used to set the vertical alignment of dimension text in relation to the dimension line. The Centered option is the default and places dimension text centered in a gap provided in the dimension line. Figure 11.34 displays this default option in the preview image. This is the dimensioning practice that is commonly used in mechanical drafting and many other fields. The dimension variable used at the Command: prompt is DIMTAD (**T**ext **A**bove **D**imension line) turned off. To change the vertical justification, pick one of the options found in the list shown in Figure 11.36. The following list explains each of the other vertical justification options:

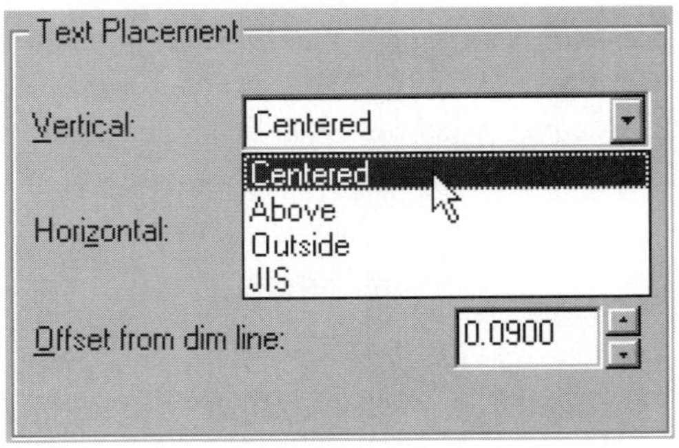

FIGURE 11.36 The list of Vertical text placement options.

- **Above** This option is commonly used for architectural drafting and building construction. This option places the dimension text horizontally and above horizontal dimension lines and in a gap provided in vertical and angled dimension lines. Architectural drafting commonly uses ***aligned dimensioning,*** in which the dimension text is aligned with the dimension lines and all text either reads from the bottom or right side of the sheet. If the dimension text is to be placed above and aligned with vertical and angled dimension lines, the Horizontal Text Alignment feature must be off. This is explained in a subsequent section. When entered at the Command: prompt, the DIMTAD setting is on.
- **Outside** This option places the dimension text outside the dimension line and either above or below a horizontal dimension line or to the right or left of a vertical dimension line depending on which way you move the cursor.
- **JIS** Use this option when dimensioning for the Japanese Industrial Standard.

An example of each of the horizontal and vertical justification options is shown in Figure 11.37. Combinations of the horizontal and vertical options can be used to create different results.

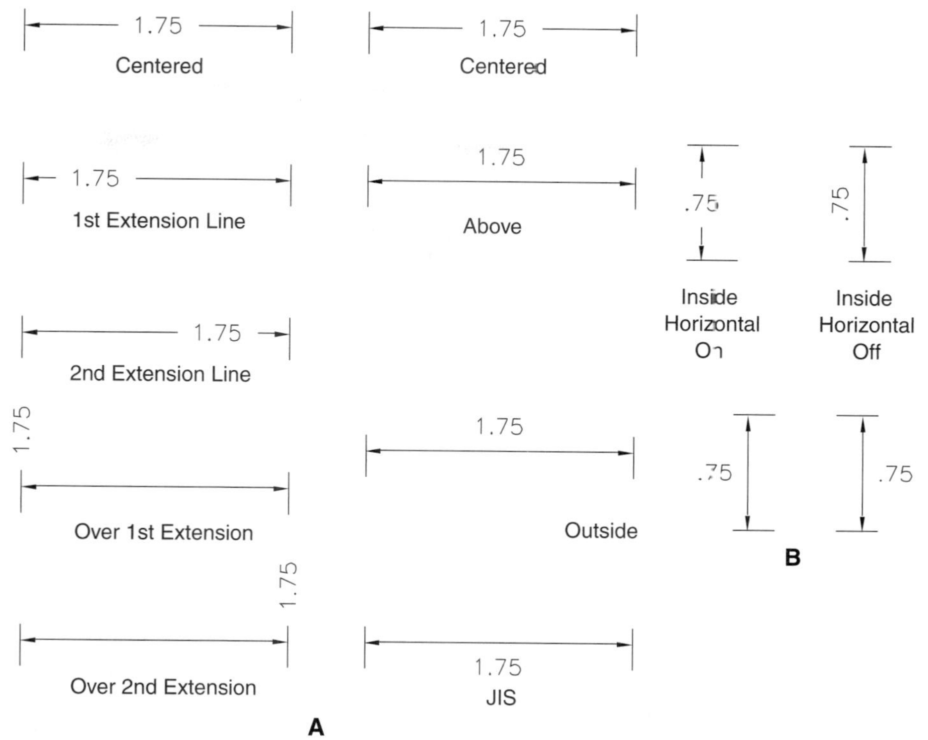

FIGURE 11.37 Actual dimensions placed using different Horizontal and Vertical placement options
(A) Horizontal options.
(B) Vertical options. Various results are possible by combining the effects of horizontal and vertical justification in different ways.

Setting the Horizontal Text Alignment

The Horizontal: list in the Text placement area is used to align the placement of the dimension text horizontally with the dimension line or extension lines. The preview image displays a representation of the current option. The Centered option is the AutoCAD LT default and is used to center text on the dimension line as shown by the preview image in Figure 11.34. Pick the down arrow to access the full list of options as shown in Figure 11.38. The horizontal placement is controlled at the Command: prompt by using the DIMJUST (**JUST**ification) variable. The following list explains each of the options:

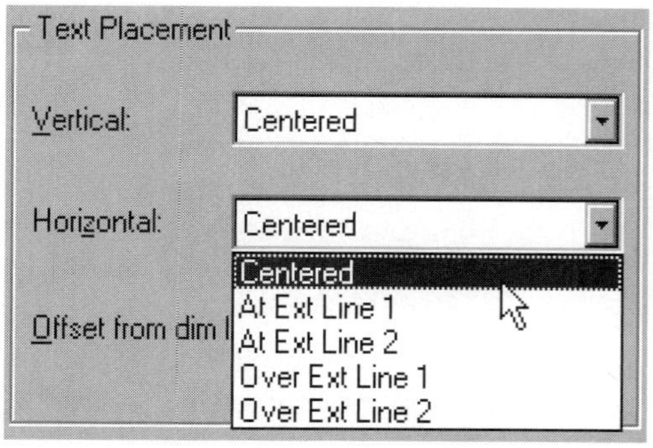

FIGURE 11.38 The list of options in the Horizontal list box.

- **At Ext Line1** This option locates the text next to the extension line that is placed first. The DIMJUST setting is 1.
- **At Ext Line2** This option locates the text next to the second extension line. The DIMJUST setting is 2.
- **Over Ext Line1** This option places the text aligned with and over the first extension line. The DIMJUST setting is 3.
- **Over Ext Line2** This option places the text aligned with and over the second extension line. The DIMJUST setting is 4.

Field Notes

The Horizontal placement options provide you with the ability to set the dimension text in a fixed position for all future dimension placement until you change to a different option. If these fixed settings do not give you enough flexibility, you might consider leaving horizontal justification at the Centered option and enable the Place text manually when dimensioning option (discussed later in this chapter) to give you flexibility when placing each dimension.

Setting the Dimension Line Gap

The Offset from dim line: setting controls the size of the text break in a dimension line. The distance value represents the distance from the broken end of the dimension line to the dimension text. This can also be set using the DIMGAP variable.

Dimension Text Alignment

The Text Alignment area on the Text tab allows you to control the alignment of dimension text. This area is used when you want to draw unidirectional dimensions or aligned dimensions. These terms were defined early in this chapter. The default is for the Horizontal radio button to be on, which draws the unidirectional dimensions that are common for mechanical drafting applications. The preview image illustrates the current setting. Aligned dimensions are typically used for architectural dimensioning. The Horizontal text alignment is controlled at the Command: prompt by the DIMTIH (**T**ext **I**nside is **H**orizontal) and the DIMTOH (**T**ext **O**utside is **H**orizontal) variables.

When doing dimensioning for mechanical drawing, it is common to have Horizontal and Vertical Justification Centered, and Horizontal alignment. For architectural drafting, it is typical to have Horizontal Justification Centered, Vertical Justification Above, and text aligned with dimension line. Figure 11.39 shows examples of these settings used for mechanical and architectural dimensioning applications. Both examples use the same objects with decimal dimensions; however, architectural drawings are usually dimensioned in feet and inches.

Exercise 11.11 — Estimated time required: 5 min.

1. Continue working in EX11.10 (or open it for editing if needed).
2. Start the Dimension Style Manager, pick the dimension style name created in EX11.10, and pick the Modify... button to continue defining the new style.
3. On the Text tab, pick the Text Style: ellipsis button to access the Text Style dialog box. Create two new text styles, one using the GDT.shx font and one using the CountryBlueprint font. Be certain to leave the text size at 0.00 to avoid problems controlling text size. Return to the Modify Dimension Style dialog box.
4. Select the appropriate text style for your dimension style.
5. Select a color for text if desired, and set the height at an appropriate value between .125 and .188.
6. Turn the Frame on and observe the results in the preview image. Turn the frame feature off again.
7. Explore the placement and alignment options. Specify settings appropriate for your dimensioning style.
8. Pick the OK button, and in the Dimension Style Manager, pick Close.
9. Save as EX11.11, and keep the drawing open for the next exercise.

FIGURE 11.39 (A) Dimensioning for mechanical drafting using unidirectional dimensioning with text placed in a space in the dimension lines. (B) Dimensioning for architectural drafting using aligned dimensioning with text placed above the dimension lines.

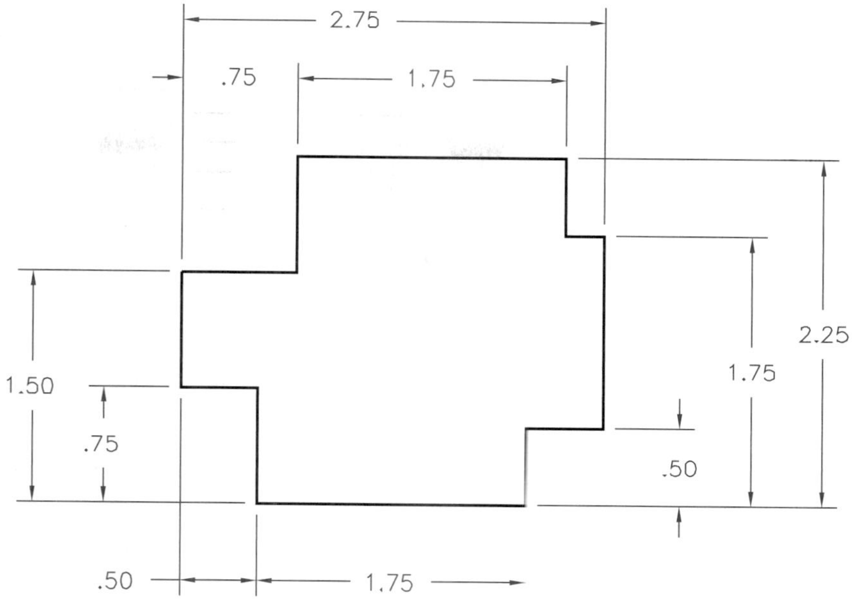

A Dimension text alignment for mechanical drafting

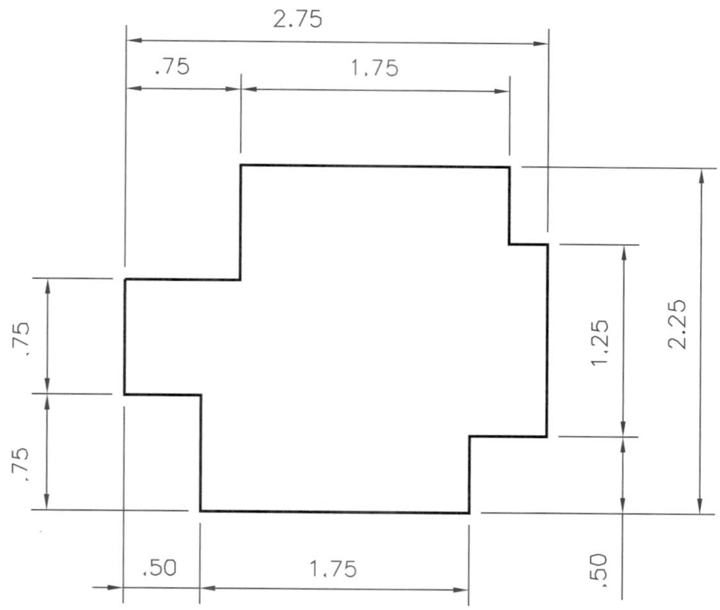

B Dimension text alignment for arch tectural drafting

Adjusting the Text Fit

The Fit tab has several options for controlling the relationship between the placement of dimension text, dimension line, and arrowheads. With the Place text manually when dimensioning feature in the Fine Tuning area toggled off, as it is by default, AutoCAD LT decides where the text is placed relative to the dimension line or leader. For example, when placing linear dimensions, AutoCAD LT automatically centers the dimension text within the dimension line, as shown in Figure 11.2. You can have maximum control over text placement if you turn the Place text manually when dimensioning feature on (see Figure 11.40). Figure 11.41 shows the difference in flexibility that can be achieved with this option off and on. As you look at Figure 11.41A, notice that the text is centered on the dimension line if the dimension is big enough. In Figure 11.41B, the text can be placed where you want it, such as moved to the side or placed outside of the extension lines. The check box acts the same as setting the DIMUPT (**U**ser **P**ositioned **T**ext) variable at the Command: prompt.

The Always draw dim line between ext lines check box causes AutoCAD LT to force the dimension line inside the extension lines even when the text and arrowheads are outside. The default application is with the dimension line and arrowheads outside the extension lines. Figure 11.42 shows the difference between

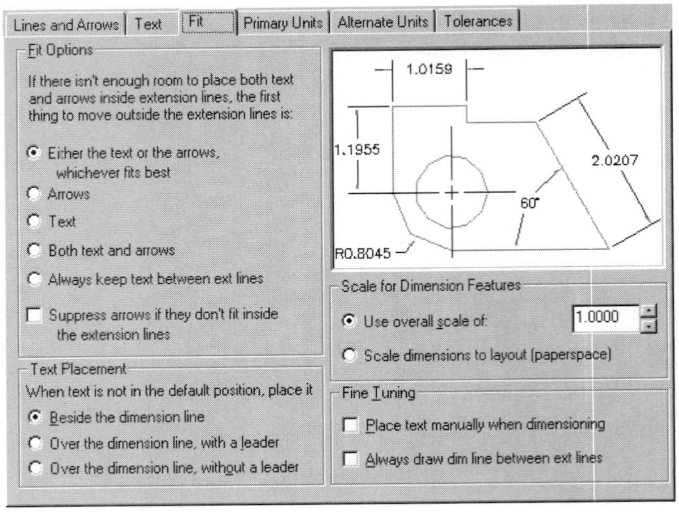

FIGURE 11.40 The Fit tab settings control the relationship between the placement of dimension text, dimension line, and arrowheads.

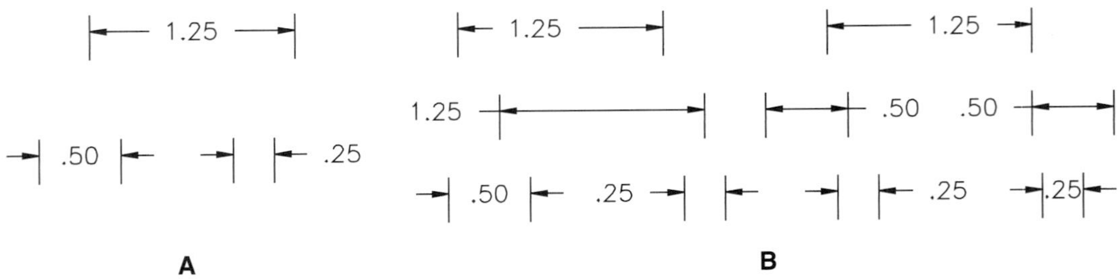

FIGURE 11.41 (A) These examples were created with the Place text manually when dimensions option off. AutoCAD LT automatically centers the dimension text on the dimension line. (B) These examples were created with this option on. This gives you control over placement of the dimension text.

turning this feature on and off. The practice used depends on the company preference. The command line dimension variable for this feature is DIMTOFL (**T**ext **O**utside, **F**orce **L**ine inside).

The Fit options area provides several options that control the way the dimension line, text, and arrowheads are formatted. The default is Either the text or the arrows, whichever fits best, which allows AutoCAD LT to place text and dimension lines with arrowheads inside of extension lines if space is available, or place the text inside and dimension line with arrowheads outside of extension lines, or place everything outside of extension lines depending on the amount of space between extension lines. Figure 11.43 shows all of the Fit options. The DIMATFIT variable has the same effect with a setting of 3 when typed at the Command: prompt. The other Fit: Options are explained in the following list:

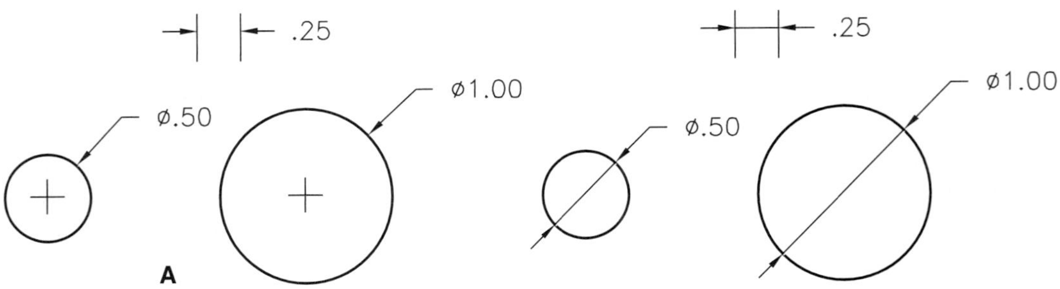

FIGURE 11.42 (A) Line representation with the Always draw dim line between ext lines option off. (B) Line representation with this option on. Notice the dimension line is drawn between the extension lines and inside the circles.

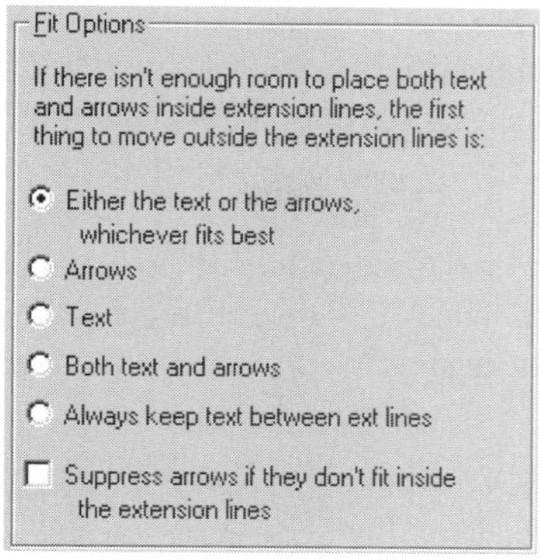

FIGURE 11.43 The options available in the Fit Options area of the Fit tab..

- **Arrows** — The text, dimension line, and arrowheads are placed inside the extension lines if there is enough space for everything. If there is enough space for only the arrowheads and dimension line inside the extension lines, then the text is placed outside. Everything is placed outside if there is not enough room for anything inside. This is a DIMATFIT setting of 2.
- **Text** — The text, dimension line, and arrowheads are placed inside the extension lines if there is enough space for everything. If there is enough space for only the text inside the extension lines, then the dimension lines and arrowheads are placed outside. Everything is placed outside if there is not enough room for the text inside. Use DIMATFIT set at 1 for this option when using the command line.
- **Both text and arrows** — When this option is used, AutoCAD LT places the text, dimension line, and arrowheads inside the extension lines if there is enough space, or everything is placed outside the extensions if there is not enough space for everything inside. This is controlled by the DIMATFIT variable set at 0.
- **Always keep text between ext lines** — This forces the text to always be placed between the extension lines, even if there is not enough room. The command line variable for this is DIMTIX (**T**ext always **I**nside e**X**tension lines).
- **Suppress arrows if they don't fit inside the extension lines** — Does not display arrowheads unless they fit inside of the extension lines. The variable name is DIMSOXD (**S**uppress **O**utside e**X**tension line **D**imension line).

Controlling Text Placement

When text is not placed manually, AutoCAD LT can control the placement of text that does not fit in the default position. The settings available in the Text Placement area of the Fit tab are as follows:

- **Beside the dimension line** — AutoCAD LT moves the dimension line to follow the text whenever the text is moved. This is a DIMTMOVE setting of 0.
- **Over the dimension line, with a leader** — AutoCAD LT places the text inside and the dimension line and arrowheads outside if space permits. If the text does not fit inside, the text is placed away from the dimension line and a leader line connects the text to the dimension line. This practice is not recommended by the ASME standard but can be used in crowded situations if all other options fail. This is the DIMTMOVE dimension variable set at 1.
- **Over the dimension line, without a leader** — This is similar to the Leader option except the text is placed away from the dimension line with no leader connecting the dimension line. This is even more unusual than using the Leader option. The DIMTMOVE setting for this option is 2.

Setting the Scale for Dimension Features

Dimension features must be scaled to match the printed scale of a drawing. When you are printing a drawing of a mechanical part at full scale, the printed dimension features should all conform to industry standard sizes. Likewise, when you are printing an architectural drawing at a scale of ¼″ = 1′, all printed dimension features should conform to industry standard sizes. This means that in such an architectural application the text height on your dimensions should be around 6″ tall. Rather than having to calculate all the various scaled sizes of features, you can adjust the overall scale. The overall scale serves as a multiplier for all dimvars, meaning that all dimension features are automatically adjusted with a single setting. The available settings are as follows:

- **Use overall scale of:** This allows you to set an overall scale that is applied to the dimensional features. Use this setting if you are doing your dimensioning in the Model tab.
- **Scale dimensions to layout (paperspace)** This is a flexible option that automatically scales dimensions based on the scale of the current floating model space viewport. Using layouts and floating model space viewports is discussed in Chapter 13.

Formatting the Dimension Units

Dimension text units can be set to meet a variety of industry standard needs. Three tabs are provided to allow precise control of the dimensional unit format and precision levels. AutoCAD LT supports dual dimensioning and allows you to specify the format for both the primary and the alternate units. Dimensional tolerances can also be configured in a variety of formats and styles.

Setting Primary Units

The ***primary units*** are the part of the dimension from which tolerances or other units are calculated or related. Tolerances are defined and explained later. The following paragraphs explain the functions of each of the options in the Primary Units tab. The Primary Units tab is shown in Figure 11.44. The elements of the Primary Units tab are grouped under Linear Dimensions and Angular Dimensions areas. The Linear Dimensions area in the Primary Units tab provides the following general settings:

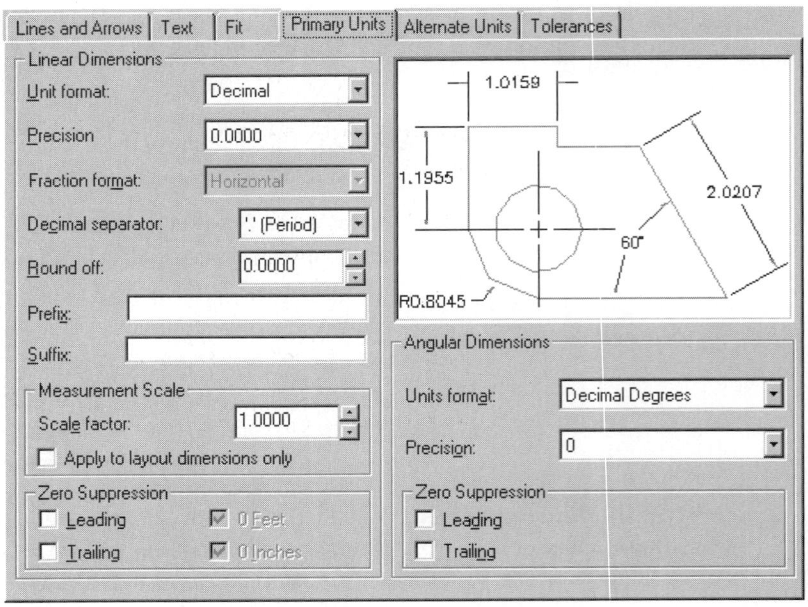

FIGURE 11.44 The Primary Units tab controls the Unit format and precision for the primary dimensioning units.

- **Unit Format:** This list is where you select the type of linear units for use as dimension text. The default is Decimal units. Pick the down arrow to access the list shown in Figure 11.45. The purpose and examples of each type of unit were explained in Chapter 2 in the discussion of drawing setup and use of the UNITS command. Linear dimension units are controlled at the Command: prompt with the DIMLUNIT variable.

- **Precision** The Precision: list allows you to decide how many zeros follow the decimal place. This is important in mechanical drafting because adding zeros after the decimal point generally tightens the tolerance for unspecified tolerance dimensions. Tolerance terminology is defined later in this section. The default is 0.0000, although 0.00 and 0.000 settings are common in inch mechanical drafting depending on the desired tolerance. Varying degrees of dimension precision can be found on the same drawing. The Precision list shows the available options based on the current Unit format: setting. If Architectural units are currently set active, then the Precision list displays its values as fractions rather than zeros behind a decimal point. The list of Precision options for Decimal units is shown in Figure 11.46A, Figure 11.46B shows the Precision list with Architectural units set. Dimension unit precision is controlled at the Command: prompt with the DIMDEC variable.

- **Fraction format:** This area is disabled unless a unit format that uses fractions is active. This controls whether fractions are presented in a stacked format, and if so whether they are stacked using a horizontal or diagonal format. This setting uses the DIMFRAC variable at the command line.

- **Decimal separator:** This area is disabled unless a unit format that uses decimal numbers is active. This allows you to change the decimal separator from the default period to either a comma or a space. This is controlled at the command line with the DIMDSEP variable.

FIGURE 11.45 The list of linear Unit formas in the Primary Units tab.

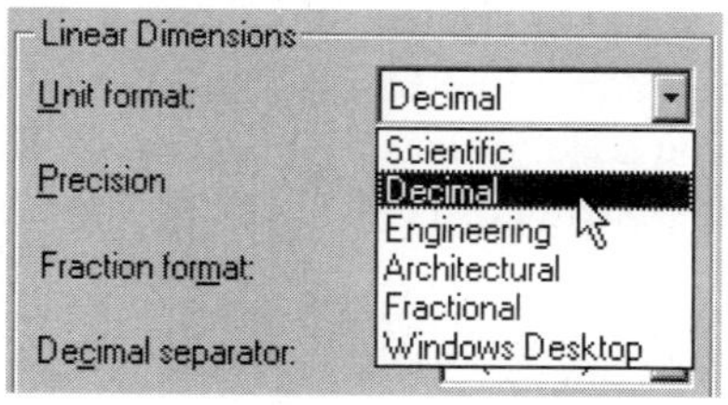

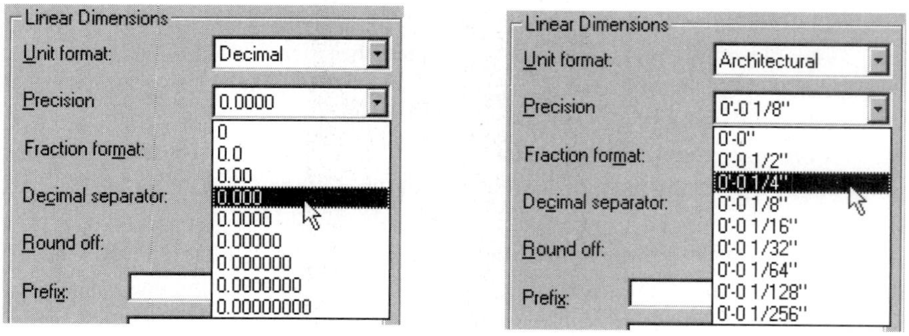

A B

FIGURE 11.46 The list of Precision options in the Linear Dimensions area. (A) Precision options for Decimal units. (B) Precision settings for Architectural units.

Rounding Off Dimension Numerals

The Round Off: box forces AutoCAD LT round off all numbers to a designated value. The default is zero as shown in Figure 11.44. Zero in the Round Off: box means that no rounding takes place and all dimensions are placed exactly as measured. If you enter a value of .1, then all dimensions are rounded to the closest .1 unit. For example, an actual measurement of 4.188 is rounded to 4.2. The Command: prompt control for this variable is DIMRND.

Setting Prefixes and Suffixes

Prefixes are special notes or applications that are placed in front of the dimension text, and ***suffixes*** are special notes or applications that are placed after the dimension text. A typical prefix might be SØ2.5, where SØ means spherical diameter. A typical suffix might be 2.5 MAX, where MAX is the abbreviation for maximum, or 2.5 MIN, where MIN is the abbreviation for minimum. The abbreviation IN. can also be used when one or more inch dimensions are placed on a metric dimensioned drawing, or a suffix of MM can be used on one or more millimeter dimensions on an inch drawing.

The desired prefix is entered in the Prefix: box and the desired suffix is entered in the Suffix: box of the Primary Units area of the Annotation dialog box. Figure 11.47A shows S%%C entered as a prefix and MAX entered as a suffix. S%%C is the code that results in SØ. Figure 11.71B shows a dimension drawn with the SØ prefix and MAX suffix. The use of the Primary Units prefix and suffix options is controlled at the Command: prompt with the DIMPOST variable. You can also set prefixes and suffixes for Alternate Units as needed when the alternate units are enabled. These are controlled at the Command: prompt with the DIMAPOST variable. Alternate units are discussed later in this chapter.

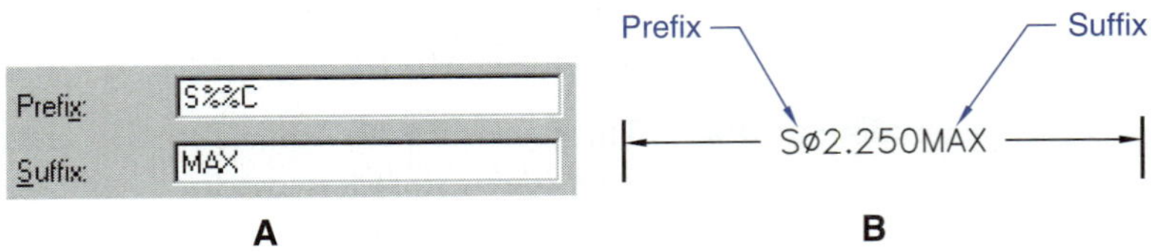

FIGURE 11.47 (A) Entering a prefix and suffix. (B) The S%%C value entered in the Prefix: box and the MAX value entered in the Suffix: box results in a dimension that looks like this.

Field Notes

> Generally a prefix or suffix is not used on every dimension in the drawing. A prefix or suffix is normally a special specification and might be used in only a few cases. Because of this, you might set up a special dimension style for these applications or just enter them when needed by using the Mtext or Text option of the related dimensioning command.

- **Measurement Scale** This area of the Primary Units tab is used to set the scale factor of linear dimensions. If the scale factor in the Scale factor: box is 1, then the dimension values are the same as their measured values. If the setting is 2, then the dimension values are twice as much as the measured amount. For example, an actual measurement of 1 in. is displayed as 1 with a linear scale of 1, but the same measurement is displayed as 2 when the linear scale is 2. This can also be set at the Command: prompt with the DIMLFAC (**L**inear units scale **FAC**tor) variable.

The *Apply to layout dimensions only* toggle sets the measurement Scale factor: to be used only when dimensioning in a Layout tab, but not when dimensioning in the Model tab. This toggle sets the DIMLFAC variable to a negative value.

Also found in the Dimension area of the Primary Units tab is the Zero Suppression area. Look at Figure 11.44, where you will see four check boxes that are used to control the display of leading and trailing zeros in the primary units. The Leading and Trailing check boxes are off by default, and the 0 Feet and 0 Inches are on by default. This is set at the Command: prompt with the DIMZIN (**Z**ero **IN**ch display) variable. The following list explains the use of each option:

- **Leading** This check box is off by default, which leaves a zero on dimension numerals less than one. This complies with the ASME standard for metric dimensions. You should check this box if you are doing inch dimensioning. The results of each application are shown in Figure 11.48. The command line variable is DIMZIN set at 4.

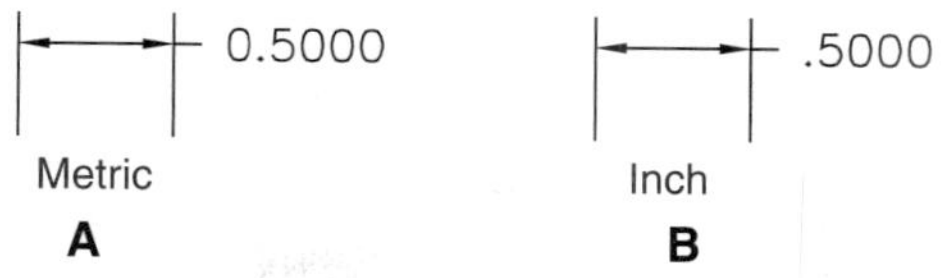

FIGURE 11.48 (A) The recommended metric dimension text application with Leading Zero Suppression off. (B) The recommended inch dimension text application with Leading Zero Suppression on.

FIGURE 11.49 (A) The recommended metric dimension text application with Leading Zero Suppression off and Trailing Zero Suppression on. (B) The recommended inch dimension text application with Leading Zero Suppression on and Trailing Zero Suppression off.

- **Trailing** This is off by default, which leaves the number of zeros after the decimal point based on the precision setting. This is usually off for inch dimensioning because the trailing zeros often imply higher precision levels for the manufacturing process. However, the ASME standard recommends that zeros be removed following decimal metric dimensions, which means that you should check this box when doing metric dimensioning. The command line setting is DIMZIN at 8. Figure 11.49 shows an example with this option off and on.
- **0 Feet** This check box is on by default which removes the zero in feet and inch dimensions when there are zero inches. For example, when 0 Feet suppression is ON a measurement reads 8". If 0 Feet suppression is OFF the same dimension reads 0′-8″. This is controlled by the DIMZIN variable.
- **0 Inches** This check box is on by default, which removes the zero when the inch part of feet and inch dimensions is less than one inch, such as 8′-3/4″. If this check box is off, the same dimension reads 8′-0 3/4″. This is controlled at the Command: prompt with a DIMZIN setting of 3.

The Angular Dimensions area of the Primary Units tab provides the following options:

- **Units format:** This area of the Primary Units tab is used to set the desired type of angular units for dimensioning. The angular unit options were discussed in Chapter 2 during the discussion of AutoCAD LT setup and the UNITS command. The UNITS command does not control the type of units used for dimensioning. These must be set here. The default is Decimal Degrees and the list of options is shown in Figure 11.50. Angular units for dimensions are set at the Command: prompt with the DIMAUNIT (**A**ngular **UNIT**s) dimension variable.

The remaining options include the Precision: setting (DIMALTD) and the Zero Suppression setting (DIMAZIN). These work exactly like the settings discussed in the Linear Dimensions area of the Primary Units tab.

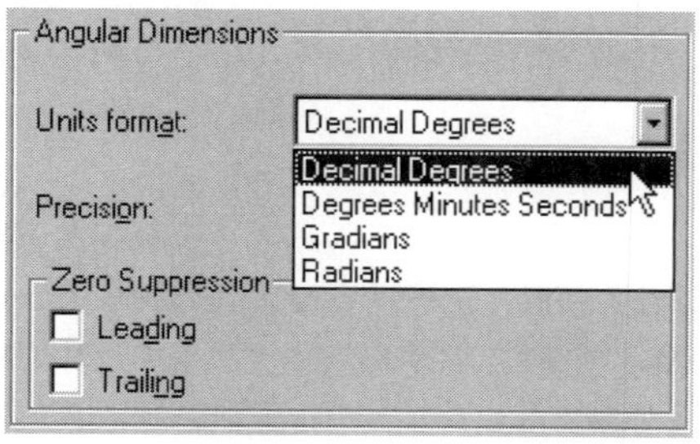

FIGURE 11.50 The Angular Dimensioning Units format: options in the Primary Units tab.

Setting Up Alternate Dimension Units

Alternate units are the secondary unit specification used in dual dimensioning. Dual dimensioning is the use of two separate unit formats in the drawing dimensions. As an example, a drawing submitted to an overseas client may need to show metric dimensions, whereas the local machine shop personnel fabricating the parts may require dimensions to be shown using inches. In a dual dimensioning system, dimensional values can be shown both in inches and in millimeters. Dual dimensioning practice is no longer a recommended ASME standard. ASME recommends that drawings be dimensioned using inches or metric units only. If you have a specialized application where dual dimensioning must be used, this feature is set up using the Alternate Units tab (see Figure 11.51).

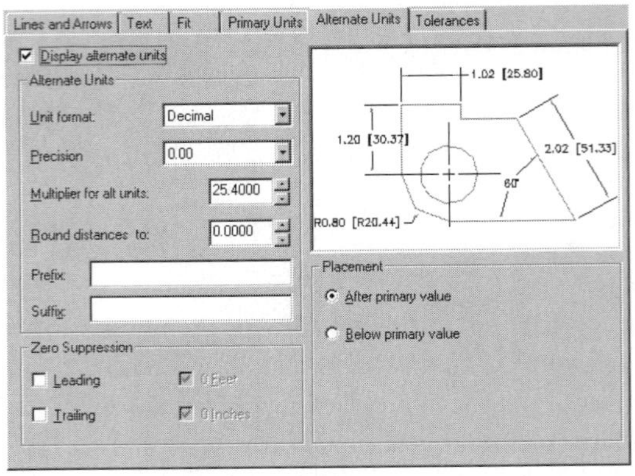

FIGURE 11.51 The Alternate Units tab provides settings related to dual dimensioning systems.

The alternate units settings are enabled by placing a check mark in the Display alternate units check box. Most of the settings are the same as the settings for the primary units. The available settings are as follows:

- **Unit format:** This allows you to select the format for the alternate units. The command line variable for this is DIMALTU.
- **Precision** Sets the precision level for the alternate units. This setting is stored in the DIMALTD variable.
- **Multiplier for alt units:** Sets the conversion factor for actual units. This number is multiplied by the primary unit value to derive the alternate units. AutoCAD LT stores this setting in the DIMALTF variable.
- **Round distances to:** Sets the rounding value used for alternate units. Use DIMALTRND at the command line to set this value.
- **Prefix:** Sets the prefix value used for alternate units display. Uses the DIMAPOST system variable.
- **Suffix:** Sets the suffix value used for alternate units display. Uses the DIMAPOST system variable.

The Zero Suppression area has the same effect on alternate units as the settings discussed earlier relating to primary units. The dimension variable used for this setting is DIMALTZ. The Placement area is used to determine whether the alternate units are placed behind or below the primary units value. This value is also stored by the DIMAPOST variable. When the alternate units are set to be displayed beneath the primary units, a value of \X is added to the end of the current Suffix: value on the Primary Units tab. The **\X** character sequence represents a carriage return keystroke (Enter).

Applying Dimension Tolerances

The Tolerances tab, shown in Figure 11.52, contains the settings for the dimensional tolerances for both primary and secondary units. The Tolerance Format area provides the settings for the primary units tolerances; selecting a dimensioning Method: from the list of options enables the settings in this area. The Alternate Unit Tolerance controls for Precision: and Zero Suppression are enabled only if alternate units are in use in the current dimension style.

FIGURE 11.52

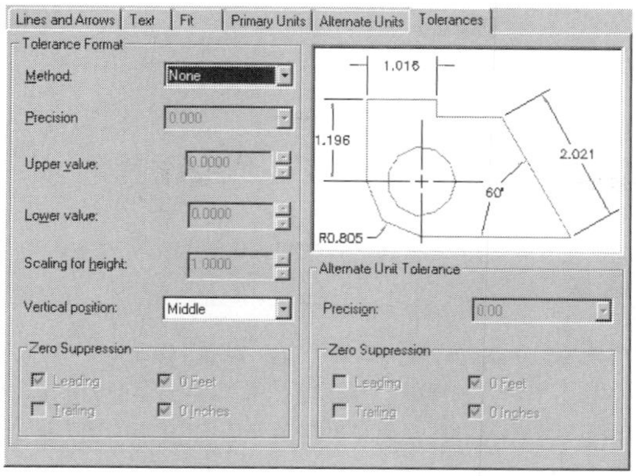

FIGURE 11.53 The Methods: options in the Tolerance Format area of the Tolerances tab

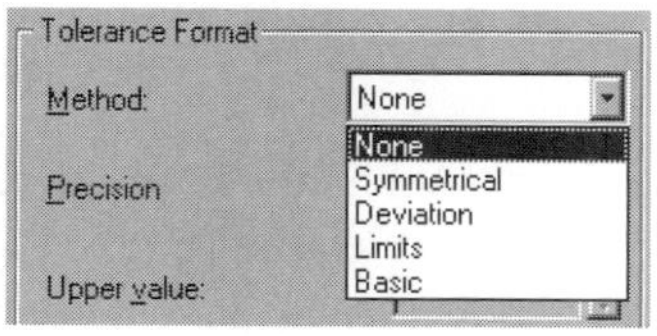

Setting Tolerance Methods

A ***tolerance*** is the total amount a specific dimension is permitted to vary. Tolerance dimensions are typically used on mechanical drawings for manufacturing. The Method: list provides None as the initial default. This means that no tolerance method is used with your dimensions and the options in this area are disabled. Pick the down arrow to see the other options in the Method: list as shown in Figure 11.53. The tolerance method options are explained in the following list:

- **Symmetrical**: This option is used to draw dimension text displaying an equal bilateral tolerance. An ***equal bilateral tolerance*** is a tolerance for which the variation is permitted equally in both directions from the specified dimension. The ***specified dimension*** is the primary units part of the dimension with tolerance. When the Symmetrical option is selected, the Preview image displays dimensions using an equal bilateral tolerance as shown in Figure 11.54A. Next, enter a value, such as .005, for the equal bilateral tolerance in the Upper value: box, as shown in Figure 11.54B. Now, draw a dimension with the ±.005 tolerance applied. Figure 11.55 shows a sample dimension and its components. The Symmetrical option can be set at the Command: prompt by turning the DIMTOL (**TOL**erance) variable on and setting the DIMTP (Tolerance **P**lus) and DIMTM (**T**olerance **M**inus) variables to the same numerical value.

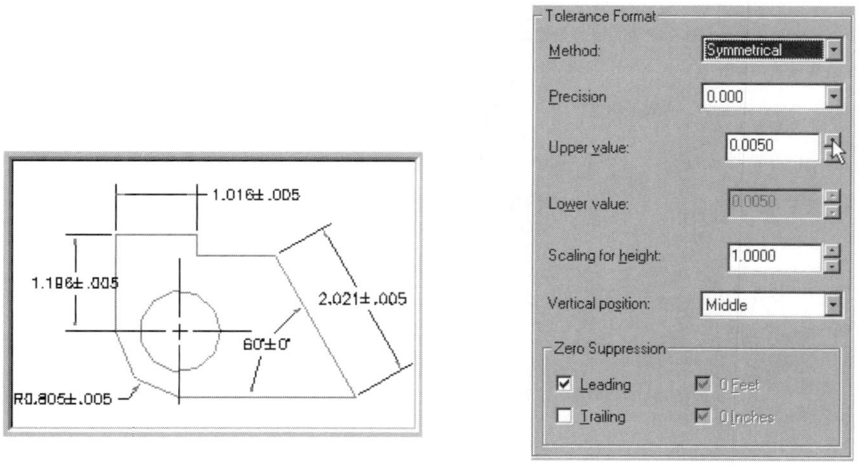

A B

FIGURE 11.54 (A) The Symmetrical tolerance method option. Enter the tolerance amount in the Upper value: box. (B) The symmetrical tolerance is illustrated in the preview area.

FIGURE 11.55 The elements of an equal bilateral tolerance dimension.

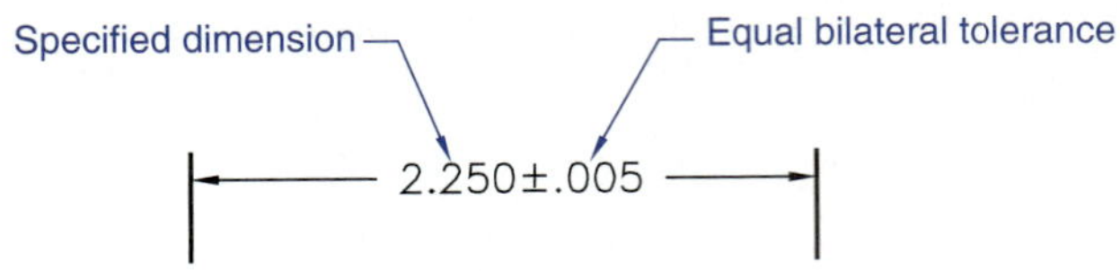

Field Notes

If your dimension tolerances do not reflect the level of precision you want, check the setting of the DIMTDEC variable. Either type **DIMTDEC** at the command line, or use the Tolerance tab of the Modify Dimension Style dialog box accessed by picking the Modify... button in the Dimension Style Manager dialog box.

- **Deviation**: AutoCAD refers to an unequal bilateral tolerance as ***deviation.*** An ***unequal bilateral tolerance*** is a tolerance for which the variation is permitted unequally in both directions from the specified dimension. When you select Deviation, the Upper value: and Lower value: text boxes are available to enter the desired upper and lower tolerance values as shown in Figure 11.56. Also, when you pick the Deviation option, the image tile in the Primary Units area changes to match a representation for this option. Figure 11.57 shows the results of drawing an unequal bilateral tolerance.

  The Deviation option can also be used to draw unilateral tolerances. A ***unilateral tolerance*** is a tolerance for which the variation is permitted in only one direction from the specified dimension. If you want a unilateral tolerance, enter zero as either the Upper Value or the Lower Value. Figure 11.58 shows an example of a unilateral tolerance dimension. When you draw a unilateral tolerance, AutoCAD LT automatically drops the + or − value from the zero part of the tolerance. This is the preferred method for a metric tolerance but is not recommended by ASME for an inch tolerance. The Deviation option can be set at the Command: prompt by turning the DIMTOL variable on and then setting the DIMTP and DIMTM variables to different numerical values.

FIGURE 11.56 The Deviation tolerance method option with values entered in the Upper Value: and Lower Value: boxes. Notice the matching preview image.

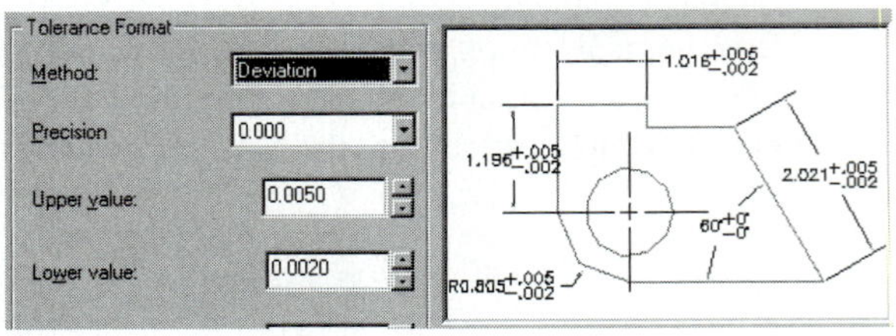

FIGURE 11.57 The elements of an unequal bilateral tolerance dimension.

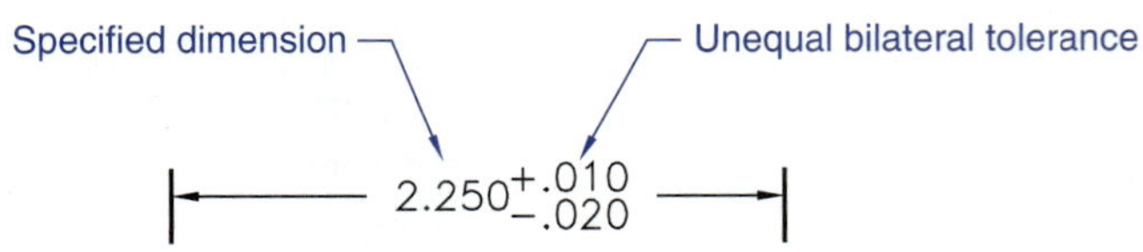

FIGURE 11.58 The elements of a unilateral tolerance dimension.

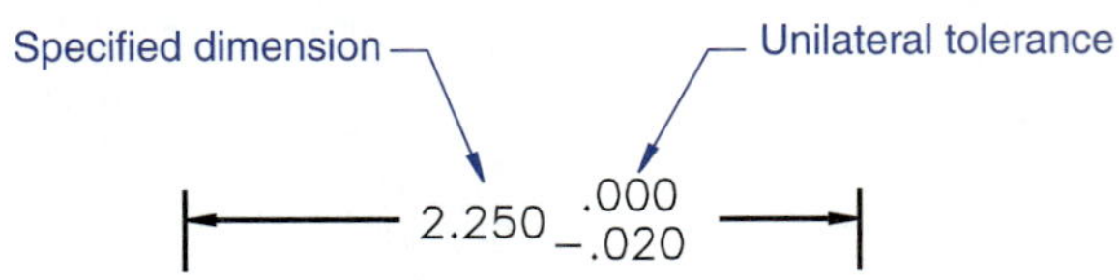

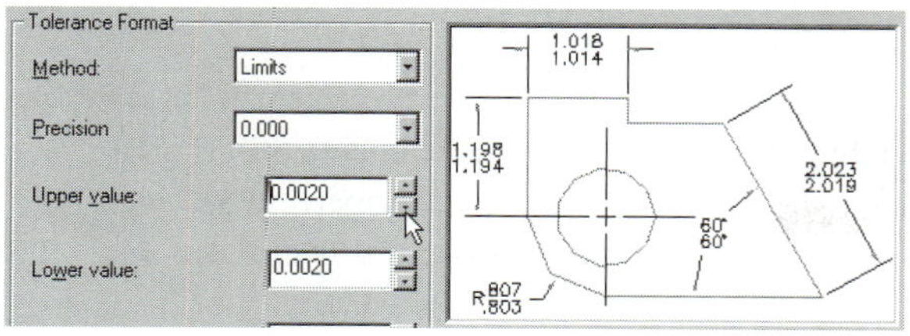

FIGURE 11.59 The Limits tolerance method option with values entered in the Upper value: and Lower value: boxes. Notice the matching image tile.

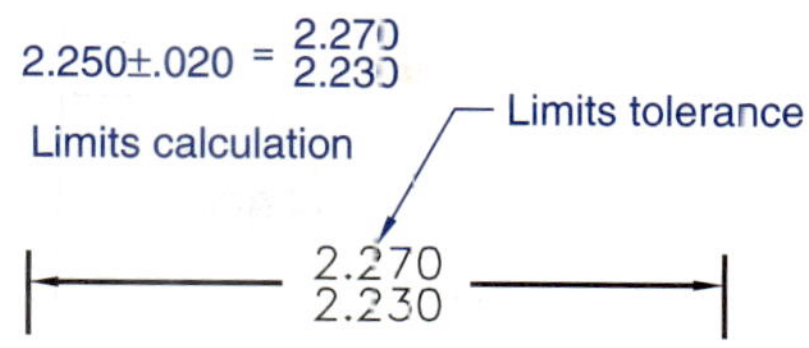

FIGURE 11.60 A sample limits tolerance dimension with the limits calculated automatically by AutoCAD LT based on the values you specify.

- **Limits:** The types of dimension shown in Figures 11.55, 11.57, and 11.58 are referred to as ***plus/minus tolerances.*** This is where a specified dimension and tolerance values are given. A ***limits tolerance*** is a tolerance for which the plus and minus part of the tolerance is calculated with the specified dimension to provide tolerance limits. When you pick the Limits option, the Upper value: and Lower value: text boxes are available to enter the desired amount you want added and subtracted from the specified dimension to create the limits. The values can be the same or different—a choice that depends on the results you expect. The Preview image is changed to represent tolerance limits as shown in Figure 11.59. A limits dimension is shown in Figure 11.60 using the values entered in Figure 11.59. The Limits option can be set at the Command: prompt by turning the DIMTOL variable off and the DIMLIM variable on, and set the DIMTP and DIMTM variables to the desired numerical values.When you turn DIMTOL on, DIMLIM is automatically turned off. Likewise, when you turn DIMLIM on, the DIMTOL variable is automatically turned off.
- **Basic:** The Basic method option is used to draw basic dimensions. A ***basic dimension*** is used in geometric dimensioning and tolerancing and is used as a value that is considered a theoretically perfect size, profile, orientation, or location dimension. When you pick the Basic option from the Method: list, other options in the Tolerance area are unavailable. A basic dimension has a box around it as displayed in the image shown in Figure 11.61. Figure 11.62 shows a sample basic dimension.

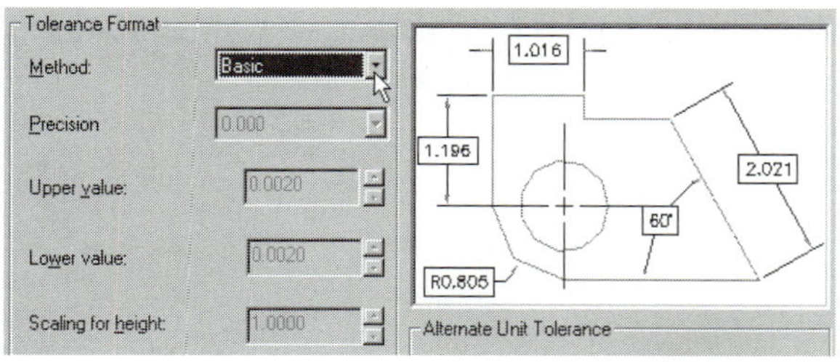

FIGURE 11.61 The Basic dimension tolerance method option. Notice the box around the dimension shown in the image tile.

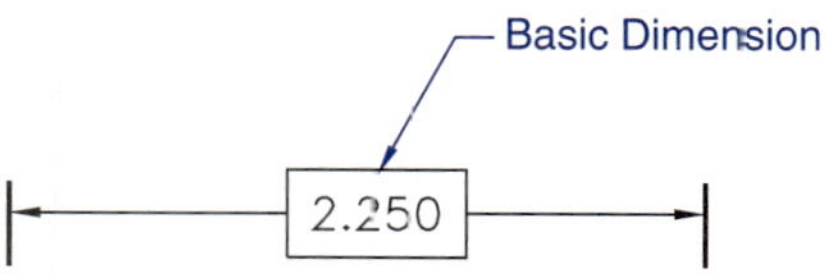

FIGURE 11.62 A sample basic dimension.

Field Notes

- Inch tolerance dimensions should have the Leading Zero Suppression box checked in the Dimension and Tolerance areas of the Primary Units tab. This allows you to properly place inch tolerance dimensions based on ASME standards without the zero before the decimal point, such as .625±.005.
- Metric tolerance dimensions should have the Leading Zero Suppression box off (not checked) in the Dimension and Tolerance areas of the Primary Units tab. This allows you to properly place metric tolerance dimensions based on ASME standards with the zero before the decimal point; for example, 12±0.2.

The tolerance property fields are enabled when they apply to the current tolerancing method. These properties control the presentation and application of the tolerance values. The settings are described as follows:

- **Precision** — Sets the number of decimal places, or precision level, of the displayed tolerance values. This value is stored in the DIMTDEC variable.
- **Upper value: & Lower value:** — As described in the previous discussion, these settings control the deviation from the dimension represented by the tolerance. Controlled using the DIMTP and DIMTM variables.
- **Scaling for height**: — Scaling for height box in the Tolerance Format area is used to set the text height of the tolerance in relationship to the text height of the specified dimension. The default is 1.00, which makes the tolerance text the same height as the specified dimension text. This is the recommended ASME practice. If you want the tolerance height three-quarters as high as the specified dimension height, enter .75 in the Height: box. Some companies prefer this practice when using unequal bilateral tolerances. Figure 11.63 shows an example of dimensions with different tolerance text
- **Vertical position**: — The vertical position: list in the Tolerance tab is used to establish how the tolerance value is placed in alignment with the specified dimension. This list is active when the Symmetrical and Deviation options are used. Middle justification is the default, and it centers the tolerance with the specified dimension. This is also the common ASME recommended practice. The other options are Top and Bottom as shown in Figure 11.64. The effect of using each of the justification methods is shown with tolerance dimensions in Figure 11.65. Tolerance justification is controlled at the Command: prompt with the DIMTOLJ variable.

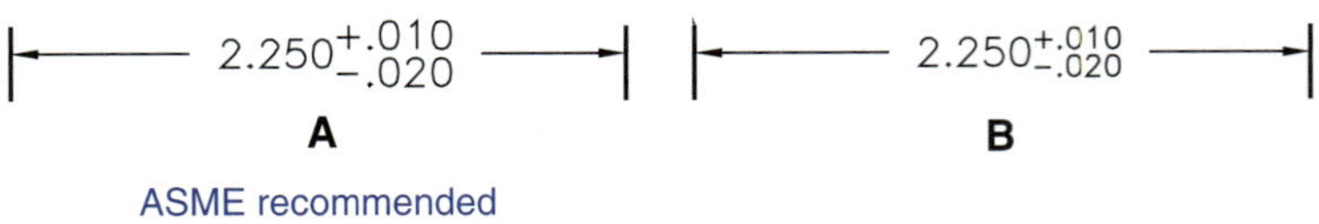

FIGURE 11.63 Examples of using different tolerance height options. (A) Tolerance height value of 1 is the default and makes the tolerance text the same height as the specified dimension text. This is the ASME recommended practice. (B) Tolerance height value of .75 makes the tolerance text height three-quarters the height of the specified dimension text height.

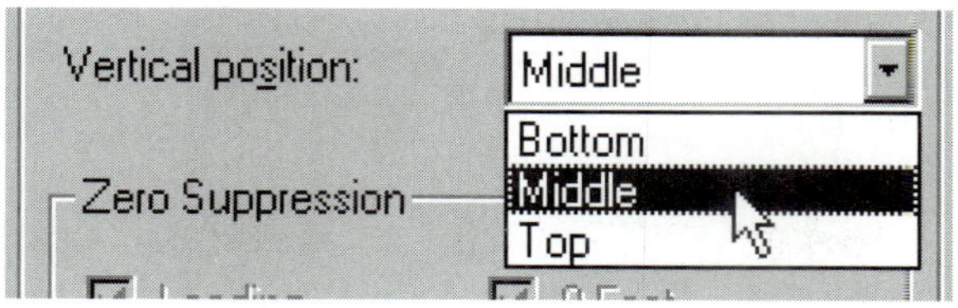

FIGURE 11.64 The Vertical position: list in the Tolerance Format area of the Tolerances tab.

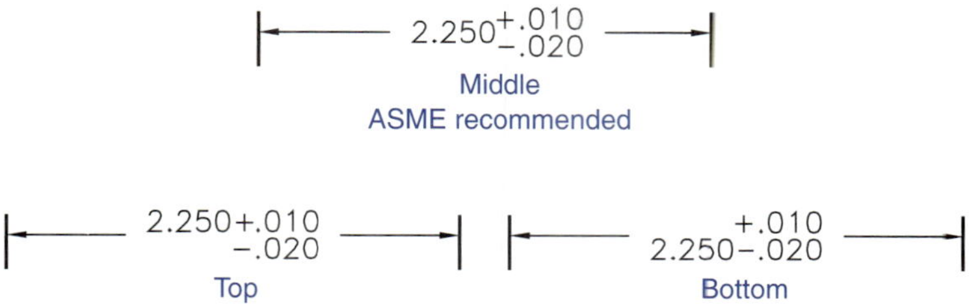

FIGURE 11.65 Examples of the different tolerance justification options. The Middle option is recommended by the ASME standard.

Once you have made all the settings to the dimension style, pick the OK button to return to the Dimension Style Manager dialog box. To make the new style active, just pick the style name from the list and pick the Set Current button. Optionally, you can double-click on the desired style name or right-click on it and pick Set current.

Field Notes

- The easiest way to set the current Dimension Style is select the desired style name from the drop-down list on the Dimension toolbar. All styles defined in the current drawing are available on this list.
- The Dimension Style drop-down list can also be used like the list features on the Object Properties toolbar to change the style used by existing dimensions. Simply grip select the dimension objects and then pick the new style to apply from the Dimension Style list.

Deleting and Renaming Dimension Styles

By right-clicking on a dimension style name in the Dimension Style Manager dialog box, you can display the Dimension Style Manager shortcut menu. This menu provides an option to rename or delete the selected dimension style. Optionally, you can pick a dimension style and press the Delete key on your keyboard to delete it.

Comparing Dimension Style Settings

The Dimension Style Manager makes it easy to find the difference between dimension styles. When a dimension style name is selected from the list, it is compared with the currently active style, and the differences are displayed in the Description area below the preview image. If not all the information is currently visible, you can pick inside the description box and use the arrow keys to move up and down through the text. By right-clicking in the Description box, you can pick Select All and then Copy to copy the information to the Windows Clipboard. The information can then be pasted into another application for printing or review.

Dimension Style comparisons can also be done by picking the Compare... button. This displays the Compare Dimension Styles dialog box (see Figure 11.66).

Pick one style name in the Compare: list and another in the With: list. The number of differences found is displayed above the list, and the list shows descriptions, the associated dimvar names, and the differing values specified for the selected styles. If you select the <none> option from the With: list or pick the same name that is displayed in the Compare: list, all the settings for that style are displayed. Picking the Copy button copies the comparison data to the Windows Clipboard, making it available for pasting into another application. The information copied to the clipboard is ***tab delimited,*** meaning that each data item, called a *field*, is separated from the next with a tab. This may produce inconsistent results if pasted into a word processor but works excellently when pasted into a spreadsheet application. In a spreadsheet, each field is placed in its own cell.

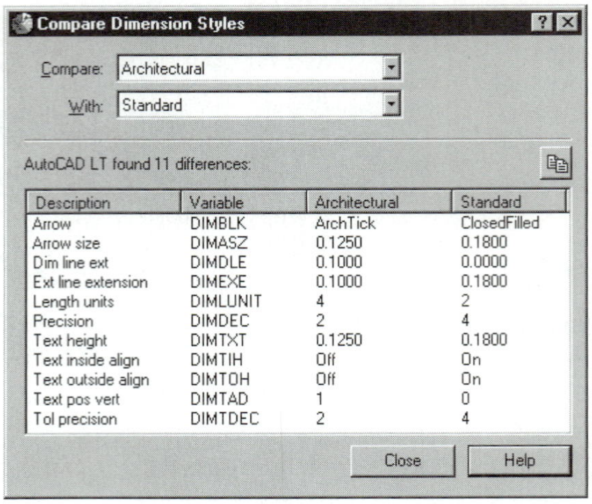

FIGURE 11.66 The Compare Dimension Styles dialog box displays the differences between two selected dimension styles.

Importing Dimension Styles Using AutoCAD DesignCenter

In a drawing started using your own template, your dimension styles should already be defined as part of the template. However, when you open an existing drawing or receive a drawing from external sources, you may need to import your company standard dimension style into the drawing. Previously in this text, the AutoCAD DesignCenter tool was used to import layer setups, linetype definitions, and text styles. You can also drag and drop dimension styles from any existing drawings using AutoCAD DesignCenter. This can speed production and helps to ensure consistent implementation of standards between drawings.

Drag-and-Drop Dimension Styles

Accessing dimension styles using AutoCAD DesignCenter uses the same procedure as described in earlier chapters for accessing layers, linetypes, and text styles. First, open the DesignCenter window and locate the content source you need—a drawing file in which the desired dimension style is defined. Open the content source file in the tree pane to display the content categories and select the desired category to display its content in the palette pane. In this case, select the Dimstyles category to display the available Dimension Style content. Figure 11.67 shows the AutoCAD DesignCenter window with a selection of dimension styles displayed in the palette pane. The fastest way to import a dimension style is to drag and drop its icon into the destination drawing, or you can use any of the other available methods for accessing DesignCenter content as described in previous chapters.

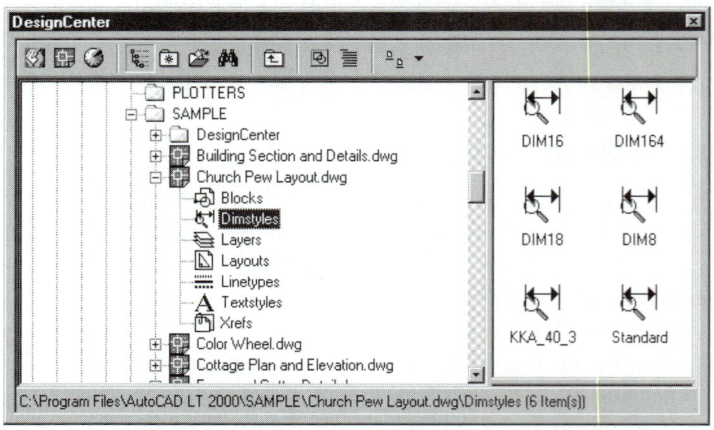

FIGURE 11.67 AutoCAD DesignCenter provides an easy way to import dimension styles from existing drawings.

Field Notes

Remember that when dragging and dropping a dimension style from the DesignCenter window, if the name is the same as a style already defined in the drawing, the new style being dragged in is ignored. For example, if you try to drag a style named Standard from an existing drawing when you already have a style named Standard, the new information is not used; therefore, the existing Standard style in the current drawing remains unchanged.

Exercise 11.12 **Estimated time required: 15 min.**

1. Continue working in EX11.11 (or open it for editing if needed).
2. Start the Dimension Style Manager, pick the dimension style name created in EX11.10, and pick the Modify... button to continue defining the new style.
3. On the Primary Units tab, change each of the settings for both Linear Dimensions and Angular Dimensions and observe the results in the preview image.
4. Set up a system of units that is appropriate for your dimension style. Check your company or school standards carefully to ensure complete compliance.
5. In the Alternate Units tab, enable alternate units and explore the setting options.
6. Disable alternate units, and select the Tolerances tab.
7. Set up tolerance options using each tolerancing method, viewing the results in the preview image.
8. Set tolerances to none.
9. Pick the OK button, and in the Dimension Style Manager pick the Compare... button and compare the new style with the Standard style.
10. Pick the Close button, and in the Dimension Style Manager, pick Close again.
11. Use AutoCAD DesignCenter to insert a desired set of layers, linetype definitions, and text styles from an existing drawing file. Close DesignCenter.
12. Save the drawing as a template file named EX11.12.**dwt** and close.
13. Start a new drawing, using EX11.12.dwt as the starting template. Check the Dimension Style Manager to see that your defined dimension style is available in the new drawing.
14. Save as EX11.12.dwg, and close the drawing.

Creating Dimension Style Families

In many drawing applications, different types of dimensions are presented using differing dimension styles. For example, linear dimensions in a mechanical drawing are frequently presented using bilateral tolerances. However, angular dimensions do not typically use tolerances. Diameter dimensions often use centerlines, but radius dimensions do not. In AutoCAD LT, each different type of dimension can be assigned specific settings that are applied to only to that type of dimension.

Dimension Style and Secondary Styles

When you first create a dimension style, you are creating what is sometimes referred to as a *parent* style. The parent defines the base characteristics from which modified secondary styles deviate; the text height, arrowhead size, and other common features are supplied by the parent style. The secondary styles, sometimes called *child* styles or substyles, can then be modified to meet any specific needs. A parent dimension style and all its substyles (children) are referred to as a di*mension family*.

In this example, a user-defined dimension style called "Mechanical-ASME" implements bilateral tolerancing in the parent style, but the tolerancing should not be used when drawing angular dimensions. The first step is to access the Dimension Style Manager dialog box. Pick the New... button to display the Create New Dimension Style dialog box. The style that was selected when you picked the New... button is offered as the default option in the Start With: list. Be certain to select the correct parent style. Specify what type of dimension you want to modify by selecting it from the Use for: list. Figure 11.68A shows the list of available options in the Use for: list. When you select something other than All dimensions, the New Style Name: box is disabled and assigned an automatically generated name using the base style name and the type of dimension being modified. The Create New Dimension Style dialog box with the New Style Name: set to *Mechanical-ASME: Angular* is shown in Figure 11.68B.

The preview image in the New Dimension Style dialog box shows only the type of dimension that you are currently modifying. All the features in the New Dimension Style dialog box work exactly as discussed previously in this chapter. The New Dimension Style dialog box as it appears when modifying the tolerance settings for angular dimension features is illustrated in Figure 11.69. After the new secondary style settings are defined for the selected dimension type, the Styles: list in the Dimension Style Manager shows the sec-

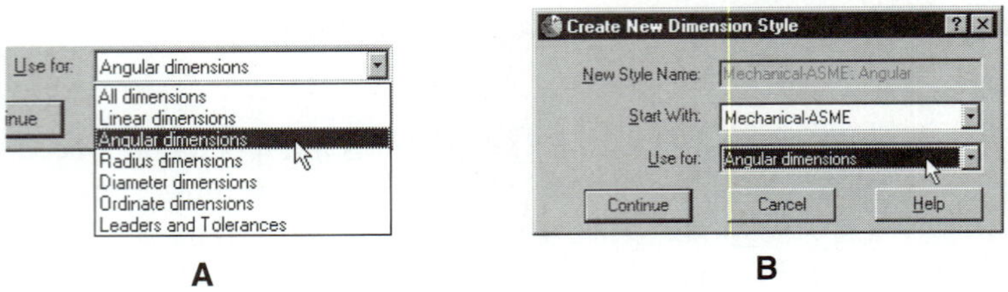

FIGURE 11.68 (A) The Use for: list specifies which type of dimension is being modified.

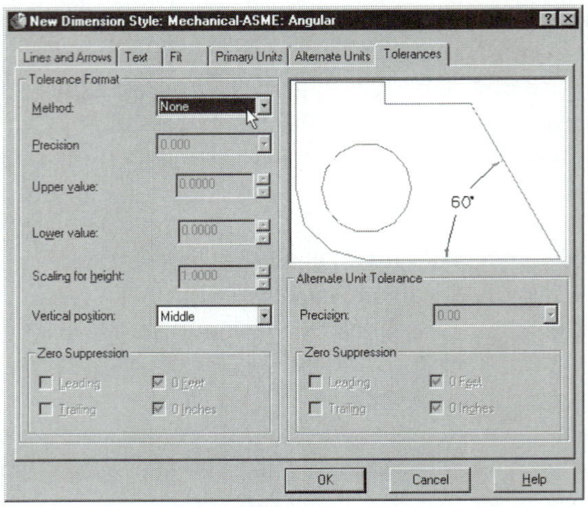

FIGURE 11.69 Tolerance values are disabled for the Angular dimension type of the Mechanical-ASME dimension style.

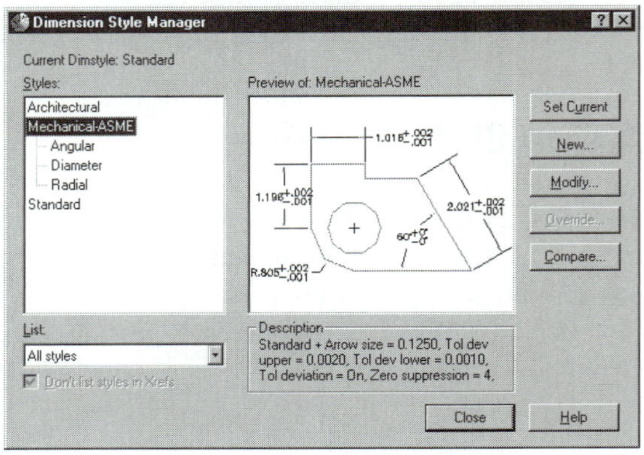

FIGURE 11.70 The dimension substyles, or secondary styles, listed in the Styles: list are shown branching off from the parent style.

ondary style branching off from the parent style name (see Figure 11.70). All subsequent modifications made to the parent style are automatically applied to the children with one exception: the specific settings that you modified to define the secondary style are no longer affected by changes to the parent style.

You cannot set a secondary style current. The secondary style settings are automatically applied to the appropriate dimensions when the parent style is used. When you want to see what the differences are between a parent style and one of its secondary styles, use the Compare… option in the Dimension Style Manager.

Using Dimension Style Overrides

Any dimensioning styles that are frequently used should be defined and permanently saved in your template files. Then, simply select the desired dimension style as you are dimensioning. If you accidentally use the incorrect style when creating a dimension, simply grip-select it and pick the correct style name from the Dimension Style drop-down list on the Dimension toolbar to change it to the correct style.

Occasionally, you will need to draw one or more dimensions that do not conform to any defined dimension style. If you will be using this style frequently, you can define a new style; otherwise, you can add temporary adjustments to your dimension style called dimension style *overrides*. Dimension style overrides can be set current so that all new dimensions use the new settings, or overrides can be applied to existing dimensions. Modifying existing dimensions is discussed later in this chapter.

Setting Running Dimension Style Overrides

You can override existing settings for the current dimension style from the Dimension Style Manager, or if you are familiar with the needed dimvar settings, you can make these changes at the command line. To set dimension style overrides from the Dimension Style Manager, select the current style from the list and pick the Override… button. The Override button is available only when the current dimension style is selected in the Styles: list. The Override Current Style: dialog box is shown in Figure 11.71.

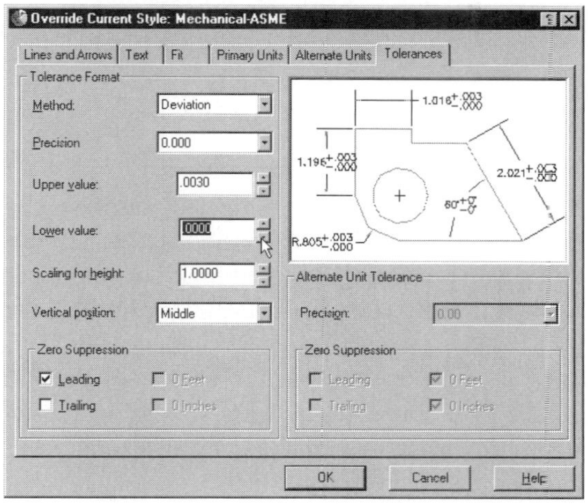

FIGURE 11.71 The Override Current Style dialog box allows you to create specialized dimensions by making temporary adjustments to defined dimension styles while you create the new dimensions.

When the Override Current Style dialog box opens, make any desired temporary changes to the currently active style. When you pick the OK button, you are returned to the Dimension Style Manager dialog box. A new entry of <style overrides> appears under the style to which the overrides were applied, as shown in Figure 11.72A. Right-clicking on the <Style overrides> listing displays a shortcut menu (see Figure 11.71B), with the following options:

- **Rename** Renaming the <style overrides> item saves these settings as a new style name. This allows you to save the style overrides for later use.
- **Delete** Deletes the <style overrides>.
- **Save to current style** Applies the settings made in <style overrides> to the current style. All dimensions that were created previously using the base style are immediately updated to match the applied override style settings.

When style overrides are active, you cannot set a different style current without deleting, renaming, or saving the <style overrides>. Attempting to set a different style current displays a dialog box indicating that the style overrides will be discarded (see Figure 11.73). If you want to save the overrides, cancel the dialog box and right-click on the <style override> to access the shortcut menu options. Discarding the style overrides does not affect the appearance of dimensions created while the overrides were active.

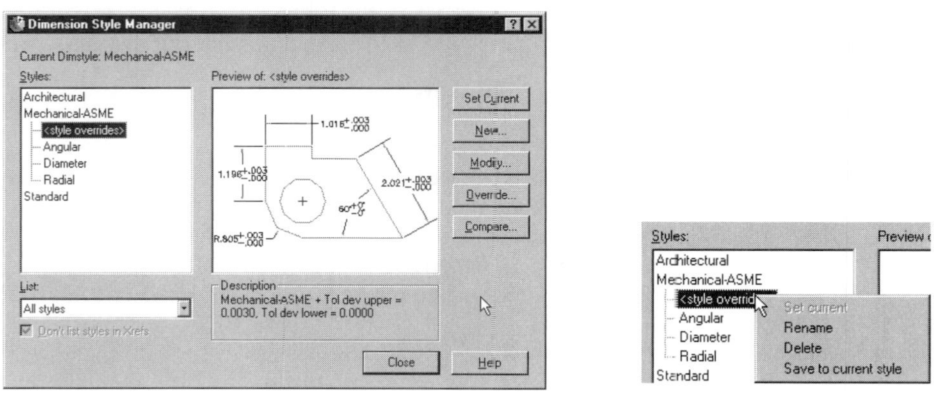

A B

FIGURE 11.72 (A) Creating a style override creates a <style overrides> entry below the primary style. (B) The style overrides shortcut menu.

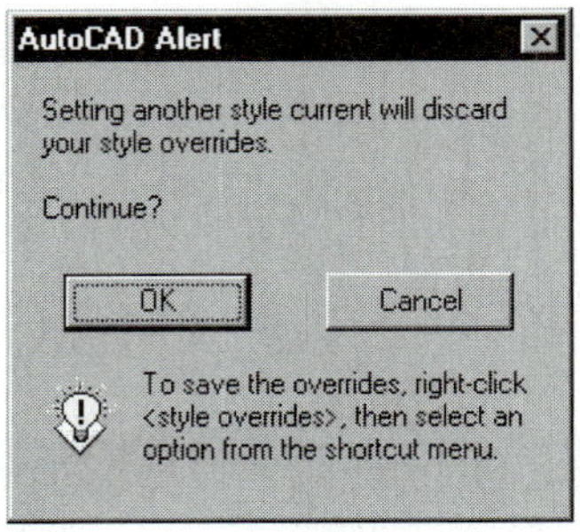

FIGURE 11.73 AutoCAD LT alerts you that setting a new style current will discard the active <style overrides>.

Field Notes

- If you currently have style overrides running and you change the active dimension style using the Dimension Style list on the Dimension toolbar, the currently active style overrides are discarded automatically. No warning is issued to allow you to cancel the process, but if you set the new style unintentionally you can use the **U** command to undo the style change and restore the overrides.
- The –DIMSTYLE command can be used to work with dimension styles at the command line. When the –DIMSTYLE command is used, dimension substyles are listed using the parent style name with a suffix made up of a dollar sign and a number. Trying to set a secondary style active causes the parent style to become active.

Setting Style Overrides at the Command Line

When you learn the names and settings of the AutoCAD LT dimension variables (dimvars), you can quickly set running overrides at the Command line by typing the name of the dimension variable and entering the override setting. For example, to turn on dimensional tolerancing and change the current bilateral tolerance settings to +.005/−.000, you would use the following Command sequence:

Command: **DIMTOL**↵
Enter new value for DIMTOL <OFF>: **1**↵
Command: **DIMTP**↵
Enter new value for DIMTP <0.0030>: **.005**↵
Command: **DIMTM**↵
Enter new value for DIMTM <0.0100>: **.000**↵
Command:

Notice that although the DIMTOL value shows ON or OFF, you can save keystrokes by entering a 1 for ON or a 0 for OFF. The previous sequence sets up a style override just as if you made the changes by picking Overrides... from the Dimension Style Manager, as discussed earlier. If you make subsequent changes to the style overrides, they do not affect dimensions that have already been drawn. The new settings are applied only to new dimensions created while the overrides are still active.

If you are currently at a prompt issued by a dimensioning command, you can omit the DIM from the variable name when you enter it. In the following sequence, extension line origins are picked, but when the dimension line is being dragged into location it is noticed that the tolerance values need to be adjusted:

Command: **DLI** or **DIMLINEAR**↵
Specify first extension line origin or <select object>: ⟨*pick first extension line origin*⟩
Specify second extension line origin: ⟨*pick second extension line origin*⟩
Specify dimension line location or [Mtext/Text/Angle/Horizontal/Vertical/Rotated]: **TP**↵
Enter new value for dimension variable <0.0030>: **.005**↵
Specify dimension line location or [Mtext/Text/Angle/Horizontal/Vertical/Rotated]: **TM**↵
Enter new value for dimension variable <0.0000>: **.005**↵
Specify dimension line location or [Mtext/Text/Angle/Horizontal/Vertical/Rotated]: ⟨*pick the dimension line location*⟩
Dimension text = 2.750
Command:

Exercise 11.13

Estimated time required: 20 min.

1. Begin a drawing using the template EX11.12.dwt.
2. Draw the shape shown in Figure 11.39. Do not add dimensions yet.
3. Draw a ∅1.0″ circle inside the shape.
4. Add an R0.5 fillet to the upper left corner of the shape.
5. Make two additional copies of the shape with the new features you added.
6. Using the Modify... option in the Dimension Style Manager, set the base style to use Center Marks. (This setting is found on the Lines and Arrows tab of the Modify Dimensions Style dialog box.)
7. Create a secondary style, based on the current style, for Diameter type dimensions. Set your diameter dimensions to use Center Lines.
8. Dimension the first shape using the dimension style you defined in your template drawing. Use a radius dimension on the fillet arc and a diameter dimension on the circle.
9. Create a secondary style, based on the current dimension style, to be used only for Angular type dimensions.
10. If the style you created is designed for:
    - **Mechanical:** Set Angular dimension precision to one decimal place.
    - **Architectural:** Set Angular dimensions to use closed-filled arrowheads and one decimal place precision.
11. Add an angular dimension to the lower right corner of the first shape. Notice the differences between the angular dimension and the linear dimensions.
12. Now, add dimensions to the second shape as described in the following steps.
13. Make the Standard dimension style current.
14. Dimension the features at the top of the shape that require linear dimensions. Use Figure 11.39 as a reference if needed.
15. If your preferred drafting field is:
    - **Mechanical:** Set style overrides to suppress leading zeros, use two decimal place precision, and use the ROMANS font for dimension text.
    - **Architectural:** Set style overrides to suppress zero feet display, use tick marks instead of arrows, set the precision at ¼″, and use the CityBlueprint font for dimension text.
16. Dimension the remaining features using the style overrides.
17. Open the Dimension Style Manager. Right-click on the <style overrides> listing and select *Save to current style*. Pick the Close button. Notice that the dimensions along the top are automatically updated to match the new dimension style settings applied from the style overrides.
18. Using the DIMTOL, DIMTP, and DIMTM variables, set an override to apply bilateral tolerances to new dimensions. Dimension the third shape using the needed dimvars to set different tolerance values for each dimension, and use no tolerancing for the angular dimension.
19. Open the Dimension Style Manager and make the Standard parent style current. Pick OK in the alert box to discard the style overrides. Close the dialog box and check your dimensions. Discarding the style overrides has not affected existing dimensions that were created using the overrides.
20. Save as EX11.13, and close the drawing.

LEARNING CHECKPOINT

- ☐ Define *dimension styles.*
- ☐ Define *dimension variables* (dimvars).
- ☐ What dimension style name is set current if you override any settings in the current style?
- ☐ Discuss the function of dimension style families, both *parents* and *children* (secondary styles).
- ☐ Name the tab where the appearance of the dimension line and extension line can be changed.

- ☐ Name the default arrowhead option that is also commonly used on mechanical drawings.
- ☐ Name the most common arrowhead option used in architectural dimensioning applications.
- ☐ Name the tab where you can adjust the size and type of center marks used.
- ☐ What is the advantage of activating the *Place text manually when dimensioning* option?
- ☐ Describe recommended *Text* tab settings for mechanical and architectural drafting applications.
- ☐ Define *primary units*.
- ☐ Give the ASME recommended Zero Suppression settings used when dimensioning in inches and in millimeters.
- ☐ Define *tolerance*.
- ☐ List the names for the tolerance method used for the following applications: Specified dimension only (no tolerance), equal bilateral tolerance, unequal bilateral tolerance, unilateral tolerance, limits tolerance, and basic dimension.
- ☐ What tolerance justification option is recommended by the ASME standard?
- ☐ What tolerance height scale factor is recommended by the ASME standard?
- ☐ Where is the gap measured when the dimension text is inserted in a space provided in the dimension line?
- ☐ Where is the gap measured when the dimension text is placed above the dimension line?
- ☐ Give an example of a dimension prefix and suffix on different dimension numerals.

Dimensioning Drawings

- Using Dimension Styles
- Overriding Dimension Styles
- Creating Dimensions with Tolerances

Drawing Leader Lines and Notes

Dimension
Quick Leader
Dimension
Leader
QLEADER
LE

Leader lines were introduced earlier when drawing dimensions for circles and arcs using the DIMRADIUS and DIMDIAMETER commands. AutoCAD LT automatically draws a leader line connected to a circle or arc when using these commands. In certain situations, you may want to draw a leader line connected to a note other than a radius or diameter dimension. These types of notes apply to specific features or processes on the drawing and are referred to as ***specific*** or ***local notes.*** When you want to use a leader for an application like this, pick the Quick Leader button in the Dimension toolbar, pick Leader in the Dimension pull-down menu, or type **LE** or **QLEADER** at the Command: prompt. The QLEADER command asks you to pick a point to start and end the leader and then add the desired text. AutoCAD LT refers to text with a leader as an ***annotation.*** An arrowhead that matches the current dimension style is added at the start and a shoulder is automatically placed at the note when appropriate. The following command sequence draws the leader and note shown in Figure 11.74 with the different elements labeled:

Command: **LE** or **QLEADER**↵
Specify first leader point, or [Settings]<Settings>: ⟨*pick the leader start point*⟩
Specify next point: ⟨*pick the leader endpoint*⟩
Specify next point: ↵
Specify text width <0.0000>: ⟨*specify a width or press* ↵ *for no wrapping*⟩
Enter first line of annotation text <Mtext>: **2 x 10 JOISTS 16″ O.C.**↵
Enter next line of annotation text: ↵
Command:

FIGURE 11.74 The leader and its related elements drawn using the QLEADER command.

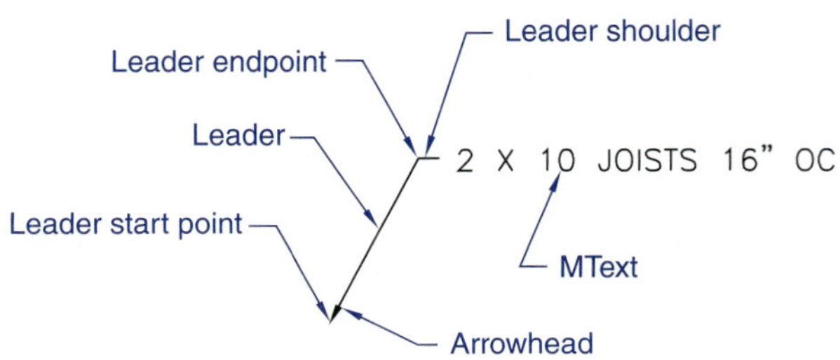

A leader in mechanical drafting normally has one line segment from the arrowhead to the shoulder. Although this is also true with architectural drafting, architectural leaders can be more flexible. Architectural leaders can have more than one segment if needed. To accomplish this, keep picking points as needed at the Specify next point: prompt. Leader text is multiline text; enter as many lines of text as needed to complete the note. When there is more than one line of text, the leader shoulder should be properly justified. Justification options are discussed later in this section. An example of a multisegment leader with more than one line of text is shown in Figure 11.75.

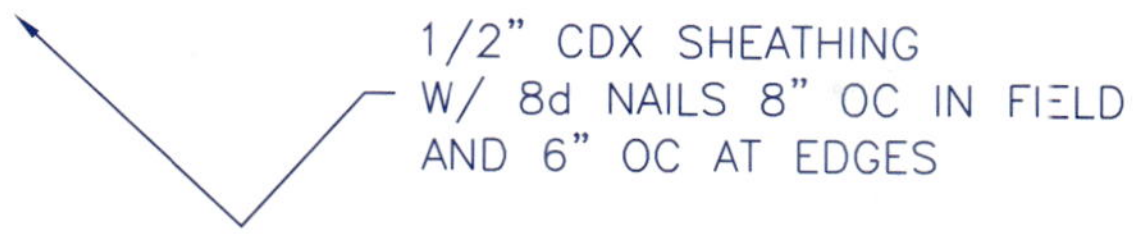

FIGURE 11.75 Leaders can have multiple line segments, but a single straight segment is recommended for mechanical drawings by the ASME standard.

You can specify any desired width for the Mtext object created with the leader. When the Mtext object has a controlled width the text content is word-wrapped as needed to stay within the defined Mtext boundary width. The text can be typed as though it were a single line. It is not necessary to define the end of each line by pressing the Enter key. If you specify a paragraph width that creates unsatisfactory results, the Mtext boundary width can be adjusted quickly and easily using grips.

If you enter a width of 0.0 at the Specify text width: prompt, the text can be any desired width and no word wrapping is applied. When entering the leader text at the command line with a zero width specification, you must press Enter at the end of each line of text in order to drop to the next line. Pressing Enter at an "Enter next line of annotation text:" prompt draws the leader and Mtext on screen and returns you to the Command: prompt.

To get the best control of the text layout, you may prefer to use the Multiline Text Editor. Working in the Multiline Text Editor provides more complete control of the final text appearance. At the "Enter first line of annotation text <Mtext>:" prompt, press Enter to start the Multiline Text Editor.

Command: **LE** or **QLEADER**↵
Specify first leader point, or [Settings]<Settings>: ⟨*pick the leader start point*⟩
Specify next point: ⟨*pick the leader endpoint*⟩
Specify next point: ↵
Specify text width <0.0000>: ⟨*specify a width or press ↵ for no wrapping*⟩
Enter first line of annotation text <Mtext>: ↵
⟨*Use the editor to define the text content, appearance, and layout; Pick OK when finished.*⟩
Command:

Leader Annotation Settings

The QLEADER command is very versatile and provides many timesaving features, which is why it is referred to as the *Quick Leader* tool. The Leader Settings dialog box is used to define the style, appearance, and functionality of the leader. The Annotation tab of the Leader Settings dialog box is shown in Figure 11.76. Pressing Enter at the first prompt of the QLEADER command displays the Leader Settings dialog box as follows:

Command: **LE** or **QLEADER**↵
Specify first leader point, or [Settings]<Settings>: ↵

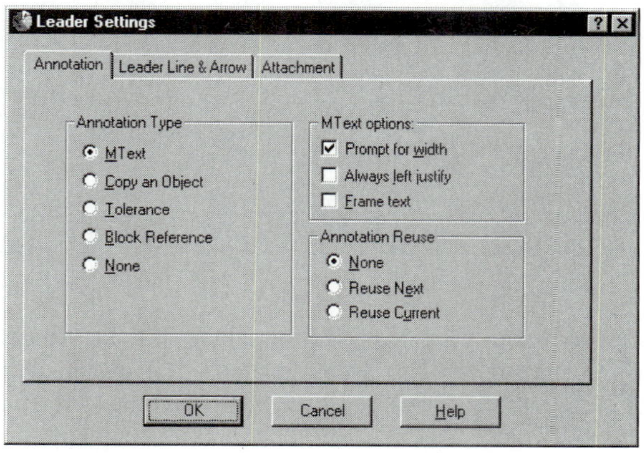

FIGURE 11.76 The Annotation tab on the Leader Settings dialog box is used to specify what type of annotation is used and to control Mtext and annotation reuse options.

Setting the Annotation Type

The settings in the Annotation Type area determine what is attached to the leader. The options offered in this area include Mtext, Copy an Object, Tolerance, Block Reference, and None. Each of these options is detailed in the following discussion.

Mtext: This option allows you to create a multiline text object with the leader. The QLEADER Mtext options were discussed previously.

Copy an Object: When the annotation object you want the leader to use is already defined in another location in your drawing, you can use this option to attach a copy of the existing object to the new leader. The objects that you can copy include multiline text, single-line text, tolerances, or block references. Block references are detailed in Chapter 12. When this option is selected, the QLEADER prompt sequence is as shown here:

Command: **LE** or **QLEADER**↵
Specify first leader point, or [Settings]<Settings>: ↵
⟨*Pick the* Copy an Object *radio button in the Annotation Type area and pick OK*⟩
Specify first leader point, or [Settings]<Settings>: ⟨*pick the leader start point*⟩
Specify next point: ⟨*pick the leader endpoint*⟩
Specify next point: ↵
Select an object to copy: ⟨*pick a text object, tolerance, or block reference to copy*⟩
Command:

The selected object is duplicated, and the copy is attached to the new leader. Existing notes or text objects that match or have similar content to the text needed for the new leader can be selected. Even if it is not an exact match, a quick edit of a similar text object can be faster than typing the entire text item from scratch. Whether copying text, tolerances, or block references, this is one of the fastest options for placing leader content.

Tolerance: After defining the leader points, the Tolerance option displays the Geometric Tolerance dialog box, where you can define a feature control frame. Enter the desired control specifications in the Geometric Tolerance dialog box, then pick OK to create the feature control frame. Although a full study of geometric tolerancing is recommended for accurate use of this feature, the following is a brief explanation of the Geometric Tolerance dialog box shown in Figure 11.77A.

The Sym area provides an image tile representing the current geometric characteristic being defined. If the image tile is blank, or you need to change the current symbol, point to the image tile and pick. This displays the Symbol dialog box (see Figure 11.77B). Picking a symbol dismisses the Symbol dialog box and places a representation of the selected symbol in the image tile. Picking the blank image in the Symbol dialog box means that no symbol is applied. In the Tolerance 1 and 2 areas there is a text box with image tiles on either side. Pick the image tile on the left to place a diameter symbol if appropriate. Picking the image tile to the right of the text box displays the Material Condition dialog box (see Figure 11.77C). Pick the desired symbol to dis-

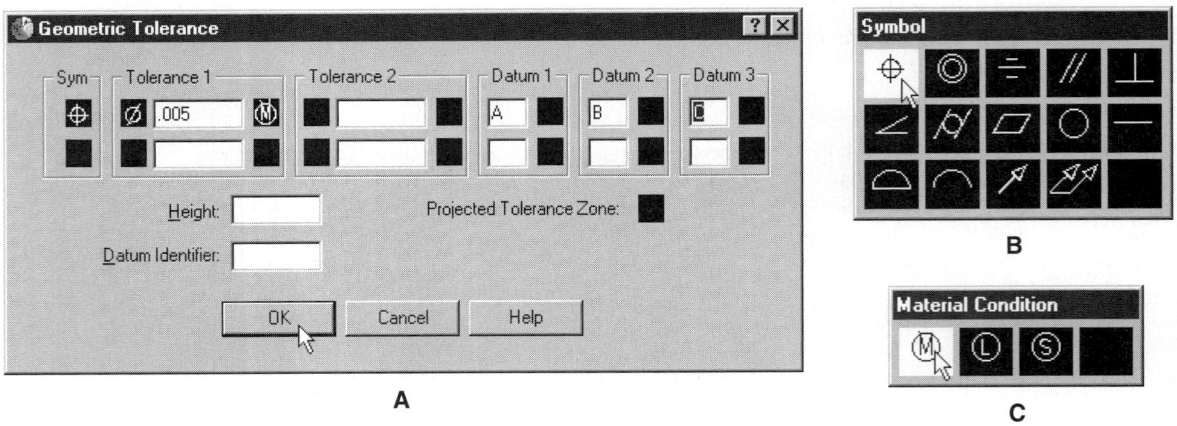

FIGURE 11.77 (A) Geometric Tolerancing feature control frames are defined using the Geometric Tolerance dialog box. (B) The Symbol dialog box allows selection of the desired geometric characteristic symbol. (C) Specify the desired Material Condition by picking the related symbol.

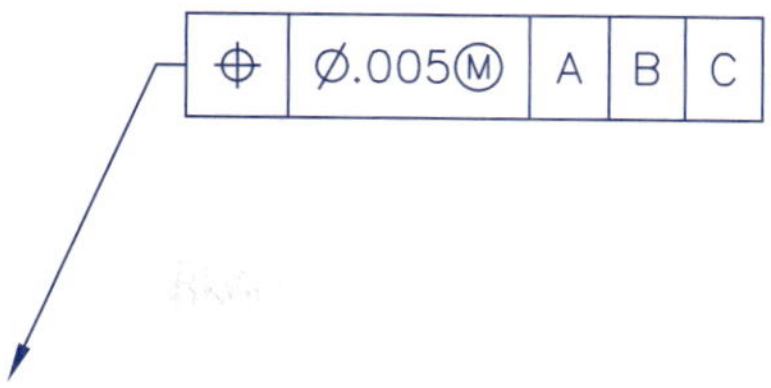

FIGURE 11.78 The results of drawing a geometric tolerance feature control frame on a leader when using the Tolerance option of the LEADER command.

play it in the image tile. The text box is where the tolerance value is entered. There are three Datum areas where you specify the datum reference and related material condition for the feature control frame. The Height: box is where you enter the value for a projected tolerance zone and then pick the image tile labeled Projected Tolerance Zone: to insert the related symbol. The Datum Identifier: box is used to establish the letter for a datum feature symbol. The resulting feature control frame using the values in Figure 11.77A is illustrated in Figure 11.78.

Block Reference: This option is used to insert a block reference at the leader location. A block reference is a special, reusable symbol. A full discussion of block references is provided in Chapter 12.

None: Using the None option allows you to create a leader without any annotation object attached. This option can be used when a single annotation item applies to multiple locations and requires leaders pointing to each location. The first leader is drawn with the appropriate annotation object. Any additional leaders required can be drawn using the None option. Draw the leader from where it points and attach the other end of the leader line to the endpoint where the leader line and shoulder meet.

Setting Mtext Options

This area is disabled unless the Mtext option is selected in the Annotation Type area. These settings are described as follows:

- **Prompt for width** — When checked, the “Specify text width <0.0000>:” prompt is issued.
- **Always left justify** — All multiline text leader annotation items are automatically left-justified.
- **Frame text** — This option places a frame around multiline text leader annotation.

Setting Annotation Reuse Options

The Quick Leader tool can speed your work by automatically reusing content that occurs in multiple locations within your drawing. When content is reused, no prompts are issued after the leader is drawn and the specified annotation object is applied to the leader. The reuse options are:

- **None** — Leader annotation is not reused.
- **Ruse Next** — The annotation specified for the next leader you create is automatically reused for subsequently drawn leaders.
- **Reuse Current** — This option is selected automatically after using the Reuse Next option. To discontinue reusing leader annotation, pick the None radio button.

Leader Line and Arrow Settings

The options found on the Leader Line & Arrow tab are used to control the appearance and application of the leader object itself. The four areas on this tab include Leader Line, Arrowhead, Number of Points, and Angle Constraints, as shown in Figure 11.79. These options are explained next:

- **Spline** — This option allows you to draw leader lines that are curved. Curved leader lines are commonly used in architectural drafting. Use the Spline option to draw the leader shown in Figure 11.80:
- **STraight** — This option is the default that draws straight leader line segments as shown in Figures 11.74 and 11.75. The LEADER command keeps the most recently used op-

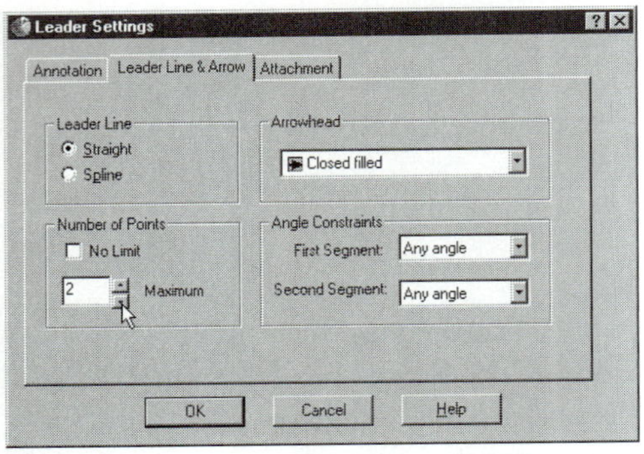

FIGURE 11.79 The Leader Line & Arrow tab in the Leader Settings dialog box.

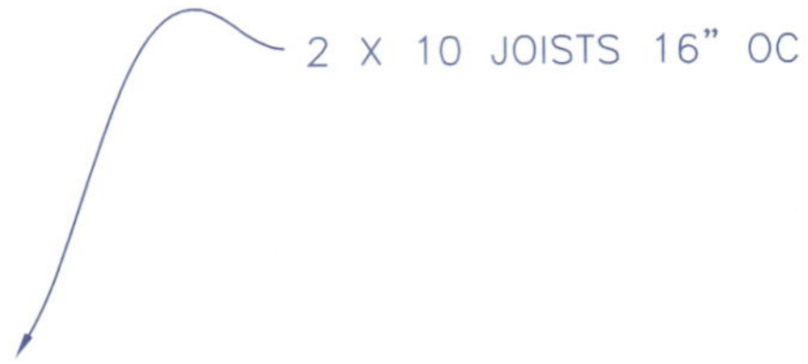

FIGURE 11.80 The Spline option of the QLEADER command is used to draw curved leader lines, which are often used in architectural drafting.

tion as a default, so if you need to go back to Straight segments, you must reset this option in the Leader Line & Arrow tab of the Leader Settings dialog box.

- **Arrowhead** The QLEADER command draws an arrowhead at the end by default. You can select a desired arrowhead from the list. If you use the None option to remove the arrowhead, you need to use the Arrow option to place arrowheads on leaders again.
- **Number of Points** If you pick the No Limit option, a leader can be drawn with any number of segments by continuing to pick points at the "Specify next point:" prompt. Setting a maximum restricts the number of "Specify next point:" prompts that are issued. If, for example, your company or school standard requires that leaders be a single segment with a shoulder and annotation, the Maximum should be set to 2. In addition to providing controls that help maintain consistent drawing standards, this also means that you save keystrokes because after you pick two points, the prompts for the annotation are displayed without your having to first press the Enter key.
- **Angle Constraints** Some company standards require that leader lines be drawn at specific angles. This feature lets you force leader lines to automatically snap to specific angles as you draw the leader. This helps to ensure uniformity and consistency in your drawing.

Annotation Attachment Settings

This tab is visible only when Mtext is selected in the Annotation Type area of the Annotation tab. These settings control the attachment style between leaders and their annotation objects. The Attachment tab is shown in Figure 11.81.

The attachment options on this tab specify where the shoulder of the leader object is drawn in relationship to the Mtext object. Some industry standards specify a variable attachment location based on the direction the leader travels and the side of the leader on which the text is placed. Use these options to draw leaders that conform with your company standards.

FIGURE 11.81 The Attachment tab controls how annotation objects are attached to leaders.

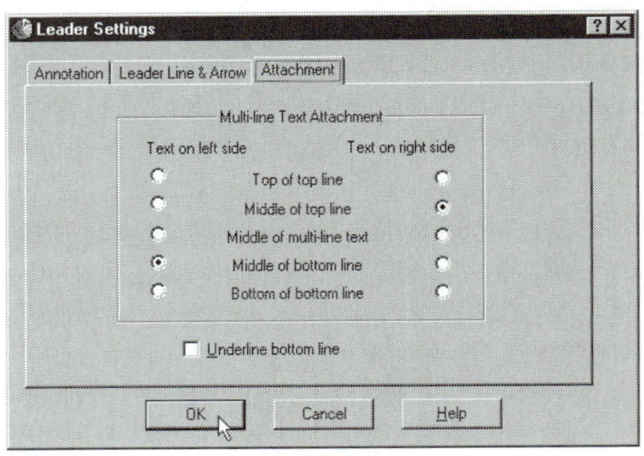

Field Notes

Geometric dimensioning feature control frames often use a special type of arrowhead called a *datum triangle*. The Arrowhead list on the Leader Line & Arrow tab provides two datum triangle options that can be used by the QLEADER command.

Drawing Geometric Tolerancing Symbols without a Leader

Dimension

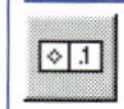

Tolerance

Dimension
Tolerance...

TOLERANCE
TOL

The TOLERANCE command works in the same manner as the Tolerance option in the LEADER command except that it places a geometric tolerancing symbol without a leader. This command is accessed by picking the Tolerance button in the Dimension toolbar, by picking Tolerance ... in the Dimension pull-down menu, or by typing **TOL** or **TOLERANCE** at the Command: prompt. When you enter the TOLERANCE command, you get the series of dialog boxes shown in Figure 11.77. Pick the desired geometric characteristic symbol enter the desired values in the Tolerance and Datum areas as needed. Enter the Height and Projected Tolerance Zone symbol, if used. Establish a Datum Identifier, if appropriate. Pick the OK button when ready. AutoCAD LT then asks you to:

Enter tolerance location: ⟨*pick the location for the symbol placement*⟩
Command:

The geometric tolerancing symbol is placed on your drawing in the location you pick. You can move it or copy it if needed. A complete introduction to geometric tolerancing is available in *Geometric Dimensioning and Tolerancing Basic Fundamentals,* by David Madsen, 1-800-323-0440.

Exercise 11.14 — Estimated time required: 5 min.

1. Begin a new drawing using the new template EX11.12.dwt.
2. Draw a note with leaders similar to those shown in Figures 11.74, 11.75, 11.78, and 11.80.
3. Use the LEADER command Copy option to draw a leader using an existing note from the drawing. Use Figure 11.78 as an example.
4. Save as EX11.14 and close the drawing.

Creating a Dimension Style for Use with Mechanical Drafting Symbols

AutoCAD LT automatically draws the diameter symbol when you use the DIMDIAMETER command and the radius symbol when using the DIMRADIUS command. However, certain symbols, such as the counterbore, countersink, and depth symbols, are not directly available for mechanical drafting applications. You can create these symbols as blocks and insert them with your dimensioning text when needed, but this is extra work. Also, symbols inserted as blocks are not part of the dimension text and cannot be edited together with the dimension text. Creating and using blocks is discussed in Chapter 12.

If you commonly use these types of symbols, you can set up a dimension style that uses one of the standard AutoCAD LT fonts to place these symbols when needed. The AutoCAD LT font that contains these symbols is gdt.shx. The symbols are drawn when you press the lowercase letter keys. The uppercase letters are displayed as normal text in a romans font, which is good for mechanical drafting. All mechanical drafting text is drawn with uppercase letters, so when you need to insert a symbol, you just press the lowercase key that matches the desired symbol. Each of the symbols, the related keyboard letters, and the symbol descriptions are given in Figure 11.82. Follow these steps when setting up a dimension style of this type:

- Use the STYLE command to create a new text style named SYMBOLS. When the Text Style dialog box opens, pick the New... button and type SYMBOLS in the Style Name: text box. Pick OK. In the Font Name: list pick the gdt.shx font and then pick the Apply or Close button.

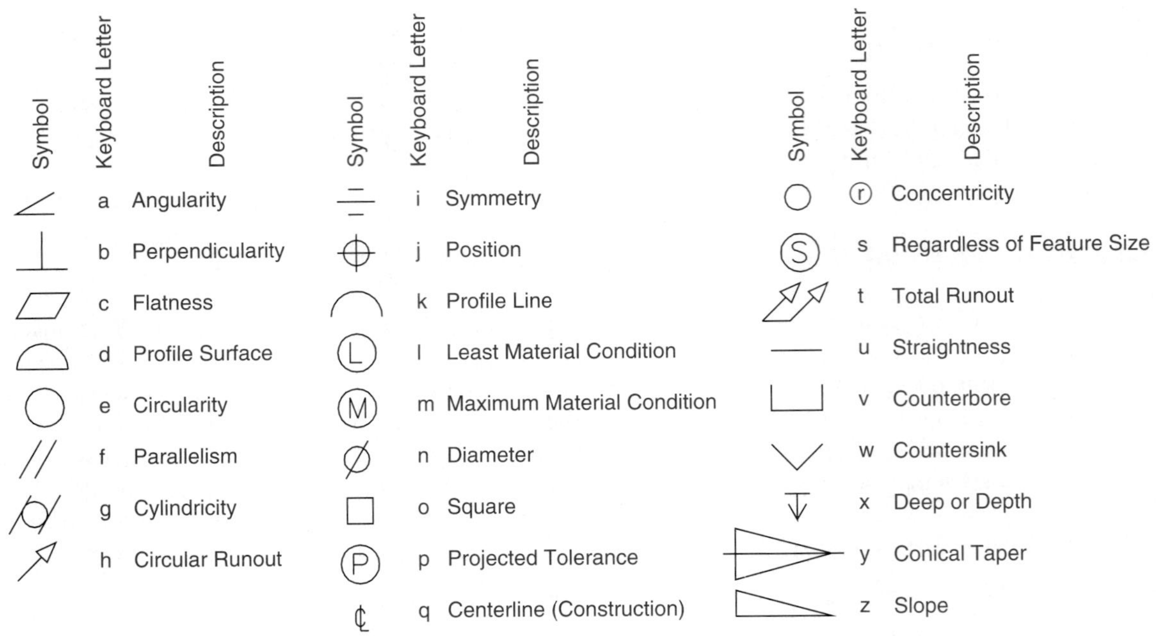

FIGURE 11.82 The keyboard letter used to draw the symbols for the SYMBOLS dimension style with the gdt.shx font. Make a copy of this figure for reference while doing your mechanical drafting to use with this dimension style.

- Open the Dimension Style Manager dialog box and define a dimension style for mechanical drafting applications. Set SYMBOLS in the Text Style: list on the Text tab. Pick OK to accept each group of settings. Pick the Close button.
- Now, you are ready to place dimension text with the symbols you need. The note shown in Figure 11.83 was drawn using this LEADER command sequence:

Command: **LE** or **QLEADER**↵
Specify first leader point, or [Settings]<Settings>: ⟨*pick the leader start point*⟩
Specify next point: ⟨*pick the second leader point*⟩
Specify next point: ↵
Specify text width <0.0000>: ↵
Enter first line of annotation text <Mtext>: **n.250 X x1.750**↵
Enter next line of annotation text: **vn.500 X x.250**↵
Enter next line of annotation text: ↵
Command:

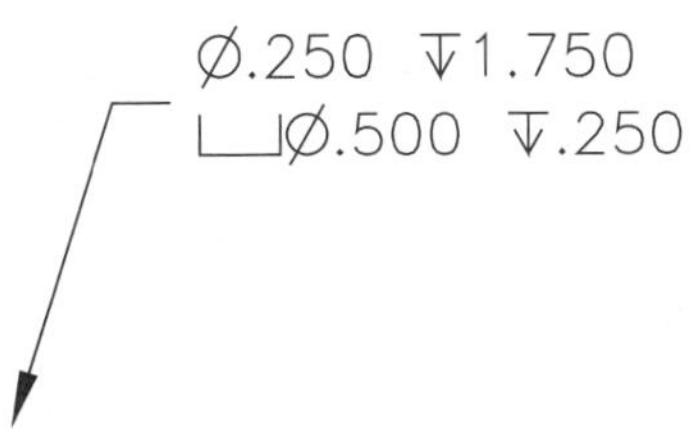

FIGURE 11.83 Using the LEADER command to place a dimension note with the symbols from the SYMBOLS dimension style.

Field Notes

The following are some possible hazards to be aware of when using the SYMBOLS dimension style that was previously discussed:

- Be sure the SYMBOLS text style is current.
- AutoCAD LT automatically places a diameter symbol that is a little smaller than recommended when using the DIMDIAMETER command. However, the diameter symbol created with the SYMBOL dimension style is correctly sized in relation to the text height. However, the only way to change the diameter symbol used by the DIMDIAMETER command is to define a custom text value for the dimension. Unfortunately, this requires changing the default dimension text—which removes the intelligence from the dimension object. If you later edit the drawing and change the size of the circle, the dimension will not automatically update to the new dimension size. To achieve consistency between the diameter symbols in your drawings, it is best to use a "%%C" entry rather than to use the lower case *n* to display a diameter symbol from the GDT font. The "%%C" version produces the same exact symbol used by diameter dimensions.
- When using the Multiline Text Editor, be sure to set the text height at the current text height used in the drawing. A text height of .125 in. (3 mm) is commonly used in mechanical drawings.

Exercise 11.15

Estimated time required: 5 min.

1. Open the EX11.12.dwt template file.
2. Create a text style using the gdt.shx font.
3. Create a dimensioning style for mechanical drafting with the gdt.shx text style.
4. Draw a dimension similar to Figure 11.83.
5. Save as EX11.15, and close the drawing.

LEARNING CHECKPOINT

- ☐ Name the command that can be used to place a leader line with a note on your drawing.
- ☐ Identify the option that can be used to draw curved leaders for architectural applications.
- ☐ Name the option used to place geometric tolerancing symbols with a leader line.
- ☐ What option is used to copy an existing note or object to a leader line?
- ☐ Name the command that is used to draw a geometric tolerancing symbol without a leader line.

Editing Dimensioned Drawings

Modify
Stretch
Modify
Stretch
STRETCH
S

AutoCAD LT dimensions are ***associative dimensions.*** This means that when a dimension object is edited, the dimension value automatically changes to match the edit. The automatic update is only applied when you accept the default value or keep the angle brackets, <>, as part of the text. This provides you with a big advantage when editing an AutoCAD LT drawing because any changes to the object are reflected in the dimensions without any extra work required of you. The STRETCH command is commonly used to either stretch or shrink an object. When using the STRETCH command, the associative dimensions are changed to match the measurement of the revised object. Figure 11.84 shows an example of an object being stretched and how the dimension changes to match. The STRETCH command used to edit the object and dimension in Figure 11.84 works like this:

Command: **S** or **STRETCH**↵
Select objects to stretch by crossing-window or crossing-polygon...
Select objects: ⟨*select both the object and the dimension with a crossing*⟩
Specify opposite corner: 2 found
Select objects: ↵
Specify base point or displacement: ⟨*pick a base point*⟩
Specify second point of displacement: **@.5<0**↵ ⟨*use any valid point specification*⟩
Command:

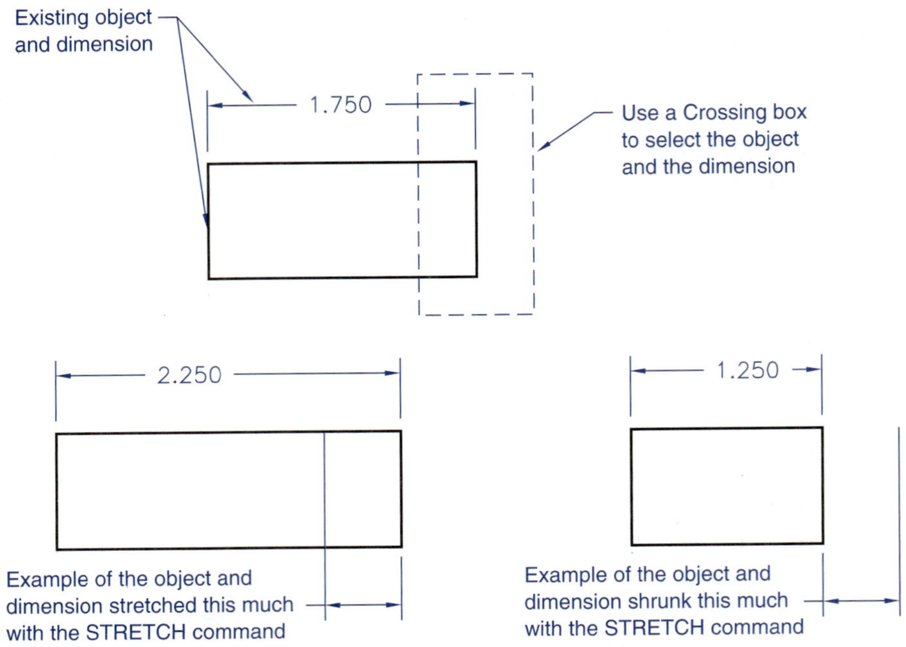

FIGURE 11.84 Using the STRETCH command to stretch an object and dimension. Notice how the dimension automatically changes to match the edit. This is referred to as an *associative dimension.*

Additional commands that can be used to edit both drawing objects and their dimensions include ROTATE, SCALE, TRIM, EXTEND, and LENGTHEN. It is important to remember to select both the drawing geometry and the dimension object when using any of these commands.

In order to properly update the value and features of an edited dimension, that dimension must be associative. The dimension variable that controls associative dimensioning is DIMASO. The initial default setting for DIMASO is on, but it can be turned off to disable associative dimensioning if desired. When you add an associative dimension to your drawing, the dimension object is constructed by AutoCAD LT using simple lines, solids, Mtext, and point objects that are subsequently combined into a single complex-dimension object. When DIMASO is off, dimensions look the same because they are still constructed using lines, solids, and text—but they are not combined to create a single dimension object. Nonassociative dimensions remain as a simple collection of lines, solids, and text. These objects do not update automatically when edited, and they cannot be converted into associative dimensions. ***Disabling associative dimensioning is not recommended for most applications.***

When you draw an associative dimension, point objects are placed at the extension line origins that were used to define the dimension. The point objects used in the construction of an associative dimension are referred to as DefPoints, which is an abbreviation for Definition Points. After an associative dimension is created in a new drawing, your layer control list shows a layer named "DefPoints" that was created automatically by AutoCAD LT. The DefPoints layer does not print, so AutoCAD LT places all the definition points on this layer. That is why these points do not show up on your plotted drawings.

The true dimensional values for all dimension objects are defined based on the location of, or the distance or angle between, its DefPoints. For example, when you apply a linear dimension to a line object, a DefPoint is placed at each endpoint of the line. You can see how definition points are applied by placing a linear dimension in an empty area in your drawing and looking closely at the extension line origin locations. Grip-selecting the linear dimension shows the DefPoints display grips, which can also be used to edit the origin points for the dimension.

When selecting objects for the STRETCH command, as you surround the endpoint of a dimensioned line with a crossing window or polygon you also surround and select the DefPoint. The stretching process then relocates the selected DefPoint. When you finish stretching the drawing geometry and the dimension object, AutoCAD LT updates the dimension value based on the new DefPoint locations. This explains why you can stretch an associative dimension object only if your crossing surrounds the extension line origin.

Field Notes

When you cannot get a dimension to appear as you want it to through working with dimension variables, you can use the EXPLODE command to break the dimension apart. This replaces the dimension object with the simpler objects used to create the dimension, including lines, solids, and text. These objects can then be edited freely, but an exploded dimension will no longer be automatically updated. Exploding dimensions should be avoided whenever possible.

Making Other Changes to Existing Dimensions

You can edit existing dimensions by changing the text value or location. You can also change dimension variables and then update existing dimensions to match the changed variables.

Aligning and Changing Dimension Text

Dimension text can be aligned to the left, right, at an angle, or moved to its original position. This is done by picking the Dimension Text Edit button in the Dimension toolbar, by picking one of the options in the Align Text cascade of the Dimension pull-down menu, or by typing **DIMTEDIT** at the Command: prompt. The Align Text cascade of the Dimension pull-down menu contains the Home, Angle, Left, Center and Right options. These options are all available when entering the DIMTEDIT command like this:

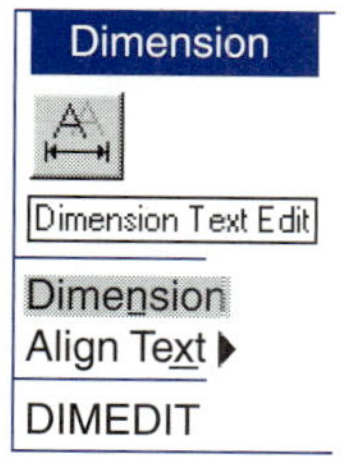

Command: **DIMTEDIT**↵
Select Dimension: ⟨*pick the dimension to edit*⟩
Specify new location for dimension text or [Left/Right/Center/Home/Angle]:

When you get the "Specify new location for dimension text or [Left/Right/Center/Home/Angle]:" prompt, the selected text is connected to the screen cursor for you to dynamically move the text and the entire dimension to any desired location. When the text and dimension are visually where you want, pick to keep that placement. If you prefer to use one of the options, they work like this:

- **Left**: This option moves horizontal dimension text to the left or vertical text down.
- **Right**: This option moves horizontal dimension text to the right or vertical text up.
- **Center**: This option centers the text on the dimension line.
- **Home**: This option moves edited dimension text to its original position. For example, if you used the Left option to move dimension text to the left, the Home option moves it back to where it was. When you stretch an object and its dimension, the dimension value is updated to match the stretch, but the text may be moved to one side of the dimension line. The Home option moves the text back to be centered on the dimension line if it was originally centered.
- **Angle**: This option allows you to place dimension text at an angle.

Figure 11.85 shows the effect of using the DIMTEDIT options.

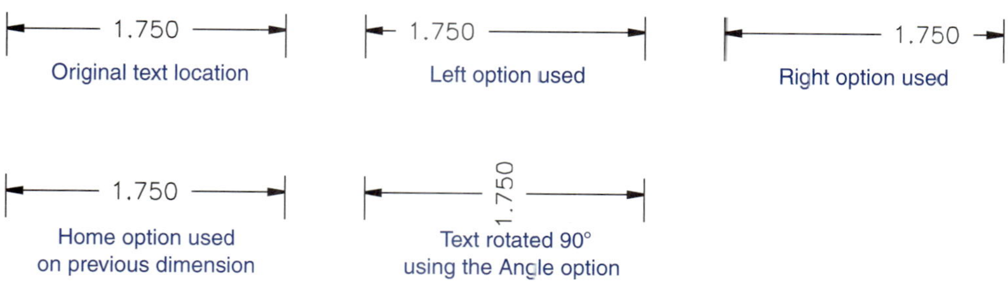

FIGURE 11.85 The results of using the DIMTEDIT options.

Dimension

Dimension Edit

Dimension Oblique

DIMEDIT
DED

The DIMEDIT command can also be used to edit dimension text. This command is accessed by picking the Dimension Edit button in the Dimension toolbar or typing **DED** or **DIMEDIT** at the Command: prompt to get these options:

Command: **DED** or **DIMEDIT**↵
Enter type of dimension editing [Home/New/Rotate/Oblique] <Home>:

The DIMEDIT options are explained next:

- **Home**: This option works just like the DIMTEDIT Home option. Home moves previously edited dimension text back to its original place. Home is the default, so you can either press Enter or type **H** and press Enter. AutoCAD LT then asks you to "Select objects:" which are the dimensions you want to edit.
- **New**: This option allows you to change dimension text values. The New option works like this:

Command: **DED** or **DIMEDIT**↵
Enter type of dimension editing [Home/New/Rotate/Oblique] <Home>: **N**↵

The New option opens the Multiline Text Editor dialog box where you change the dimension text as desired and pick the OK button to get this prompt:

Select objects: ⟨*select the dimension or dimensions to edit*⟩
Select objects: ↵
Command:

- **Rotate**: This option allows you to rotate existing dimension text to a designated angle.
- **Oblique**: The Oblique option was discussed earlier in this chapter under the topic of creating oblique dimensions. See Figure 11.19.

Modifying Dimensions

A dimension style controls the appearance and application of dimensions created while the style is current. Because each dimension object maintains a link to the dimension style with which it is associated, revising dimension settings for every dimension object in a drawing can be as simple as adjusting the settings for the associated dimension style. Understanding how to use dimension styles effectively within your drawings allows much greater control and flexibility when working with dimensions.

Understanding Dimension Styles and Dimension Style Overrides

When you modify a dimension style, all dimensions associated with that style may be affected. Any settings that were not applied using a style override are still controlled by the current dimension style settings. However, dimension settings established using style overrides are not affected by subsequent modifications to the dimension style settings. Earlier in this chapter, you learned to set up temporary dimension style overrides in order to draw dimensions that do not conform with the current dimension style settings. Modifying a setting using style overrides severs the connection between that setting and the current dimension style definition.

The relationship between dimensions and dimension styles can be compared with the relationship between drawing objects and layers. Consider the effect of drawing a line on layer 0 using BYLAYER settings. When you change the color, linetype, or lineweight assigned to layer 0 the properties of the line object are immediately updated to match. However, if you change the color setting of the line from BYLAYER to Red, the line stays red, ignoring any changes made to the layer color setting. Assigning a new linetype or lineweight specification still affects the line, but its color assignment is now absolute.

With dimensions, the effect of using a style override on a dimension is similar to the effect of assigning an absolute color setting on the line. A setting established by an override is an absolute setting that does not change when the dimension style settings are modified. Any settings that have not been established using style overrides are still connected to the dimension style and are updated to match any style modifications.

In Figure 11.86A, the current style uses a text height of 0.125. A single dimension using a text height of 0.188 is desired, so a style override is created using the larger text (see Figure 11.86B). After the nonconforming dimension is drawn, the style override is deleted. Later, it is decided that all dimensions should use .25-tall blue text and .25 arrowheads, so the dimension style itself is modified to these new settings. Figure

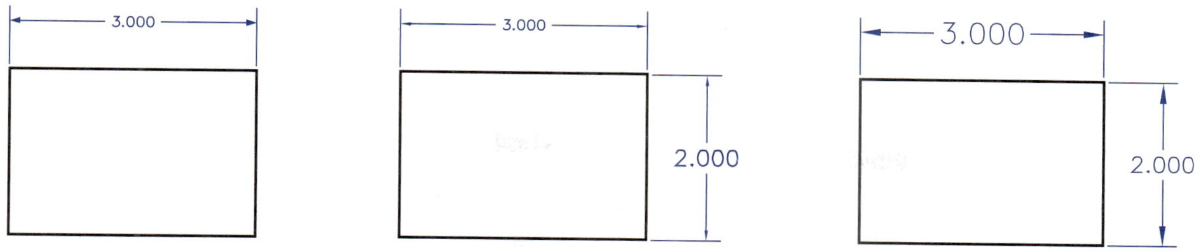

A B C

FIGURE 11.86 Dimension settings established using style overrides are not affected by modifications to the dimension style. (A) The first dimension is drawn using the current dimension style. (B) Style overrides are set to increase text size for one dimension, which is drawn and the style overrides are discarded. (C) The dimension style is modified to use larger arrowheads and blue text at double the previous size. All settings are applied to both dimensions except for the text height that was established with a style override.

11.86C shows that the modified arrowhead size and text color for the dimension created using the style override is updated, but the new text size setting is ignored.

Redefining Dimensions that Have Style Overrides

Dimensions that do not reflect recent dimension style modifications because of previous settings made using style overrides can still be correctly modified using other dimension editing options. You can redefine selected dimension objects using any available dimension style. This discards the current dimension settings and creates a new definition for the dimension object based on the specified dimension style settings.

The Dimension Style drop-down list on the Dimension toolbar can be used to apply any available dimension style to selected dimensions. As discussed earlier in this chapter, the Dimension Style list can be used to apply a dimension style to selected objects in the same way that the lists on the Object Properties toolbar are used to set object properties. For example, you can grip-select the troublesome dimension object from Figure 11.86 and then open the Dimension Style list and pick the name of the dimension style whose settings you want to apply. All the current settings in the specified style definition are then applied to the selected dimension. This works even if the dimension style name you pick is the same style already referenced by the dimension object, because the previous style information is discarded and the dimension settings are completely redefined from scratch using the settings from the selected dimension style. Using the Dimension Style list on the Dimension toolbar is illustrated in Figure 11.87.

FIGURE 11.87 The Dimension Style list on the Dimension toolbar can be used to apply new style settings to selected dimension objects. Applying a style name that is already referenced by the dimension discards the previous style information and redefines the dimension object from scratch using the current settings for the selected style.

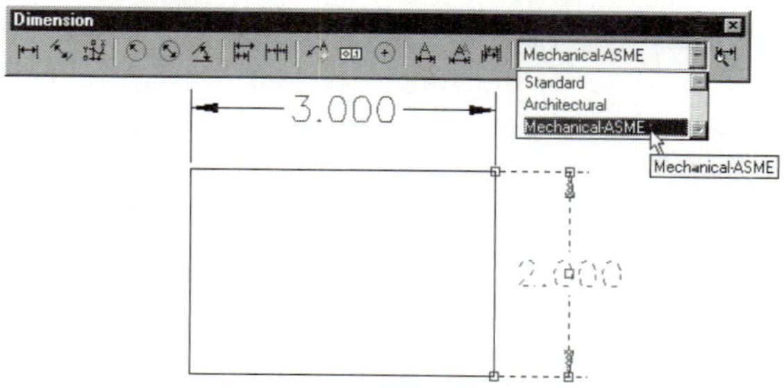

Updating Dimensions Using the Current DimVar Settings

The Dimension Update tool applies all the currently active dimension settings to the selected dimensions. The currently active dimension settings are defined by all the current dimension variable settings. In addition to the settings from the current style, the Dimvar settings also contain all the currently active dimension style overrides. Because it applies *all* the current dimvar values to the selected dimensions, the Dimension Update tool can occasionally produce unexpected results.

To access the Dimension Update feature, pick the Dimension Update button from the Dimension toolbar or pick Update from the Dimension pull-down menu. Select the dimension objects to update at the Select objects: prompt.

Dimension

Dimension Update

Dimension
Update

DIM1
D1
UPDATE
UP

Using Style Overrides on Existing Dimensions

Dimension
Override

DIMOVERRIDE
DOV

Previous discussions regarding dimension style overrides focused on setting style overrides that are used by newly created dimension objects. You can also use style overrides to modify existing dimension objects in your drawings. The DIMOVERRIDE command allows you to apply style overrides to existing dimension objects. You can access the DIMOVERRIDE command by picking Override from the Dimension menu or by typing **DOV** or **DIMOVERRIDE** at the Command: prompt. You are first prompted for the names and settings of the variables to override, then you select any number of dimension objects to which to apply the overrides. The command sequence looks like this:

Command: **DOV** or **DIMOVERRIDE**↵
Enter dimension variable name to override or [Clear overrides]: **TXT**↵
Enter new value for dimension variable <0.2500>: **.125**↵
Enter dimension variable name to override: **ASZ**↵
Enter new value for dimension variable <0.2500>: **.125**↵
Enter dimension variable name to override: **CLRT**↵
Enter new value for dimension variable <5 (blue)>: **BYBLOCK**↵
Enter dimension variable name to override: ↵
Select objects: ⟨*pick dimension objects to override*⟩
Select objects: ↵
Command:

As with any prompt from a dimensioning command, the "DIM" can be omitted from the dimvar names you enter. The DIMOVERRIDE command allows you to specify any number of dimension variables for the style override. To remove any overrides currently applied to a dimension object, type **C** at the first prompt to access the Clear option.

Dimension Editing Using Shortcut Menu Options

Right-clicking when a dimension object is grip-selected displays a shortcut menu that provides fast and convenient access to frequently needed dimension editing options. These tools are grouped into three categories, with each category displayed on a cascading menu. When you pick an option, the specified setting is instantly applied to all the selected dimension objects. The available options on the shortcut menu are described here:

- **Dim Text position ▸**
- **Above dim line** Places the dimension text above the dimension line.
  - **Centered** Center-justifies the dimension text on the dimension line.
  - **Home text** Moves the dimension text to the home (default) position.
  - **Move text alone** Lets you move the text without affecting the dimension line location.
  - **Move with leader** Lets you move the text to a new position with a leader drawn from the text to the dimension line.
  - **Move with dim line** Lets you move both the text and the dimension line at the same time.
- **Precision ▸** Pick the desired precision level to apply to the selected dimensions. The options provided on this cascade range from 0 to 6 decimal places.
- **Dim Style ▸** In addition to the following options, this cascade displays the names of two defined dimension styles. Picking a dimension style name applies the style to the selected dimensions.
  - **Save as New Style…** Displays the Save As New Dimension Style dialog box, where you can define a new dimension style based on the settings used by the selected dimension. This option does not work when more than one dimension object is selected.
  - **Other…** Displays the Apply Dimension Style dialog box with a list of all available dimension styles. Pick a dimension style name to apply it to the selected dimension objects.

Field Notes

The following dimension features cannot automatically be updated to new settings:

DIMDLI (**D**imension **L**ine **I**ncrement) controls the spacing between the dimension lines of baseline dimensions. To modify the baseline dimension spacing manually, try this:

1. Using grips, drag the first dimension into place.
2. Using the Rotate option of the SNAP command, set the snap base point where the dimension line of the first dimension intersects the baseline (datum). Specify a rotation angle of 0.
3. Use SNAP again and set the snap distance to match the desired spacing.
4. Toggle SNAP off and grip the next dimension using the grip where the dimension line meets the baseline.
5. Toggle SNAP on and drag the dimension into place.
6. Repeat steps 4 through 6 for each baseline dimension.

Circle and arc center marks and centerlines drawn using the **DIMCENTER** command are created from simple line objects and are not associative dimensions—and therefore do not automatically update. Center marks and centerlines drawn as part of a Diameter or Radius dimension are associative and can automatically be updated.

Exercise 11.16 — Estimated time required: 8 min.

1. Start a new drawing using the template EX11.12.dwt.
2. Draw an object with dimensions similar to the existing object and dimensions shown in Figure 11.84. Copy the object and dimensions to two new places below the existing object.
3. Use the STRETCH command on one of the copies to stretch the object and dimension.
4. Use the STRETCH command on the other copy to shrink the object and dimension. The results should look similar to those of Figure 11.84.
5. Draw a dimension similar to the original text location shown in Figure 11.85.
6. Copy the dimension to four places similar to the layout shown in Figure 11.85.
7. Use the DIMTEDIT command options to create results similar to the dimensions given in Figure 11.85.
8. Use the DIMEDIT command's Home option to place the previously rotated dimension back to its original position. Use the Undo command to undo this edit.
9. Draw a dimension of your own choosing. Use the DIMEDIT command's New option to change the dimension text.
10. Make a change to a couple of dimension variables. For example, change the arrowhead type and length, and change the dimension text height.
11. Update a few of the dimensions on this drawing to reflect the changes you just made to the variables. Observe the results and then Undo the effect if you wish.
12. Save as EX11.16, and close the drawing.

Dimensioning at the Command Line

AutoCAD LT provides maximum flexibility by giving you command access with toolbar buttons and pull-down menus. Many commands open dialog boxes for you to have the most interaction with the process. You can also enter commands using the keyboard. The dimensioning practices that have been discussed throughout this chapter can be accessed at the command line by putting AutoCAD LT into the ***dimensioning mode.*** Many of the commands that have been introduced and commands from earlier AutoCAD LT releases can be entered while in the dimensioning mode. The dimensioning mode is used by typing either **DIM** or **DIM1** at the Command: prompt. The DIM command allows you to enter as many consecutive dimensioning commands as you want until you decide to exit the command. The DIM1 command allows you to use only one dimensioning command before automatically returning you to the Command: prompt. When you type the DIM or DIM1 command, you enter the dimensioning mode like this:

Command: **DIM** or **DIM1**↵
Dim:

If you want to leave the dimensioning mode, type **E** or **EXIT** and press Enter, or press the Esc key. Dimensioning commands, with names that are different from what you have already learned, are used at the Dim: prompt while you are in the dimensioning mode. The following list shows the AutoCAD LT commands and the same dimensioning mode commands:

AutoCAD LT Command	*Dimensioning Mode Commands*
DIMALIGNED	ALIGNED
DIMANGULAR	ANGULAR
DIMBASELINE	BASELINE
DIMCENTER	CENTER
DIMCONTINUE	CONTINUE
DIMDIAMETER	DIAMETER
DIMEDIT (Home)	HOMETEXT
DIMLINEAR (Horizontal)	HORIZONTAL
LEADER	LEADER
DIMEDIT (Text)	NEWTEXT
DIMEDIT (Oblique)	OBLIQUE
DIMORDINATE	ORDINATE
DIMOVERRIDE	OVERRIDE
DIMRADIUS	RADIUS
DIMSTYLE (Restore)	RESTORE
DIMLINEAR (Rotated)	ROTATED
DIMSTYLE (Save)	SAVE
DIMSTYLE (Status)	STATUS
DIMEDIT	TEDIT
DIMEDIT (Rotate)	TROTATE
DIMSTYLE (Apply)	UPDATE
DIMSTYLE (Variables)	VARIABLES
DIMLINEAR (Vertical)	VERTICAL

To give you an example of how the DIM command works, try drawing a horizontal linear dimension and a couple of datum dimensions similar to Figure 11.10 using this command sequence:

Command: **DIM**↵
Dim: **HOR** or **HORIZONTAL**↵
Specify first extension line origin or <select object>: ⟨*pick the first extension line origin*⟩
Specify second extension line origin: ⟨*pick the second extension line origin*⟩
Specify dimension line location or [Mtext/Text/Angle]: ⟨*pick the dimension line location*⟩
Enter dimension text <1.50>: ↵
Dim: **BAS** or **BASELINE**↵
Specify a second extension line origin or [Select] <Select>: ⟨*pick the origin of the next dimension's second extension line*⟩
Enter dimension text <2.75>: ↵
Dim: **BAS** or **BASELINE**↵
Specify a second extension line origin or [Select] <Select>: ⟨*pick the origin of the next dimension's second extension line*⟩
Enter dimension text <4.00>: ↵
Dim: **E** or **EXIT**↵ ⟨*or press the Esc key to exit*⟩
Command:

Exercise 11.17

Estimated time required: 5 min.

1. Start a new drawing using the template EX11.12.dwt.
2. Use the DIM command to draw an object with dimensions similar to those of Figure 11.10.
3. Save as EX11.17, and close the drawing.

LEARNING CHECKPOINT

- ☐ Define associative dimensions.
- ☐ Explain the advantage of having associative dimensions.
- ☐ What function does the Home option of the DIMTEDIT or DIMEDIT command perform?
- ☐ Name the DIMTEDIT options.
- ☐ What is the purpose of the DIMEDIT command's New option?
- ☐ How do you change the dimension variables on existing dimensions in a drawing?
- ☐ Describe the benefits of an effective implementation of dimension styles in your drawings.
- ☐ How can dimension styles be used to revise all the dimensions in a drawing in a single operation?
- ☐ How do dimension style overrides affect the relationship between a dimension and its associated dimension style?
- ☐ If a dimension has one style override set, what happens when multiple changes are made to the dimension style settings?
- ☐ Explain how all the settings in a style definition can be applied to a selected dimension even when style overrides are in place.
- ☐ Describe the function of the Dimension Update tool.
- ☐ How can the DIMOVERRIDE command be used to remove all style overrides from a dimension object?
- ☐ What is the fastest way to change the precision setting for an existing dimension?
- ☐ Name the dimension features that cannot automatically be updated.
- ☐ Name the command to use if you want to perform one dimensioning task in dimensioning mode.
- ☐ Name the command to use if you want to create several consecutive dimensions while in dimensioning mode.

Dimensioning Drawings

- Modifying Dimension Text and Creating Geometric Tolerances
- Creating Center Marks and Leaders

MULTIPLE CHOICE

Instructions: Circle the choice or enter your response on an answer sheet by selecting the option that most closely completes or answers the given statements.

1. The command used for drawing straight line dimensions:
a. DIMANGULAR **c.** DIMLINEAR
b. DIMRADIUS **d.** DIMDIAMETER

2. The option used to select objects directly for dimensioning:
a. Select **c.** Object
b. <select object> **d.** Linear

3. This command is used to draw arrowless dimensions:
a. DIMARROWLESS **c.** DIMORDINATE
b. DIMTABULAR **d.** DIMBASE

4. Saved sets of variables that determine the appearance of the dimensions:
a. dimension variables **c.** dimension styles
b. dimension settings **d.** dimension controls

5. This tab in the New Dimension Style dialog box is used to change the dimension line, extension line, arrowhead, and center mark presentation is called:
a. Text **c.** Lines and Arrows
b. Fit **d.** Tolerances

6. Variables that control the way dimension text appears on the drawing and the relationship with the positioning of dimension lines and arrowheads are adjusted in this dialog box:
   a. Text
   b. Fit
   c. Lines and Arrows
   d. Tolerances
7. The dimension variable that provides maximum flexibility in the placement of dimension text, dimension line location, extension line length, and arrowhead placement:
   a. DIMUPT
   b. DIMUD
   c. DIMUPC
   d. DIMUP
8. Architectural drafting applications typically use this Vertical Justification option:
   a. Centered
   b. Outside
   c. Above
   d. JIS
9. When a dimension object is edited and the dimension automatically changes to match the edit the dimension is described as:
   a. Update
   b. DIMEDIT
   c. DIMTEDIT
   d. associative
10. This DIMEDIT option is used to change the value of dimension text:
   a. Home
   b. Change
   c. New
   d. Edit

MATCHING

Match each term to the correct description by writing the appropriate number in each box at the left.

- ☐ Associative
- ☐ DIMLINEAR
- ☐ DIMCONTINUE
- ☐ DIMBASE
- ☐ DIMANG
- ☐ DIMALIGNED
- ☐ DIMDIAMETER
- ☐ DIMRADIUS
- ☐ DIMORDINATE
- ☐ Lines and Arrows
- ☐ DIMCENTER
- ☐ Text

1. This tab of the New Dimension Style dialog box is used to change the dimension line, extension line, arrowhead, and center mark presentation.
2. This command is used to draw straight line dimensions.
3. Circles should be dimensioned with this command.
4. Changes can be made to the appearance of dimension text in this tab of the New Dimension Style dialog box.
5. Dimensions that automatically update when editing changes are made.
6. This command is used to draw arrowless dimensions.
7. This command is used to draw dimensions beside a slanted object.
8. Arcs should be dimensioned with this command.
9. Chain dimensioning is performed with this command.
10. This command is used to dimension angles in degrees.
11. Center marks are placed on arcs and circles with this command.
12. Datum dimensioning is performed with this command.

WORD SCRAMBLE

Unscramble the five scrambled words below, one letter to each square, to form five AutoCAD LT–related words:

MRDEIANIL

OETCSVAIAIS

TEIDTIMD

ADELRE

TANAONIOTN

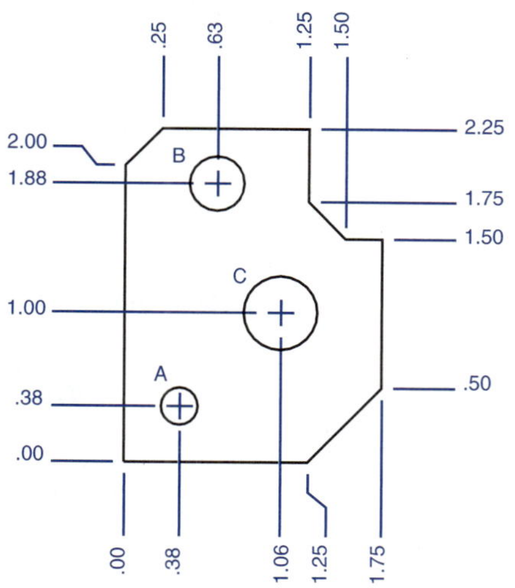

KEY	DIAMETER	DEPTH
A	.26	THRU
B	.38	THRU
C	.50	THRU

Unscramble the circled letters above to form the special answer, as suggested by the illustration.

PROJECTS

Set up the following drawing projects with the dimensions placed on a specific layer. Review Chapter 5 if needed. Establish dimension styles based on the type of drafting, such as mechanical, architectural, or electrical. Review this chapter and plan the dimension style to match the project before beginning work on the project. The following are some basic recommended guidelines to follow unless otherwise specified by your instructor or company (Values are given in inches. Convert to millimeters as needed):

Mechanical	*Setting*
Dimension line spacing	.50 minimum
Extension line offset	.0625
Extension line extension	.125
Arrowhead	Closed Filled
Dimension text height	.125 (should match balance of drawing)
Gap	.06
Dimension text style	ROMANS (should match balance of drawing)
Dimension text centered	
Unidirectional dimensioning	

Zero Suppression for inch or metric as outlined in this chapter and in compliance with ANSI/ASME dimensioning standards.

Architectural	*Setting*
Dimension line spacing	.50 minimum
Extension line offset	.0625
Extension line extension	.125
Arrowhead	Architectural Tick, Dot, or Closed Filled
Dimension text height	.125 (should match balance of drawing)
Gap	.06
Dimension text style	CityBlueprint or Stylus BT (should match balance of drawing)
Dimension text above	
Aligned dimensioning	

Zero Suppression for feet and inches as outlined in this chapter and in compliance with AIA dimensioning standards.

11.1 Open P3.4 and dimension as shown in the original layout. Save as P11.1. INCH

11.2 Open P3.5 and dimension as shown in the original layout. Save as P11.2. METRIC

11.3 Open P3.6 and dimension as shown in the original layout. Save as P11.3. INCH

11.4 Open P3.7 and dimension as shown in the original layout. Save as P11.4. METRIC

11.5 Open P5.2 and dimension as shown in the original layout. Save as P11.5. INCH

11.6 Open P5.3 and dimension as shown in the original layout. Save as P11.6.

11.7 Open P6.3 and dimension as shown in the original layout. Save as P11.7.

11.8 Open P6.4 and dimension as shown in the original layout. Save as P11.8. INCH

11.9 Open P6.5 and dimension as shown in the original layout. Save as P11.9. METRIC

11.10 Open P6.6 and dimension as shown in the original layout. Save as P11.10. INCH

11.11 Open P6.9 and completely dimension by placing the appropriate dimensions on the right side view. Save as P11.11. INCH

11.12 Open P6.8 and properly dimension the views. Save as P11.12. INCH

11.13 Open P6.9 and properly dimension the views. Save as P11.13. INCH

11.14 Open P6.12 and properly dimension the views. Save as P11.14. INCH

11.15 Open P7.3 and dimension as shown in the original layout. Save as P11.15. INCH

11.16 Open P7.7 and dimension the completed object. Save as P11.16. INCH

11.17 Open P7.8 and dimension as shown in the original layout. Save as P11.17. INCH

11.18 Open P8.9 and properly dimension the partial floor plan. Save as P11.18.

11.19 Open P8.10 and properly dimension the partial floor plan. Save as P11.19.

11.20 Open P10.1 and properly dimension the views. Save as P11.20. INCH

11.21 Open P10.2 and properly dimension the views. Save as P11.21. METRIC

11.22 Open P10.3 and properly dimension the views. Save as P11.22. INCH

11.23 Open P10.4 and properly dimension the views. Save as P11.23. INCH

11.24 Open P10.5 and dimension as shown in the original layout. Save as P11.24.

11.25 Open P10.5 and dimension as shown in the original layout. Save as P11.25.

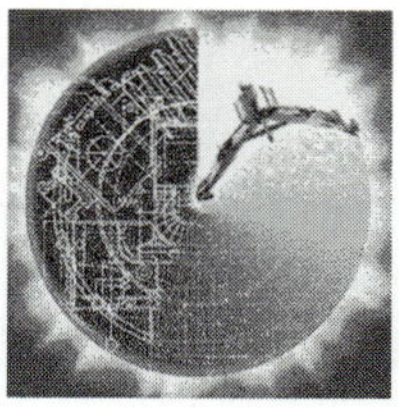

CHAPTER 12

Designing and Using Your Own Symbols, Using Externally Referenced Drawing Files

LEARNING GOALS

- Group objects together for easier editing
- Use the BLOCK command to create reusable symbols
- Save blocks as individual drawing files for use in any drawing
- Use the Insert command to insert predrawn symbols
- Create and use a symbol library
- Use the Content Explorer to manage symbols and symbol libraries
- Use attributes to store additional information with symbols
- Extract attribute information to generate a bill of materials
- Import clip art into a drawing
- Access information contained in external drawing files
- Overlay multiple drawing files to create a combined drawing database
- Reference external drawing files in the current drawing session
- Use each of the XREF command options
- Incorporate information contained in externally referenced drawing files

Grouping Objects

In most drawing applications, several objects in a drawing are used to represent a more complex shape. For example, in a multiview drawing, a collection of drawing objects is used to depict the front, top, or side view of an object. In a schematic application, several simpler objects are used to represent specific symbols. Many assembly drawings may consist of several smaller subassemblies. In each of these cases, your drawing contains sets of objects that you may need to select and edit as a unit. You may need to relocate a view or duplicate a symbol or subassembly. AutoCAD LT provides a way to group these objects together so that they can be selected and edited as though they were a single object. Objects within a group can also be edited individually if needed. The following section covers grouping and ungrouping objects, plus management of object groups.

The Group Manager

Group
Group Manager
Tools
Group Manager...
GROUP
G

The GROUP command opens the Group Manager. You can access the GROUP command by selecting Group Manager ... from the Tools pull-down menu, by picking the Group button from the Group toolbar or by typing **G** or **GROUP** at the Command: prompt. The Group Manager is similar to the AutoCAD LT toolbars; it can be docked at the top or bottom, or it can be placed in a floating position. The Group Manager cannot be docked on either side of the AutoCAD LT program window. Figure 12.1 shows the Group Manager in a floating position (A) and a docked position (B). The Group Manager can be closed by dragging it to a floating position and picking the Close button in the upper right corner.

When you first start the Group Manager in a drawing with no groups defined, only one of its buttons is selectable. Just below the row of control buttons on the right side of the Group Manager is the Group Manager sta-

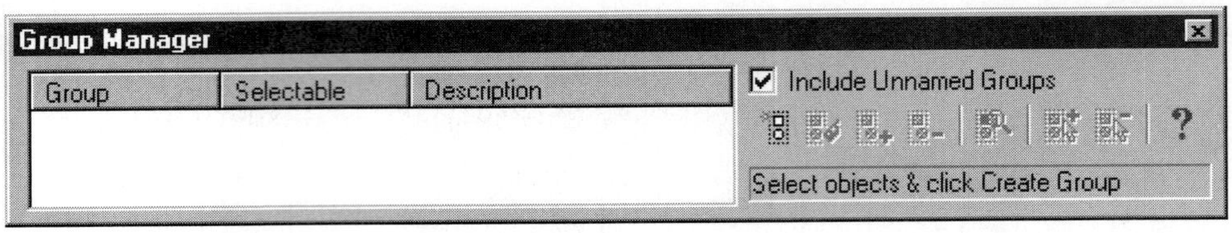

A

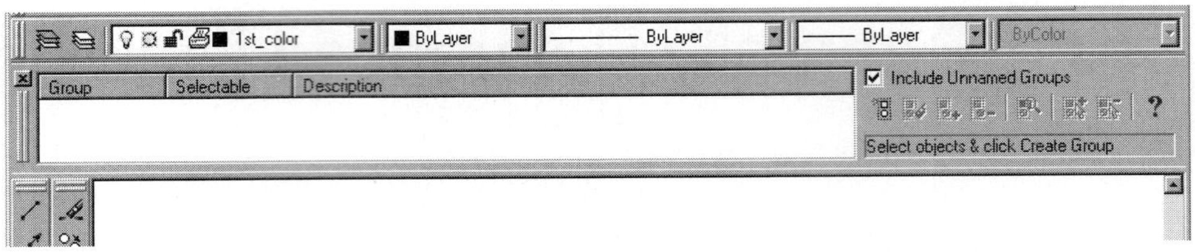

B

FIGURE 12.1 The Group Manager can be placed in a floating position (A), or it can be docked at the top or bottom of the AutoCAD LT program window (B).

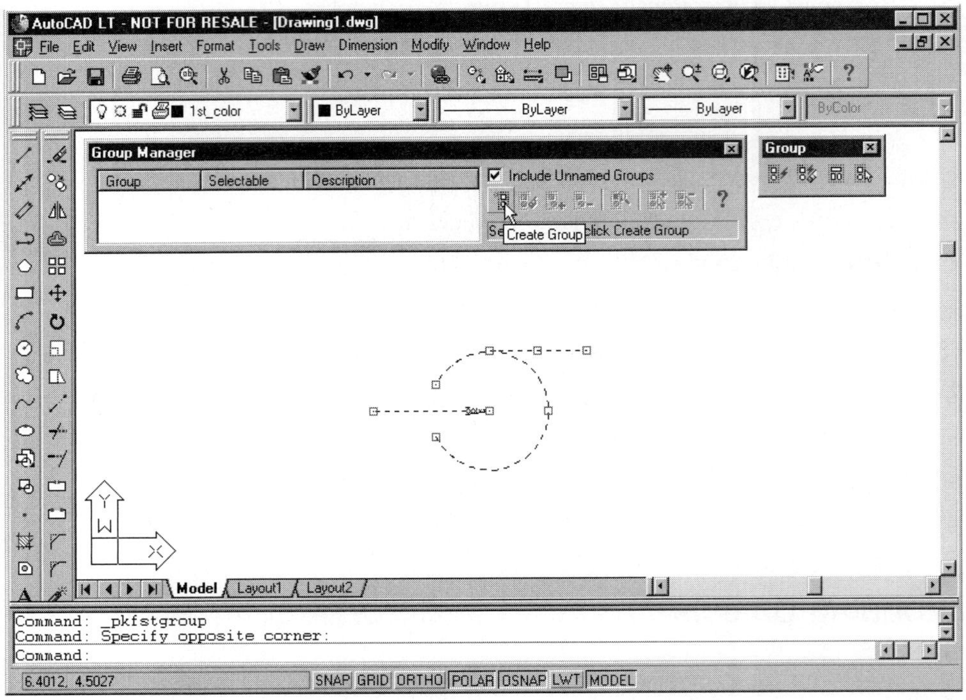

FIGURE 12.2 Grip-select the objects you want to group, then pick the Create Group button in the Group Manager.

tus bar. This area provides supplementary information when you are working with groups. The initial message, "Select objects & click Create Group," refers to using the noun/verb selection method of grip-selecting the objects and then picking the Create Group button, as shown in Figure 12.2. No prompts are issued in the floating command window.

When items have been selected for grouping and the Create Group button is picked, the items are grouped and an active edit box appears in the Group column on the left side of the Group Manager. You may enter a group name that is up to 31 characters long. As in naming other objects such as layers and views, you can use dollar signs ($), hyphens (-), and underscores (_), but cannot use blank spaces or other restricted characters.

After you have named the new group, you can adjust other settings as needed. First, you can specify whether the group is selectable. When a group is selectable, picking any component of the group also selects all other objects that are part of the group. Objects in a group that is not selectable can be picked and edited individually without affecting the rest of the group. When the light bulb in the Selectable column is on (yellow), the group is selectable. Click on the light bulb icon itself to turn it on or off.

You can also enter a description of up to 64 characters to provide supplementary information about a group. This information can provide helpful reminders about the nature and content of your groups. The description can be entered, deleted, or edited at any time. Figure 12.3 shows a description being entered for a currently unselectable group containing three objects.

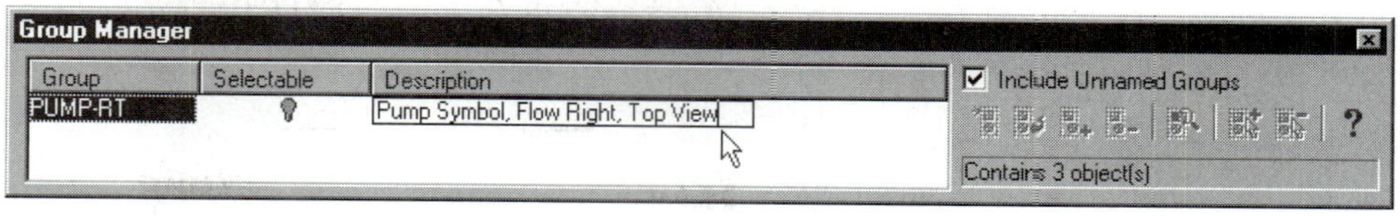

FIGURE 12.3 The group description may contain up to a 64-character description for each group. The status bar provides additional information about the currently selected group in the group list.

Every group requires a unique name. You cannot have multiple groups with the same name. If you copy an existing group with the COPY command, the new set of objects is assigned to an *unnamed* group. Unnamed groups are assigned a sequential name with the first unnamed group being named "*A1," the second "*A2," and so on. These groups will appear in the Group Manager list only if the Include Unnamed Groups toggle is checked.

The group control buttons allow you to add new objects to a group, remove existing objects, ungroup, and more. The function of each of these buttons is as follows:

- **Create Group** — If objects are currently grip-selected, they are added to a new group. You may enter a name for the new group or press Enter to create a new unnamed group. If no objects are currently selected, an empty group is created. 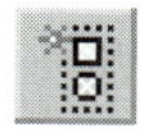
- **Ungroup** — Discards the group definition and removes the association between the objects that composed the group. The objects remain in the drawing as they were before they were grouped. 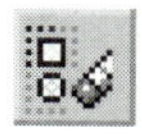
- **Add to Group** — Adds the currently selected objects to the highlighted group name in the group list. This button is available only when objects in the drawing are grip-selected. 
- **Remove from Group** — Removes the currently selected objects from the specified group. If the group is selectable, all objects are selected when you pick one component. You can use the Shift key to unselect components, but you may find it easier to simply turn off selectability while specifying which objects to remove. 
- **Details** — Displays the Group Manager - Details dialog box shown in Figure 12.4. The details for all highlighted group names appear in the listing. When a group name is selected, the number of objects it contains and the space they are in is displayed, along with the description field. Additionally, the group is highlighted on the screen to show its location. 
- **Select Group** — Selects the objects that compose the highlighted group name or names. You can use this button to find groups by highlighting them or to make noun/verb selections. 
- **Deselect Group** — Deselects any currently selected objects that are components of the highlighted group name. You can select objects by any standard means and then conveniently remove the grouped objects from the selection set. 
- **Help** — Displays context-sensitive help associated with the GROUP command. 

Field Notes

Groups can be selected automatically at a Select objects: prompt by using the Group option. The following example shows the MOVE command being used, but most Select objects: prompts allow this option. This option can be used only to select groups that currently have the Selectable option enabled.

Command: **MOVE↵**
Select objects: **G↵**
Enter group name: **PUMP-RT↵**
3 found
Select objects:

FIGURE 12.4 The Group Manager - Details dialog box.

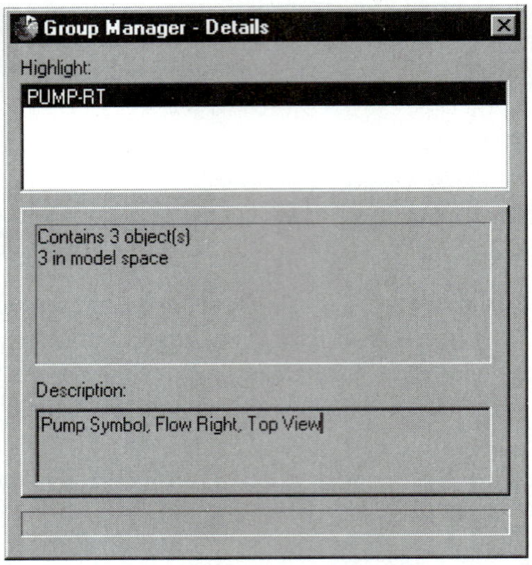

The Group Toolbar

In addition to the GROUP command, other options are also found on the Group toolbar. Using the group toolbar provides a fast and convenient means of using groups that do not require names and descriptions. In many cases, this is the most productive way to use object groups. Right-click on a currently visible toolbar button, then select Group from the popup cursor menu to display the Group toolbar.

Group

Group

Tools
Group

-GROUP
-G

The Group button on the Group toolbar automatically creates an unnamed group from the selected objects. This option is also found on the Tools menu. If it is picked when no objects have been selected, you are prompted to select the objects to group. The next sequential "*A_" name is used for the new unnamed group. This option provides a convenient way to group associated objects without having to name and describe the group. This toolbar button actually uses the command line version of the GROUP command. When objects are currently grip-selected, using this option displays the following at the command line:

```
Command: _-pkfstgroup
Enter a group option [?/Add/Remove/Ungroup/REName/Selectable/Create] ⟨Create⟩:
? /* (unnamed group) / Group name: * Enter a group description:
9 found
Command:
```

Group

Ungroup

Tools
Ungroup

-GROUP
-G

To ungroup objects without having to find the group name in the Group Manager, use the Ungroup tool from the Group toolbar or the Tools pull-down menu. If the group has been grip-selected, it is ungrouped with no further prompts. If no objects have been selected, you are prompted to select the group to ungroup.

```
Command: _qkungroup
Command:
```

Group

Group Selection On/Off

PICKSTYLE
[Ctrl] + [H]

The Group Selection On/Off option toggles the current setting for the PICKSTYLE system variable, which controls whether selecting a member of a group selects all objects within the group. You can also toggle this setting by pressing CTRL+H or by using the Object Selection Settings dialog box. This global setting overrides the Selectable setting for individual groups within the Group Manager.

Field Notes

- The **GROUP** and **–GROUP** commands are actually command aliases, similar to entering **L** to start the **LINE** command. Picking the Group option on the Tools pull-down menu starts the Group Manager dialog box and shows the command name **PKFSTGROUP** in the floating command window, and picking the Group toolbar button uses the command line version: **–PKFSTGROUP**. You can type **PKFSTGROUP** at the Command: prompt to start this command if you want, but it is much faster just to type **G** (or **–G** for the command line version).
- Erasing the objects that make up a group does not remove the group from the drawing; rather, it results in an empty group. To remove the group name, you must use the Ungroup option.
- Groups can be nested, meaning that one set of grouped objects can be part of another group.

Exercise 12.1

Estimated time required: 10 min.

1. If it is not already visible, display the Group toolbar.
2. Start the Group Manager using the GROUP command. Make sure that "Include Unnamed Groups" is checked.
3. Draw a symbol similar to the one shown in Figure 2.2.
4. Grip-select the objects in the symbol and pick the Create Group button.
5. Name the group PUMP-RT, make it selectable, and give it a description.
6. Start the MOVE command, and at the Select objects: prompt, pick the group using the pickbox. Complete or cancel the MOVE command.
7. Start the COPY command, and at the Select objects: prompt, type G for Group, then enter the group name. Complete the COPY command by placing one copy of the group. Notice the new group name that appears in the Group Manager.
8. Make the PUMP-RT group unselectable.
9. Grip-select the arc segment, then pick Remove from Group.
10. Make the group selectable again, and ERASE it. Notice that the Group Manager now reports this group as having 0 objects. Use OOPS to bring the group back.
11. Grip select the line segment you removed from the group, and pick Add to Group.
12. Highlight the PUMP-RT group name in the Group Manager and pick the Details button.
13. Use the Select Group button to select a group, then pick Deselect Group.
14. Draw a shape of your own design using several objects.
15. Use the Group button from the Group toolbar to group the new objects. Select the new group and pick the Ungroup button.
16. Save as EX12.1.dwg, and close the drawing.

LEARNING CHECKPOINT

- ☐ Why is it useful to group objects?
- ☐ What command starts the Group Manager?
- ☐ The Group Manager can be docked or floating. Where can you not dock the Group Manager?
- ☐ What limitations apply to Group names?
- ☐ Describe the features of the Group Manager - Details dialog box.
- ☐ How can the Group and Ungroup toolbar buttons on the Group toolbar be faster and more convenient than using the Group Manager?
- ☐ Group selection is controlled globally using what system variable? What is the shortcut key to toggle this variable?

Viewing, Selecting, and Using Precision Drawing Tools

- Using Groups to Edit Multiple Objects

Using Drafting Symbols in AutoCAD LT

In drafting, the term ***symbol*** refers to a simplified graphic image used to represent specific elements of a drawing. Most drafting disciplines make use of symbols in one form or another to illustrate many of the common features within a drawing. The use of standard symbols can clarify and simplify many types of technical drawings. For example, an architectural drawing uses many standard symbols to represent various features of a floor plan. To draw views of specific doors, windows, or other architectural features as they actually appear is a long and unnecessary process. Instead, simplified symbols are used to describe the style, position, and orientation of such features. This reduces drafting time, and the lower detail level helps to prevent overcrowding in complex drawings.

A manual drafter uses tools such as templates or sticky-backs to speed up the process of using symbols. ***Templates*** are plastic guides that provide an easy-to-follow outline, allowing the drafter to draw uniform symbols quickly wherever needed in a drawing. *Sticky-backs* are predrawn symbols printed on transparent media with an adhesive backing. When a symbol is needed, it is simply placed in the appropriate location and then held in place by the adhesive. This allows a manual drafter to insert symbols into a drawing without having to actually draw them in each location.

Using AutoCAD LT, you can use the concept of sticky-backs in an electronic format. Predrawn symbols are referred to as ***blocks*** within AutoCAD LT. Once a symbol is drawn, using its geometry to define a block allows the symbol to be used over and over again as needed within a drawing—without having to redraw it or copy the original to each new location. And, if you need to use the same symbol in more than one drawing, it can be saved to disk and inserted as desired in any subsequent drawing session. Frequently needed symbols can be incorporated into a standard symbol library for yourself or your company.

Typically, in a drawing that uses symbols, several of the symbols are likely to occur in many different locations within the drawing. However, some symbols can vary in what they represent. For example, electronic components, such as fixed-value resistors, can have properties that vary from one resistor to the next. Some resistors may come from different manufacturers and have varied resistance values. Even so, in an electronic schematic drawing, the same standard symbol is used to represent each fixed-value resistor. In AutoCAD LT, blocks can be assigned certain properties called ***attributes.*** These attributes can be assigned individually to each occurrence of the block to distinguish it from all of the others. The attributes can be displayed as visible text on the drawing, or they can be invisible and stored only within the block itself. Block attributes can even be extracted from a drawing and used to automate the creation of a bill of materials.

You should always remember that the primary productivity gain from using a CAD application comes from never having to draw the exact same thing twice. When you draw something that you are going to need again in the future, you can save it in a form that makes it easily accessible to all future drawing sessions. Mastering the use of drawing symbols, or blocks, in AutoCAD LT can greatly increase your drafting productivity. AutoCAD LT 2000 provides a powerful tool called the AutoCAD DesignCenter for working with symbols and symbol libraries. It provides an easy "drag-and-drop" interface for use and management of your symbols. This chapter discusses the creation, management, and use of symbols and symbol libraries through the use of the DesignCenter and other AutoCAD LT tools.

Creating and Inserting Blocks in a Drawing

Creating Blocks

A ***block*** is a collective representation of any number of regular AutoCAD LT objects that is stored and used as a single object. Blocks can be created within a specific drawing and used only in that drawing, or you can make a block available for use in other drawings. This section discusses the basics of defining a block.

The first step in creating any block definition is to draw the geometry that represents the required symbol or component. This is done using normal drawing and editing commands. If what you are drawing is to be used as a standard drafting symbol, you should always refer to the appropriate reference material to ensure that the symbol complies with accepted industry standards. When creating a block to represent a nonstandard symbol, such as a frequently used part or subassembly, be sure that the symbol complies with all applicable company standards.

Field Notes

The descriptions and definitions of accepted industry standard symbols can be found in documents published by a variety of organizations. Some of the most widely recognized standards organizations include these:

- **ASME**—American Society of Mechanical Engineers
- **AIA**—American Institute of Architects
- **IEEE**—Institute of Electrical and Electronics Engineers
- **ISO**—International Standards Organization
- **MIL-STD**—United States Military Standards
- **SAE**—Society of Automotive Engineers

All symbols should comply with pertinent drafting standards. The standards documents that you need to reference are usually based on the final destination of the drawing you are creating. Usually, it is your customer who will specify the standards by which a project is to be completed.

Depending on the scope of your business, it may be necessary to maintain multiple drawing templates and symbol libraries to meet the needs of a diverse customer base.

Additional information regarding standards documents and organizations is found in Appendix B.

Draw
Make Block
Draw
Block ▸
Make
BMAKE
BLOCK
B

In preparation for the following example, create a piece of geometry to represent the electronic schematic symbol for an NPN transistor like the one shown in Figure 12.5. Based on a standard symbol height of 0.125 units, the circle in this symbol is defined as being 0.375 units in diameter. The rest of the features are drawn proportionately to match the example in Figure 12.5.

Once you have completed the geometry that defines the new symbol, start the BMAKE command to display the Block Definition dialog box. The BMAKE command is accessed by picking the Make Block button in the Draw toolbar, selecting Make ... from the Block cascade on the Draw pull-down menu, or by typing **B** or **BMAKE** at the Command: prompt. The Block Definition dialog box is shown in Figure 12.6. This dialog box starts out with the Name: field active. You can enter this information first, or you can proceed to other areas of the dialog box and return to this field later if you wish.

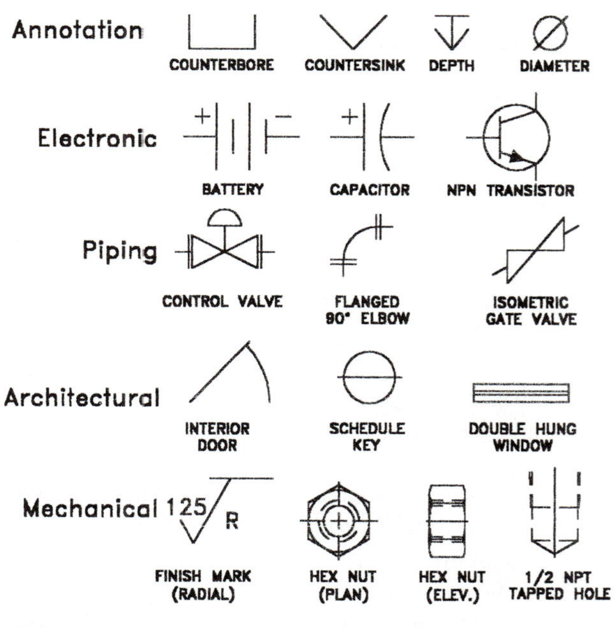

FIGURE 12.5 Standard drafting symbols are used in almost every drafting discipline.

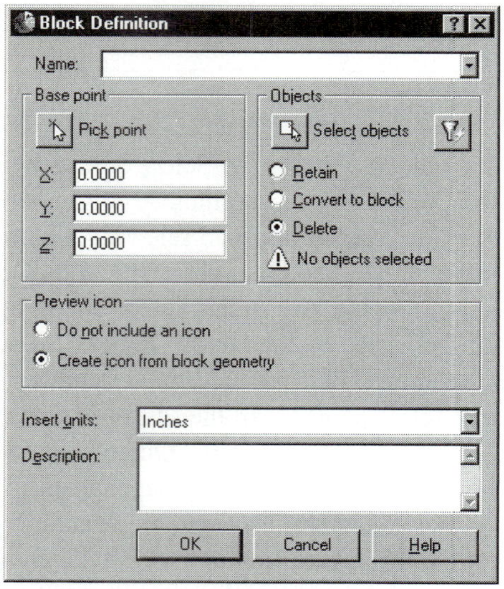

FIGURE 12.6 The Block Definition dialog box is used for creating new block definitions.

In this example, the block Name: value is entered first. The name specified for a block is up to you, as long as it complies with the AutoCAD LT conventions for block names. The block name can be up to 255 characters in length and can contain spaces, periods, and some special characters. Reserved characters that cannot be used in a block name are shown here inside the parentheses: (< > / \ " : ? * | , = `). When you specify a block name, the letter case you entered it with is preserved. When the block name is displayed, it is presented exactly as you originally typed it. Even so, block names are not case sensitive. A block name originally entered as "NPN Transistor" can be accessed as "NPN TRANSISTOR" or "npn transistor".

Although block names can be up to 255 characters in length, it is usually best to stay well below this maximum length. Extremely long block names can be cumbersome to work with, and can cause complications when creating permanent symbol libraries and using external references as discussed later in this chapter.

Another consideration when specifying block names is to use a clearly recognizable name. Keep in mind that you may not be the only person to edit this drawing. If a client or coworker opens this drawing at a later date, the block names you have defined should be easily recognizable to them as well.

Since the symbol in Figure 12.5 represents an NPN transistor, an acceptable option for a short, descriptive name might be NPNTRANS. Or, to make it easier to read, you can separate the individual parts of the description using an underscore character, as in NPN_TRANS. AutoCAD LT 2000 supports long symbol names and allows the use of spaces and punctuation characters as well. Using these features, you might name the block "NPN Transistor - .125" so that the block name provides added information about the symbol.

Field Notes

In a professional environment you may occasionally need to share drawings with a client or vendor who uses a different, and maybe older, computer system and software. Some older operating systems do not support long file names. Older versions of the AutoCAD LT software do not support long symbol names. For example, previous versions of the AutoCAD LT software allow symbol names to be a maximum of 31 characters long, and spaces or special characters cannot be used. In such a situation, you may decide to avoid possible problems by using naming conventions that are fully supported by the older systems.

However, when naming blocks using multiple words or designations, readability is enhanced by separating the individual naming components. If you are not using spaces in the symbol names, you can use the hyphen and underscore characters to achieve the same result. For example, when generating a name (using no spaces) for the radial finish mark symbol shown in Figure 12.5, you might decide to name it something like FINMARKRAD. Adding a hyphen, an underscore or both can help make the name much easier to read:

FIN_MARK-RAD

In most cases, it is best to use the shortest possible name that effectively communicates the nature of the symbol. Avoid the use of long descriptive sentences for block names. Use the separator characters only when readability is improved by doing so.

The Objects area is where you tell AutoCAD LT which objects in your drawing are to be used to define the new block. Picking the Select objects button temporarily hides the Block Definition dialog box and displays a Select objects: prompt. Any standard object selection method can be used to select the desired objects. When you are finished selecting the objects that define the new block, press the Enter key to return to the Block Definition dialog box. If you prefer, you can pick the Quick Select button to access the specialized selection tools in the Quick Select dialog box. When you are finished selecting objects and return to the Block Definition dialog box, a preview image of the block, based on the objects you selected, is displayed in the Preview icon area. If this image is not what you expected, pick one of the selection options to discard the current selection and start the selection process over.

The radio buttons in the Objects area determine what happens to the objects selected for the block definition. The option you select depends on what your plans are. The Retain option keeps the original objects in the drawing after the current block definition is complete. This option is useful when you are creating several symbols that are similar to one another or have duplicate features. For example, when designing a series of plumbing symbols for different styles of valves you are likely to realize that the geometry for the valve you are currently defining can be easily modified to match the next valve on the list. Picking Retain keeps you from having to start the next symbol from scratch. If you do not need to keep the original objects, you can pick Convert to block or Delete. The Convert to block option removes the source geometry and inserts the first copy of the block in its place. This is useful when the original geometry used to define the block was drawn in a location where one of the block references will need to be inserted. If you do not need to keep the original objects and do not want the objects converted to a block, pick the Delete radio button, and the objects used in the block definition will be deleted.

Field Notes

It is recommended that you turn on the Delete option to delete the selected objects after completing the block creation and use the OOPS command to restore the objects if you have further need for them. Seeing which objects disappear can be a helpful checkpoint in the block definition process, because otherwise it may not be obvious if any objects were missed in the selection process. The block preview image is very small and may not always provide an accurate enough image.

One such situation is in a drawing where one or more layers are locked. During the selection process, surrounding the desired objects with a window or crossing can lead you to believe that all of the objects have been selected, when in fact, any objects on locked layers were not selected. If the Delete option is used, the objects not successfully selected are immediately obvious because they are still visible.

The Base point area is where you specify the insertion *base point*. The ***insertion base point*** represents a meaningful reference point that is used to position the symbol accurately when it is being inserted into a drawing. Figure 12.7 shows a variety of symbols with an appropriate insertion base point for each symbol indicated by a filled circle. The rationale for the insertion base points shown in this figure becomes clear when you consider how each of the symbols is used. For example, electronic schematic symbols and single line piping diagram symbols are ordinarily connected to the end of a line object that designates a circuit pathway or a section of pipe. Looking at the electronic and piping symbols, you can see that the defined insertion base point makes it a quick and easy process to connect the symbol to an existing line using an ENDPoint object snap setting. An insertion base point located somewhere in the middle of the symbol would make it more difficult to position accurately.

The mechanical symbols shown specify the most commonly referenced point for locating the feature as the insertion base point. For example, a finish mark is located by placing the bottom point directly on the surface being described. The insertion base point shown for the finish mark in Figure 12.7 makes this an easy process. The hex nut symbol is typically positioned by centering it on a bolt or stud—so the center of the nut

FIGURE 12.7 The specified insertion point of a block should always reference the feature or location that is most commonly used as a base point when positioning the symbol in a drawing. The filled circles indicate appropriate insertion points for the symbols shown.

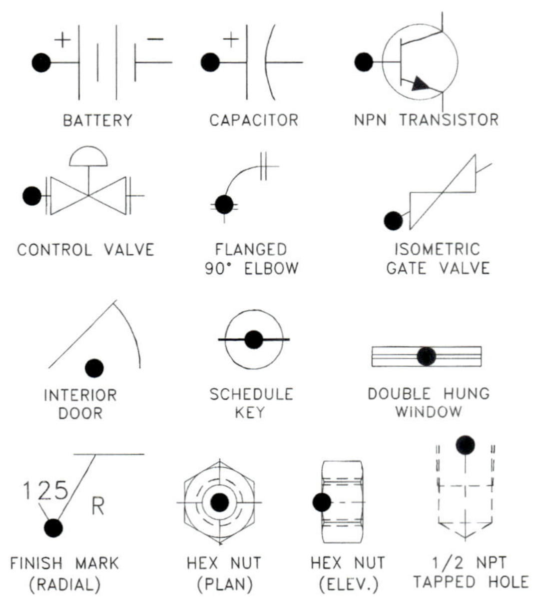

is the insertion base point. The NPT thread symbol insertion base point is where the surface profile and the hole center line intersect. Doors and windows are typically dimensioned to the center line of the opening, so an insertion base point that corresponds to the dimensioned position may work best.

To specify the desired insertion base point for the new block, pick the Pick Point button in the Base point area. The Block Definition dialog box is temporarily hidden while you pick the desired point. For the transistor block, a simple pick using the ENDpoint object snap mode accurately sets the desired insertion point.

After selecting an insertion base point, the Block Definition dialog box reappears and the selected coordinate location is displayed in the X:, Y:, and Z: text boxes. If you are not satisfied with the specified point, pick the Pick Point button again to specify a different insertion base point.

Alternatively, if you already know the exact coordinate location of the desired insertion base point, you can directly enter the X, Y, and Z values in the appropriately labeled text boxes. Regardless of the method used to enter the coordinates for the insertion base point of a block, be certain that the specified point is completely accurate. If you are picking the point with your cursor, be sure to use a suitable precision drawing aid such as the snap grid or an applicable object snap mode.

The Preview icon area displays an image of the block based on the current selection. The two radio buttons in this area control whether or not a preview image is created with the block. In most cases it is best to create a preview icon. Creating blocks that include preview image icons makes it possible to browse through your blocks visually in AutoCAD DesignCenter. Accessing blocks from DesignCenter is discussed later in this chapter.

Use the Insert units: list to select the desired insertion units for scaling when dragging and dropping blocks from DesignCenter. This provides automatic scaling based on a comparison of the unit type referenced by the inserted blocks and the unit type referenced by the drawing where the block is being inserted. The insertion units setting referenced by the destination drawing is found in the Drawing Units dialog box displayed by the UNITS command. There are many different styles of units available, from millimeters to light years. When the Drawing Units setting for DesignCenter blocks is set as *unitless*, the values used are based on the current settings found in the Source Content Units and Target Drawing Units settings in the User Preferences tab of the Options dialog box. If these are also set to unitless, no automatic scaling takes place. As an example of how this automatic scaling works, consider a situation where the source content units are specified as inches and the target drawing units are millimeters. When a 1″ square shape is inserted from the Source conent, it is automatically scaled to 25.4 units (mm) in the Target drawing.

The last field in this dialog box is the Description: text box. This optional field can be used to store a detailed description of the symbol, along with any other desired comments. Allowing a maximum of 30,000 characters, this field can be viewed when using the DesignCenter.

Figure 12.8 shows the appearance of the Block Definition dialog box on completion of this block definition. The block name is set to NPN_TRANS, the coordinates for the endpoint of the transistor's base lead are displayed, eight selected objects are to be used in the definition, and the Delete radio button is active. Pick the OK button to complete the block definition process.

When you select the OK button, the block definition data is checked for validity. If the block name you have specified duplicates an existing block name, a warning message is issued, as shown in Figure 12.9. To avoid redefining the existing symbol name with the new block definition, pick the Cancel button and specify a new block name. Redefining and renaming existing symbols is covered later in this chapter.

Once a symbol, or block, is defined in a drawing, it can be quickly and easily inserted into each desired location. Inserting symbols in a drawing is covered in the next section.

FIGURE 12.8 The appearance of the Block Definition dialog box on completion of the definition for the NPN_TRANS block.

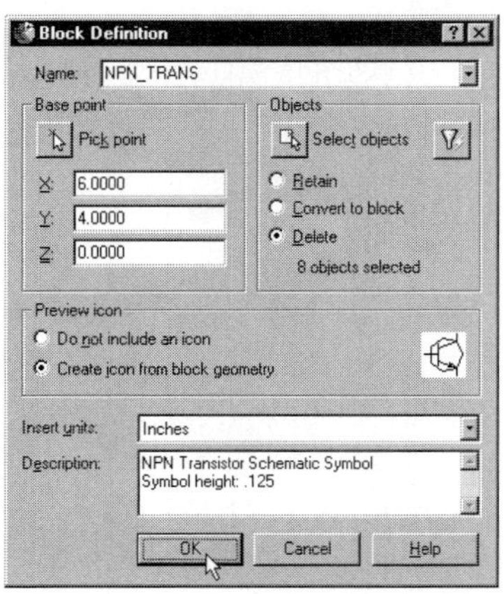

FIGURE 12.9 This warning is displayed if the specified block name duplicates an existing block name.

Field Notes

- For unique symbols that are particular to your business, you may need to simply create the required symbols on an "as-needed" basis. When a project requires a new symbol, create it and save it in your custom symbol library. Creating and managing custom symbol libraries is discussed later in this chapter.
- For standard drafting symbols, it can be advantageous to buy predrawn commercial symbol libraries to save yourself valuable drafting time. The Autodesk company markets symbol library packages designed specifically for use with AutoCAD LT, or you may find other companies that market a similar product.

Exercise 12.2 — Estimated time required: 20 min.

1. Start a new drawing using the Quick Setup defaults. Draw the geometry to describe an NPN transistor, as shown in Figure 12.7, and use it to define a block named NPN_TRANS specifying the insertion base point as shown in the illustration.
2. Draw four more symbols of your choice from Figure 12.7. Generate new block definitions for each symbol, and assign a short and descriptive name to each block. Use the insertion base points as shown in the illustration.
3. Save as EX12.2, and close the drawing.

LEARNING CHECKPOINT

- ☐ What are the advantages of using drafting symbols?
- ☐ Describe the primary productivity gain from using a CAD application.
- ☐ What is the first step in creating any block definition?
- ☐ Detail the block name conventions required by AutoCAD LT.
- ☐ What should be considered when defining a block insertion base point?
- ☐ What is the function and significance of the Delete option in the objects area?
- ☐ What are the recommended guidelines for specifying block names?

Working with Text and Symbols

- Creating and Maintaining Symbols and Drawing Files

Inserting Blocks

In the previous section you learned how to create block definitions. The term ***block*** is a generic term often used in reference to *block definition* and *block reference* objects. Both of these objects are needed to apply a block within a drawing. Once a block definition has been created, it remains available in the current drawing unless it is removed from the drawing database. A ***block definition*** object is a complete description of all of the objects that were used to create the initial block representation. To use a block definition in a drawing, the

Insert

Insert Block

Insert
Block...

DDINSERT
INSERT
I

INSERT command is used to insert a block reference object. A ***block reference***, also called an ***instance***, is a special type of object that is inserted into a drawing and displays data stored in the associated block definition.

The INSERT command can be accessed by picking the Insert Block button from the Draw toolbar, by picking Block... from the Insert pull-down menu, or by typing **I** or **INSERT** at the Command: prompt. The Insert dialog box is shown in Figure 12.10.

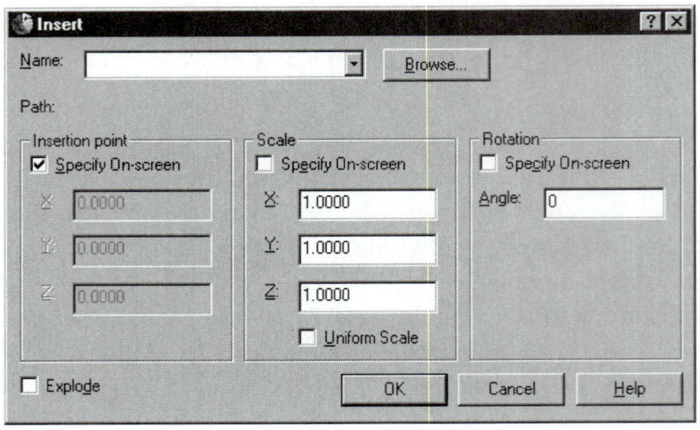

FIGURE 12.10 The Insert dialog box is accessed by using the INSERT command.

The Insert dialog box provides an easy interface for inserting block references into a drawing. To insert a locally defined block, pick the desired block name from the Name: drop-down list. A ***locally defined block*** refers to a block that is defined within the current drawing. For example, the sequence in the previous section creates the block definition named NPN_TRANS as a locally defined block. The Name: list shows the names of all the block definitions found in the current drawing (see Figure 12.11).

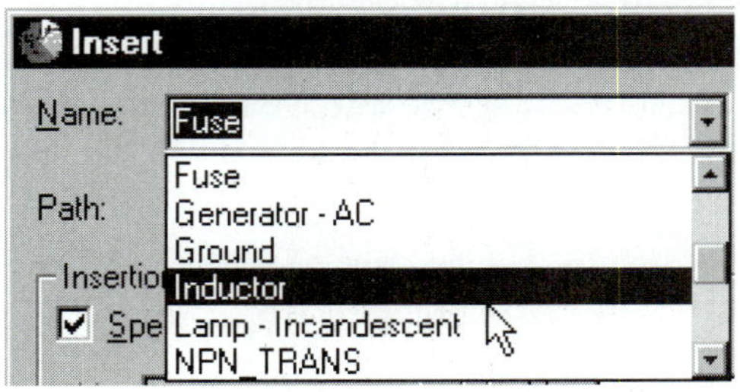

FIGURE 12.11 All blocks defined in the current drawing are listed in the Name: drop-down list.

To select a block name for insertion, select the desired block name from the list. If the current drawing has more than six block names defined, a scroll bar is added to the Name: drop-down list.

The Insert dialog box is where you indicate where and how to insert the block reference. The three boxed areas in the middle of the Insert dialog box are used to specify the Insertion point, the insertion Scale factor, and the Rotation angle to apply. At the top of each of these areas is a check box labeled Specify On-screen. When the Specify On-screen option is checked, the text boxes in that area are disabled. The initial default setting offers the Insertion point as the only setting to be specified on-screen. To follow along with the text and fully explore all of the on-screen insertion options, place a check in the Specify On-screen box for Insertion point, Scale, and Rotation. To continue with the block insertion process using this default option, pick the OK button. The Insert dialog box is dismissed and you will see the selected symbol attached to your cursor by its defined insertion base point. AutoCAD LT then issues the following prompt:

Command: **I** or **INSERT**↵
Specify insertion point or [Scale/X/Y/Z/Rotate/PScale/PX/PY/PZ/PRotate]: ⟨*pick the location for the block insertion base point*⟩

The NPN_TRANS block is attached to the specified insertion point by its insertion base point as specified in the block definition. Figure 12.12 shows the block attached to the cursor, with the ENDpoint object snap active, while picking an existing line. Using an applicable precision drawing aid, such as the snap grid or object snap, when inserting your block ensures that it is positioned accurately.

After specifying the location of the symbol within the drawing, you are prompted for an insertion scale factor. The insertion scale factor allows you to adjust the size of the symbol as needed for any specific appli-

FIGURE 12.12 The block is dragged with the cursor by its defined insertion base point. Picking an insertion point attaches the block to the selected point—also by its defined insertion base point.

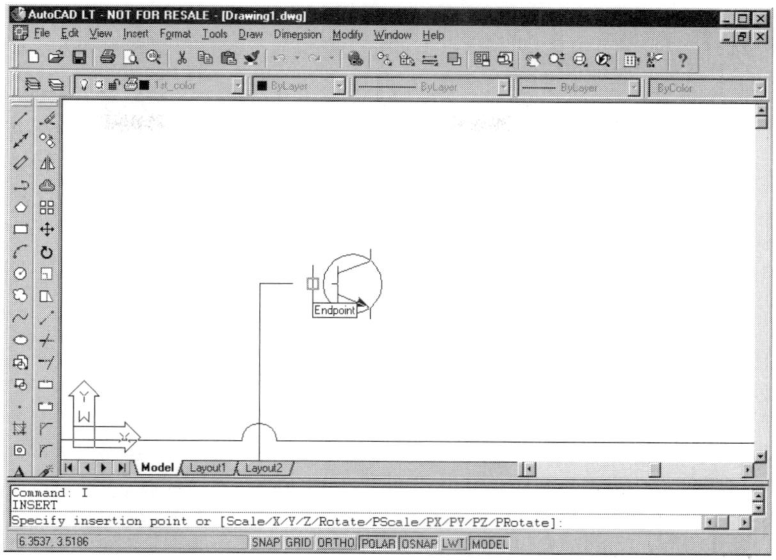

cation. Many symbols, such as those used in schematic diagrams, are drawn at a standard size and are typically inserted at the default scale factor of 1. Some symbols may vary in size depending on the application. Symbols that vary in size are often drawn based on a unit of 1, and the size is adjusted as needed during the insertion process. The example in Figure 12.13 uses a standard-sized schematic symbol, therefore the defined block is already the correct size. The following prompts are displayed at the command line to determine scale factors:

Enter X scale factor, specify opposite corner, or [Corner/XYZ] <1>: ↵
Enter Y scale factor <use X scale factor>: ↵

Pressing Enter at the X scale factor prompt accepts the default of 1 as displayed in the angle brackets: <1>. The next prompt asks for the Y scale factor and defaults to the value used for the X scale factor. Pressing Enter at this prompt accepts the default scale factor of 1.

Finally, you are prompted for a rotation angle. This allows you to reorient the block as needed for each placement in your drawing. The prompt is as follows:

Specify rotation angle <0>: ↵

Again, pressing Enter accepts the default of zero degrees rotation. This is appropriate in this case, because the symbol is already oriented correctly for this application. The result of inserting the block NPN_TRANS using the default values for each of the insertion parameters is shown in Figure 12.13.

FIGURE 12.13 The NPN_TRANS block as it appears after being inserted at a specified point using the default values for insertion options.

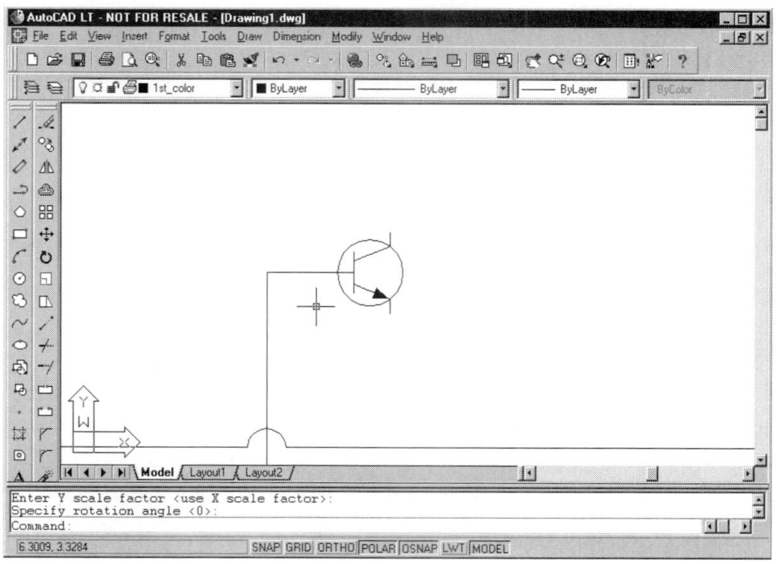

Field Notes

A distinct advantage to using blocks within a drawing is decreased drawing file size. A block definition is maintained as a singular record in the drawing database. Every insertion of the block in a drawing references the original definition and therefore does not duplicate information regardless of how many times the block is used in the drawing. Each individual block insertion stores only unique information such as its insertion point, scale factors, and rotation angle.

When working with schematic diagram drawings, inserted symbols often need to be rotated into the proper orientation. The rotation angle prompt can be used to adjust the orientation of a symbol when inserting it. To try this, use the INSERT command again. Notice that the last block inserted is presented as the default—the NPN_TRANS block name appears in the text box to the right of the Block ... button. Pick the OK button to accept the default and insert another copy of this block.

For the following example, pick any desired location on the screen for the insertion point and accept the default values for the X and Y scale factors. When prompted for the rotation angle, enter an angle of 90 degrees. Note that, similar to using the ROTATE command, a rotation angle can be specified by entering a numeric value using the keyboard or you can pick the angle using your cursor. If you enter the value using your keyboard, the prompt sequence looks like this:

Command: _ddinsert
Insertion point: ⟨*pick a point on the screen*⟩
X scale factor <1> / Corner / XYZ: ↵
Y scale factor (default=X): ↵
Rotation angle <0>: **90**↵

The inserted symbol is rotated 90 degrees and appears as shown in Figure 12.14. Notice that the insertion base point is also the rotation base point. For symbols that are frequently rotated when used, this can be an important consideration when defining the location of the block insertion base point.

Each of the previous examples shows a block inserted using the default values for the insertion scale factors. The insertion scale factors serve as direct multipliers for the sizes of the objects as they were drawn in the original block definition. By adjusting the values of the X and Y scale factor options, the size and aspect ratio of a symbol can be modified as needed, allowing for added flexibility when using symbols in your drawings. The term ***aspect ratio*** refers to the ratio of width to height, or in this case the ratio of X to Y scale factors.

Changing the X scale factor resizes the block based on the X axis of the original block definition geometry. Likewise, the Y and Z scale factors resize the block based on the Y and Z axes of the objects used in the original block definition. Additionally, a block can be mirrored upon insertion by specifying a negative insertion scale factor value. To mirror the symbol horizontally, indicate an X scale factor of −1; to mirror vertically, specify a Y scale factor of −1. Figure 12.15 shows several examples of various X and Y scale factors.

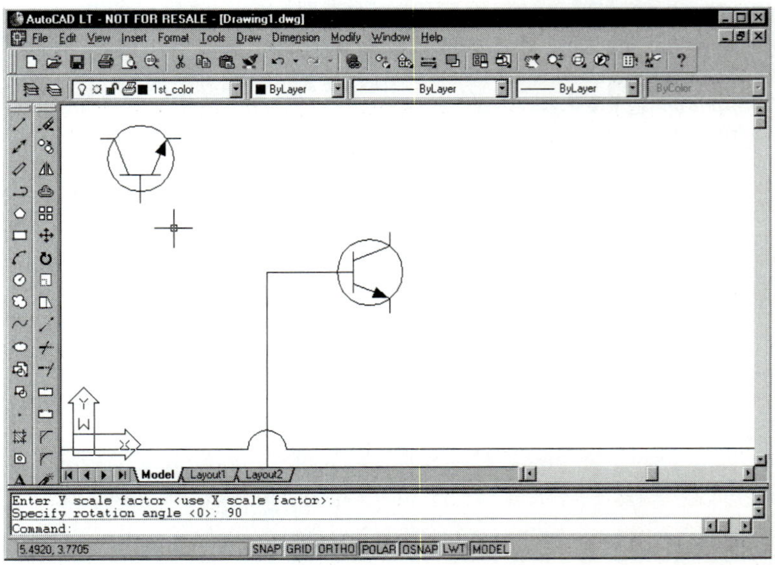

FIGURE 12.14 The second insertion of the NPN_TRANS block is rotated about the insertion base point 90 degrees.

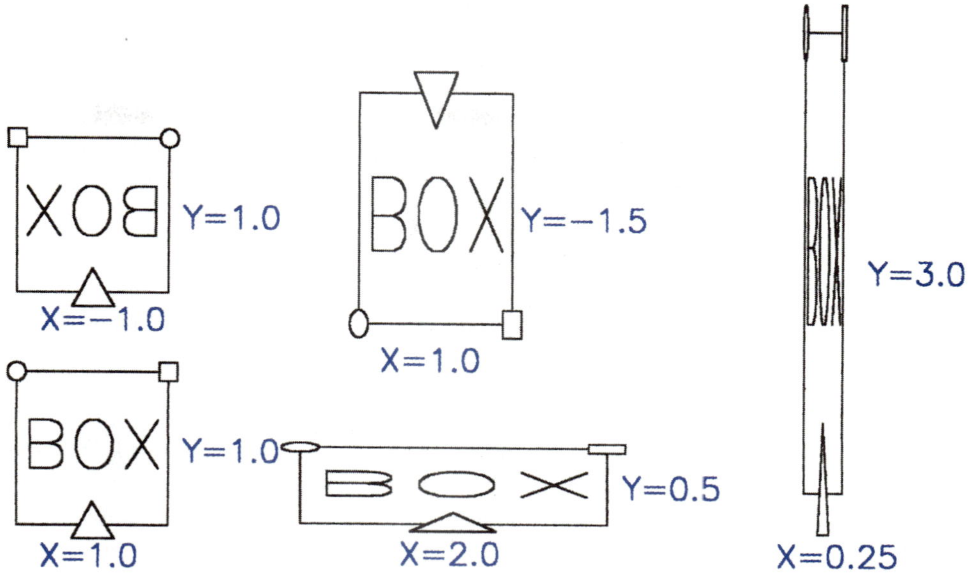

FIGURE 12.15 Various insertion scale factors can be used to alter the overall size or the aspect ratio of an inserted block. Negative values can be used to mirror a symbol on one or both axes during insertion.

Notice the effects of the negative values and the positive values both greater than and less than one. The Z axis value has no effect unless the block being inserted contains 3-D objects that have a Z axis dimensional value. Drawing 3-D objects is covered in Chapter 14.

As stated earlier, some symbols are defined as being a specific size. These symbols are drawn full size for the block definition and then inserted at a scale factor of 1. Other symbols, however, may vary in size or aspect ratio from one application to the next.

One example of a symbol that can vary in overall size from one application to the next includes annotation symbols, as shown in Figure 12.5. An ***annotation symbol*** is a symbol used in combination with text. The definitions of annotation symbols change based on the height of the text with which they are being used. Figure 12.16 shows the definition of a depth symbol as specified in ASME Y14.5M-1994. The "h" used in the dimensions references the height of the text with which the symbol is being used. The dimensions are not part of the symbol.

When creating a symbol that varies in size, the best approach is to create the block definition based on a unit of 1. This means that to create the definition for the annotation symbol shown in Figure 12.16, substitute a distance of 1 unit for the "h" dimension. Because the "h" dimension is drawn at 1 unit, the scale factor corresponds to the height of the text where the symbol is to be used. For example, in a mechanical drawing that uses 1/8-in. annotation text, the depth symbol is inserted using equal X and Y scale factors of 0.125. Because the scale factor is a multiplier, the defined symbol height of 1 unit is multiplied by 0.125, resulting in an inserted height of 0.125 units—the same as the text. If the text height is 5/32, use an insertion scale factor of 0.15625 (or 5/32). Whatever the text height is indicates what the insertion scale factor for the annotation symbol needs to be.

FIGURE 12.16 Annotation symbols will vary in size depending on the height of the text with which they are used. The "h" in the specified dimensions is a reference to the height of the accompanying text.

Field Notes

> Remember that many of the most commonly accessed annotation symbols are available as part of the text when using the GDT.shx font. Even if you need to use a different font, using the MTEXT editor enables you to create text objects that use more than one font file. If the symbol you need is not available as part of the text, then use the methods described here to create the needed annotation symbol.

An example of using symbols that vary in aspect ratio could include different types of block diagrams, such as a simplified floor plan that uses appropriately sized rectangles to depict various furnishings. A possible application for this type of drawing is for space planning in a building or office, where floor space is the concern rather than furniture details. To prepare for this task, create a simple 1-unit square for a block definition and name it very generically. For example, you could name the block FURN as a nonspecific reference to furniture.

When inserting a symbol to represent a desk measuring 30 in. deep by 60 in. wide, set the X scale factor at 30 and the Y scale factor at 60 and indicate the desired rotation angle. The same symbol can then be used to represent a conference room table measuring 42 in. × 96 in. by using X and Y scale factors of 42 and 96, respectively. This type of an application has one major disadvantage, which is the fact that all the symbols have the same name. So unless you insert some text labels, you may not remember what each insertion represents. A good solution for this problem is to use block attributes, which are discussed later in this chapter.

Other Insertion Scale Factor Options

When using the Specify Parameters on Screen option, two additional options are available for specifying insertion scale factors. To explore these options, use the INSERT command to insert the NPN_TRANS block. Pick any desired insertion point on screen and study the additional available options shown at the X scale factor prompt:

Command: **I** or **INSERT**↵
Specify insertion point or [Scale/X/Y/Z/Rotate/PScale/PX/PY/PZ/PRotate]: ⟨*pick a point*⟩
Enter X scale factor, specify opposite corner, or [Corner/XYZ] <1>: **C**↵
Specify opposite corner:

To use the corner option, type **C** and press Enter at the prompt, as shown above. The next prompt asks for the "Other corner:" of a user-specified rectangle. The implied First corner is automatically assigned to the block insertion point. The other corner can be an arbitrarily picked point, or specified using any valid coordinate entry method. AutoCAD LT then measures the X and Y axis distances between two corners of the rectangle. The distance on the X axis is used for the X scale factor and the distance on the Y axis is supplied for the Y scale factor. If the X coordinate of the second point is greater than that of the insertion point, the X scale factor is positive. An X axis value for the second corner that is less than the X axis value of the block insertion point results in a negative X scale factor. This is also true of the Y axis values. The Corner option is not very accurate when picking the other corner manually. This option can be more accurately controlled if you type a coordinate specification or use appropriate precision drawing aids.

After specifying the other corner, you are prompted for a rotation angle:

Specify rotation angle <0>: ↵

Typically, the Z scale factor is defaulted to the value of the X scale factor. If you need to use a specific Z scale factor that is not the same as the X scale factor, and you are specifying parameters on screen, the XYZ option is used. This option allows specification of different scale factors for all three axes if desired. This is how it works:

Command: **I** or **INSERT**↵
Specify insertion point or [Scale/X/Y/Z/Rotate/PScale/PX/PY/PZ/PRotate]: ⟨*pick a point*⟩
Enter X scale factor, specify opposite corner, or [Corner/XYZ] <1>: **X** or **XYZ**↵
Specify X scale factor or [Corner] <1>: ⟨*enter the X scale factor*⟩
Enter Y scale factor <use X scale factor>: ⟨*enter the Y scale factor*⟩
Specify Z scale factor or <use X scale factor>: ⟨*enter the Z scale factor*⟩
Specify rotation angle <0>: ↵

Alternately, after activating the XYZ option, you can use the Corner option to indicate the X and Y scale factors and you are then prompted for the Z scale factor.

Regardless of the application, specifying block insertion parameters can also be done using the settings in the Insert dialog box. After specifying the block name to insert, remove the checks from the Specify On-screen toggle. The text boxes are now enabled and can be modified as needed, as shown in Figure 12.17.

To use the Options area of the Insert dialog box effectively, you must already know the correct coordinates for the block insertion point. After indicating the insertion point coordinates, you can specify individual or common X, Y, and Z scale factors and a rotation angle. Notice that when you set the X scale factor, the Y and Z default values are automatically set to match. If this is not correct, you then need to adjust the Y and Z values individually.

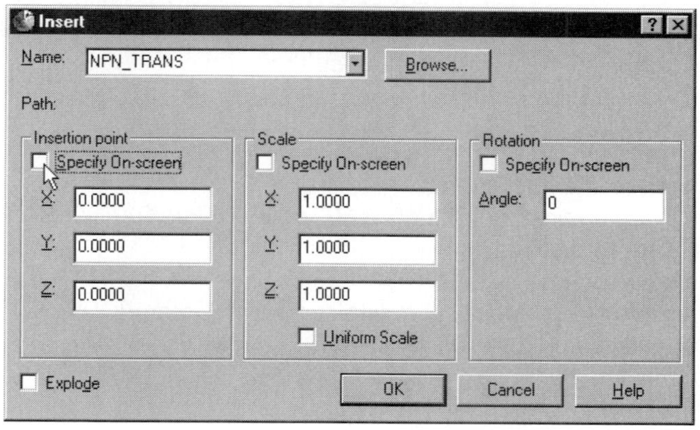

FIGURE 12.17 Turning off the Specify On-screen toggle enables the text boxes.

Presetting Block Insertion Parameters

When inserting a block, as you move the cursor, you drag along a representation of the block as it appears using the default insertion parameters. After picking an insertion point, the block is then stretched as you move your cursor to show the insertion scale factors indicated by the current X and Y distances from the selected point to the current cursor location. While entering the rotation angle, you can drag the cursor to point to any angle from the insertion point and the block representation is actively rotated to show the results.

In some cases, it can be helpful to see the block representation in its final form, according to the scale factor or rotation angle (or both) that you intend to use. This can be done using block insertion parameter presets. Presetting any or all of the insertion parameters allows AutoCAD LT to display the dragged block representation according to actual values you specify. Depending on which preset options you use, AutoCAD LT can use the preset values for inserting the block with no further prompting, or you can give a temporary preset value for the display only and you are then presented with the normal prompts.

Presets can only be used on screen, using the -INSERT command or the INSERT command with the Specify On-screen toggles turned on. To enter a preset scale factor, type **S** at the Insertion point: prompt.

Command: **I** or **INSERT**↵
Specify insertion point or [Scale/X/Y/Z/Rotate/PScale/PX/PY/PZ/PRotate]: **S**↵
Specify scale factor for XYZ axes: **2**↵
Specify insertion point: ⟨*specify the insertion point*⟩
Specify rotation angle <0>: ⟨*specify a rotation angle*⟩
Command:

When you are dragging the cursor at the second Insertion point: prompt, the block representation is displayed at a scale factor of 2. Notice that when using this method, only a single scale factor is requested and is used for both the X and Y values and no default values are given. Also, the preset value is automatically applied to the final inserted block reference with no further prompts. The rotation angle is then requested.

Another option is to preset the rotation angle:

Command: **I** or **INSERT**↵
Specify insertion point or [Scale/X/Y/Z/Rotate/PScale/PX/PY/PZ/PRotate]: **R**↵
Specify rotation angle: **45**↵
Specify insertion point: ⟨*specify the insertion point*⟩
Enter X scale factor, specify opposite corner, or [Corner/XYZ] <1>: ↵
Enter Y scale factor <use X scale factor>: ↵

And if desired, you can preset both the scale factor and the rotation angle:

Command: **I** or **INSERT**↵
Specify insertion point or [Scale/X/Y/Z/Rotate/PScale/PX/PY/PZ/PRotate]: **S**↵
Specify scale factor for XYZ axes: **2**↵
Specify insertion point: **R**↵
Specify rotation angle: **45**↵
Specify insertion point: ⟨*specify the insertion point*⟩
Command:

It is also possible to preset individual X, Y, and Z scale factors in the same manner by typing **X, Y,** or **Z** at the Insertion point: prompt.

If you want to use the presets as a reference only, but you also want an opportunity to enter a value different from the preset, you can use a temporary preset. Temporary presets are used in the same manner as the presets just described, but you are still issued the normal scale factor and rotation angle prompts after picking the insertion point. To make the preset temporary, precede the preset option with a P. For example, the next sequence is used to set a temporary preset scale factor:

Command: **I** or **INSERT**↵
Specify insertion point or [Scale/X/Y/Z/Rotate/PScale/PX/PY/PZ/PRotate]: **PS**↵
Specify preview scale factor for XYZ axes: **2**↵
Specify insertion point: ⟨*specify the insertion point*⟩
Enter X scale factor, specify opposite corner, or [Corner/XYZ] <1>: ⟨*specify a scale factor*⟩
Enter Y scale factor <use X scale factor>: ⟨*specify a scale factor*⟩
Specify rotation angle <0>: ⟨*specify a rotation angle*⟩
Command:

Field Notes

AutoCAD LT also provides command line versions of the BMAKE and INSERT commands for making and inserting blocks.

- The -BLOCK command is used to create new block definitions using text entry at the command line.
- The -INSERT command (alias = -I) is used to insert blocks using text entry at the command line.

The BMAKE and INSERT commands provide a more effective interface for creating and using blocks than these command line versions. However, the command line versions are necessary when employing advanced automation techniques such as command scripts. The use of command scripts is detailed in Chapter 17.

Exercise 12.3

Estimated time required: 10 min.

1. Open the drawing EX12.2.
2. Use the INSERT command to insert the NPN_TRANS block using default insertion options.
3. Insert additional copies of NPN_TRANS and experiment with changing the values for the X and Y scale factors and rotation angles. Try both positive and negative values.
4. Create the geometry for the DEPTH symbol, as shown in Figure 12.16, substituting a distance of 1 unit for the "h" dimension.
5. Insert the DEPTH symbol in conjunction with a text object to create a note specifying a 0.25 diameter by a depth of 1.75 units.
6. Save as EX12.3, and keep the drawing open for subsequent activities.

LEARNING CHECKPOINT

- ☐ To what does the term *locally defined block* refer?
- ☐ How can you display a list of the blocks defined for the current drawing?
- ☐ What are the advantages of using the Specify On-screen options?
- ☐ Describe each of the prompts issued when specifying parameters on screen.
- ☐ How does the definition process differ for a symbol that may vary in size?
- ☐ Name the command line versions of BMAKE and INSERT.
- ☐ What is meant by defining a block based on a unit of 1?
- ☐ Describe the use of the Corner option for specifying insertion scale factors.

Drag-and-Drop Block Insertion Using DesignCenter

The single most powerful tool for accessing drawing content is AutoCAD DesignCenter. Drawing content such as blocks can also be accessed using the easy DesignCenter interface. Using DesignCenter provides added flexibility, allowing you to access blocks defined in current drawings as well as any blocks defined in virtually any drawing to which you have access. You can quickly browse through folders full of drawings to find needed block definitions, plus benefit from easy access to the DesignCenter symbol library that comes with AutoCAD LT.

Start the DesignCenter window using either the ADC command or by pressing Ctrl + 2. Pick the Open Drawings button to display only content from the currently open drawings. In the Tree View pane, locate the Blocks content source for the current drawing. Pick the Blocks icon in the Tree View pane to display the available block content in the palette pane. In Figure 12.18, the block content from the exercise drawing EX12.3.dwg is displayed in the DesignCenter window.

The icons in the palette pane representing blocks are typically displayed as a small preview image. These smaller preview icons are usually adequate for recognizing smaller or less detailed blocks. Preview icons are displayed only when the view is set to display Large Icons. Blocks that were not saved with a preview icon are displayed using a generic block icon. When you create new block definitions, remember to save the preview icon and try to take a moment to enter a concise text description. These features can be very helpful when you are trying to locate and identify content sources. Use the Preview and Description buttons to display larger preview images and text descriptions attached to selected content items. You can adjust the size of the preview image area by pointing to the border and dragging it with the resizing cursor.

Blocks are inserted from DesignCenter using the same drag-and-drop method and shortcut menu options practiced previously with other types of drawing content. If you drag and drop a block into your draw-

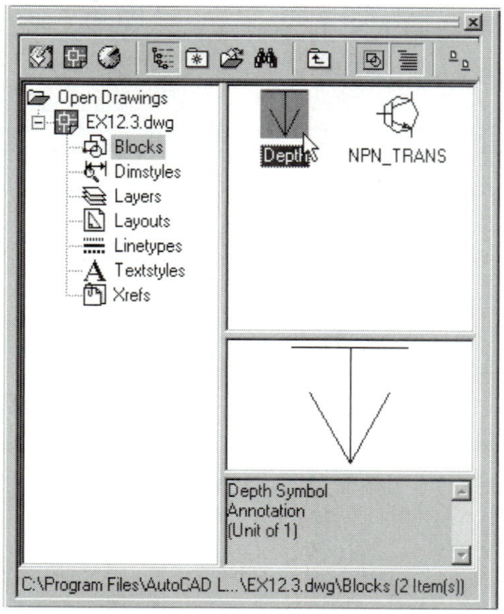

FIGURE 12.18 AutoCAD DesignCenter provides easy and convenient access to all types of drawing content, including Blocks. The Preview and Description features provide additional information about the selected item.

ing using the pick button, no prompts are displayed. The blocks are inserted using a default scale of 1 and a rotation angle of 0. You can pick the inserted block and use the Properties window to modify the settings as needed. Right-clicking on a content item displays a shortcut menu. Picking the Insert Block... option displays the Insert dialog box with the block name already specified. Use this method if you want to insert the block using specific settings. Picking the Copy option from the shortcut menu copies the selected block object to the Windows clipboard; you can now paste the block into one or more drawings.

Accessing the DesignCenter Symbol and Resource Library

Using AutoCAD DesignCenter, you can access content from a small library of symbols and other valuable resources supplied as part of the AutoCAD LT 2000 software package. The library is provided in the form of sixteen drawing files, each one providing different content. One of the drawing files provides predefined text style and linetype content ready to drag and drop wherever it is needed. The rest contain small symbol libraries with an average of around twenty common symbols related to a specific field of drafting and design.

These files are located in the **AutoCAD LT 2000\Sample\DesignCenter** folder. Access the Desktop in the Tree View pane of DesignCenter, then find and open the DesignCenter folder. Figure 12.19 shows the Blocks content found in the *Welding.dwg* file.

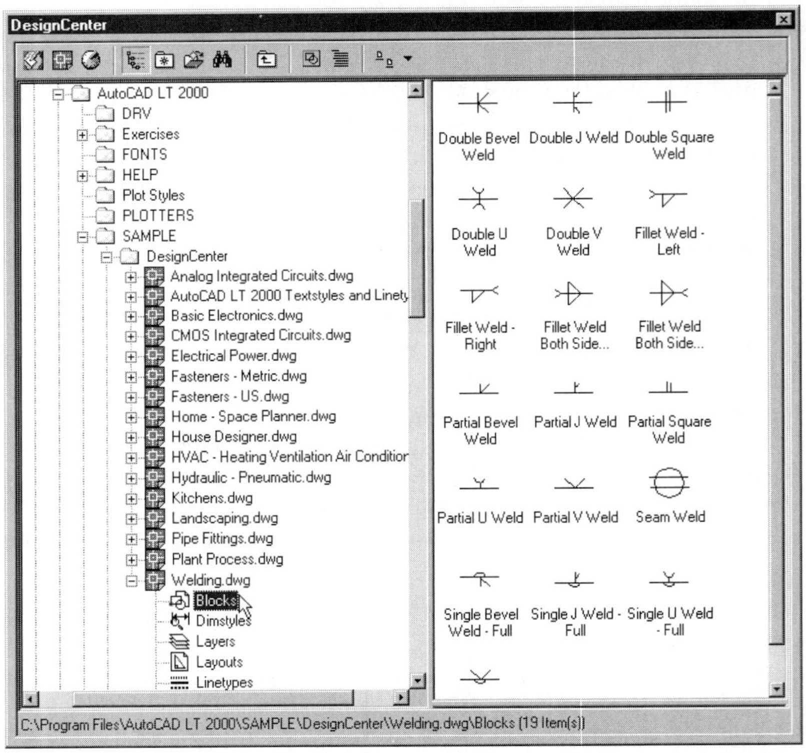

FIGURE 12.19 AutoCAD DesignCenter provides easy access to this library of resources that comes with the AutoCAD LT software.

Field Notes

- When content is dragged and dropped into a drawing from DesignCenter, the command line does not show any commands being entered. However, if you view the Undo list on the Standard toolbar you will see the DROPGEOM command listed.
- The DesignCenter resource library illustrates an effective way to keep your reusable drawing content well organized and easily accessible. Think about ways that you could organize your own specific drawing content using this model as a guide.
- Content source locations you visit frequently should be added to your Favorites list in DesignCenter.
- The ADCNAVIGATE command opens DesignCenter if it is not yet open and takes you directly to a specified folder location, file, or network UNC address. But if you are still learning basic keyboarding skills, typing a long path name may take longer than picking your way through the Tree View. However, the ADCNAVIGATE command and the desired path name can be added to a new toolbar button that requires only a single click of the mouse. Creating new toolbar buttons is covered in Chapter 17.

Working with Blocks

A block that has been inserted into a drawing is known as a block reference. It is called a ***block reference*** because that is exactly what it does—it references a block definition. Each insertion of a specific block references the same stored block definition data, and has no actual definition of its own. Relevant information that is specific to a block reference includes its insertion point, scale factors, and rotation angle, plus a reference to the layer on which it was inserted.

Editing a Block

Blocks are not like other objects in an AutoCAD LT drawing. A block is a complex object, meaning that regardless of how many objects are used in the block definition, a block is still handled like a single object. Selecting a block reference at a Select objects: prompt highlights all of the component objects, but the prompt reports only one object found. This is similar to a polyline object, which can be composed of multiple line and arc segments, but is still handled as a single object.

Block editing capabilities are very limited. The only editing commands that can be used are those that affect the entire block rather than individual components within the block reference. For example, duplication commands can be used with a block reference, including COPY, MIRROR, and ARRAY. Commands that change the size, position, or orientation of the block can be used, such as MOVE, SCALE, and ROTATE. Certain properties associated with a block reference can be changed using PROPERTIES and DDCHPROP. Additionally, any block reference can be removed from a drawing using the ERASE command.

When editing block references, object snap modes can be used to increase accuracy. The INSert object snap mode snaps to the block's defined insertion base point. All object snap modes work the same on objects that are components of a block reference as they do with individual objects.

Standard

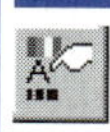

Properties (Ctrl+1)

Modify
Properties

PROPERTIES
[Ctrl] + [1]

When you need to change the location, scale factors, or rotation angle of a block reference, the PROPERTIES command provides a one-step method to change any or all of the block insertion parameters. PROPERTIES is accessed by picking the Properties button from the Standard toolbar, by right-clicking and picking Properties ..., by selecting Properties ... from the Modify pull-down menu, or by typing **PROPERTIES** or by pressing Ctrl+1 at the Command: prompt.

Grip select one or more block references to access the desired settings in the PROPERTIES window, as shown in Figure 12.20. Several of the properties of block references can be modified using this window. Of the items in the area labeled General at the top of the property list, the only option that is likely to have any noticeable effect is changing the Layer setting. The color, linetype, and individual object linetype scale properties of a block are dependent on how the original block definition was created. Techniques for controlling these properties within block references are detailed later in this section.

The Geometry area in the Properties window provides options for modifying the insertion point, and the X, Y, and Z scale factors. The block rotation angle is listed in the Misc area. The insertion point can be

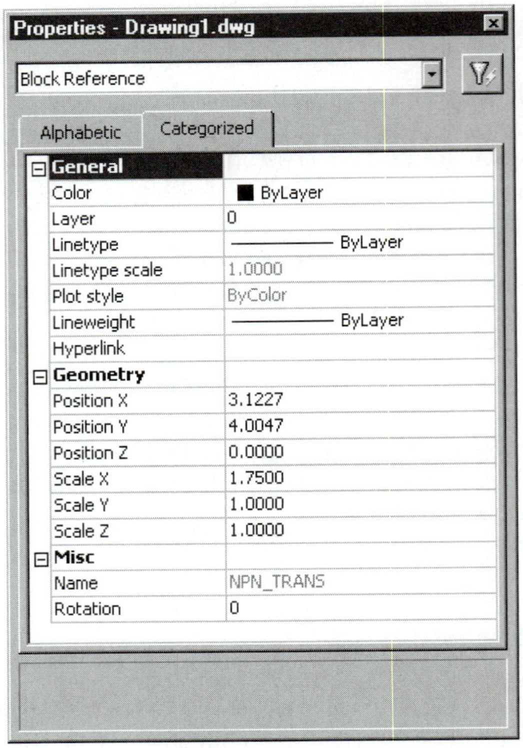

FIGURE 12.20 The Properties window provides a convenient means to change the insertion parameters of an existing block reference.

picked on screen or entered directly as individual X, Y, and Z coordinate values. Alternately, the CHANGE command can be used to quickly modify the insertion point and rotation angle of a block reference using the command line. Note that any changes to scale factors and rotation angles in this manner use the insertion point as the base point for the scaling or rotation.

As mentioned earlier, any command that attempts to edit individual components within the block reference cannot be used. Commands such as BREAK, TRIM, LENGTHEN, FILLET, and CHAMFER have no effect on blocks. For example, in the NPN_TRANS block, it is not possible to separately modify the circle, lines, or the polyline object that comprise the block reference. To do this type of editing, the block reference must first be exploded.

Exercise 12.4 **Estimated time required: 5 min.**

1. Open the drawing EX12.3.
2. Use the INSERT command to insert the NPN_TRANS block using default insertion options.
3. Try using editing commands, such as TRIM, EXTEND, or FILLET to modify the component geometry of the block reference. Notice the messages issued by AutoCAD LT.
4. Edit the block using editing commands such as COPY, MOVE, and ROTATE to duplicate, reposition, and reorient the block reference.
5. Use the Properties command to change the scale factors, insertion point, and rotation angle of the block reference.
6. Save as EX12.4, and close the drawing.

Modify

Explode

Modify
Explode

EXPLODE
X

Exploding a Block

When you need to edit individual elements of a block in your drawing, you can disassemble the block reference using the EXPLODE command:

Command: **X** or **EXPLODE**↵
Select objects: ⟨*select a block reference*⟩
Select objects: ↵
Command:

Exploding a block reduces it to its component objects. This means that the block reference is replaced with individual objects that represent the block definition. AutoCAD LT modifies these individual objects to match the exploded block's scale factors and rotation angle so that the size, position, and orientation of the displayed geometry remain the same.

Once a block reference has been exploded, it is no longer a complex object, and it loses all association with the original block definition. For example, exploding the NPN_TRANS block replaces the singular block reference object with one circle, six lines, and one polyline. Now the component objects can be freely edited with no effect on other NPN_TRANS block references in the drawing.

Field Notes

Exploding a block that was inserted using unequal scale factors can sometimes result in the creation of different object types than were used in the original block definition. For example, unequal insertion X and Y scale factors cause a circle object to appear elliptical in the inserted block reference. In order to preserve the appearance of the geometry when the block is exploded, AutoCAD LT substitutes an appropriate ellipse in place of the circle used in the original definition. Additionally, arc objects within such a block reference are converted to elliptical arcs when the block is exploded.

Inserting an Exploded Block

If you know prior to inserting a block that you are going to need to edit the geometry, you can turn on the Explode toggle in the Insert dialog box. The Explode toggle is located at the bottom left corner of the Insert dialog box. Toggling this on causes a block to be inserted as component objects and not as a block reference. Essentially, the block is automatically exploded while it is being inserted. To do this using the -INSERT command, precede the specified block name with an asterisk. For example:

Command: **-INSERT**↵
Enter block name or [?] <NPN_TRANS>: ***NPN_TRANS**↵
Specify insertion point for block: Specify scale factor for XYZ axes: ↵
Specify rotation angle <0>: ↵
Command:

When a block is exploded during insertion, unequal scale factors cannot be specified. Notice that the prompt is for a single scale factor, which is then applied equally to the X, Y, and Z axes. Similarly, if the Specify On-screen toggles are off when the Explode toggle is on, you will notice that the Y and Z scale factor options are disabled, allowing you to enter only a single scale factor that is applied to X, Y, and Z.

Exercise 12.5 — Estimated time required: 5 min.

1. Open the drawing EX12.4.
2. Before beginning, ensure that inserted block references exist using both equal and unequal X and Y scale factors.
3. Use the EXPLODE command to explode several of the blocks.
4. Insert a new copy of a block using -INSERT with the Explode toggle on and the Specify On-screen toggles off.
5. Insert a new copy of a block using -INSERT and precede the block name with an asterisk.
6. Using the LIST command, list the properties of the component circle objects of the exploded blocks. Notice the difference in object type, depending on the insertion scale factors of the original block reference.
7. Save as EX12.5, and close the drawing.

Redefining a Locally Defined Block

One very powerful aspect of using blocks in your drawings comes from the ability to revise every copy of a specific block in a drawing by simply revising the block definition. Inserted block references have no actual definition of their own. All insertions of a block reference within a drawing display the geometry described in the current block definition.

To redefine a symbol, first insert an exploded block reference of the block you are redefining. Alternately, you can insert the block reference and then explode it prior to editing. Which method you use is not important, but it is crucial that the block be exploded before you do any editing.

After exploding the block, perform all of your desired edits. Once you are finished editing the block and are satisfied with the new symbol, start the BMAKE command. In the Name: field, enter the same name that the block used previously. Specify the insertion base point and select the objects to use for the block definition. When you pick OK, AutoCAD LT warns you that the block name you specified already exists. This warning dialog box, shown in Figure 12.21, presents a yes-or-no option: pick the Yes button to redefine the block or No to cancel.

FIGURE 12.21 Picking the Yes button revises the block definition and, on exiting the Block Definition dialog box, updates all previously inserted block references using the new definition.

Block Redefinition Problems

If you forget to explode a block reference before revising it, you may encounter some unexpected difficulties when trying to redefine the existing block definition. If you need to remove or change some of the objects that comprise the definition, you will find that you cannot edit the individual components of a block reference prior to exploding it. Even if all you need to do is add some new objects to the definition, you are still required to explode the reference in order to use its component geometry in the revised definition. Otherwise, as shown in Figure 12.22, the message "Block references itself." is displayed in an alert box when you pick the Yes button to complete the redefinition.

AutoCAD LT permits existing block references to be used in the creation of *other* block definitions. This practice is called ***nesting*** and is discussed in the next section. However, AutoCAD LT does not allow an inserted block reference to be used as part of the block definition that has the same name as the reference. To demonstrate this concept, the following example shows the definition of a block named SIGN, followed by one successful and one unsuccessful attempt to redefine it using the component geometry of the block reference as part of the new definition.

FIGURE 12.22 An error message is displayed when a block is specified as part of its own definition.

All block definitions consist of a descriptive listing of the objects selected to represent the block geometry. As an example, in Figure 12.23A, the block named SIGN has been created using the three listed line objects to comprise the block definition. Each of the lines selected is clearly defined in the drawing database, and AutoCAD LT uses this information in the definition for the block named SIGN.

As with any block reference, an inserted SIGN block simply reads the source definition in order to know what component geometry to display. The source definition of SIGN lists the descriptions of the three component lines.

In Figure 12.23B, the block is successfully redefined. To use the geometry comprising the current definition as part of the new definition, an insertion of the block reference SIGN is placed in the drawing. Explode the block during insertion as practiced in Exercise 12.5, or after insertion, use the EXPLODE command. This removes the block reference and replaces it with individual objects that represent the existing

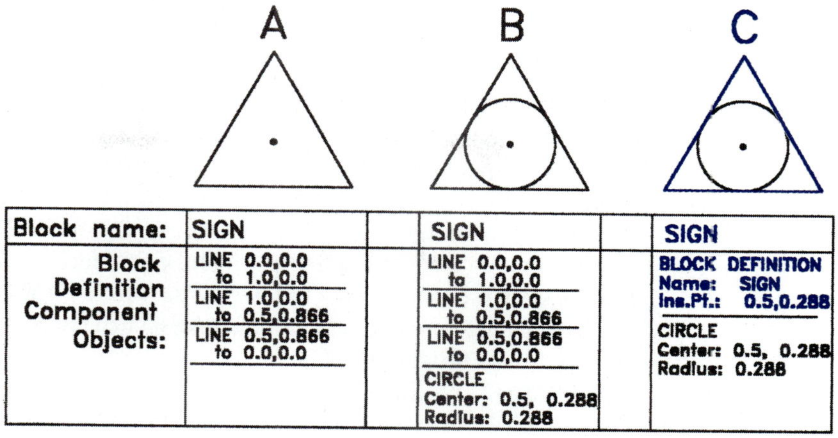

FIGURE 12.23 (A) The original SIGN block is defined using three line objects. (B) The correct approach is to explode the block reference before trying to redefine a block. This example successfully redefines the block SIGN as being comprised of three line objects and a circle. (C) An error is produced when the existing block SIGN is used as part of the definition for the new SIGN block.

block definition. Edits can now be made to the existing geometry, and in this example, a circle is placed inside of the triangle formed by the three lines.

Now that the revisions to the symbol are complete, use the BMAKE command to change the block definition. The objects selected as the definition are three line objects and a circle object. As with the previous definition of SIGN, these objects are clearly defined in the drawing database and AutoCAD LT uses this information in the new definition for the block named SIGN. Additionally, any other occurrences of a reference to this block definition are immediately updated.

An error situation is produced in Figure 12.23C, where an attempt is made to revise the definition of the block named SIGN using an existing reference to the block as part of its new definition. In this case, the block reference has not been exploded and is therefore still just a reference to the block definition of SIGN. As in Figure 12.23B, the revision edit consists of a circle being placed in the triangle. When the BMAKE command is used and the descriptive geometry is selected, this time only two objects are found: the circle and an inserted reference to the definition of the block named SIGN. To determine how to display a representation of the component objects, AutoCAD LT finds the drawing database records of the selected objects. The circle is clearly defined, but the block reference SIGN is now defined as comprising two objects, a circle and the block named SIGN. At this point, the block named SIGN does not have a complete definition. It is defined as being comprised of an inserted reference to itself and a circle.

The final result is that when the inserted block *reference* named SIGN looks to the new block *definition* to find out what geometry to display, it finds that the *definition* of the block SIGN contains an inserted block *reference* named SIGN. Any attempts to resolve the definition of the SIGN block result in another reference to a block named SIGN. This creates an endless loop and prevents AutoCAD LT from being able to determine what geometry to use to display the new definition. A block definition that uses an inserted reference to itself as part of its own definition is what is referred to by the message "Block references itself." So if you see this message while redefining a locally defined block, exit the Block Definition dialog box and explode the existing block reference. Now you should be able to proceed without any further problems.

Renaming a Block

To change the name of a block definition, use the RENAME command. You can access the RENAME command by typing **REN** or **RENAME** at the Command: prompt or by picking Rename ... from the Format menu. To rename a block, pick Blocks from the Named Objects list and highlight the name of the block you want to rename. The old name then appears in the Old Name: text box. Enter the new name in the Rename To: text box and pick the Rename To: button. Now pick OK. If you forget to pick the Rename To: button before picking OK, the block will not be renamed.

Format
Rename...
RENAME
REN

Exercise 12.6 **Estimated time required: 10 min.**

1. Start a new drawing session.
2. Create a 1-unit square using LINE objects. Use these four lines as a definition for a block named TILE, using the lower left corner as the insertion base point.
3. Insert one TILE block reference using default values. Insert four others using any desired insertion parameters.
4. Draw a circle within the first inserted TILE block reference.
5. Using the BMAKE command, try to redefine the block TILE. When selecting objects, pick both the inserted block reference and the circle. Notice the message issued by AutoCAD LT when you pick the OK button.
6. Cancel the BMAKE command and use the EXPLODE command to explode the block reference. Try using BMAKE again to redefine the block TILE, and select all four lines from the exploded block and the circle object.
7. Notice the changes made to the other inserted TILE block references.
8. Save as EX12.6, and close the drawing.

☑ LEARNING CHECKPOINT

- ☐ What are the limitations regarding editing inserted block references?
- ☐ Which properties of a block reference can be changed with PROPERTIES?
- ☐ Name the command that reduces a block to its components.
- ☐ What two methods can be used to explode a block while inserting it?
- ☐ What happens to block references when the block definition is modified?
- ☐ What is meant by a block referencing itself?
- ☐ How can you avoid a block referencing itself when redefining it?

Nesting Blocks

Block references can be used as needed in other block definitions, this practice is called ***nesting.*** One situation for which a nested block is useful is within a subassembly that occurs in multiple locations within a drawing or within multiple drawings. In many cases, the parts of the subassembly may be represented as symbols that were created using blocks. For example, in the piping subassembly shown in Figure 12.24A, several individual blocks representing valves, tanks, gauges, and other components were inserted and connected by lines as appropriate to form the subassembly representation. The resulting geometry is then used as the definition for another block that represents the full subassembly. This procedure allows you to insert the entire subassembly as needed, rather than constructing it from individual blocks in each required location. Figure 12.24B shows the use of the subassembly in a piping diagram. Notice that the block on the right has been inserted using a negative X scale factor, and therefore appears mirrored.

Blocks and Layers

Blocks have a special relationship with layers in an AutoCAD LT drawing, and certain considerations need to be made both when creating and when inserting block references. The objects that are used in the block definition can be created on any desired layer, or can even have any desired color and linetype assignments apart from layer settings. The most appropriate layer, color, and linetype settings for the component geometry of a block definition are determined by the desired appearance of the actual inserted block reference.

Objects created using "bylayer" color and linetype settings ignore any absolute color and linetype settings that are active when the block reference is inserted. These bylayer objects behave differently in the actual inserted block reference depending on whether they were created on layer 0 or on a user-defined layer. If created on layer 0, an object acquires the properties of the layer on which the block reference exists. This means that the objects initially take on the properties of the layer that the block reference is inserted on, but if the block reference is moved to a different layer these objects are updated to the settings for the new layer. However, if the object is created on any user-defined layer, they maintain the properties associated with that layer regardless of what layer the block reference exists on. This concept is demonstrated in Figure 12.25. The objects used to define the threaded hole symbol shown in Figure 12.25A were created using the settings listed in Table 12.1.

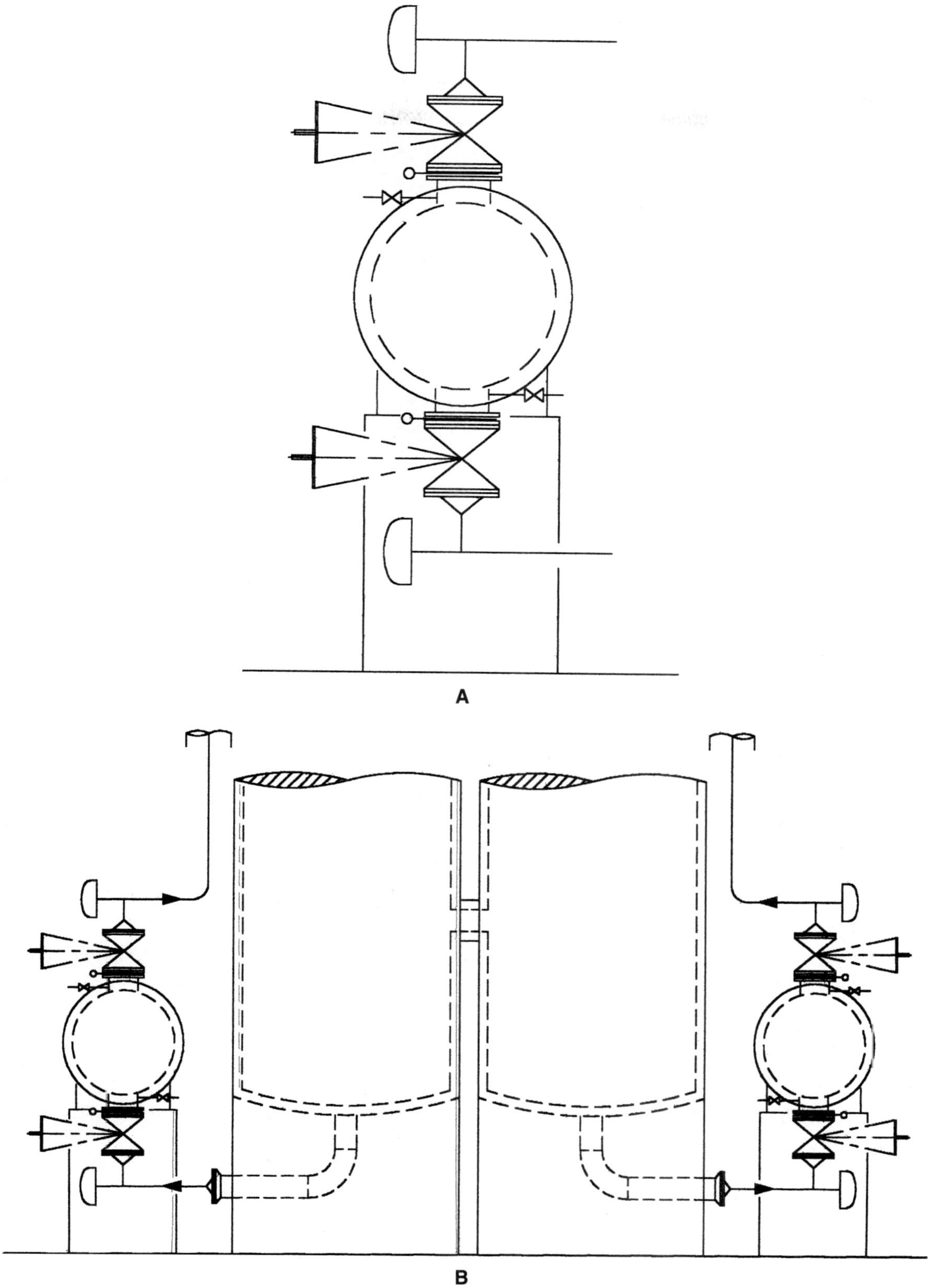

FIGURE 12.24 (A) Block references can be used as part of the definition of other blocks. (B) Inserting the block representing the subassembly can save a great deal of time if the subassembly is a commonly used feature.

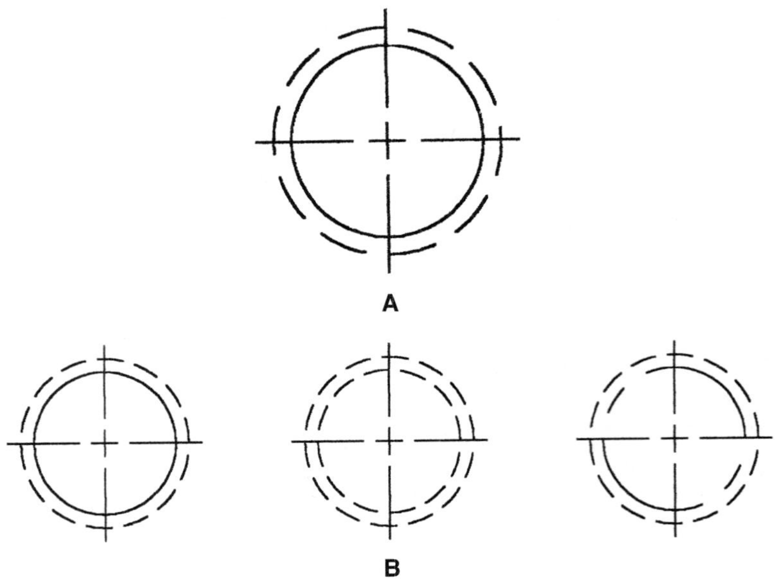

FIGURE 12.25 (A) These objects were created on varying layers using a bylayer setting. (B) Objects created on layer 0, using bylayer settings, take on the properties of the layer on which the block reference is inserted. Objects created on other layers, using bylayer settings, are displayed according to their individual layer settings.

TABLE 12.1 Threaded hole settings

	Solid Circle	Dashed Circle	Center Lines
Current layer setting	"WHITE"	"HID"	"CEN"
Current layer color	BYLAYER	CYAN	GREEN
Current layer linetype	CONTINUOUS	HIDDEN	CENTER
Current color setting	BYLAYER	BYLAYER	BYLAYER
Current linetype setting	BYLAYER	BYLAYER	BYLAYER

In Figure 12.25B, the block reference has been inserted on each of the three layers 0, HID, and CEN as indicated. Notice that the primary circle, which was created on layer 0, has taken on the properties of the layer on which the block reference was inserted. The objects that were created on layers other than layer 0 are displayed according to the current settings of that layer, regardless of the layer on which the block reference is inserted.

If you need the inserted block always to maintain the exact same appearance with regard to colors and linetypes, you can assign permanent settings to some or all of the objects within a block definition. Using the Objects Properties tool bar, you can set an absolute color or linetype setting for all new objects. Any objects used in a block definition that are created using absolute settings for color or linetype (or both) maintain those same settings regardless of the layer on which the block reference is inserted. When absolute settings are used, it does not matter on which layer the objects were created.

A specialized setting exists, for both the color and linetype options, called ***byblock.*** This can be set using the Object Properties tool bar, or any of the available commands for changing absolute color and linetype settings. When the byblock setting is active, any objects drawn are displayed using color number 7 and continuous lines. But when these objects are used in a block definition, they are treated like any other newly created object when the block reference is inserted. If the currently active color or linetype is bylayer, the objects are displayed according to the settings of the layer on which the block reference is inserted. When an absolute color or linetype is set, the objects are displayed accordingly. All byblock objects respond in this manner, regardless of the layer on which they were created.

Note that the color and linetype of component objects created using byblock settings can also be changed within the inserted block reference. You can use the Properties command to change the layer, the absolute color, or even the linetype of the block reference. Remember that only the objects in the block definition that were created using byblock settings are affected by these changes.

Field Notes

- When a block reference is exploded, each component object reverts to the layer on which the same object in the original block definition was created. This means that component objects created on layer 0, using bylayer settings, no longer use the color and linetype settings of the layer on which the block reference was inserted. If this is not desirable, you can easily move the objects back to the appropriate layer. A simple way to do this is to pick the Properties toolbar button to start the PROPERTIES command and make the required changes.
- Objects created as "byblock," when the block reference is exploded, revert to continuous white (or black) lines and are placed on the layer on which they were created.

Block References and Layer Controls

When you insert a block reference, it is always inserted on the current layer. This means that the block reference is affected by the visibility controls and other settings for the layer on which it is inserted. As an example, in Figure 12.25, a block definition of a threaded hole was created using objects on layers 0, CEN, and HID, and the resulting block has been inserted while layer 0 is current. Although the component geometry references other layers in the drawing, the block reference is created on layer 0. This means that freezing layer 0 makes the entire inserted block invisible, regardless of the status of the layers referenced by the component geometry. Likewise, if layer 0 is visible, but the layer named HID is frozen, all objects in the block referencing layer HID are invisible. However, even if some of the components of a block reference are currently invisible, they are still affected by edits made to the visible geometry.

In the Figure 12.25 example, if layer 0 is locked the block cannot be edited regardless of the current status of layers CEN and HID. Since component geometry cannot be directly edited without exploding the block reference, locking one or more layers referenced by the component geometry does not limit your editing options for the block reference itself.

Exercise 12.7 — Estimated time required: 20 min.

1. Start a new drawing session using the Quick Setup default options.
2. Set up a layer system as follows:

0	Color—7	Linetype—Continuous
OBJ	Color—5	Linetype—Continuous
HID	Color—4	Linetype—Hidden
CEN	Color—3	Linetype—Center

3. Create a block definition of a threaded hole, as shown in Figure 12.25, according to the following parameters:

Primary circle	Layer—0	∅0.865
Hidden circle	Layer—HID	∅1.0
Center lines	Layer—CEN	DIMCEN=−0.09

   The block insertion base point should be at the center of the circles, and name the block 1-8UNC-2B_P to indicate a ∅1-in. hole, 8 threads per inch, internal thread, and a plan view.
4. Insert one copy of this block on each layer. Notice the display of the primary circle on each layer.
5. Change the color of layer HID to color 2 and layer 0 to color 6. Study the effects on each insertion of the block reference.
6. Draw three ∅1.0 circles and create new block definitions as indicated:

Name—C-BYL	Color—Bylayer	Linetype—Bylayer
Name—C-ABS	Color—Blue	Linetype—Phantom
Name—C-BYB	Color—Byblock	Linetype—Byblock

7. Using current color and linetype settings of bylayer, insert each of the three blocks created in Step 6 on each layer in your drawing.
8. Change the current color and linetype to absolute settings of your choice, and insert each of the blocks again as in Step 7. Compare the results with the settings used for drawing the circles in the block definitions.
9. Save as EX12.7, and close the drawing.

LEARNING CHECKPOINT

- ☐ What is meant by the term *nesting blocks?*
- ☐ Describe the behavior of bylayer block components when inserted.
- ☐ What is the effect of using absolute properties in block components?
- ☐ How are byblock objects displayed when inserted in a block?
- ☐ How does layer visibility affect the display of inserted blocks?

Creating and Managing a Symbol Library

A block definition created within any specific drawing is available only within that drawing or through DesignCenter. To save your individual blocks permanently for use in other drawings, you can save the block definitions in separate container drawing files on disk and drag them into any other drawing as needed using DesignCenter.

As you create blocks to represent commonly used symbols, establish a standard procedure for saving them in a symbol library. The term ***symbol library*** is used to describe an organized collection of drafting symbols and other commonly used drawing elements saved in categorized AutoCAD LT drawing files. A procedure for symbol library development should include correctly and accurately drawing each symbol conforming to drafting standards. Additionally, it is important to provide adequate documentation. Professionally developed symbol libraries include documentation with a graphic representation of each symbol, its file name, and the directory where the drawing file is located.

The folder and file structure for your symbol library should be uncomplicated and easy to understand, and it should allow for organized storage of symbols associated with each drafting discipline practiced by your organization. In Figure 12.26, the DesignCenter library files are organized within a folder structure using a simple, easy-to-understand arrangement.

1. A main folder named *Symbol Libraries* is created to establish a standardized location where all symbol library related files are located.
2. A single level of folders, one representing each applicable drafting discipline, is created under the *Symbol Libraries* folder.
3. Each of the container files contains a specific category of related symbols associated with a particular drafting discipline.
4. The container drawings are placed in the folder representing the applicable drafting discipline.

FIGURE 12.26 A symbol library folder and file structure should be simple in nature and easy to understand, and it should use short, descriptive names.

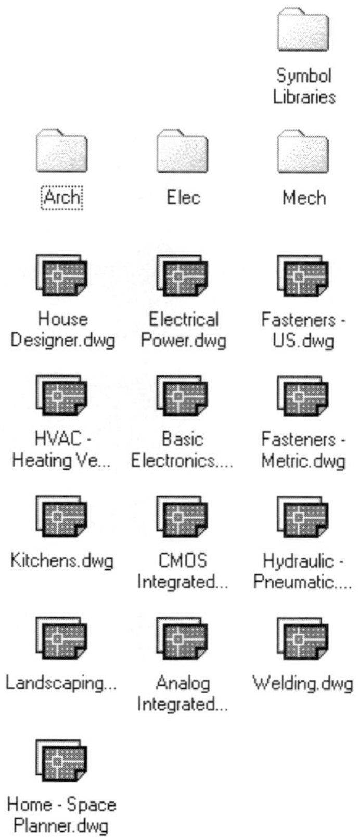

Using Container Drawings

The term *container drawing* refers to a drawing file that is used for storing a collection of related, reusable resources. For example, in Figure 12.26, the container drawing *Welding.dwg* holds a collection of standard welding symbols. By keeping many resources in a single location, container drawings simplify resource control and management issues. Additionally, accessing content from container drawings is fast and easy using AutoCAD DesignCenter. DesignCenter provides a simple yet effective interface for copying content between different drawings. DesignCenter can be used both to add new content to your containers and to access existing content for use in current drafting projects.

Creating a container drawing is simply a matter of placing related reusable content into a single drawing file. Using DesignCenter to drag and drop content into the container simplifies this process. A good way to get started is to place a partially complete container, or even an empty drawing, in your library and just continue to drop new content into the file whenever possible. This approach allows you to develop the resource content over a longer period of time. Well-developed container drawings can be rich resources that provide easy access to more than just symbol libraries.

Using the WBLOCK Command

WBLOCK
W

The command used to save a block as a separate drawing file is the WBLOCK command. WBLOCK stands for Write-BLOCK, and it writes a specified block definition as a separate drawing file. The WBLOCK command is accessed by typing **W** or **WBLOCK** at the Command: prompt. When you start the WBLOCK command, the Write Block dialog box is displayed, as shown in Figure 12.27.

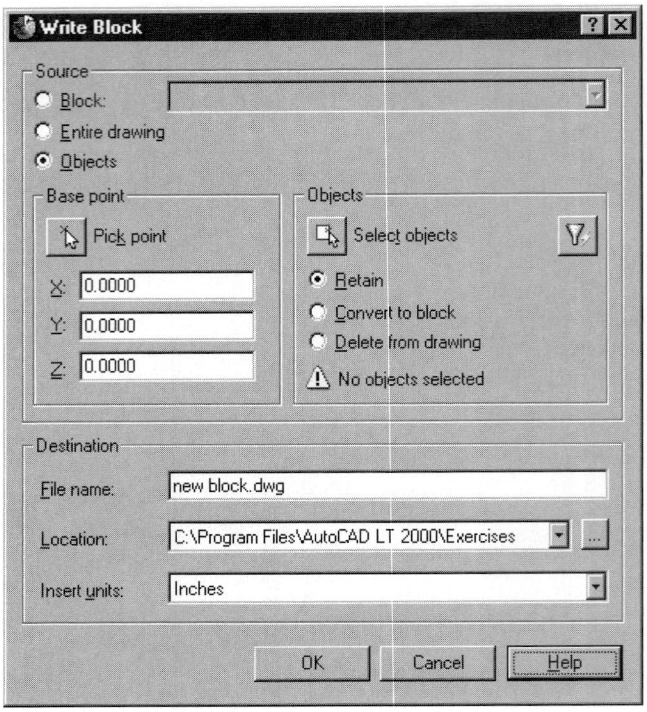

FIGURE 12.27 The Write Block dialog box is used to create a separate drawing file based on an existing block definition or specified drawing objects.

Defining the Source

Use the radio buttons near the top of the Source area to specify the data source for the new drawing file. The WBLOCK command copies the source data and saves it in a new drawing file. The available Source options are as follows:

- **Block:** Use this option to save a locally defined block as a separate drawing file. This selection is available only if the current drawing contains a block definition. Picking this option activates the Block: drop-down list where you select the name of the source block. The Destination File name: is set to match the name of the selected block. It is not necessary for the file and block to have the same name.
- **Entire drawing** Use this to save a copy of the entire drawing in a separate file.
- **Objects** Allows you to select objects in the drawing as the source for the new drawing file. Selecting this option enables the Base point and Objects areas. These settings in these areas are the same as in the Block Definition dialog box. Use the Base point area to define the insertion base point for the new drawing. The Objects area provides selection tools and lets you specify what happens to the selected objects after the new file has been saved.

Defining the Destination

Use the Destination area to specify where the new file is saved and what it is named. Specify the desired filename in the File name: box. The Location: list shows the most recently used locations. Pick the ellipsis button to use the Browse for Folder dialog box. The Insert units sets the Source contents units referenced when using DesignCenter to insert the drawing.

After the Source and Destination have been defined, pick the OK button to create the new drawing file. As the new file is being written, the WBLOCK Preview dialog box flashes on screen and then quickly disappears.

When you insert a drawing into another drawing, AutoCAD LT uses the value stored by a system variable named INSBASE as the insertion base point. The default value for this variable is 0,0. If you used a block for the source, the value for INSBASE was set to the insertion base point of the specified block, or the point you specified for the Base point if you selected individual objects in your drawing.

You have two choices for resolving the base point of a drawing created using SAVE or SAVEAS. One option is to move all of the geometry so the desired insertion point is located at the 0,0 coordinate point. An easier approach is to use the BASE command. The BASE command allows you to specify an insertion point that is not located at 0,0. To use the BASE command, type **BA** or **BASE** at the Command: prompt.

Command: **BA** or **BASE**↵
Base point <0.0000,0.0000,0.0000>: ⟨*specify desired insertion point*⟩

Field Notes

Self-referencing drawing files: A drawing that contains a block definition with the same name as the drawing file cannot be inserted into another drawing because AutoCAD LT converts the data in the drawing file into a block definition when it is inserted. In the previous discussion regarding self-referencing blocks, we explained that a block definition that contains a reference to itself cannot be resolved.

When you try to insert a drawing file containing a block reference with the same name as the drawing file, AutoCAD LT issues the message:

Block ⟨*filename*⟩ references itself

(The drawing name you specified is displayed in place of ⟨*filename*⟩.)

Exercise 12.8 — Estimated time required: 5 min.

1. Using the appropriate file management tools, create the directory \SYM-LIB\MECH. If you need assistance, ask your instructor or refer to the Windows documentation.
2. Open the drawing file EX12.7 for editing in AutoCAD LT.
3. Using the WBLOCK command, write the block definition for the block named 1-8UNC-2B_P to a drawing file of the same name in the directory created in step 1.
4. Draw a 1-unit square with a circle inside of it. Using the WBLOCK command, create a new drawing file using these two objects to define it. Specify the lower left corner as the insertion point.
5. Save as EX12.8, and close the drawing.

Inserting a Drawing File

Inserting a drawing file works much the same as inserting any other block. The INSERT command provides a flexible way of finding and inserting other drawing files in the current drawing. Using the INSERT command displays the Insert dialog box as shown in Figure 12.10. To insert a drawing file, pick the Browse ... button. This displays the Select Drawing File dialog box. Use this file dialog box to locate the drawing file you want to insert. The Select Drawing File dialog box works similar to the Select File dialog box when using the OPEN command.

When you pick a file name and select the Open button, you are returned to the Insert dialog box and the selected file name appears in the Name: box. Notice also that the file name appears in the Path: listing along with the path and drawing file extension. After specifying any other desired options in the Insert dialog box, pick the OK button. You can now insert the selected file the same as any other block, specifying any desired insertion point, scale factors, and rotation angle.

Once you insert a drawing file, that block name is now defined in the current drawing. The drawing is available from the defined block list by picking the Name: button in the Insert dialog box.

If you want the name of the block to be different from the drawing name, you can use the Name: text box to edit the block name as needed. When the block is inserted, it is renamed accordingly and added to the block list with the specified name.

Field Notes

- The -INSERT command can be used from the command line to start an automated search for a block name. If the specified block name is found in the current drawing, it is inserted without looking further. If the specified block name is not found in the current drawing, then the AutoCAD LT *library search path* is scanned for a drawing file matching the specified block name. The library search path includes the current working folder, the drawing folder, all folders specified in the *support file search path,* and the folder containing the AutoCAD LT program file (aclt.exe). As soon as a matching file name is found, the search stops and the file is inserted into the current drawing. In an AutoCAD LT file dialog box, pick the Locate button to search the library search path for the file specified in the File name: box.
- The support file search path is specified using the Files page of the Options dialog box and can be edited to include any desired folders. The easiest way to add a new folder is to pick Add... and then pick the Browse... button. In the Browse for Folder dialog box, go to the desired folder, highlight the appropriate folder, then select the OK button. Unneeded folders can be deleted from the path if desired. Placing your symbol library folders on the support path forces AutoCAD LT to search the specified folders automatically if the block name specified is not yet defined in the current drawing.

Inserting a Drawing File using the DesignCenter

The drag-and-drop interface in AutoCAD DesignCenter can be used to access any available drawing content, including complete drawing files. However, you cannot drag content from the Tree View pane. The desired content must be displayed in the palette pane to be accessible. In the Tree View find and open the folder where the drawing file is located. Opening a folder displays its content in the palette pane. The drawing files displayed in the palette pane can now be accessed like any other content. Figure 12.28 shows a drawing file being inserted using the drag-and-drop method.

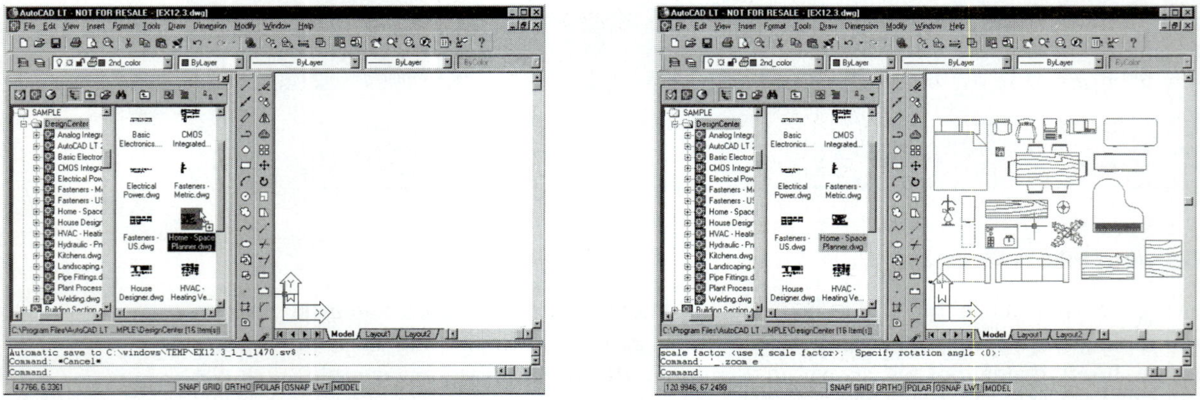

A B

FIGURE 12.28 The drag-and-drop interface in DesignCenter allows easy access to virtually any type of drawing content—even entire drawing files. (A) To be accessible, the content item must be displayed in the palette pane. Open the folder in the Tree View to display its contents in the palette. (B) The drawing file was successfully inserted.

Defining or Redefining Block Definitions from the Symbol Library

If a symbol has been revised and you need to update the block references in the current drawing, you can force a quick and easy redefinition at the command line using the -INSERT command. When prompted for the block name to insert, enter the block name, an equals sign, and the name of the file to read for the updated information. In a case where the existing block name is the same as the file name, and the block name is G-VALVE, the prompts appears as follows:

Command: **-I** or **-INSERT**
Enter block name or [?] <dims>: **G-VALVE=G-VALVE**
Block **"G-VALVE"** already exists. Redefine it? [Yes/No] <N>: **Y**
Block **"G-VALVE"** redefined
Regenerating model.
Specify insertion point or [Scale/X/Y/Z/Rotate/PScale/PX/PY/PZ/PRotate]:

If you need another copy of the specified block in your drawing, you can continue with the -INSERT command. Otherwise you can press the Esc key to cancel the insertion because the block definition has already been updated. All inserted references to the specified block are automatically revised according to the new definition.

The preceding example shows the block name and file name as being the same, but this is not necessary. This technique works exactly the same even if the block name is different from the file name.

Exercise 12.9 — **Estimated time required: 10 min.**

1. Using the OPTIONS command, update the support path to include the \SYM-LIB\MECH directory you created in Exercise 12.8.
2. Start a new drawing using the Quick Setup defaults.
3. Use the -INSERT command and type the block name 1-8UNC-2B_P. Notice that AutoCAD LT automatically searched your symbol library path to find the drawing file.
4. Save the current drawing as EX12.9.
5. Open the file 1-8UNC-2B_P.DWG for editing. Change the primary circle to the layer named OBJ and then save the file.
6. Open EX12.9 for editing.
7. Insert several copies of 1-8UNC-2B_P on various layers in the drawing. At this time you may notice that the layers defined in the 1-8UNC-2B_P drawing were brought in when it was inserted.
8. Use the -INSERT command and specify the block name as 1-8UNC-2B_P=1-8UNC-2B_P.
9. Notice the effects of the block redefinition.
10. Save as EX12.9, and close the drawing.

☑ LEARNING CHECKPOINT

- ☐ When should you consider developing a symbol library?
- ☐ What methods can be used to save a block as a drawing file?
- ☐ Describe some basic guidelines for a symbol library directory structure.
- ☐ How can one drawing be inserted into another?
- ☐ List three ways to use the WBLOCK command.
- ☐ How can a block be updated to match an existing drawing file?

Using Block Attributes

Blocks are complex objects that can be defined using many different object types. Any desired information can be stored as part of a block reference. The term ***attributes*** is used to describe information stored within a block reference.

Visible block attributes can be used to generate simple text labels to identify specific information regarding a symbol. For example, a resistor symbol on an electronic schematic diagram is often labeled with a resistor number, such as R1 or R27. Another visible label on a resistor symbol might include the resistance value.

Other information about these components is often required, but is not frequently used as part of a text label. This information is stored as ***invisible block attributes*** and might include the manufacturer, part number, and price. Invisible block attributes can be used to store data associated with a component when you do not want the information to be displayed on the drawing.

Defining Attributes

Define Attribute

Draw
Block ▶
Define
Attributes

DDATTDEF
DAD
AT

An ***attribute definition*** is a special type of object that is included as part of a block definition. The properties you set up in an attribute definition determine how the attribute acts when it is inserted as part of a block reference. Use the DDATTDEF command to create new attribute definitions. DDATTDEF is accessed by typing **AT**, **DAD** or **DDATTDEF** at the Command: prompt, by picking the Define Attribute button, or by picking Define Attributes… from the Block cascade of the Draw pull-down menu. Optionally, you can use the command line version by typing -**AT** but the DDATTDEF command provides an easy-to-use dialog interface and is usually preferred.

Command: **DAD** or **DDATTDEF**↵

The Attribute Definition dialog box is shown in Figure 12.29. This dialog box is used to define the characteristics of an attribute. A leader bubble provides a simple example of a block with an attribute. A ***leader bubble*** is a circle attached to a leader and with a numeric value inside. They are often used to reference an item in a bill of materials listing or parts list. An example of a leader bubble is shown in Figure 12.30. To create this symbol from scratch each time it is needed, you have to first draw the circle, then specify the desired text properties, and finally enter the appropriate text for each occurrence of the bubble in your drawing. Creating a block that uses an attribute automates the process, making it fast and simple.

FIGURE 12.29 The Attribute Definition dialog box is used to create an attribute definition and specify the desired characteristics of the inserted attribute.

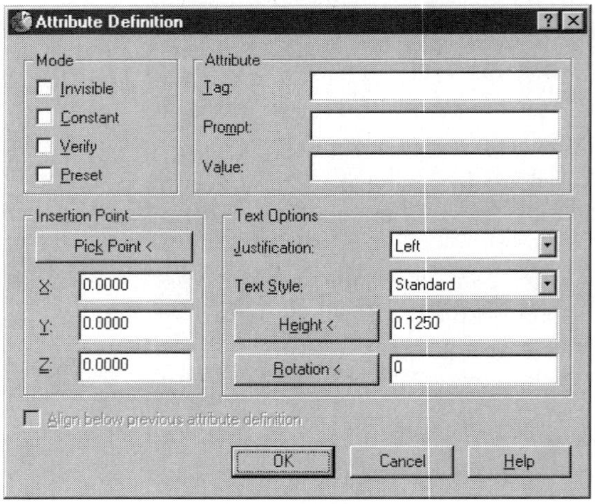

FIGURE 12.30 By creating a block from a circle and an attribute definition, the process of creating a leader bubble is greatly simplified.

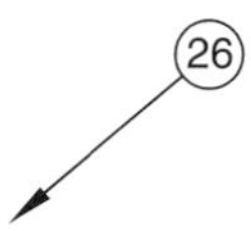

The first step in defining a block with attributes is to create the actual geometry that represents the symbol. In this case, a circle is drawn with a 5/16-in. diameter. Now, it is time to create the attribute definition using the DDATTDEF command.

An attribute can act in many different ways when inserted, depending on what settings you use in this dialog box. The settings you use typically depend on the nature of the attribute you are defining. First, look at the options in the Mode area of the Figure 12.31 Attribute Definition dialog box.

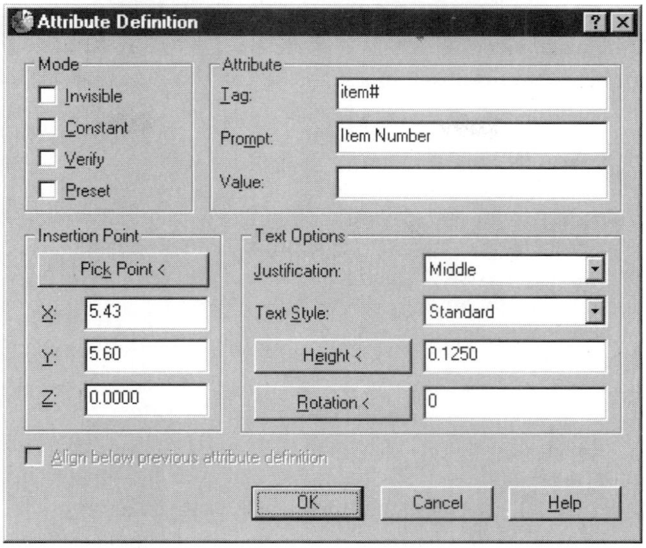

FIGURE 12.31 The Attribute Definition for the leader bubble attribute.

- **Invisible**: If this toggle is checked, the inserted attribute is not displayed in the drawing. It does not appear on screen and it is not plotted.
- **Constant**: Turning on this toggle forces the attribute to use the default value and does not prompt you for a new value. A constant attribute cannot be edited later.
- **Verify**: After the initial prompts for attributes are entered, the values are verified by prompting the user again and presenting the entered value as a default.
- **Preset**: A preset attribute accepts the default value without prompting, but can be edited later if necessary.

A leader bubble with an invisible number would not be of much use, so this attribute should be visible. The value changes with each bubble so it should not be constant or preset. And since the value is only one to three characters in length and is not a particularly critical feature of the drawing, verification is not necessary.

The next critical data fields are found in the area labeled Attribute. The items that are defined here include the following:

- **Tag**: The tag is a dual-purpose feature. First, the text entered here is used to represent the attribute definition so that you have an object to select when you are defining the block. Second, it provides a means of access for extracting attribute values from a drawing. The tag can consist of any numbers or characters but cannot include spaces. Although a tag can be almost any length, it is recommended that they be short and descriptive.
- **Prompt**: This is the text prompt that appears to the user each time a block is inserted, if the constant or preset modes are not set. This should be a clear message to the user that communicates the exact nature of the information to be entered. A colon (:) is automatically attached to the end of the prompt you enter when the block is inserted. If you do not provide a prompt for a nonconstant attribute, the tag text is used as the prompt.
- **Value**: This is a standard default value that is offered with the prompt. As with other default values in AutoCAD LT, the default is offered in angle brackets: ⟨*default value*⟩.

The tag should be unique and clearly related to the attribute definition it represents. A prompt should be simple and clear, and a default value should be supplied if a specific value is commonly used. Because the leader bubble has a different value for each insertion in a given drawing, there is no appropriate default value.

Now it is time to set the properties for the attribute text. Attribute text is displayed like any other text in AutoCAD LT, referencing a defined text style and allowing you to specify the insertion point, height, rotation angle, and justification method. These values must be specified even if the attribute is to be invisible. The properties you give to the text are based on the desired appearance of the inserted symbol. For example, with the leader bubble block, the numeric value should be middle justified at the center point of the circle with a 0.125 text height and 0 rotation angle.

The completed attribute definition for the leader bubble is shown in the Attribute Definition dialog box of Figure 12.31.

When you pick OK, the tag for the newly defined attribute appears on screen at the specified location. To define the block named BUBBLE, use the BMAKE command and select both the circle and attribute definition. Now you can insert the block and see how the attribute works. One special note is that attribute definitions act like any other component object of a block with regard to layers and color settings.

Command: **-I** or **-INSERT**↵
Enter block name or [?] <>: **BUBBLE**↵
Specify insertion point or [Scale/X/Y/Z/Rotate/PScale/PX/PY/PZ/PRotate]: ⟨*specify an insertion point*⟩
Enter X scale factor, specify opposite corner, or [Corner/XYZ] <1>: ⟨*specify a scale factor*⟩
Enter Y scale factor <use X scale factor>: ⟨*specify a scale factor*⟩
Specify rotation angle <0>: ⟨*specify a rotation angle*⟩
Enter attribute values
Item Number: **15**↵
Command:

The block appears at the insertion point and displays the specified attribute text. When you work with symbols that require more than one text label, you can create as many attribute definitions as you need. Additionally, each individual attribute definition can be assigned appropriate characteristics depending on the requirements for the symbol. In Figure 12.32, the resistor symbol is supplied with various attributes, some used for labels and some to store information that is not displayed on the drawing. Study each of the attribute definition properties shown in the table in Figure 12.32.

The symbol attributes defined for the resistor symbol shown in Figure 12.32 can be used to demonstrate the reasoning for when it is appropriate to use each of the available attribute modes.

Whether an attribute is defined as visible or invisible depends completely on how the attribute information is to be used. Attributes defined as invisible for a block typically represent pieces of information that are not needed within the drawing but are useful outside of the drawing. For example, the supplier name and part number of a resistor is not necessary to understand the content or nature of the schematic diagram. The geometry used in the symbol clearly shows that it is a fixed-value resistor, so the RTYPE attribute is also nonessential information within the drawing. After the drawing is complete, however, this information can be useful in scheduling and planning or in the creation of an accurate bill of material.

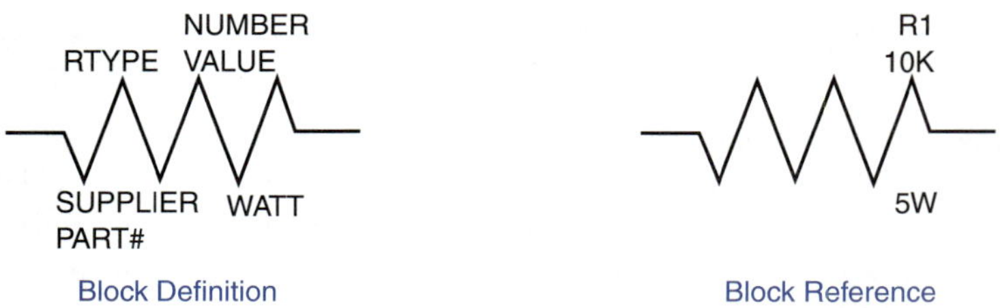

FIGURE 12.32 Attribute definition properties that might be used for a resistor symbol.

Tag	Prompt	Default	Mode
RTYPE		FIXED	INVISIBLE, CONSTANT
NUMBER	Resistor designation		
VALUE	Resistance value	1K	
WATT	Wattage rating	5W	
SUPPLIER	Supplier name	ACME	INVISIBLE, PRESET
PART #	Part number		INVISIBLE, VERIFY

If a value never changes, it should be set as constant. A constant attribute does not prompt when inserted and always uses the default value. The symbol geometry used to define the block in this example represents a fixed-value resistor; if a variable resistor is needed then a different resistor is used. Therefore, the RTYPE attribute can be set to constant.

A preset attribute, like one that is constant, does not prompt when inserted. The difference between preset and constant is that a preset attribute value can be easily changed if necessary, providing added flexibility. Use the preset mode when an attribute almost always uses a particular value, but you want to reserve the option of editing it at a later date. Presetting the supplier in this example implies that these parts are typically ordered from Acme, Inc., but that another supplier can be used if desired.

Attribute values that vary frequently should not be constant or preset. If you can identify one value that is used very frequently, you can set a default value. This saves you a little time in each case where the default is applicable.

Verification can be useful in some cases, but if used too often it can slow down your drawing productivity. An attribute value should be verified if the value represents a critical feature in the drawing, or has a long or complex value where a mistake can easily be made. The part number for the resistor is fairly critical, since ordering an incorrect part number means that the wrong part is installed and the integrity of the design is compromised. Verifying the part number allows the drafter to quickly double-check that the number was entered correctly.

The prompt sequence when inserting the resistor block is as follows:

Command: **I** or **INSERT**↵
⟨*use the dialog box to specify the block name* ⟩
Specify insertion point or [Scale/X/Y/Z/Rotate/PScale/PX/PY/PZ/PRotate]: ⟨*specify an insertion point* ⟩
Enter X scale factor, specify opposite corner, or [Corner/XYZ] <1>: ↵
Enter Y scale factor <use X scale factor>: ↵
Specify rotation angle <0>: ↵
Enter attribute values
Resistor designation: **R1**↵
Resistance value <1K>: **10K**↵
Wattage rating <5W>: ↵
Part number: **R17N10-5**↵
Verify attribute values
Part number <R17N10-5>: ↵
Command:

Using the Enter Attributes Dialog Box

By default, attribute prompts are issued at the command line. This method requires you to answer each prompt in sequence and does not provide much flexibility. Defining attribute values using a dialog box is usually the preferred option. The ATTDIA (**ATT**ribute **DIA**log) system variable controls this behavior. The initial default value for ATTDIA is 0; set this variable 1 to use the Enter Attributes dialog box for entering attribute values (see Figure 12.33). The ATTDIA value is set as follows:

Command: **ATTDIA**↵
Enter new value for ATTDIA <0>: **1**↵
Command:

Even when one or more attributes have the Verify option active, no additional prompts are given, and the Enter Attributes dialog box is not displayed a second time for verification values. However, in a dialog interface, you can quickly verify all entered values prior to picking OK.

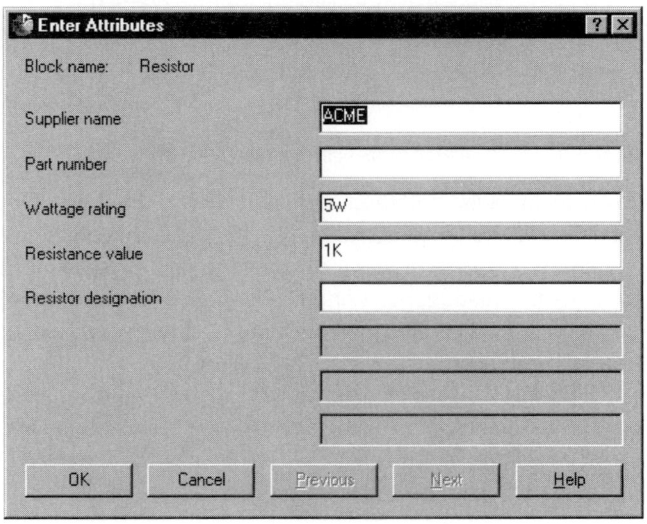

FIGURE 12.33 The Enter Attributes dialog box provides more flexibility than entering attribute values at the command line.

Field Notes

- When designing a block with attributes, if you select the Convert to block option in the Objects area of the Block Definition dialog box, the attribute prompts for the new block are displayed in a dialog box.
- Carefully designing a prompt and offering an appropriate default value can greatly simplify the insertion process. One aspect of designing a prompt is capitalization. The prompts issued by AutoCAD LT are never displayed as all capital letters. Look at the following prompts. Notice that the sentence case prompt looks more like a standard AutoCAD LT prompt:

```
RESISTANCE VALUE:
Resistance value <1K>:
```

Another consideration is the wording. A concise prompt is best, but it must be completely clear as to what the user is expected to enter. Study the following three prompts. The first does not offer a default, and the second may not be clear enough. The third prompt is clear, offers a default value, and appears to be the best choice.

```
What's the resistance?:
Value <1>:
Resistance value <1K>:
```

Always keep in mind that the symbols you create may be part of a symbol library for many years to come. Thoughtfully designed symbols and attributes present a professional appearance and work very effectively.

- The order of presentation of attribute prompts depends on the selection method used when creating the block. If you pick the attributes one at a time, the order in which you select them is the order in which the prompts are issued. If you use a window selection, the attribute definitions are selected in the order of their closeness to the 0,0 point, with the closest one selected first, and the farthest selected last. Because the prompts are issued in the order in which the attribute definitions are selected, window selections can result in attribute prompts being presented out of order.

Exercise 12.10 — Estimated time required: 10 min.

1. Start a new drawing using the Quick Setup defaults.
2. Use the example shown in Figure 12.32 to define a block named RESISTOR that uses the attribute definitions shown in the table.
3. Insert the block in three separate locations in your drawing, supplying varied values for attributes.
4. Save as EX12.10, and close the drawing.

Automating Drawing Procedures Using Attributes

Certain text-based features are common to most technical drawings. One such item is a drawing title block. An engineering drawing title block usually has many different data fields that are often unique values in each drawing you create. Here, the term *data field* refers to the individual areas that are filled in with information in a drawing title block. Creating, positioning, sizing, and justifying a large number of text objects can take a significant amount of time. If you have to repeat this task in every drawing you create, it can lower your drafting productivity level considerably.

An effective way to handle your title block is to place appropriate attribute definitions in each of the areas where text information is required and then save the title block as a separate drawing file. Now, when you insert the title block into another drawing the attributes will prompt you for the appropriate values and automatically position, justify, and size the text according to the characteristics you assigned to the attribute definitions. In addition to simplifying the process of filling in the title block, this method ensures that the title block will maintain the same standard appearance from one drawing to the next.

Some other features that can be automated using blocks and attributes include revision blocks, parts lists, item schedules, general notes, and any other text-based information systems in your drawings.

Modifying Attribute Definitions

Modifying an attribute definition before you create the block is a simple process. You can use the DDEDIT command to edit the tag, prompt, and default values. Figure 12.34 shows the DDEDIT dialog box after selecting an attribute definition. It is important to note that an attribute *definition* has been selected, as opposed to an attribute that is part of an inserted block reference.

If you need to change other characteristics of the attribute definition, such as the text size, insertion point, or mode settings, use the PROPERTIES command. The Properties window is shown, after picking an attribute definition, in Figure 12.35.

After you have defined a block, you cannot directly edit the attribute definitions. If you want to modify the characteristics or behavior of the attributes associated with a defined block, you must redefine the block. As with any other block, exploding a block reference replaces it with the component objects of the current block definition. Any attribute values in the block are replaced by the attribute definitions, and the tags are visible again. Now you can use either DDEDIT or PROPERTIES to make the required changes and then redefine the block. Any future insertions of the block reflect the modifications made to the attribute characteristics.

Unfortunately, when redefining a block in AutoCAD LT, only the geometry is updated in any existing block references. Attributes in the existing blocks are unaffected by any changes you make to the block definition.

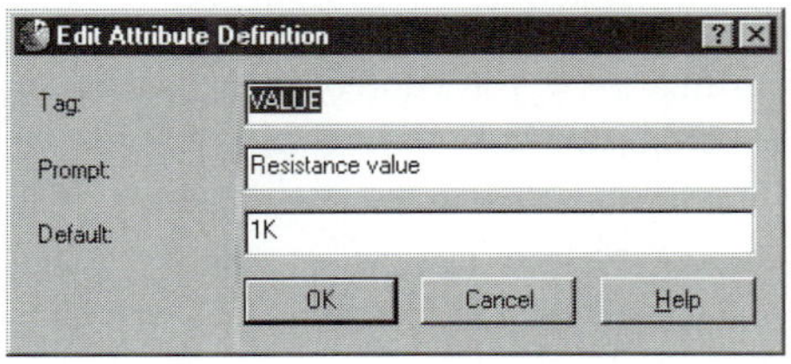

FIGURE 12.34 Some attribute definition properties can be changed using the DDEDIT command.

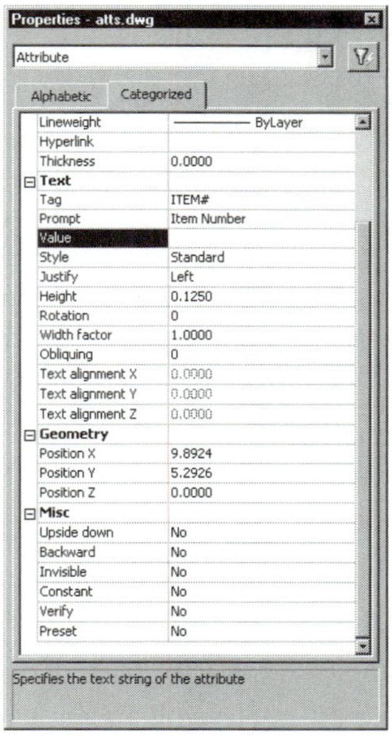

FIGURE 12.35 The PROPERTIES command allows you to change any characteristic of an attribute definition.

Editing Attribute Values in a Single Block Reference

Modify II

Edit Attribute

Modify
Object ▶
Attribute ▶
Single

DDATTE
AE

The values of the attributes in an inserted block reference can be modified as long as the attribute was not defined as a constant. You can edit individual attribute values or, if needed, you can edit many attribute values at one time. To edit the attribute values within a single block, you can use the DDATTE command by typing **AE** or **DDATTE** at the Command: prompt, picking the Edit Attribute button from the Modify II toolbar, or by selecting Attribute from the Object cascade of the Modify pull-down menu and then picking the Single … option. At the Select block: prompt, pick the block containing the attributes you need to edit. You can pick anywhere on the block or pick any visible attribute. When you select a block that has one or more nonconstant attributes, the Edit Attributes dialog box is displayed as shown in Figure 12.36.

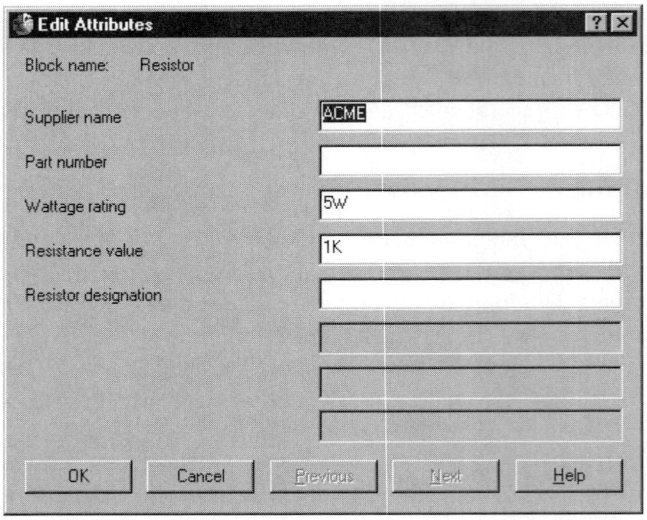

FIGURE 12.36 The Edit Attributes dialog box.

The name of the block you select appears in the upper left corner of the dialog box, and all of the attribute prompts are displayed along with their current values. This dialog box also displays all preset attributes. The preset values can be changed as needed. Pick any text box to edit the displayed value. If the block contains more than eight attributes, the Next button is enabled. Pick Next to see the next page of attributes, or Previous to go back. When you are finished editing the attributes, pick OK to complete the operation. Be aware that if you pick Cancel, all of the changes you made in the dialog box are discarded and the attributes are not modified.

Editing Attribute Values Globally

Edit Attribute Globally

Modify
Object ▸
Attribute ▸
Global

ATTEDIT
AE

Sometimes, you may need to do a global edit on specific attribute values. Doing a ***global edit*** means that you are changing every occurrence of a specific attribute value in the current drawing. As an example, if you completed an electronic schematic drawing and then determined that you were going to buy fixed-value resistors from a different supplier than ACME, you would need to change every attribute value that referenced ACME to the name of the new supplier. The -ATTEDIT command is used to edit attribute values globally, and can be accessed by typing **-ATE** or **-ATTEDIT** at the Command: prompt, by picking the Edit Attribute Globally button, or by selecting Attribute from the Objects cascade of the Modify pull-down menu and then picking the Global option. The ATTEDIT command displays the following prompts:

Command: **-ATE** or **-ATTEDIT**↵
Edit attributes one at a time?[Yes/No] <Y> **N**↵

Answering "No" to editing attributes one at a time allows global editing. Now you can edit every attribute contained in every block reference in the drawing, or you can use the next prompts to limit editing to specific blocks, tags, or even to attributes having a specified value:

Performing global editing of attribute values.
Edit only attributes visible on screen? [Yes/No] <Y> **N**↵
Drawing must be regenerated afterwards.

By entering a "No" to editing only attributes visible on screen, you can force AutoCAD LT to automatically select and edit every attribute in the drawing that matches the values entered at the subsequent prompts. You can force the search for matching values to be limited to a specific block name by typing that name as shown here:

Enter block name specification <*>: **RESISTOR**↵

This limits the search to only blocks with the name RESISTOR. To limit the search to two or more specific block names, enter the block names separated by commas. Additionally, wild card parameters can be used for convenience. The default is an asterisk wild card, which means *all* block names.

The search can also be limited to particular tag names for attributes found in the previously specified blocks. As with the block names, a single tag name can be entered, or you can specify multiple tag names and wild cards. Refer back to Chapter 8 if you need to review the use of wild card characters. The following entry limits the search to attributes with a tag name of SUPPLIER:

Enter attribute tag specification <*>: **SUPPLIER**↵

You can further limit the selection of the specified attributes found in the designated blocks to only those attributes with a particular value. Again, single values, multiple values, and wild cards can be used. This example specifies only attributes whose value is ACME:

Enter attribute value specification <*>: **ACME↵**

The drawing database is now searched, and every insertion of RESISTOR is checked for an attribute with the tag name SUPPLIER and a value of ACME. In this example, ten matching attributes are found in the drawing:

10 attributes selected.
String to change: **ACME↵**
Enter new string: **ZENITH↵**

After reporting the number of matching attributes, the prompt asks you to enter the text string that you want to change. In the previous example, the entire string is replaced. If you only want to change part of an attribute value you can enter just the text to change. For example, to change an attribute string of "Logn Attribute Text" to "Long Attribute Text," the string to change would be "gn" and the new string is "ng." In this way, you can avoid having to completely retype long text values. If the specified string to change occurs more than once in the selected attribute, only the first occurrence is modified. As you might imagine, this is a terrific time saver in a drawing where you need to change 50, 60, or even 100 or more existing attribute values.

You can also edit attributes one at a time. A common way of using this option is to accept the default values for each of the prompts. This leaves you at a Select Attributes: prompt with the freedom to pick any desired attribute. You can window a group of blocks or you can pick individual attributes. When you pick individual attributes, the selection process is like the "multiple" selection option because nothing is highlighted until you finish the selection process by pressing Enter at the Select Attributes: prompt. Regardless of how you select attributes, the following prompt is displayed:

Enter an option Value/Position/Height/Angle/Style/Layer/Color/Next <N>:

Looking at the selected attributes on your screen, you see that one is highlighted and has a small X-shaped marker. Changing the position, rotation angle, text style, layer, and color work just as you would expect them to. However, when changing the value of an attribute, you have the option to replace the existing text or to just change specific parts:

Enter an option [Value/Position/Height/Angle/Style/Layer/Color/Next] <N>: **V↵**
Enter type of value modification [Change/Replace] <R>: ↵
Enter new attribute value: **10W↵**
Enter an option [Value/Position/Height/Angle/Style/Layer/Color/Next] <N>: **V↵**
Enter type of value modification [Change/Replace] <R>: **C↵**
Enter string to change: **10↵**
Enter new string: **5↵**
Enter an option [Value/Position/Height/Angle/Style/Layer/Color/Next] <N>: ↵
Enter an option [Value/Position/Height/Angle/Style/Layer/Color/Next] <N>:

The default option Next moves the X marker to the next attribute if more than one was selected. Any modifications that you make are applied only to the currently marked attribute.

Field Notes

When selecting single attributes to edit using the -ATTEDIT command, it is important to be aware that invisible attributes cannot be selected. If the attribute you need to edit is currently invisible, you can force AutoCAD LT to display all attributes whether they are defined as visible or invisible. To do this, use the ATTDISP command as follows:

Command: **ATTDISP↵**
Enter attribute visibility setting [Normal/ON/OFF] <Normal>: **ON↵**
Regenerating model.

Turn the attribute display on to see invisible attributes. Turn it off to hide all attributes, and use the Normal setting to display visible attributes but not invisible ones.

Exercise 12.11 **Estimated Time Required: 10 min.**

1. Open the drawing EX12.10.
2. Insert additional copies of RESISTOR until you have a total of 10 occurrences in your drawing. Use any available default values while inserting the blocks.
3. Turn ATTDISP on.
4. Use the DDATTE command to edit the attributes in three of the resistor blocks.
5. Change the wattage rating of each of the three blocks to 10W.
6. Start the ATTEDIT command, select global editing, enter NO to editing only visible attributes, and specify a block name of RESISTOR, a tag of SUPPLIER, and a value of ACME.
7. Change the string "ACME" to "Zenith."
8. Set ATTDISP back to Normal.
9. Save as EX12.11, and close the drawing.

LEARNING CHECKPOINT

- ☐ What is an attribute?
- ☐ Describe applications for each of the four modes for an attribute.
- ☐ What is an attribute tag? prompt? default value?
- ☐ How are attributes included in a block?
- ☐ What is the purpose of invisible attributes?
- ☐ What commands can be used to modify an attribute definition?
- ☐ What commands are used to edit an attribute?
- ☐ Describe the procedure for global editing.
- ☐ How can invisible attributes be made temporarily visible for selection?

Working with Text and Symbols

- Attaching Data to Symbols

Suppressing Attribute Prompts

In some situations, you may not want to answer attribute prompts when inserting blocks. During the initial phases of a design, you may not be ready to assign final attribute values. Having to repeatedly divert your attention away from the design process to answer unnecessary prompts can interrupt your concentration and adversely affect your creativity. At such a time, it may be more convenient simply to insert symbols where they go and then come back and fill in the specific attributes later.

To turn off all attribute prompts, set the ATTREQ system variable to 0 by typing **ATTREQ** at the Command: prompt as follows:

Command: **ATTREQ**↵
Enter new value for ATTREQ <1>: **0**↵

ATTREQ is short for ATTribute REQuest, and controls whether or not AutoCAD LT issues attribute prompts when they are inserted. When ATTREQ is set to 0 no prompts are issued, and if a default value was specified in the attribute definition, that value is automatically used.

Set ATTREQ back to 1 when you are ready for attribute prompts to once again be issued normally. Any blocks that were inserted at default values can then be edited as needed to assign the appropriate values.

Extracting Attribute Values from a Drawing

Using AutoCAD LT, you can gather any or all of the available information regarding blocks and attributes in a drawing and save it in a text file. Before the attributes can be extracted from a file, some preparations are required. First, a special kind of text file, called a ***template file,*** is created to specify what information AutoCAD LT is to extract from the blocks and attributes. This makes it possible to extract only specific information as required for particular uses.

Field Notes

> Accessing the values of attributes is termed *attribute extraction.* The word *extract* implies that the attributes are being removed from the drawing, but this is not the case. The drawing and the attributes it contains are in no way affected by the attribute extraction process.

A template file can be created using any normal text editor program. Windows provides a basic text editor called *Notepad.* This program creates what is known as an ASCII file (American Standard Code for Information Interchange), which means that the file contains text characters only. Files created with a word processing program such as Microsoft Word or Word Perfect often contain special printer codes that AutoCAD LT does not understand. If you use a word processor to generate a template file, be sure to save the file as "text only."

A template file uses special types of notations that tell AutoCAD LT which information to extract and the format in which to present it. The tag name for the attribute to extract is used, along with the formatting information. As an example, to extract the value associated with the attribute whose tag is SUPPLIER, the following specification could be used in the template file:

```
SUPPLIER      C008000
```

The tag name is indicated followed by formatting codes for the extracted information. All values assigned to attributes are stored as text-based information in the drawing. This can be inconvenient when importing the information into a spreadsheet application because text and numbers are handled differently. You can control whether the extracted information is stored as text or as numerical data with the first character in the formatting code. In the preceding example, the supplier information is expected to be text so a "C" is used to specify "Character" data. If the value is numerical data, the formatting code is preceded with an "N" for "Numerical." In the following example, the value for the WATT attribute is specified:

```
WATT      N006002
```

The rest of the formatting code is comprised of two three-digit numbers that determine the appearance and content of the data extracted. The first three digits are used to specify the total field width for the extracted value. The term ***field width*** indicates the number of character positions used. So, the previously shown specification for the SUPPLIER attribute extracts up to eight characters. The last three digits are always required, but their value is ignored if the attribute value is specified as being character data.

If the extracted data are specified as numeric data, the first three digits are still used for field width and the second three digits of the formatting code indicate how many decimal places to use in the number. Note that the field width indicates the total number of character positions including the decimal numbers and the decimal point. Therefore, the WATT specification given earlier indicates that two decimal places are to be used in a number that can use up to six character positions. Since two decimals are specified, and the decimal point takes one position, only three positions are left for numbers to the left of the decimal point. Figure 12.37 shows an illustrated explanation of the formatting code options.

In addition, you can extract information specific to the block references. This can include the block names, insertion points, scale factors, rotation angles, and more. An information code is used, preceded by a "BL:" designation, but the formatting codes are exactly the same as for attribute data. The BL: designation stands for "Block." The table in Figure 12.38 shows each information category available for extraction, the specification method, and whether it is character or numeric data.

Some of these options are of little use for most applications, but information such as the block name, location, rotation, and scale can frequently be useful. These items are listed in the template file in the same manner as attribute extraction designations, substituting the item listed in the Template Specification column instead of an attribute tag name. For example, the following listing might be useful for the drawing created in Exercise 12.11 to extract the information regarding each of the attributes and to select block information:

```
RTYPE         C008000
NUMBER        C004000
VALUE         C006000
WATT          C004000
SUPPLIER      C008000
PART#         C016000
BL:NAME       C012000
BL:X          N006003
```

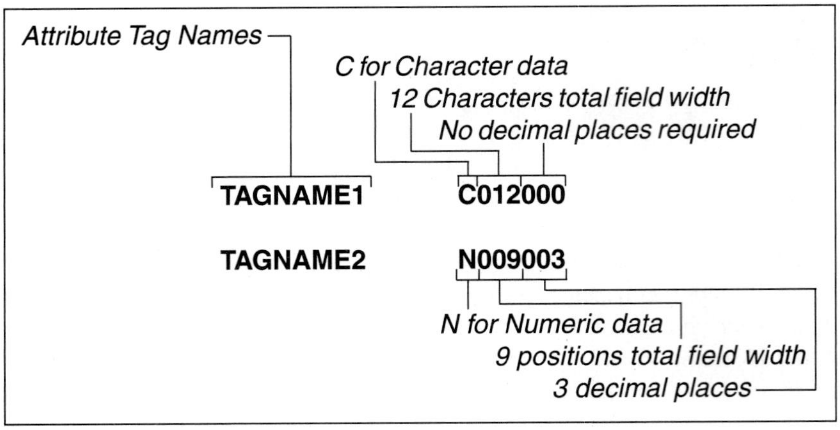

FIGURE 12.37 Attribute extraction field formatting codes.

FIGURE 12.38 Useful block information can also be extracted.

Template Specification	Type	Description
BL:NAME	C	Block name
BL:X	N	X coordinate of block insertion point
BL:Y	N	Y coordinate of block insertion point
BL:Z	N	Z coordinate of block insertion point
BL:NUMBER	N	Block counter (Incremented for each block found)
BL:HANDLE	C	Block Handle (Unique object name)
BL:LAYER	C	Block insertion layer
BL:ORIENT	N	Block rotation angle
BL:XSCALE	N	Block insertion X scale factor
BL:YSCALE	N	Block insertion Y scale factor
BL:ZSCALE	N	Block insertion Z scale factor
BL:XEXTRUDE	N	Block extrusion direction X value
BL:YEXTRUDE	N	Block extrusion direction Y value
BL:ZEXTRUDE	N	Block extrusion direction Z value
BL:LEVEL	N	Block nesting level

```
BL:Y          N006003
BL:NUMBER     N004000
BL:LAYER      C032000
```

This template file listing provides each of the attribute values, the block name and location, and the layer on which the block is located. Additionally, using the NUMBER field provides a quick count of the total number of blocks with attributes in the drawing. Figure 12.39 shows this template being created in the Windows Notepad program.

FIGURE 12.39 Notepad is an easy-to-use text editor that can be used to create attribute extraction template files.

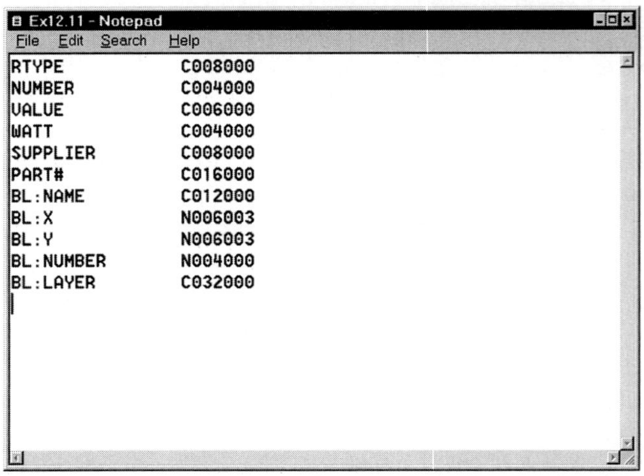
Ex12.11 - Notepad
File Edit Search Help

```
RTYPE         C008000
NUMBER        C004000
VALUE         C006000
WATT          C004000
SUPPLIER      C008000
PART#         C016000
BL:NAME       C012000
BL:X          N006003
BL:Y          N006003
BL:NUMBER     N004000
BL:LAYER      C032000
```

Through the Window...

Creating template files is easy to do using the Notepad text editor available in Windows. Finding and starting this application is done somewhat differently in each operating system. From the Start menu on the Taskbar, pick Programs, then Accessories, and select the Notepad program. Once the editor has opened, you can begin typing and enter all of the information required in your template file.

Once you save the file and exit the Notepad program, it is very easy to reopen the file if you need to edit it. From the Start menu on the Taskbar, pick Documents. The name of your template file should appear in the cascading submenu that appears. Picking the file name automatically starts Notepad and preloads the template file.

Field Notes

- You can only place one extraction specification per line in the template file.
- Although the sample template files show the field formatting codes as all beginning in the same column, this is not necessary. This is done in the text examples for readability, and for that same reason, it is recommended that you format your files in this manner. When each of the fields is aligned, it is easier to spot any errors.
- One easy mistake to make when creating a template file is to use an uppercase "O" instead of a 0 (zero) in the formatting code. They are not always easy to spot, but they do appear slightly wider and should be visible under close inspection.
- The AutoCAD LT User's Guide recommends that you always include at least one space (using the space bar) between the field or attribute name and the field formatting code rather than using the [TAB] key.
- The most common mistake made when creating a template file is forgetting to press Enter at the end of the last line in the file. Forgetting to do this causes an error during the attribute extraction process.

Exercise 12.12

Estimated time required: 10 min.

1. Start the Windows Notepad Program.
2. In Notepad, enter the following template file information as shown:

```
RTYPE        C008000
NUMBER       C004000
VALUE        C006000
WATT         C004000
SUPPLIER     C008000
PART#        C016000
BL:NAME      C012000
BL:X         N006003
BL:Y         N006003
BL:NUMBER    N004000
BL:LAYER     C032000
```

3. Be sure to press Enter at the end of the last line (the BL:LAYER line).
4. Save as EX12.12.TXT, and close the Notepad program.

Tools
Attribute
Extraction

ATTEXT
AX

After creating the template file, you are ready to proceed with extracting the attributes from a drawing. The primary command used to extract attributes is the ATTEXT command. To access ATTEXT you can type **AX or ATTEXT** at the Command: prompt or pick Attribute Extraction... from the Tools pull-down menu.

Command: **AX or ATTEXT↵**
⟨the Attribute Extraction dialog box is displayed . . .⟩

Starting the ATTEXT command displays the Attribute Extraction dialog box as shown in Figure 12.40. The File Format area of the Attribute Extraction dialog box allows you to specify how the attribute information is formatted in the output file. The format used depends primarily on how you intend to use the output file. The most common use of attribute extraction files is as input to spreadsheet or database programs. Many such applications can read the CDF, or Comma Delimited File format. The term ***delimit*** means "to establish the limits of," and indicates that individual fields within each record are separated from each other. This ensures that the application you are importing into knows where one field ends and the next begins. In a CDF file the fields are each separated by commas inserted in the output file as it is written. The second option is SDF, or Space Delimited File format. This format does not actually insert any characters, spaces or otherwise, into the file. When using an SDF format, you must specify field widths containing more characters than the values actually require. Any character positions not filled in by the value are left as empty spaces and are considered the field delimiters. Most applications, such as the Microsoft Excel spreadsheet program, are very flexible with regard to the types of files they can read and can import files of either type. Database applications such as dBase IV can easily read SDF formats. Regardless of which of these formats you use, each block occurrence and all of its attributes is considered a single record and is written on a single line. Each individual data item extracted from the block and each attribute make up separate fields within a record.

The DXF Format Extract File (DXX) setting writes a very unique file with a .DXX file extension, which is a subset of the DXF file format discussed in Chapter 15. This selection does not utilize a template file, and automatically writes all block and attribute data to the output file. This setting is only for very specialized needs, and is not commonly used for exporting data to spreadsheets or databases.

The Select Objects < button allows you to select only specific blocks for the extraction process. The number of objects selected appears to the right of the button. If the Number found: value is 0, the specified data is extracted from all of the blocks within the drawing that contain attributes. In a drawing with many different blocks defined, you can limit the extract file output by selecting the blocks to use. As a special note, if you have inserted different symbols on specific layers, the selection process is made easier by freezing the unneeded layers.

Enter the name of the template file in the Template File … field. A file extension of .TXT is expected and is the default. When no file extension is entered AutoCAD LT automatically looks for the specified file name with a .TXT extension. If an extension other than .TXT is entered, it is automatically changed when you pick the OK button. To use a file dialog box to select the template file, pick the Template File … button.

The Output File … field works the same with regard to the file extension. Only .TXT can be used here as well. And again, to use the file dialog box for specification of the output file name, select the Output File … button. If you specify the same name for both the template and the output, you are requested to change the name of one of the files.

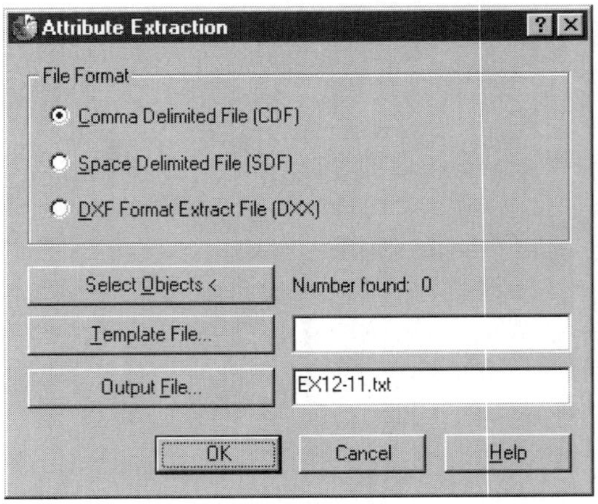

FIGURE 12.40 The Attribute Extraction dialog box provides an intuitive interface for extracting attribute values from a drawing.

Picking OK will then start the attribute extraction process, and any errors encountered are listed on the screen. If the error is not too serious, the extract file is still created, but may not be as you expect. Always be sure to press the F2 key to examine your text screen and read any messages after doing an attribute extraction. A completely successful extraction results in a message that specifies how many records were created in the output file:

Command: **AX or ATTEXT↵**
10 records in extract file.

The command line version of this command is the ATTEXT command, which is available at the Command: prompt only, by typing **-ATTEXT.** The command line version does not provide the same convenience or safeguards as the dialog version.

Error messages you may encounter can be caused by any of several possible problems in your template file. If, for example, a specification in a template file does not allow enough characters to hold the value assigned to an attribute, an error message is displayed. This situation is reported as a field overflow, and the message is repeated for each time the problem is encountered:

```
**Field overflow in record 1
**Field overflow in record 2
**Field overflow in record 3
**Field overflow in record 4
**Field overflow in record 5
**Field overflow in record 6
**Field overflow in record 7
**Field overflow in record 8
**Field overflow in record 9
**Field overflow in record 10
10 records in extract file.
```

This error situation does not halt the creation of the output file. To correct this problem, check that each listing in the template file includes the correct field width and look in the output file to see what field appears incomplete.

Another possible problem is when a duplicate field definition exists in the template file. Each field can be defined only once, so this produces an error and the output file is not created. This message is produced when trying to write an extract file named C:\CHAP_12.TXT using a template containing a duplicate definition:

Command: **ATTEXT↵**
**Duplicate field specification:
RTYPE C009000

This can be corrected by removing the duplicate definition from the Template file and saving it again.

Specifying a field that does not exist creates no problems, but if a field listing is not constructed correctly, then no output file is created and an error message is issued. In the next example, the formatting code is not entered completely and an error message is produced:

Command: **ATTEXT↵**
**Invalid field specification:
BL:NUMBER N004

When you get this message, check each item in the template file carefully to ensure that each field specification is complete and correct. Also, another reason this message might appear is if you forgot to press Enter at the end of the last line in the template file. After correcting the problem, save the updated template file and try the extraction again.

If a field is specified as numeric but actually contains text characters, you may get two possible results. If a number is in the first character position, then the text that follows is not extracted. A text character in the first position causes the field value to be entered as 0 (zero) or another inappropriate numeric value. Either way, an error message is issued for each incorrect item encountered:

```
**Bad numeric value for field RTYPE, record 1
**Bad numeric value for field RTYPE, record 2
**Bad numeric value for field RTYPE, record 3
```

**Bad numeric value for field RTYPE, record 4
**Bad numeric value for field RTYPE, record 5
**Bad numeric value for field RTYPE, record 6
**Bad numeric value for field RTYPE, record 7
**Bad numeric value for field RTYPE, record 8
**Bad numeric value for field RTYPE, record 9
**Bad numeric value for field RTYPE, record 10
10 records in extract file.

Field Notes

- Any tag names listed in the template file that do not exist are still written to the output file. If the listing indicates a character field, it is written as an empty field. A numeric specification results in a value of 0 (zero) being written to the output file. When you are using an SDF file, this can be used to your advantage.

  One problem with a space delimited file is that the numeric entries are right justified and the character entries are left justified. Because no delimiting characters are inserted in an SDF file, this means that a numeric field followed directly by a character field has no separation. To fix this problem, enter the name of a nonexistent attribute tag and specify it as character data with a width of 1. Now the nonexistent tag is written as a single blank space, which separates the fields.
- If any tag name appears more than once in a template file, only the first listing is recognized. When you need more than one blank field, be sure to specify different names in each location in the template file.

Once you have successfully created an extract file, it should look similar to one of the files shown in Figures 12.41 and 12.42. One shows a CDF file and the other, an SDF file.

FIGURE 12.41 An attribute extract file created using CDF format and opened using Notepad.

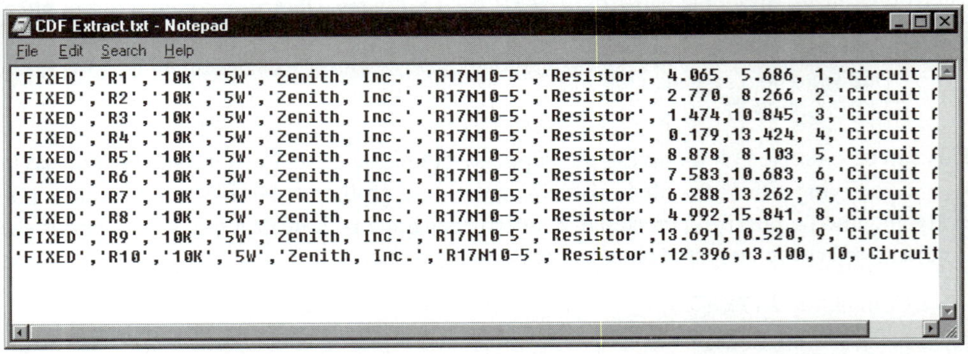

CDF Extract.txt - Notepad

File Edit Search Help

```
'FIXED','R1','10K','5W','Zenith, Inc.','R17N10-5','Resistor', 4.065, 5.686, 1,'Circuit
'FIXED','R2','10K','5W','Zenith, Inc.','R17N10-5','Resistor', 2.770, 8.266, 2,'Circuit
'FIXED','R3','10K','5W','Zenith, Inc.','R17N10-5','Resistor', 1.474,10.845, 3,'Circuit
'FIXED','R4','10K','5W','Zenith, Inc.','R17N10-5','Resistor', 0.179,13.424, 4,'Circuit
'FIXED','R5','10K','5W','Zenith, Inc.','R17N10-5','Resistor', 8.878, 8.103, 5,'Circuit
'FIXED','R6','10K','5W','Zenith, Inc.','R17N10-5','Resistor', 7.583,10.683, 6,'Circuit
'FIXED','R7','10K','5W','Zenith, Inc.','R17N10-5','Resistor', 6.288,13.262, 7,'Circuit
'FIXED','R8','10K','5W','Zenith, Inc.','R17N10-5','Resistor', 4.992,15.841, 8,'Circuit
'FIXED','R9','10K','5W','Zenith, Inc.','R17N10-5','Resistor',13.691,10.520, 9,'Circuit
'FIXED','R10','10K','5W','Zenith, Inc.','R17N10-5','Resistor',12.396,13.100, 10,'Circuit
```

FIGURE 12.42 An attribute extract file created using SDF format and opened using Notepad.

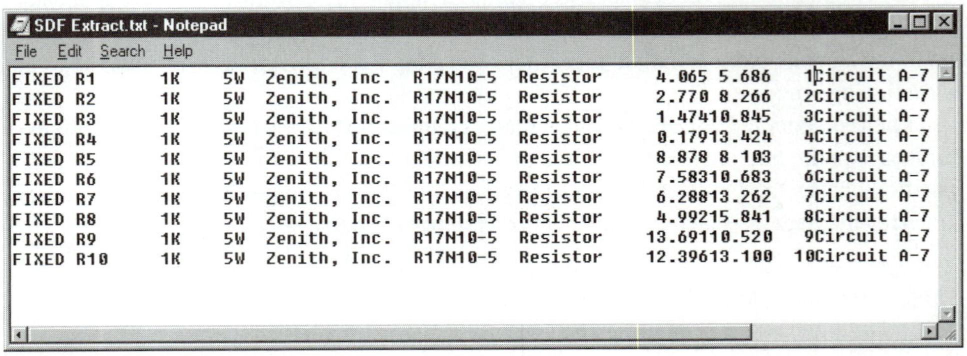

SDF Extract.txt - Notepad

File Edit Search Help

```
FIXED R1     1K    5W  Zenith, Inc.  R17N10-5  Resistor     4.065 5.686    1Circuit A-7
FIXED R2     1K    5W  Zenith, Inc.  R17N10-5  Resistor     2.770 8.266    2Circuit A-7
FIXED R3     1K    5W  Zenith, Inc.  R17N10-5  Resistor     1.47410.845    3Circuit A-7
FIXED R4     1K    5W  Zenith, Inc.  R17N10-5  Resistor     0.17913.424    4Circuit A-7
FIXED R5     1K    5W  Zenith, Inc.  R17N10-5  Resistor     8.878 8.103    5Circuit A-7
FIXED R6     1K    5W  Zenith, Inc.  R17N10-5  Resistor     7.58310.683    6Circuit A-7
FIXED R7     1K    5W  Zenith, Inc.  R17N10-5  Resistor     6.28813.262    7Circuit A-7
FIXED R8     1K    5W  Zenith, Inc.  R17N10-5  Resistor     4.99215.841    8Circuit A-7
FIXED R9     1K    5W  Zenith, Inc.  R17N10-5  Resistor    13.69110.520    9Circuit A-7
FIXED R10    1K    5W  Zenith, Inc.  R17N10-5  Resistor    12.39613.100   10Circuit A-7
```

Special Extract File Formats

Some database applications may require specific file formats other than CDF or SDF. If you are using such an application, you can customize your extract files using two special template file modifiers. As an example, all character fields written to the output file are surrounded with single quote (') characters by default. Some applications, like Microsoft Excel, import these characters as part of the text string in character fields. However, text surrounded in double quotes (") is brought in without the surrounding quotes, reducing the amount of editing that must be done. You can force AutoCAD LT to surround text in the output file with whatever character you wish by specifying a C:QUOTE field. This field is followed by the character you want used, so to specify the use of double quotes, the following line is included in the template file:

C:QUOTE "

You may also wish to use a special character as a delimiter, depending on which application you are taking your data into. This is done using the C:DELIM field specification. For example, to use a forward slash as a field delimiter, enter the following line into the template:

C:DELIM /

These specifications are entered on a line by themselves, anywhere in the template file. Before using these fields, you should be certain of the requirements for importing information into the spreadsheet or database application you are using.

Exercise 12.13 **Estimated time required: 20 min.**

1. Open drawing EX12.11 There should still be 10 occurrences of the block RESISTOR present in your drawing. If not, insert them now using the attribute values as specified in Exercise 12.10.
2. Start the ATTEXT command, and specify a comma delimited file format.
3. Specify a global attribute extraction (by not using the Select Objects < button).
4. Use the template file EX12.12.TXT.
5. Specify the output file as EX12.13C.TXT and start the extraction.
6. Check your text screen for error messages. If you see any error messages, make the necessary corrections as described earlier in this section and run the extraction again.
7. Use Notepad to open and view the output file EX12.13C.TXT.
8. Start the ATTEXT command again, specifying a space delimited file format.
9. Using the Select Objects < button, pick five occurrences of the RESISTOR block.
10. Use the template file EX12.12.TXT again.
11. Specify the output file as EX12.13S.TXT and start the extraction.
12. Check your text screen for error messages. If you see any error messages, make the necessary corrections as described earlier in this section and run the extraction again.
13. Use Notepad to open and view the output file EX12.13S.TXT.

☑ LEARNING CHECKPOINT

- ☐ How can attribute prompts be suppressed? Why is suppression sometimes desirable?
- ☐ What is meant by the term *attribute extraction?*
- ☐ What is the purpose of a template file?
- ☐ Detail the use of the field formatting codes used in a template file.
- ☐ What are some of the most common BL: codes used in a template file?
- ☐ Describe the use of the ATTEXT command.
- ☐ What file extension is required for template and extract files?
- ☐ Define the CDF and SDF extract file formats.
- ☐ List the causes and fixes for some common attribute extraction errors.
- ☐ What are the purposes of C:QUOTE and C:DELIM in a template file?

Using Clip Art

Insert

Import

Insert
Windows MetaFile

IMPORT
IMP

Technical images such as drafting symbols are usually constructed in AutoCAD LT using standard drawing geometry, such as lines, arcs, circles, and polylines. AutoCAD LT provides precision drawing tools necessary for creating these technically accurate images.

Some applications may require the use of nontechnical images within a drawing project, or you may have other uses for drawings that use artistic symbols or images. These artistic symbols and images are called ***clip art.*** You can import these images into AutoCAD LT in a manner similar to that of inserting blocks in a drawing.

Clip art takes many forms, and a very commonly used format is the .WMF file—or Windows MetaFile. These files, unlike bitmap images used by paint programs, support both raster and vector information. ***Raster information*** is a record of the assigned colors of pixels within a defined area. Although it can be imported, this type of information cannot be directly edited in AutoCAD LT. ***Vector information*** is a record of distances, angles, and properties associated with distinct drawing objects.

As an example, a line recorded in a paint program is raster information. This means that the entire line cannot be selected as a single object and edited. The only record kept is a listing of which pixels are colored and what color they are. The fact that they look like a line is not recognized by a raster-based program. Changing the appearance of the line is done by changing the color assigned to the pixels.

On the other hand, a line recorded in AutoCAD LT is vector information. The line can be selected and modified as a unit. It has two defined endpoints with a single vector drawn between them. The appearance of this object can be changed by modifying its properties. Its location can be changed by moving the endpoints.

A Windows MetaFile can store both raster and vector information. If it does contain raster information, the only way it can be directly edited once it has been imported is to be resized. A Windows MetaFile that contains only vector information comes in as a block, and can therefore be exploded. The actual object type used for the vectors within an exploded .WMF file is polylines.

A Windows MetaFile can be imported into any AutoCAD LT drawing using either the IMPORT command or the WMFIN command. The IMPORT command is accessed by typing **IMP** or **IMPORT** at the Command: prompt, picking the Import button from the Insert toolbar, or picking Windows Metafile… from the Insert pull-down menu. The Import File dialog box is shown in Figure 12.43. The Files of type: pull-down list offers only the option to import a WMF file.

Any existing WMF file names are shown in the file name area. The Preview area on the right displays a preview of the currently highlighted .WMF file name. As with many file dialog boxes, this one also offers a Find File … option that allows you to search your local disk drive or network drives for available files and a Locate option to scan the Support File Search Path.

When a .WMF file is imported using this dialog box, the insertion point, scale factors, and rotation angle are entered automatically. After insertion, however, you can edit the image as you would any block. The insertion point, scale factors, and rotation angle can be changed, or you can explode it and edit it further.

More control is available when you import clip art using the WMFIN command. You can specify the insertion point, scale factors, and rotation angle. This command is accessed by typing **WI** or **WMFIN** at the Command: prompt, and it starts the Import WMF dialog box. This dialog box works just like the Import File dialog box. The Import WMF dialog box is shown in Figure 12.44.

Importing .WMF files can bring a significant amount of overhead into a drawing. AutoCAD LT offers certain controls that can be set to control the display of wide lines and fill areas in an imported .WMF file.

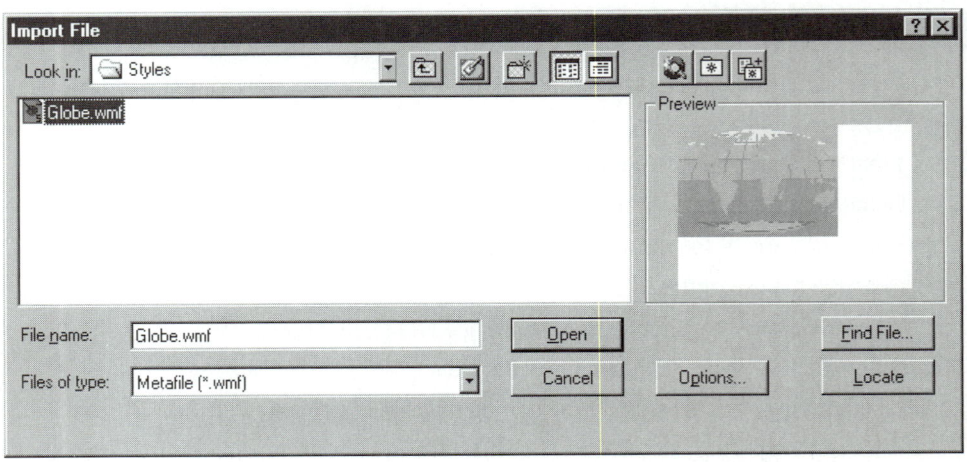

FIGURE 12.43 The Import File dialog box can be used to import .WMF files.

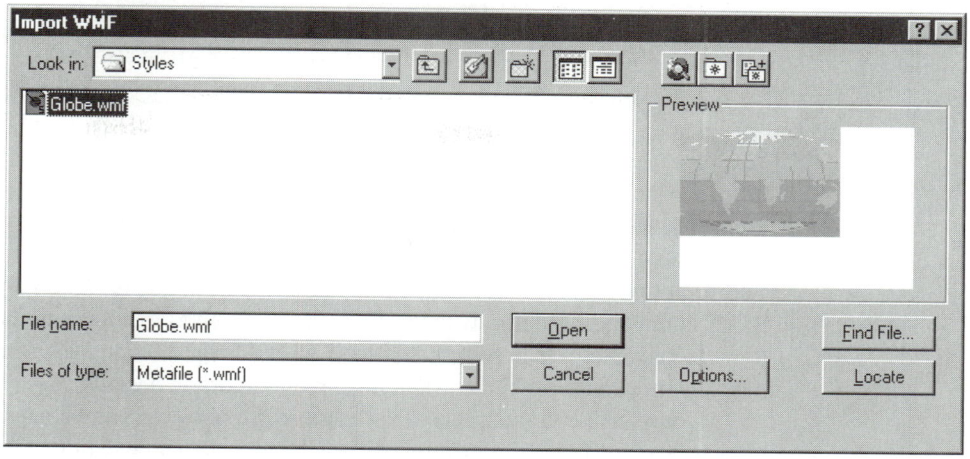

FIGURE 12.44 The WMFIN command starts the Import WMF dialog box and offers more flexibility when importing .WMF files.

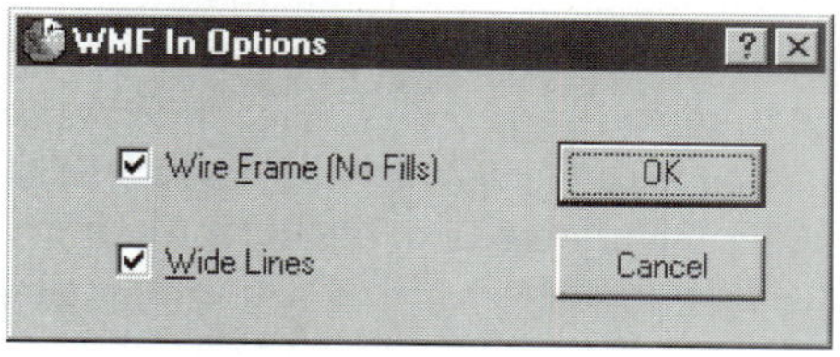

FIGURE 12.45 The WMF Import Options dialog box provides controls for how imported .WMF files are displayed.

The WMF options are set using the WMFOPTS command. You can type **WMFOPTS** at the Command: prompt or select Options ... from the Import File dialog box to display the WMF Import Options dialog box as shown in Figure 12.50.

Two toggles are available under WMF Import Options: Wire Frame (No Fills) and Wide Lines. If Wire Frame (No Fills) is set, all .WMF files are imported as outlines and all filled areas are left empty. When Wide Lines is set, the width of wide lines within the .WMF file is maintained when the file is imported.

Exercise 12.14 — **Estimated time required: 5 min.**

1. Start a new drawing using the default options for Quick Setup.
2. Set Wire Frame (No Fills) to ON using the WMF Import Options dialog box, and Wide Lines to OFF.
3. Start the IMPORT command and import a .WMF file if one is available. Ask your instructor or system administrator for assistance if needed.
4. Use the LIST command to get additional information about the object. Notice that it is shown as a "BLOCK REFERENCE" object.
5. Explode the new object and LIST one of its components.
6. Save as EX12.14, and close the drawing.

LEARNING CHECKPOINT

- ☐ What is clip art?
- ☐ What are the differences between using IMPORT and WMFIN?
- ☐ What is a .WMF file?
- ☐ In what ways can a .WMF file be edited inside of AutoCAD LT?
- ☐ When can a .WMF file not be exploded?
- ☐ Name the command that helps limit the overhead of .WMF files.

Field Notes

Other image file types can also be inserted into AutoCAD LT drawings using OLE (Object Linking and Embedding). Using OLE is covered in Chapter 15.

Externally Referenced Drawings

Earlier in this chapter, you learned that any drawing can be inserted into any other drawing by using the INSERT command. One disadvantage to inserting another drawing into the current drawing is that the inserted drawing becomes a locally defined block and no longer maintains any connection with the original drawing file. This can cause problems when it is time to update a design.

Consider the drawing update process required by a design change on a particular subassembly that is used in many different drawings. If in each case, the subassembly drawing has been inserted into another drawing, you not only need to open and update the original drawing, you must also open and update every other drawing where the subassembly had been used. This can be a long and time-consuming process.

An alternative exists that is known as *referencing* an external drawing. A drawing database that is stored outside of the current drawing is called an ***external drawing.*** The term ***referencing*** means that AutoCAD LT refers to the source file for the information, rather than storing it in the current drawing. Therefore, an ***external reference*** is a source drawing outside of the current drawing that AutoCAD LT refers to for information displayed in the current drawing. Using an external reference works much like inserting drawings, except that the information is not added to the current drawing database. Instead, each time you open a drawing, AutoCAD LT reads the source file for each external reference and displays the geometry in the current drawing.

Using external references has many advantages over inserting drawings. One advantage is that the information is not permanently added to the current drawing and the drawing file size can be kept from getting unnecessarily large. Another advantage of external references is that any number of drawings can reference a specific drawing file. Also, AutoCAD LT reads the source drawing file for each external reference every time you open a drawing that uses external references. So, all drawings that reference external drawings automatically reflect the latest state of the referenced drawing files.

Attaching an External Reference

Insert

External Reference

Insert
Xref Manager

XREF
XR

The primary command used for working with externally referenced drawing files is the XREF command. In fact, an external reference is most commonly referred to as an *"Xref."* The Xref Manager dialog box is accessed by picking Xref Manager ... from the Insert pull-down menu, from the Insert toolbar, or by typing **XR** or **XREF** at the Command: prompt. The Xref Manager dialog box is shown in Figure 12.46.

The basic XREF option is the Attach ... option. This option attaches an Xref to the current drawing. When an Xref is attached, it is displayed in the current drawing at each specified location. The definition of

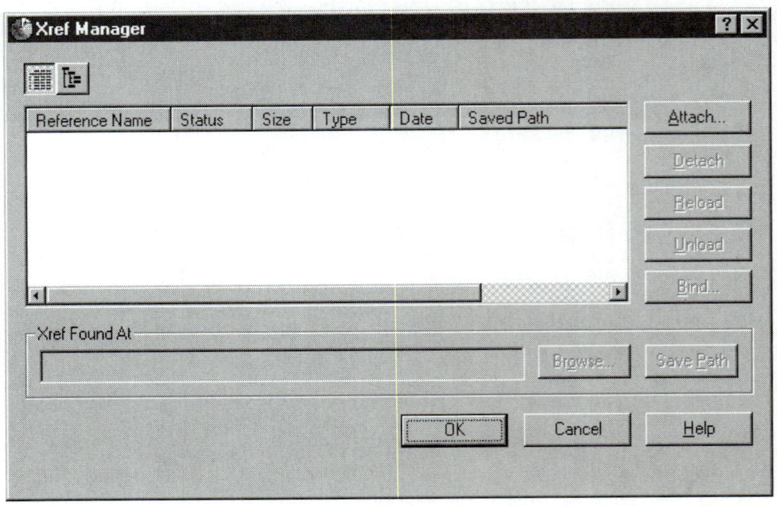

FIGURE 12.46 The Xref Manager dialog box provides an intuitive interface for working with Xrefs.

the Xref is automatically updated each time you open the current drawing. Additionally, an attached Xref can be nested. The term ***nested*** means that an Xref can contain other Xrefs. So if an Xref is attached to a drawing, and that drawing is then referenced by another drawing, the nested Xref is also displayed.

Your first step when using Xrefs is to create the drawing that will be referenced. Next, open the drawing that is to reference it and use the XREF Attach option. This is accessed by picking Attach… in the Xref Manager dialog box.

Picking the Attach... button displays the Select Reference File dialog box (see Figure 12.47). Use this dialog box as you do any file dialog to go to the desired folder, preview, and select an existing drawing file. In Figure 12.47, the file named "Eave and Gutter Detail" found in the AutoCAD LT 2000\Sample folder is selected and its preview is displayed. Picking the Open button displays the External Reference dialog box where you specify the reference and insertion parameters for the selected file. The External Reference dialog box is shown in Figure 12.48.

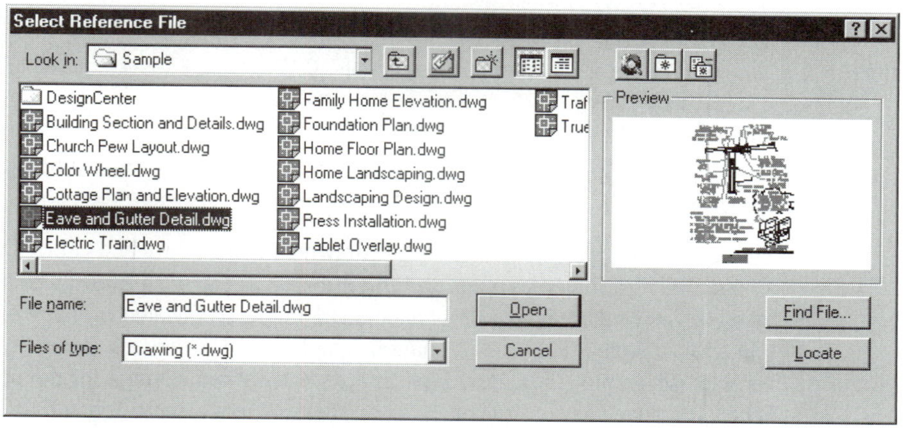

FIGURE 12.47 The Select Reference File dialog box allows you to preview and select a file to reference.

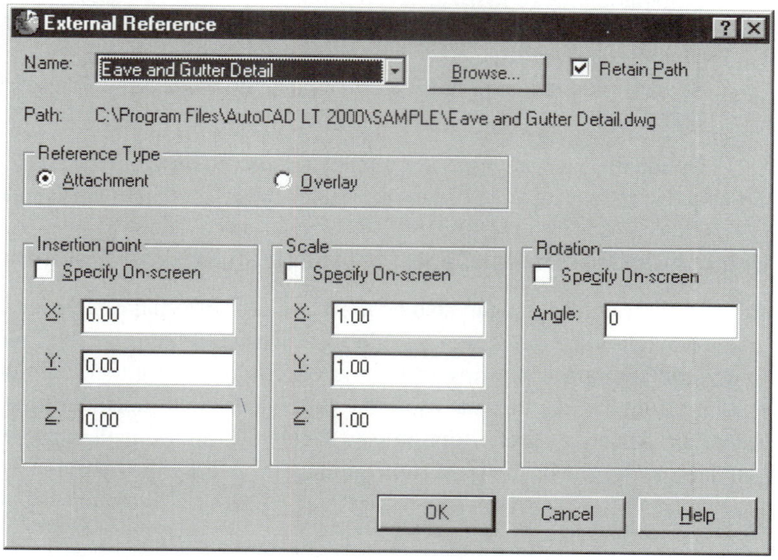

FIGURE 12.48 The External Reference dialog box is used to specify the insertion parameters for the referenced file.

Field Notes

The XATTACH command provides greater convenience for attaching external references. XATTACH displays the Select Reference File dialog box immediately, without your needing to first access the Xref Manager and then pick the Attach… button. The XATTACH command is accessed by picking External Reference… from the Insert pull-down menu or by typing **XA** or **XATTACH**.

The External reference dialog box displays the name and path of the currently selected file in the area near the top. If you need to return to the Select Reference File dialog box, pick the Browse ... button.

In the area labeled Reference Type, select the Attachment option. External Reference Attachments and Overlays are handled differently and have different applications. Xref overlays are discussed later in this chapter.

Typically, the toggle labeled Retain Path is checked. This option controls whether the full path to the Xref is saved in the current drawing. If the path is not saved, the next time the current drawing file is opened, AutoCAD LT will look for the referenced file only in the AutoCAD LT Support File Search Path, as set in the Files tab of the Options dialog box.

The insertion parameters are specified in the Insertion point, Scale and Rotation areas. When an externally referenced file is brought into a drawing, its placement, sizing, and orientation are handled similar to when you use the INSERT command. To be prompted for the insertion location, scale factors, or rotation angle at the command line, pick the Specify On-screen toggles for the appropriate options. Otherwise, indicate the desired values in the text boxes. When all parameters are specified, pick the OK button. In this example, the insertion point is specified on-screen, and the scale and rotation are specified in the dialog. The following appears at the command line:

Command: **XR** or **XREF**↵
Attach Xref "Eave and Gutter Detail": C:\Program Files\AutoCAD LT 2000\SAMPLE\Eave and Gutter Detail.dwg
"Eave and Gutter Detail" loaded.

Specify insertion point or [Scale/X/Y/Z/Rotate/PScale/PX/PY/PZ/PRotate]: **4,4**↵
Command:

The result is that a representation of the drawing named "Eave and Gutter Detail" appears in the current drawing. To place additional copies of an Xref in a drawing, you can duplicate an existing copy using any duplication command or you can use the Xref Manager again. In the Xref Manager dialog box, pick the name of the existing Xref you need and pick the Attach... button. The External Reference dialog box is displayed with the selected Xref name preset in the Name: text box. Specify the desired settings for the new instance and pick the OK button. When you attach a new instance of an existing reference, the command line displays the following:

Command: **XR** or **XREF**↵
Xref "Eave and Gutter Detail" has already been defined.
Using existing definition.
Specify insertion point or [Scale/X/Y/Z/Rotate/PScale/PX/PY/PZ/PRotate]: ⟨*specify a point*⟩
Command:

Optionally, you can select any already referenced file from the Name: drop-down list. To select a file that is not already referenced, you need to pick the Browse ... button to display the Select Reference File dialog box.

Using AutoCAD DesignCenter to Attach an External Reference

AutoCAD DesignCenter can also be used to attach external references using its simple drag-and-drop interface. As when inserting a drawing file from DesignCenter, use the Tree View pane to locate and select the folder containing the drawing to be referenced. You can either right-click on the drawing file or drag the drawing from the Palette pane using the right mouse button. Both of these methods display a shortcut menu. Select the Attach as Xref... option (see Figure 12.49) to display the External Reference dialog box, where you can specify the desired insertion parameters as described previously.

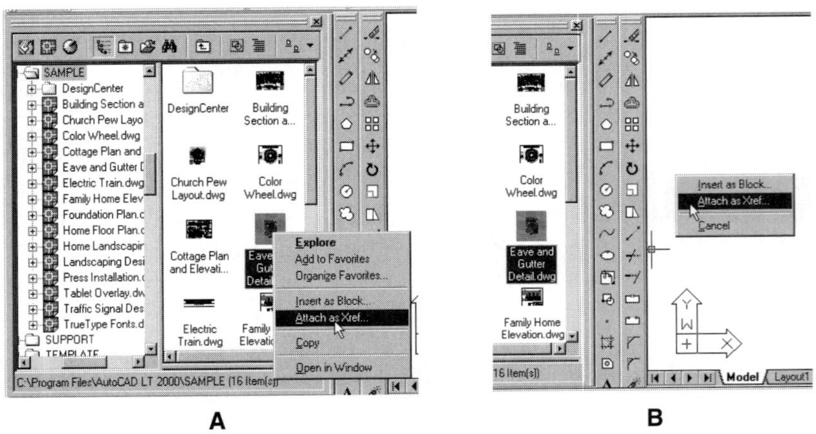

FIGURE 12.49 The shortcut menus from DesignCenter provide the option to attach a drawing file as an Xref. (A) Right-click on a drawing in the Palette pane to get this shortcut menu. (B) When you drag a drawing from DesignCenter using the right mouse button, this shortcut menu is displayed when you drop the drawing.

Dependent Symbols

Xrefs are very different from blocks. When you insert a block, all the nonduplicated named objects are then defined in the current drawing. Styles and definitions are stored and referenced within a drawing by name, and are called ***named objects***. The types of named objects discussed so far include text styles and dimension styles, plus layer, linetype, view, and block definitions. The named objects defined in an Xref are brought in as dependent symbols. The term ***dependent symbol*** is used to describe any named object defined in an externally referenced drawing.

To explore the nature of dependent symbols, first start a new drawing from scratch using English settings. A drawing started from scratch has only the default named objects, such as layer 0 and the Standard text and dimension styles. No other layers, linetypes, or any other named objects are currently defined. Take a moment to verify this by opening the Layer Properties Manager, Linetype Manager, and Dimension Style Manager.

Next, attach a reference to the file "Building Section and Details.dwg" found in the Sample folder. In the External Reference dialog box, specify an insertion point of 0,0. Set the Scale to 1 and the Rotation to 0, then pick OK. This Xref file is much larger than the initial display area of the drawing. Use ZOOM Extents to view the instance of the referenced file.

The styles and definitions, which are named objects in the "Building Section and Details.dwg" drawing file, are now stored in the current drawing as dependent symbols.

For example, the Layer Properties Manager dialog box shown in Figure 12.50 shows a variety of layer names defined in the current drawing. Notice that the layer names, except for layer O, are all preceded by the name of the externally referenced drawing file on which they are dependent. These layers are dependent on the referenced drawing in which they were originally defined. The symbol used to separate the dependent symbol name from the Xref it is dependent on is the "|" symbol, called a ***vertical bar.*** Experienced DOS users may also call this the ***pipe*** symbol.

Attaching this particular external drawing has created many different dependent layer names, linetypes, text styles, and even a new dimstyle. Many of these dependent symbols can be brought permanently into the current drawing, as discussed later.

AutoCAD LT uses this type of naming system for dependent symbols to ensure that no conflicts are produced by duplicate named objects. For example, a text style named Standard exists in the current drawing, and a style of the same name exists in the drawing file "Building Section and Details.dwg". If the Standard style in the current drawing is modified to reference the Romans.shx font file, then a conflict exists because the Standard style in the "Building Section and Details" drawing uses the Txt.shx font file. Naming the dependent style "Building Section and Details|Standard" allows the two separate definitions to coexist with no problems.

In the current drawing, the layers 0 and DefPoints, and the linetype Continuous override entries of the same name in the attached Xref. This is why a layer named "Building Section and Details|0" and a linetype named "Building Section and Details|Continuous" is not added to the current drawing. Any objects in the

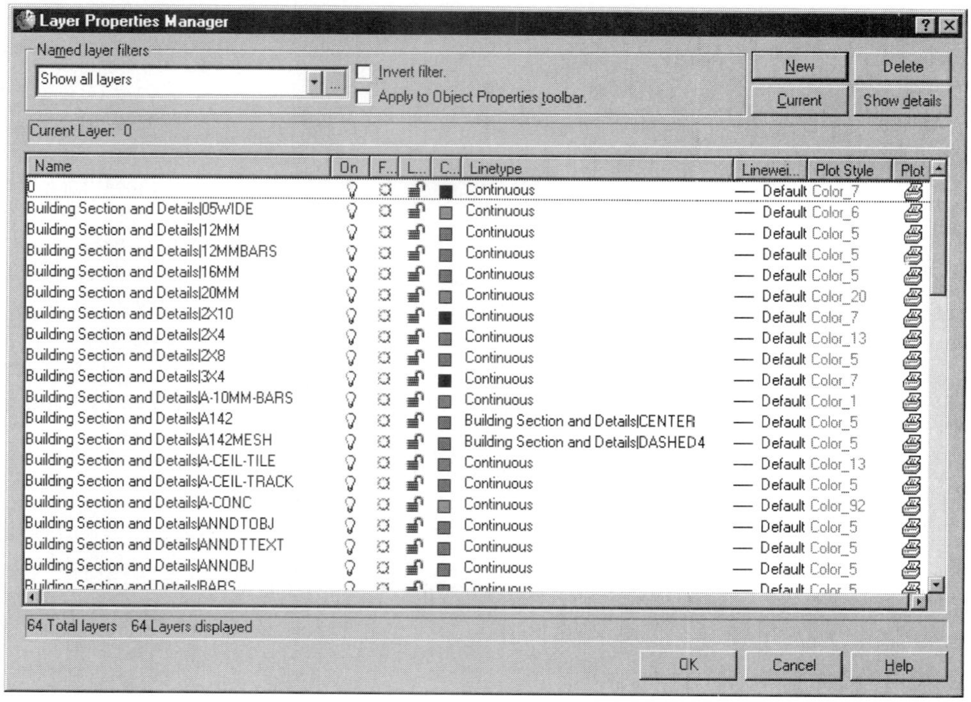

FIGURE 12.50 The shown layer names are dependent symbols, defined in the externally referenced drawing named "Building Section and Details."

Xref that were on layer 0 or DefPoints and use Bylayer settings in the original drawing are displayed using the active settings applied to these layers in the current drawing.

Because dependent symbols may change, or even disappear the next time the Xref is loaded, you cannot directly use dependent symbols. You cannot make a dependent layer current, nor can you rename a dependent layer. Additionally, you cannot rename or delete any dependent symbol.

Visibility changes can be made to dependent layers as desired, but by default, all of those changes are discarded the next time you load the Xref on which the layers are dependent. For example, if the layer "Text" is thawed in the drawing "Building Section and Details" and you freeze the layer "Building Section and Details|Text" in the current drawing, it is thawed again the next time you open the current drawing and the Xref is reloaded. In addition to visibility settings, you can also change the layer property settings including color, linetype, lineweight, lock status, and Plot/Don't Plot setting for Xref dependent layers.

To retain the layer property settings of dependent layers, you can set an AutoCAD LT system variable named VISRETAIN (VISibility RETAIN). The default setting for this variable is 1, which means ON. To turn it off, type **VISRETAIN** at the Command: prompt and enter a value of 0. Set it to 1 again to turn this variable back on:

Command: **VISRETAIN↵**
Enter new value for VISRETAIN <1>: **0↵**

The VISRETAIN setting can also be changed in the Options dialog box. This is done using the check box labeled Retain changes to Xref layers found in the External References (Xref's) area on the Open and Save tab. The effects of VISRETAIN become apparent the next time you load the Xref, because any visibility changes you have made to dependent layer names are preserved.

Field Notes

- If the layer DefPoints does not yet exist in the current drawing, referencing an external file that has an existing DefPoints layer defines the layer also in the current drawing. The new DefPoints layer in the current drawing uses the default settings, regardless of any changes to the settings in the referenced file.
- The word *resolve* is frequently used with regard to external references. It refers to the process of finding the referenced file and reading the drawing information it contains.
- When a drawing that has external references is opened, if an XREF cannot be *resolved* it is displayed as a text item in the drawing. The text shows the drive letter, directory path, and drawing file name for the Xref.

Exercise 12.15

Estimated time required: 10 min.

1. Begin a new drawing, starting from scratch.
2. Use the XREF Attach option to attach the drawing \AutoCAD LT 2000\SAMPLE\Building Section and Details to the current drawing. Use 0,0 for the insertion point and default scale and rotation values, use ZOOM ALL to see the entire drawing.
3. Open the Layer Properties Manager and try to set a dependent layer to be current. Then try to rename a dependent layer. Close the Layer Properties Manager.
4. Copy the Xref instance to a new location in the current drawing.
5. Use the XREF command again to insert another copy of Building Section and Details.
6. Use the Layer Properties Manager to freeze the layer Building Section and Details|TEXT in the current drawing.
7. Save the current drawing as EX12.15, and close it.
8. Use the OPEN command to reopen EX12.15.
9. Check the visibility of the Building Section and Details|TEXT layer.
10. Freeze the Building Section and Details|TEXT again, and set VISRETAIN to 0.
11. Repeat Steps 7, 8, and 9.
12. Turn VISRETAIN on and save the current drawing as EX12.15. Close the drawing.

LEARNING CHECKPOINT

- ☐ What are the advantages of Xrefs compared to inserting drawings?
- ☐ Describe three ways in which the XREF command is accessed.
- ☐ What command directly displays the Select Reference File dialog box?
- ☐ How can DesignCenter be used to attach an Xref?
- ☐ What methods are available to attach a second instance of an existing reference?
- ☐ What is a dependent symbol?
- ☐ What limitations apply to dependent symbols?
- ☐ What is the function of the VISRETAIN system variable?

Sharing Data and Drawing Files

- Using Reference Files to Work with Others

Concept Animations

- External Reference Files

Overlaying an External Reference

One potential problem with Xrefs comes from what is called ***circular referencing.*** This is what happens when two drawings reference each other. Consider the possibility in which a floor plan of an office is created in order to do office layout planning and maintenance of records. To plan for placement of equipment, the electrical layout for the building is attached as an external reference. Then at a later date, the electrical wiring of the building is revised. To plan the electrical layout to match the needs of the office, the office floor plan is attached to the electrical drawing as an external reference. Attaching the electrical layout that was previously attached to the office floor plan back to the electrical layout creates the situation defined as a *circular reference.*

When attaching an external reference that references the current drawing, AutoCAD LT 2000 displays the warning dialog box shown in Figure 12.51 and allows you to continue or cancel the operation.

Selecting Yes to continue attaches the Xref and produces the following message:

```
Command: XR or XREF↵
Attach Xref "XR1": C:\Program Files\AutoCAD LT 2000\Sample\Floorplan.dwg
"Floorplan" loaded.

Breaking circular reference from "Floorplan" to "current drawing".
Command:
```

This indicates that the actual data from this drawing are being used, not the data referenced by the attached file. Although this method can be used, there is a much better way to handle this type of situation.

The way to avoid this situation is to overlay external references instead of attaching them. An attached Xref travels with the drawing it is attached to, but when the Overlay option is used, the external reference is not attached to the current drawing and does not travel with it as a nested Xref. This prevents the problem of circular referencing from occurring. The Overlay option can be accessed by picking the Overlay radio button from the Reference Type area of the External Reference dialog box, as shown in Figure 12.52.

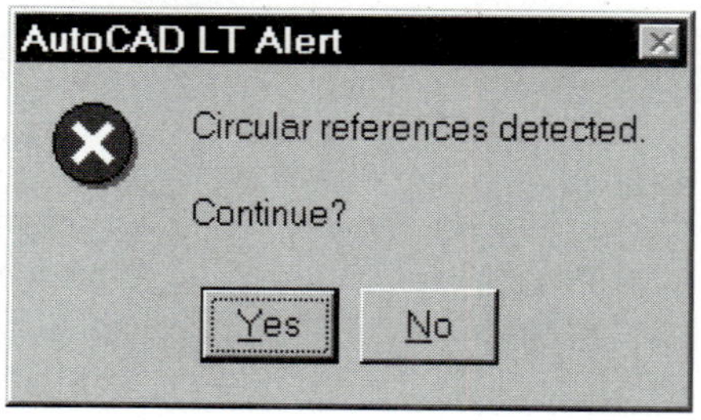

FIGURE 12.51 Attaching a reference file that references the current drawing creates what is called a circular reference.

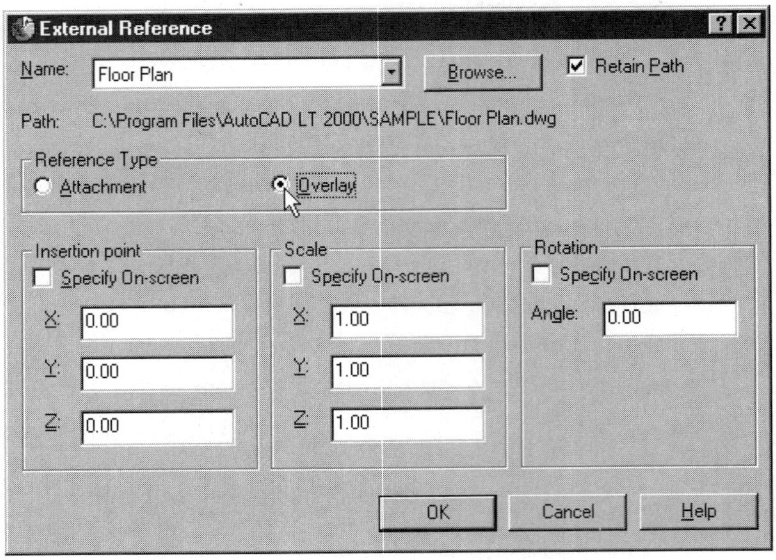

FIGURE 12.52 Using the overlay option prevents circular referencing between referenced files.

In this example, even when overlaying Floorplan into Elecplan, the circular referencing alert will still be displayed, because Elecplan is *attached* to Floorplan. However, when the Floorplan drawing is again opened, it does not have a circular reference back to itself, because the overlaid copy of Floorplan does not travel with the attached Elecplan reference.

Exercise 12.16 **Estimated time required: 10 min.**

1. Begin a new drawing.
2. Use the XREF Attach option to attach the drawing \AutoCAD LT 2000\SAMPLE\Building Section and Details to the current drawing. Use 0,0 for the insertion point and default scale and rotation values. Use ZOOM ALL to see the entire drawing.
3. Save the drawing as EX12.16-ATTACH, and close.
4. Open the drawing \AutoCAD LT 2000\SAMPLE\Building Section and Details.
5. Use the XREF command, and attempt to attach the drawing EX12.16-ATTACH. Notice the error message. Cancel the operation.
6. Begin a new drawing. Close, but DO NOT save changes to \AutoCAD LT 2000\SAMPLE\Building Section and Details.
7. Use the XREF Overlay option to overlay the drawing \AutoCAD LT 2000\SAMPLE\Building Section and Details in the current drawing. Use 0,0 for the insertion point and default scale and rotation values. Use ZOOM ALL to see the entire drawing.
8. Save the drawing as EX12.16-OVERLAY, and close.
9. Open the drawing \AutoCAD LT 2000\SAMPLE\Building Section and Details.
10. Use the XREF command, and attach the drawing EX12.16-OVERLAY. Use the default insertion parameters.
11. DO NOT save changes to \AutoCAD LT 2000\SAMPLE\ Building Section and Details. Use SAVEAS to save the drawing as EX12.16 and close the drawing.

Detaching an External Reference

Although you can erase an external reference, doing so does not remove the actual reference from the current drawing. All dependent symbol names remain defined even after erasing all copies of an Xref. The XREF Detach option is used to remove completely an Xref and all its dependent symbols. This is accessed by picking Detach in the Xref Manager dialog box. The currently highlighted Xref names are then detached.

External References and Demand Loading

AutoCAD LT 2000 provides an Xref feature called demand loading. ***Demand loading*** increases the performance of AutoCAD LT by loading only the portion of a referenced drawing that is required to regenerate the current drawing. This means that information on layers that are frozen in the referenced drawing is not loaded with the xref.

In order to benefit from demand loading, the referenced drawing must first be saved with a layer index. To save a drawing with a layer index, the system variable named INDEXCTL is set to 1. As discussed in earlier chapters, any AutoCAD LT system variable can be adjusted by typing the variable name at the command line, as follows:

Command: **INDEXCTL↵**
Enter new value for INDEXCTL <0>: **1↵**

The available settings for INDEXCTL are as follows:

Value	Index Type	Effect
0	None	No indexes are saved.
1	Layer	Layer states are indexed.
2	Spatial	Xref Clipping data are saved.
3	Layer and Spatial	Layer states and Xref Clipping data are saved.

Field Notes

Drawings created in AutoCAD 2000 are able to create clipping boundaries so that only a specified portion of an externally referenced file is visible. AutoCAD LT 2000 cannot create these boundaries, but if you are working with AutoCAD 2000 drawings using AutoCAD LT 2000, you should set INDEXCTL to save a spatial index.

When working in an AutoCAD 2000 drawing that contains clipped xrefs, set the XCLIPFRAME variable to 1 if you want to see the clipping boundaries.

Once INDEXCTL has been set in the referenced drawing, demand loading must be enabled in the drawing you are bringing the referenced file into. Demand loading is enabled under the Open and Save tab in the Preferences dialog box or by directly setting the XLOADCTL system variable. The settings for XLOADCTL are as follows:

Value	Effect
0	Demand load disabled.
1	Demand load enabled. Referenced file is kept open.
2	Demand load enabled. Copy of referenced file is opened.

When demand loading is disabled, AutoCAD LT 2000 opens the referenced drawing, reads the entire file, and then closes it. With demand loading enabled, AutoCAD LT reads the file and loads the necessary information. However, the drawing is kept open in case more data must be loaded from the referenced file. While the drawing is kept open, it cannot be edited by anyone else. A setting of 2 forces AutoCAD LT to make a copy of the referenced file and keep the copy open. Thus, the original referenced file can be opened and edited by another user if necessary. This situation is often required in a networked environment where several CAD drafters are working on a single project and, therefore, sharing files.

Updating an External Reference

Each time you open a drawing with external references, the source files are read and the referenced drawing is displayed in its latest state. However, depending on your demand load settings, it may be possible for someone else to modify the referenced drawing while you are working in your current drawing. This is possible in a networked environment, where computers are interconnected and drawing files are shared. However, even on a stand-alone workstation, it is possible for you to have more than one session of AutoCAD LT active at once, so you could possibly change the definition of an Xref being referenced by a currently open drawing.

If an externally referenced drawing has been changed and you want to update the reference without having to reopen the current drawing, you can reload the referenced file by picking the Reload button in the Xref Manager dialog box. Highlight the files that you want to reload and pick reload. The file is not actually reloaded until you pick OK in the Xref Manager dialog box. The dependent symbols are automatically updated along with any changed drawing geometry or visibility adjustments to layers. All instances of this XREF in the current drawing are updated when the definition is reloaded.

The External Reference Directory Path

If the Retain Path toggle in the External Reference dialog box is checked when referencing, an external reference is remembered by the drawing to which it is referenced by using the drive letter, directory path, and drawing file name of the Xref. If your directory structure changes or you move or rename the externally referenced file, any drawings referencing it cannot find the file where it is expected and AutoCAD LT is unable to resolve the Xref. As discussed earlier, when an Xref cannot be resolved, a text object representing the drive path and name of the Xref is displayed at the insertion point of the Xref to show that it exists in the drawing but was not resolved.

When this happens, you can change the path associated with an external reference by using the Save Path button in the Xref Found At area in the Xref Manager dialog box. If you know the path for the new location, you can simply type it in the text box. Otherwise, use the Browse ... button to display the Select new path dialog box. Go to the new folder and select the file name to use for the referenced file. Note that this can be a completely new file name, or it can even be a completely different file if desired. Pick the Open button and you are returned to the Xref Manager dialog box. Pick the Save Path button; then pick OK. The drawing is then updated using the new reference file.

Although the original Xref is given the same name as the file referenced, if you change the path of an Xref, the name stays the same. Even when the name of the source file has changed, the name of the Xref in the drawing does not change in the current or in any future session. Once the path of an Xref is successfully changed, the new definition is immediately displayed in the drawing.

If the new path and file name cannot be resolved, the AutoCAD LT message dialog box is displayed, as shown in Figure 12.53.

FIGURE 12.53 This warning appears when AutoCAD LT cannot find the specified external drawing file.

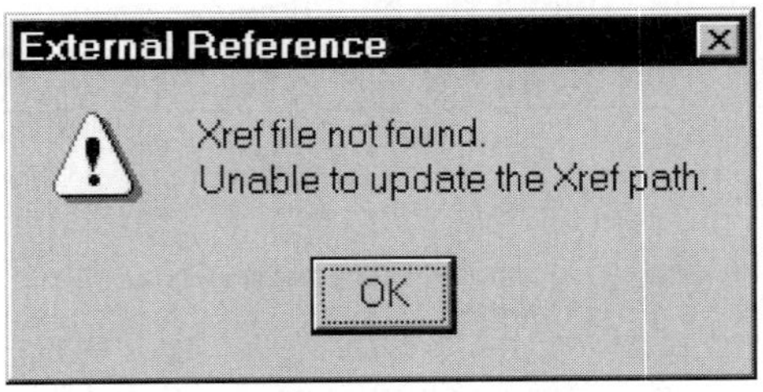

Unloading External References

The Unload button in the Xref Manager dialog box allows you to suppress the display and regeneration of the Xref definition. It does not remove it from the drawing, as with the Detach option. This is used primarily to speed up performance by reducing the amount of drawing information that needs to be regenerated. To restore the Xref in the drawing, use the Reload option.

Obtaining Information About External References

The Xref Manager dialog box has two display modes. The default display mode is the List View, which displays text information about the referenced files. Figure 12.54 shows an example of the Xref Manager dialog box in List View. The text information displayed includes the Reference Name, Status, file Size, attachment Type, Date modified, and the Saved Path. Similar to other Windows dialog boxes, the category buttons at the top of the list can be selected to sort the listing based on the information in that column.

Alternatively, the listing can be shown as a Tree View. This is very useful for quickly identifying the status and relationships of the Xrefs in your drawing. Figure 12.55 shows the same dialog box as Figure 12.54, with Tree View active. Using this mode, you can quickly determine the nesting levels of your Xrefs, plus their current status. Note that Home Landscaping is a nested attachment to Home Floor Plan, and Eave Gutter Detail is a currently unloaded overlay. An arrow is displayed on the icon if an Xref is to be reloaded (up arrow) or unloaded (down arrow). If a question mark is displayed on an icon, it indicates that the Xref has been orphaned. An Xref is orphaned if the Xref it is nested in is unloaded.

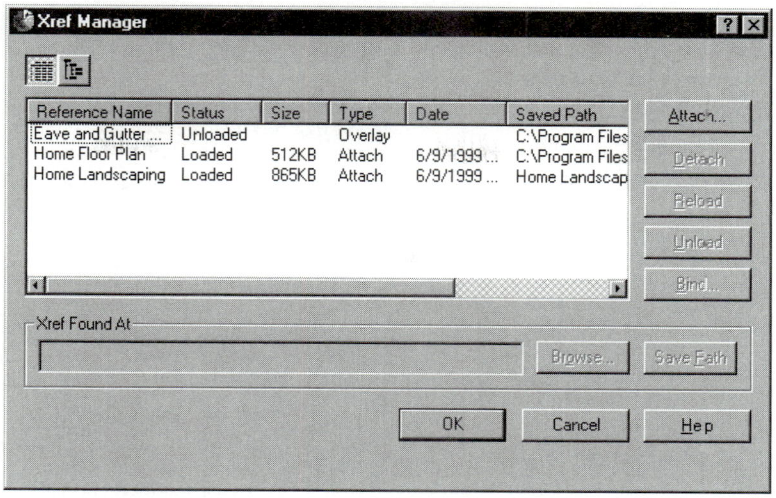

FIGURE 12.54 The Xref Manager dialog box in List View.

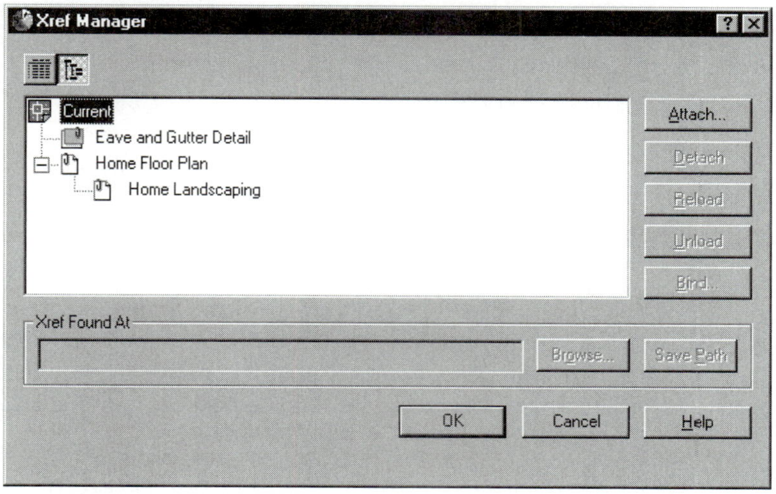

FIGURE 12.55 The Xref Manager dialog box in Tree View.

Field Notes

When sharing a drawing that has external references, it is necessary to include all of the Xref files as well as the actual drawing. Otherwise, any of the Xrefs that are not available will be unresolved when the drawing is opened, which may leave the drawing incomplete.

Using the Xref Log File

To assist you in keeping track of Xrefs, AutoCAD LT can generate an Xref log file. To turn this feature on, set the system variable XREFCTL to 1. By default, this variable is set to 0 and no log file is maintained. When this feature is activated, it is then active for all drawings—not just the one in which it is activated.

The file that is created is a standard ASCII text file that is given the same name as the drawing, but has an .XLG file extension. The Xref log file is created in the same directory location where the drawing file is found.

To set the XREFCTL variable, type **XREFCTL** at the Command**:** prompt:

Command**: XREFCTL↵**
Enter new value for XREFCTL <0>**: 1↵**

To turn this feature back off, set XREFCTL to 0 again. When you need to view or print this file, it can be opened with the Notepad text editing program. Figure 12.56 shows the Notepad program with an Xref log file loaded.

When XREFCTL is on, the Xref log file for any given drawing is updated each time an Xref command option is used to attach, overlay, reload, or detach an Xref, and each time the Xrefs in a drawing are resolved.

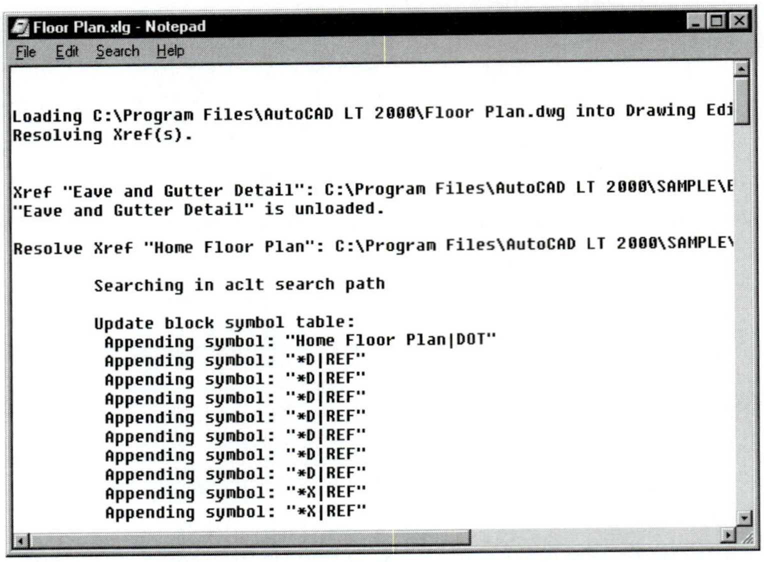

```
Floor Plan.xlg - Notepad
File  Edit  Search  Help

Loading C:\Program Files\AutoCAD LT 2000\Floor Plan.dwg into Drawing Edi
Resolving Xref(s).

Xref "Eave and Gutter Detail": C:\Program Files\AutoCAD LT 2000\SAMPLE\E
"Eave and Gutter Detail" is unloaded.

Resolve Xref "Home Floor Plan": C:\Program Files\AutoCAD LT 2000\SAMPLE\

        Searching in aclt search path

        Update block symbol table:
         Appending symbol: "Home Floor Plan|DOT"
         Appending symbol: "*D|REF"
         Appending symbol: "*D|REF"
         Appending symbol: "*D|REF"
         Appending symbol: "*D|REF"
         Appending symbol: "*D|REF"
         Appending symbol: "*D|REF"
         Appending symbol: "*D|REF"
         Appending symbol: "*X|REF"
         Appending symbol: "*X|REF"
```

FIGURE 12.56 The Notepad text editor program can be used to open the Xref log file for viewing or printing.

A title block is written to the file as it is updated. For example, the following is a title block from the Xref log file shown in Figure 12.56:

```
================================
Drawing: C:\Program Files\AutoCAD LT 2000\Floor Plan.dwg
Date/Time: 02/19/00 11:37:36
Operation: Attach Xref
================================
```

This title block confirms the drawing file name, provides a time and date stamp, and indicates what type of operation took place. Following this title block is a listing of the updates performed to each of the symbol tables. The term ***symbol table*** is used to describe the information stored regarding named objects such as blocks, linetypes, and text styles. Additionally, the Xref log indicates the nesting level of all Xrefs.

Field Notes

If XREFCTL is ON, and a drawing that is opened contains no external references, the .XLG file is not created. After the last Xref is detached, the .XLG file is no longer updated unless another Xref is attached.

Exercise 12.17

Estimated time required: 5 min.

1. Open the drawing EX12.16-OVERLAY for editing.
2. Set the XREFCTL variable to a value of 1.
3. Use the open command again to open EX12.16-OVERLAY.
4. Enter the XREF command and the Reload option.
5. Access the Save Path option in the Xref Manager, and change the Building Section and Details external reference path to \AutoCAD LT 2000\SAMPLE\Eave and Gutter Detail.DWG.
6. Use the Detach option of XREF to detach the Xref named Building Section and Details.
7. Use the NOTEPAD program to open and view the Xref log file named EX12.16-OVERLAY.XLG.
8. Set XREFCTL to a value of 0.
9. Save the current drawing file as EX12.17. Close the drawing.

LEARNING CHECKPOINT

- ☐ What are the advantages of an Xref Overlay compared to an Attached Xref?
- ☐ Which option is used to list the current external references in a drawing?
- ☐ How can an Xref be updated without reopening your drawing?
- ☐ Describe the purpose and use of the XREF Detach option.
- ☐ What is an Xref log file?
- ☐ What variable controls the creation of Xref log files?
- ☐ What program can be used to open an Xref log file?
- ☐ How is an Xref log file named and where is it stored?
- ☐ What system variables control demand loading features?

Sharing Data and Drawing Files

- Updating Reference Links and Binding Drawings to Files

Binding Xrefs

Sometimes, you might want to make an Xref a permanent part of the current drawing. This is a convenient way to share your drawings with others. Rather than including a base drawing and the source drawings for several different Xrefs, you can simply bind the Xrefs to make them a permanent part of the current drawing. This way, anyone else who needs to use your drawing has only one file to deal with instead of several. The process of permanently adding an Xref to the current drawing is called ***binding.*** Whether an Xref is attached or is an overlay, the Bind option can be used to bind it to the current drawing.

When you bind an Xref, all of the external drawing's dependent symbols also become part of the current drawing. The XREF Bind option is used when you want to bind an entire drawing. This option is accessed in the External Reference dialog box by highlighting the names of the Xrefs you want to bind and picking the Bind ... button. Note that when nested Xrefs are selected without their parent drawing, the Bind ... button is disabled and a message is displayed in the lower left area of the dialog box. If you bind an Xref that has nested Xrefs attached, the nested Xrefs are also bound to the current drawing. You can bind both attached and overlaid Xrefs.

When you select references to bind, the Bind Xrefs dialog box is displayed. See Figure 12.57. Here you must specify how the Xrefs are to be bound. The two options are Bind and Insert.

FIGURE 12.57 The Bind Xrefs dialog box allows you to specify how the Xref is brought in to the current drawing.

When an Xref is bound to the current drawing using the Bind option, all its dependent symbols are brought in also. To prevent possible conflicts, the names use a format similar to that used when they are dependent. The vertical bar character is replaced with a "0" (dollar sign, zero, dollar sign) sequence. So the dependent layer named XREF1|TEXT is renamed to XREF1$0$TEXT when it is permanently added to the current drawing. This is true of all dependent symbols; however, once added to the current drawing these items can be renamed as desired. The easiest way to rename named objects is to use the Rename dialog box accessed with REN or RENAME. The Layer Properties Manager shown in Figure 12.58 shows a list of layer names added to the current drawing as part of an XREF command Bind option.

Once bound to the current drawing, the external reference is removed and the source geometry is added to the current drawing as a new block definition. Using the list option after binding an Xref shows that the external reference name does not show up anymore. However, the externally referenced drawing is now a block definition and acts like one in every way. Additional copies can be freely inserted using the INSERT command and, if needed, it can be exploded.

Using the Insert option in the Bind Xrefs dialog box brings in the geometry and dependent symbols but maintains no reference to the original Xref file. The results are similar to what would happen if you detached

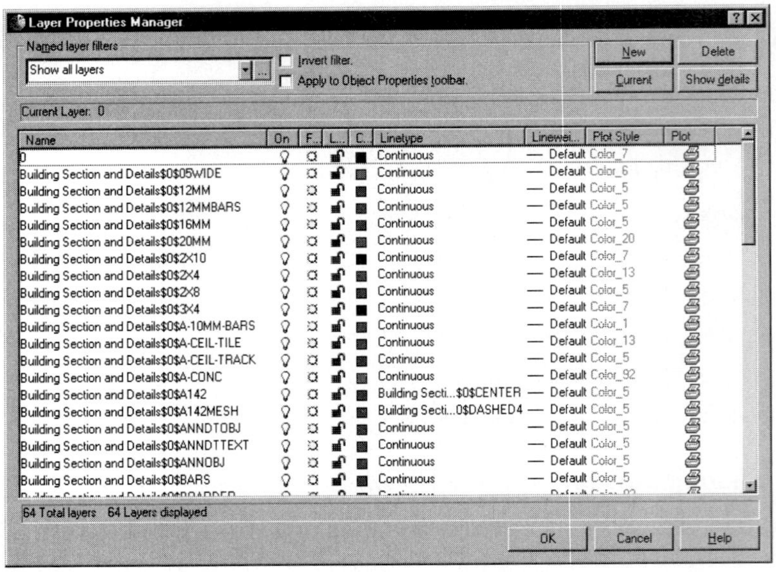

FIGURE 12.58 The Layer Properties Manager dialog box displays the new names of the bound layers.

the Xref and inserted the file using INSERT. What this means is that the dependent symbols are stripped of the Xref name. When symbol names match, then the definition in the current drawing overrides that of the incoming definition.

Binding Dependent Symbols

Modify Object ▸ External Reference Bind
XBIND XB

Oftentimes, a text style, dimension style, layer, linetype, or a block that you want to use exists in the current drawing as an Xref dependent symbol. As discussed earlier, dependent symbols cannot be used while they are dependent on an Xref. Rather than bind an entire Xref when you only need one or two items from it, you can bind dependent symbols into the current drawing on an individual basis. Doing this helps to decrease drawing file size. Binding an entire drawing brings all named objects with it and can also define the Xref as a block in the current drawing just as if you used the INSERT command. The XBIND command allows you to pick specific elements from an external reference drawing to import into the current drawing.

The XBIND command can be accessed by typing XB or XBIND at the Command: prompt. Optionally, you can select External Reference Bind ... from the Object cascade of the Modify menu. The XBIND command displays the Xbind dialog box, as shown in Figure 12.59. All Xrefs, whether attached or overlaid, are displayed in a tree view in the Xrefs list on the left side of the dialog box. Expand and collapse the branches of the Xrefs and Symbol Tables Categories by double-clicking or picking the "+" or "–" symbol. Empty categories cannot be expanded. Use the Add and Remove buttons to build your list of Definitions to Bind, and pick OK when you are finished.

In Figure 12.59, a layer named Building Section and Details|TEXT was added to the Definitions to Bind list.

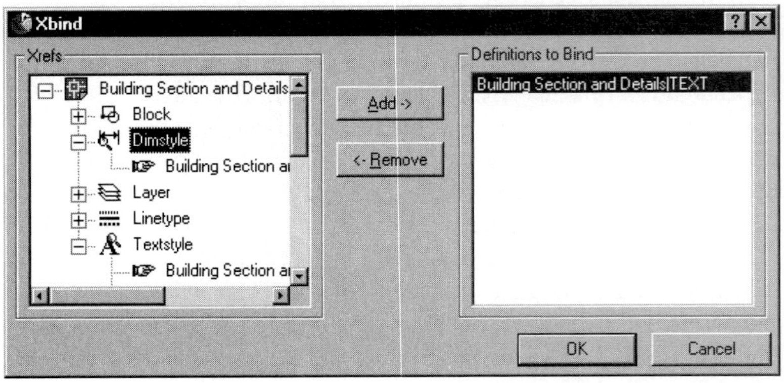

FIGURE 12.59 The Xbind dialog box provides an intuitive interface for making Xref dependent symbols available in the current drawing session.

The binding process makes a dependent symbol a permanent part of the current drawing, even if the Xref is later detached. If the bound symbol is a layer, that layer becomes available for use. If the bound symbol is a block, the block becomes defined in the current drawing and is then available for insertion. Text styles, dimension styles, and linetypes can be made current and used as needed.

The previously dependent layer is now renamed Building Section and Details0TEXT in the current drawing. This does not affect the source file for the external reference. Additionally, the next time you resolve the Xref by either opening the current drawing or reloading the Xref, the previously assigned name is again listed in any inquiries you make. So, for example, after binding the layer just as shown and reloading the Xref, both layer names Building Section and Details|Text and Building Section and Details0Text now exist.

Figure 12.60 shows the text screen of AutoCAD LT with a listing of the defined blocks displayed. The listing shows that the Xref named Building Section and Details is still externally referenced, and the dependent symbols are appropriately labeled. In this case, the entire external reference named Church Pew Layout has been bound and all its dependent symbols have been defined in the current drawing. Any of the items not listed as Xref (External Reference) or Xdep (Externally dependent) are now defined as blocks in the current drawing.

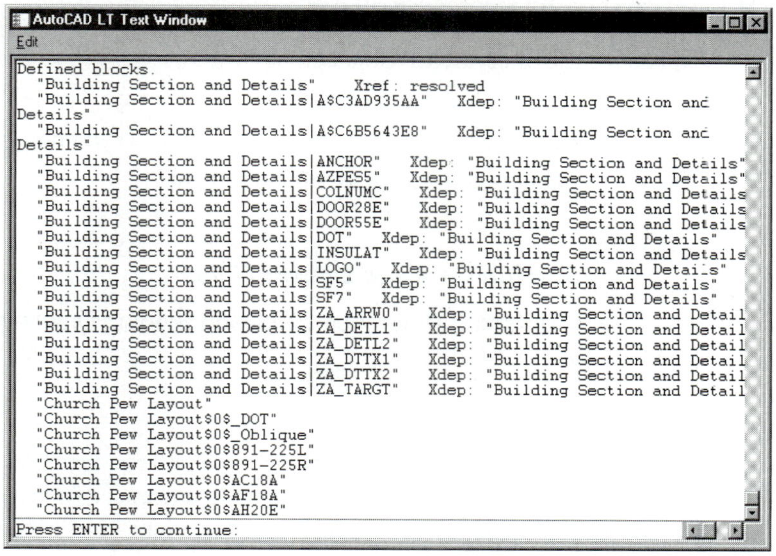

FIGURE 12.60 Once a dependent symbol is bound, AutoCAD LT changes its name and makes it available in the drawing in which it is bound.

Field Notes

- When a particular dimension style, layering convention, text style, linetype, or block definition exists in another drawing, it can be quickly and easily defined in the current drawing even if you do not need to reference the drawing for any other reason. Here's how:

  1. XREF (Attach OR Overlay) the source drawing. Use the default settings.
  2. XBIND the needed items into the current drawing.
  3. XREF Detach the drawing.

  Now, the items you need are defined in the current drawing without unneeded overhead generated by inserting drawings.
- Whether listing blocks, text styles, or another dependent symbol, you can focus your search by specifying a pattern using the Xref name followed by an asterisk. For example, to list dependent symbols of XREF1 at the search prompt, use the following search pattern:

  XREF1|*
- Binding dependent symbols leaves them with long and cumbersome names. The RENAME command can be used to remove the unnecessary part of the name.

Exercise 12.18 — Estimated time required: 8 min.

1. Start a new drawing.
2. Examine the current setup layers, text styles, dimension styles, blocks, and linetypes.
3. Use XREF Attach to \AutoCAD LT 2000\SAMPLE\Building Section and Details.DWG.
4. Reexamine the layers, text styles, dimension styles, blocks, and linetypes.
5. Bind the entire Building Section and Details drawing to the current drawing using XREF Bind.
6. Reexamine the layers, text styles, dimension styles, blocks, and linetypes.
7. Use XREF Overlay to overlay \AutoCAD LT 2000\SAMPLE\XREF2.DWG.
8. Use XBIND to bind the Church Pew Layout/Pewchair dependent block.
9. Rename Church Pew Layout/Pew chair to Pewchair1.
10. Save as EX12.18 and close the drawing.

LEARNING CHECKPOINT

- ☐ Explain the use of the XREF Bind option.
- ☐ How does XREF Bind differ from XBIND?
- ☐ What is an advantage of selectively binding dependent symbols?
- ☐ Describe the naming convention for bound symbols.

Sharing Data and Drawing Files

- Updating Reference Links and Binding Drawings to Files

Field Notes

Drawings can be opened, inserted, or externally referenced from a local disk drive, an intranet, or the Internet. Accessing files from the Internet is covered in Chapter 16.

MULTIPLE CHOICE

1. This command allows a collection of any number of regular AutoCAD LT objects to be selected and handled as a single object:
   a. FILE
   b. COLLECTION
   c. GROUP
   d. SHAPE
2. The common name for a group of objects that compose a named definition that is represented in the drawing by a *reference*:
   a. file
   b. group
   c. block
   d. object
3. This command is used to add the answer to question 2 into a drawing:
   a. SYMBOL
   b. INSERT
   c. GROUP
   d. REFERENCE
4. To simplify the process of inserting symbols that may vary in size and proportion, the definition should be based on:
   a. a unit of one
   b. ASME standards
   c. a unit of ten
   d. your intuition
5. A specialized setting for color and linetype that provides the greatest flexibility when defining the answer to question 2 is called:
   a. Byblock
   b. Bylayer
   c. Bygosh
   d. Bycolor
6. This is not an available option in the Mode area of the Attribute Definition dialog box:
   a. Invisible
   b. Constant
   c. Off
   d. Preset
7. This variable allows attributes to be entered using a dialog box:
   a. ATTDISP
   b. ATTDIA
   c. ATTREQ
   d. ATTDLG
8. This command displays information from another drawing without adding the objects to the current drawing:
   a. INSERT
   b. INSREF
   c. DISPLAY
   d. XREF
9. This type of the answer to question 8 can be used to prevent circular references:
   a. Overlay
   b. Insertion
   c. Attachment
   d. Orphan
10. This command permanently attaches the information from a referenced file into the current drawing:
    a. XATTACH
    b. XKEEP
    c. XBIND
    d. XREF

MATCHING

Match each term to the correct description by writing the appropriate number in each box at the left.

- ☐ Byblock
- ☐ XREF
- ☐ ATTREQ
- ☐ ATTDIA
- ☐ BMAKE
- ☐ INSERT
- ☐ WBLOCK
- ☐ Constant
- ☐ Verify
- ☐ Preset
- ☐ wmf
- ☐ Tag
- ☐ Nesting
- ☐ XATTACH
- ☐ XBIND

1. Using one block as part of the definition of another block.
2. When ON, displays a dialog box for entering attributes.
3. An attribute with this property does not prompt but can be edited later.
4. Creates a drawing file from a block definition.
5. Permanently adds an Xref to the current drawing.
6. A "handle" with which to select attribute definitions.
7. Controls whether or not attributes prompt the user.
8. Special color setting useful when defining blocks.
9. An attribute with this property does not prompt and cannot be edited later.
10. An attribute with this property prompts twice.
11. This command is used to create a block.
12. This command places a block reference in the drawing.
13. The command that starts the Xref Manager.
14. The Windows Metafile extension.
15. A faster way to attach an Xref.

WORD SCRAMBLE

Unscramble the six scrambled words below, one letter to each square, to form six AutoCAD LT–related words:

RETITATUB

LETIPYEN

NOTSTANC

TRACEXT

MOPRTP

INXBD

Unscramble the circled letters above to form the special answer as suggested by the illustration.

PROJECTS

12.1 Draw the figure below. Create two block definitions as shown, one named BOX and the other ARROW, and create the figure below. Save the drawing as P12.1.

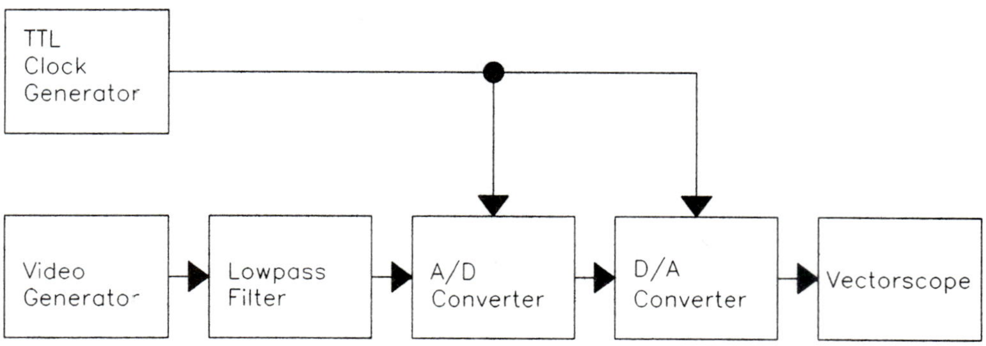

12.2 Create blocks for each of the symbols in the figure below and draw the figure using the new blocks. Save the drawing as P12.2.

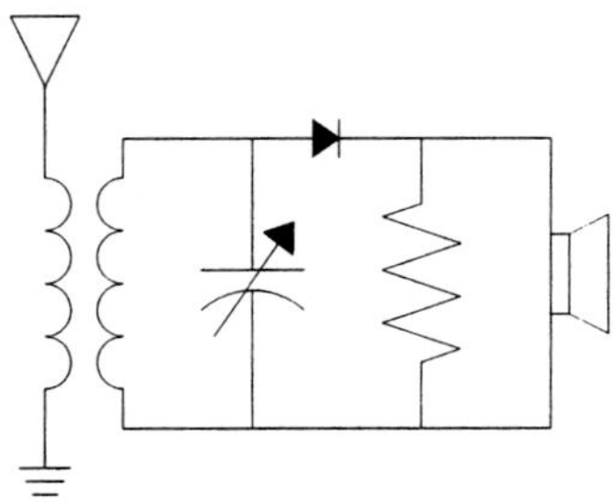

12.3 Create blocks for the doors and each of the legend symbols in the figure below and draw the figure using the new blocks. Save the drawing as P12.3.

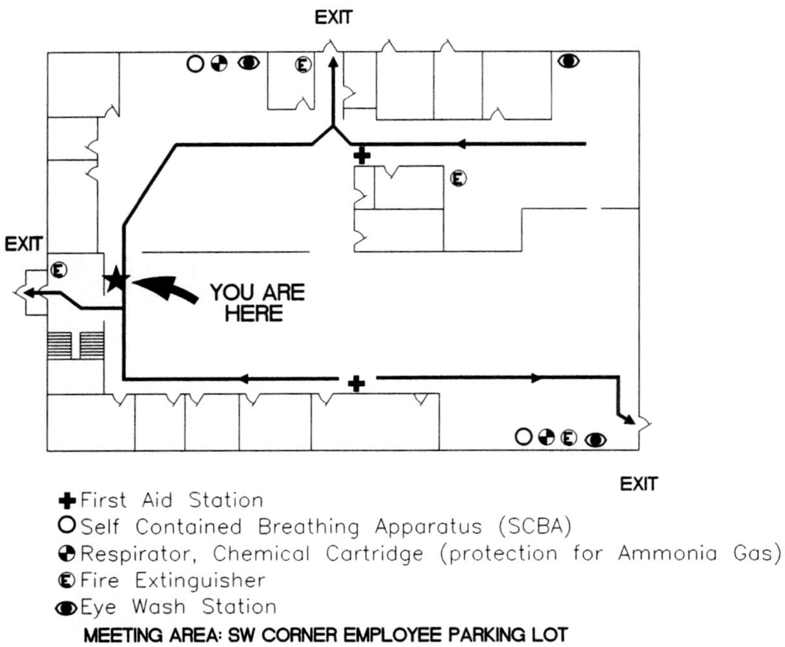

12.4 Create blocks for each of the symbols in the figure below and draw the figure using the new blocks. Save the drawing as P12.4.

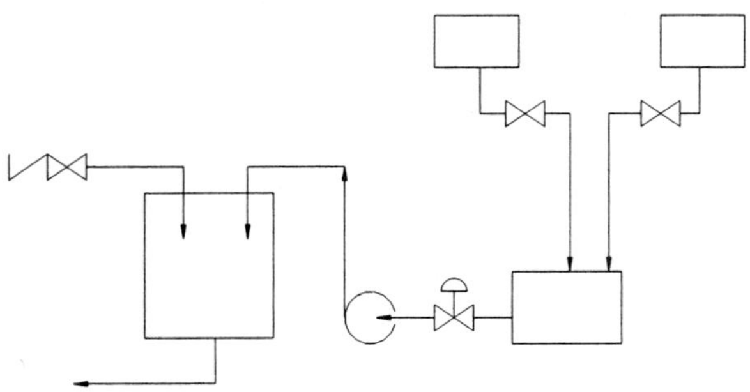

12.5 Create blocks for each of the symbols shown in the figure below using attribute definitions to prompt the user for the appropriate labeling. Use attribute editing to change the orientation of the text, where required. Save the drawing as P12.5.

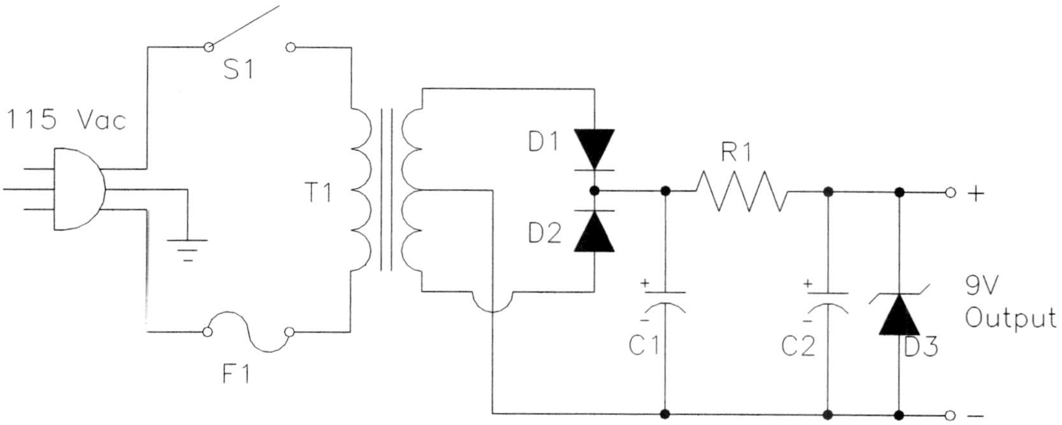

12.6 Create proportionately sized blocks representing office furniture. The symbols you create are to include a standard desk, corner desk, office chair, house plant, 4′ × 8′ table, a computer workstation, printer, and office telephone. Using the blocks, design an office layout suitable for four workstations and a receptionist. Save the drawing as P12.6.

12.7 Create the following block definition with attribute definitions as shown. The block name should be VALVE. When defining the attributes, use the table below as a guide. Save the drawing as P12.7.

TAG	DEFAULT	VERIFY	INVISIBLE	PRESET	CONSTANT
MFGR	ACME				Y
PARTNO	SV112-10	Y			
SIZE	4″		Y	Y	
PRICE	72.00		Y		

12.8 Open a suitable text editor for creating an attribute extraction template file. Use the following as a guide for creating the template file, and save it as P12.8.TXT.

FIELD	CHARACTERS	DECIMAL PLACES
MFGR	8	0
PARTNO	8	0
SIZE	6	0
PRICE	6	2

12.9 Open the drawing P12.7 for editing. Insert the block VALVE in 10 locations within the drawing using differing values in some of the insertions. Extract the attribute values to both a CDF and an SDF file using the template file P12.8. Name the output files P12.9C.TXT and P12.9S.TXT.

12.10 In a new drawing, import one or more of the WMF images if available. Check with your instructor or system administrator for assistance if necessary. Save the drawing as P12.10.

12.11 Start a new drawing, using the Start from Scratch option. Set up the drawing with the following settings:

Layer Name	Color	Linetype
0	BLUE	Continuous
OBJ	WHITE	Continuous
CEN	50	Center
HID	CYAN	Hidden
DIM	RED	Continuous

Text Styles	Properties
Standard Annotation Label	Use three different font files. Assign properties as desired.

Dimension Styles	Properties
Standard	Default properties.
Mechanical Architectural	Assign properties as appropriate for the specific dimension style.

Save the drawing file as P12.11.

12.12 Start a new drawing, using the Start from Scratch option. Using the XREF Attach option, create a reference to P12.11. When prompted to supply a block name, enter **P12-11.** Use the XBIND command to bind all of the named objects shown in the tables in Project 12.11. Use the DDRENAME command to remove the **P12-11$0$** from each symbol name if possible. Save the drawing as P12.12.

12.13 Start a new drawing, using the Start from Scratch option. Attach an external reference to the drawing file P12.11. When prompted to supply a block name, enter **P12-11.** Using XBIND, bind the "Architectural" dimension style. Detach the external reference to P12.11. Use DDRENAME to remove the **P12-11$0$** from the dimension style name. Save this drawing as P12.13.

12.14 Start a new drawing, using the Start from Scratch option. Attach an external reference to the drawing file P12.11. When prompted to supply a block name, enter **P12-11.** Using Layer Control, freeze the layers named P12-11|DIM and P12-11|HID. Set VISRETAIN to 1, and save the drawing as P12.14. Reopen the drawing file to be sure that the visibility changes have been retained.

12.15 Start a new drawing, using the Start from Scratch option. Save the drawing as P12.15. Now, set the variable XREFCTL to 1, in order to generate an Xref log file. Repeat the steps listed in Project 12.12. Turn the Xref log file off by setting XREFCTL to 0. Open the file named P12.15.XLG using Notepad. Exit the XLG file without saving, and save the drawing file as P12.15.

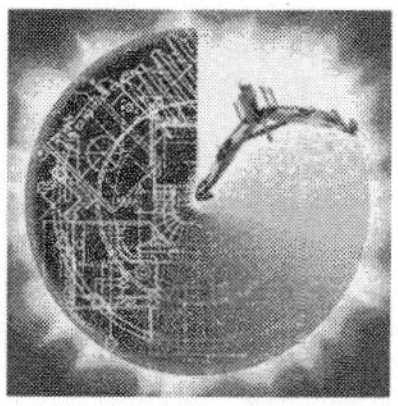

CHAPTER 13

Multiview Drawing Layout, Plotting, and Plot Styles

LEARNING GOALS

- Create and manage drawing layouts
- Set up and control layout viewports
- Control individual viewport layer visibility
- Manage linetype, associative hatch pattern, and dimension scales within a layout
- Configure a plotting device
- Plot multiview layouts from a layout tab
- Create and edit color-dependent and named plot styles
- Assign plot style tables to match desired plotting standards

Multiview Drawing Layout

While a drawing is being created onscreen, the layout is very flexible because you can use display change options such as Pan and Zoom to view any portion of the drawing you need to see. All the geometry you create in a CAD drawing is always drawn on a 1:1 scale. This means that one AutoCAD LT drawing unit represents one real-world measurement unit. You may frequently be drawing objects that are much larger than the paper on which you will be producing your final plotted drawing, particularly if you are doing architectural drafting or any other large-format drawings.

Engineering and architectural drawings often require several views of the part or building you are drawing, and these views are usually presented at varying scale factors for the best clarity. On a small mechanical part, an enlarged detail, for example, a 4:1 scale may be needed in order to dimension the part adequately. In an architectural drawing, the floor plan is presented at a specific scale (for example, 1/4″=1′0″). The stair and footer details look better when plotted at a slightly larger scale, such as 1/2″=1′0″. Finally, a title block and border are placed around the completed views and the composite image is plotted at a scale of 1″=1″. The term ***composite*** refers to the combination of views, border, and title block. In a manual drawing, the final composite image must be drawn using varied scales. In a CAD drawing all of the geometry is created at full size, but it can be displayed at different scale factors when creating the final multiview layout. The term ***multiview layout*** is used to describe a drawing that shows more than one view of the object drawn. Multiview layouts are commonly used in most drafting disciplines to communicate all of the required information.

Presenting varied views of a drawing at differing scales, all on the same sheet, is achieved using an AutoCAD LT feature known as paper space. ***Paper space*** is a special drawing environment intended only for creating a final layout of your drawing for plotting purposes.

This section discusses the differences in concepts and applications of paper space and model space. The term ***model space*** refers to space where you create the geometry that defines your model, or drawing. Regardless of whether the drawing you are working on is a two-dimensional or a three-dimensional representation of an object, the geometry you create to define the object is referred to as the ***model.***

Model Space Concepts

There are two named spaces in which AutoCAD LT objects can exist, model space and paper space. From the drawing tabs at the bottom of the graphics screen area, select the Model tab to draw in tiled model space. The Model tab is current by default when you start a drawing using a Wizard or from scratch. Model space provides a three-dimensional coordinate system and a practically unlimited area for the construction of two- and three-dimensional drawings of objects that can be virtually any size. Although you can draw many types of objects in paper space, the drawing model should be created within model space. In addition to allowing for more flexibility when generating the final drawing layout, model space offers some distinct advantages when creating a drawing.

When working in model space, you have access to some commands and options that are not available in paper space. For example, AutoCAD LT does not allow three-dimensional display change commands to be used in paper space. Three-dimensional display changes are discussed in Chapter 14. The UCSFOLLOW system variable is ignored when paper space is active.

All of the drawing exercises and problems you have done so far have been done in model space. When you start a new drawing from scratch, using quick setup or either of the wizards, you automatically start out in model space. This makes sense, because your first task is usually to draw the model; then you annotate and plot it later.

Most of the supplied templates start you out in a drawing layout (paper space). Although it is possible to work in model space while paper space is still visible, it can be a waste of valuable screen space to the have paper space layout visible while you are still creating your model. It is recommended that you simply work in model space until it is time to work on the final layout of your drawing, or time to create a hardcopy image.

Although it is possible to have multiple layout tabs, there is only one Model tab in each drawing. The Model tab cannot be copied, moved, renamed, or deleted. When model space is accessed from the Model tab, it is considered to be ***tiled model space***. This is because the viewports created in the Model tab are displayed in a tiled arrangement, edges touching with no gaps or overlapping. Tiled model space viewports were introduced in Chapter 4 and are discussed fully in Chapter 14.

Paper Space Concepts

When the model is complete, it is time to enter paper space and do the drawing layout. Paper space is accessed by picking one of the drawing layout tabs. Because AutoCAD LT provides automatic scaling features for dimensions, it is usually a good idea to wait until after you complete the layout to finish dimensioning the part.

As previously discussed, the primary function of paper space is to provide an area to set up the drawing layout and generate a plotted hardcopy. Essentially, paper space is used to represent the "paper" on which you lay out your views, set up a title block, and provide the appropriate annotation after completing the actual model. Consider placing an object on your desk and then holding a sheet of paper in front of the object. You would not be able to see the object through the paper. This is the case with paper space also. When you enter paper space, you can no longer see your model, because you have placed a sheet of "paper" between you and the drawing. To see the object on your desk you need to cut a hole in the paper that you can look through to see the model. In paper space, you can create "holes" called ***layout viewports*** that look through the "paper" into model space. Figure 13.1 demonstrates this concept.

Each viewport can display the same or different views of model space. Varied scale factors can be used. In the case of a 3-D drawing, you can even set up each viewport to look at the model from a different 3-D viewing angle. Additionally, layer visibility can be controlled for individual viewports so that some view-

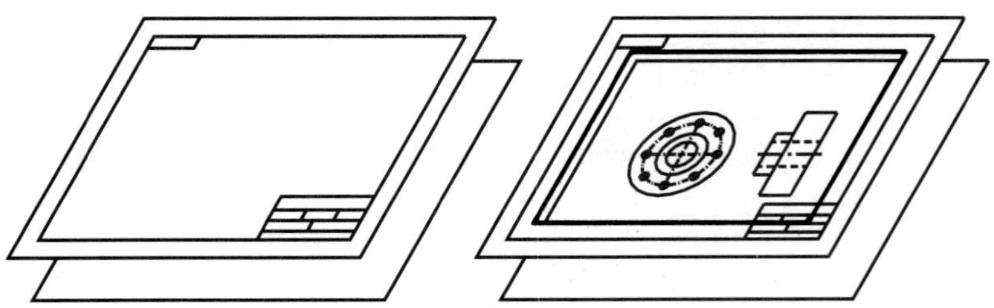

FIGURE 13.1 Paper space is where you create a drawing layout for plotting purposes. To see through the "paper" (the layout tab) into the model space, "holes" called *layout viewports* are cut from the paper.

ports only display objects on specific layers. The use and control of floating model space viewports as part of designing an effective drawing layout is discussed later in this chapter.

You can have multiple layout tabs in a drawing to meet all your plotting needs for any given project. Most drafting projects have multiple applications for prints. For example, in a mechanical application where a mechanical part drawing is created, a drafter might set up one layout tab for generating quick check prints on a small format printer with no title block. Another layout might be set up for generating full-size dimensioned prints on a large-format plotter, to be supplied to the project engineer or drawing checker. A smaller layout might be used to generate a half-scale dimensioned print for easier handling on the shop floor, and the sales department might prefer nondimensioned drawings produced on a color printer for presentation purposes.

Architectural drafting projects often require individual prints for each of the many different aspects of a single drawing. To simplify the print requirements in such a project, any needed number of layouts can be created. An architectural drawing might utilize an individual layout for each of these applications: Plot Plan, Foundation Plan, 1st Floor Plan, 2nd Floor Plan, Basement Plan, HVAC, Roof Plan, Electrical Layout, Plumbing Layout, Reflected Ceiling Plan, and any other layouts necessary to meet printing requirements.

A piping drawing might have one layout for each floor of a building. A mechanical assembly drawing might have one layout showing the full assembly, and individual layouts for each of the assembly components. Using multiple layouts increases the versatility and usefulness of a drawing. Even so, in some projects you will need to create only a single layout. Whatever your specific needs for any project, it is important to understand how to create and use drawing layouts effectively.

Laying Out Your Drawing

Each layout in a drawing is set up to use a specific printing device and provides paper size options that are supported by the selected printer or plotter. A layout is initially set up by specifying the paper size to use, plot style, and any desired plotting parameters. You can then define what areas of the drawing are printed and at what scale, how the views are arranged on the sheet, and what layers are visible in each view. For many applications, you will also place a border and title block on the paper. This section covers setup, editing, and management of drawing layouts in an AutoCAD LT drawing.

Initial Page Setup

Once you have completed the drawing model in the Model tab, it is time to begin setting up the needed layouts. When a drawing is started from scratch or a setup wizard is used to begin the drawing, the available tabs are the Model, Layout1, and Layout2 tabs. Figure 13.2 shows these default drawing tabs with the Model tab currently active.

Layout
Page Setup
File
Page Setup...
PAGESETUP

To begin setting up a layout, pick the desired layout tab. This activates the selected tab; if the layout has not yet been defined, the Page Setup dialog box is displayed. The Page Setup dialog box has two tabs, described in the following discussion. The Plot Device tab is used to select and configure the desired plotting device and to select a plot style table to use (see Figure 13.3). The Layout Settings tab is where the plot parameters, paper size, and other settings are defined.

FIGURE 13.2 A drawing started from scratch or using a setup wizard shows the Model, Layout1, and Layout2 tabs by default.

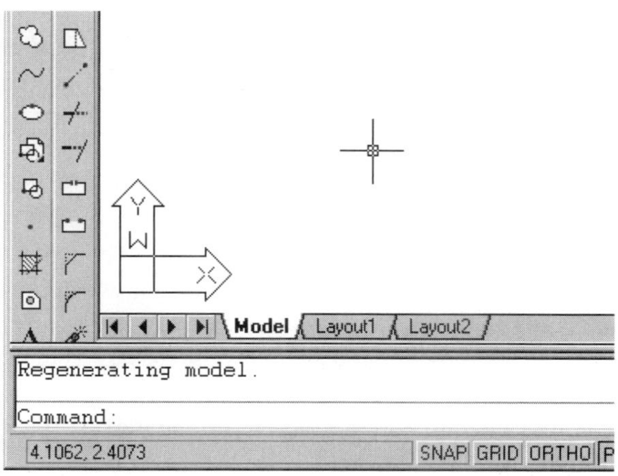

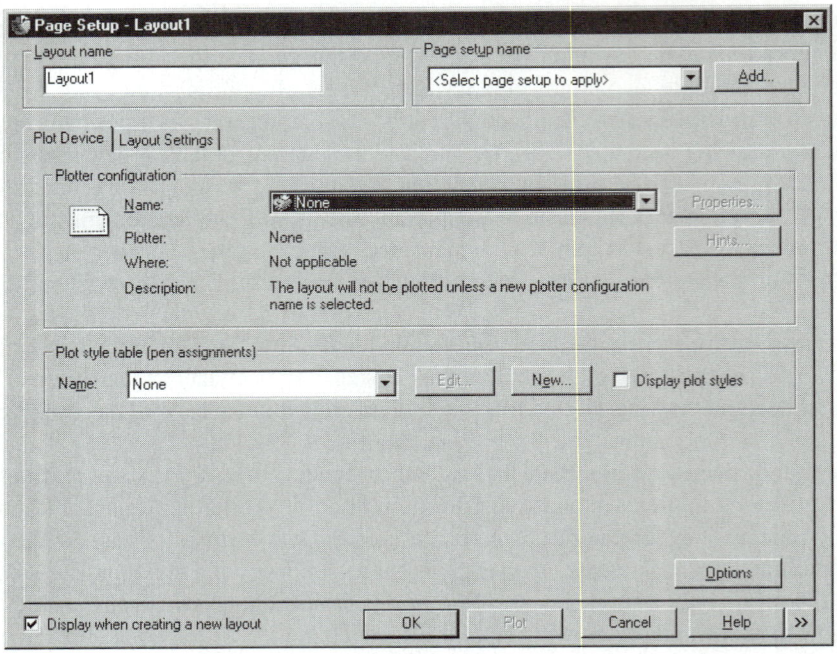

FIGURE 13.3 The Plot Device tab in the Page Setup dialog box is used to select the printer or plotter and specify a plot style table to use.

Field Notes

If the Page Setup dialog box is not displayed when you pick the Layout1 tab, you can start the PAGESETUP command by one of the following methods:

1. Right-click on the layout tab and pick the Page Setup… option from the shortcut menu.
2. Pick Page Setup… from the File pull-down menu.
3. Type **PAGESETUP** at the Command: prompt

In the Page Setup dialog box, use the check box in the lower left corner labeled "Display when creating a new layout" to control whether this dialog is displayed automatically when you pick a layout tab for the first time.

If your screen resolution is set to 1024 × 768 or higher, the Page Setup and Plot dialog boxes display a small button at the lower right corner with two arrows pointing right. Pick this button to expand the dialog box and display a window area with a dynamic help system. This area dynamically displays information about the feature to which your cursor is currently pointing. The window area uses the standard hypertext interface used by the on-line help system. Pick a more… link to display additional information on a topic, as shown in Figure 13.4A. As you move your cursor in the Page Setup dialog box the window continuously updates to show information about the feature you are currently using or to which you are pointing (see Figure 13.4B). If your screen resolution is set to 800 × 600, this button does not appear in the dialog box. At this resolution you can still get limited help information by picking the question mark button on the title bar of the Page Setup dialog box and picking the desired feature. Appendix A has a tutorial to help you set the screen resolution on your computer if you need assistance.

At the top of the Page Setup dialog box is the Layout name text box, where you can specify a desired layout name. Although you can leave the name as the default, Layout1, it is best to rename it. By establishing a unique name, it is easier to access this resource in other drawings using AutoCAD DesignCenter. If the name is left as Layout1, it cannot be accessed from a drawing where the default layout of the same name is still present. A layout name should be short and descriptive, to make it easily recognizable.

The Page setup name list provides access to any saved page setups available in the drawing. Like text and dimension styles, page setups can be saved with a name so they can be reused whenever needed. Additionally, these pages setups can be imported from existing drawings. Working with named page setups is discussed later in this chapter.

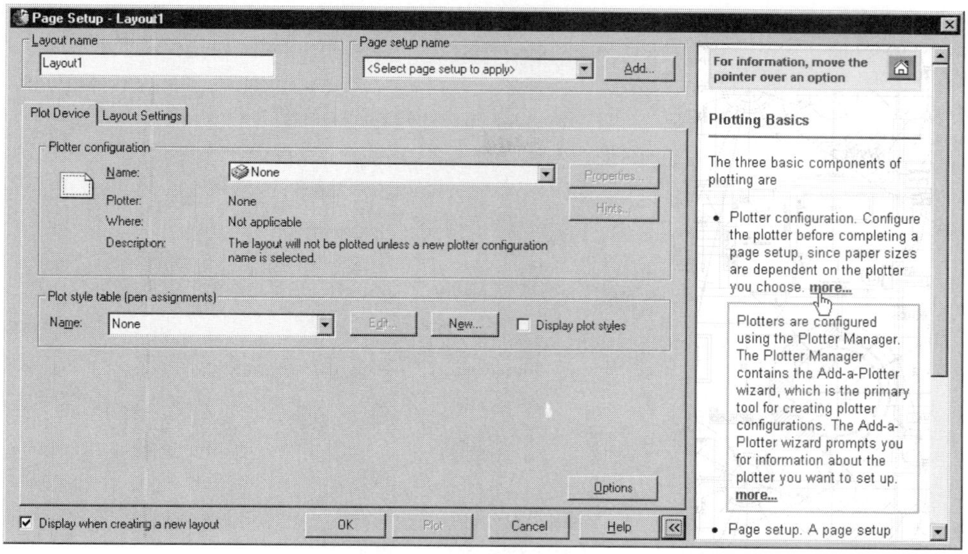

A

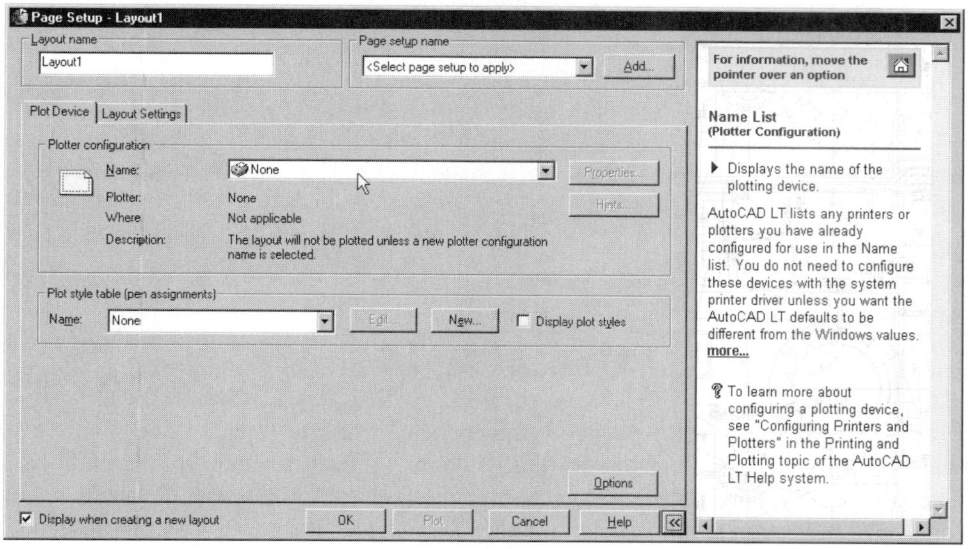

B

FIGURE 13.4 (A) The Page Setup dialog box expands to show a dynamic help window. (B) When you move your cursor, the help window updates to show information on each feature to which you point.

The Plotter configuration area at the top of the Plot Device tab is where you select a printer or plotter from the list of currently available devices. Any printers or plotters that you have access to through Windows are displayed in the drop-down list. You can select any available device, or if you want to specify the device later, you can use select None from the list. When a device is selected from the list, information about the device is displayed below the list. The Properties... and Hints... buttons can now be used to set up the device or to get more information. Picking Properties... displays the Device and Document Settings tab on the Plotter Configuration Editor dialog box shown in Figure 13.5. The device settings are the current defaults as used by Windows and usually do not require adjustment. The User-defined Paper Sizes & Calibration category allows you to modify standard paper sizes to your standards, set up a custom paper size that does not exist, and to calibrate your printer or plotter. The Plotter Calibration option plots a rectangle at a specified size. You measure and input the actual size of the rectangle, and AutoCAD LT then adjusts all future plots on this device based on this information. Additional discussion on configuring plotters is provided later in this chapter. Picking the Hints... button in the Page Setup dialog box displays a help window with additional information about the currently selected printer driver.

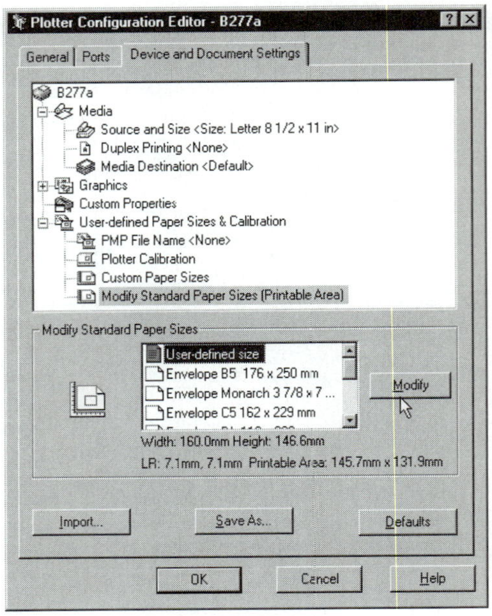

FIGURE 13.5 The Plotter Configuration Editor can be used to fine-tune the settings of your printer or plotter and to modify the printable area of standard paper sizes or to define custom paper sizes.

The Plot style table (pen assignments) area in the Page Setup dialog box is where the desired plot style table is selected. A plot style table determines how drawing objects are plotted. When a plot style table is selected, the Edit... button becomes active. Creating and editing plot style tables is discussed later in this chapter. Place a check in the Display plot styles check box if you want the layout tab to display its contents based on the active plot style.

Field Notes

- When a drawing is started from scratch or with a wizard, AutoCAD LT's initial default is a color-dependent plot style.
- Which plot style table you should use depends on your application and the capabilities of your printing device. If you are using a monochrome (black ink only) printer or plotter, you should use the *monochrome.ctb* plot style table or, if you prefer, the *Grayscale.ctb* option. If you are using a color printer and want to print in color, use the *acad.ctb* plot style table. Later in this chapter you will learn to create, edit, and use custom plot style tables to meet your specific needs.

Use the Options button to display the Plotting tab of the Options dialog box, where plotting options can be configured. This is where default values for many of the plot settings are set. Specifying default plot settings and configuring plotters is discussed later in this chapter.

The Layout Settings tab is where paper size, plotting scale, and other options are specified. The Layout Settings tab is shown in Figure 13.6. The Paper size and paper units area shows the currently selected Plot device and the paper size. Use the Paper size: list to select from any paper size supported by the current plot device. If the current plot device is None, all standard ANSI and ISO paper sizes are available for selection. You can also select from Letter size or Legal size paper, or from additional options specified in pixel sizes. The Printable area: setting determines whether layout units represent inches or millimeters. Select the appropriate radio button.

For now, the two areas that need to be set up are the Paper size and paper units area and the Drawing orientation area. Other areas can be adjusted as needed when you are ready to plot. Once you have selected a plot device and a plot style table and have set up paper size and orientation, you can pick the OK button to close the Page Setup dialog box and view the layout tab. The layout tab shown in Figure 13.7 has been set up on an "A" size sheet in landscape orientation.

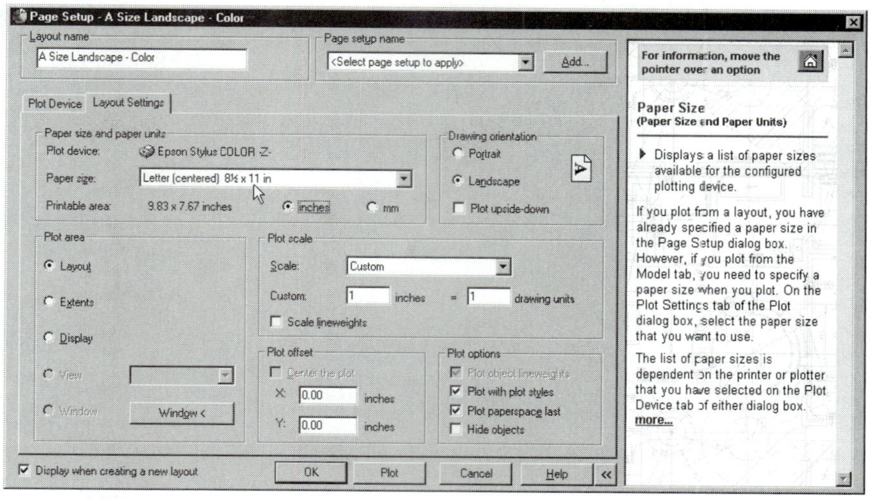

FIGURE 13.6 The Layout Settings tab in the Page Setup dialog box is used to specify paper size and plotting parameters.

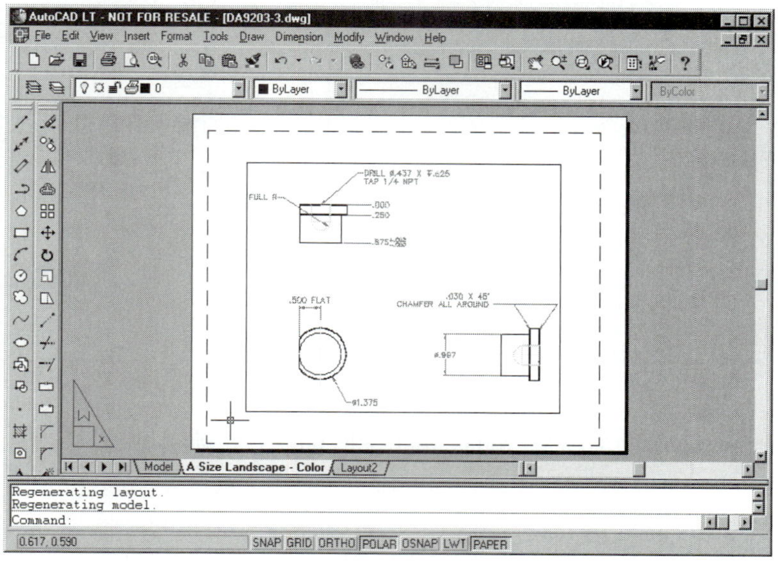

FIGURE 13.7 The specified paper size is represented on the layout, and a single floating viewport is created in the layout. The model space drawing extents are shown in the viewport.

Field Notes

When AutoCAD LT is first installed, the initial default setting for the layout tab background color is black. To change this to white as shown in the illustrations in this chapter, or to any other desired color, access the Options dialog box. On the Display tab, pick the Colors... button to display the Color Options dialog box, where you can change the color used for Layout tabs.

Using the Layout Wizard

Insert
Layout ▸
Layout Wizard
Tools
Wizards ▸
Create Layout...
LAYOUTWIZARD

AutoCAD LT provides the Layout Wizard for automating the creation of drawing layouts. This powerful tool provides an easy-to-use interface that leads you through the setup options found in the Page Setup dialog box. You can access the Layout Wizard by picking Layout Wizard from the Layout cascade on the Insert menu, by picking Create Layout... from the Wizards cascade on the Tools menu, or by typing **LAYOUTWIZARD** at the Command: prompt.

The LAYOUTWIZARD command displays the Create Layout - Begin dialog box, where you name the new layout (see Figure 13.8A). Enter the desired name in the textbox and pick the Next > button to continue. Remember to assign a short and descriptive name.

The next step is to select the plotter that will be used for this layout. This is done in the Create Layout - Printer dialog box, shown in Figure 13.8B. The list shows all plotting devices currently configured on your system, including local and network plotters and printers. Pick the desired device and select the Next > but-

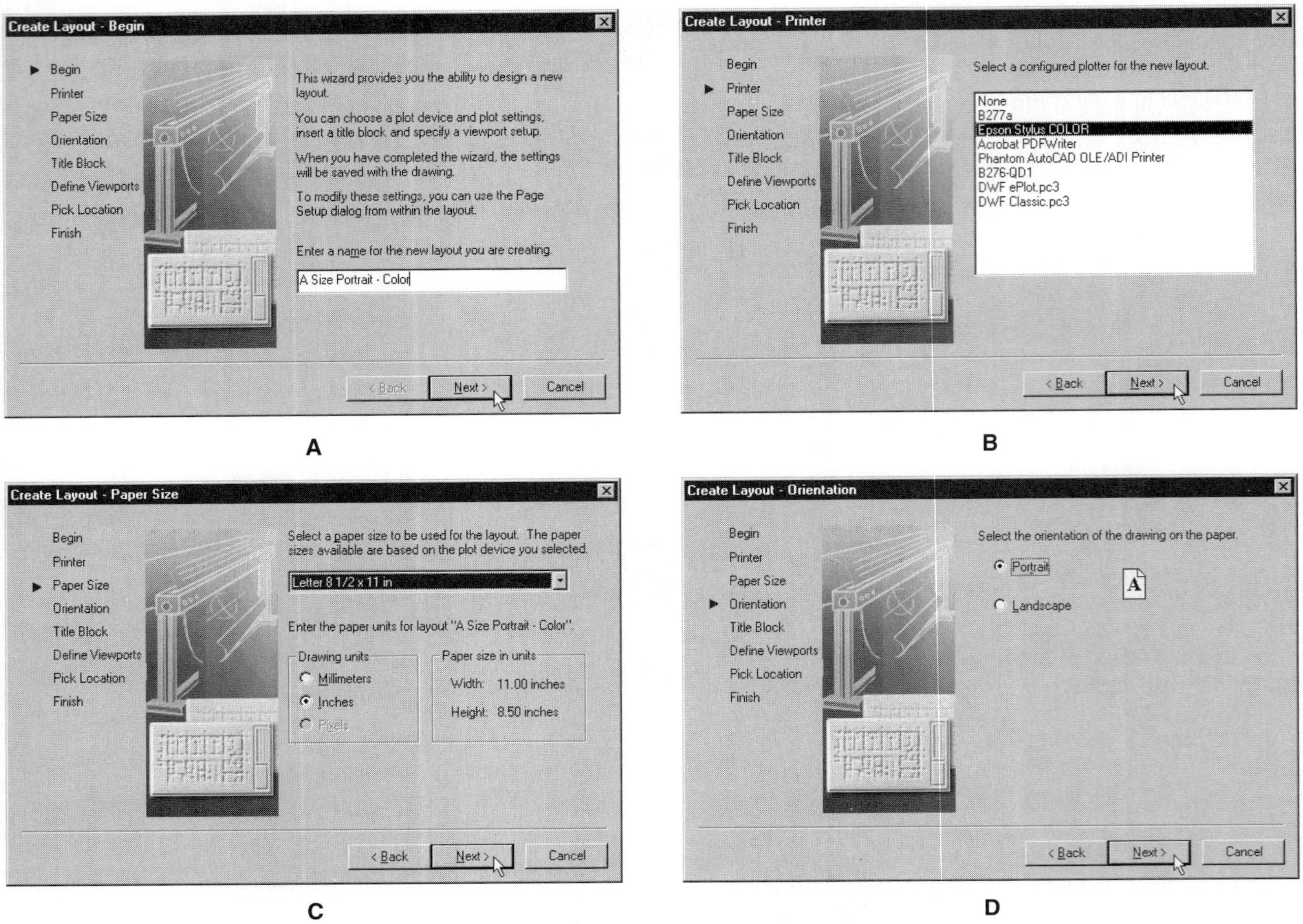

FIGURE 13.8 The Layout Wizard guides you through setting up a drawing layout.

ton. As with the Page Setup dialog box, you can pick None and select a plotting device at a later time. Additionally, if you select a specific plotter, you can still change it later if needed.

Use the Create Layout - Paper Size dialog box to set up the desired paper size (see Figure 13.8C). If you selected a specific plotting device in the previous step, the paper size drop-down list shows all paper sizes supported by the selected device. If you selected the None option, this list offers a selection of standard ANSI, Architectural, and ISO paper sizes. Select the desired layout units in the Drawing units area, and pick the Next > button.

Specify the desired paper orientation in the Create Layout - Orientation dialog box, shown in Figure 13.8D. The available options are either Portrait or Landscape. The image to the right of the radio buttons shows a representation of the current orientation.

The Layout Wizard provides a convenient way to set up a title block, using the Create Layout - Title Block dialog box (see Figure 13.8E). This allows you to select from any of the title block drawings currently found in the AutoCAD LT 2000\Template folder. The default options provided with AutoCAD LT include ANSI, ISO, DIN, and JIS standard title blocks. You can specify whether to insert the title block as a block or to attach it as an external reference.

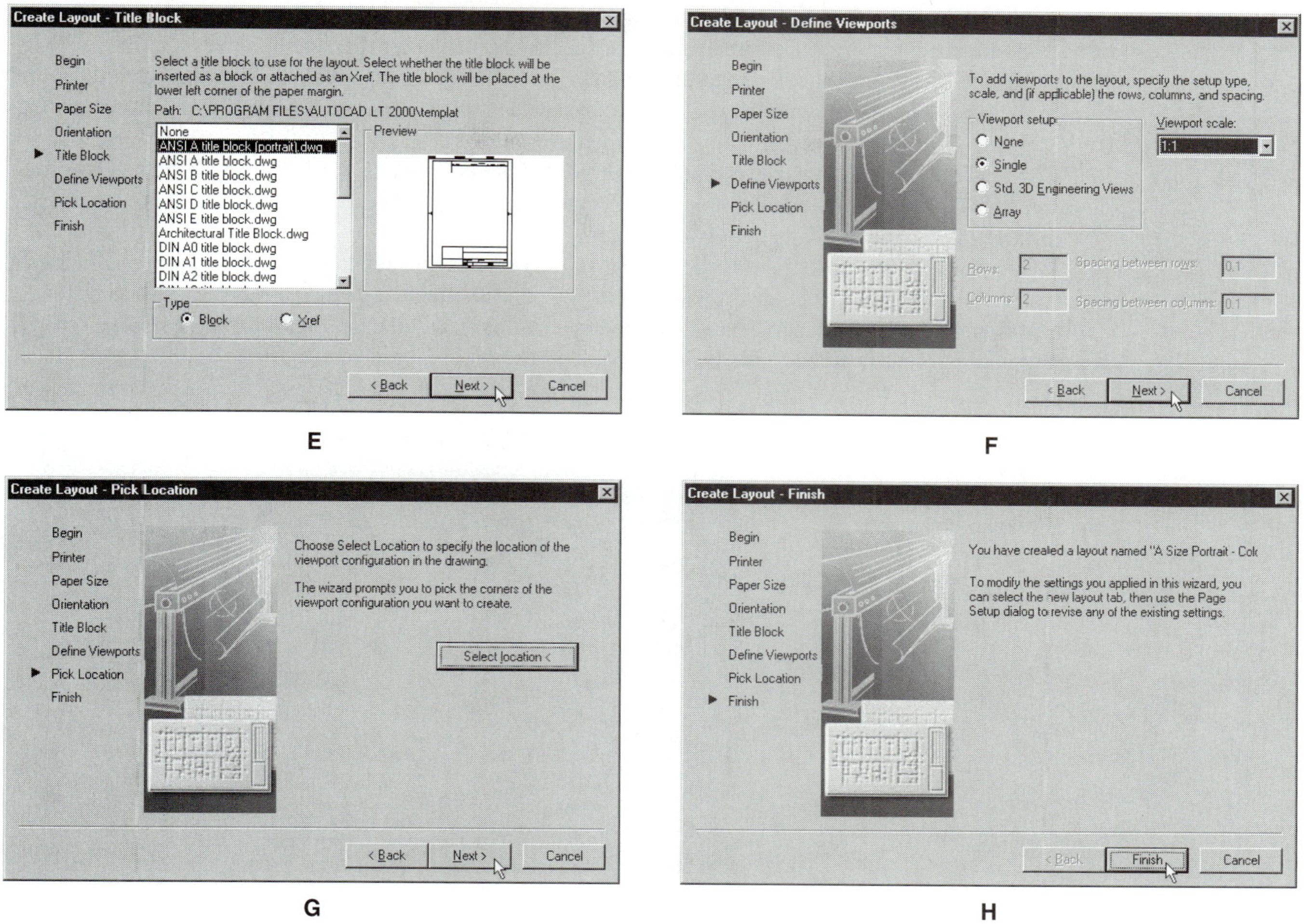

FIGURE 13.8 *continued*

Field Notes

- To access your school or company title blocks using the Layout Wizard, copy the desired drawing files to the AutoCAD LT 2000\Template folder. All drawings in this folder are displayed in the list shown in the Create Layout - Title Block dialog box.
- Block attributes in your customized title block drawings use default values and do not display prompts when the title block is inserted using the Layout Wizard. After completing the Layout Wizard, use the ATTEDIT, or AE, command to edit the default values as needed.

The next dialog box displayed by the wizard is the Create Layout - Define Viewports dialog box (Figure 13.8F). You can select from one of the preset viewport options listed in the Viewport setup area. If none of the preset options meet your needs, or you have not yet decided what the viewport setup should be, use the None option. The Single option is the same as the default used by the PAGESETUP command; this places a single viewport in the layout, sized a little smaller that the paper size. The Std. 3D Engineering Views option creates four viewports based on standard views of a three-dimensional part. The viewports are arranged in an orthographic layout that shows the front, top, and right sides, plus a fourth view showing an isometric view. This option does not work for 2D drawings but simplifies the layout process for a 3D model. Finally, you can create a rectangular Array of viewports, specifying how many rows and columns of viewports to create. If you select an option that creates more than one viewport, you can also specify the spacing between rows and columns of viewports. Creating and working with viewports is covered later in this chapter.

The Create Layout - Pick Location dialog box shown in Figure 13.8G allows you to select a custom area where the specified viewports are created. To specify an area other than the default, pick the Select location < button. The dialog box is temporarily hidden, and you are prompted to pick two corners that define the overall area where the viewports are placed. If you selected the None option in the Create Layout - Define Viewports dialog box, this dialog box is not displayed.

The final dialog box displayed by the Layout Wizard is the Create Layout - Finish dialog box shown in Figure 13.8H. This shows the name of the layout you created and displays information about how to modify these settings later using the Page Setup dialog box.

When you pick the Finish button, the Layout Wizard creates the layout according to your specifications and displays the contents of the new layout tab. If you need to make any changes, you can use the PAGESETUP command at any time. Modifying layout viewports is discussed later. Figure 13.9 shows a layout created using the settings specified in the Layout Wizard as shown in Figure 13.8.

FIGURE 13.9 After completing the Layout Wizard as shown in Figure 13.8, the layout tab is completed and displayed.

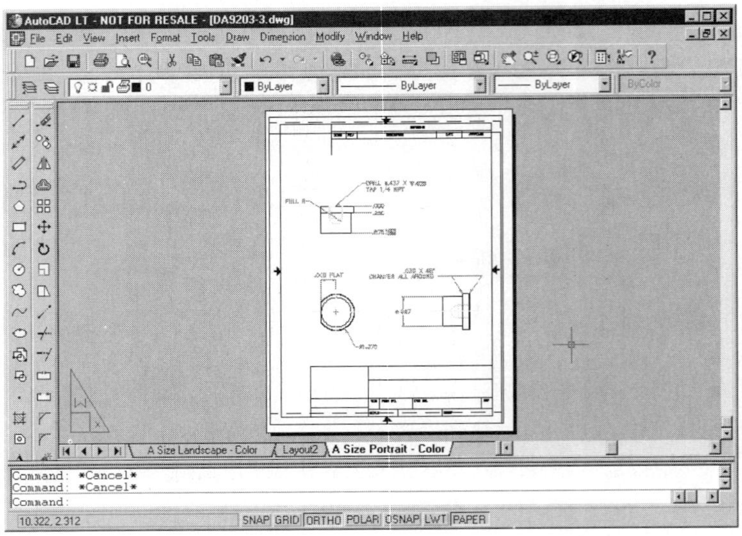

Managing Layouts

To manage your layouts using a text interface on the command line, type **LO** or **LAYOUT** at the Command: prompt. The LAYOUT command provides options to create, copy, delete, and rename layouts as shown here:

Command: **LO** or **LAYOUT**↵
Enter layout option [Copy/Delete/New/Template/Rename/SAveas/Set/?] <set>:

Picking the New Layout button on the Layouts toolbar starts the LAYOUT command and automatically enters the New option. You are then prompted for the layout name as follows:

Command: _-layout
Enter layout option [Copy/Delete/New/Template/Rename/SAveas/Set/?] <set>: _n
Enter new Layout name <Layout1>: ⟨*type a name for the new layout or press* ↵ *to accept the default*⟩

Tools for managing layouts can also be accessed using the layout shortcut menu (see Figure 13.10). Right-click on any layout tab to display this menu with all the options available. Right-clicking on the Model tab displays the same menu, but you cannot rename, move, copy, or delete the Model tab, so these options are disabled. This menu offers easy access to most of the options of the LAYOUT command and provides a more intuitive interface.

FIGURE 13.10 Right-click on any layout tab to display the layout shortcut menu.

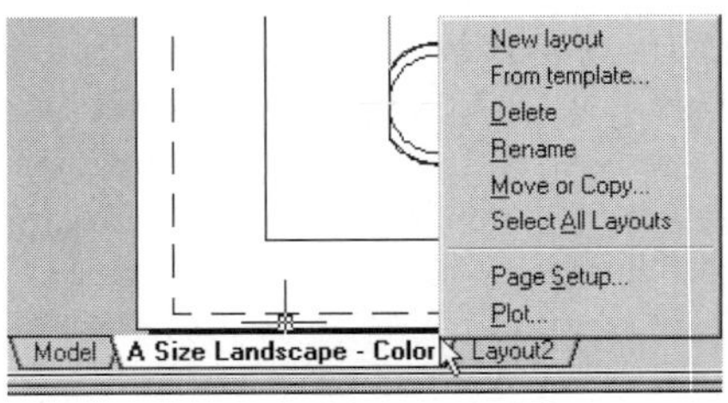

The options available on the layout shortcut menu are described as follows:

- **New Layout** Creates a new layout. The layout is assigned an incrementally numbered default name such as *Layout3*. This option is also available on the Layout cascade of the Insert menu or can be accessed using the New option of the LAYOUT command.
- **From template...** Creates a new layout using settings from a selected existing layout found in a template file. This option also can be accessed by picking Layout from Template... on the Layout cascade of the Insert menu or by using the Template option of the LAYOUT command. Creating a layout from a template is covered later in this chapter.
- **Delete** Deletes the selected layout tab. The dialog box shown in Figure 13.11A is displayed, where you can confirm the deletion or cancel it. You cannot delete the Model tab, and if you delete the last layout tab in a drawing, a new and unmodified Layout1 tab is created.
- **Rename** Displays the Rename Layout dialog box, where you can rename the selected layout tab (see Figure 13.11B). You cannot rename the Model tab.
- **Move or Copy...** Displays the Move or Copy dialog box. Using this dialog box is explained in the following discussion.
- **Select All Layouts** Highlights all layout tabs. As when working with files, you can use the Shift and Ctrl keys in combination with picking to select or deselect one or more tabs.
- **Page Setup** Starts the PAGESETUP... command using the current layout.
- **Plot...** Starts the PLOT command using the current layout.

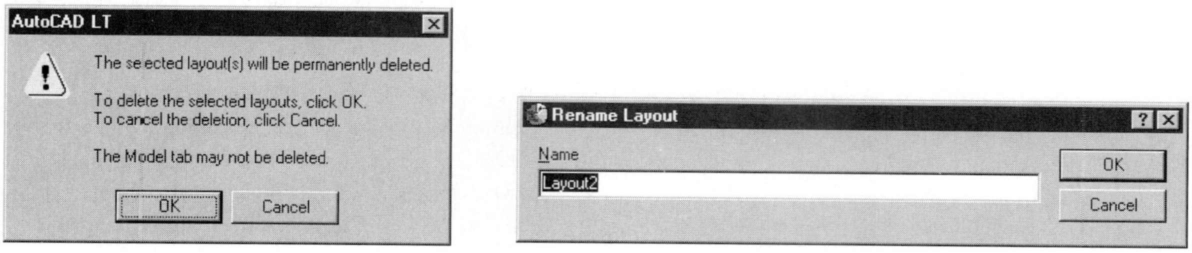

A B

FIGURE 13.11 (A) This warning is displayed when you select the Delete option from the Layout shortcut menu; You can Cancel the deletion or pick OK to confirm. (B) Use the Rename Layout dialog box to rename the selected layout tab.

You can move or copy layouts within a drawing. If a layout already existing in the current drawing uses some or all of the same settings required in a new layout, copy the existing layout and make the needed changes to the new copy. Additionally, you can control the order in which your layout tabs are organized using the Move or Copy... option. This displays the Move or Copy dialog box, as shown in Figure 13.12. The new placement of the selected layouts is specified relative to an existing layout. The existing layout names are displayed in the Before layout list. The selected layouts are placed *before*, or directly to the left of, the layout name selected from the list. Selecting the (move to end) option places the selected layouts at the far right of all other tabs. If multiple tabs are selected for moving, the left-to-right order of the selected layouts is preserved in the new location.

Place a check mark in the Create a copy checkbox to create copies of the selected layouts in the specified location rather than moving the existing layouts. When you copy a layout, a default name is assigned that consists of the name of the original and an incremental number in parentheses. For example, copying a layout named Layout1 creates a new layout named Layout1 (2). Likewise, copying Layout1 (2) creates Layout1 (3).

FIGURE 13.12 The Move or Copy dialog box allows you to rearrange or copy existing layouts.

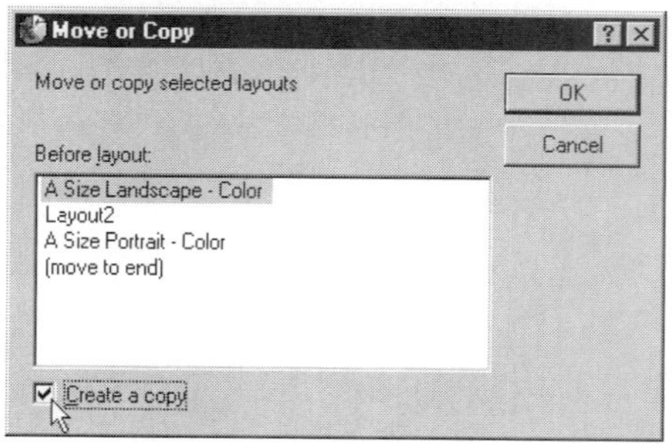

When multiple layouts have been created, there may not be enough room on the screen to display all the layout tabs at the same time. The set of four arrow buttons on the left side of the display tabs are used to move the tab display left or right to show hidden tabs (see Figure 13.13). The two arrow buttons in the middle move the display area one tab at a time in the direction of the arrow. The outside buttons move the display all the way to the left or all the way to the right. Another option is to use the resizing cursor to adjust the size of the horizontal scroll bar area as needed to increase the available tab display space. Point at the vertical bar on the left side of the scroll bar to display the resizing cursor.

FIGURE 13.13 You can display hidden tabs using the arrow buttons, or increase the size of the tab display area by sizing the horizontal scroll bar down.

Exercise 13.1 — Estimated time required: 20 min.

1. Open a completed dimensioned drawing from a previous chapter that uses varied layer and layer color assignments.
2. Pick the tab named Layout1 to display the Page Setup dialog box, or use the PAGESETUP command if necessary.
3. If your screen resolution is 1024 × 768 or higher, pick the button with two right arrows at the lower right corner to display the dynamic help system. Explore the Page Setup dialog box by pointing to features and viewing the dynamic help content.
4. *If your screen resolution is 800 × 600 and you want to increase it, ask your instructor or system administrator for guidance* ***before*** *referring to the tutorial in Appendix A on setting screen resolution. When finished, start again at step 1 of this exercise.*
5. In the Plot Device tab, select a plotter to use for this layout. Ask your instructor or system administrator for assistance if needed.
6. Select the *monochrome.ctb* option from the Name: list in the Plot style table (pen assignments) area.
7. Pick the Layout Settings tab to access its options.
8. Select an appropriate paper size from the Paper size: list, and specify paper units as either inches or millimeters as appropriate. Select either Portrait or Landscape orientation as desired.
9. Pick OK and view the layout. Right-click on the Layout1 tab and pick Page Setup... from the shortcut menu. On the Plot Device tab, place a check mark in the box labeled Display plot styles. Pick OK and view the changes to the layout.
10. Right-click on the Layout1 tab and pick Rename from the shortcut menu. Rename the layout *Monochrome*.
11. Start the Layout Wizard using any desired method.
12. Using the Layout Wizard, set up two different layouts using any appropriate layout options.
13. Delete the layout named Layout2 from your drawing.
14. Copy the *Monochrome* layout using the Move and Copy dialog box. Keep the default layout name for the new copy.
15. Save as EX13.1.dwg.
16. Use SAVEAS to save the drawing as a template file named EX13.1.dwt and close the drawing.

LEARNING CHECKPOINT

- ☐ How can the Page Setup dialog box be accessed if it is not displayed automatically when you pick a layout tab? Which setting in the Page Setup dialog box controls this behavior?
- ☐ What screen resolution is required for the dynamic help window to be available in the Page Setup dialog box?
- ☐ What option in the Name: list in the Plotter configuration area of the Plot Device tab allows you to specify a plotter later?
- ☐ What plot style table is recommended when using a plotting device that has only black ink?
- ☐ Which option displays the layout exactly as it will be plotted based on the current plot style?
- ☐ Name the settings that should be made in the Layout settings tab when first defining a new layout.
- ☐ Describe three ways to access the Layout Wizard tool. Discuss the advantages of using the Layout Wizard to create a new layout.

Laying Out Drawings

- Creating a New Drawing Layout

Concept Animations

- Layouts

Layout Templates

One or more defined drawing layouts can be saved in custom drawing templates, as is done with other drawing elements like layer settings, text styles, and dimension styles. Unfortunately, you do not always know what size layout will be needed when you are initially starting a drawing project. It is possible to define all your standard layouts in each of your standard templates and just delete any that are unused when the drawing and all required layouts are complete. However, it is not always practical to define all your standard layouts in a template file that is used to begin your drawings. If a title block drawing is inserted into each layout, this can increase the size of your drawing unnecessarily. For most applications, the best option is to save drawing templates and layout templates as separate files.

Various drawing templates can be created and used to store standardized drawing settings such as layer settings, text and dimension styles, and other required drawing content. Use an appropriate template when beginning each new drawing to save setup time and ensure consistent implementation of required drafting standards.

Layout templates are created and used to store commonly used standard drawing layouts; a template file can contain any number of layouts. Each individual layout template file should store only related layouts that are based on particular applications or specific sets of drafting standards. When you complete a drawing and are ready to define a layout, you can import predefined layout settings from an appropriate layout template file.

Creating a Template from a Layout

The LAYOUT command allows you to save a template file that contains the definition for a single selected layout. When your drawing is complete, create a desired drawing layout using either the Page Setup dialog box or the Layout Wizard. Next, start the LAYOUT command by typing **LO** or **LAYOUT** at the Command: prompt. Use the SAveas option to create a new template file that contains a specified layout as defined in the current drawing:

Command: **LO** or **LAYOUT** ↵
Enter layout option [Copy/Delete/New/Template/Rename/SAveas/Set/?] <set>: **SA** ↵
Enter layout to save to template <A Size Portrait - Color>: ↵
Command:

At the "Enter layout to save to template <*current*>:" prompt, enter the name of the layout to save or press Enter to save the current layout shown as the default. If the name that you enter does not match the name of a defined layout in the current drawing, the following message is displayed:

Layout *"nosuch"* does not exist.

If a valid layout name is specified, the Create Drawing File dialog box is displayed with the default option in the Save as type: list specified as Drawing Template File (*.dwt) (see Figure 13.14). You may elect to save the file as a drawing if desired. The currently open folder is the configured template folder location based on the settings in the Files tab of the Options dialog box. You can specify a file name that matches the name of the layout or enter a different name if desired. Pick the Save button to save the new template file. The Model tab in the resulting template file is empty, and the only layout tab created is the one that was saved to the template. It has the same name and properties as the original layout, including plot device, plot style, and plot settings. Named object definitions such as layers and text styles are saved in the new layout template only if they are referenced (current or in use). A template created from a layout does not save a drawing preview.

The SAveas option of the LAYOUT command provides a convenient way to save a single layout in a template file, but using this method requires that you create an individual template for each different layout that you want to save. Creating templates that store multiple layouts is covered later in this chapter.

The SAVEAS command can also be used to create a template from the current drawing, but this method saves all aspects of the drawing in the new template file, including the contents of model space and all named object definitions. Using the SAVEAS command also changes the name, location, and file type of the current drawing.

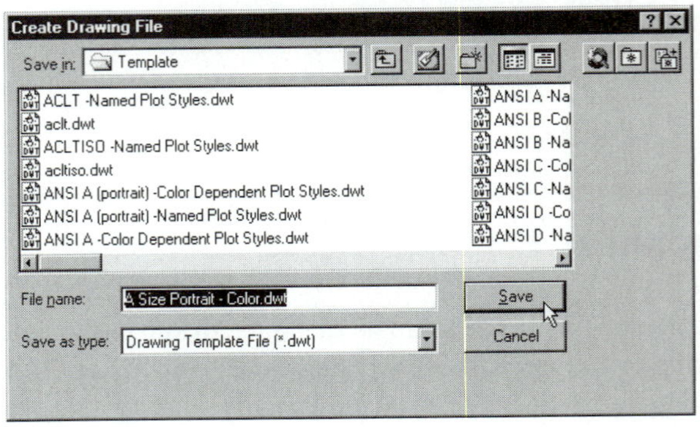

FIGURE 13.14 Specify a template file name in which to save a layout using the Create Drawing File dialog box.

Field Notes

You can change the default location where AutoCAD LT saves and looks for template files using the Files tab of the Options dialog box. In the "Search paths, file names, and file locations:" list, expand the Drawing Template File Location folder and pick the current path name (1). Pick the Browse... button (2) to display the Browse for Folder dialog box, where you can locate and select the desired folder location (3) (see Figure 13.15).

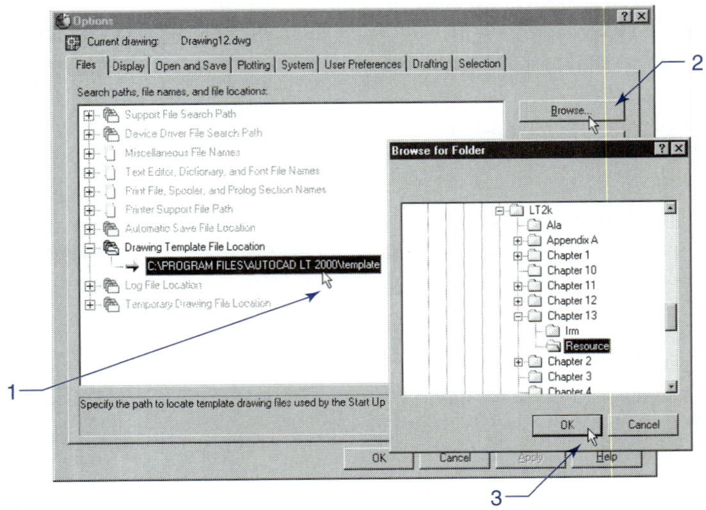

FIGURE 13.15 Change the default template file using the Browse for Folder dialog box.

Creating a Layout from a Template

When you have completed your drawing and are ready to create a layout, you can import layout settings from a template file. To create a layout from a template using the Command line interface, start the LAYOUT command and use the Template option:

Layout
Layout from Template
Insert
Layout ▸
Layout from
Template...
LAYOUT
LO

Command: **LO** or **LAYOUT** ↵
Enter layout option [Copy/Delete/New/Template/Rename/SAveas/Set/?] <set>: **T** ↵

The Select File dialog box is displayed, showing the files in the default template folder. Double-click on the desired template file name, or select a file and pick the Open button. This opens the selected template and returns you to the command line. At the "Enter layout name(s) or [?]:" prompt, enter a question mark to see a listing of the available layouts on the AutoCAD LT text screen. To import a selected layout, enter the layout name at the prompt, as shown in the following sequence:

Enter layout name(s) or [?]: **?**↵

Layout(s) in drawing:
A Size Portrait - Color
Enter layout name(s) or [?]: **A Size Portrait - Color** ↵
Command:

An easy way to enter a layout name and avoid typographical errors is to use your cursor to highlight the desired layout name, then right-click on the highlighted text and pick Paste To CmdLine from the shortcut menu.

You can use a more intuitive dialog box interface by right-clicking on a drawing tab and picking the From template... option from the Layout shortcut menu, or by picking Layout from Template... from the Layout cascade on the Insert menu. This method also displays the Select File dialog box for picking the desired template file. After a template is selected, the Insert Layout(s) dialog box is displayed. You can select one or more layouts to insert into the current drawing in a single operation. Use the Shift and Ctrl keys in combination with picking to select multiple layouts. The Insert Layout(s) dialog box is shown in Figure 13.16.

FIGURE 13.16 The Insert Layout(s) dialog box provides a more flexible interface than the command line. You can select one or more layouts to insert into the current drawing.

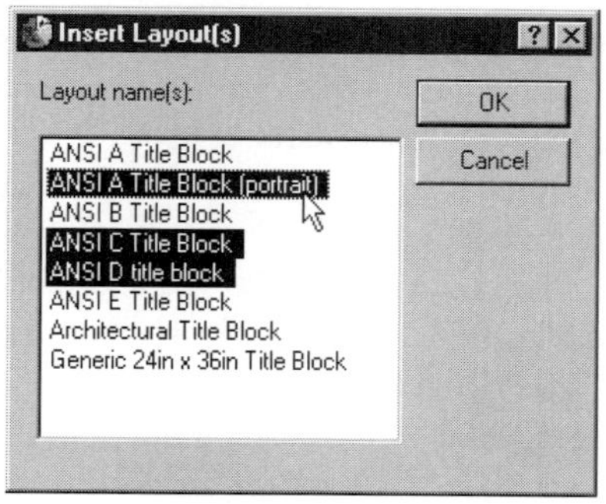

The templates supplied with the AutoCAD LT software include an assortment of files that contain single viewport layouts based on several industry standards, including ANSI, ISO, DIN, and JIS. These layouts use appropriate title blocks and standard sheet sizes, but the plotting device and plot style are set to None. The predefined Layout Settings use generic settings. You can open these files and customize the existing layouts as needed to meet your needs.

For convenient access, the available layouts are divided into two general categories: *ANSI Layouts* and *Metric Layouts*. All the inch-based predefined drawing layouts are found in the file ANSI Layout templates.dwt located in the AutoCAD LT 2000\Template folder. The file named Metric Layout templates.dwt, also found in this folder, contains all the metric-based predefined drawing layouts. The layouts available in these files are shown in Table 13.1.

TABLE 13.1

ANSI Layout templates.dwt	Metric Layout templates.dwt
ANSI A title block	DIN A0 title block
ANSI A title block (portrait)	DIN A1 title block
ANSI B title block	DIN A2 title block
ANSI C title block	DIN A3 title block
ANSI D title block	DIN A4 title block
ANSI E title block	ISO A0 title block
Architectural Title Block	ISO A1 title block
Generic 24in × 36in Title Block	ISO A2 title block
	ISO A3 title block
	ISO A4 title block (portrait)
	JIS A0 title block
	JIS A1 title block
	JIS A2 title block
	JIS A3 title block
	JIS A4 title block (landscape)
	JIS A4 title block (portrait)

Copying Layouts Using AutoCAD DesignCenter

Layouts, blocks, and drawings are named objects that can be copied from existing drawings by dragging and dropping them from AutoCAD DesignCenter. Open the DesignCenter window by picking the AutoCAD DesignCenter toolbar button, by picking AutoCAD DesignCenter from the Tools menu, by typing **ADC** at the Command: prompt, or by using the accelerator keystroke Ctrl+2. To copy a layout from an existing drawing, first locate the existing drawing in the Tree View pane and double-click on it, or pick the plus sign next to the drawing icon. Pick the Layouts icon below the selected drawing to display the accessible content in the Palette pane. The layout content from a drawing in the Sample folder is displayed in the DesignCenter Palette pane in Figure 13.17. Now, just drag and drop the desired layouts into the target drawing. Optionally, you can select any number of layouts in the Palette pane, right-click on one of the highlighted layouts, and pick Add Layout(s). To quickly import a single layout, just double-click on the layout icon.

Drawing template files (*.dwt) are not displayed in the DesignCenter window. If you open the Template folder in the Tree View pane, you will find drawing files (*.dwg) corresponding to the template file names. The layouts in these drawing files do not contain title blocks like the template files. The title block geometry is created in the Model tab so that the title block can be inserted into other drawings as a block object.

To access both the layout and the title block from these drawings using DesignCenter requires two operations. First, import the layout using your preferred method. Next, pick the Template folder in the Tree view to view the drawing file content in the Palette pane. Right-click on the desired drawing and pick Insert as Block… from the shortcut menu. In the Insert dialog box, remove the check marks from the Specify On-screen boxes, and insert the drawing at 0,0 using a scale factor of 1 and 0 rotation.

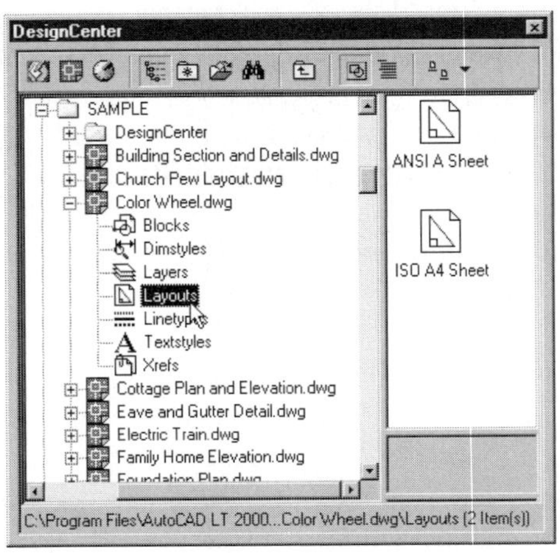

FIGURE 13.17 Using DesignCenter, you can access layouts from existing drawings and use a simple drag-and-drop operation to import them into other drawings.

Named Page Setups

A layout is defined by its settings, including the plot device, plot style table, and each of the various layout settings. When you are creating a new layout, the Layout Wizard helps automate the setup process. A new layout created from a template automates the layout setup by using the same settings as the original layout in the source drawing. So far, each of the tools introduced for automating layout settings has been used only for the initial setup of a new layout. Using the Page Setup dialog box, you can manually adjust any desired layout settings as needed to meet new requirements. However, making a variety of adjustments manually each time your plotting needs change can be tedious and time consuming.

Consider a situation in which you repeatedly need to plot the same layout using several different plotting devices. After setting up the layout to plot correctly on one device, you immediately need to adjust the settings to work on a different device. Finally, after plotting on each of these devices, you need to restore the original settings. As another example, you may plot varied sheet sizes using a color printing device. When producing a drawing for the engineering department, you plot a specific layout full size in landscape orientation using black ink only. Other departments needing a print of the same layout prefer portrait-style, half-size prints using vivid colors. Using named page setups is an effective way to manage diverse page setup issues like these. Like other reusable resources in AutoCAD LT, page setups can be named and saved for future use. Any page setup that may need to be reused should be saved and assigned an appropriate name.

The first step in creating a named page setup is to establish the desired settings in the Page Setup dialog box. Then, pick the Add... button in the Page setup name area in the top right corner of the Page Setup dialog box (see Figure 13.18A). In the User Defined Page Setups dialog box, specify a concise descriptive name in the New page setup name: box and pick the OK button, as shown in Figure 13.18B.

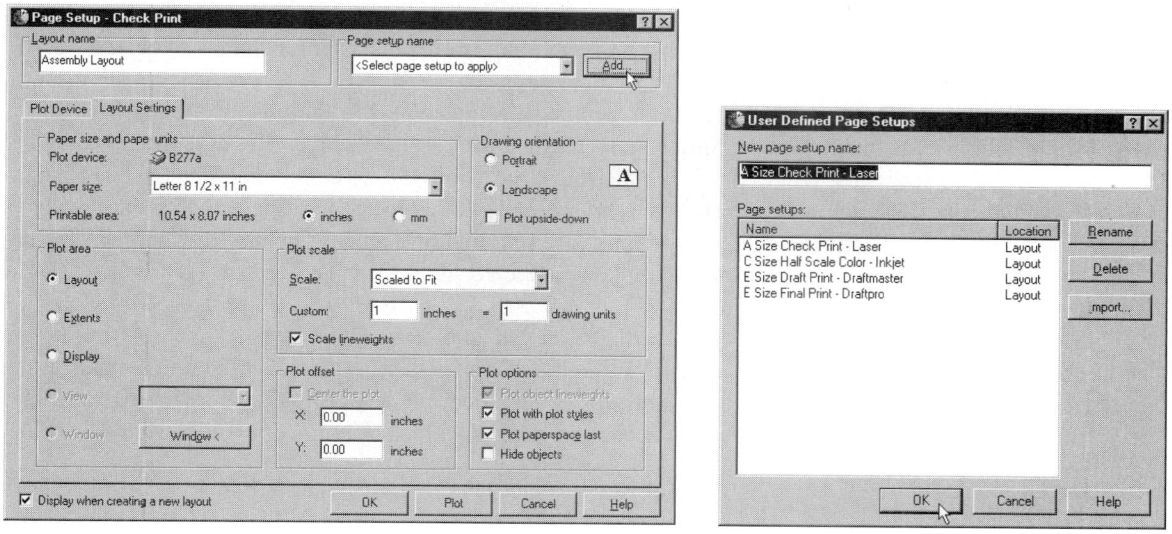

A B

FIGURE 13.18 (A) After defining the desired settings, pick the Add... button to save the page setup with a name. (B) Assign a concise descriptive name to the new page setup in the User Defined Page Setups dialog box and pick OK.

To apply the settings from a named page setup to the current layout, select it from the Page setup name: drop-down list. The settings are applied immediately after you pick an option from the list. Figure 13.19 shows the Page setup name: drop-down list. In addition to named page setups, this list shows the name of all active drawing layouts with the exception of the current layout. An active layout is any layout to which any settings have been applied. This means that you can copy the settings used by one layout in a drawing and apply them to another layout. This is useful for creating new layouts that are similar to existing layouts with just minor differences.

You can save a named page setup for virtually any plotting needs. The named page setups are saved in the drawing file in which they were defined, so they are available each time you work in that drawing. You can also import named page setups found in other drawings by picking the Import... button in the User Defined Page Setups dialog box to display a Select File dialog box. Locate and select a drawing or template file that contains named page setups, and pick the Open button to display the available named page setups in the Import user defined page setup(s) dialog box. In Figure 13.20 the template file named *ANSI Layout templates.dwt* in the Template folder was selected. This template file has a wide variety of named page setups available.

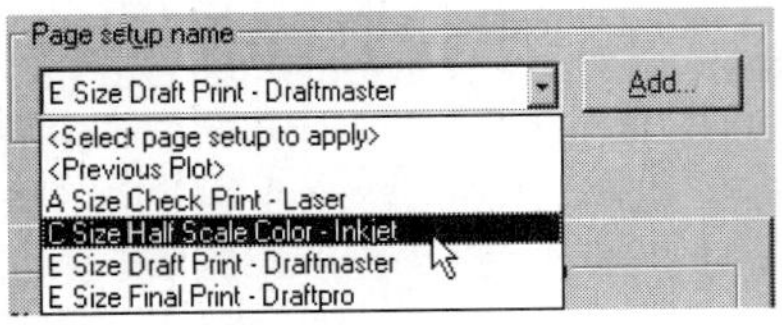

FIGURE 13.19 Select a named page setup from the drop-down list to apply its settings to the current pages setup.

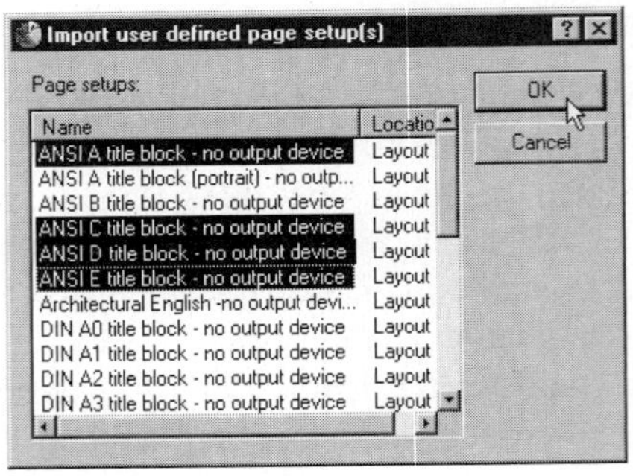

FIGURE 13.20 The Import user defined page setup(s) dialog box displays all existing named page setups found in the selected drawing or template file.

Inserting a Title Block into a Layout

The most common application of a title block in an AutoCAD drawing is to insert it as a block object. This allows the title block to be handled as a single object rather than as a multitude of lines, text, and other objects. Additionally, this approach allows you to add attribute definitions to the block or drawing. You are then prompted for required text values when you insert the title block. This makes it much faster and easier to fill in the title block information and ensures a consistent appearance.

As discussed in Chapter 12, the title block geometry and attribute definitions must be created in the Model tab to allow insertion into another drawing. Each title block design can be saved as a separate drawing file, allowing you to access the required title block using either the INSERT command or AutoCAD DesignCenter. Another common approach is to store a group of related title blocks in a single container drawing as part of a symbol library, using DesignCenter to insert the required title block. The use of the INSERT command and related DesignCenter applications were also covered in Chapter 12. Refer to this information if you need an in-depth review of these topics.

If you use the Layout Wizard, a selected title block can automatically be inserted as the layout is created. When a layout is created from a template, a title block comes in with the new layout if it exists in the layout template. But if you are creating a layout from scratch or editing an existing drawing in which the layouts do not already have title blocks, you may need to insert a title block using the INSERT command or DesignCenter, as appropriate.

Field Notes

When you are creating container drawings for title blocks or storing multiple layouts in a layout template, use AutoCAD DesignCenter to help you quickly locate and insert the desired content into these reusable resource files.

Twenty-four title block drawings are provided with the AutoCAD LT software. Like the drawing template files, these drawings provide standard title block sizes using ANSI, Architectural, ISO, DIN, and JIS standards. You can insert any of these drawings as needed into your layouts, or you can insert a title block drawing of your own design. Layouts are set up so that the 0,0 origin point occurs near the lower left corner of the printable area of the paper. Title block drawings are usually drawn in correct orientation using the lower left corner as the insertion base point. Because the paper size is represented at 1:1, title blocks are typically inserted at 0,0 using a scale factor of 1 and 0 rotation. The easiest way to use the Insert dialog box in this case is to disable the Specify On-screen option and to specify the correct insertion parameters in the text boxes. When using DesignCenter, right-click on the drawing or block definition and pick Insert as Block... from the shortcut menu to access the Insert dialog box. An example is shown in Figure 13.21.

In some applications, title blocks are inserted into a drawing as an external reference. This allows the title block geometry to automatically be updated when revisions are made. A title block that is externally referenced cannot be equipped with attributes to automate the text entry. One solution is to Xref the title block geometry and insert a block composed only of attribute definitions correlated to the title block. When attaching or overlaying an externally referenced title block, use the same insertion guidelines as when using the Insert dialog box.

FIGURE 13.21 Inserting a title block into a layout using the Insert dialog box.

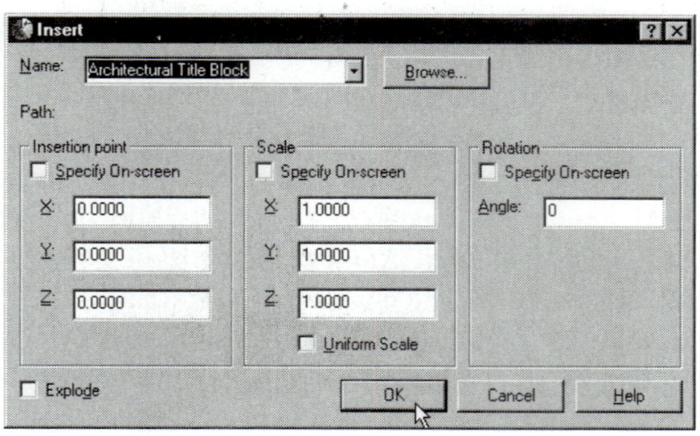

Exercise 13.2

Estimated time required: 20 min.

1. Open EX13.1.dwg for editing.
2. Enter the LAYOUT command using the keyboard; use the SAveas option of the LAYOUT command to save the *Monochrome* layout to a template named EX13.2.dwt.
3. Close EX13.1.dwg. Do not save any changes.
4. Begin a new drawing using the template file EX13.2.dwt. Look at the *Monochrome* layout tab, then check the layout properties in the Page Setup dialog box.
5. Save the current drawing as EX13.2A.dwg.
6. Delete the *Monochrome* layout.
7. Pick the From template... option on the Layout shortcut menu.
8. In the Select File dialog box, pick the template file EX13.2.dwt.
9. Using the Insert Layout(s) dialog box, insert the layout named *Monochrome*.
10. Save the current drawing as EX13.2B.dwg.
11. Delete the *Monochrome* layout.
12. Enter the LAYOUT command using the keyboard, and use the Template option. In the Select File dialog box, pick the EX13.2.dwt template again.
13. Use the "?" option at the "Enter layout name(s) or [?]:" prompt to list the available layouts.
14. Use your cursor to highlight the *Monochrome* layout.
15. Right-click on the highlighted text and pick the Paste To CmdLine option from the shortcut menu, then press the ↵ key to enter the response.
16. Save the current drawing as EX13.2C.dwg.
17. Create four additional layouts from templates, import two from *ANSI Layout templates.dwt* and two from *Metric Layout templates.dwt*. Use your preferred method of accessing layouts from templates.
18. Save the current drawing as EX13.2D.dwg.
19. Delete all layout tabs. When you delete the last layout tab, a new Layout1 tab will automatically be created.
20. Use DesignCenter to drag and drop the layout named *ANSI C Title Block* from the *ANSI C title block.dwg* drawing found in the Template folder into the current drawing.
21. Drag another copy of the *ANSI C Title Block* layout from the *ANSI C title block.dwg* drawing into the current drawing. Notice that no additional layout is created.
22. Right-click on the *ANSI C Title Block* layout in the Palette pane and pick the Add Layout(s) option. Look at the name of the new layout that was created. Delete this new layout.
23. Make the *ANSI C Title Block* layout tab current, and specify a "C" size sheet in the Page Setup dialog box. If your printer does not support "C" size sheets, use the None option for the plotter name. When the new layout tab is displayed, notice that no title block is present.
24. Use either the INSERT command or DesignCenter to insert the drawing file *ANSI C title block.dwg* into the *ANSI C Title Block* layout using the Insert dialog box. Disable the Specify On-screen options. Enter 0,0 as the insertion point, and use a scale factor of 1 and a rotation angle of 0.
25. Import three named page layouts of your choice from the template *ANSI Layout templates.dwt* in the Template folder. Restore the settings from one of these named page setups, pick OK in the Page Setup dialog box, and look at the layout. Repeat this for all three setups.
26. Create two named page layouts of your own design that use different paper sizes. Restore the settings from your first named page setup, and look at the layout.
27. Restore the settings from the second named page setup and look at the layout again.
28. Save as EX13.2E.dwg and close the drawing.

LEARNING CHECKPOINT

- □ Discuss the value of saving drawing templates and layout templates as separate files.
- □ Describe the features of the resulting file when a template is created from a layout using the SAveas option of the LAYOUT command.
- □ What is the path for the default drawing template file location?
- □ Describe the procedure for changing the default drawing template file location.
- □ What are the advantages of picking the option of creating a layout from a template from a shortcut or pull-down menu?
- □ What are the respective names of the templates that store all the inch-based and metric-based drawing layouts? In which folder are these found by default?
- □ Describe the process of copying a layout from an existing drawing using DesignCenter.
- □ List some advantages of inserting title blocks as block objects.

Laying Out Drawings

- Creating a New Drawing Layout
- Using Layout Templates and Copying Layouts

Layout (Floating) Viewports

In preparation for the following discussion, open a completed drawing from a previous chapter and create a new layout using the Page Setup dialog box. After defining the page setup settings for a new layout and closing the Page Setup dialog box, the new layout tab is displayed. The content of the layout tab, by default, shows two rectangles drawn on a representation of the selected paper size (see Figure 13.22). The first rectangle, which is drawn with a dashed line, represents the printable area. This shows what area of the paper can be printed on based on the paper size and the currently selected plot device. The second rectangle which is drawn with a continuous line is a layout viewport. ***Layout viewports*** are also called ***floating viewports***. These terms are used interchangeably in this text. Creating a new layout using the Page Setup dialog box places a single layout viewport near the center of the paper. Although the Layout Wizard offers limited options for setting up additional viewports, much more flexibility is afforded using the Viewports dialog box, which is discussed later in this section.

When a new layout is first displayed, the paper space environment is active. The purpose of the layout is to show what the plotted drawing will look like based on the current page setup and layout features. Having a representation of the paper boundary and printable area helps you more effectively plan the organization and arrangement of the final printed drawing. Another unique feature of model space and paper space is that the UCS icon has a different appearance in each. In the Model tab or inside a layout viewport, the UCS icon appears as shown in Figure 13.23A. In a layout tab with paper space active, the UCS icon appears as shown in Figure 13.23B.

The UCS icon is on by default and set to display at the drawing origin. The UCS icon is fully covered in Chapter 14, but for now you can control the UCS icon display options using the UCS Icon cascade found on the Display cascade of the View menu. The default setting places a check mark next to both options on this menu.

The Model tab is used only for drawing the geometry that defines the model. The model can represent a two-dimensional mechanical part or architectural plan, or a complex three-dimensional assembly. When you finish drawing the model, it is time to set up the required drawing layouts.

The default appearance of the layout tabs is managed by a group of settings in the Layout elements area of the Display tab of the Options dialog box. All these options are enabled by default. Disabling these features makes AutoCAD LT 2000 look and feel more like the older software versions. It is recommended that you leave all these features enabled. The available settings are as follows:

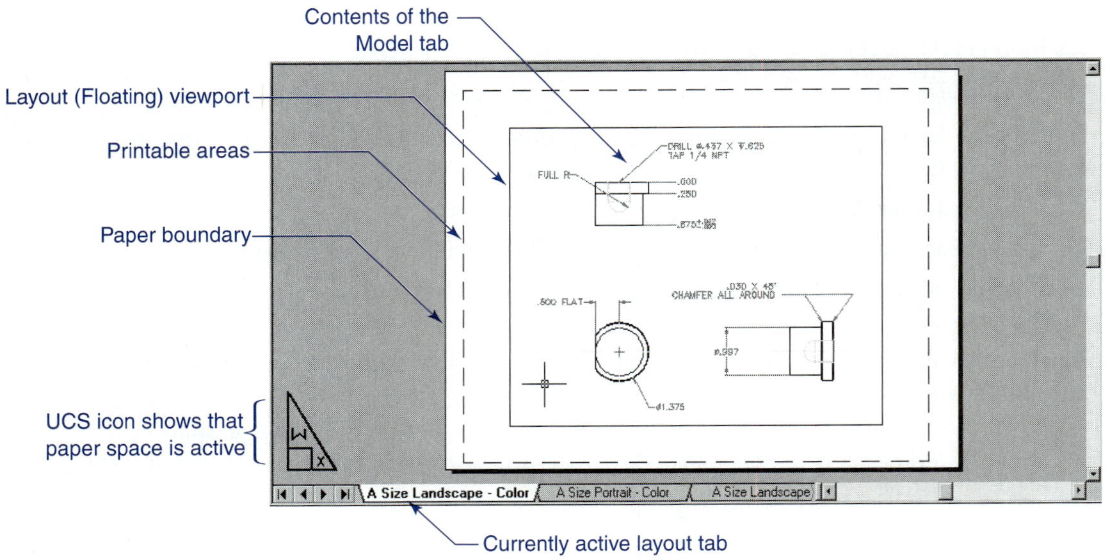

FIGURE 13.22 A layout tab shows a representation of the actual plotted paper drawing, which is used to plan, organize, and arrange the elements of the final printed drawing layout.

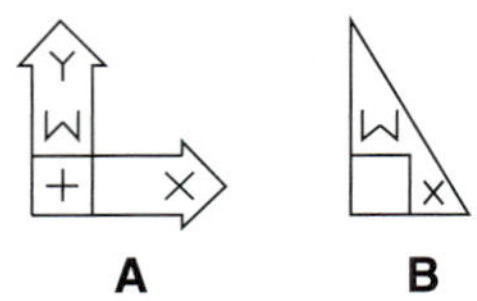

FIGURE 13.23 (A) The UCS icon in the Model tab, and (B) the UCS icon in paper space in a layout tab.

- **Display Layout and Model tabs** — Controls display of Model and layout tab elements along bottom of drawing area.
- **Display margins** — Margins show the printable area on the paper.
- **Display paper background** — Displays representation of selected paper size.
- **Display paper shadow** — Controls display of paper shadow representation; active only if paper background is enabled.
- **Show Page Setup dialog for new layouts** — Controls whether Page Setup dialog is automatically displayed when a layout tab is picked the first time.
- **Create viewport in new layouts** — Controls whether the single default layout viewport is automatically created.

The layout tab is where a title block is inserted and all its required text fields are completed. Any needed notes and annotations are also placed in the layout, and this is where the planning and organization of the final printed drawing takes place. The next step is to display the required views of the model geometry in accordance with standard drafting practices.

In order to view the model geometry in the layout tab, layout viewports must be added to the layout. Earlier in this chapter, layout viewports were described as "holes" cut into the paper through which the model can be viewed. When you finish setting up a layout using the Page Setup dialog box, and the default layout viewport is placed on the paper, the objects in the Model tab can be seen through the new "hole" in the paper. Refer to Figure 13.1 for an illustration of this concept.

One or more layout viewports can be placed in a layout tab and arranged so that all required views of the model are displayed in their correct position and orientation and at the correct drawing scale. Many drawing projects can be displayed adequately using a single viewport. If you want to use the initial viewport created by the PAGESETUP command, you may need to adjust the viewport size and location for the best results. Layout viewports are AutoCAD LT drawing objects, similar to lines, arcs, and circles. Therefore, layout viewports can be freely edited, with a few limitations. Layout viewports are referred to as *floating* because you can move them as needed in the layout using the MOVE command to position them as desired.

Floating viewports can be resized horizontally or vertically using the STRETCH and SCALE commands. In a layout with multiple viewports, each viewport is a separate objects and can be edited independently of the others. Resizing a viewport does not affect the size of the model, nor does it change the apparent size of the geometry displayed within the viewport. An easy way to adjust the size of a layout viewport is to use grip editing to quickly drag the corners into the desired location. Figure 13.24 shows a viewport being resized using a corner grip.

You can create copies of layout viewports using standard AutoCAD LT duplication commands. Layout viewports can be copied, mirrored, and even arrayed, but they cannot be rotated. Rotating a viewport moves it around the specified base point but does not change its actual orientation.

Layout viewports can be erased when they are no longer needed in the drawing. Regardless of what kind of edit you perform on a layout viewport, the model space objects displayed in it are completely unaffected.

FIGURE 13.24 Resizing layout viewports is very easy using grips.

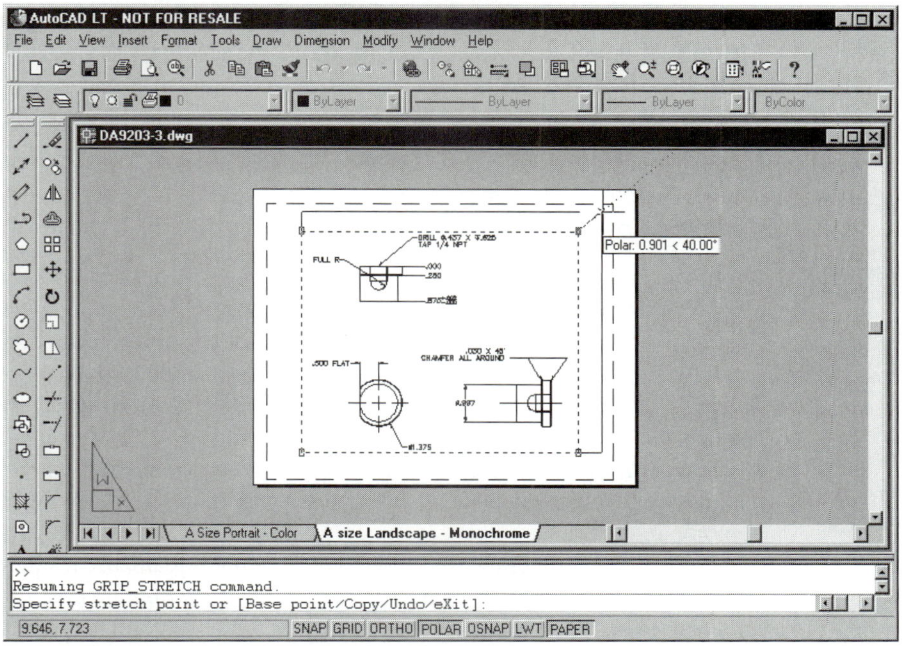

Field Notes

- Grip-selecting a single corner grip on a floating viewport provides a fast and easy way to resize viewports. With ORTHO off, you can freely move the corner to resize the viewport both horizontally and vertically at the same time. Toggling ORTHO on restricts the movement of the cursor to horizontal or vertical movements, allowing you to resize it on only one axis at a time.
- Editing a layout viewport does not affect the model space objects in any way.
- Irregularly shaped viewports can be simulated by copying a viewport and locating the copy in the same place as the original. Use grip editing to move the corners of the copy to the new desired location. Using this technique keeps the model in the same apparent position and allows you to create L-shaped viewports. With additional copies you can make even more complex shapes when needed to show a very specific view.

Moving between Model Space and Paper Space

TILEMODE
TM

In a new layout you are initially placed in the paper space environment, but you can freely move between paper space and model space whenever necessary. Using the drawing tabs at the bottom of the drawing area lets you move to a different layout or into the Model tab if desired. Optionally, you can type **TM** or **TILEMODE** at the Command: prompt and set the TILEMODE variable to 1 to move directly to the Model tab. Setting TILEMODE back to 0 returns to the most recently used layout tab. When TILEMODE is 1, you are placed in

tiled model space, otherwise known as the Model tab. It is called tiled model space because viewports created in the Model tab are tiled neatly into place, each edge just touching and not overlapping.

While in a layout tab you can work on the drawing model by entering the layout viewport. To work inside a layout viewport while the layout tab is still visible, double-click anywhere inside the desired viewport. The floating viewport border is accented, becoming wider and bolder. The drawing cursor changes to a Windows system cursor when it is moved outside the active viewport boundary. Additionally, if the model space drawing origin is visible in the viewport, the model space UCS icon is displayed in the viewport. Refer to the model space and paper space UCS icon illustrations in Figure 13.23. While working in model space inside a layout viewport you can use the ZOOM and PAN commands as needed to adjust the display area.

Status Bar
MODEL
PAPER
MSPACE
MS
PSPACE
PS

To leave model space in the layout viewport and return to paper space in the layout tab, double-click anywhere in the layout that is not inside a layout viewport. This returns the viewport border to its normal display, and the paper space UCS icon is displayed again.

Another way to toggle between model and paper space is by picking the Model or Paper Space button on the AutoCAD LT status bar. The current space is always indicated by the label on this button. If the button is labeled PAPER, picking it activates model space, and the label is updated to match. When the button reads MODEL, it means that model space is active, and picking the button returns to paper space. This button uses the MSPACE and PSPACE commands to make the switch. You can also type these commands, or you can use the command aliases MS and PS. When you use this method to enter model space in a drawing with multiple floating viewports, you are placed in the most recently used viewport.

Creating Layout Viewports

Viewports

Display Viewports Dialog
View
Viewports▸
New Viewports...
VPORTS

Determining how many viewports are required for a layout and how they are to be used is an important first step toward working effectively with layout viewports. You can complete a layout for many routine drafting projects using only a single layout viewport. As an example, consider a typical 2D mechanical part drawing using two to five orthographic/auxiliary views, with all views plotted at the same scale. In this type of project, one large viewport in the layout can adequately display all required drawing views. More involved drafting projects can require two to eight viewports in the layout. For example, in a complex drafting application where one or more scaled detail views are used, one viewport is established for each specific drawing scale used in the layout. Very specialized projects may require even more viewports in a layout, but this is not a common requirement.

When an entire drawing is plotted at a common scale, use a single viewport. Whenever possible, use a single viewport. In drawings where multiple drawing scales are employed, create only one viewport for each unique drawing scale being used. Keep in mind that using too many layout viewports can complicate the layout process and slow down productivity.

While working with viewports it can be helpful to have ready access to the Viewports toolbar. To display the Viewports toolbar, right-click on any toolbar button to display the Toolbars shortcut menu, and pick Viewports.

Layout viewports can be added to a layout using the Viewports dialog box (see Figure 13.25). The Viewports dialog box can be accessed by picking the Display Viewports dialog button found on both the Layouts and the Viewports toolbars, by picking New Viewports... from the Viewports cascade of the View menu or by typing **VPORTS** at the Command: prompt. The Viewports dialog box simplifies the creation of layout viewports in a layout by providing a list of several predefined standard viewport configurations that can be applied to your layout. ***Viewport configuration*** is the term used in reference to a viewport layout, the number of viewports, and their associated settings.

The features of the Viewports dialog box are described as follows:

- **Current name:** Shows the name of the currently selected option.
- **Standard viewports:** A list of the predefined standard viewport configurations.
- **Preview** Shows the appearance of the currently selected option.
- **Viewport Spacing:** Specifies size of space between viewports.
- **Setup:** 2D setup defaults to *Current* view in all viewports. 3D applies standard orthogonal 3D views to viewports.
- **Change view to:** If Setup: is 2D, lists named views to apply to viewports. If Setup: is 3D, lists standard orthogonal 3D views to apply to viewports.

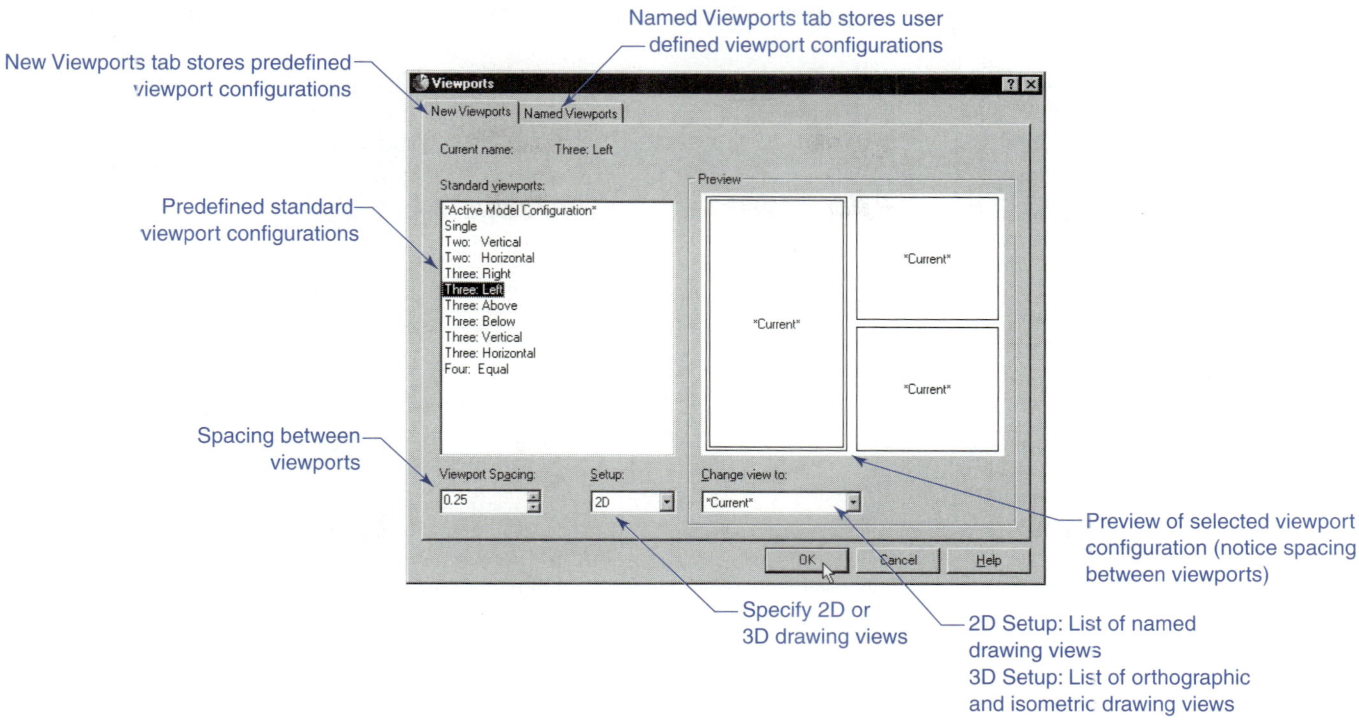

FIGURE 13.25 The Viewports dialog box can be used to set up a viewport configuration in a layout.

When you highlight an option in the Standard viewports: list, a preview of the selected configuration is displayed in the Preview image. Each of the standard viewport configuration options creates an arrangement of between one and four viewports. The Viewport Spacing: box is used to specify the distance between each pair of new viewports.

If the Setup is defined as 2D, the current view is displayed in each new viewport by default. When you use a 2D setup, the currently defined named drawing views are listed in the Change view to: list. You can specify what is displayed in each viewport by picking the viewport in the Preview window and then picking the desired named view from the list. A 3D Setup automatically assigns 3D orthographic views to the viewports. To change the default assignment, pick the viewport and select the new view name from the list.

After selecting a standard viewport configuration from the Standard viewports: list and specifying any desired options, pick the OK button to apply the selected viewport configuration to the current layout. You are then prompted to draw a rectangle to define the area where the viewports are to be placed. The default option is Fit, which uses the maximum available area by filling the printable area of the layout. The Three: Left viewport configuration using the Fit option produces the results shown in Figure 13.26. The prompt sequence is shown here:

```
Command: _vports
Specify first corner or [Fit] <Fit>: ↵
Regenerating layout.
Regenerating model.
Command:
```

If you have created a set of named views while working on the model, you can set up each viewport to display a specific view. In this example, named views were defined while working on a multiple-part composite drawing. When the drawing is complete and it is time to create the layout, the views can then be used to define the view location of each for the layout viewports. The views are assigned to the viewports by picking the desired viewport in the Preview window and then picking the view name to assign to that viewport. Notice that in Figure 13.27 the view names are displayed in the preview area, indicating that the view was successfully assigned. Figure 13.28 shows the resulting viewports as displayed in the drawing layout.

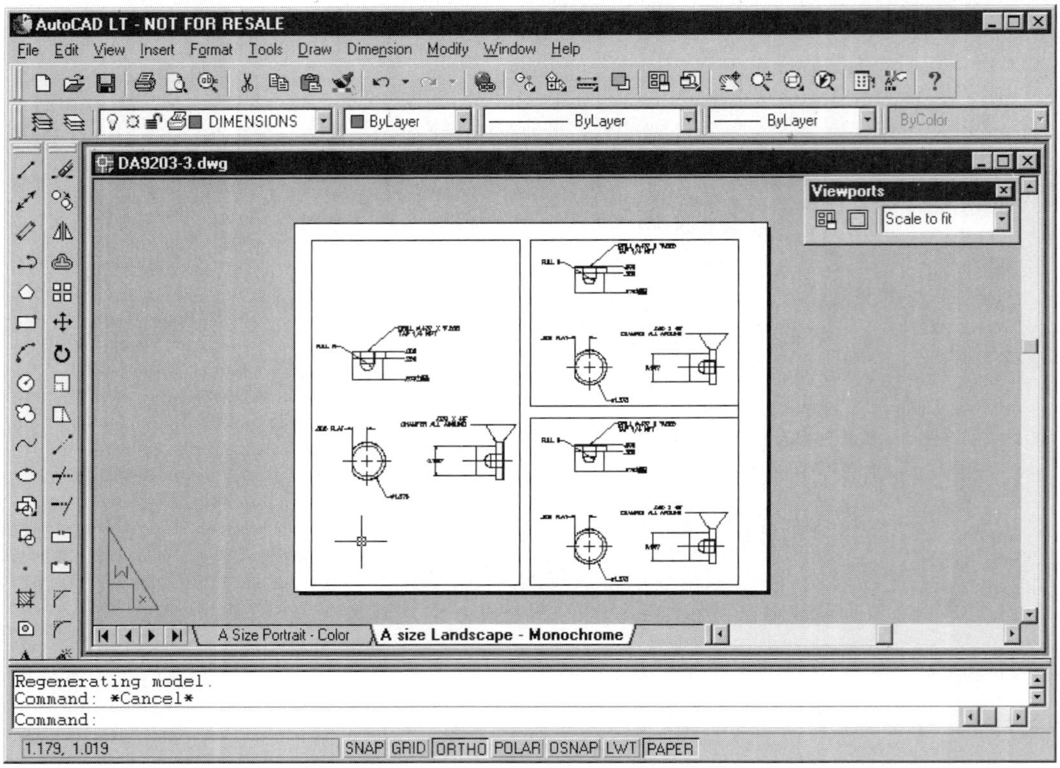

FIGURE 13.26 This shows the results of selecting the Three: Left viewport configuration with 0.25 viewport spacing and the Fit option to place the viewports.

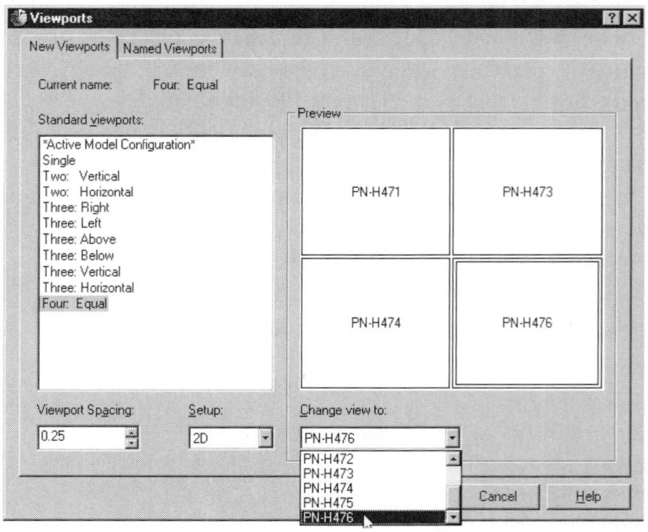

FIGURE 13.27 Named drawing views can be assigned to each layout viewport by picking the viewport preview and selecting a named view from the Change view to: list.

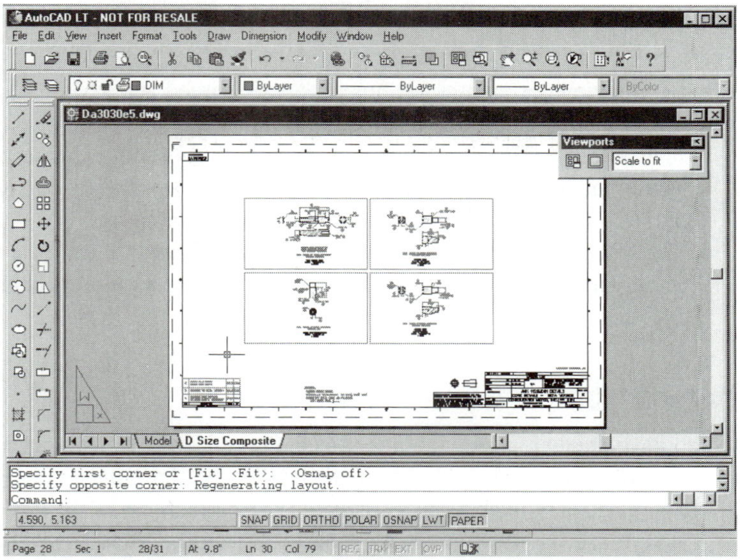

FIGURE 13.28 Each layout viewport displays the named drawing views as assigned in Figure 13.27.

The Viewports dialog box can be used to create a limited set of predefined viewport configurations, but keep in mind that the layout viewports it creates can be edited as needed to meet your specific requirements. You can quickly grip-edit these viewports, changing location and position to achieve the desired results.

Even so, you may find it is much simpler to just define your viewports one at a time. You can select the Single option from the Viewports dialog box or type **-VPORTS** at the Command: prompt. The fastest way to define a single layout viewport is to pick the Single Viewport button from the Viewports toolbar and pick two points on screen to place the viewport. Picking the Single Viewport button displays the following prompt sequence:

Standard
Single Viewport
View
Viewports ▸
1 Viewport
-VPORTS

Command: _-vports
Specify corner of viewport or [ON/OFF/Fit/Hideplot/Lock/Restore/2/3/4] <Fit>: ⟨*pick first corner*⟩
Specify opposite corner: ⟨*pick second corner*⟩
Regenerating model.
Command:

Virtually any number of layout viewports can be created in a drawing. Although there is no specific limit to the number of viewports that can be created in a drawing, there is a limit to the number that can be active at the same time. A viewport is referred to as *active* when it is on and displaying an area of model space.

The maximum number of viewports that can be active at the same time is determined by your operating system and the display driver. The maximum number of active viewports can also be controlled by setting the MAXACTVP system variable. The initial default value for MAXACTVP is 64. This number should be more than sufficient for virtually any situation. As with most system variables, MAXACTVP can be set by typing its name at the Command: prompt:

Command: MAXACTVP ↵
Enter new value for MAXACTVP <64>: **32**↵

The MAXACTVP variable cannot be set to any value that is beyond the capabilities of your system. If you try to set a value that is too high, you get the following message:

Command: **MAXACTVP**↵
Enter new value for MAXACTVP <32>: **65**↵
Requires an integer between 2 and 64.
Enter new value for MAXACTVP <32>: **64**↵
Command:

Field Notes

- Layout viewport configurations cannot be named and saved.
- Saved model space viewport configurations can also be applied to a layout, so if you want to save a frequently used layout viewport configuration, define the same configuration in the Model tab and save it. You will then be able to use the saved viewport configuration in a layout!
- The MAXACTVP variable can be set to a low value to increase your system performance. Inactive viewports are left blank, and their contents are not regenerated.

Controlling Layout Viewport Display Scales

Once you have created, sized, and positioned all the layout viewports required for your drawing layout, you are ready to adjust the settings that control viewport behavior and appearance. One of the first items to adjust is the viewport display to show its contents at the correct scale. The easiest way to control the viewport display scale is to use the Viewport Scale Control list on the Viewports toolbar. The Viewports toolbar and the Viewport Scale Control list are shown in Figure 13.29. This list works like the lists on the Object Properties toolbar. You can check the existing display scale of a layout viewport either by double-clicking inside it to make it active or by grip-selecting it. The current scale of the selected viewport is displayed in the Viewport Scale Control list. You can open the list and select a new display scale from the preset options, or you can type a custom scale in the edit box. The specified scale is assigned to the viewport, and the viewport display scale is updated. In Figure 13.30A the selected viewport shows a current display scale of 0.73 (0.73:1). A new scale of 1:1 is picked and assigned to the viewport in Figure 13.30B.

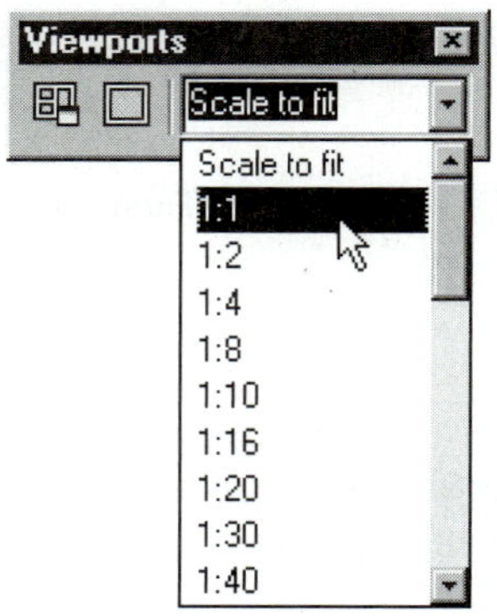

FIGURE 13.29 The Viewport Scale Control list on the Viewports toolbar.

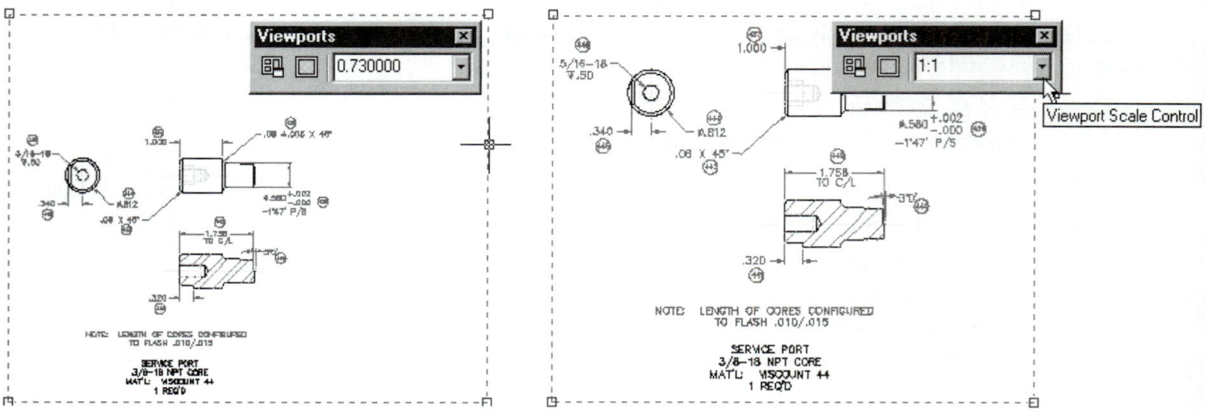

A B

FIGURE 13.30 (A) The current display scale of the selected viewport is displayed. (B) Select the new scale to assign it to the selected viewport.

Another way to adjust the display scale viewports is to use the XP option of the ZOOM command. The designation *XP* means *times paper space*. Using an XP option displays the viewport contents at a scale directly relative to paper space, and paper space represents the real-world paper size, since it is plotted at 1:1. First, double-click inside the viewport to make it the active viewport. To display the viewport contents at half scale, use the ZOOM command and enter 0.5XP or 1/2XP. The model space area is displayed at double scale, or 2:1, by using ZOOM 2XP. The ability to use direct fractions makes it easy to set up the scale using this option. For example, to set the viewport display at 1/4″=1′0″ scale, use 1/48XP. This is because there are four 1/4″s in 1″, and there are twelve 1″s in 1′, so the equation is $4 \times 12 = 48$, and the resultant XP factor is 1/48. To present another example, consider setting a viewport to display at 1/8″ = 1′0″. There are eight 1/8″s in 1″, and, again, twelve 1″s in 1′, so the equation is $8 \times 12 = 96$, so the resultant XP factor is 1/96XP.

Controlling Layout Viewport Display and Plotting Options

Grip-select a layout viewport and right-click to display a shortcut menu with several viewport-related options available. These options allow you to control display and plotting options for the selected layout viewports. The shortcut menu actually accesses various options of the -VPORTS command (the command-line version of VPORTS).

Viewport displays can be turned off when they are not needed. To turn off the selected viewport, pick No from the Display Viewport Objects cascade on the shortcut menu. When a viewport display is turned off, it does not display its model space objects, appearing empty instead. Turning off unneeded viewports can help boost system performance on slower computer systems. A viewport that has been turned off can no longer be made current. To turn a viewport display back on, pick Yes from the Display Viewport Objects cascade on the shortcut menu.

You can also lock a viewport display to prevent the display area or scale from being changed inadvertently. When you enter model space in a layout viewport to revise or edit model space geometry, any display changes that are made can alter the display scale or display area for the viewport. When the display is locked, AutoCAD LT goes to paper space to respond to display change commands, and when the display change is complete, you are returned to model space. To lock the display of the selected viewport, pick the Yes option from the Display Locked cascade on the shortcut menu. Pick No to unlock the viewport display. Zooming while in model space in a locked viewport displays the following messages at the command line:

Command: **ZOOM**↵
Viewport is view-locked. Switching to Paper space.
Specify corner of window, enter a scale factor (nX or nXP), or
[All/Center/Dynamic/Extents/Previous/Scale/Window] <real time>: ⟨*pick first corner*⟩
Specify opposite corner: ⟨*pick other corner*⟩
Switching back to Model space.
Command:

The third cascade menu is the Hide Plot menu. This controls whether hidden lines (lines on a 3D part that are not visible from the current viewing angle) are removed from the model space objects displayed in a viewport when you plot from paper space.

The PROPERTIES command provides complete control of all layout viewport properties in one convenient location. The Properties window can be used to turn viewports on or off, change the display scale, lock or unlock the display, and more. Figure 13.31 shows the Properties window with a layout viewport selected. The special properties unique to viewports are listed in the Misc section of the Properties window.

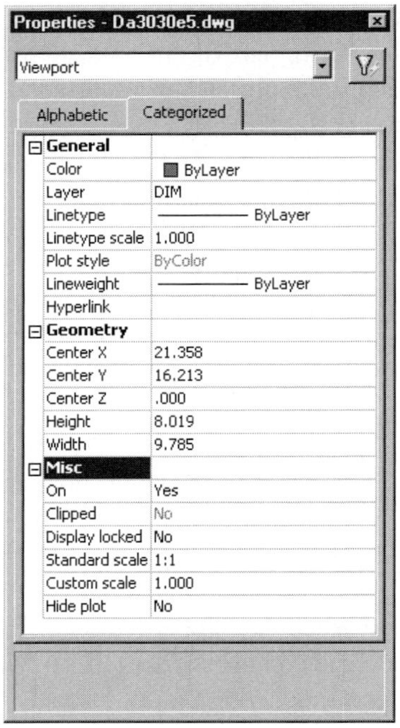

FIGURE 13.31 The Properties window provides a complete and convenient means to modify the special properties of layout viewport objects.

Field Notes

- Drawings created in AutoCAD 2000 can use nonrectangular floating viewports. These can be edited using AutoCAD LT, but you cannot create new nonrectangular viewports except by copying an existing one. You can copy nonrectangular viewports within a single drawing or from one drawing to another. You can also rotate nonrectangular viewports.
- The "Clipped" property listed in the Misc section of the Properties window for layout viewports reports whether a viewport is clipped. Viewport *clipping* is the process used in AutoCAD 2000 to create nonrectangular viewports. You cannot change this property in AutoCAD LT.
- When a layout viewport is initially created, it uses the current Grid and Snap settings of the model tab. The Grid and Snap features can be set to different values in each layout viewport in a layout without affecting the settings in other viewports.

Exercise 13.3 — Estimated time required: 15 min.

1. Open a completed dimensioned drawing from a previous chapter.
2. Use the Page Setup dialog box to set up the layout settings using an appropriate plot device and paper size. Name the layout EX13-3. Close the Page Setup dialog box when you are finished.
3. Examine the layout tab, identify the printable area and the layout viewport.
4. Check for the paper space UCS icon. Double-click inside of the layout viewport. Find the model space UCS icon. Double-click outside the viewport to activate paper space again. Use the Model or Paper Space button to toggle to model space and then back to paper space. Try the MS and PS option. Which option works best for you?
5. Adjust the current settings in the Layout elements area of the Display tab in the Options dialog box. Exit the Options dialog box and check the results. Reset all the features to the default of ON.
6. Use Grip editing options to resize and relocate the default viewport object.
7. Erase the viewport. Use the OOPS command to restore it. Erase it one more time.
8. Explore the Viewports dialog box. Look at the preview for each option in the Standard viewports: list
9. Use the Viewports dialog box to place the Three: Left viewport configuration in the EX13-3 layout using the Fit option.
10. Erase the viewports created in step 9. Create two named drawing views in the current drawing. In the Viewports dialog box select the Two:Vertical option, and assign the named views to a viewport. Save the drawing as EX13.3A.dwg.
11. Erase the viewports created in step 10. Use the Single Viewport button to create an arrangement of at least six viewports.
12. Set MAXACTVP to 4. Look at your viewports. How many are active? Change MAXACTVP back to 64. Use the REGENALL command to regenerate all viewports.
13. Use the Viewport Scale Control list to set varying scales for each of the layout viewports in your drawing.
14. Enter model space in one of your layout viewports. Use the ZOOM XP option to set various display scales.
15. Turn two of your viewports off.
16. Lock the display on one of your viewports. Enter model space in the display-locked viewport. Use the ZOOM IN and ZOOM OUT options and view the command line.
17. Grip-select a viewport object and start the PROPERTIES command.
18. Review the Misc area of the Properties window.
19. Save as EX13-3B.dwg and close the drawing.

☑ LEARNING CHECKPOINT

- ☐ Describe the features and appearance of a layout tab.
- ☐ What is the purpose of the layout tab?
- ☐ What is significant about the UCS icon in model space and paper space environments?
- ☐ Describe the layout feature settings found in the Layout elements area of the Display tab of the Options dialog box.
- ☐ Describe the display controls used with layout viewports.
- ☐ What is the fastest and easiest way to resize a layout viewport?
- ☐ Name three different ways to toggle from model space to paper space and back again.
- ☐ Define a viewport configuration.

Laying Out Drawings

- Laying Out Your Drawing
- Creating a New Drawing Layout

Layout Viewport Applications

Layout viewports provide tremendous flexibility for setting up multiview drawing layouts. Any number of viewports can be created and arranged as needed on the final layout. Each viewport in the layout can be set up to display a specific area of model space at any required scale. Different Grid and Snap settings can be applied to individual viewports without affecting other viewports. Viewport displays can be turned on or off, or even locked, to prevent unintentional changes to the set display scale. Additional tools and techniques for working effectively with layout viewports are introduced in this section.

AutoCAD LT 2000 allows you to control the visibility and plotting of the rectangular viewport border displayed in the layout. You can prevent viewport borders from being plotted, or you can hide the viewport object while still displaying its contents. Another very powerful feature of layout viewports is the capability to control what is displayed in each viewport through layer visibility settings. You can specify which layers are visible and which are not visible in each individual viewport. AutoCAD LT can automatically apply the correct scale factor for hatch patterns that are created inside a layout viewport. Dimension styles can be set to automatically set the dimension scale to match the display scale of the current viewport. Even the linetype scale of objects displayed in layout viewports can be controlled automatically. Learning to take advantage of these capabilities can help you create better quality layouts in less time.

Hiding Layout Viewport Borders

Viewport borders show the location and size of each layout viewport, and they are used to select a viewport when necessary for editing operations. In most professional applications, these borders should not be shown on your final printed drawings. You can prevent these from showing up on plots using layer control options.

In most professional drafting applications, it is standard practice to place layout viewport objects on their own layer. This is an effective means of controlling both visibility and plotting for viewports. To suppress the display of a viewport border and prevent plotting, you can turn off or freeze the layer containing the viewport. This does not affect the display area of the viewport; only the viewport border is hidden. The area of model space displayed by the viewport is still visible, and double-clicking within the viewport area still allows access to model space. When you enter model space within a layout viewport, a boundary is shown regardless of layer settings. Figure 13.32 shows a drawing with four layout viewports on a frozen layer, with model space active in one of the viewports. Notice the graphics cursor and UCS icon inside the active viewport.

FIGURE 13.32 Freeze or turn off the viewport layer to hide the viewport border. The viewport display area is not affected by layer visibility settings.

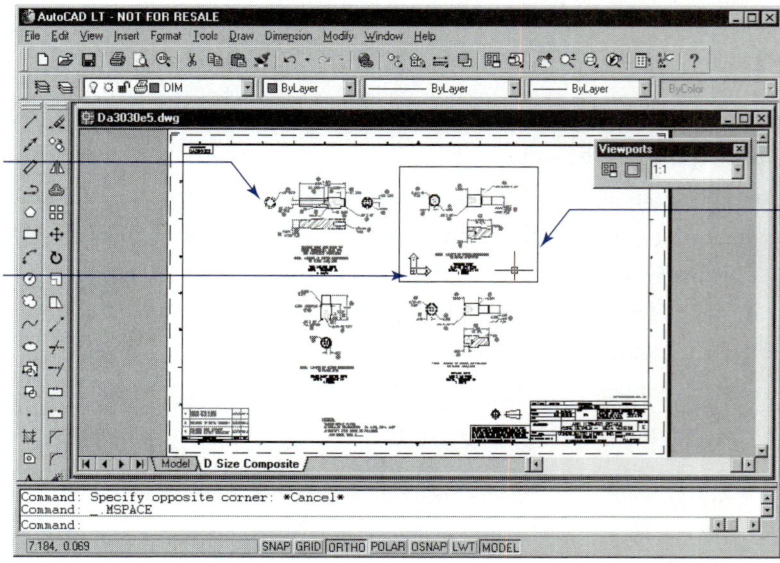

Keep in mind that a viewport can be selected by picking only when its border is visible. The frozen viewport layer must be thawed to allow options such as grip editing. Even when on a frozen layer, you can still select the viewports using the Quick Select tool.

If you want to prevent plotting while keeping the viewport border visible on screen, you can turn off the Plot / Don't Plot property for the viewport layer. You can do this in the Layer Properties Manager or by using the Layer Control list on the Object Properties toolbar, by picking the printer icon for the viewport layer (see Figure 13.33).

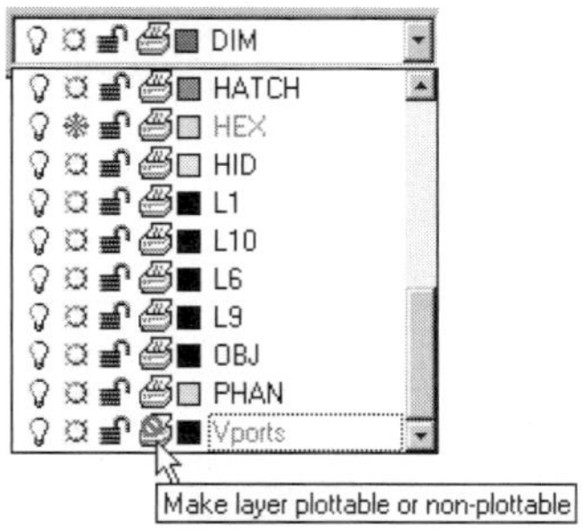

FIGURE 13.33 Turning off plotting for the viewport layer allows the viewport to be displayed but not plotted.

Controlling Layer Visibility in Layout Viewports and Scaling Dimensions to the Layout (Paper Space)

The capability to control layer visibility in specific viewports provides tremendous flexibility for setting up your multiview layouts. One very common application of this feature is in drawings where some of the drawing views are presented using varying scale factors. For example, in Figure 13.34 the sectioned part shown in the layout viewport has a very small feature that can be described most effectively using an enlarged detail view. The following discussion walks through the process of creating an appropriate layout for this part.

The default view in the layout viewport is zoomed to the extents of the model. Changing the viewport to the desired display scale more accurately shows the relationship between the model and the layout. In this drawing, the desired scale for the primary view is 1:1. The Viewport Scale Control list on the Viewports toolbar can be used to set the display scale.

When planning a layout, it can be easier to visualize if the title block is already in place. After the title block is inserted, the layout viewport size and position can be adjusted to fit within the preferred drawing area. Figure 13.35 shows the layout with the title block inserted, the viewport display set at 1:1, and the viewport boundaries adjusted to fit in the preferred drawing area.

If this drawing was started using a customized template file, your standard layers and dimension styles should already be defined in this drawing. Otherwise, you can use DesignCenter to import the appropriate content into the current drawing. Also, check your dimension style to verify that dimensions are being scaled to the layout (paper space). This setting is found on the Fit tab in the Modify Dimension Style dialog box.

Before beginning to apply dimensions, be sure to set the appropriate layer and dimension style current. Select the viewport and use the shortcut menu to lock the viewport display. Finally, activate model space inside the layout viewport, and dimension the view as needed. Figure 13.36 shows the part drawing with di-

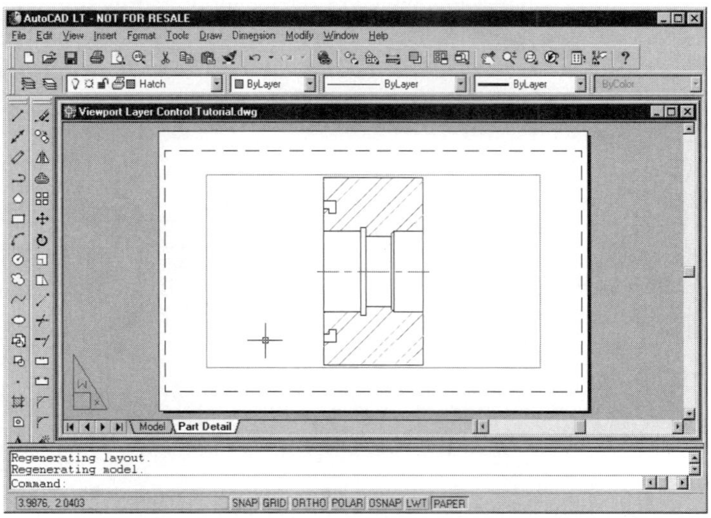

FIGURE 13.34 The Page Setup dialog box was used to create this layout. The model is visible through the default layout viewport. A larger scale detail view is needed to show the smaller feature shown on the left side of the part, near the top and bottom.

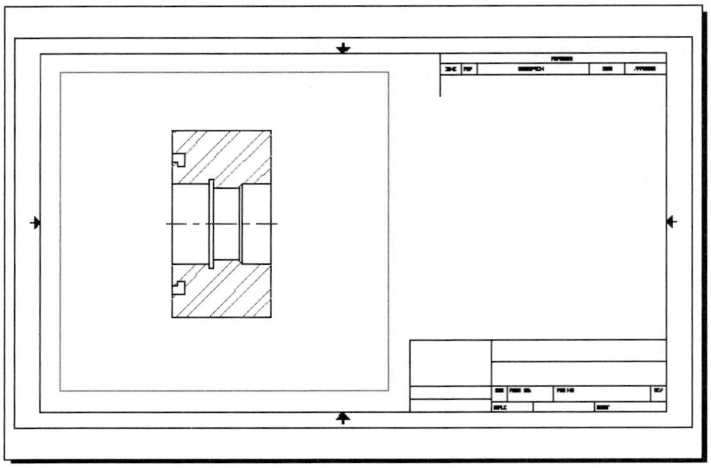

FIGURE 13.35 The layout viewport is adjusted to a 1:1 scale, a title block is inserted, and the viewport is resized and relocated appropriately.

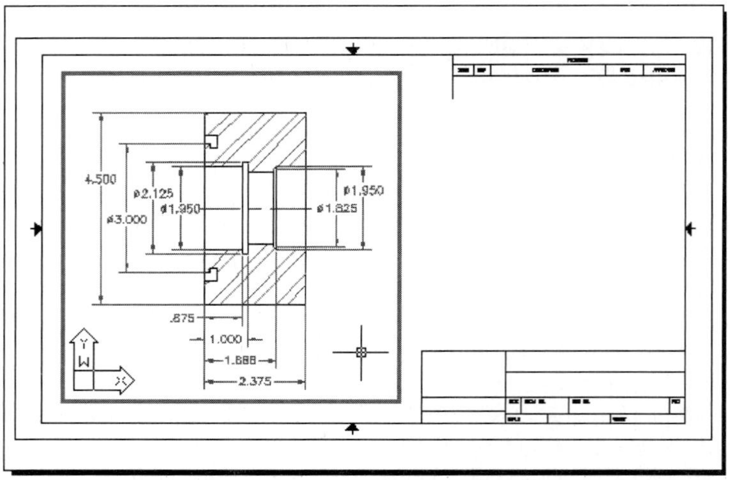

FIGURE 13.36 When you are dimensioning in model space from inside the layout viewports, you should scale the dimension style to the layout. This way, all dimensions are automatically drawn at the correct scale.

mensions applied to the primary view. Notice that at this scale it is not practical to apply dimensions to the small feature on the left side of the part.

Next, create a new layout viewport to display an enlarged detail view of the small feature that could not be dimensioned effectively in the primary view. Use the Single Viewport button on the Viewports toolbar or any preferred method. Use the Viewport Scale Control list to set the viewport display scale at 4:1, then pan the drawing as needed to position the feature within the viewport (see Figure 13.37).

A noticeable problem with the new detail view at this point is that parts of the dimensions created in the other view are also visible in this viewport. The solution to this situation is to freeze the dimension layer in the smaller view. You can use the Layer Properties Manager dialog box to specify the layer visibility settings for a layout viewport. The viewport visibility settings made in the Layer Properties Manager affect only the

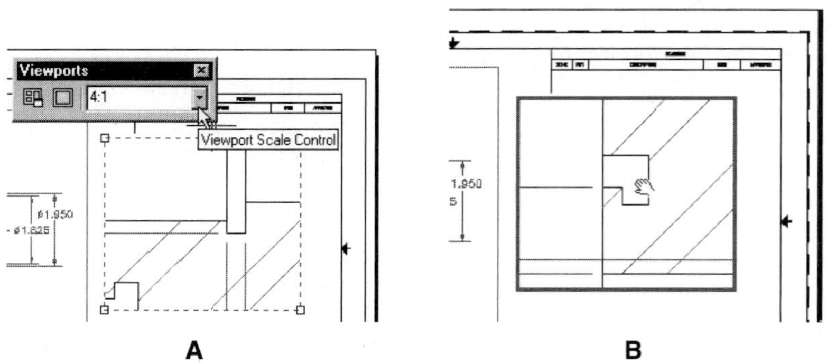

FIGURE 13.37 (A) Create a viewport for the detail view and set the display scale to 4:1. (B) Pan the display to position the feature in an appropriate location.

current viewport or viewports that have not been created yet, so be sure that you are in model space inside the viewport to which you want the settings to apply.

When you access the Layer Properties Manager from a layout tab, two additional columns appear in the layer property listing. One column is labeled Active…, and the other is shown as New…. If you use your resizing cursor to expand the columns, the labels are displayed in full as Active VP Freeze and New VP Freeze. Figure 13.38 shows the Layer Properties Manager dialog box with the two additional property columns. The new icons show the familiar sun or snowflake in combination with a representation of a viewport. The icon for New viewports shows its viewport as being blank. The setting in the Active… column affects only the currently active viewport. If you forget to enter model space inside a layout viewport before making changes, the new settings are applied to paper space. The New… column sets the default layer visibility in any new viewports created after the setting is made.

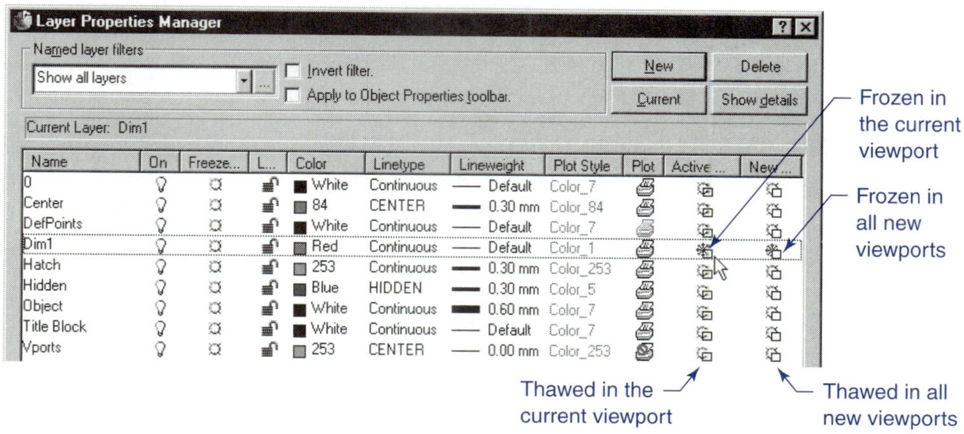

FIGURE 13.38 Two new layer properties are available when you access the Layer Properties Manager from a layout tab. The settings you make are applied to the current viewport.

In this example the dimensions applied in the primary view were created on the Dim1 layer. Picking the property icon toggles it from one state to the other. In Figure 13.38 the DIM1 layer is frozen in the current viewport and in all new viewports. Although this project should not require any additional viewports, if one is created, then the Dim1 layer will already be frozen in the new viewport.

Because the primary dimension layer is not visible in the current viewport, the dimensions will have to go on a different layer. A new layer is created for the dimensions in this viewport. The name selected in this example is Dim4. Any naming system can be used. In this example the Dim1 layer is for the full-scale dimensions in the primary view, and Dim4 will contain the dimensions scaled for the 4:1 detail view. After setting the new layer current, it is time to finish dimensioning the drawing. Remember to lock the viewport display to keep the display scale at the correct setting. Figure 13.39 shows the layout after the dimensions are completed in the detail view.

In Figure 13.39 the dimensions created in the small viewport are now visible in the large viewport as well. The Dim4 layer needs to be frozen in the large viewport. To use the Layer Properties Manager dialog box to freeze the layer, you must first set the large viewport current. You can double-click inside the large

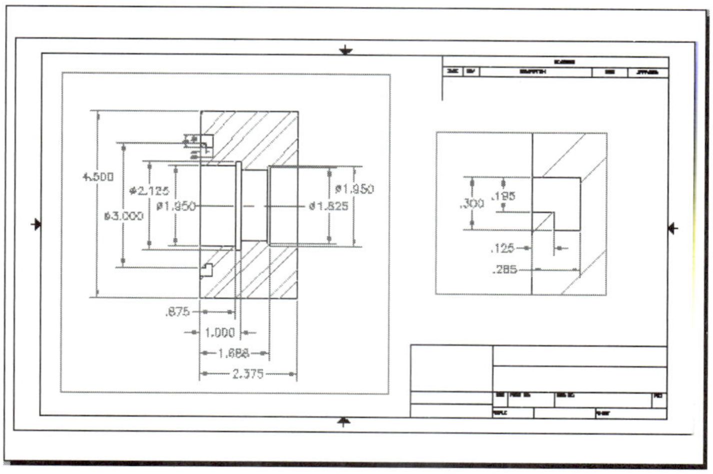

FIGURE 13.39 The 4:1 scale view is now dimensioned. Because the dimensions are scaled to the layout, they are automatically created at the correct scale.

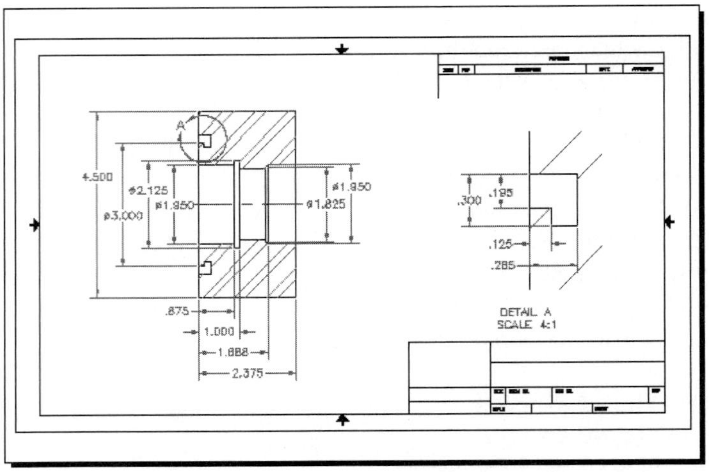

FIGURE 13.40 The completed layout.

viewport or use the Ctrl+R accelerator keystroke if preferred. Figure 13.40 shows the completed layout. The viewport layer has been frozen to show how the printed drawing will look.

The Layer Properties Manager provides an easy-to-use interface for managing viewport layer visibility settings. The primary disadvantage of using the Layer Properties Manager is that the settings you make are applied only to the current viewport or to viewports that do not yet exist. In a drawing with very few layout viewports this is not a problem. However, when you are trying to manage layer settings in a drawing that uses several viewports, it can be faster to use the VPLAYER command. Although it uses a command-line interface, the VPLAYER command provides the capability to apply settings to all viewports or to use your cursor to pick the desired viewports. The VPLAYER command also offers an option to create a new layer that is frozen in all existing or new layout viewports using the individual viewport visibility setting.

VPLAYER
VL

The VPLAYER command is accessed by typing **VL** or **VPLAYER** at the Command: prompt. The available options for the VPLAYER command are described here:

- **?** Displays the names of layers that are frozen in the current viewport.
- **Freeze** Freezes one or more layers in one or more layout viewports.
- **Thaw** Thaws one or more layers in one or more layout viewports.
- **Reset** Resets layer visibility settings in specified viewports to their current default. The default setting is specified using the Vpvisdflt option of VPLAYER.
- **Newfrz** Creates new layers that are frozen in all viewports.
- **Vpvisdflt** Sets the default visibility for specified layers in subsequently created viewports.

One of the most powerful features of the VPLAYER command is the capability to set visibility options for any number of layers and to apply the settings to any number of viewports. When changing the visibility of multiple layers, use commas to separate the individual layer names. The options for specifying the viewports to which to apply the settings include All, Select, and Current. The All option affects all layout viewports in the current layout, or you can use the Select option to pick the desired viewports. The following example uses VPLAYER to freeze five layers in four selected viewports:

Command: **VL** or **VPLAYER**↵
Enter an option [?/Freeze/Thaw/Reset/Newfrz/Vpvisdflt]: **F**↵
Enter layer name(s) to freeze: **HATCH,DIMENSIONS,DETAIL,BOR,Title Block**↵
Enter an option [All/Select/Current] <Current>: **S**↵
Select objects: ⟨*pick a viewport*⟩ 1 found
Select objects: ⟨*pick a viewport*⟩ 1 found, 2 total
Select objects: ⟨*pick a viewport*⟩ 1 found, 3 total
Select objects: ⟨*pick a viewport*⟩ 1 found, 4 total
Select objects: ↵
Enter an option [?/Freeze/Thaw/Reset/Newfrz/Vpvisdflt]: ↵
Command:

Field Notes

- Another common application of controlling layer visibility in individual viewports can be found in drawings where multiple external references are placed in a single composite drawing.
- When specifying layer names for the VPLAYER command, you can use wildcards to simplify specification of multiple layer names.
- To specify all layers introduced by a particular Xref, use the wildcard specification XrefName|*, substituting the actual name of the external reference for "XrefName". For example, all of the dependent layers in the Xref named StairDetail.dwg can be specified using StairDetail|*.

Using Paper Space Linetype Scaling

In many drawing applications, the layout shows the drawing model using multiple viewports that use varying display scales. Scaling linetype representations based on paper space units ensures a consistent appearance in the layout regardless of the magnification levels used in each viewport. When paper space linetype scaling is disabled, the linetype representations are based on the actual units of the space in which the objects were created (model or paper).

Both viewports in Figure 13.41A show the exact same drawing objects using different display scales. With paper space linetype scaling enabled, the dashed linetypes have a consistent appearance and are able to conform with appropriate drafting standards. The same viewports are shown in Figure 13.41B, with paper space linetype scaling disabled. Because the linetype appearance is based on model space units, a larger display scale results in longer dash lengths. Inconsistent representations of the same line linetype can cause a drawing to deviate from proper drafting standards.

Paper space linetype scaling can be set in the Details area of the Linetype Manager dialog box using the checkbox labeled Use paper space units for scaling. Optionally, you can set the PSLTSCALE system variable to 1 to enable paper space linetype scaling, or set it to 0 to disable this feature. The PSLTSCALE variable can be set at the Command: prompt as follows:

Command: **PSLTSCALE**↵
Enter new value for PSLTSCALE <0>: **1**↵
Command:

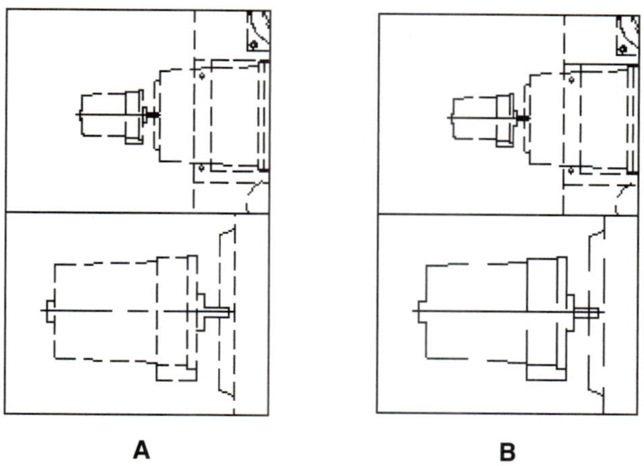

FIGURE 13.41 (A) With paper space linetype scaling enabled, linetype representations are consistent in each viewport. (B) Disabling paper space linetype scaling can result in varied representations of the same linetypes.

Field Notes

- Even when paper space linetype scaling is enabled, the current LTSCALE setting and object linetype scales can cause incorrect linetype representations. The dashed linetype definitions used by AutoCAD LT are created at actual size based on accepted drafting industry standards, so if the linetypes in your layout are not displayed correctly even with paper space linetype scaling enabled, try setting the global linetype scale (LTSCALE) and object linetype scales to a value near 1.
- Linetypes scaled to paper space are not automatically updated when you change the display scale in a layout viewport. Additionally, changes to the PSLTSCALE setting are not shown until the viewport is regenerated. To update a single viewport, make it current and use the REGEN command. To update all viewports at the same time, use the REGENALL command.
- Paper space linetype scaling does not affect the representation of linetypes in the Model tab. While you are working in the Model tab, use the LTSCALE variable to control the display of linetypes.

Scaling Hatch Patterns Relative to Paper Space

The appearance of hatch patterns, just like linetypes and other drawing elements, should be consistent in each application within a layout. Scale your hatch pattern based on paper space units to achieve a uniform appearance in each viewport and to ensure that the hatch pattern scale used is appropriate for the layout.

The paper space scaling option is provided in the boundary hatch dialog box on the Quick tab, shown in Figure 13.42A. Place a check mark in the box labeled Relative to paper space to enable this feature. An application of hatching scaled relative to paper space is illustrated in Figure 13.42B. The top viewport shows the relative sizes of the circles shown in the two bottom viewports. The actual hatch scale as applied in paper space is very different between these two objects, yet in the layout the patterns are identical. The display scale in the viewport on the left is 10:1, and the one on the right is shown at 1:1. Because the Relative to paper space option was used, the hatch patterns were scaled to look correct based on the display scale of the viewport where the hatch was performed. Unlike linetype scales, hatch pattern scales are not updated based on a change in the viewport display scale.

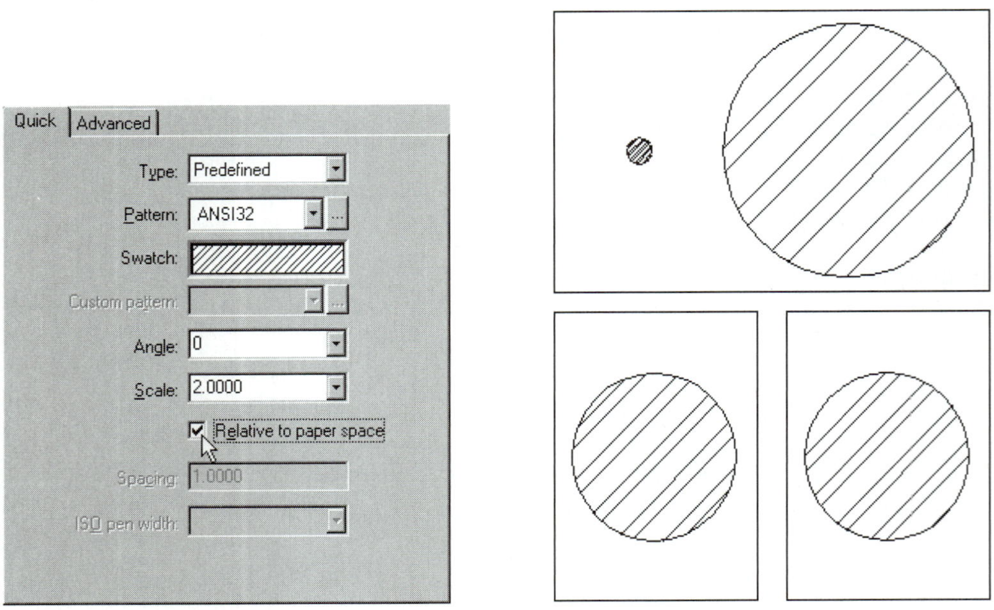

A B

FIGURE 13.42 (A) Check the Relative to paper space option to automatically scale a pattern correctly for your layout. (B) Scaling hatch patterns relative to paper space produces hatch patterns that are scaled appropriate to your layout, regardless of the actual size of the hatch area.

Exercise 13.4

Estimated time required: 15 min.

1. Open EX13-3B.dwg for editing.
2. Turn all layout viewports on.
3. Create a layer named *Vports*, and change all the layout viewports to the new layer.
4. Freeze the Vports layer. Double-click inside one of the viewports to activate model space.
5. Use the Ctrl+R accelerator keystroke to move to a different viewport.
6. Freeze several layers in the Active viewport using the Layer Properties Manager. Close the Layer Properties Manager and observe the results.
7. Open the Layer Properties Manager again and freeze several layers in New viewports. Close the Layer Properties Manager.
8. Create a new viewport and make it current. Open the Layer Properties Manager and check the layer settings.
9. Use the VPLAYER command to thaw all layers in all viewports.
10. Set the PSLTSCALE variable to 1 to enable paper space linetype scaling. Verify that the LTSCALE variable is also set to 1.
11. In one of your viewports, set the display scale at 1:1. Draw a simple shape using the CENTER linetype.
12. Switch to a different viewport. Zoom or pan if necessary to view the shape you created in step 11.
13. Change the viewport display scale to 1:4. Use the REGENALL command to regenerate all viewports.
14. Create a viewport arrangement using the example illustrated in Figure 13.42 as a guide. Draw one circle with a diameter of 1 unit and a second circle with a diameter of 10 units. Adjust the display scale as needed to look like the example.
15. Use the BHATCH command to apply a hatch pattern in each circle using the Relative to paper space option.
16. Save as EX13.4 and close the drawing.

LEARNING CHECKPOINT

- □ What options are available to prevent viewport borders from being displayed or plotted?
- □ What dimension scale setting should be used when dimensioning in a viewport?
- □ Discuss the tools in the Layer Properties Manager for controlling layer visibility in layout viewports.
- □ What is the primary disadvantage of using the Layer Properties Manager to control viewport layer visibility?
- □ What are the options of the VPLAYER command?
- □ What is the name of the variable that controls paper space linetype scaling? Name two ways to set this variable.
- □ What are the benefits of scaling linetypes and hatch patterns relative to paper space?

Laying Out Drawings

- Controlling the Visibility of Objects in Layout Viewports
- Controlling the Scale of Dimensions in Drawing Views

Plotting Your Drawing

Basic plotting concepts and procedures were introduced in Chapter 2 of this text. Topics covered included the primary features of the Plot dialog box, setting basic plot parameters, and using the partial and full preview features to check your results before sending the plot to the plotting device. The following discussion covers plotter configurations and additional topics related to plotting.

Configuring Printers and Plotters

AutoCAD LT automatically lists the currently configured system printers in the Plotter configurations area on the Plot Device tab of the Page Setup and Plot dialog boxes. ***System printers*** are printers or plotters configured for use with Windows. A device that is supported by AutoCAD LT but not by Windows is referred to as a ***non-system printer***. The Plotter Manager is used to add non-system printers to the list of available devices in AutoCAD LT.

You can access the Plotter Manager by picking Plotter Manager... from the File menu or by typing **PLOTTERMANAGER** at the Command: prompt. The Plotter Manager is displayed as a Windows Explorer window showing the contents of the AutoCAD LT 2000\Plotters folder (see Figure 13.43). Its appearance may vary slightly depending on your operating system.

FIGURE 13.43 The Plotter Manager window is a Windows Explorer window where you can access the Add-A-Plotter Wizard or modify existing plotter configurations.

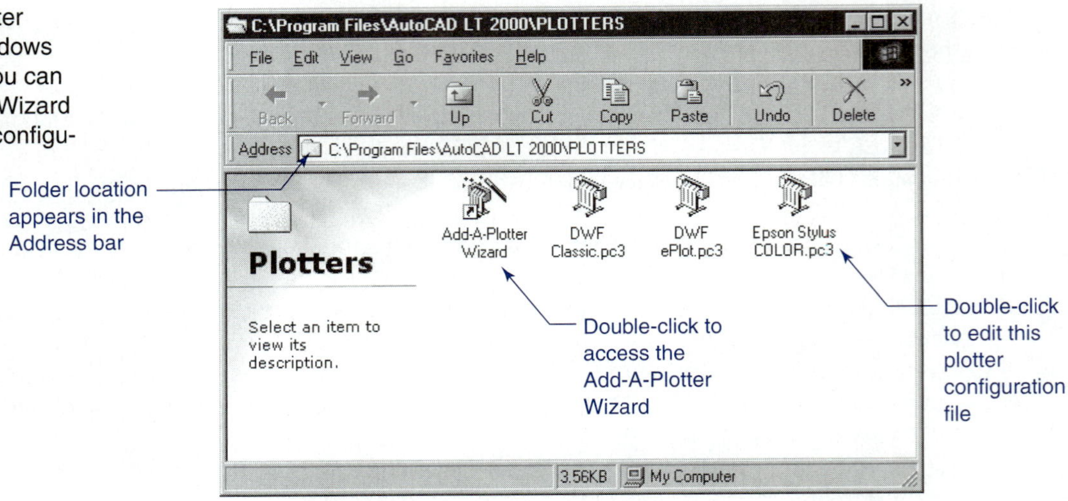

Double-click on the Add-A-Plotter Wizard icon to add a non-system printer to your list of available plot devices. The Add-A-Plotter Wizard guides you step by step through the process of configuring the new device. In a school or work environment, always ask your instructor or system administrator for authorization and assistance before configuring new plot devices.

The other icons in this window represent custom plotter configuration files. When you need the AutoCAD LT default printing properties to be different from the Windows defaults, you can create a new custom plotter configuration or modify an existing configuration. You do this from the Plot Device tab by selecting the desired Plotter configuration from the Name: list and picking the Properties... button to display the Plotter Configuration Editor dialog box (refer to Figure 13.5). If you modify the default print settings for AutoCAD LT, the new settings are saved in a custom plotter configuration file. You are prompted for a name and location, and a .pc3 file extension is automatically assigned. The default and recommended location for a new .pc3 file is the Plotters folder so that it is displayed when you open the Plotter Manager window. When configuration changes are made from the Plot dialog box, you are given the option of applying the changes to the current plot only or of saving them in a .pc3 file. Existing custom plotter configurations can also be modified by double-clicking on the .pc3 file icon in the Plotter Manager window.

If you calibrate the plotter or change any of the default paper sizes, a Plotter Model Parameters file is saved in the AutoCAD LT 2000\Drv folder using a .pmp file extension.

Field Notes

- Do not modify any existing .pc3 files without proper authorization and guidance. Incorrectly configuring a plotter can produce undesirable results.
- The Custom Properties category in the Plotter Configuration Editor dialog box displays the Custom Properties... button. Picking the Custom Properties... button displays the device-specific user interface. This refers to the configuration software supplied with the device (or an aftermarket driver software) and used to control printing options in Windows.

If you have used previous versions of AutoCAD LT, or your company has upgraded to AutoCAD LT 2000, you can import plot configurations originally created in the earlier software version. Depending on which version of AutoCAD LT was used, plot settings saved to a file were assigned either a .pcp or a .pc2 file extension.

AutoCAD LT provides Wizard tools to guide you through each step. From the Wizards cascade on the Tools menu, pick Import AutoCAD R14/LT97/LT98 Plot Settings... to import settings for paper size and for plot area, scale, origin, and offset. The imported settings are applied to the current model or layout tab. Pen assignment settings can be imported from a .pcp or a .pc2 file using the Add-A-Plot Style Table Wizard covered later in this chapter.

When configuring a new non-system printer, you can import default settings from a .pcp or .pc2 file in the Add-A-Plotter Wizard. To import the settings into an existing plotter configuration, pick the Import... button in the Plotter Configuration Editor dialog box; this displays the Plotting Components dialog box to show how the imported settings are used in AutoCAD LT 2000 (see Figure 13.44). Pick OK to display the Import file dialog box, and select the file to import.

FIGURE 13.44 The Plotting Components dialog box illustrates how imported plotter configuration information is implemented in AutoCAD LT 2000.

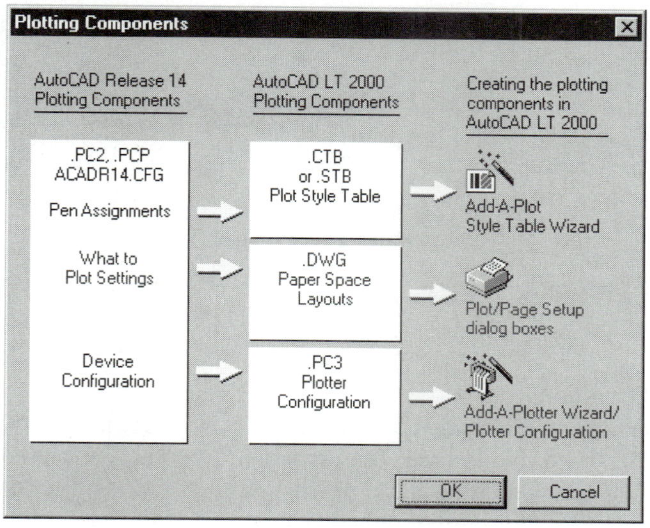

Using the Plot Dialog Box

File
Plot...

PLOT
PRINT
PP
[Ctrl] + [P]

Basic layout settings were established in the Page Setup dialog box, which also provided access to set up the default plotting options for your layout. When you are ready to plot your layout, these default values are presented in the Plot dialog box. You can use the plot default settings or modify them as needed for the current plotting application. The Plot dialog box is displayed by the PLOT command. You can access the PLOT command by picking the Plot button from the Standard toolbar, by picking Plot... from either the File menu or the layout tab shortcut menu, by typing **PLOT, PRINT,** or **PP** at the Command: prompt, or by using the Ctrl+P accelerator keystroke.

The Plot dialog box and the Page Setup dialog box look very similar and present many of the same options. The Plot dialog displays additional options related to plotting that do not affect the page setup. These include all general settings that can apply to any layout, such as the plot device, plot style tables assignment, and plot settings. Settings that are specific to a particular layout such as the layout name cannot be changed in this dialog box. The Plot Device tab of the Plot dialog box is shown in Figure 13.45.

Layout name

The name of the current layout is displayed in this area. The Save changes to layout checkbox is used to specify whether any changes you make to the plot settings are saved as defaults for this layout.

Page setup name

You can select a named page setup from which to import plot settings, or you can save the current settings as a named page setup. Saving and using named page setups was covered earlier in this chapter.

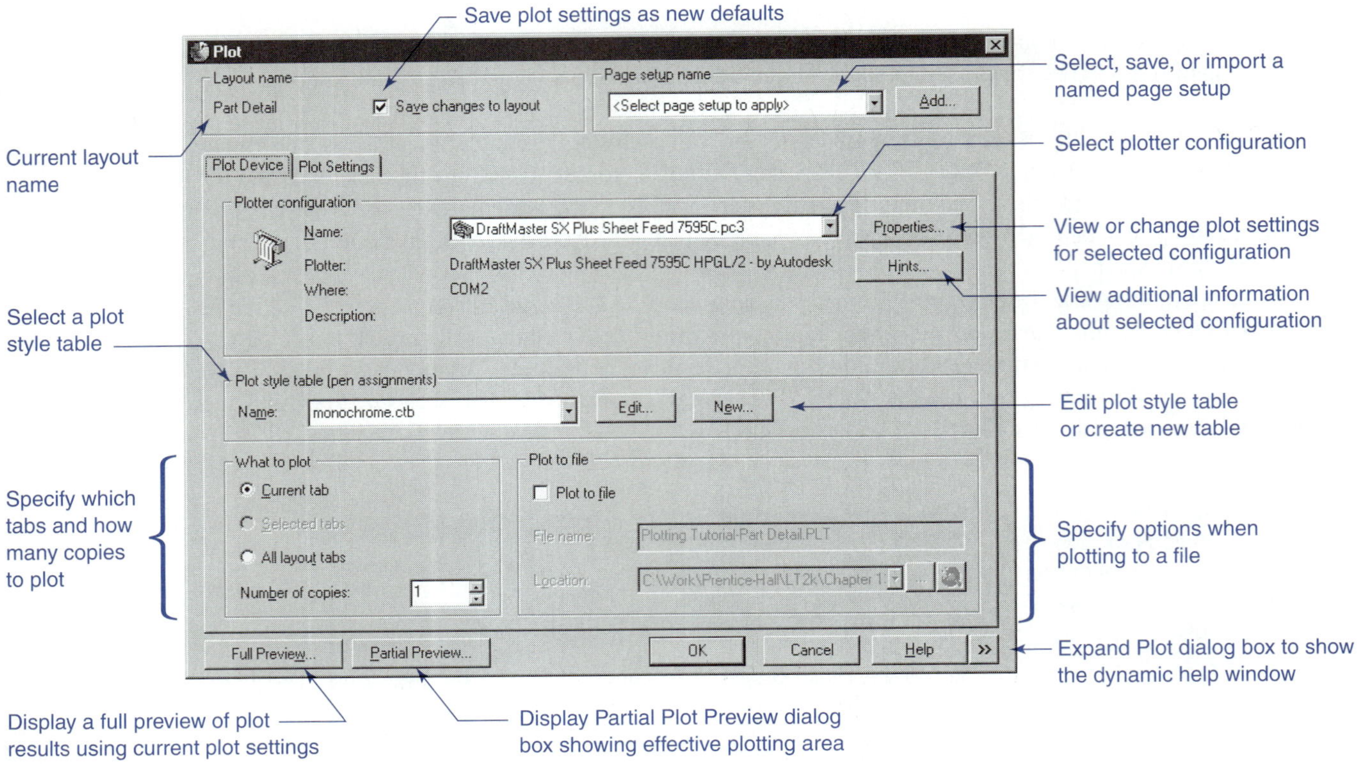

FIGURE 13.45 The Plot Device tab of the Plot dialog box.

Plotter configuration

The default current plotter configuration for this layout is shown in the Name: list. You can use the default device or select a new one as desired. The Properties... button can be used to modify the selected plotter configuration. Configuration changes can be applied to the current plot only or saved in a .pc3 file. Use the Hints... button to get additional information about the current plot configuration if needed.

Plot style table (pen assignments)

AutoCAD LT provides several plot style table options. If the current drawing is set to use color-dependent plot styles, the options show a .ctb file extension. In a drawing using named plot styles, the file extension is .stb. Unless the default plot style setting has been changed or you started your drawing using a template with named plot styles, then color-dependent plot styles are used. Using named plot styles and working with plot style tables is covered later in this chapter. Until you learn to work with plot styles, it is recommended that you select *aclt.ctb* when using color printing devices and *monochrome.ctb* for black-ink-only devices.

What to plot

The default option is to plot only the Current tab. You can also specify that All layout tabs are to be plotted, or just the currently Selected tabs. The Selected tabs option is available only if more than one tab is selected when you start the PLOT command and can be used to plot only tabs that already have plot settings established. After you specify what to plot, you can specify the Number of copies to plot.

Plot to file

You can save the plot information in a plot file by checking the Plot to file box. This enables the File name: box and the Location: list, so that you can specify where the plot file is to be saved and to assign a desired name. Use the ellipsis button to use the Browse for Folder dialog box to specify the location, or pick the Search the Web button to save the plot file to a Web location. Plot files are saved with a .plt file extension.

When all of the desired options have been set in the Plot Device tab, pick the Plot Settings tab to finish configuring the plot. The Plot Settings tab displays the exact same options as the Layout Settings tab of the Page Setup dialog box. The Plot Settings tab is shown in Figure 13.46.

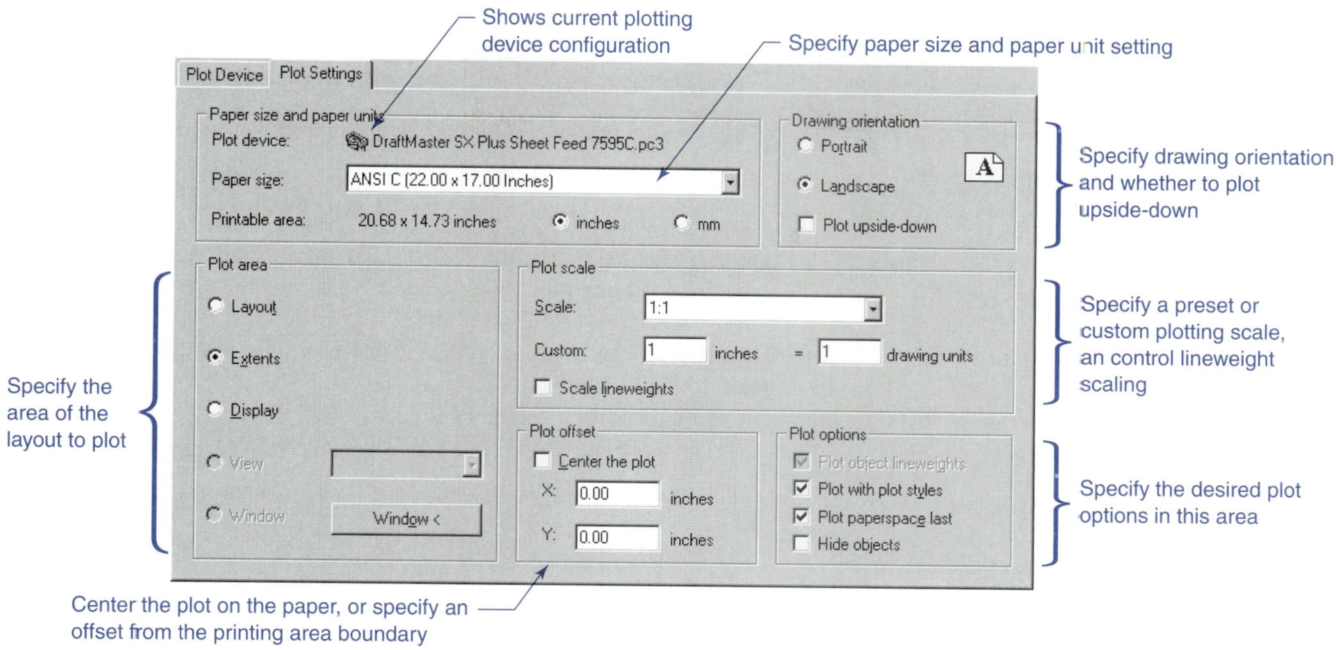

FIGURE 13.46 The Plot Settings tab in the Plot dialog box.

Paper size and paper units

The current plot device configuration is displayed in this area. The default paper size and paper units settings can be changed if desired. All available paper sizes supported by the current plot device are shown in the Paper size: list.

Plot area

This determines what part of the layout is printed. The available options are as follows:

- **Layout** Plots everything in the printable area in the layout. When you are plotting from the Model tab, this option changes to Limits, which plots the current drawing limits. In a 3D view that is not a plan view, the drawing extents are plotted.
- **Extents** Plots the calculated drawing extents. The drawing extents are defined as the smallest possible rectangle that can surround all objects in the current tab.
- **Display** This option plots the area of the drawing that is currently displayed in the drawing window.
- **View** This option is enabled only if named views are defined in the current space. All available named views are shown in the drop-down list.
- **Window** Plots a user-defined area of the drawing. To enable this selection or to change the current window definition, pick the Window < button. Specify the corners of the window either by using the keyboard or by picking with the cursor.

Drawing orientation

Specify either Portrait or Landscape orientation. Placing a check in the checkbox creates the plot upside-down. This has the same effect as rotating 180°.

Plot scale

The scale for plotting a layout is typically 1:1. All scaling of geometry is done in the layout viewports by setting the viewport display scale. If you need to plot at a different scale, select from the preset options, or enter a custom value. Using the Scaled to Fit option plots the specified plot area as large as possible on the selected paper size; the calculated scale displayed in the text boxes show the ratio of plotted units to drawing units. If you are plotting a layout at a scale other than 1:1, you may want to scale the lineweights so that the drawing presentation does not change. For example, if you are plotting an "E" size layout on an "A" size paper, full-size lineweights may make the drawing difficult to read.

Plot offset

You can position the plot on the paper by centering it or by specifying an offset from the origin. The default origin offset is 0 on both the X and Y axes. This means that the lower left corner of the plotted area is positioned at the lower left corner of the printable area.

Plot options

The Plot options are used to control plotting results. These options are described as follows:

- **Plot object lineweights** This option is enabled only if the Plot with plot styles option is disabled. When you are not using plot styles to specify pen widths, this option plots each object using its assigned lineweight.
- **Plot with plot styles** This option plots objects based on the current plot style settings and is the best option for most applications.
- **Plot paperspace last** Specifies that paper space geometry is plotted last.
- **Hide objects** Plots model space views with hidden lines removed in 3D applications.

Field Notes

- Using the plot preview options can help you avoid having to plot a layout more than once to get the desired results. In the full preview mode you can view the plot exactly as it will appear on the paper, allowing you to spot any possible problems and correct them before actually sending the plot. This practice increases productivity and reduces paper waste.
- If you have plotted a layout previously and do not need to change the active settings, you can plot the drawing without using the Plot dialog box. Pick the Plot Preview button to display a full preview, and if the settings are correct, right-click and pick Plot from the shortcut menu.
- The Layer Properties Manager or Layer Control list can be used to turn plotting on or off for specific layers.

Exercise 13.5 — Estimated time required: 15 min.

1. Open a completed dimensioned drawing from a previous chapter.
2. Plot the drawing extents from the Model tab.
3. Define a layout that is appropriate for the drawing if one is not already defined. Set up the default plot parameters in the Page Setup dialog box. Ask your instructor or system administrator if you need assistance selecting or setting up a plotter configuration.
4. Plot the layout at a scale of 1:1.

LEARNING CHECKPOINT

- ☐ Define system and non-system printers.
- ☐ How is the Plotter Manager used?
- ☐ How can plot settings from earlier versions of AutoCAD LT be used in AutoCAD LT 2000?
- ☐ Name six different ways to display the Plot dialog box.
- ☐ What are the primary differences between the Page Setup dialog box and the Plot dialog box?
- ☐ What feature in the Plot dialog box saves the current plot settings as default values for the current layout?
- ☐ What setting must be active for plot styles to be used in a plot?

Plotting Your Drawing

- Configuring Your Plotter
- Basic Plotting

Plot Styles

Plot styles are saved settings that control how drawing geometry is plotted. A ***plot style table*** stores defined plot styles, which are assigned to drawing objects to control plotting features like color, lineweight, linetype, and screening. Existing plot style settings can be modified to produce different plotting results. When a plot style is assigned to a layer or to an object, the plot style definition is not added into the drawing database. Instead, AutoCAD LT reads the plot style table each time you plot and uses the current plot style definitions. By editing plot style definitions in a plot style table, you change the way that all drawings using that table are plotted.

Plot styles are not device dependent, so they can be used to control the plotting results on every device to which you plot. Any specific plot style features that are not supported by a device are simply ignored. Effective use of plot styles enables you to consistently produce professional quality prints of your drawing layouts.

Plot Style Control Features

The primary properties of an object that affect its plotted appearance include color, linetype, and lineweight. When plot styles are not used for plotting, objects are plotted using their assigned color and linetype, and the Plot Options area of the Plot Settings tab controls whether object lineweights are used for plotting. If you use different colors in a drawing and plot to a monochrome (black-ink-only) printer without using plot styles, the printer may try to simulate the object colors using various shades of gray.

Plot style assignments override object properties for plotting but do not affect the assigned properties for objects in the drawing. The Display plot styles checkbox is found in the Plot style table (pen assignments) area of the Plot Device tab on the Plot and Page Setup dialog boxes. When this box is checked, the layout is displayed on screen using the current plot style settings. This allows you to view the drawing exactly as it will be printed while you are designing the layout. Plot style properties cannot be displayed in the Model tab, so this option is enabled only when the current tab is a layout.

Besides controlling color, linetype, and lineweight characteristics, plot styles have additional property settings that provide more complete control over plotting results. Plot style control features include the following aspects:

- **Color** Specifies the plotted object color. If object colors are used with a black-ink-only device, object colors are simulated using various shades of gray (if this feature is supported by the plotter).
  Default: Use object color
- **Dither** This setting refers to the approximation of colors using dot patterns. If your plotter does not support dithering, this setting is ignored. On thin-lineweight objects, dot patterns can change the linetype appearance. Turning dithering off prevents this from happening.
  Default: On.
- **Grayscale** Allows you to produce a grayscale drawing on a color printing device, if this feature is supported by the device. Two hundred fifty-five different shades of gray are used to represent the 255 colors supported by AutoCAD LT (see Figure 13.47).
  Default: Off.

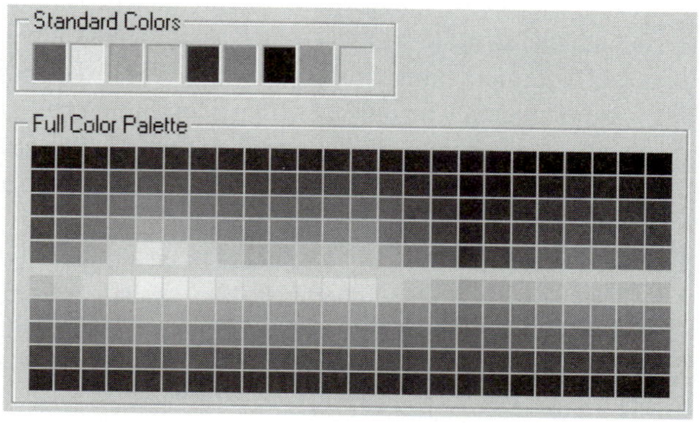

FIGURE 13.47 The AutoCAD LT Color Index (ACI) represented as grayscale colors.

- **Pen number** This setting is used only for pen-style plotters. You can assign up to 32 pen numbers, depending on how many pens the plotter actually uses. This value cannot be changed in a color-dependent plot style or if the Color setting is set to *Use object color*. The *Automatic* setting determines the appropriate pen for each color based on the Physical Pen Characteristics settings in the Plotter Configuration Editor.
Default: Automatic.
- **Virtual pen** A ***virtual pen*** is a color setting used by a non-pen plotter so it can plot based on pen assignments. If your plotter supports this feature, it can be set to use virtual pens in the Plotter Configuration Editor using the Color Depth setting under the Graphic > Vector Graphics option. Many plotting devices that support this feature also allow the virtual pens to be assigned specific properties, such as lineweight or color, using controls on the front panel of the device. The *Automatic* setting makes pen assignments from the AutoCAD Color Index (ACI).
Default: Automatic.
- **Screening** ***Screening*** is an effect used to plot objects using varying color intensities by controlling the amount of ink applied when plotting. Screening can be used to *fade* parts of the drawing to make other areas stand out more. For example, in a remodeling project, the existing structure can be faded to the background for contrast, so that the new geometry can be clearly identified. The screening value represents a percentage of ink intensity; 0 is white (no ink), and 100 plots using complete color density.
Default: 100.
- **Linetype** This setting is used to override an object's assigned linetype and plot using a different linetype. Set this to *Use object linetype* to plot object linetypes as represented in the drawing.
Default: Use object linetype.
- **Adaptive** Adjusts linetype patterns so that objects display complete linetype representations and do not end in the middle of a linetype. On screen, AutoCAD LT does this by default. You can turn this off for plotting if exact linetype scales are more important than complete linetype representations.
Default: On.
- **Lineweight** Plots objects at a specified lineweight, overriding the lineweight used in the drawing. Set this to *Use object lineweight* to plot object lineweights as assigned in the drawing.
Default: Use object lineweight.
- **Line end style** Controls the plotting of object ends. The available line end styles are illustrated in Figure 13.48. Line end styles are visible only on objects with a lineweight greater than 0.
Default: Use object end style.

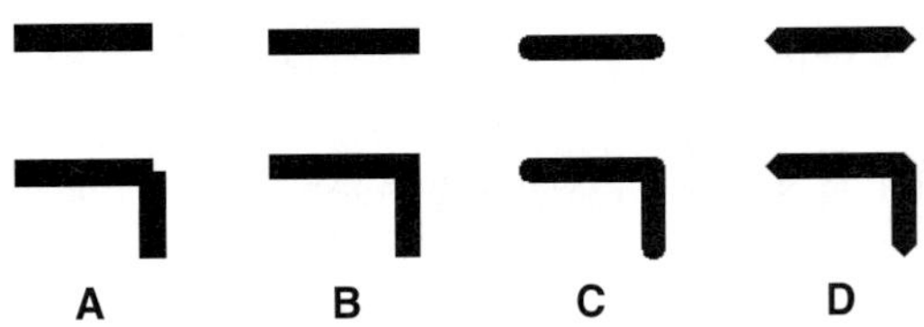

FIGURE 13.48 Available line end style options: (A) butt, (B) square, (C) round, and (D) diamond.

- **Line join style** Controls the way that object ends are joined. This setting works only for complex objects with two or more segments, such as polylines or text characters. The line join style does not affect individual line objects that meet at the endpoints, and the effects of this setting are visible only on objects with a lineweight greater than 0. The four available line join styles (miter, bevel, round, and diamond) are illustrated in Figure 13.49 as they appear when applied to a closed polyline with 0 width and an assigned lineweight of 2.0.
Default: Use object join style.
- **Fill style** A custom fill style can be selected to be applied to objects using fill, such as wide polylines or solid fill hatch patterns. You can select from nine options (see Figure 13.50), or you can use the object's assign fill style. In a drawing with many wide polylines or solid fill areas, this option can be used on your check plots to conserve ink.
Default: Use object fill style.

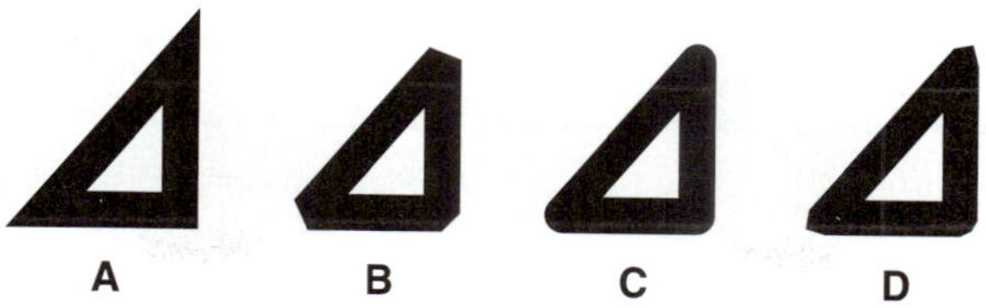

FIGURE 13.49 Available line join style options: (A) miter, (B) bevel, (C) round, and (D) diamond.

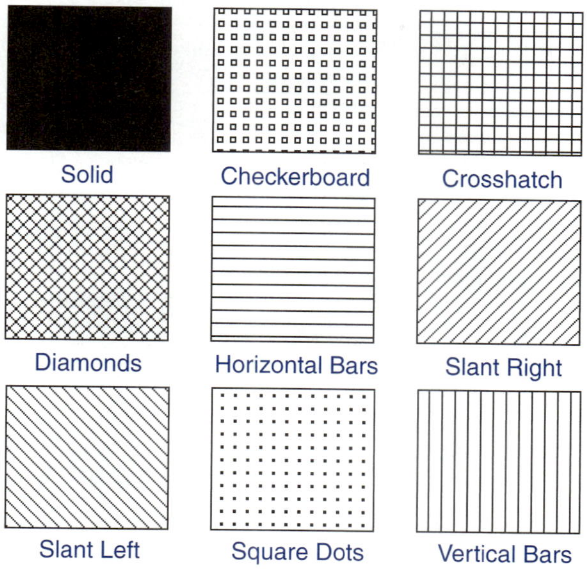

FIGURE 13.50 Optional fill styles can be used when plotting filled objects like polylines or solid hatch patterns.

Field Notes

Object lineweights are ignored by polylines drawn with the PLINE Width option set to a value greater than 0. This includes polylines whose width has been set above 0 using the PEDIT Width option. This means that the Lineweight, Line End Style, and Line Join Style settings have no effect on either the display or plotted appearance of wide polylines.

The features described in the previous list give you an idea about how aspects of plotted object appearance can be controlled using one or more customized plot styles. You can define multiple plot styles, each of which is set up using a different combination of values, to flexibly manage the results of a variety of plotting applications.

Related plot styles are stored in individual plot style tables, which are saved in a file. Plot style tables can be either *Color-dependent plot style tables* or *Named plot style tables*. Color-dependent plot style tables provide a familiar approach to managing plots for users of previous releases of AutoCAD LT and can easily be defined by importing established standard plot settings saved in an earlier software version. Named plot style tables provide the greatest flexibility and can be easier to set up, apply, and manage in your drawings. The following discussion gives complete descriptions of both types of plot style tables.

Color-Dependent Plot Style Tables

Color-dependent plot style tables control plotting characteristics based on object color. All objects in a drawing of any particular color are plotted using the same style settings. Because AutoCAD LT supports 255 different object colors, a color-dependent plot style table contains 255 plot styles—one for each color. You can edit color-dependent plot styles, but you cannot add plot styles to the table or remove them. Color-dependent plot style tables are similar to the plotting controls used in earlier versions of AutoCAD LT, which also used object color to control plotting characteristics.

In a drawing that uses color-dependent plot styles, the Plotstyle Control on the Object Properties toolbar list is disabled (see Figure 13.51A). When one or more objects are selected, the Plot style value in the

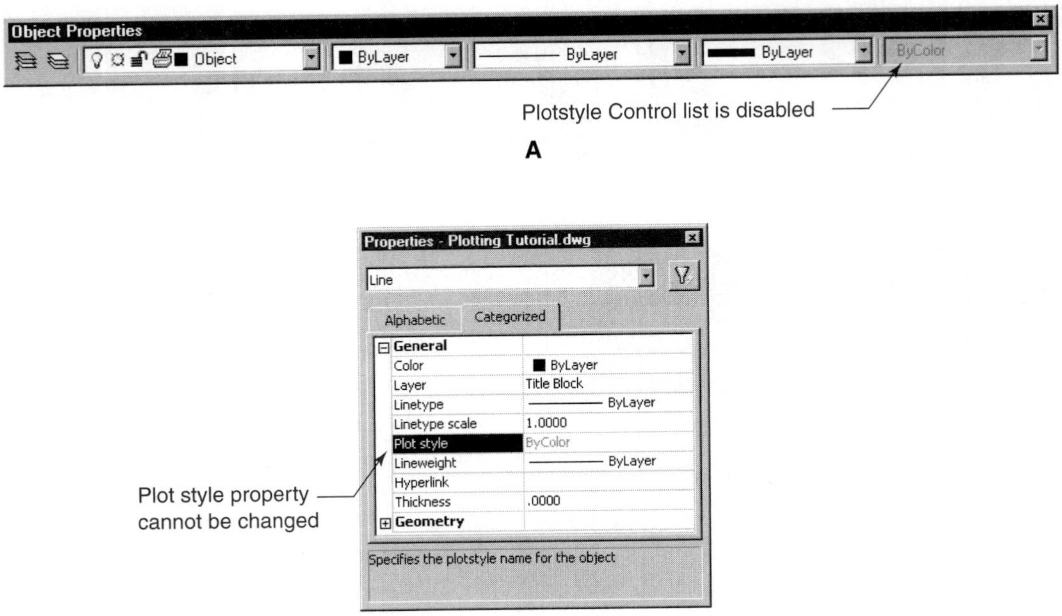

FIGURE 13.51 In a drawing using color-dependent plot styles, (A) the Plotstyle Control list is disabled and (B) the *ByColor* Plot style property cannot be changed.

Properties window is set to ByColor and cannot be changed, as shown in Figure 13.51B. In the Layer Properties Manager dialog box, the Plot Style value for each layer matches the current color of that layer. Changing the color setting of a layer also updates the Plot Style setting. To change the plotting characteristics of an object in a color-dependent application, you must change the object's color, edit the plot style defined for its current color, or assign a different plot style table.

Each layout in a drawing can reference a different plot style table. The default plot style table is specified in the Page Setup dialog box when a layout is defined and can be changed later using either the Page Setup or the Plot dialog box. Setting the plot style assignment was discussed previously in this chapter. AutoCAD LT provides several predefined color-dependent plot style tables that you can assign to your layouts, as described in Table 13.2. You can use these styles as they are, or you can use an existing table as a template and define a completely new style to match your plotting needs. Creating and editing plot style tables is covered later in this chapter.

TABLE 13.2 Predefined color-dependent plot style descriptions

Table	Description
Aclt.ctb	The default plot style table; all properties set to defaults.
Fill Patterns.ctb	First 9 colors use first 9 fill patterns; all others use object's fill. All other style properties set to defaults.
Grayscale.ctb	Plot all colors using grayscale; all other properties set to defaults.
Monochrome.ctb	Plots all colors as black; all other properties are set to default values.
None	No plot style table is used.
Screening 100%.ctb	Uses 100% ink density for all colors; all other properties set to defaults.
Screening 75%.ctb	Uses 75% ink density for all colors; all other properties set to defaults.
Screening 50%.ctb	Uses 50% ink density for all colors; all other properties set to defaults.
Screening 25%.ctb	Uses 25% ink density for all colors; all other properties set to defaults.

Field Notes

- Color-dependent plot style tables restrict how and where colors can be applied in a drawing. The colors assigned to the objects in your drawing are determined by the desired plotting results.
- AutoCAD LT actually supports 256 different colors, one of which is the drawing window background color. You can select only from 255 colors for drawing objects, because anything drawn using the same color as the background will not be visible. This is also why the color White is displayed either as white or black, depending on the current background color.

Named Plot Style Tables

Named plot style tables allow you to define one or more named plot styles that control plotting characteristics independent of the object color. In a drawing using named plot styles, the plot style setting is a simple object property—just like the color or linetype setting. You can assign plot style names to layers and use a *ByLayer* plot style setting as you draw. When you need to override layer settings you can set an active plot style name that is applied to the objects you draw. The current plot style property of any number of selected objects can be changed instantly using the Object Properties toolbar or the Properties window. Named plot style tables provide complete and flexible control of your plotting results.

Like object color, linetype, and lineweight, plot style name properties are most effectively managed using layers. Using the ByLayer setting for objects allows the plot style assignments to be controlled using layer property settings. The currently active plot style is displayed in the Plotstyle Control list in the Object Properties toolbar. Figure 13.52A shows the available list of options, which can also be used to modify the plot style assigned to selected objects. The Properties window provides the same list of settings (see Figure 13.52B).

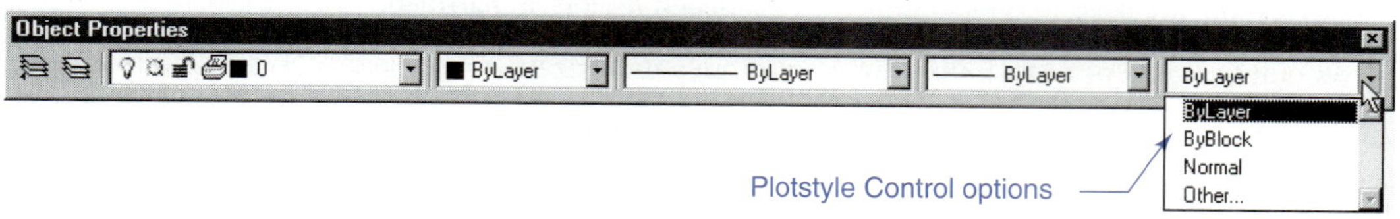

A

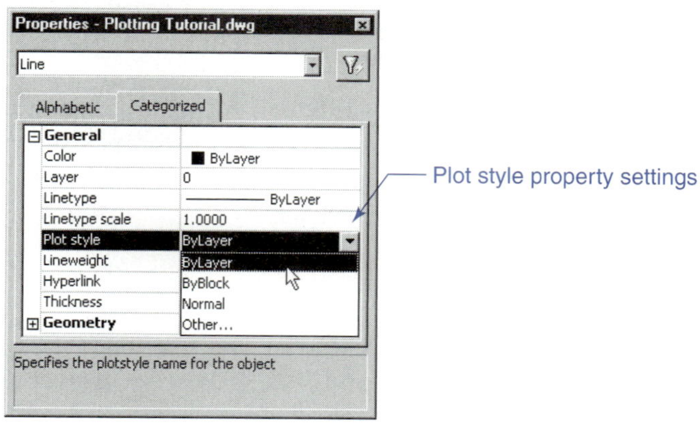

B

FIGURE 13.52 Named plot styles are assigned as object properties and, like color and linetype properties, should typically be set to ByLayer for most applications. The named plot style property can be set or changed using (A) the Plotstyle Control list or (B) the Plot style list in the Properties window.

Plot Style Tables

The first step toward successful plotting using plot styles is to define one standard plot style table for each set of drafting standards used in your company. These *standard* plot style tables are used to store each of the plot styles needed to plot the typical drawings produced by you or your department according to the required standards.

Before beginning to create and edit plot style tables, it is important to understand exactly what plot style tables are and how they are used by AutoCAD LT. Plot style tables are dynamic control centers for managing plotting results. AutoCAD LT does not store any plot style information with a saved drawing file except for the style names in use and the name of the plot style table in which they are found. Each time you open a drawing, the plot style table is located, and the style information is loaded. If any of the plot style definitions have changed since the last time you plotted, your results may be different this time. A single plot style table may directly control the plotting results for dozens or possibly hundreds of individual drawing files.

It is a fairly common practice in a networked environment for all drafters within a department to access standard resource libraries stored on the network. Plot styles that conform to established plotting standards are saved in a common plot style table that is located on the network for easy access by all members of the design team. This helps to ensure consistent plotting results that conform with established plotting standards. However, when a single plot style table is used by everyone, any changes to the plot styles it contains can affect everyone's plotting results.

When new plot style definitions are needed, evaluate the applications for the new standards. If these new styles are used in typical drawings produced in your department and will be needed on a continuing basis, place the new definitions in an appropriate standard plot style table. If the new styles are needed only on a temporary basis, or if they pertain to an unusual application, place them in a separate table.

Because of the potential of significantly affecting the plotting results for any number of drawings, it is important to follow proper procedure when working with plot style tables. Following these basic guidelines for working with plot style tables can help you avoid some of the potential problems related to plot style tables:

- Limit the content of standard plot style tables to plot styles that conform to the appropriate standard and styles that are used in typical drawings produced in your department.
- Never edit standard plot style tables without proper authorization.
- Always create a backup copy of a standard plot style table *before* editing it. Save backup copies in a secure location.
- Document the settings for each plot style in a standard plot style table; revise the documentation when changes are made.
- When making changes to a standard plot style table, promptly communicate the nature of the changes to everyone who uses the table.

AutoCAD LT provides several powerful tools for creating, editing, and managing your plot style tables. The Plot Style Manager window is used to access existing plot style tables or to create new ones. Easy-to-use wizard tools are also available to guide you through each step in creating new style tables. Each of these features is discussed in the following section.

Using the Plot Style Manager

File
Plot Style Manager...
STYLESMANAGER

The Plot Style Manager is a Windows Explorer window that shows the contents of the currently configured Plot Style Table Search Path. By default, this is the C:\Program Files\AutoCAD LT 2000\Plot Styles folder. The Plot Style Table Search Path specifies the folder where AutoCAD LT searches for plot style table files. This location is set on the Files tab of the Options dialog box, under the Printer Support File Path > Plot Style Table Search Path setting. Color-dependent plot style tables are saved with a .ctb file extension, and named plot style tables use a .stb extension. The Add-A-Plot Style Table Wizard is also found in this folder. You can access the Plot Style Manager by picking Plot Style Manager... from the File menu or by typing **STYLESMANAGER** at the Command: prompt. The Plot Style Manager window is shown in Figure 13.53.

To be guided through the process of creating a new plot style table, double-click on the Add-A-Plot Style Table Wizard. This wizard can also be accessed by picking Add Plot Style Table... from the Wizards

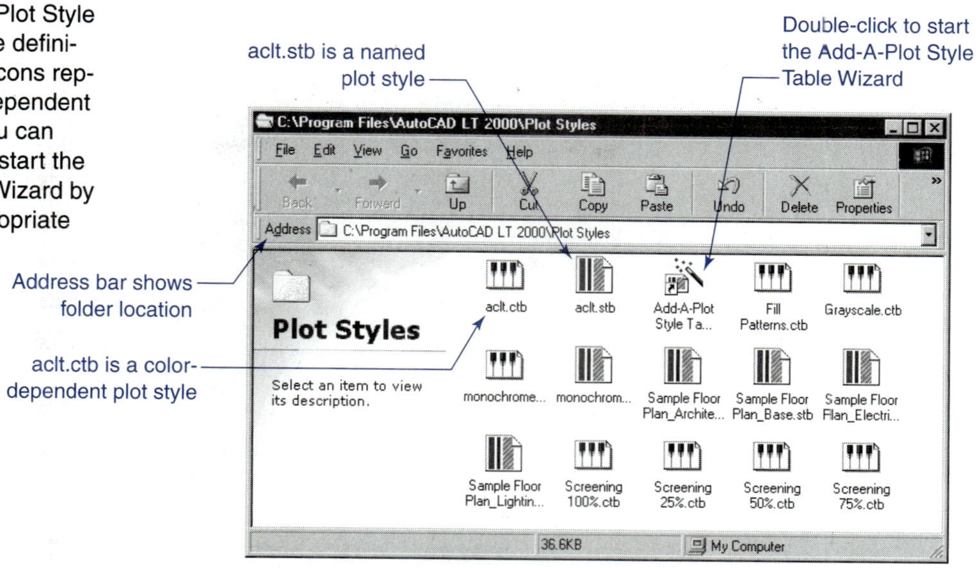

FIGURE 13.53 In the Plot Style Manager, plot style table definition files are shown as icons representing either color-dependent or named plot styles. You can edit a plot style table or start the Add-A-Plot Style Table Wizard by double-clicking the appropriate icon.

cascade on the Tools pull-down menu. When you start this wizard, the Add Plot Style Table dialog box is displayed. This first page provides a very general overview of plot style tables and the purpose of the wizard tool. Read through the information, then pick the Next > button to begin creating the new style.

The Wizards cascade on the Tools menu also displays an option listed either as Add Named Plot Style Table… or Add Color-Dependent Plot Style Table…; the listed option always matches the plot style table type used in the current drawing. Selecting this option also accesses the Add-A-Plot Style Wizard, but you are restricted to creating only the indicated table type.

On the Begin page of the Add Plot Style Wizard dialog box, shown in Figure 13.54, you first need to specify how the new table is to be created. Your options are as follows:

- **Start from scratch** This option allows you to create a new table that has only the initial default settings. If you are creating a color-dependent plot style table, it will have the required 255 styles all using default settings. A named plot style started from scratch is empty except for the Normal plot style, which cannot be modified, renamed, or deleted.
- **Use an existing plot style table** Use this option to start a new plot style table using the settings from an existing plot style table. This is helpful when the plot style table you are defining uses some of the settings as existing ones.
- **Use My R14 Plotter Configuration (CFG)** Use this option to import pen mapping information from an AutoCAD or AutoCAD LT configuration file; these were saved with a *.cfg* extension. Although this option references AutoCAD R14, you can also import from AutoCAD LT 97 or 98. The AutoCAD LT 98 configuration file name was *aclt5.cfg*, AutoCAD LT 97 used the *aclt4.cfg* file, and AutoCAD R14 saved as *acad14.cfg*. AutoCAD LT 2000 creates a file named *aclt2000.cfg*, but most of its configuration data are now saved in the Windows system registry.
- **Use a PCP or PC2 file** Importing .pcp and .pc2 files was introduced previously in this chapter. These files were used in earlier releases of AutoCAD LT to save plotter configuration information and pen settings. In addition to pen mapping, this option imports configuration information such as pen optimization settings, plot to file configurations, paper size and orientation, resolution, device name, and plot destination.

To review the Plotting Components dialog box illustration showing the relationship between .cfg, .pcp, and .pc2 files and AutoCAD LT 2000 plotting components, refer to Figure 13.44.

After you specify the option you want to use on the Begin page, select the Next > button to continue. The Table Type page is used to select the type of plot style table you want to create (see Figure 13.55). The

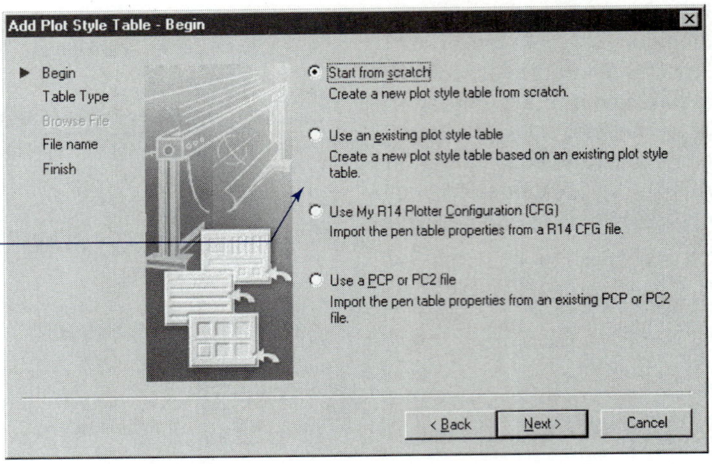

FIGURE 13.54 Select one of the four options to indicate how you want to create the new plot style table.

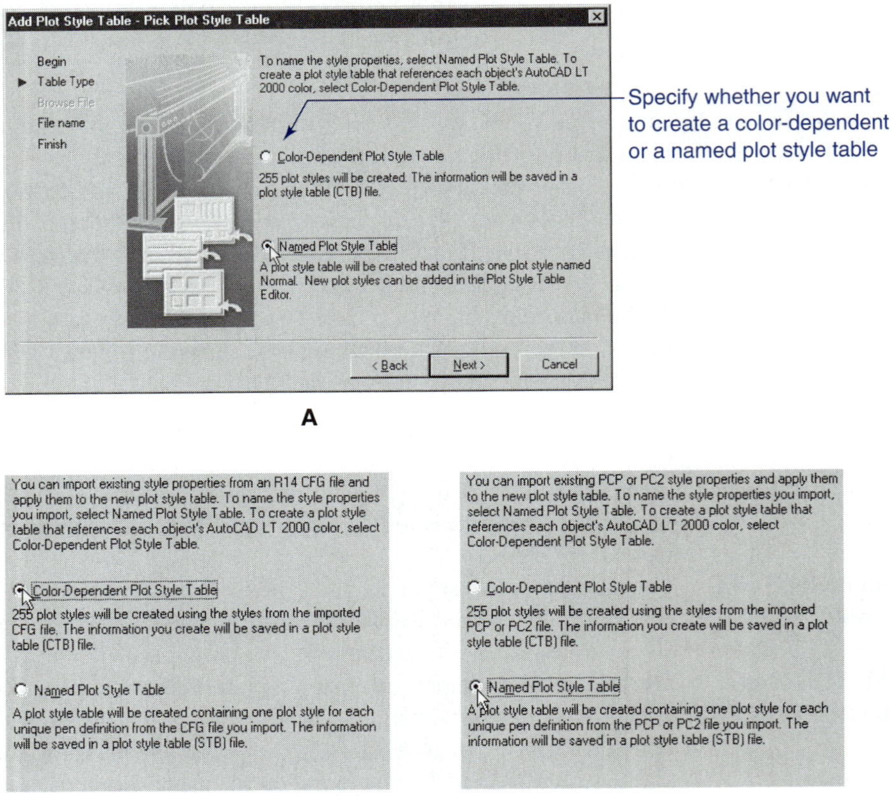

FIGURE 13.55 The Table Type page is used to specify the type of plot style table you want to create. This information displayed on this page varies depending on the method you selected for creating the new table, (A) Start from scratch, (B) Use My R14 Plotter Configuration, or (C) Use a PCP or PC2 file.

information displayed on this page varies based on the option selected on the Begin page. You can indicate whether to create a color-dependent or a named plot style. This dialog box is not displayed if you selected the Use an existing plot style table option because the new table will automatically be the same type as the existing one with which you started.

In the next step, the Browse File name page is used to select the file you are using to define the new plot style. Depending on the option you specified in the Begin page, you will need to select an existing plot style table, an AutoCAD/AutoCAD LT configuration file, or a plot configuration file. The information and options on this page depend on the Begin option that was specified. If you are starting from scratch, this page is not displayed at all. When you select an existing plot style table, the drop-down list displays all the plot style tables found in the current plot style table support path location, as shown in Figure 13.56A. If you prefer, you can pick the Browse... button to access the Select File dialog box to select a .ctb or .stb file from another location. The wizard appears as shown in Figure 13.56B if you selected the Use My R14 Plotter Configuration option. You can enter the location and name of a .cfg file to use or pick the Browse... button to display the

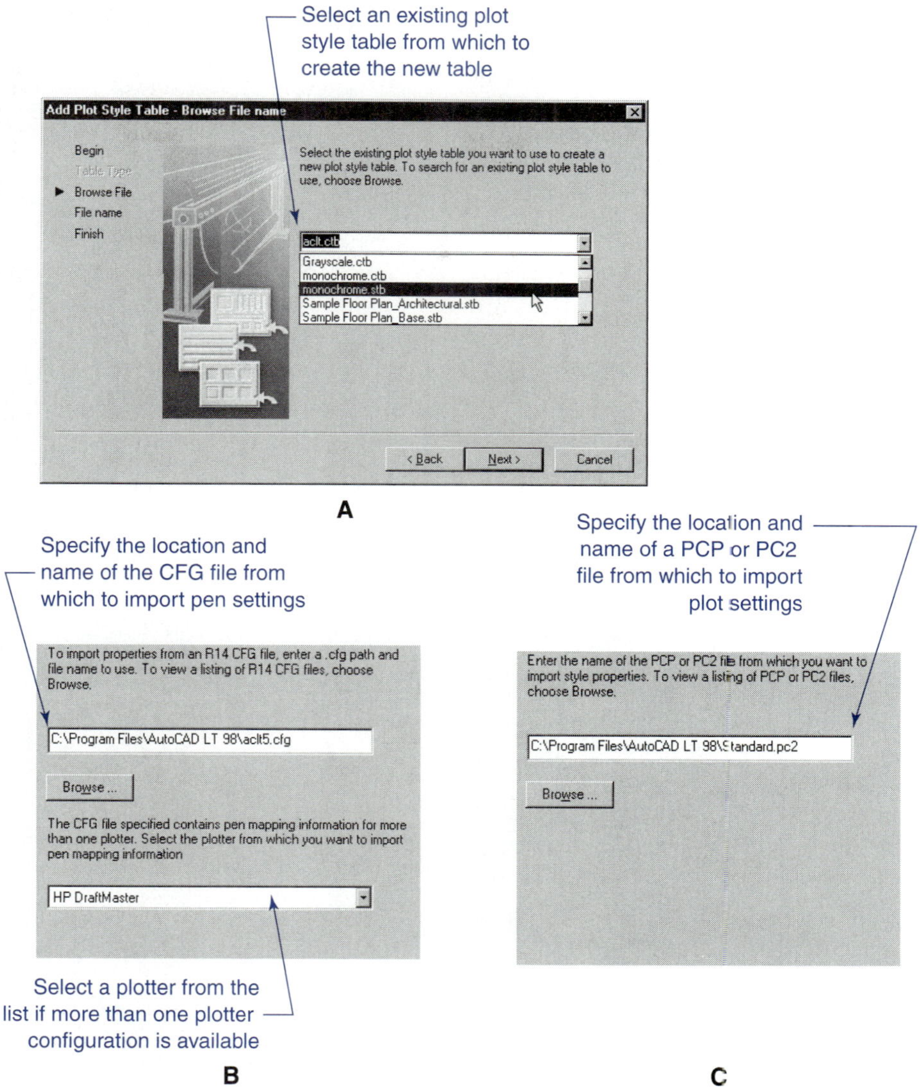

FIGURE 13.56 The Browse File name dialog options, based on the method you are using to create the new plot style table, allow you to specify (A) an existing plot style table, (B) an R14/LT97/LT98 configuration file, or (C) a PCP or PC2 file.

Import dialog box. If more than one plotter configuration is defined in the selected file, use the drop-down list to select from a list of the available plotter configurations. Creating the new table with the Use a PCP or PC2 file method requires specification of an existing .pcp or .pc2 file name and displays the dialog box shown in Figure 13.56C. Enter the desired file location and name, or pick the Browse… button to select a file using the Import dialog box.

Figure 13.57 shows the next page of the Add-A-Plot Style Wizard, where you specify the File name for the new .stb or .ctb file you are creating. You are not prompted for a location. It is automatically stored in the folder specified by the current Plot Style Table Search Path setting.

The final step shows the Finish page of the wizard (see Figure 13.58). This provides additional information based on the options you used to define the new plot style table. The Plot Style Table Editor… button can be used to start the Plot Style Table Editor so you can edit the new plot style table to define new styles or modify existing ones, as required. You can start the editor from here or pick the Finish button and modify the new plot style table later, as shown in the discussion that follows. Place a check mark in the check box if you want to set this as the default plot style table applied to new drawings and drawings you open that were created in an earlier release of AutoCAD LT. This option is available only when the plot style type you created matches the default setting specified in the Options dialog box. Setting default plot style behavior is covered later in this chapter.

The Finish page reports that the new style has been created, but it is not actually saved as a file until you pick the Finish button. This closes the Add-A-Plot Style Wizard dialog box and saves the new plot style table in the default Plot Styles folder using the file name you specified. Figure 13.59 shows the new plot style table definition icon displayed in the Plot Style Manager window. Double-click on any plot style table icon to open it for editing using the Plot Style Table Editor.

FIGURE 13.57 Specify the name of the plot style table file. The .ctb or .stb file extension is automatically applied, and the file is saved in the folder specified in the current Plot Style Table Search Path setting.

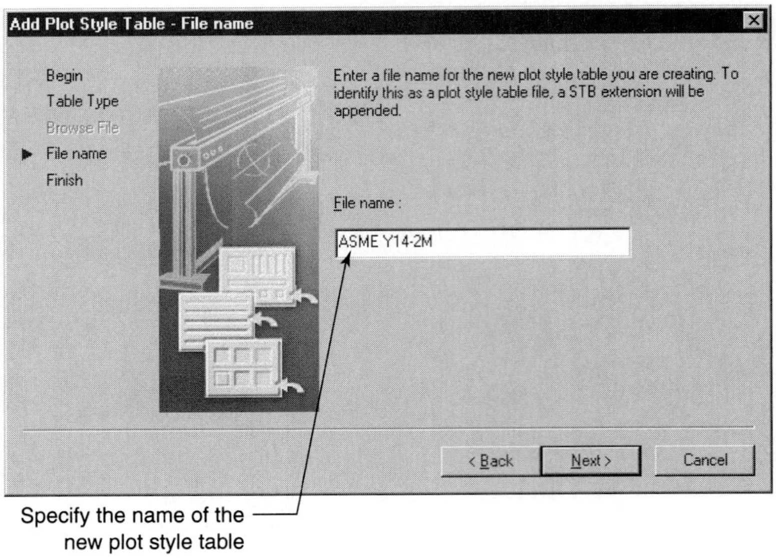

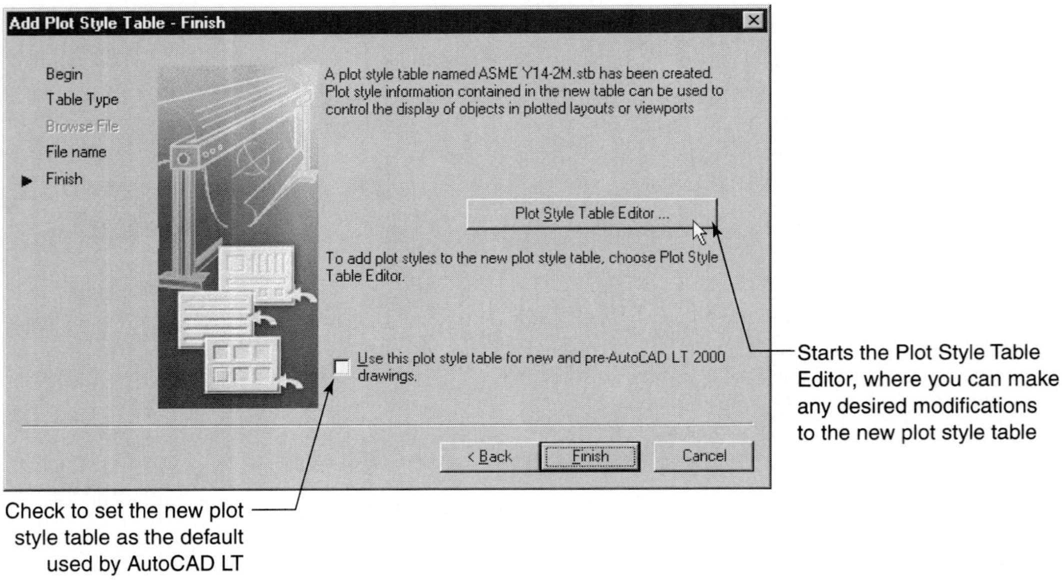

FIGURE 13.58 The Finish page displays the message that the new plot style table was saved as a file. Pick the Plot Style Table Editor... button to edit the new plot style table. The check box can be used to set the new plot style as the AutoCAD LT default.

FIGURE 13.59 (A) The new plot style table is displayed in the Plot Style Manager window.

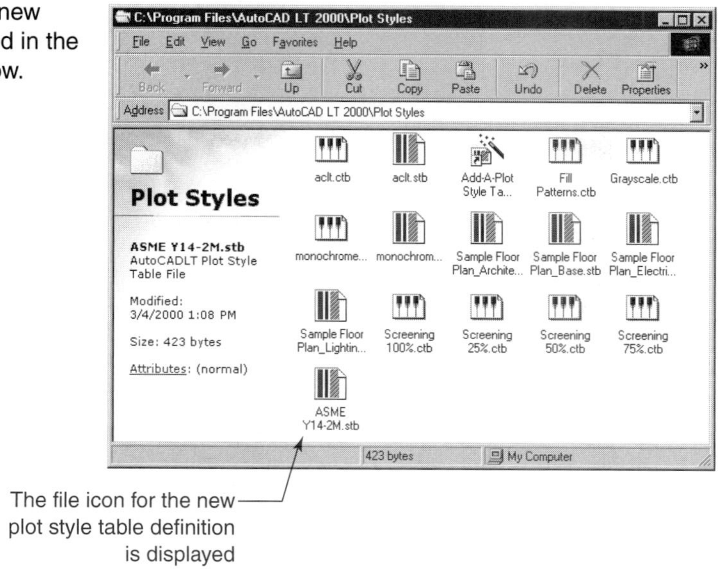

The Plot Style Table Editor

The Plot Style Table Editor dialog box displays three tabs. The General tab, as shown in Figure 13.60, displays general information about the plot style table such as the path and file name where it is saved, how many styles definitions it contains, and the version number of the Plot Style Table Editor being used. The Description box can be used to provide a description using up to 1024 characters that is saved with the style.

Pick the *Apply global scale factor to non-ISO linetypes* check box to automatically scale non-ISO linetypes and fill patterns when plotting objects using this plot style table. The *Scale factor* box is used to set the desired scale factor.

The Table View and Form View tabs are used to edit styles and set style properties. You can modify plot style settings in either one of these tabs, but they provide two different interface styles. The Table View presents plot style settings in columns within a table. The horizontal scroll bar is used to move the display to the left or right as needed to access the desired style name. Figure 13.61 shows a named plot style table being edited in the Table View tab.

FIGURE 13.60 Double-click on a Plot Style Table icon in the Plot Style Manager window to open the table for editing using the Plot Style Table Editor.

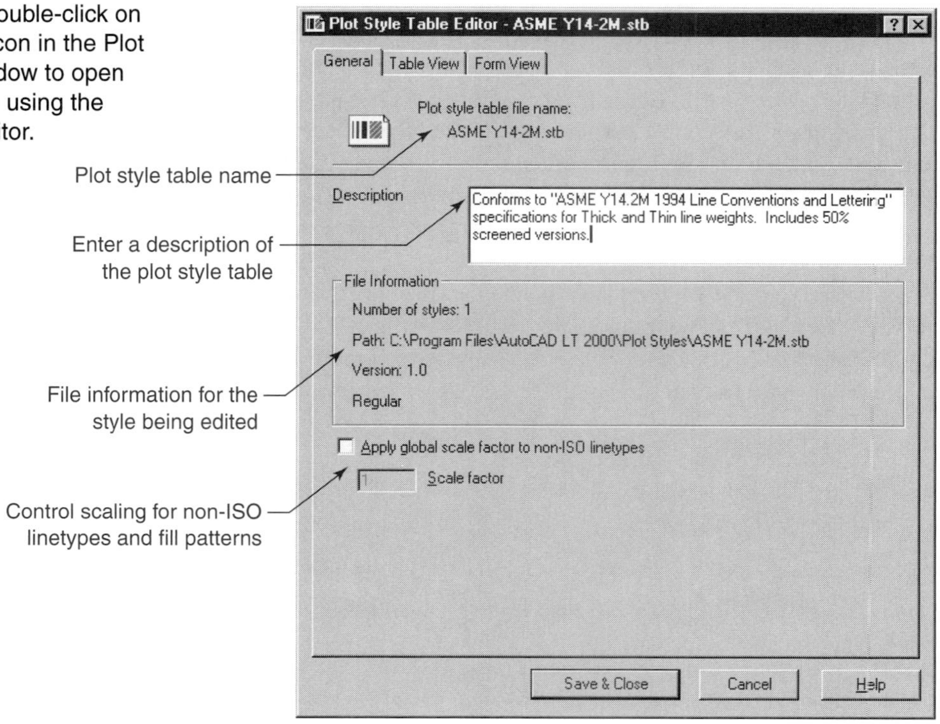

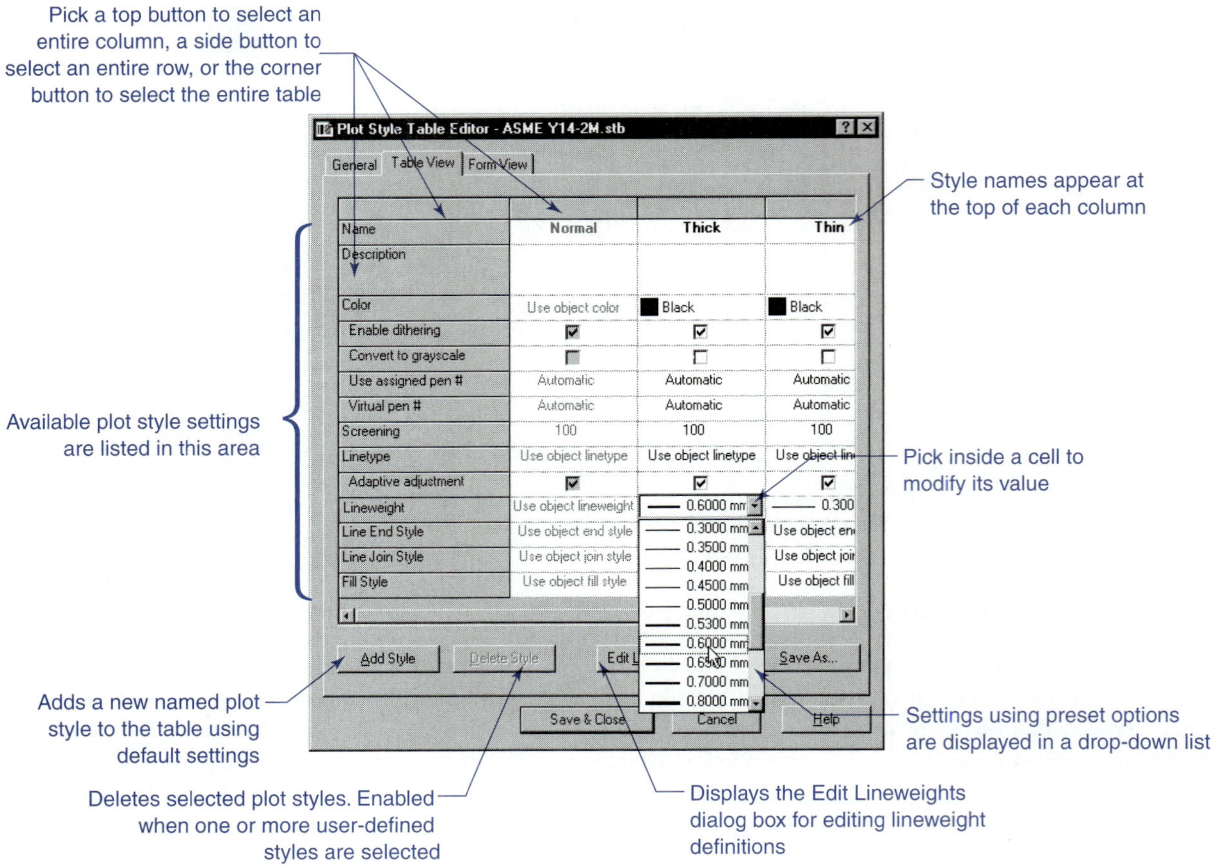

FIGURE 13.61 The Table View tab presents plot style properties arranged in columns within a table.

Like most Windows features, the rows, columns, and even the entire dialog box can be resized as needed to display more or less information. Shortcut menus are also available by right-clicking to conveniently add or delete styles or to copy and paste values from one style to another. Right-click on any setting and pick the Paste to All Styles option from the shortcut menu to apply that setting to all styles in this table.

Pick inside any cell in the table to activate its interface. If you pick an item that has a preset list of options, the available options are presented on a drop-down list. Look at the list for setting lineweight in Figure 13.61. Picking in some cells displays a set of arrow buttons for adjusting numeric values, or you can just pick inside the box and type a desired value. In the pen assignments areas, a setting of 0 is the same as the "Automatic" setting.

The Table View tab works well enough when you are working with a small number of plot styles, but the Form View tab can be much easier to use when working with a larger number of styles. A color-dependent plot style table is shown in the Form View tab in Figure 13.62. It has all the same options and settings as the Table View but provides an interface that allows easier editing of multiple items.

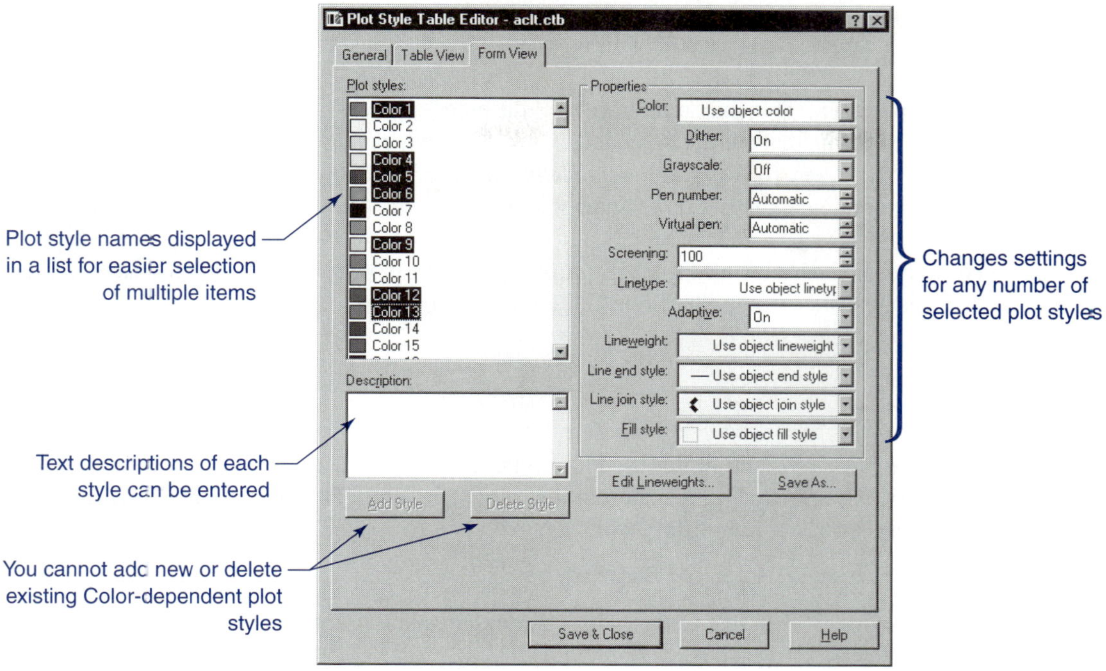

FIGURE 13.62 The Form View can be easier to use when modifying multiple style definitions.

Defining Plot Styles

A new color-dependent plot style table created from scratch starts with 255 individual plot styles. Each style definition controls the plotted appearance for all objects of a single color. All objects in the drawing of a particular color are plotted using the same plot style settings.

When new color-dependent plot style tables are defined, they should be based on established layer and color standards. Correlating desired plot results with existing layer and color standards makes it easier for other drafters in a department to use the new plot style successfully. In a multidisciplinary environment where the type of project determines the standard that is used, you can create plot style tables based on each standard.

For users of previous AutoCAD LT versions, working with color-dependent plot styles may help facilitate a smoother integration into the new plot control methods introduced with the AutoCAD LT 2000 software. Color-dependent plot style tables use object color to control plotting characteristics. In this way they are comparable to the plotting controls used in previous versions of AutoCAD LT. Additionally, you can directly import previous plotter configuration information from existing .pcp and .pc2 files when creating a new color-dependent plot style table. This allows you to easily maintain established plotting standards in your AutoCAD LT 2000 drawings.

Named plot style tables are not as restrictive as color-dependent tables. You can define as many or as few styles as you need, and you can control plotting results without limiting the use and application of color. When you create a new named plot style table, a single plot style named *Normal* is automatically defined in the table. This style represents the default properties of an object; it cannot be modified, renamed, or deleted. This is the initial default plot style name assigned to layer 0 in new drawings.

To add a new style to the table, pick the Add Style button, as illustrated in Figure 13.61. This adds a new style definition, which is assigned the default name of "Style *n*", where *n* represents its column number. When the record is added, the name is already selected, so you can begin typing the new style name.

As discussed previously, the plot styles defined within your standard plot style tables should be based on required drafting standards. For example, to comply with the ASME Y14.2M-1992 *Line Conventions and Lettering* standards document, at least two plot styles are required. This standard defines line conventions using two drafting lineweights, described as Thick and Thin. The plot style used for *Thick* lines uses a 0.6-mm lineweight, and the second style plots *Thin* lines with a 0.3-mm lineweight. In most standard production style applications, both these styles are set to use black ink. All the additional plot style features are left at default values. For specialized applications, two additional styles can be defined with the same lineweights, but using the screening feature. Screening is used for fading some drawing elements on the plot to draw attention to other features.

An architectural plot style table may require several different style definitions. Architectural standards define four standard lineweights that are applied in black ink. The style names and lineweights include *Light* (0.025″), *Medium* (0.035″), *Heavy* (0.050″), and *Very Heavy* or *Punch* (0.070″). A selection of several colors using the medium lineweight, and a selection of screened plot styles are often used in architectural applications.

When you have finished defining all the styles required in a new plot style table, pick the Save & Close button to save your changes and exit the Plot Style Table Editor.

Field Notes

Changing the default location setting for the Plot Style Table Search Path can cause undesirable results when AutoCAD LT cannot locate a required plot style table. For most applications it is best to maintain the initial default setting, which is:

C:\Program Files\AutoCAD LT 2000\Plot Styles

Storing new plot style tables in this folder helps ensure that AutoCAD will be able to locate the style definitions referenced in each of your drawings.

Default Plot Style Behavior

Every new drawing is started using either color-dependent plot style mode or named plot style mode. The default plot style mode for new drawings is set in the *Default plot style behavior for new drawings* area in the Plotting tab of the Options dialog box (see Figure 13.63).

The two radio buttons at the top of this area control what happens when a drawing without a plot style assignment is opened. This includes both new drawings and existing drawings that were created using an earlier version of AutoCAD LT. The initial default setting is *Use color dependent plot styles*. This means that every new drawing you begin from scratch and any drawings created in a previous version of AutoCAD LT are automatically set to use color-dependent plot styles. When this setting is active, the *Default plot style table:* drop-down list shows the names of all the currently available color-dependent plot style tables. The initial default setting for this is None, which plots objects the way they are drawn and does not apply any plot

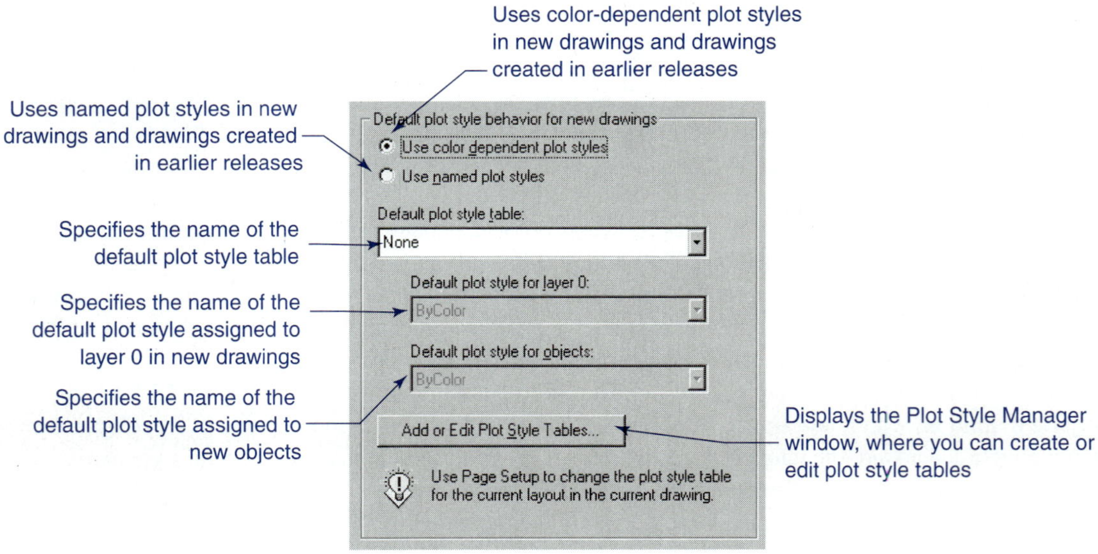

FIGURE 13.63 By default, AutoCAD LT uses color-dependent plot style tables in new drawings and drawings created using earlier versions of AutoCAD LT.

style settings. Pick one of the listed color-dependent plot styles to use as the default plot style table to attach to new drawings. A predefined table can be used if it provides the desired plotting results, but a customized plot style table defined to match established drafting and plotting standards is usually the best option. To review the descriptions of the predefined color-dependent plot style tables included with AutoCAD LT, refer to Table 13.2.

Picking the *Use named plot styles option* configures AutoCAD LT to use named plot styles in new drawings and when opening drawings created in previous versions. Select an appropriately named plot style table from the *Default plot style table:* list, or create an appropriate style if necessary.

When the default setting uses a named plot style, the *Default plot style for layer 0:* and *Default plot style for objects:* lists are enabled. The initial default named plot style assigned to layer 0 is the "Normal" style, or you can select another style name from the list. The default plot style applied to objects should be set to ByLayer for most applications.

Attaching Plot Styles to Layouts

Attaching a plot style table to a layout controls the way that both the paper space and the visible model space objects are plotted from that layout. A plot style table can be attached to a layout from the Plot Device tab on the Page Setup dialog box (refer to Figure 13.45). From the Name: list in the Plot style table (pen assignments) area, select the name of the plot style table to apply. Check the Display plot styles check box if you want to view the layout as it will be plotted.

The type of plot style table displayed in the list is determined by the current plot style mode setting used in the drawing. If the drawing is currently in Color-dependent mode, then the list displays only color-dependent plot styles. Likewise, if the drawing is currently in Named plot style mode, the list displays the available named plot style tables. The plot style mode of your drawing is initially determined by the default plot style behavior settings specified in the Options dialog box.

The Edit... button opens the currently selected plot style table for editing in the Plot Style Table Editor. Pick the New... button if you want to create a new plot style table using the Add-A-Named Plot Style Table Wizard. As indicated previously, accessing the wizard from the Page Setup dialog box restricts you to creating a table type matching the current plot style mode.

A different plot style table can be attached to each layout in your drawing, but all layouts must use the same type of table. You cannot attach a color-dependent plot style table in one layout and a named plot style table in another. A plot style table can also be applied to the Model tab if you need to create check prints from tiled model space.

Field Notes

The current plot style mode is saved in a "read only" system variable named PSTYLEMODE. The term *read only* indicates that you cannot change the value of this variable by typing a new value at the command line, but you can read the current value. When the drawing is set to Color-dependent mode, the PSTYLEMODE = 1. When PSTYLEMODE = 0, the drawing is currently in Named plot style mode.

```
Command: PSTYLEMODE↵
PSTYLEMODE = 0 (read only)
```

Applying Plot Styles

Attaching a plot style table provides access to the plot styles defined within the table. If you are using a color-dependent plot style, you cannot attach plot styles to objects or to layers. Drawing objects are automatically associated to a defined plot style based on the current color of the object. To change the style with which an object is plotted, you change its color. To change the style associated with a color, you can open the plot style table using the Plot Style Table Editor and modify the style settings as needed.

Named plot styles are much more flexible. Named plot styles are managed in the same ways as are other object properties such as the linetype setting. For example, when the current linetype is set to *Hidden*, all new objects you draw are drawn using the *Hidden* linetype, and the linetype property of the current layer is ignored. If the current linetype setting is *ByLayer*, all new objects are drawn using the linetype setting assigned to the layer on which they are created. If moved to a different layer, the object with the ByLayer setting now displays the linetype setting for the new layer. The named Plot Style property is used and applied in the same ways as is the linetype property.

The *Default plot style for objects:* setting in the Plotting tab on the Options dialog box controls the initial default Plot style setting, but this can be changed at any time. The Plot style property can be set to any style name defined in the current plot style table, or it can be set to ByLayer (or even ByBlock). As with other layer properties, using a ByLayer Plot style setting for drawing objects allows Plot styles to be managed using layer property settings.

The Layer Properties Manager, Figure 13.64, shows the Plot Style property in the column between Lineweight and Plot. The default Plot Style property assigned to a layer is *Normal*, which has no effect on the plotted appearance. To change the Plot Style property of a layer, point to the existing setting and press the pick button. This displays the Select Plot Style dialog box, as shown in Figure 13.65.

In this example, most of the layers use the Plot style named *Thin*. When assigning Plot style properties to multiple layers, you can select any number of layers and then pick one of the property values that you want to change. All the selected layers are changed to the new value in a single operation, as shown in Figure 13.66.

FIGURE 13.64 The default Plot Style setting for drawing layers is *Normal*.

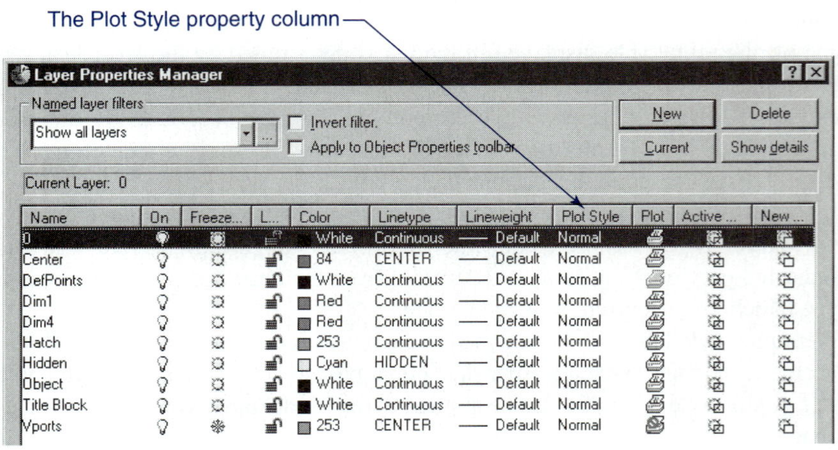

FIGURE 13.65 The Select Plot Style dialog box.

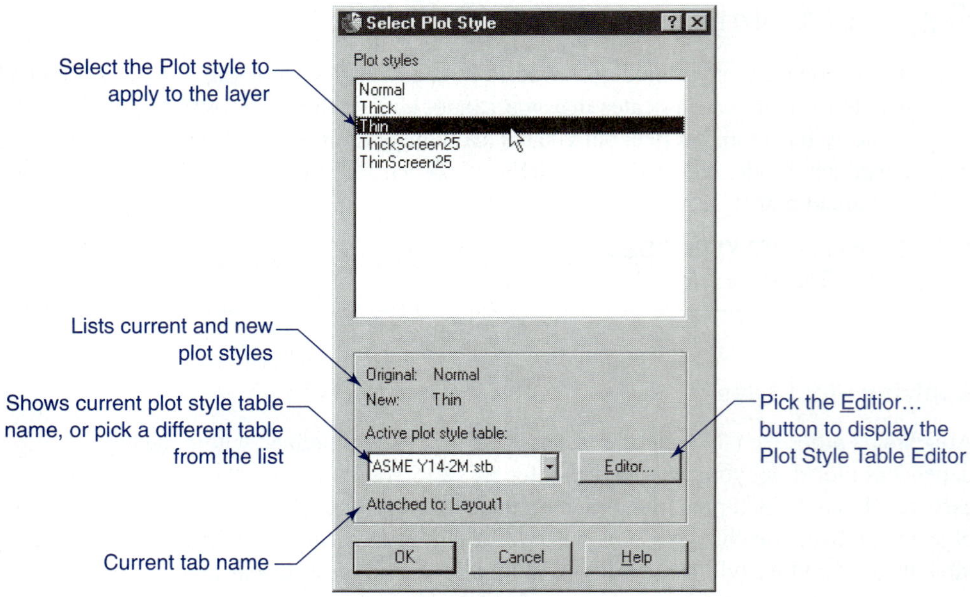

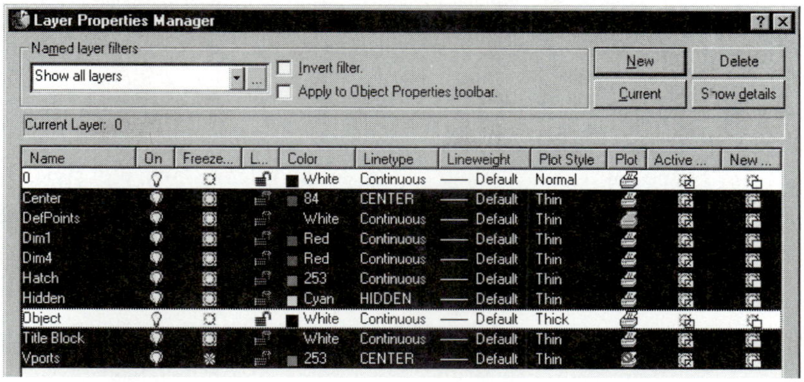

FIGURE 13.66 The selected layers are updated to use the new Plot style property setting.

The Plot style property assigned to any number of objects can be changed as needed. The easiest way to change any property displayed on the Object Properties toolbar is to grip-select the objects and then select the new setting from the property control list. The Plotstyle Control list (refer to Figure 13.52) can be used to change the Plot style setting for all the currently selected objects.

Field Notes

- With the flexibility given by AutoCAD LT 2000 to assign different plot style tables to each layout, and because each named style table may contain any number of plot style definitions, it is possible to end up with an object or layer using a plot style that is not defined in every plot style table. The Plot Styles list in the Select Plot Style dialog box reports these styles as (missing) and plots the affected objects using the default object properties.
- If required, the plot style table type used by an existing drawings can be switched using the **CONVERTPSTYLES** command. The considerations are as follows:
  - When a drawing is converted from color-dependent to named plot style tables, all color-dependent plot style tables attached to layouts are removed and replaced with named plot styles. Color-dependent plot styles should first be converted to named plot style tables using the **CONVERTCTB** command.
  - Converting from a named plot style table to a color-dependent table results in a loss of the plot style names assigned to drawing objects.

Exercise 13.6 — Estimated time required: 20 min.

1. In the Options dialog, set AutoCAD LT to start a new drawing using the named plot style mode. Close any open drawings. Start a new drawing from scratch using English settings.
2. From the Plot Style Manager window, open the Add-A-Plot Style Wizard and define a Named Plot Style Table using the Start from scratch option, and name the style "Exercises.stb". Launch the Plot Style Table Editor from the Finish page of the wizard.
3. Define named plot styles with settings needed to draw Figure 13.48 using Line objects.
4. Define named plot styles with settings needed to draw Figure 13.49 using Polyline objects.
5. Define named plot styles with settings needed to draw Figure 13.50 using the SOLID hatch pattern for each square.
6. Save the plot style and close the Plot Style Editor.
7. Create a layout named EX13-6A with three floating viewports. Draw the figures referenced in items 2, 3, and 4, drawing one figure in each viewport. Make any settings needed to display the objects correctly.
8. Check the current value for PSTYLEMODE.
9. Save as EX13.6.dwg and close the drawing.

LEARNING CHECKPOINT

- □ Define *plot styles* and *plot style tables.*
- □ Describe the two plot style table types.
- □ Name the twelve plotting feature settings defined in a plot style.
- □ How do lineweight settings in a plot style affect wide polyline objects?
- □ How many plot styles are in a color-dependent plot style table?
- □ How many plot styles can be defined in a named plot style table?
- □ What are the disadvantages of color-dependent plot styles?
- □ What problems can result from editing a plot style table?
- □ What measures can be taken to avoid problems when editing plot style tables?
- □ Name the command that starts the Plot Style Manager, and describe its appearance and function.
- □ Which tab in the Plot Style Table Editor works better for editing multiple styles at the same time?
- □ Describe the contents of a plot style table that complies with ASME Y14.2 standards.
- □ Describe the contents of a plot style table used for architectural applications.
- □ How are color-dependent plot styles referenced by drawing objects? What about named plot styles?

Plotting Your Drawing

- Creating and Assigning Plot Style Tables
- Migrating Previously Saved Pen Settings

Model (Tiled) Viewports

By default, the display in the Model tab is shown in a single model viewport that fills the entire tab. Using standard display control methods, you can display any area of the drawing at any desired magnification. For added versatility, the Model tab can be divided into separate viewports to display two or more views of the drawing at the same time. These separate view areas are called ***model viewports*** and are sometimes referred to as ***tiled*** viewports, which describes the way they are displayed in the Model tab. The active model viewports are arranged edge to edge without overlapping, and fill the entire Model tab.

As with layout viewports, the display in each model viewport is controlled separately, allowing you to zoom, pan, or restore named views. The grid, snap, and UCS icon display settings can be set differently in each model viewport, but layer visibility cannot be set for individual model viewports. Model viewports, unlike layout viewports, are not objects and cannot be selected or edited. When setting up model viewports, you can select from a number of preset viewports configurations or define custom viewport configurations that can be saved and restored whenever needed.

New Viewports

Viewports
Display Viewports Dialog
View
Viewports ▸
New Viewports...
VPORTS

Model viewport configurations can be set up quickly and effectively using the New Viewports tab in the Viewports dialog box. The VPORTS command displays the Viewports dialog box. You can access the VPORTS command by picking the Display Viewports Dialog button on the Viewports toolbar or by typing **VPORTS** at the Command: prompt. Selecting the New Viewports… option on the Viewports cascade of the View pull-down menu starts the Viewports dialog box and automatically displays the New Vewports tab (see Figure 13.67). Most of the available options are the same as when setting up layout viewports, which was discussed previously in this chapter.

The Standard viewports: list provides several predefined viewport configurations that will meet the display requirements for most applications. A representation of the currently selected option is displayed in the Preview image. Selecting the first item in the Standard viewports list, shown as *Active Model Configuration*, shows the current Model tab viewport arrangement in the Preview image. When you select or design a viewport configuration, always use the fewest number of viewports possible for your application. There is a limited area on the Model tab, so using more viewports means using smaller viewports. It can be difficult to work effectively in a viewport that is too small.

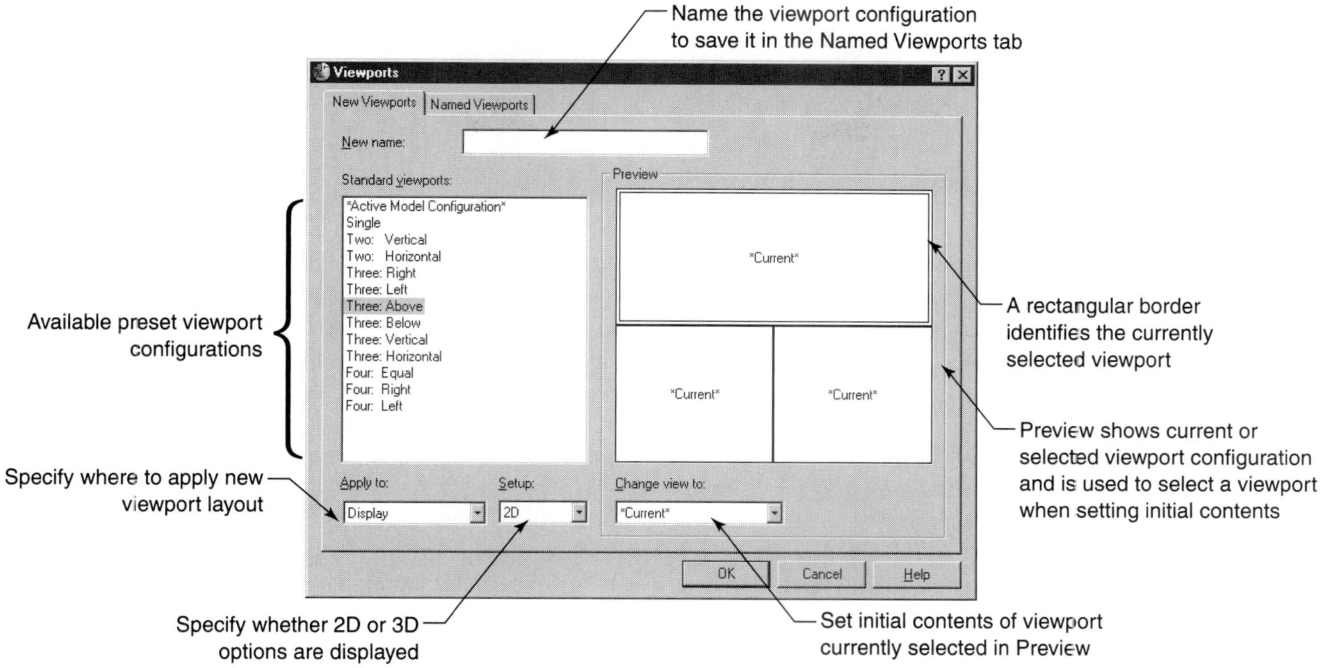

FIGURE 13.67 The New Viewports tab in the Viewports dialog box can be used to set up a model viewport layout.

When multiple model viewports are used, a thick dark border is displayed around the currently active viewport. The cursor is displayed as the standard AutoCAD LT crosshairs inside the active viewport and as a system cursor (arrow) when pointing to an inactive viewport. Use the Ctrl+R accelerator keystroke to toggle the active viewport, or to switch to a specific viewport, just point to it and press the pick button.

You can actively work among all the available model viewports. For example, you can begin drawing a line in one viewport and finish it in another. In Figure 13.68, a polyline is started in the lower left viewport and finished in the lower right viewport.

FIGURE 13.68 Actively working among Model viewports can simplify many drawing tasks.

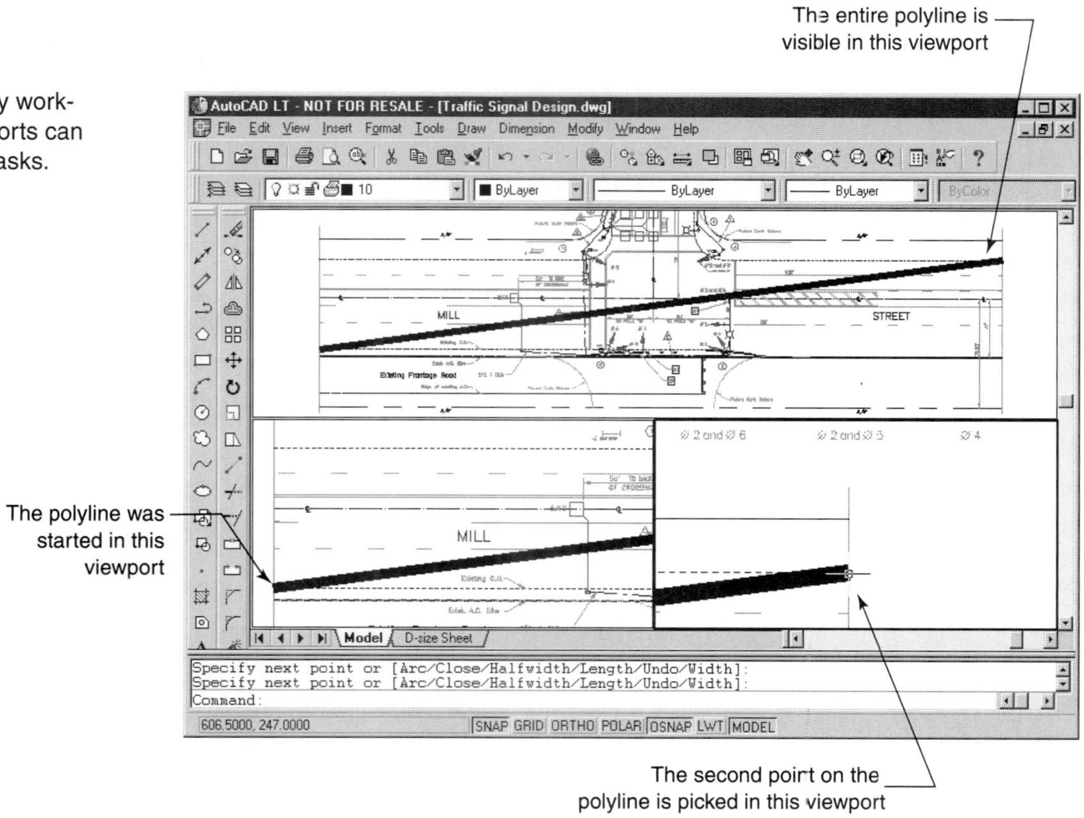

The Apply to: list is enabled when you select an option from the Standard viewports: list. The default option is *Display*, which means that the current viewport configuration will be replaced with the selected option. Selecting *Current viewport* from the list applies the selected viewport configuration to the currently active model viewport, allowing you to divide an existing model viewport into even more viewports.

Named Viewports

When you set up model viewports from the Model tab, the New Viewports tab displays a text box labeled New name:. To name and save a model viewport configuration, select the desired configuration from the Standard viewports: list, and enter a name in the New name: box, then Pick OK. To save the configuration currently displayed in the Model tab, be sure that *Active Model Configuration* is currently selected. If you define a new configuration that assigns named drawing views to specific viewports, that information is also saved. In Figure 13.69, picking the OK button saves the selected viewport configuration with the specified name.

Named viewport configurations are managed from the Named Viewports tab of the Viewports dialog box. You can start the VPORTS command using previously discussed options, or pick Named Viewports… from the Viewports cascade of the View pull-down menu. Existing named viewport configurations can be deleted or renamed. Right-clicking on a name in the Named viewports: list displays a shortcut menu, as shown in Figure 13.70. To restore a named viewport configuration, pick the desired name and pick OK. The Viewports dialog box is dismissed, and the selected viewport configuration is restored. Any named views associated with the viewport configuration are restored as well (see Figure 13.71).

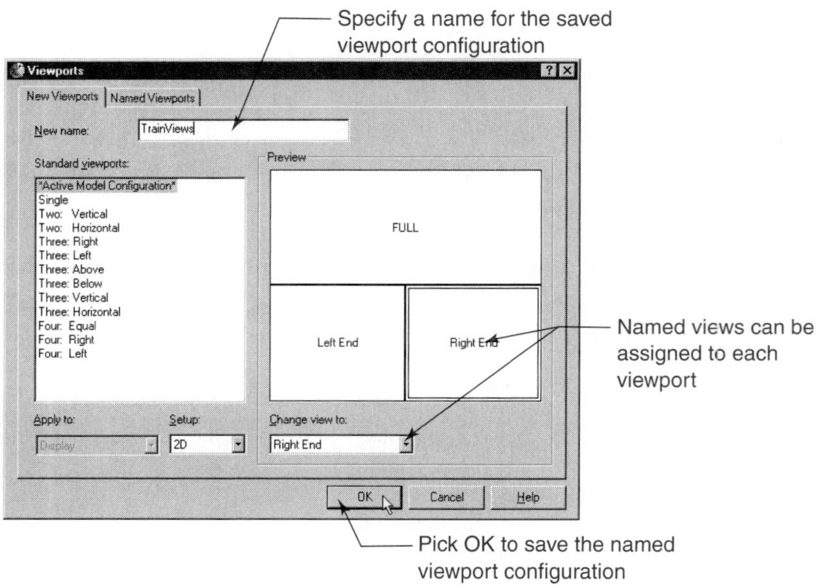

FIGURE 13.69 Customized viewport configurations can be named and saved for later use.

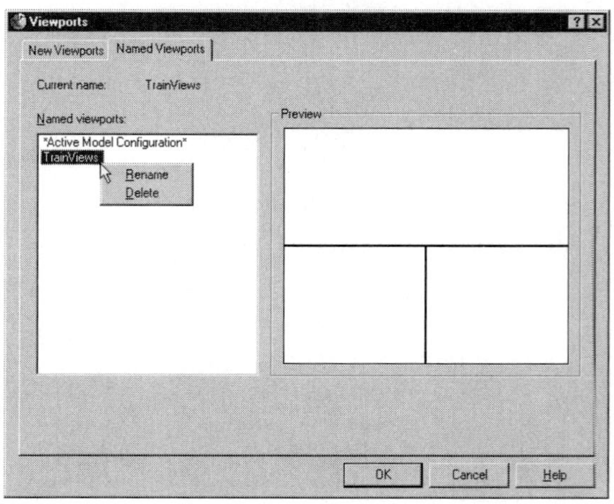

FIGURE 13.70 The Named Viewports tab of the Viewports dialog box.

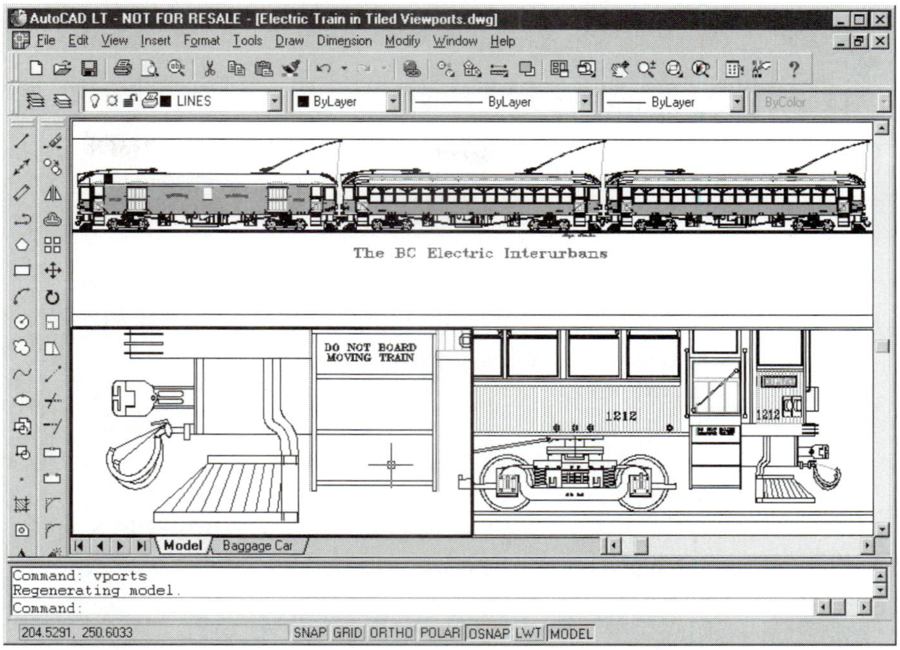

FIGURE 13.71 Restoring a named viewport layout also restores any associated drawing views.

Field Notes

- Named viewport configurations can be saved only for model viewports; however, named viewport configurations can be restored in a layout tab to create an arrangement of layout viewports.
- Model viewports are very useful in 3D drafting applications, which are covered in Chapter 14.

Exercise 13.7 — Estimated time required: 20 min.

1. Open the drawing *Electric Train.dwg* in the Sample folder for editing.
2. Create three named drawing views using the VIEW command. Refer to Figures 13.69 and 13.71.
3. In the Viewports dialog box, define a viewport configuration named *TrainViews* using Figure 13.69 as a guide.
4. Restore the *Single* viewport configuration from the Standard viewports: list.
5. Restore *TrainViews* from the Named Viewports tab in the Viewports dialog box.
6. Save the drawing as EX13.7 if required by your instructor.

LEARNING CHECKPOINT

- ☐ What display feature of layout viewports is not available for model viewports?
- ☐ What options are available for changing the active model viewport?
- ☐ Describe how named drawing views can be associated with model viewports.

MULTIPLE CHOICE

Circle the choice or enter your response on an answer sheet by selecting the option that most accurately completes or answers the given statements.

1. This dialog box is used to initially set up a layout.
- **a.** Layout
- **b.** Layset
- **c.** Page Setup
- **d.** PS

2. This command automates the creation of drawing layouts.
- **a.** AUTOLAYOUT
- **b.** PAGETSETUPWIZARD
- **c.** PAGEWIZARD
- **d.** LAYOUTWIZARD

3. Setting this variable to 1 makes the model tab active.
- **a.** MODELTAB
- **b.** TILEMODE
- **c.** MODELSPACE
- **d.** TILESPACE

4. The command that starts the Viewports dialog box is:
- **a.** VIEWPORT
- **b.** VPORT
- **c.** VPORTS
- **d.** VIEWPORTS

5. The initial default value for MAXACTVP is:
- **a.** 64
- **b.** 32
- **c.** 128
- **d.** 100

6. This accelerator keystroke toggles the active viewport:
- **a.** Ctrl+V
- **b.** Ctrl+M
- **c.** Ctrl+R
- **d.** Ctrl+P

7. The command used to control viewport layer visibility is:
- **a.** VPVIS
- **b.** LAYERVIS
- **c.** VPLAYER
- **d.** VPLAYVIS

8. This setting controls linetype scaling in layout viewports:
- **a.** LTSCALE
- **b.** VPLTSCALE
- **c.** CELTSCALE
- **d.** PSLTSCALE

9. The command that displays a window where you can add or modify plotter configurations is:
- **a.** PLOTTERCONFIG
- **b.** PLOTTERMANAGER
- **c.** PLOTTERWIZARD
- **d.** PLOTMAN

10. The command that displays a window where you can add or modify plot style tables is:
- **a.** PLOTSTYLES
- **b.** STYLESMANAGER
- **c.** STYLESWIZARD
- **d.** STYLEMAN

MATCHING

Match each term to the correct description by writing the appropriate number in each box at the left.

- ☐ VPLAYER
- ☐ TILEMODE
- ☐ VPORTS
- ☐ UCS icon
- ☐ Grips
- ☐ Options
- ☐ INSERT
- ☐ DesignCenter
- ☐ PSLTSCALE
- ☐ STB
- ☐ Model
- ☐ PAGESETUP
- ☐ Tiled
- ☐ PROPERTIES
- ☐ Layout
- ☐ Floating
- ☐ MAXACTVP
- ☐ PSTYLEMODE
- ☐ Layout Templates
- ☐ CTB

1. The default tab where you start a drawing using a Wizard or from scratch.
2. The tab where the final plotted drawing arrangement is set up.
3. Starts the Page Setup dialog box.
4. Files that store commonly used layouts.
5. Used to drag and drop layouts.
6. Place a title block in a layout using this command.
7. Describes layout viewports.
8. Describes model viewports.
9. Displayed differently in model space and paper space.
10. An easy way to resize viewports.
11. In the Model tab, this variable is set to 1.
12. Displays the Viewports dialog box.
13. Limits number of active viewports.
14. Command that provides complete control of all layout viewport properties.
15. Command that controls layer visibility in viewports.
16. Scales linetypes to a layout.
17. File extension for color-dependent plot style tables.
18. File extension for named plot style tables.
19. Set the default plot style behavior in this dialog box.
20. This variable shows the current plot style mode.

WORD SCRAMBLE

Unscramble the six scrambled words below, one letter to each square, to form six AutoCAD LT–related words:

SODALEMPEC

SAPPECERAP

STWEVPORI

PALMETTE

PARVLEY

SUPPEGATE

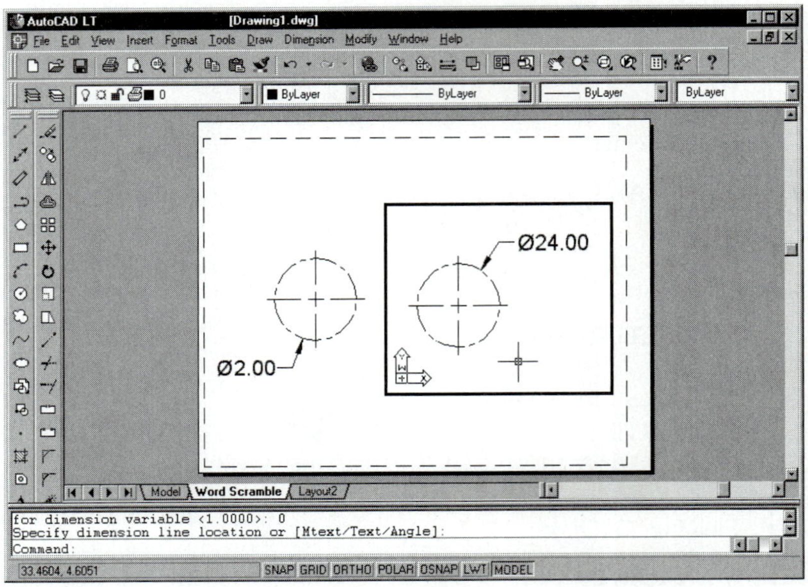

Unscramble the circled letters to form the special answer, as suggested by the illustration.

&

PROJECTS

If you do not have access to a plotter that supports the listed paper size in an assigned project, select the DWF ePlot.pc3 plot device. This plot configuration supports all standard ANSI and ISO paper sizes.

1. Open AutoCAD LT and pick the Cancel button in the Startup dialog box. Access the Plotting tab on the Options dialog box and set the default plot style behavior to start new drawings using color-dependent plot styles. Start a new drawing from scratch using English settings. Design a layout as follows:
   A. Pick the Layout1 tab to start the Page Setup dialog box.
   B. Select an appropriate plot device for a "B" size layout, use the *aclt.ctb* plot style table, and display the plot style on the layout.
   C. Specify the paper size as an ANSI "B" size, plotting the "Layout" at a scale of 1:1.
   D. Name the layout *Color,* and save a named page setup as *B – Final Print – Color.*
   E. Use the same options to set up Layout2, with the following differences: Use the *monochrome.ctb* plot style table, name the layout *Monochrome,* and save the named page setup as *B – Final Print – Monochrome.*
   F. Save the drawing as a template named *Layout B - CTB.dwt.*

2. Start a new drawing from scratch using English settings. Use the Create Layout Wizard to create two "C" size layouts, each using a single default viewport. One will use the *aclt.ctb* plot style table, and the other will use *monochrome.ctb*. Save each layout as named page setups using the names *C – Final Print – Color* and *C – Final Print – Monochrome*. Save the drawing as a template named *Layout C - CTB.dwt.*

3. Start the Add-A-Plot Style Table Wizard from the Plot Style Manager window. Define a color-dependent plot style table that implements lineweight standards as specified in the ASME Y14.2M standard. Define the table to be used with currently established layer and color standards. Save the plot style table as ASME.ctb.

4. Start the Add-A-Plot Style Table Wizard from the Plot Style Manager window. Define a color-dependent plot style table that implements lineweight standards appropriate for architectural applications. Use your school or company standards as a guide, or refer to the discussion of architectural plot styles applications provided in Chapter 13. Define the table to be used with currently established layer and color standards. Save the plot style table as Architectural.stb.

5. Define a color-dependent plot style table based on a drafting standard of your choice that is currently used in industry by professional drafters in your selected drafting discipline. Define the table to be used with currently established layer and color standards. Save the table as P13-5.ctb, or use an appropriate name specified by your instructor.

6. Start a new drawing using the Layout B - CTB.dwt template created in Project 1. Using the SAveas option of the LAYOUT command, save both layouts as individual template files named P13.7ColorCTB.dwt and P13.7MonoCTB.dwt. Close the new drawing without saving.

7. Start a new drawing from scratch using English settings. Use the From template... option on the Layout shortcut menu to import two layouts from the templates created in Project 7. Save the drawing as P13.7.dwg.

8. Start a new drawing from scratch using English settings. Pick the Layout1 tab to display the Page Setup dialog box. In the Page Setup dialog box, import the named page setups from the template Layout C.dwt created in Project 2. Apply the imported named page setups to two new layouts. Save the drawing as P13-8.dwg.

9. Open AutoCAD LT and pick the Cancel button in the Startup dialog box. Access the Plotting tab on the Options dialog box, and set the default plot style behavior to start new drawings using named plot styles. Start a new drawing from scratch using English settings. Design a layout as follows:
   A. Pick the Layout1 tab to start the Page Setup dialog box.
   B. Select an appropriate plot device for a "B" size layout, use the *aclt.stb* plot style table and display the plot style on the layout.
   C. Specify the paper size as an ANSI "B" size, plotting the "Layout" at a scale of 1:1.
   D. Name the layout *Color* and save a named page setup as *B – Final Print – Color.*
   E. Use the same options to set up Layout2, with the following differences: Use the *monochrome.stb* plot style table, name the layout *Monochrome,* and save the named page setup as *B – Final Print – Monochrome*.
   F. Save the drawing as a template named *Layout B - STB.dwt.*

10. Start a new drawing from scratch using English settings. Use the Create Layout Wizard to create two "C" size layouts, each using a single default viewport. One will use the *aclt.stb* plot style table, and the other will use *monochrome.stb*. Save each layout as named page setups using the names *C – Final Print – Color* and *C – Final Print – Monochrome*. Save the drawing as a template named *Layout C - STB.dwt.*

11. In a new drawing that uses named plot styles, draw the mechanical part shown below. Using the material in Chapter 13 as a guide, create a layout using two viewports to lay out the part. One viewport will use a scale of 1:1, and the second viewport will display an enlarged detail at 4:1. Dimension the part using the appropriate dimension scale. Apply layer and viewport settings to complete this drawing to match the results of the chapter tutorial as shown in Figure 13.40. Save the drawing as P13.11.dwg.

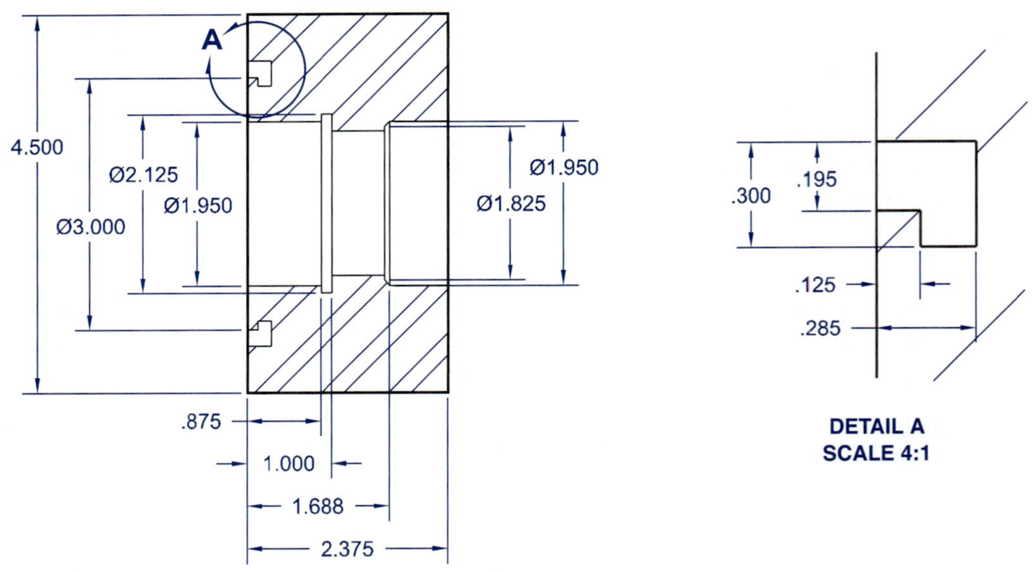

12. Start the Add-A-Plot Style Table Wizard from the Plot Style Manager window. Define a named plot style table that implements lineweight standards as specified in the ASME Y14.2M standard. Save the plot style table as ASME.stb.

13. Open P3.11.dwg for editing. Attach the ASME.stb table to the layout and assign the appropriate plot styles to the drawing layers. Set the plot style for all objects to be ByLayer. Save the drawing as P13.13.dwg and produce a full-size plot.

14. Start the Add-A-Plot Style Table Wizard from the Plot Style Manager window. Define a named plot style table that implements lineweight standards appropriate for architectural applications. Use your school or company standards as a guide, or refer to the discussion of architectural plot styles applications provided in Chapter 13. Save the plot style table as Architectural.stb.

15. Define a named plot style table based on a drafting standard of your choice that is currently used in industry by professional drafters in your selected drafting discipline. Save the table as P13-14.stb, or use an appropriate name specified by your instructor.
16. Start a new drawing using the Layout B - STB.dwt template created in Project 1. Using the SAveas option of the LAYOUT command, save both layouts as individual template files named P13.7ColorSTB.dwt and P13.7MonoSTB.dwt. Close the new drawing without saving.

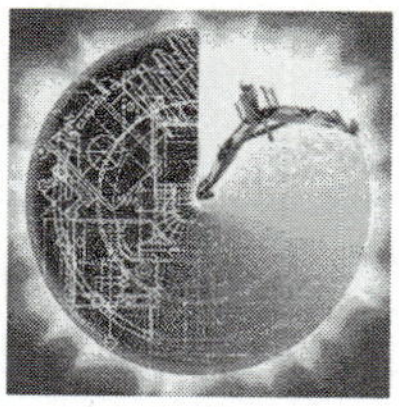

CHAPTER 14

3D Drafting with AutoCAD LT

LEARNING GOALS

- Apply the right-hand rule to determine three-dimensional fundamentals
- Utilize three-dimensional coordinate systems
- Utilize the User Coordinate System (UCS) when working in three dimensions
- Use Elevation and Thickness values to simulate surfaces
- Effectively use tiled viewports for 3D display options
- Change 3D views dynamically
- Create automatic perspective views of 3D models
- Remove hidden lines and display shaded views
- Simulate 3D models using isometric drawing tools

3D Drafting

Creating three-dimensional, or 3D, drawings can be a very effective way to communicate an idea. A complete 3D object is often much easier to visualize than two-dimensional, or 2D, views of an object. When you look at a multiview drawing, you must then assemble each of the separate 2D views in your mind to visualize the final 3D shape. Seeing objects already constructed in 3D can help you to better visualize the finished product.

AutoCAD LT 2000 is primarily a 2D drafting program. This means that it is used principally for producing flat drawings, similar to those drawn on a sheet of paper. However, AutoCAD LT software is capable of basic 3D functions. Most of the applications earlier in this text use 2D coordinates that represent values on the X and Y axes of the Cartesian coordinate system. In this chapter, you will learn to work with the 3D coordinate system by specifying X, Y, and Z axis values. An illustration of the three axes of the Cartesian coordinate system is shown in Figure 14.1.

Both 2D and 3D objects can be placed anywhere in three-dimensional space by supplying a Z coordinate location. The Z coordinate location is called the ***elevation.*** Although AutoCAD LT does allow some objects to be either drawn with or to be given a ***thickness*** to simulate 3D surfaces, it does not allow the creation of true 3D solid objects. The 3D objects you can create in AutoCAD LT give the appearance of being 3D. It is even possible to produce a view that looks like a solid model and has shading to make the object appear more realistic. Although these objects can be used to determine spatial information and better visualize a final product, they do not contain information such as mass, center of gravity, or surface area.

AutoCAD LT can directly share drawings with AutoCAD 2000, which is a full-featured package that can create 3D solid objects. When such objects are present in a drawing, AutoCAD LT can be used to do simple editing, and even make copies of existing solid objects—but no new solid objects can be defined.

Whether sharing an AutoCAD 2000 drawing or creating a simple 3D drawing of your own, it is important to understand the use of the 3D coordinate system. The coordinate system in AutoCAD LT is extremely powerful and provides you with a great deal of flexibility for working in two or three dimensions. You were introduced to the concept of modifying the User Coordinate System, for creating ordinate dimensions, in Chapter 11. In this chapter, you will learn new ways to use the UCS to make working in 3D much easier.

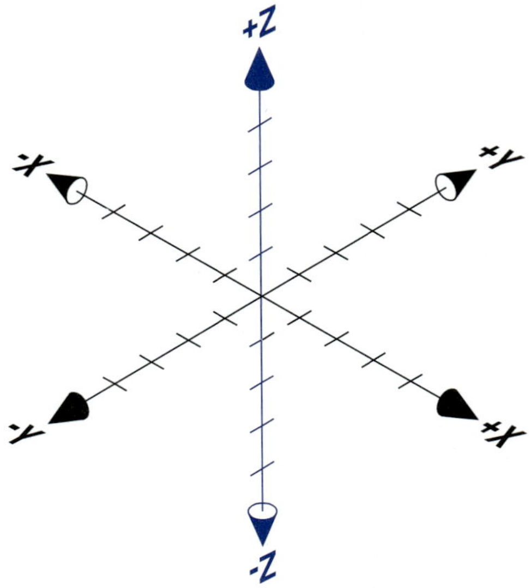

FIGURE 14.1 The Z axis adds elevation and depth concepts to the drafting process. The Z axis is perpendicular to the X,Y plane.

Another effective way of communicating 3D information is by creating an *isometric* view of your drawing. ***Isometric drawings*** create a 3D pictorial in which the three axes are true measurements of the object and form equal angles. Isometric drawings are commonly used when the creation of an actual 3D model is not practical. Sometimes an isometric drawing is combined with a standard orthographic drawing to assist in the visualization process. A very common use for isometric drawings is in the field of technical illustration. AutoCAD LT provides several powerful tools for use in creating isometric drawings.

Using X,Y,Z Point Coordinates

The coordinate systems presented up to this point in the text have been 2D coordinates, specifying point coordinate locations on the X,Y plane of the World Coordinate System. The World Coordinate System, or WCS, was defined in Chapter 11 as a fixed coordinate system used by default in AutoCAD LT. You were also introduced to the concept of the movable User Coordinate System, or UCS, which is covered in greater detail in this chapter.

In the WCS, the X axis is horizontal, the Y axis is vertical, and the Z axis is perpendicular to the X,Y plane. Specifying a 2D absolute point coordinate is done by supplying an X,Y value. A 2D coordinate specification defaults to a 0 value for the Z axis. This means that the coordinate specification 6,4 is interpreted as 6,4,0. To specify a 3D point coordinate that does not lie on the X,Y plane, a nonzero Z axis value is supplied. Figure 14.2 shows a representation of the point coordinate 6,4,2. Notice that the point is found 6 units along the positive X axis, 4 units along the positive Y axis, and 2 units on the positive Z axis.

The X,Y,Z coordinate specifications work the same as standard X,Y coordinates with regard to absolute and relative specifications. This means that a coordinate point entered as X,Y,Z indicates an absolute location in 3D space. When the coordinate point is preceded by the "@" symbol, the coordinate entry is interpreted as being relative to the last point entered. The first example in the following sequence uses absolute coordinate entry. The results are shown in Figure 14.3A. The second example uses relative coordinate entry, and its results are shown in Figure 14.3B:

Command: **L** or **LINE**↵
Specify first point: **6,4,2**↵
Specify next point or [Undo]: **-2,0,3**↵
Specify next point or [Undo]: ↵

Command: **L** or **LINE**↵
Specify first point: **6,4,2**↵
Specify next point or [Undo]: **@-2,0,3**↵
Specify next point or [Undo]: ↵

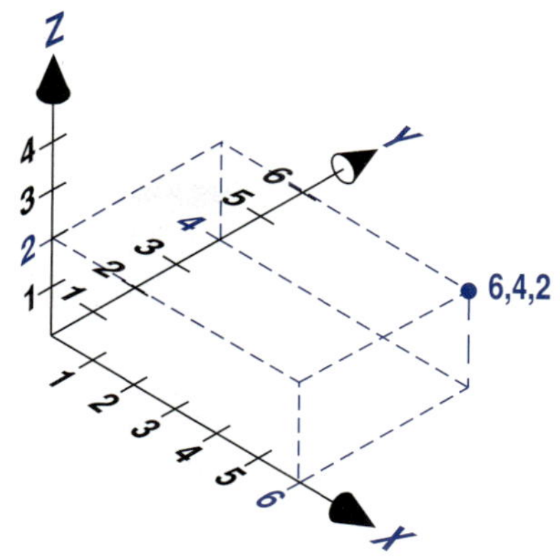

FIGURE 14.2 A 3D point coordinate uses a Z value that indicates its elevation. The elevation is the distance of the point from the X,Y plane of the current UCS.

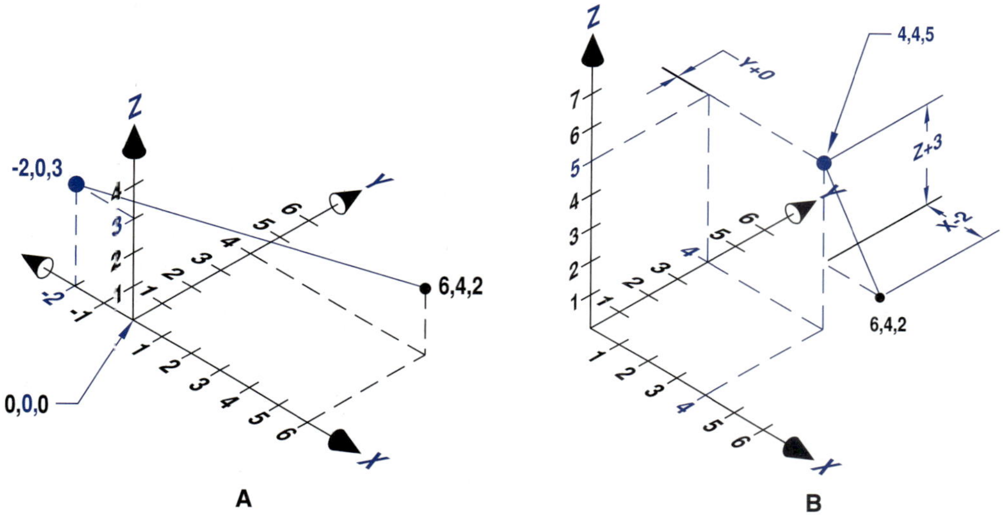

FIGURE 14.3 As with 2D coordinate entry, preceding a 3D coordinate with the "@" symbol makes it relative to the last point entered. (A) In this figure, a line is drawn from the point 6,4,2. (A) An entry of **-2,0,3** indicates an absolute coordinate location. (B) An entry of **@-2,0,3** indicates a point that is relative to the current location, resulting in a line drawn to 4,4,5.

Field Notes

Even when you are working with 3D objects in a drawing, many operations are completed in the current X,Y plane. For these tasks, it is not necessary to specify 3D coordinates. For example, to move a 3D object 2 units in the positive X direction and 1 unit in the negative Y direction with no change in the Z axis, you do not need to specify the Z coordinate:

Command: **M** or **MOVE**↵
Select objects: *<select desired objects>*
Select objects: ↵
Specify base point or displacement: **@2,1**↵
Specify second point of displacement or <use first point as displacement>: ↵

In such a situation, any acceptable method of 2D coordinate entry can be used, including absolute, relative, polar, or even direct distance entry.

The Right-Hand Rule

The ***right-hand rule*** provides an easy-to-understand reference to determine the positive and negative directions of the X, Y, and Z axes. Knowing how to use this simple reference makes it easier to visualize the relationships of the X, Y, and Z axes in 3D space. This helps to ensure that objects you create and edit are placed in the correct location in your drawing. But don't worry, if you do place something incorrectly, you can always *undo* it!

Figure 14.4 shows the first point of the right-hand rule. Hold your right hand so your thumb points in the positive direction of the X axis and your index finger points in the positive direction of the Y axis. When you are using the default WCS, the back of your hand is toward the screen, your thumb points right, and your index finger points up. Now, extending your middle finger as shown in Figure 14.4 shows you the positive direction of the Z axis. In the WCS, the positive direction of the Z axis is toward you. This method still works when you are using a UCS; rotate your hand appropriately to match the setting of the UCS.

The second point of the right-hand rule allows you to determine the direction of positive rotation around each axis. Figure 14.5 illustrates this concept. Point your right thumb in the positive direction of any axis, then curl your fingers as shown. The direction in which your fingers curl indicates the positive rotation angle. For example, using the example shown in Figure 14.4, you know that the positive direction of the Z axis of the WCS points toward you. With your right hand, point your thumb toward yourself. The curl of your fingers is in the counterclockwise direction, which is the positive rotation direction around the Z axis. This agrees with what you have already learned about rotating objects in the X,Y plane.

FIGURE 14.4 The right-hand rule helps you to better visualize the positive and negative directions of the X, Y, and Z axes.

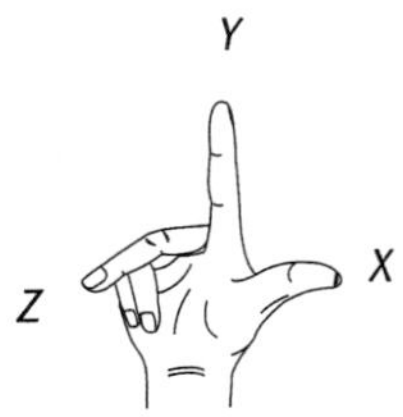

FIGURE 14.5 Point your right thumb in the positive direction of any axis. The curl of your fingers shows the positive rotation angle.

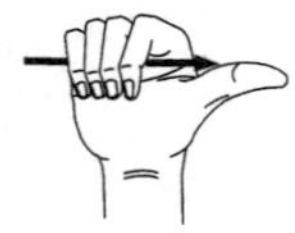

3D Polar Coordinate Entry

The 2D coordinate entry system in AutoCAD LT provides a flexible interface for indicating distances and directions for creating and editing objects. Rather than requiring just absolute or relative coordinate entry, the polar method is provided for use when you know a distance and an angle rather than an X and Y location or displacement value. AutoCAD LT also provides similar options for working in a 3D drawing environment. There are two variations of the polar coordinate entry system that provide much greater flexibility when entering 3D point coordinates. These variations are called *cylindrical* coordinates and *spherical* coordinates.

Cylindrical coordinates are a simple variation of polar coordinate entry that use a standard polar coordinate entry followed by a Z axis value. A cylindrical coordinate entry looks like this:

2<90,6

This coordinate entry is interpreted as *Distance<Angle,Z-axis.* The *Distance<Angle* entry of 2<90 is measured in the X,Y plane of the current UCS and the *,Z-axis* value of **,6** is the Z coordinate. In this form, the coordinate entry is relative to the 0,0,0 origin point. It is more often used in the following form:

@2<90,6

Preceding the coordinate entry with the "@" symbol makes it relative to the last point entered. An example of entering a cylindrical coordinate is shown in the following example:

Command: **L** or **LINE**↵
Specify first point: **2,2**↵
Specify next point or [Undo]: **@2<90,6**↵
Specify next point or [Undo]: ↵

In this example, the line object is started at 2,2 in the current X,Y plane. Because no Z coordinate is specified, the point is interpreted as 2,2,0. The first part of the *To point:* coordinate entry, **@2<90**, works in the X,Y plane, just like its 2-D equivalent. The **,6** value that follows indicates a Z axis value. Because this is preceded by the "@" symbol, all of the values are calculated from the last point entered: 2,2,0. The resulting point location is 2 units at 90° in the X,Y plane, or **2,4,0,** and 6 units in the positive Z direction for a result of **2,4,6.** Figure 14.6 demonstrates the results of this example.

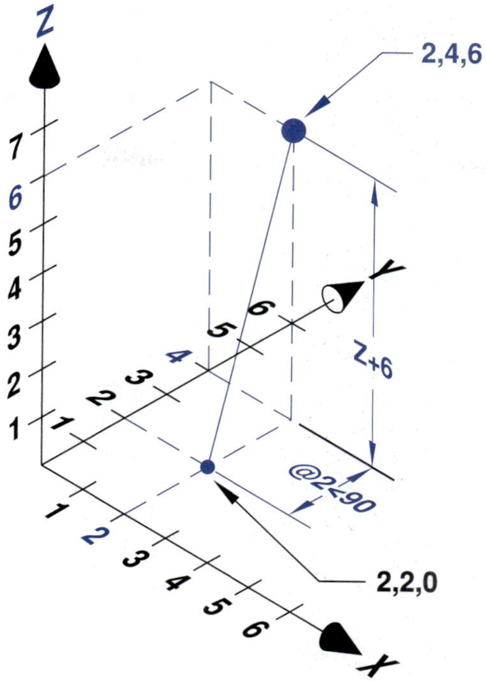

FIGURE 14.6 The cylindrical coordinate entry specifies a polar value in the X,Y plane and a Z axis distance.

The spherical coordinate system provides a true 3D polar coordinate entry option. This coordinate entry method allows you to specify the distance from the point of origin followed by the angle *in* the X,Y plane and the angle *from* the X,Y plane. A spherical coordinate specification looks like this:

2<45<60

This entry is defined as *Distance<Angle from X axis<Angle from X,Y plane.* The specification indicates a point that is 2 units from the origin at an angle of 45° in the X,Y plane and 60° from the X,Y plane. This format establishes the point relative to 0,0,0. The following format is more commonly used:

@2<45<60

This format establishes the new point relative to the last point entered. For example, the following sequence creates the line shown in Figure 14.7:

```
Command: L or LINE↵
Specify first point: 2,2↵
Specify next point or [Undo]: @2<45<60↵
Specify next point or [Undo]: ↵
```

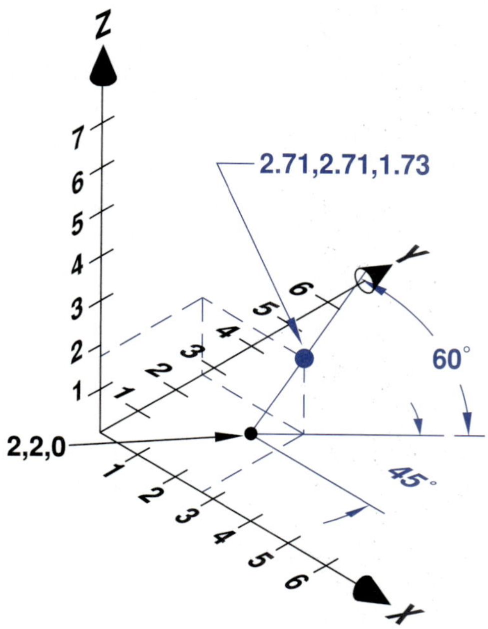

FIGURE 14.7 The spherical coordinate entry specifies a polar value both in and from the X,Y plane.

Field Notes

- When using cylindrical or spherical coordinates, the individual values can be specified as either positive or negative to get the desired results.
- Point filters can be very valuable in any 3D application. By entering **.XY** at a point prompt, you can select a point in the drawing and then type or pick a separate Z value. These filters include .XY, .XZ, .YZ, .X, .Y and .Z.

Applying 3D Coordinates

AutoCAD LT does not provide a great deal of 3D functionality. The 3D coordinate system allows you to place objects anywhere you want in the drawing; however, AutoCAD LT does not provide the capability to create any true 3D solid objects. A common application for working with advanced 3D coordinate systems such as cylindrical and spherical coordinates is found when AutoCAD LT is used in an office to supplement an installation of AutoCAD 2000. In such a case, AutoCAD LT may be used to edit 3D drawings created in AutoCAD. 3D drawings created in AutoCAD LT are typically of 2D objects that have been assigned a thickness. Placement of these objects is best handled through working with a User Coordinate System. Working with User Coordinate Systems and assigning 3D properties are covered later in this chapter.

Like using 2D coordinate entry, deciding which 3D coordinate entry method to use depends on what information is available and what is most effective. For example, the next sequence uses a variety of coordinate entry methods to draw a simple wire frame shape. The term *wire frame* is used to describe a 3D shape that uses 2D lines and curves to describe its outline.

As you work through this example, change the current object creation color as indicated. A fast and easy option is to use the Color Control list on the Object Properties toolbar. The first command in this sequence is VPOINT, which is described later in this chapter and is used to display the drawing area at a 3D viewing angle so you can see the effect of each coordinate entry.

```
Command: VPOINT↵
Current view direction: VIEWDIR=0.000,0.000,1.000
Specify a view point or [Rotate] <display compass and tripod>: -1.1,-2.2,3.1↵
Regenerating model.
<set object color to White(Black)>
Command: REC or RECTANGLE↵
Specify first corner point or [Chamfer/Elevation/Fillet/Thickness/Width]: 0,0↵
Specify other corner point: 6,4↵
Command: L or LINE↵
LINE Specify first point: 3,0,2↵                          <3D Absolute>
Specify next point or [Undo]: 3,4,2↵                      <3D Absolute>
Specify next point or [Undo]: ↵
```

The rectangle is created on the XY plane of the WCS and can therefore be defined using only 2D coordinate specifications. The line defines a profile that will be connected to the geometry created subsequently in this section.

The following lines are drawn starting at 0,0 and use 2D and 3D relative coordinate entries to draw part of this wire frame shape. Watch the effect of 2D coordinate entries on 3D lines. Even when the start point of a line is not located on the XY place of the WCS, specifying the other end using a 2D coordinate entry method draws the line parallel to the XY plane.

```
<set object color to Blue>
Command: L or LINE↵
Specify first point: 0,0↵                                 <2D Absolute>
Specify next point or [Undo]: @0,0,4↵                     <3D Relative>
Specify next point or [Undo]: @1,0↵                       <2D Relative>
Specify next point or [Close/Undo]: @2,0,-2↵              <3D Relative>
Specify next point or [Close/Undo]: @2,0,2↵               <3D Relative>
Specify next point or [Close/Undo]: @1,0↵                 <2D Relative>
Specify next point or [Close/Undo]: @0,0,-4↵              <3D Relative>
Specify next point or [Close/Undo]: ↵
Command:
```

The next sequence draws the same profile on the other side of the shape, starting at 0,4 and using a mix of absolute, relative, polar and cylindrical coordinate entries.

```
<set object color to Red>
Command: L or LINE↵
Specify first point: 0,4↵                                 <2D Absolute>
Specify next point or [Undo]: @0,0,4↵                     <3D Relative>
Specify next point or [Undo]: @1<0↵                       <2D Polar>
Specify next point or [Close/Undo]: @2<0,-2↵              <Cylindrical>
Specify next point or [Close/Undo]: @2<0,2↵               <Cylindrical>
Specify next point or [Close/Undo]: @1<0↵                 <2D Polar>
Specify next point or [Close/Undo]: @0,0,-4↵              <3D Relative>
Specify next point or [Close/Undo]: ↵
Command:
```

The next sequence gets closer to the object with ZOOM Extents and uses absolute and spherical coordinates to continue defining the wire frame shape.

```
Command: Z or ZOOM↵
Specify corner of window, enter a scale factor (nX or nXP), or
   [All/Center/Dynamic/Extents/Previous/Scale/Window] <real time>: E↵
Command:
```

```
<set object color to Magenta>
Command: L or LINE↵
Specify first point: 0,0,4↵                               <3D Absolute>
Specify next point or [Undo]: @1<90↵                      <2D Polar>
Specify next point or [Undo]: @1.4142<90<-45↵             <Spherical>
Specify next point or [Close/Undo]: @1.4142<90<45↵        <Spherical>
Specify next point or [Close/Undo]: @1<90↵                <2D Polar>
Specify next point or [Close/Undo]: ↵
Command: ↵
LINE Specify first point: 0,1,4↵                          <3D Absolute>
Specify next point or [Undo]: @1<0↵                       <2D Polar>
Specify next point or [Undo]: ↵
Command: ↵
LINE Specify first point: 0,3,4↵                          <3D Absolute>
Specify next point or [Undo]: @1<0↵                       <2D Polar>
Specify next point or [Undo]: ↵
Command: ↵
LINE Specify first point: 0,2,3↵                          <3D Absolute>
Specify next point or [Undo]: @2<0↵                       <2D Polar>
Specify next point or [Undo]: ↵
Command:
```

The wire frame shape now looks like the illustration in Figure 14.8A. The next profile of the shape is completed by picking points using a running ENDPoint object snap (Figure 14.8B). Many of the standard AutoCAD LT editing commands used to increase drawing productivity can be applied in either 2D or 3D drafting projects. For example, the profiles drawn in the magenta color can now be duplicated on the other side of the wire frame shape using the MIRROR command.

Although AutoCAD LT can create and edit simple 3D drawings, many of the available editing commands are designed primarily for 2D drafting needs. Commands such as MOVE, COPY, STRETCH, and SCALE are flexible and can use 3D coordinate specifications. Other commands, such as OFFSET, ROTATE, and MIRROR, work in a plane parallel to the current XY plane.

When the points defining the mirror line for the MIRROR command are specified, the points are projected onto the XY plane of the current coordinate system. No matter how or where the mirror line points are specified, AutoCAD LT changes the specified points to use a Z coordinate value of 0. Objects are mirrored in a 2D manner, using the same Z axis values as the original objects. In this example, the mirror line is defined using a MIDpoint on one of the rectangle's X-axis lines. The second point is picked using a polar snap vector, as shown in Figure 14.8C. The MIRROR command completes the shape. The final results are shown in Figure 14.8D.

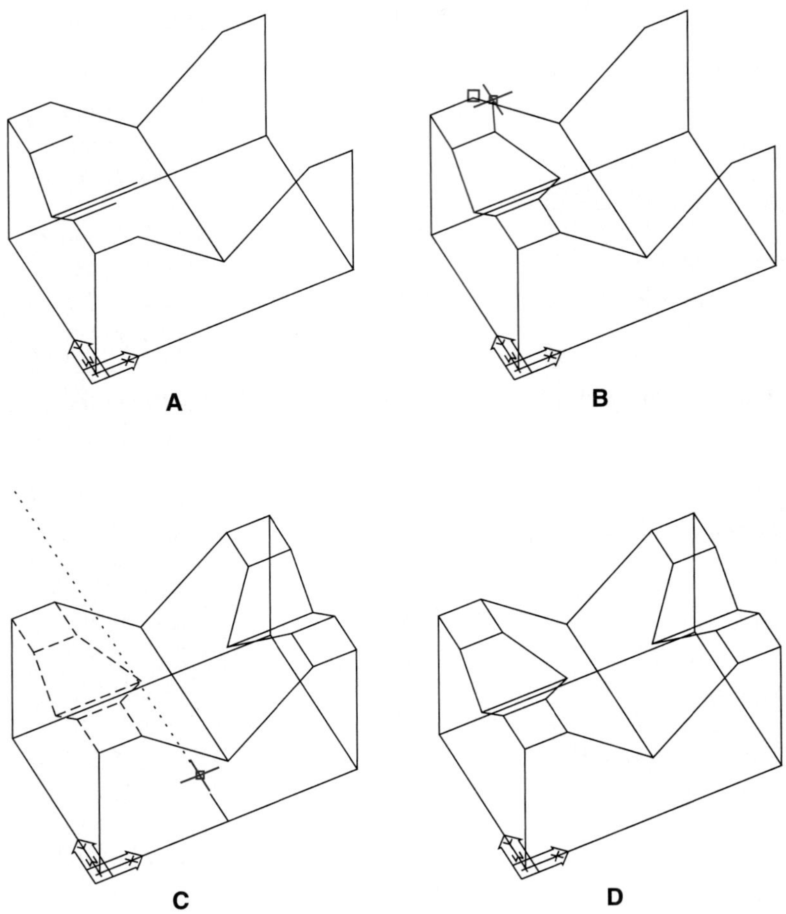

FIGURE 14.8 A wire frame object displays 3D object profiles using 2D objects such as lines and arcs. (A) 3D objects can be defined with a variety of coordinate entry methods or (B) using Osnap and picking points. (C) When MIRROR is used, the mirror line is defined in the current XY plane. (D) 2D editing commands such as MIRROR can also be productively applied when working in common 3D applications in order to simplify typical 3D construction procedures.

Exercise 14.1

Estimated time required: 10 min.

1. Start a new drawing from Scratch, using English settings.
2. For best viewing, use the VPOINT command and specify a setting of **−1.1,−2.2,3.1** at the prompt, as illustrated in the text example for the construction of the geometry in Figure 14.8.
3. Using simple Line objects, draw a wire frame representation of the 3D shape defined in this exercise, using the guidelines described in the following steps.
4. **Important:** To begin this exercise, define the bottom of the 3D shape using the RECTANGLE command with the first corner placed at 0,0,0 and the opposite corner located at 7.5,5.0,0.0. This places the base of the part directly on the XY plane of the WCS, with the long edge oriented along the X axis and the short side oriented along the Y axis. The rest of the part geometry is constructed in the direction of the positive Z axis (check the right-hand rule!). The correct location and orientation of this geometry is required for successful completion of subsequent exercises.
5. Use a variety of 2D and 3D coordinate entry methods to define the Lines. For each typed coordinate specification, try to use the coordinate entry method that is best suited for each coordinate specification.
6. Use the Extents option of the ZOOM command if needed to fully display the completed shape in the drawing area (or double-click with the wheel button if you are using a wheel mouse).
7. *Note:* For step-by-step guidance and a quick review of the previous discussion, refer to the example command sequence used to create the shape in Figure 14.8, which is a smaller version of the shape shown in this exercise. The specific coordinate values for this larger shape are different, but you can follow the same steps in the construction process and use the same coordinate entry methods as were used in the text example.
8. When you are finished drawing the wire frame shape, save as EX14.1.dwg and close the drawing.

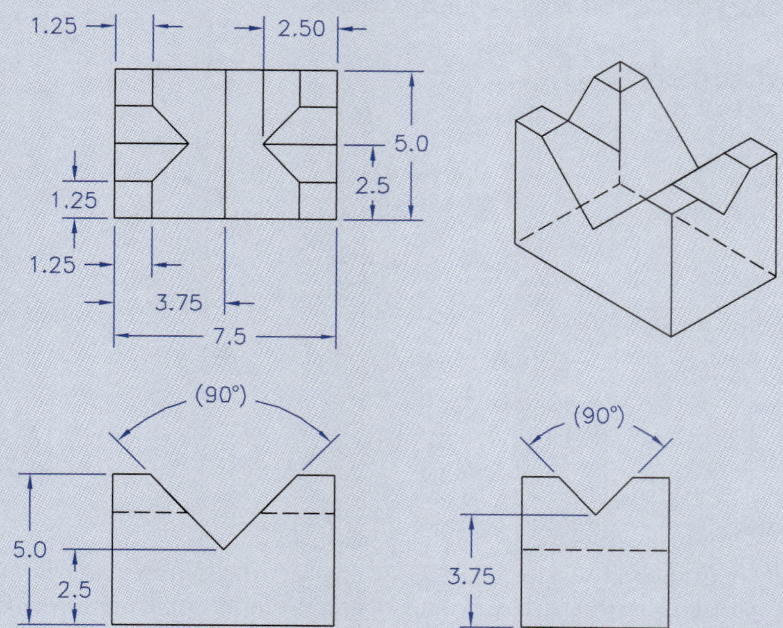

LEARNING CHECKPOINT

- ☐ Why do 3D drawings present an idea more effectively than 2D drawings?
- ☐ Where is the Z axis found in the Cartesian coordinate system?
- ☐ How can a 3D coordinate be specified as relative to the last point entered?
- ☐ Describe the WCS.
- ☐ What are the two points of the right-hand rule?
- ☐ Describe how cylindrical and spherical coordinates are used.
- ☐ Give a summary of the 3D capabilities of AutoCAD LT.

Concept Animations

- Coordinate System—Right-Hand Rule

Customizing the User Coordinate System

The World Coordinate System, or WCS, and User Coordinate System, or UCS, were introduced in Chapter 11. The WCS is the default coordinate system used by AutoCAD LT. This coordinate system is based on Cartesian coordinates. It exists on the plane parallel to the X and Y axis at the zero point of the Z axis, as shown in Figure 14.9.

The UCS is a custom coordinate system that can be relocated as needed in 3D space. All User Coordinate Systems are based on the WCS. Defining a new UCS to meet your needs can greatly simplify your work, whether you are drawing in two or three dimensions.

When you relocate the UCS, the 0,0 location can be placed anywhere in your drawing and the current UCS plane can be rotated to any desired angle. The uses that were explored earlier included placement of the 0,0 point for use in ordinate dimensioning and rotating it to match the orientation of an auxiliary view. 3D applications for customizing the UCS are discussed in this section.

FIGURE 14.9 The World Coordinate System is the default coordinate system on which all User Coordinate Systems are based.

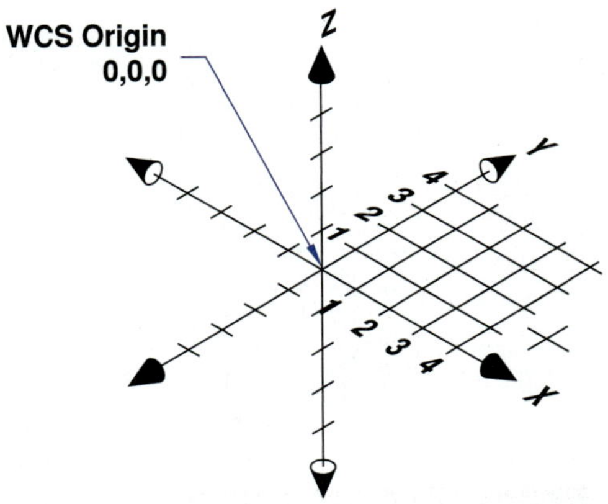

Controlling the UCS Icon

Also discussed briefly in Chapter 11 was the UCSICON command. You learned to use the ON and OFF options, as well as Origin and Noorigin. It is very important to understand the use of the UCS icon when working in 3D. The UCS icon helps you to keep track of where you are in 3D space. Figure 14.10 shows the various ways in which the UCS icon is displayed.

Descriptions for each of the UCS icon configurations are given here:

A The W in the icon indicates that the WCS is active and this is displaying its current orientation.

B When the W is not present, a UCS is currently active.

C The UCS icon appears deformed when the current 3D viewing angle is not perpendicular to the active UCS.

D When the UCS is rotated, the icon shows the positive directions for the X and Y axes.

E The plus sign (+) means that the icon is displayed at the origin (0,0 point) of the current UCS. If the origin is not visible in the current view, the icon will be displayed in the lower left corner of the viewport without the plus sign.

F This icon is intended to look like a broken pencil. The broken pencil is used to indicate that the viewing angle is almost parallel to the X,Y plane of the current UCS. When this icon is displayed, specifying point locations with your cursor may produce unexpected results.

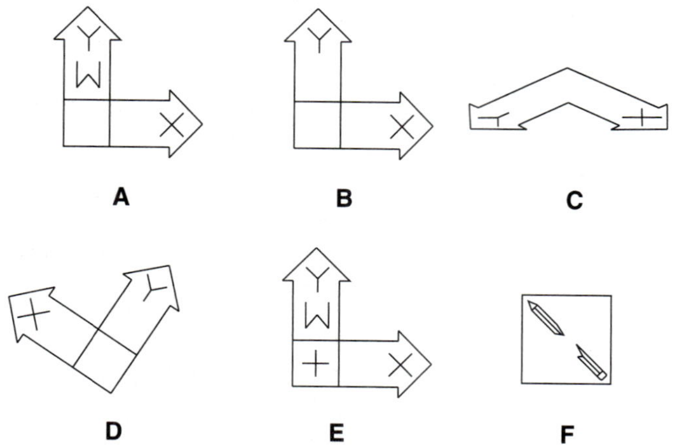

FIGURE 14.10 The UCSICON is used to help keep track of where you are in a 3D drawing.

View
Display▶
UCS Icon▶
UCSICON

The options for the UCS icon are set using the UCSICON command. To use the UCSICON command, pick the desired option from the UCS Icon cascade on the Display cascade on the View pull-down menu, or type **UCSICON** at the Command: prompt. When used this way, any settings you change affect only the current viewport.

The two primary options available for the UCS icon are turning it on and off, and controlling whether or not it is displayed at the UCS origin. When you access the pull-down menu, a check mark is displayed next to the option that is currently active. One advantage to typing UCSICON is that the settings can be applied to all viewports at the same time. The following example turns the UCS icon off, then on again and then places it at the origin in all viewports:

Command: **UCSICON↵**
Enter an option [ON/OFF/All/Noorigin/ORigin] <ON>: **A↵**
Enter an option [ON/OFF/Noorigin/ORigin] <ON>: **OFF↵**
Command: ↵
UCSICON
Enter an option [ON/OFF/All/Noorigin/ORigin] <OFF>: **A↵**
Enter an option [ON/OFF/Noorigin/ORigin] <OFF>: **ON↵**
Command: ↵
UCSICON
Enter an option [ON/OFF/All/Noorigin/ORigin] <ON>: **A↵**
Enter an option [ON/OFF/Noorigin/ORigin] <ON>: **OR↵**
Command:

Field Notes

The UCS icon is on, by default, in AutoCAD LT. When you are using the WCS, the UCS icon may be considered to be unnecessary clutter on the screen. However, it should always be turned on when you are working with a UCS. This helps to keep you properly oriented in your drawing.

Relocating the UCS

Any coordinate system that is not the WCS is called a UCS. The current UCS controls the placement of objects that you create in your drawing, because coordinates that you enter are interpreted based on the current UCS, not the WCS. Also, the location and orientation of the current UCS affects operations performed by pointing with the cursor.

Several tools are available for relocating the UCS. The coordinate system can be rotated, its origin can be changed, it can even be set to match the UCS of an object in your drawing or to match the current 3D viewing angle. After creating a new UCS, it can be named and saved and restored as desired. If a saved UCS is no longer needed, it can be deleted from the named UCS list. AutoCAD LT even provides dialog boxes that allow you to restore a selected predefined UCS.

UCS
UCS
Tools
New UCS ▶
UCS

Most of the available options are provided in the UCS command. The UCS command options can be accessed from the UCS toolbar found on the Standard toolbar, by picking the UCS cascade on the Tools pull-down menu, or by typing **UCS** at the Command: prompt. To actively display the UCS toolbar without using the flyout button, right-click on any toolbar button to display the Toolbars shortcut menu, then pick the UCS option.

The default option for the UCS command is World, which restores the World Coordinate System. Although you can type W to access this option, it is not necessary because World is the default:

UCS
World UCS
Tools
New UCS ▶
World
UCS

```
Command: UCS
Current ucs name: *WORLD*
Enter an option [New/Move/orthoGraphic/Prev/Restore/Save/Del/?/World] <World>: ↵
Command:
```

The Origin option of the UCS command sets a new UCS origin point. No rotation is applied to the UCS using this option; rather the X,Y origin point (0,0) is moved to a new location. This movement can be in the current X,Y plane, or it can be used to move the current UCS up or down the Z axis while maintaining the current rotation. The UCS Origin Zdepth option is used in the following sequence to move the UCS by sliding it a specified positive or negative distance along the Z axis. The Zdepth specification represents a relative change in the Z axis from the current location of the UCS origin; it does not describe an absolute (fixed) Z axis location. In the following sequence, the specified Zdepth distance is positive 3; this slides the UCS origin location three units in the positive direction along the Z axis relative to the current UCS origin location, as shown in Figure 14.11:

UCS
Move UCS Origin
Tools
Move UCS
UCS

```
Command: UCS↵
Current ucs name: *WORLD*
Enter an option [New/Move/orthoGraphic/Prev/Restore/Save/Del/?/World] <World>: M↵
Specify new origin point or [Zdepth]<0,0,0>: Z↵
Specify Zdepth<0>: 3↵
Command:
```

UCS
Origin UCS
Tools
New UCS ▶
Origin

The Zdepth provides an easy way to slide the UCS origin point up or down along the Z axis while maintaining a constant placement in the X,Y plane for each new origin location that is applied. Look at Figure 14.11 again to review a clear illustration of the effects of changing the Zdepth to define a different UCS origin point. The XY plane defined by the new UCS is parallel to the XY plane in the previous UCS and maintains the same orientation.

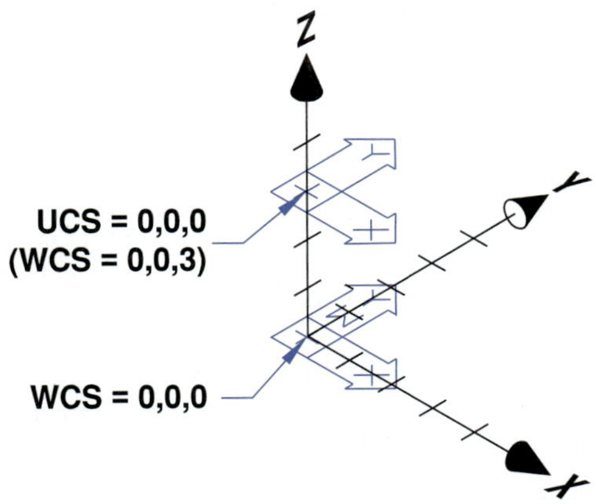

FIGURE 14.11 The Origin option of the UCS command sets the location of the 0,0 point while maintaining the current rotation and orientation. This example shows the UCS origin point being moved 3 units in the positive Z axis direction using the Z depth option.

For greater flexibility, you can specify a new UCS origin point using any valid coordinate entry method, by specifying a point on the screen by picking unassisted or using an appropriate object snap mode, or you can define a location as an absolute coordinate location specified using any desired combination of X,Y, and Z axis values to describe the new coordinate location. When a new origin point is specified by picking a point or using an absolute coordinate specification, the new location of the UCS Origin is an absolute location based on the previous UCS configuration and is not located relative to the previous UCS origin location. The Specify new origin point method is used in the following sequence to locate the UCS origin point at an absolute coordinate location specified as **8,2.5,-1.75**. In the subsequent UCS command, the WCS is set current using the default option *World:*

```
Command:  UCS↵
Current ucs name:  *NO NAME*
Enter an option [New/Move/orthoGraphic/Prev/Restore/Save/Del/?/World] <World>:  M↵
Specify new origin point or [Zdepth]<0,0,0>:  8,2.5,-1.75↵
Command:  ↵
UCS
Current ucs name:  *NO NAME*
Enter an option [New/Move/orthoGraphic/Prev/Restore/Save/Del/?/World] <World>:  ↵
Command:
```

When setting UCS options, you can use either absolute or relative coordinates. The definition for the WCS given earlier states that it is the basis for all User Coordinate Systems. However, all coordinate specifications given for drawing or editing objects, as well as relocating the UCS are relative to the *current* UCS. Preceding the coordinate specification with the @ symbol makes it relative to the last point entered. Alternately, absolute coordinate points can be entered.

The ZAxis option of the UCS command allows you to select a new origin point and specify the direction for the new Z axis. The UCS is automatically rotated as necessary around either the X or Y axis as necessary to place the Z axis in the specified direction from the origin points. The following example shows the ZAxis option being used. After the new UCS Origin point is specified, you are prompted to specify a point that lies on the positive Z Axis. The default point matches the origin point and adds 1 to the Z Axis value, which maintains the existing direction as the positive Z Axis direction. The result of setting a new Zaxis direction is illustrated in Figure 14.12.

```
Command:  UCS↵
Current ucs name:  *WORLD*
Enter an option [New/Move/orthoGraphic/Prev/Restore/Save/Del/?/World] <World>:  N↵
Specify origin of new UCS or [ZAxis/3point/OBject/Face/View/X/Y/Z] <0,0,0>:  ZA↵
Specify new origin point <0,0,0>:  4,2,6.5↵
Specify point on positive portion of Z-axis <4.0000,2.0000,7.5000>:  <specify a point or accept the
   default>
Command:
```

The UCS icon indicates the new origin and orientation of the UCS. If you discover that the new UCS is not what you actually want, simply undo the change using the UNDO command.

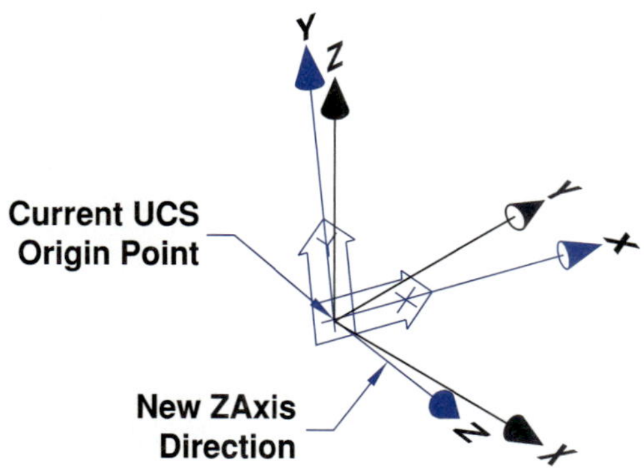

FIGURE 14.12 The ZAxis option of the UCS command sets the location of the 0,0 point and allows you to change the current rotation and orientation by specifying a new Z axis direction. This example shows a new UCS origin and Z axis direction being specified.

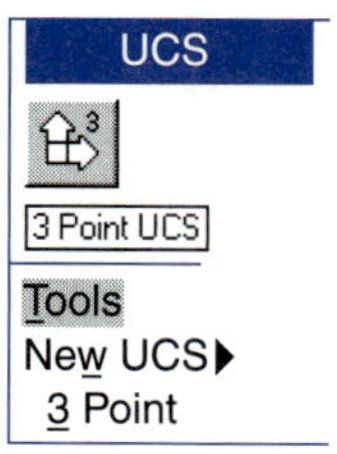

The 3point option provides a flexible UCS tool for setting up a coordinate system that aligns with existing features in the drawing. Similar to the ZAxis option, you are prompted to enter an origin point. The difference is that with this option you are prompted for the positive directions for both the X and Y axes.

The following sequence shows the prompts issued when using the 3point option:

```
Command:  UCS↵
Current ucs name:  *NO NAME*
Enter an option [New/Move/orthoGraphic/Prev/Restore/Save/Del/?/World] <World>:  N↵
Specify origin of new UCS or [ZAxis/3point/OBject/Face/View/X/Y/Z] <0,0,0>:  3↵
Specify new origin point <0,0,0>:  ENDP↵
of  <pick UCS origin point>
```

Specify point on positive portion of X-axis <3.00,2.00,3.00>: **ENDP↵**
of *<pick point on positive X axis>*
Specify point on positive-Y portion of the UCS XY plane <2.00,3.00,3.00>: **ENDP↵**
of *<pick point on positive Y axis>*
Command:

UCS
Object UCS
Tools
UCS ▶
Object

This example shows object snap modes being used for point selection for accuracy. Any valid point entry is acceptable, including relative, polar, spherical or cylindrical coordinates, or direct distance entry. Figure 14.13 illustrates the three points that would be picked to create a UCS on the inclined plane as shown.

The Object option provides a convenient way to establish a UCS that matches an existing object in the drawing. Simply select an object and the UCS is set to match:

Command: **UCS↵**
Current ucs name: *NO NAME*
Enter an option [New/Move/orthoGraphic/Prev/Restore/Save/Del/?/World] <World>: **N↵**
Specify origin of new UCS or [ZAxis/3point/OBject/Face/View/X/Y/Z] <0,0,0>: **OB↵**
Select object to align UCS: *<select an object>*

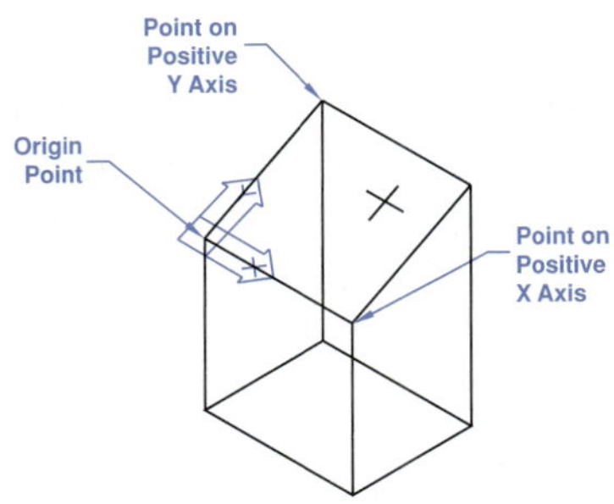

FIGURE 14.13 The 3point option of the UCS command sets the location of the 0,0 point and allows you to change the current rotation and orientation by specifying both a new X axis and Y axis direction. This example shows the new UCS based on the three points selected.

The determination of how the UCS is interpreted depends on the type of objects selected. The following explains how different objects are used to set up the UCS. Note that the following applies to each object as viewed from the positive side of the X,Y plane.

Object Type	UCS Definition Description
Arc	Origin is at arc center. The X axis passes through endpoint of arc closest to pick point.
Circle	Origin is at circle center. The X axis passes through pick point.
Dimension	Origin is at midpoint of dimension text. Direction of new X axis is parallel to X axis direction in effect when the dimension was created.
Line	Origin is at endpoint closest to pick point. The X axis is defined so that line lies on XZ axis of the new UCS. Second endpoint of line defines the Y axis coordinate of 0.
Point	Origin is placed at point location.
2D Polyline	Origin is at pline start point. The X axis passes through the next pline vertex.
2D Solid	Origin is placed at first solid definition point. First two definition points define the X axis.
Text, Block Reference, or Attribute Definition	Origin is placed at insertion point. X axis is defined by rotation angle applied to object. Because the object rotation defines the positive X axis direction, the object has a 0 rotation angle in the new UCS.

UCS
View UCS
Tools
New UCS ▶
View

Some objects, such as splines, ellipses, and elliptical arcs cannot be used to define a coordinate system.

Using the View option of the UCS command sets the X,Y plane of the UCS parallel to the current view of the drawing. The current origin point is unchanged. This method is simple and effective when you establish a 3D view that you wish to use to define your UCS.

Command: **UCS↵**
Current ucs name: *NO NAME*
Enter an option [New/Move/orthoGraphic/Prev/Restore/Save/Del/?/World] <World>: **N↵**
Specify origin of new UCS or [ZAxis/3point/OBject/Face/View/X/Y/Z] <0,0,0>: **V↵**
Command:

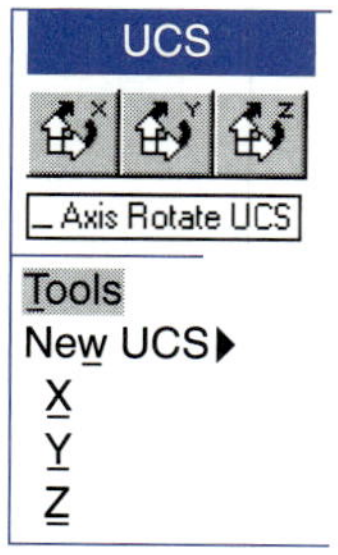

The X, Y, and Z options are commonly used options that allow you to rotate the UCS around the specified axis. For example, Figure 14.14A shows the beginning of the construction of a 3D wire frame shape. The first rectangle is drawn in the WCS, then the UCS is rotated 90° around the X axis for the construction of the second rectangle. When using these options, refer to the second step of the right-hand rule to determine whether the angle should be specified as positive or negative. The following sequence illustrates the procedure used in Figure 14.14B:

Command: **REC** or **RECTANGLE**↵
Specify first corner point or [Chamfer/Elevation/Fillet/Thickness/Width]: **0,0**↵
Specify other corner point: **4,4**↵
Command: **UCS**↵
Current ucs name: *WORLD*
Enter an option [New/Move/orthoGraphic/Prev/Restore/Save/Del/?/World] <World>: **N**↵
Specify origin of new UCS or [ZAxis/3point/OBject/Face/View/X/Y/Z] <0,0,0>: **X**↵
Specify rotation angle about X axis <90>: ↵
Command: **REC** or **RECTANGLE**↵
Specify first corner point or [Chamfer/Elevation/Fillet/Thickness/Width]: **0,0**↵
Specify other corner point: **4,4**↵

The construction (XY) plane where the next rectangle is to be drawn is parallel to the XY plane of the current UCS. The Zdepth option for defining the UCS Origin is designed expressly for this type of application. Applying the right-hand rule confirms that the Zdepth distance must be specified using a negative value to get the desired results. The following sequence slides the XY plane –4 units to locate the new UCS Origin point as required for drawing the next rectangle. The results are shown in Figure 14.14C:

Command: **UCS**↵
Current ucs name: *NO NAME*
Enter an option [New/Move/orthoGraphic/Prev/Restore/Save/Del/?/World] <World>: **M**↵
Specify new origin point or [Zdepth]<0,0,0>: **Z**↵
Specify Zdepth<0>: **-4**↵
Command: **REC** or **RECTANGLE**↵
Specify first corner point or [Chamfer/Elevation/Fillet/Thickness/Width]: **0,0**↵
Specify other corner point: **6,4**↵

As before, the VPOINT command is used here to set up a 3D viewing angle to display the drawing in a more understandable format. 3D drawing display commands are covered later in this chapter.

Command: **VPOINT**↵
*** Switching to the WCS ***
Current view direction: VIEWDIR=0.0000,0.0000,1.0000
Specify a view point or [Rotate] <display compass and tripod>: **1.1,-1.1,1.5**↵
*** Returning to the UCS ***
Regenerating model.
Command:

Several of the options for creating a new UCS require the new UCS to be defined in terms of the active settings in the current UCS. In some cases it can be difficult to create a new UCS definition when working in an unusual UCS with unfamiliar settings. The definition of a new UCS can be easier if you first restore the familiar environment and the default coordinate system used by the WCS. In the following sequence, the World Coordinate System is restored first to simplify the needed absolute coordinate specifications supplied to the UCS 3point option to define a UCS parallel to the inclined plane of the object. The new UCS is represented with the UCS icon, as shown in Figure 14.14D.

Command: **UCS**↵
Current ucs name: *NO NAME*
Enter an option [New/Move/orthoGraphic/Prev/Restore/Save/Del/?/World] <World>: ↵
Command: **UCS**↵
Current ucs name: *WORLD*
Enter an option [New/Move/orthoGraphic/Prev/Restore/Save/Del/?/World] <World>: **N**↵
Specify origin of new UCS or [ZAxis/3point/OBject/Face/View/X/Y/Z] <0,0,0>: **3**↵
Specify new origin point <0,0,0>: **0,0,4**↵
Specify point on positive portion of X-axis <1.0000,0.0000,4.0000>: **4,0,4**↵
Specify point on positive-Y portion of the UCS XY plane <0.0000,1.0000,4.0000>: **0,4,6**↵

In the previous example, a new UCS was defined to match the inclined plane, providing a 2D construction plane to simplify the creation of any planar drawing objects. A ***planar*** object is a 2D object that can be created only in an orientation that is parallel to the current construction plane. The XY plane of the current UCS is the active construction plane. Examples of planar objects include circles, arcs, and even rectangles—which are actually created from 2D polyline objects. The construction plane also controls the plane of operation used for planar style editing commands such as TRIM, EXTEND, OFFSET, and ROTATE.

As indicated previously, the AutoCAD LT software is designed primarily for 2D drafting applications. Appropriately defined and positioned construction planes allow standard 2D drawing and editing commands to be used in the construction of 3D geometry. Effective use of 2D construction planes is critical to working productively in most typical 3D drawing projects created in AutoCAD LT. The wire frame model created in this example illustrates how the appropriate use and application of 2D construction planes makes it possible to use simple 2D planar objects in the production of an accurate 3D wire frame representation of a product, a design, or any other desired application. The following sequence creates the final rectangle and draws the circle on the construction plane made available by the new UCS definition.

Command: **REC** or **RECTANGLE↵**
Specify first corner point or [Chamfer/Elevation/Fillet/Thickness/Width]: **0,0↵**
Specify other corner point: **END↵**
Of *<pick endpoint to define location for opposite corner>*
Command: **C** or **CIRCLE↵**
Specify center point for circle or [3P/2P/Ttr (tan tan radius)]: **2,2.25↵**
Specify radius of circle or [Diameter] <1.00>: **D↵**
Specify diameter of circle <2.00>: **2↵**
Command:

Field Notes

Some AutoCAD LT commands, such as the UCS command, present the available options in a hierarchical structure. A hierarchical structure refers to "layered" command options that, when accessed, present a subsequent group of related options. For example, accessing the New option of the UCS command displays a listing of the available options for defining a new UCS.

Accessing the ZAxis option of the UCS command using the available options as presented in the Floating Command Window works like this:

Command: **UCS↵**
Current ucs name: *NO NAME*
Enter an option [New/Move/orthoGraphic/Prev/Restore/Save/Del/?/World] <World>: **N↵**
Specify origin of new UCS or [ZAxis/3point/OBject/Face/View/X/Y/Z] <0,0,0>: **ZA↵**
Specify new origin point <0,0,0>: *<continue with desired options>*

Many commands allow direct access to an option if you know the name and the required character entry for the desired option. For example, you can skip the hierarchical command structure of the UCS command and directly access the access the ZAxis option by entering the ZAxis option at the first prompt, as follows:

Command: **UCS↵**
Current ucs name: *NO NAME*
Enter an option [New/Move/orthoGraphic/Prev/Restore/Save/Del/?/World] <World>: **ZA↵**
Specify new origin point <0,0,0>: *<continue with desired options>*

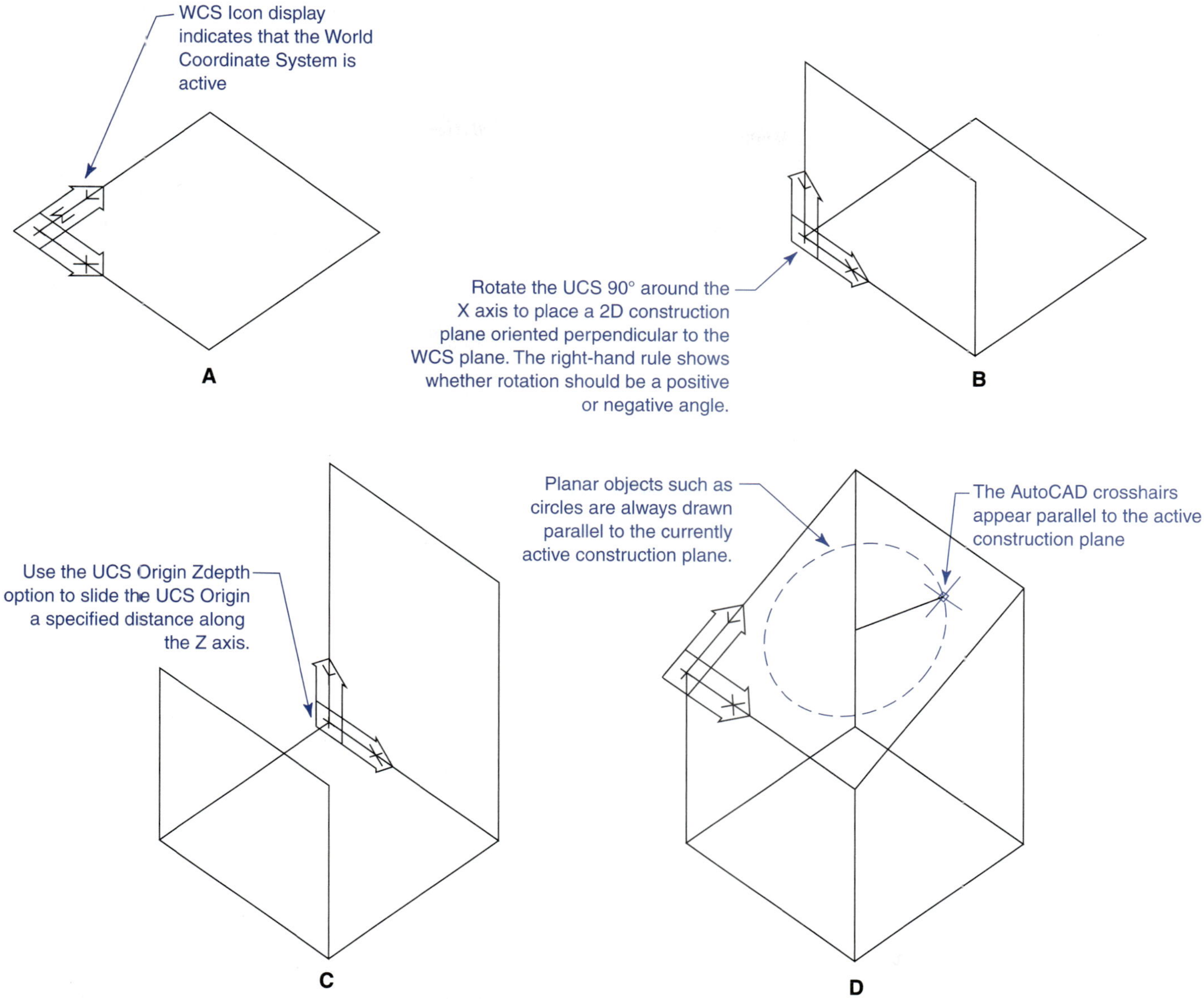

FIGURE 14.14 (A) The first rectangle is created in the WCS. (B) Rotating the UCS 90° on the X axis defines a construction plane perpendicular to the WCS for creation of the next rectangle. (C) Use the UCS Origin Zdepth option to "slide" the UCS origin −4 units along the Z axis to place the construction plane as needed to draw the next rectangle. (D) Use the UCS 3point option to define a new construction plane that is used to define 2D planar objects on the inclined top plane of the part.

Displaying the Current UCS

When you change the UCS, your current viewing angle does not automatically change to match. Sometimes it is helpful to view your work from a 3D angle, rather than a flat plan view. Therefore, the UCS and viewing angle are handled separately. When you want to view your drawing from a plan view of either the WCS or any existing UCS, use the PLAN command. The PLAN command is accessed by typing **PLAN** at the Command: prompt, or by picking an option from the Plan View cascade under the 3D Views cascade on the View pull-down menu. A very common use of the PLAN command is to quickly set your view to the plan view of the current UCS. The following example shows how this is done:

View
3D Views ▸
Plan View ▸
Current UCS
World UCS
Named UCS
PLAN

```
Command: PLAN↵
Enter an option [Current ucs/Ucs/World] <Current>: ↵
Regenerating model.
Command:
```

The default option is Current, referring to the current UCS. Pressing Enter at the prompt displays its plan view. Use the **W** option to display the plan view of the WCS. The UCS option allows you to enter the name of a saved UCS to view. Working with named User Coordinate Systems is discussed in the next section.

Field Notes

- To specify a point in the WCS without making it the current coordinate system, precede the point coordinate with an asterisk. For example, the following entry specifies a coordinate in the WCS:

  To point: ***2,4,0↵**

  All coordinate entry methods can be used this way. For example, an absolute cylindrical coordinate would be:

  ***2<30,4**

  When the coordinates are relative to the last point entered, the asterisk follows the @ symbol:

  @*2.25<60 or **@*3<45<60** or **@*2<30,4**

- Paper space does not allow the use of certain commands discussed in this chapter. The PLAN command is one of the commands that can only be used in model space.

Working with Named UCSs

The basic philosophy behind any CAD software is that if you are going to need something again, save it. If you have done it once, there is no need to do it again. This is true of blocks, named views, layering systems, and any other feature of a drawing that can be saved. It is also possible to assign a name to a UCS so that you can immediately restore it at any time in the future. This keeps you from having to define the UCS each time you need it.

The first step in this process is to create a needed UCS. After creating it, if you feel you may need to use it again, it should be saved with a recognizable name. To name and save a UCS, use the Save option of the UCS command:

```
Command: UCS↵
Current ucs name: *WORLD*
Enter an option [New/Move/orthoGraphic/Prev/Restore/Save/Del/?/World] <World>: S↵
Enter name to save current UCS or [?]: FRONT↵
Command:
```

To get a listing of the currently saved coordinate systems, use the question mark option of the UCS command. Similar to listing most named objects, AutoCAD LT prompts for a search string, where a specific name can be entered, or wild card characters can be used. In the following example, the default asterisk wild card is accepted to get a listing of all saved coordinate systems:

```
Command: UCS↵
Current ucs name: FRONT
Enter an option [New/Move/orthoGraphic/Prev/Restore/Save/Del/?/World] <World>: ?↵

Enter UCS name(s) to list <*>: ↵
Current ucs name: "FRONT"
Saved coordinate systems:

"FRONT"
  Origin = <0.0000,0.0000,0.0000>, X Axis = <1.0000,0.0000,0.0000>
  Y Axis = <0.0000,1.0000,0.0000>, Z Axis = <0.0000,0.0000,1.0000>

Enter an option [New/Move/orthoGraphic/Prev/Restore/Save/Del/?/World] <World>:
```

The numbers displayed will be more familiar to you as you become accustomed to working in 3D. The Origin coordinate, as implied, indicates the location of the UCS origin with respect to the current UCS. The X, Y, and Z axes coordinates indicate a point, based on the current UCS, that the specified axis passes through in its positive direction. When a UCS is current, it always shows the same description found in the preceding example. In the next listing, a new UCS has been defined and is now current:

Enter UCS name(s) to list <*>: ↵
Current ucs name: "NEW-UCS"
Saved coordinate systems:

"FRONT"
Origin = <0.0000,0.0000,0.0000>, X Axis = <0.5766,-0.3787,0.7240>
Y Axis = <0.8171,0.2672,-0.5109>, Z Axis = <0.0000,0.8861,0.4634>
"NEW-UCS"
Origin = <0.0000,0.0000,0.0000>, X Axis = <1.0000,0.0000,0.0000>
Y Axis = <0.0000,1.0000,0.0000>, Z Axis = <0.0000,0.0000,1.0000>

Enter an option [New/Move/orthoGraphic/Prev/Restore/Save/Del/?/World] <World>:

To make a saved UCS current, use the Restore option. The Restore option is accessed by typing **R** at the prompt as follows:

Command: **UCS**↵
Current ucs name: *WORLD*
Enter an option [New/Move/orthoGraphic/Prev/Restore/Save/Del/?/World] <World>: **R**↵
Enter name of UCS to restore or [?]: **FRONT**↵ *<enter the name of any saved UCS>*
Command:

Field Notes

When you restore a saved UCS, remember that even though the UCS is restored, your view may not be parallel to the X,Y plane of the UCS. Be sure to check your UCS Icon, and use the PLAN command if necessary.

If you have incorrectly created a saved UCS, or simply no longer need it, use the Delete option of the UCS command to remove it. Wild card characters can also be used at the UCS name prompt when you need to delete more than one UCS. If you accidentally delete the wrong UCS name, you can use the U command to undo the deletion. The following example shows the prompts issued when deleting a UCS:

Command: **UCS**↵
Current ucs name: *WORLD*
Enter an option [New/Move/orthoGraphic/Prev/Restore/Save/Del/?/World] <World>: **D**↵
Enter UCS name(s) to delete <none>: **NEW-UCS**↵
Deleted 1 UCS name.
Command:

UCS

UCS Previous

The UCS Previous option provides the same kind of convenience as the ZOOM PREVIOUS command. This allows you to step back through the last 10 coordinate systems created in the current space. Also like ZOOM PREVIOUS, this movement through coordinate systems is one way only. This option can be accessed through the Previous option of the UCS command or by picking the UCS Previous button on the UCS toolbar:

Command: **UCS**↵
Current ucs name: FRONT
Enter an option [New/Move/orthoGraphic/Prev/Restore/Save/Del/?/World] <World>: **P**↵
Command: ↵
UCS
Current ucs name: *WORLD*
Enter an option [New/Move/orthoGraphic/Prev/Restore/Save/Del/?/World] <World>:

UCS & UCS II

Display UCS Dialog

Tools
Named UCS...

UCSMAN
UC

The DDUCS command displays the UCS dialog box. This provides an easy way to work with named coordinate systems. The DDUCS command is accessed by typing **UC** or **DDUCS** at the Command: prompt, by picking Named UCS ... from the Tools menu, or by picking the Display UCS Dialog button from either the UCS or UCS II toolbar. The Named UCSs tab of the UCS dialog box is shown in Figure 14.15.

The UCS dialog box contains three tabs used for managing various settings related to UCS control. The Named UCSs tab is displayed by default when this dialog box is accessed by picking the Display UCS Dialog toolbar button or by picking Named UCS... from the Tools pull-down menu. All named UCSs are displayed in the list box, including the World Coordinate System. The current UCS displays an arrow to its left, and its name is listed above the list in the *Current UCS:* field. The Previous option is displayed only when it is a valid option. Previous is available after changing the active UCS, but only when one or more of the Previous UCSs have not been restored in this drawing session.

The Named UCSs tab of the UCS dialog box provides a limited set of basic management tools for working with named UCSs. The available options are as follows:

- **Set Current** Sets the highlighted UCS name to be current. This option is available as a button on the Named UCSs tab or from the shortcut menu, as shown in Figure 14.15. Double-clicking on a named UCS in the list also sets the selected UCS to be current.
- **Rename** Opens the highlighted UCS name for editing, allowing you to change the currently assigned UCS name. The Rename option is available only on the shortcut menu (see Figure 14.15). If preferred, you can pick a UCS name once to highlight it, pause briefly, and pick the name again to open it for editing. The brief pause prevents the two picks from being interpreted as a double click. You cannot rename the World or Previous items.
- **Delete** Deletes the highlighted UCS name. If the current UCS is deleted, it is renamed Unnamed and remains current. You cannot delete the World Coordinate System, the Previous option, or an Unnamed UCS that is current. The Delete option is available only on the shortcut menu (see Figure 14.15), or you can pick a UCS name and press the Delete key on your keyboard.
- **Details...** Displays the UCS Details dialog box (Figure 14.16), which describes the location of the UCS origin and lists the axis direction for the highlighted UCS name. This option is available as a button on the Named UCSs tab or from the shortcut menu (see Figure 14.15).

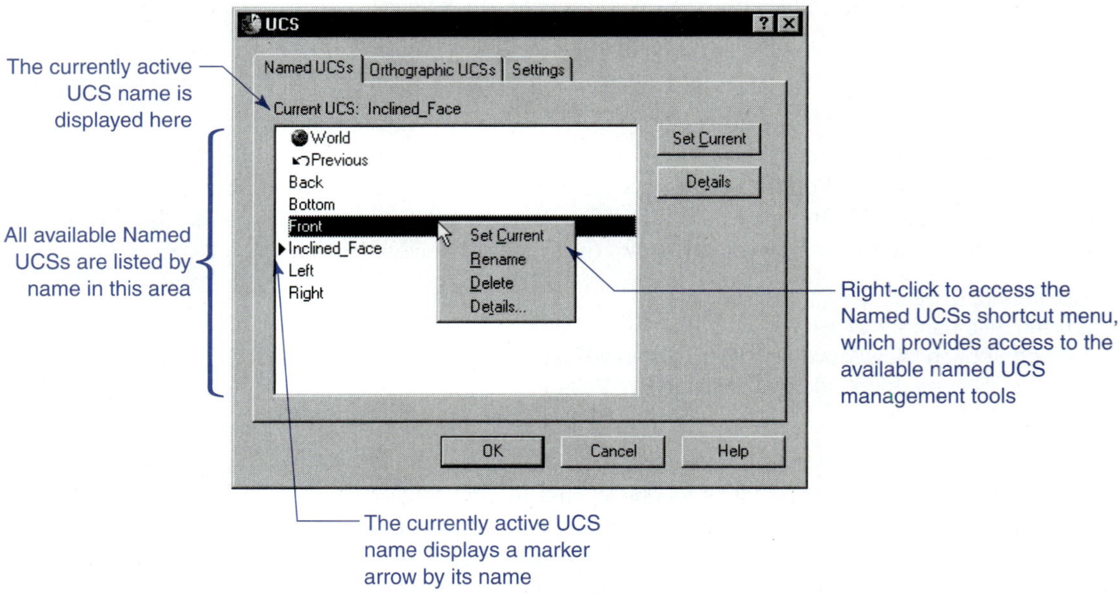

FIGURE 14.15 The Named UCSs tab of the UCS dialog box lists all named UCSs and provides a limited set of management tools for working with your named UCSs.

FIGURE 14.16 The UCS Details dialog box describes the UCS origin point and axis directions for the currently selected UCS name. The base coordinate system used to calculate locations can be selected from the available named UCSs listed in the Relative to: drop-down list.

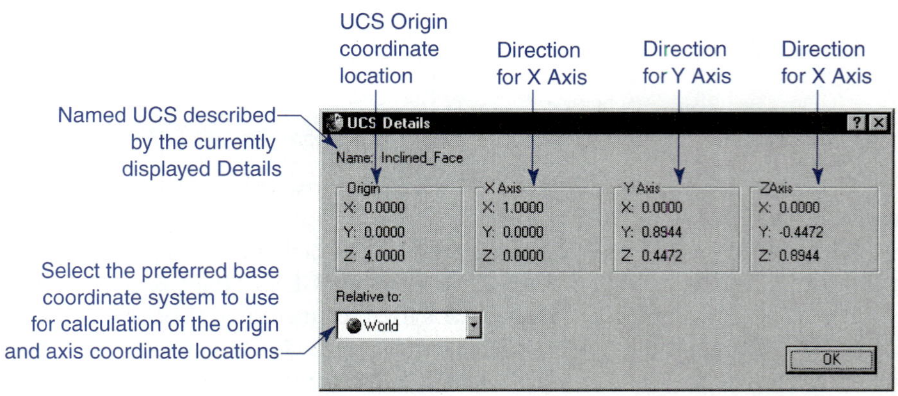

UCS Presets

UCS & UCS II

Display UCS Dialog

Tools
Orthographic UCS ▶
Preset...

DDUCSP
UCP

Several preset UCS settings are available by using the Orthographic UCSs tab of the UCS dialog box. This tab is displayed by using the DDUCSP command. To access this command, type **UCP** or **DDUCSP** at the Command: prompt, pick Preset ... from the Orthographic UCS cascade of the Tools pull-down menu, or pick the Display UCS Dialog button on the UCS or UCS II toolbar, and pick the Orthographic UCSs tab.

The preset UCS selection provides six coordinate system orientations that match the six sides of a cube. This includes front, back, top, bottom, left, and right. Just like when you set the UCS by any other means, the view does not change. To switch to the plan view of any current UCS, use the PLAN command and accept the default of *Current UCS.*

The images in the UCS Orientation dialog box show a colored face on one side of the cube to describe each of the available UCS options. This tab of the UCS dialog box is shown in Figure 14.17A.

There are two ways to use these presets, absolute and relative. The absolute method works in reference to the WCS, and is specified by selecting the world option from the Relative to: list. With this method, the Top is the default WCS, and the other five options rotate the UCS around the appropriate axes to generate the described view. The WCS option, indicated by the UCS Icon with the W, and the current view options are automatically established by this method when the World option is selected in the Relative to: List.

The Named UCS management options available in the Orthographic UCSs tab include some of the same options as are listed in the Named UCSs tab (see Figure 14.17A). Two additional options are provided on the shortcut menu and are described as follows:

- **Reset** Resets the currently assigned Depth value for the highlighted named UCS to 0.000.
- **Depth** Displays the Orthographic UCS depth dialog box (Figure 14.17B), for specification of the value for the UCS Depth property. When a preset orthographic UCS is applied, the UCS origin is then moved on the Z axis for the distance assigned to the depth property.

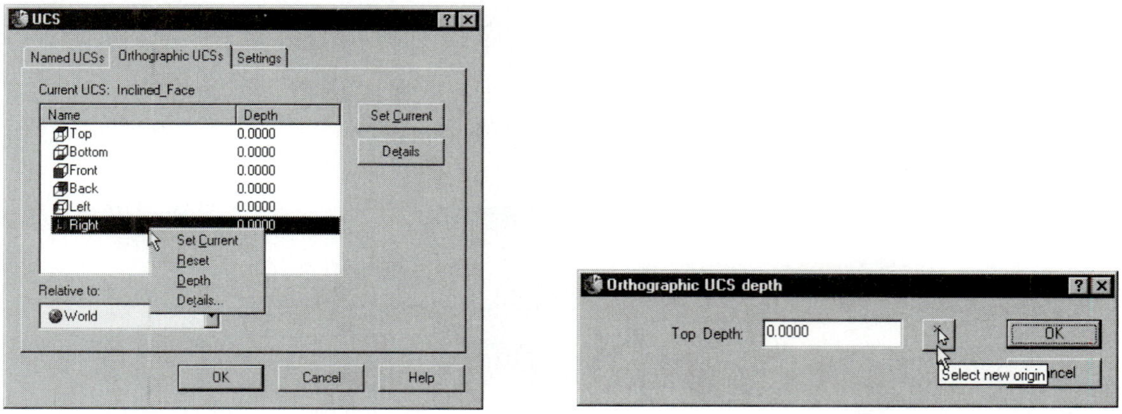

A B

FIGURE 14.17 (A) The predefined orthographic UCSs are specifically designed to provide fast and convenient access to the six orthographic coordinate systems and are very useful when constructing a 3D representation of your design. (B) The Depth setting specifies the distance that the Origin point of the applied UCS is moved along the Z axis from the UCS base.

The Settings tab in the UCS dialog box provides convenient access to the UCS icon display settings and to the UCSFOLLOW setting (see Figure 14.18). The UCS Icon settings area controls whether the UCS Icon is displayed in the current viewport and whether it is displayed at the UCS origin location. Checking the Apply to all active viewports box works like the All option of the UCSICON command. When this box is checked, the current settings are applied to all active viewports.

The check box provided in the UCS settings area is labeled "Update view to Plan when UCS is changed." When this box is checked, changing the UCS automatically displays the plan view of the new active UCS. Enabling this has the same effect as using the PLAN command every time you change the current UCS. In some cases, enabling this setting can be helpful, but in many typical 3D applications it may be preferable to have a 3D viewing angle that is not parallel to the active UCS.

FIGURE 14.18 The Settings tab in the UCS dialog box manages settings for the UCS icon and controls the UCSFOLLOW option. Changing the current UCS when UCSFOLLOW is enabled automatically displays the plan view of the new UCS.

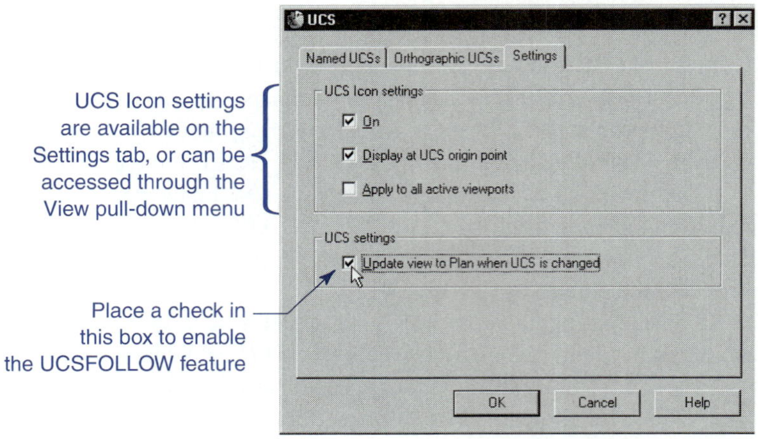

In typical 3D drawing projects, it is can be helpful to define and work with multiple Named UCS applications. When it is necessary to change the active UCS frequently, you may prefer working with the UCS II toolbar rather than the UCS dialog box. Figure 14.19 shows the UCS II toolbar with the Named UCS Control list open for selection of a Named UCS to restore. Picking an item from this list immediately restores the Named UCS settings in your drawing. The list displays all custom-defined UCSs as well as the preset orthographic UCS options, and it is an excellent solution when you need a fast and convenient means to restore Named UCSs frequently.

FIGURE 14.19 The Named UCS Control list on the UCS II toolbar provides fast and convenient access to Named UCSs.

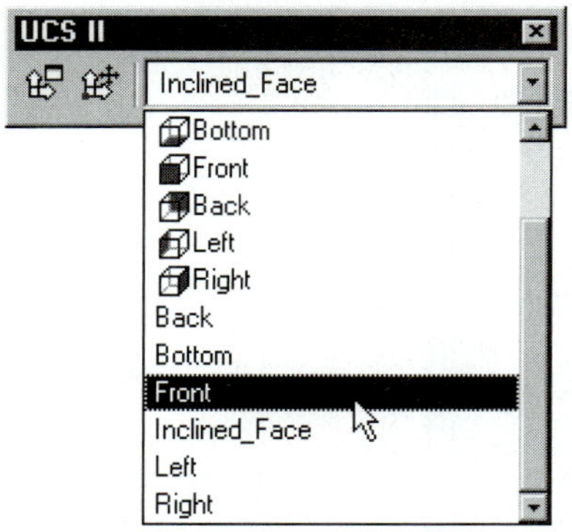

Field Notes

When using a preset UCS, all rotations are made with respect to the current UCS origin point (0,0,0). Use the UCS Origin option to move the origin point to a more appropriate location, if necessary.

Exercise 14.2

Estimated time required: 15 min.

1. Open EX4.1.dwg for editing.
2. Set the World Coordinate System to be current if it is not already. Use the PLAN command to display the plan view of the WCS.
3. Use the X option of the UCS command and rotate the UCS +90° around the X axis.
4. Save the current UCS as UCSFront.
5. Restore the WCS. From the Settings tab of the UCS dialog box, place a check mark in the box labeled *Update to Plan when UCS is changed*. This sets UCSFOLLOW to 1.
6. Access the UCS II toolbar, and restore the Named UCS *UCSFront*. The display should now show the plan view of this UCS.
7. Use the BHATCH command and apply a hatch pattern of your choice to this drawing view. When specifying the hatch area, use the Pick Points option and pick inside the part profile as required to hatch the entire profile.
8. Use the VPOINT command and set the viewpoint to **−1.1,−2.2,3.1**. Look at the hatching results. Does the hatch pattern appear to be a *planar* object?
9. Type UCSFOLLOW at the Command: prompt and change the setting to 0.
10. Save as EX14.2A.dwg and close the drawing.
11. Begin a new drawing.
12. Confirm that the UCS icon is currently on and set to display at the UCS origin. Disable the UCSFOLLOW feature by setting it to a value of 0.
13. Draw two lines, two arcs and two circles any size and location. Use the RECTANGLE command to draw a 4 × 2 rectangle placing the corners at 0,0 and 4,2.
14. Use the OBject option of the UCS command to create varied UCSs by picking different points on each of the objects. Use the Previous option of the UCS command to go back through several UCS settings.
15. Restore the WCS and display the Plan view.
16. Use the X option of the UCS command and rotate the UCS +90° around the X axis. Save the new UCS as *UCSFront* and use the PLAN command to display the plan view of the new UCS. Draw another rectangle with corners at 0,0 and 4,2 in the new UCS.
17. Move the UCS origin to the top left corner (endpoint) of the rectangle. Use the X option of the UCS command and rotate the UCS −90° around the X axis. Save the new UCS as *UCSTop,* and display the plan view of the new UCS. Draw another rectangle, again placing the corners at 0,0 and 4,2 in the current UCS.
18. Move the UCS origin to the top left corner (endpoint) of the rectangle. Use the X option of the UCS command and rotate the UCS −90° around the X axis. Save the new UCS as *UCSBack,* and display the plan view of the new UCS. Draw another rectangle, again placing the corners at 0,0 and 4,2 in the current UCS.
19. Move the UCS origin to the top left corner (endpoint) of the rectangle. Use the X option of the UCS command and rotate the UCS −90° around the X axis. Save the new UCS as *UCSBottom,* and display the plan view of the new UCS. Draw a fourth rectangle, again placing the corners at 0,0 and 4,2 in the current UCS.
20. Use the VPOINT command and set the viewpoint to **−1.1,−2.2,3.1.**
21. Access the UCS II toolbar, and observe the display of the UCS icon as you restore each of the Named UCSs using the Named UCS Control list.
22. Next, restore the four named UCSs one at a time and apply hatching to each rectangle using patterns of your choice.
23. Save as EX4.2B and close the drawing.

☑ LEARNING CHECKPOINT

- ☐ Where and what is the WCS?
- ☐ What is a UCS?
- ☐ How can using UCSs make 3D drafting tasks easier?
- ☐ Describe the use and value of named coordinate systems.
- ☐ In the preset UCS options, which coordinate system is displayed by selecting the preset Orthographic UCS named Top?

Setting Up 3D Viewing Angles

VPOINT
-VP

In the previous sections you used the VPOINT command to establish a 3D viewing angle to be able to better see the results of your 3D drawing efforts. When your view is parallel to the plane in which the objects you are viewing were created, you can only see two of the available three dimensions. The PLAN command allows you to set your viewing angle parallel to any available UCS, but allows no real flexibility for viewing from different angles. 3D viewing angles are easiest to create using the VPOINT command. The VPOINT command cannot be used in paper space.

To access the VPOINT command, type **-VP** or **VPOINT** at the Command: prompt. When this command is activated while the WCS is current, the following prompt sequence is displayed:

Command: **-VP** or **VPOINT**↵
Current view direction: VIEWDIR=0.0000,0.0000,1.0000
Specify a view point or [Rotate] <display compass and tripod>:

This prompt awaits a direction vector. A ***vector*** is a line describing distance and direction. The vector is described as a line from the 3D coordinate point that you enter to the 0,0,0 point of the UCS. To better visualize this concept, imagine looking at the drawing through a camera. The camera is positioned at the coordinate location you specify and pointed directly at 0,0,0. Figure 14.20 illustrates this concept using the settings specified in the following sequence:

Command: **-VP** or **VPOINT**↵
Current view direction: VIEWDIR=0.0000,0.0000,1.0000
Specify a view point or [Rotate] <display compass and tripod>: **-1.5,-1.5,3.47**↵
Regenerating model.
Command:

The viewpoint is always set in reference to the WCS. Any time you specify a vector to describe the viewpoint, the coordinates and origin point always reference the WCS. If the WCS is not current, the prompt sequence tells you that it is switching to the WCS to apply the specified setting. After adjusting the viewpoint, the UCS is then restored, as shown in the following example:

Command: **-VP** or **VPOINT**↵
*** Switching to the WCS ***
Current view direction: VIEWDIR=-1.5000,-1.5000,3.4700
Specify a view point or [Rotate] <display compass and tripod>: **2,2,5**↵
*** Returning to the UCS ***
Regenerating model.

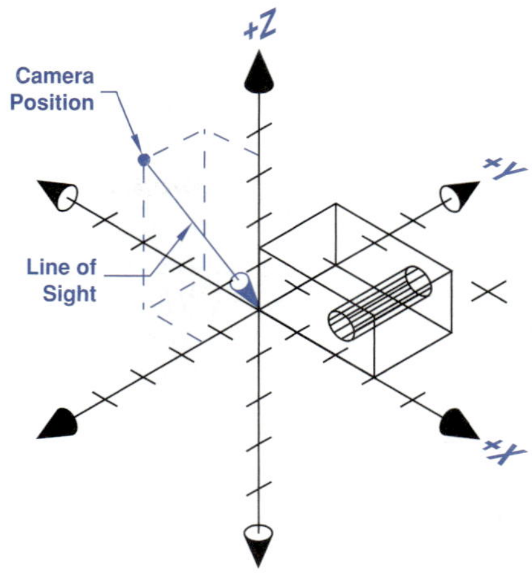

FIGURE 14.20 The vector determines the distance and direction of the viewing plane from the WCS origin.

Field Notes

- When the vector point is specified, running object snap modes can affect the point you specify. Although the difference in the current X,Y plane may be small, the difference in elevation can be significant.
- Once you have a clear understanding of 3D views, you may wish to specify your viewpoints with respect to the current UCS instead of the WCS. To make this possible, you need to set the WORLDVIEW system variable to 0. When WORLDVIEW is set to 0, the WCS is not made current during the VPOINT and DVIEW commands. DVIEW is discussed later in this chapter. To change the value of WORLDVIEW, just like any other system variable, type it at the Command: prompt:

  Command: **WORLDVIEW**↵
  Enter new value for WORLDVIEW <1>: **0**↵

Important: The examples in this chapter all use the WORLDVIEW default value of 1.

This method works very well once you have a solid understanding of 3D coordinate systems and can visualize 3D viewpoints accurately. Another method that can be used is the Compass and Axis Tripod, accessed by picking VPOINT from the 3D Views cascade on the View pull-down menu, or by pressing Enter at the "Specify a view point or [Rotate] <display compass and tripod>:" prompt:

Command: **-VP** or **VPOINT**↵
Current view direction: VIEWDIR=2.0000,2.0000,5.0000
Specify a view point or [Rotate] <display compass and tripod>: ↵
<specify the new 3D viewpoint>
Regenerating model.

The Axis Tripod is a visual display of the current orientation of the X, Y, and Z axes. Use this, combined with the Compass, to define a 3D viewing angle. See Figure 14.21. This provides additional visual clues to the resulting 3D viewpoint. As you move your cursor, you will see a small set of crosshairs moving within the compass circles. The resulting viewpoint is further demonstrated by the position of the Axis Tripod.

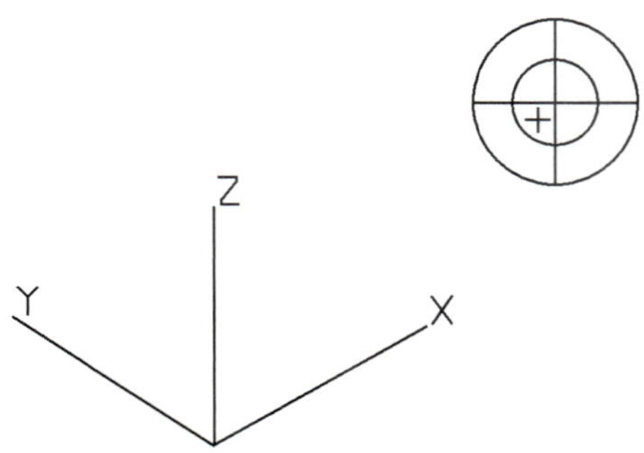

FIGURE 14.21 The Compass and Axis Tripod can be used to help visualize the desired viewing angle.

The compass represents a globe, flattened out so that you can see all of it. The center point is the North Pole, the inner circle is the Equator, and the outer circle is the South Pole. Pointing directly at the North Pole represents the Top view in the WCS. Keep this in mind as you adjust the viewpoint.

The compass is very sensitive to cursor movements. You can point more accurately by turning Snap on while adjusting the viewpoint. Do this by pressing the F9 key, Ctrl+B, or by picking the SNAP button on the status bar.

Although the Axis Tripod shows the relative positions of the X, Y, and Z axes, it is still a two-dimensional display and may not be completely clear. For example, with Snap on, move the cursor to the North Pole and then downward and to the left a couple of clicks. The Z axis appears shorter than the rest to imply that it is now pointing either toward you or away from you. Without the compass display, it would be impossible to tell which way it is actually pointing. Since you know that it is pointing directly at you when the cursor was on the North Pole, it can be determined that it is still pointing toward you, but not directly toward you. Continue to move the cursor downward and to the left, at approximately 225° from the North Pole. When you reach the equator, the Z axis is at its full length. As you continue movement beyond the Equator, the Z axis again becomes shorter. Now it is pointing away from you. By using both of these visual aids, it is easier to determine the results of the display change you are describing.

Because the Z axis is inclined toward you while it is within the inner circle, this indicates that the viewpoint you are describing is looking from above the X,Y plane of the WCS. When the cursor is between the Equator and the South Pole, the viewing angle you are describing is looking from below the X,Y plane.

Using the Rotate Option

An alternate method of adjusting the 3D viewing angle using VPOINT is the Rotate option. This allows you to specify a relative rotation both *in* the X,Y plane and *from* the X,Y plane of the WCS. To fully understand this option, it is helpful to know that the angle specifications are the same as they are for spherical coordinate specifications. Figure 14.22 shows the results from the following example:

Command: **VP** or **VPOINT**↵
Current view direction: VIEWDIR=0.0000,0.0000,1.0000
Specify a view point or [Rotate] <display compass and tripod>: **R**↵
Enter angle in XY plane from X axis <270>: **225**↵
Enter angle from XY plane <90>: **45**↵
Regenerating model.

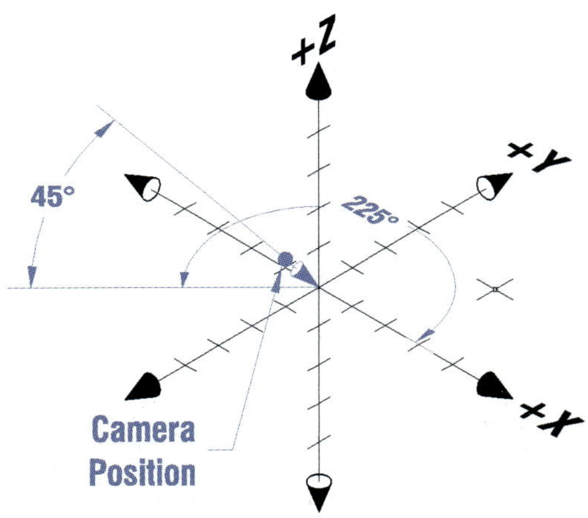

FIGURE 14.22 The Rotate option allows specification of the viewing angle in terms of the rotation angle both in and from the X,Y plane. The angles used are the same as those used when specifying spherical coordinates.

Exercise 14.3 — **Estimated time required: 5 min.**

1. Open EX14.2B.
2. Using the VPOINT vector option, set the current viewpoint to **−1,−1,1**. Use ZOOM PREVIOUS to return to the previous view and the U command to undo the ZOOM PREVIOUS. Using these two commands, switch back and forth to compare the views.
3. Use the Axis Tripod and Compass to change the viewpoint again.
4. Use the Rotate option, set the viewpoint rotation angle to be 225° in the X,Y plane and 45° from the X,Y plane.
5. Save as EX14.3 and close the drawing.

Field Notes

When working with 3D viewpoints, you can work more effectively by saving viewpoints that you need to work with again. Named views, as discussed in Chapter 4, can also be used to save 3D viewpoints. Always use names that are clearly recognizable to avoid confusion in later drawing sessions.

3D Viewpoint Presets

Similar to the UCS presets, AutoCAD LT also provides 3D viewpoint presets. These are predefined views that are commonly used and are already defined to allow you to switch immediately to the desired view. To see the available 3D viewpoint options, look at the 3D Views cascade on the View pull-down menu or use the View toolbar.

The top, bottom, left, right, front, and back views are the same as the UCS options when specified as absolute to the UCS. The isometric options provide 3D vantage points that are not parallel to any of the cube faces. Although it is often easier to work with your view parallel to the current UCS, the isometric options can sometimes provide a better perspective for viewing the results of your efforts. Table 14.1 shows the available isometric view toolbar buttons and their corresponding VPOINT vector and rotation.

When using the preset viewpoints, the vector entries are specified with an asterisk preceding them. This indicates that the coordinate entries are in the WCS. However, this is unnecessary, because the VPOINT command automatically switches to the WCS before applying the viewpoint change. After the viewpoint change is made, if a UCS was active when the command was used, it is then restored.

TABLE 14.1 Isometric view toolbar buttons

Toolbar Button	View Name	Vector	Rotation *IN* X,Y Plane	Rotation *FROM* X,Y Plane
	SW Isometric	−1,−1,1	225°0′	35°16′
	SE Isometric	1,−1,1	315°0′	35°16′
	NE Isometric	1,1,1	45°0′	35°16′
	NW Isometric	−1,1,1	135°0′	35°16′

Field Notes

- The term *isometric* is used to describe two different drafting techniques. One is an isometric projection, and the other is an isometric drawing. The preset isometric views in AutoCAD correspond to an isometric projection.

  Isometric projection: This method is seldom used for 2D drafting in industry because it represents the *true appearance* of the model as though it were tilted 35°16′ toward you, and thus requires the drafter to scale each line correctly.

  Isometric drawing: This method is commonly used for 2D drafting in industry because the isometric lines are drawn actual length and require no scaling.

- When using the VPOINT command options or presets, the extents of the drawing are displayed when the viewpoint is changed. Depending on the desired view, you may need to zoom in or out. To still see the drawing as large as possible, without touching the edges of your display area, use a ZOOM scale option such as 0.9X.

Exercise 14.4 **Estimated time required: 5 min.**

1. Begin a new drawing.
2. Set the UCS Icon to ON and ORigin.
3. Draw a 2-unit square using the RECTANG command. The lower left corner should be at 0,0,0.
4. Use each of the 3D Viewpoint Presets to look at the drawing from each available preset.
5. Set the SW Isometric viewpoint to be current and set the UCS to the current view.
6. Draw a horizontal line from 0,0 to 2,0.
7. Create an angular dimension that shows the 30° angle of projection.
8. Rotate the UCS 90° around the Y axis and use the PLAN command to view the new UCS.
9. Draw a horizontal line from 0,0 to 2,0.
10. Set angular dimension units to Degrees/Minutes/Seconds, and Precision to 1 place. Create an angular dimension that shows the 35°16′ incline.
11. Save as EX14.4, and close the drawing.

Giving Objects Thickness

In a 2D environment, objects have two dimensions, height and width. The third dimension is thickness, or depth. AutoCAD LT 2000 allows you to simulate 3D objects by giving 2D objects a thickness property. In a true 3D system, an object is solid and has properties such as mass. Some 3D systems allow the creation of surface models. A ***surface model*** is a visual representation of a 3D object created by describing the surfaces only. Such objects do not have the same properties as solid objects. 3D objects in AutoCAD LT simulate 3D surface models. There are no true 3D surface objects in AutoCAD LT, but an object with thickness can present the appearance of a 3D surface model. With a bit of creativity and imagination, fairly complex 3D drawings can be created with the available tools.

Format
Thickness
THICKNESS
TH

There are two ways to give objects thickness in AutoCAD LT. The first is to set the current object thickness using the THICKNESS command. This is just like setting the current object linetype or color—all objects drawn will use the specified value, if applicable. The THICKNESS command is accessed by typing **TH** or **THICKNESS** at the Command: prompt. For example:

Command: **TH** or **THICKNESS**↵
Enter new value for THICKNESS <0.0000>: **1.25**↵

Figure 14.23 shows different object types drawn with the thickness at 1.25 as set previously. Notice that some objects do not observe the thickness setting. Objects that can be drawn with thickness include lines, arcs, circles, polylines, 2D solids, hatches, and points. Shapes created using polylines can also be drawn with thickness, including rectangles, spline-fit polylines, polygons, boundaries, and donuts. The viewpoint setting used in Figure 14.23 is the SW Isometric view.

Text objects are automatically drawn at zero thickness regardless of the current object thickness setting. The thickness property of text objects can be changed after they are drawn, in order to create 3D text. This can be done using any of the commands for changing object properties. Figure 14.24 shows a text object after changing the thickness with the following sequence:

Command: **CHPROP**↵
Select objects: 1 found
Select objects: ↵
Enter property to change [Color/LAyer/LType/ltScale/LWeight/Thickness/PLotstyle]: **T**↵
Specify new thickness <0.0000>: **.5**↵
Enter property to change [Color/LAyer/LType/ltScale/LWeight/Thickness/PLotstyle]: ↵

Some objects cannot be given a thickness at any time. These objects may reflect a nonzero thickness property but still do not appear thick. Others may show the thickness property edit box disabled in the Properties window.

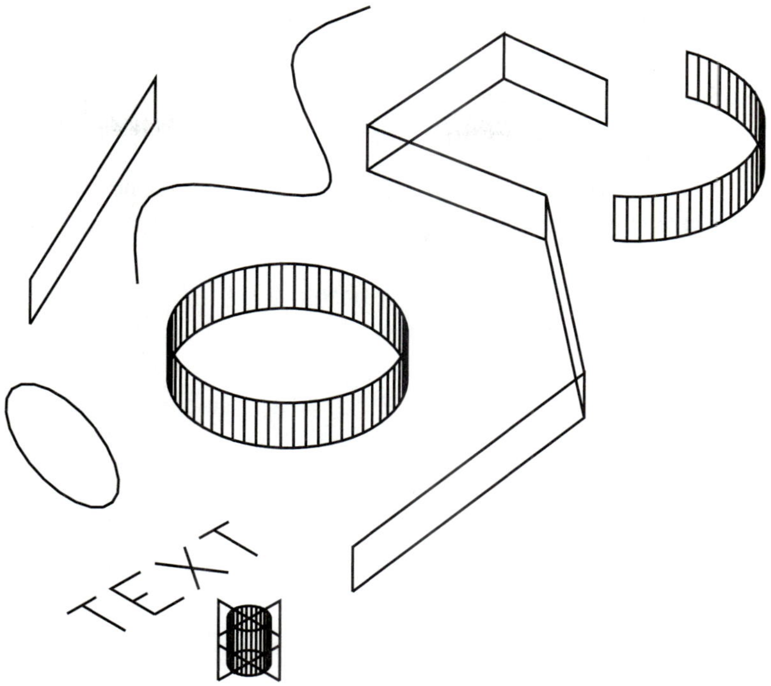

FIGURE 14.23 The current object thickness setting determines the thickness for newly drawn objects. Not all object types observe the thickness setting.

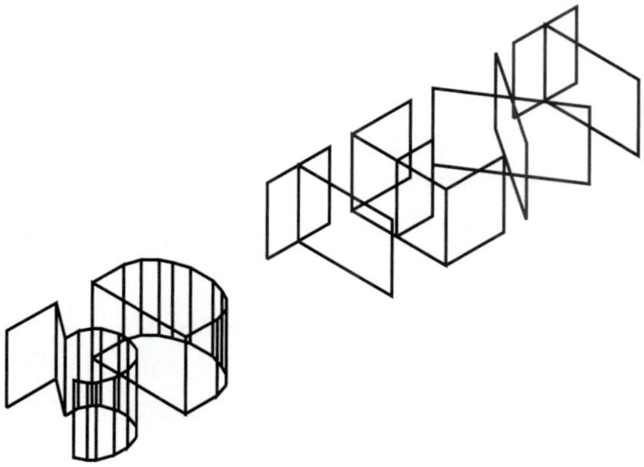

FIGURE 14.24 Text is drawn with a thickness of zero even when the current object thickness setting is nonzero. The thickness property can be changed to create 3-D text.

Field Notes

The current object thickness can be set to either a positive or negative value. When set to positive, the thickness extends in the positive Z axis direction. When set to negative, the thickness extends in the negative Z axis direction.

Exercise 14.5

Estimated time required: 10 min.

1. Begin a new drawing.
2. Set the current viewpoint to SW Isometric.
3. Set the current object thickness to 1.5.
4. Draw each of the object types shown in Figure 14.23.
5. Save the drawing as EX14.5.

Using Elevation

ELEV

The term ***elevation*** refers to the Z axis value of the current drawing plane. For example, if the elevation is zero, then you are drawing *on* the X,Y plane of the current UCS. If the elevation is 2, then you are drawing 2 units *above* the X,Y plane of the current UCS. Essentially, the elevation is simply the current Z axis value. The elevation can be positive or negative.

The current elevation is set using the ELEV command. This command can be accessed by typing **ELEV** at the Command: prompt. The following example sets the current elevation to 2.5:

Command: **ELEV**↵
Specify new default elevation <0.0000>: **2.5**↵
Specify new default thickness <1.2500>: ↵
Command:

When accessed using the ELEV command, an opportunity is presented to set the current thickness also. The result is the same as that produced using the THICKNESS command.

Setting the elevation is an alternative to moving objects on the Z axis or defining a new UCS origin. A very important note is that the elevation setting defines the current construction plane in reference to the current coordinate system. The elevation setting remains in effect even when you change to a different UCS, which can cause confusion. Such confusion can be avoided by leaving the elevation at zero and setting a new UCS origin when you need to draw at a new elevation.

Because the UCS is a more reliable and straightforward method of controlling your current construction plane, it is recommended that the UCS Origin option be used rather than the ELEV command.

Exercise 14.6

Estimated time required: 5 min.

1. Begin a new drawing.
2. Set the current viewpoint to SW Isometric.
3. Set the current object thickness to 0.15.
4. Draw a hexagon, with the center at 2,2 and a .25 radius.
5. Make two copies of the hexagon, one centered at 3,2 and the other at 4,2.
6. Zoom in a little closer to your work.
7. Set the elevation to 0.15, and the thickness to .75. Draw a circle at the center of the first hexagon, using the point coordinate 2,2 and a .15 radius.
8. Set the UCS Origin to 0,0,0.15. Draw a circle at the center of the second hexagon, using the point coordinate 3,2 and a .15 radius.
9. Set the elevation to 0. Draw a circle at the center of the third hexagon, using the point coordinate 4,2 and a .15 radius.
10. Save as EX14.6, and close the drawing.

☑ LEARNING CHECKPOINT

- ☐ What primary command is used to change the 3D viewing angle?
- ☐ By default, what coordinate system is used when changing 3D viewpoints?
- ☐ Describe the function of the Axis Tripod and Compass.
- ☐ How does the Rotate option work to change the 3D viewing angle?
- ☐ Describe each 3D viewpoint preset option.
- ☐ What is thickness?
- ☐ What is the effect of thickness on text objects?
- ☐ What object types does thickness affect?
- ☐ What are the disadvantages of using ELEV instead of UCS?

Simulating 3D Surfaces

In a true 3D CAD environment, AutoCAD 2000 for example, a 3D surface is a 2D solid object. This means that it has height and width but no thickness. A 3D surface can be located and oriented anywhere in 3D space. These objects are used to define the "skin" of a 3D object, also known as a surface model.

AutoCAD LT does not have a 3D surface object type. However, 2D objects that have been given a thickness property can be used to simulate 3-D surfaces. The term *simulate* means to look like, or give the appearance of.

When objects are drawn on screen, whether using 2D coordinates or 3D coordinates, they do not appear to be truly three-dimensional. This is because the objects are represented as a wire frame. A wire frame drawing does not appear to be 3D because you can see lines that would not normally be visible because they are on the back side of the object. For example, in Figure 14.25, two circles have been drawn with thickness to give the appearance of cylinders. However, although they are displayed as wire frame objects, all the lines used to define them are completely visible. This does not give a true 3D appearance. Additionally, it is difficult to be sure of the orientation of the cylinders—are they standing on end or lying flat?

FIGURE 14.25 Objects shown as wire frame do not give a clear 3D appearance.

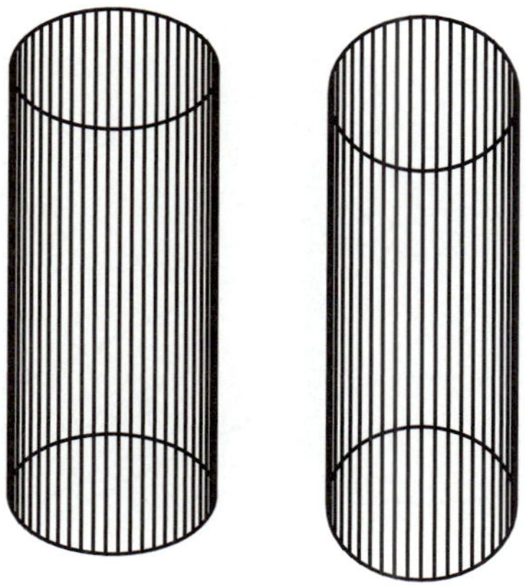

Removing Hidden Lines

View
Hide

HIDE
HI

In drafting, lines that would not be seen in the view being drawn are called *hidden lines*. Hidden lines are drawn in a different linetype to avoid confusion. To make a 3D drawing easier to understand, you can view it with the hidden lines removed from the view. The HIDE command is used to remove these hidden lines. After removing the hidden lines, you can continue to work or you can restore the previous appearance of your drawing by using the REGEN command. The HIDE command is accessed by picking Hide from the View pull-down menu or by typing **HI** or **HIDE** at the Command: prompt. Depending on how many 3D objects are in your drawing and the speed of your computer, this may take only a moment or it can take several minutes.

```
Command: HIDE↵
Regenerating model.
```

The HIDE operation affects only the current viewport. The current status of the hide operation is displayed on the status line as a percentage starting at 0% and dynamically reports the progress of the operation. If you feel the operation is going to take too long, you can cancel by pressing the Escape key.

Figure 14.26 shows the circles drawn previously, this time with the hidden lines removed. With the hidden lines removed, the circles appear to be a solid cylinder. The orientation of the cylinder in 3D space also becomes obvious.

Another point that becomes obvious only after hidden lines are removed is the relative position of objects in 3D space. In Figure 14.27A, the relative positioning of each of the objects is difficult to determine. The removal of the hidden lines in Figure 14.27B clears up any confusion.

The hidden image remains visible until the next regeneration occurs in that viewport. Notice that in Figure 14.27B the circles simulate surfaces not only on the thickness, but also on the ends—in the X,Y plane. The polyline object, however, only simulates a surface along its thickness. This is true also of lines, arcs, and

FIGURE 14.26 With the hidden lines removed, the true nature of the 3D objects becomes apparent.

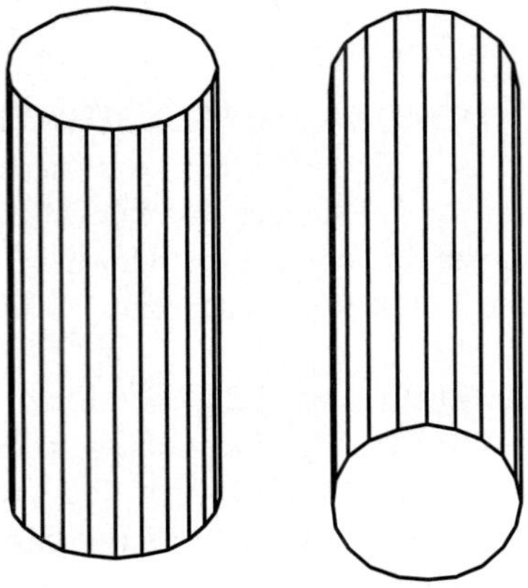

FIGURE 14.27 Removing hidden lines clarifies both the orientation and the relative positioning of objects in 3D space.

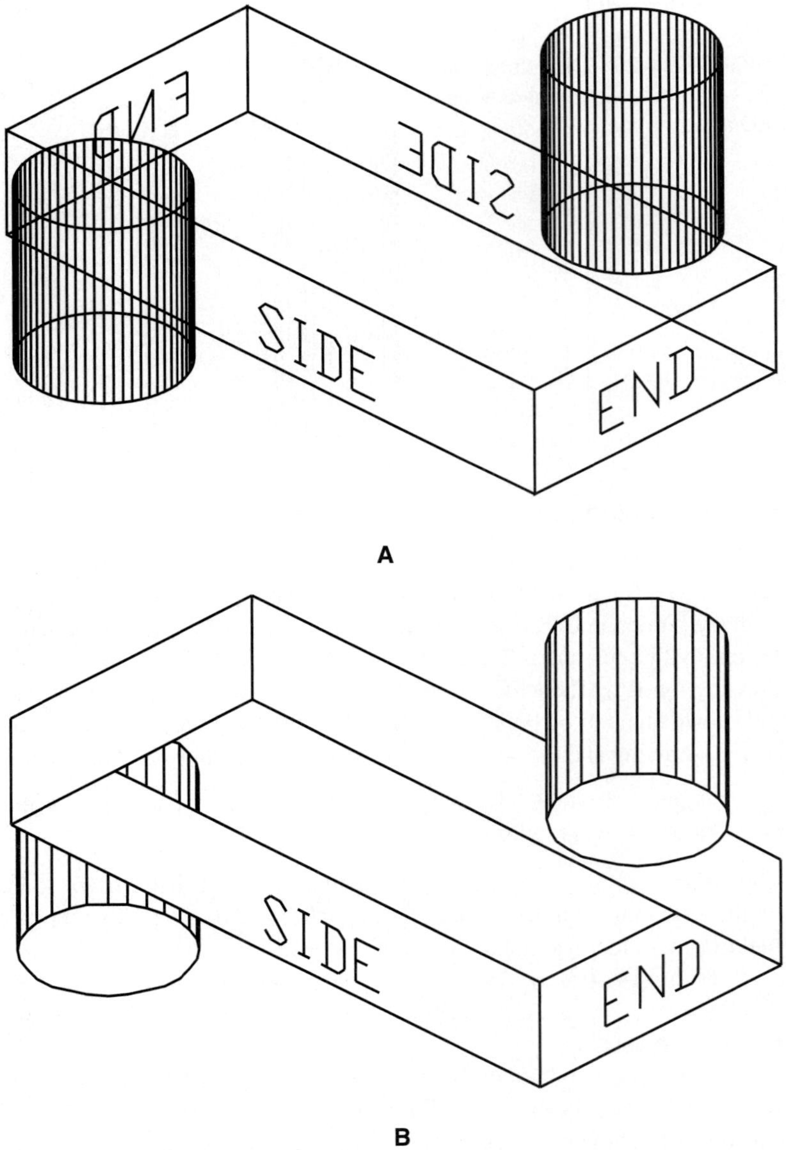

spline-fit polylines. Therefore, a complete box cannot be made by simply giving a rectangle a thickness value. This means that in order to create a convincing 3D image, you must exercise some creative imagination.

The following example creates a surfaced cube using line objects. First, the four sides are drawn, then the UCS is rotated and the top and bottom are added. The results are shown in Figure 14.28:

Command: **TH↵**
Enter new value for THICKNESS <0.0000>: **2↵**
Command: **L↵**
LINE Specify first point: **0,0↵**
Specify next point or [Undo]: **2,0↵**
Specify next point or [Undo]: **2,2↵**
Specify next point or [Close/Undo]: **0,2↵**
Specify next point or [Close/Undo]: **C↵**

Command: **UCS↵**
Current ucs name: *WORLD*
Enter an option [New/Move/orthoGraphic/Prev/Restore/Save/Del/?/World] <World>: **X↵**
Specify rotation angle about X axis <0>: **-90↵**
Command: **PLAN↵**
Enter an option [Current ucs/Ucs/World] <Current>: ↵
Regenerating model.

Command: **L↵**
LINE Specify first point: **0,0↵**
Specify next point or [Undo]: **2,0↵**
Specify next point or [Undo]: ↵
Command: ↵
LINE Specify first point: **0,-2↵**
Specify next point or [Undo]: **2,-2↵**
Specify next point or [Undo]: ↵
<set the current viewpoint to SW Isometric>
Command: **HIDE↵**
Regenerating model.

FIGURE 14.28 This cube appears to be a complete surface model. Each face is covered by a line object with a thickness property.

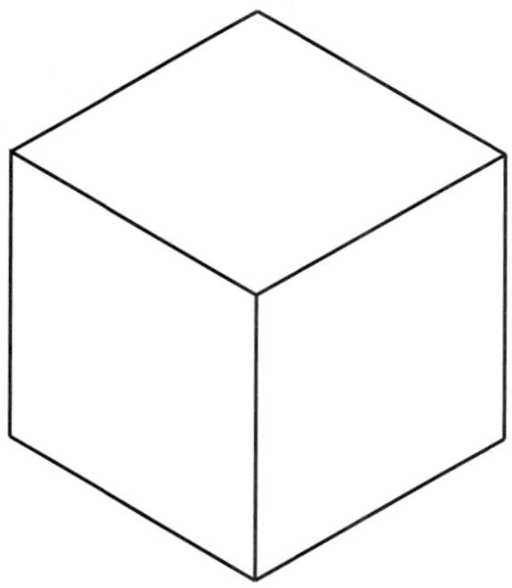

Very complex models can be created using a combination of thick objects created in varied coordinate systems. In the model shown in Figure 14.29, lines were created using varied coordinate systems and thickness values. Next, the direct hatch option was used because the thickness of an object is not hatchable by selecting the area or the object. Prior to creating each hatch pattern, the UCS was set to match the plane of the objects being hatched.

FIGURE 14.29 Creativity and imagination can be valuable when constructing a 3D model. Even with AutoCAD LT's limited 3D tool set, complex 3D floor plans and other 3D models can be simulated.

Field Notes

Although AutoCAD cannot create true 3-D surfaces, one of its object types can be used in a similar manner. When viewed from a 3-D angle, the SOLID object type does not appear filled in, but when the HIDE command is used, any lines behind the solid are not visible.

Adding Color to Surfaces

View Shade
SHADE SHA SH

The term ***rendering*** is used to describe the process of applying colors to the surfaces in a drawing. The simplest form of rendering is called ***shading.*** This applies simple colors to all of the surfaces, without allowing for lighting, shadows, or reflections. See Figure 14.30.

AutoCAD LT shades all simulated surfaces, such as thick objects and solids. Shading can be applied to any object that responds to the HIDE command. The SHADE command is accessed by typing **SH** or **SHADE** at the Command: prompt, or by picking an option from the Shade cascade on the View pull-down menu:

```
Command: SH or SHADE↵
Regenerating model.
```

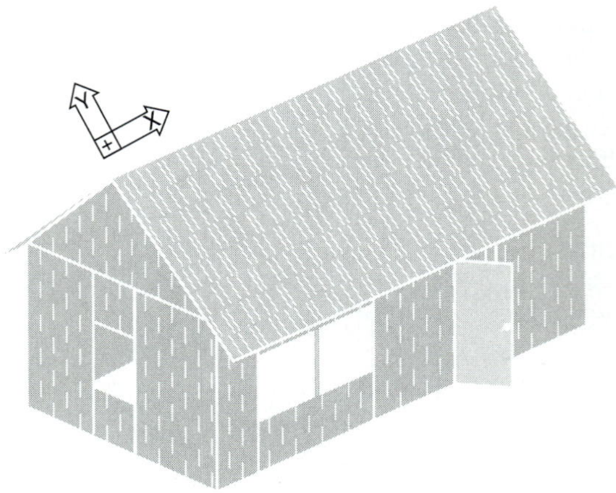

FIGURE 14.30 A shaded drawing applies simple colors to the surfaces in the drawing.

Similar to the HIDE command, there are no prompts to answer. The shaded image remains until a regeneration occurs in that viewport. Shaded objects cannot be selected for editing, so you need to regenerate the viewport to continue working. Shaded images can only be displayed on screen; they cannot be plotted.

The SHADE command uses the current settings for two system variables, SHADEDGE and SHADEDIF, to determine the final appearance of the shaded image. The SHADEDGE variable controls the shading of edges and can be adjusted by typing **SHADEDGE** at the Command: prompt. The four SHADEDGE settings are available automatically from the Shade cascade on the View pull-down menu. These four options, a brief explanation, and the SHADEDGE value used are shown in Table 14.2. A sample shaded image, using each of these settings, is shown in Figure 14.31. Looking at these images, you can see that the 256-

TABLE 14.2 The SHADEDGE options

Option	Description	SHADEDGE setting
256 Color	Shades faces using a 256-color palette; does not show face edges.	0
256 Color Edge Highlight	Shades faces using a 256-color palette; highlights edges using background color.	1
16 Color Hidden Line	Shades the edges, not the faces. Looks similar to results obtained when using the HIDE command.	2
16 Color Filled	Fills faces using object color; highlights edges using background color.	3

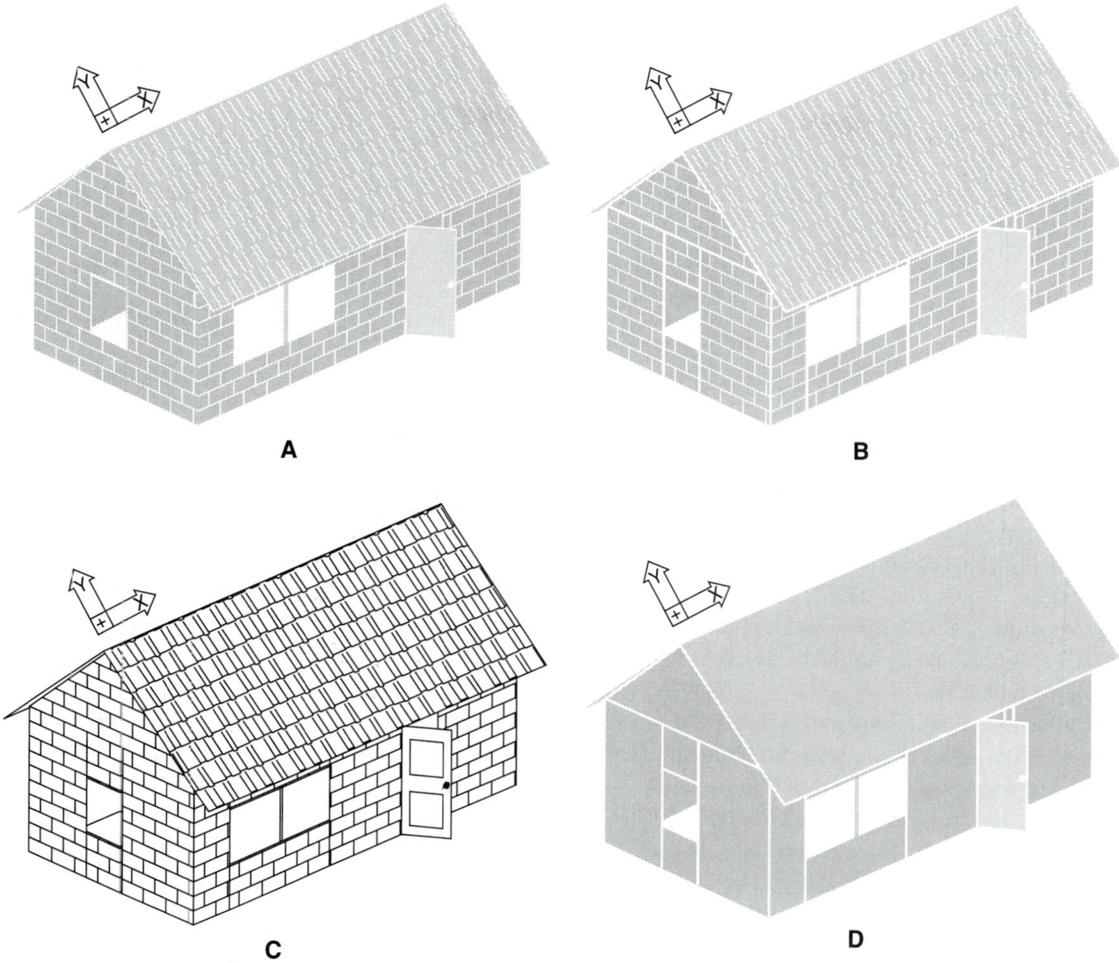

FIGURE 14.31 (A) SHADEDGE=0, (B) SHADEDGE=1, (C) SHADEDGE=2, and (D) SHADEDGE=3.

color shade with highlighted edges, where SHADEDGE=1, shows the most accurate representation of the model being shaded. This model relies on the display of edges as well as faces to show the most detail. To achieve more refined results, you can adjust the value of the SHADEDIF variable.

SHADEDIF controls the way AutoCAD LT uses lighting in the shaded image. Two different types of lighting are used, ambient and diffuse reflective. *Ambient light* refers to the surrounding light, which produces a uniform light reflection level. *Diffuse reflective light* produces varied reflection levels. The light source is always considered to be a single source from directly behind your eye. SHADEDIF controls the percentage of light used in the shading process that is considered to be diffuse reflective, and can be set between 0% and 100%. The default is 70%, which means that the other 30% is ambient light. Figure 14.30 used the default value for SHADEDIF. In Figure 14.32, the SHADEDIF value has been set to 85% so the edges show up better.

Field Notes

- In order for SHADEDIF to have an effect, the SHADEDGE value must be set to 0 or 1.
- Hatch lines in an image are considered to be edges, and will only be visible when viewed from a suitable viewing angle with an appropriate SHADEDIF value.

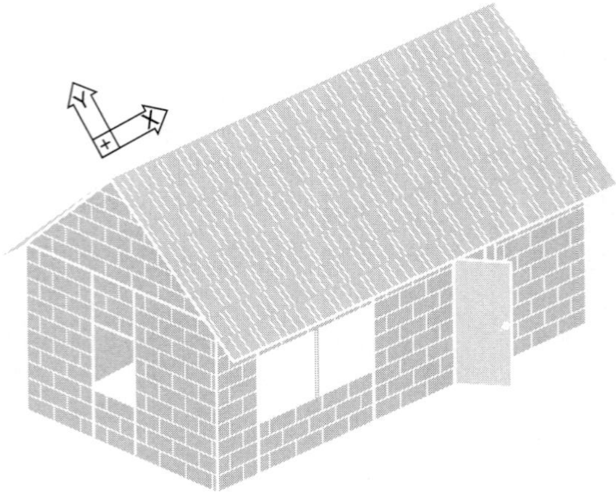

FIGURE 14.32 The SHADEDIF value and the viewing angle affect the appearance of edges in a shaded image.

Editing AutoCAD 2000 Shaded Drawings Using AutoCAD LT 2000

Display options for the full AutoCAD 2000 software incorporate powerful visualization tools such as full-time shading or hidden line removal. The shading can be displayed in flat colors, similar to the shading method used by AutoCAD LT, or it can be set to present a more realistic appearance that even applies lighting variations. In AutoCAD 2000, objects can be selected and edited whether shading is on or off. With AutoCAD LT 2000, however, a shaded drawing must be regenerated to remove the shading before objects can be selected or edited.

The AutoCAD 2000 and AutoCAD LT 2000 programs are able to use drawings created in either software version. In a company where both AutoCAD and AutoCAD LT are used, drawings may sometimes be created in one version and edited in the other. When using AutoCAD LT to edit a drawing created in AutoCAD, you may need to work in a drawing that was saved with full-time shading enabled. In this situation, the shading settings are still active when you open the drawing in AutoCAD LT. These drawings are displayed accurately in AutoCAD LT and can be edited just like any other drawing. Additionally, new objects added to the drawing in LT are also displayed using the AutoCAD 2000 shading options.

The SHADEMODE command is used to control shading options in both AutoCAD and AutoCAD LT. The SHADEMODE command available in AutoCAD LT presents two options listed as "2D wireframe" and "Hidden." The 2D wireframe option is used to disable specialized display options and display 3D drawing objects using a simple wire frame representation. The following sequence is used to turn off the shading in an AutoCAD drawing opened in AutoCAD LT:

Command: **SHADEMODE**
Current mode: Gouraud
Enter option [2D wireframe/Hidden] <2D wireframe>: ↵
Command:

AutoCAD LT can turn the shading off but cannot turn it back on. The AutoCAD 2000–based shading features can be turned back on using only the AutoCAD 2000 software.

The Hidden option of the SHADEMODE command enables full-time hidden line removal, which does work in AutoCAD LT 2000. Unlike the HIDE command, the SHADEMODE effect is continuous and allows you to create, select, and edit drawing objects with no restrictions. The following sequence enables full-time hidden line removal:

Command: **SHADEMODE↵**
Current mode: 2D wireframe
Enter option [2D wireframe/Hidden] <2D wireframe>: **H↵**
Command:

When any of the advanced display options are enabled, including the hidden line removal feature, the UCS icon is displayed in a 3D format. Figure 14.33 shows a 3D box in a drawing where hidden line removal is enabled. The UCS icon is displayed at the current UCS origin located at one corner of the box.

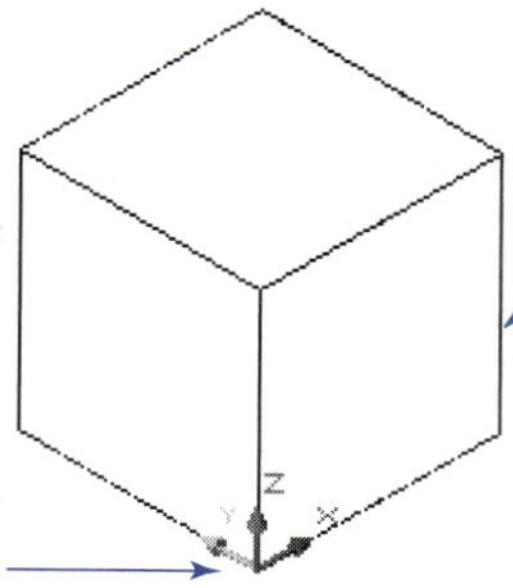

FIGURE 14.33 The UCS icon is presented in a 3D representation when SHADEMODE display features are enabled.

Exercise 14.7 **Estimated time required: 5 min.**

1. Start a new drawing from scratch.
2. Create a simulated solid cube, as shown in Figure 14.28.
3. Set up a SE Isometric viewpoint.
4. Shade the image using each of the available shading options, by adjusting the value of SHADEDIF and SHADEDGE.
5. Save as EX14.7, and close the drawing.

LEARNING CHECKPOINT

- ☐ What part of a 2D object can be used like a surface?
- ☐ Describe the effects of SHADEDGE and SHADEDIF.

Dynamic 3D Viewing Options

View
3D Dynamic View
DVIEW
DV

With standard 3D viewpoint options, it may be necessary to try several various settings until you find one that suits your needs. AutoCAD LT offers a way to change the view dynamically. This means that you can see the results as you change the settings, similar to the real time pan and zoom features. The DVIEW command, short for Dynamic VIEW, is accessed by typing DV or DVIEW at the Command: prompt, or by picking 3D Dynamic View from the View pull-down menu.

The DVIEW command offers a number of options. You can define a viewing angle as with other 3D viewing options, termed a ***parallel projection.*** You can also create perspective views. In drafting, a ***perspective view*** is defined as the most realistic form of pictorial illustration. It presents objects as though they were being viewed in the real world, with closer objects being larger and distant objects being smaller.

There are two primary ways to use the DVIEW command. When this command is started, a Select objects: prompt is displayed. Because the DVIEW command is dynamic, it needs a way to display the results of the view changes as you make them. You can select objects in your drawing for AutoCAD LT to use for this purpose. A word of caution: Selecting too many objects can cause the dynamic display to be very slow. Also, too many selected objects can make the resulting display difficult to interpret. It is best to select as few objects as possible, as long as the selected objects present a clear representation of the current view. Alternatively, pressing Enter without selecting any objects displays a simple wire frame model of a house to represent the current view results. Figure 14.34 shows this image.

Field Notes

The wire frame house used by the DVIEW command is actually a block named DVIEWBLOCK. You can create your own customized DVIEWBLOCK. Create the geometry you want to use, then use the BLOCK command and specify the block name as DVIEWBLOCK. When asked if you want to redefine it, pick Yes. The geometry you create should fit within a 1 × 1 × 1 cube.

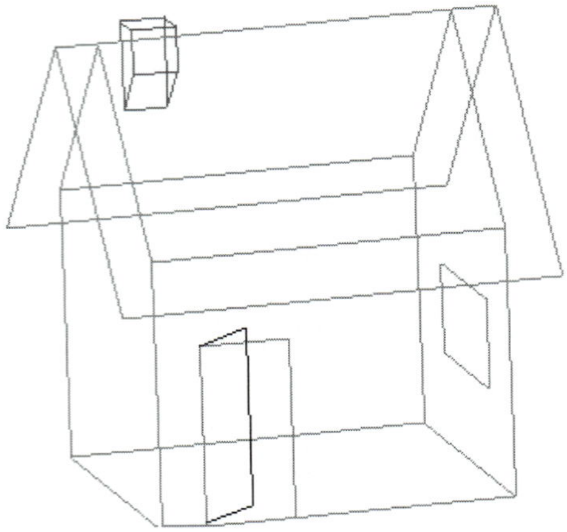

FIGURE 14.34 The default image used by DVIEW is a simple wire frame house. This is used when you press Enter instead of selecting objects in your drawing.

After specifying what the DVIEW command is to display at the Select objects: prompt, you are returned to the WCS to begin making your adjustments. Both parallel projections and perspective views require that you set up an appropriate viewing angle. The following describes the options that are used to define your viewing angle.

At the DVIEW option line prompt, you can select an option or simply pick a point on screen. The point you select becomes the base point for a dragging operation. As you move your cursor, the view onscreen updates continuously. The first point you pick becomes the base point for the drag line. Use the status line display as a reference for your next pick. The items listed Dir: and Mag:, for Direction and Magnitude, represent the direction of rotation (Dir:) and how far (Mag:) to rotate the viewing angle. For example, dragging your cursor upward, you can see that the apparent position of the model is rotated the same direction. If you continue to drag until the Mag: value is 180 and pick, the view is now from the back of the model and it appears to be upside-down.

The Dir: value can be confusing at first, because the camera is actually rotated in the opposite direction. For example, if you are looking at the front of a house and you specify Dir:270 and Mag:90, the resulting view is from the top instead of the bottom as you might expect.

Another means of entering the Dir: and Mag: values is by simply typing them in, separated by a comma. This is shown in the following example:

Command: **DV** or **DVIEW**↵
Select objects or <use DVIEWBLOCK>: ↵
*** Switching to the WCS ***
Enter option [CAmera/TArget/Distance/POints/PAn/Zoom/TWist/CLip/Hide/Off/Undo]: *<pick a point>*
Enter direction and magnitude angles: **270,90**↵
Enter option [CAmera/TArget/Distance/POints/PAn/Zoom/TWist/CLip/Hide/Off/Undo]: ↵
*** Returning to the UCS ***
Regenerating model.

Field Notes

The AutoCAD LT on-line Help states that when using the Dir: and Mag: values, you are *rolling the view under the camera.* It is important to understand that the objects in a drawing are not reoriented; rather, the camera position is changed. Therefore, rolling the view 90° downward is actually accomplished by rotating the camera 90° upward.

Using the CAmera Option

This adjusts the position of the camera by rotation around the target point. The ***target point*** defines an anchor point in the drawing and is set using the Target option. The CAmera option does not alter the distance from the target point. When CAmera is selected, the following prompt is displayed:

> Command: **DV** or **DVIEW**↵
> Select objects or <use DVIEWBLOCK>: ↵
> Enter option [CAmera/TArget/Distance/POints/PAn/Zoom/TWist/CLip/Hide/Off/Undo]: **CA**↵
> Specify camera location, or enter angle from XY plane, or [Toggle (angle in)] <90.0000>: **45**↵
> Specify camera location, or enter angle in XY plane from X axis, or [Toggle (angle from)] <90.00000>: **45**↵
> Enter option [CAmera/TArget/Distance/POints/PAn/Zoom/TWist/CLip/Hide/Off/Undo]: ↵
> Regenerating model.

The option line for the DVIEW command is repeated until the EXIT option is used or the command is canceled. The Toggle angle option allows you to switch between the two angle input modes. Similar to entering spherical coordinates, you are specifying angles either *in* or *from* the X,Y plane. Typing **T,** for Toggle, at the prompt toggles you between these two input modes.

When entering the angle, you can either move the cursor and pick, or you can type an angle value. If you pick a point at the first prompt, AutoCAD LT accepts the input and rotates the camera in the appropriate plane. The Toggle option allows you to switch between entering angles *in* the X,Y plane and *from* the X,Y plane. If an angle is typed at the first prompt, you are then prompted for the other angle.

All adjustments in the DVIEW command are made with respect to the WCS. If the WCS is not active when you use DVIEW, it will be made current while your view adjustments are made:

> Command: **DV** or **DVIEW**↵
> Select objects or <use DVIEWBLOCK>: ↵
> *** Switching to the WCS ***
> Enter option [CAmera/TArget/Distance/POints/PAn/Zoom/TWist/CLip/Hide/Off/Undo]: **CA**↵
> Specify camera location, or enter angle from XY plane, or [Toggle (angle in)] <45.0000>: **T**↵
> Specify camera location, or enter angle in XY plane from X axis, or [Toggle (angle from)] <45.0000>: **T**↵
> Specify camera location, or enter angle from XY plane, or [Toggle (angle in)] <45.0000>: **45**↵
> Specify camera location, or enter angle in XY plane from X axis, or [Toggle (angle from)] <45.0000>: **60**↵
> Enter option [CAmera/TArget/Distance/POints/PAn/Zoom/TWist/CLip/Hide/Off/Undo]: ↵
> *** Returning to the UCS ***
> Regenerating model.

The previous UCS is restored when you exit the DVIEW command and the drawing is regenerated. Figure 14.35 illustrates the concept of rotating the camera around the target.

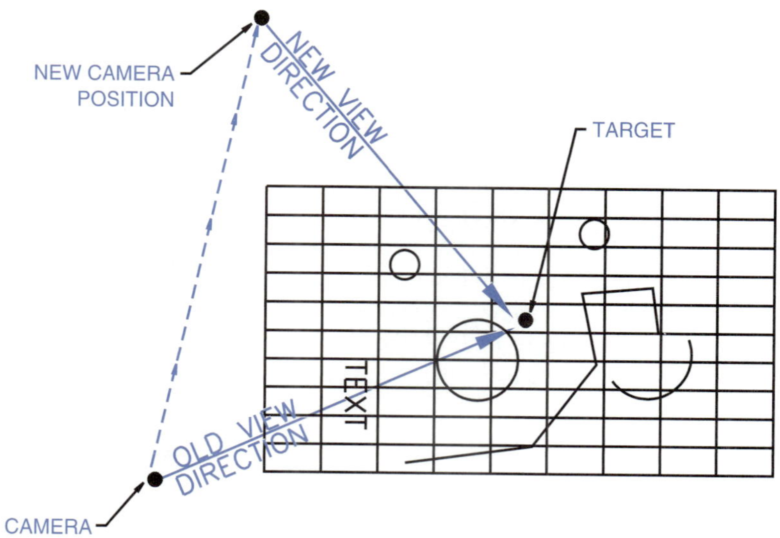

FIGURE 14.35 Adjusting the camera changes the direction from which you are looking; the target position remains the same.

Using the TArget Option

The TArget option allows you to change the rotation angle of the target point in reference to the camera position. The target indicates the point at which your camera is looking. This point is used as the base point for DVIEW options. The position of the target is adjusted by specifying the angles of rotation in and from the X,Y plane:

Command: **DV** or **DVIEW**↵
Select objects or <use DVIEWBLOCK>: ↵
*** Switching to the WCS ***
Enter option [CAmera/TArget/Distance/POints/PAn/Zoom/TWist/CLip/Hide/Off/Undo]: **TA**↵
Specify camera location, or enter angle from XY plane, or [Toggle (angle in)] <45.0000>: **30**↵
Specify camera location, or enter angle in XY plane from X axis, or [Toggle (angle from)] <45.00000>: **55**↵
Enter option [CAmera/TArget/Distance/POints/PAn/Zoom/TWist/CLip/Hide/Off/Undo]: ↵
*** Returning to the UCS ***
Regenerating model.

This option also allows you to pick the angle and toggle the input mode, as with the CAmera option. Figure 14.36 shows the effect of rotating the target point.

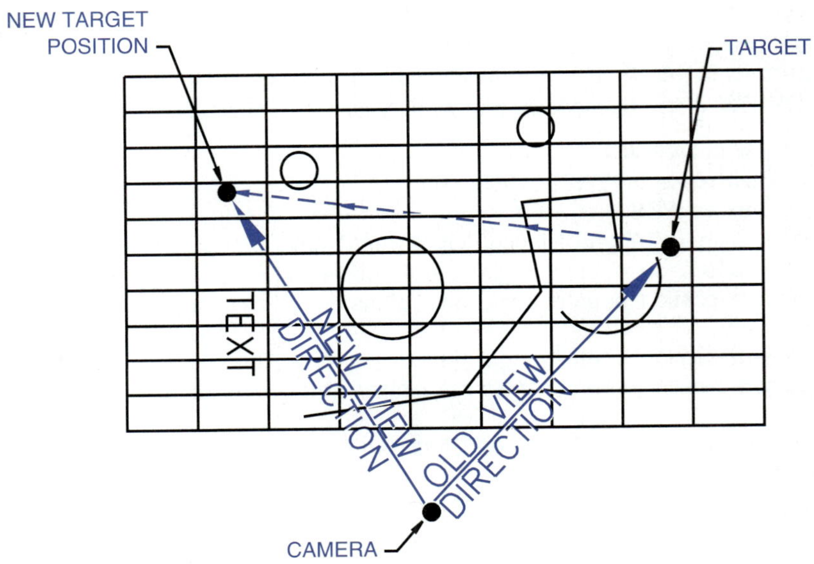

FIGURE 14.36 Adjusting the target changes the location at which the camera is looking. The camera position stays the same and the distance from camera to target does not change.

Using the Distance Option

This option turns perspective viewing mode on, and allows you to adjust the distance between the camera and the target along the line of sight. The term ***line of sight*** refers to an imaginary line of infinite length that passes through the camera location and the target point. When this option is used, AutoCAD LT displays a ***slider bar*** at the top of the graphics screen area. This feature is shown in Figure 14.37. Moving your cursor to the right or left will increase or decrease the distance between the camera and the target by the multiple shown.

Often, when you start the Distance option, only part of the drawing is visible. To correct this, increase the distance between camera and target. The numbers on the slider are used as multiplier values, so anything over 1 increases the distance and anything under 1 decreases the distance. Sometimes it is more convenient to simply type in a number. When typed, a number is taken as an absolute distance, not a multiplier.

When the current view is in perspective, AutoCAD LT replaces the UCS icon with a special perspective icon, shown in Figure 14.38. If the UCS icon is turned off, this icon is not visible. Figure 14.39 shows a perspective view defined using the Distance option.

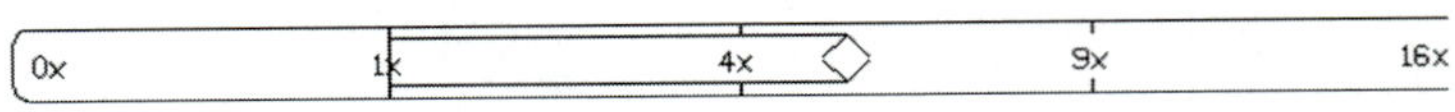

FIGURE 14.37 The slider bar allows you to change your distance dynamically.

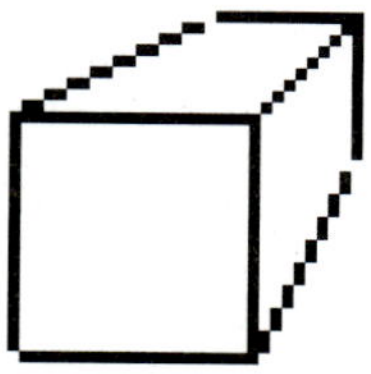

FIGURE 14.38 This icon indicates that your view is currently in a perspective view.

FIGURE 14.39 Perspective views look more realistic than parallel projections.

Field Notes

- Many standard AutoCAD LT options are disabled when perspective view is active. These include zooming, panning, and sketching. Additionally, picking points using your pointing device is not allowed in some cases.
- When in perspective view, you cannot ZOOM PREVIOUS. Using the DVIEW OFF option does not help, because a ZOOM PREVIOUS restores the dynamic view and, again, you cannot restore previous views. Be sure to save the current view as a named view prior to creating the perspective, so you can easily restore that view.
- When working with the DVIEW command, it is best to make adequate use of named views. Saving unique viewpoints allows you to restore them immediately without having to remember all of the settings for that view.

Using the POints Option

This option allows you to locate the camera and target points using absolute X,Y,Z coordinates. The current locations are displayed as default values and can be used as a reference point. You can specify the new point through any acceptable coordinate entry method. Polar and relative coordinates are in reference to the current location. The prompt sequence looks like this:

Command: **DV** or **DVIEW**↵
Select objects or <use DVIEWBLOCK>: ↵
*** Switching to the WCS ***
Enter option [CAmera/TArget/Distance/POints/PAn/Zoom/TWist/CLip/Hide/Off/Undo]: **PO**↵
Specify target point <5.7264, 4.5948, 4.0908>: **4,2,7**↵
Specify camera point <-4.7898, -10.4239, -6.4946>: **@4<30<15**↵
Enter option [CAmera/TArget/Distance/POints/PAn/Zoom/TWist/CLip/Hide/Off/Undo]: ↵
*** Returning to the UCS ***
Regenerating model.

Using the PAn Option

The PAn option moves the image without changing the magnification. This command actually moves the target and camera points, but maintains the same distance and angle between them. In a perspective view, the image will change as the angles of perspective change. The actual image does not change in a parallel projection view, it is simply relocated.

The movement is similar to a PAN command, requiring a base point and second point of displacement. This option is performed with respect to the current view. The following example shows the prompt sequence:

Command: **DV** or **DVIEW**↵
Select objects or <use DVIEWBLOCK>: ↵
*** Switching to the WCS ***
Enter option [CAmera/TArget/Distance/POints/PAn/Zoom/TWist/CLip/Hide/Off/Undo]: **P**↵
Ambiguous response, please clarify...
PAn or POints? **PA**↵
Specify displacement base point: *<pick first point>*
Specify second point: *<pick next point>*
Enter option [CAmera/TArget/Distance/POints/PAn/Zoom/TWist/CLip/Hide/Off/Undo]: ↵
*** Returning to the UCS ***
Regenerating model.

Several of the DVIEW options share the same first character with another option and therefore require that the first two characters be typed to access them. As with all option prompts in AutoCAD LT, the required entry is shown in uppercase characters.

Using the Zoom Option

When the current view is a parallel projection, this option works similar to the scale option of the ZOOM command. The value typed represents the scale factor to be applied to the current magnification. It can be entered as a simple number, or it can be followed by an **X.** Both methods produce the same results. The slider bar can also be used to specify the zoom scale factor. The slider bar is the same as the one shown in Figure 14.37.

If a perspective view is currently displayed, the Zoom option adjusts the lens length of the camera. This is similar to changing the length of a lens on a real camera; the distance between the camera and the object does not change but the field of view does. The default setting is 50mm, which displays the drawing as though it were being viewed using a 35mm camera and a 50mm lens. A longer lens, similar to a telephoto lens, displays the model larger but narrows the field of vision. Shorter lens lengths widen the field of vision, similar to a wide-angle lens on a real camera.

Through working with a combination of the Distance setting and the lens length using Zoom, you can display a drawing using varied lines of perspective. Be careful to avoid displaying extreme lines of perspective, as shown in Figure 14.40. To return to a more conventional perspective view, increase both the lens length and distance values.

Using the TWist Option

The TWist option rotates the view around the line of sight. This means that the axis of rotation is the line between the camera and the target point. The twist angle is absolute, relative to zero, and is not cumulative. Therefore, specifying a twist angle of 15° twice in a row leaves the twist at 15°, not 30°. The angle can be specified by dragging the cursor and picking, or by typing the angle directly at the prompt.

FIGURE 14.40 Too short a distance and lens length can produce extreme angles of perspective, resulting in a drawing that appears distorted.

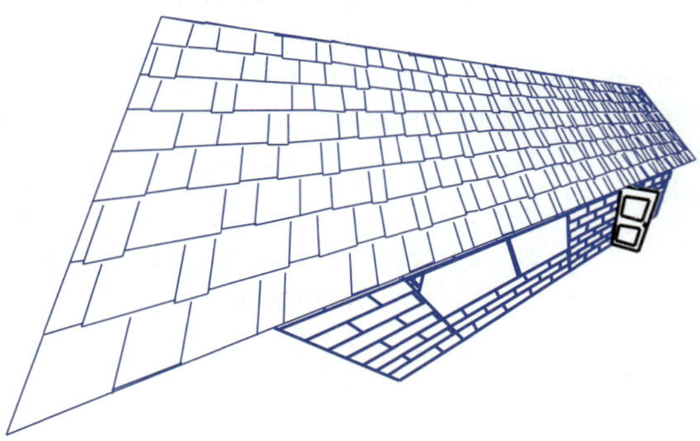

Using the CLip Option

To view only part of the model, clipping planes can be positioned in the drawing. A ***clipping plane*** is an imaginary plane that hides part of the drawing. There are two clipping planes, the front and the back. Objects and parts of objects that occur in front of the front clipping plane or behind the back clipping plane are not drawn. These options are used to create cutaway sections or simply to reduce drawing clutter. Clipping planes are parallel to the current view, and they move when the view is changed. Figure 14.41 shows an illustration of the function of clipping planes.

Selecting the CLip option presents the following option line:

Enter option [CAmera/TArget/Distance/POints/PAn/Zoom/TWist/CLip/Hide/Off/Undo]: **CL↵**
Enter clipping option [Back/Front/Off] <Off>:

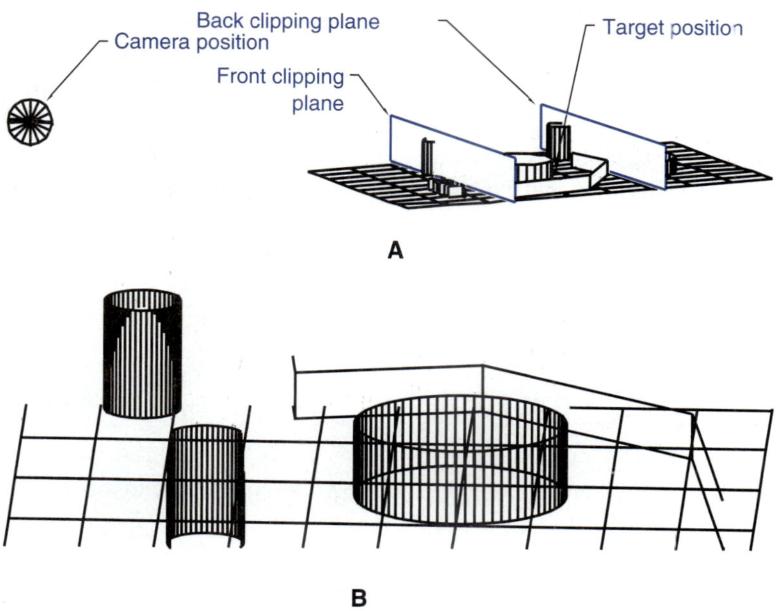

FIGURE 14.41 The front and back clipping planes control which objects in a view are drawn.

The default option, Off, turns both clipping planes off. The Back and Front options access additional options for the selected plane. The following options are the same for both the front and back clipping planes:

- **ON** Turns on clipping in the current clipping plane location.
- **OFF** Turns off the clipping for the specified plane.
- **Distance from target** Positions the clipping plane at the specified distance from the target point, along the line of sight.

The Front plane provides an additional option:

- **Eye** Sets the front clipping plane to its default location, at the camera point.

Using the Hide Option

This option works just like the HIDE command. Hidden lines are removed from the display to provide a clear and understandable image of the model. This option works whether you have selected objects with DVIEW or the DVIEWBLOCK is being used.

Using the Off Option

The Off option is used to turn perspective viewing off, which restores the model to a parallel projection. Perspective viewing is turned on when the Distance option is used.

Using the Undo Option

This is very valuable when working with DVIEW. You can undo one option at a time, all the way back to the beginning of this DVIEW command.

Exiting the DVIEW Command

The eXit option exits the DVIEW command and implements the view changes made within the DVIEW command. The entire drawing is regenerated according to the viewpoint and camera options specified.

Field Notes

- If you have made several adjustments to the view using DVIEW and do not wish to save them, you can press the Esc key at any time to cancel the effects of the DVIEW command.
- As discussed at the beginning of this chapter, you cannot create 3D surface objects in AutoCAD LT. However, you can import, duplicate, and edit 3D surfaces. The object type in AutoCAD 2000 for a 3D surface is called a 3DFACE. By opening or inserting a drawing containing 3DFACE objects, you have the opportunity to experiment with these object types in AutoCAD LT. Inserting and exploding the block named DVIEWBLOCK leaves its component objects in your drawing. Because this block definition uses 3DFACEs, it is now possible to duplicate and grip edit these objects for your own project.

Exercise 14.8 **Estimated time required: 5 min.**

1. Open EX14.7 for editing.
2. Use each of the DVIEW command options. Be sure to use the HIDE option frequently to clarify the results.
3. Produce a perspective view.
4. Save as EX14.8, and close the drawing.

LEARNING CHECKPOINT

- ☐ What does the term *camera* refer to?
- ☐ Define the term *target.*
- ☐ Which DVIEW option creates a perspective view?
- ☐ What are clipping planes?

Model Viewports and 3D Drawings

Viewports
Display Viewports Dialog
View
Viewports ▸
New Viewports...
VPORTS

Model viewports, introduced in Chapter 13, can be very useful for 3D drafting. The biggest problem in 3D drafting is visualization. Designers and drafters must be able to visualize what they are drawing in order to create accurate drawings. The problem comes from viewing 3D objects through a 2D screen. This gets back to the same concept of communicating 3D ideas on 2D paper. The most effective way to do this is by using several different views from various angles.

When model viewports are used, each viewport can be set to view the model from different angles and at any desired scale factors. Additionally, various grid and snap settings can be used. Some views can show hidden lines removed or even shaded images. Figure 14.42 shows an example of a working model viewport layout.

The Viewports dialog box can be accessed from the Viewports cascade on the View pulldown menu or at the Command: prompt using the VPORTS command. The features of the Viewports dialog box are discussed in Chapter 13.

Creative use of the VPORTS command allows you great flexibility in designing your working layout. The basic guideline for generating viewport layouts is not to make viewports so small that you cannot easily edit objects within them.

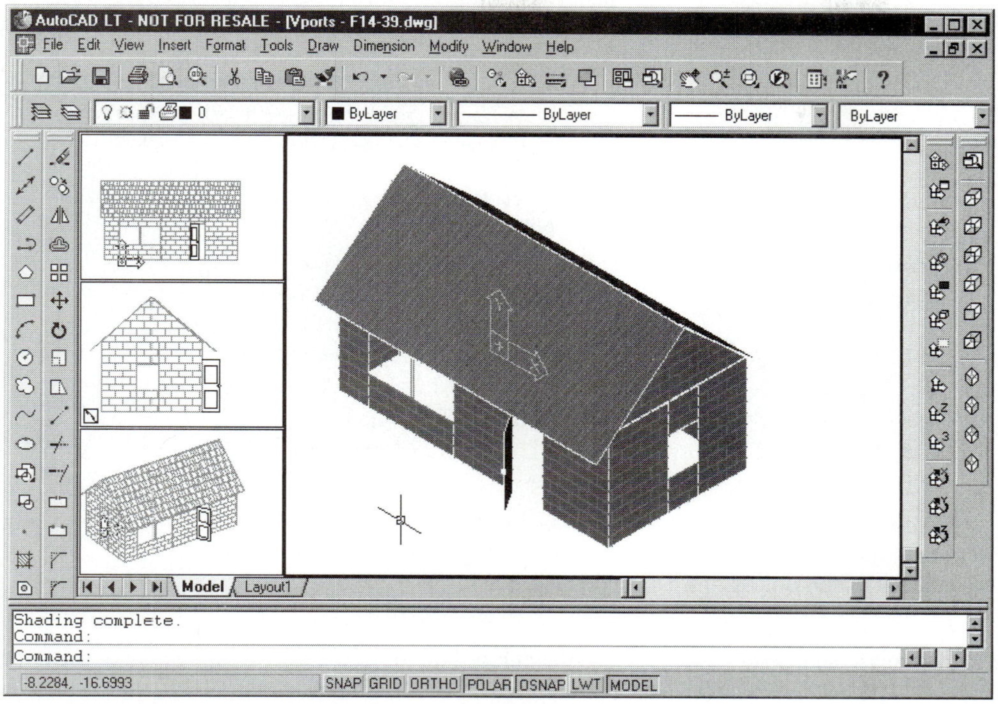

FIGURE 14.42 Model viewports can be used to create a versatile environment for working in 3D drawings.

Exercise 14.9 **Estimated time required: 5 min.**

1. Open EX14.8.
2. Create the viewport layout shown in Figure 14.42.
3. Save the drawing as EX14.9.

LEARNING CHECKPOINT

☐ What is the basic guideline for creating tiled viewports?

Creating Isometric Drawings

An isometric drawing can be used to simulate a 3D view of an object. In some cases, this may be much quicker than actually creating a full 3D drawing. Because true 3D solids cannot be created in AutoCAD LT, drawings created in 3D are simulations and are primarily useful for visualization only. Therefore, it is often more productive to generate an isometric representation of a part.

AutoCAD LT provides some basic isometric drawing tools to assist you when creating isometric views. The first of these tools is the isometric snap and grid. The isometric snap and grid properties are set in the Snap type & style area on the Snap and Grid tab of the Drafting Settings dialog box. You can access the Drafting Settings dialog box by typing **DS** or **DSETTINGS** at the Command: prompt or by picking Drafting Settings… from the Tools pull-down menu. Picking Settings… from the status bar SNAP or GRID button shortcut menus starts the Drafting Settings dialog box and automatically displays the Snap and Grid tab.

The Rectangular and Isometric snap style radio buttons are not accessible when the current snap type is set to Polar snap (see Figure 14.43A). Setting the snap type to Grid snap enables the snap style options. Picking the Isometric snap option sets the current snap style to Isometric. When the snap style is set to isometric, the appropriate X spacing for the Grid and Snap is calculated from the current Y spacing values and entered automatically.

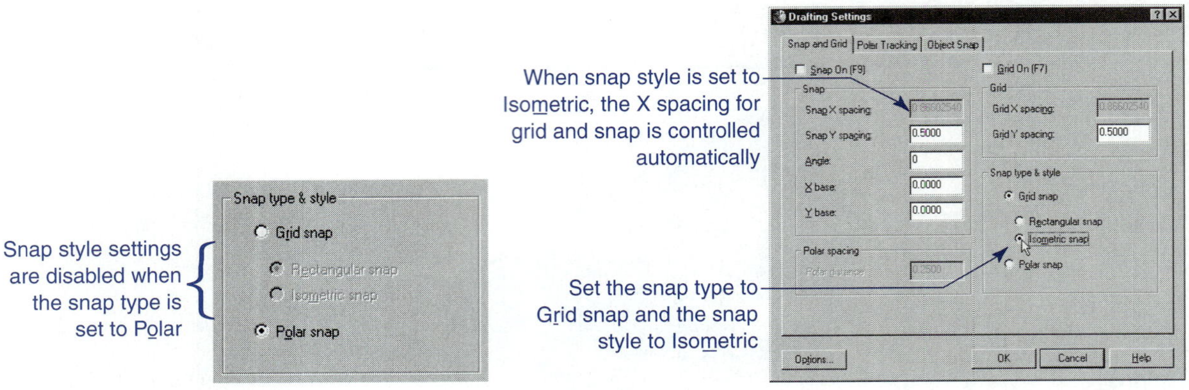

FIGURE 14.43 (A) The snap style settings are not available when the snap type is set to Polar. (B) When the current snap style is set to Isometric, the X spacing for grid and snap is controlled automatically based on current Y spacing values.

ISOPLANE
IS

Enabling the isometric snap/grid mode changes the cursor into an isometric cursor. An isometric cube is shown in Figure 14.44, with the three isometric planes labeled. While isometric mode is on, the cursor can be set to the correct configuration for each of these isometric planes as needed. The F5 or Ctrl+E keystrokes are used to toggle through the three settings. The IS or ISOPLANE command can also be used, but this is the long way around. Each of the plane toggling options can be used transparently. An example of using ISOPLANE is shown here:

Command: **IS** or **ISOPLANE**
Current isoplane: Left
Enter isometric plane setting [Left/Top/Right] <Top>: ↵
Current isoplane: Top
Command:

Ortho mode restricts some movement to be parallel to the cursor. This is also true in isometric mode. Figure 14.45 shows the third segment of a line sequence being drawn using an isometric snap/grid mode, with Ortho on.

FIGURE 14.44 The three isometric planes are Left, Right, and Top. The cursor is modified for each of these planes when isometric mode is being used.

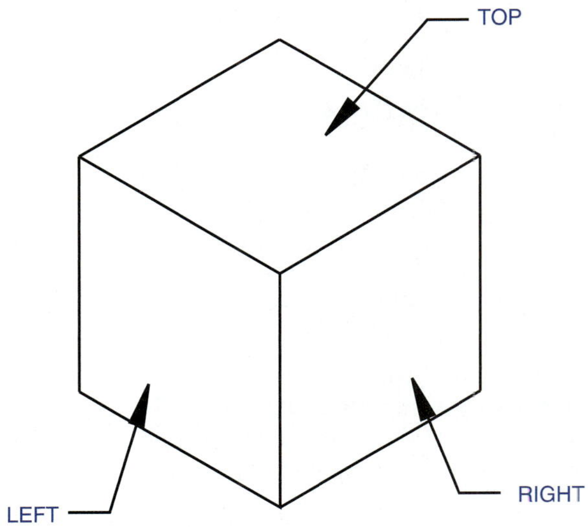

FIGURE 14.45 The isometric cursor also responds to Ortho settings.

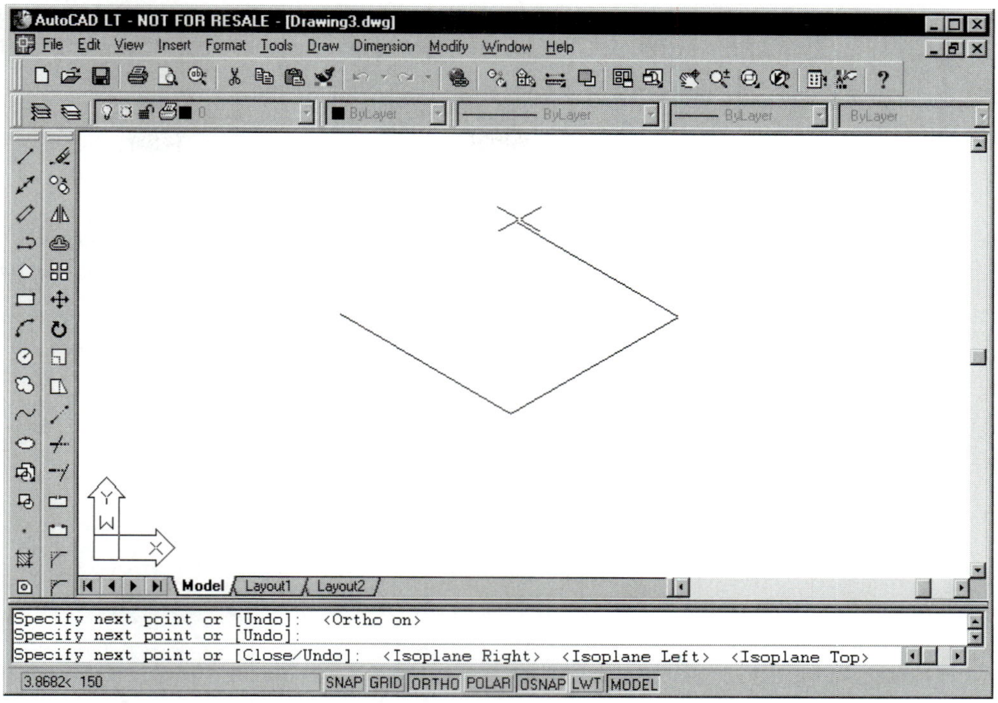

Although the snap and grid orientation changes in isometric mode, the coordinate system is not changed. You can define a new UCS at any time, but you cannot create a UCS that matches a 2D isometric snap/grid. Figure 14.46 shows an isometric drawing environment with Grid turned on and example coordinate locations labeled.

Drawing Isometric Circles and Arcs

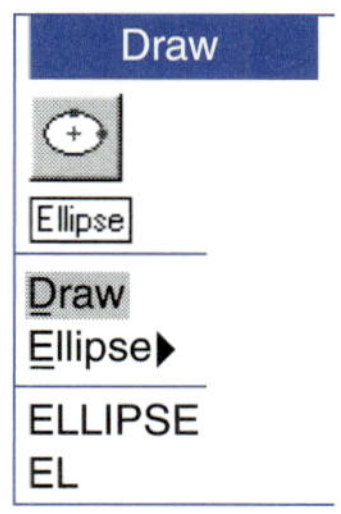

Because an isometric plane is rotated and not viewed flat, an isometric circle appears as an ellipse. When in isometric mode, the ELLIPSE command offers the Isocircle option to assist in drawing isometric circles and arcs:

Command: **EL** or **ELLIPSE**↵
Specify axis endpoint of ellipse or [Arc/Center/Isocircle]: **I**↵
Specify center of isocircle: *<pick center point for isocircle>*
Specify radius of isocircle or [Diameter]: *<specify a radius or* **D** *for diameter>*

FIGURE 14.46 The isometric snap/grid mode does not affect the UCS.

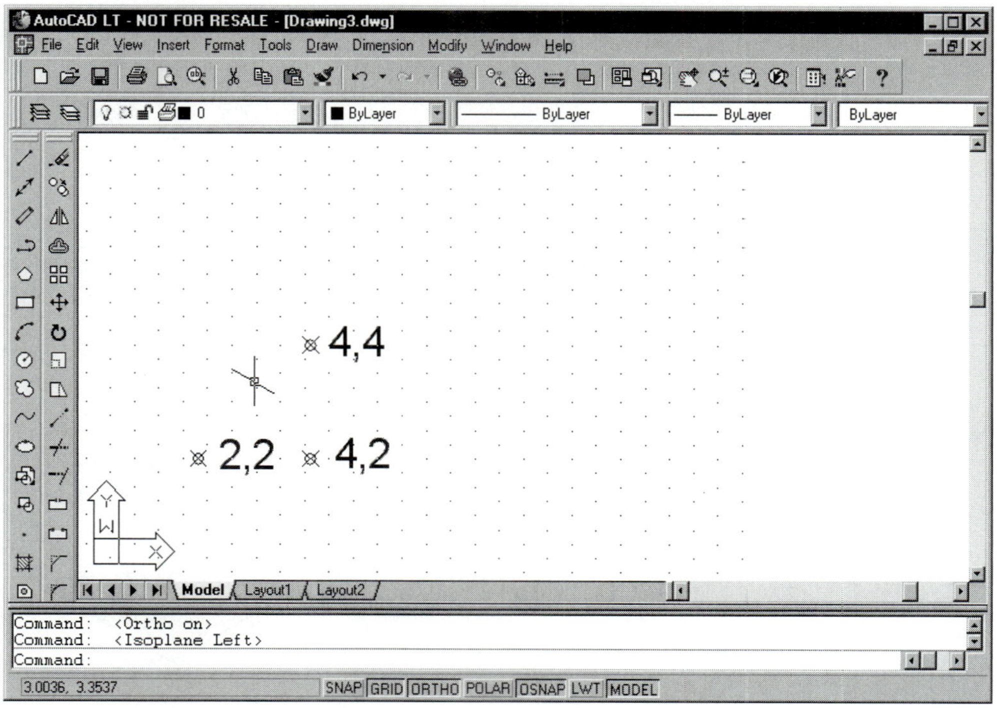

Isometric arcs can be created either by editing isometric circles or they can be drawn directly with the ELLIPSE command. The ELLIPSE Arc option line also presents an option for isometric mode:

Command: **EL** or **ELLIPSE**↵
Specify axis endpoint of ellipse or [Arc/Center/Isocircle]: **A**↵
Specify axis endpoint of elliptical arc or [Center/Isocircle]: **I**↵
Specify center of isocircle: *<pick center point for isocircle>*
Specify radius of isocircle or [Diameter]: **.25**↵
Specify start angle or [Parameter]: *<specify start angle or parameter>*
Specify end angle or [Parameter/Included angle]: *<specify angle or option>*

The isometric circle or arc is automatically created as it should appear in the currently active isometric plane. Figure 14.47 shows an isometric circle in each of the isometric planes.

FIGURE 14.47 Isometric circles are automatically drawn to appear correct in the currently active isometric plane.

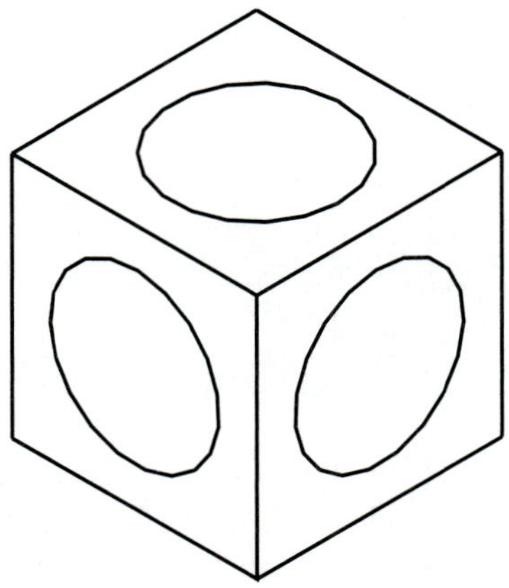

Isometric Text

Using the text obliquing angle within the STYLE command, and rotation angle when creating text, text can easily be made to appear to be drawn on any isometric plane. The cube in Figure 14.48 shows the settings for the text shown on each face. The obliquing angle is defined in the text style, but the rotation can be specified for each line of text. If you create two text styles, one obliqued +30° and the other −30°, the rotation angle can be specified as you create text to create it on the desired isometric plane.

FIGURE 14.48 Settings for isometric text

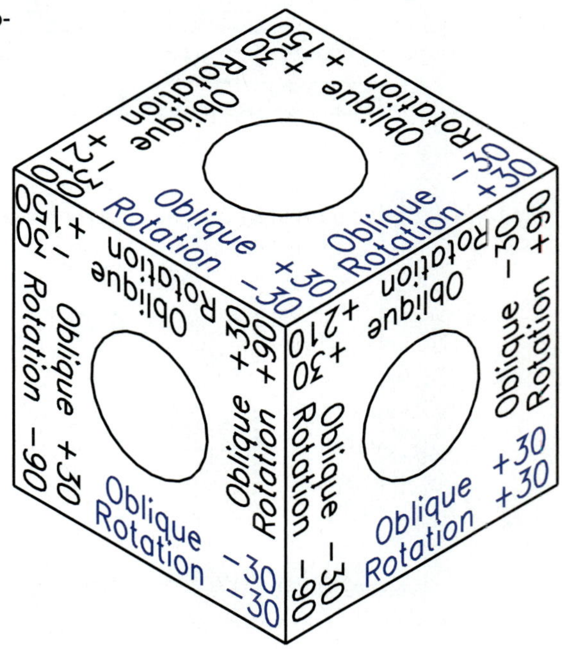

Isometric Arrowheads

It is not a common practice to fully dimension isometric drawings. However, it is sometimes necessary to dimension specific features or use a leader for pointing in an isometric drawing. AutoCAD LT does not have any isometric arrowheads available in its standard dimensioning features. You can, however, create your own, and AutoCAD LT can use them while dimensioning.

Isometric arrowheads can be created using the SOLID command. It may be helpful to draw an outline for the arrowhead first as a guide for the SOLID command. In Figure 14.49, all the isometric arrowheads are shown.

FIGURE 14.49 Isometric arrowheads.

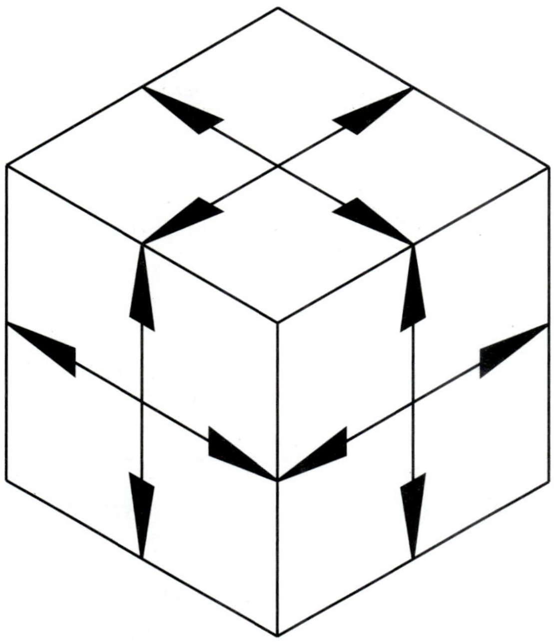

As you create isometric arrowheads, keep in mind that the DIMASZ setting is a multiplier for the *length.* In order for DIMASZ to have the correct effect, the original geometry must be drawn at one unit long. That way, a DIMASZ value of 0.125 creates a 1/8″-long arrowhead because 0.125 × 1″ = 0.125″ (1/8″).

After creating the arrowheads, you must then make them into blocks. Use a simple, yet effective naming system. For example, the left horizontal arrowhead on the right plane could be named RHL, the one on the right might be RHR. The vertical arrowheads could be RVB and RVT for Right-Vertical-Bottom and Right-Vertical-Top. Any naming system that makes sense to you can be used.

To use isometric arrowheads in AutoCAD LT dimension objects, it is necessary to adjust the DIMBLK1 and DIMBLK2 settings according to the isometric plane you are working on. Additionally, you need to set the DIMTXSTY variable to the appropriate setting for the plane and direction of the dimensions. A more effective means would be to define an individual dimension style for vertical and horizontal dimensions on each plane. This way you only need to change one setting rather than three when you need a different type of dimension.

When drawing the dimensions, the DIMALIGNED option can be used because most isometric lines are drawn true length. DIMVERTICAL can be used for the vertical lines. To adjust the dimensions to appear to be in an isometric plane, the OBLIQUE option is used. Figure 14.50A shows an isometric drawing dimensioned using DIMALIGNED and DIMVERTICAL. In Figure 14.50B, the OBLIQUE command has been used to make the dimensions appear correctly. The obliquing angle used appears next to each dimension.

Field Notes

If you plan to do more than one isometric drawing in your career, it is best to define all your isometric options in an isometric template, or prototype drawing. This template should have all of the appropriate text styles, arrowhead blocks, and dimension styles already defined.

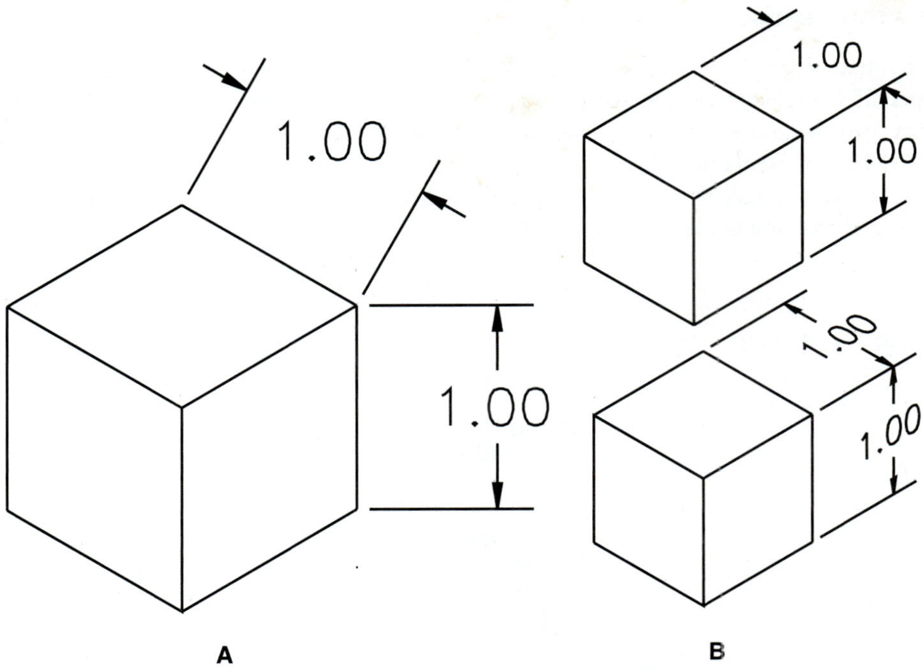

FIGURE 14.50 (A) Dimensions before obliquing. (B) Dimensions after obliquing.

Exercise 14.10 **Estimated time required: 10 min.**

1. Start a new drawing.
2. Draw an isometric cube using the appropriate isometric environmental settings.
3. Place an isometric circle at the center of each face of the cube.
4. Place an isometric fillet at each corner using the ELLIPSE Arc Isometric option.
5. Save as EX14.10, and close the drawing.

LEARNING CHECKPOINT

- ☐ What are the ways to change the current isometric plane? Which is best?
- ☐ How does Ortho respond to isometric settings?
- ☐ What is the effect of isometric snap on the coordinate system?
- ☐ How is isometric text created?
- ☐ Describe how isometric dimensions are created.
- ☐ Why is an isometric template valuable?

MULTIPLE CHOICE

Circle the choice or enter your response on an answer sheet by selecting the option that most closely completes or answers the given statement.

1. The fixed coordinate system used by default in AutoCAD LT is called the:
a. default coordinate system **c.** world coordinate system
b. user coordinate system **d.** object coordinate system

2. This simple reference makes it easier to visualize the relationships of the X, Y, and Z axes in 3D space:
a. the coordinate display **c.** object snap
b. the right-hand rule **d.** the status bar

3. This variation of polar coordinate entry uses a standard polar coordinate followed by a Z-axis value:
- **a.** relative coordinates
- **b.** absolute coordinates
- **c.** spherical coordinates
- **d.** cylindrical coordinates

4. **2<45<60** represents an example of:
- **a.** relative coordinates
- **b.** absolute coordinates
- **c.** spherical coordinates
- **d.** cylindrical coordinates

5. A custom coordinate system that can be relocated as needed in 3D space is called:
- **a.** default coordinate system
- **b.** user coordinate system
- **c.** world coordinate system
- **d.** object coordinate system

6. This command is used to set up 3D viewing angles:
- **a.** VIEW
- **b.** ZOOM dynamic
- **c.** VPOINT
- **d.** RTZOOM

7. This term refers to the Z-axis value of the current drawing plane:
- **a.** elevation
- **b.** height
- **c.** UCS origin
- **d.** thickness

8. This system variable controls the way that AutoCAD LT uses lighting in the shaded image:
- **a.** SHADEDGE
- **b.** SHADEDIF
- **c.** LIGHTS
- **d.** SHADELIGHT

9. Which keystroke is used to toggle the isometric plane?
- **a.** Ctrl+A
- **b.** Ctrl+E
- **c.** Ctrl+B
- **d.** Ctrl+P

10. What is the name of the command used to draw an isometric circle?
- **a.** ISOCIRCLE
- **b.** ELLIPSE
- **c.** ISOELLIPSE
- **d.** CIRCLE

MATCHING

Match each term to the correct description by writing the appropriate number in each box at the left.

- ☐ SHADEDGE
- ☐ VPOINT
- ☐ HIDE
- ☐ SHADE
- ☐ SHADEDIF
- ☐ Camera
- ☐ Target
- ☐ THICKNESS
- ☐ ELEVATION
- ☐ DVIEW
- ☐ UCS
- ☐ WCS
- ☐ PLAN
- ☐ VPORTS
- ☐ CLIPPING

1. Coordinate system defined by the user.
2. Removes hidden lines.
3. Where the camera looks.
4. Can be used to create a perspective view.
5. Applies color to 3D objects.
6. The default coordinate system.
7. The variable that controls edge shading.
8. The variable that controls lighting in a shaded image.
9. Command to change your viewpoint.
10. Command to change your view dynamically.
11. Front and back planes control what part of the drawing is displayed.
12. Command to set up tiled viewports.
13. View perpendicular to a coordinate system.
14. The Z-axis coordinate.
15. The Z-axis dimension.

WORD SCRAMBLE

Unscramble the six scrambled words below, one letter to each square, to form six AutoCAD LT-related words:

VOSTRIPEW

PREALLLA

EPCORTINOJ

MECIRITOS

EINVALETO

EDVWI

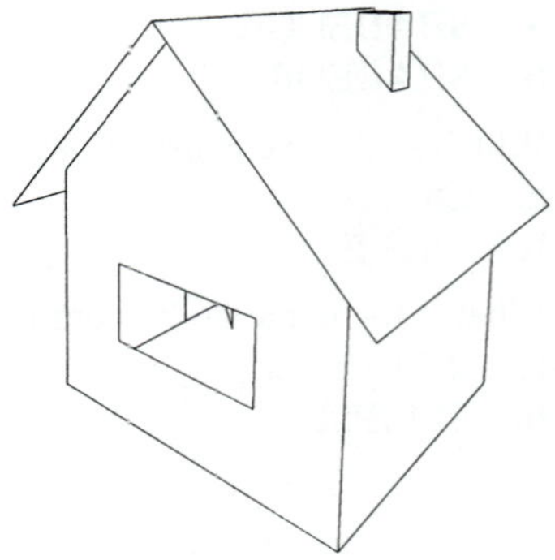

Unscramble the circled letters above to form the special answer, as suggested by the illustration.

PROJECTS

14.1 Start a new drawing using the Start from Scratch option. Construct a 3D wire frame cube, two units per side, with the bottom-left corner at the 0,0,0 origin. Use the LINE command, and supply only *absolute* coordinates. Construct two more cubes, one using *spherical* coordinates with a bottom-left corner at 3,0,0, and the other using *cylindrical* coordinates and a bottom-left corner at 0,3,0. Use the VPOINT command to setup a 3D viewing angle of your choice. Save the drawing as P14.1.

14.2 Open P14.1 for editing. Using the UCS command, create and save two user coordinate systems. Create one on the Y,Z plane with an origin of 0,0,0 in the World Coordinate System and assign a name of YZ. Create the other on the X,Z plane, with an origin of 4,2,9 in the WCS and name it XZ. Restore the WCS and save the drawing file as P14.2.

14.3 Start a new drawing using the Start from Scratch option. Create a cube that simulates a surface model by drawing lines and giving them a thickness. The cube should be one unit on a side and the bottom-left corner at 2,2,0. Save the drawing as P14.3.

14.4 Open P14.3 for editing. Create five named views, with the viewing angle being appropriate for the view name. The views should be TOP, FRONT, RIGHT, SW-ISO, and SE-ISO. Restore the SW-ISO view, use the HIDE command, and save the drawing file as P14.4.

14.5 Start a new drawing using the Start from Scratch option. Set the current THICKNESS value to 2.0. Draw a circle, an arc, a line, a polyline, a spline, and a line of text. Each should be appropriately sized within an area of about 12 × 9 units. Change the current view to a SW Isometric view. Use the HIDE command and save the drawing as P14.5.

14.6 Open P14.5 for editing. Change the properties of the text object so that the thickness is 0.5 units. Use the HIDE command and save the drawing as P14.6.

14.7 Open P14.4 for editing. Create six named user coordinate systems: TOP, BOTTOM, LEFT, RIGHT, FRONT, and BACK. Each UCS should have an origin and alignment on the appropriate face of the cube. Now, place a different hatch pattern on each face of the cube. Change the view to SW Isometric and use the HIDE command. Save the drawing as P14.7.

14.8 Open P14.7 for editing. Adjust the value of the SHADEDIF and SHADEDGE system variables to produce the best image when using the SHADE command. Try different values and use the one you think looks best. Use the SHADE command and save the drawing as P14.8.

14.9 Draw the following figure. Use standard drawing tools for the orthographic portion, and use isometric tools to create the isometric view. Save the drawing as P14.9.

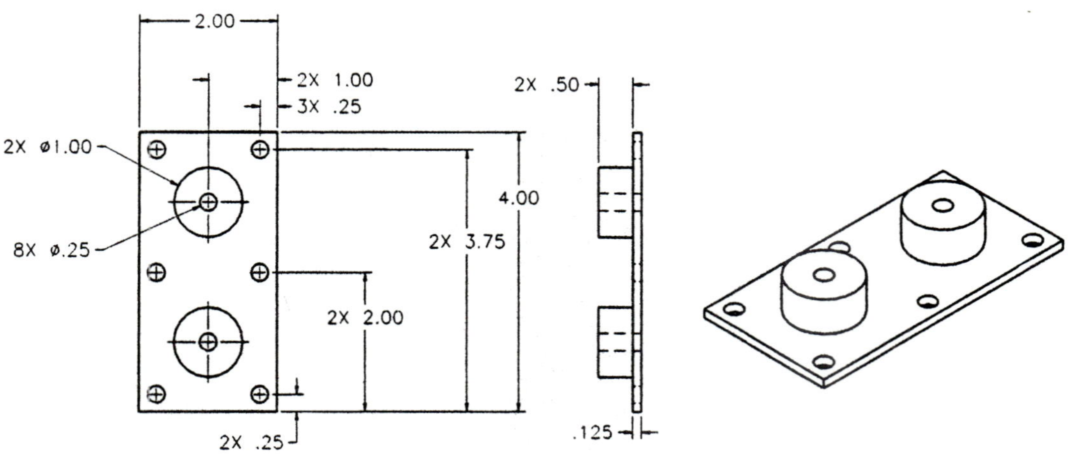

14.10 Create an isometric view of the following figure. Save the drawing as P14.10.

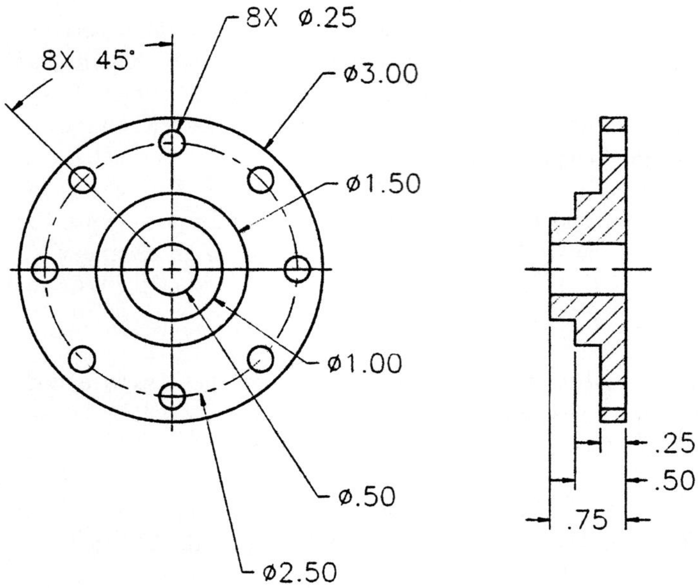

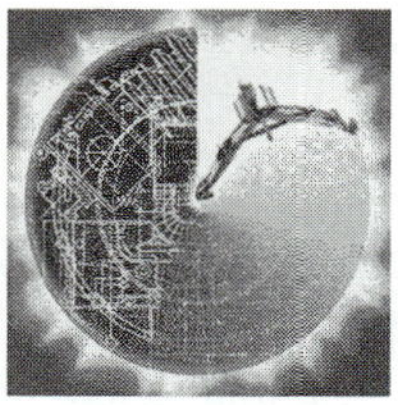

CHAPTER 15

File Management and Data Exchange

LEARNING GOALS

- Optimize drawing files for minimum size.
- Manage AutoCAD LT files in a networked environment.
- Import and export AutoCAD LT drawing information.
- Print drawings to a file.
- Create live documents using OLE.
- Use the Windows Clipboard for data exchange.

AutoCAD LT Files

In a CAD environment, computer files are at the very heart of everything you do. The programs you use rely on information stored in files that the computer evaluates and executes. Many of the features of AutoCAD LT such as linetype and hatch pattern definition are also stored in files. Most importantly, the drawings you create in AutoCAD LT are stored as drawing files. Understanding proper file management techniques allows you to maximize the potential of your workstation and saves you time when working in AutoCAD LT.

Managing Drawing File Size

The size of the drawing you are working in can affect the speed of your workstation. Used in this sense, the term *size* does not refer to the area displayed within the drawing; rather, it reflects the amount of information contained in the drawing. Recall from Chapter 1 that computer files are measured in size by the number of *bytes* required to store all of the information in the file. A byte is approximately equal to one character. A single line object needs to store a record of its coordinate locations, layer, color, linetype, elevation, thickness, linetype scale, and more. Therefore, this simple line object can require several hundred bytes of storage space within the drawing. Considering the number of lines, arcs, circles, and other objects in a typical drawing, it is easy to see how files can become large in a short time.

In addition to the objects on the screen that you can see, other types of information within drawings can add unnecessarily to the overall file size. For example, block definitions are not visible on your drawing—just the block reference. If a block definition exists within your drawing, but has not been inserted anywhere, that definition is consuming valuable space for no reason. Some drafters will load all of the linetype definitions for convenience when working. When the drawing is complete, however, the unused linetype definitions are also unnecessary. All unnecessary information in a drawing makes the file larger than it needs to be.

Earlier chapters discussed the value of using blocks and Xrefs to help keep drawing file size at a minimum. Another technique for maintaining efficient drawing sizes is through purging unnecessary data out of the drawing.

Removing Unused Data from a Drawing

File
Drawing Utilities▸
Purge...

PURGE
PU

AutoCAD LT 2000 provides an easy dialog interface for purging unreferenced drawing data. The term *unreferenced* indicates data that defines something that is not used within the drawing. For example, when a block definition exists in a drawing but the block has not been inserted anywhere, that block definition is unreferenced. A layer that contains no objects and is not associated with existing block definitions is another example of unreferenced data. Use the PURGE command to remove unreferenced data from a drawing.

Using the PURGE Command

You can access the PURGE command by picking Purge ... from the Drawing Utilities cascade on the File pull-down menu or by typing **PU** or **PURGE** at the Command: prompt. The PURGE command displays the Purge dialog box, as shown in Figure 15.1.

The graphic list in the center of the Purge dialog box displays icons and labels representing the types of information that can be purged from a drawing. The categories are as follows:

- **All items** This category represents the whole drawing. Picking Purge with this option highlighted will purge all unused information listed in each of the categories below it.
- **Blocks** Block definitions can be purged when they define blocks that are not currently inserted anywhere in the drawing, are not referenced by a dimension style, and are not referenced by other block definitions.
- **Dimension styles** Dimension styles can be purged when they are not referenced by existing dimension objects and are not referenced in any block definitions. The STANDARD dimension style cannot be purged.
- **Layers** A layer can be purged when it is not the current layer, contains no objects, and is not referenced by objects that comprise existing block definitions. Layer 0 cannot be purged.
- **Linetypes** A currently loaded linetype definition can be purged when it is not used by any objects in the drawing and is not referenced by objects that are part of an existing block definition. The linetypes named CONTINUOUS, BYLAYER, and BYBLOCK cannot be purged.
- **Mline styles** Multiline styles can be purged when they are not referenced by existing multilines. AutoCAD LT cannot create multilines or multiline styles, so this category will contain only items other than STANDARD if the drawing has been edited using AutoCAD. The style named STANDARD cannot be purged.
- **Plot Styles** Plot style definitions can be purged when they are not assigned to layouts or objects in the drawing. The default plot styles, BYLAYER, BYBLOCK, NORMAL, and the current plot style cannot be purged.
- **Shapes** Shape definition files (.shx) can be purged when no shapes defined by the file are used in the current drawing, and the shape definitions are not referenced by any linetype definitions. In AutoCAD LT, shape definitions are used only as part of complex linetype definitions (such as Fenceline1 and Tracks). A drawing edited previously in AutoCAD may contain additional shape definitions.
- **Text styles** A text style definition can be purged when it is not used by any existing text, mtext, or attribute object and is not referenced by any block definition, dimension style, or complex linetype. The text style named STANDARD cannot be purged.

The radio buttons at the top of the Purge dialog box control whether the list displays items that can be purged from the drawing. When you select the *View items you can purge* button, the list title reads "Items not used in drawing:" and the appropriate items are listed (see Figure 15.1A).

The list appears in a tree-style view that shows the drawing at the root of the tree and branches into categories of data. A category with a plus sign next to it indicates that the category contains items that can be purged. Categories without a plus sign have no items available for purging. In some drawings you may find no listing of unused data, which means that nothing can be purged.

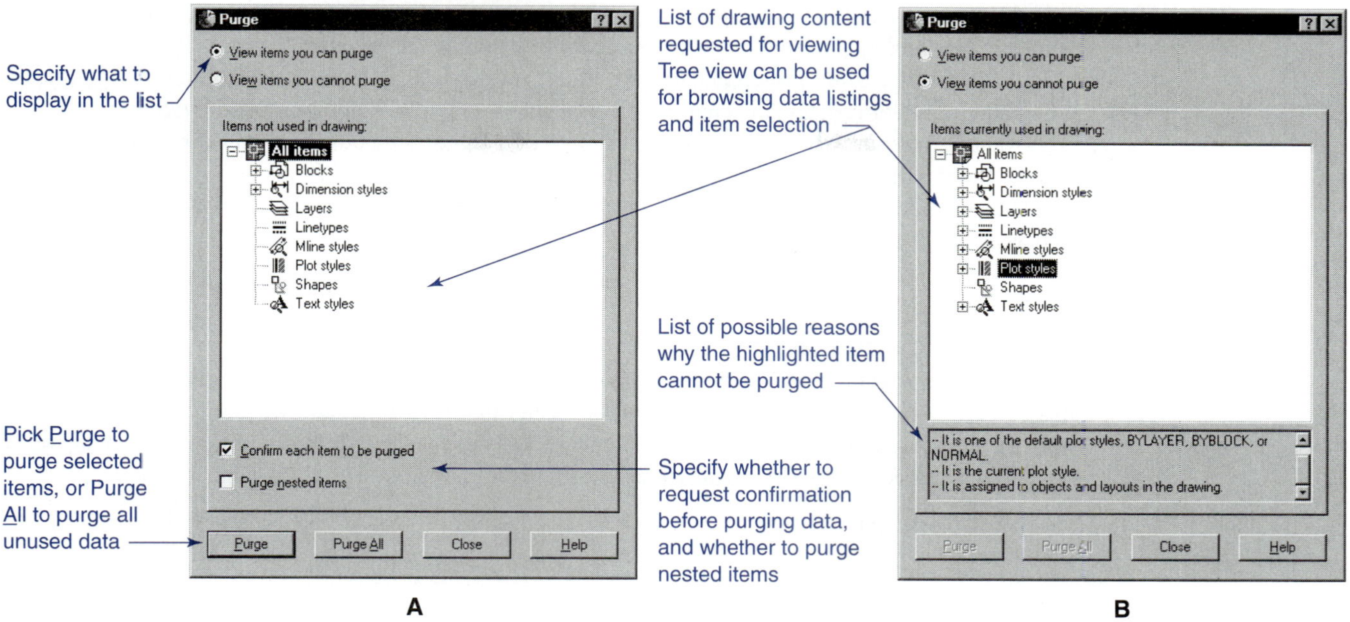

FIGURE 15.1 The list in the Purge dialog box lets you either (A) View items you can purge or (B) View items you cannot purge.

Purging Selectively

The Purge dialog box allows you to select specific items for purging. In Figure 15.1, a plus sign is displayed next to the icons of categories that have unused data. The drawing used in this example is Church Pew Layout.dwg, found in the Sample folder. Notice that this drawing currently contains unused block and dimension style data. Expanding the Blocks category shows one block definition that is not used in the drawing. To remove the unused definition, pick that definition and select the Purge button. By default, the *Confirm each item to be purged* option is active, and the Confirm Purge dialog box is displayed for each item to be purged.

To suppress this confirmation, remove the check next to this option. The Confirm Purge dialog box is shown in Figure 15.2, asking for confirmation before purging the block definition named "_Oblique."

FIGURE 15.2 The Confirm Purge dialog box.

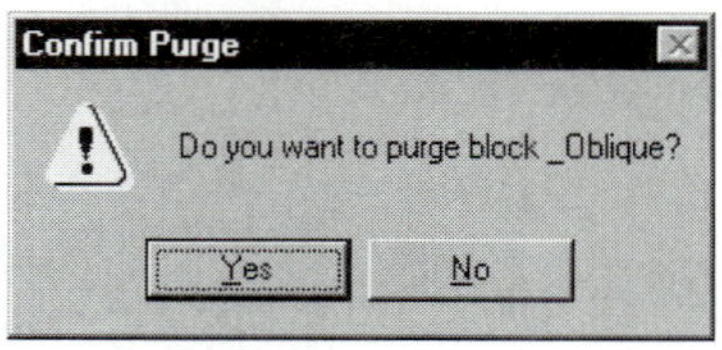

The list in the Purge dialog box has standard Windows functionality, and allows you to select multiple items in different categories by using the Shift and Ctrl keys in combination with picking. Alternatively, you can purge all items within a specific category by highlighting its icon and picking Purge. To select multiple categories, use the Shift or Ctrl keys when picking.

Purging All Unused Data

To purge all unused elements from your drawing, either select the Purge All button at the bottom of the dialog box or highlight the drawing icon labeled All items and pick the Purge button. It is best to purge all unused data when a drawing project is finished.

When you select the Purge All button, the Confirm Purge dialog box is displayed even if you have not checked the Confirm each item to be purged option. The Confirm Purge dialog box allows you to pick Yes to purge the item or Yes to All to purge all remaining items with no further confirmations. Picking No skips the listed item and continues to the next item. The default button is Cancel, which stops the purging operation and returns you to the Purge dialog box.

Checking the *Purge nested items* toggle allows removal of definitions that are nested, or contained as part of the definition of other items. This option works only when you pick the Purge button when *All items* or *Blocks* is selected, or when you select the Purge All button. A nested item is available for purging only after the definition in which it is nested has been purged. For example, each of the original objects selected as part of a block definition carries a reference to a specific layer name. Any layer names referenced by objects within a block definition are nested and cannot be purged unless the block definition is purged first.

If you want to find out why a particular item cannot be purged, select the *View items you cannot purge* radio button at the top of the Purge dialog box. This changes the list title to "Items currently used in drawing:" and displays named items that cannot be purged. Picking any item displays a possible reason why it cannot be purged (refer to Figure 15.1B).

Field Notes

Drawing files can become unexpectedly large when inserting other drawings. Objects such as dimensions are created as *unnamed blocks.* This means that they have a block definition stored within the drawing. Even if the insertion of the block has been erased, the definition remains. Unnamed blocks are named with an asterisk preceding them. For example:

```
Purge block *D0? <N>:
```

When an unnamed block is presented for purging, it means that the definition is no longer needed and that it is safe to purge the definition.

AutoCAD LT 2000 Drawing File Management

Throughout this text, you have seen many examples of the flexible nature of the AutoCAD LT 2000 software. Almost all aspects of the AutoCAD LT software can be set up, configured, and customized to work the way that you work. This discussion introduces the configuration options related to your drawing files.

File Safety Precautions

Data loss can be very costly to design professionals. Drawing files typically represent a significant investment of time, effort, and money. AutoCAD LT provides configuration options that can help reduce your risk of data loss. The File Safety Precautions settings are accessed from the Open and Save tab on the Options dialog box (see Figure 15.3).

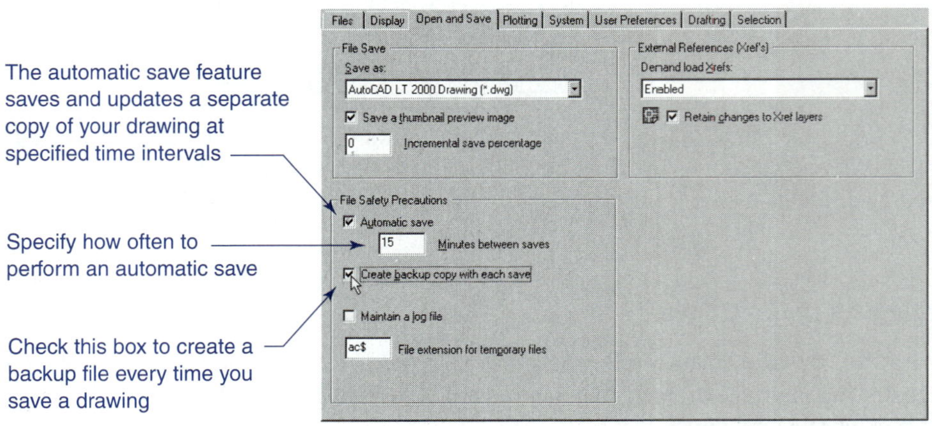

FIGURE 15.3 Proper configuration of the File Safety Precautions settings can help reduce the possibility of data loss.

Create backup copy with each save

It is strongly recommended that the *Create backup copy with each save* option be enabled. Place a check mark in the check box to enable this feature, as shown in Figure 15.3. Here's how this feature actually works:

The first time you save a new drawing file, AutoCAD LT saves the drawing data in a file assigned a user-specified name and the file extension .DWG. To provide a clear example in this discussion, a file name of *MyDrawing* is used, so the complete name of the file created by AutoCAD LT is *MyDrawing*.**dwg**.

The second time you save the drawing, AutoCAD LT changes the file extension of the first file from .DWG to .BAK (a common file extension for backup files). So *MyDrawing*.**dwg** becomes *MyDrawing*.**bak**, and the latest version of the drawing is saved in a new *MyDrawing*.**dwg**. This all occurs in the same folder where the original drawing was saved.

The third (and beyond…) time you save your drawing, AutoCAD LT deletes *MyDrawing*.**bak**, renames *MyDrawing*.**dwg** to *MyDrawing*.**bak** and then saves the newest version as *MyDrawing*.**dwg**.

Automatic save

The *Automatic save* setting provides an additional layer of protection from data loss (see Figure 15.3). Place a check mark in the box to enable this feature, which automatically saves your drawing information in a separate file at a specified number of *Minutes between saves*. It is important to understand that the automatic save feature does not update or overwrite the actual drawing file or any existing backup files.

It is recommended that the automatic save feature be enabled using an appropriate setting for the time between saves. A general guideline for determining an appropriate time between saves is to set the interval based on how much work you are willing to repeat in the event of a power outage or computer crash. Keep in mind that if you are working in extremely large drawing files that are slow to save, setting too short an interval can be counterproductive.

The folder location for the automatic save file is specified in the Files tab of the Options dialog box. Open the item labeled Automatic Save File Location to see the current location (see Figure 15.4). If you want to change the default folder, you can edit the path directly or pick the Browse… button to use the Browse for Folder dialog box.

An automatic save file uses the original name of the drawing file as a base and adds a combination of underscores and numbers to the end of the name as a unique identifier. The file is saved with the file extension .SV$. For example, the automatic save file for a drawing named *F14-39.dwg* was named as follows:

F14-39_1_1_6299.sv$

The time between saves can also be set using the SAVETIME variable. The **TIME** command can be used to see when the next automatic save will be performed. The SAVETIME timer is reset when the drawing is saved using SAVE, QSAVE, or SAVEAS. The timer is not started again until you make a change to the drawing. If an automatic save finds an existing .SV$ file, it is renamed with a .BAK extension, and the new save file is created. Saving the drawing manually deletes the last automatic save file but does not affect backup versions of the automatic save file. In the event of a power failure or system crash, the automatic save file is not deleted.

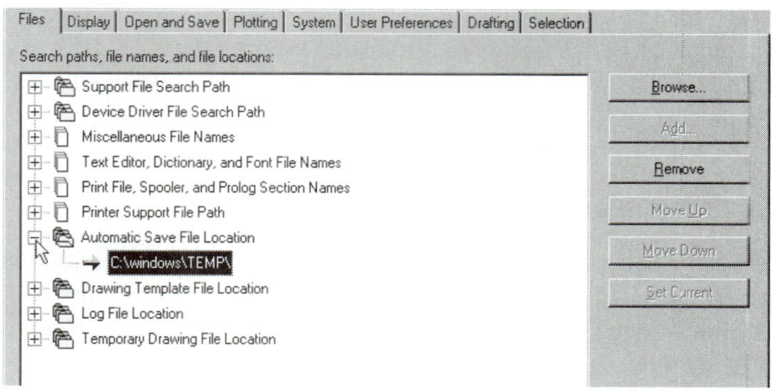

FIGURE 15.4 The default location for the automatic save file can be set in the Files tab on the Options dialog box.

Field Notes

- Backup files and automatic save files are valuable safety features, but remember that the single most important practice to avoid data loss is:

  Save your work frequently.

- Anyone who uses computers on a professional level should perform regular scheduled backups of all data files to reliable and well organized media. An inexpensive and versatile option is a writable (or rewritable) CD-ROM.

Disaster Recovery Options

There are many ways that a drawing file (or any other file) can be corrupted, lost, or destroyed. Files can be damaged by a minor computer malfunction, by loss of power during a save operation, or by media failure (such as a bad floppy disk). A drawing file is referred to as being ***corrupt*** when part or all of the drawing data contained in the file has become unreadable by AutoCAD LT.

Corrupt drawings can sometimes be recovered in part or even completely if the damage to the file was not severe. If AutoCAD LT reports an error in reading a file, you can try to open it with the RECOVER command. You can type **RECOVER** at the Command: prompt, or pick Recover... from the Drawing Utilities cascade on the File menu. Use the file dialog box to select the file needing recovery. After the recovery, an audit of the drawing is performed to evaluate the integrity of the drawing. AutoCAD LT reports the results in the text window (see Figure 15.5):

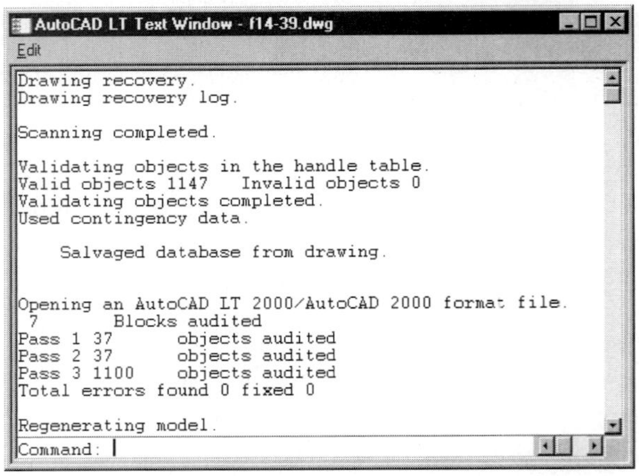

FIGURE 15.5 The results of the RECOVER command are displayed in the text window.

When a file is lost, the first step you should take is to perform a complete search of all local and network disk drives using the Windows Explorer. When a file is found to be missing, it may be due to something as simple as being dropped in the wrong folder. Always be sure to search the Recycle bin as well. If a thorough search produces no results, then you can take the next step.

After making the determination that the required file is actually lost or destroyed, it is time to see what can be recovered from other sources—beginning with the backup file. To open a .BAK file in AutoCAD LT, you must first rename it with a .DWG file extension.

If the data loss was due to a power outage or a sudden failure of your computer system, you should be able to access a recent drawing version in an automatic save file. Like the backup files, an automatic save file must be renamed with a .DWG file extension before AutoCAD LT can open it. Additionally, if necessary, you may be able to locate a backup of the automatic save file. These files are saved in the same folder as the .SV$ file, but they use a .BAK extension.

File Save Settings

The File Save area on the Open and Save tab of the Options dialog box provides options related to how AutoCAD LT saves drawing files. The available settings allow control of file formats and performance controls.

When it is necessary to save the majority of your drawing files in a format other than the AutoCAD LT 2000 default, you can set the required format as the default file format. In the File Save area, shown in Figure 15.6, select the desired option from the Save as: list. The selected option is used as the default file save format and is the active option in the Save Drawing As dialog box.

If for any reason you need to save your drawing files without a thumbnail preview, this feature can be disabled by removing the check mark from the box.

Incremental saves can be a much faster option for extremely large drawing files. Setting the Incremental save percentage to 0 disables incremental saves, meaning that every save is performed as a "full" save. An incremental save reduces the time required to save by quickly appending any new or changed drawing data to the end of the current file. Although incremental saves can be much faster, they can also produce unnecessarily large files. The value entered for the Incremental save percentage defines the maximum allowable wasted space in a drawing file. When the file reaches the specified percentage of wasted space, the next save is performed as a full save. A full save rewrites the entire file and eliminates all wasted space from a drawing file.

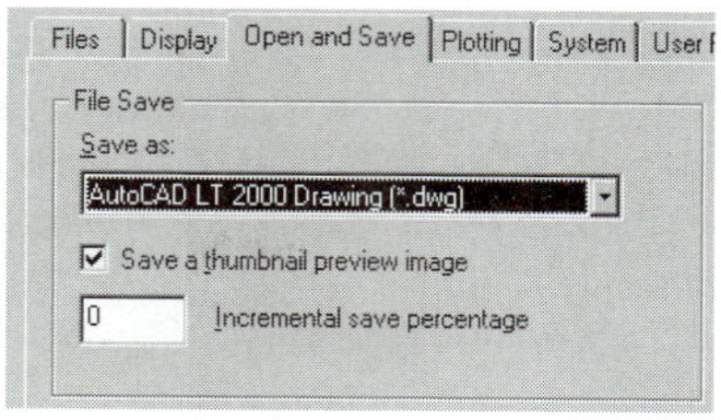

FIGURE 15.6 The File Save options control format, method, and content for saved files.

Managing File Properties

The **DWGPROPS** command can be typed at the Command: prompt, or you can pick the Drawing Properties... option from the File menu. The DWGPROPS command displays the file Properties dialog box, where the file properties can be reviewed, modified, or appended. The file Properties dialog box contains four tabs. Figure 15.7 shows the Summary tab, which is used to add relevant text information to a drawing in a form that can be searched using Windows Explorer.

The General tab provides general information such as file size, location, and relevant dates. File statistics are presented on the Statistics tab, and the Custom tab provides a location for entering custom fields and values.

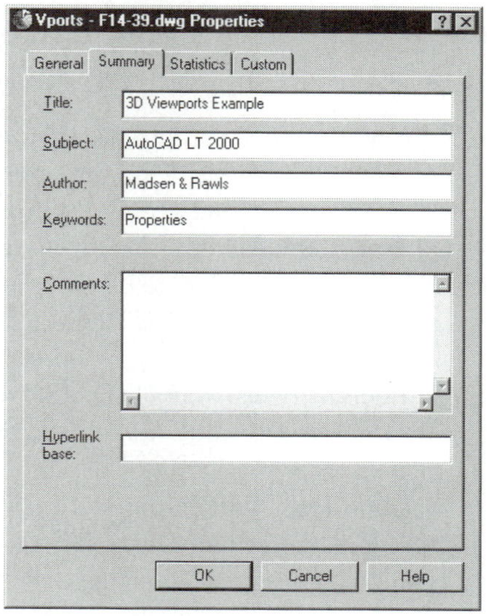

FIGURE 15.7 The file Properties dialog box can be used to add text information to a drawing that can be searched using Windows Explorer.

Networked Environments and File Sharing

In a networked environment, the drawing files are typically stored on a central computer known as a ***file server.*** These files may be accessible from many different workstations. This can create a problem if the same file is accessed by more than one user at the same time. Imagine what could happen, for example, if the same drawing was opened by two different users. When the first user decided to save, the changes this user made would then be saved. Now, when the second user saved, the changes made by this user would overwrite the changes made by the first user. The last user to save the file would write the last version of the drawing according to the changes made on that workstation. This means that all the changes made by the other user would be completely lost. To prevent multiple user file access with AutoCAD LT, the Windows file locking system is used.

A write-locked drawing can still be opened for reading by another user. A drawing opened in read-only mode can be edited normally, but the changes cannot be saved to the original file. Opening a file that is already open displays the dialog box shown in Figure 15.8. The SAVEAS command can, however, be used to save the drawing under a different name.

FIGURE 15.8 This alert is displayed when you open a file that is already open.

LEARNING CHECKPOINT

- ☐ Why is it important to manage file sizes for AutoCAD LT drawings?
- ☐ What command removes unreferenced data from a drawing file?

Exchanging Drawing Information with Other Applications

Drawing data can be imported into or exported from AutoCAD LT in order to share data with other applications. Several file formats are supported, including both vector and raster formats. In earlier chapters you learned that vector information is composed of actual objects, such as lines or polylines. A raster file is a record of pixels, and each pixel is separate from all of the others. The type of file used depends on the type of application. CAD-based applications usually create vector files, and paint programs usually create raster files.

Exchanging Drawing Files

AutoCAD LT can read files directly from many other Autodesk software programs. For example, drawing files (.DWG extension) created using AutoCAD Release 12, 13, or 14 or AutoCAD LT Release 2, AutoCAD LT for Windows 95, and AutoCAD LT 97/98 can be read directly by AutoCAD LT 2000. A drawing file created in an older version of AutoCAD LT or AutoCAD is automatically converted to AutoCAD LT 2000 format when it is opened, but the original file does not change unless you save the file using the same name. Once a file has been converted and saved in the AutoCAD LT 2000 format, it can no longer be read by the older application.

Drawing files can be exchanged freely between AutoCAD 2000 and AutoCAD LT 2000. This means that if you open an AutoCAD 2000 drawing using AutoCAD LT and then save the drawing, it can still be opened and edited using AutoCAD 2000.

If you need to communicate back and forth with earlier software versions, you can use the SAVEAS command to save your drawings in a compatible format. The SAVEAS command can be typed at the Command: prompt or it can be selected from the File menu. When the Save Drawing As dialog box appears, select the desired drawing file format from the Save as type: drop-down list, as shown in Figure 15.9.

The OPEN command is used to open DWG files with AutoCAD LT, regardless of the software version with which they were created.

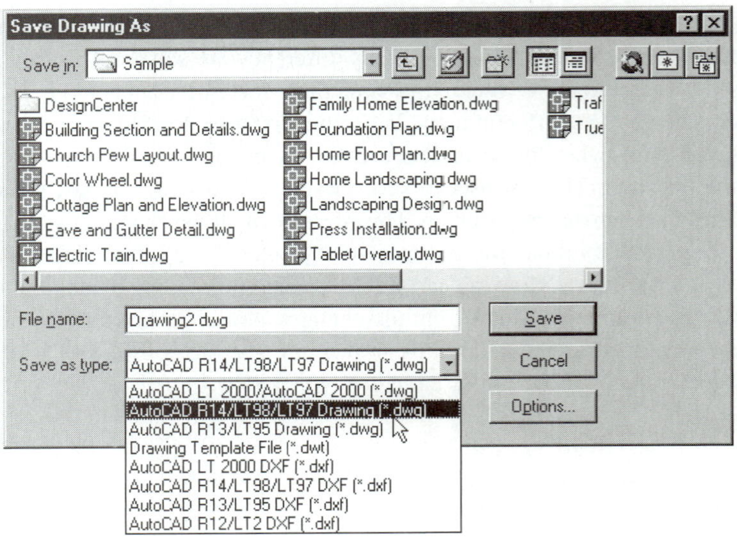

FIGURE 15.9 AutoCAD LT 2000 can save drawings in a format readable by earlier software versions by using the SAVEAS command.

Importing Drawing Interchange File Information

DXFIN
DN

The Drawing Interchange File (.DXF extension) is a proprietary file format created by Autodesk for exchanging drawing file information. Many applications can read DXF files and convert them to their own format. Most applications that can read a DXF file can also create DXF files.

DXF files are imported into AutoCAD LT by using the OPEN command. The OPEN command can be accessed by picking Open … from the File pull-down menu, and specifying DXF (*.DXF) in the Files of type drop-down list. You can also type **DN** or **DXFIN** at the Command: prompt. If you use the OPEN command, the Select File dialog box is displayed (see Figure 15.10). However, no preview is shown for a DXF file. The DXFIN command displays the Select DXF File dialog box. Using DXFIN displays the Select DXF file dialog box. Both dialog boxes are used the same way: Navigate to the appropriate directory, select the desired file, and pick the Open button.

When a DXF file is imported, two results are possible, depending on the state of the current drawing and how the DXF file was created. A DXF file can be created to store only the definition of selected objects or it can store all of the drawing information, as discussed further in the section on exporting DXF files. When only selected objects are stored in the DXF file, importing it results in the definition of those objects in the current drawing with no changes to the system variable settings. However, in AutoCAD LT 2000, DXF files can be imported only into a new, and blank, drawing file. An exception is DXF files that were created with AutoCAD Release 12 or earlier versions. These files can be imported into existing AutoCAD LT drawings. To access a DXF file created with R13 or R14, you must use the OPEN (or DXFIN) command in a new drawing file created using the Start from Scratch option.

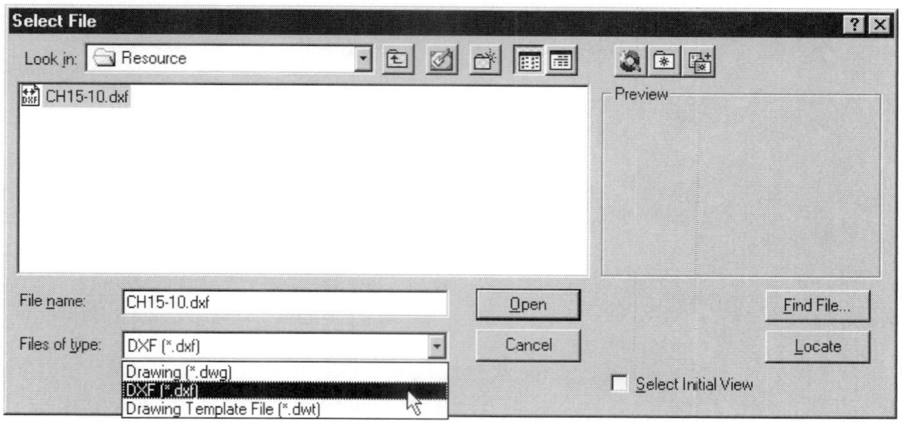

FIGURE 15.10 The Select File dialog box displayed by the Open command allows DXF files to be opened directly.

Creating DXF Files

DXFOUT
DX

Many applications can read DXF files, so this is a common format to use when transferring your AutoCAD LT drawings into another application. The DXFOUT command is used to create a DXF file. This command is accessed by typing **DX** or **DXFOUT** at the Command: prompt. The DXFOUT command displays the Save Drawing As dialog box (see Figure 15.11). Navigate to the desired directory and specify the desired file name. A DXF file uses the .DXF file extension.

Selecting the Options ... button displays the Save as Options dialog box, where you can specify the desired file format, the precision level, and what is to be written to the exported file. The Save as Options dialog box is shown in Figure 15.12.

If you want to want to select objects in your drawing to save in the DXF file, place a check mark in the Select Objects toggle. If this is not checked, the entire drawing file is exported to the DXF file.

The next step is to specify the accuracy level of the DXF file. The number of decimal places of accuracy should be set no higher than needed. The default of 6 is sufficient for most applications, but AutoCAD LT accepts values from 0 to 16. The number of decimal places you specify can significantly affect the final DXF file size. To demonstrate this, a sample drawing was saved as a DXF file using 3 decimal places and then using 16 decimal places. The 16-decimal-place version was 23% larger than the 3-decimal place version (1.7 MB versus 2.1 MB). Typical applications for this drawing would not apply accuracy beyond 3 decimal places, so a more accurate version is of no additional benefit. After you specify the number of decimal places, the DXF file is created and you are returned to the Command: prompt.

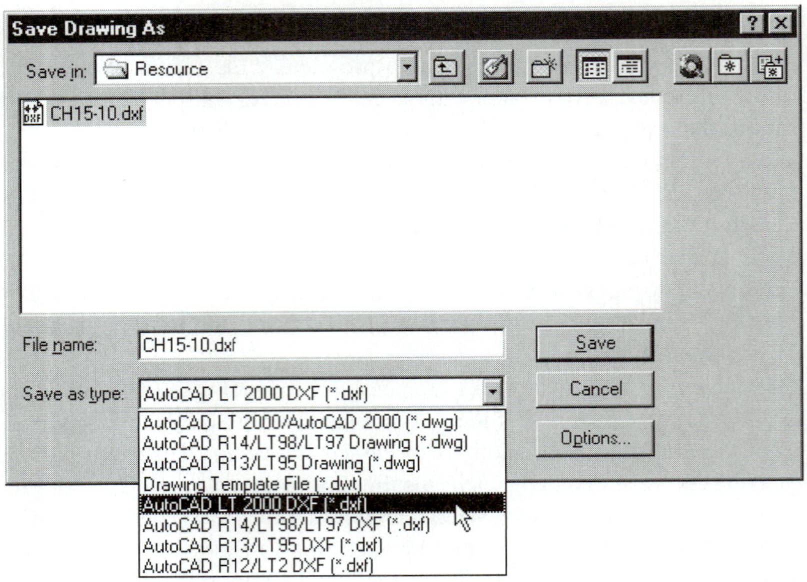

FIGURE 15.11 The Save Drawing As dialog box allows DXF files to be saved in formats compatible with either current or older AutoCAD releases.

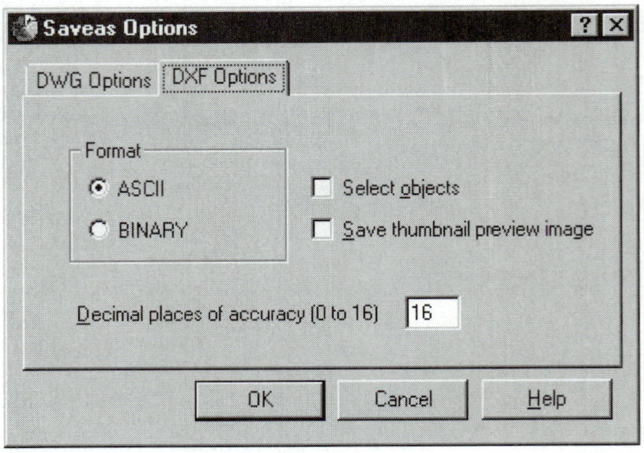

FIGURE 15.12 Use the Save as Options dialog box to specify format and precision level for the DXF file being created.

The default option for creating a DXF file generates an ASCII file. The term *ASCII* (pronounced "askee") stands for American Standard Code for Information Interchange and refers to alphabetical characters and numbers. The other possible file format is ***binary,*** in which information is stored as 1's and 0's. A binary DXF file can be significantly smaller than its ASCII equivalent and can be read faster. To create a binary DXF, pick the Binary option from the Format area of the Export Options dialog box.

Notice that the Binary option disables the accuracy level setting. This is because the binary option always uses the maximum accuracy level. Even so, using the binary option on the sample drawing results in a file size of 1.23 MB. When compared with the ASCII equivalent, which uses 16-decimal-place accuracy, the resulting binary file is just over half the size of the ASCII file. Therefore, in an application requiring the highest level of precision, a binary DXF file is smaller and, therefore, may be preferred.

Field Notes

DXF files are often much larger than the original DWG file and, therefore, should only be used when taking the drawing information to an application that cannot read DWG files. To provide a contrast, the DWG file for the sample drawing referenced in the previous examples was only 677K in size. The smallest DXF file was created by the binary option, which was still nearly double the size of the original drawing file.

Exercise 15.1 **Estimated time required: 5 min.**

1. Open a drawing, from a previous chapter, that contains drawing objects.
2. Create three DXF files as follows:
3. Create one from the whole drawing, using 3-decimal-place precision.
4. Create one by selecting all of the objects in the drawing, and specify 16-decimal-place precision.
5. Create the third using the binary option.
6. Open the Windows Explorer (or File Manager) and check the relative sizes of the three DXF files.
7. Start a new drawing.
8. Import the DXF file created in step 3.
9. Save the drawing as EX15.1

LEARNING CHECKPOINT

- ☐ When transferring drawing files between CAD systems, what is the best file format to use?
- ☐ Describe how DWG files can be shared between different versions of AutoCAD and AutoCAD LT.
- ☐ Explain each of the DXFIN and DXFOUT option settings.

Concept Animations

- Drawing Exchange Files (DXF)

Exchanging Bitmap Files

Bitmap files (.BMP extension) are the simplest sort of graphics files. A ***bitmap*** is a record of pixel colors that make up an image. This is the type of file used by non-object-oriented programs such as paintbrush-style applications. An image is recorded as a number of small rectangles arranged in rows and columns, with the color being listed for each. Bitmap files, by nature, produce a very coarse image in any application. Bitmaps are seldom used for detailed or accurate graphics applications. AutoCAD LT is an object-oriented program, and does not have a means to directly edit a bitmap image. AutoCAD LT does not directly import bitmap files, but the image displayed in the graphics screen area can be saved as a bitmap file.

The command used in AutoCAD LT to export a BMP file is the BMPOUT command. This command can be accessed by typing **BMPOUT** at the Command: prompt. AutoCAD LT creates what is called a *device-independent bitmap.* The file name has the extension .BMP. This type of file can be used by almost any Windows software that imports or exports graphics.

The screen determines the size and shape of the bounding box, and only the selected objects are included in the exported image. After specifying the name and location of the new BMP file, a Select objects: prompt is issued. Also, only the visible portions of the objects are saved in the exported file.

Field Notes

Many graphics files use what is termed as a bounding box. A bounding box defines the size of the area in which the image is contained. When a BMP file is created in AutoCAD LT, the bounding box is defined by the edges of the graphics screen area. This means that actual image size is the size of the graphics screen. Therefore, before creating a BMP file, it is often best to zoom in so the selected geometry fills the graphics area.

The graphics screen area not only defines the image size, it also defines the image shape. This means that you can resize the AutoCAD LT program window until the graphics screen area is the size and shape you want, then zoom the image to an appropriate size, to avoid padding your image with a lot of empty space.

Exercise 15.2 **Estimated time required: 5 min.**

1. Open a drawing of your choice.
2. Create a BMP file named EX15.2.BMP using all the objects visible on the screen.

Exporting PostScript Files

The EXPORT command allows EPS formats for exporting drawing data. EPS format is an *encapsulated PostScript* file. When the contents of your drawing are to be imported into an application such as a desktop publishing, presentation, or illustration program, this is often the best choice. The EPS format offers high-resolution print capability utilizing the same language that PostScript printers use. Rather than communicating pixel information, an EPS file communicates in an object-oriented manner. A PostScript file has descriptions for PostScript objects such as ***path objects,*** text that references PostScript fonts, and fill patterns. This allows PostScript printers to print at resolutions of 600 dpi and higher, for a crisp, clean print.

An EPS file is produced using the PSOUT command. The PSOUT command can be accessed by typing **PSOUT** at the Command: prompt. Use the file dialog box to specify the directory folder and file name. The name will use an .EPS file extension.

Because an EPS file is written in the PostScript printer language, the PSOUT command works much like plotting a drawing. Producing a PostScript file is considered *plotting to a file,* because the drawing information is the same as would be sent to the printer, but it is being stored in a file instead. PostScript is object oriented, and drawing data to be exported does not have to be visible on the screen. Like plotting, rather than select objects to export, you specify an area of the drawing, and objects or portions of objects that are outside of the area to export are not included.

Select the Options ... button to display the PostScript Out Options dialog box for PostScript output, as shown in Figure 15.13.

The first field is for specification of the prolog section name. This is for specialized printing needs and can be left blank for most applications. The What to plot area allows specification of what part of the drawing is to be included in the PostScript file. If you select Window ... and use the Pick option, a message appears indicating that you will be prompted for the window after all other specifications have been made.

The user-defined window exports all drawing information contained within the window. You may also choose to export the currently displayed area, the drawing extents, the preset limits, or even an area previously saved as a named view. Many graphics applications offer an option to preview graphics files just like

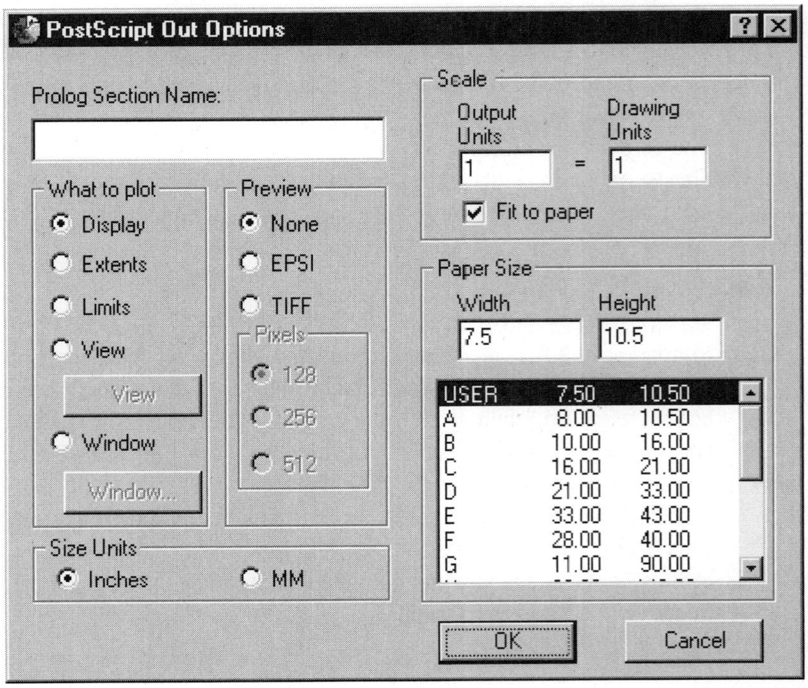

FIGURE 15.13 Exporting an .EPS file is very similar to using the PLOT command to plot to a file.

AutoCAD LT displays previews of drawing files. If the destination of the file is to be a printer, there is no need to increase the size of the file by including a preview image. A PostScript printer cannot use a file that has been given a TIFF preview. TIFF stands for tagged image file format, and is a widely used graphics file format. The TIFF format for image previews is used by applications such as Microsoft Word.

The size units and scale determine the size of the final image. If you need a specific scale, it should be entered appropriately. When a specific scale is not required, using the Fit to paper option ensures that the selected area will fit within the printed area.

Select the appropriate paper size to indicate the final output. When the final output is intended to fill an entire sheet, the appropriate sheet size can be specified. If the image you wish to generate does not match one of the listed options, you can enter a custom width and height. For example, to specify an area 6 units wide by 4 units high, enter these values in the Width and Height fields. Pick OK when you are finished, and the EPS file is created.

Plotting to a File

One of the options for producing a plot is plotting to a file. Instead of sending the output from the PLOT command directly to a printer or plotter, it is stored in a file. A plot file can be easily transported or stored for later use.

If you need to get a hardcopy of a drawing produced at home and wish to use a large-format plotter or high-resolution printer at work or school, a plot file can be more convenient to take than the actual drawing file. Plot files can be sent out to a plotting service, and many plot spoolers use plot files. A ***plot spooler*** is a piece of hardware or software that sends plot files to a plotting device. A spooler can be set up to run overnight or during weekends and holidays for unattended plotting.

There are two different ways to plot to a file using the PLOT command. The first is to plot to a PLT file. To create a PLT file, use the Plot dialog box, displayed by the PLOT command. On the Plot Device tab set the Plot to file ... toggle ON by placing a check in the box. Just below, the File name: and Location: are specified as shown in Figure 15.14.

A PLT file uses a .PLT file extension. All the other features of the Plot Configuration dialog box are used exactly in the same way as when you are plotting to a file. When you select OK, the plot information is written to disk and given the specified name.

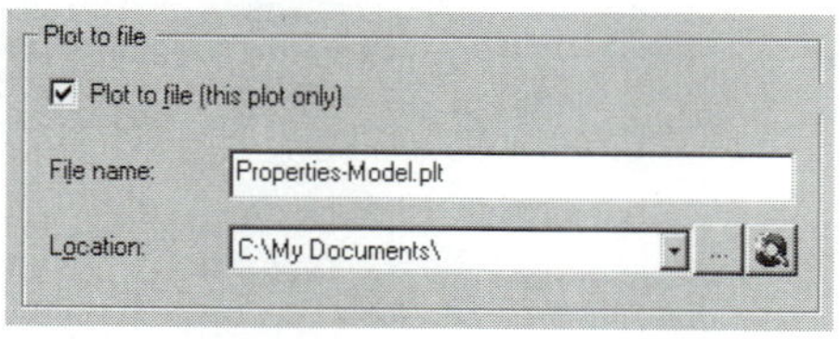

FIGURE 15.14 Pick check box, then specify the name and location of your plot file.

Exercise 15.3 — **Estimated time required: 8 min.**

1. Open a completed drawing from a previous chapter.
2. Plot to a file to produce a .PLT file of the current display.
3. Save the plot file as EX15.3.PLT.

LEARNING CHECKPOINT

- ☐ What file formats can AutoCAD LT exchange with other applications?
- ☐ What is meant by "plotting to a file"?
- ☐ In what ways can a PLT file be used? An EPS?

Using Object Linking and Embedding

Object Linking and Embedding, or OLE, is a feature of the Windows operating systems that allows information from different applications to be combined into a single document or drawing. OLE is often used to produce technical documents that combine descriptive text with technical drawings or illustrations. Most Windows applications support object linking and embedding. The term ***object application*** is used to describe the source application, and the destination is called the ***container application.*** The terms ***server application*** and ***client application*** are also used in some references to describe the source and destination.

The AutoCAD LT software provides powerful drafting tools, but like most drafting programs, it provides few tools for creating complex or artistic style graphic images. Additionally, AutoCAD LT does not handle large quantities of text as well as a word processor. OLE provides great flexibility, however, allowing you to share data created in two or more different applications.

The shared information is handled differently, depending on whether it has been linked or embedded. The difference between linking and embedding is much like the difference between the XREF and the INSERT commands in AutoCAD LT. Similar to the results of the INSERT command, the ***embedding*** of information makes a copy of the external information but maintains no further connection with the original data. Similar to external references made using XREF, a ***linked object*** is connected to the original data and is updated when the source file changes.

Embedding Objects in AutoCAD LT Drawings

When it is not necessary to maintain a link to a separate original data file, information can be embedded within a drawing. In the following example, a bitmap image is embedded into an AutoCAD LT drawing. The bitmap is a logo graphic designed in the Paint program, which is found in the Accessories group of Windows. This software is included with the Windows operating system. In this case, the object application is Paint, and the container application is AutoCAD LT. Figure 15.15A shows the Paint program being selected from the Accessories group on the Windows Start menu. In Figure 15.15B, a logo graphic has been designed.

The Windows Clipboard can be easily used to embed objects. After selecting the desired area of the graphic, press [Ctrl]+[C] or pick Copy from the Edit pull-down menu. The selected objects are copied to the Clipboard. Now they can be pasted into another application, such as AutoCAD LT.

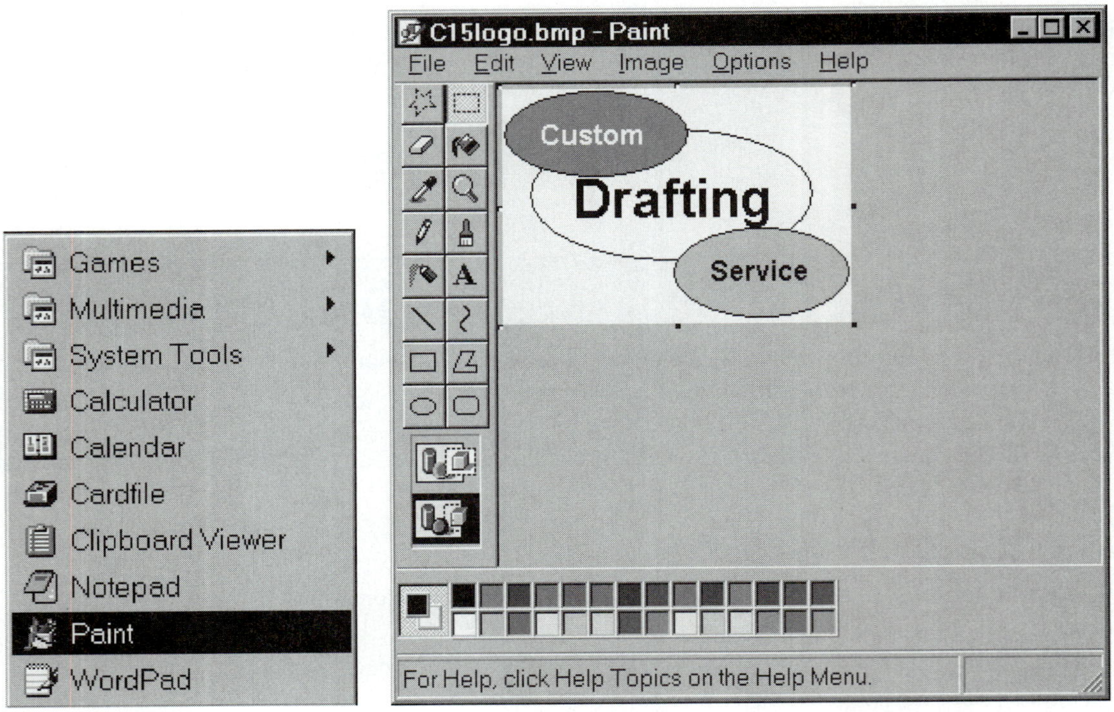

A B

FIGURE 15.15 (A) The Paint program is started from the Accessories group. (B) Bitmap editors can be used to make colorful graphic images.

The PASTECLIP command is used to paste the contents of the Clipboard into the current drawing. To access the PASTECLIP command, press Ctrl+V or pick Paste from the Edit pull-down menu. The contents of the Clipboard are placed in the upper left corner of the drawing area, and the OLE Properties dialog box is displayed (see Figure 15.16). The OLE Properties dialog box can be used to control the appearance of an OLE object placed in an AutoCAD LT drawing. The Size area of the OLE Properties dialog box is used to specify the object size in AutoCAD units, or the Scale area can be used to scale the object relative to its current display size. If the object contains text, any font definitions present in the OLE object are displayed in the list along with available point sizes. The third box at the far right of the Text size area sizes text in OLE objects based on AutoCAD units. Select an option from the OLE plot quality list that best describes the primary content type. Pick OK when you are finished.

The INSERTOBJ command can be used to embed an object, but PASTECLIP is faster and easier. If the INSERTOBJ command is used, the Link toggle should be turned off to embed an object. The Insert Object dialog box is detailed later in this chapter in the discussion on creating links.

Once it is embedded, a limited number of ways are available in which AutoCAD LT can edit an object, including deleting, repositioning, and resizing. To change the content of an embedded object, the source application must be used, but the very nature of an embedded object simplifies this process. An embedded object maintains no link to the original source data, but it does maintain an association with the source application. This means that when you need to edit the embedded object, the source application can be started automatically.

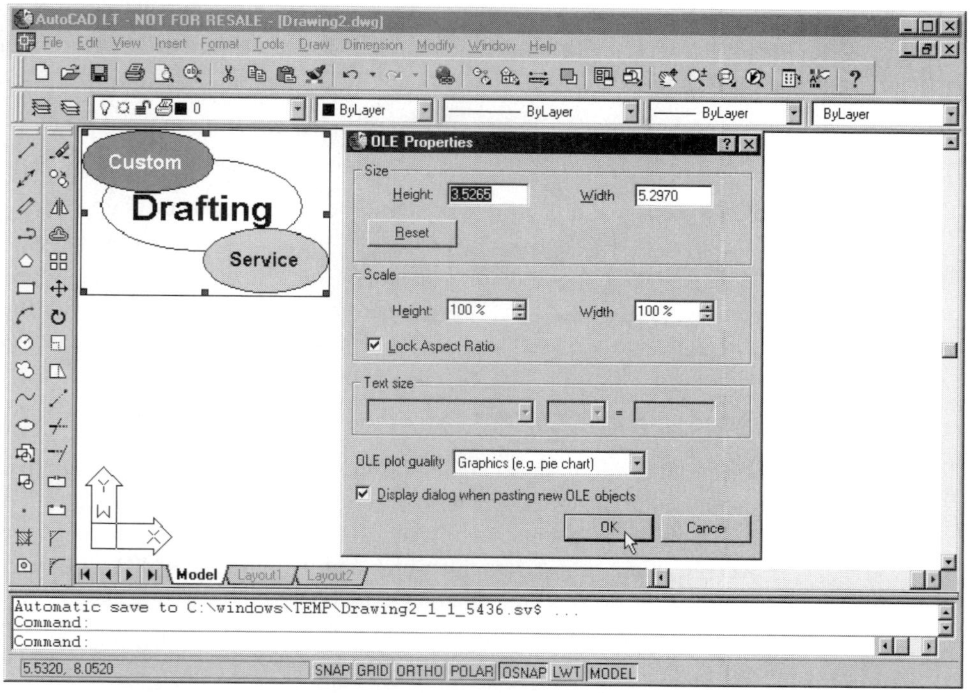

FIGURE 15.16 The embedded object is placed in the upper left corner of the drawing area by default, and the OLE Properties dialog box is displayed.

The grip selection technique is used to select an embedded object. At the Command: prompt, point to the object with the cursor and pick. When selected, the object shows a boundary line and eight squares around the border. The cursor changes to an appropriate system arrow, depending on what feature of the object you point to. Pointing within the image displays the move cursor. With this cursor visible, press and hold the pick button to drag the image to a new position. Pointing to the squares at the four corners displays the diagonal resize button. Press and hold the pick button to resize the object. The top, bottom, and side squares allow vertical and horizontal resizing. Figure 15.17 shows these features. To start the application associated with the object, double-click on it. The application is automatically started with the object already open for editing.

Another option is to display a cursor menu by right-clicking on the embedded object. This allows you to conveniently select from the available options. The options on this menu, shown in Figure 15.18, are as follows:

- **Cut** Copies the image to the clipboard and removes it from the drawing.
- **Copy** Copies the image to the clipboard.
- **Clear** Removes the image from the drawing.

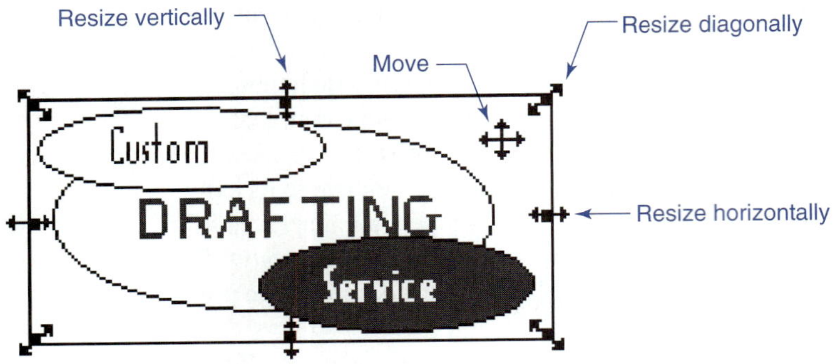

FIGURE 15.17 Embedded objects are resized and repositioned in a manner similar to that used for program windows.

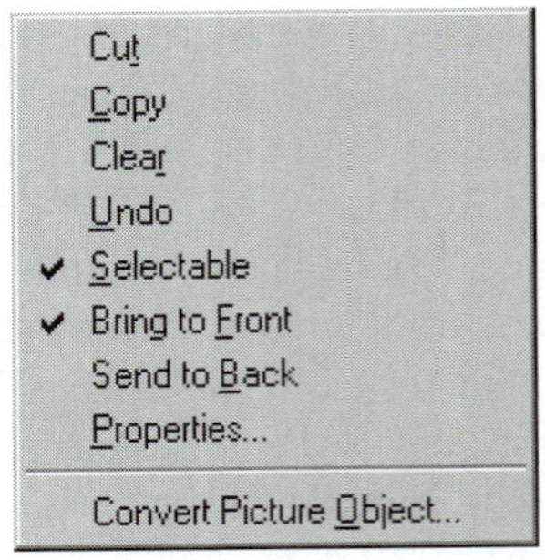

FIGURE 15.18 The OLE shortcut menu.

- **Undo** — The standard AutoCAD LT UNDO command has no effect on embedded objects. This allows you to undo the last actions performed on the image. Each image stores its own Undo record and the Undo option can be used repetitively, as with the AutoCAD LT UNDO command. All actions after the object was embedded can be undone. However, there is no Redo option.
- **Selectable** — Turns the object's frame on or off to control selection options.
- **Bring to Front** — Brings object to the front of the display.
- **Send to Back** — Sends the object to the back of the display.
- **Properties...** — Displays the OLE Properties dialog box.
- **Convert Picture Object...** — This option allows you to convert the object from an embedded OLE object to an AutoCAD LT object. For example, with a Paint image, the Convert dialog box offers you the option of converting a file to a device-independent bitmap. Doing this removes all OLE associations.

Embedding AutoCAD LT Drawings in Other Applications

As with embedding objects in AutoCAD LT drawings, the primary advantage over importing is that the object maintains an association with the source application. This makes it easy to edit the object at a later time. The simplest way to embed an AutoCAD LT drawing in another application is to use the Clipboard. In AutoCAD LT, select the objects to embed, and then use the COPYCLIP command by pressing [Ctrl]+[C]. The AutoCAD LT objects are copied to the Clipboard.

In the destination application, use the PASTE option to embed the AutoCAD LT drawing. In most Windows applications, this is done by pressing [Ctrl]+[V] or by picking Paste from the Edit pull-down menu. Once it is embedded, the object can be edited in AutoCAD LT by double-clicking on it. Because no connection is maintained to the original source file, if there is one, editing the object has no effect on the source data.

Field Notes

When AutoCAD LT is used as an object application, the current display size and shape control the appearance of the image brought into the container application. If a selected object is only partially visible, this is how it is displayed in the OLE object. Additionally, all of the empty space around the selected objects is also displayed in the OLE object.

For the best final image quality, use the program window resizing options to shape the drawing area as desired and zoom so that the objects to be selected fill the drawing area.

One very common application for embedding AutoCAD LT drawings is placing them within a technical document created in a word processor. Figure 15.19 shows an AutoCAD LT drawing embedded in a WordPad document.

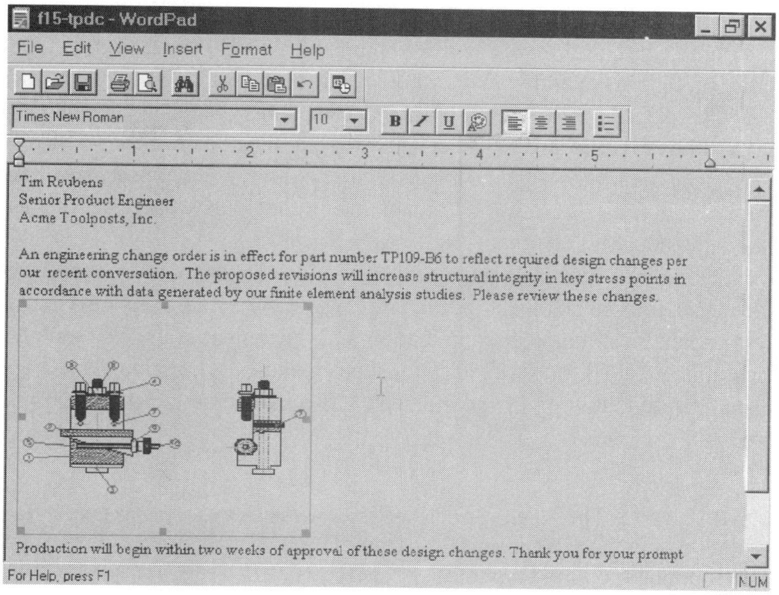

FIGURE 15.19 Embedding drawings within a word processor document is a common use of OLE.

Linking Objects in AutoCAD LT Drawings Using the Clipboard

When it is necessary to maintain a continued relationship between the object and the original source data file, a link can be established. The link can only be made to a file, so the data must first be saved to a file on disk. Linking is most useful when more than one document uses the same information, and that information may change in the future. Each time a container application opens a document with links, the original object data file is read to get the latest version of the data. This means that when the information changes, editing the source data file automatically updates all documents and applications that are linked to that file.

It is not a common practice to link word processing documents in drawings. However, other types of data, such as spreadsheets and graphic images can be very useful in an AutoCAD LT drawing. Spreadsheet applications, such as Microsoft Excel, are powerful tools for managing table data. In Figure 15.20, a dimension table has been created that specifies the dimensional values for different configurations of the same design. After saving the file to disk, it can be linked within an AutoCAD LT drawing.

Each piece of information in a spreadsheet is stored in a box called a *cell*. Using the standard features of the spreadsheet, the desired cells can be selected and the information can be copied to the clipboard by pressing [Ctrl]+[C]. After switching to AutoCAD LT, the link can be established by using the PASTESPEC command. PASTESPEC is an abbreviation for Paste Special, and allows objects to be either embedded or linked. The PASTESPEC command is accessed by selecting Paste Special ... from the Edit pull-down menu.

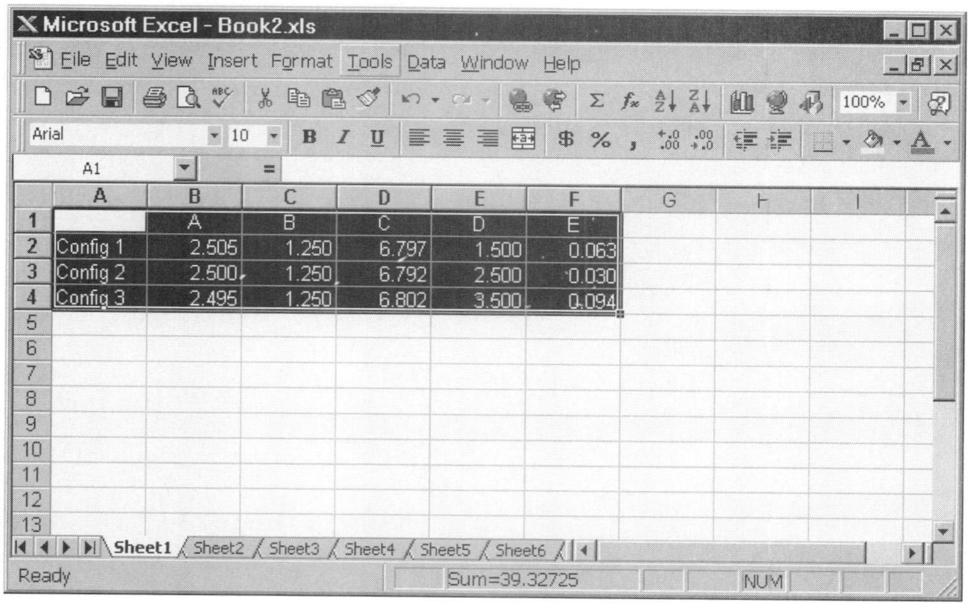

FIGURE 15.20 Table data is easily managed within spreadsheet programs.

The options in the Paste Special dialog box vary depending on the source of the information currently held in the Clipboard. Because the contents of the Clipboard are from Excel, the options in the Paste Special dialog box in this example are as shown in Figure 15.21.

The default option in the Paste Special dialog box is to embed the object into the drawing. To ensure that a link is established, the Paste Link toggle must be checked as shown in Figure 15.22.

Once the linked object is placed into the drawing, it appears just like an embedded object does. The difference is that a connection is kept between the source data and the OLE object. Figure 15.23 shows the linked spreadsheet cells in an AutoCAD LT drawing.

Now that a link has been established, any changes made in the source spreadsheet data are immediately reflected in the linked object. For example, in Figure 15.24, a change has been made to one cell in the spreadsheet. When both the object application and the container application are active at the same time, linked object status is polled, or checked every few seconds, to determine if changes have been made. Within a matter of seconds, the drawing file is updated to match the changes made in the spreadsheet.

FIGURE 15.21 The Paste Special dialog box offers different options depending on the source of the Clipboard data.

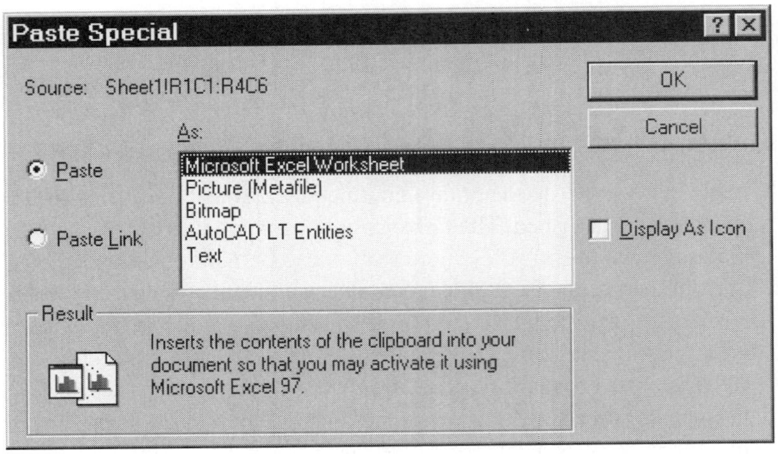

FIGURE 15.22 Selecting Paste Link allows a link to be established to the source data file.

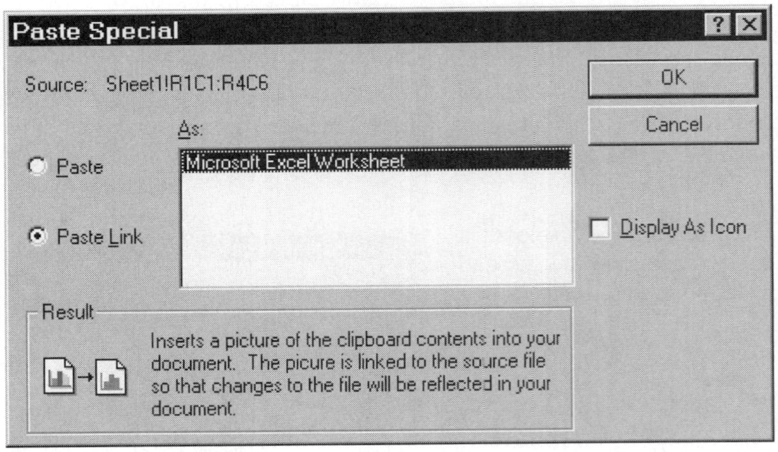

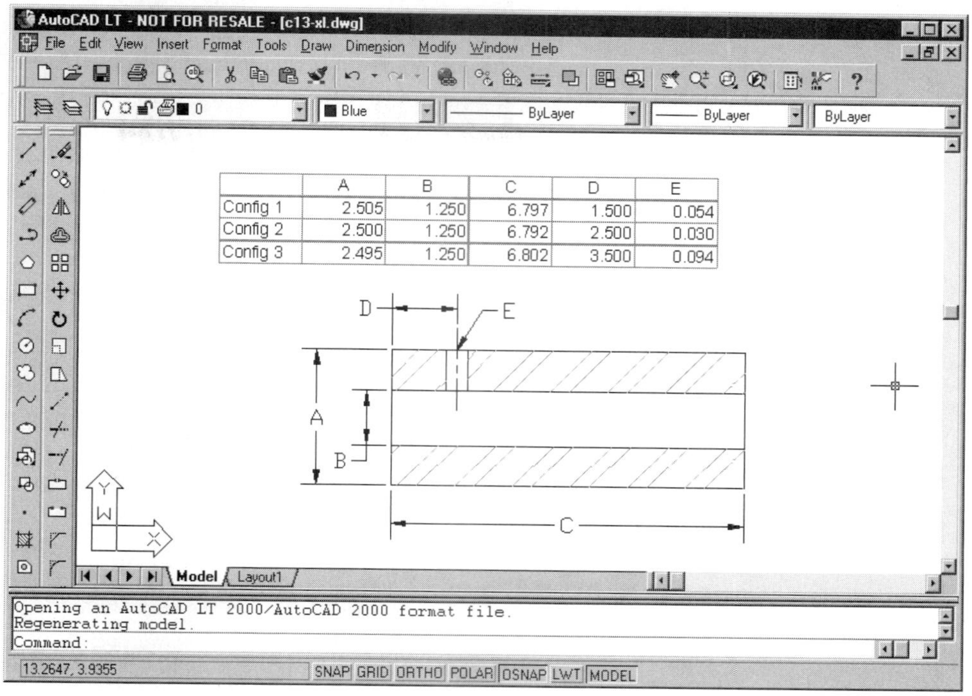

FIGURE 15.23 Linked and embedded objects appear the same but are much different functionally.

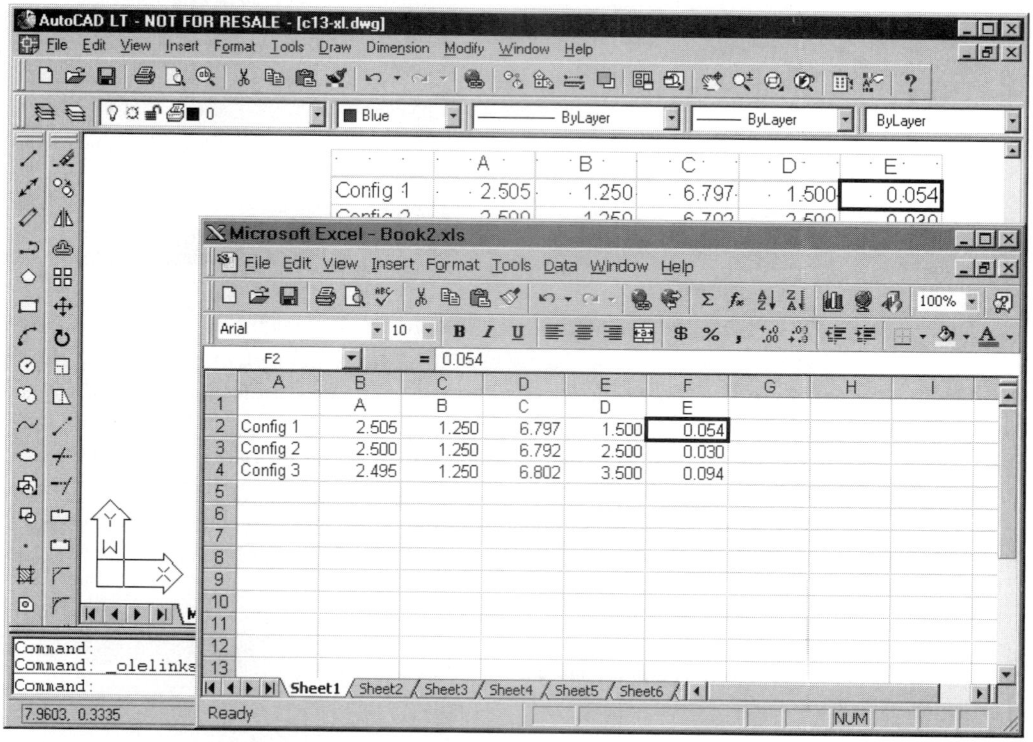

FIGURE 15.24 The changes made in the object application are reflected in the container application.

Field Notes

Links require that a file exists to link to. If the data copied to the Clipboard have not yet been saved as a file, the Paste Link ... option in the Paste Special dialog box is not enabled. To correct this, save the file in the source application and again copy the data to the Clipboard.

Linking Objects in AutoCAD LT Drawings Using Data Files

When the data you need to link do not yet exist or exist in a file but the object application is not open, then the Clipboard cannot be used to transfer the data using PASTESPEC. Instead, the INSERTOBJ command is used to insert a new or existing object into the drawing. The INSERTOBJ command is accessed by picking OLE Object ... from the Insert pull-down menu or by typing **INSERTOBJ** at the Command: prompt.

The INSERTOBJ command displays the Insert Object dialog box, as shown in Figure 15.25. By default, the selected option is Create New, which is used to start the appropriate source application in order to generate the OLE object. The options displayed in the Object Type list box show the applications and object types currently registered on your system. Most software ***registers*** the type of files that it uses during the installation process. The listing that appears in the Object Type list box depends on the software and system drivers currently installed on your computer.

In Figure 15.25, the Paintbrush Picture option is highlighted. Selecting this option starts the Paintbrush program with a temporary file listed as "Paintbrush Picture in *drawingname* drawing." Because this is a temporary file, and no longer exists after exiting the Paintbrush program, there is no option to link to this object. The Create New option can, therefore, only be used to create embedded objects; it cannot be used to establish a link.

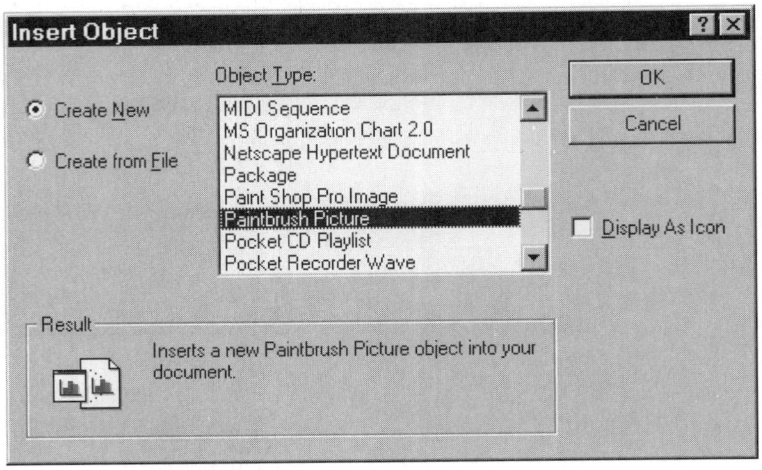

FIGURE 15.25 The Insert Object dialog box with the Create New toggle checked.

Selecting the Create from File option changes the layout of the Insert Object dialog box, as shown in Figure 15.26. This can also be used to embed an object, or the Link toggle can be checked to establish a link to the original data file. If you know the directory folder location and file name, it can be typed in the File: text box. To find a file, use the Browse ... button to display the Browse File dialog box.

Any type of file that is a registered object type can be linked using INSERTOBJ. If the contents of the file can be displayed, such as text or a graphic image, a picture of the file is displayed appropriately in the drawing. Some objects, such as multimedia sound recordings, can be linked or embedded, but cannot be displayed. In this case, the icon representing the object application is displayed instead.

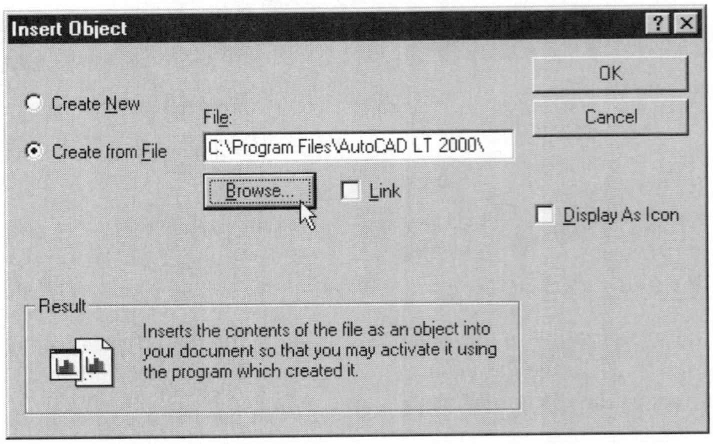

FIGURE 15.26 When creating an object from a file, a link can be established.

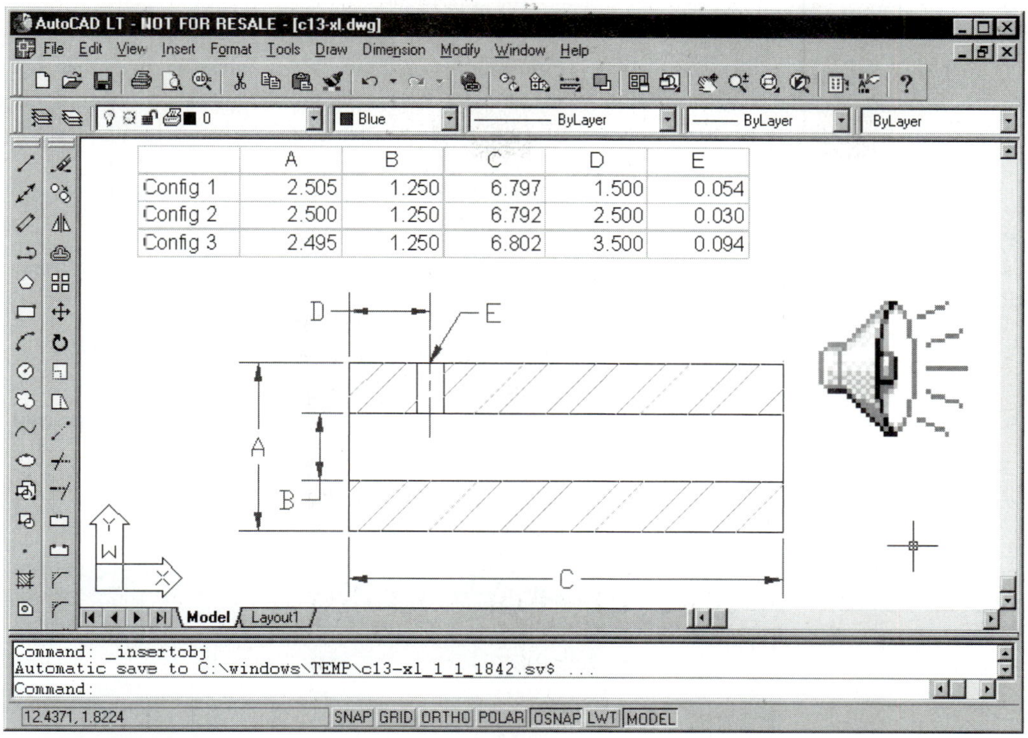

FIGURE 15.27 An embedded sound file is displayed as an icon within the drawing.

Multimedia features are becoming more widely used to enhance drawings now that most computer systems are sold as multimedia capable. If your system has a sound card, you can record and play sounds. Voice messages can be used to help clarify information in a drawing. Figure 15.27 shows a drawing with a sound file placed within it. Double-clicking on the icon causes the object application to start and the sound file to play.

Field Notes

When using sound files in a drawing, the file size can be significantly increased. To keep drawing size manageable, keep voice messages short and to the point. Additionally, your sound recording software provides settings to control sound quality. A sound that is recorded using a CD Quality setting will result in a much larger file than the same recording using the Telephone Quality setting.

Also, sound files are unlikely to be used in multiple locations requiring synchronized updates. It is usually unnecessary to maintain a link with a sound file in a drawing.

Linking AutoCAD LT Drawings in Other Applications

The COPYLINK command is accessed by picking Copy Link from the Edit pull-down menu. This option is available in an unnamed drawing, however a link can only be established once a file has been saved. This command copies the current view to the clipboard, with all visible objects selected. To place this in another application, use the Paste Special ... option on the Edit pull-down menu, or whatever method is normally used to establish a link in the software you are using. When the drawing object in the container application is double-clicked, AutoCAD LT is started and the drawing object is loaded automatically.

Managing Links in AutoCAD LT

Once a link has been established, it may occasionally require maintenance in special circumstances. If a link is disconnected because the original file was relocated or renamed, it must be updated and reconnected. Or, if a link is no longer necessary, it can be broken. The Links dialog box is displayed by the OLELINKS command, which is accessed by picking OLE Links ... from the Edit pull-down menu.

All links associated with this drawing are displayed in the Links: list box. Picking a link enables the option buttons, shown in Figure 15.28, and described as follows:

- **Update Now** This reads the file and updates the linked object according to the current information.
- **Open Source** Opens the source file using the object application.
- **Change Source ...** Allows the link to be changed to reference a new file. This option is also used when the source file has been relocated or renamed.
- **Break Link** Removes link information from an OLE object, converting it to an embedded object.

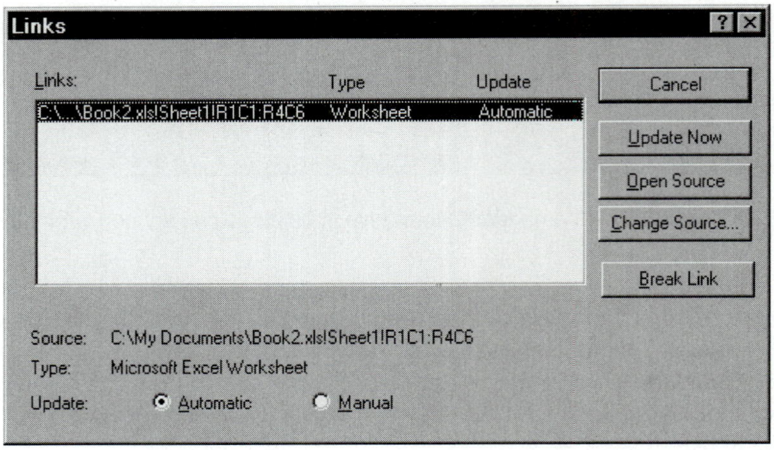

FIGURE 15.28 Selecting a link enables the option buttons.

Field Notes

OLE objects cannot be plotted using non-Windows drivers. This includes plotting devices that utilize HPGL, HPGL/2, PCX, GIF, TIFF, and BMP plot data formats. If your printer or plotter is set as the system printer by Windows, and you are configured to plot to the system printer, then OLE objects are also plotted.

Exercise 15.4 **Estimated time required: 20 min.**

1. Using the Paintbrush program, create a simple graphic and name it EX15.4.BMP.
2. Start a new AutoCAD LT drawing from scratch.
3. Use the INSERTOBJ command with Create from File specified, and do not check the Link: option.
4. Use the Browse dialog box to find the file named EX15.4.BMP.
5. After the object has been embedded, use the cursor to resize and reposition the object.
6. Double-click on the object to start the Paintbrush program. Edit the object, save it, and exit Paintbrush.
7. Save the drawing as EX15.4E.
8. Open Paintbrush and create a simple graphic. Save it to a file named EX15.4L.BMP and copy the image to the Clipboard.
9. Use the PASTESPEC command to insert the object with a link to the original file.
10. Arrange your desktop so that both Paintbrush and AutoCAD LT are visible.
11. Edit the paintbrush image and observe the automatic updates.
12. Save the drawing file as EX15.4L.
13. Start the WordPad program to create a simple word processor document.
14. Start a new drawing from scratch in AutoCAD LT.
15. Create a simple drawing in AutoCAD LT and save it as EX15.4O.
16. In AutoCAD LT, use the COPYLINK command.
17. From WordPad, use Paste Special … option from the Edit pull-down menu to paste the AutoCAD LT drawing link.
18. Save the WordPad file as EX15.4.

☑ LEARNING CHECKPOINT

- ☐ How can OLE be used with AutoCAD LT for technical documentation?
- ☐ What is the difference between linking and embedding?
- ☐ What are some other useful applications for OLE?

Sharing Data and Drawing Files

- Importing Data Using OLE Applications

Concept Animations

- OLE: Object Linking and Embedding

Working with Slide Files

In AutoCAD LT, a ***slide*** is a "picture" of a drawing. This is a special type of file that records the current drawing display so it can be viewed later. Slide files (.SLD extension) contain no geometry and cannot be edited. Slide files have different applications, from drawing management to presentation portfolios. In drawing management applications, slides can be used to create and view full-screen previews of drawings. Viewing a slide file is much faster than opening a drawing file. Slide files can be used to create a portfolio to show to prospective employers. Slide files are much smaller than the original drawing files. Where 20 or 30 large drawings might not fit on a diskette, the same number of slides fits very easily on a single diskette.

To make a slide file, use the MSLIDE command. The MSLIDE command is accessed by typing **MSLIDE** at the Command: prompt. Use the Create Slide File dialog box, shown in Figure 15.29, to specify the name and location of the slide file.

To view a slide file, the VSLIDE command is used. Access the VSLIDE command by typing **VS** or **VSLIDE** at the Command: prompt. Use the Select Slide File dialog box, shown in Figure 15.30, to select the slide file.

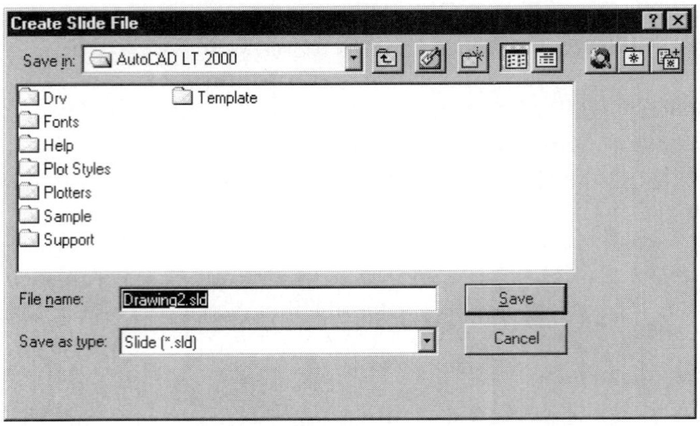

FIGURE 15.29 The Create Slide File dialog box.

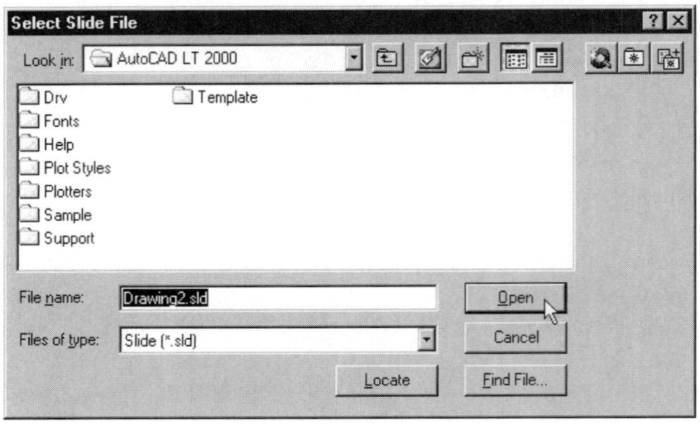

FIGURE 15.30 The Select Slide File dialog box.

You can view a slide at any time, even while you are editing a drawing. Viewing a slide replaces the current display with the contents of the slide file, but does not actually affect the geometry in your drawing. To remove the slide from your display and restore the view of the current drawing, use the REDRAW command.

Exercise 15.5 **Estimated time required: 5 min.**

1. Open a drawing from a previous problem or exercise.
2. Create a slide file named EX15.5 using MSLIDE.
3. Open a different drawing file.
4. View the EX15.5 slide file using VSLIDE.
5. Use the REDRAW command to remove the slide.

Creating a Slide Library

Slide files that are used in a group, such as for a portfolio demonstration or other purposes, are easier to manage if they are combined into a single slide library file. A slide library is a special type of tile that stores any number of individual slide files in it. This allows you to work with a single file even when your particular application requires a large number of slides.

To create a slide library, you must first create the individual slides that you want to incorporate into the library. This is done using the MSLIDE command as discussed earlier. Next, use Notepad to create a text file listing of the name of each slide file you intend to use, placing only one slide name on each line. Save this file, using any desired name, in the same directory location as the slide files.

Now, you need to use the SLIDELIB command at the OS prompt. The *OS prompt* refers to the MS DOS prompt available by opening an MS DOS window by picking MS DOS Prompt from the Start menu.

Once at the MS DOS prompt, navigate to the directory where the slide files are that you want to put into the library file. Ask your instructor or system administrator or consult the appropriate documentation if you need assistance. From within the directory location where the slide files are located, you need to access the SLIDELIB.EXE file found in the AutoCAD LT folder. This is done by typing the following at the OS prompt:

"C:\Program Files\AutoCAD LT 2000\SLIDELIB" ***LibraryName*** **<** ***SlideListFileName***

If your installation of AutoCAD LT is on a different drive letter or in a different directory folder name, change the drive and path name to match. The *LibraryName* is the file name you want to assign to the new slide library. Used in this manner at the OS prompt, the less than symbol is called a *redirection* symbol. The *SlideList-FileName* entry refers to the name and file extension you assigned to the list of slides created in Notepad.

To put this into effect, the following example creates a slide library file named LIB001. The slide list file name in this example is SLDLIST.TXT.

"C:\Program Files\AutoCAD LT 2000\SLIDELIB" LIB001 < SLDLIST.TXT

This creates a file named LIB001.SLB. If any errors are reported, no slide library is created and you must correct the error and try again. The most common error encountered is an improperly spelled slide file name or a nonexistent file.

Viewing slides from a slide library is somewhat different than using a standard slide file. For example, to view a slide named SLIDE01 that is in the LIB001 slide library, a slide name is entered as:

LIB001(SLIDE01)

The slide library name is entered first, followed by the slide name in parentheses. There are no spaces in this entry.

Field Notes

Slides that are in slide libraries cannot be viewed using the Select Slide File dialog box displayed by the VSLIDE command. The entry is only accepted at the command line, so prior to using VSLIDE, the system variable CMDDIA must be set to 0. This is only true when viewing the slides manually; most standard applications for slide files are not affected by the CMDDIA setting. Remember to set CMDDIA back to 1 before continuing with other tasks.

If, at a later time, you wish to add, remove or change a slide from the library, you cannot do so. Instead, the slide library must be recreated. Therefore, it is advisable to keep the slides and the slide list on file for such a need.

Exercise 15.6

Estimated time required: 20 min.

1. Create four different slide files. Name them SLIDE01 through SLIDE04.
2. Using Notepad, create a text file that lists the names of each of the slides, one name per line, and save it in the directory that holds the slide files.
3. Open a DOS window and go to the directory folder that holds the slides.
4. Use the SLIDELIB command to create a slide library named EX15.6.SLB.
5. Close the DOS window and return to AutoCAD LT.
6. Turn CMDDIA off by setting it to 0, and view each of the slides in the slide library.
7. Turn CMDDIA back on.

MULTIPLE CHOICE

Circle the choice or enter your response on an answer sheet by selecting the option that most closely completes or answers the given statement.

1. What is the name of the command that allows you to remove unreferenced data from a drawing?
   a. REDUCE **c.** COMPRESS
   b. PURGE **d.** REMOVE
2. This feature of the Windows operating system allows information from different applications to be combined into a single document or drawings:
   a. cut and paste **c.** object linking and embedding
   b. multitasking **d.** external references
3. In OLE, this term describes the source application:
   a. source document **c.** container application
   b. object application **d.** clipboard
4. The destination application, in OLE, is called the:
   a. destination document **c.** container application
   b. object application **d.** clipboard
5. To create a link to external data as it is brought into AutoCAD LT, this command is used:
   a. PASTESPEC **c.** LINKOBJ
   b. PASTELINK **d.** NEWLINK
6. This command is used to manage links in an AutoCAD LT drawing:
   a. LINKEDIT **c.** OLELINKS
   b. LINKS **d.** EDITLINK

MATCHING

Match each term to the correct description by writing the appropriate number in each box at the left.

☐	PURGE	**1.**	Command to output a drawing in an alternate file format or for use with a different software version.
☐	DXF	**2.**	Drawing Interchange File extension.
☐	Object application	**3.**	Command to review or modify drawing file properties.
☐	PSOUT	**4.**	This command lets you manage linked objects in a drawing.
☐	Slide	**5.**	This command is used to repair damaged drawing files.
☐	BMPOUT	**6.**	Storage place for cut data.
☐	RECOVER	**7.**	Removes unreferenced data from a drawing.
☐	Link	**8.**	A connection to the object application.
☐	OLELINKS	**9.**	The source application for an OLE object.
☐	Clipboard	**10.**	A "picture" of a drawing file.
☐	DWGPROPS	**11.**	Creates a PostScript output file.
☐	SAVEAS	**12.**	Creates a bitmap (.BMP) file.

WORD SCRAMBLE

Unscramble the six scrambled words below, one letter to each square, to form six AutoCAD LT–related words:

RUGEP

PORPSTICTS

ANINORECT

LEDIS

BOETJC

PIMTAB

Unscramble the circled letters above to form the special answer, as suggested by the illustration.

PROJECTS

15.1 Open a project drawing file from Chapter 13. Use the PURGE command as many times as necessary to remove all unreferenced data from the file. Save the drawing as P15.1.

15.2 Open P15.1 for editing. Create a DXF file named P15.2.DXF.

15.3 Start a new drawing using the Start from Scratch option. Import the file P15.2.DXF. Save the drawing as P15.3.

15.4 Start a new drawing using the Start from Scratch option. Draw an object such as a line or a circle. Import the file P15.2.DXF. Note the message on the command line. Save the drawing as P15.4.

15.5 Open P15.1 for editing. Using the Plot to File option, create the following Plot file: P15.5.PLT.

15.6 Open a word processing application such as WordPad, Write, or Word. Write a paragraph describing the drawing file P15.1, and embed the drawing in the document with no links. Save the document as P15.6.

15.7 Open a word processing application such as WordPad, Write, or Word. Write a paragraph describing the drawing file P15.1, and embed the drawing in the document with a link to the original file. Save the document as P15.7.

15.8 Use the Paint Brush program to create a small bitmap image. Select and copy the image. Start a new drawing in AutoCAD LT and paste the image in with no links. Save the drawing as P15.8.

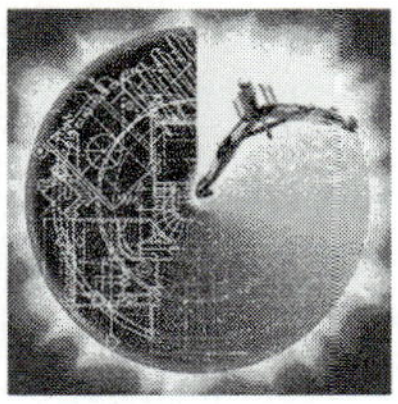

CHAPTER 16

AutoCAD LT and the Internet

LEARNING GOALS

- Identify Internet-related terminology.
- Utilize the WWW to access drawing content, files, and valuable resources.
- Attach hyperlinks to drawing objects.
- Use hyperlinks to open drawings, documents, or URLs.
- Create electronic plot files for viewing with a Web browser.
- Publish Drawing Web Format files in a Web page to share drawing data.

New technologies are rapidly changing the way things are done in industry. One of the most influential technologies in today's design industry is the Internet. The ***Internet*** is a worldwide network of computers connected to one another through telecommunication lines. One of the more popular uses of the Internet is for fast and convenient communications through the medium of e-mail. ***E-mail***, or electronic mail, uses the Internet to transmit messages and computer files anywhere in the world in a matter of minutes.

The ***World Wide Web*** is probably the most widely known application of Internet technologies. The World Wide Web, or WWW, provides an easy-to-understand interface for the Internet. You may also see the WWW referred to as W3, or just the Web. This powerful medium uses HyperText Markup Language (HTML) files to present information. When viewed with a piece of software known as a Web browser, HTML files provide a graphical user interface (GUI) to the Internet, similar to the way that the Windows operating system simplifies complex computer processes using buttons, icons, and menus. The term ***HyperText*** describes text items that are *linked* to other resources, but links are often attached to images, icons, and menus as well. Items in HTML documents that are *linked* to other Web resources are called ***hyperlinks***.

Web technologies are now widely used in the design industry. Because this industry is driven by information, the Web is a perfect medium for presenting and accessing information quickly and easily. AutoCAD LT 2000 provides a powerful tool set for incorporating Web-based technologies into your design process. Using these tools, you can share your drawings with anyone, anywhere in the world. AutoCAD LT 2000 can plot drawing files electronically so they can be viewed using just a Web browser. This means that clients or coworkers can now view your AutoCAD LT drawings in an electronic format even if they do not have AutoCAD or AutoCAD LT software.

This chapter covers the AutoCAD LT 2000 Internet-related tools and how to integrate Internet- and Web-based technologies into your design process. Maximum benefit from this chapter will require Internet access and a Web browser.

The Internet Connection

Conceived in 1969 by the Advanced Research Projects Agency of the U.S. government, the Internet began as a network consisting of four computers. Today, the Internet is a publicly accessible communications system that consists of literally millions of computers worldwide that are interconnected through the use of existing public telecommunications networks—in other words, standard telephone lines.

Many large companies, schools, and governmental agencies use a high-speed connection to the Internet known as the *T-Carrier* digital transmission system. The two types of T-Carrier connections commonly used are referred to as T-1 and T-3 lines, with T-3 being much faster than T-1. Another common means of accessing the Internet is through the use of a modem and a standard telephone line. A ***modem*** is a translation device that allows a computer to transmit and receive digital information through telephone lines. A modem modulates, or converts, digital computer data into sounds. The sounds are transmitted through your telephone lines to another modem that then demodulates the sound back into digital computer information.

If you are using a computer at work or school, ask your instructor or system administrator how to gain access to the Internet. If you are working at home or in a company not yet connected to the Internet, a telephone line and a modem may be a workable solution.

When selecting a modem, speed is the primary concern. Web pages consist not only of text but also graphic images, sounds, and many other large data files. All these files must be sent to your computer through your modem, and a slower modem means more time spent waiting for files to be downloaded to your system. The term ***download*** refers to the process of receiving files from a remote site through your modem or network connection. As a rule, you should not consider anything less than a 28.8-Kbps modem. A 56-Kbps (*kilobits per second*) modem is a better option for a standard telephone line connection.

For faster transmission speeds at an affordable rate for home and small businesses, you may wish to consider an ISDN line. Offering transmission speeds of up to 128 Kbps, the Integrated Services Digital Network requires an ISDN adapter rather than a modem. Not yet available in all areas, an ISDN connection requires installation of a special ISDN line and is subject to an installation charge and monthly fee. This cost can quickly be recovered in reduced wait times when accessing Web resources or transmitting and receiving large data files.

Another option for Internet access is called a Digital Subscriber Line, or DSL. A DSL system also communicates through your telephone line, but the signal is not converted to analog first. This system sends digital signals across your telephone line using a splitter that allows digital and analog communication at the same time—meaning that you use your computer and your telephone on the same line at the same time. Some DSL systems provide data transmission speeds of up to 6.1 Mbps (*megabits per second*) or higher, but the typical speed offered by most providers is 1.544 Mbps, which is the same speed as a T-1 carrier.

Table 16.1 shows the most common carrier technologies used for Internet access, with speeds and typical applications listed.

TABLE 16.1

Carrier Technology	Speed	Medium	Typical Application
Modem with regular telephone service	56 Kbps	Standard telephone line	Home and small business
ISDN (basic rate interface)	128 Kbps	Standard telephone line	Home and small business needing higher speeds
ISDN (primary rate interface)	1.544 Mbps 2048 Mbps	T-1 Line E1 Line	Medium-sized and large enterprise access
T-1	1.544 Mbps	Standard telephone line, coaxial cable, or optical fiber	Large company to ISP, and ISP to Internet infrastructure
DSL	512 Kbps to 8 Mbps	Standard telephone line	Home and small business
Cable modem	512 Kbps to 10 Mbps	Coaxial cable	Home, business, and school access
T-3	44.736 Mbps	Coaxial cable	ISP to Internet infrastructure

Once you have decided on a means for connecting your computer system to the Internet, you will need to contact an Internet Service Provider, or ISP. You can select an ISP from your phone book, but it is usually the best idea to ask for a recommendation from a friend or associate who already has Internet access. Another option is an on-line service provider such as America On-Line®, which also provides Internet access. Most ISPs will provide you with the required software and instructions for accessing the Internet and the Web. Additionally, your ISP typically provides you with e-mail access and assigns a personal e-mail address.

Included with your Windows operating system is an Internet browser package called Internet Explorer. A popular alternative is the Netscape Communicator software, which is a powerful and versatile Web browser package. This browser software can be purchased at a local software store or downloaded from the Netscape Web site at no charge. Additionally, you can download an evaluation version of Netscape to try it before you decide to purchase it. Whatever your browser software choice is, be certain that it is the latest version available and that it is Java-enabled.

Field Notes

- The information in Table 16.1 was adapted from information provided courtesy of www.Whatis.com. This Web site currently contains more than 2000 definitions of acronyms and terms associated with the ever-changing world of computers and the Internet. This site is a highly recommended resource for all students and professionals working in computer-related industries.
- AutoCAD LT 2000 requires Microsoft Internet Explorer 4.0 or later, or Netscape Navigator 4.0 or later to use the AutoCAD LT Internet feature.

Accessing Web Resources

Your Web browser can be launched from within AutoCAD LT 2000 by selecting any of the options from the Autodesk on the Web cascade on the Help menu or by picking the Browse the Web button from the Web toolbar. The options on the *Autodesk on the Web cascade* access Web locations that provide AutoCAD LT–related resources that were discussed in Chapter 1. Picking the Browse the Web button from the Web toolbar, like picking the AutoCAD LT Home Page option from the Autodesk on the Web cascade, displays the AutoCAD LT 2000 home page on the Autodesk Web site. This is the initial default URL. A ***URL*** (uniform resource locator) is the term that describes the location, or *address*, of a file found on the Internet. Alternatively, you can enter the BROWSER command directly at the Command: prompt. When you enter the command this way, AutoCAD LT allows you to specify an alternate URL, or press the Enter key to accept the default:

Command: **BROWSER**↵
Enter Web location (URL) <http://www.autodesk.com/acltuser>: ↵

Help
Autodesk on the Web ▸
AutoCAD LT Home Page ▸
BROWSER

If you enter a different location, AutoCAD LT launches the browser and opens the specified location, but this does not change the default URL. This default should be set to the Web locations that you most frequently access when you start your browser. This could be your company Web site, a client's Web site, a Web search engine, or any other site that you access frequently. The system variable named INETLOCATION is used to store the value for the default URL. If you would like your browser to start at a different location, you can change the value of this variable at the command line:

Command: **INETLOCATION**↵
Enter new value for INETLOCATION <"http://www.autodesk.com/acltuser">:
http://atc.clackamas.cc.or.us↵

Command: **BROWSER**↵
Enter Web location (URL) <http://atc.clackamas.cc.or.us>: ↵

The AutoCAD LT 2000 Web site is a dual-purpose site. It offers sales-oriented information for prospective customers as well as technical assistance for current users. Figure 16.1 shows the AutoCAD LT 2000 Home Page in the Netscape Communicator Web browser.

FIGURE 16.1 The AutoCAD LT 2000 Home Page is the initial default location accessed when launching your Web browser from within AutoCAD LT.

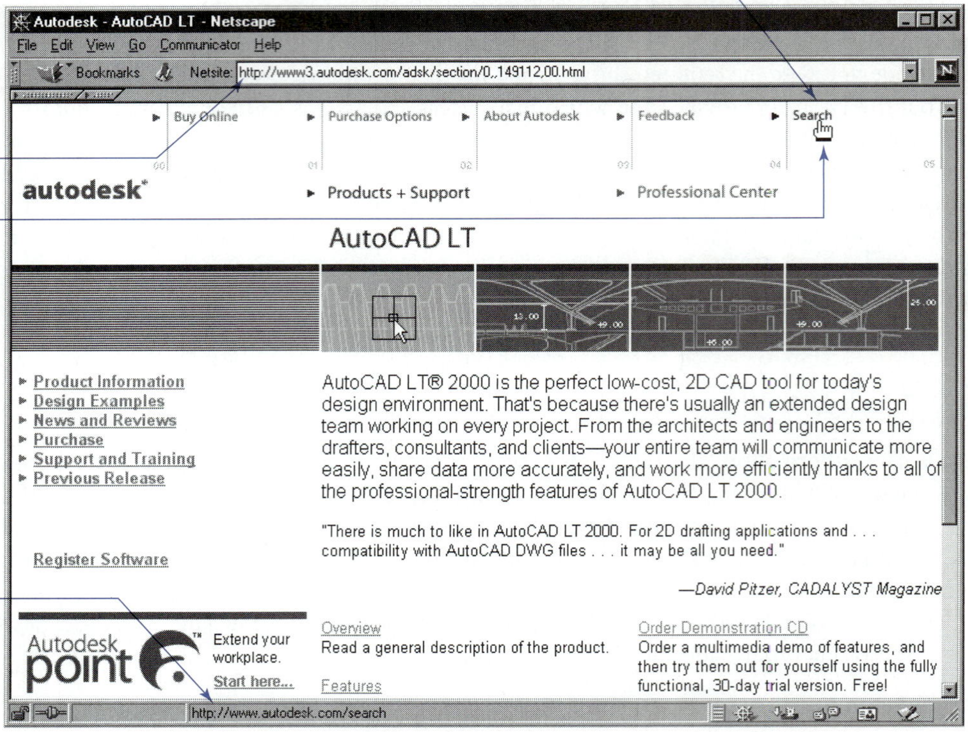

Field Notes

Like most professionally maintained Web sites, the AutoCAD LT 2000 Web site is frequently revised and updated. Therefore, the current appearance may differ from that shown in the illustrations found in this chapter.

There are several categories of information shown on the AutoCAD LT 2000 home page. As you move your cursor around the page, it will change to a hand and pointing finger as you move across various images and text items. This indicates the presence of a hyperlink, and picking the item will take you to a new location or document with related information.

Although most of the information on this site is concise and well organized, it is still very easy to get lost within any large Web site. The most effective selection you can make from the AutoCAD LT 2000 home page is the Search link. Using a search tool, or *search engine*, to find the specific information you are looking for can greatly reduce the amount of time spent at a Web site. Figure 16.2 shows the Search page for the AutoCAD LT 2000 Web site.

In the example in Figure 16.2, a search is entered for documents related to the Internet. When you enter the search, the entire Web site is searched for documents related to the words you indicate. The search results are displayed followed by a list of all the documents that are relevant to your specified search criteria (see Figure 16.3). The document titles are presented as hyperlinks that can be picked to display the document. Scrolling down the results page may display links to additional pages of related document links.

Another valuable resource that is accessible through the AutoCAD LT 2000 Web site is the discussion groups. The Autodesk *Discussion Groups* are open-forum areas where you can post questions or messages for others to read and respond to. This forum is read by many AutoCAD LT 2000 users as well as Autodesk staff members. If you have an unexplained software problem or have a question on using the software effectively, posting your questions in these forums can often get you a fast solution. To access the Autodesk News Groups, select the link labeled Support and Training on the AutoCAD LT 2000 Home Page (see Figure 16.1). On the Support and Training page, pick the Discussion Groups link, then pick the AutoCAD LT Discussion Groups link. This takes you to the AutoCAD LT Discussion Groups page, shown in Figure 16.4, where you can select the news group that you want to participate in. The best newsgroup for AutoCAD LT 2000 information is autodesk.autocadlt.2000general.

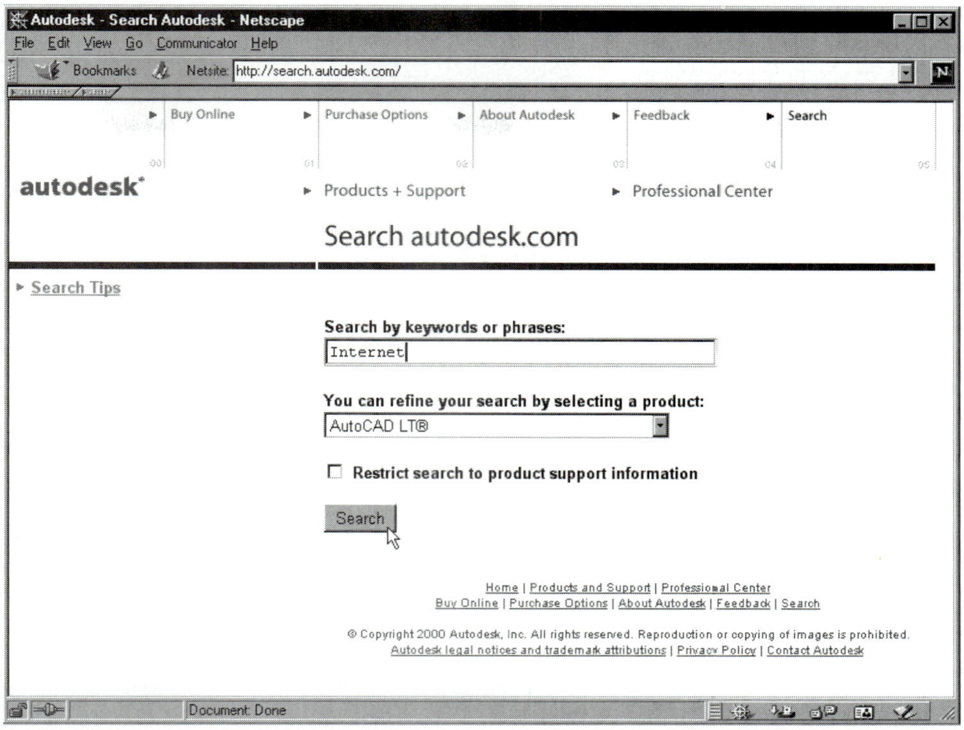

FIGURE 16.2 Using search engines will reduce the amount of time spent browsing a Web site.

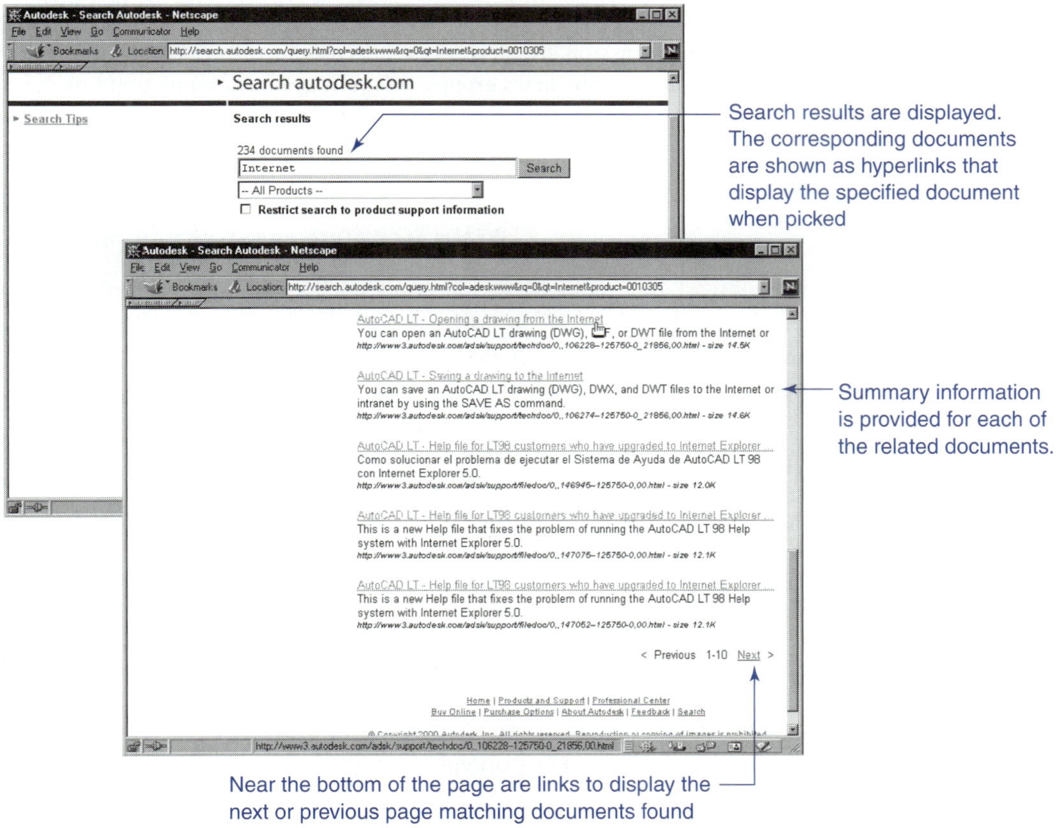

FIGURE 16.3 Search results are displayed as links that can be picked to display Web pages related to the information for which you are searching.

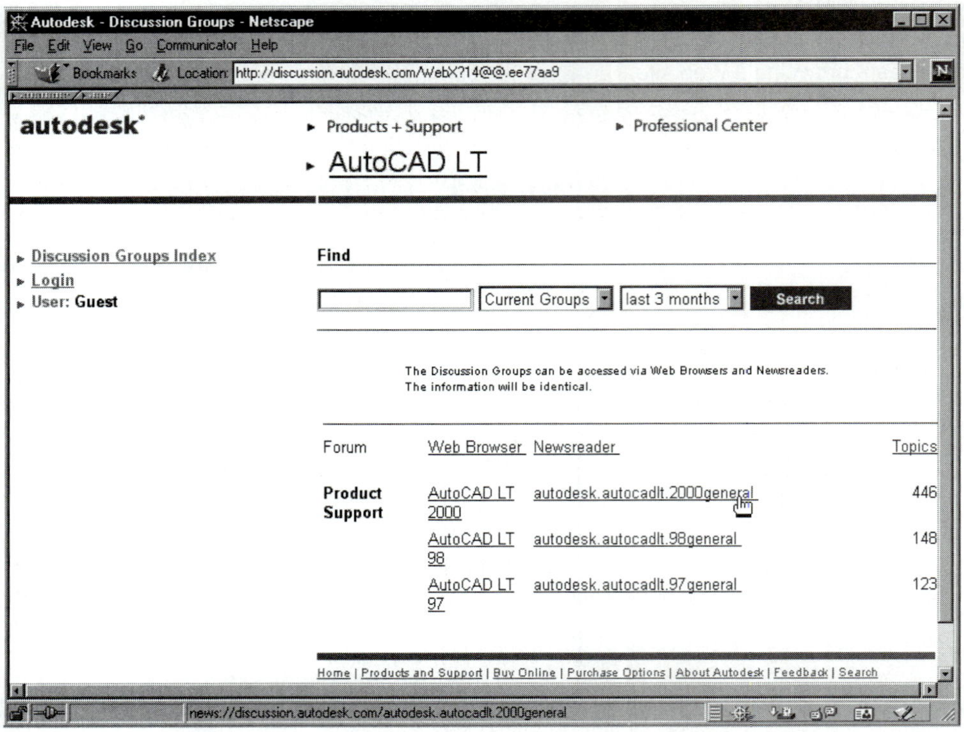

FIGURE 16.4 The Autodesk Newsgroups offer fast answers and lots of valuable information.

Field Notes

Netscape Communicator has a built-in discussion group viewer that is activated by picking a discussion group link. If you are unable to access the news groups, ask your system administrator or instructor for assistance.

Exercise 16.1 — Estimated time required: 10 min.

1. If you are using a computer at work or at school, ask your system administrator or instructor for assistance in gaining Web access.
2. Determine what your default Web browser software is.
3. Use the BROWSER command to start your browser and go to the AutoCAD LT 2000 Home Page.
4 Use the search engine to search for documents on two or more topics.

LEARNING CHECKPOINT

- ☐ What are the most widespread uses of the Internet?
- ☐ Define the terms *HyperText* and *hyperlink.*
- ☐ Name three ways to connect to the Internet.
- ☐ Where is the default Internet location in AutoCAD LT 2000?
- ☐ What is a discussion group?

Internet-Aware File Handling

Having access to a global distribution network for sharing files and resources offers tremendous flexibility and effectively overcomes geographical restrictions on collaborative design efforts. The Internet provides the global communications framework needed for effective communication among members of a design team who are at remote locations. Also, in a company that has multiple locations, standard resource files can be managed as a single collection that is accessible from all sites. In almost any application, the Internet provides easy access to standard resources with no geographical restrictions.

Understanding URLs

The Uniform Resource Locator, or URL, was introduced previously in this chapter as being the means of specifying a file name and location on the Internet. Transferring files from your computer to an Internet location (***uploading***) or from an Internet location to your computer (***downloading***) requires a correct specification of a valid URL. You can specify a URL for the filename when opening, saving, inserting, or externally referencing files.

URLs can point to several different types of Internet resources, and they use different prefixes to identify the protocol application used to access the desired resource. The term ***protocol*** refers to a set of rules and data formats used when exchanging information. The two primary protocols used for file transfer across the Internet are HTTP (HyperText Transfer Protocol) and FTP (File Transfer Protocol). HTTP is typically used for text, graphics, or multimedia files accessed through Web browser software. FTP is used for simple file transfers and supports file maintenance controls such as moving, renaming, or deleting files. FTP transfers may be restricted if you access the Internet through a proxy server. Your instructor or system administrator should be able to provide guidance in this area.

Although files can typically be read from an Internet location using HTTP access, most transfers of files to an Internet location are handled using FTP. The format for a URL in an FTP transaction is as follows:

ftp://servername/pathname/filename

The *servername* refers to the name or location on the Internet of the computer with which you are communicating. The *pathname* specifies the folder or folder structure found on the *servername* to or from which you are transferring files. As an example, to specify a file named **Example.dwg** stored in a folder structure of **\Public\Drawings** located on a Web server named **atc.Clackamas.cc.or.us**, the following specification is used:

ftp://atc.clackamas.cc.or.us/Public/Drawings/Example.dwg

When transferring files to or from an FTP site, always check with your instructor or system administrator to ensure you have the correct URL information.

Secure FTP Access

To maintain security on Web servers, an FTP site that is not intended for public use will have a login requirement before files can be accessed. Depending on the security requirements, permissions may be needed to download files, upload files, or both. Some servers may incorporate multiple levels of security, allowing read-only access to some users and full access to others. With read-only access, you can download files, but you cannot change or delete the files on the server.

When specifying a URL to open or save a file using AutoCAD LT on a secure site, you are prompted for the login information, which is authenticated before the file transfer request is processed. If preferred, you can directly access the file with no further prompts by entering the login information as part of the file name. For example, to open or save the file Example.dwg from the previous example on a secure site, you can specify the filename as:

ftp://**LoginName:Password**@atc.clackamas.cc.or.us/Public/Drawings/Example.dwg

Some servers may have publicly accessible or anonymous FTP sites. When files are accessed from an anonymous site, the login name is typically specified as *anonymous,* and any password is accepted.

Opening a Drawing from a URL

The **OPEN** command is used to open a drawing file from a URL. The OPEN command displays the Select File dialog box, where the file specification is entered. You can enter an FTP specification directly in the File name: text box as described previously, including the login name and password if the FTP site is secure. Figure 16.5A shows a URL entered using an FTP specification. Pick the OK button to access the specified URL. If the login information was not included as part of the file name, the Enter Network Password dialog box requests authentication information (see Figure 16.5B). If the specified file is located and your user name and password are accepted, the file transfer is started. In Figure 16.5C, the File Download dialog box reports the status of the current download and estimates how much longer it will take. Transfer times will vary based primarily on file size and the speed of your Internet access.

FIGURE 16.5 (A) A URL can be entered in the File name: text box using an FTP specification. (B) A secure FTP site will require a correct user name and password to be entered for file access. (C) The download status also displays the estimated time required to complete the transfer.

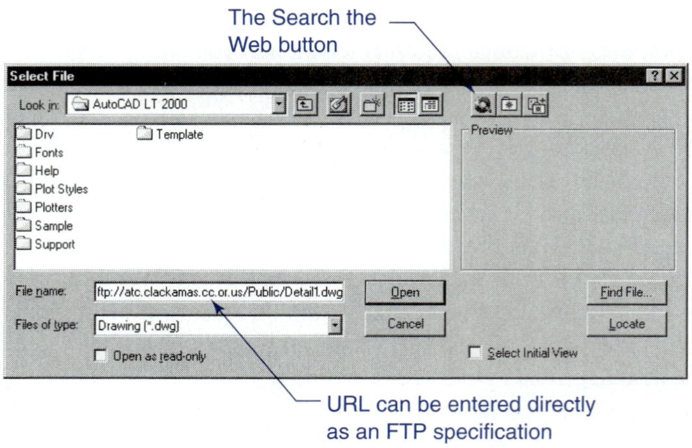

A

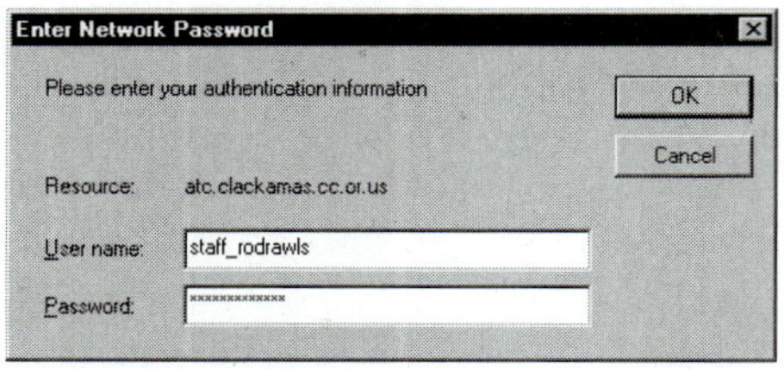

B

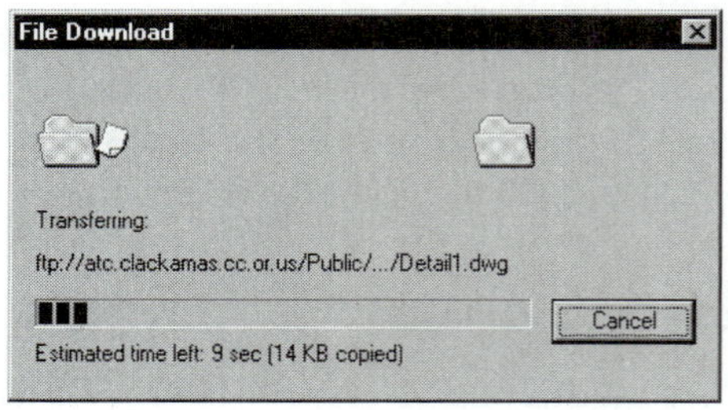

C

If either the server name or any other component of the URL is incorrectly specified, a message is displayed indicating that the server name cannot be located as it is currently typed (see Figure 16.6A). Pick the OK button and then check your entry for typographical errors or an incorrect server name. If the entry is verified and there are no errors but you still get an error message, ask your instructor or system administrator for assistance.

Once AutoCAD LT finds the server and requests file access, the server may ask for login information which AutoCAD LT then prompts you for using the Enter Network Password dialog box (refer to Figure 16.5B). If either the login name or the password you specify is incorrect, the dialog box shown in Figure 16.6B is displayed. Pick the OK button to return to the Select File dialog box. Pick the Open button again and enter your user name and password carefully to ensure that it is entered correctly this time. Some logins may also be case-sensitive.

Specifying the folder path incorrectly displays the error message shown in Figure 16.6C. Pick OK to return to the Select File dialog box, edit the path as needed and pick Open to try again. When opening a drawing file in AutoCAD LT using a path and drawing name existing on a local disk drive or on your local area network (LAN), it is not necessary to type the .DWG file extension in the File name: box. However, when specifying a file name to open from an FTP site, you must enter the .DWG extension as part of the file name. In Figure 16.6C, an error message reports that the specified file cannot be found because the file extension was not added. All the file types that can be opened or accessed in AutoCAD LT use a specific file extension.

FIGURE 16.6 The error messages indicate: (A) The server name cannot be located. (B)The Login user name/password combination was not accepted. (C) The folder path was not found on the server. (D) The file name was not found at the specified location.

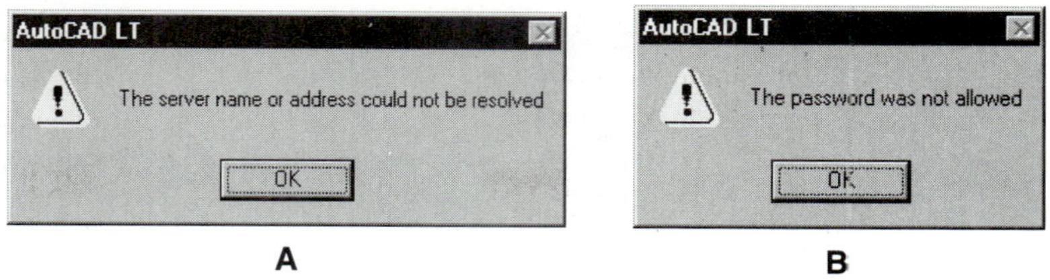

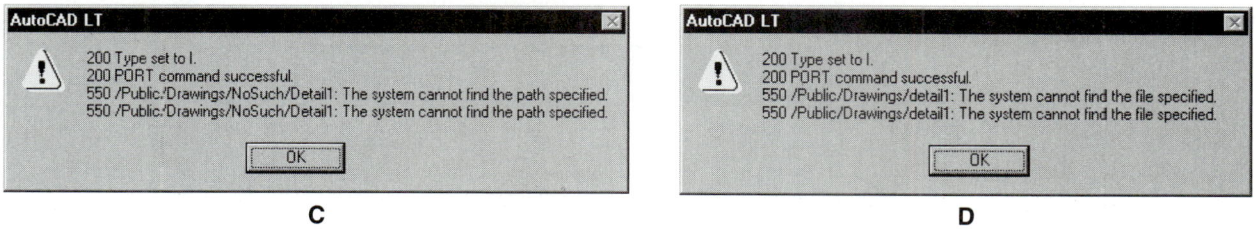

Be sure to include the correct file extension for all Internet file transfers. When the file name specified is not found in the URL location you entered, the dialog box in Figure 16.6D is displayed.

Field Notes

Some of the Internet file access dialog boxes display select standard FTP numeric codes to indicate the results of various elements of the file transfer process. The meanings of the codes listed in the dialog boxes in Figure 16.6 are shown here.

Code	*Meaning*
200	OK
550	File unavailable

Once you have completed a file transfer, if you are using a dial-up connection to the Internet, AutoCAD LT asks if you want to close the connection. You can pick Yes to close the connection, or No to keep it open. The Disconnect dialog box is shown in Figure 16.7.

FIGURE 16.7 The Disconnect dialog box can be used to close your current dial-up connection to the Internet.

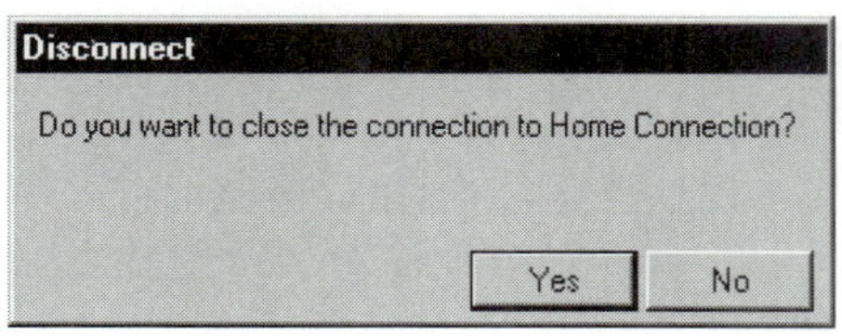

If you prefer, you can use the built-in browser interface in AutoCAD LT to locate a file. To display the Browse the Web dialog box, pick the Search the Web button, as shown in Figure 16.5A. The Browse the Web dialog box displays the text Open or Save on the title bar depending on whether you are attempting to download or upload a file. The Browse the Web dialog box displays your current default Internet location saved in the INETLOCATION variable (see Figure 16.8).

Use the Browse the Web dialog box as you would Netscape or Internet Explorer to search through Web sites using HTTP access. This allows you to access Web pages that provide links to resource files that you can pick to access. In Figure 16.9, the Browse the Web dialog box is being used to select a file to Open using a link to the actual drawing.

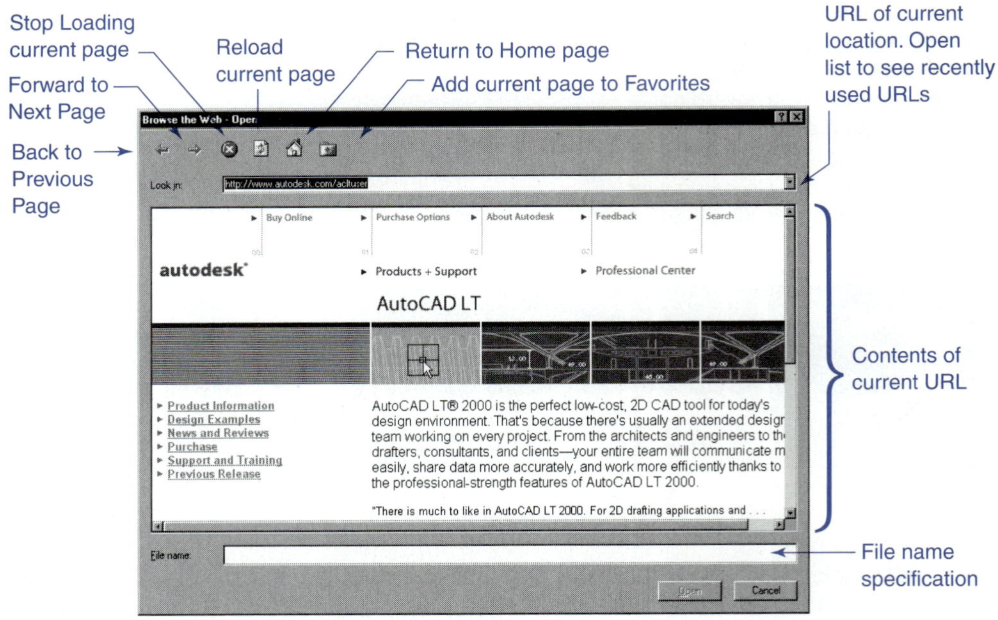

FIGURE 16.8 The Browse the Web dialog box can be used to browse for a desired file.

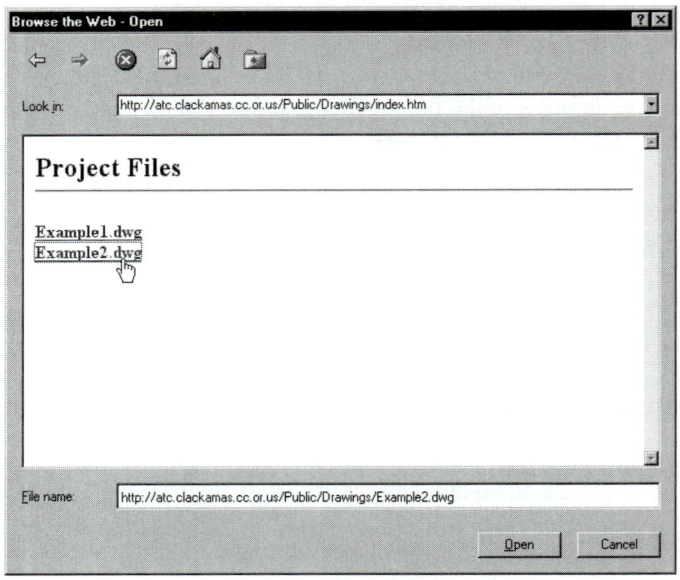

FIGURE 16.9 Links can be placed on Web pages to provide easy access to files and resources.

Inserting or Externally Referencing a Drawing from a URL

Once you access the Select Drawing File (INSERT) or Select Reference File (XREF) dialog box, the process of inserting or referencing a drawing from the Internet is exactly the same as described previously for opening a file. Specify the desired URL and pick the Open button, or use the Browse the Web dialog box to locate and select the file.

If you are inserting the drawing file, it is assigned a unique name and saved first in the **C:\Windows\temp\Internet** folder. The name the drawing was saved as now appears in the Insert dialog box. The naming format looks like this: **AC$C305**. You can rename the block, if desired, using the RENAME command. The rest of the insertion process is the same as when inserting any drawing. You must specify the insertion point, a scale factor, and a rotation angle.

When a drawing is referenced from the Internet, the file is also copied to the Internet folder and assigned a unique name. The first Xref name in the drawing is assigned the default name XREF1, and subsequent Xrefs are incremented numerically. When the file is reloaded, a new drawing is downloaded from the Internet location, and the Xref is updated to use the new file. The following appears at the command line when an Xref is attached from the Internet:

```
Command: XR↵
Attach Xref "XREF1": C:\windows\TEMP\Internet\AC$B101.dwg
"XREF1" loaded.
```

Field Notes

- *Caution:* Renaming or deleting files from the C:\Windows\temp\Internet folder can cause unexpected results in drawings that reference these files.
- If you have particular URLs where you frequently access files, add the location to your list of Favorites for easier access.

Accessing the Internet with DesignCenter

To access content sources from the Internet with DesignCenter, pick the Load button from the DesignCenter toolbar. In the Load DesignCenter Palette dialog box, use the same methods specified previously to access a desired file. The selected file is copied to the Internet folder and assigned a unique name. The file can then be opened in DesignCenter to access any of its content in the same way that content is accessed from a local file.

Saving Drawings to a URL

If the file you are working on was opened from the Web, it is automatically updated on the Web when you save it. To save a new drawing to a URL, use the Save Drawing As dialog box. You can enter a URL directly using an FTP specification, or you can use the Browse the Web dialog box if desired. The file is saved in the Internet folder and copied to the specified URL. You must have the appropriate permission and any needed login. Subsequent saves of the file will automatically update both the local file and the Internet file.

Accessing Other Files from the Internet

Virtually all the AutoCAD LT input and output commands that access files will recognize any valid URL path to an AutoCAD LT file. Support files can also be accessed from a URL, including Linetype files, Hatch pattern definition files, menu files, and more.

Sending Drawings as E-mail Attachments

If you currently have a system e-mail tool, such as Microsoft Outlook®, the Send... option on the File pull-down menu in AutoCAD LT 2000 can be selected. Otherwise, it appears grayed out and cannot be selected. Picking this option starts your e-mail tool and automatically attaches the current drawing to the e-mail. In Figure 16.10, the drawing file icon shows up in the e-mail message composer to indicate that the file has been attached.

Although this option represents a simple and convenient method for sending drawings to another location, it does have one major disadvantage. This option sends the drawing file as is, meaning at full size. Usually, when sending a drawing electronically, it is best to compress the file using some type of file compression utility. A good file compression tool can reduce the file size for a drawing to less than half of the actual size. This is especially valuable when sending larger drawings.

Field Notes

Many file compression utilities are available in today's market. Many, such as WinZip, can be tested before they are purchased. This powerful, yet inexpensive, utility can create self-extracting archive files for the convenience of the recipient. To try the shareware version of WinZip, you can visit their Web site at WWW.WINZIP.COM.

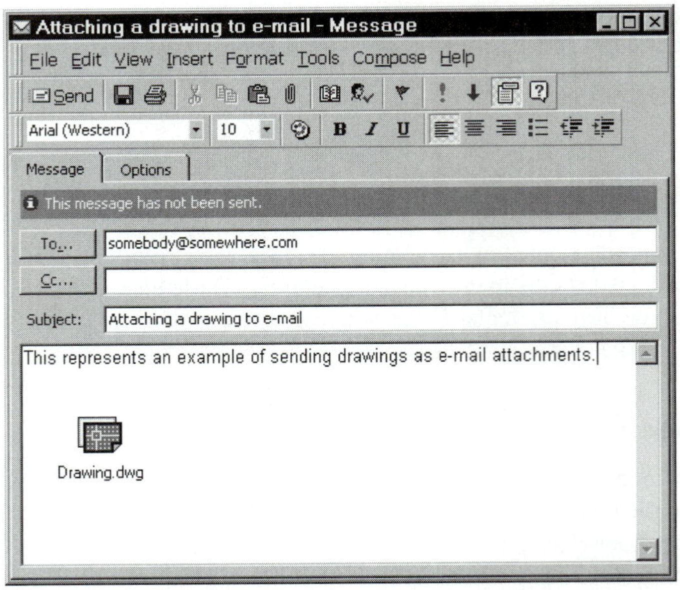

FIGURE 16.10 The Send... option on the File menu starts your e-mail tool and attaches the current drawing to the message.

Exercise 16.2

Estimated time required: 10 min.

1. Check with your instructor to find a safe FTP location that is available to you for practicing Internet file access. While you are first learning, the location provided should not contain or allow access to any critical files.
2. Create a simple drawing of your own design. Use SAVEAS to save the file to the provided FTP site. Enter the URL using an FTP specification defined fully in the File name: text box. Name the drawing EX16.2A.dwg.
3. Close the drawing.
4. Use the OPEN command to reopen the file EX16.2A.dwg from its Internet location.
5. Close the drawing.
6. Start a new drawing, then use the INSERT command to insert EX16.2A.dwg into the current drawing.
7. Save the current drawing as EX16.2B.dwg.
8. Use Windows Explorer to look at the contents of the C:\Windows\temp\Internet folder. Compare the file name with the name that was assigned to the inserted file.
9. Close EX16.2B.dwg and Explorer.

LEARNING CHECKPOINT

- ☐ What are the two primary file transfer protocols?
- ☐ Show how a login name and password can be included in a specified file URL.
- ☐ List four common errors reported when trying to access a file from the Internet.
- ☐ What is the Windows\temp\Internet folder used for?

Concept Animations

- Internet Utilities

Using Hyperlinks in AutoCAD LT Drawings

Hyperlinks provide a way to link related information within a drawing. AutoCAD LT 2000 allows you to attach hyperlinks to drawing objects that can provide access to related documents or to even other drawings. For example, you can link a word processing document to an object to provide comprehensive information about that object or assembly. Spreadsheets, databases, and even Web locations can also be linked to drawing objects. Each component in an assembly drawing might feature a link to the relevant detail drawing.

Adding Hyperlinks to Drawing Objects

Standard

Insert
Hyperlink

HYPERLINK
[Ctrl] + [K]

The command used to add a hyperlink to an AutoCAD LT drawing object is HYPERLINK. You can access the HYPERLINK command by picking the Insert Hyperlink button from the Standard toolbar, by picking Hyperlink… from the Insert pull-down menu, by typing **HYPERLINK** at the Command: prompt, or by using the accelerator keystroke Ctrl+K.

You should name and save a drawing before creating hyperlinks in it. Starting the HYPERLINK command in a drawing that has not yet been saved displays the Hyperlink – Save Drawing dialog box, shown in Figure 16.11. Pick the Yes button to display the Save Drawing As dialog box, where you can save the drawing and continue. If the current drawing has been saved and named already, the HYPERLINK command prompts you to select one or more objects to which to attach the hyperlink. Press Enter after selecting the desired objects to display the Insert Hyperlink dialog box (see Figure 16.12).

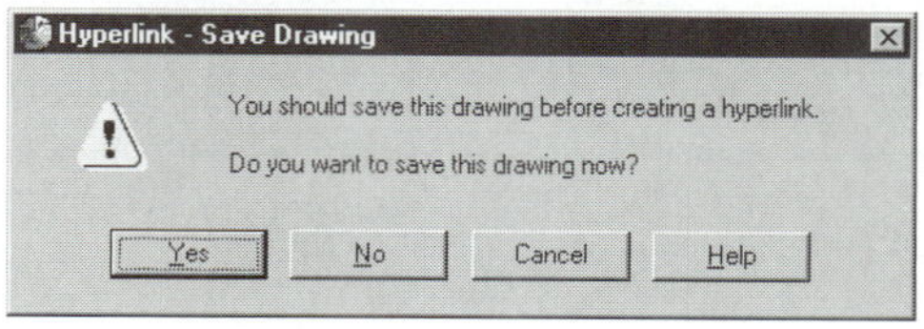

FIGURE 16.11 A drawing should be saved before hyperlinks are attached to objects in the drawing.

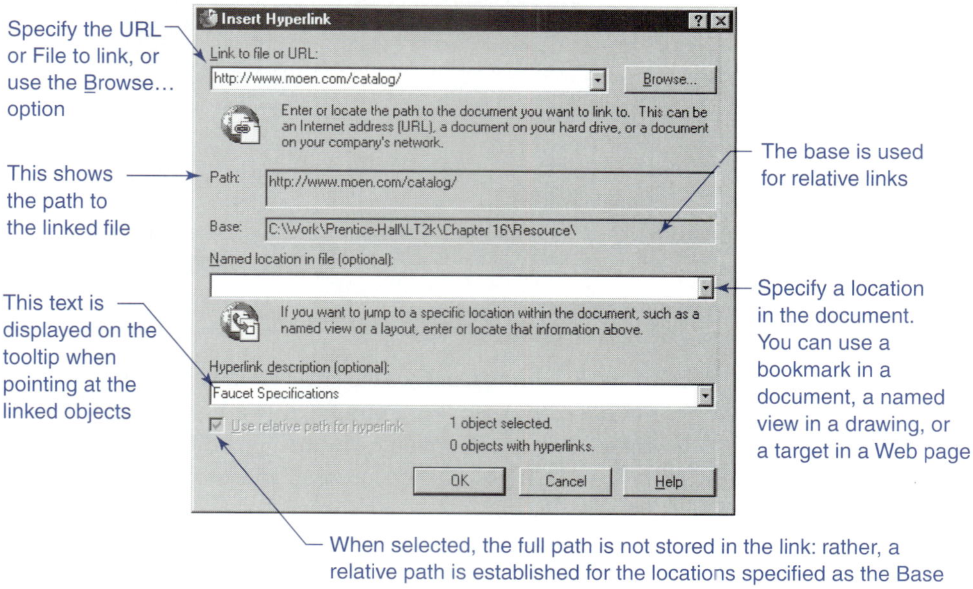

FIGURE 16.12 The Insert Hyperlink dialog box.

When an object has a hyperlink attached, AutoCAD LT shows the hyperlink cursor and tooltip when you point to it. This behavior can be turned on or off in the Hyperlink area of the User Preferences tab on the Options dialog box, or you can use the HYPERLINKOPTIONS command. Figure 16.13 shows the appearance of the hyperlink cursor and the tooltip displayed.

To access the hyperlink shortcut menu, grip-select the linked object and then right-click in the drawing area. This displays the shortcut menu, which now shows a cascade at the bottom labeled Hyperlink. This cascade is shown in Figure 16.14.

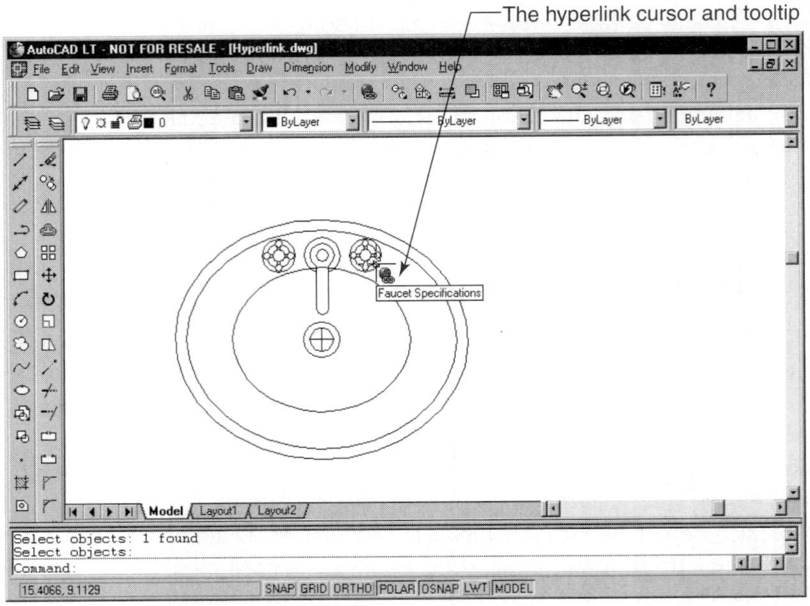

FIGURE 16.13 The hyperlink cursor and tooltip identify linked objects in a drawing.

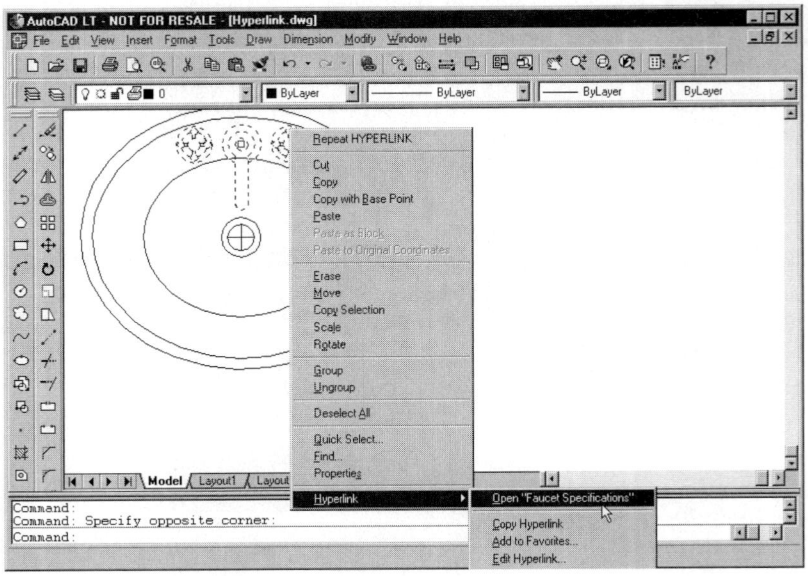

FIGURE 16.14 The Hyperlink cascade on the shortcut menu provides access to hyperlink-related options.

Opening the hyperlink launches the attached file using the application normally used to view or edit the specific type of file referenced. For example, if you link the URL of a Web site as in the previous example, picking the Open "*linkname*" option from the Hyperlink cascade launches your default Web browser and loads the specified site. If you link a document, your word processor software is launched when you open the linked file.

If any of the objects selected at the Select objects: prompt of the HYPERLINK command already has an attached hyperlink, the Edit Hyperlink dialog box is displayed. This dialog lists the number of linked objects and provides a Remove Link button to clear the existing links. You also can enter a new link to replace any existing links for the selected objects. You may attach only one link to any one drawing object. The Edit Hyperlink dialog box is shown in Figure 16.15. The Properties window can also be used to edit Hyperlinks.

Use the Copy Hyperlink option from the Hyperlink cascade to copy the definition of an existing hyperlink to Windows Clipboard. Next, pick the Paste as Hyperlink option from the Edit menu and select any number of objects to which to copy the link. The Hyperlink attached to the selected objects will have all the same properties as the copied hyperlink. You also can enter the PASTEASHYPERLINK command directly at the command prompt to start this command.

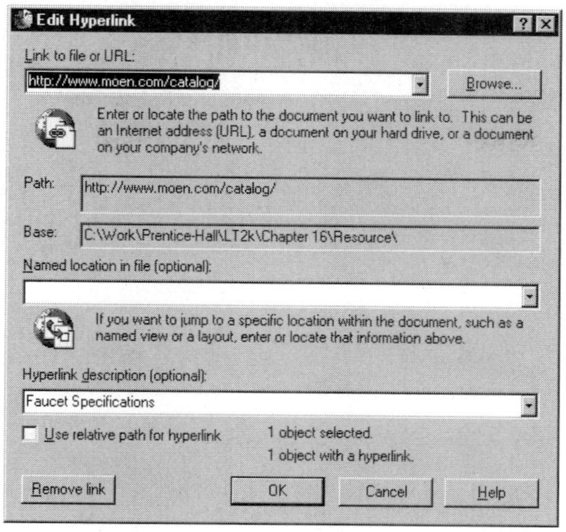

FIGURE 16.15 The Edit Hyperlink dialog box can be used to edit or remove existing hyperlinks.

Adding a Hyperlink to an Area of a Drawing

To use the command line version of the HYPERLINK command, enter **-HYPERLINK** at the Command: prompt. The command line version allows you to define an area of the drawing that is linked to a file or URL without selecting any objects. A rectangle is added to the drawing on a layer called URLLAYER. This layer is on and plots by default, so you may need to change the settings for the layer URLLAYER. In the drawing, the rectangle must be picked to open its linked document. However, the rectangles used to define a hyperlink area actually define an entire area of the drawing that is linked when you create an electronic plot. Electronic plots are covered later in this chapter. Here is how the command line version of the HYPERLINK command works:

Command: **-HYPERLINK↵**
Enter an option [Remove/Insert] <Insert>: ↵
Enter hyperlink insert option [Area/Object] <Object>: **A↵**
First corner: *<pick first corner of area>*
Other corner: *<pick second corner of area>*
Enter hyperlink <current drawing>: *<specify file name to link to>*
Enter named location <none>: *<specify named location (bookmark, named view, etc.)>*
Enter description <none>: *<specify text to appear on tooltip>*
Command:

This option also allows for easy removal of all links in a drawing. To clear all hyperlinks from a drawing, use the Remove option of the -HYPERLINK command and when prompted to select objects, specify ALL.

Setting the Hyperlink Base

The base location is used for relative hyperlinks in a drawing. This value is stored in the HYPERLINKBASE system variable. If no value is specified, the relative path is set to match the current drawing location. The HYPERLINKBASE variable is set as follows:

Command: **HYPERLINKBASE↵**
Enter new value for HYPERLINKBASE, or for none <"">: *<specify new location>*

Navigating through Linked Documents

When you open a linked file from another application, that application is launched and the linked file is loaded. In a Microsoft Office–compliant application, a Web navigation toolbar is automatically displayed that includes Back and Forward buttons to allow you to move easily between applications. Figure 16.16A shows the Web toolbar in Microsoft Word 2000, and the Web toolbar in AutoCAD LT is shown in Figure 16.16B. Use the back and forward buttons to move through any number of linked documents.

FIGURE 16.16 The Web toolbar in (A) Microsoft Word 2000 and in (B) AutoCAD LT 2000.

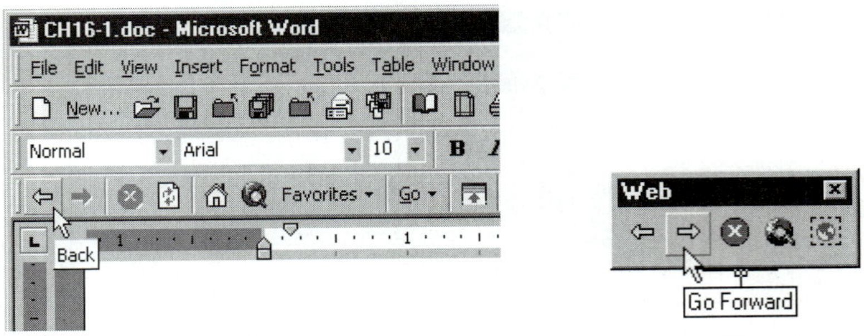

A B

Displaying Hyperlinked Objects in a Drawing

To grip-select and highlight all objects that have hyperlinks in a drawing, use the SELECTURL command. You can type **SELECTURL** at the Command: prompt, or pick the Select URLs button from the Web toolbar. Once the objects are grip-selected, you can then activate any desired editing command to work with the selected objects, just as you would with any other noun-verb selection. To remove the highlighting and grips, press the Escape key twice, or pick Deselect All from the shortcut menu.

Exercise 16.3 **Estimated time required: 10 min.**

1. Open an existing drawing from a previous chapter.
2. Use the HYPERLINK command to link another drawing file to an object in the drawing.
3. Pick the object with the hyperlink and right-click to open the linked file.
4. Close the linked drawing and return to the original drawing.
5. Create a document in another application such as a text file, a word processing document, or a spreadsheet.
6. Link the new document to an object in your drawing.
7. Use the Copy link option to copy the link to Windows Clipboard.
8. Pick Paste a Hyperlink from the Edit menu, and select several objects to which to attach the copied link.
9. Use the -HYPERLINK command to attach a link to an area of drawing.
10. Display the Web toolbar in AutoCAD LT.
11. Open the hyperlink to the new document. In the application that was opened to edit the new document, use the Web toolbar to go Back to AutoCAD LT. In AutoCAD LT pick the Go Forward button to return to the other application. Return to AutoCAD LT, save as EX16.3.dwg, and close the drawing.

LEARNING CHECKPOINT

- ☐ Describe some possible applications for hyperlinks in a drawing.
- ☐ List the available ways to start the HYPERLINK command.
- ☐ What is the hyperlink base, and how is it set?
- ☐ Describe how to attach a hyperlink to an area of the drawing.
- ☐ How can the Web toolbars be used to navigate between linked documents?

Sharing Data and Drawing Files

- Placing Hyperlinks in Drawing Files

Plotting AutoCAD LT Drawings Electronically

AutoCAD LT 2000 has a feature called ***ePlot***, which creates electronic plot files. These files are produced in the form of DWF (Drawing Web Format) files that can be viewed using a Web browser, allowing you to share your drawings with customers, clients, and vendors even if they do not have AutoCAD or AutoCAD LT. Because ePlots are vector format files and not raster images, they are much more flexible and accurate for presenting CAD drawings. Although DWF files can be viewed and printed they cannot be opened or edited. Additionally, no data can be extracted from a DWF file. These files are intended for viewing only.

The PLOT command is used to create ePlots, or DWF files. Select the DWF ePlot.pc3 option from the Name: list in the Plotter configuration area of the Plot Device tab in the Plot dialog box (see Figure 16.17).

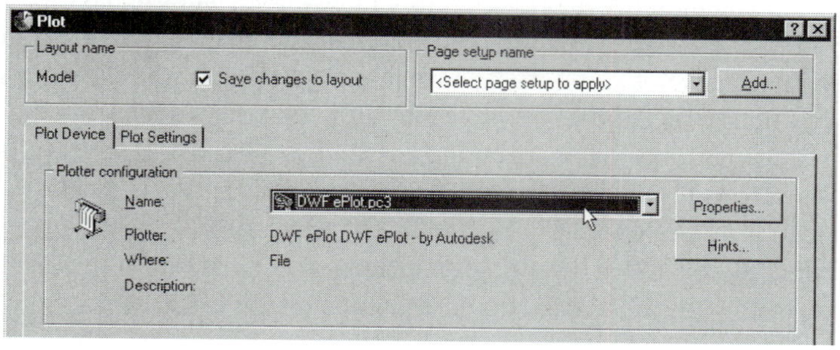

FIGURE 16.17 The DWF ePlot.pc3 plotter configuration is set up to plot drawings electronically into a DWF file.

To customize the DWF file settings, pick the Properties… button. This displays the Plotter Configuration Editor, where you can select the Custom Properties… button to customize the output for the ePlot in the DWF Properties dialog box (see Figure 16.18).

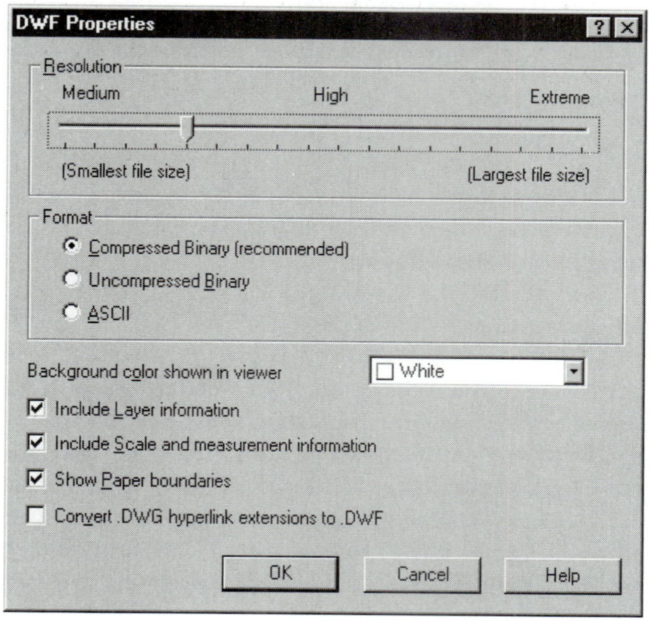

FIGURE 16.18 The DWF Properties dialog box is used to customize the ePlot output.

The DWF Properties settings control the size, format, and appearance of the file. The available settings are as follows:

- **Resolution** Allows you to increase or decrease plotting resolution for ePlots; higher resolution produces higher files, and lower resolution produces smaller files. Smaller file sizes are desirable when your files are delivered over the Internet. Use the slider bar to set a desired value.

Format

■ **Compressed Binary**	Recommended setting. Generates smaller binary files.
■ **Uncompressed Binary**	Binary files again, but larger because they are not compressed.
■ **ASCII**	Files are uncompressed plain text information.
■ **Background...**	Sets color of drawing background in browser software.
■ **Include Layer info...**	Controls whether layer data is saved in the DWF file. This allows the viewer to freeze and thaw layers in the ePlot.
■ **Include Scale and...**	Includes information on scale and measurement.
■ **Show Paper boundaries**	Display the paper size on the plot, just like in the layout.
■ **Convert DWG to DWF...**	Converts any hyperlinks to other drawings to reference a DWF extension from DWG.

When you plot, if you do not specify lineweight values in the Layer Properties Manager, a default value of 0.06 in. is used for all drawing objects. This may change the appearance of your drawings when zooming in close. You can plot using no lineweights by removing the check mark from the Plot with Lineweights check box option on the Plot Settings tab of the Plot dialog box.

Also, hyperlinks that were created in model space will not be available in a drawing plotted from paper space. Be sure to place your hyperlinks in paper space if that is where you plot from and you want your links available in the DWF file.

You will also need to specify a file name and location for the DWF file. If you are plotting to a secure FTP site, follow these steps to successfully upload the ePlot:

1. Enter the Plot command.
2. Select the ePLot device from the list.
3. Enter the name of the DWF file to create in the File name: text box.
4. Select the Browse the Web button to display the Browse the Web dialog box.
5. Delete the Look in: entry (at the top).
6. Enter **ftp://LoginName:Password@servername/pathname/** on the File name line.
7. Pick Save.
8. Pick the Plot button.

The DWF file is now available for viewing but requires either a browser and an add-on known as a *WHIP!* driver, or it can be viewed with the Volo View Express DWF viewer. Both of these software items are free on the Autodesk Web site.

The *WHIP!* Driver

The *WHIP!* driver is a software add-on for your Web browser software that lets you open and view DWF files. You can obtain it free, and it will install automatically on your system. To find the *WHIP!* download page, first go to www.Autodesk.com and pick the Products & Support link. From one of the product categories, pick the *WHIP!* Viewer link, which takes you to the *WHIP!* home page, shown in Figure 16.19.

Pick the Download *WHIP!* link to go to the download page, which is shown in Figure 16.20. After filling out the form, pick the Get *WHIP!* button to move to the next page, shown in Figure 16.21. Here, you will see two options, the top one is used to "auto-install the plug-in," and the next one down simply downloads the executable file. Using the "auto-install the plug-in" option allows for an easy installation. If you download the executable file, you will need to execute it after downloading; do this by double-clicking on the downloaded file.

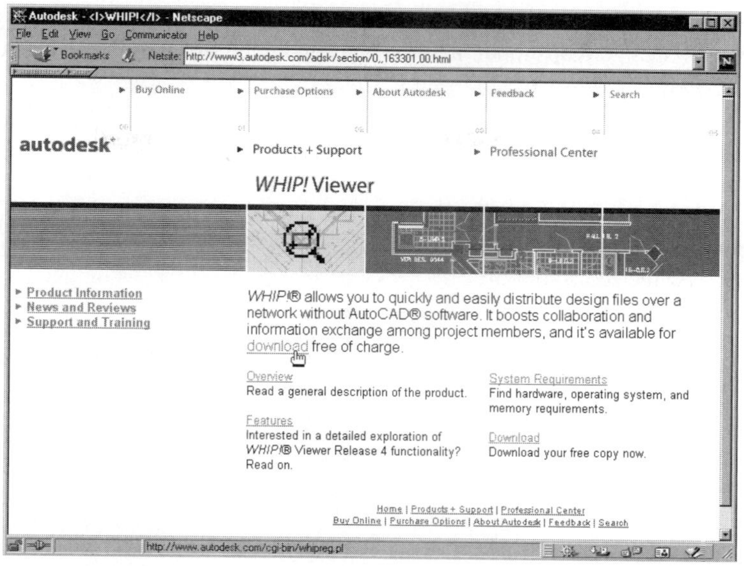

FIGURE 16.19 The *WHIP!* home page on the Autodesk Web site.

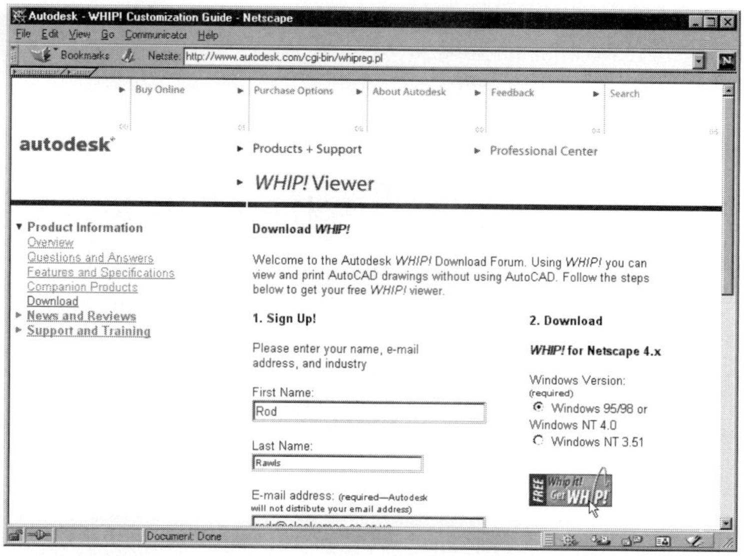

FIGURE 16.20 The Download *WHIP!* page requires you to supply some information to Autodesk.

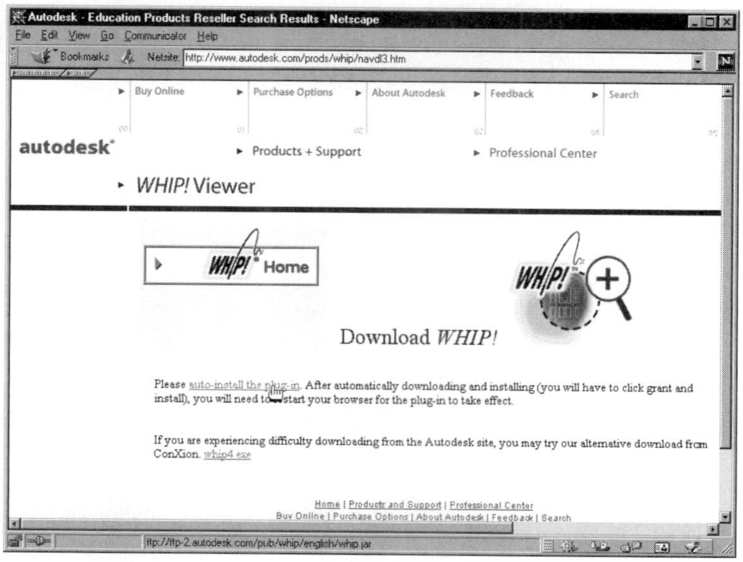

FIGURE 16.21 Select the auto-install option for an automated and typically trouble-free installation.

The next step is to download the software. This is about a 3.3 Mb download and can take around 20 minutes on a 56 Kbps modem. If you have selected the auto-install, the download progress dialog appears as illustrated in Figure 16.22.

When the download is completed, the auto-install displays a JavaScript Security dialog box that requests permission to do the install. Picking Grant allows the software to be installed. You can pick Deny to stop the install or Details to find out more.

If you grant permission for the installation to continue, the *WHIP! Setup* screen appears, as shown in Figure 16.24. For most applications, you should be able to just pick the default options for any of the prompts issued by the setup routine.

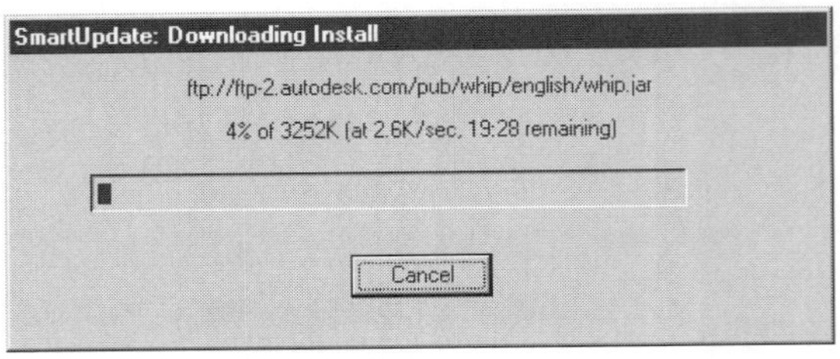

FIGURE 16.22 The file download progress is tracked, and the time remaining is estimated.

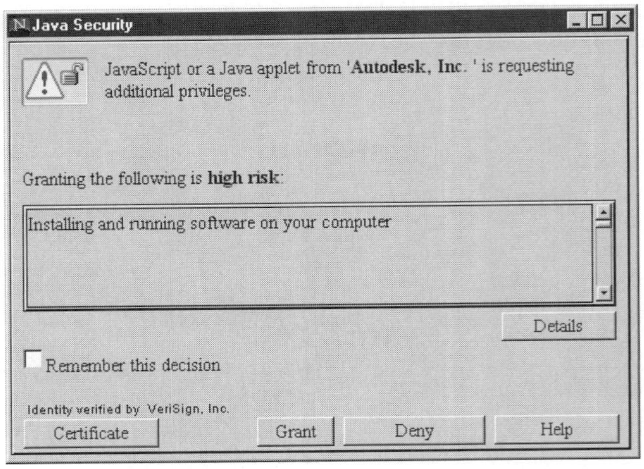

FIGURE 16.23 The JavaScript Security window requests permission to install your software.

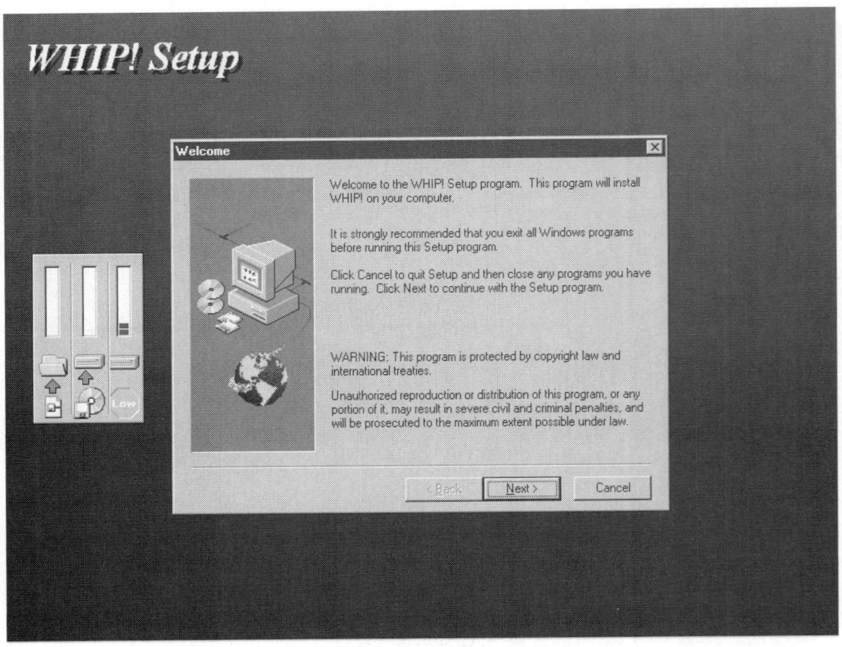

FIGURE 16.24 The *WHIP! Setup* screen.

One the setup is complete, a message is displayed indicating that the *WHIP!* driver is now available to your browser (see Figure 16.25). You will need to close your browser and restart it to be able to use the *WHIP!* driver.

You can now open DWF files for viewing in your browser. Figure 16.26 shows the Netscape Navigator software with a DWF file (ePlot) loaded for viewing. If you have a wheel mouse, you will be able to zoom in and out by simply rolling the wheel. Right-clicking in the drawing area displays the *WHIP!* shortcut menu, which provides access to the many available features of the *WHIP!* driver.

FIGURE 16.25 After setup is complete, you will need to close and restart your browser.

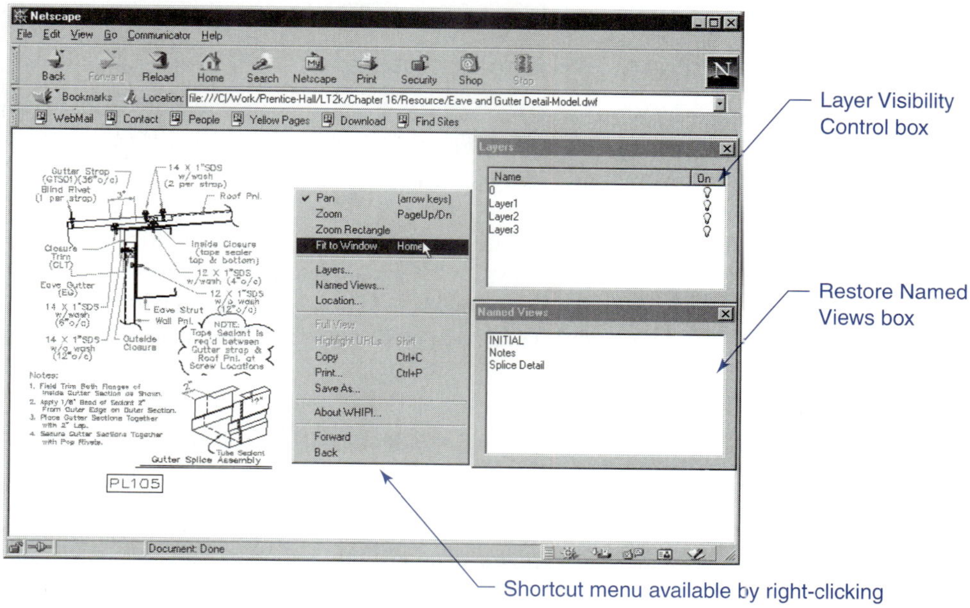

FIGURE 16.26 The *WHIP!* viewer provides many tools for viewing DWF files. You can pan, zoom, control layer visibility, and even restore named drawing views.

Field Notes

The intent of the DWF drawings is to provide a secure method to share your drawings with others, even if they do not have AutoCAD. Even so, DWF files are not completely secure. Although AutoCAD and AutoCAD LT provide no way to convert DWF files back into drawings, some third-part vendors are now marketing software that does this—meaning that DWF files may not provide the full level of security needed in some applications.

Volo View Express

The Volo View Express software can also view DWF files, but it does not work as part of your Browser software. Like the *WHIP!* viewer, it can be obtained free from the Autodesk Web site. To find the *Volo View Express* download page, first go to www.Autodesk.com and pick the Products & Solutions link. From the Design + Drafting category, pick the Volo™ View link, which takes you to the Volo View Express home page, shown in Figure 16.27.

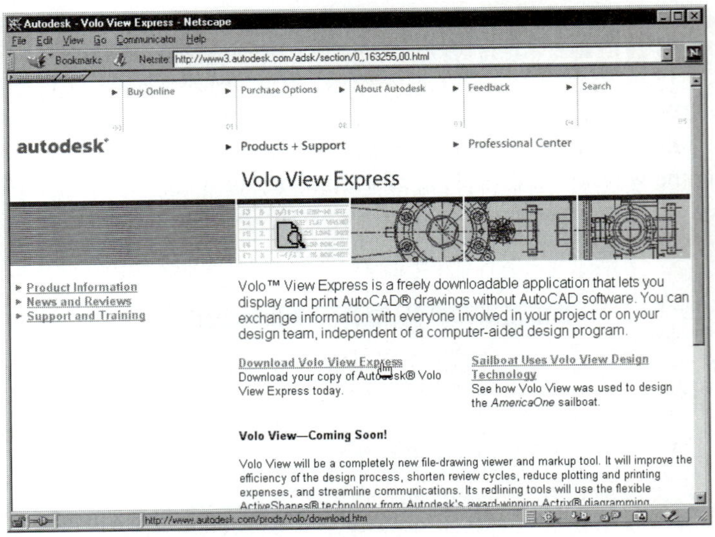

FIGURE 16.27 The Volo View Express home page on the Autodesk Web site.

Embedding a DWF File in a Web Page

Once the *WHIP!* viewer is installed, you can open a DWF file directly with your browser. You can select the DWF file type selected from the Files of Type list in your Browser's Open dialog box. However, in some cases you may want to embed a DWF file in a Web page to communicate a variety of information in the same document.

The Autodesk Web site has a full array of technical documents and tutorials on how to use DWF files. Refer to these resources as needed for additional information. This section provides a template that can be adapted to most applications of embedding a DWF file in a Web page.

The following HTML code defines a simple Web page that includes an embedded DWF file.

```
<html>
<head>
 <title>Template for an Embedded DWF File</title>
</head>
<body>
<center>
<h2>This shows an application of an embedded DWF file in a web page.</h2>
<hr>
<object
   id="FILEREFERENCE"
   classid="clsid:B2BE75F3-9197-11CF-ABF4-08000996E931"
   codebase="ftp://ftp.autodesk.com/pub/whip/english/whip.cab#version=4,0,42,102"
   width=300
   height=400>
   <param name="Filename" value="FILENAME.dwf">
   <embed
   name="FILEREFERENCE"
   pluginspage="http://www.autodesk.com/products/whip"
   width=300
   height=400
   src="FILENAME.dwf">
</object>
</body>
</html>
```

After creating this file, save it with any desired name using a standard .HTM or .HTML file extension. For simplicity, this basic template uses a minimum of options. The items that you can change to make this work in your application are shown in blue. Here are the definitions of the changeable items:

- **FILEREFERENCE** A name that you decide on, so that you can refer to this object from other locations in your Web page.
- **FILENAME** The actual name of your DWF file. If the DWF file and the HTML file are in the same folder, no path is necessary. If they are in separate locations, you will need to specify a path as well.
- **Height & Width Values** Set any desired height and width, measured in pixels.

Exercise 16.4

Estimated time required: 20 min.

1. Open an existing drawing from a previous chapter.
2. Use the DWF ePlot.pc3 plot configuration to create a DWF file named EX16.4A.dwf.
3. If the *WHIP!* driver is not available on your system, ask your system administrator or instructor for permission to install it and for guidance if necessary.
4. After *WHIP!* is installed, restart your browser software.
5. Use your browser to open the DWF file you created. Use each of the tools from the *WHIP!* shortcut menu to see how they work.
6. In a text editor such as Notepad, enter the HTML code shown in the preceding template, substituting the appropriate values where necessary to reference your DWF file. Save the file as EX16-4.HTML and open it in your browser. Explore the DWF interface to see how it works when embedded in a Web page.
7. Close your browser.

LEARNING CHECKPOINT

- ☐ What does DWF stand for?
- ☐ When sending an ePlot to a secure FTP site, how and where are the user name and password entered?
- ☐ Describe the display features of the *WHIP!* viewer.
- ☐ Name the viewer for AutoCAD LT that does not work from a browser.

Sharing Data and Drawing Files

- Placing a Drawing Web Format File on a Web Page

MULTIPLE CHOICE

1. Which term is not an acronym or term used to describe the World Wide Web?
   a. WWWeb c. W3
   b. WWW d. the Web
2. Which term does not describe an Internet connection?
   a. modem c. coaxial
   b. ISDN d. T-1
3. The term ISP stands for:
   a. Information Services Protocol c. Intranet Systems Project
   b. Internet Service Provider d. Internet System Protocol
4. A software package used to view World Wide Web documents is called a(n):
   a. Browser c. CAD Package
   b. Web viewer d. Internet editor
5. The AutoCAD LT command used to start the software described in Question 4 is:
   a. GotoURL c. BROWSER
   b. INETLOCATION d. OPENURL
6. The command used to set the default Internet location is:
   a. SETURL c. DEFAULTURL
   b. INETLOCATION d. OPENURL
7. The initial default Internet location is:
   a. Autodesk Home Page c. AutoCAD LT 2000 Home Page
   b. http://www.yahoo.com/www.Yahoo.com d. Netscape Home
8. The tool used to quickly find the information you are looking for on a Web site is called a(n):
   a. QuickFinder c. search engine
   b. Internet locator d. thesaurus
9. An open forum area where questions and messages can be posted for others to read is called a:
   a. chat room c. Web site
   b. FTP site d. discussion group
10. In order to use the Send... option on the File menu, you must first have a(n):
    a. e-mail tool c. Web browser
    b. ISDN line d. recycle bin
11. The command used to save a drawing file to an FTP site is:
    a. SAVEAS c. SEND
    b. SAVE d. ATTACHURL
12. To open a drawing from a Web site, this command is used:
    a. OPEN c. GOTOURL
    b. OPENFROMURL d. INSERT
13. The command used to insert a drawing from a remote location on the Internet is:
    a. OPENURL c. GOTOURL
    b. OPENFROMURL d. INSERT
14. DWF stands for:
    a. dynamic Web file c. drawing With flair
    b. drawing Web format d. drawing Web file
15. To attach a link to an object or area, this command is used:
    a. ATTACHLINK c. INSERTURL
    b. HYPERLINK d. OPENURL
16. To remove a link from an object, use this command:
    a. DETACH c. DETACHURL
    b. HYPERLINK d. DELETEURL
17. This command is used to find the linked objects and areas in a drawing:
    a. FINDURL c. GETURL
    b. FINDLINK d. SELECTURL

MATCHING

Match each term to the correct description by writing the appropriate number in each box at the left.

☐	URL	1.	Standard drawing file extension.
☐	HTTP	2.	World Wide Web.
☐	HTML	3.	T-Carrier connections.
☐	WWW	4.	Internet Service Provider.
☐	FTP	5.	Kilobytes per second.
☐	ISDN	6.	HyperText Transfer Protocol.
☐	ISP	7.	Modulator/Demodulator.
☐	DWF	8.	Hypertext Markup Language.
☐	Kbps	9.	Integrated Services Digital Network.
☐	T-1/T-3	10.	Uniform Resource Locator.
☐	Modem	11.	Drawing Web Format.
☐	dwg	12.	File Transfer Protocol.

WORD SCRAMBLE

Unscramble the six scrambled words below, one letter to each square, to form six AutoCAD LT–related words:

WIERDWELDBO

NINETRET

THYEXPERT

PERKYNIHLS

DEMOM

Unscramble the circled letters above to form the special answer as suggested by the illustration.

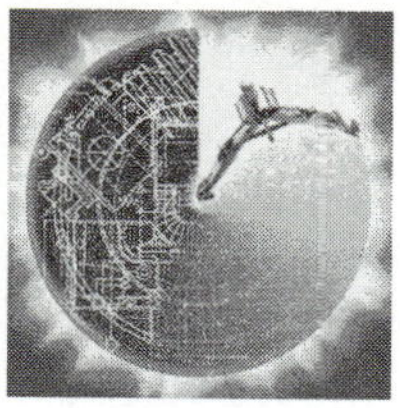

CHAPTER 17

Customizing AutoCAD LT

LEARNING GOALS

- Create custom command alias definitions.
- Automate AutoCAD LT using command scripts.
- Create and modify toolbars and toolbar buttons.
- Modify the AutoCAD LT pull-down menu system.
- Incorporate DIESEL strings in custom menu entries.
- Define custom linetypes and hatch patterns.

Why Customize?

One very important reason for the popularity of the AutoCAD and AutoCAD LT software packages is ease of customization. Within the technical drafting and design area there are many different methods and standards. Technical drawing fields include mechanical, architectural, electronic, civil, and other categories, with many highly specialized applications in each category. Some CAD software packages are very specialized, working most effectively within one specific discipline. AutoCAD LT is capable of working productively in each of these fields to meet almost any technical drawing need. This is because the AutoCAD LT software allows custom tools to be developed to meet specific needs. These custom tools automate repetitive tasks and can quickly finish even very complex tasks.

There are many ways to customize the AutoCAD LT software package to help you be more productive. You have already done simple customization of the interface by placing and positioning toolbars and setting up the drawing environment. Screen layout and drawing setup are two very important aspects of customizing your drafting environment; however, many other aspects of this software can be customized as well. You can customize the initialization files to control how AutoCAD LT starts up. Command scripts can be written and used for automating procedures. Custom menus can be built from scratch or the existing menu system can be modified to meet your needs. Your menu picks can be made "intelligent" through the use of DIESEL strings. You can create new command aliases for frequently used commands, and even design new linetype and hatch pattern definitions.

When you learn to customize AutoCAD LT, you are learning how to get the most out of your software. This chapter shows you how to be more productive and meet specialized needs through customizing the AutoCAD LT software.

Creating Your Own Command Aliases

Command aliases are shortened names for commands that allow you to access commands more easily from the keyboard. All command alias definitions are created and stored in an AutoCAD LT support file called ACLT.PGP. The term ***support file*** refers to files that are not part of the core program that are used to enhance or modify the way AutoCAD LT works. The ACLT.PGP file is used to modify the way AutoCAD LT works, but because it is not a part of the core program, it is not required in order for AutoCAD LT to run. The file extension PGP stands for ProGram Parameters.

All the existing command aliases you have learned so far are defined in the ACLT.PGP file. For example, the alias L for the LINE command, C for the CIRCLE command, and E for ERASE are all command aliases that are set up in the ACLT.PGP file.

The ACLT.PGP file is found in the \AutoCAD LT 2000\support folder. It is a standard ASCII text file and can be edited using the Notepad text editing software. Notepad is a simple text editing program that comes with the Windows operating system. To open the ACLT.PGP file using Notepad, start Notepad from the Accessories group and pick Open ... from the File pull-down menu. Using the Open dialog box, go to the \AutoCAD LT 2000\support folder and select the ACLT.PGP file. Figure 17.1 shows the ACLT.PGP file loaded in the Notepad text editor.

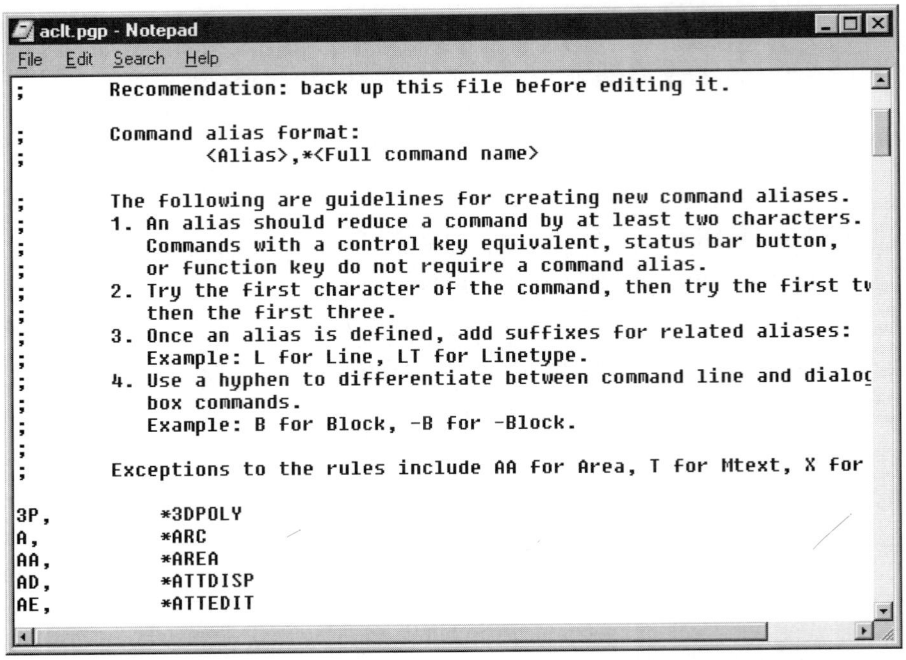

FIGURE 17.1 Notepad can be used to edit the ACLT.PGP file.

The introductory text at the top of the ACLT.PGP file explains how to create a command alias. Notice that the informative lines begin with a semicolon (;). Any line in the ACLT.PGP file that starts with a semicolon is considered a comment. Comments in files are ignored by AutoCAD LT. Comments in files are typically used for informative purposes and can be placed anywhere in the file as long as the first character on the comment line is a semicolon.

The introductory statement shows that the listing that defines a command alias is in this format:

<Alias>, *<Full command name>

This means that the alias, or shortened command name, is listed first, separated by a comma from the full command name. The full command name is preceded by an asterisk (*). The command alias can be any combination of alphanumeric characters. The term ***alphanumeric*** refers to any letters of the alphabet and the numbers 0 through 9. For example, a command alias could be named "1," "A," or even "A1." Any number of characters can be used in a command alias, but the purpose of an alias is to reduce typing requirements so the name should typically be shorter than the full command name. Another guideline that can be helpful is to stick with a shortened version of the actual command name. This makes the alias easier to remember. For example, the MSLIDE command does not have an alias listed in the ACLT.PGP file. If you were to create one, a logical choice for an alias name might be MSL. The choice of MS might be preferred, but this has already been assigned to MSPACE. It is best to avoid redefining existing aliases. An unrelated alias, M7 for example, could be used, but might not be as easy to remember.

When adding a new alias, it is a good idea to place your custom alias listings in the appropriate alphabetical position with the existing alias definitions. This helps you avoid accidentally redefining an existing command alias. If more than one listing is present in the PGP file for a single alias name, the last one encountered is the one that is used. If you prefer to do so, you can group your custom alias definitions in a separate area of the PGP file.

To use Notepad to add the alias MSL for MSLIDE, move the cursor to the line where you wish to enter the new definition. If there is already an entry on that line, press the Enter key to move it down one line and then use the arrow keys to move back up to the new blank line. Now, enter the following:

MSL, *MSLIDE

The modified ACLT.PGP file is shown in Figure 17.2. The number of spaces between the comma and the asterisk does not matter. You can have no spaces, one space, or any number of spaces. The primary factor is keeping the file neat and easy to read. Next, save the file by picking Save ... from the File pull-down menu.

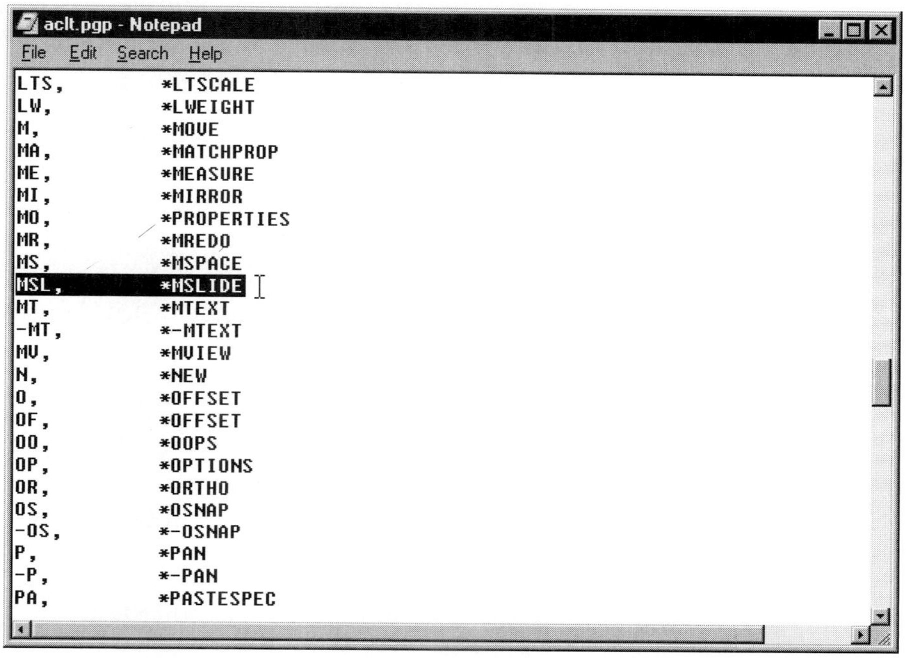

FIGURE 17.2 The new line in the ACLT.PGP file is highlighted. This creates a command alias named MSL for the MSLIDE command.

If AutoCAD LT has not already been started, the new PGP file is automatically loaded when you do start it. If AutoCAD LT is already active, you need to use the REINIT command to ***reinitialize,*** or reload, the PGP file. This command is started by typing **RI** or **REINIT** at the Command: prompt. The REINIT command displays the dialog box shown in Figure 17.3.

REINIT
RI

After reloading the PGP file, the new command alias is ready to use:

Command: **MSL**↵
MSLIDE
⟨*the Create Slide File dialog box is displayed*⟩

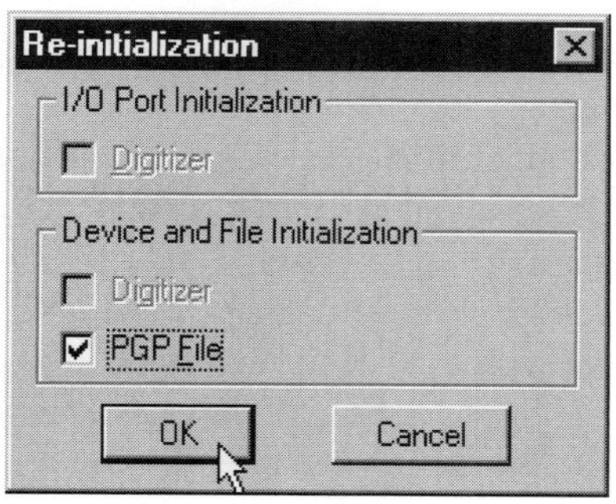

FIGURE 17.3 The REINIT command displays the Re-initialization dialog box. This allows you to reload the PGP file after making changes.

Command aliases can be defined only for starting commands, and they cannot access any of the options of that command. This means that although the Z alias can start the ZOOM command, it is not possible to define a command alias that automatically does a ZOOM Window or ZOOM Previous. Although command aliases have this limitation, you may still find that an effectively designed command alias list can help you be much more productive. Once you learn to use the keyboard effectively, it can be much faster than picking commands from the menus.

Field Notes

Existing command aliases can be redefined as desired. However, if your workstation is also used by others, you should not change the existing alias definitions.

When editing a support file, it is often a good idea to first create a backup version of the file you are editing. For example, before editing the PGP file you may wish to copy it to a file such as ACLT.PGP.BACKUP. This way, if you make changes that you do not like, you can always refer back to the original file.

Through the Window ...

When AutoCAD LT is installed, it automatically associates the PGP file with the Notepad text editing program. This means that if you double-click on the PGP file from Windows Explorer or File Manager, the Notepad program is automatically started with the PGP file loaded.

Exercise 17.1

Estimated time required: 5 min.

1. Using your file management application, make a copy of ACLT.PGP and name it ACLT.PGP.BACKUP.
2. Using the Notepad editor, open the ACLT.PGP file for editing.
3. Add three custom command alias definitions to the PGP file.
4. Save the ACLT.PGP file.

LEARNING CHECKPOINT

- ☐ Define the term *command alias.*
- ☐ In what file are command alias definitions created?
- ☐ What type of software application is used to edit the command alias file?
- ☐ Show how the alias DXI could be defined to start the DXFIN command.
- ☐ What command reloads the command alias file?

Automating AutoCAD LT Using Command Scripts

A simple, yet effective means of customizing the AutoCAD LT software is through the use of command scripts. A ***command script*** is a text file that contains a list of commands and options that AutoCAD LT reads and performs. It is called a script because the file tells AutoCAD LT what to do and what sequence to do it in. In essence, a script is a plain English programming language for AutoCAD LT.

A script file is an ASCII text file with a .SCR file extension. You can create a script file with any text editing software, but if you use a word processor, be certain to save the file as a *text* file. One easy way to create a script file is by using the Notepad program, found in the Accessories group. Within the script file, there are a few things you need to keep in mind as you create a script. First, any blank spaces in the file are interpreted as an [Enter] keystroke—just like when you press the space bar at the AutoCAD LT Command: prompt. Additionally, the end of each line is considered an [Enter] keystroke.

If the command script has any errors, it will run to the point where the error is encountered and then stop. Possible command script errors include misspelled commands or options, and incorrectly answering an AutoCAD LT prompt. Also, the use of spaces should be kept to a minimum, because spaces are not easy to count, and if you have one too many or one too few, it can cause your script file to produce an error.

Applications for script files vary widely. They can be used for doing drawing setups, unattended plotting, or even for running automated script shows using slide files. Creating and viewing slide files was discussed in Chapter 15. The following example shows a simple script file that does a brief setup procedure:

```
LIMITS
0,0
36,24
GRID
.5
SNAP
.25
ZOOM
ALL
```

The file can have any valid file name but must have a file extension of .SCR. A reasonable name for this might be SETUP-D.SCR because it performs a setup sequence for a D size sheet. Loading a script file into AutoCAD LT is done using the SCRIPT command. The SCRIPT command is accessed by Run Script ... from the Tools pull-down menu or by typing **SCR** or **SCRIPT** at the Command: prompt. The SCRIPT command displays the Select Script File dialog box. Use this file dialog box to go to the correct directory and select the desired script file name. The Select Script File dialog box is shown in Figure 17.4.

Tools
Run Script...
SCRIPT
SCR

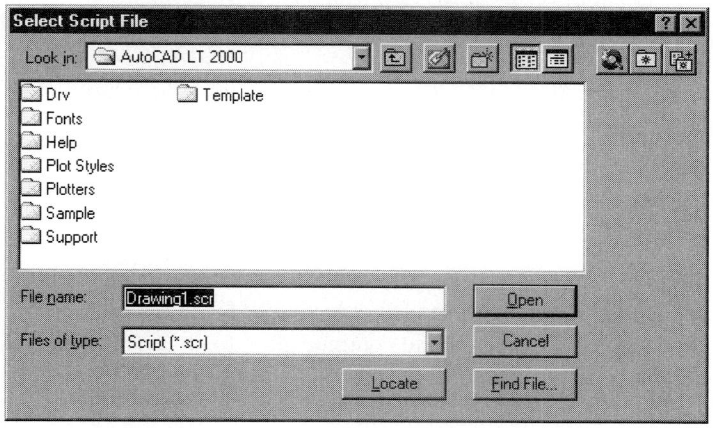

FIGURE 17.4 The Select Script File dialog box.

As the script file is processed, each entry is shown at the command line. This is useful for troubleshooting the script if it malfunctions. The term ***troubleshooting*** is used to describe the process of figuring out what went wrong. The command line entries for the SETUP-D script file are shown in the following example as they appear on the text screen:

```
Command: LIMITS
Reset Model space limits:
Specify lower left corner or [ON/OFF] <0.0000,0.0000>: 0,0
Specify upper right corner <12.0000,9.0000>: 36,24
Command: GRID
Specify grid spacing(X) or [ON/OFF/Snap/Aspect] <0.5000>: .5
Command: SNAP
Specify snap spacing or [ON/OFF/Aspect/Rotate/Style/Type] <0.5000>: .25
Command: ZOOM
Specify corner of window, enter a scale factor (nX or nXP), or
   [All/Center/Dynamic/Extents/Previous/Scale/Window] <real time>: ALL
Regenerating model.
```

A more complex script file might set up layers, insert title sheets, or automate almost any desired task. Keep in mind, however, that the best and easiest way for setup procedures is often through the use of drawing template files. Another common use for script files is to create a running "slide show" for any number of purposes. A ***slide show*** in AutoCAD LT, similar to a presentation given using standard slides and a projector, displays a sequence of graphic images. An AutoCAD LT slide show can display a comprehensive portfolio or proposal to a prospective client, and slide shows are often used at trade shows and product demonstrations.

To create a portfolio using a slide show, you first need to create all of the slides you wish to display. These slide files might be of various drawing projects on which you have worked. Unless you have a laptop computer to run the show, it is likely that you will be transporting the slide show files on a floppy diskette. With this in mind, the following example assumes that the slide files have been placed on a floppy diskette that occupies the A: drive.

Once you have created and stored your slide files, it is time to write the script file. In this example, four slide files have been created using a simple naming system of PFS001.SLD through PFS004.SLD. The command used to view a slide file is VSLIDE, so this is the first command, followed by a space for an Enter and then the file name entry. This example shows the use of spaces, but it also works the same with each entry on its own line. It is not necessary to specify the .SLD file extension. When running a script file, the command line versions of commands are used, with no dialog boxes being displayed. Here is how the script file starts:

```
VSLIDE A:\PFS001
```

At this point, it is necessary to pause the script file for a short time. Allowed to run unchecked, the slides are displayed as quickly as AutoCAD LT can process the script file. This does not allow any viewing time for the slides being viewed. For this purpose, AutoCAD LT provides the DELAY command. The DELAY command does just as its name suggests—it delays before processing the next command. The DELAY command prompts for the amount of time to delay, and the input is read as *milliseconds,* or thousandths of a second. So, a delay time of 500 is 500/1000 s, or 1/2 s. A delay time of 4000 produces a 4-s delay. The DELAY command accepts delay times up to 32,767 ms, which is just over 30 s.

Before placing the DELAY command in the script, the next slide file to be viewed can be preloaded. This causes the next script file to be read from disk and stored in memory while the previous slide is being viewed. This helps the script file to run smoother. To preload a slide file, use the VSLIDE command and precede the slide file name with an asterisk:

```
VSLIDE A:\PSF001
VSLIDE *A:\PSF002
DELAY 2000
```

Now, the slide show starts by displaying PSF001, then it preloads PSF002 and delays for 2 s of viewing time. When a slide file has been preloaded, it is viewed by entering the VSLIDE command again without specifying a file name. So for the script to continue after the delay, another VSLIDE command is necessary:

```
VSLIDE A:\PSF001
VSLIDE *A:\PSF002
DELAY 2000
VSLIDE
```

The preload and delay sequence is now repeated. The completed script file is shown here with comments to clarify the purpose of each line:

```
;Display PSF001.SLD
VSLIDE A:\PSF001
;Preload PSF002.SLD
VSLIDE *A:\PSF002
;Delay 2 seconds for viewing time of PSF001.SLD
DELAY 2000
;Display the preloaded PSF002.SLD
VSLIDE
;Preload PSF003.SLD
VSLIDE *A:\PSF003
;Delay 1.5 seconds for viewing time of PSF002.SLD
DELAY 1500
;Display the preloaded PSF003.SLD
VSLIDE
;Preload PSF004.SLD
```

VSLIDE *A:\PSF004
;Delay 4 seconds for viewing time of PSF003.SLD
DELAY 4000
;Display the preloaded PSF004.SLD
VSLIDE

Comments can be placed in a script file on a line that begins with a semicolon, similar to the PGP file. Each comment listed in the preceding script example explains the function of the line that follows.

The previous example shows one run-through of the script file. The delay times you set up in your slide show should be based on how much viewing time is necessary for the viewer to absorb the intent of each slide. A simple introductory slide, such as a lead-in title slide, might require only a second or two. A more complex slide that shows many important details might require four or five seconds or even longer.

If you want to interrupt a script without canceling the command, press the Backspace key. The Esc key can also be used, but the Backspace key does not print *CANCEL* on the command line. To resume the script processing where it left off, enter the RESUME command at the Command: prompt.

There are also specialized commands available for your script files that allow added flexibility. Here is a listing of those commands:

- **RSCRIPT** This command can be placed at the end of a script file to repeat the script. This creates a self-running script file that runs until interrupted.
- **TEXTSCR** The TEXTSCR command displays the AutoCAD LT text window.
- **GRAPHSCR** This displays the AutoCAD LT graphics window.

Field Notes

- In a script file, you must press Enter after the final entry on the last line or the entry will not be processed.
- When creating a script file, the best technique is to walk through the commands and options manually and write down each command and option as you go. This helps you to avoid errors that can occur from not addressing a prompt sequence correctly.

Exercise 17.2

Estimated time required: 15 min.

1. Create a selection of four slide files from drawings you have completed so far.
2. Create a script file that runs a *repeating* slide show of these four slides.
3. Be sure to preload slides when appropriate and allow for sufficient viewing time for each slide.
4. Save the script file as EX17.2.SCR.

LEARNING CHECKPOINT

- ☐ What is a script file?
- ☐ How can script files be used to increase drafting productivity?
- ☐ Describe how slide shows can be created using script files.
- ☐ What special commands are available in script files? What do they do?

Customizing Toolbars and Toolbar Buttons

Toolbar buttons provide top-level access to many frequently used commands and options. Rather than having to first pick a menu and then pick an option from the menu, many toolbar buttons can access the same options with a single pick. In addition to providing a wide variety of toolbars and toolbar buttons for you to use, AutoCAD LT also allows you to modify the existing tools or even to create your own completely new tools.

Having a custom tool set for different types of drafting needs can greatly enhance your productivity levels. Using toolbars and toolbar buttons, you can create buttons that start commands and create menu macros. A ***macro*** is a set of multiple commands and options that runs automatically when started. For example, a selection that starts the ZOOM command is not considered a macro. A selection that starts the ZOOM command and then enters the Previous option is a macro because it does more than one thing.

The simplest way to work with toolbars is to control toolbar visibility and location. Right-clicking on any existing toolbar button accesses the Toolbars cursor menu. As shown in Figure 17.5, the toolbars menu shows a checkmark by the names of the toolbars that are currently visible. To change the current visibility of any toolbar listed, just pick its name. The next time you display this menu, the toolbar name displays a checkmark, indicating that it is currently visible.

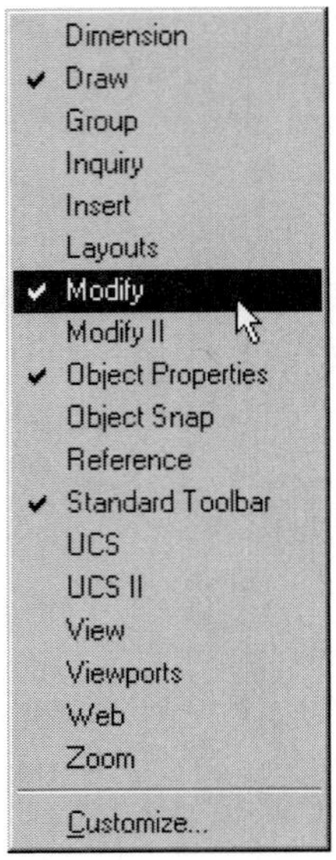

FIGURE 17.5 Right-click on any toolbar button to display the Toolbar cursor menu.

You can place toolbars anywhere on the screen in either a floating or a docked state. A docked toolbar appears as though it were part of the program window, attached near the top, bottom, or sides of the window. By default, the Standard and Object Properties toolbars are docked at the top of the screen; the Draw and Modify toolbars are docked on the left side of the screen. To change the Modify toolbar to a floating state, point to the grab bars; then press and hold the pick button on your mouse. When you move your cursor, you will see the outline of a toolbar. A bold outline indicates that if you release the pick button, the toolbar will drop into a floating state. When your cursor approaches the edge of the window, the outline becomes thin and may change shape or orientation, which indicates that the toolbar will be docked on the edge to which you are pointing. Figure 17.6 illustrates the differences in the dragged outline. While you are dragging a toolbar the helpstring displayed on the status bar at the bottom of the AutoCAD LT window indicates that you can prevent docking by holding the Ctrl key as you drag the toolbar. This is useful when you want to move a toolbar near an edge but you do not want it to be docked.

A docked toolbar defaults to a single row or column and cannot be resized. When a toolbar is floating, it can be resized as desired. Resizing toolbars is limited to adjusting the number of rows or columns in which the buttons are displayed. Toolbars are resized just like program windows. Move your cursor to an edge and when you see the resizing cursor, press and hold the pick button. Drag the toolbar into the desired shape and release the pick button. Toolbars can be resized only horizontally and vertically, not diagonally.

To begin working with toolbars, select Toolbars … from the View pull-down menu or right-click on any toolbar button and select Customize...from the cursor menu. Both of these methods results in the display of the Customize dialog box, which is shown in Figure 17.7.

The toolbar listings in the Toolbars list show the names of the toolbars preceded by a check box used to display or hide the toolbar.

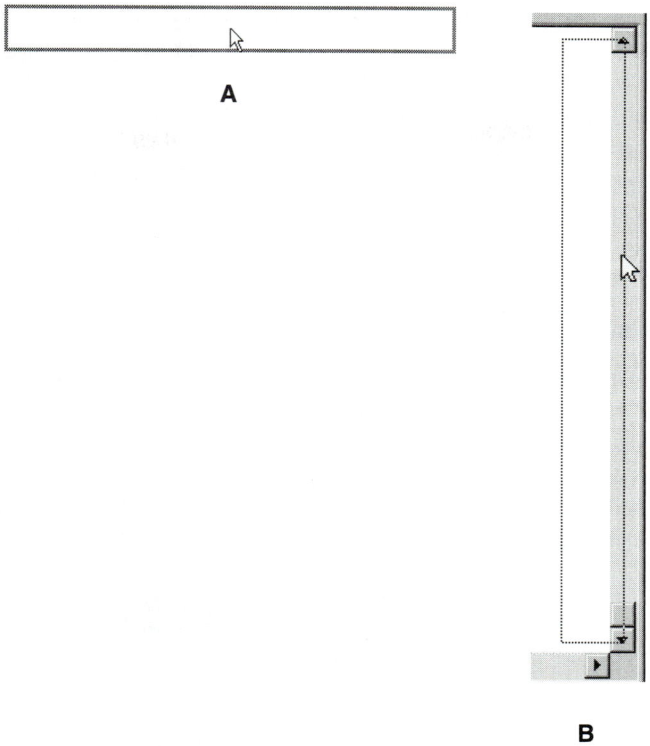

FIGURE 17.6 The outline of the toolbar indicates whether the toolbar will be (A) Floating or (B) Docked when the button is released.

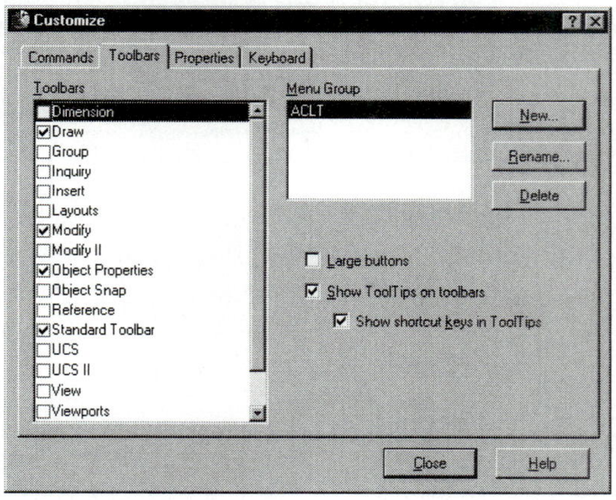

FIGURE 17.7 The Toolbars tab on the Customize dialog box.

Field Notes

As you customize the AutoCAD LT tools, it is usually a good idea to maintain the standard tool set unchanged. Place your new and modified tools in new toolbars. This keeps the basic AutoCAD LT interface in the same condition as described in the documentation and reduces relearning requirements for the drafters using the new tool set.

The Customize Dialog Box

AutoCAD LT 2000 provides an easy-to-use interface for creating and modifying toolbars and toolbar buttons. Figure 17.7 shows the Customize dialog box with the Toolbars tab in front. This dialog box has four tabs. The Toolbars tab is displayed by default when you pick Toolbars… from the View pull-down menu. As indicated previously, the checkboxes next to the names in the Toolbars list allow you to control toolbar visibility. The Menu Group field selection determines the menu file whose toolbars are displayed in the Toolbars list. Loading multiple menus and using menu groups is covered later in this chapter.

The settings in the lower right area control the appearance and functionality of the toolbar buttons. The default size of toolbar buttons is 16 pixels wide by 15 pixels high. You can increase the size of the toolbar buttons to 24×22 pixels by checking the Large buttons checkbox. You will need to have your screen resolution set higher than 800×600 to use this setting effectively, because some of your toolbars will be too long to fit vertically on the screen. This means that the buttons at the bottom of these toolbars will not be visible when they are docked on the sides of the window.

It is highly recommended that you leave the Show ToolTips on toolbars option active. Even experienced users will benefit from having ToolTips displayed when using unfamiliar toolbars. The Show shortcut keys in ToolTips option helps you become familiar with all the shortcut keys available in AutoCAD LT.

The three buttons on the right side allow you to create new toolbars and rename or delete existing toolbars. These options are detailed in the next section.

Creating a New Toolbar

To create a new toolbar, pick the New... button from the Toolbars tab in the Customize dialog box. The New Toolbar dialog box, shown in Figure 17.8, prompts you for the name and menu group of the new toolbar. The toolbar name can contain spaces and a maximum of 128 characters. It is usually best to use shorter, descriptive names for your new toolbars. If you do not provide a specific name for the toolbar, it is named Toolbar1. A second unnamed toolbar defaults to the name Toolbar2, and so on. Unless you have more than one menu loaded already, the Save toolbar in menu group: list shows only the default ACLT menu group.

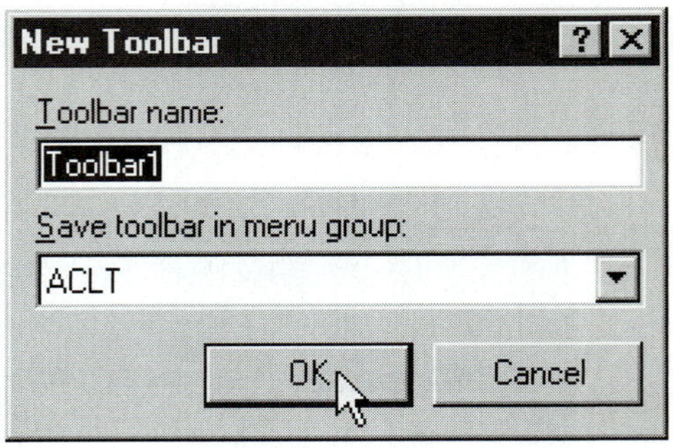

FIGURE 17.8 The New Toolbar dialog box.

After specifying the new toolbar name and group information, pick OK and the new toolbar will appear on the screen near the top of the AutoCAD LT window. Because the new toolbar is empty, it may not be wide enough to display the assigned name on its title bar. Figure 17.9 shows a new toolbar named Custom Tools as it appears when first created.

FIGURE 17.9 The new toolbar appears without any buttons in it.

Field Notes

Unneeded toolbars can be deleted using the Toolbars dialog box. Highlight the name of the toolbar to delete and pick the Delete button. Before you delete any toolbar, be absolutely certain that you have selected the correct toolbar name and be sure that you actually want to delete it. There is no OOPS command for toolbars, and the UNDO command does not affect any changes made to toolbars, so ***deleted toolbars cannot be automatically restored!***

Adding Buttons to a Toolbar

Existing toolbar buttons can be placed in the new toolbar to form your own specific grouping of existing AutoCAD LT tools, or you can create completely new buttons. To place an existing AutoCAD LT toolbar button on the toolbar, pick the Commands tab in the Customize dialog box. The Commands tab is shown in Figure 17.10.

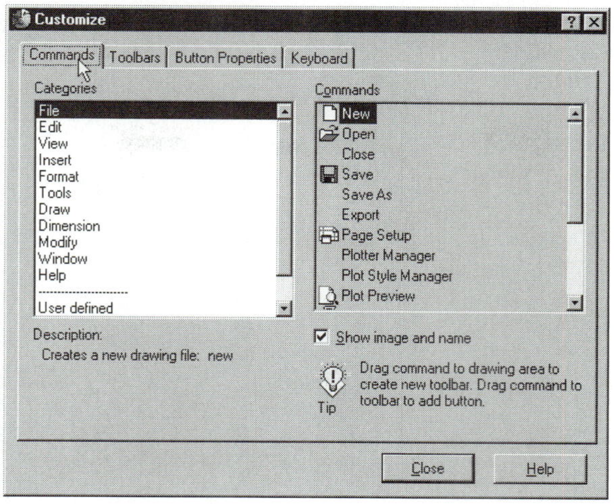

FIGURE 17.10 The Commands tab on the Customize dialog box.

When adding components to the new toolbar, you can select from any existing toolbar buttons or define completely new buttons. Two lists are displayed on this tab, labeled Categories and Commands. The Commands list displays the existing toolbar button definitions based on the current specification in the Categories list. The commands that do not display a button icon do not have a corresponding toolbar button defined.

The command categories are the same as the pull-down menus, which makes it easier to find the button you are looking for. Optionally, you can select All Commands from the category list to display all the AutoCAD LT commands. The User Defined category is discussed later in this chapter. Scrolling the list downward displays the Flyouts category, which contains all the existing flyout button definitions. In all categories, when you highlight a command, a short text description appears below the Categories list.

To select a command to place on the new toolbar, point to it with the cursor; then press and hold the pick button. When the cursor is moved away from the selected tool, an outline appears that is then dragged to the desired toolbar. Drag the toolbar button inside of the toolbar where you want it and then release the pick button. Figure 17.11 shows the toolbar button for the Real-Time Zoom tool being selected, dragged, and then dropped into the new toolbar.

When placing additional buttons into a toolbar, they are added on the side where they are dropped. Once placed, the toolbar buttons can be relocated by picking and dragging them to the desired new location.

When dragging buttons from the Modify Toolbars dialog box to a toolbar, be sure that the dragging image is within the boundary of the toolbar before dropping it. If it is not within the boundary, it automatically creates a new toolbar. The new toolbar is given a generic name using the format "Toolbar1." Each time you create a toolbar using this method, the number is increased by one, so the second one is named "Toolbar2." If you do accidentally create a toolbar, it can be deleted using the Delete button on the Toolbars tab in the Customize dialog box, or you can pick Rename… and change the name.

In addition to placing buttons from the Customize dialog box, you can copy buttons from other toolbars. This works similar to other drag-and-drop type operations in Windows. Select the button from one toolbar, press and hold the pick button, then press and hold the Ctrl key on the keyboard.

To remove a button from a toolbar, drag it away from the toolbar it is on and release it in the drawing area. Make sure the dragged button is not over a different toolbar, or it is simply moved to the toolbar whose boundaries it falls within. Dropping it in the drawing area displays a warning dialog where you can confirm or cancel the delete operation (see Figure 17.12).

Field Notes

One common application for creating new toolbars is to group commonly used commands into one convenient location. You may have several tools that you use very frequently that are located across several different toolbars. Having all of these toolbars visible at the same time can take up too much valuable screen space. The solution is to create a new toolbar and place each of the desired tools within that single toolbar.

FIGURE 17.11 The drag-and-drop method is used to place toolbar buttons in a toolbar. (A) Select the desired tool, (B) press and drag to the new toolbar, and (C) drop it into the new toolbar.

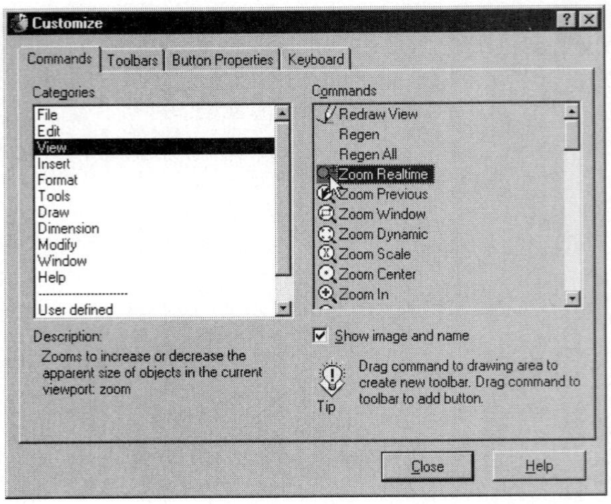

A

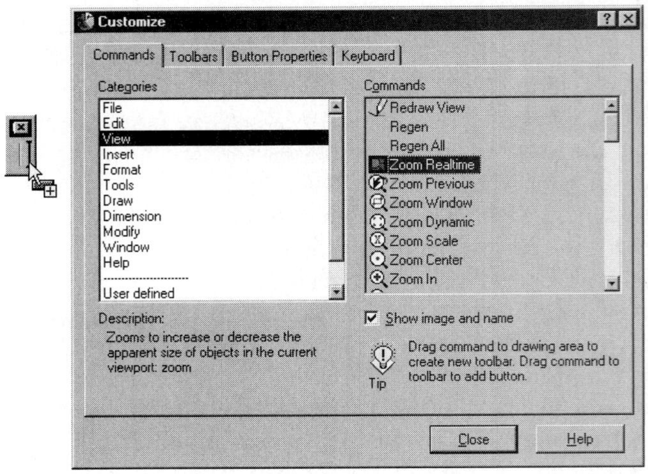

B

C

FIGURE 17.12 A warning is given along with an opportunity to confirm or cancel toolbar button deletion.

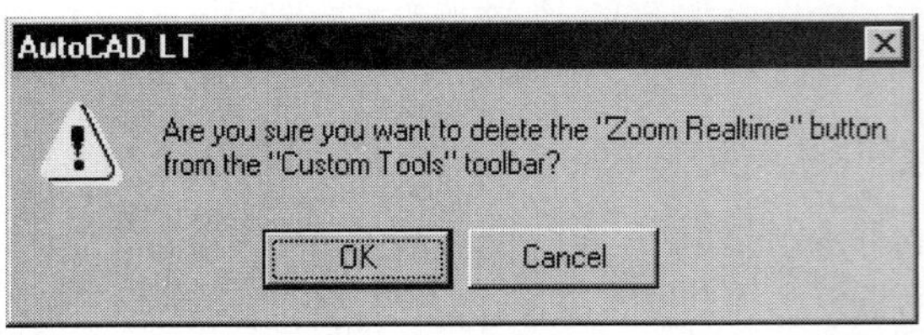

Exercise 17.3 **Estimated time required: 10 min.**

1. Create a new toolbar using the New... button in the Toolbars tab of the Customize dialog box.
2. In the New Toolbar dialog box, name the new toolbar Custom Tools and pick OK.
3. Display the Commands tab.
4. Think about five toolbar buttons that you use frequently. Place these five buttons on the new toolbar.
5. Remove a button from the toolbar by dragging it off of the toolbar.
6. Drag a button out of the Customize dialog box and drop it on the graphics screen area, outside of any toolbar boundaries.
7. Find the item "Toolbar1" on the Toolbars: listing or the Toolbars tab.
8. Remove the unwanted toolbar by highlighting its name and picking the Delete button. Be sure that the correct name is highlighted before picking the Delete button.

Working with Toolbar Buttons

Toolbar buttons can be created and modified as desired, to do any specific set of tasks available within the AutoCAD LT command structure. Most of the existing tools either start a command or supply one or two options to the command. This is just the tip of the iceberg with regard to the powerful tools you can create using menu macros.

To begin working with toolbar buttons, you need to learn a few special codes that are used within the menu system, but the rest is all plain English. Once you have become familiar with these special codes, menu customization can be very easy to master. One of the best ways to begin learning is by looking at what is already there. Once the Customize dialog box is visible, you can use the Button Properties tab by picking any button. Optionally, you can right-click on the button and pick Properties... from the pop-up cursor menu. Figure 17.13 shows the Button Properties tab with the Line toolbar button properties displayed. The Name: text box shows the name of the toolbar button. This text is displayed in the tooltip when you point at the button with the cursor and the text in the Description: text box is displayed on the status bar. The entry in the Macro associated with this button: area shows the menu code that is activated when you select the button. Finally, the Button Image area shows the graphic image that is displayed on the button.

The content and function of the button name and help are self-explanatory. In the Macro associated with this button: area is the actual functionality of the button. In the case of the Line tool, the function is fairly simple. The entry is as follows:

FIGURE 17.13 The Button Properties for the Line toolbar button.

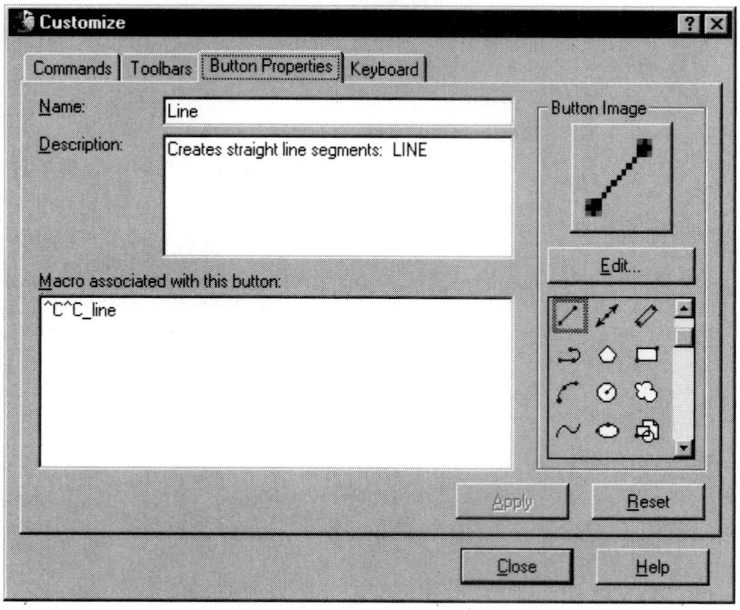

```
^C^C_line
```

The function of the ^C is a cancel, as if you pressed the Esc (Escape) key. If you have configured AutoCAD LT to recognize AutoCAD LT standard keystrokes using the User Preferences tab of the Options dialog box, then the Ctrl+C keystroke is a cancel also. In the menu file, the ^ character is known as a *caret,* and it indicates the use of the Ctrl key. So, the ^C code is called *Control C,* which is simply a cancel. This is true regardless of any settings in the Preferences dialog box.

Notice that there are two ^C's in sequence in the preceding entry. This ensures that the rest of the code starts at the Command: prompt. If, for example, you are in Dim: mode and start a Horizontal subcommand, the first ^C returns you to the Dim: prompt and the next ^C returns you to the Command: prompt before issuing the LINE command. Unless a menu macro is intended to be transparent, it should always begin with ^C^C.

Next is the actual command. In this case, the command is preceded with an underscore character (_). The underscore character is not necessary unless you are producing menu that may be used on non-English versions of AutoCAD LT. The underscore character causes the commands and options to be translated automatically so they can work on any foreign language version of AutoCAD LT. The actual command text is entered the same as it would be at the Command: prompt. AutoCAD LT automatically adds an Enter to the end of the menu macro in most cases. The exceptions are discussed later. This is the simplest form of menu macro, and represents the type of content for most of the toolbar buttons.

Field Notes

Do not use command aliases in toolbar or menu macros. Always use the full command name.

More complex macros require some additional special codes. The next example is of the Break 1 Point button found in the All Commands category in the Commands tab. The Button Properties dialog box for this tool is shown in Figure 17.14.

The menu code entered in the macro listing for the Break 1 Point tool is:

```
^C^C_break \@
```

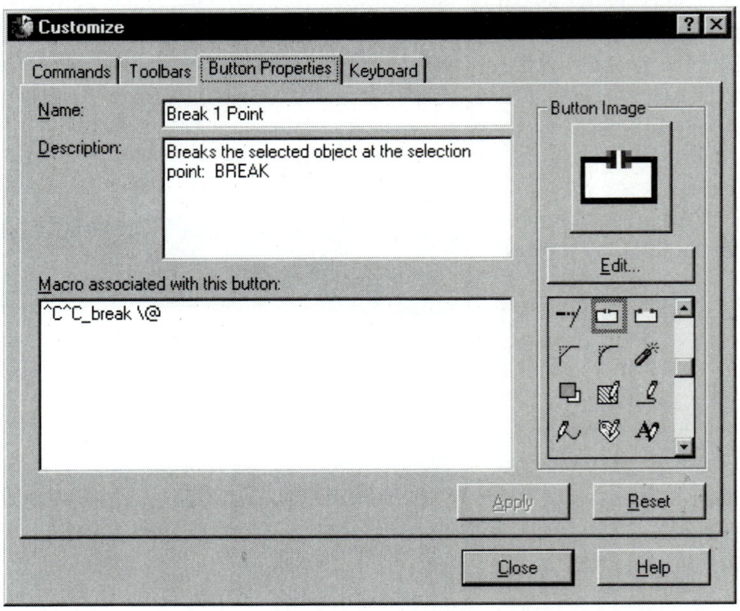

FIGURE 17.14 The Button Properties for the Break 1 Point tool.

Again, to ensure that the Command: prompt is available, ^C^C is the first entry. The underscore characters are for international versions and do not affect the basic functionality of the macro.

Field Notes

A ***transparent*** command or macro is one that can be processed without canceling the currently active command. If a macro is to be transparent, do not use the ^C^C characters. Any commands used in the macro should start with an apostrophe. For example, to do a transparent ZOOM Previous, the macro appears as:

```
'ZOOM;P
```

A macro can only be transparent if all of its commands are commands that can be used transparently.

Although this macro works normally when an object is properly selected at the prompt, it can have unexpected results if no object is selected. First, let's take a look at how it works and then explore how to make it work better.

As it is written now, the first command in the macro after the double cancel is the BREAK command, followed by a single space. As when entering commands at the Command: prompt, a space is used as an Enter keystroke. Optionally, you may use a semicolon character to indicate an Enter keystroke in a menu macro. It is strongly recommended that you use semicolons instead of spaces, because it is much easier to count semicolons than it is to count spaces. If your macro has an extra space or is missing one, your macro may not function properly. Trying to find the source of the problem can be much easier when you can see and count the Enter keystrokes in your macro.

The next item encountered after issuing the BREAK command is a backslash character. The backslash pauses the macro and allows user input—in this case, a pick point. Once the user picks a point, the BREAK command issues the prompt

Enter second point (or F for first point:):

The macro supplies an F and a space (Enter) to the prompt to use the first point option and then follows with another backslash to allow the user to pick a point for the first break point. The final prompt for this command is

Enter second point:

The macro uses the last point variable by supplying the "@" symbol, indicating that the first and second break points are the same. An automatic Enter is issued at the end of the macro. The result is the object is broken at a single point. Although this macro works when an object is properly picked by the user, it can produce unexpected prompts if you accidentally miss the object on your first pick attempt. Here is an example:

Pick the menu button
Command: _break Select object: *Pick a point not on an object*
No object found
Select object: @ No object found
Select object: *If you pick the object now...*
Specify second break point or [First point]: *Press Escape to cancel*

Because the anticipated object was not selected, this macro fails and issues unexpected prompts and error messages. This next example shows a simple, yet effective, means of preventing this problem. The improved version of the macro looks like this:

```
^C^C_select;_single;\_break;@;_f;\@
```

The first command issued in this macro is the SELECT command, which is used to create a selection set. The character following the SELECT command is a semicolon. As previously discussed, the semicolon is the same as an Enter keystroke. Spaces can also be used as an Enter, but spaces are not as easy to count. The use of semicolons makes it easier to design and troubleshoot menu macros.

The SELECT command issues the Select objects: prompt, and the option entered is SINGLE. The SINGLE selection mode is commonly used in menu macros because it limits the selection set to a single selection. The BREAK command can only break a single object, so this helps to ensure that a single object is selected. This is also followed by an Enter (semicolon).

A backslash character is placed next. In a menu macro, the backslash pauses for user input. In this macro, after SINGLE is entered at the Select objects: prompt, the Select objects: prompt is issued again. Here is where the menu macro pauses for user input, allowing the user to select the object to be broken. However, if no object is picked, the SELECT command reissues the Select objects: prompt. Additionally, if the user presses Enter at the prompt, the macro halts, instead of starting the FILLET command (as does the first version). Because SINGLE selection mode is being used, the SELECT command is complete and the Command: prompt is returned. The rest of this macro works in the same way as the first version.

This macro provides an excellent example of combining automated procedures with user input to accomplish a complex task. Using AutoCAD LT's existing tools as examples helps you to learn valuable techniques like this.

Field Notes

The BREAK command requires a point selection. You can prevent the user from using an implied window or crossing at the selection by setting the PICKAUTO variable to a value of 0. This can be part of the menu macro. The following example temporarily disables PICKAUTO for the selection sequence:

^C^C**_pickauto;0**;select;_single;**_pickauto;1**;_break;@;_f;\@

When you begin to create macros for toolbar buttons, it is important to be certain that you address each prompt as it occurs at the command line. If you provide an incorrect response to a prompt, the macro will not work properly. The best way to ensure that each prompt is answered correctly is to walk through the entire procedure one step at a time, writing down the appropriate command or option entries as you go. Then, reference this listing as you develop the macro.

The next step in creating a custom toolbar button is to place a blank button on the toolbar. A blank button can be found in the User Defined category. Two buttons are available in this category; one is a blank button, the other is a *flyout* button and is discussed later. Figure 17.15 shows a blank button placed within the new toolbar.

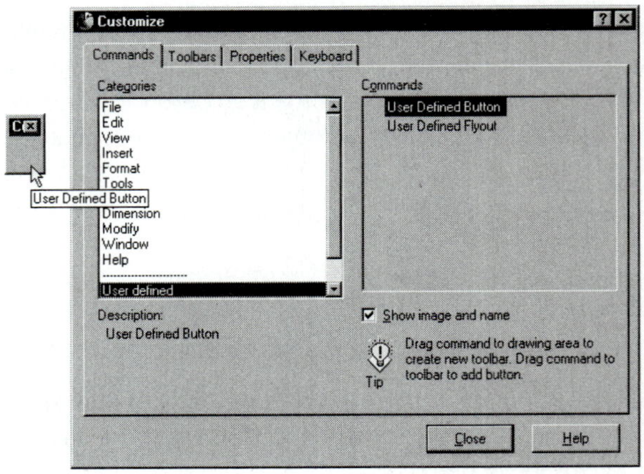

FIGURE 17.15 Blank buttons can be used to create completely new toolbar buttons.

After placing the button, pick it to access the Button Properties. The Button Properties fields reads "User Defined Button," and the macro area displays the familiar ^C^C , as shown in Figure 17.16. This example creates a macro designed to perform basic setup procedures for a multiple viewport model tab. The intent is that before creating a drawing, this macro moves to the Model tab, sets up the snap, grid, and display, and creates an arrangement of model viewports. As suggested earlier, it is best to walk through the process step by step first in order to determine the required command and option entries. The command sequence is shown here:

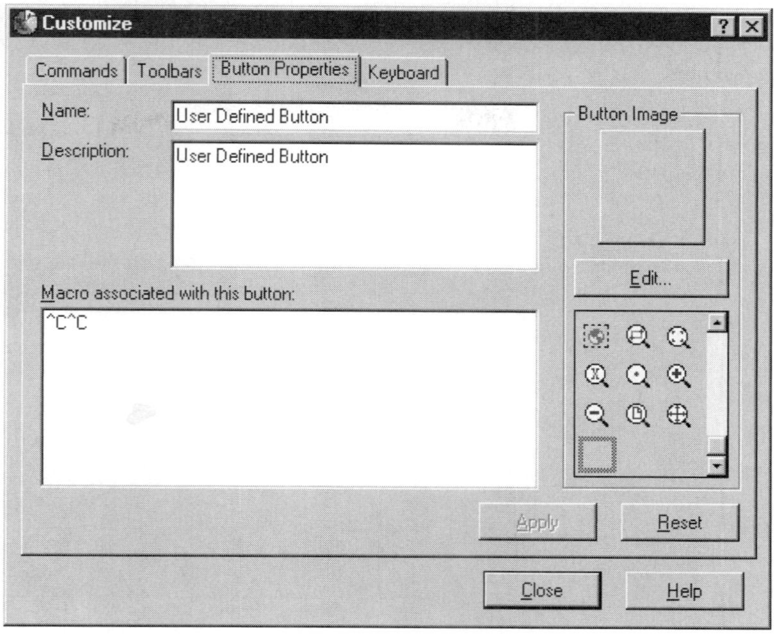

FIGURE 17.16 The default Button Properties for a User Defined Button.

Command: **TILEMODE**
Enter new value for TILEMODE <1>: **1**
Command: **LIMITS**
Reset Model space limits:
Specify lower left corner or [ON/OFF] <0.0000,0.0000>: **0,0**
Specify upper right corner <12.0000,9.0000>: **48,36**
Command: **GRID**
Specify grid spacing(X) or [ON/OFF/Snap/Aspect] <0.5000>: **2**
Command: **SNAP**
Specify snap spacing or [ON/OFF/Aspect/Rotate/Style/Type] <0.5000>: **.25**
Command: **ZOOM**
Specify corner of window, enter a scale factor (nX or nXP), or
[All/Center/Dynamic/Extents/Previous/Scale/Window] <real time>: **ALL**
Regenerating model.
Command: **-VPORTS**
Enter an option [Save/Restore/Delete/Join/SIngle/?/2/3/4] <3>: **3**
Enter a configuration option [Horizontal/Vertical/Above/Below/Left/Right] <Right>: **R**
Regenerating model.

Using the AutoCAD LT text screen is an easy way to reference the step-at-a-time procedure. Now, with this information, a macro can be constructed by simply entering the command sequence in as a macro and substituting semicolons where Enter was pressed:

^C^Ctilemode;1;limits;0,0;48,36;grid;2;snap;.25;zoom;all;-vports;3;r

Other elements to define include the name and help text for the button. Figure 17.17 shows the Button Properties tab with all of the entries completed.

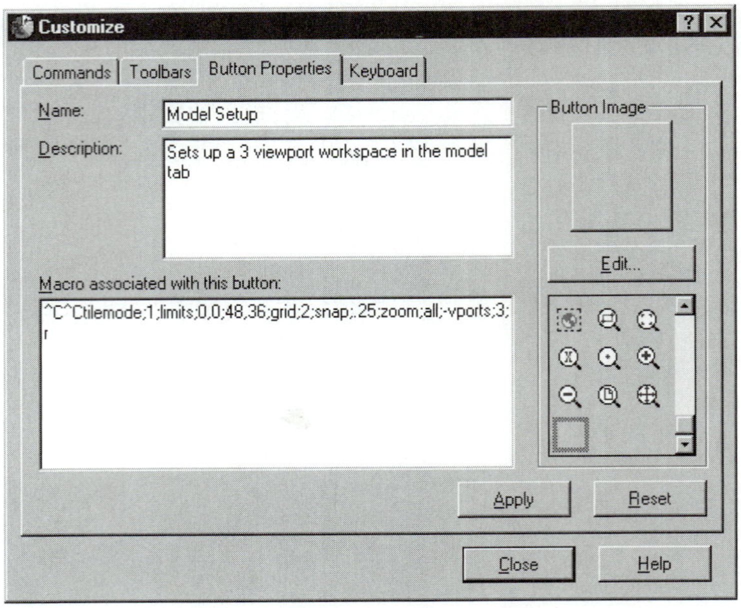

FIGURE 17.17 The custom Model Setup toolbar button properties.

Field Notes

At the end of a macro, AutoCAD LT issues an automatic Enter. If, however, the last character of the macro is a semicolon, this is not true. Therefore, if you want more than one Enter at the end of the macro, it is necessary to place one semicolon for each Enter needed. For example, when using an option of the LAYER command, an Enter is required for the option, and another is used to return to the Command: prompt:

```
^C^CLAYER;MAKE;DIM;;
```

where the DIM; returns you to the Layer option line, and the next Enter returns the Command: prompt.

The final property to define is the icon, or graphic image, for the button. The Button Image area of the Button Properties tab offers three options for defining the appearance of a button. First, the scrolling image list displays all of the currently defined buttons. Although you are free to select any existing button, this can cause confusion if the icon looks the same as a familiar icon that starts a different command or macro. The next option is to select an existing button and then pick the Edit ... button to alter its appearance. Or, you can select a blank button image and pick the Edit ... button to define the button image from scratch. In this case, a blank button image is selected and the Edit ... button is picked. This displays the Button Editor dialog box, shown with its features labeled in Figure 17.18.

The drawing area of the editor is in the center of the dialog box and is composed of a grid of squares, or pixels. If the AutoCAD LT buttons are currently displayed at the small size, this grid is 16×15 pixels. If the Large buttons toggle has been set in the Toolbars tab, the image is displayed at 24×22 pixels. To see this grid visibly displayed, select the Grid toggle in the Button Editor dialog box.

The four basic drawing tools are in a row across the top of the dialog box. The current color used by these tools is set by picking the desired color swatch from the Colors column on the right side of the Button Editor dialog box. The available drawing tools include Pencil, Line, Circle, and Erase and are used as follows:

- **Pencil** The Pencil tool colors one pixel at a time in the current color by pressing the pick button on your pointing device. Holding the pick button down while you move the Pencil colors each grid that is touched.

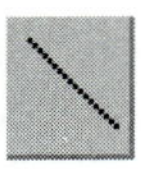

- **Line** The Line tool draws straight lines in the current color. To draw a line, move the cursor to the location where the line is to start, then press and hold the pick button while moving the cursor to the other end of the desired line. Similar to drawing lines in AutoCAD LT, a rubberband line is displayed to show where the line is to be drawn. Releasing the pick button causes the line to be drawn.

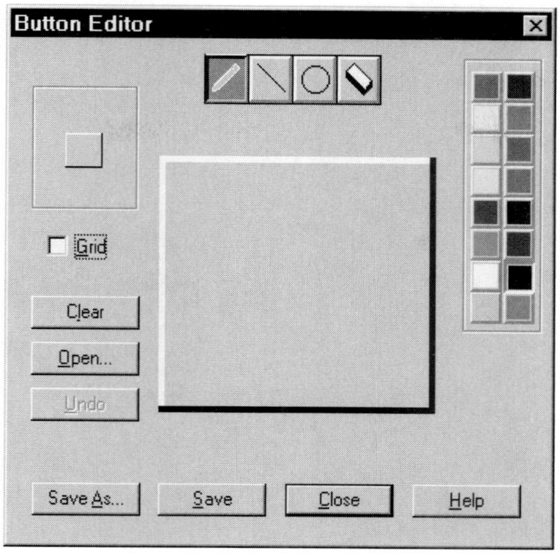

FIGURE 17.18 The Button Editor dialog box can be used to create or modify button icon images.

- **Circle** Although the AutoCAD LT documentation refers to this as a Circle tool, it would be more accurate to call it an Ellipse tool. The first point picked is the center of the circle or ellipse. Then the final shape of the object is determined by the second pick. Both circles and ellipses can be created, but it may take some practice to create truly round circles.

- **Erase** The Erase tool returns pixels back to the background color. The functionality is much like the Pencil tool; individual pixels can be erased or you can hold the pick button and move the eraser to affect each pixel it touches.

A preview of the image being created is displayed actual size in the upper left corner of the Button Editor dialog box. This changes size depending on the currently configured size of the toolbar buttons in AutoCAD LT. The other options available in the Button Editor dialog box are as follows:

- **Clear** This is used to completely clear the image from the drawing area. This is your basic "start over" button.
- **Open** The Open button allows you to open an existing bitmap file. You can only open files that are the appropriate size, either 16×15 or 24×22 pixels. The Paintbrush program and other software that produces bitmaps can be used to create button images, but the image size must be correct.
- **Undo** This works like the U command in AutoCAD LT, but you can only undo one operation. You can even undo a Clear.
- **Save As . . .** This allows you to save the created image as bitmap files.
- **Save** This button saves the current image using the current file name if it has been named. If the image has not been saved to a file, then it is saved in the menu resource file, which is discussed later.
- **Close** The Close option closes the Button Editor. If you have unsaved changes, a prompt is issued to allow you to save changes before exiting.
- **Help** This offers help for the dialog box.

Figure 17.19A shows an image created in the Button Editor for the Model Setup tool. After picking the Save and then the Close buttons, the Button Properties dialog box now displays the newly created icon, as shown in Figure 17.19B.

The Apply button must be selected before any of the changes are actually applied to the button being edited. If you dismiss this dialog box without picking Apply, all of your changes are lost and cannot be recovered. Any time that the Apply button is enabled, it means that you currently have unsaved changes. After picking the Apply button, it is again disabled until further changes need to be saved. Once the changes have been applied, the new image appears on the toolbar button and the macro is associated with it.

To complete the process, close the Customize dialog box. A message then appears on the status line telling you that AutoCAD LT is compiling menu files, and lists various file names. The term ***compiling*** refers to a process in which the menu files are rewritten, with the latest changes, in a way that provides the fastest access to the information by AutoCAD LT. Once the menu is compiled and the Command: prompt reappears, the new toolbar button is ready to use.

FIGURE 17.19 (A) After an image has been designed for the toolbar button, (B) it appears in the Button Properties dialog box where it can be applied to the button.

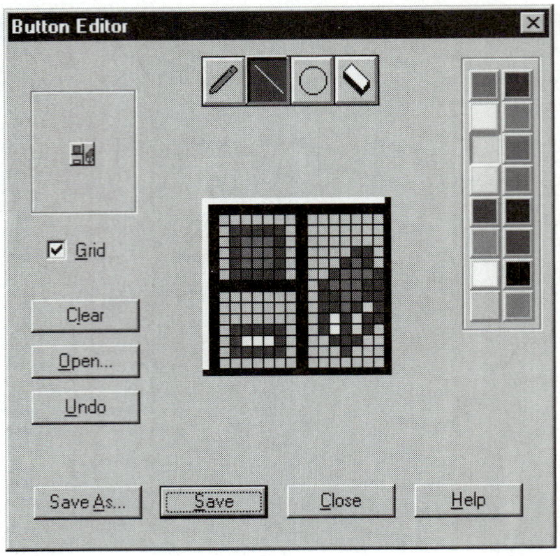

A

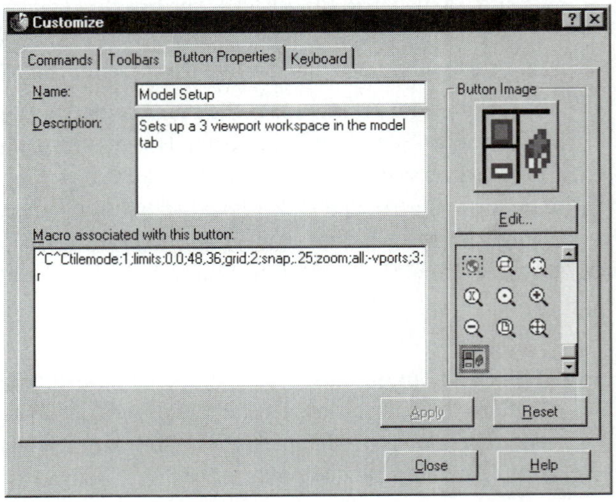

B

Field Notes

When a macro is finished processing, control reverts back to the command line. This means that you can use a macro to start a command, or even supply some of the options, and then return control to the user. When a block with attributes is inserted using a macro, the attribute prompts can be answered in the macro, or control can be returned to the user after the block is placed.

Exercise 17.4

Estimated time required: 20 min.

1. Place a blank button from the Custom category on the Custom Tools toolbar.
2. Create a custom macro, similar to Model Setup, that does a setup routine using a viewport configuration of your choice. Assign an appropriate name and help text.
3. Create an image in the Button Editor that somehow communicates the intent of the button.
4. Apply the changes to the button and test it to be certain it works properly.

LEARNING CHECKPOINT

- ☐ What should all macros start with if they are not intended to be transparent?
- ☐ What character pauses a macro for user input?
- ☐ Which two characters can be used for an Enter keystroke? Which is best?
- ☐ How is a new toolbar created?
- ☐ Describe how a new toolbar button is created.
- ☐ How is the Button Editor used?
- ☐ What is the requirement for using bitmap files not created with the Button Editor?
- ☐ Why must two images be created for each new button?
- ☐ How are toolbar buttons moved and copied?
- ☐ What happens if you forget to pick the Apply button after making changes?

Creating Toolbar Flyouts

Toolbar flyouts allow you to hide an entire toolbar behind a single toolbar button. As an example, when you open the Insert flyout from the Draw toolbar, what you are actually seeing is the Insert toolbar. To see the contents of a toolbar associated with a flyout, pick the flyout button when the Customize dialog box is visible. This displays the Flyout Properties tab. To see the actual toolbar, place a check next to the toolbar name in the list on the Toolbars tab. The insert toolbar is shown with the insert flyout on the Draw toolbar in Figure 17.20.

The advantage of flyouts is that you can conserve valuable screen space while keeping the maximum number of tools immediately available. This is why there are several flyouts within the built-in AutoCAD LT tool set.

To create a flyout, you must first have a toolbar created that the flyout is to display. Figure 17.21A shows a toolbar with the Model Setup and other buttons as well. To assign a toolbar to a flyout button, you must know the name of the toolbar. This toolbar has been named Setups, and the name is highlighted in the Toolbars listing on the Toolbars tab in Figure 17.21B.

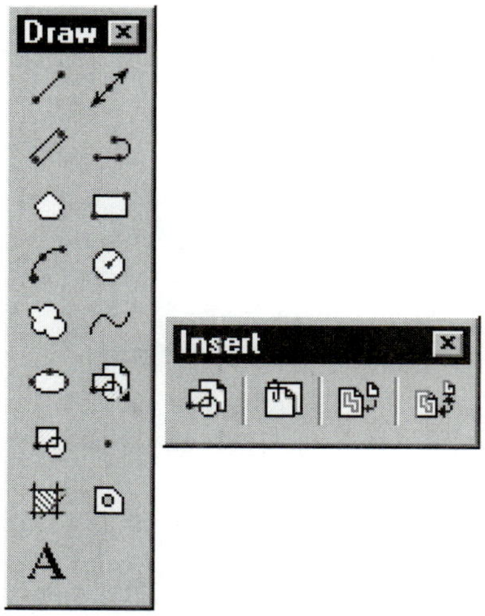

FIGURE 17.20 The Insert toolbar.

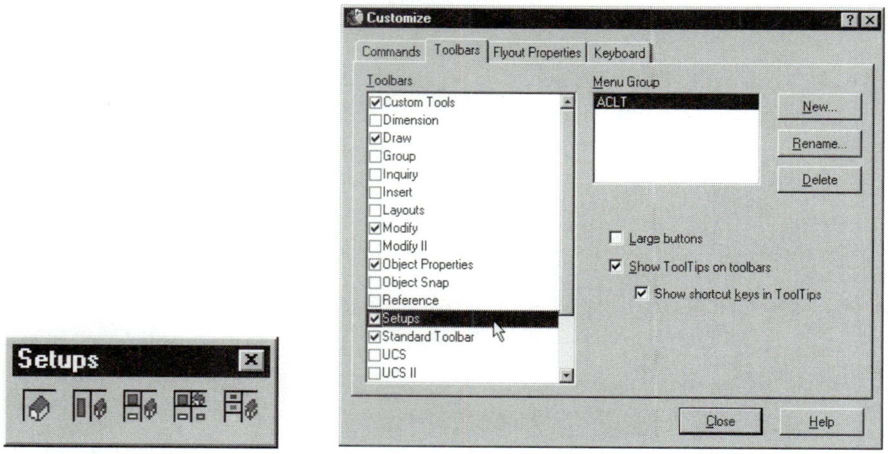

A B

FIGURE 17.21 (A) To create a flyout, you must have a toolbar available to assign to the flyout. (B) Toolbar names are displayed in the Customize dialog box.

The next step is to have a toolbar in which to place the flyout button. Do not place a flyout button *in* the toolbar that it displays, this creates what is called a ***recursive toolbar.*** Once you have a toolbar to place the flyout in and a toolbar for the flyout to display, you are ready to create the flyout button.

From the User defined category in the Commands tab, drag a blank flyout button to its destination toolbar. Next, pick the new flyout button. A warning dialog box is displayed indicating that the associated toolbar cannot be found. Pick the OK button to continue. The Flyout Properties tab is shown in Figure 17.22.

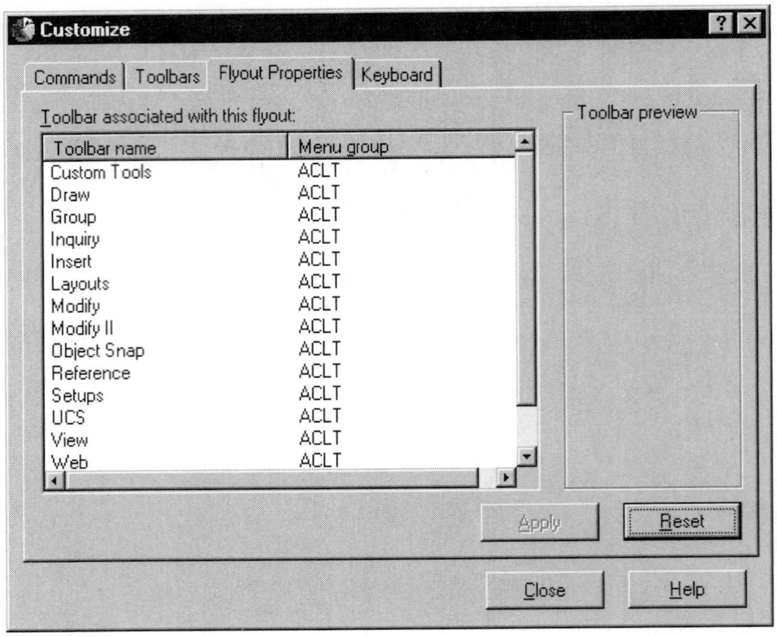

FIGURE 17.22 The Flyout Properties dialog box.

To associate the desired toolbar with the flyout button, the toolbar's name must be highlighted in the Toolbar associated with this flyout list box, as shown in Figure 17.23. To complete this operation, pick the Apply button and close the Customize dialog boxes.

When the changes are applied to the flyout button, it then displays the first button from the toolbar it is associated with. When you press and hold the pick button while pointing at the flyout button, it expands to show the entire toolbar. If one of the tools is picked, that button's icon is then displayed by the flyout. Figure 17.24 shows the Setups toolbar as an expanded flyout.

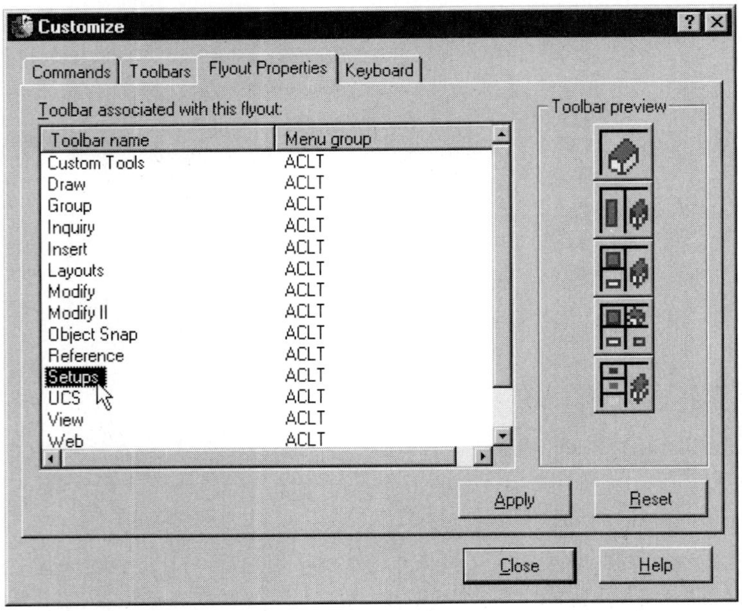

FIGURE 17.23 The completed Flyout Properties dialog box for the Setups flyout.

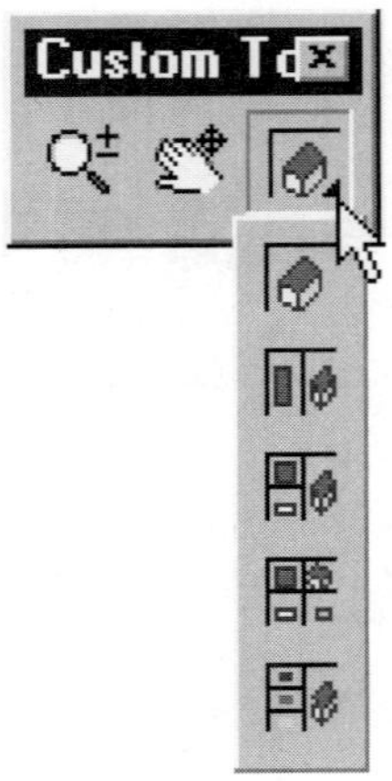

FIGURE 17.24 The Setups flyout.

Exercise 17.5 **Estimated time required: 20 min.**

1. Create a new toolbar named Setups.
2. Using the Model Setup button as a template, create setup macros for four other viewport configurations, and place them on the Setups toolbar.
3. Create a new toolbar named Custom Tools.
4. Place a flyout button on the Custom Tools toolbar.
5. Set the properties of the flyout button so it displays the Setups toolbar.

☑ LEARNING CHECKPOINT

- ☐ What is a flyout?
- ☐ How are toolbars associated with flyout buttons?
- ☐ What image is displayed on the flyout button?
- ☐ How do flyout buttons work when displaying their own icons?

Customizing the AutoCAD LT Menu System

The AutoCAD LT menu system is a combination of several different interfaces. You have already worked with toolbars and toolbar buttons, which are also part of the menu system. Other features of the menu system include digitizer button menus, pull-down and cursor menus, image tile menus, keyboard accelerators, help strings, and the tablet menu.

Menus are defined using ASCII text files that associate a particular menu action with a command or macro, in the same way that commands and macros are associated with toolbar buttons. Several different files are used by the AutoCAD LT menu system, with each one serving a special function. The default menu files included with AutoCAD LT are named ACLT, with various file extensions depending on what the file does. Each of the menu file types and their purpose is listed in the following list by file extension:

- **.MNU** The .MNU file is called a *template* file. It is referred to as a template because it is what the actual menu source file is based on. The ACLT.MNU file contains menu code and comments that can be referenced when you are learning to work with the menu system. The .MNU file is typically only edited when it is desirable to make your changes a permanent part of the menu system.
- **.MNS** This is the menu *source* file. The .MNS file is the primary file that you edit when making changes to the AutoCAD LT menu system. Any changes you make to the toolbar menus are stored in this file.
- **.MNC** The .MNC file is the *compiled* version of the source file. This file cannot be read and edited directly, but it is a much faster file for AutoCAD LT to work with than the ASCII version (.MNS).
- **.MNR** This file is the menu *resource* file. All bitmap images for toolbars and image tile menus are stored in this file for easy access and fast retrieval. This helps to avoid unnecessary delays when displaying graphic menus.

To edit the menu source file, you must use a text editor that can edit larger files. When trying to open the .MNS file with Notepad, you may get the message that the file is too large to open with Notepad. The prompt asks if you would like to open the file with WordPad instead. It is OK to open the file and edit it using WordPad, but you need to be certain that if you save the file, you save it as a text-only file. Similar to script files, discussed earlier, a menu source file must be saved in ASCII format. If you use any word processor to edit your menu, be sure that you save it as a text-only file.

It is not recommended that you directly edit the ACLT menu files. It is not necessary to edit these files when adding new features to the menu system; edit them only if you wish to change something about the built-in menus. If you do edit the ACLT menu files, be sure that you create a backup copy of the menu to refer to if you have problems. You can do this using Windows Explorer.

Menus in the Workplace

When modifying a menu system in a professional environment, certain considerations must be made. With any new interface, the users will need time to learn to use it effectively. This process is often referred to as a *learning curve*. In the workplace, time is money, so it is important to keep the learning curve as short as possible. One of the best methods for assisting users in this process is to maintain a base menu that is common to each workstation. It is also easier for new employees to integrate into a department when the AutoCAD LT default menu is used as the base menu system.

Frequently, the menu system is modified only by adding to it rather than by removing or relocating existing features. The best approach for making these additions is to start a completely new menu file where your additions will be stored. You can then load the new menu file in addition to the existing base menu and even specify which elements of any currently loaded menus are visible. Loading and unloading of menu files is covered later in this chapter.

Another aspect of menus in the workplace is usability. All the new elements should be easy to recognize and to use. Graphic images, labels, and helpstrings should be clear and concise. Always keep in mind that users of varied experience levels may use your custom menus. If your menu is designed to meet the needs of less experienced users, then it will be usable by all.

Menu Sections

When you open the .MNS file, you see that it is divided into several sections. Figure 17.25 shows the ACLT.MNS file opened using WordPad. Each section can be identified easily because the section names have three asterisks in front of them. For example, the first section in the menu file is listed as:

***MENUGROUP=ACLT

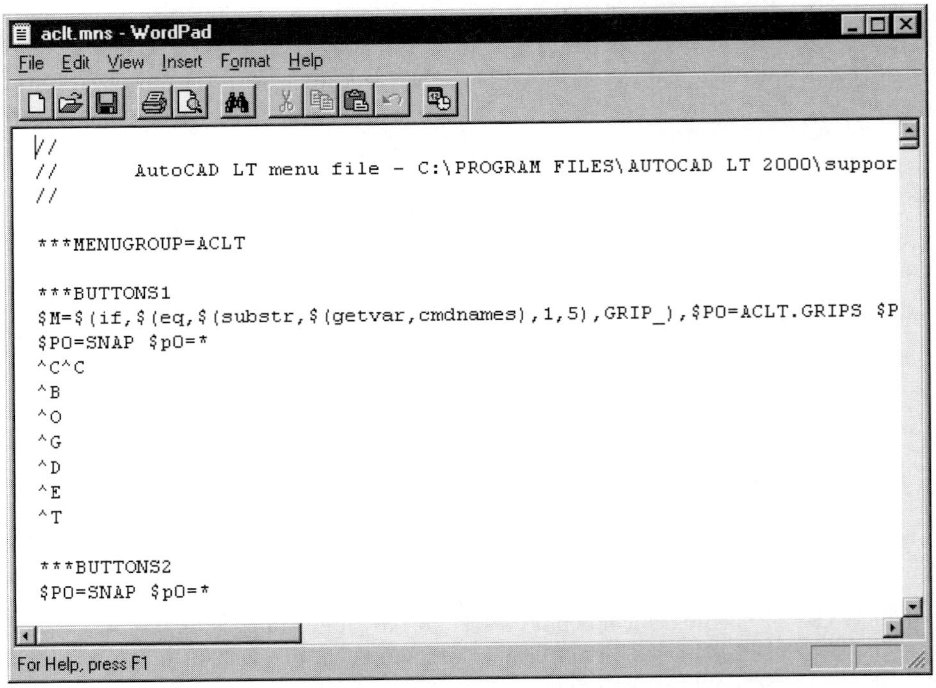

FIGURE 17.25 The ACLT.MNS file can be edited using WordPad.

Group names are used when loading partial menu files, which is discussed later in this section. The MENUGROUP section supplies the group name, but does nothing else. Prior to this first group listing are three lines that start with the characters //. The double-slash indicates that the line is a comment line and is ignored by AutoCAD LT.

The next section in the menu file is listed as:

***BUTTONS1

The BUTTONS1 section describes the function of each button on your pointing device, with the exception of the pick button. Although you can use this section to redefine your second and third mouse buttons, it is actually intended for multibutton pointing devices such as digitizers. Many digitizers have anywhere from 4 to 16 buttons. Editing this section allows you to assign special functions to each of these buttons.

Using the text search feature in your editor, searching for three asterisks is an easy way to locate menu sections within the menu file. The following listing provides a brief description of each of the sections found in the menu:

- *****BUTTONS1 and ***BUTTONS2** These sections are used if your computer does not use a system pointing device, such as the system mouse in Windows. The term ***system mouse*** can refer to either a mouse or a digitizer and indicates that the pointing device is used not only by AutoCAD LT but also by the operating system. Although there are only two buttons sections in the default menu, you can have up to four buttons menu sections. The purpose of each section is detailed later.
- *****AUX1 and ***AUX2** These menus are equivalent to the buttons sections when you are using a system mouse. Windows uses a system mouse by default, but can be configured to use another pointing device. There can also be up to four AUX sections.
- *****POP0** This defines the cursor menu, which is accessed by using the middle button on a three-button mouse, or by pressing the Shift key and right-clicking. The default cursor menu displays the object snap override menu.
- *****POP1–***POP10** These are the standard pull-down menus. AutoCAD LT can support POP menus up to POP16 within a single menu file. Additional POP menus are used by the system.
- *****POP500–***POP999** These are the menu sections where context-sensitive shortcut menus are created.
- *****TOOLBARS** Toolbars can be edited manually from the menu file, but it is much easier to edit them as explained previously in this chapter.
- *****IMAGE** This section defines your image tile menus.
- *****ACCELERATORS** If Keystrokes Accelerators is set to Customizable in the Preferences dialog box, you are able to use keystrokes like [Ctrl+C] for COPYCLIP and [Ctrl+V] for PASTECLIP. These are referred to as accelerator keystrokes and are defined in this section.
- *****HELPSTRINGS** Help strings, also referred to as help text, for toolbars are defined in the Description text box within the Button Properties dialog box. For pull-down menus, the help strings are defined here.
- *****TABLET1–***TABLET4** These sections define a menu system for use with a digitizer tablet. The default configuration allows for four menu areas and a screen pointing area.

Exercise 17.6 **Estimated time required: 10 min.**

1. Open the ACLT.MNS file using WordPad.
2. Using the Find option, locate each of the menu sections.
3. Using the Save As... option, save the menu file with the name CHAP17.MNS.
4. Close the text editor.

MENUGROUP Names and Partial Menus

AutoCAD LT supports the use of multiple menus, allowing you to combine menu elements from different menu source files. Whether you load all elements of an additional menu file or just some elements, it is referred to as a *partial* menu. Each partial menu file to be loaded must have a unique menu group name. As shown previously, the menu group name for a menu file is specified in the main menu section labeled ***MENUGROUP. A menu group name cannot have spaces or punctuation marks and can be up to 32 characters in length. The menu group name for the default AutoCAD LT menu is ACLT.

There are different ways to start a menu project. In many cases, the best way is to create a new menu file and assign it a menu group name. You can do this by opening any text editor application and creating a new file. As the first line of text in the file, enter the following:

***MENUGROUP=MYMENU

Be certain to press the Enter key after entering this line, otherwise AutoCAD LT may not be able to read the file correctly. This menu group uses the name MYMENU, but you can specify any desired named as long as it complies with the naming conventions indicated earlier.

Save the file in a *text only* format and name it as desired, but you must specify a file extension of **.MNS**. This menu file is now ready to load and use in AutoCAD LT. Once loaded, any new toolbar additions can be added to this menu file by selecting the menu group name in the New Toolbar dialog box (refer to Figure 17.8).

If you choose to, you can begin editing a copy of the existing menu file rather than creating a brand new file. This enables you to work within the existing menu structure, which can be very helpful for learning how the menu works. For working through the pull-down menu discussion later in this chapter, it is recommended that you use this method. To update the menu group information within the new menu file, you will need to do two things. First, change the entry in the MENUGROUP field to a new menu group name. This example uses the menu group name **CHAP17**. The second step is to replace all references to the menu group name in the menu from ACLT to match the CHAP17 specification in the MENUGROUP field. Menu calls are discussed later in this chapter, but for now you should know that menu calls within the menu file specify a menu group name, period, and then the actual menu name. So all menu calls in this file will currently read ACLT.*menuname*. To update this file, you need to change the "ACLT." into "CHAP17." in each occurrence within the menu. The easiest way to do this is to use your editor's Find & Replace tool to find the text **ACLT**. and replace it with **CHAP17**. Selecting a Replace All option makes all the replacements in a single operation. Be certain to include the period for both the find and replace values.

Exercise 17.7 **Estimated time required: 5 min.**

1. Use Wordpad to open the file CHAP17.mns you created in Exercise 17.6 for editing.
2. Use the Find & Replace tool to update all menu group references in the menu file by placing "ACLT." in the *Find what:* field, and "CHAP17." in the *Replace with:* field. Use the Replace All option to make all the replacements in a single operation.
3. Save the menu file and close the text editor.

Loading the Menu

Once a menu file has been created or modified, it must be loaded into AutoCAD LT before it can be used. The command used to load menus is MENULOAD. The MENULOAD command can be accessed by picking Menus... from the Customize cascade on the Tools pull-down menu, or by typing MENULOAD at the Command: prompt. The MENULOAD command displays the Menu Customization dialog box, as shown in Figure 17.26.

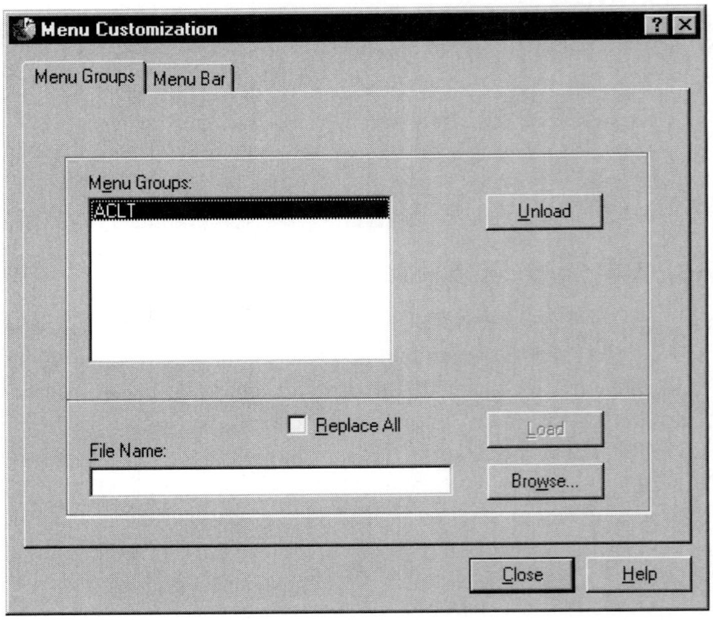

FIGURE 17.26 The Menu Customization dialog box is used to load menu files.

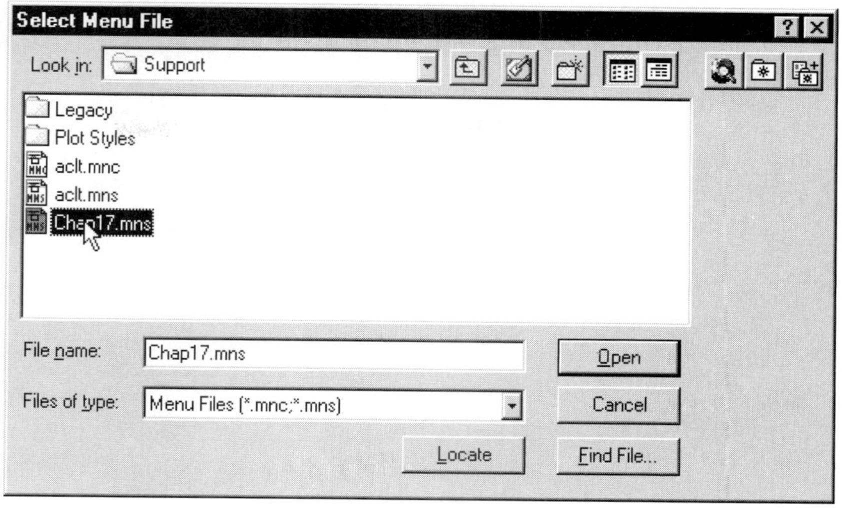

FIGURE 17.27 The Select Menu File dialog box provides an easy way to specify the name and location of a menu file to load.

To load a menu file, either type the full directory path and file name in the File name: text box, or select the Browse... button to use a file dialog box. It is usually easier to use the file dialog box, which is displayed in Figure 17.27.

Notice that the Files of type: list defaults to *Menu Files (*.mns, *.mnc).* This is the correct setting, and should not be changed unless you intend to load a template file (.MNU). Be aware that loading a menu template file automatically overwrites any changes you have made to the toolbars, because toolbar changes and additions are stored in the .MNS file. Loading an .MNU file creates a new .MNS file, thereby discarding all of your toolbar modifications. If you do try to load a menu template file, a strong warning is issued to ensure that you really want to go through with it before the file is actually loaded. The warning dialog box is shown in Figure 17.28.

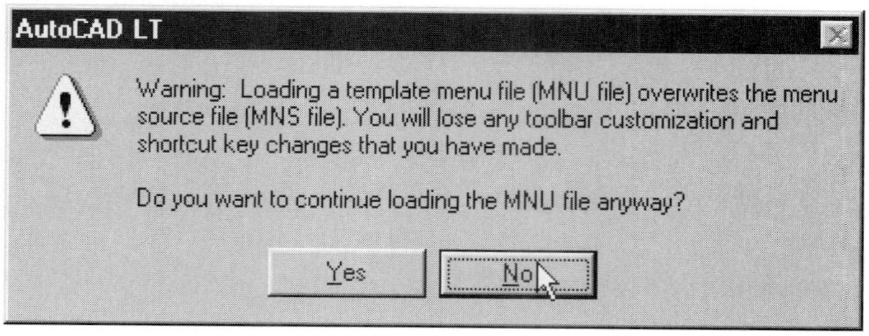

FIGURE 17.28 Loading a menu template file overwrites any changes you have made to the toolbar menu system. If loaded by accident, it can destroy many hours of toolbar modification work in just a few short seconds.

Once you find and select the .MNS file to be loaded, you are returned to the Menu Customization dialog box. AutoCAD LT cannot load multiple menus that use the same MENUGROUP name. If you attempt to reload the ACLT.MNS file, an error message is displayed, as shown here:

Unable to load menu: C:\Program Files\AutoCAD LT 2000\support\aclt.mns
A menu with that MENUGROUP name already exists.

To reload an existing menu regardless of the MENUGROUP name, check the Replace All toggle. This causes the menu currently loaded in memory to be redefined based on the newly loaded menu.

When loading a menu with a different MENUGROUP name, the toolbars and pull-down menus from both menus are then available. This allows you to continue using your standard menu while being able to use tools from other menu files also. Figure 17.29 shows the Menu Customization dialog box with both the ACLT menu and the CHAP17 menu loaded.

When more than one MENUGROUP name is currently loaded, you can specify which features you want available from each menu system. To set up the toolbars, select Toolbars ... from the View pull-down menu. Specify the MENUGROUP name for which you want to adjust the toolbars by selecting it from the Menu Groups: list as shown in Figure 17.30.

To adjust the pull-down menus, use the Menu Customization dialog box. The Menu Bar tab of this dialog box, shown in Figure 17.31, allows you to insert, remove, and relocate pull-down menus from the currently loaded MENUGROUP names.

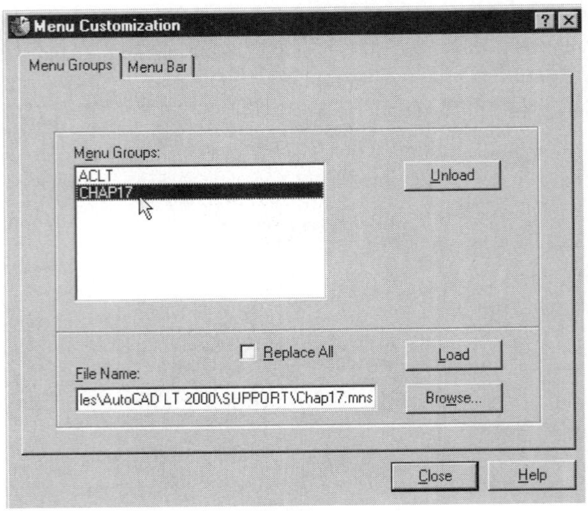

FIGURE 17.29 More than one menu can be loaded at a time using MENULOAD.

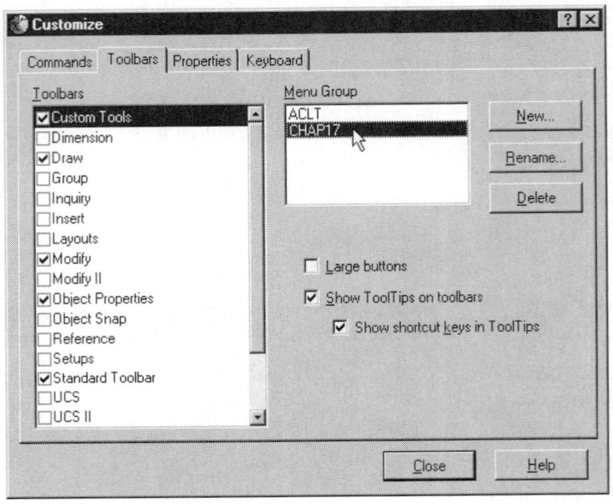

FIGURE 17.30 All the currently available MENUGROUP names are listed in the Toolbars tab. You can select the toolbars from each menu that you want to be visible.

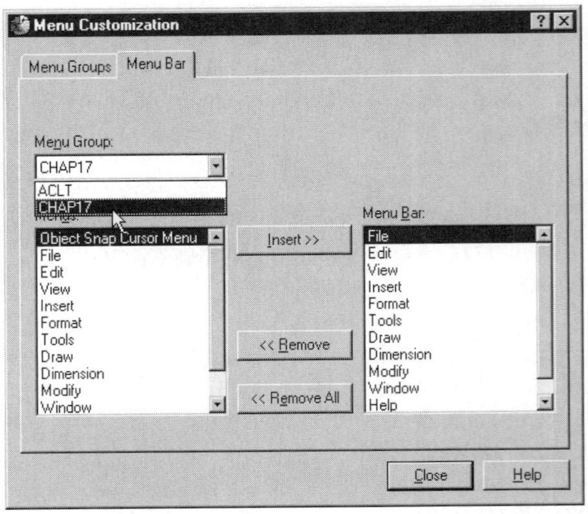

FIGURE 17.31 Pull-down menus from more than one menu can be made available on your menu bar.

To insert a new pull-down menu, first select the appropriate MENUGROUP name from the Menu Group: drop-down list. Next, highlight the name of the menu to insert in the Menus: list box. Finally, select the name of the menu to the left of which you want it inserted from the Menu Bar: list box, and pick the Insert>> button. Repeat this procedure for each menu that you need to insert.

Removing a menu from the menu bar is even easier. Pick the appropriate name from the Menu Bar: list and pick the <<Remove button. Removing a menu does not delete it from the menu file; it simply removes it from the menu bar. Picking the <<Remove All button clears the menu bar of all menus.

When a menu is no longer needed, it should be unloaded. This reduces the amount of memory required by AutoCAD LT and speeds up your menu system. To unload a menu, go to the Menu Groups tab of the Menu Customization dialog box. In the Menu Groups: list, highlight the MENUGROUP name that you wish to remove and pick the Unload button.

Field Notes

- The buttons menus, accelerators, and tablet menus are not changed when loading additional menus, unless the Replace All toggle is checked.
- The MENUUNLOAD command also displays the Menu Customization dialog box.
- The UNDO and U commands have no effect on menu changes made using MENULOAD or MENUUNLOAD.

Exercise 17.8 **Estimated time required: 10 min.**

1. Use MENULOAD to load the CHAP17.MNS file. Do not check Replace All.
2. Use the Menu Bar tab to insert pull-down menus from the CHAP17 menu group and remove one or two existing pull-down menus.
3. In the Toolbars tab on the Customize dialog box, adjust the visibility of various toolbars from each menu group.
4. Use MENULOAD to load CHAP17.MNS. This time, check the Replace All toggle and see how the results differ from previously.
5. Use the Unload option to remove CHAP17.MNS and reload ACLT.MNS.

Working with Buttons Menus

The default buttons menu section provides preset functions for 9 buttons. Therefore, if you have a 10-button pointing device, the pick button remains unchanged, and the second through tenth buttons are given the appropriate function assignments as listed, and in the order provided, in the menu. You can freely edit these to change the default assignments, and you can add additional functions if you have a 12- or 16-button pointing device.

To show how the buttons menu system works, this example references the AUX1 menu as used by the Windows system mouse. Because the first button on the mouse is the pick button, the first listing in the menu section is applied to the second button. This means the rightmost button, unless you are using a left-handed mouse. The buttons are reversed on a left-handed mouse. In the AutoCAD LT environment, the right-click is an Enter. Looking at the AUX1 menu section, you see a complex-looking macro that controls the function performed when you right-click through the use of something called DIESEL code. An introduction to DIESEL code is provided later in this chapter. This code determines the current drawing status before determining what to do on a right-click. For example, when a grip is currently hot, right-clicking displays the grips cursor menu. When no command is active, the standard popup menu is displayed. If a command is active but a grip is not hot, right-clicking is equivalent to an Enter keystroke. Although it is not visible on this page, if you look at this line in the menu file, you will see that the rightmost character is a semicolon. Just as when working with toolbars, a semicolon in the menu file is an Enter. Also like the toolbar buttons, an automatic Enter is issued by AutoCAD LT at the end of each menu pick, unless the last character is a semicolon. The AUX1, AUX2, AUX3 and AUX4 menu sections are listed here:

```
***AUX1
$M=$(if,$(eq,$(substr,$(getvar,cmdnames),1,5),GRIP_),$P0=CHAP17.GRIPS$PO=* );
$P0=SNAP $p0=*
^C^C
^B
^O
^G
^D
^E
^T

***AUX2
$P0=SNAP $p0=*

***AUX3
$P0=SNAP $p0=*

***AUX4
$P0=SNAP $p0=*
```

Take a close look at the second listing in AUX1. The $P0=SNAP $p0=* is a menu call. A ***menu call*** is a special code that displays a menu or makes it active. All menu calls start with a dollar sign ($). In this menu call, the "p0" tells AutoCAD LT that it is referring to the ***POP0 menu, which is the cursor menu. The "=*" part tells AutoCAD LT to display the menu on screen *now.*

If you are using a three-button mouse, the middle button displays the object snap cursor menu. This makes sense, because the second listing in the menu is applied to the third button. However, to display the cursor menu using a two-button mouse, it is necessary to press the Shift key while right-clicking. The Shift key modifier tells AutoCAD LT to use AUX2 instead of AUX1. Notice that the listing for the second button in the AUX2 menu is the cursor menu call. The AUX3 and AUX4 menus use other modifiers. Figure 17.32 shows a table with the available key and button combinations and their effects listed.

FIGURE 17.32 Available button and key combinations and their effect.

Key and Button Sequence	Menu Used
Button only	AUX1 (or BUTTONS1)
Shift + Button	AUX2 (or BUTTONS2)
Ctrl + Button	AUX3 (or BUTTONS3)
Shift + Ctrl + Button	AUX4 (or BUTTONS4)

Therefore, it is possible to get four separate functions from the second button of the mouse if the AUX3 and AUX4 sections are added to the menu. With a three-button mouse, this provides for up to eight different functions besides picking.

The added items in the default AUX and BUTTONS menus include the ˆCˆC, which is a cancel, and several other control codes. These control codes are only available at the keyboard if you are configured for AutoCAD classic keystrokes in the Preferences dialog box, but they work from the menu file regardless of this setting. The function of these codes is as follows:

ˆB	SNAP Toggle
ˆO	ORTHO Toggle
ˆG	GRID Toggle
ˆD	COORDS Toggle
ˆE	IsoPlane Toggle
ˆT	Tabletmode Toggle

Any or all of these codes can be changed to a command or macro, as desired. The rules for working within menu files is much the same as working with toolbar buttons. To assign the LINE command to a Shift+RightClick, modify the AUX2 menu section to read as follows:

```
***AUX2
ˆCˆCLINE
```

Field Notes

In the BUTTONS and AUX menu sections, the first backslash character accepts the current screen coordinates of the cursor location rather than waiting for user input. This can be used to begin a command at the current location, for example:

```
^C^CLINE;\
```

When this macro is accessed, the LINE command is started using the current cursor location as the first input item. The first prompt for the LINE command is From point:, so the line is started at the cursor location.

Exercise 17.9

Estimated time required: 10 min.

1. Open CHAP17.MNS with WordPad.
2. Find the third and fourth buttons menu sections (AUX3 and 4 or BUTTONS3 and 4, as appropriate).
3. Edit your menu so CTRL + right-click starts the U command transparently and CTRL + SHIFT + right-click starts the REDO command.
4. Close the file and save your changes.

Customizing Pull-Down Menus

Pull-down menus can be modified as desired, removed, and new ones added. In a single menu file, AutoCAD LT supports up to 16 pull-down menus. The default ACLT menu defines 10 pull-down menus. It is generally recommended that the primary menu system remain as is, and that any modified menus be additions from a partial menu file. This keeps the AutoCAD LT documentation accurate, and ensures that all levels of AutoCAD LT users can function productively with the menu system.

To avoid the need to write an entire menu file from start to finish, AutoCAD LT allows the use of partial menu files. A ***partial menu file*** is one that has only specific items in it, such as a set of specialized pull-down menus or toolbars. All that is required in a partial menu file is a unique MENUGROUP name and the definitions for the items you want included.

To begin constructing pull-down menus, whether in a full menu file or a partial one, you need to understand what the necessary elements of a pull-down menu are. This example builds a partial menu file, one step at a time, that has a single pull-down menu in it. Except for the requirement for a unique MENUGROUP name in the partial menu file, the procedures and techniques are exactly the same.

Because it is a partial menu file and will be loaded separately from the primary menu, the menu must have its own unique menu group name. This name is placed in the MENUGROUP section as follows:

```
***MENUGROUP=Example
```

If you wish to place comments in the file, they can go on any blank line, as long as they are preceded with two forward slashes. The top of your partial menu file might look like this:

```
//
// Partial menu file name: Chap17A.mns
// This file holds custom drafting macros in a single pull-down menu.
//

***MENUGROUP=Example
```

Comments are not required, but they can be useful to help explain the intent of specific items, or to record information such as revision dates and author's name. The next required element is a POP menu name assignment. Even though there are already 10 pull-down menus in the default menu file, this is a unique file and its pull-down menu sequence should begin at POP1. POP1 is a main menu section, so it is preceded by three asterisks:

```
***POP1
```

The first line below the pull-down menu name is for the label that is to appear on the menu bar. The term ***label,*** as used here, refers to an item of text that is visible to the user on a given menu feature. The labels on the menu bar are the only means of accessing the menu underneath, so this is a required element. Labels are enclosed in square brackets and should be 14 characters or less. The following example assigns the label "Custom" to this new pull-down menu:

```
***POP1
[Custom]
```

All menu bar items in the default menu have a menu shortcut key associated with them. A ***menu shortcut key*** is the underlined character that gives keyboard access to the menu item. For example, in the File menu, the F is the menu shortcut key, so the File menu can be accessed by pressing [Alt+F]. To assign a menu shortcut key to a menu label, place an ampersand (&) in front of the character to use. For example, to make the Custom label appear as Custom on the menu bar, the label is written as:

```
***POP1
[&Custom]
```

All shortcut keys should be unique in the area of the menu that they are a part of, whenever possible. Ideally, the menu bar and each individual menu or cascade should not have duplicate shortcut keys. This helps prevent unnecessary conflicts when trying to access a menu item. The shortcut key C does not conflict with any of the menu shortcut key in the default ACLT menu. If, however, you want to make the "u" the mnemonic, as in Custom, the ampersand is placed in front of the "u" like this:

```
[C&ustom]
```

The next step is to place the new menu selections in the pull-down menu. Unlike toolbar buttons, pull-down menus do not display graphics and so they require a text label to pick when activating the desired menu selection. The menu item labels are created just like the menu bar label. The first item on this menu is a macro that erases the last object drawn. Pull-down menus expand to match the width of the widest label they contain, but as a rule of thumb, label names should be no longer than needed. If additional information is required, it can be supplied as a help string, which is discussed later.

This next menu macro erases the last object drawn, so a suitable label might be "Erase Last," so this is now added to the menu:

```
***POP1
[&Custom]
[Erase &Last]
```

The menu code for an Erase Last macro is fairly simple, but all menu codes should be checked and verified at the command line to avoid errors. At the command line, erasing the last object looks like this:

```
Command: Erase↵
Select objects: L↵
1 found
Select objects: ↵
Command:
```

To write this as a menu macro, simply duplicate the keystrokes, substituting semicolons for Enters, like this:

```
erase;l;;
```

The actual macro needs to begin with ^C^C to ensure that the macro always starts at the Command: prompt. So far, the custom pull-down menu looks like this:

```
***POP1
[&Custom]
[Erase &Last]^C^Cerase;l;;
```

It is possible to make menu items automatically repeat, working until the user cancels the macro. This is done by placing an asterisk in the first position within the actual macro code. For example, the following defines a macro that draws single line objects by starting the line command, asking the user for two input points, canceling the LINE command, and repeating:

```
[&1 LINE]*^C^CLINE;\\;
```

The label uses the "1" for the shortcut key character. An asterisk as the first character of the macro code tells AutoCAD LT to repeat the macro until the user cancels. The ^C^C ensures that the macro starts at the Command: prompt, and LINE; starts the LINE command. Two backslashes allow for two items of user input, which in this case is a From point: and a To point: for the line. Finally, the last semicolon serves the same purpose as pressing Enter at the To point: prompt, which returns you to the Command: prompt.

```
***POP1
[&Custom]
[Erase &Last]^C^Cerase;l;;
[&1 LINE]*^C^CLINE;\\;
```

Another use for the SINGLE selection mode in menus comes with specialized functions that are only intended to work with one selection. Placed in a repeating command, this option allows the command to execute as soon as you make a selection. For example, the next macro is an Erase 1 macro that erases objects as they are picked:

```
[&Erase 1]*^C^Cerase;si;
```

When the repeating macro starts, the ERASE command is issued, followed by the SINGLE selection option. When an object is selected, the command executes with no further input. The effect is that when you pick an object, it is immediately erased without the need to press Enter to finalize the selection set.

This macro, however, ignores the current setting of PICKAUTO. That means that you cannot select objects using an implied window. To allow for implied windowing, add the AUTO selection mode as follows:

```
[&Erase 1]*^C^Cerase;si;au;
```

Field Notes

When using repeating macros, do not use a ^C^C sequence other than in the initial *^C^C. Doing so causes the repeating macro to be canceled.

The current partial menu file, with each of the edits in this example, now looks like this:

```
***MENUGROUP=EXAMPLE
***POP1
[&Custom]
[Erase &Last]^C^Cerase;l;;
[&1 LINE]*^C^CLINE;\\;
[&Erase 1]*^C^Cerase;si;au;
```

One very important aspect of creating menus is to keep the menu selections organized and easy to use. Most of the built-in menus group similar commands together, often separating them from other groups with dividing lines. This example menu is presented in a more logical fashion if the Erase macros are grouped and separated from the other items on the menu. The following listing reorganizes the menu selections and incorporates a dividing line. The dividing line is placed in a menu using a label of two hyphens, or dashes, as shown in this sequence:

```
***MENUGROUP=EXAMPLE

***POP1
[&Custom]
[Erase &Last]^C^Cerase;l;;
[&Erase 1]*^C^Cerase;si;au;
[--]
[&1 LINE]*^C^CLINE;\\;
```

To load the partial menu, the Menu Customization dialog box is used. After browsing and locating the file, the Load button is picked and the new MENUGROUP name appears in the Menu Groups: listing. On the Menu Bar page, the Example menu group is selected, and the Custom pull-down menu is inserted into the menu bar, as shown in Figure 17.33A. The actual pull-down menu is shown in Figure 17.33B.

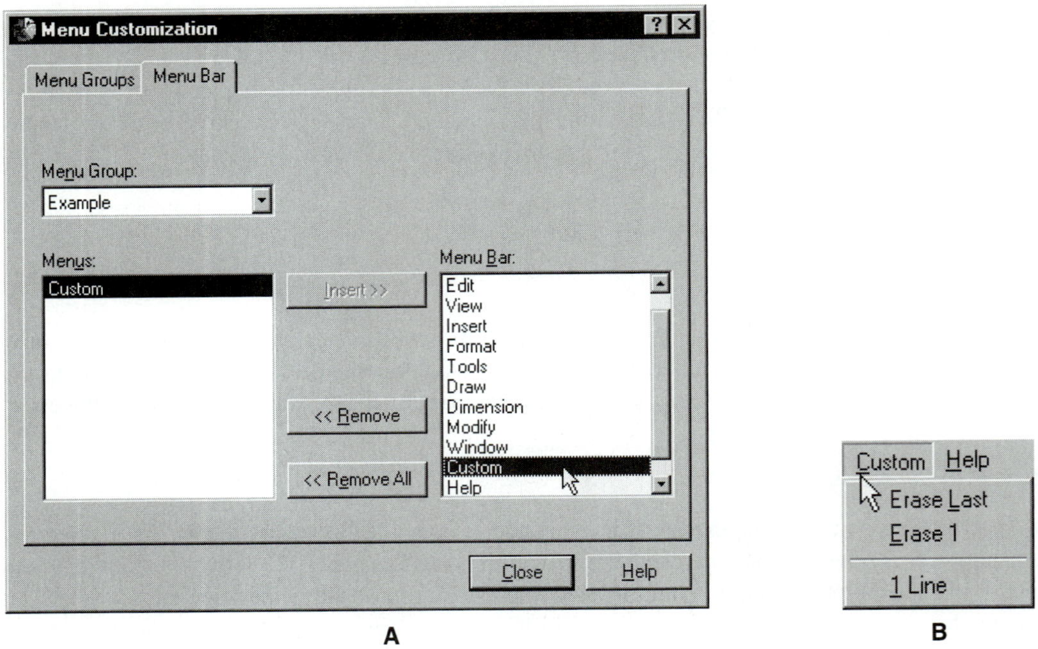

FIGURE 17.33 (A) Pull-down menus from partial menu files can be inserted into the menu bar using the Menu Customization dialog box. (B) The Custom pull-down menu.

Field Notes

Modifying the menu system is not covered within the AutoCAD LT User's Guide. The only built-in documentation is found using the on-line help system.

Exercise 17.10 — Estimated time required: 15 min.

1. Start a new file with Notepad or WordPad.
2. Create a partial menu, using the previous examples as a guideline. The menu group name should be CHAP17A and the pull-down menu name should be Custom.
3. Design a pull-down menu that has two drawing commands or macros, two editing commands or macros, and two display commands or macros.
4. Use separator lines to group similar menu selections.
5. Save the file as CHAP17A.MNS and use MENULOAD to load the partial menu file and place it on the menu bar.
6. Check your menu to ensure that everything works properly.

LEARNING CHECKPOINT

- ☐ What is a partial menu file?
- ☐ How are comments separated from menu code in the menu file?
- ☐ What is the maximum number of pull-down menus that can be defined in a single menu file?
- ☐ How is a label specified in a pull-down menu?
- ☐ What is a menu shortcut key and how is it specified?
- ☐ Describe the creation of a repeating menu macro.
- ☐ How is a separator line placed in a menu?

Creating Cascading Submenus

Similar to the concept of a Toolbar Flyout, a cascading submenu allows more menu items to be accessible from the same menu. Because using a cascading submenu requires an additional pick, these menus are often reserved for macros as opposed to simple commands. Menu selections that simply start a command are generally kept at the top level; otherwise it is quicker and easier to use the keyboard. Figure 17.34 shows the Arc cascading submenu on the Draw menu. Notice that commands on the top level are those such as Line, Polyline, and others that simply start a command. The options on these cascades run macros of varying complexity.

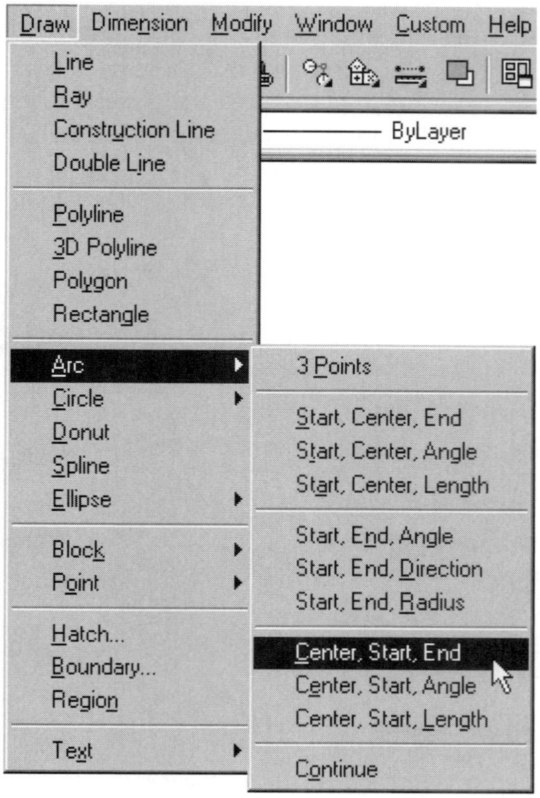

FIGURE 17.34 Cascading submenus require an additional pick, and therefore are most frequently used for macro items that do more than simply start a command.

Cascade sections are created by inserting special labels into the menu. The label that opens a cascading submenu cannot be assigned its own macro. Picking it only displays the cascading menu underneath. The characters used in the label to begin and end cascade sections are the *less than* (<) and *greater than* (>) symbols combined with a hyphen to form an arrow shape (-> <-). The *begin cascade* symbol is ->, an arrow that points to the right, the *end cascade* symbol <- points to the left. As you use these symbols in labels to define cascades, it may help to think of these symbols as directional arrows. The following listing shows the format used for cascade menu sections:

```
[->Begin Cascade]
[Submenu Item 1] macro code . . .
[Submenu Item 2] macro code . . .
[Submenu Item 3] macro code . . .
[etc. . . .] . . .
[<-Last Submenu Item on cascade] macro code . . .
```

The last item on the cascade has the End Cascade character placed in the label. To put this technique into use with the Custom pull-down menu, the next example groups the two Erase macros together in a cascading submenu. The first step is to insert a new label with the Begin Cascade character and then place the End Cascade character in the label of the last item on the cascade, like this:

```
***MENUGROUP=EXAMPLE

***POP1
[&Custom]
[->&Erase Macros]
  [Erase &Last]^C^Cerase;l;;
  [<-&Erase 1]*^C^Cerase;si;au;
[- -]
[&1 LINE]*^C^CLINE;\\;
```

As you study this example, notice that the Begin Cascade label can also have a shortcut key, and that the last cascade item is not changed except for the placement of the End Cascade character as the first character in the label. Figure 17.35 shows the Custom menu with the cascading submenu expanded.

A cascading submenu can also be placed on another cascading submenu. This practice, called ***nesting,*** should be avoided, when possible, to keep menu picks as close to the top level as possible. When nesting must be done, you should never nest more than two cascades.

FIGURE 17.35 The cascading submenu for the Custom menu.

Exercise 17.11 **Estimated time required: 15 min.**

1. Open CHAP17A.MNS for editing using a text editor.
2. Define three cascading submenus, one for the drawing commands, one for the editing commands, and one for the display commands.
3. Using MENULOAD, unload the previous version of CHAP17A, and load the new version.
4. Check each of the menu features to see if they work.

Working with Image Tile Menus

The default ACLT menu does not utilize any image tile menus, but AutoCAD LT still supports their use. An image tile menu is similar to a dialog box, and it can display graphic items for menu picks. These graphic images are created using the MSLIDE command, and are stored in slide libraries created using SLIDELIB. Creating slide libraries is introduced in Chapter 15. Figure 17.36 shows an example of an image tile menu.

An image tile menu offers the capability to display up to 20 images. All 20 boxes are displayed regardless of how many are actually used in any given application. The unused boxes remain blank. If more than 20 are specified, the Next button is enabled and the images tiles are continued on the next page. Because it displays slide images, an image tile menu is often a preferred method of presenting symbol libraries to the user for easy selection.

All image tile menus are actually submenus found in the IMAGE section. The default ACLT menu has no IMAGE section, but you can place one in the menu file. The IMAGE section uses three asterisks, because it is the main section name. Each of the actual image tile menus is a submenu of the IMAGE section, and submenus are designated using only two asterisks. An IMAGE section and a title for a submenu named SYMBOL1 are shown in the following listing, placed in the EXAMPLE partial menu:

```
***MENUGROUP=EXAMPLE

***POP1
[&Custom]
[->&Erase Macros]
  [Erase &Last]^C^Cerase;l;;
  [<-&Erase 1]*^C^Cerase;si;au;
[- -]
[&1 LINE]*^C^CLINE;\\;

***IMAGE
**SYMBOL1
```

FIGURE 17.36 An image tile menu displays custom graphics images as menu selections and offers a text-based version of the menu in the list on the left.

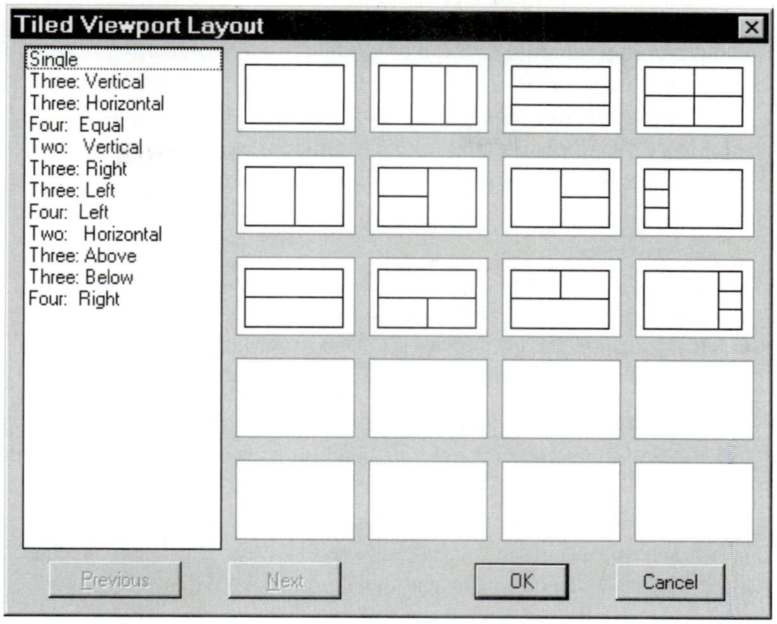

The first item in an image tile menu description is the text that appears at the top of the image tile menu. Each subsequent listing describes one of the image tile options. The description of an individual image tile is done in the label, and the menu code that follows the label is executed when either the image or the corresponding text listing in the list box is selected.

The actual image tile is described by naming the slide image that is to be used in the tile. A slide *may* be part of a slide library, or you can use individual slide files in an image tile menu. The label determines what is displayed both in the image tile and in the text list. The four ways to set up the image tile label depend on the slide name, library name, and the text that you want displayed in the list box, and are as follows:

- **[SlideName]:** The name of the slide file that is to be displayed. When used this way, the slide file name also appears in the text listing.
- **[SlideName,Label Text]:** The name of the slide file to display and a custom text label to appear in the text listing.
- **[LibName(SlideName)]:** The slide SlideName, found in the LibName slide library, is displayed, and the text SlideName is displayed in the text listing.
- **[LibName(SlideName,Label Text)]:** The slide SlideName, found in the LibName slide library, is displayed, and the text Label Text is displayed in the text listing.

Although it is acceptable to use individual slide files in your image tile menus, it is highly recommended that you use the slide library method instead. A slide library provides a single file that stores all the image tiles associated with your menu. Managing a multitude of individual slide files can be a formidable challenge. The examples in this text use the slide library method.

Field Notes

When creating slides to use in an image tile menu, be certain to optimize the space on the screen. First, the image tiles are created at a ratio of 1.5 to 1. To best visualize the end result, go to a layout tab and create a layout viewport that is 1.5 units wide and 1 unit tall. Zoom in close around the viewport. Now access model space through the viewport. Image tile menus are very small and can be difficult to see if the image is small when you make the slide. A good rule of thumb is to zoom the geometry so that it is centered and completely fills the viewport, then ZOOM .95X. In this way, the geometry is centered and fills the viewport without touching the very edges.

Wide polylines and solid objects are displayed as outlines on image tiles. To create an area that appears filled, create a dense hatch pattern in the area, but be careful not to do this too often, because these patterns can slow down the display of the image tile menu.

For the purposes of this example, three symbols have been defined, and slides were made of each symbol and incorporated into a slide library named SYMBOLS. The symbols are annotation symbols used in mechanical drafting, including the depth symbol, and symbols for countersinks and counterbores. The slide and symbol names are the same as follows: DEPTH, CSINK, and CBORE. The next example shows the construction of the labels for this image tile menu, and the menu code inserts the appropriate defined symbol. The first label is for the text that appears at the top, and then each of the three image tiles is defined:

```
***IMAGE
**SYMBOL1
[Select a Symbol to Insert:]
[symbols(depth,Depth)]^C^Cinsert;depth;
[symbols(csink,CounterSink)]^C^Cinsert;csink;
[symbols(cbore,CounterBore)]^C^Cinsert;cbore;
```

This code has sufficiently defined an image tile menu, but there is not yet a way to display this menu. Unlike the toolbars and pull-downs, there are no buttons or menu bars that activate image tile menus. An image tile menu is displayed by a menu call activated by a menu pick on an accessible menu system, such as a toolbar or a pull-down menu. A menu call always begins with a dollar sign, followed by the type of menu to display, an equals sign, and the menu specification. For example, the next listing makes an image tile menu named SYMBOL1 active. Notice the required placement of the MENUGROUP name in front of the menu name, separated by a period in the following:

```
$i=EXAMPLE.SYMBOL1
```

The act of making an image tile menu current does not actually display the menu. An image tile menu is displayed, similar to the display of pull-down and cursor menus, using an asterisk as the menu specification like this:

```
$i=EXAMPLE.SYMBOL1 $i=*
```

Sequential menu calls are separated by a single space. Placing a semicolon between menu calls makes them unusable, and an extra space reactivates the last command used. This menu call must now be placed on an accessible menu, such as the Custom pull-down menu as follows:

```
***POP1
[&Custom]
[->&Erase Macros]
   [Erase &Last]^C^Cerase;l;;
   [<-&Erase 1]*^C^Cerase;si;au;
[--]
[&1 LINE]*^C^CLINE;\\;
[--]
[&Symbols]$i=EXAMPLE.SYMBOL1 $i=*
```

Now, when the menu is reloaded, the new selection makes SYMBOL1 the current image tile menu and causes it to be displayed. This image tile menu appears as shown in Figure 17.37.

Field Notes

Image tile menu selections can issue menu calls that display other image tile menus.

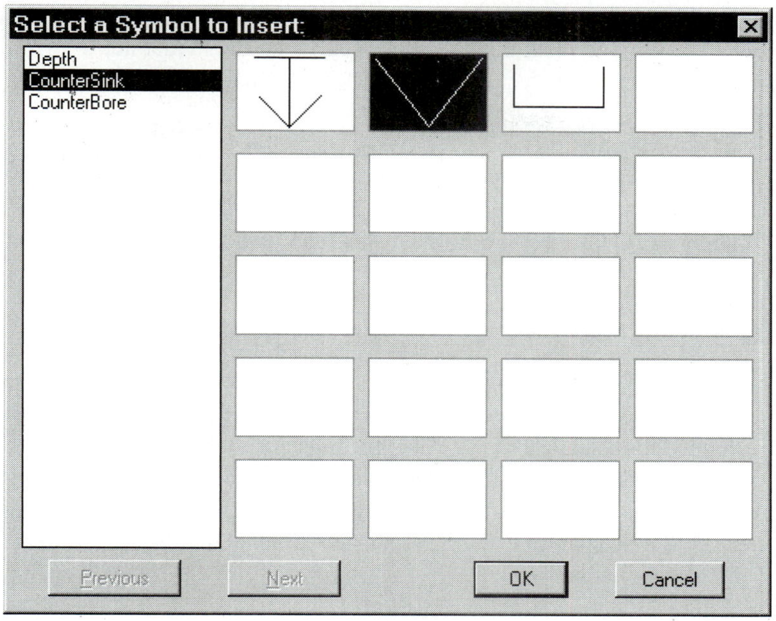

FIGURE 17.37 An image tile menu is useful for insertion of symbols.

Exercise 17.12 **Estimated time required: 20 min.**

1. Define three symbols, create slides of each of the symbols, and store them in a slide library named EX17-12.SLB.
2. Open CHAP17A.MNS for editing and create an IMAGE section.
3. Place a definition for an image tile menu named EX17-12 in the menu. Each image tile should insert one of the symbols.
4. Save CHAP17A.MNS and reload it into AutoCAD LT.
5. Check your new image tiles to be sure they work.

LEARNING CHECKPOINT

- ☐ Describe an image tile menu. Why is it often used for inserting blocks?
- ☐ How many tiles are available in one menu?
- ☐ What happens when there are more or less tile listings than the image tile menu displays?
- ☐ Can individual slides be used in creating image tile menus? What method is preferred?
- ☐ Where is the title text for an image tile menu defined?
- ☐ How are image tile menus displayed? Show an example.
- ☐ What must be in front of the image tile menu name in the actual menu call?

Defining Help Strings

Help strings, the text items that appear on the status line when a menu selection is pointed to or highlighted, help users of all levels to be certain of what action is to be performed. There are many different toolbar button images and menu picks, and new ones can be defined at any time. It would not be an easy task to memorize every button image and menu pick so that they are all instantly recognized. Help strings, however, can help avoid this obstacle by providing quick descriptions of the menu items on the status line.

Help strings are defined in the HELPSTRINGS section. To create a help string, you must define an ID Tag, plus the actual help text. An *ID Tag* is a unique name that begins with ID_, and allows menu items to reference the help string. For example, the following listing is found in the ACLT.MNS file:

```
ID_ERASE     [Removes objects from a drawing: ERASE]
```

The actual text displayed by this help string is placed in square brackets, much like menu labels. The ID Tag is the unique identifier referenced by menu items that are to display this particular help string. The Erase option in the Modify pull-down menu looks like this:

```
ID_Erase      [&Erase]^C^C_erase
```

The help string reference is placed prior to the label. Now, whenever this menu item is highlighted, the associated help string is displayed on the status line. The text in a help string should be as concise as possible. A short and clear message is understood at a glance, and this is the goal for all help strings.

Field Notes

Help strings can be referenced only if they are defined in the same menu file. For example, a partial menu cannot reference help strings defined in the base menu. The help strings must also be defined in the partial menu. Also, ID Tags cannot be duplicated in the same file, but an ID Tag in a partial menu file can have the same ID Tag as a help string listed in the base menu—even if the actual help text is different. Each menu item knows which help string to use.

If a help string is duplicated in the same menu file, the last definition encountered in the file is the one that is used.

Exercise 17.13 — Estimated time required: 15 min.

1. Open CHAP17A.MNS for editing.
2. Create help strings for each menu item on the pull-down menu.
3. Create and place ID Tags so that each menu pick references its help string.
4. Save and exit. Then reload the menu in AutoCAD LT.
5. Test your help strings.

LEARNING CHECKPOINT

- ☐ Why are help strings such a vital part of any menu file?
- ☐ What section are help strings defined in?
- ☐ Describe an ID Tag and its function.
- ☐ Why should help strings be as clear and concise as possible?

Defining Custom Accelerator Keys

Accelerator keystrokes are key combinations that activate a command or macro. For example, the [Ctrl+C] keystroke accesses the COPYCLIP command and [Ctrl+V] accesses PASTECLIP. These keys can be redefined or new keystrokes can be added. Accelerators are defined only in the base menu, and are not affected by any listings in a partial menu.

Accelerator keys can be defined in either of two ways, through supplying a macro or through referencing an ID Tag. The first method is much like the construction of a pull-down menu item. The difference is that the label specifies the accelerator keystroke. For example, the next listing, placed in the ***ACCELERATORS section, defines the [Ctrl+M] keystroke as the MOVE command:

```
[CONTROL+"M"]^C^Cmove
```

Accelerator macros cannot pause for user input; any backslash characters are passed directly to the command line and do not cause the macro to pause. You can, however, create longer macros as long as they do not require user input.

The next way to define accelerator keys is called mapping to a command. By placing an ID Tag in front of the accelerator key label, the keystroke is mapped to the command or macro in the menu file that references that ID Tag. For example, the following accelerator definition maps the Ctrl+W keystroke to the macro in the menu file that uses the ID Tag ID_UCSWORLD:

```
ID_UCSWorld      [CONTROL+"W"]
```

The following listing within the POP6 menu is accessed now by a [Ctrl+W] keystroke:

```
ID_UCSWorld      [&World]^C^C_ucs_w
```

Accelerator keys cannot use Alt key combinations, because the Alt key accesses Windows system functions. They can, however, use Ctrl, Shift, and [Ctrl+Shift] combinations. All of the letter keys are used by placing the letter of the key in quotation marks as shown in the previous examples. Any of the function keys can be used in the same manner. The following example makes the [Shift+F7] key run a macro that sets up your grid and snap:

```
[SHIFT+"F7"]^C^Cgrid;.5;snap;.25
```

To use a numeric keypad number, use "NUMPAD0" for the 0 key, "NUMPAD1" for the 1 key and so on. The following accelerator definition sets a [Ctrl+2] on the numeric keypad to zoom using a 2X option:

```
[CONTROL+"NUMPAD2"]'ZOOM;2X
```

If you want to access the "2" key found above the alphabetical keys on your keyboard, leave out the "NUMPAD" part and just specify which number like this:

```
[CONTROL+"2"]'ZOOM;2X
```

Other keys that can be referenced are listed here:

"HOME"	HOME key	"UP"	UP ARROW key
"END"	END key	"DOWN"	DOWN ARROW key
"INSERT"	INS key	"LEFT"	LEFT ARROW key
"DELETE"	DEL key	"RIGHT"	RIGHT ARROW key
		"ESCAPE"	ESC key

The Ctrl and Shift keys are called modifiers. To use two modifiers, place a plus sign between them as follows:

```
[CONTROL+SHIFT+"M"]
```

You can add accelerator keys directly to the menu or use the Keyboard tab of the Customize dialog box. You can access the Customize dialog box as you have previously by picking the Keyboard tab or by selecting Keyboard... from the Customize cascade on the Tools pull-down menu. The Customize dialog box provides a simpler method for working with your keyboard macros, but it has some limitations. The Keyboard tab is shown in Figure 17.38 with a menu group named EXAMPLE.

The Categories drop-down list shows a listing of the names of the pull-down menus in the current menu group as specified in the Menu Group list. At the bottom of the Categories list is the AutoCAD LT Commands option, where you can select the built-in AutoCAD LT Commands option. This allows you to assign keyboard shortcuts to any existing AutoCAD LT pull-down menu selection.

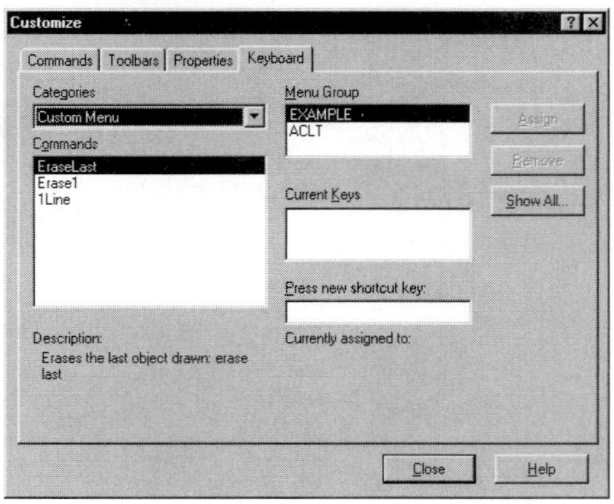

FIGURE 17.38 The Keyboard tab on the Customize dialog box provides an easy way to create, edit, and remove accelerator key definitions.

The labels for each of the menu options are displayed in the Commands category. The contents of the EXAMPLE menu group used in Figure 17.38 are shown here:

```
***MENUGROUP=EXAMPLE

***POP1
                [&Custom]
ID_ERASELAST    [Erase &Last]^C^Cerase;l;;
                [&Erase 1]*^C^Cerase;si;
                [--]
                [&1 Line]*^C^Cline;\\;

***HELPSTRINGS
ID_ERASELAST    [Erases the last object drawn: ERASE;L;;]
```

To assign a new menu short-cut key to one of the commands in the Commands list, first highlight its name. Below the Commands list, the helpstring for the highlighted command will appear if one has been defined. Any existing accelerator keystrokes associated with that command are shown in the Current Keys category. Pick the edit box labeled Press new shortcut key: to make it active. Now, press the keystroke combination you want to assign to this command. If you select a keystroke that is already being used, this is indicated in the Currently assigned to: area. For example, in Figure 17.39 the keystroke [CTRL+E] has been selected for the Erase Last command. A message indicates that this is currently assigned to *Cycles through isometric planes*. Selecting the Assign button makes the new assignment and places a description of the keystroke in the Current Keys list. Keep in mind that if you use a previously assigned keystroke, AutoCAD LT recognizes the one whose menu group was loaded first. Also, AutoCAD LT and Windows both have certain key assignments that cannot be changed. In the previous assignment of [CTRL+E] to the Erase Last tool, testing the keystroke after leaving the Customize dialog box reveals that it still activates the Isoplane toggle. If the keystroke that you want is already in use, try adding a Shift key to the combination. Instead of [CTRL+E], try [CTRL+Shift+E] or maybe something totally different, like [Shift+F2]. To remove an unwanted shortcut key definition, highlight the key in the Current Keys list and pick the Remove button. Figure 17.40 illustrates this procedure.

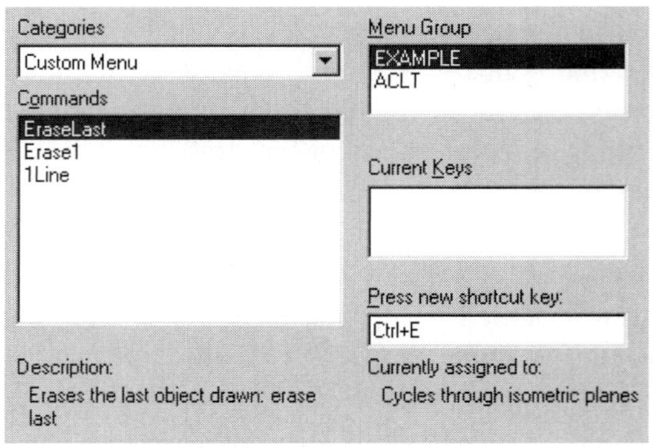

FIGURE 17.39 If a selected keystroke has already been defined, its current assignment is shown below the Currently assigned to: label.

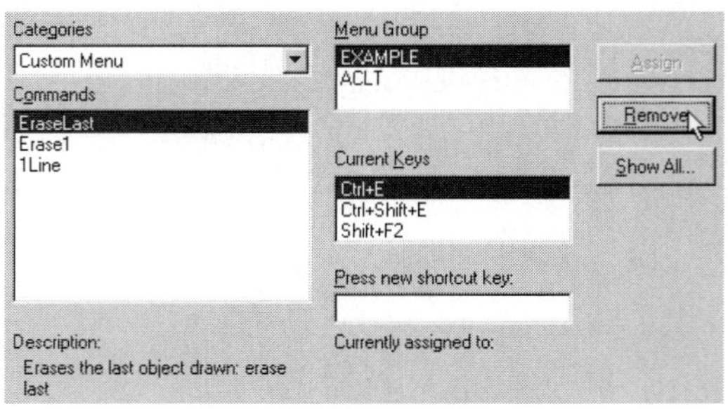

FIGURE 17.40 Unwanted shortcut key definitions can be removed from a menu group.

When the changes are applied, you can reopen the MNS file to see the changes that AutoCAD LT has added to your ***ACCELERATORS menu section. You will also find that any menu items that did not previously have ID tags now have a tag that relates to the label for the menu item:

```
***MENUGROUP=EXAMPLE

***POP1
                    [&Custom]
ID_ERASELAST        [Erase &Last]^C^Cerase;l;;
ID_Erase1_0         [&Erase 1]
                    [--]
ID_1Line_0          [&1 Line]*^C^Cline;\\;

***TOOLBARS

***ACCELERATORS
ID_ERASELAST        [CONTROL+SHIFT+"E"]
ID_ERASELAST        [SHIFT+"F2"]

***HELPSTRINGS
ID_ERASELAST        [Erases the last object drawn: ERASE;L;;]
```

Field Notes

Always be very careful when editing a menu file from a text editor and within AutoCAD LT at the same time. If you are not careful, you can lose all the changes you have made in one of the two processes. For example, if you currently have the MNS file open in a text editor and you make some changes in AutoCAD LT, then the version that is open in the text editor is no longer up to date. AutoCAD LT has rewritten the menu file on disk, but those changes are not automatically made in the text editor. You must close the file and reopen the new version to see the changes. An easy way to avoid this type of problem is to simply close the MNS file in your text editing application while you are making changes from within AutoCAD LT.

Similarly, each time you save the file with the text editor, you must unload the menu and reload it to see the changes. If you forget to unload and reload the menu and then make changes in AutoCAD LT, the saved changes are not incorporated in the new version of the file that AutoCAD LT creates. Always be sure that the first thing you do after editing your menu file in a text editor is to unload and reload the menu. For your convenience, you can even make a toolbar button that does this with a simple pick. The following example provides the menu macro for unloading and reloading a menu file named Chap17.mns that uses the menugroup name EXAMPLE.

```
^C^Cmenuunload;EXAMPLE;menuload;CHAP17
```

Exercise 17.14

Estimated time required: 10 min.

1. Open the CHAP17.MNS file for editing.
2. Add three new accelerator keystroke definitions.
3. Save and exit the menu file.
4. Reload the menu file in AutoCAD LT.
5. Check the functionality of the new accelerators.
6. Use the Keyboard tab on the Customize dialog box to define two new keyboard shortcuts.
7. Close the Customize dialog box and test your new keystrokes.
8. Open your menu file to see the changes entered by AutoCAD.

LEARNING CHECKPOINT

- ☐ What is an accelerator keystroke?
- ☐ Describe the two ways to define an accelerator.
- ☐ Can accelerators be defined in partial menu files?
- ☐ What is a modifier?

Customizing Tablet Menus

A tablet menu is a menu that is accessed using a digitizer tablet. Because of the many difficulties often associated with getting a reliable WinTab driver, fewer companies are using digitizer menus today. A ***WinTab driver*** is a piece of software that allows AutoCAD LT to utilize a tablet while working in the Windows environment. With all of the toolbars available, plus pull-down menus and accelerator keys, digitizer tablets are often unnecessary. If you are using a tablet and a tablet menu, and you would like to modify it, the process is much the same as modifying any other area of the menu system with regard to actual menu code. Like the Buttons menus, labels are not displayable and are not required. However, placing your menu macros in the proper location requires an understanding of the structure of the tablet menu section.

The tablet menu is very large and has many repeated items. This is because the tablet itself is divided into grid squares whose position is reported to the system as a set of X,Y coordinates. The menu itself is also divided into grid squares that tell AutoCAD LT what menu item you have selected based on the X,Y coordinates returned to the system.

Configuring the tablet is detailed in the AutoCAD LT 2000 on-line help. The default row and column settings can be changed, but the ACLT menu system is set up for the default configuration. If you have a tablet, you can print the tablet menu template that has been supplied in the Sample directory folder in the drawing named TABLET.DWG. This drawing is shown in Figure 17.41.

Although any area of the tablet menu is subject to modification as desired, the area that is actually intended for user modification is the top menu area defined on the template. This area is set up in the default menu as a group of rectangular areas, called cells, defined as 25 columns by 9 rows. This means that you could have as many as 225 separate menu items placed in this area. The section of the menu file that represents this menu area is:

```
***TABLET1
**TABLET1STD
```

In the default menu, each cell is provided with a semicolon, which issues an Enter. Cells can be modified as desired to hold menu macros of your choice. If you have a menu template, you will see that the rows are labeled alphabetically and the columns are labeled numerically. This helps you to reference the cell position in the menu file. For example, the first entry under TABLET1STD is for cell A1, the next is for A2 and so on. After getting to A25, the next menu listing is assigned to cell B1 and the cycle continues.

Additionally, multiple cells can be set to the same macro to create larger selection areas. For example, setting cells A1, A2, B1, and B2 to the same macro creates a square selection area that is four times the area of a single cell.

Finally, using the TABLET drawing as a guide, you can draw the upper area menu template using AutoCAD LT. Then, plot the entire drawing, including your additions. Place this template on your tablet and use the TABLET command to configure the tablet menu areas. Use Appendix H in the User's Guide as a reference for setting up the tablet menu.

An Introduction to DIESEL Code

The term *DIESEL* stands for Direct Interpretively Evaluated String Expression Language. DIESEL allows menu macros to be given decision-making abilities, effectively creating "smart" menu picks. Using DIESEL, you can determine the current settings of system variables and act based on this information. DIESEL code greatly increases the capabilities of your menu macros.

A DIESEL code expression is preceded by a dollar sign ($) similar to a menu call. If compared with a menu call, the menu specification is "M"; on the other side of the equals sign is the actual macro code. For example, the following DIESEL expression could be added to an image tile macro created earlier to get the current values for the DIMSCALE and TEXTSIZE variables, multiply them, and supply the product as the scale factor for the insertion of the symbol:

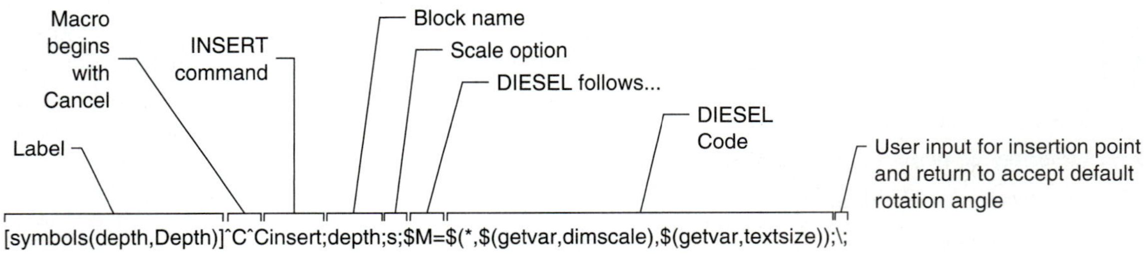

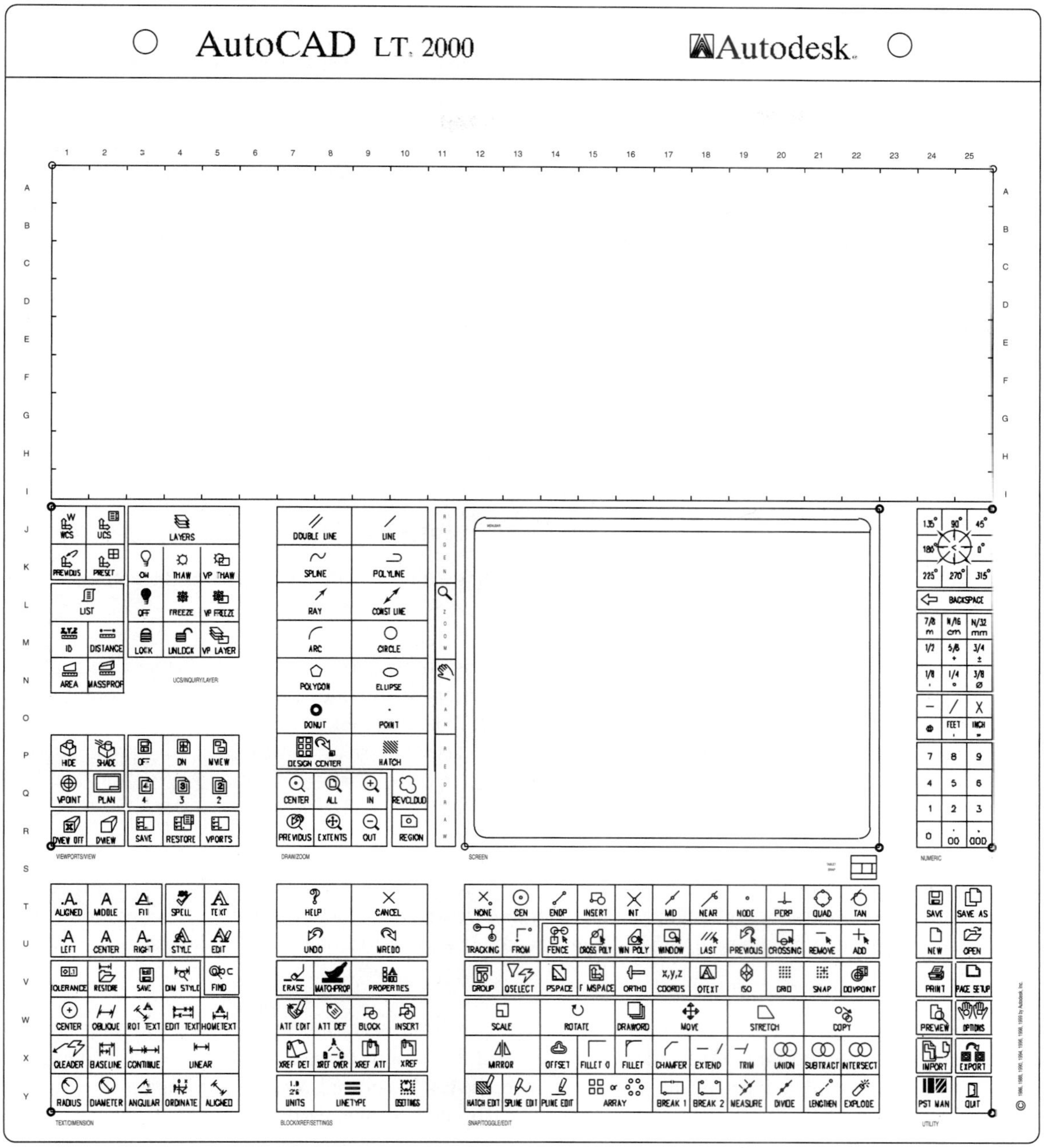

FIGURE 17.41 The drawing TABLET.DWG can be printed so you can use the menu template on your tablet.

To prepare for this insertion method, the original symbol is drawn 1 unit tall, so if DIMSCALE is 1.0, and TEXTSIZE is 0.125, the symbol is also 0.125 units tall, because $1.0 \times 0.125 = 0.125$.

The label specifies the image tile appearance, and the actual macro begins here with the ^C^C. The INSERT command is issued, the block name specified, and the Insertion point is answered with the S option to preset the scale factor. When the command line prompts for the scale factor, the macro evaluates the DIESEL expression and returns the result to the prompt. The $M= tells AutoCAD LT that the information to follow is a DIESEL macro. Each individual DIESEL expression, even nested expressions, is preceded by a dollar sign. The first expression in this macro is multiplication, indicated by the asterisk. The syntax, or correct layout, for any DIESEL expression is for the function to be listed, followed by any required arguments, with each item separated with a comma. The term ***argument*** refers to data provided for the function to operate on or with. For example, the arguments for a multiplication expression are the numbers to multiply. Therefore, a multiplication expression is always written as:

(*, *arg1*[, *arg2*, . . ., *arg9*])

In this listing, the items shown in square brackets are optional. All DIESEL expressions have a maximum limit of 10 parameters, including the function name. The term ***parameter,*** as used here, refers to any item in the DIESEL expression—functions and arguments alike. According to this limit, a multiplication function can be supplied with one, two, three, or more arguments up to a total of nine. If only one argument is provided, that same value is returned. The expression in the previous example provided two arguments, which are also DIESEL expressions. A DIESEL expression inside of another expression is a nested expression. The nested expressions are evaluated first and the values they return are used by the upper level expression. In this example, the GETVAR expression is used to get the value of the two variables that are used to determine the insertion scale factor for the symbol, DIMSCALE and TEXTSIZE. The GETVAR expression accepts a single argument, which is the variable name to get. So, the values returned by these two expressions are multiplied and the returned value is used by the INSERT command as a preset scale factor:

```
$(getvar,dimscale)
$(getvar,textsize)
```

Exercise 17.15 — Estimated time required: 20 min.

1. Create two block definitions for annotation symbols, such as a depth symbol, and a countersink or counterbore symbol.
2. Open the partial menu file CHAP17A.MNS for editing.
3. Set up the appropriate menu picks on either an image tile menu or on the pull-down menu.
4. Use DIESEL code to preset the scale factors for insertion to match the current dimensioning text size by referencing the DIMSCALE and TEXTSIZE variables.
5. Save and exit the file. Reload the partial menu and test your menu entries.

In addition to modifying specific macros, a DIESEL expression can be used to make decisions in a macro. For example, the DIESEL language provides an IF function. The classic IF-THEN-ELSE model is a fundamental of all programming languages, allowing one course of action to be taken if a condition exists, and a different course if not. In the DIESEL language, the IF expression syntax is as follows:

$(if,*test,do-if-true*[, *do-if-false*])

The IF function requires a test and an expression to perform if the test is positive (the THEN item). The expression to do if the test fails (the ELSE item) is optional. If no value or zero is returned by the test expression, then the test has failed. If a nonzero value is returned, the test has passed. As a sample implementation, the next set of code uses DIESEL to construct a toggle for the Blipmode system variable as a pull-down menu item:

```
[Blip&mode]$M=$(if,$(getvar,blipmode),blipmode;0;,blipmode;1;)
```

The test expression is $(getvar,blipmode), which returns 1 if Blipmode is on and 0 if Blipmode is off. A positive result, meaning that Blipmode is on, causes the *do-if-true* expression to be evaluated. The *do-if-true* expression is blipmode;0, which turns Blipmode off. The *do-if-false* expression is blipmode;1, which turns Blipmode on. Notice that the setting is not followed with an Enter because an automatic Enter is issued at the end of the macro. This sample represents but one minor example of decision making using DIESEL code.

Exercise 17.16 — Estimated time required: 20 min.

1. Open the partial menu file CHAP17A.MNS for editing.
2. Create a cascading submenu on the Custom pull-down menu. Label it "Toggles."
3. Place three menu selections on the cascade that toggle any three variables of your choice. These variables must have 0 and 1 values to apply this technique.
4. Save and exit the menu file. Reload the menu and test your new menu entries.

While making decisions about what to do the DIESEL codes can also decide how to display the menu selection itself. Menu displays can be modified in simple ways to communicate more effectively with the user. For example, items that are not available at the current time can be "grayed out," or settings that are currently active can have check marks placed by them.

Using DIESEL code within the actual label allows testing for conditions and modification of the display based on the results. The two most common sequences used to modify menu labels are the tilde (~) and an exclamation point–period combination (!.). The tilde character, placed in the first position in the label, grays out the menu item. The !. sequence places a check mark in front of the item.

As a working example of graying items out, the View pull-down menu grays out items specific to paper space when model space is active, and grays out model space items when paper space is active. It does this by checking the value of the TILEMODE system variable and implementing the tilde using DIESEL. Study the label in the following menu macro:

```
[$(if,$(getvar,tilemode),~)MView]^C^Cmview
```

Because the DIESEL code here is part of the label, and not part of the macro, the $M= prefix is not required. The test expression gets the value of tilemode and returns it to the IF function. When TILEMODE is set to 1, the MVIEW command cannot be used. Therefore, the *do-if-true* expression supplies a tilde as the first character when TILEMODE is 1. This has the effect of graying out the item, which disables it so that it cannot be picked.

Exercise 17.17

Estimated time required: 15 min.

1. Open the partial menu file CHAP17A.MNS for editing.
2. Create a menu entry for the VPORTS command.
3. Using DIESEL code, gray out the menu item when Tilemode is 0; enable the item when Tilemode is 1.
4. Save and exit. Reload the menu and test your entries.

Placing a check mark in front of a menu item is done in exactly the same way as graying an item out, except that the !. is used instead of the ~. A test is performed to find the appropriate course of action and it is executed using DIESEL. In the next example, the entry made earlier for the Blipmode toggle is modified so that if Blipmode is on, a check mark is displayed in front of the label:

```
[$(if,(getvar,blipmode),!.)Blip&mode]$M=$(if,$(getvar,blipmode),'blipmode;0,'blipmode;1)
```

The test returns 1 if Blipmode is on, which places the !. at the beginning of the label, causing a check mark to be displayed. The remainder of the code does not change; it still toggles the current setting. Figure 17.42 shows a pull-down menu with a grayed out item and a check mark placed in front of another item.

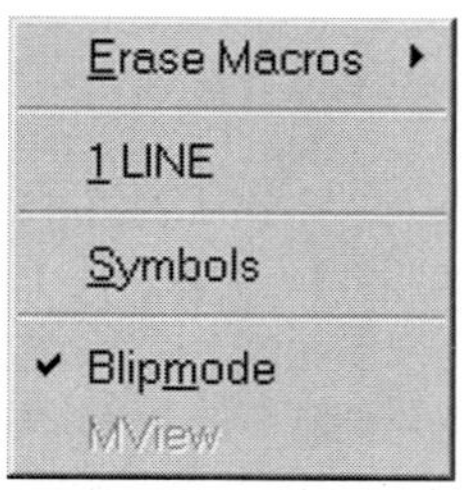

FIGURE 17.42 DIESEL code can be used to control both the function and the appearance of menu items.

Exercise 17.18

Estimated time required: 20 min.

1. Open the partial menu file CHAP17A.MNS for editing.
2. Edit each of the menu picks on the Toggles cascade on the Custom pull-down menu so that a check mark is displayed when the current setting is 1, or ON.
3. Save and exit. Reload the menu and check your entries.

Creating Custom Linetypes

AutoCAD LT provides a wide variety of linetypes, but this represents only a small portion of the many different linetypes used in technical drawings. The linetypes included with AutoCAD LT include the ASME and ISO standard linetypes. Additionally, a number of complex linetypes are included to represent fencing, batting, water lines, and more. Still, there are many other linetypes used in industry that are not included with AutoCAD LT. To allow the greatest degree of flexibility possible, AutoCAD LT allows you to create your own custom linetypes as desired.

The two basic categories of linetypes in AutoCAD LT are simple linetypes and complex linetypes. A ***simple linetype*** is one that is made up only of lines and spaces, like CENTER lines and HIDDEN lines. A ***complex linetype*** often incorporates text or symbols into the line pattern to supply additional information or to be instantly recognizable.

Simple linetypes can be created directly at the Command: prompt using the -LINETYPE command. When the -LINETYPE command is entered, the following prompt is displayed:

```
Command: -LINETYPE↵
Current line type: "ByLayer"
Enter an option [?/Create/Load/Set]:
```

The Create option allows new linetypes to be defined. When accessed, the Create option asks you to name the new linetype that you are about to create. This option can be used to your advantage to see how existing linetypes are defined. Reviewing the definitions for the existing linetypes can help you to better understand how to create the new linetype you need. For example, the linetype to be created in this example is very similar to the DIVIDE2 linetype, which displays a long dash, two dots and then repeats. The new linetype is to have a long dash, one dot, a short dash, another dot and then repeat. Looking first at the definition of DIVIDE2 can be very helpful, as shown in the following example:

```
Enter an option [?/Create/Load/Set]: C↵
Enter name of linetype to create: DIVIDE2↵
⟨use the Create or Append Linetype File dialog box to pick the ACLT.LIN file⟩
Wait, checking if linetype already defined...
"DIVIDE2" already exists in this file. Current definition is:
  *DIVIDE2, Divide (.5x) __..__..__..__..__..__..__..__
  A,0.25,−0.125,0,−0.125,0,−0.125
Overwrite? <N> ↵
Enter name of linetype to create:
```

All the built-in simple linetypes are defined in the file named ACLT.LIN. New linetypes can be stored here also or placed in a different file. The ACLT.LIN file must be specified here in order to get the current definition of DIVIDE2 to be displayed. The current definition is listed as:

```
*DIVIDE2,__..__..__..__..__..__..__..__..__..__..__..__..
A,0.25,−0.125,0,−0.125,0,−0.125
```

The first line of the definition is the name of the linetype followed by a keyboard-generated approximation of the appearance of the linetype. This approach is optional; you can use a simple text description instead if you wish. A reasonable description might be "Long dash, two dots, long dash," or something along these lines. Any description should stay under 47 characters in length.

The second line is the actual descriptive code for the linetype. Every linetype definition starts with the "A," which specifies the alignment style. AutoCAD LT only supports A type alignment. This ensures that lines and arcs made using noncontinuous lines both start and end on a dash sequence, and not on an empty space. When constructing linetypes at the command line, A type alignment is automatically entered. The sequence of numbers in the description represents the PEN DOWN and PEN UP distances used as a model for the linetype. Positive numbers are Pen Down, and negative numbers are Pen Up distances. The terms Pen Down and Pen Up may be easier to understand by observing a pen plotter. *Pen Down* means that your pen is in contact with the media and you are drawing. *Pen Up* indicates that the pen is not in contact with the paper, so it is moving but not drawing. To put it in simple terms, pen down distance is dash length, and pen up distance is gap length.

A careful look at the DIVIDE2 linetype shows that the specification indicates a 0.25 dash, a 0.125 gap, a 0 length dash (dot), another 0.125 gap, another dot, and finally a 0.125 gap before the sequence repeats. Using this information as a model, this example places a short dash between the two dots in a new linetype named SAMPLE:

```
Enter name of linetype to create: SAMPLE↵
Wait, checking if linetype already defined...
Descriptive text: An example of creating simple linetypes.
Enter linetype pattern (on next line):
  A,.25,-.125,0,-.125,.125,-.125,0,-.125↵
New linetype definition saved to file.
Enter an option [?/Create/Load/Set]: ↵
Command:
```

Figure 17.43 shows the two linetypes side by side for an easy comparison. Study this figure, along with the actual linetype definitions shown above.

FIGURE 17.43 A comparison between the DIVIDE2 and SAMPLE linetypes.

Once a linetype has been defined, it is saved in a linetype file and can be loaded in any drawing as desired.

Field Notes

- Linetype definition files are simple ASCII text files and can be directly edited using Notepad or any other text editor.
- The ACLT.LIN file is the primary linetype definition file, and the ACLTISO.LIN file is provided for those using ISO drafting standards.

Exercise 17.19 — Estimated time required: 15 min.

1. Use the LINETYPE command to create a new linetype that has a long dash, short dash, dot, short dash and repeats, as follows:

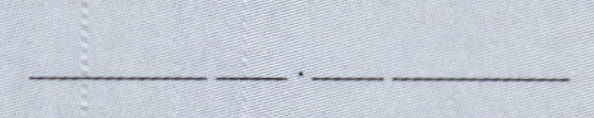

2. Find a linetype to use as a template and list its definition for reference.
3. Call the new linetype EX17.19, and save it in a linetype definition file named CHAP17.LIN.

Complex linetypes are not quite as easy to create as simple linetypes, but the Pen Up/Pen Down information is handled exactly the same. To work with complex linetypes, you must open the linetype definition file with a text editor. The complex linetype section of the ACLT.LIN file is shown here:

```
;; Complex linetypes
;;
;; Complex linetypes have been added to this file.
;; These linetypes were defined in LTYPESHP.LIN in
;; Release 13, and are incorporated in ACAD.LIN in
;; Release 14.
;;
;; These linetype definitions use LTYPESHP.SHX.
;;
*FENCELINE1,Fenceline circle ,----0,----0,----0,----0,----0,----0,----
A,.25,-.1,[CIRC1,ltypeshp.shx,x=-.1,s=.1],-.1,1
*FENCELINE2,Fenceline square ,----[],----[],----[],----[],----[],----
A,.25,-.1,[BOX,ltypeshp.shx,x=-.1,s=.1],-.1,1
*TRACKS,Tracks -|-|-|-|-|-|-|-|-|-|-|-|-|-|-|-|-|-|-|-|-|-|-|-|-
A,.15,[TRACK1,ltypeshp.shx,s=.25],.15
```

```
*BATTING,Batting
SSSSSSSSSSSSSSSSSSSSSSSSSSSSSSSSSSSSSSSSSSSSS
A,.0001,–.1,[BAT,ltypeshp.shx,x=–.1,s=.1],–.2,[BAT,ltypeshp.shx,r=180,x=.1,s=.1],–.1
*HOT_WATER_SUPPLY,Hot water supply —— HW —— HW —— HW ——
A,.5,–.2,["HW",STANDARD,S=.1,R=0.0,X=–0.1,Y=–.05],–.2
*GAS_LINE,Gas line ,----GAS,----GAS,----GAS,----GAS,----GAS,----GAS,----
A,.5,–.2,["GAS",STANDARD,S=.1,R=0.0,X=–0.1,Y=–.05],–.25
*ZIGZAG,Zig zag /\/\/\/\/\/\/\/\/\/\/\/\/\/\/\/\/\/\/\/\/\/\/
A,.0001,–.2,[ZIG,ltypeshp.shx,x=–.2,s=.2],–.4,[ZIG,ltypeshp.shx,r=180,x=.2,s=.2],–.2
```

In addition to simple Pen Up/Pen Down information, complex linetypes also allow for text elements and shapes from shape definition files. Shapes and the shape definition file are discussed later.

The easiest way to begin creating your own complex linetypes is to start by modifying existing linetypes. The following example helps to explain the various elements of a complex linetype definition:

```
*HOT_WATER_SUPPLY,----HW----HW----HW----HW----HW----
A,.5,−.2,["HW",STANDARD,S=.1,R=0.0,X=−0.1,Y=−.05],−.2
```

The first line is exactly the same as in a simple linetype definition. The linetype name and a text description. When creating a linetype at the command line, some of the entries are made automatically by AutoCAD LT. The asterisk in front of the linetype name, for example. This, along with the A specification for alignment, is one of the required elements that is automatically entered in the definition for you when you define the linetype at the command line. When you are directly editing the definition file, none of these entries is made automatically. Pay special attention to each detail to make sure that nothing is overlooked as you define new complex linetypes.

The second line starts out with the A for the alignment specification, and then defines the appearance of the linetype. A 0.5 pen down is followed by a 0.2 pen up. Within the square brackets is the text item definition, followed by another gap of 0.2 before the pattern repeats. The required elements within the text definition are the actual text, in quotation marks, and the text style name to use. Five additional parameters can be used to assign the desired properties to the text, as follows:

- **S=** Specifies a scale factor.
- **R=** Specifies a relative rotation angle.
- **A=** Specifies an absolute rotation angle.
- **X=** Specifies an offset distance in the X axis to aid in locating the text. The text is inserted lower-left justified, and the offsets are used to center the text within a gap.
- **Y=** Specifies an offset distance in the Y axis.

Based on this format, the text defined in the Hot_Water_Supply linetype places the text "HW" using the STANDARD text style. The text height is 0.1 times the height described in the style definition. If a height of 0 is used for the style definition, the scale value becomes an absolute height. Whether relative or absolute, text size is scaled using the current object and global linetype scales. The relative rotation of 0 degrees ensures that the text maintains its orientation relative to the line direction. The X and Y offset values help to center the text properly.

```
["HW",STANDARD,S=.1,R=0.0,X=−0.1,Y=−.05]
```

To create a similar linetype that can be used for the cold water lines, the first step is to copy the existing HW linetype definition. For this example, the rest is easy. Simply change the H to a C. However, few modifications are this simple. To demonstrate a more challenging example, the next sequence creates a linetype to represent sewage lines. This new linetype is to use the text SEWER in the line gaps. If the HW line is modified by simply changing the HW to SEWER, the resulting linetype does not look correct, as shown in Figure 17.44. Two adjustments need to be made to this linetype. First, the gap is widened to fit the longer text string, and the dash length is increased proportionately so as not to change the appearance of the line too much. Next, the text offsets must be adjusted to center the longer text string. The new linetype definition looks like this:

```
*SEWER_LINES,----SEWER----SEWER----SEWER----SEWER----
A,.7,−.3,["SEWER",STANDARD,S=.1,R=0.0,X=−0.25,Y=−.05],−.3
```

Compare this with the definition of the Hot_Water_Supply linetype. Figure 17.45 shows the Sewer_Lines linetype after the changes are made to accommodate the longer text string. Almost any requirements can be met for creating new linetypes by using an existing linetype as a template and adjusting it as needed to make the necessary changes.

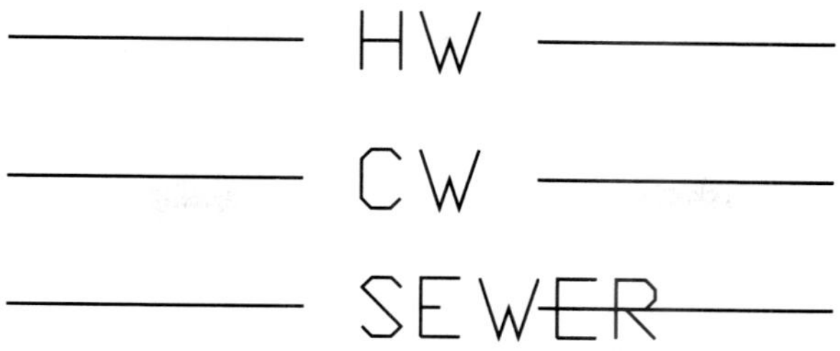

FIGURE 17.44 Some modifications require more work than simply changing the text value.

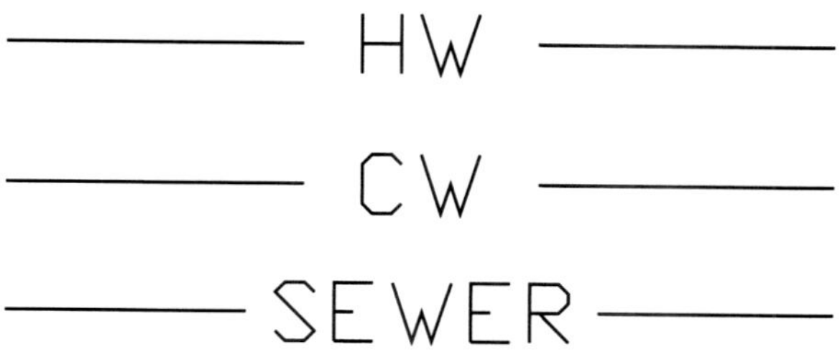

FIGURE 17.45 Adjusting the parameters of existing linetype definitions is the fastest and easiest way to create new linetypes.

Exercise 17.20 — Estimated time required: 15 min.

1. Using the GAS linetype as a template, create a new linetype by substituting the text string "CABLE" for "GAS."
2. Make the necessary adjustments to the gap and modify the dashes to maintain the correct appearance for the linetype.
3. Adjust the X and Y offset values to center the text in the gap.
4. Load the new linetype and draw several objects using it.
5. Save the drawing as EX17.20.

A shape is a special type of object that is defined using the same system used to define text fonts. AutoCAD LT comes with a shape definition file named LTYPESHP.SHX, which defines the shapes used by some of the complex linetypes. This shape file contains only five shapes, named as follows:

TRACK1
ZIG
BOX
CIRC1
BAT

This does not allow for a large number of options for creating linetypes using shapes. The following example creates a third fence line linetype, using both the BOX and the CIRC1 shapes. Because the existing parameters work well in the other two fence line linetypes, they are reused here:

```
*FENCELINE3,----0----[]----0----[]----
A,.25,[CIRC1,ltypeshp.shx,s=.1],-.2,1.25,[BOX,ltypeshp.shx,s=.1],-.2,1
```

The first entry in the shape specification is the name of the shape followed by the name of the shape file that contains its definition. Shapes use the same type of modifiers as text strings, including Scale, Rotation, X-Offset, and Y-Offset. Figure 17.46 shows the appearance of this linetype.

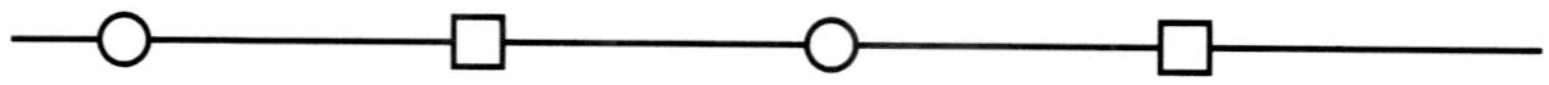

FIGURE 17.46 The FENCELINE3 linetype uses elements of both the FENCELINE1 and FENCELINE2 linetype definitions.

Field Notes

If your office or school also has installations of AutoCAD, you can design new shapes and compile new shape definition files. Check the AutoCAD documentation regarding creating shapes, and look into these commands: SHAPE, LOAD, and COMPILE.

Exercise 17.21 **Estimated time required: 20 min.**

1. Open the file ACLT.LIN for editing using Notepad.
2. Using the FENCELINE1 and 2 definitions as a reference, create a new linetype named FENCELINE3 that uses a pattern of dash, circle, dash, circle, dash, square, and repeats:

——o——o——[]——o——o——[]——

3. Save the linetype in a new linetype definition file named CHAP17C.LIN.
4. Load the new linetype and draw several objects. Save the drawing as EX17.21.

LEARNING CHECKPOINT

- ☐ What is the difference between simple and complex linetypes?
- ☐ Explain what PEN UP and PEN DOWN distances refer to and how they are specified in a linetype definition.
- ☐ What are the two primary linetype definition files?
- ☐ What parameters are available to control the appearance of text and shapes in a complex linetype?
- ☐ Define A type alignment.
- ☐ What is a shape and where are they found?

Defining Custom Hatch Patterns

AutoCAD LT comes with an extensive library of hatch patterns but, like linetypes, a multitude of applications exist that require specialized applications. The capability to create new hatch patterns is just one additional way in which AutoCAD LT can be customized to meet almost any need. AutoCAD LT's default hatch patterns are stored in the file ACLT.PAT. The .PAT file extension is used for all hatch pattern definition files. Custom patterns can be defined within the ACLT.PAT file or in a separate file. A .PAT file is an ASCII text file and can be edited with your text editor. If defined in a separate file, only a single pattern is defined in each file and the pattern name and file name must match. As an example, a pattern named TESTPAT needs to be defined in a file named TESTPAT.PAT.

The format for a hatch pattern listing is similar to a linetype definition file: The name is preceded by an asterisk, and a text-based description follows. One of the simplest pattern definitions in the ACLT.PAT file is for the following ANSI31 pattern:

```
*ANSI31, ANSI Iron, Brick, Stone masonry
45, 0,0, 0,.125
```

where the *ANSI31 entry indicates the pattern name, and the ANSI Iron, Brick, Stone masonry provides a brief text description of what the pattern represents. The additional lines represent that actual pattern definition, which in this case fits all on one line. Each line of the definition for a pattern describes one of its vectors. The ANSI31 pattern has only one vector, which is repeated as needed to fill a specified area.

The first entry in the pattern definition (45,) specifies the angle for drawing the vector being described. The next entry is an X,Y coordinate, in this case 0,0. The snap base setting is what AutoCAD LT uses to determine where the pattern fill should begin, and this determines where this particular vector is drawn from in relationship to the snap base. Finally, the third entry in this definition is another X,Y coordinate value that determines the offset for the next instance of this vector. In other words, with a setting of 0,0.125, the next vector begins at the same X coordinate as the previous vector, but the Y axis distance is 0.125 units from the start point of the previous instance. For this offset calculation, the direction of the line is considered to be the X axis. Therefore, the Y offset specifies the distance between parallel copies of the vector, and the X offset is meaningful only when working with dashed hatch lines. Figure 17.47 demonstrates this concept.

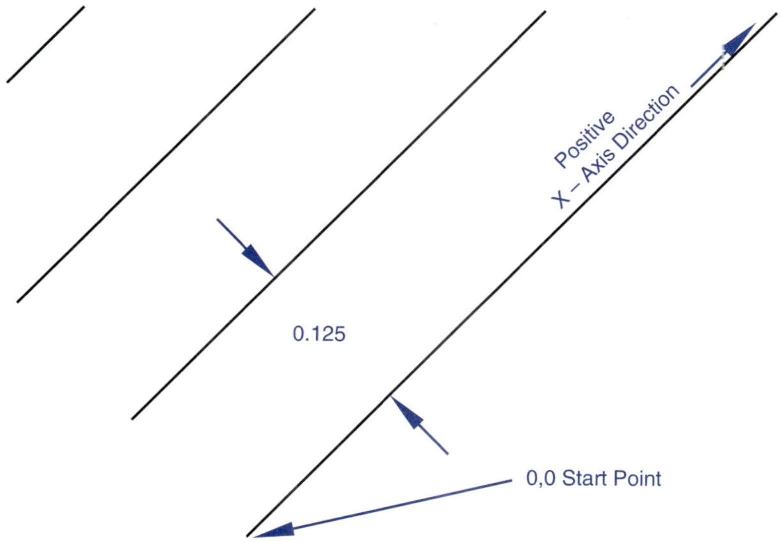

FIGURE 17.47 The starting point for the vector and the offset distance for a hatch pattern control its final appearance.

All hatch patterns are defined as vectors. A ***vector*** is a distance and angle that describe a straight line. By combining lines of various lengths at the appropriate angles, virtually any pattern can be created. Most patterns, however, do not have only continuous lines as with the ANSI31 pattern. Most patterns require a Pen Down and Pen Up style description to allow for dashed hatch lines. The dash length specifications are appended to the pattern definition after the offset values. For example, to draw a dashed version of the ANSI31 pattern that is the same angle and spacing but has 0.75 dashes separated by 0.25 gaps, the following is added to the pattern definition:

```
*45D, A 45 degree dashed pattern
45, 0,0, 0,.125, 0.75,–0.25
```

The circle in Figure 17.48 is hatched using the 45D pattern defined. Notice that, like linetype definitions, Pen Down is a positive number and Pen Up is a negative number. A maximum of six dash length specifications can be used in a single line of the pattern definition.

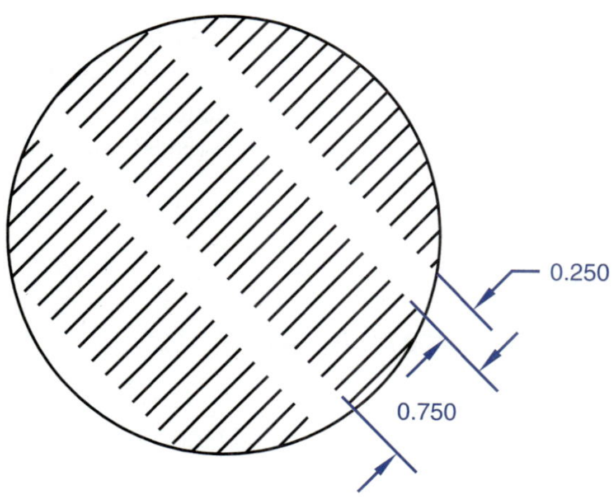

FIGURE 17.48 Adding a Pen Up and Pen Down specification to the ANSI31 pattern creates a dashed pattern.

The pattern name is specified as 45D, so the definition is saved in a file named 45D.PAT that has been placed in one of the AutoCAD LT support directories.

Now that a dashed pattern is being used, the effect of an X offset value can be seen. The 45D pattern definition is changed as follows to produce the pattern shown in Figure 17.49.

```
*45D, A 45 degree dashed pattern
45, 0,0, 0.5,.125, 0.75,-0.25
```

By using X and Y offset distances, Pen Up and Pen Down specifications, and a combination of lines at different angles, very complex hatch patterns can be created. The easiest way to get started creating a hatch pattern is to first draw the intended pattern in AutoCAD LT. Using AutoCAD LT inquiry commands, the lengths, angles, and distances can be easily determined and placed in a pattern file.

For example, using the POLYGON command, the hexagon shown in Figure 17.50 can easily be constructed as the basis for a tiled hexagonal like the standard pattern named "Honeycomb." After drawing it, use the EXPLODE command to reduce it to individual line objects for easier inquiries.

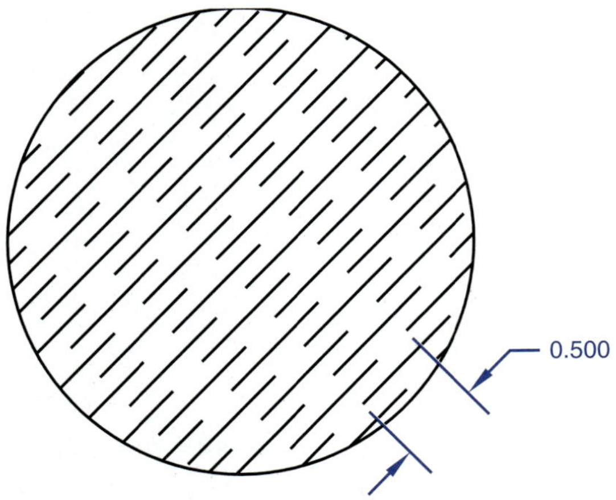

FIGURE 17.49 The X offset values can be used in dashed line pattern definitions.

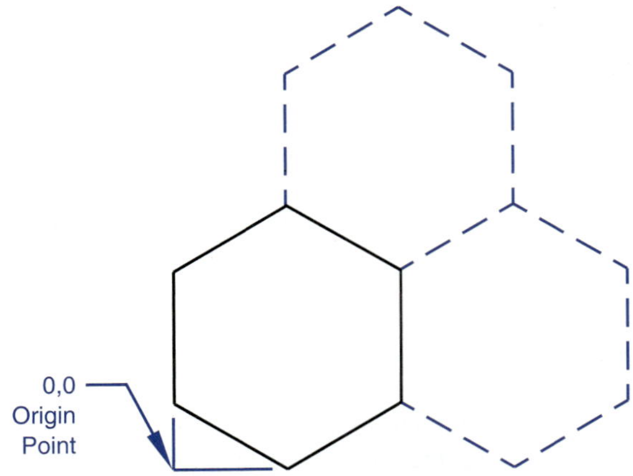

FIGURE 17.50 Drawing the hatch pattern first makes it easier to create because you can use the AutoCAD LT inquiry tools instead of a calculator to determine the required data for the pattern.

In the following example, a file named HEXAGON.PAT is to be created with a definition for a hatch pattern also named HEXAGON. The first line of the pattern definition names the pattern and provides a brief description. The description should be 80 characters or less in length:

```
*HEXAGON, A tiled hexagon pattern.
```

The order in which the lines are listed in a pattern definition is not critical. The important factor is to be sure that all of the data are entered and entered correctly. In Figure 17.50, notice the placement of the hexagon in relationship to the 0,0 origin point. This makes it easier to work with the numbers received from inquiry commands. The added hexagons are shown to help determine offsets and dash lengths, but it is only necessary to define the first hexagon. The rest are automatically calculated based on offsets and dash length.

The first objective in this example is to define the vertical line on the left. Using the LIST command in AutoCAD LT, the following information is provided:

```
LINE Layer: 0
Space: Model space
Handle = 3BB
from point, X= 0.0000 Y= 0.8660 Z= 0.0000
to point, X= 0.0000 Y= 0.2887 Z= 0.0000
Length = 0.5774, Angle in XY Plane = 270
Delta X = 0.0000, Delta Y = -0.5774, Delta Z = 0.0000
```

The information needed in the hatch pattern definition is shown in bold text, and includes the start point, length, and angle of the line. So, the first part of the definition looks like this:

```
*HEXAGON, A tiled hexagon pattern.
270, 0,0.866,
```

The next entries in the pattern definition are for the offsets. Figure 17.51 shows how the offsets for this line are determined. After adding the X and Y offsets to the pattern definition, the dash lengths are specified. From the previous LIST command, it is known that the Pen Down length for this line is .5774. Using the DIST command, the Pen Up distance can be determined. Figure 17.52 shows where the 1.1547 measurement for the Pen Up distance was determined.

Completing the definition for this line, the pattern definition now appears as follows:

```
*HEXAGON, A tiled hexagon pattern.
270, 0,0.866, 0.866,0.5, 0.5774,-1.1547
```

Because of the combination of offsets and dashes, this first line definition actually creates two of the parallel lines for the hexagon. To see what the pattern looks like so far, it can be saved and used as is. Figure 17.53 shows the partial hatch pattern created by this definition.

FIGURE 17.51 To determine offsets, find the position where this line is repeated in the pattern and measure the X and Y offset values.

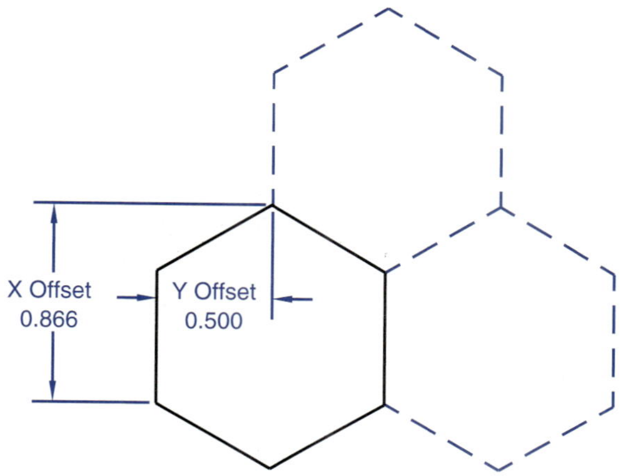

FIGURE 17.52 Use the DIST command to determine the Pen Up distances.

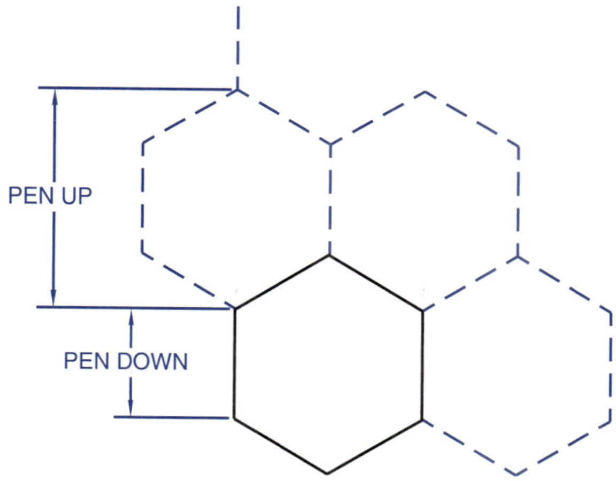

FIGURE 17.53 It can be helpful to check hatch pattern definitions one line at a time, in order to avoid errors. This is the effect of the first line of the HEXAGON pattern definition.

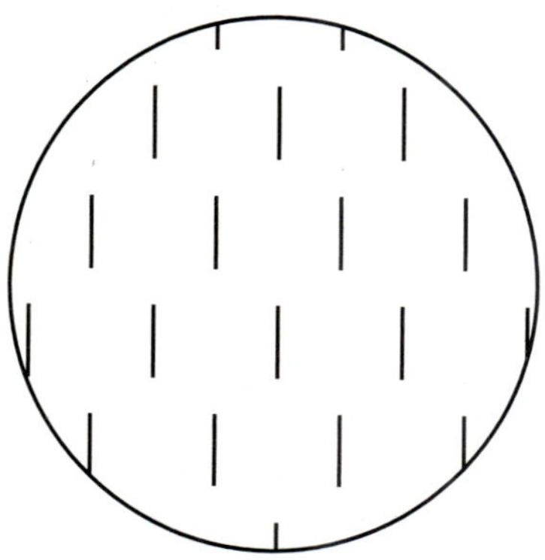

Field Notes

When constructing a hatch pattern, testing as you go is a good idea. Hatch a simple shape in the drawing editor using the new pattern definition and specifying an *associative* hatch. Each time you make a modification and save the definition file, return to AutoCAD LT and pick a grip point to make a minor adjustment in the boundary. When AutoCAD LT updates the pattern, it reads the definition file again and automatically implements your latest changes.

Using the LIST command for the next line provides this information:

LINE Layer: 0
Space: Model space
Handle = 3BA
from point, X= 0.5000 Y= 1.1547 Z= 0.0000
to point, X= 0.0000 Y= 0.8660 Z= 0.0000
Length = 0.5774, **Angle in XY Plane= 210**
Delta X = −0.5000, Delta Y = −0.2887, Delta Z = 0.0000

Each line in a hexagon is the same length, and all of the offsets and dash lengths are the same. The necessary information from this listing is the start point and the angle of the line. Modifying the pattern definition as follows produces the pattern shown in Figure 17.54.

```
*HEXAGON, A tiled hexagon pattern.
270, 0,0.866, 0.866,0.5, 0.5774,-1.1547
210, 0.5,1.1547, 0.866,0.5, 0.5774,-1.1547
```

FIGURE 17.54 Updating the hatch pattern in the drawing produces this result.

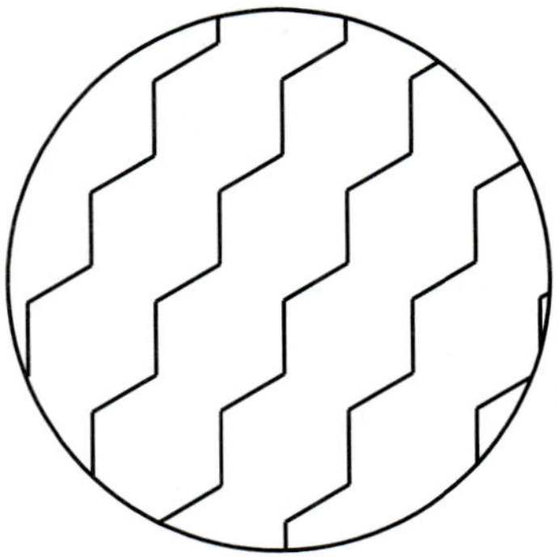

Finally, listing the third line provides the information needed to complete the pattern definition as shown here:

```
*HEXAGON, A tiled hexagon pattern.
270, 0,0.866, 0.866,0.5, 0.5774,-1.1547
210, 0.5,1.1547, 0.866,0.5, 0.5774,-1.1547
330, 0,0.2887, 0.866,0.5, 0.5774,-1.1547
```

Saving the pattern file and updating the pattern in the drawing produces the results shown in Figure 17.55.

FIGURE 17.55 The final appearance of the HEXAGON hatch pattern definition.

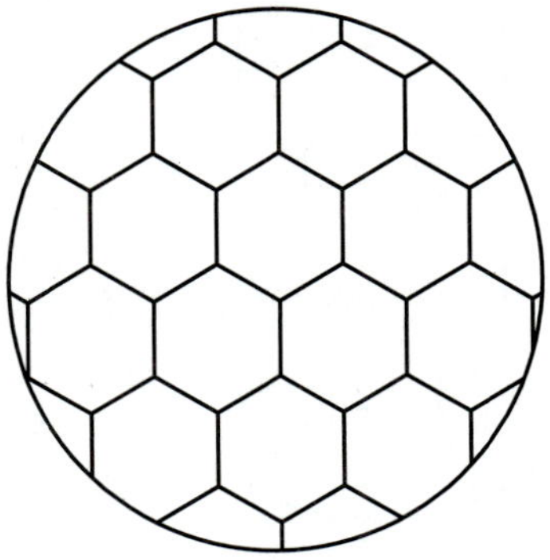

To use the new custom hatch pattern, first select the Custom option from the Type: list on the Quick tab of the Boundary Hatch dialog box. Next, select the ellipsis button next to the Custom pattern: list and pick the pattern file from the Custom tab in the Hatch Pattern Palette dialog box. Pick OK to return to the Boundary Hatch dialog box, where you can define the boundary by picking points or selecting objects. Apply the pattern as you would a built-in pattern.

Exercise 17.22 — Estimated time required: 30 min.

1. Create a hatch pattern definition called OFFSQR in a file of the same name.
2. The pattern will be of a 1-unit by 1-unit square, offset by .5 units, as shown in the following illustration:

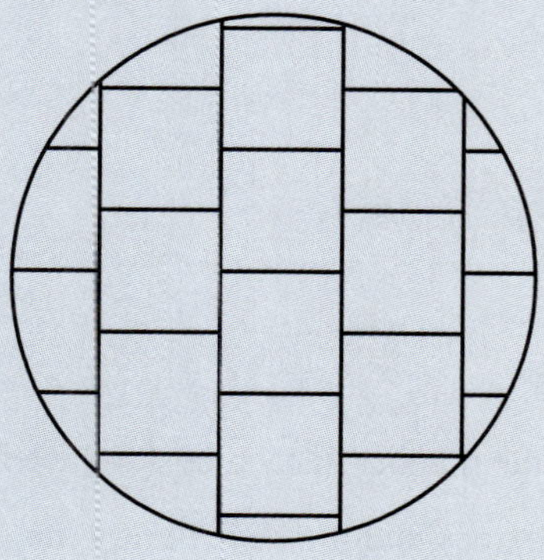

3. Save the file and test the new hatch pattern.

MULTIPLE CHOICE

Circle the choice or enter your response on an answer sheet by selecting the option that most closely completes or answers the given statements.

1. Files that are not part of the core program that are used to enhance or modify the way AutoCAD LT works are called:

a. support files **c.** initialization files
b. drawing files **d.** backup files grid

2. The PGP file stores definitions for:

a. pull-down menus **c.** command aliases
b. toolbar buttons **d.** hatch patterns

3. A text file that contains a list of commands and options that AutoCAD LT reads and performs is called a(n):

a. menu file **c.** command script
b. option list **d.** text file

4. This is the file extension for the primary file that is edited when making changes to the AutoCAD LT menu system:

a. MNU **c.** MNC
b. MNS **d.** MNR

5. This command is used in AutoCAD LT to load menu files:

a. MENU **c.** LOADMENU
b. MENULOAD **d.** LOAD

6. When loading menus, the menu file with this file extension is typically avoided:

a. MNU **c.** MNC
b. MNS **d.** MNR

7. AutoCAD LT cannot load multiple menus that use the same:

a. file name **c.** buttons menu
b. MENUGROUP name **d.** icon images

8. The menu section named POP0 contains the code for which menu?

a. the buttons menu **c.** the first pull-down menu
b. the cursor menu **d.** the help menu

9. The characters used in the menu label to begin and end cascade sections are:

a. -/ /- **c.** ( )
b. >> << **d.** -> <-

10. A linetype definition file has this file extension:

a. .ltd **c.** .ldf
b. .lin **d.** .lts

MATCHING

Match each term to the correct description by writing the appropriate number in each box at the left.

☐ DIESEL
☐ Cascade
☐ Macro
☐ .MNR
☐ .MNU
☐ .MNC
☐ .MNS
☐ Partial menu
☐ POP
☐ IMAGE
☐ .LIN
☐ .PAT
☐ .SCR
☐ .SLD
☐ .SLB

1. File extension for a slide library file.
2. Menu resource file extension.
3. Menu template file extension.
4. Compiled menu file extension.
5. A supplementary menu file.
6. Menu section for pull-down menus.
7. Menu section for image tile menus.
8. File extension for a linetype definition file.
9. File extension for a menu source file.
10. File extension for a script file.
11. A pull-down menu feature.
12. A menu selection that does more than one task.
13. File extension for a slide file.
14. Direct Interpretively Evaluated String Expression Language.
15. Hatch pattern definition file extension.

WORD SCRAMBLE

Unscramble the six scrambled words below, one letter to each square, to form six AutoCAD LT–related words:

ZITUSCOME

CROMA

EIZNITRIALIE

TEGPSHLIRN

DESCACA

FOULTY

Unscramble the circled letters above to form the special answer as suggested by the illustration.

PROJECTS

17.1 Open the ACLT.PGP file with Notepad. Add six new command aliases of your choice to the file. As you consider your options for the alias definitions, select the options that will best benefit you in your day-to-day drafting needs. Save the PGP file and use the REINIT command to reinitialize the PGP file. Test each of your alias definitions and make any necessary corrections.

17.2 Using Notepad, create a script file for a C size drawing setup. The script file should set units, limits, grid, snap, all layer settings, and any other settings that you think should be included. Then it should insert the correct title block in paper space. Save the script file as P17.2.SCR and test it in a new drawing. Make any necessary corrections and save the file again.

17.3 Create block definitions for the symbols shown in the figure below. Now, create a toolbar with a button for each of the symbols. Use a value of 1.0 for "h." When selected, the toolbar button should insert the symbol, allowing the user to specify the insertion point, scale factors, and rotation angle. Create an appropriate graphic on the toolbar buttons for both large and small buttons. Name the toolbar P17–3.

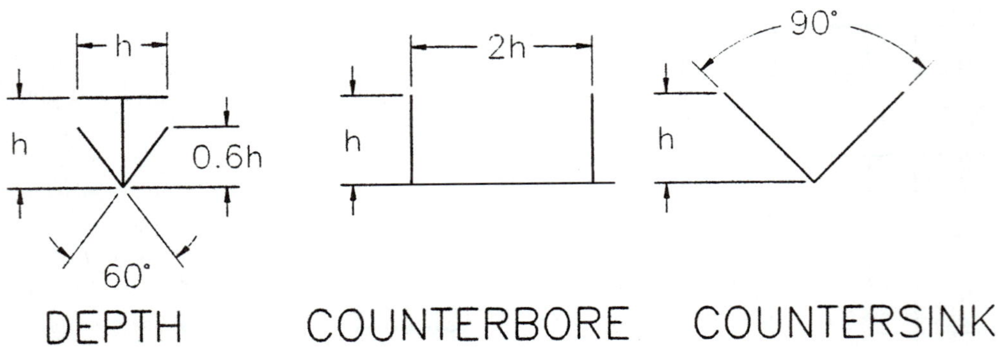

17.4 Create a flyout button and place it on the Dimensioning toolbar. When picked, it should display the P17–3 toolbar you created in Project 17.3.

17.5 Create a partial menu file named P17.MNS using Notepad. The MENUGROUP name should be P17. Create a new pull-down menu named CUSTOM. On the new menu, place four drawing options and four editing options. Include at least one macro in each category. Set up appropriate labeling and mnemonics for each item. Load the partial menu file in a drawing and test each menu option. Make any necessary corrections and save the file again as P17.MNS.

17.6 Open the file P17.MNS for editing in Notepad. Place an IMAGE section in the file, and create appropriate image tiles for at least four common architectural symbols. You will need to create both the geometry and slide images for each of the symbols. Place a menu call in your Custom pull-down menu that displays the image tile menu. Save the file as P17.MNS. Load the partial menu file in a drawing and test each menu option. Make any necessary corrections and save the file again as P17.MNS.

17.7 Using a file manager such as Windows Explorer, make a backup copy of the file ACLT.MNS named ACLT.MNS.BAK. If you need assistance, ask your instructor or system administrator. Open the file ACLT.MNS for editing. Create two new accelerator keystroke definitions in the ACCELERATORS section. Save the file and test the accelerator keystrokes. Make any necessary corrections and save the file again.

17.8 Using Notepad, create a new file named P17–8.LIN. Create a simple linetype definition in this file that has three dashes then three dots. Test the linetype and make any necessary corrections.

17.9 Using Notepad, open P17–8.LIN. Create a complex linetype definition in this file that has a text entry of "P17." Test the linetype and make any necessary corrections.

17.10 Using Notepad, create a file named P17.PAT. Enter a hatch pattern definition for a hexagon pattern. Test the pattern and make any necessary corrections.

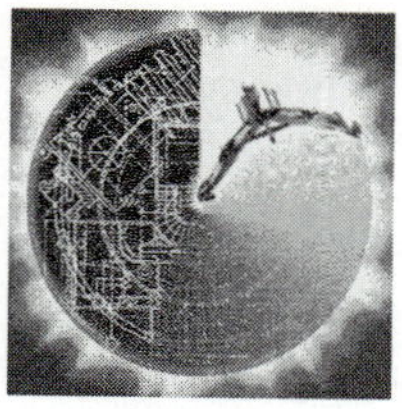

APPENDIX **A**

AutoCAD LT 2000 and Learning Assistance:

SYSTEM CONFIGURATION

SOFTWARE INSTALLATION

UPDATE PATCHES

As with most programs designed for the Windows operating systems, the installation of AutoCAD LT 2000 and the Autodesk Learning Assistance is automated. This means that the transfer of files from the original software CD to the hard disk of your computer is done automatically. The installation system creates all the appropriate directory folders and places the necessary files in the proper locations.

Before you begin installation of the AutoCAD LT 2000 or AutoCAD LT Learning Assistance software, you should first check the minimum system requirements listing to be certain that your workstation hardware and configuration meets or exceeds the specifications. A system that meets the minimum hardware requirements may still need specific Windows system configuration settings to be modified in order for the software to work properly. These settings should be adjusted before you install the AutoCAD LT or AutoCAD LT Learning Assistance software.

This appendix leads you through the process of checking the specifications and Windows configuration settings of your workstation. Short tutorial guides are also provided to help you adjust important system configuration settings when necessary.

Minimum System Requirements

Table A.1 shows the minimum hardware and operating system requirements for your system to run AutoCAD LT 2000 and AutoCAD LT 2000 Learning Assistance. A system configured at the minimum levels provides minimum performance and does not allow access to some specialized features of the software. For example, the dynamic help feature in the Page Setup dialog box is not available on a system configured at the specified 800 × 600 minimum resolution setting. Computer workstation components, including the meanings and effects of system configuration settings such as display resolution, are discussed in the first chapter of this textbook. If any terms or concepts in this appendix are unfamiliar to you, review the discussion in Chapter 1 as needed before proceeding.

In all applications, a faster processor and more memory (RAM) will result in better software performance and contribute to increased productivity. In some areas, the absolute minimum specification is shown with a recommended minimum. Use the recommended minimums, if possible, for better system performance and complete feature accessibility.

TABLE A.1 Minimum System Requirements

	AutoCAD LT 2000	Learning Assistance
CPU class and clock Speed	Pentium®-based PC (or compatible) *Minimum:* 133 MHz *Recommended:* Best Possible	Pentium (or compatible) 200 MHz
Display resolution	*Minimum:* 800×600 *Recommended:* 1024×768 or higher	1024×768 (64K or more colors)
Operating System	Windows 2000®, Windows 98®, Windows95®, Windows NT 4.0® *Note:* Windows NT 4.0 must have Service Pack 3 or greater installed for Learning Assistance to operate correctly.	
Audio		16-bit sound card
CD-ROM speed		8X
Memory (RAM)	*Minimum:* 32MB minimum, *Recommended:* 64MB or more	4 MB
Hard disk space used for Installation	73 MB for 45 MB for Microsoft Internet Explorer 4.01 (if IE is not already present)	
Swap space (used by system)	*Minimum:* 64 MB *Recommended:* 100 MB or more	
Pointing Device	Mouse or other pointing device A *wheel mouse* is recommended.	

Optional Hardware

- Printer or plotter
- Network interface card *if connected to LAN* (recommended: 100 Megabit or higher)
- Modem *if using a dial-up connection* (recommend 56K or higher)
- *Wintab* digitizer tablet

Special Requirements

- Microsoft Internet Explorer 4.01 or later is required for the HTML-based on-line help system and the dynamic help system in the Page Setup and Plot dialog boxes. **Internet Explorer will automatically be installed or updated during the AutoCAD LT 2000 installation, if required.** Although Internet Explorer is required by AutoCAD LT, you can still use any preferred Web browser for accessing the Internet.
- The *WHIP!*® Browser Accessory 4.0 is needed in order to view DWF (Drawing Web Format) files from intranet or Internet locations using your Web browser. *WHIP!* is available as either a Netscape Navigator plug-in or as a Microsoft Internet Explorer ActiveX™ control. For a complete discussion of downloading and installing *WHIP!*, refer to Chapter 16. You can also find information on the Web about *WHIP!* at http://www.autodesk.com/products/whip/index.htm
- AutoCAD LT 2000 can use only a digitizer that is supported by Windows through the Wintab interface. Contact the digitizer manufacturer, or visit their Web site, to obtain a Wintab driver specific to your version of Windows.

Operating System Versions

The most recent version of the Windows operating system at the time of this writing is Windows 2000. AutoCAD LT 2000 is reported to be qualified as "Windows 2000 Ready," meaning that Autodesk has conducted internal testing to determine its compatibility with the Windows 2000 platform (operating system). This also means that Autodesk will provide the same level of product support to customers on the Windows 2000 platform as they do with customers using any other supported version of Windows.

AutoCAD LT 2000 can also be run on the Windows 98, Windows 95, or Windows NT4.0 operating systems. If your operating system is Windows NT4.0, you will need Service Pack 3 or greater installed to run AutoCAD LT 2000 Learning Assistance properly. At the time of this writing, Service Pack 6A for Windows NT4.0 is listed as the most current release available on the Windows NT Service Packs information page at the Microsoft Web site:

http://support.microsoft.com/Support/NTServer/Content/ServicePacks/Default.asp

If your system does not have the correct service pack installed, contact your instructor or system administrator for assistance. The service pack can be freely downloaded from the Microsoft web site, or you can order it on a CD. You can get the latest information regarding the currently available service packs from the URL shown previously, or you can access the main Microsoft Web site at

http://www.microsoft.com

Field Notes

At this time, AutoCAD LT 2000 is not known to have problems on any particular version of Windows 95 or Windows 98. However, both of these operating systems have service packs available. As a rule, your system administrator or instructor will review the information on the Microsoft Web site regarding the operating system being used and the available service packs to determine if an update is appropriate. At work or school, never update an operating system without proper authorization and adequate guidance. Your system administrator or instructor may also be able to offer guidance for updating a home system. Never apply a service pack unless you have completely read and fully understand all relevant documentation.

System Configuration Issues

The primary configuration settings in your operating system that affect AutoCAD LT are the display properties (including resolution and color palette) and the system swap space setting. You will need to have administrative rights in your computer's security settings to make some of these configuration changes. This section discusses the effects and control options for these system configuration issues.

Configuring the Display Properties

AutoCAD LT 2000 can run at an 800 × 600 resolution, as indicated by the minimum specifications. However, some program features, such as the dynamic plotting help, require a minimum of 1024 × 768 resolution. The range of values is 640 × 480 through 1600 × 1200. Most modern monitors can be set as high as 1280 × 1024 but may not function if set to 1600 × 1200. Keep in mind that not all the values displayed in this list can be used by your monitor.

Higher screen resolution means that more pixels are used to display the same physical area; items on your screen are represented using smaller pixels, resulting in a crisper, cleaner display appearance. One consideration regarding screen resolution is that this setting directly affects the size of the Windows desktop features. Most of these features are represented using a specific number of pixels. For example, a toolbar button in AutoCAD LT is displayed at a default size of 16 × 15 pixels. Because higher resolution means smaller pixels, standard program features such as buttons and menus appear smaller. Increasing the size of desktop features to compensate for higher resolutions is also covered in this section.

Another aspect of the display configuration that can affect the AutoCAD LT 2000 and Learning Assistance software is the number of colors used in the Windows color palette. In the Windows 95 and Windows 98 operating systems, display problems can occur in AutoCAD LT 2000 (specifically, with DesignCenter) when your color palette is set to display 256 colors. To correct this problem, the color palette must be set to display more than 256 colors. Typical palette color display options usually include 256, 32K, 64K, 16M, and True Color If you are installing the Learning Assistance software, the color palette must be set to 64K or higher to work properly. The more colors you set your system to display, the more accurate the appearance of colors on your screen. The optimum setting is for true color, but resolution, color, and refresh frequency are interdependent and are collectively subject to the limitations of your display hardware.

Setting the screen resolution is easy to do, but an incorrect display setting can cause a failure in your display system. When your display system fails, it may display incorrectly or not at all. Because you cannot pick what you cannot see, it can be difficult or even impossible to fix the incorrect settings without restarting your system.

Never Apply **any** changes to the settings on the Settings tab of the Display Properties dialog box until after you have successfully tested them and you are **certain** that they are working properly.

Configuring Display Resolution and Color Palette Settings

First, read through the following tutorial completely. Next, to change your display properties, return to the beginning and follow each of these steps carefully and completely.

1. Access the Display Properties dialog box using one of these methods:
   a. From My Computer on the Desktop…
      i. On the Windows Desktop, double-click the My Computer icon.
      ii. Double-click the Control Panel icon in the My Computer window.
      iii. Double-click the Display icon.

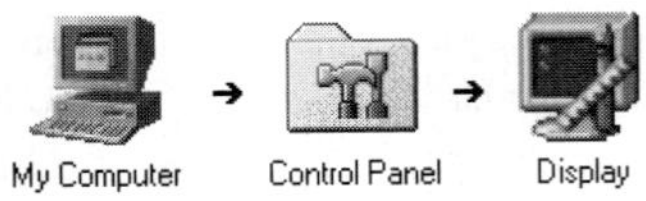

   b. From the Start menu…
      i. Pick the Settings cascade.
      ii. Pick Control Panel.
      iii. Double-click the Display icon.

   c. From the Desktop Shortcut menu…
      i. Right-click on a blank area of the Desktop.
      ii. From the Shortcut menu, pick Properties.

2. In the Display Properties dialog box, pick the Settings tab, shown in Figure A.1. The appearance of the Display Properties dialog box, and the available property settings accessible on the Settings tab, may vary depending on the brand and model of your display system hardware (video adapter card) and software (video drivers). The possible values shown for each of these properties represent the capabilities of your video adapter card, but *your monitor may not be able to support all these settings.*
3. First, check to see if the recommended minimum settings are supported by your display system by making the following settings:
   a. Set the Color Palette to 65536 Colors (64K).
   b. Set the Desktop Area (resolution) to 1024 × 768 using the slider bar.
   c. Set the Refresh Frequency to 72 Hertz.

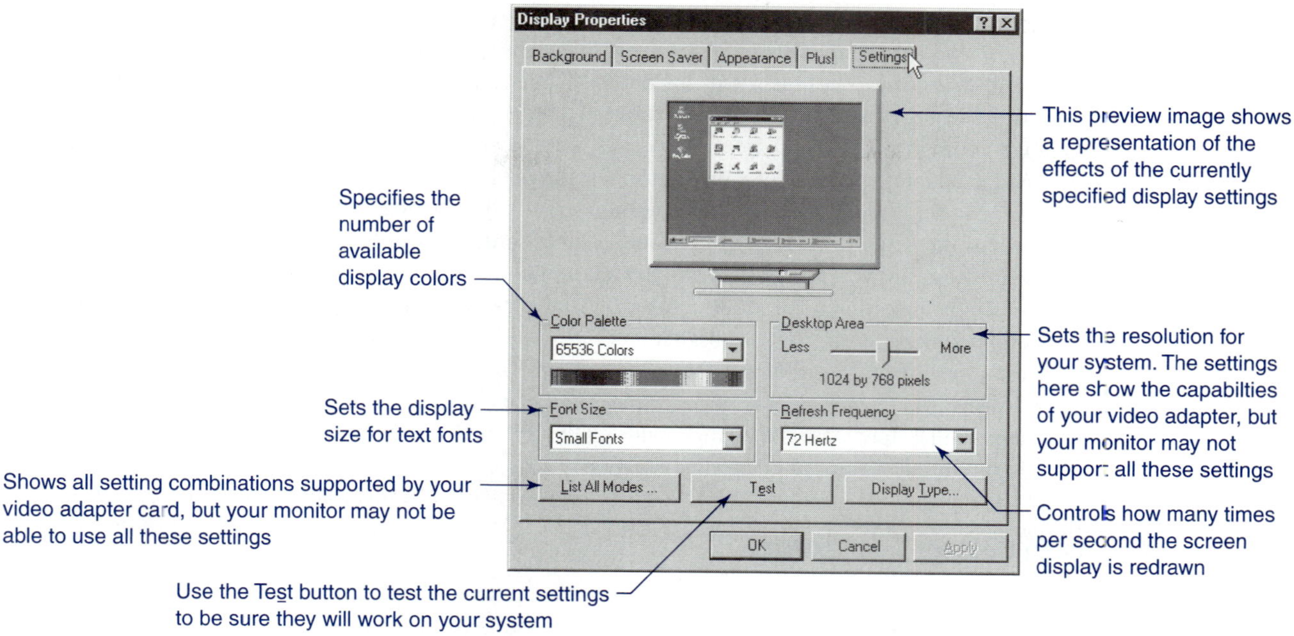

FIGURE A.1 The Settings tab on the Display Properties dialog box provides control options for the display resolution and color palette. *Never apply settings that have not been successfully tested.*

   d. Check the settings to ensure that they are set as defined in 3a, 3b, and 3c.
   e. If *any* of these settings is not available, or if they *cannot all be set at the same time,* skip directly to step 7.
4. Pick the Test button.
   a. In the Testing Mode dialog box, pick OK to begin the 5-second test.
   b. *Watch the screen to see if a test pattern is displayed.* Whether or not this is successful, you will be returned to the desktop with your previous settings after 5 seconds.
   c. In the Testing Mode dialog box, pick Yes if the pattern was displayed properly, or pick No if it was not.
5. If the test pattern *was not* displayed properly, skip directly to step 7.
6. If the test pattern *was* displayed properly, skip directly to step 9.
7. These settings cannot be used on your system. Your best choice is to upgrade your hardware as soon as you can. If you cannot wait for an upgrade to your display system and you need to install AutoCAD LT 2000 now, follow these steps to establish the best possible settings:
   a. Set the Refresh Frequency to 60 Hertz, and pick Test. If the test pattern is displayed, use these settings temporarily. This will run both AutoCAD LT 2000 and Learning Assistance properly; the 60 Hz setting may cause your screen to "flicker" if you use fluorescent lighting, which can cause eye fatigue and even headaches. The best setting for refresh frequency is 70 Hertz and above. Use the 60 Hz setting only as long as absolutely necessary. If the pattern was not displayed, go to 7b.
   b. Set the Color Palette to 32768 Colors(32K), and pick Test. If the test pattern is displayed, use these settings temporarily. This will run AutoCAD LT 2000 but will not run Learning Assistance properly. If the pattern was not displayed, or you need to run Learning Assistance, go to 7c.
   c. Set the Color Palette back to 64K Colors, set the resolution to 800 × 600, and pick Test. If the test pattern is displayed, use these settings temporarily. This will disable certain features in AutoCAD LT 2000, but you will be able to use both AutoCAD LT 2000 and Learning Assistance for now. If the pattern was not displayed, go to 7d.
   d. Set the Color Palette to 32K Colors, and pick Test. If the test pattern is displayed, use these settings temporarily. This resolution will disable certain features in AutoCAD LT 2000, and you will not be able to run Learning Assistance properly. If the pattern was not displayed, go to 7e.
   e. Set the Color Palette to 256 Colors, and pick Test. If the test pattern is displayed, use these settings temporarily. This resolution will disable certain features in AutoCAD LT 2000 and

may cause display problems in some cases. You will not be able to run Learning Assistance properly with these settings. If the pattern was not displayed, go to Step 8.

8. You will need to upgrade your display system before you can install or use AutoCAD LT 2000 or Learning Assistance. If all the recommended settings are listed in the property settings found on Settings tab of the Display Properties, but they do not display properly, it indicates that your video adapter card supports the required settings but your monitor does not. In this case, you will need to replace the monitor. If the settings are not listed or cannot all be set to recommended values at the same time, then your video adapter card needs to be upgraded. Be sure that any new hardware that you install supports the recommended minimum specifications.
9. Once the recommended minimum settings have been successfully tested, you can test other possible configurations that use higher resolution or more colors or both. When you specify a combinations of settings that are not supported, one or more of the settings is automatically adjusted downward to a setting that works. Every time you change a setting, check all the other settings to ensure that they were not changed automatically. In all configurations, be certain to keep the Refresh Frequency set to 70 Hertz or higher.

Increasing Desktop Feature Size

The size of desktop icons, text, and menus can be increased to compensate for higher resolution settings. This enables you to get the best possible display quality and yet still see the desktop features well enough to work productively. The size of desktop features is also controlled in the Display Properties dialog box. The Appearance tab on the Display Properties dialog box allows individual control of the color and size of all primary desktop features. You can set each item as desired, or you can use one of the predefined desktop schemes.

In Figure A.2A, the default *Windows Standard* scheme is selected, and the preview shows the elements at their actual size. To change any element of the screen, pick it in the preview, or select its name from the Item: list, then change the value displayed in the Size, Color, or Font boxes. Windows provides two predefined schemes that use the default Windows color scheme but display the text menu elements at a larger size. One is named *Windows Standard (Large),* and the other is *Windows Standard (Extra Large).* Figure A.2B shows the preview in the Appearance tab with the *Windows Standard (Extra Large)* scheme selected. This helps to make desktop features much easier to read at higher resolution settings.

Figure A.3 illustrates the difference in appearance in the AutoCAD LT 2000 program window with the settings shown in Figure A.2 applied. Pick the *Use large icons* toggle on the Plus! Tab of the Display Properties dialog box to increase the size of the desktop icons, and the *Large Icons* representing folders and files as displayed in Windows Explorer and all standard file dialog boxes. In some systems, this tab may be named Effects instead of Plus!. After installing AutoCAD LT 2000, you can also increase the size at which its toolbar buttons are displayed. This procedure is discussed in Chapter 2 under the topic *Setting Interface Options.* Finally, you can even increase the size at which the cursor is displayed on screen using the Pointers tab of the Mouse Properties dialog box, which is accessed through the Control Panel. The mouse pointer settings also have various schemes which can be set, including *Windows (Large)* and *Windows (Extra Large).*

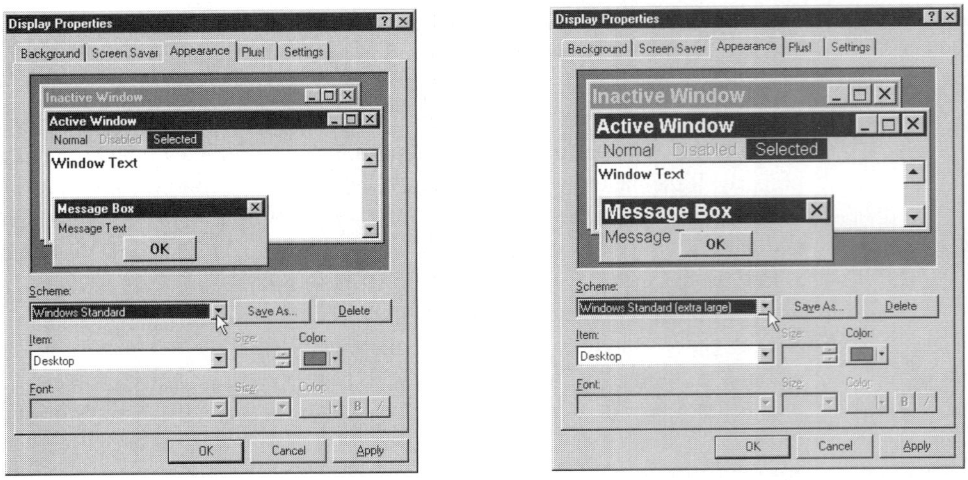

A B

FIGURE A.2 (A) The Windows Standard scheme represents the initial default settings in Windows. (B) Using the Windows Standard (Extra Large) option helps compensate for the reduction in desktop feature size at higher resolution settings.

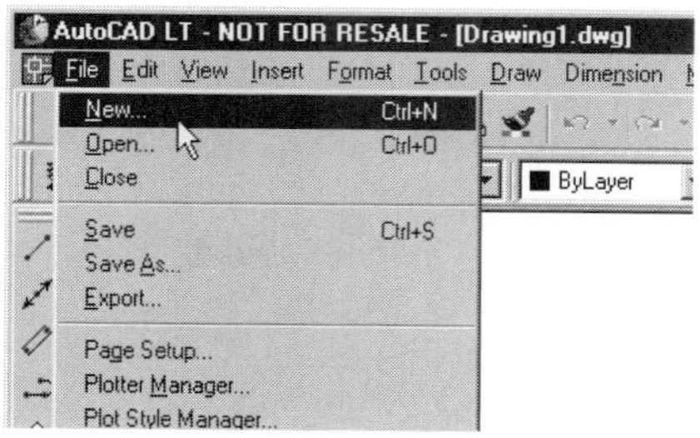

A

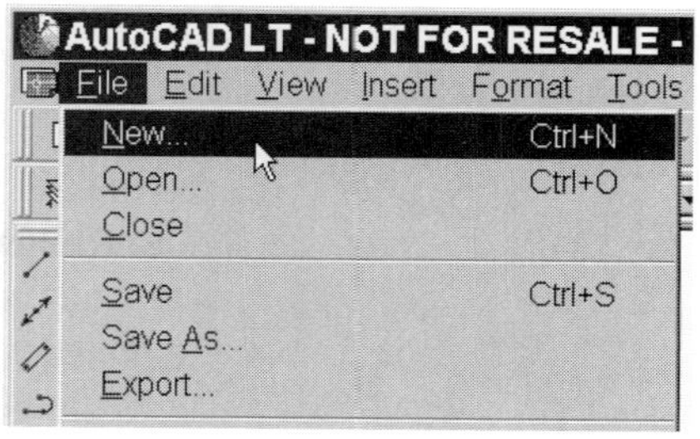

B

FIGURE A.3 (A) Standard desktop feature sizes used by default. (B) Extra large Windows features applied in the AutoCAD LT 2000 program window.

Setting System Swap Space

The Windows 98 and Windows 95 operating systems automatically manage the swap file space, and in most cases this is the best option. You can override the automatic management of swap file space, but it is not recommended in most cases. Windows NT 4.0, however, requires that you specify the swap space to make available to the system. Before making any changes to the swap space settings, always check with your instructor or system administrator for assistance.

In each of these operating systems, you can check the current swap space settings by double-clicking on the System icon in the Control Panel. This opens the System Properties dialog box, which will vary in appearance based on your operating system. The Performance tab on the System Properties dialog box shown in Figure A.4A is from the Windows NT 4.0 operating system. The swap space setting is also referred to as *Virtual Memory*. The current swap (or *paging*) file size is shown here in the NT4 version of this dialog box. Pick the Change... button (the Virtual Memory... button in 95/98) to access the Virtual Memory dialog box, and adjust the currently specified file sizes. Figure A.4B shows the Virtual Memory dialog box in Windows NT 4.0.

For the best performance in Windows NT4.0, it is recommended that you select a fast drive with plenty of available space, and specify an Initial Size (MB): that is equal to or greater than your recommended setting. The recommendation in this dialog box is for Windows only and does not take your other software into account. Since the AutoCAD LT 2000 recommended minimum swap space setting is 100 MB, this should be specified as the new value in the Initial Size (MB): text box. You will need to restart your system after changing this setting in order for it to take effect. Once all your configuration changes have been made and you have verified that your system hardware and configuration now meets or exceeds all the minimum system requirements, it is time to install your software.

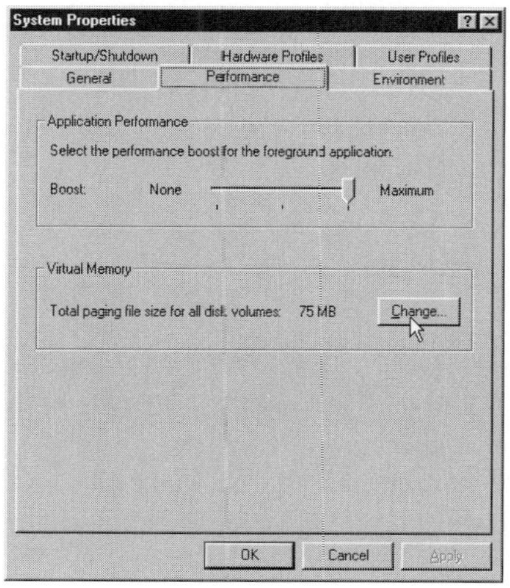

A

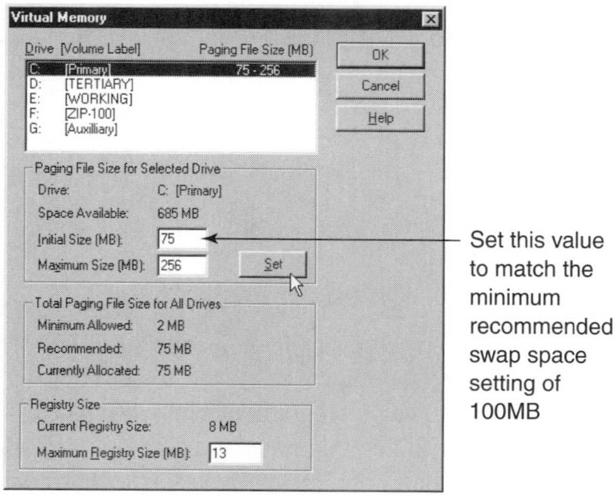

B

FIGURE A.4 (A) The Performance tab of the System Properties dialog box. (B) The Virtual Memory dialog box is used to change the swap space settings.

Before You Begin Installation...

AutoCAD LT 2000 is shipped on a single CD-ROM disk, accompanied by your AutoCAD LT 2000 Learning Assistance CD. The AutoCAD LT 2000 CD packaging has a label containing your serial number and the CD "key." Be sure to transcribe this information to a safe and secure location to maintain a permanent record copy. This information is required to be able to install the AutoCAD LT 2000 software; keep a copy handy so you can enter it when requested during the installation.

You will need to have proper permissions to add and modify system files in several key areas on your workstation. Make sure that with your current login you have write permission in these locations:

- Folder where AutoCAD LT 2000 is to be installed
- Windows System folders
- System registry

Before starting the installation, you need to exit from any other software applications that are currently running. Having another application open and running may prevent the installation program from replacing or modifying one or more of the necessary system files. The installation process can be slowed down significantly by some virus protection software packages. You may also wish to temporarily disable virus checking during the installation.

In Windows NT4.0, this means that you must have Administrator privileges and be authorized to modify the system registry. To check your rights and permissions in NT, pick User Manager from the Administrative Tools (Common) group on the Programs cascade of the Start menu on the Windows taskbar. Check with your instructor or system administrator for assistance if needed.

Installing the AutoCAD LT 2000 Software

The installation process is automated but not fully automatic. The installation program creates all the required folders and copies the necessary AutoCAD LT 2000 program files from the CD into the appropriate folder locations. However, you will be required to supply some input during the installation process, including security and personalization information. You will also need to specify the type of installation you want, and you will be asked for information such as the drive and location into which the program is installed plus the program folder into which the shortcuts are installed. This section leads you through the process of installing the AutoCAD LT 2000 software on your computer. You can cancel the software installation at any time, if necessary, by pressing either the F3 or the Esc key.

Field Notes

> If you intend to use AutoCAD 2000 and AutoCAD LT 2000 on the same workstation, it is important to *install AutoCAD 2000 prior to installing AutoCAD LT 2000.* If AutoCAD 2000 is installed on a system where AutoCAD LT 2000 was already installed, you should *reinstall* the AutoCAD LT 2000 software after completing the AutoCAD 2000 installation.

Getting Started

Place the AutoCAD LT 2000 CD in your CD-ROM drive. This CD has an AutoRun feature that automatically starts the installation process when you load the disk into your CD-ROM drive. If it does not start up by itself after a minute or two, you may need to start the installation program manually.

Setup.exe

To start the installation program manually, you need to execute the file named Setup.exe on the CD. Pick the Start menu on the Windows taskbar and pick Run... from the menu to display the Run dialog box. Pick the Browse... button to display the Browse dialog box, where you can open the CD and select the Setup.exe file. Pick the Open button, and when you return to the Run dialog box, pick OK to run the selected application.

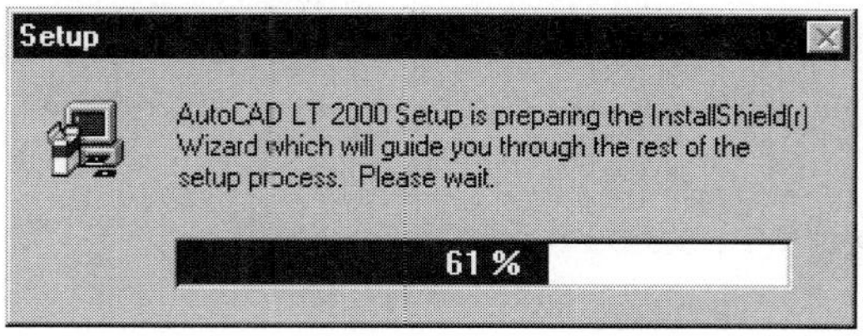

The Setup dialog box indicates that the InstallShield® Wizard is being loaded to guide you through the rest of the setup process. The progress is reported as it loads. The setup process begins as soon as the wizard is finished loading.

Security, Licensing, and Personalization

The Welcome dialog box indicates that the AutoCAD LT 2000 software will be installed on your computer, and reminds you with a strong recommendation that you exit from all other Windows applications before running the Setup program. You can use the Alt+Tab keystroke to see if there are any other active applications. Just switch to any other active programs, save your files if desired, and close the applications. If you prefer, you can pick the Cancel button to stop the installation process and close the active programs, and restart the AutoCAD LT 2000 installation when you are done. Pick Next > to continue.

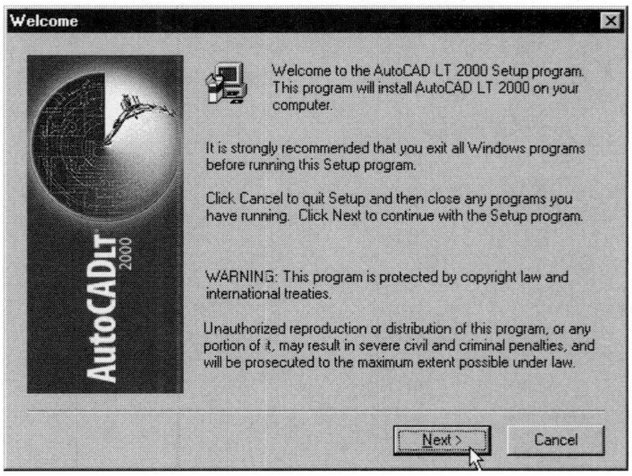

The Software License Agreement displayed in the subsequent dialog box is a very important part of your software because it governs the terms and conditions of the license granted to you. You should read this document fully and work to gain a complete understanding of the terms of the agreement you are accepting. You may not proceed beyond this point in the installation without picking the I accept button and then the Next > button.

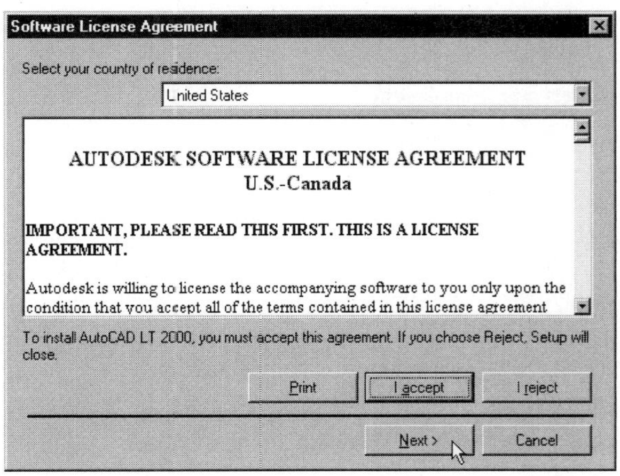

Some of the key issues that you should be aware of include the following:

- You may create only one archive copy of the CD. It is illegal to create any additional copies beyond the terms of the agreement.
- This software is *licensed* to you; you do not own it.
- If the software is an educational version, it can be used only by the student who originally acquired it, and only for study and instruction. It may not be used for commercial purposes.
- You may install and use a second copy of the software provided that the software is used only by you and only in one location at a time. This allows you to install a copy in your office computer and your home computer so that you can work in either location.

This listing should not be considered a substitute for reading the complete agreement before accepting the terms it defines. The agreement discusses copyright conditions, liabilities, warranties, and restrictions that are important to you. If desired, pick the Print button to produce a printed copy that you can read and keep on file. However, this information is available for review at any time after installing AutoCAD LT 2000 with a single menu pick.

The Serial Number dialog box now prompts you to enter the serial number of your software and the CD "key" that was printed on the CD package. You may not continue past this point without a valid serial number and CD key. Be certain that you file this information in a safe and secure location for your permanent records. Pick Next > to continue.

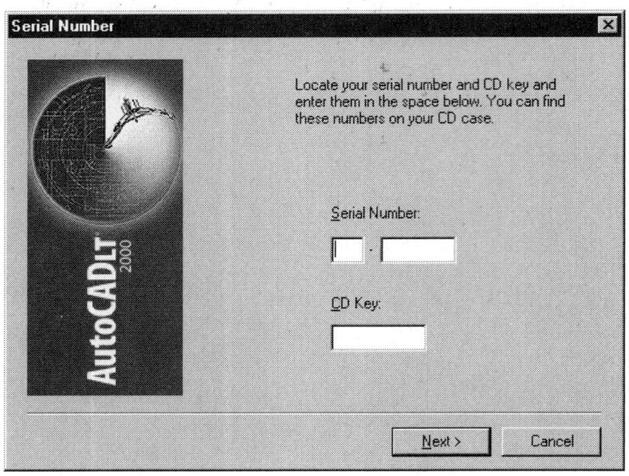

Next, the Personalization dialog box personalizes your software to identify you as the licensed user. A confirmation is provided in the second Personalization dialog box to allow you to check your settings. Pick < Back to go to the previous dialog box to make any needed changes, or pick Next > if everything is already correct.

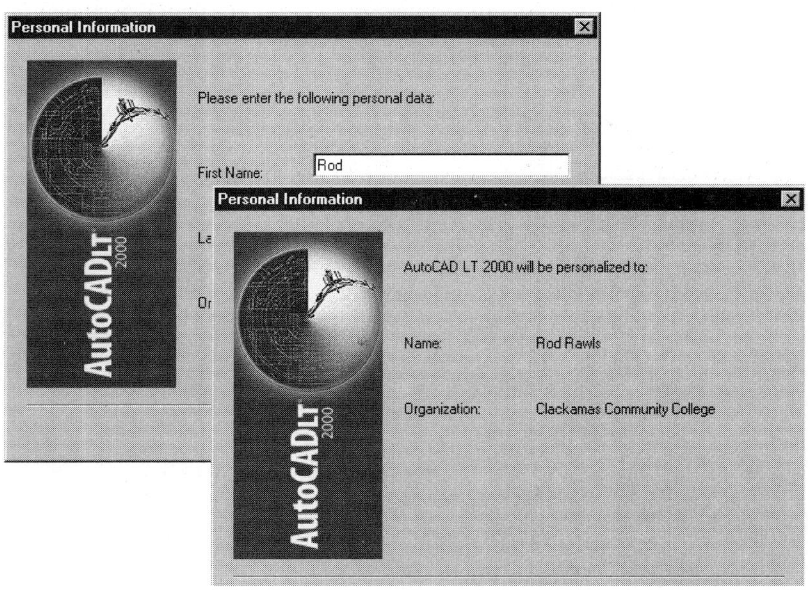

Defining Installation Parameters

The Destination Location dialog box shows the default installation location for the AutoCAD LT 2000 program files. The default path is suitable for most applications. If you do not need to change the default location, pick Next > to continue. If you need to install it in an alternative location, pick the Browse... button and use the Choose Directory dialog box to browse your local and network disk drives. Specify any desired disk drive and folder location. Be sure that the target drive has sufficient disk space available.

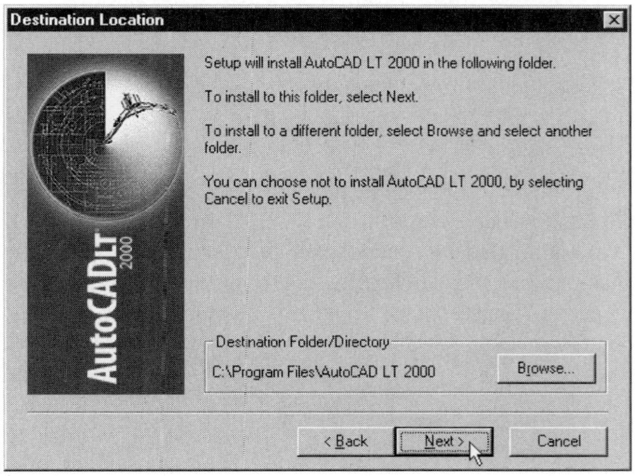

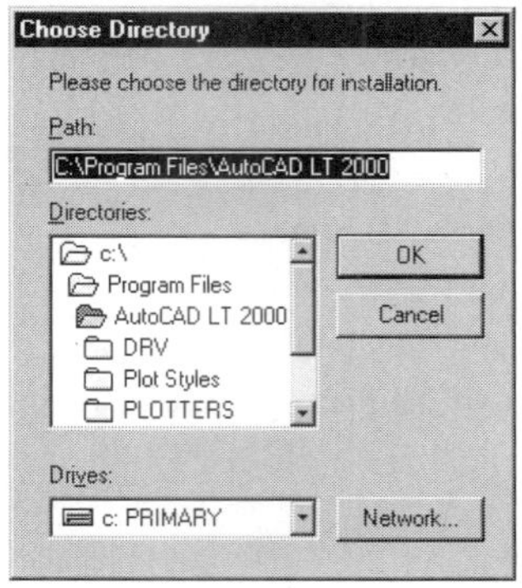

If the specified folder does not yet exist, the AutoCAD LT 2000 Setup dialog box confirms the folder location that you specified and asks if the folder should be created for you. This identifies the location of the base program folder. Several subfolders are also created below this one for better organization of the various support and sample files. Pick Yes to create the folder, or pick No to return to the Destination Location dialog box.

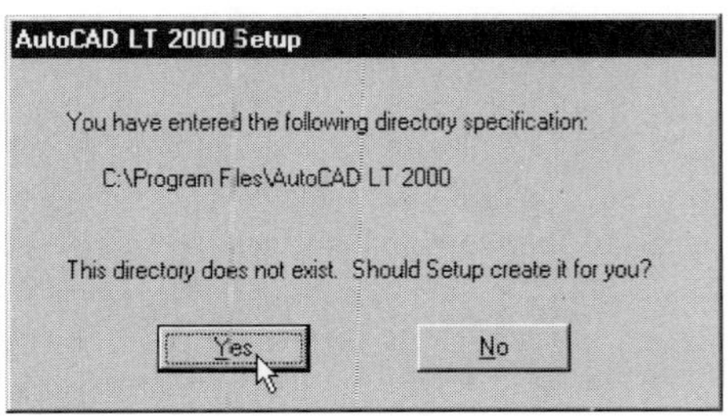

The Setup Type dialog box allows you to specify the type of installation you want. You can choose from three options, Typical, Compact, or Custom. The option you select depends primarily on the type of application in which you will be using the AutoCAD LT 2000 installation. For example:

Setup Type	Files Installed	Typical Application
Typical	Executables Support files Additional support files Templates TrueType fonts Sample drawings and images Main dictionary On-line help and support files What's New and Help drawings	The typical setup installs the most commonly used files for most applications. Additional support files, complete on-line help resources, templates, sample drawing files including the DesignCenter resource drawings, the main dictionary, and TrueType fonts constitute most of the files needed in a typical AutoCAD LT 2000 professional desktop workstation installation
Compact	Executables Support files On-line help	A compact installation omits sample files and non essential resource files to create the smallest possible footprint. This type of installation is used when file storage space is limited (e.g., notebooks, laptops) and all that is needed is the basic software functionality.
Custom	All files are installed except those you exclude.	This approach allows complete control over what components of the software are installed on your system. Excluding no files results in a full install. A full install is valuable for educational purposes and for users wanting access to every available tool and feature. Custom installation allows the user to determine which files to install and displays a running total of the disk space required/available statistics.

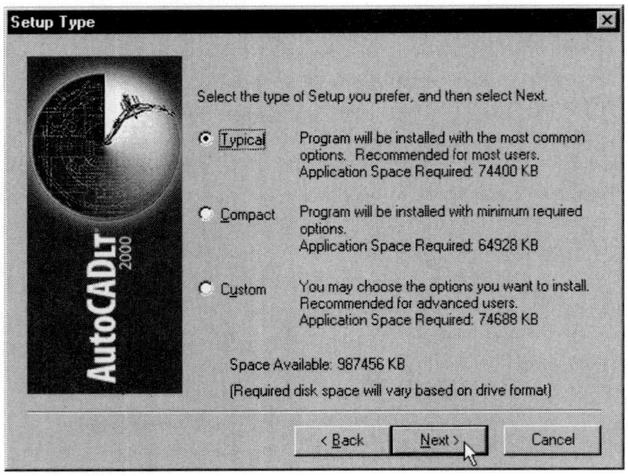

If the setup type is specified as Custom, picking the Next > button in the Setup Type dialog box displays the Custom Components dialog box. In the Components list, pick a category to list the optional components in the list on the right. Each optional component displays a check box that is already checked by default. Pick the check box to remove the check mark and exclude that file from installation. In this example, the French-Canadian dictionary file is removed from the list of files to install.

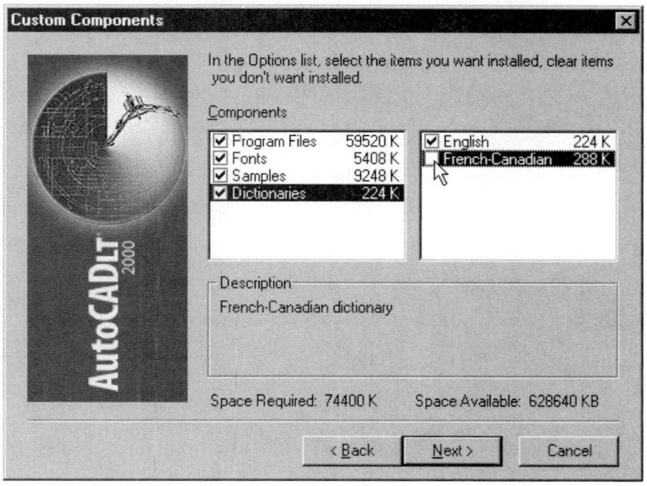

The Custom Components dialog box also displays a running total of the amount of disk space required to install the currently selected files along with the current amount of available disk space, letting you optimize your installation when necessary. After selecting all the files that should not be installed, pick the Next > button to continue. The installation program checks the available disk space to see if the files you want to install will fit on the destination drive.

Once the available disk space has been verified as being available, the Folder Name dialog box prompts you for the name of the Program folder where the AutoCAD LT 2000 related links will be installed. This refers to the program folders (presented as cascading menus) displayed on the Program cascade on the Start menu accessed from the Windows taskbar. The default program folder name is AutoCAD LT 2000, which is recommended for most applications. If you have your program folders organized differently, you can specify a different folder name or path to use.

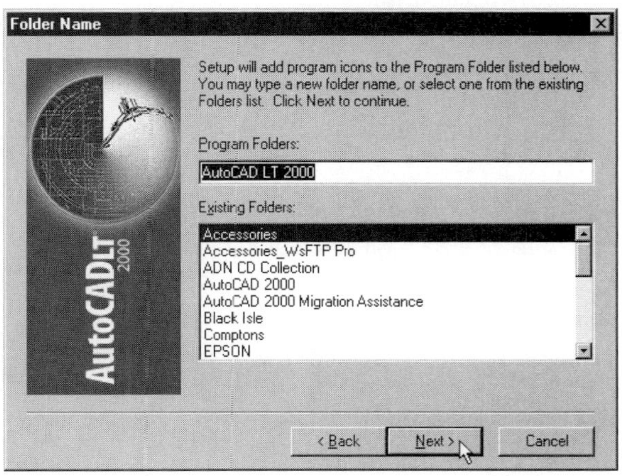

The Setup Confirmation dialog box indicates that AutoCAD LT has gathered enough information to begin copying the files required for the specified installation. Review the Current Settings: list to evaluate all the setup parameters that you specified. Use the scroll bars as necessary to view all the information. If anything is incorrect, you cannot edit it in this dialog box. You will need to use the < Back button to return to the dialog box where that setting was made and continue from that point. Pick the Next > button to confirm that all the current settings are correct.

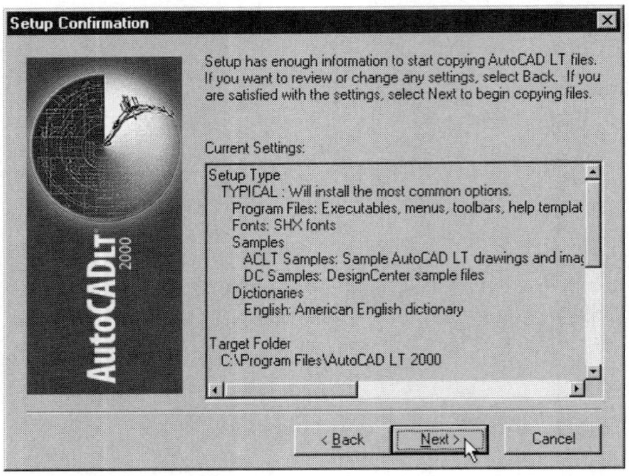

The installation is now underway. A progress meter representing the current percent completion of the software installation and the tasks in progress is displayed. Various banners are displayed that tell you about software features and installation tasks in progress.

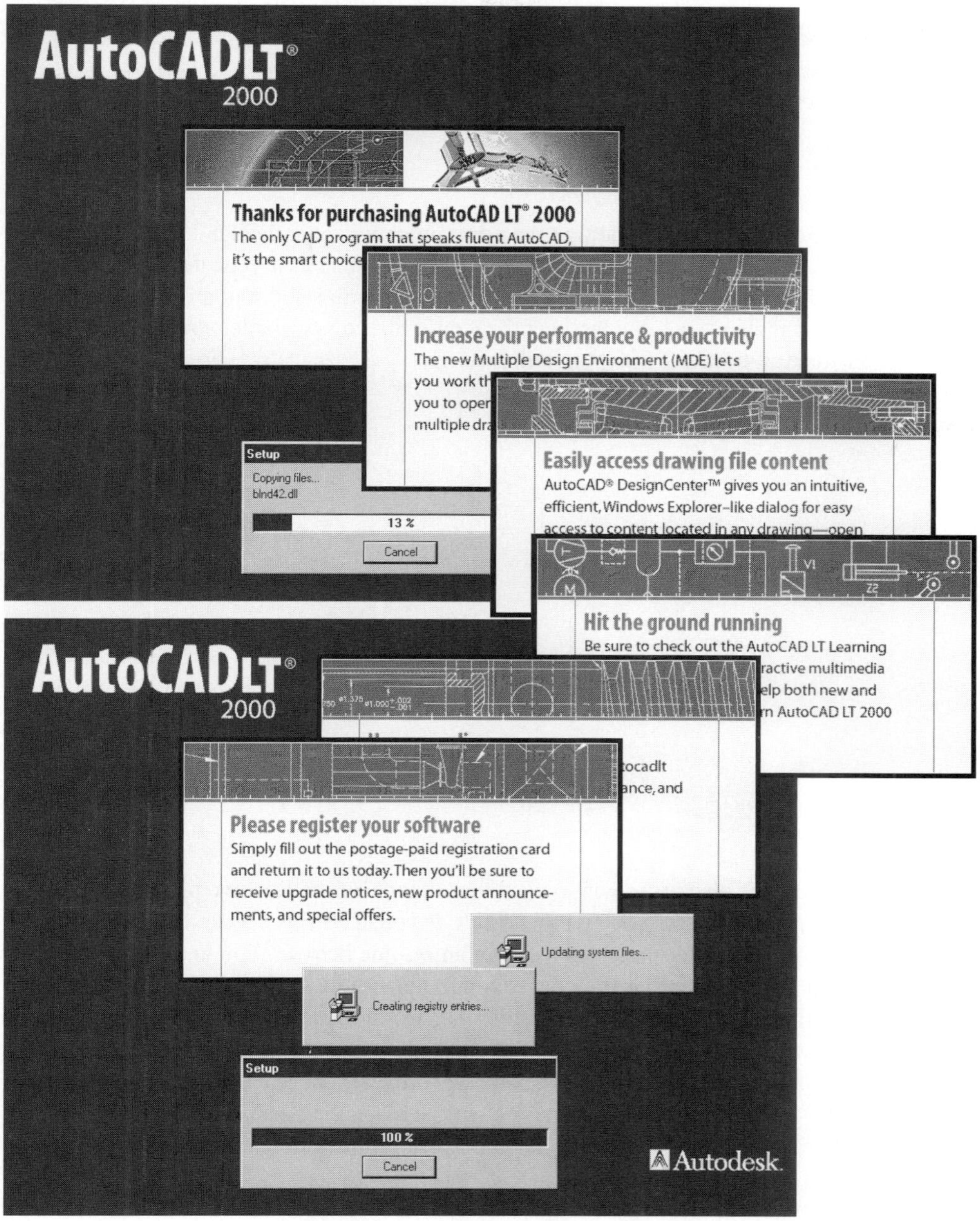

Readme, Reboot, and Results

If the installation routine prompts you regarding installation of the AutoCAD LT 2000 version of TrueType Fonts, choose Yes to All. The final banner encourages you to register your AutoCAD LT 2000 software. Registering your software is highly recommended. Registration protects your investment. Additionally, registering enables you to receive any incremental upgrades that are issued and also allows you to receive occasional product information mailings.

When installation is complete, the AutoCAD LT 2000 Setup dialog box is displayed and asks if you want to restart your computer system now or later. The dialog box displays a message indicating that your computer must be rebooted (restarted) before AutoCAD LT 2000 will work properly. If you pick *Yes, I want to restart my computer now*, any active applications are closed and the computer system is restarted. If you pick *No, I will restart my computer later*, the Setup Complete dialog box is displayed.

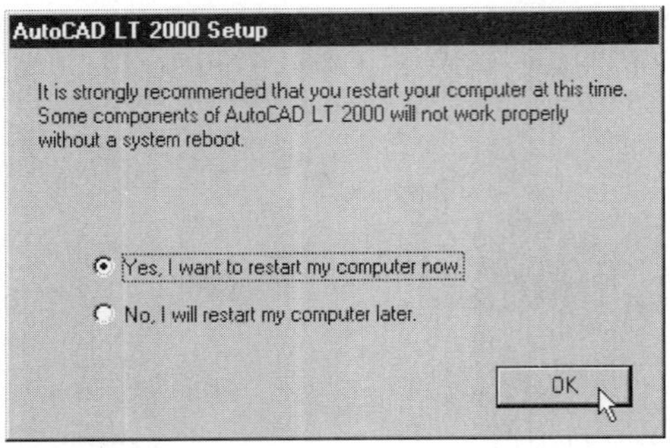

The Setup Complete dialog box informs you that the setup process is complete and that you can start AutoCAD LT 2000 by double-clicking on the program icon that was installed on your desktop. The AutoCAD LT 2000 program icon on your desktop appears as the LT logo art with a shortcut arrow and is labeled AutoCAD LT 2000. Despite this message and the fact that the icon is already available, you will still need to restart your system in order for AutoCAD LT 2000 to work properly.

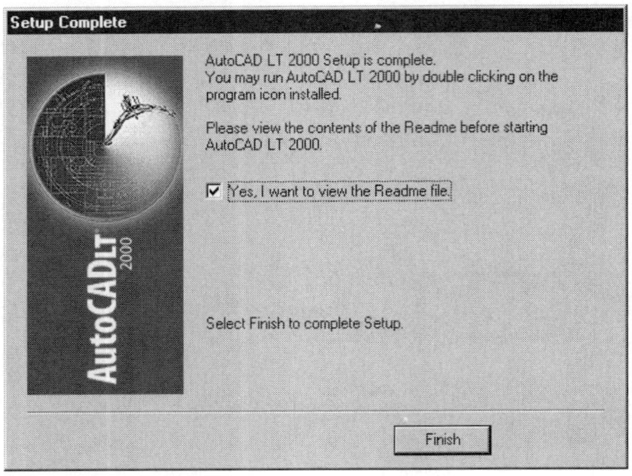

The Setup Complete dialog box also urges you to view the contents of the Readme file, and checks the *Yes, I want to view the Readme file* so that it is enabled by default. If you leave this checked and pick the Finish button, the AutoCAD LT 2000 Readme file is displayed in an on-line help window interface. There are several categories of important information that provides last-minute additions to the software documentation plus any necessary corrections to the existing documentation. When installing any type of software on your computer, you should always take time to review the Readme file. Some of the information in the Readme may not have any context until you learn more about the software, but other information may be of immediate benefit to you. You can review the Readme file at any time by picking AutoCAD LT 2000 Readme from the AutoCAD LT 2000 program group on the Programs cascade of the Start menu.

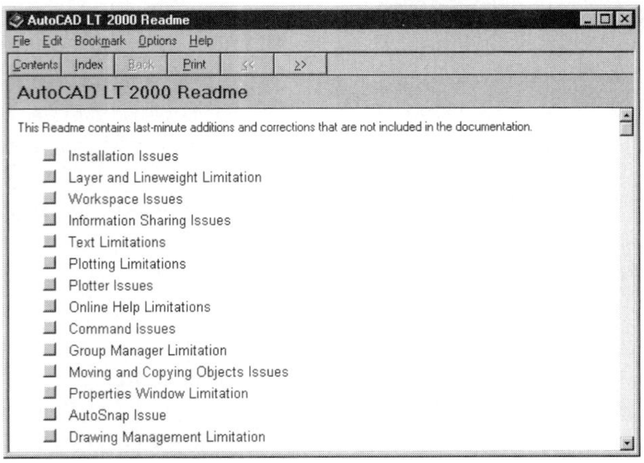

When you are ready to continue, restart your system as you would at any other time. You can pick Shut Down… from the Windows Start menu, and select the Restart the computer option from the Shut Down Windows dialog box. When Windows reboots and starts up again, the Windows Setup dialog box is displayed while the Windows System Settings are updated. When the system settings update is completed, Windows finishes loading.

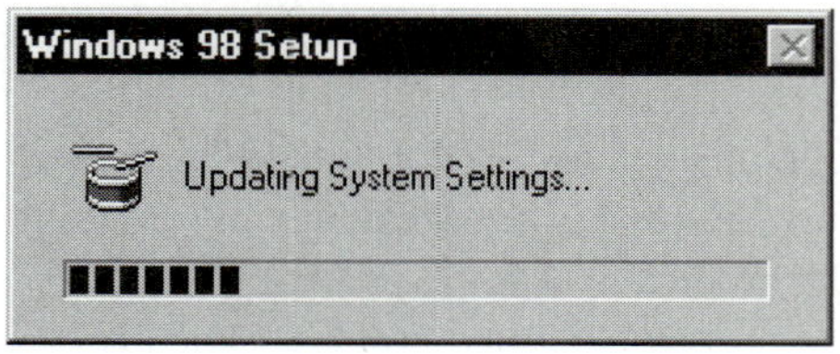

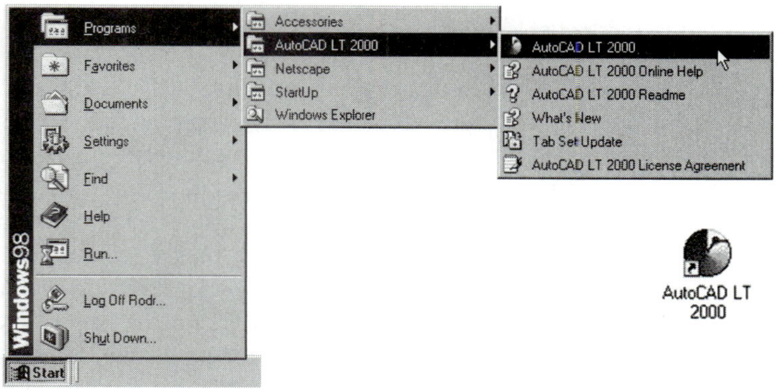

Now you can start AutoCAD LT 2000 if desired. Either pick AutoCAD LT 2000 from the Programs cascade on the Windows Start menu, or double-click the desktop shortcut icon for AutoCAD LT 2000. The AutoCAD LT 2000 program group contains the following shortcuts:

- **AutoCAD LT 2000** Starts the AutoCAD LT 2000 program
- **AutoCAD LT 2000 Online Help** Starts the Online Help System without starting AutoCAD LT 2000
- **AutoCAD LT 2000 Readme** Displays the Readme file as shown previously
- **What's New** Interactive presentation highlighting the differences between AutoCAD LT 98 and AutoCAD LT 2000
- **Tab Set Update** Converts tab sets created with AutoCAD LT 97 or 98 to folder shortcuts in the Favorites folder for use with AutoCAD LT 2000
- **AutoCAD LT 2000 License Agreement** Starts the Windows Wordpad application and loads the file containing the Software License Agreement (license.rtf) that you accepted when you installed AutoCAD LT 2000.

AutoCAD LT 2000 Installation Notes

The following section provides supplementary information regarding functionality issues with the AutoCAD LT 2000 software.

Restoring Your Default Browser

If the MSIE (Microsoft Internet Explorer) application was installed on your system during the AutoCAD LT 2000 installation, MSIE took the opportunity to set itself up as your default Web browser. If you prefer to use a different Web browser software, you can restore it as your default browser.

After installation is complete and you have restarted your computer, open your preferred Web browser as you would normally. When it opens, the browser should display a dialog box indicating that it is no longer the default browser. The Netscape Navigator dialog box shown here asks if you want to register it as your default browser. Picking Yes restores Netscape Navigator as your default browser.

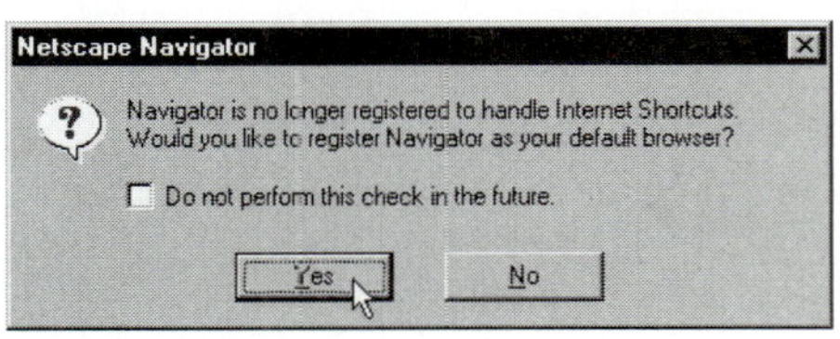

If your preferred browser is Netscape, and this dialog box is not displayed because the *Do not perform this check in the future* toggle was checked in a previous session, the process is a bit more involved. Netscape provides a step-by-step tutorial on their Web site at this URL:

http://help.netscape.com/kb/consumer/19971009-21.html

Wheel Mouse Functionality in AutoCAD LT 2000

Using a wheel mouse product with AutoCAD LT 2000 is highly recommended because of the extended functionality of the wheel available while working in a drawing. The wheel button is used to initiate fast and easy display changes and can represent a significant productivity tool for design and drafting professionals.

Many wheel mouse products come with sophisticated software drivers that increase the available options for configuring the mouse functionality in a variety of applications. In many cases, however, these retail and aftermarket software drivers may prevent your wheel mouse from functioning correctly in AutoCAD LT. It has been the experience of the authors of this text that installing a generic wheel mouse driver provided by your operating system typically provides full wheel functionality in AutoCAD LT as well as in other Microsoft Windows logo–compliant programs. If you prefer the fully customizable functionality afforded by your software driver products, updating to a more recent version of the driver may resolve any conflicts and allow the AutoCAD LT 2000 features to be used as well.

If you use a Microsoft IntelliMouse®, you will need to install the latest available driver on your system in order for the device to be fully functional in AutoCAD LT 2000. The latest IntelliMouse drivers are posted on the Microsoft Web site at this URL:

http://microsoft.com/products/hardware/mouse/driver/default.htm

If you use a Logitech Wheel Mouse, and you have installed the Logitech drivers, you must press the Ctrl key while rolling the wheel to use the dynamic zooming function. Without the Ctrl key, rolling the wheel pans the drawing. For this feature to work as described here, you should have the Logitech Mouseware 8.62 or later installed on your system. You can download the latest Logitech drivers from the Logitech Web site. At the time of this writing, updated drivers can be freely downloaded from the following URL:

http://www.logitech.com/cf/support/mousefiles.cfm

The URL for the main Logitech Web site is

http://www.logitech.com

AutoCAD LT 2000 Network Version

Autodesk has indicated that a network version of AutoCAD LT 2000 is not available. For network users requiring multiple seats of AutoCAD LT, licenses can be purchased through the Autodesk Open License Program. The Open License Program provides a more cost effective method for deploying multiple seats of AutoCAD LT 2000.

AutoCAD LT 2000 to AutoCAD 2000 Drag-and-Drop Results in Unintentional OLE

When both programs are installed on the same operating system and workstation, dragging or pasting objects from AutoCAD LT 2000 to a drawing open in AutoCAD 2000 results in unintentional OLE (object linking and embedding) operations. This means that the resulting objects in the AutoCAD software are *linked* to the LT drawing. To successfully place objects in AutoCAD from LT, create a block in LT and insert the block into the AutoCAD drawing.

Dragging or pasting drawing objects from AutoCAD into the LT software works normally, inserting the objects as intended—without any links.

Uninstalling AutoCAD LT 2000

The following discussion introduces some issues and considerations associated with uninstalling the AutoCAD LT 2000 software from your workstation.

How To Uninstall AutoCAD LT 2000

Add/Remove Programs

To uninstall the AutoCAD LT 2000 software, open the Control Panel window and double-click on the Add/Remove Programs icon. This displays the Install/Uninstall tab of the Add/Remove Programs dialog box. This dialog box displays a list of software applications that can automatically be removed by Windows. To remove any application, highlight the name of the software and pick the Add/Remove... button. The Confirm File Deletion dialog box asks you to confirm that you want to remove the program. Pick Yes to continue with the uninstall.

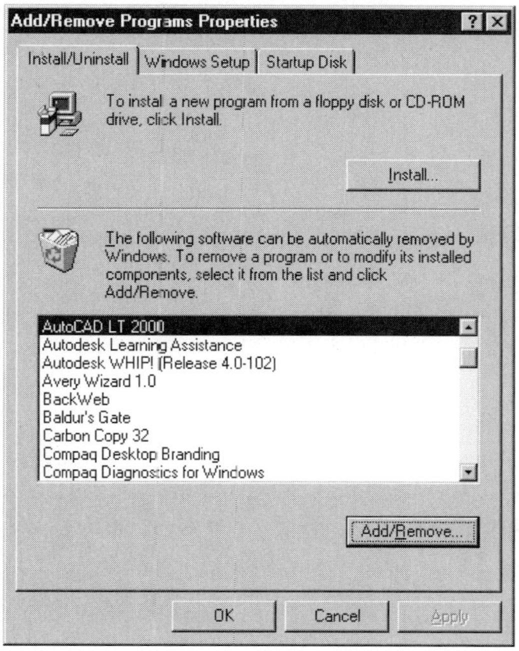

The Remove Programs From Your Computer dialog box lists the removed components. If any files that were not part of the original installation were added to the AutoCAD LT 2000 folders, those files will not be removed. A message is displayed under the progress bar indicating that the files will need to be removed manually. After removing the AutoCAD LT 2000 software, you will need to restart your system.

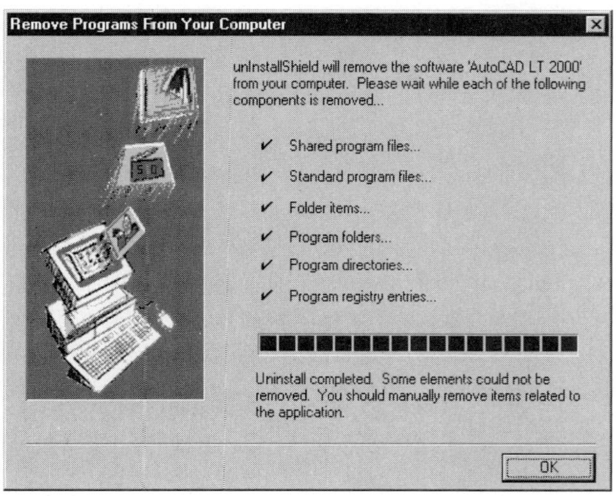

Preserving Your Customized Files

Uninstalling AutoCAD LT 2000 removes all files, including customized files, from your system. If you have customized AutoCAD LT 2000 files, such as the Menu, Hatch Pattern, or Linetype files, you should save backup copies of these files in a secure location before uninstalling the software. You only need to copy files that you have actually customized. Some of the primary user customizable files in AutoCAD LT 2000 are listed here:

aclt.pat	aclt.dwt	aclt.mnr	aclt.unt
acltiso.pat	acltiso.dwt	aclt.mns	sample.cus
aclt.lin	aclt.mnu	aclt.pgp	
acltiso.lin	aclt.mnc	aclt.psf	

WHIP! Plug-In Problems

After the AutoCAD LT 2000 software is uninstalled, the *WHIP!* plug-in may not function properly when used with other Autodesk programs. You can avoid this problem by reinstalling the *WHIP!* driver after you have uninstalled AutoCAD LT 2000.

Installation Maintenance

When the setup program is run on a system that already has AutoCAD LT 2000 installed, the Welcome dialog box is displayed followed by the Setup Choices dialog box. This dialog box is part of the AutoCAD LT 2000 Installation Maintenance Program. Two setup choices are offered, which are displayed as the Add and Reinstall buttons.

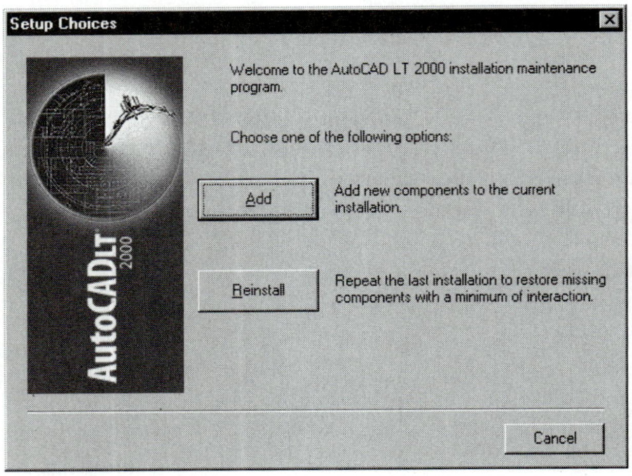

To add components to the installation that have not already been installed, pick the Add button to display the Custom Components dialog box. In this dialog box you can select any of the listed elements that you want to add to the existing installation. All items that have not been installed previously are already checked for your reference.

Pick the Next > button in the Custom Components dialog box when you have selected all the components you want to add. The Setup Confirmation dialog box is displayed to show you what will be installed. You are not prompted for the location; the current installation folders are automatically used. Pick the Next > button in the Setup Confirmation dialog box to begin the installation of the new components.

Field Notes

> If you pick the < Back button in the Custom Components dialog box, you do not return to the Setup Choices dialog box. Instead, you are returned to the Setup Type dialog box just as if you were performing a new installation.

The Reinstall option in the Setup Choices dialog box can be used to restore the original versions of any program files that have been deleted or altered. All the program components included in the initial installation and any that have been added subsequently are replaced with the original versions from the software CD. A dialog box asks if you want to back up the configurable files first. If you pick No, all the AutoCAD LT 2000 files are reinstalled with no further prompts, and all the configurable files are replaced. Pick Yes if you have modified one or more configurable files and do not want to lose your modifications.

The Select Files to Backup dialog box is used to specify which configurable files should be backed up. Initially, all the files are selected, and you are prompted to clear the selection of the files you do not want to be backed up. Any files that are backed up are saved in the folder ...\AutoCAD LT 2000\backup.000. If a folder with this name already exists from a previous reinstall, the new folder is named incrementally as ...\AutoCAD LT 2000\backup.001. All the files left highlighted in the list are copied to the backup folder before they are replaced. If there are other files you have modified and want to keep, you should take the time to copy those files to a safe location as well before reinstalling the software.

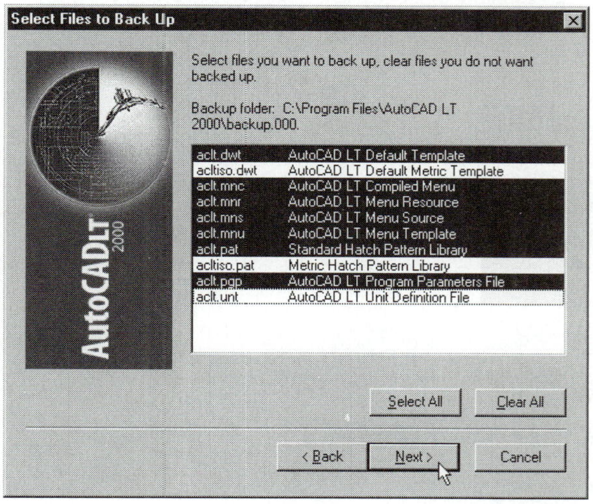

Installing AutoCAD LT Learning Assistance

Earlier discussion covered minimum hardware and operating system requirements as well as relevant system configuration issues for both AutoCAD LT 2000 and AutoCAD LT Learning Assistance. If required, refer to the beginning of this appendix to check the recommended minimum requirements and review system configuration options.

Getting Started

Like the AutoCAD LT 2000 installation CD, the Learning Assistance software also has an AutoRun feature and should automatically run when you place the CD in your CD-ROM drive.

If it does not start automatically, you can start the installation program manually. Access the file named Ala.exe from the CD. You can pick Run... from the Start menu on the Windows taskbar to display the Run dialog box. Pick the Browse... button, then open the CD and select the Setup.exe file using the Browse dialog box. Pick Open, and when you return to the Run dialog box, pick OK to run the installation program. The first ALA *(Autodesk Learning Assistance)* dialog box offers two options, Install or Run.

You are not required to install the ALA software on your local hard drive. If you prefer, you can run it directly from the CD whenever it is needed. However, running ALA from the CD or from a network installation does not allow you to use a number of ALA features. When ALA is installed on a local hard drive, you can save your software preferences, create bookmarks, and track which documents you have viewed. This

option also allows those who use more than one Autodesk product to add and use additional volumes of instructional content.

Defining Installation Parameters

The ALA installation is automated and is very similar to the AutoCAD LT 2000 installation. Installing ALA, however, does not require security codes or personalization settings. The Setup dialog box is displayed first, providing a recommendation to close all other software applications before starting the installation.

You must indicate that you accept the terms of the Software License Agreement by picking the I accept button before you can install the ALA software.

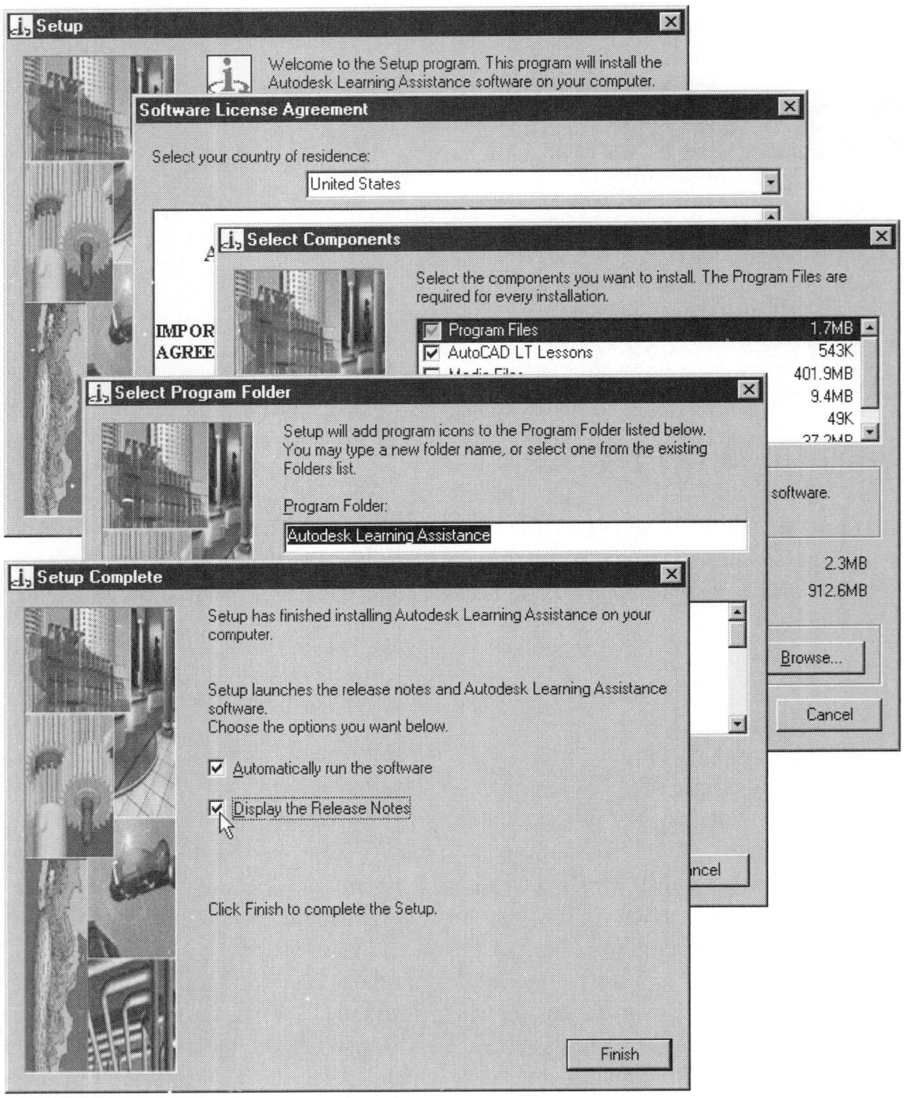

The Select Components dialog box is used to specify what program components are installed. A default installation includes only the Program Files, AutoCAD LT Lessons, and Help Files and requires just 2.3 MB of disk space. If you have a large hard drive with sufficient available disk space, you can install all the ALA files on your hard drive. This requires 450 MB of disk space but gives the best possible performance for the Learning Assistance multimedia components.

Autodesk Learning Assistance

In the Select Program Folder dialog box you can use the default name for the ALA program group on the Windows Start menu or specify a different name if you desire. For most applications, the default values can be used for all the ALA installation settings. Use the *Create shortcut on the desktop* check box to indicate whether a Learning Assistance shortcut icon should be created on your desktop.

In the Setup Complete dialog box, you can select the option to Display the Release Notes, which is the same type of document as a Readme file. The Release Notes for ALA contain detailed information on system requirements and include step-by-step guides for troubleshooting any audio- or video-based problems you may encounter with the multimedia presentations. Place a check in the *Automatically run the software* box to launch the Autodesk Learning Assistance program. Pick the Finish button to continue with your selected options.

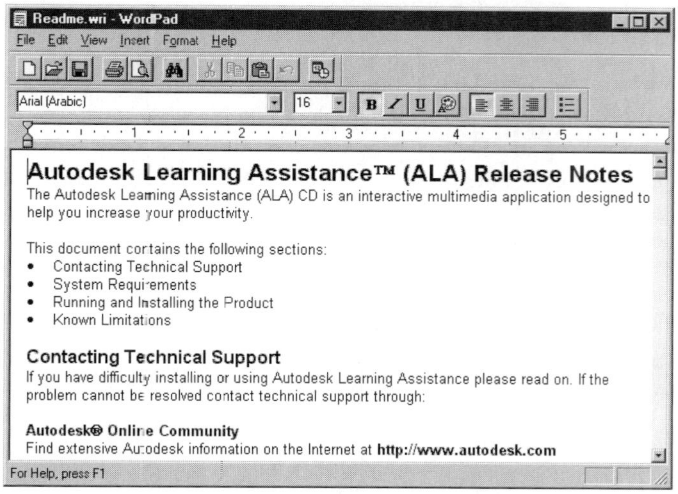

Installing and Running ALA on a Network Drive

Installing the AutoCAD LT Learning Assistance on a network drive makes it conveniently accessible to multiple users. Depending on your network configuration, you can either make the CD accessible from a CD-ROM drive on your server or simply do a full installation to a network hard drive. This can be done either on a mapped drive or a UNC path.

Autodesk Learning Assistance

Running the ALA software from a network drive works the same as running it from a local CD-ROM drive—it does not install any files on your local hard drive. This also means that you cannot save bookmarks or preferences or track your progress within the software. To run ALA from a network drive, you can use the Run dialog box or Windows Explorer to access the folder where ALA is installed, and double-click on the Ala.exe file. When the Autodesk Learning Assistance start screen is displayed, pick the Run button.

To install Learning Assistance from a network drive, again locate and double-click Ala.exe. Pick the Install button to start the installation process, which works the same as installation from a local CD-ROM drive. You can specify what components to install, and because you are installing it, you are able to save preferences and bookmarks and document tracking information.

Installing the Media Player Software

The Microsoft Media Player is required in order for Autodesk Learning Assistance to play video and sound files. If you do not have the media player installed yet, you can install it directly from the Learning Assistance CD. On the CD, find the file named MPINSTALL.EXE and double-click it. Follow the instructions in the dialog boxes to complete this installation.

Field Notes

- The Release Notes list this file as MPFULL.EXE; however, the AutoCAD LT 2000 Learning Assistance CD received by the authors shows the file name as MPINSTALL.EXE.
- If the ALA media files are not playing correctly, in terms of either video or audio, review the Release Notes document carefully for troubleshooting procedures and supplementary information.

Update Patches

Update patches are files that modify your original AutoCAD LT installation. An update patch may fix a bug that was discovered after the software was released, or it may add new capabilities, improve performance, or all the above. For example, at the time of this writing, there are two update patches available that are applicable to the English version of AutoCAD LT 2000. These can be freely downloaded from the Autodesk Web site.

AutoCAD® 3D Graphics System Update (01/00)

This update provides significant performance improvements and fixes some critical bugs. As the name of this patch suggests, several of the issues that it addresses are related to the 3D graphics display system. However, this patch provides other benefits not related to working in 3D drawings. For example, this patch reduces memory consumption by 30–80% and significantly improves the performance of the BLOCK command and Autodesk DesignCenter. It also fixes some bugs that can cause AutoCAD LT 2000 to crash.

AutoCAD 2000 Plotting Update Patch

This same patch is used for both AutoCAD 2000 and AutoCAD LT 2000. This patch updates all plotter drivers to improve plot quality for vector and OLE plotting, fixes several known plotting problems associated with specific drivers, and adds support for several new plotting devices. The crashing problem with some Windows system printers has also been fixed.

Accessing and Installing Patch Updates

The URL for the Patches and Maintenance Releases page on the Autodesk Web site was shown previously in this section. Access this page with your Web browser to get complete information about the available patches, and download the ones you need.

Be sure to completely review the documentation for each patch before installing it. When you install a patch, always follow the directions very carefully. The patch releases may not have an uninstall feature, so you may be advised to back up specific critical files before installing the patch. It is highly recommended that you take all the suggested precautions listed in the installation instructions.

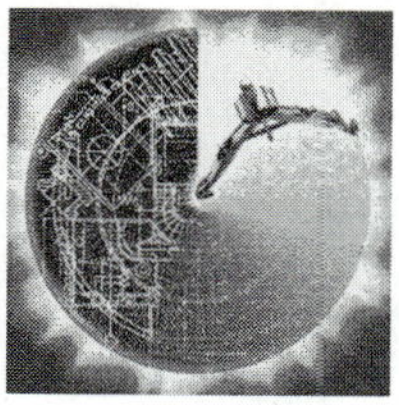

APPENDIX B

Drafting Standards

The following lists provide some of the national drafting standards that are recommended for a variety of disciplines:

Architectural

Architectural Graphic Standards, American Institute of Architects (AIA), John Wiley and Sons, New York.

CAD Layer Guidelines, AIA Press, 1735 New York Avenue, NW, Washington D.C. 20006

Mechanical

American National Standards Institute (ANSI)
11 West 42nd Street
New York, NY 10036

American Society of Mechanical Engineers (ASME)
345 East 47th Street
New York, NY 10017

ANSI Y14.1	*Drawing Sheet Size and Format*
ASME Y14.1M	*Metric Drawing Sheet Size and Format*
ASME Y14.2M	*Line Conventions and Lettering*
ANSI Y14.3	*Multi and Sectional View Drawings*
ASME Y14.5M	*Dimensioning and Tolerancing*
ANSI Y14.6	*Screw Thread Representation*
ANSI Y14.6aM	*Screw Thread Representation Metric Supplement*
ANSI Y14.13M	*Mechanical Spring Representation*
ASME Y14.35M	*Revision of Engineering Drawings and Associated Documents*
ANSI Y14.36	*Surface Texture Symbols*
ANSI/AWS A2.4	*Standard Symbols for Welding, Brazing and Nondestructive Examination*

Technical Illustration

ASME Y14.4M	*Pictorial Drawing*

Electrical and Electronic

ANSI Y14.15	*Electrical and Electronic Diagrams*
ANSI Y31.9	*Graphical Symbols for Electrical Wiring and Layout Diagrams Used in Architecture and Building Construction*

Piping

ASME Y32.2.3	*Graphical Symbols for Pipe Fittings, Valves and Piping*

The following illustrations display the standard inch sheet sizes based on ANSI Y14.1, Drawing Sheet Size and Format, and metric sheet sizes based on ASME Y14.1M, Metric Drawing Sheet Size and Format.

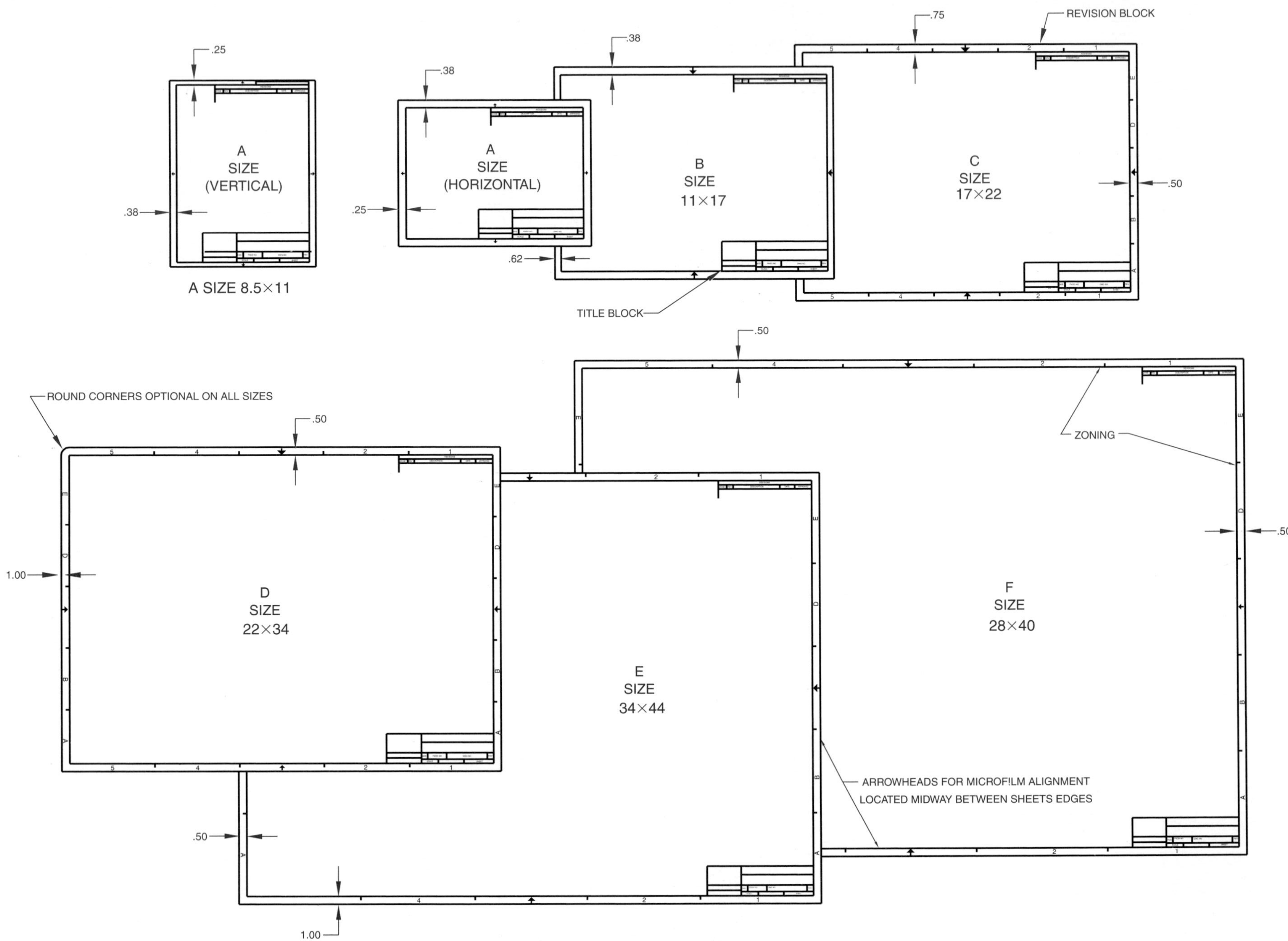

Standard ANSI inch sheet sizes

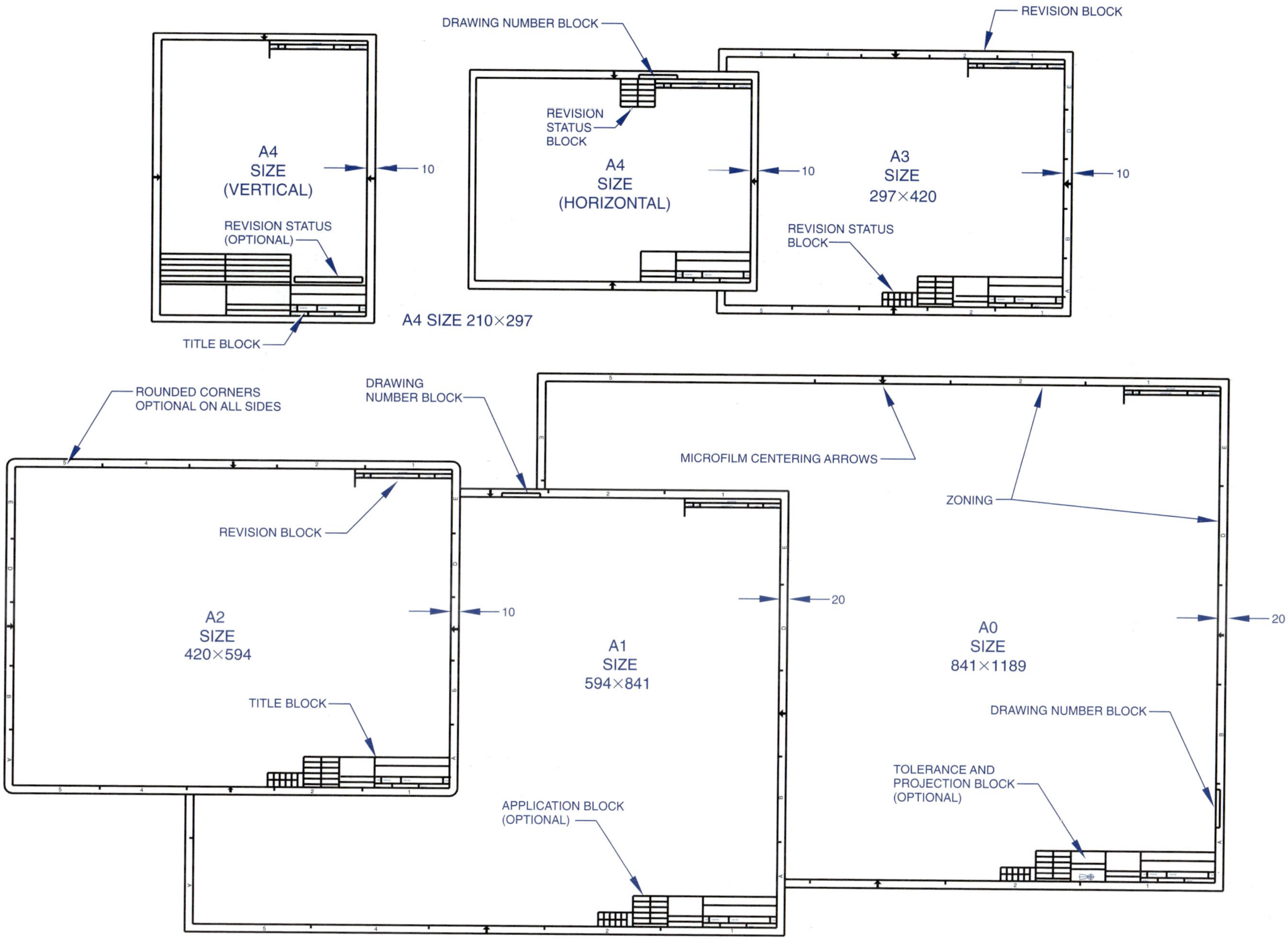

Standard ANSI metric sheet sizes

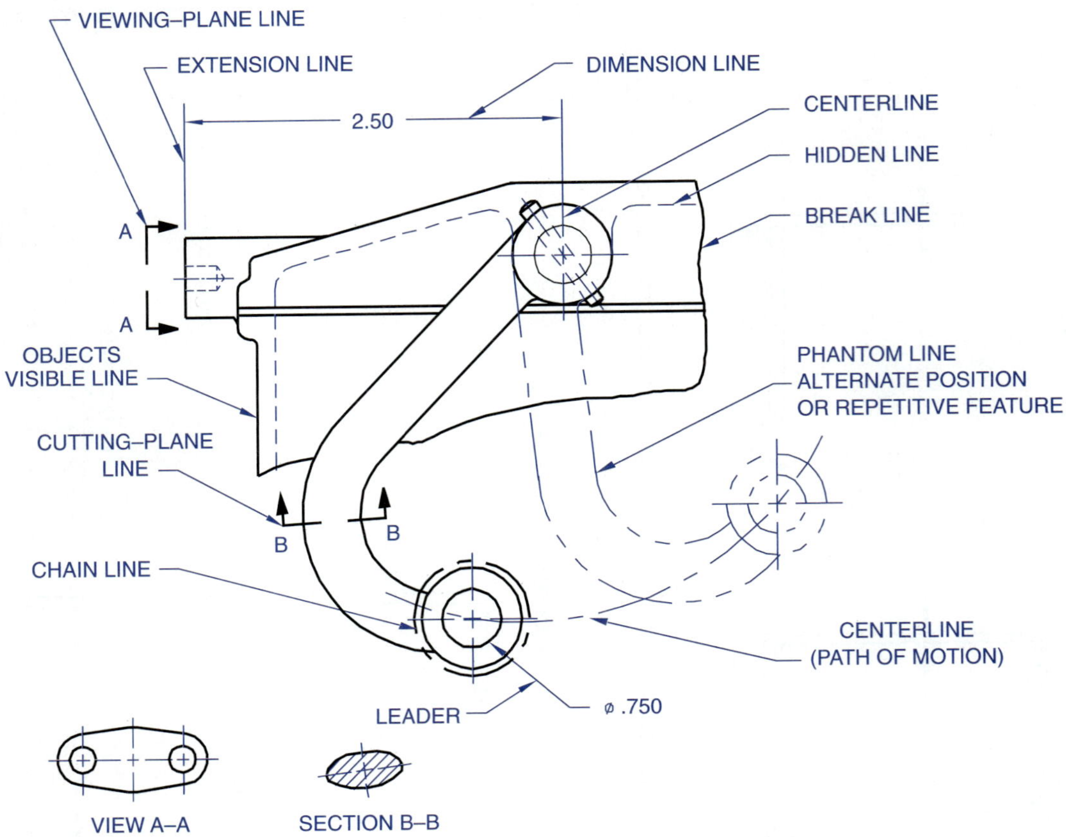

Applications of lines

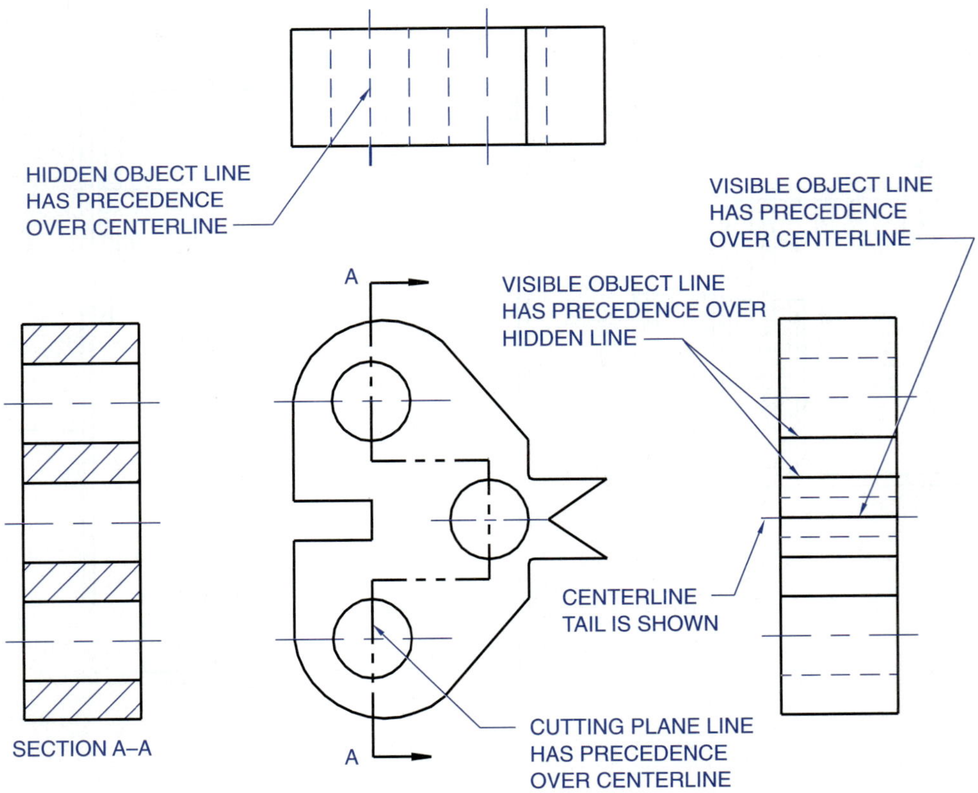

Line precedence

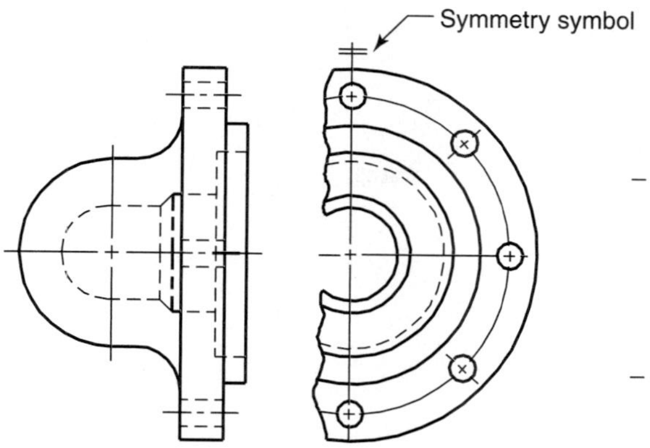

Symmetry line applications

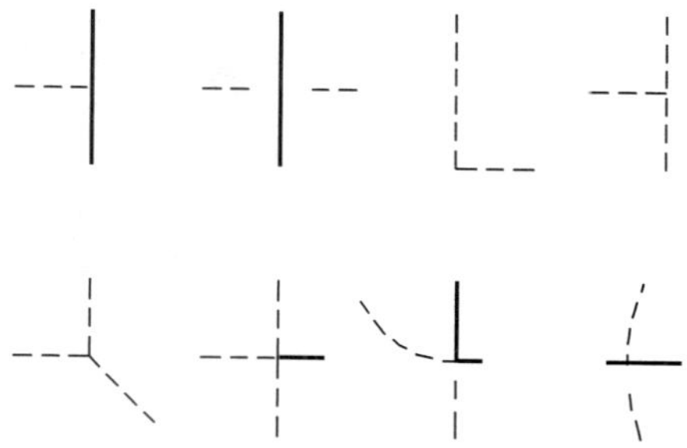

Hidden line techniques

(Some preferred hidden line techniques are difficult to obtain with AutoCAD LT.)

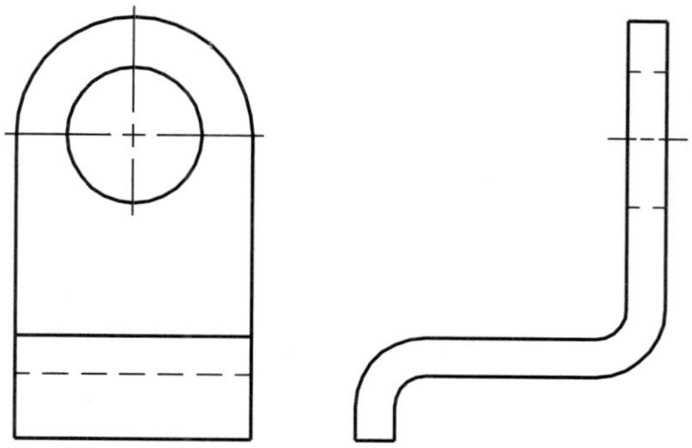

Two view drawings

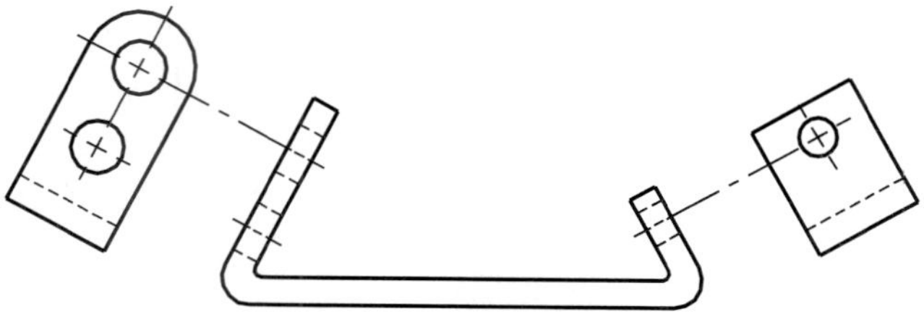

Auxiliary views

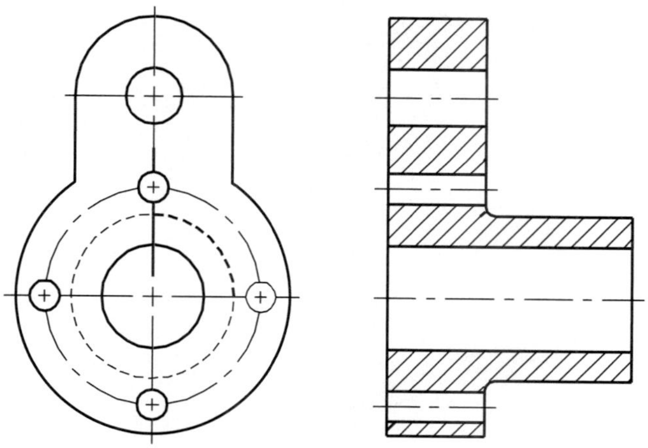

Full section

(Cutting plane line not required if section is obvious.)

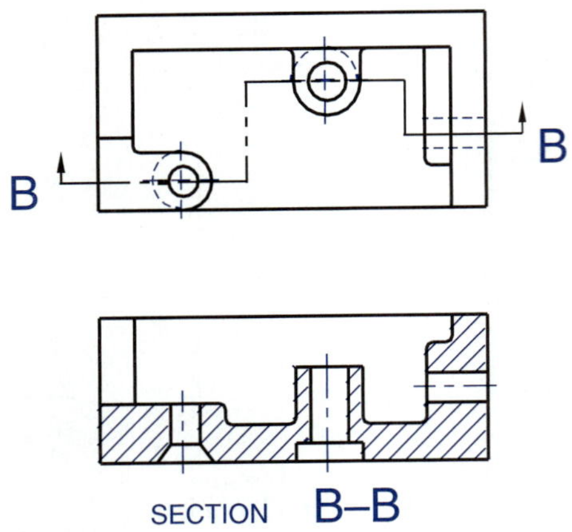

Offset section

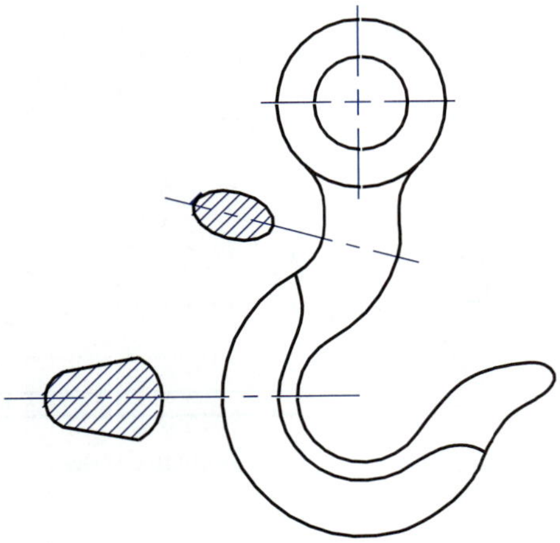

Alternate removed section method

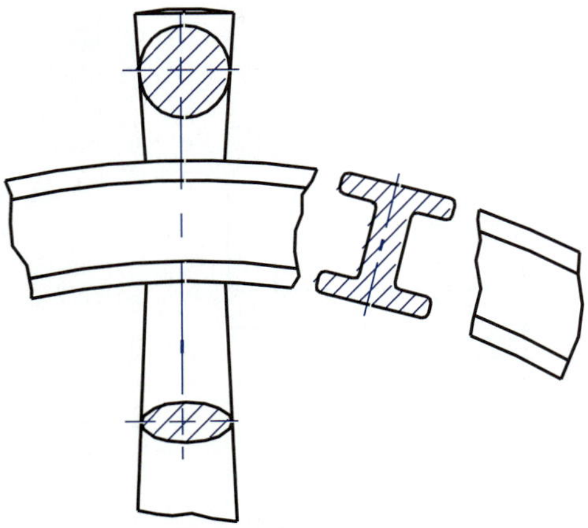

Revolved sections

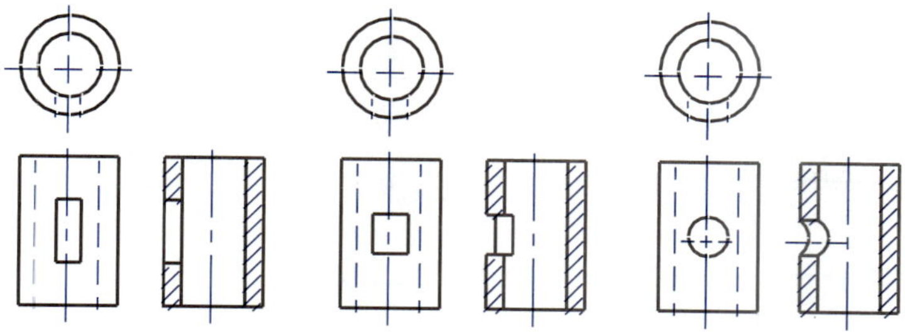

Intersections in section

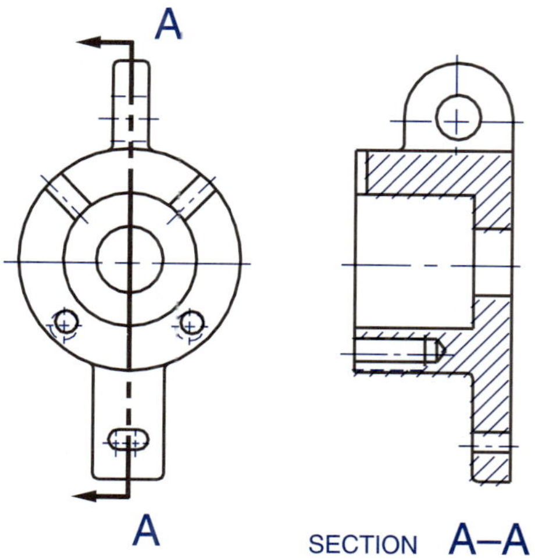

Conventional representation of ribs and rotated details

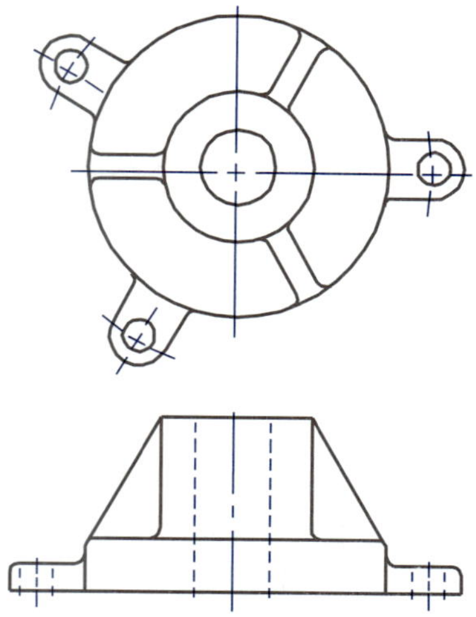

Rotated features conventional practices

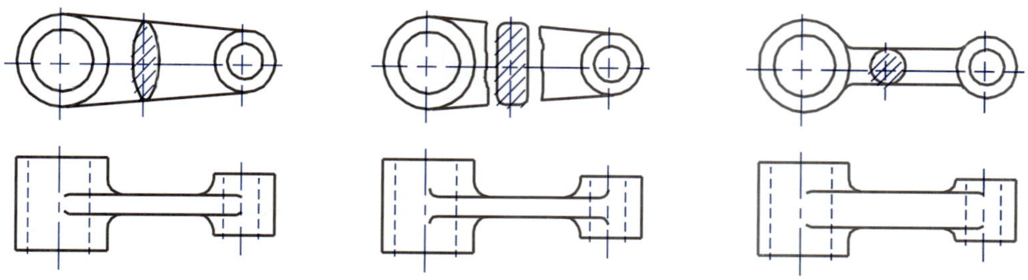

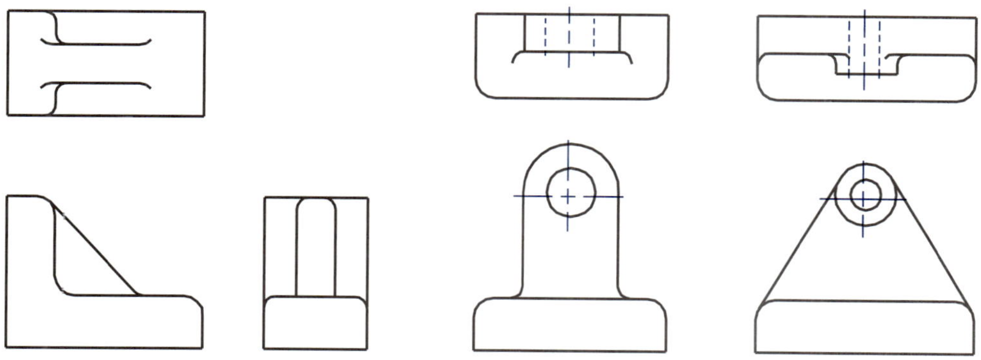

Conventional representation of fillets and runouts

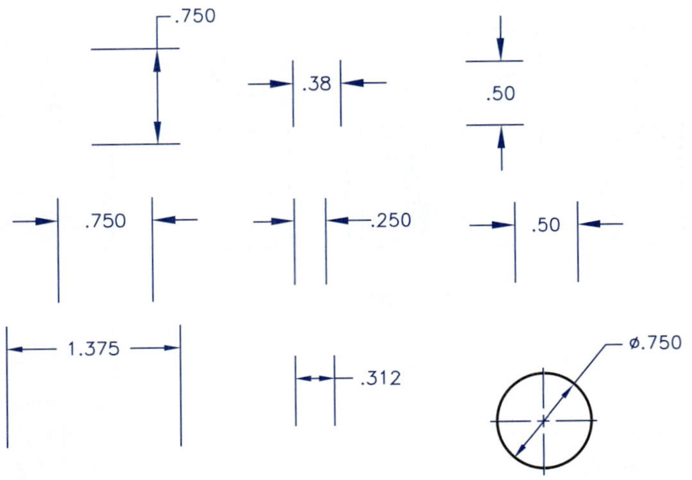

Decimal inch dimensions

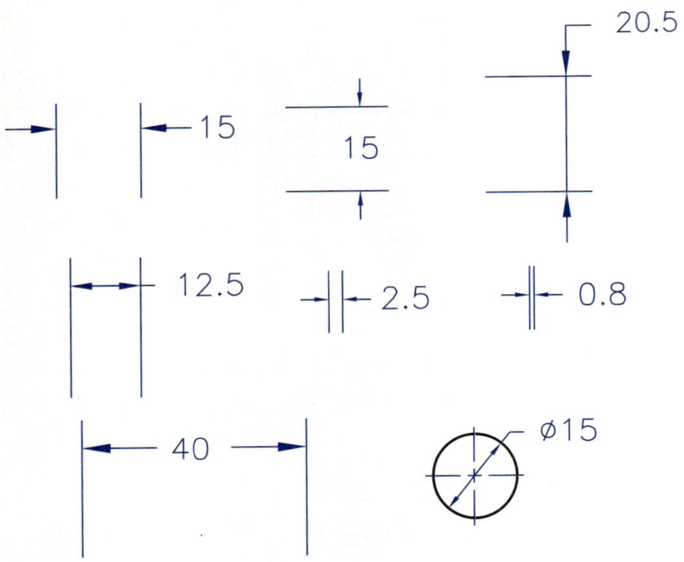

Millimeter dimensions

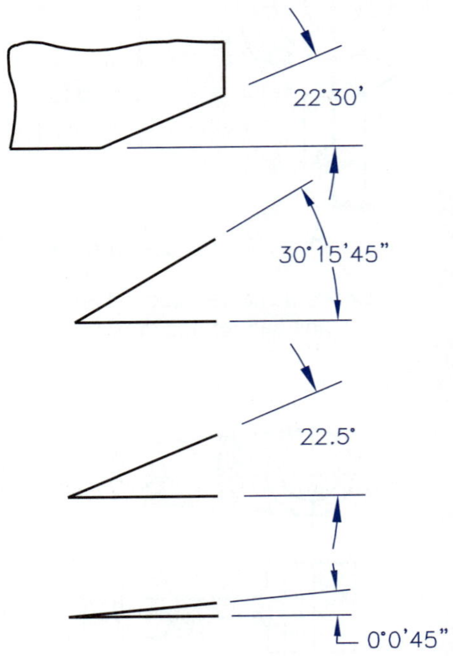

Angular dimensions

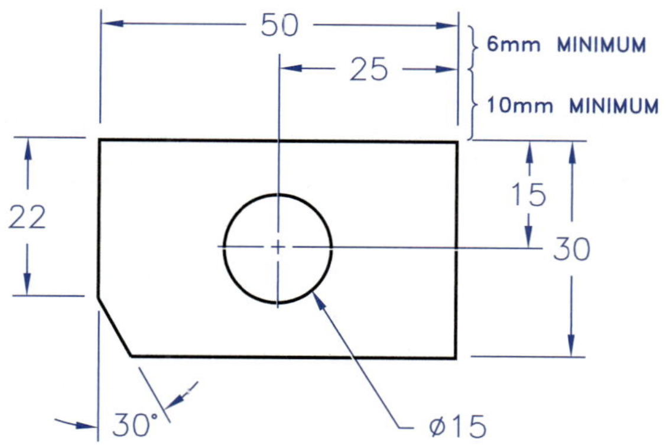

Applications of dimensions

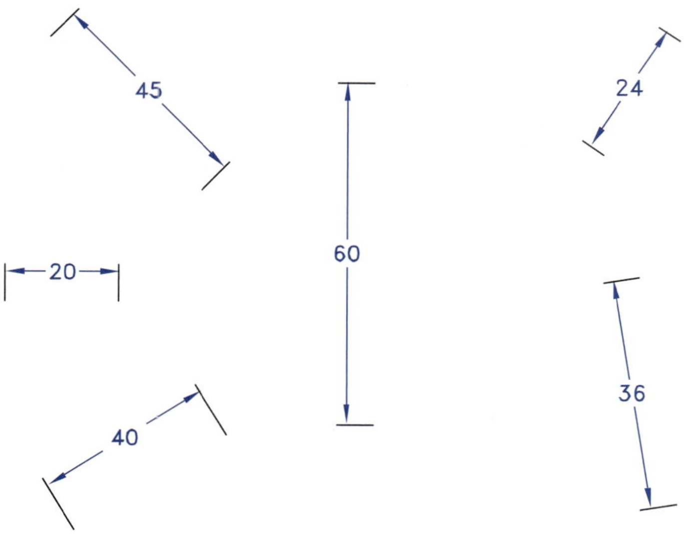

Reading direction for unidirectional dimensions

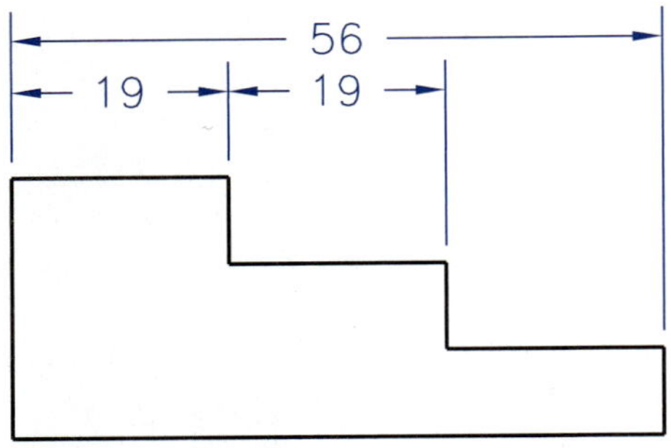

Grouping of dimensions

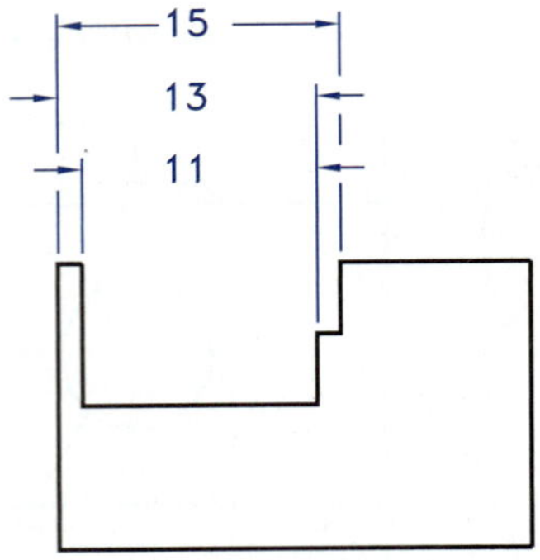

Breaks in extension lines

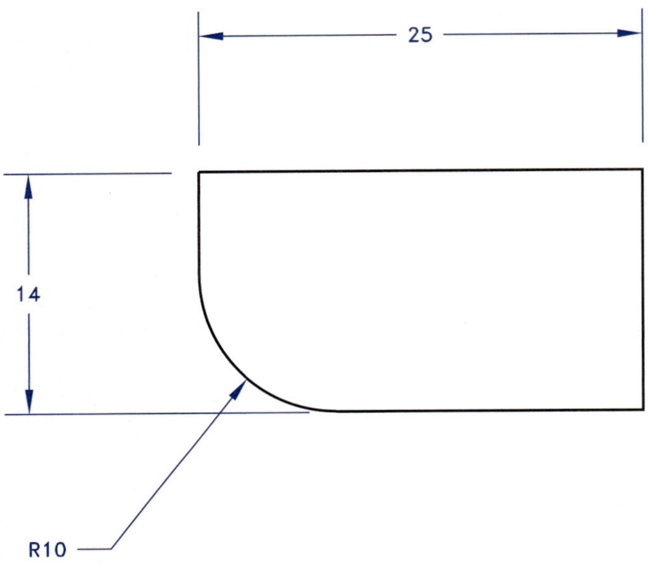

Rounded corners

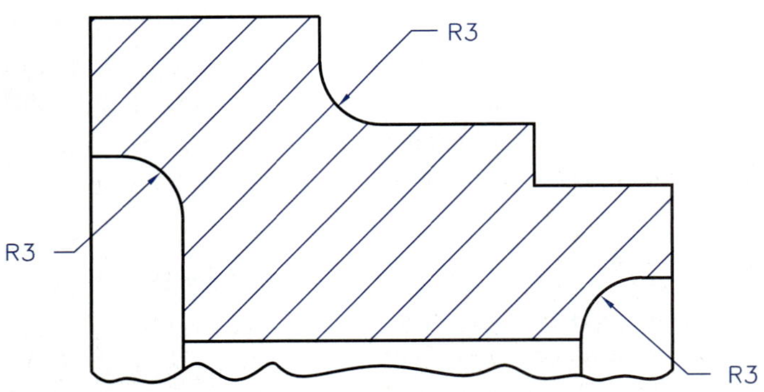

Leader-directed dimensions

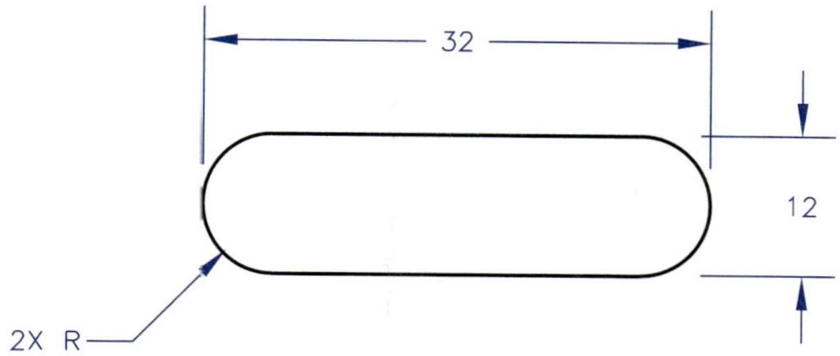

Fully rounded ends

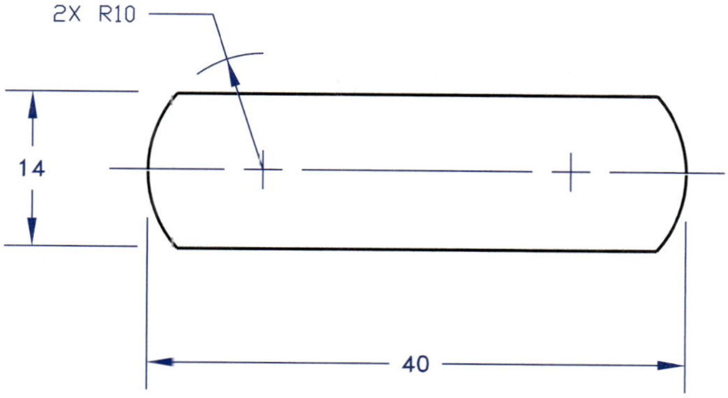

Partially rounded ends

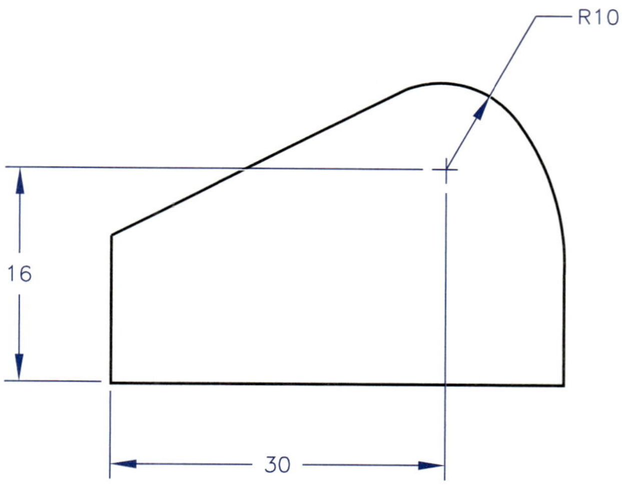

Radius with located center

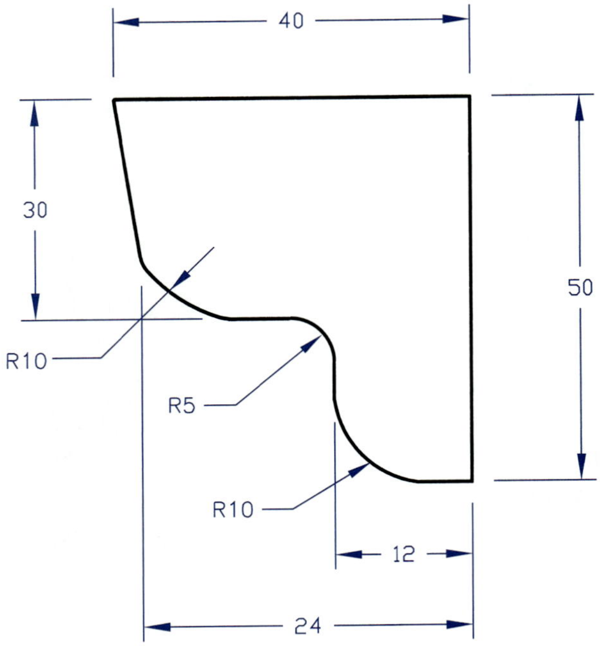

Radii with located centers

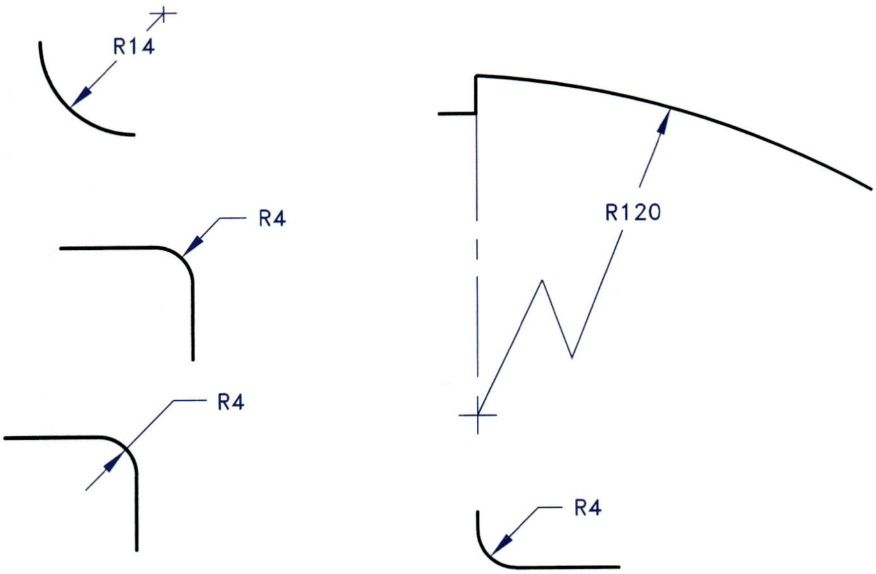

Radii

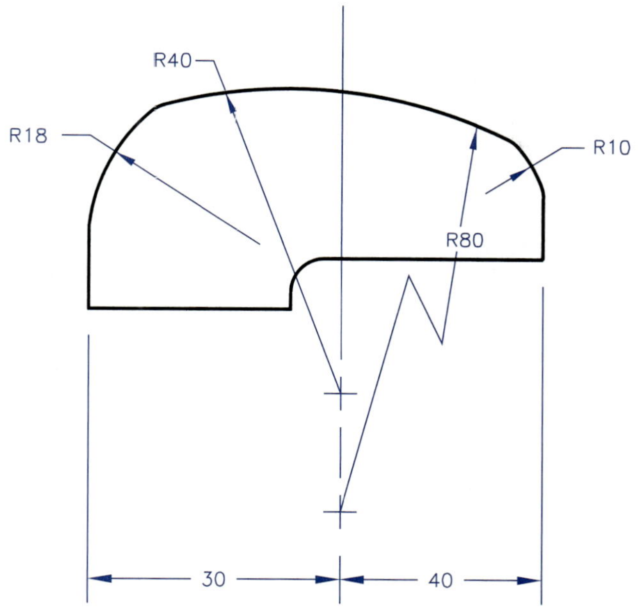

Circular arc outline

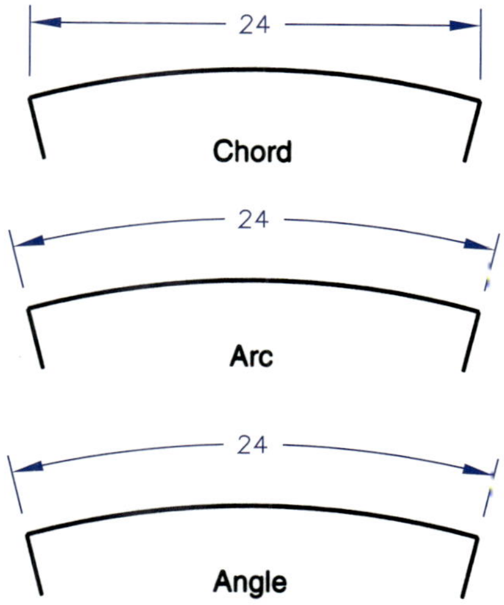

Dimensioning chords, arcs, angles

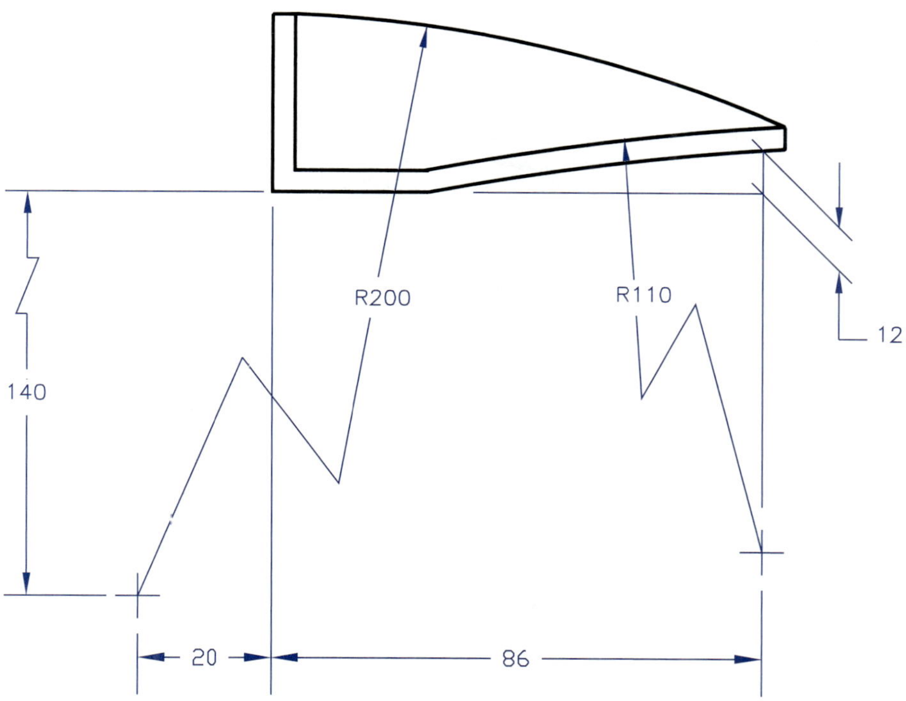

Foreshortened radii

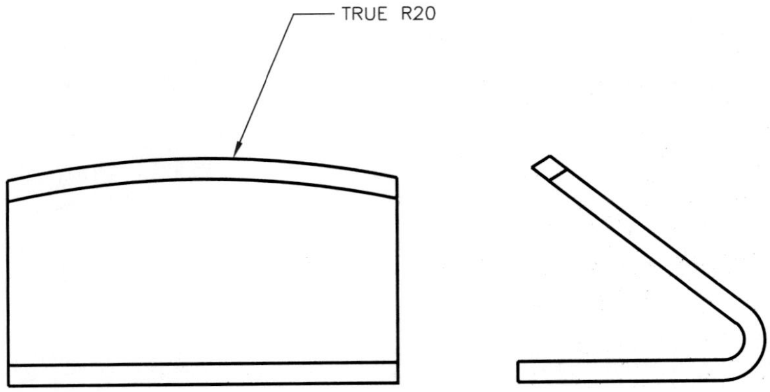

True radius

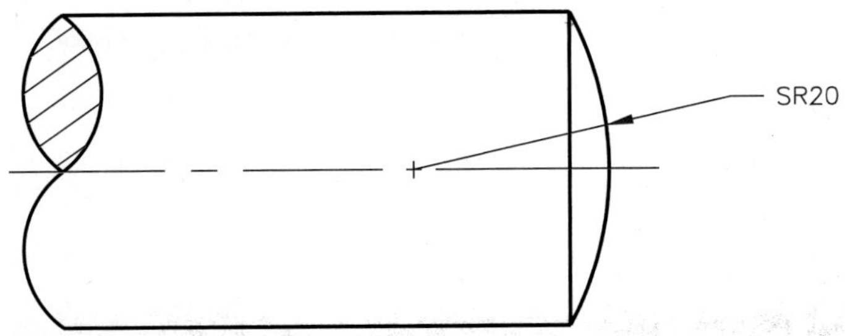

Spherical radius

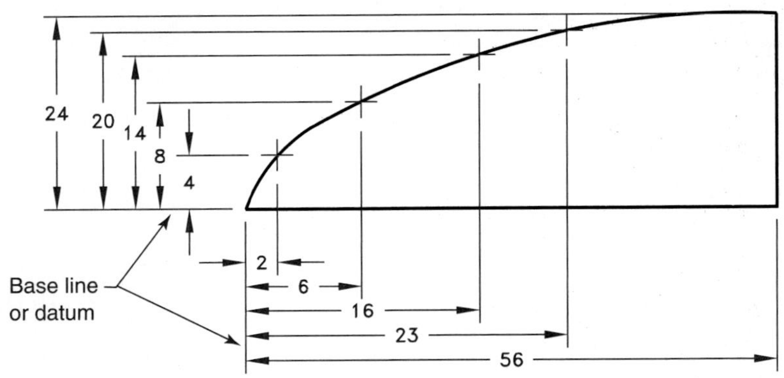

Coordinates of offset outline

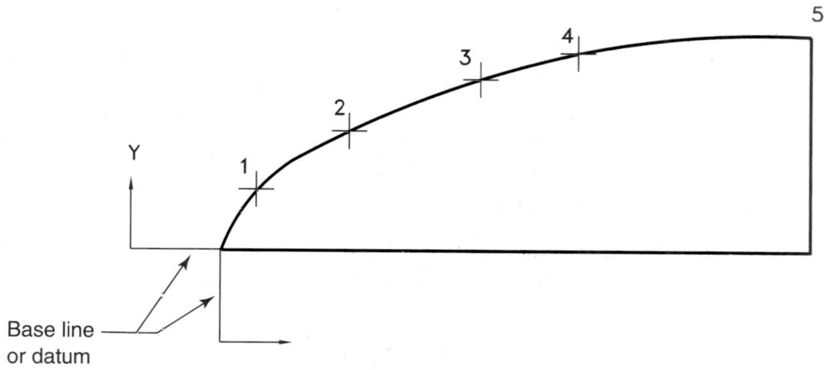

STATION	1	2	3	4	5
X	2	5	15	25	55
Y	4	8	15	20	24

Arrowless tabular dimensioning of offset outline

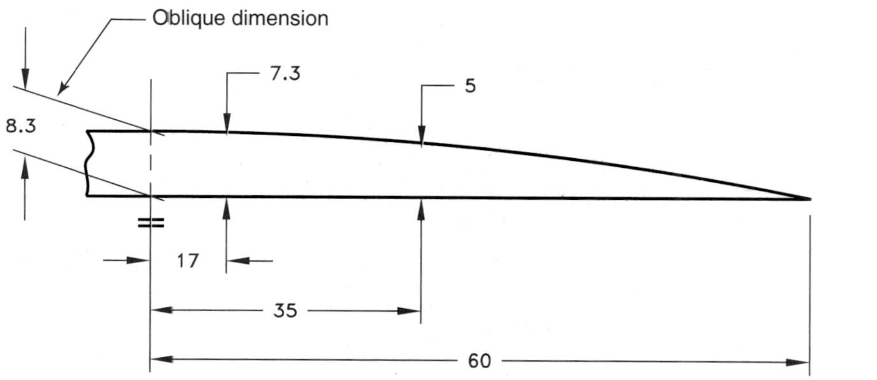

Symmetrical outlines

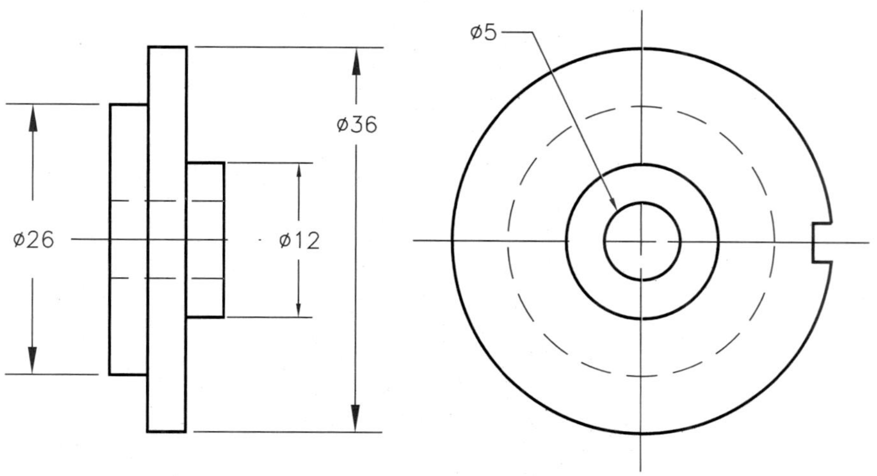

Diameters of cylindrical features and holes

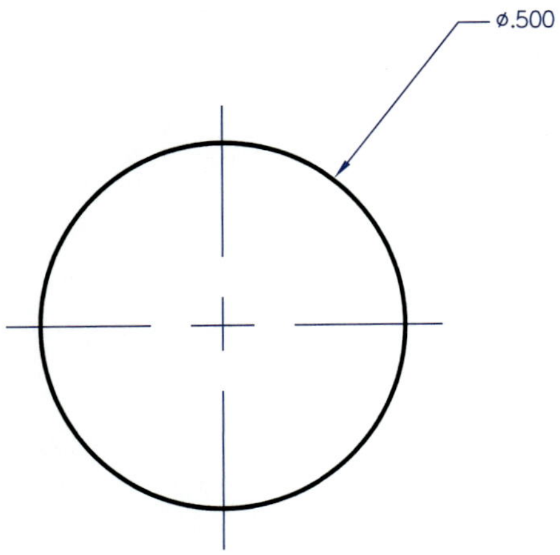

Leader direction

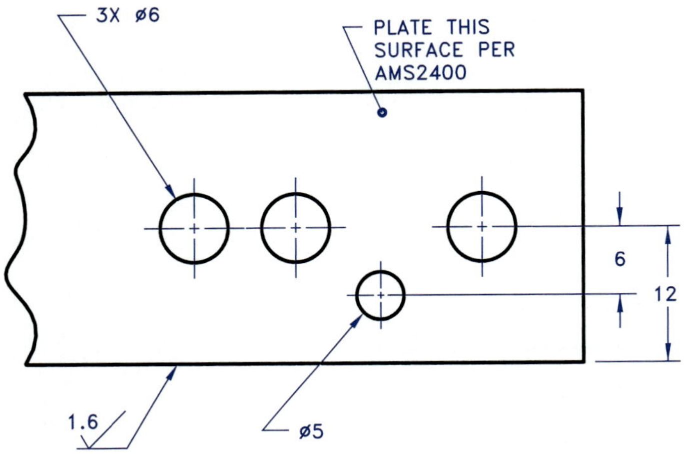

Leader usage

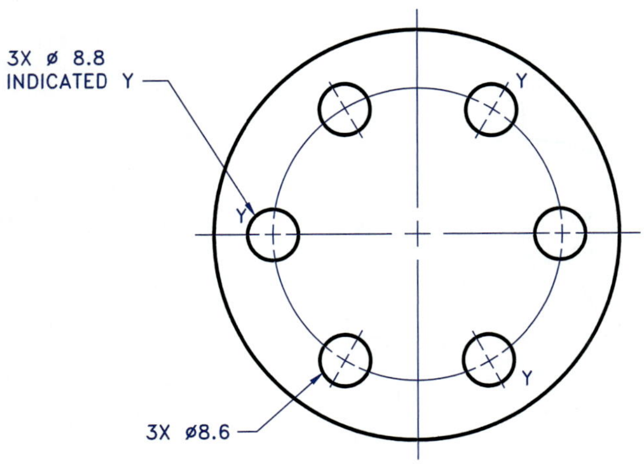

Minimizing leaders

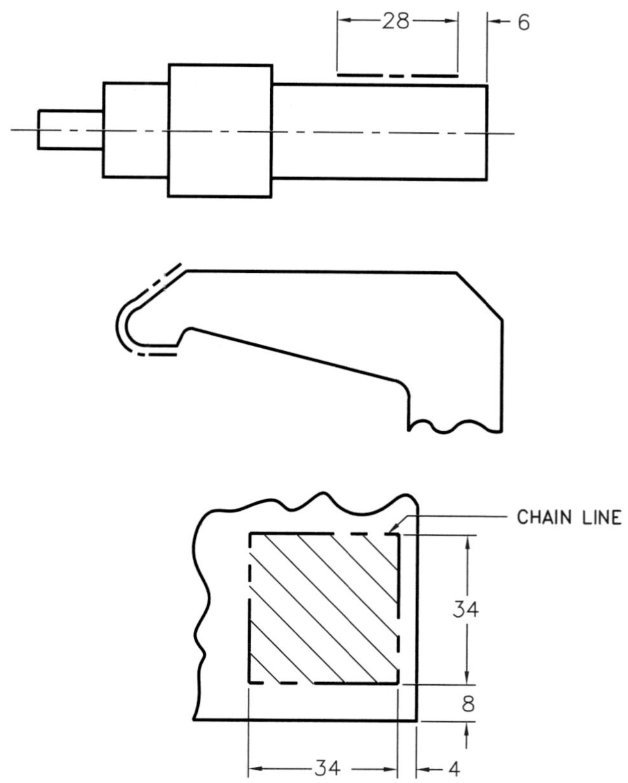

Limited length or area indication

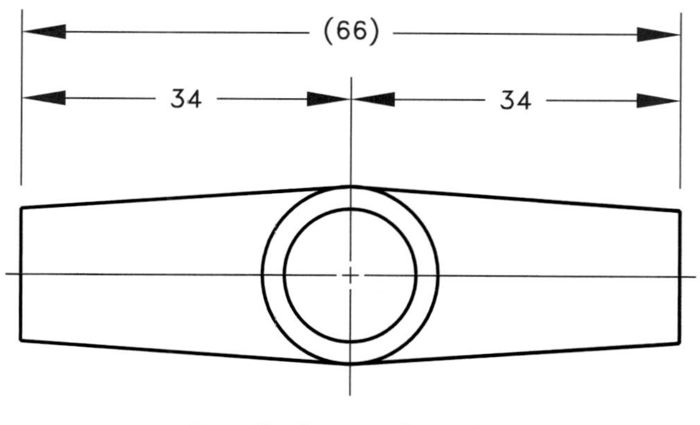

Overall reference dimension

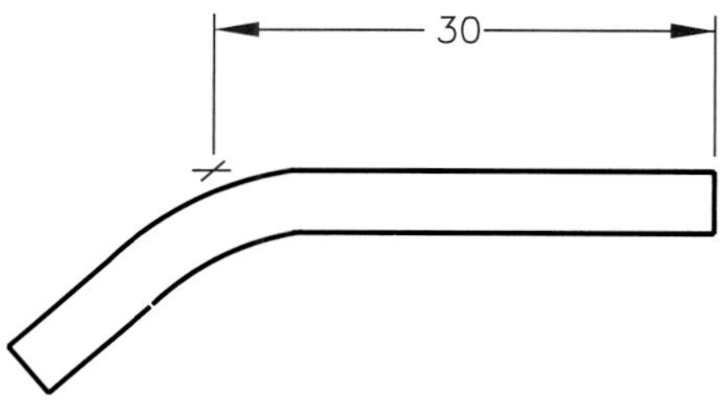

Point location

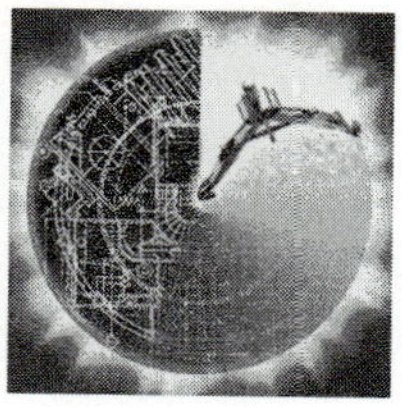

APPENDIX C

Standard Support Libraries

AutoCAD LT provides standard library files for you to define linetypes, hatch patterns, text fonts, and symbols for dimensioning. This appendix illustrates or describes

- Linetypes included in the *aclt.lin* file
- Standard hatch patterns included in the *aclt.pat* file
- Standard text and symbol fonts *(.shx)*
- TrueType fonts *(.ttf)*
- Geometric characteristic symbols

*Courtesy of Autodesk, Inc.

Standard Linetypes

AutoCAD LT provides a library of standard linetypes in the *aclt.lin* file.

Acad_iso02w100
Acad_iso03w100
Acad_iso04w100
Acad_iso05w100
Acad_iso06w100
Acad_iso07w100
Acad_iso08w100
Acad_iso09w100
Acad_iso10w100
Acad_iso11w100
Acad_iso12w100
Acad_iso13w100
Acad_iso14w100
Acad_iso15w100
Batting
Border
Border2
Borderx2
Center
Center2
Centerx2
Continuous
Dashdot
Dashdot2
Dashdotx2
Dashed
Dashed2
Dashedx2
Divide
Divide2
Dividex2
Dot
Dot2
Dotx2

FenceLine1

FenceLine2

Gas_Line

Hidden

Hidden2

Hiddenx2

Hot_water_supply

Phantom

Phantom2

Phantomx2

Tracks

Zigzag

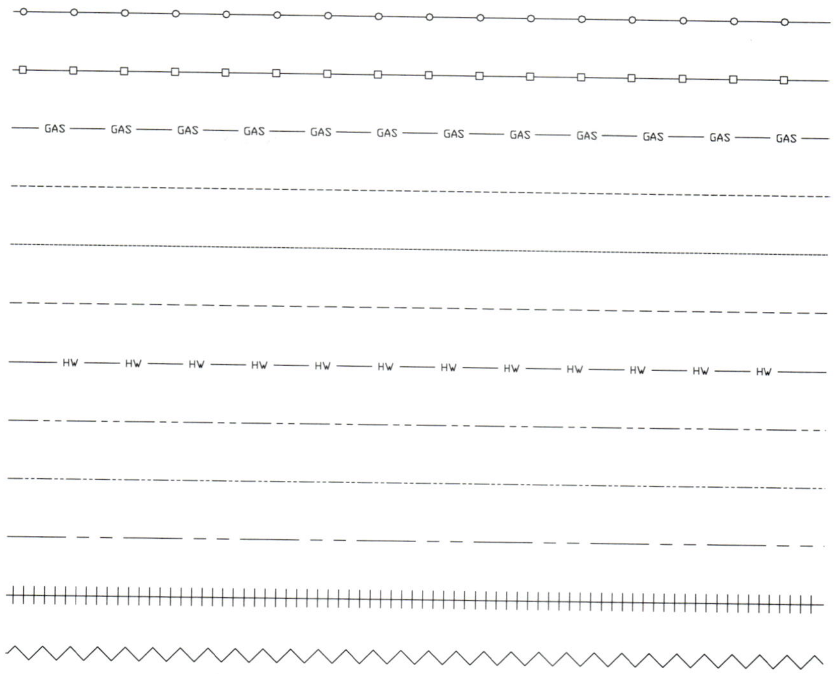

Standard Hatch Patterns

AutoCAD LT provides a library of standard hatch patterns in the *aclt.pat* file.

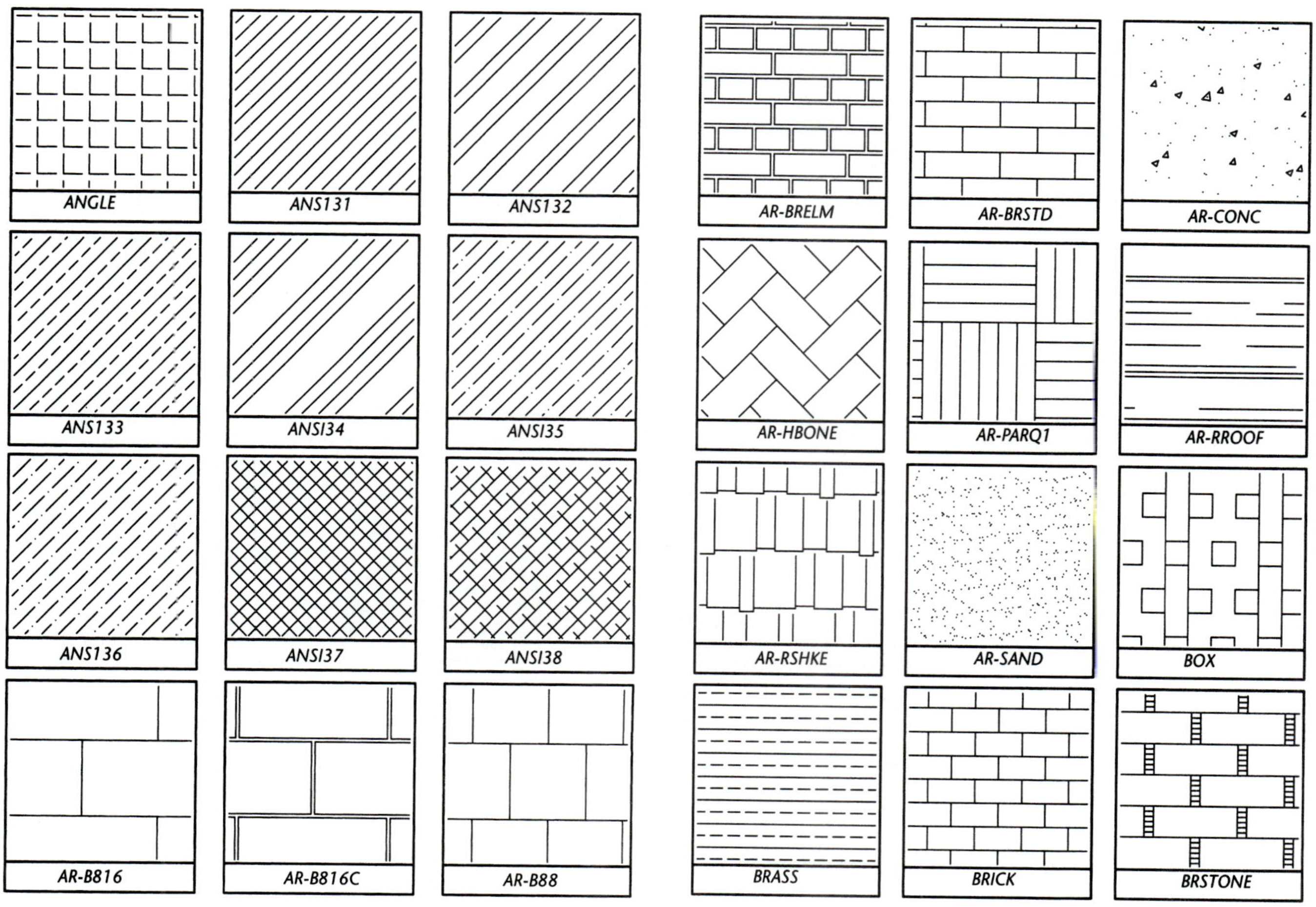

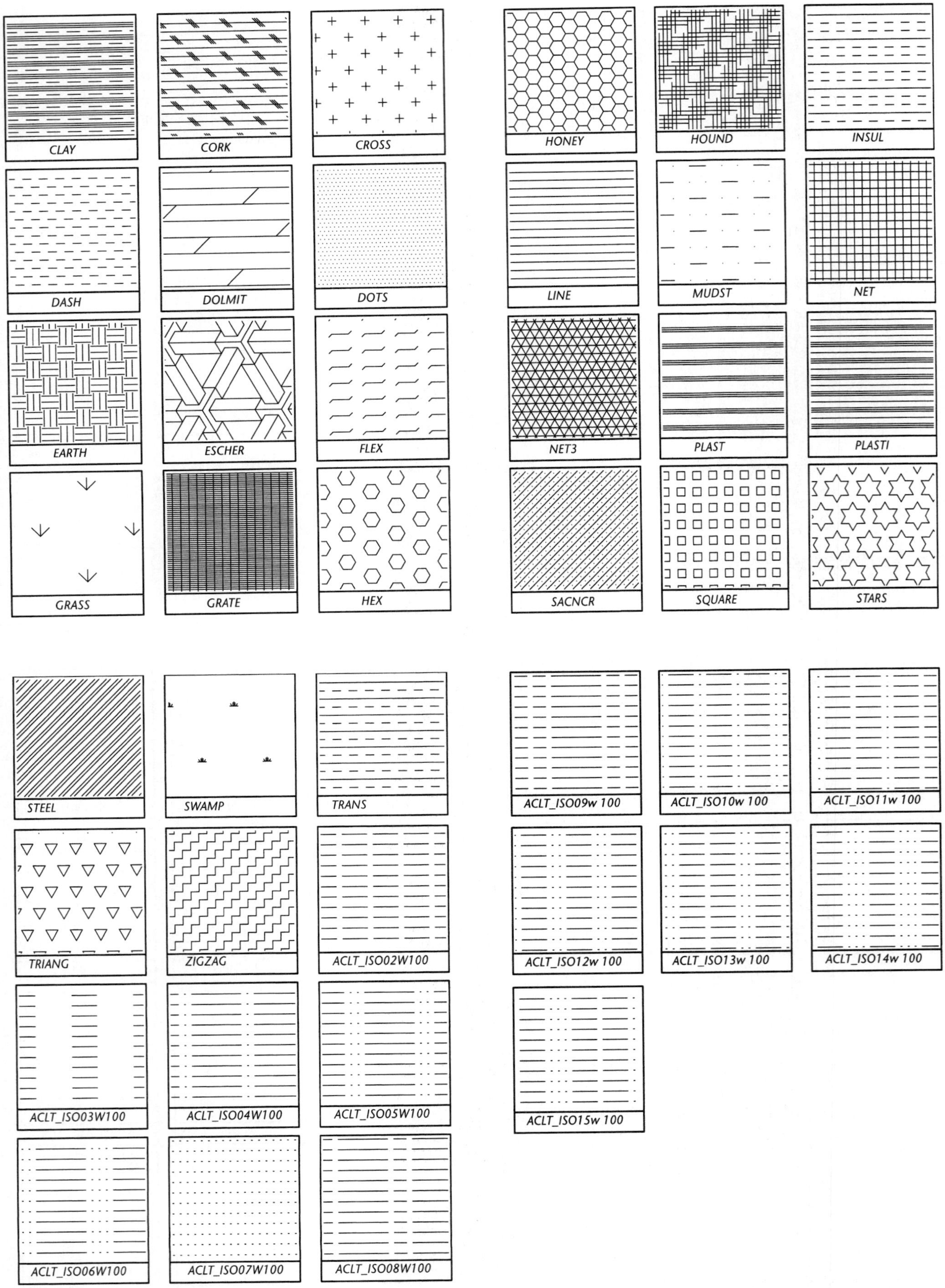
CLAY
CORK
CROSS
HONEY
HOUND
INSUL
DASH
DOLMIT
DOTS
LINE
MUDST
NET
EARTH
ESCHER
FLEX
NET3
PLAST
PLASTI
GRASS
GRATE
HEX
SACNCR
SQUARE
STARS
STEEL
SWAMP
TRANS
ACLT_ISO09w 100
ACLT_ISO10w 100
ACLT_ISO11w 100
TRIANG
ZIGZAG
ACLT_ISO02W100
ACLT_ISO12w 100
ACLT_ISO13w 100
ACLT_ISO14w 100
ACLT_ISO03W100
ACLT_ISO04W100
ACLT_ISO05W100
ACLT_ISO15w 100
ACLT_ISO06W100
ACLT_ISO07W100
ACLT_ISO08W100

Standard Text and Symbol Fonts

AutoCAD LT provides a variety of text and symbol fonts available for use in your drawings. Using commands and techniques discussed in Chapter 9, you can customize the appearance of these text fonts to meet specialized needs. The width factor of text can be adjusted, you can slant the text to the right or left, and you can even apply horizontal or vertical orientation. Text creation commands allow further controls, such as text height and baseline rotation angle.

In all but the monospaced text font (monotxt), characters are proportionally spaced; that is, the space needed for the letter *l* is narrower than that for the letter *m*. AutoCAD LT 2000 supports the use of compiled shape/font files as well as standard Windows TrueType® fonts. Compiled shape/font files have a .shx file extension, and are unique to AutoCAD products.

The following table lists the font names and samples of the AutoCAD LT compiled shape (.shx) fonts, and the Windows TrueType fonts that ship with AutoCAD LT 2000. Most of the .shx fonts are also available as TrueType fonts, for increased flexibility while working within AutoCAD LT 2000 or within other Windows applications.

AutoCAD LT 2000 (.SHX) Shape/Font Listing

✓ - *A checkmark in the TT column indicates the font is also available as a TrueType font.*

Font Name	*TT*	*Font Sample*
gdt	✓	ABCD ∠ ⊥ ▱ ⌓ ○ // ⌭ ↗ ⌯ ⌖ ⌒ Ⓛ Ⓜ ∅ □ Ⓟ ℄ ◎ Ⓢ ⌰ — ⌴ ⌵ ↧ ⌲ ⌳ 1234567890
gothicg	✓	ABCDEFGHIJKLMNOPQRSTUVWXYZ abcd 1234567890
gothici	✓	ABCDEFGHIJKLMNOPQRSTUVWXYZ abcd 1234567890
greekc	✓	ΑΒΧΔΕΦΓΗΙϑΚΛΜΝΟΠΘΡΣΤϒ∇ΩΞΨΖ αβχδ 1234567890
greeks	✓	ΑΒΧΔΕΦΓΗΙϑΚΛΜΝΟΠΘΡΣΤϒ∇ΩΞΨΖ αβχδ 1234567890
isoct	✓	A B C D E F G H I J K L M N O P Q R S T U V W X Y Z a b c d 1 2 3 4 5 6 7 8 9 0
isocp	✓	ABCDEFGHIJKLMNOPQRSTUVWXYZ abcd 1234567890
isocp2	✓	ABCDEFGHIJKLMNOPQRSTUVWXYZ abcd 1234567890
isocp3	✓	ABCDEFGHIJKLMNOPQRSTUVWXYZ abcd 1234567890
isoct2	✓	A B C D E F G H I J K L M N O P Q R S T U V W X Y Z a b c d 1 2 3 4 5 6 7 8 9 0
isoct3	✓	A B C D E F G H I J K L M N O P Q R S T U V W X Y Z a b c d 1 2 3 4 5 6 7 8 9 0
italict	✓	***ABCDEFGHIJKLMNOPQRSTUVWXYZ abcd 1234567890***
italicc	✓	*ABCDEFGHIJKLMNOPQRSTUVWXYZ abcd 1234567890*
italic	✓	*ABCDEFGHIJKLMNOPQRSTUVWXYZ abcd 1234567890*
ltypeshp		Not a text font file. Contains shapes used in complex linetypes.
monotxt	✓	ABCDEFGHIJKLMNOPQRSTUVWXYZ abcd 1234567890
romanc	✓	ABCDEFGHIJKLMNOPQRSTUVWXYZ abcd 1234567890
romand	✓	ABCDEFGHIJKLMNOPQRSTUVWXYZ abcd 1234567890
romans	✓	ABCDEFGHIJKLMNOPQRSTUVWXYZ abcd 1234567890
romant	✓	**ABCDEFGHIJKLMNOPQRSTUVWXYZ abcd 1234567890**
scriptc	✓	*ABCDEFGHIJKLMNOPQRSTUVWXYZ abcd 1234567890*
scripts	✓	*ABCDEFGHIJKLMNOPQRSTUVWXYZ abcd 1234567890*
simplex	✓	ABCDEFGHIJKLMNOPQRSTUVWXYZ abcd 1234567890
syastro	✓	⊙☿♀⊕♂♃♄♅♆♇☾☄✶☊☋♈♉♊♋♌♍♎♏♐♑♒♓ ✶"C 1234567890
symap	✓	1234567890
symath	✓	ℵ'‖|±∓×·÷=≠≡<>≦≧∝~√⊂∪⊃∩∈→↑ ←↓∂∇ 1234567890
symeteo	✓	1234567890
symusic	✓	♯♮♭ 𝄞 𝄢 1234567890
txt	✓	ABCDEFGHIJKLMNOPQRSTUVWXYZ abcd 1234567890

AutoCAD LT 2000 TrueType Font Listing

Font Name	*Font Sample*
BankGothic Lt BT	ABCDEFGHIJKLMNOPQRSTUVWXYZ ABCD 12345
BankGothic Md BT	ABCDEFGHIJKLMNOPQRSTUVWXYZ ABCD 1234
CityBlueprint	ABCDEFGHIJKLMNOPQRSTUVWXYZ abcd 1234567890
CommercialPi BT	±°′″∅+ − × ÷ = ±°′″ ℞♀♂· ©®©® ●●■■○○□★
Complex	ABCDEFGHIJKLMNOPQRSTUVWXYZ abcd 1234567890
CommercialScript BT	ABCDEFGHIJKLMNOPQRSTUVWXYZ abcd 1234567890
CountryBlueprint	ABCDEFGHIJKLMNOPQRSTUVWXYZ abcd 1234567890
Dutch801 Rm BT	ABCDEFGHIJKLOMNOPQRSTUVWXYZ abcd 1234567890
Dutch801 Bd BT	ABCDEFGHIJKLMNOPQRSTUVWXYZ abcd 1234567890
Dutch801 Bi BT	ABCDEFGHIJKLMNOPQRSTUVWXYZ abcd 1234567890
Dutch801 XBd BT	ABCDEFGHIJKLMNOPQRSTUVWXYZ abcd 1234567890
EuroRoman	ABCDEFGHIJKLMNOPQRSTUVWXYZ abcd 1234567890
GothicE	ABCDEFGHIJKLMNOPQRSTUVWXYZ abcd 1234567890
Monospac821 BT	ABCDEFGHIJKLMNOPQRSTUVWXYZ abcd 1234567890
Proxy 1	ABCDEFGHIJKLMNOPQRSTUVWXYZ abcd 1234567890
Proxy 2	ABCDEFGHIJKLMNOPQRSTUVWXYZ abcd 1234567890
Proxy 3	ABCDEFGHIJKLMNOPQRSTUVWXYZ abcd 1234567890
Proxy 4	ABCDEFGHIJKLMNOPQRSTUVWXYZ abcd 1234567890
Proxy 5	ABCDEFGHIJKLMNOPQRSTUVWXYZ abcd 1234567890
Proxy 6	ABCDEFGHIJKLMNOPQRSTUVWXYZ abcd 1234567890
Proxy 7	ABCDEFGHIJKLMNOPQRSTUVWXYZ abcd 1234567890
Proxy 8	ABCDEFGHIJKLMNOPQRSTUVWXYZ abcd 1234567890
Proxy 9	ABCDEFGHIJKLMNOPQRSTUVWXYZ abcd 1234567890
PanRoman	ABCDEFGHIJKLMNOPQRSTUVWXYZ abcd 1234567890
Romantic	ABCDEFGHIJKLMNOPQRSTUVWXYZ abcd 1234567890
SanSerif	ABCDEFGHIJKLMNOPQRSTUVWXYZ abcd 1234567890
Stylus BT	ABCDEFGHIJKLMNOPQRSTUVWXYZ abcd 1234567890
SuperFrench	ABCDEFGHIJKLMNOPQRSTUVWXYZ abcd 1234567890
Swis721 BT	ABCDEFGHIJKLMNOPQRSTUVWXYZ abcd 1234567890
Swis721 BdOul BT	ABCDEFGHIJKLMNOPQRSTUVWXYZ abcd 1234567890
Swis721 BdCnOul BT	ABCDEFGHIJKLMNOPQRSTUVWXYZ abcd 1234567890
Swis721 Cn BT	ABCDEFGHIJKLMNOPQRSTUVWXYZ abcd 1234567890
Swis721 BlkCn BT	ABCDEFGHIJKLMNOPQRSTUVWXYZ abcd 1234567890
Swis721 LtCn BT	ABCDEFGHIJKLMNOPQRSTUVWXYZ abcd 1234567890
Swis721 Ex BT	ABCDEFGHIJKLMNOPQRSTUVWXYZ abcd 1234567890
Swis721 BlkEx BT	ABCDEFGHIJKLMNOPQRSTUVWXYZ abcd 1234567890
Swis721 LtEx BT	ABCDEFGHIJKLMNOPQRSTUVWXYZ abcd 1234567890
Swis721 Blk BT	ABCDEFGHIJKLMNOPQRSTUVWXYZ abcd 1234567890
Swis721 BlkOul BT	ABCDEFGHIJKLMNOPQRSTUVWXYZ abcd 1234567890
Swis721 Lt BT	ABCDEFGHIJKLMNOPQRSTUVWXYZ abcd 1234567890
TechnicBold	ABCDEFGHIJKLMNOPQRSTUVWXYZ ABCD 1234567890
TechnicLite	ABCDEFGHIJKLMNOPQRSTUVWXYZ ABCD 1234567890
Technic	ABCDEFGHIJKLMNOPQRSTUVWXYZ ABCD 1234567890
UniversalMath1 BT	ΑΒΨΔΕΦΓΗΙΞΚΛΜΝΟΠΘΡΣΤΘΩ6ΧΥΖ αβψδ + − × ÷ = ± ∓°′″
Vineta BT	ABCDEFGHIJKLMNOPQRSTUVWXYZ abcd 1234567890

Geometric Characteristic Symbols

The following table shows the geometric characteristic symbols used in geometric tolerancing. Unless otherwise stated, these symbols adhere to ANSI standards. AutoCAD LT 2000 automatically creates and places these symbols within feature control frames when using the TOL (Tolerence) command. These symbols can be accessed directly by entering lower-case characters while using the GDT.shx font file (or GDT .ttf).

Geometric characteristic symbols

Symbol	*Name*
⌖	Position
◎	Concentricity/coaxiality
⌯	Symmetry
//	Parallelism
⊥	Perpendicularity
∠	Angularity
⌭	Cylindricity
⏥	Flatness
○	Circularity or roundness
—	Straightness
⌓	Profile of a surface
⌒	Profile of a line
↗	Circular runout
⌰	Total runout
⌀	Diameter
Ⓜ	Maximum material condition (MMC)
Ⓛ	Least material condition (LMC)
Ⓢ	Regardless of feature size (RFS)
Ⓟ	Projected tolerance

Using the GDT Font

The GDT font file provided with AutoCAD LT 2000 gives you the capability to create text objects that use symbols such as countersink, counterbore, depth, or geometric characteristic symbols. This font file is provided both as a .shx file and as a TrueType font file (.ttf).

Uppercase character entries using this font produce standard uppercase text characters that resemble the RomanS font (which is highly suited for a variety of drafting applications). All lowercase character entries produce GDT and drafting-related symbols. The following table lists the results obtained for both upper- and lowercase keystrokes.

Key Entry	*GDT Font Character*	*Key Entry*	*GDT Font Character*	*Key Entry*	*GDT Font Character*
A	A	S	S	k	⌒
B	B	T	T	l	Ⓛ
C	C	U	U	m	Ⓜ
D	D	V	V	n	Ø
E	E	W	W	o	□
F	F	X	X	p	Ⓟ
G	G	Y	Y	q	℄
H	H	Z	Z	r	◎
I	I	a	∠	s	Ⓢ
J	J	b	⊥	t	⌰
K	K	c	▱	u	⏤
L	L	d	⌓	v	⌴
M	M	e	○	w	⌵
N	N	f	//	x	↧
O	O	g	⌭	y	⌲
P	P	h	↗	z	⌳
Q	Q	i	⌯		
R	R	j	⌖		

APPENDIX D

Accessibility Features

Effective use of a CAD workstation can present significant challenges to users with impaired vision or hearing, or with restricted physical mobility. Both AutoCAD LT 2000 and the Windows operating systems provide options for customizing the user interface to meet specialized needs. Additionally, the availability of adaptive technologies such as voice input, magnified displays, specialized keyboards, and alternative pointing devices create many new possibilities for all computer users. This appendix introduces many of the available options for increasing computer accessibility, both in the Windows operating systems and in the area of adaptive technologies.

Windows Accessibility Options

The Windows NT 4, Windows 95, and Windows 98 operating systems have built-in accessibility options that can make it easier to work in the Windows environment. In Windows 98, the Accessibility Wizard provides a simple guided process for adjusting the system appearance and behavior to meet individual needs. To access this feature, select the Start button on the task bar, pick Programs > Accessories > Accessibility, and then pick the Accessibility Wizard option. If you do not have Windows 98, or if you prefer not to use the wizard, you can use the Control Panel to make adjustments. To access the Control Panel, pick the Start button on the task bar, then select Settings and Control panel. The following section discusses both methods of setting up your system accessibility.

Display Options

The Welcome page is displayed when you start the Accessibility Wizard. Here, the first settings you make are for the text size used in window titles and menus. Three sizes of text are presented and you are asked to select the smallest size of text that you can read (see Figure D.1).

FIGURE D.1

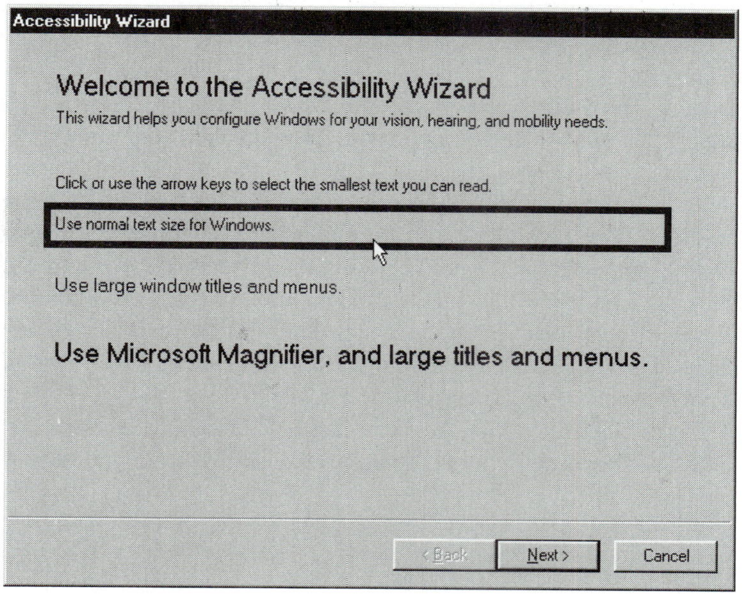

Based on the default Windows system settings, if you select the smallest size of text displayed, then no changes are made to the text size. Selecting the larger text increases the size of text used in window titles and menus. If you select the largest of the text sizes displayed, the *Microsoft Magnifier* is used. The Microsoft Magnifier displays an area of your desktop based on the current settings and lets you specify a magnification factor of up to nine times the standard display size. Also, title and menu sizes are increased for greater visibility. Figure D.2 shows the Microsoft Magnifier being used at a magnification of 4X, with the Magnifier dialog box visible. You can adjust the behavior and appearance of this feature in the Magnifier dialog box. One of these options is a high-contrast color scheme. The Microsoft Magnifier is not available in Windows 95 or Windows NT4.

FIGURE D.2

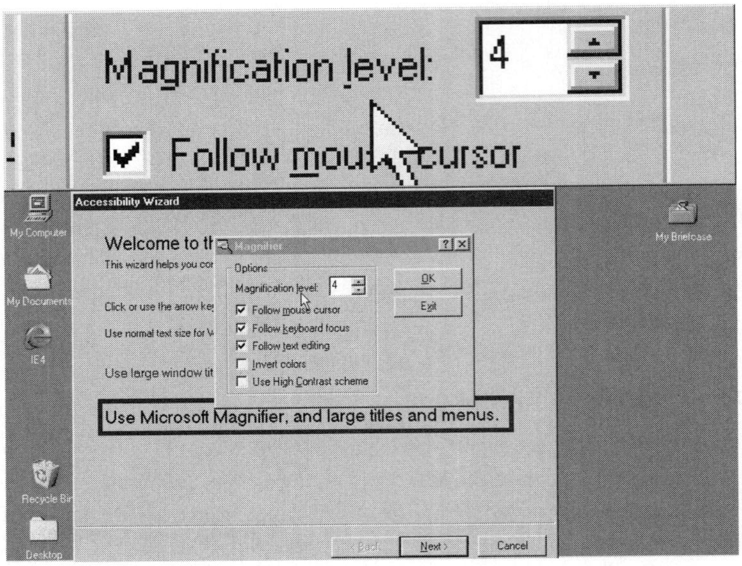

The next step in the wizard is the Text Size page in which you specify whether you want to increase the standard font size, switch to a lower screen resolution, or use the Microsoft Magnifier. The settings will be preset to recommended values based on the font size you selected on the previous screen. You can keep these values or specify new settings if desired.

The Set Wizard Options page of the wizard is displayed next. The settings you make here control what accessibility options are offered through the remainder of the Accessibility Wizard. Select each applicable option in the list. In this discussion of the Accessibility Wizard, each of the available options has been selected so that all features are presented.

The next few pages of the wizard allow you to set desired sizes for scroll bars, window borders, and program icons as well as to set your desired color scheme. If you indicated that you have difficulty hearing sounds from the computer, you are offered options that supplement system sounds with visual cues. The SoundSentry allows you to set up the system to display visual warnings of system events that normally produce a sound. The ShowSounds feature can be set to display captions for speech and sounds in applications that support this option. Some multimedia programs have the capability to display captions when playing speech or other sound files.

With the exception of the Microsoft Magnifier, each of these options is available in Windows 95 and Windows NT4. The Control Panel is used to make the appropriate settings, using the Display and Accessibility Options applications. Figure D.3 shows these icons within the Control Panel.

Pick the icon labeled Display, as shown in Figure D.3, to change the display settings. The first step is typically to set the display resolution, which controls the overall size of on-screen features. Keep in mind that a resolution of 800×600 is the minimum resolution possible for using AutoCAD LT 2000. To set the resolution, pick the tab labeled Display as shown in Figure D.4.

The area labeled Desktop Area provides a slider bar that allows you to choose from the available resolution settings. **Never apply any changes to this setting until you have successfully tested it.** Lower reso-

FIGURE D.3

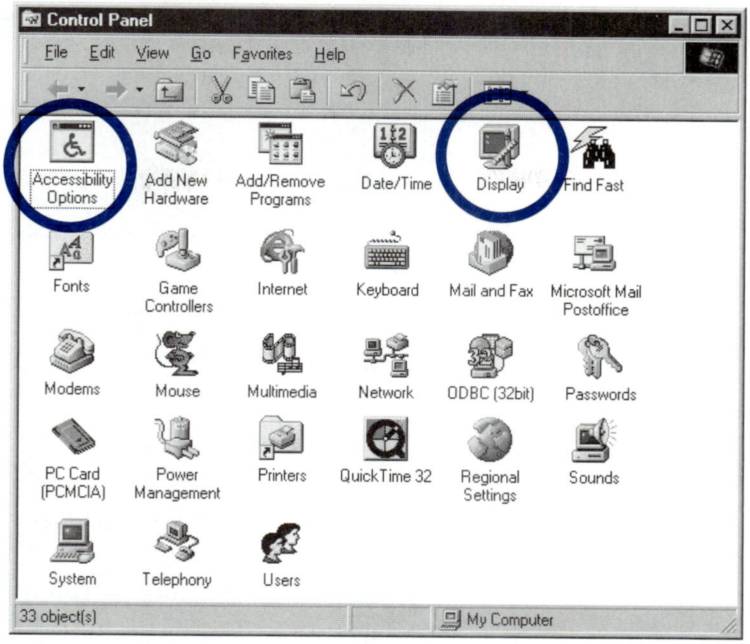

FIGURE D.4

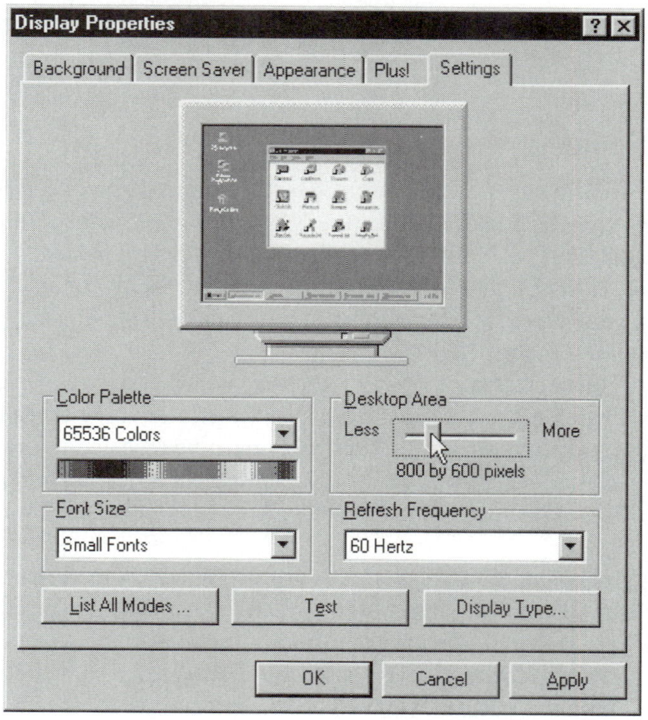

lution settings result in larger on-screen features. As you adjust the resolution you may also need to change the number of colors in the Color Palette settings or the Refresh Frequency rate. Again, as you make adjustments always test each setting before trying to use it. Incorrect settings can disable your display, requiring you to reboot your system in "safe mode." The primary font size can also be adjusted using the Font Size list. If you do adjust the font size, you may be required to restart your system before the changes take effect

To adjust the size of individual screen features and text elements, pick the Appearance tab. The Appearance tab of the Display Properties dialog box is shown in Figure D.5 with the Scheme: list open. Although you can adjust each element on the screen individually, you may find it more convenient to select a predesigned scheme from this list. The display area at the top of this tab shows the results of any settings you make. Schemes are available for both size and color adjustments. Finally, you can adjust the sizes of desktop icons from the tab labeled "Plus!"

FIGURE D.5

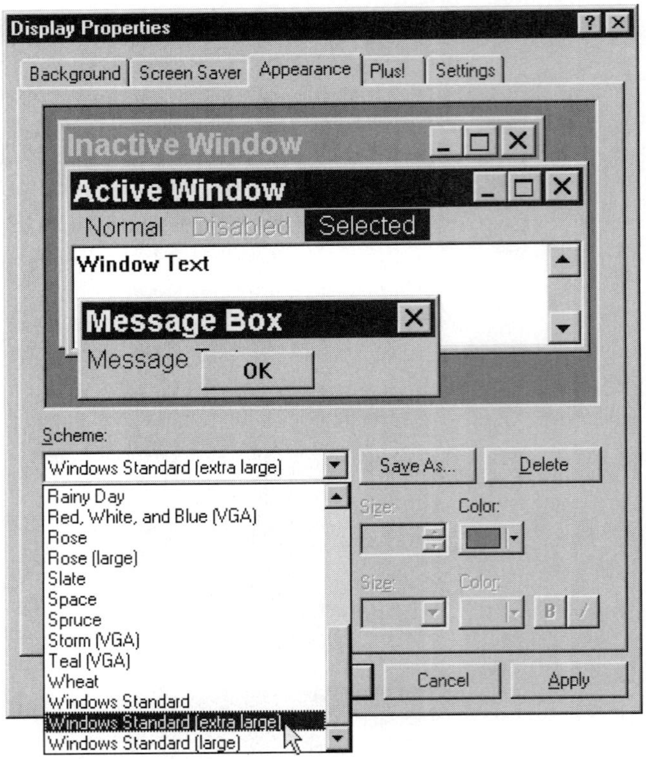

Keyboard Options

Keyboard accessibility features are presented by the wizard if you indicated that you have difficulty using the keyboard or mouse. The Sticky Keys feature is helpful for keystroke combinations that you need to use, such as Ctrl+(key), Alt+(key) or Shift+(key). When Sticky Keys is enabled, you can press one key at a time. For example, in AutoCAD LT the Ctrl+N keystroke starts the NEW command. Normally, you have to press and hold Ctrl, then press N and release both keys. With Sticky Keys, you can press and release the Ctrl key, then press the N key for the same effect.

The BounceKeys feature is useful if your hands shake and you sometimes press a key more times than you intend to. Enabling BounceKeys causes the system to ignore repeated keystrokes. In the BounceKeys settings you can specify how fast the keystrokes must be repeated in order to be ignored, and you can also have Windows play a beep when the keys are accepted. A test area is provided where you can test your BounceKey settings. This feature is called FilterKeys when accessed from the Accessibility Properties dialog box.

The ToggleKeys options allow you to instruct Windows to play a sound when you press Caps Lock, NumLock, or Scroll Lock. The sound differs depending on whether you are turning the toggle on or off. Keep in mind that if you have told Windows to display a visual warning, your screen will also flash.

The MouseKeys feature allows you to use the keyboard numeric keypad instead of your mouse for pointing. If this option is enabled, you will be prompted to set the speed of the pointer.

You can select a custom mouse cursor for better visibility and you can specify both its size and colors. Other mouse settings you can choose include the button to be used for the pick button, the speed of the cursor on screen, and mouse trails. When mouse trails are enabled, moving the cursor leaves behind a temporary trail to make it easier to locate the cursor.

Finally, Windows allows you to configure your system for a multiple-user environment by setting automatic time-outs for the accessibility features and specifying whether the current settings are automatically applied to all new user accounts on the workstation. Windows also allows you to save your settings in a file so you can restore them at any time or even take them with you to other workstations.

If you are using Windows 95 or NT4, all these settings can be made in the Accessibility Options dialog box. The Windows 98 Accessibility Properties dialog box is shown in Figure D.6.

FIGURE D.6

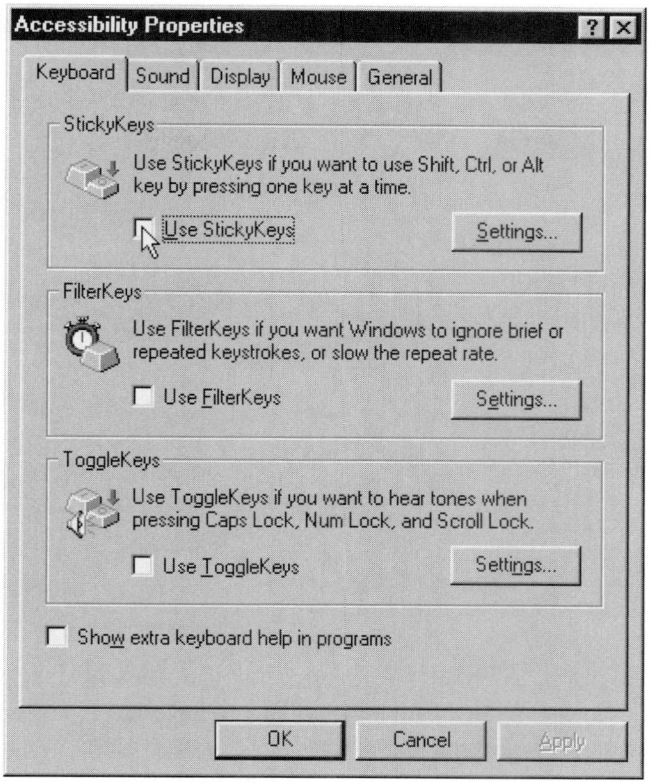

Adaptive Technology

Adaptive technology refers to equipment used in conjunction with a computer to assist people with disabilities in the use of the computer. Adaptive technology includes devices that are designed to assist those with impaired vision, hearing, or motor skills.

The purpose of the following discussion is to increase your awareness of the types of adaptive technology devices that are currently available. You should always consult with your physician, physical therapist, or other appropriate medical professional prior to making decisions regarding the use of such devices.

Display Options

In addition to the Windows Accessibility Options discussed previously, different display technologies are available to assist visually impaired users. Common solutions include larger display areas, audible feedback, and even tactile output using a Braille system.

Depending on the severity of the visual impairment, a simple increase in the size of the display may be a workable solution. The most common size for display monitors used in modern CAD industry is between 17″ and 19″. Larger display sizes are available from many different manufacturers. A 21″ monitor provides more than 1½ times the area of a 17″ monitor and monitor sizes up to 35″ are now available, providing more than four times the area of a 17″ monitor.

Very large computer monitors can be very expensive and so may be cost-prohibitive. One alternative is to use a dual monitor system. If your video adapter supports multiple display monitors, you can place two smaller monitors side by side to increase the display area at a much more affordable price.

Audible feedback systems can augment the display through tools such as *screen readers*. A screen reader converts text on your screen into speech, but it has no option for displaying geometric information such as a CAD drawing.

Braille output systems can also output text in a nonvisual format, typically one to four lines of up to 80 characters per line, but like audible feedback systems, cannot yet display geometric or graphical information.

Keyboard Options

A variety of adaptive technology options are available to provide enhanced accessibility to computer keyboards. One of the simplest options is to configure your keyboard to match your style of use. Earlier discussion introduced many of the options for keyboards that are set using the Accessibility Wizard (or Accessibility Options). Other options are available from the Keyboard Properties dialog box. For example, if you tend

FIGURE D.7

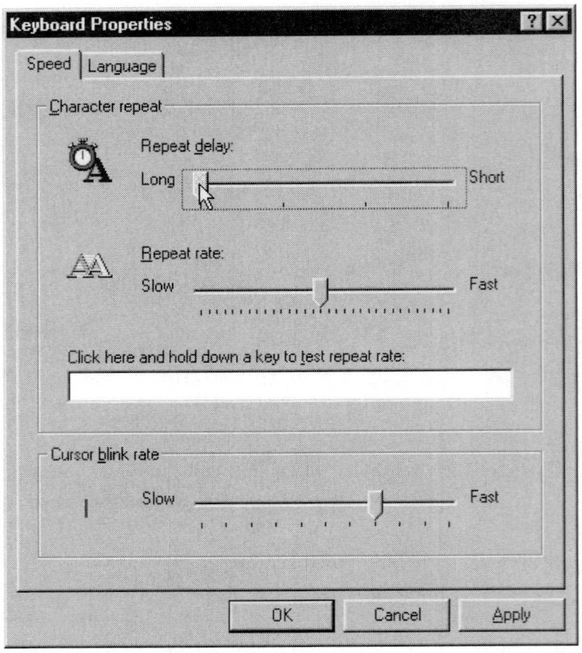

to press keys too slowly, the keyboard may switch into repeat mode and enter multiple characters when you intended to enter only one. To modify the behavior of your keyboard, pick the Start button from your task bar, then pick Settings Control Panel. In the Control Panel window, pick the Keyboard icon to display the Keyboard Properties dialog box, as shown in Figure D.7.

The Repeat Delay slider controls how long you must continue to press a key before it begins to repeat. Four incremental settings are shown along the slider bar. When the slider is moved all the way to Short, the delay is one-half second; all the way toward Long sets the delay at 2 seconds. The Repeat Rate slider controls how fast Windows enters the repetitive characters. If the slider is moved all the way to Fast, approximately 40 characters per second are printed when repeating; the Slowest speed prints out about 2 or 3 characters per second.

If this option does not work or does not produce consistent results, a *key guard* may be a better choice. A key guard is a plastic or metal overlay that covers the keyboard and has holes in it that allow only the keys positioned directly below them to be pressed. This device helps prevent accidental pressing of more than one key at a time with either a finger or a typing stick. This cover also helps improve accuracy and minimizes accidental keystrokes. Additionally, it allows users to rest their hands on the key guard without fear of accidentally pressing keys. These features make the keyboard much more accessible to users with stress injuries or motor coordination impairments.

For those users with very minor difficulties using the keyboard, a good solution might be to use an ergonomic keyboard. The Keyboard Properties dialog box also allows the keyboard to be reconfigured for the DVORAK keyboard layout. The DVORAK keyboard layout is a much more efficient layout that requires significantly fewer motions than the standard (or QWERTY) keyboard. To make this change, pick the Language tab in the Keyboard Properties dialog box. Highlight the English (United States) selection in the list and pick the Properties button. In the Language Properties dialog box, pick the United States — Dvorak option. Changing the function of specific keys on the keyboard is referred to as *remapping* the keys. Keep in mind that remapping the keys does not change the letters that appear on the keyboard; it changes only which characters appear on screen when you press the keys. You will need to learn the DVORAK keyboard layout before you can begin to use this configuration effectively.

Some companies currently manufacture single-handed keyboards, which are designed to provide quick and comfortable access to all the available keys. Figure D.8 shows an example of single-handed keyboards for right- and left-handed users. Notice the curved design that keeps all the keys within reach at the same time, allowing easier access for users who have limited mobility or who are able to use only a single hand. The manufacturer of the keyboard shown in this illustration indicates that experienced users have demonstrated the ability to input up to 60 words per minute in word-processing applications. Other considerations made for single-handed users include "Push-On" and "Push-Off" functions for the Shift, Ctrl, and Alt keys to assist with pressing key combinations with one hand. Another unique product for single-handed users implements a foot pedal that allows one-finger input for combined keystrokes.

FIGURE D.8 For computer users who are able to use only one hand for keyboarding, adaptive single-handed keyboards provide easier and faster access than conventional keyboards. [Photos courtesy of PCD Maltron, Ltd. (www.Maltron.com)]

Other keyboard designs are available for users who can use only a one-finger pointing method or who cannot use their hands to operate a keyboard. These keyboards use a gently curved profile that helps minimize motion requirements for better accessibility. Figure D.9 shows an example of this style of keyboard and shows a user working with a mouth-stick to access the keys. Users working with a mouth-stick need to minimize motions to prevent neck and shoulder fatigue.

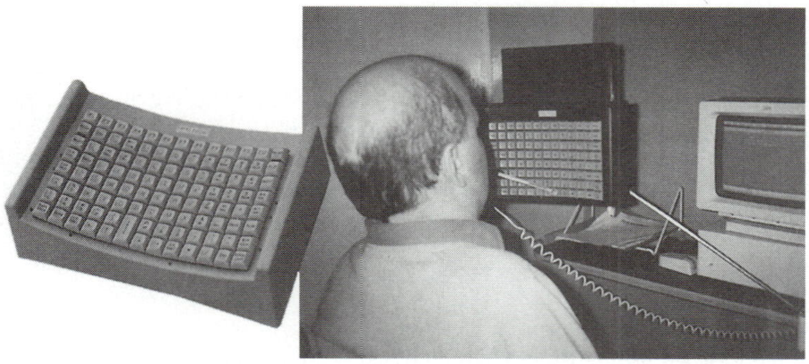

FIGURE D.9 The mouth-stick style keyboard provides easy access for users who cannot use their hands to operate a keyboard. [Photo courtesy of PCD Maltron, Ltd. (www.Maltron.com)]

Expanded keyboards are oversized keyboards with larger keys, "sticky" buttons, and other accessibility features. Some expanded keyboards use slightly recessed keys to help prevent entry errors due to convulsive movement or muscular spasms.

Software applications can be used to manage a *virtual keyboard* — a simulated keyboard that is displayed on the monitor and accessed with a pointing device or speech recognition system. Many of these applications assist the user through *word prediction*, which reduces typing requirements by automatically finishing many of the words or commands being typed.

Some systems provide a comprehensive speech recognition interface that allows the user to input software commands by speaking. Speech recognition systems are much better today than they were a few years ago, but they still present certain challenges to working effectively. Inconsistencies in speech patterns, background noises, and the system's difficulty in understanding contiguous speech can increase the possibilities that voice commands will be misunderstood. Modern speech recognition systems may have a 30,000- to more than a 50,000-word vocabulary. Software can be "trained" to recognize new commands or words, such as technical terms or even vendor names. Optionally, custom voice command libraries containing many words specific to specific trades or industries can be purchased.

Pointing Devices Options

Pointing devices come in many different configurations. Users who have difficulty working with a mouse can find a variety of alternative pointing devices. One of the most common mouse alternatives is the trackball. Both the mouse and the trackball translate the movement of a ball into cursor movement on screen. When using a mouse, you must continually move your hand, rotate your wrist, and extend your arm. A trackball, however, allows you to rest your hand and arm in a comfortable position and roll the ball with your fingers or thumb to move the cursor. Many different sizes and styles of trackballs have been designed to assist with a diverse range of needs.

Joysticks are frequently thought of primarily as a gaming accessory; however, many companies manufacture joystick and software combinations that provide all the functionality of a two- or three- button mouse.

Many computer users who experience difficulty using a mouse are able to use a joystick effectively. Much like a trackball, a joystick allows you to rest your arm and hand comfortably in a set position.

Some of the additional adaptive technologies that address pointing device accessibility include touch screens and touch tablets. With a touch screen, users can point to what they want directly on the display and tap it to pick. A touch tablet works according to the same principle, but rather than a display monitor, a flat tablet device is used. The tablet can lie flat or it can be inclined as needed. Some of these devices, though, require as much or more motion than even a mouse.

Users who require a hands-free-style interface may be able to utilize eye-control technology as their primary interface option. Some systems are able to track the motion of the eyes and apply that motion to the on-screen cursor. Others track head movement to guide the cursor. An intentional blink is used to specify a cursor pick. Blinking twice signifies a double-click. Because text input is fundamental to much of what we do with computers, these types of adaptive technologies are often used in conjunction with an on-screen keyboard and integrated word prediction.

Earlier, we described how a mouth-stick can provide keyboard accessibility. This same type of interface can be applied as a pointing device and used with a virtual (on-screen) keyboard. Many mouth-stick pointing device systems use a breath switch system referred to as sip and puff. A "sip" (drawing air in) through the mouth-stick activates one mouse button function, such as a pick. A "puff" (pushing air out) through the mouth-stick activates the second mouse button function. Some sip-and-puff systems have additional control features that respond to lip pressure or other user actions.

Resources for Further Study

The following is a list of some available resources on the World Wide Web for gathering further information on accessibility features and adaptive technology.

Center for Information Technology Accommodation (CITA)
http://www.itpolicy.gsa.gov/cita

Alliance For Technology Access
http://www.ataccess.org

Vendor Members of the Alliance for Technology Access
http://www.ataccess.org/MemberDirectory/atavendors.html

The National Institute on Disability and Rehabilitation Research —
U.S. Department of Education "AbleData" Website
http://www.abledata.com

Center for Applied Special Technology
http://www.cast.org

Equal Access to Software and Information
http://www.isc.rit.edu/~easi

Family Guide to Assistive Technology
http://www.pluk.org/AT1.html

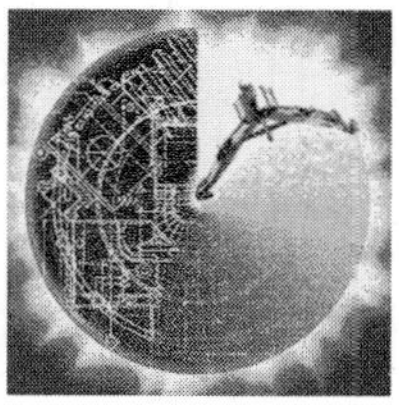

Glossary

absolute coordinates A point specification method based on the Cartesian coordinate system that indicates locations in a drawing relative to the origin, 0,0. Absolute coordinates are entered as X axis and Y axis values separated by a comma (X,Y) or, in a 3D point specification, X,Y, and Z axis values (X,Y, Z).

accelerator keystrokes Key combinations provided for easy access to commonly used functions and commands.

actual size When referring to an AutoCAD LT drawing, the scale is 100% or full size. The AutoCAD term for this is *World Size.*

ADI® Autodesk Device Interface™. An Autodesk interface specification for device drivers that support equipment used with Autodesk products.

alert box Used to display an error or warning message.

alias A shorter name for an AutoCAD LT command. Predefined command aliases include L, which is the alias for LINE, and E for ERASE. Command aliases are defined in the aclt.pgp file.

aligned dimensioning Type of dimensioning in which text for horizontal dimensions is placed horizontally and reads from the bottom of the sheet, text for vertical dimensions is placed vertically and reads from the right side of the sheet, and dimensions placed at an angle have the text placed at the same angle.

alphanumeric characters Letters and numbers.

alternate units The second set of units shown when dual dimensioning is used. Dual dimensioning shows inch measurements followed by millimeter measurements in brackets or vice versa. Dual dimensioning is no longer a recommended ASME standard.

angular dimension Type of dimension that shows the angular measurement between linear profiles or arc segments.

angular unit The unit of measurement used to represent angular measure. AutoCAD LT supports the following angular units: decimal degrees, degrees/minutes/seconds, grads, and radians.

annotation Any text, notes, dimensions, and text symbols on a drawing.

annotation symbol A symbol used in combination with text.

anonymous block An unnamed block created by AutoCAD LT, such as the blocks used to represent associative dimension objects.

ANSI American National Standards Institute. Coordinator of the United States private sector voluntary standardization system. ANSI standards are inclusive of information technology, and govern several aspects of drafting and computer standards.

aperture A box on the screen cursor that allows the user to easily pick an object. Also known as a *target box.*

approximation point A point that a curve or surface follows, but might not pass through. Compare with *interpolation point.*

argument Data provided to a function that operates on the data.

array In AutoCAD LT, a rectangular or circular pattern formed using multiple copies of selected drawing objects.

arrowhead Often used as a generic reference to a terminator at the end of a dimension line and used to indicate where a dimension begins and ends. AutoCAD LT supports many varieties, such as filled or unfilled triangular shapes, ticks (angled slashes), and dots.

ASCII American Standard Code for Information Interchange. Refers to a set of standard alphabetical characters and numbers.

aspect ratio The ratio of width to height.

associative dimensions Dimensions whose values automatically change to match those of an edit.

associative hatch pattern A hatch that is automatically revised to fit a new boundary if the hatch boundary is changed.

attribute Information stored within a block reference that describe the characteristics of the block. See also *invisible block attributes* and *visible block attributes.*

attribute definition Special type of object that is included as part of a block definition.

attribute extraction file A standard text file containing attribute data extracted from a drawing using DDATTEXT.

attribute extraction template file A template file identifies attributes to be extracted and controls formatting of the attribute data that are saved in the attribute extraction file.

attribute prompt When an attribute is inserted into a drawing, this is the text string that is displayed to request a value to assign to the attribute. The attribute prompt, mode, default, and tag are part of the attribute definition.

attribute tag A text string that serves as a "handle" for an attribute or attribute definition. Attribute tags are used to select attribute definitions when defining a block and are used in the attribute extraction process. The attribute prompt, mode, default, and tag are part of the attribute definition.

attribute value The text information associated with an attribute. The value specified during the attribute definition process is used as the default when inserting an attribute. The attribute prompt, mode, default, and tag are part of the attribute definition.

AutoCAD LT library search path The defined locations where AutoCAD LT searches for needed support files. This includes the current folder, the AutoCAD LT program folder, the drawing folder, and all folders specified in the Support File Search Path in the Files tab of the Options dialog box.

AutoSnap A feature of AutoCAD that works with object snaps to display a marker at the object snap location when you move the cursor to indicate the desired object or snap point.

axis tripod Displayed during the VPOINT command, this graphic helps visualize the relative directions of the X, Y, and Z axes as the viewpoint is changed.

baseline dimensioning See *datum dimensioning.*

base point A point specified as an original reference point in many different types of editing operations in AutoCAD LT. Base points are needed to control the results of operations such as moving, copying, rotating, scaling, or creating polar array patterns. Text, block objects, Xrefs, and inserted drawings use a base point to identify their location in a drawing.

basic dimension Value that is considered a theoretically perfect size, profile, orientation, or location dimension.

bearing The direction of a line with respect to one of the quadrants of a compass. Bearings are measured either clockwise or counterclockwise depending on the quadrant and beginning from either north or south.

big font An Asian or other large-format font. A big font cannot be specified as a primary font file.

binary file format Format in which information is stored as a series of 1's and 0's.

binding The process of permanently adding an Xref to the current drawing.

bitmap A record of colors that comprises an image.

blip Temporary screen marks that are displayed when you pick a point.

block A generic term for a named object defined from one or more other drawing objects, which is handled as a single object. This term is commonly used in reference to both block definitions and block references. See also *block definition* and *block reference*.

block definition The named record of geometry and related data used to define a complex drawing object. References to this definition can be displayed in one or more locations within a drawing. A block definition typically consists of a name, an insertion base point, a record of one or more drawing objects defining the geometric appearance, and any number of block attributes. See also *block* and *block reference*.

block reference A reference to a named block definition that is inserted in a drawing and displays the data stored in that block definition. Individual block references are also referred to as an *instance*. See also *block* and *block definition*.

boundary set A group of objects that AutoCAD LT analyzes for the boundary definition when you specify a point on the drawing.

bounding box Defines the size of the area in which a drawing is contained.

B-spline An approximate curve. Also known as a *nonuniform rational B-spline (NURBS).*

button menu The menu defining the function of the buttons on a pointing device having multiple buttons. The AutoCAD LT menu file uses the BUTTONS*n* section for digitizers and the AUX*n* section for system pointers.

ByBlock A specialized linetype and color setting that allows objects that are part of a block to reflect current drawing or layer settings.

ByLayer A specialized object property setting that applies layer properties settings to the object. The ByLayer setting can be assigned to properties such as color, linetype, lineweight, and plot style.

byte The approximate space required by a computer to store one text character. A byte is eight bits, which are electronic on/off signals that are put together to make a message for the computer to interpret.

Cartesian coordinate system Coordinate system used to locate points within a drawing relative to two intersecting axes (2D), or three intersecting axes (3D). In 2D coordinate specifications, the X and Y axes are used, and in 3D coordinates the third Z axis is also referenced.

cascading menu Groups of selected commands that are accessed by picking a pull-down menu item.

central processing unit (CPU) Primary component of computer that processes the data and numerical calculations needed to run software applications.

centroid The center of mass of an object. The MASSPROP command is used to find the centroid of a region in AutoCAD LT.

chain dimensioning Type of dimensioning in which the next dimension continues from the previous dimension. Also called *continuous dimensioning* and *point-to-point dimensioning.*

chamfer In mechanical drafting for manufacturing, chamfers are slightly angled corners. AutoCAD LT lets you make any desired angled corner using the CHAMFER command.

circular referencing The situation that occurs when a drawing is externally referenced that, in turn, externally references the current drawing.

circumference Perimeter line of a circle.

client application See *container application.*

clip art A collection of artistic symbols and images.

clipping plane An imaginary plane that hides part of a drawing.

CMYK Cyan, Magenta, Yellow and blacK. The ink color system used by most color printers. The ink colors can be applied using *dithering* to produce other colors. Display systems use an RGB color system, which is why colors on printed output often differ slightly from the colors displayed on-screen.

command Instructions given by the user of a computer program.

command alias A shortened version of a command name that allows you to enter commands more quickly at the keyboard.

command line Refers to the text interface provided in the floating command window.

command script A text file that contains a list of commands and options that AutoCAD LT reads and performs.

compact disk See *optical disk.*

compile The process by which menu files are rewritten, with the latest changes, in a way that provides the fastest access by AutoCAD LT to the information.

complex linetype A linetype that incorporates text or symbols into the basic line pattern to supply additional information.

composite The final drawing that is a combination of views, border, and title block.

computer-aided design (CAD) Area of CADD that is associated with the creation and editing of technical drawings.

computer-aided design and drafting (CADD) Computer technology that provides powerful engineering tools used for the creation and analysis of precision technical drawings.

construction lines Lines that extend into infinity in one or two directions. Also referred to as *xlines* and *rays.*

construction plane The XY plane of the current UCS on which planar geometry is constructed.

container application The destination application, or software package, for an OLE object. Also called *client application.*

continuous dimensioning See *chain dimensioning.*

control code Combinations of text characters used to add special characters to a text object, such as a degree or diameter symbol.

control frame A linear path of point locations that define the shape of a B-spline. The SPLFRAME system variable is used to display or hide control frames.

coordinate Numbers assigned to points so they can be located on a grid in the Cartesian coordinate system.

coordinate display Indicates where the cursor is in relation to the drawing origin.

coordinate filters See *point filters.*

crosshairs Vertical and horizontal line combination cursor.

crossing polygon A selection area defined as an irregular polygonal shape that selects everything it surrounds or touches. Enter CP or CPolygon at a Select objects: prompt to use this feature. See also *crossing selection* and *window polygon.*

crossing selection A rectangular selection area that selects everything it surrounds or touches. See also *crossing polygon.*

cubic curve An extremely smooth curve with the elements of the curve passing through the first and last control points and close to the other control points. Compare with *quadratic curve.*

cursor Computer onscreen symbol to indicate location on the screen. It moves with the movement of the mouse or arrow keys.

cylindrical coordinate A coordinate specification that uses a standard polar coordinate entry followed by a Z-axis value.

data field Individual areas that are filled in with information in a drawing title block.

datum dimensioning Dimensioning in which every dimension begins at the same starting place. Also called *baseline dimensioning.*

default Command prompt options and values that are set by AutoCAD LT until changed. The changed option or value is then used.

definition points Also called *defpoints*, these are the defining points that are used to calculate the value of an associative dimension. Definition points are stored on the special layer DEFPOINTS, which does not plot.

delimit To separate individual objects or fields within a group or series; some text files use spaces or commas to separate and identify each field.

demand loading A feature that increases the performance of AutoCAD LT by loading only the portion of a referenced drawing that is required to regenerate the current drawing.

dependent objects Named objects that are defined in an externally referenced drawing.

dependent symbol Any named object defined in an externally referenced drawing.

desktop Refers to the layout of icons and features on the operating system screen.

deviation See *unequal bilateral tolerance.*

dialog box Provides the means for entering instructions or settings for a software program.

diameter The distance across a circle that passes through the center of a circle.

DIESEL Direct Interpretively Evaluated String Expression Language. A macro language used to create smart menu items.

digitize To trace the information on a paper drawing or image with a digitizer to create a computer file. Topographical map data is a common application of digitizing.

digitizer tablet Device used to track the position of the pointing device on its surface.

dimension styles Saved sets of dimension variable settings that determine the appearance of the dimensions.

dimension text The text part of a dimension representing its dimensional value.

dimension variables AutoCAD LT system variables that help you control the way dimensions look. Also called *dimvars.*

dimensioning Measurements given on a drawing. See also *aligned dimensioning, chain dimensioning, datum dimensioning,* and *unidirectional dimensioning.*

dimensioning mode AutoCAD LT dimensioning at the command line using the DIM or DIM1 commands.

dimensions Numerical values expressed in appropriate units of measure and indicated on a drawing and in other documents. See also *associative dimensions, linear dimensions, location dimensions, oblique dimensions, ordinate dimensions,* and *size dimensions.*

dimvar See *dimension variable.*

direct distance entry Feature that allows the user to point the cursor in the direction in which the next point should be placed and simply specify the distance.

direct hatching Used to define a hatch boundary and hatch pattern placement. The user then instructs AutoCAD to remove or retain the hatch boundary during the hatching process.

dithering A process used by printers to combine color dots to emulate colors that are not available.

docked Placement of a toolbar that removes the title bar and embeds it in the program window.

donut In AutoCAD LT, a filled circle or ring. Also known as a *doughnut.*

dot matrix printer Low-quality printer often used for check prints rather than final drawings.

double line Pairs of parallel lines and arcs.

double-click Mouse action of clicking a mouse button twice very quickly.

download The process of receiving files from a remote site through your modem or network connection.

drawing database The information stored by AutoCAD LT to define the objects in a drawing file.

drawing extents The area of a drawing that contains objects.

drawing limits The user-defined rectangular drawing area where grid dots are displayed when the grid is active. Also called *grid limits.*

drawing origin Located at coordinates 0.0000,0.0000 and found at the lower left corner of the screen when you start AutoCAD. Also referred to simply as *origin.*

DWF Drawing Web Format. The file extension for a compact drawing file format that can be viewed in a web browser.

DWG The file extension for the default AutoCAD LT file format.

DXF™ Drawing interchange Format. A proprietary Autodesk file format that can be created using either an ASCII or a binary file format, which is used to import and export drawing information between AutoCAD LT and other CAD applications.

edit The process of erasing, moving, copying, or altering objects.

edit box A box that provides a means for entering text or number values into a dialog box. Also referred to as a *text box.*

electrophotographic plotter A plotter used for large-volume plots. The process uses a line of closely spaced, electrically charged wire nibs to produce dots on coated paper. Pressure or heat is then used to attach ink to the charged dots. It is much faster than a pen plotter. Also known as an *electrostatic plotter.*

elevation The Z-coordinate location.

ellipse An object drawn by a curve that has a constant value equal to the sum of its distance from two fixed points.

e-mail Shortened version of *electronic mail,* this is a means of communication via computer.

embedding The process of placing an OLE object in a container application.

equal bilateral tolerance Tolerance for which variation is permitted equally in both directions from the specified dimension. Compare with *unequal bilateral tolerance.*

ergonomic With reference to computers, refers to the science of adapting a workstation to fit the user's body comfortably.

extended intersection The point at which one object would intersect another if both objects were extended far enough along their natural paths of extension.

extension The distance a dimension line extends beyond the extension line.

external reference A source drawing outside of the current drawing that AutoCAD LT refers to when information is needed. Referred to as an *Xref.*

family member In terms of dimensions, this is one of the specific dimension types, including linear, radial, angular, diameter, ordinate, and leaders.

fast font A font that can be drawn and regenerated very quickly.

feature control frame An arrangement of geometric tolerance data applied to drawing features that displays applicable geometric characteristic symbols and associated tolerance values. Feature control frames are created automatically with the TOLERANCE command.

fence A single-line crossing selection specified by defining a series of linear segments that touch the objects to be selected.

field width Number of character positions used in a field.

file server A central computer with a large amount of storage space that is used for storing files from many workstations within a network.

fill Refers to the solid color that fills wide objects such as polylines and donuts, or can refer to areas filled with the SOLID command or using the SOLID hatch pattern.

fillet In mechanical drafting for manufacturing, fillets are slightly rounded inside corners, and rounds are slightly rounded outside corners. AutoCAD LT lets you make any desired rounded corner using the FILLET command.

filters Used to remove or combine certain values to create a new value.

fit points Points used to define a B-spline. See also *interpolation points* and *approximation points.*

fit tolerance The setting that controls the maximum distance that a B-spline can be drawn from each of the fit points that define it.

floating viewports See *layout viewports.*

freeze A layer setting that can shorten regeneration time by suppressing the display of objects associated with the frozen layer. Any objects on a frozen layer are not displayed, regenerated, or plotted. See also *thaw.*

flyout A toolbar button that displays additional related commands. This is like a toolbar within a toolbar.

font See *text font.*

font file A font definition resource in which a complete font is available for use.

From An option that allows you to specify a point that is a specific location from a given point.

general notes Notes that supply information that applies to the entire drawing.

global edit The process of changing every occurrence of a specific attribute value in the current drawing.

global setting A type of setting that affects an entire drawing. Compare with *individual setting,* which affects a single object or group of objects.

gradient A unit of angular measure. A circle has 400 grads.

graphics cursor See *crosshairs* and *cursor.*

grid A pattern of dots displayed on the screen in increments established by the user.

grips Squares that are automatically displayed on a line when you move the cursor to the line and pick it.

group Any number of individual drawing objects that are combined into a named or unnamed set for easier handling.

hard disk Magnetic drive for storage of computer programs and files. Also referred to as a *nonremovable drive.*

hardcopy A printed version of a computer file.

hardware Physical computer equipment.

hatch A pattern used to fill in areas of a drawing.

hatch boundary The shape that encloses a hatch pattern.

hatchable Capable of being hatched. An object must be closed to be hatchable, or be part of a set of objects that form a closed boundary.

HDI driver Heidi® Device Interface. An Autodesk interface specification for device drivers that support equipment used with Autodesk products.

healing A situation in which an area becomes filled with a hatch pattern.

help strings The items that appear on the status line when a menu selection is pointed to or highlighted. They allow users to be certain of what action is to be performed.

home page The primary Web page, or a central navigation page, for a Web site.

hyperlink Items in HTML documents that are linked to other Web resources.

HyperText Text items that are linked to other resources.

implied windowing The ability to automatically place a window around an object or objects to select by picking and moving the mouse.

included angle The angle formed between the start point, endpoint, and center of an arc.

individual setting A type of setting that affects only an individually drawn object or group of objects without changing the entire drawing. Compare with *global setting,* which affects the entire drawing.

ink-jet printer Printer that is capable of producing a high-quality image but at slower rates than a laser printer, by spraying ink droplets onto paper to produce dot matrix images.

insertion base point A meaningful reference point that is used to position a symbol when it is inserted into a drawing after a block definition has been created.

interactive layer A logical grouping of data; akin to transparent overlays on a mechanical drawing.

interface The method by which users communicate with a computer program, which is referred to as the user interface. The hardware interface is where the computer works with other parts of the system. The software interface is the programming that allows the computer applications to work with the operating system.

Internet A worldwide network of computers connected to one another through telecommunication lines.

interpolation point A point through which a curve or surface passes to define the curve or surface. Compare with *approximation point.*

intuitive interface A method by which users communicate with a computer program in a clear, easy-to-understand manner. Also see *interface.*

invisible block attribute Attribute that is part of the block reference but not displayed on the drawing as part of a text label. Compare with *visible block attributes.*

island An enclosed area within a hatch pattern.

isometric drawing A 3D pictorial in which the three axes are true measurements of the object and form equal angles.

isometric projection The true appearance of the model as though it were tilted toward the viewer.

isometric snap style A snap setting that aligns the cursor with two of three isometric axes and displays a customized grid point conforming to the isometric planes.

justification Determines how text is aligned with the insertion point.

keyboard Input device for a computer, with keys that are similar to a typewriter and additional keys such as numeric keys and function keys.

label An item of text that is visible to the user on a given menu.

laser printer Printer capable of producing high-quality images using a laser, which draws lines on a revolving plate that is charged with high voltage. The laser light causes the plate to discharge as an ink toner adheres to the images and ink is bonded to paper by pressure or heat.

layer A logical grouping of data within a drawing that can be visualized as being like one or more transparencies overlaid on a drawing. Layers can be assigned specific properties and visibility settings.

layer visibility The property that determines if an object that has been drawn on a layer is visible or invisible.

layout The combination of views, annotation, and other drawing data arranged as required for producing a plot. Also refers to any of the available paper space layout tabs in a drawing.

layout viewports Rectangular areas defined in a layout tab that display model space drawing content. See also *paper space.*

leader bubble A circle attached to a leader and with a numeric value inside.

limits tolerance Tolerance for which the plus and minus part of the tolerance is calculated with the specified dimension to provide tolerance limits. Compare with *plus/minus tolerance.*

line of sight An imaginary line of infinite length that passes through the camera location and the target point.

line text See *single-line text.*

linear dimensions Dimensions that are placed in a straight line that is either horizontal, vertical, or at an angle.

linetype Types of drafting lines. Recommended linetypes have been identified by the American National Standards Institute. See Appendix B for examples.

linetype scale Scale used to determine the length of dashes in linetypes such as hidden and center lines.

lineweight An object property that controls the pen width applied to the display or the plotted drawing.

linked object An object that is connected to the original data and is updated when the source file changes.

list box A box that provides several options from which to choose.

locally defined block A block that is defined within the current drawing.

location dimensions Used to locate features and objects.

lock file When a file is being edited, AutoCAD LT creates a lock file to prevent the file from being simultaneously opened and edited by another user. Drawing lock files have a .DWK file extension.

logical extents The area of the drawing that AutoCAD LT is currently keeping within video memory.

macro A set of multiple commands and options that runs automatically once started.

major axis The length of an ellipse.

marker A special symbol used to indicate the correct object snap mode and point on an object on screen.

mass properties Displayed by the MASSPROP command, these refer to the calculated characteristics of 2D regions including the area, perimeter, centroid, and moments of inertia.

memory Temporary storage space in a computer.

menu List of available options and commands from which to choose.

menu call A special code that displays a menu or makes it active. All menu calls start with a dollar sign ($).

minor axis The width of an ellipse.

mirror To produce a mirror image, or a backward copy, of one or more existing objects by reflecting it symmetrically with respect to a user-defined line.

mnemonic Underlined character in a menu bar and each menu option that provides keyboard access to the pull-down menus and menu items, rather than use of a mouse pick item.

mode A setting or operating condition controlled by the user.

model AutoCAD LT name for a drawing. The geometry that is created to define the object drawn.

model space The space in which the geometry is created that defines your model, or drawing.

model viewport A viewport displayed in the Model tab. One or more viewports can be configured to allow simultaneous access to multiple areas of a drawing. See also *layout viewports*.

modem A translation device that allows a computer to transmit and receive digital information through telephone lines.

monitor Display device for a computer.

mouse Pointing device used to control the onscreen movement of the cursor.

multiline text Letters and numbers on a drawing that are entered and edited in paragraph form. Compare with *single-line text.* Also called *paragraph text.*

multiview layout A drawing that shows more than one view of the object drawn.

named object Any item that is assigned a name, such as layers, blocks, linetypes, and text styles.

named view An area of the drawing that is defined and named and can be restored at a later time.

nested Xref Any Xref contained within another Xref.

nesting The practice of permitting existing block references to be used in the creation of other block definitions.

node A point object.

nonassociative hatch pattern A hatch that is not automatically revised to fit a new boundary if the hatch boundary is changed.

notes Information provided on a drawing. See also *general notes* and *specific notes.*

noun/verb selection The process of picking objects to be edited prior to selecting the editing command.

NURBS See *B-spline.*

object The geometric elements of a drawing, including text, dimensions, lines, circles, or polylines, that are handled as a single element for creation, manipulation, and modification. Also called *entity.*

object application The source application, or software package, for an OLE object. Also called *server application.*

object properties The settings that control the appearance and geometric characteristics of objects, such as color, layer, linetype, linetype scale, lineweight, and plotstyle.

object snaps Allow commonly referenced points on an object to be selected easily and accurately.

oblique dimensions Dimensions that have the extension lines placed at an angle from the feature being dimensioned.

OLE Object Linking and Embedding. An operating system feature that allows information from different applications to be combined into a single document or drawing. Data from one application can be linked or embedded in a file used by another application.

on-line help Help supplied by a computer program while a user is working.

operating system Software that controls the basic operation of a computer.

optical disk Storage device for computer program files that has large amounts of storage, typically 4 GB or more. Also referred to as a *compact disk.*

option line The available options for the currently active command.

ordinate dimensions Dimensions drawn without the traditional dimension lines and arrowheads. Also called *arrowless dimensions.*

origin See *drawing origin.*

orphaned The situation describing an Xref when the Xref in which it is nested is unloaded.

Ortho When Ortho is enabled, cursor movements in dragging operations are restricted to only horizontal or vertical relative to the current UCS and Snap rotation angle. A dragging operation is described as a specification of drawing or editing parameters by pointing with the cursor while dragging a rubber-band line from a base point.

orthogonal Having perpendicular slopes or tangents at the point of intersection.

pan Changing the location of a view without changing its size.

paper space A special drawing environment intended only for creating a final layout of your drawing for plotting purposes.

paragraph text See *multiline text.*

parallel projection A 3D view that does not show perspective.

parameter A value, name, option, or characteristic. Also defines the boundaries of an object when used as part of an AutoCAD LT command.

parent style In terms of dimensions, this is a general style that applies to all the family members, or each type of dimension.

partial menu file One that contains only specific items, such as a set of specialized pull-down menus or toolbars.

path objects An object type used in the creation of PostScript files.

peripherals Computer input and output devices.

perpendicular At right (90°) angles.

perspective view View of objects that makes them appear as if they are being viewed in the real world, with closer objects being larger and distant objects being smaller.

pick box A small box to which the cursor changes when you get the Select objects: prompt.

pick button Button on a mouse, puck, or stylus that is used to cause an action.

picture elements See *pixels.*

pipe symbol. See *vertical bar.*

pixels An acronym for *picture elements,* these are the small discrete elements that together make up an image on a monitor.

plan view A view of the current construction plane from a point in the positive Z-axis direction and perpendicular to the X,Y plane of the current UCS.

pline See *polyline.*

plot spooler A piece of hardware or software that sends plot files to a plotting device.

plotter Output device used to print large-format drawings. *Pen plotters* and *pencil plotters* are available. Plotters use a liquid ink, felt tip, or pencil to place images on paper by traversing. Also see *electrophotographic plotter.*

plus/minus tolerance Tolerance for which a specified dimension and tolerance values are given. Compare with *limits tolerance.*

point (1) A location in 3D space specified by X, Y, and Z coordinate values. (2) A specialized AutoCAD LT object defined by a single set of coordinate values and displayed according to the current point display mode settings (PDMODE and PDSIZE).

point filter Used to extract the X, Y, and Z coordinate values from individual points in order to create a new combined point. Also referred to as *coordinate filters.*

point-to-point dimensioning See *chain dimensioning.*

polar array A method of copying objects into a partial or complete circular pattern arrangement by specifying a center point, the number of objects, and the included or total angle for the pattern.

polar coordinates A point specification method based on the Cartesian coordinate system that indicates locations in a drawing relative to the current location. Polar coordinates are entered as a distance and angle preceded by the @ symbol and separated by the < symbol (@distance<angle).

PolarSnap A feature that allows you to draw or edit objects using specific angles and increments without typing values at the keyboard.

Polar tooltip An AutoCAD LT feature that tells you the distance and angle being entered.

polar tracking A more flexible version of the Ortho control that allows specification of angular increments that can be used to control the direction of cursor movements.

polygon A planar geometric object with three or more sides.

polygon window See *window polygon.*

polyline An object composed of one or more line segments or circular arcs that are treated as a single object. Also referred to as a *pline.*

prefix A special note or application that is placed in front of the dimension text.

primary units That part of the dimension from which tolerances or other units are calculated or related.

printer Output device for a computer that provides hard copy.

prompt A request by a program for input.

properties See *object properties.*

puck Specialized type of pointing device for cursor control. Used with a digitizer tablet.

pull-down menu A menu that is accessed by picking a menu name. The menu displayed appears to be pulled down from the menu bar.

purge To remove unused (unreferenced) named object definitions from a drawing, such as block definitions, layers, plotstyles, and text styles from a drawing using the PURGE command.

quadrant One quarter of the circle in the polar coordinate system.

quadratic curve Not as smooth as a cubic curve because the curve passes through the first and last control points but the rest of the curve is tangent to the polyline segments at intermediate control points. Compare with *cubic curve.*

radian An angular unit, arc, or rotational measure in which pi (3.14159…) radians equals 180°.

radius The distance from the center of a circle to its circumference.

raster information A record of the assigned colors of pixels within a defined area.

ray casting The process of sending out an invisible ray. When the ray hits an object, it turns counterclockwise and follows the object to trace the hatch boundary.

read-only memory (ROM) Memory that allows files to be read, but not changed and no additional data can be added.

rectangle A geometric figure with four sides and four right angles.

recursive toolbar Used when a flyout toolbar button displays the toolbar that the flyout is on.

referencing The process by which AutoCAD LT refers to the source file to obtain information, rather than storing it in the current drawing.

regenerate To update drawing objects and the drawing display based on the currently active drawing settings.

region A 2D solid object.

regular polygon A planar geometric object with three or more equal length sides and equal included angles.

reinitialize To reload a support file or restart a device driver.

relative coordinates A point specification method based on the Cartesian coordinate system that indicates locations in a drawing relative to the current location. Relative coordinates are entered as the total change in X- and Y-axis values preceded by the @ symbol and separated by a comma (@change in X, change in Y).

rendering The process of applying shape and color to the surfaces in a drawing.

resolution Term used to indicate display quality. The more pixels, the higher the resolution and sharper the image. Also refers to the quality of a printed image.

rewritable Capable of storing, erasing, and replacing files.

RGB Red, Green, and Blue. The three primary colors used by computer display systems. Different colors are defined and displayed using varying percentages of red, green, and blue content.

right-hand rule Provides an easy-to-understand reference to determine the positive and negative directions of the X, Y, and Z axes.

rubber-band cursor Temporary dashed line between a chosen point and the current cursor location; shows the user how the line will be placed if a particular point is chosen in relation to the preceding point.

running object snap An object snap option or group of options that is set to run continuously.

scale factor Determines the final size of characteristics such as text height, dimension features, and linetype appearance for a plotted drawing.

script file A listing of commands and options in a text file with an .SCR extension that AutoCAD LT reads and executes sequentially from beginning to end.

search area The area searched by AutoCAD's DLINE Snap option when attempting to snap to another object.

selection set The objects selected for editing become part of a selection set.

serifs Fine artistic lines projecting from, generally, the top and bottom of a letter.

server application See *object application.*

shading The process of applying simple colors to all drawing surfaces without consideration being given to lighting, shadows, or reflections.

sheet size The size of the paper on which a drawing is printed or plotted. When printed or plotted, units are scaled to fit the sheet size. Appendix B shows standard ANSI/ASME inch and metric sheet sizes.

shortcut menu A context-sensitive menu that is displayed at the cursor location when you right-click in the command window, text window, or drawing window

simple linetype A linetype that is made up only of lines and spaces.

single-line text Short text entries of letters and numbers on a drawing. Each line of text can be edited individually. Compare with *multiline text.* Also called *line text.*

size dimensions Used to provide the measurements for the size of features and objects.

slide A special type of file that records the current drawing display so it can be viewed later. A "picture" of a drawing.

slide library A single file with an .SLB extension used to store any number of individual slide files for convenient retrieval and display. Slide library files are created with the *slidelib.exe* utility.

slide show Displays a sequence of graphic images created from slide files.

slider Used to change values interactively by picking the arrows at either end of a bar and moving them along the bar.

snap An invisible grid that forces the cursor to move in exact increments as established by the user.

snap angle The current rotation angle applied to the snap grid.

snap grid See *snap.*

Snaptip A feature that identifies the name of the object snap that has been activated.

software Computer programs.

spec Abbreviation for *specification.*

specific notes Notes that apply to specific features on a drawing and may be connected to the features with a leader line. Also known as *local notes.*

specified dimension Primary units part of the dimension being toleranced.

spherical coordinate A coordinate specification that uses a standard polar coordinate entry to specify distance and angle *in* the X,Y plane, followed by an angle specification *from* the X,Y plane.

spline-fit curve The curve created when using the Fit and Spline options of the PEDIT command.

sticky-back Predrawn symbol that is printed on a transparent media that has an adhesive backing. When a symbol is needed, it is simply placed in the appropriate location on the drawing and held in place by the adhesive.

stylus Specialized type of pointing device for cursor control. Used with a digitizer tablet.

subdialog box A box that is displayed and made active without hiding or ending the previous dialog box.

suffix A special note or application that is placed behind the dimension text.

support file A file that is not part of the core program that is used to enhance or modify the way AutoCAD LT works.

surface model A visual representation of a 3D object created by describing the surfaces only. Such objects do not have the same properties as solid objects.

symbol A simplified graphic image used to represent specific elements of a drawing.

symbol library An organized collection of drafting symbols and other commonly used drawing elements that is saved as an individual AutoCAD LT drawing file.

symbol table The information stored regarding named objects such as blocks, linetypes, and text styles.

system mouse Refers to either a mouse or digitizer and indicates that the pointing device is used by AutoCAD LT as well as the operating system.

system variable A named setting maintained by AutoCAD LT that is related to or controls an aspect of a drawing or the drawing environment. Most system variables can be adjusted by entering the variable name at the command line, but some are "read-only" and cannot be modified directly.

2D Two-dimensional; a flat drawing method where objects are drawn on the X,Y plane and have no Z-axis value (thickness).

3D Three-dimensional; a drawing that represents objects on the X, Y, and Z axes to give a real-world appearance. Three-dimensional objects have height, width, and thickness.

Tab Set A series of shortcuts to drawings containing blocks or to folders containing drawings.

tangent The characteristic of a line, arc, or circle touching another arc or circle at only one point without intersecting or crossing each other and a line from the center of the arc or circle is 90° to a line at the point of tangency, or a line between the centers of tangent arcs or circles passes through the point of tangency.

target box See *aperture.*

target option An anchor point in a drawing; used with the CAmera option.

template A drawing file with preestablished settings. Also referred to as a *prototype.*

tessellation lines Incremental lines placed along a curved 3D surface for better visualization.

text The AutoCAD LT term for letters and numbers.

text boundary Establishes the width of the paragraph text.

text font A complete set of characters, including letters, numbers, marks, and symbols, that is of unique proportion and design.

text style The settings that determine the appearance of text characters. The user controls what the computer does by sending it commands via keyboard or other input device.

thaw A layer setting that removes the effect of a previous freeze and restores the display of objects on that layer. See also *freeze.*

thermal plotter A plotter that uses tiny heat elements to burn dot matrix characters into treated paper. Produces high-quality hardcopy.

thickness The extrusion distance applied to a 2D object to give a 3D appearance.

tiled model space The active area of a drawing when TILEMODE is set to 1 (on).

tiled viewports See *model viewport.*

title bar Area across the top or bottom of a program window that lists the program and name of the currently opened file.

tolerance Total amount by which a specific dimension is permitted to vary. See also *equal bilateral tolerance, limits tolerance, plus/minus tolerance, unequal bilateral tolerance,* and *unilateral tolerance.*

toolbar The component of the AutoCAD LT interface that contains one or more buttons for accessing commands or features.

tooltip A small text box displayed next to the cursor that shows the name of the button at which the cursor is pointing.

tracking A process in which a point is located relative to other points on the drawing.

transparent command A transparent command can be used without interrupting a currently active command as long as it does not require a drawing regeneration and it does not change the drawing database. Transparent commands are entered by typing an apostrophe (') before the command name.

tree view A hierarchical list used for more effective access to various types of information. Branches, or categories of information, can be expanded or collapsed to control what is displayed. Tree views are available in AutoCAD® DesignCenter™, the Purge dialog box, the External Reference dialog box, and the on-line help system. Windows Explorer also presents a tree view for accessing disk drives and folder locations.

troubleshooting The process of trying to figure out what went wrong, for example, if a script file does not execute properly.

UCS icon A graphic icon displayed in the current viewport that can show the origin and orientation of the current UCS.

undo To return to the condition a drawing was in prior to execution of the last command.

unequal bilateral tolerance Tolerance for which variation is permitted unequally in both directions from the specified dimension. Compare with *equal bilateral tolerance.* Also known as *deviation.*

ungraceful exit An unplanned exit from AutoCAD LT that is caused by system crashes and power failures.

unidirectional dimensioning Type of dimensioning in which all of the dimension numbers are placed horizontally on the drawing and read from the bottom of the sheet.

unilateral tolerance Tolerance for which variation is permitted in only one direction from the specified dimension.

unreferenced data Data that define something that does not exist or is not used in a drawing.

URL Uniform Resource Locator; a feature that describes the location, or address, of a file found on the internet.

User Coordinate System (UCS) User coordinate systems are user-defined variations from the World Coordinate System. A UCS can simply define a new drawing origin for applications such as ordinate dimensioning, or it can define a completely new orientation for the *X*, *Y*, and *Z* axes in 3D space. The X,Y plane of the current UCS is the active construction plane, which determines the results of drawing planar objects or using planar editing commands. See also *World Coordinate System.*

variable A text item that represents a value which is stored for later use.

vector A line that describes distance and direction.

vector information A record of the distances, angles, and properties associated with distinct drawing objects.

vertex The point at which polyline segments meet. Plural: *vertices.*

vertical bar Symbol (|) used to separate the dependent symbol name from the Xref on which it is dependent. Also called the *pipe symbol.*

video adapter card One of a computer's printed circuit boards that controls the graphic display on a monitor.

viewpoint A point used to define a 3D orientation for viewing a drawing.

viewport configuration An arrangement of tiled viewports that has been saved with a name so it can be restored when needed.

virtual screen An area of memory in which AutoCAD LT stores the current drawing so the user can change the display area without having to regenerate the drawing.

visible block attribute Attribute that is used to generate simple text labels to identify specific information regarding a symbol. Compare with *invisible block attributes.*

Web server A computer system that stores and sends requested files on the World Wide Web.

wild card An asterisk (*) symbol that is used to match anything that is similar.

window Graphical user interface–type operating system in which a rectangular frame or frames on the screen allow the user to work on applications or files. Allows the user to run different applications at the same time, each in its own window.

window polygon A selection area defined as an irregular polygonal shape that selects everything it surrounds completely. Enter WP or WPolygon at a Select objects: prompt to use this feature. See also *window selection* and *crossing polygon.*

window selection A rectangular selection area that selects everything it surrounds completely. See also *window polygon.*

WinTab driver A piece of software that allows AutoCAD LT to utilize a tablet while working in the Windows environment.

wire frame A 3D shape that uses lines and curves to describe its outline.

wire frame model The representation of a 3D object by using lines and curves to represent its profiles.

word wrapping The process by which words that exceed the boundary width are automatically moved, or "wrapped," to the next line.

working drawing A drawing for manufacturing or building purposes.

workstation Powerful personal computer set up to do work applications. Provides quality graphics, has high-capacity hard drive, and can be networked.

world coordinates Coordinates expressed in relation to the World Coordinate System.

World Coordinate System (WCS) The core coordinate system in AutoCAD LT upon which all objects and user coordinate systems are based.

World Wide Web An easy-to-understand interface to the Internet.

Xref See *external reference.*

zoom To change the apparent size of an object for viewing.

Index